Lecture Notes in Computer Science

Lecture Notes in Artificial Intelligence 16617

The series Lecture Notes in Artificial Intelligence (LNAI) was established in 1988 as a topical subseries of LNCS devoted to artificial intelligence.

The series publishes state-of-the-art research results at a high level. As with the LNCS mother series, the mission of the series is to serve the international R & D community by providing an invaluable service, mainly focused on the publication of conference and workshop proceedings and postproceedings.

Raymond Chi-Wing Wong · Hanghang Tong ·
Hua Lu · James Kwok · Flora Salim ·
Yuanfeng Song · Man Lung Yiu
Editors

Data Science: Foundations and Applications

30th Pacific-Asia Conference
on Knowledge Discovery and Data Mining, PAKDD 2026
Hong Kong, China, June 9–12, 2026
Proceedings, Part I

Springer

Editors
Raymond Chi-Wing Wong
Hong Kong University of Science and Technology
Hong Kong, China

Hanghang Tong
University of Illinois Urbana-Champaign
Urbana, IL, USA

Hua Lu
Aalborg University
Copenhagen, Denmark

James Kwok
Hong Kong University of Science and Technology
Hong Kong, China

Flora Salim
University of New South Wales
Sydney, NSW, Australia

Yuanfeng Song
ByteDance
Shanghai, China

Man Lung Yiu
Hong Kong Polytechnic University
Hong Kong, China

ISSN 0302-9743 ISSN 1611-3349 (electronic)
Lecture Notes in Artificial Intelligence
ISBN 978-981-92-1925-4 ISBN 978-981-92-1926-1 (eBook)
https://doi.org/10.1007/978-981-92-1926-1

LNCS Sublibrary: SL7 – Artificial Intelligence

This Springer imprint is published by the registered company Springer Nature Singapore Pte Ltd.
The registered company address is: 152 Beach Road, #21-01/04 Gateway East, Singapore 189721, Singapore

Foreword

On behalf of the Organizing Committee, we are delighted to welcome all participants to the 30th Pacific-Asia Conference on Knowledge Discovery and Data Mining (PAKDD 2026). Since the first PAKDD conference in 1997, PAKDD has established itself as one of the leading international conferences on data mining and knowledge discovery. PAKDD provides an international forum for researchers and industry practitioners to share their new ideas, original research results, and practical development experiences across all areas of data mining. This year, after its previous edition in Hong Kong (2001), PAKDD was held for the second time in the fascinating city of Hong Kong, during June 9–12, 2026.

We extend our sincere gratitude to the researchers who submitted their research work to the PAKDD 2026 conference. The main conference of PAKDD 2026 had three tracks, namely Main Track, Survey Track, and Special Track on LLMs for Data Science. Following the initial practice of PAKDD 2025, this year, we organized a Special Session on Data Science Foundations and Applications (DSFA). The conference program was further enriched with an AI forum (involving 11 invited speakers), ten high-quality tutorials, six workshops on cutting-edge topics, and a doctoral consortium. We would like to express our sincere thanks to all authors for their efforts in research, as well as in preparing high-quality presentations. We also express our appreciation to all the collaborators and sponsors for their support, trust, and cooperation. We were honored to have five distinguished keynote speakers joining the conference: Zhi-Hua Zhou (Nanjing University), Geoff Webb (Monash University), Xin Luna Dong (Meta Reality Labs), Xia "Ben" Hu (Shanghai AI Laboratory), and Qingsong Wen (Squirrel AI Learning), each with high reputations in their respective areas. Moreover, we had three award talks, namely (1) PAKDD Distinguished Research Contributions Award Talk (by Jian Pei (Duke University)), (2) PAKDD Most Influential Paper Award Talk (by Truyen Tran (Deakin University)), and (3) PAKDD Early Career Research Award Talk (by Guansong Pang (Singapore Management University)). We enjoyed their participation and talks, which made the conference one of the best academic platforms for knowledge discovery and data mining. We also included a panel session, moderated by Flora Salim (University of New South Wales), involving the following panelists: Geoff Webb (Monash University), Jian Pei (Duke University), Cyrus Shahabi (University of Southern California), and Xia "Ben" Hu (Shanghai AI Laboratory).

We would like to express our sincere gratitude for the contributions of the members and reviewers in the Senior Program Committee and the Program Committee, led by program chairs Raymond Wong, Hanghang Tong, and Hua Lu, and the track chairs including Elena Baralis and Guandong Xu on the Survey Track, and Carl Yang and Xiang Li on the Special Track on LLMs for Data Science. It is through their untiring efforts that the conference had an excellent technical program. We are also thankful to the other Organizing Committee members: including the Chairs of the DSFA Special Session: Guansong Pang, Xuyun Zhang, and Xin Wang; Workshop Chairs Cheng Long,

Jieming Shi, and Yuxuan Liang; Tutorial Chairs Jianliang Xu, Gao Cong, and Sinno Jialin Pan; Doctoral Consortium Chairs Xiao Huang and Byron Choi; Publicity Chairs Chen Ma, Yixiang Fang, and Huiping Cao; Industrial Chairs Xiaoli Li, Jason Zhang, and James Cheng; Proceedings Chairs Yuanfeng Song and Man Lung Yiu; Finance Chair Xin Huang and Yuchen Li; Web and Content Chairs Wenqi Fan and Chenhao Ma; Registration Chairs Haibo Hu and Harry Chan; and Sponsorship Chairs Yangqiu Song, Amelia Jing Li, Wei Bi, Mi-Yen Yeh, and Lu Hou. We would like to particularly thank the Local Arrangement Team, Hong Va Leong and Sibo Wang. The conference would not have been successful without their dedication, commitment, and efforts. We are also grateful to the PAKDD Steering Committee for their guidance, the hosting organizations, and all our sponsors for continuously providing institutional and financial support to PAKDD 2026.

Finally, we hope that you found our program interesting and thought-provoking and will preserve a cherished memory of the conference and Hong Kong. Once again, our warmest welcome to you all!

June 2026

James Kwok
Flora Salim

Preface

It is our great pleasure to present the 30th Pacific-Asia Conference on Knowledge Discovery and Data Mining (PAKDD 2026) as Program Committee Chairs. PAKDD is one of the longest-established and leading international conferences in the areas of data mining and knowledge discovery. It provides an international peer-reviewed forum for presenting and sharing new ideas, original research results, and practical development experiences from all data science areas, including data mining, data warehousing, machine learning, artificial intelligence, databases, statistics, knowledge engineering, visualization, decision-making systems, and emerging applications.

The PAKDD 2026 technical program featured three tracks, the Main Track, the Survey Track, and a Special Track on Large Language Models in Data Science. The Main Track continued its tradition of being the premier forum for the presentation of research results and experience reports on knowledge discovery, data science, and machine learning. The Survey Track was introduced in 2025 for the first time, to promote the dissemination of insightful survey papers: survey papers are intended to provide a structured synthesis of a particular topic in the area of data mining, including but not limited to theoretical foundations of mining, inference, and learning, big data technologies, as well as security, privacy, and integrity, for the perusal of junior researchers and of experts from other research fields. As the rapid advancements in Large Language Models (LLMs) have opened new avenues for innovation and research across various domains, particularly in the field of data science, we introduced the Special Track on LLMs, which aimed to explore the transformative potential of LLMs for data science, bringing together researchers, practitioners, and industry experts to discuss the latest developments, challenges, and opportunities in this rapidly growing area.

This year's conference was highly competitive. The three tracks received 728 submissions with 552 to the Main Track, 39 to the Survey Track, and 137 to the Special Track on LLMs. The selection process was competitive, rigorous, and thorough, involving 532 PC and 206 Senior PC (SPC) members. Each submission was double-blindly reviewed by at least 3 reviewers with many receiving 4 or more reviews, followed by a discussion, and then further evaluated by a designated SPC member, the Track chairs, and the PC program co-chairs. The final selection considered multiple factors such as novelty, technical depth, experimental validation, and relevance to the conference. We accepted 139 papers in the Main Track, 12 in the Survey Track, and 33 in the LLM Track, thus having an acceptance rate of approximately 25% for the main conference. Following the practice of PAKDD 2025, in PAKDD 2026, considering the high quality of some of the rejected submissions, we decided to have a Special Session on Data Science – Foundations and Applications (DSFA), to which we recommended 125 of the original submissions. 281 of all submissions accepted to the main conference program

---

The original version of the book has been revised. A correction to this book can be found at https://doi.org/10.1007/978-981-92-1926-1_50

and to the DSFA Special Session were presented orally during the conference. We would like to thank the Chairs of the Survey Track (Elena Baralis and Guandong Xu) and the Chairs of the LLM Track (Carl Yang and Xiang Li), the SPC members, PC members, and external reviewers, together with the Chairs of the DSFA special session (Guansong Pang, Xuyun Zhang, and Xin Wang), for their invaluable efforts in ensuring a timely, fair, and highly effective paper review and selection procedure. We formed the PAKDD 2026 Best Paper Selection Committee, involving all PC co-chairs, all chairs of the Survey Track and the LLM Track and two new members, namely De-Nian Yang and Xintao Wu, for selecting the best paper award, the best student paper award, and the best survey paper award. Their diligence, dedication, and expertise helped produce the high-quality program for PAKDD 2026.

In addition to the exciting technical presentations, our program also featured five outstanding keynotes, a panel session, three award talks, the AI forum, ten high-quality tutorials, six workshops, and a doctoral consortium. We hope our PAKDD 2026 program provided a wonderful journey for researchers, users, practitioners, and developers.

June 2026

Raymond Chi-Wing Wong
Hanghang Tong
Hua Lu

Organization

Organizing Committee

General Chairs

James Kwok	Hong Kong University of Science and Technology, China
Flora Salim	University of New South Wales, Australia

Program Committee Chairs

Raymond Wong	Hong Kong University of Science and Technology, China
Hanghang Tong	University of Illinois Urbana-Champaign, USA
Hua Lu	Aalborg University, Denmark

Sponsorship Chairs

Yangqiu Song	Hong Kong University of Science and Technology, China
Amelia Jing Li	Hong Kong Polytechnic University, China
Wei Bi	Tencent AI Lab, China
Mi-Yen Yeh	Academia Sinica, Taiwan
Lu Hou	Huawei, China

Best Paper Selection Committee

Raymond Wong	Hong Kong University of Science and Technology, China
Hanghang Tong	University of Illinois Urbana-Champaign, USA
Hua Lu	Aalborg University, Denmark
Elena Baralis	Politecnico di Torino, Italy
Guandong Xu	Education University of Hong Kong, China
Carl Yang	Emory University, USA
Xiang Li	East China Normal University, China
De-Nian Yang	Institute of Information Science, Academia Sinica, Taiwan
Xintao Wu	University of Arkansas, USA

Local Arrangement Chairs

Hong Va Leong	Hong Kong Polytechnic University, China
Sibo Wang	Chinese University of Hong Kong, China

Industrial Track Chairs

Xiaoli Li	Agency for Science, Technology and Research, Singapore
Jason Zhang	Hong Kong Polytechnic University, China
James Cheng	Chinese University of Hong Kong, China

Survey/Vision Track Chairs

Elena Baralis	Politecnico di Torino, Italy
Guandong Xu	Education University of Hong Kong, China

Special Track on Large Language Models in Data Science Chairs

Carl Yang	Emory University, USA
Xiang Li	East China Normal University, China

Special Session on Data Science: Foundations and Applications (DSFA) Chairs

Guansong Pang	Singapore Management University, Singapore
Xuyun Zhang	Macquarie University, Australia
Xin Wang	University of Calgary, Canada

Tutorial Chairs

Jianliang Xu	Hong Kong Baptist University, China
Gao Cong	Nanyang Technological University, Singapore
Sinno Jialin Pan	Chinese University of Hong Kong, China

Workshop Chairs

Cheng Long	Nanyang Technological University, Singapore
Jieming Shi	Hong Kong Polytechnic University, China
Yuxuan Liang	Hong Kong University of Science and Technology (Guangzhou), China

Doctoral Consortium Chairs

Xiao Huang	Hong Kong Polytechnic University, China
Byron Choi	Hong Kong Baptist University, China

Publicity Chairs

Chen Ma	City University of Hong Kong, China
Yixiang Fang	Chinese University of Hong Kong (Shenzhen), China
Huiping Cao	New Mexico State University, USA

Financial Chairs

Xin Huang	Hong Kong Baptist University, China
Yuchen Li	Singapore Management University, Singapore

Proceedings Chairs

Yuanfeng Song	ByteDance, China
Man Lung Yiu	Hong Kong Polytechnic University, China

Web Masters

Wenqi Fan	Hong Kong Polytechnic University, China
Chenhao Ma	Chinese University of Hong Kong (Shenzhen), China

Registration Chairs

Haibo Hu	Hong Kong Polytechnic University, China
Harry Chan	University of Sheffield, UK

PAKDD Steering Committee

Chair

Longbing Cao	University of Technology Sydney, Australia

Vice Chair

Gill Dobbie	University of Auckland, New Zealand

Treasurer

Longbing Cao	University of Technology Sydney, Australia

Working Group

Longbing Cao (Chair)	University of Technology Sydney, Australia
Ming-Syan Chen (Senior Award Chair)	National Taiwan University, Taiwan
Gill Dobbie (Vice Chair and Treasurer)	University of Auckland, New Zealand
Hady W. Lauw (Diversity, Equity, and Inclusion Chair)	Singapore Management University, Singapore
Jaideep Srivastava (Strategy Chair)	University of Minnesota, USA
Raymond Chi-Wing Wong (Junior Award Chair)	Hong Kong University of Science and Technology, China
Min-Ling Zhang (Engagement Chair)	Southeast University, China

Members

Ramesh Agrawal	Jawaharlal Nehru University, India
Gill Dobbie	University of Auckland, New Zealand
Joao Gama	University of Porto, Portugal
Zhiguo Gong	University of Macau, China
Hisashi Kashima	Kyoto University, Japan
Hady W. Lauw	Singapore Management University, Singapore
Jae-Gil Lee	Korea Advanced Institute of Science & Technology, South Korea
Dinh Phung	Monash University, Australia
Kyuseok Shim	Seoul National University, South Korea
Geoff Webb	Monash University, Australia
Raymond Chi-Wing Wong	Hong Kong University of Science and Technology, China
De-Nian Yang	Institute of Information Science, Academia Sinica, Taiwan
Xintao Wu	University of Arkansas, USA

Life Members

Longbing Cao	University of Technology Sydney, Australia
Ming-Syan Chen	National Taiwan University, Taiwan
David Cheung	University of Hong Kong, China
Joshua Z. Huang	Shenzhen Institutes of Advanced Technology, Chinese Academy of Sciences, China
Masaru Kitsuregawa	Tokyo University, Japan
Rao Kotagiri	University of Melbourne, Australia
Ee-Peng Lim	Singapore Management University, Singapore
Huan Liu	Arizona State University, USA
Hiroshi Motoda	AFOSR/AOARD and Osaka University, Japan
Jian Pei	Simon Fraser University, Canada
P. Krishna Reddy	International Institute of Information Technology, Hyderabad, India
Jaideep Srivastava	University of Minnesota, USA
Thanaruk Theeramunkong	Thammasat University, Thailand
Tu-Bao Ho	Japan Advanced Institute of Science and Technology, Japan
Vincent S. Tseng	National Yang Ming Chiao Tung University, Taiwan
Takashi Washio	Osaka University, Japan
Kyu-Young Whang	Korea Advanced Institute of Science & Technology, South Korea
Graham Williams	Australian National University, Australia
Chengqi Zhang	University of Technology Sydney, Australia
Ning Zhong	Maebashi Institute of Technology, Japan
Zhi-Hua Zhou	Nanjing University, China

Past Members

Arbee L. P. Chen	Asia University, Taiwan
Hongjun Lu	Hong Kong University of Science and Technology, China
Takao Terano	Tokyo Institute of Technology, Japan

Senior Program Committee

Albert Bifet	Université Paris-Saclay, France
Amparo Alonso-Betanzos	University of A Coruña-CITIC, Spain
Anirban Dasgupta	IIT Gandhinagar, India

Arianna Dagliati	University of Pavia, Italy
Aris Anagnostopoulos	Sapienza University of Rome, Italy
Binbin Hu	Ant Group, China
Bo Han	Hong Kong Baptist University, China/RIKEN, Japan
Bo Yuan	University of Queensland, Australia
Branislav Kveton	Adobe Research, USA
Byung Suk Lee	University of Vermont, USA
Chang Tang	China University of Geosciences, Wuhan, China
Chang-Tien Lu	Virginia Tech, USA
Chao Chen	RMIT University, Australia
Chao Huang	University of Hong Kong, China
Chao Lan	University of Oklahoma, USA
Chen Gong	Nanjing University of Science and Technology, China
Chen Wang	Huazhong University of Science and Technology, China
Chen Zhao	Baylor University, USA
Cheng Wang	Amazon, USA
Chenhao Ma	Chinese University of Hong Kong (Shenzhen), China
Christan Grant	University of Florida, USA
Chuxu Zhang	University of Connecticut, USA
Da Yan	Indiana University Bloomington, USA
De-Nian Yang	Academia Sinica, Taiwan
Depeng Xu	University of North Carolina at Charlotte, USA
Di Jin	Tianjin University, China
Dongjin Song	University of Connecticut, USA
Dongxiao He	Tianjin University, China
Dongxiao Yu	Shandong University, China
Eirini Ntoutsi	University of the Bundeswehr Munich, Germany
Elio Masciari	University of Naples, Italy
Elisa Bertino	Purdue University, USA
Fabrizio Marozzo	Università della Calabria, Italy
Feiping Nie	Northwestern Polytechnical University, China
Feng Chen	University of Texas at Dallas, USA
Feng Xia	RMIT University, Australia
Fenglong Ma	Pennsylvania State University, USA
Fu-lai Chung	Hong Kong Polytechnic University, China
Gan Sun	South China University of Technology, China
Gang Li	Deakin Univeristy, Australia
Giancarlo Sperlì	University of Naples Federico II, Italy

Gianlorenzo D'Angelo	Gran Sasso Science Institute, Italy
Giovanni Montana	University of Warwick, UK
Grigorios Loukides	King's College London, UK
Guanfeng Liu	Macquarie University, Australia
Guansong Pang	Singapore Management University, Singapore
Guodong Long	University of Technology Sydney, Australia
Guo-Sen Xie	Nanjing University of Science and Technology, China
Hady W. Lauw	Singapore Management University, Singapore
Hai Lan	University of Queensland, Australia
Haipeng Dai	Nanjing University, China
Hamid Bouchachia	Bournemouth University, UK
Hao Liao	Shenzhen University, China
Hao Wang	Sichuan University, China
Hao Wang	Xidian University, China
Heitor M. Gomes	Victoria University of Wellington, New Zealand
Hengshu Zhu	Computer Network Information Center, Chinese Academy of Sciences, China
Hisashi Kashima	Kyoto University, Japan
Hongkai Xiong	Shanghai Jiao Tong University, China
Hongsheng Hu	University of Newcastle, Australia
Hongyan Liu	Tsinghua University, China
Hongzhi Yin	University of Queensland, Australia
Hua Wei	Arizona State University, USA
Huaming Du	Southwestern University of Finance and Economics, China
Huawen Liu	Shaoxing University, China
Hung-Yu Kao	National Cheng Kung University, Taiwan
Ioanna Miliou	Stockholm University, Sweden
Jae-Gil Lee	KAIST, South Korea
James Jianqiao Yu	Harbin Institute of Technology, China
Jeffrey Chan	RMIT University, Australia
Jerry Chun-Wei Lin	Silesian University of Technology, Poland
Jian Kang	Mohamed bin Zayed University of Artificial Intelligence, United Arab Emirates
Jiangchao Yao	Shanghai Jiao Tong University, China
Jianxin Li	Beihang University, China
Jiapu Wang	Hefei University of Technology, China
Jiaying Lu	Emory Univesity, USA
Jicong Fan	Chinese University of Hong Kong (Shenzhen), China
Jie Shao	University of Electronic Science and Technology of China, China

Jie Wen	Harbin Institute of Technology, China
Jie Yin	University of Sydney, Australia
Jing Jiang	University of Technology Sydney, Australia
Jingrui He	University of Illinois Urbana-Champaign, USA
Jinyu Tian	Macau University of Science and Technology, China
Johannes Fürnkranz	Johannes Kepler University Linz, Austria
Jose Machado	University of Minho, Portugal
Jose M. Alvarez	NVIDIA, USA
Jun Wang	Shandong University, China
Junbo Zhang	JD Intelligent Cities Research, China
Junchi Yan	Shanghai Jiao Tong University, China
Jundong Li	University of Virginia, USA
Kai Shu	Emory University, USA
Kaiqi Zhao	Harbin Institute of Technology (Shenzhen), China
Kamalakar Karlapalem	IIIT Hyderabad, India
Ke Liang	National University of Defense Technology, China
P. Krishna Reddy	IIIT Hyderabad, India
Kui Yu	Hefei University of Technology, China
Kunpeng Liu	Portland State University, USA
Laizhong Cui	Shenzhen University, China
Lan-Zhe Guo	Nanjing University, China
Leandro Minku	University of Birmingham, UK
Lei Zou	Peking University, China
Leopoldo Bertossi	Carleton University, Canada
Lianhua Chi	La Trobe University, Australia
Lianyong Qi	China University of Petroleum (East China), China
Lili Su	Northeastern University, USA
Lin Li	Wuhan University of Technology, China
Lina Yao	University of New South Wales, Australia
Lisi Chen	University of Electronic Science and Technology of China, China
Longbing Cao	Macquarie University, Australia
Luca Romeo	University of Macerata, Italy
Ludovico Boratto	University of Cagliari, Italy
Mahardhika Pratama	University of South Australia, Australia
Masashi Sugiyama	RIKEN/University of Tokyo, Japan
Meikang Qiu	Augusta University, USA
Meng Jiang	University of Notre Dame, USA
Miao Xu	University of Queensland, Australia

Ming Li	Nanjing University, China
Mingbo Zhao	Donghua University, China
Mingming Gong	University of Melbourne, Australia
Min-Ling Zhang	Southeast University, China
Mirco Nanni	CNR-ISTI Pisa, Italy
Mi-Yen Yeh	Academia Sinica, Taiwan
Muhammad Aamir Cheema	Monash University, Australia
Nan Ye	University of Queensland, Australia
Neil Shah	Snap Inc., USA
Nizar Bouguila	Concordia University, Canada
Noseong Park	KAIST, South Korea
Panagiotis Papapetrou	Stockholm University, Sweden
Pang-Ning Tan	Michigan State University, USA
Paul Honeine	University of Rouen Normandy, France
Paulo Cortez	University of Minho, Portugal
Pengpeng Zhao	Soochow University, China
Qi Yu	Rochester Institute of Technology, USA
Qiang Cheng	University of Kentucky, USA
Qinghua Hu	Tianjin University, China
Quanming Yao	Tsinghua, China
Rajeev Raman	University of Leicester, UK
Rajiv Khanna	Purdue University, USA
Ranga Raju Vatsavai	North Carolina State University, USA
Ricardo J. G. B. Campello	University of Southern Denmark, Denmark
Riccardo Guidotti	University of Pisa, Italy
Sang-Wook Kim	Hanyang University, South Korea
Sen Wang	University of Queensland, Australia
Shirui Pan	Griffith University, Australia
Shui Yu	University of Technology Sydney, Australia
Shuo Wang	Shanghai Jiao Tong University, China
Siyu Huang	Clemson University, USA
Slawomir Nowaczyk	Halmstad University, Sweden
Suhang Wang	Pennsylvania State University, USA
Sung-Bae Cho	Yonsei University, South Korea
Tingting Wang	RMIT University, Australia
Tong Chen	University of Queensland, Australia
Tru Hoang Cao	UTHealth, USA
Tsuyoshi Ide	IBM Research, T. J. Watson Research Center, USA
Tzung-Pei Hong	National University of Kaohsiung, Taiwan
Uday Kiran Rage	University of Aizu, Japan
Wei Fan	University of Oxford, UK

Wei Ju	Sichuan University, China
Wei Emma Zhang	University of Adelaide, Australia
Weiqing Wang	Monash University, Australia
Wei-Shinn Ku	Auburn University, USA
Wenbin Zhang	Florida International University, USA
Wenqi Fan	Hong Kong Polytechnic University, China
Wenqing Lin	Tencent, China
Xia Ning	Ohio State University, USA
Xiang Deng	Harbin Institute of Technology (Shenzhen), China
Xiangyu Zhao	City University of Hong Kong, China
Xiao Huang	Hong Kong Polytechnic University, China
Xiaoning Liu	RMIT University, Australia
Xiaowei Jia	University of Pittsburgh, USA
Xin Cao	University of New South Wales, Australia
Xindong Wu	Hefei University of Technology, China
Xintao Wu	University of Arkansas, USA
Xun Zhou	Harbin Institute of Technology (Shenzhen), China
Xuyun Zhang	Macquarie University, Australia
Yanchang Zhao	CSIRO, Australia
Yanchao Tan	Fuzhou University, China
Yang Cao	Institute of Science Tokyo, Japan
Yibing Zhan	JD Explore Academy, China
Yinbin Miao	Xidian University, China
Ying Li	AwanTunai, Indonesia
Yingxia Shao	Beijing University of Posts and Telecommunications, China
Yipeng Zhou	Macquarie University, Australia
Yiqun Xie	University of Maryland, USA
Yongkai Wu	Clemson University, USA
Yu Zhang	Southern University of Science and Technology, China
Yuan Luo	Northwestern University, USA
Yue Xu	Queensland University of Technology, Australia
Yufei Han	Inria, France
Yu-Feng Li	Nanjing University, China
Yunjun Gao	Zhejiang University, China
Yunlong Yu	Zhejiang University, China
Yunyun Wang	Nanjing University of Posts and Telecommunications, China
Yuxuan Liang	Hong Kong University of Science and Technology (Guangzhou), China

Zhao Kang	University of Electronic Science and Technology of China, China
Zheng Wang	University of Leeds, UK
Zhengming Ding	Tulane University, USA
Zhengzhang Chen	NEC Laboratories America, USA
Zhong Ji	Tianjin University, China
Zhongfei Zhang	Binghamton University, USA
Zimu Zhou	City University of Hong Kong, China
Ziwei Zhu	George Mason University, USA
Ziyu Jia	Chinese Academy of Sciences, China

Program Committee

Abdur Rehman Khan	Queensland University of Technology, Australia
Abheek Dhingra	University of the Bundeswehr Munich, Germany
Akhlaque Ahmad	Indiana University Bloomington, USA
Akihiro Yamaguchi	Toshiba Corporation; Kyushu University, Japan
Akira Sakai	Fujitsu Laboratories Ltd., Japan
Alex Memory	Johns Hopkins University Applied Physics Laboratory, USA
Alfredo Cuzzocrea	University of Calabria, Italy
Amir Gandomi	University of Technology, Sydney, Australia
Andrzej Skowron	University of Warsaw, Poland
Ankit Sharma	University of Minnesota, USA
Anne Denton	North Dakota State University, USA
Antonela Tommasel	ISISTAN, CONICET-UNICEN, Argentina
Anushka Vidanage	Australian National University, Australia
Arindam Pal	TechSoftX, Australia
Aris Gkoulalas-Divanis	Merative, USA
Arnab Sharma	Paderborn University, Germany
Aryya Gangopadhyay	University of Maryland, Baltimore County, USA
Ashwin Viswanathan Kannan	Amazon, USA
Ashwini Kodipalli	RV University, India
Atsuhiro Takasu	National Institute of Informatics, Japan
Augusto A. Santos	Instituto de Telecomunicações, Portugal
Bang An	University of Akron, USA
Baodi Liu	China University of Petroleum (East China), China
Beibei Li	Chongqing University, China
Bijay Prasad Jaysawal	University of Southampton, UK
Bijaya Adhikari	University of Iowa, USA

Binbin Zhou	Hangzhou City University, China
Bingqiao Luo	National University of Singapore, Singapore
Bi-Ru Dai	National Taiwan University of Science and Technology, Taiwan
Bo Jin	Dalian University of Technology, China
Bo Peng	Ohio State University, USA
Boqi Li	Wuhan University, China
Bozhen Hu	Zhejiang University and Westlake University, China
Bradley Malin	Vanderbilt University Medical Center, USA
Brendon J. Woodford	University of Otago, New Zealand
Bruno Veloso	INESC TEC and FEP, Portugal
Buyue Qian	Xi'an Jiaotong University, China
Canyu Chen	Illinois Institute of Technology, USA
Carson K. Leung	University of Manitoba, Canada
Chandra Mohan Dasari	Indian Institute of Information Technology, Design and Manufacturing, Kurnool, India
Chandrasekar Ramachandran	Carnegie Mellon University, USA
Chang Ge	University of Minnesota, USA
Chaobo He	South China Normal University, China
Chaoran Cui	Shandong University of Finance and Economics, China
Chaoxiang He	Shanghai Jiao Tong University, China
Chen Zhao	Baylor University, USA
Chen-Chen Zong	Nanjing University of Aeronautics and Astronautics, China
Cheng Long	Nanyang Technological University, Singapore
Cheng-Wei Wu	National Ilan University, Taiwan
Chengyang Ying	Tsinghua University, China
Chengyuan Zhang	Hunan University, China
Chih-Chieh Hung	National Chung Hsing University, Taiwan
Chih-Hua Tai	National Taipei University, Taiwan
Chih-Ya Shen	National Tsing Hua University, Taiwan
Chihyun Park	Kangwon National University, South Korea
Chong Zhang	Hunan University, China
Chotirat Ann Ratanamahatana	Chulalongkorn University, Thailand
Chowdhury Farhan Ahmed	University of Dhaka, Bangladesh
Chuan-Wei Kuo	National Yang Ming Chiao Tung University, Taiwan
Chul-Ho Lee	Texas State University, USA
Chunchun Chen	Tongji University, China
Cristiano Landi	University of Pisa, Italy

Dai Hai Nguyen	Hokkaido University, Japan
Dalin Zhang	Hangzhou Dianzi University, China
Dan Simovici	University of Massachusetts Boston, USA
Daokun Zhang	Monash University, Australia
De-Chuan Zhan	Nanjing University, China
Deguang Kong	Yahoo Research, USA
Delvin Ce Zhang	Singapore Management University, Singapore
Derui Lyu	University of Science and Technology of China, China
Dharmalingam Muthusamy	Bharathiar University, India
Dong Li	Baylor University, USA
Dong-Dong Wu	University of Tokyo, Japan
Dongqi Fu	Meta, USA
Dongyuan Li	Tokyo Institute of Technology, Japan
Dugang Liu	Shenzhen University, China
Edouard Fouché	Karlsruhe Institute of Technology, Germany
Eduardo Ogasawara	Federal Center for Technological Education of Rio de Janeiro, Brazil
Ekta Gujral	University of California, Riverside, USA
Eliana Pastor	Politecnico di Torino, Italy
Enea Vincenzo Napolitano	University of Naples Federico II, Italy
Erhu He	University of Pittsburgh, USA
Esra Akbas	Georgia State University, USA
Fali Wang	Penn State University, USA
Fan Wu	Central South University, China
Fanglan Chen	Virginia Tech, USA
Fei Zhao	University of Alabama at Birmingham, USA
Felipe R. Azúa	University of Edinburgh, UK
Feng Xiao	Chinese University of Hong Kong (Shenzhen), China
Fengxin Li	Renmin University of China
Florent Masseglia	Inria, France
Francesco Marcelloni	University of Pisa, Italy
Francesco Spinnato	University of Pisa, Italy
Fuqiang Yu	Qilu University of Technology, China
Fuyuan Cao	Shanxi University, China
Giovanna Nicora	University of Pavia, Italy
Giuseppe Albi	University of Pavia, Italy
Guangyan Huang	Deakin University, Australia
Guimu Guo	Rowan University, USA
Guixian Zhang	China University of Mining and Technology, China

Guodu Xiang	Hefei University of Technology, China
Guoyin Wang	Chongqing University of Posts and Telecommunications, China
Guozhong Li	King Abdullah University of Science and Technology, Saudi Arabia
Hadi Talal Jaafar	University of Birmingham, UK
Haidong Kang	Northeastern University, China
Haifang Li	Baidu Inc., China
Hailiang Zhao	Zhejiang Univerisity, China
Haiquan Chen	California State University, Sacramento, USA
Hanchen Wang	University of New South Wales, Australia
Hang Yu	Shanghai University, China
Hao Xue	University of New South Wales, Australia
Hao Zhen	University of Georgia, USA
Hao Zheng	Central South University, China
Haomin Yu	Aalborg University, Denmark
Haoran Duan	Wuhan University, China
Haoran Luo	Nanyang Technological University, Singapore
He Kong	Jilin University, China
He Li	Xidian University, China
Heitor M. Gomes	Victoria University of Wellington, New Zealand
Hezhe Qiao	Singapore Managment University, Singapore
Hoang H. Nguyen	University of Tennessee at Chattanooga, USA
Hongchao Qin	Beijing Institute of Technology, China
Hongliang Zhang	Nanjing University of Science and Technology, China
Hongtao Wang	North China Electric Power University, China
Hongzu Su	University of Electronic Science and Technology of China, China
Huaiyuan Yao	Arizona State University, USA
Huan Li	Zhejiang University, China
Huan Wang	University of Wollongong, Australia
Huan Zhang	Zhengzhou University, China
Huaxiang Zhang	Shandong Normal University, China
Hui Fang	Shanghai University of Finance and Economics, China
Huifang Ma	Northwest Normal University, China
Huiping Cao	New Mexico State University, USA
Huizhong Wang	Chinese University of Hong Kong (Shenzhen), China
Ickjai Lee	James Cook University, Australia, Australia
Jae Oh Woo	Samsung SDS America, USA

Kunpeng Xu	University of Sherbrooke, Canada
Kun-Ta Chuang	National Cheng Kung University, Taiwan
Kun-Yang Yu	Nanjing University, China
Lam Ngo	RMIT University, Australia
Lecheng Zheng	Virginia Tech, USA
Lei Chen	Tsinghua University, China
Lei Duan	Sichuan University, China
Lei Gu	Nanjing University of Posts and Telecommunications, China
Lei Li	Hong Kong University of Science and Technology (Guangzhou), China
Lei Zhang	Nanjing Normal University, China
Li Hu	Hong Kong Polytechnic University, China
Li Tang	Yunnan University, China
Liang Hong	Wuhan University, China
Liang Li	National University of Defense Technology, China
Liang Qu	Edith Cowan University, Australia
Libin Wang	Northwestern Polytechnical University, China
Lihui Liu	Wayne State University, USA
Lijing Wang	New Jersey Institute of Technology, USA
Likang Wu	University of Science and Technology of China, China
Lin Zhang	IDEA.EDU, USA
Ling Ding	Tianjin University, China
Ling Zheng	Fujian Provincial Maternity and Children's Hospital, China
Lingwei Chen	Rochester Institute of Technology, USA
Lingyang Chu	McMaster University, Canada
Liu Xichao	Yunnan University, China
Liwei Deng	Aalborg University, Denmark
Lizhong Ding	Beijing Institute of Technology, China
Lo Pang-Yun Ting	National Cheng Kung University, Taiwan
Longxu Sun	Hong Kong Baptist University, China
Lu Jiang	Dalian Maritime University, China
Luca Cagliero	Politecnico di Torino, Italy
Lujun Li	Hong Kong University of Science and Technology, China
Lulwah AlKulaib	Kuwait University, Kuwait
Luyuan Yang	University of Oklahoma, USA
Luzhi Wang	Dalian Maritime University, China
Lyu Xu	Nanyang Technological University, Singapore

Lyuheng Yuan	Indiana University Bloomington, USA
Maciej Grzenda	Warsaw University of Technology, Poland
Mandar Chaudhary	eBay, USA
Man-Sheng Chen	Sun Yat-sen University, China
Maolin Wang	City University of Hong Kong, China
Marc Plantevit	EPITA, France
Marcellin M Atemkeng Teufack	Rhodes University, China
Maria Luisa Sapino	Università di Torino, Italy
Marzena Kryszkiewicz	Warsaw University of Technology, Poland
Masahiro Nakano	NTT Communication Science Laboratories, Japan
Matej Mihelčić	University of Zagreb, Croatia
Matjaž Gams	Jožef Stefan Institute, Slovenia
Melike Yildiz Aktas	Virginia Tech, USA
Meng Wang	Tongji University, China
Mengdi Huai	Iowa Sate University, USA
Menghan Wang	eBay, USA
Miao Hu	University of Southampton, UK
Miguel Rodriguez	Google, USA
Milos Radovanovic	University of Novi Sad, Serbia
Milos Savic	University of Novi Sad, Serbia
Min Gao	Chongqing University, China
Ming Yang	Nanjing University, China
Minglai Shao	Tianjin University, China
Minglong Lei	Beijing University of Technology, China
Mingyu Yang	Hong Kong University of Science and Technology (Guangzhou), China
Mingyue Cheng	University of Science and Technology of China, China
Mingzhong Wang	University of the Sunshine Coast, China
Minh-Hao Van	University of Arkansas, USA
Minhua Lin	Pennsylvania State University, USA
Min-Te Sun	National Central University, Taiwan
Mohamad El-Hajj	MacEwan University, Canada
Mohammad M. Masud	United Arab Emirates University, United Arab Emirates
Morteza Saberi	University of Technology Sydney, Australia
Moshe Eliasof	University of Cambridge, UK
Mrinal Das	IIT Palakkad, India
Muhammad Abulaish	South Asian University, India
Muhammad Daffa Robani	AwanTunai, Indonesia
Nannan Wu	Tianjin University, China
Nassim Belmecheri	Simula Research Laboratory, Norway

Nathan S. Gavenski	King's College London, UK
Nian Liu	National University of Singapore, Singapore
Ning Liu	Shandong University, China
Ou Wu	Tianjin University, China
P. Radha Krishna	National Institute of Technology, Warangal, India
Panagiotis Liakos	Athens University of Economics and Business, Greece
Paolo Garza	Politecnico di Torino, Italy
Pedro G. Ferreira	University of Porto, Portugal
Peer Kröger	Christian Albrechts University Kiel, Germany
Peiliang Zhang	Wuhan University of Technology, China
Peng Li	Dalian University of Technology, China
Peng Qian	Zhejiang University, China
Pengfei He	University of Washington, USA
Pengpeng Zhao	Soochow University, China
Pengyang Wang	University of Macau, China
Pinhan Fu	Shanxi University, China
Pranjal Shankhdhar	Meta Platforms, USA
Praveen Kumar Donta	Stockholm University, Sweden
Primoz Kocbek	University of Maribor, Slovenia
Purushottam Panta	University of Kentucky, USA
Qian Li	Curtin University, Australia
Qian Sun	Hong Kong University of Science and Technology, China
Qiang Gao	Southwestern University of Finance and Economics, China
Qiang Tang	Luxembourg Institute of Science and Technology, Luxembourg
Qiange Wang	National University of Singapore, Singapore
Qianying Ren	University of Connecticut, USA
Qiao Xue	Nanjing University of Aeronautics and Astronautics, China
Qiheng Sun	Hong Kong Polytechnic University, China
Qing Liao	Harbin Institute of Technology (Shenzhen), Singapore
Qing Liu	Zhejiang University, China
Qing Tian	Nanjing University of Information Science and Technology, Singapore
Qingxiang Liu	Chinese Academy of Sciences, China
Qiqi Wang	Nankai University, China
Qisen Cheng	Samsung Display America Lab, USA
Qixu Gong	New Mexico State University, USA
Qizhou Wang	Monash University, Australia

Quangui Zhang	Liaoning Technical University, China
Qun Liu	Louisiana State University, USA
Rajatsubhra Chakraborty	University of North Carolina at Charlotte, USA
Ravi Chhabra	Nvidia, USA
Renchi Yang	Hong Kong Baptist University, China
Renqiang Luo	Jilin University, China
Robert J. Churchill	Georgetown University, USA
Rong Du	Taiyuan University of Technology, China
Rosalba Giugno	University of Verona, Italy
Ru Wang	Shandong Normal University, China
Ruiqi Zheng	University of Queensland, Australia
Ruliang Xiao	Fujian Normal University, China
Rundong Zuo	Hong Kong Baptist University, China
Runlong Yu	University of Alabama, USA
Sadok Ben Yahia	Southern Denmark University, Denmark
Senzhang Wang	Central South University, China
Shafiq Alam	Massey University Auckland, New Zealand
Shangqing Zhao	University of Oklahoma, Oklahoma
Shao-Yuan Li	Nanjing University of Aeronautics and Astronautics, China
Shengchao Chen	University of Technology Sydney, Australia
Shengda Zhuo	Jinan University, China
Shengkun Wang	Virginia Tech, USA
Shen-Shyang Ho	Rowan University, USA
Shichao Zhang	Central South University, China
Shifei Ding	China University of Mining and Technology, China
Shiyu Yang	Guangzhou University, China
Shi-Yu Tian	Nanjing University, China
Shridhar B Devamane	Amrita Vishwa Vidyapeetham, India
Shu Wang	Chinese University of Hong Kong (Shenzhen), China
Shuai Li	University of Cambridge, UK
Shubham Jain	Visa Research, USA
Shuichi Miyazawa	Graduate University for Advanced Studies, Japan
Shuo Li	Guangxi University, China
Shuo Yu	Dalian University of Technology, China
Siddhartha Bhattacharyya	University of Illinois Chicago, USA
Simone Monaco	Politecnico di Torino, Italy
Siqi Liang	Amazon, USA
Siqing Li	Unversity of New South Wales, Australia

Siru Zhong	Hong Kong University of Science and Technology (Guangzhou), China
Siyang Liu	Nanjing University, China
Song Wu	Aalborg University, Denmark
Sungsu Lim	Chungnam National University, South Korea
Tadashi Nomoto	National Institute of Japanese Literature, Japan
Tai Le Quy	University of Koblenz, Germany
Tao Chen	China University of Geosciences, Wuhan, China
Tao Meng	Central South University of Forestry and Technology, China
Tao Wang	University of Chinese Academy of Sciences, China
Tetsuya Yoshida	Nara Women's University, Japan
Thi Huyen Nguyen	L3S Research Center, Germany
Thilina N Ranbaduge	Australian National University, Australia
Tianrui Li	Southwest Jiaotong University, China
Tiantian Liu	Aalborg University, Denmark
Tianyi Li	Aalborg University, Denmark
Tiejin Chen	Arizona State University, USA
Tim Oates	University of Maryland, Baltimore County, USA
Tong Chen	University of Queensland, Australia
Trung-Hoang Le	Nanyang Technological University, Singapore
Tsunenori Mine	Kyushu University, Japan
Tuan Le	New Mexico State University, USA
Tung Kieu	Aalborg University, Denmark
Vahid Taslimitehrani	PhysioSigns Inc., USA
Vana Kalogeraki	Athens University of Economics and Business, Greece
Wanfu Gao	Jilin University, China
Wang Lizhen	Yunnan University, China
Waqas Jamil	Bournemouth University, UK
Wei Chen	Beihang University, China
Wei Wang	Fudan University, China
Wei Ye	Tongji University, China
Wei Emma Zhang	University of Adelaide, Australia
Weifeng Liu	China University of Petroleum, China
Weiwei Jiang	Beijing University of Posts and Telecommunications, China
Wenbo Shang	Hong Kong Baptist University, China
Wen-Chao Hu	Nanjing University, China
Wenda Zhang	Walmart Inc., USA
Wengen Li	Tongji University, China

Wenjian Xu	Zhejiang University of Science and Technology, China
Wenjie Xi	George Mason University, USA
Wenke Du	Cornell University, USA
Wenlu Wang	Texas A&M University-Corpus Christi, USA
Wensheng Luo	Hunan University, China
Wensheng Wu	University of Southern California, USA
Wentao Fan	Nanjing University, China
Wentao Li	University of Leicester, UK
William Hsu	Kansas State University, USA
Xi Chen	Soochow University, China
Xiang Lian	Kent State University, USA
Xiangmin Zhou	RMIT University, Australia
Xiangyang Gou	University of New South Wales, Australia
Xiao Cheng	University of New South Wales, Australia
Xiaobo Zhang	Southwest Jiaotong University, China
Xiaocao Ouyang	Southwestern University of Finance and Economics, China
Xiaoguang Guo	University of Connecticut, USA
Xiaohui Chen	Baylor University, USA
Xiaojuan Cheng	Deakin University, Australia
Xiaoou Liu	Arizona State University, USA
Xiaoping Zhou	Beijing University of Civil Engineering and Architecture, China
Xiaoshan Yu	Anhui University, China
Xiaoyang Li	Adelaide University, Australia
Xiaoyang Wang	University of New South Wales, Australia
Xiaoyu Ding	University of Technology Sydney, Australia
Xin Li	Macquarie University, Australia
Xin Luo	Shandong University, China
Xin Peng	National University of Defense Technology, China
Xin Sun	City University of Macau, China
Xin Wang	University of Calgary, Canada
Xin Zheng	RMIT University, Australia
Xing Xing	Tongji University, China
Xingbo Fu	University of Virginia, USA
Xinghao Yang	China University of Petroleum (East China), China
Xinguo Feng	University of Queensland, Australia
Xingyu Zhao	Nanjing University of Aeronautics and Astronautics, China

Xinyu Su	University of Melbourne, Australia
Xinyu Wu	Baylor University, USA
Xinyue Sun	Harbin Institute of Technology, China
Xiuling Wang	Stevens Institute of Technology, USA
Xiwen Chen	Clemson University, USA
Xu Zhang	Macquarie University, Australia
Xuliang Zhu	Shanghai Jiao Tong University, China
Xuyun Zhang	Macquarie University, Australia
Yan Cao	University of Texas at Dallas, USA
Yan Ru Pei	NVIDIA, USA
Yanchao Liu	Communication University of China, China
Yanchao Tan	Fuzhou University, China
Yang Cao	Great Bay University/Tsinghua University, China
Yang-Sae Moon	Kangwon National University, South Korea
Yanhao Wang	East China Normal University, China
Yanwei Yu	Ocean University of China, China
Yaqian Zhang	University of Waikato, New Zealand
Yi Zhang	University of Queensland, Australia
Yibing Zhan	JD Explore Academy, China
Yifan Wang	University of Hawaii, USA
Yifeng Gao	University of Texas Rio Grande Valley, USA
Yi-Hui Chen	Chang Gung University, Taiwan
Yijun Lin	University of Minnesota, USA
Yimin Wen	Wuyi University, China
Yiming Tang	Hefei University of Technology, China
Yin Xian	Hong Kong Baptist University, China
Yingjie Wang	Nanyang Technological University, Singapore
Yingli Zhou	Chinese University of Hong Kong (Shenzhen), China
Yiran Li	University of Toronto, Canada
Yi-Shin Chen	National Tsing Hua University, Taiwan
Yixin Liu	Monash University, Australia
Yongcan Huang	University of Georgia, USA
Yongjie Wang	Nanyang Technological University, Singapore
Yongjing Hao	Suzhou University of Science and Technology, China
Yongmin Yoo	Macquarie University, Australia
Yongpan Sheng	Southwest University, China
Yongyu Wang	Michigan Technological University, USA
Yu Li	Hangzhou Dianzi University, China
Yu Liu	Beijing Jiaotong University, China
Yuanbo Xu	Jilin University, China

Zhichun Guo	University of Washington, USA
Zhiguo Gong	University of Macau, China
Zhiwei Liu	University of Illinois Chicago, USA
Zhiwei Zhang	Pennsylvania State University, USA
Zhiwen Xiao	Southwest Jiaotong University, China
Zhiyu Chen	Chinese University of Hong Kong (Shenzhen), China
Zhong Chen	Southern Illinois University, USA
Zhongkui Ma	University of Queensland, Australia
Zhun Zhou	MobiusVision, USA
Zhuo Huang	University of Sydney, Australia
Zichong Li	Rensselaer Polytechnic Institute, USA
Zihan Feng	Hong Kong Baptist University, China
Zi-Jian Cheng	Nanjing University, China
Zijie Pan	University of Connecticut, USA
Ziming Li	University of Connecticut, USA
Ziwen Wang	Anhui University, China
Ziyan Wang	Georgia Institute of Technology, USA
Ziye Zhu	Nanjing University of Posts and Telecommunications, China
Ziyue Li	University of Cologne, Germany
Zong Ke	National University of Singapore, Singapore
Zongqian Wu	University of Electronic Science and Technology of China, China

External Reviewers

Abdul Wahid	IIIT Dharwad, India
Adam Pazdor	University of Manitoba, Canada
Akhlaque Ahmad	Indiana University Bloomington, USA
Alessio Cascione	University of Pisa, Italy
Baha Rababah	University of Manitoba, Canada
Baobao Song	University of Technology Sydney, Australia
Binhao Wang	City Univerisity of Hong Kong, China
Blaise Delattre	Institute of Science Tokyo, Japan
Boris Sedlak	Universitat Pompeu Fabra, Spain
Cássio Prazeres	Federal University of Bahia (UFBA), Brazil
Chao Yan	Vanderbilt University Medical Center, USA
Chaudhary Muhammad Shaheer Yasir	Rowan University, USA
Chunyang Li	Xidian University, China

Congning Ni	Vanderbilt University Medical Center, USA
Cristiano Mesquita Garcia	Instituto Federal de Santa Catarina, Brazil
Dazhi Fu	Chinese University of Hong Kong (Shenzhen), China
Enea Vincenzo Napolitano	University of Naples Federico II, Italy
Eric Inae	University of Notre Dame, USA
Fangwei Ye	Nanjing University of Aeronautics and Astronautics, China
Feng Xiao	Chinese University of Hong Kong (Shenzhen), China
Fuhong Song	Guizhou University of Finance and Economics, China
Gözde Tataroglu Özbulak	University of Lausanne, Switzerland
Hadi Al-Kadhimi	University of Birmingham, UK
Hao Yuan	Northeastern University, China
Hoang Hai Nguyen	University of Manitoba, Canada
Huan Wang	University of Wollongong, Australia
Huy-Son Nguyen	TU Delft, Netherlands
Hy Dang	University of Notre Dame, USA
Ichsan Budiman	University of Birmingham, UK
Jaime Hieu Do	Singapore Management University, Singapore
Jianzhe Li	East China Normal University, China
Jiaqi Zhao	China University of Mining and Technology, China
Kan Guo	Beijing University of Technology, China
Kexin Meng	Zhengzhou University, China
Liqun Deng	China University of Petroleum (East China), China
Lorenzo Peracchio	University of Pavia, Italy
Lorenzo Corso	University of Pavia, Italy
Ludovico Ferreri	University of Pavia, Italy
Lyuheng Yuan	Indiana University Bloomington, USA
Manuel Tognon	Verona University, Italy
Marco De Luca	Politecnico di Torino, Italy
Matteo Berta	Politecnico di Torino, Italy
Miguel Rodriguez	Google, USA
Mong Yuan Sim	Adelaide University, Australia
Moshe Eliasof	University of Cambridge, UK
Nan Zhang	East China Normal University, China
Padipat Sitkrongwong	National Institute of Informatics, Japan
Paolo Garza	Politecnico di Torino, Italy
Peiliang Zhang	Wuhan University of Technology, China

Pengpeng Qiao	Institute of Science Tokyo, Japan
Qi Wen	East China Normal University, China
Qing Tian	Nanjing University of Information Science and Technology, China
Qingyuan Song	Vanderbilt University, USA
Quanjiang Guo	University of Electronic Science and Technology of China, China
Renxuan Hou	Hong Kong Polytechnic University, China
Ritabrata Chakraborty	Manipal University Jaipur, India
Ruimin Dai	Clemson University, USA
Saranya Maneeroj	Chulalongkorn University, Thailand
Show-Jane Yen	Ming Chuan University, Taiwan
Siqing Li	University of New South Wales, Australia
Tingzheng Jia	Beijing University of Technology, China
Tung Doan	Hanoi University of Science and Technology, Vietnam
Vyshnavi Gutta	Georgia Institute of Technology, USA
Wajid Manzoor	Rowan University, USA
Weixin Liu	Vanderbilt University, USA
Wengang Guo	Tongji University, China
Wenke Du	Cornell University, USA
Xiaoyang Li	Adelaide University, Australia
Xin Ai	Northeastern University, China
Xuanting Xie	University of Electronic Science and Technology of China, China
Yanwei Xu	Peking University, China
Yijun Lin	University of Minnesota, USA
Ying Li	Northeastern University, China
Yiyang Zhang	East China Normal University, China
Yongmin Yoo	Macquarie University, Australia
Yue Deng	Michigan State University, USA
Yuhong Dai	Shenzhen University, China
Yunhe Feng	University of North Texas, USA
Yushan Jiang	University of Connecticut, USA
Yutong Ye	Beihang University, China
Zhen Wu	East China Normal University, China
Zhiyu Chen	Chinese University of Hong Kong (Shenzhen), China
Zifeng Zhou	Jinan University, China

Sponsors

Exclusive Diamond Sponsor

王寬誠教育基金會
K. C. WONG EDUCATION FOUNDATION

Gold Sponsors

香港科技大學
THE HONG KONG UNIVERSITY OF SCIENCE AND TECHNOLOGY

AsianArk

Silver Sponsor

THE HONG KONG POLYTECHNIC UNIVERSITY
香港理工大學

Bronze Sponsors

香港浸會大學
HONG KONG BAPTIST UNIVERSITY

香港教育大學
The Education University of Hong Kong

香港中文大學（深圳）
The Chinese University of Hong Kong, Shenzhen

Publication

Springer

Contents

Main and LLM Track

Main and LLM Track

EUR-GAN: Enhanced URes-Net Generative Adversarial Network for CT Image Super-resolution

Yubin Wei[1,2], Xiao Yu[1,3], and Jinting Guan[1,2](✉)

[1] Department of Automation, Xiamen University, Xiamen, Fujian, China
jtguan@xmu.edu.cn

[2] Key Laboratory of System Control and Information Processing, Ministry of Education, Shanghai, China

[3] Institute of Artificial Intelligence, Xiamen University, Xiamen, Fujian, China

Abstract. Deep learning-based image super-resolution methods have achieved certain successes, while when being applied to computed tomography (CT) medical images, they still encounter problems including blurry imaging, loss of high-frequency information, and unclear edge details. We propose EUR-GAN (Enhanced URes-Net Generative Adversarial Network), an innovative GAN model for CT image super-resolution. In the generator of EUR-GAN model, we integrate the ResNet152 network with the encoder structure of U-Net network, forming a dual-branch structure termed URes-Net. This integration effectively addresses issues related to gradient vanishing and long-range information learning. Furthermore, a residual block and self-attention mechanism are incorporated with URes-Net module to better preserve global information and local texture details in CT images. Compared with various existing methods, EUR-GAN demonstrates outstanding high-resolution reconstruction performance across various organs and scaling levels. It emerges as a reliable deep learning model for medical image super-resolution, facilitating the diagnosis, screening and monitoring processes in clinical practice.

Keywords: Super-resolution · CT image · EUR-GAN · URes-Net · GAN

1 Introduction

Medical imaging technology, especially computed tomography (CT) imaging, plays a crucial role in modern medicine. With the continuous advancement of CT technology, its clinical benefits in disease diagnosis and treatment planning have significantly improved, allowing physicians to better understand the internal structures and abnormalities of patients' bodies with greater precision. However, in practice, due to various factors such as the constraints of acquisition equipment and environment, network transmission media and bandwidth, and the inherent degradation models of images, we often cannot directly obtain ideal high-resolution CT images with clear edges and no chunky blurring. The balance between image resolution and radiation dose remains a major challenge in the field of CT imaging.

R. C.-W. Wong et al. (Eds.): PAKDD 2026, LNAI 16617, pp. 3–15, 2027.
https://doi.org/10.1007/978-981-92-1926-1_1

Single-image super-resolution is a highly ill-posed problem in computer vision, aiming to reconstruct a high-resolution (HR) image from a low-resolution (LR) image. Super-resolution reconstruction can generate multiple high-resolution images from a single low-resolution image, meaning the results are not unique. Additionally, when the scaling factor of the image is large, recovering the lost high-frequency information in the low-resolution image becomes more difficult. Therefore, developing an algorithmic technology that achieves higher resolution and restores more precise and detailed texture features has become an urgent technical issue to be addressed.

Currently, methods for image super-resolution can be broadly categorized into three types: interpolation-based methods, reconstruction-based methods, and machine learning-based methods. Among them, interpolation-based methods are the most direct, simplest, but effective approaches, including nearest-neighbor interpolation [1], bicubic interpolation [2], bilinear interpolation [3], and others. These methods are straightforward and fast but tend to lose high-frequency information during the reconstruction process, resulting in blurry images lack of detailed information. Reconstruction-based methods, such as maximum a posteriori methods [4] and convex set methods [5], can recover images with higher quality when sufficient prior information is available. However, in the real world, it is difficult to obtain a large amount of prior information. In recent years, deep learning has made significant progress in the field of super-resolution. Methods such as EDSR [6], ESPCN [7], SRCNN [8], SRGAN [9], and ESRGAN [10] are representatives. EDSR enhances the deep network structure to improve super-resolution performance; ESPCN utilizes efficient sub-pixel convolution for image upsampling; SRCNN reconstructs high-resolution images using convolutional neural networks (CNNs); SRGAN combines the concept of generative adversarial networks (GANs) [11] to make images more realistic and detailed; and ESRGAN further enhances the super-resolution performance of SRGAN. Although these super-resolution methods have improved the accuracy of single-image super-resolution, in the field of CT imaging demanding higher image quality and stricter detail requirements, effectively restoring finer texture details remains challenging.

As to the development of image enhancement technologies in medical image processing, CNN is one of the essential tools. The successful implementation of the U-Net architecture [12] is considered as a revolutionary breakthrough in the field of medical image segmentation. Its outstanding feature capturing ability has garnered widespread attention and brought new research and application possibilities to the other fields of medical imaging processing.

In this context, to address the issues of low restoration quality, unclear texture details, and significant noise impact in CT image super-resolution, we propose a novel network model called EUR-GAN (Enhanced URes-Net Generative Adversarial Network). The encoding part of the generator network in this model integrates the ResNet152 [13] residual network with the encoder structure of the U-Net network, forming a dual-branch network structure called URes-Net, to effectively overcome the challenges of gradient disappearance and long-distance information learning, thereby enhancing network performance. Additionally, a residual module and self-attention mechanism are incorporated after the U-Net network decoder output to enable the network to better preserve global information while focusing on local texture details of CT images. After multiple rounds of experimentation and comparison, it has been demonstrated that our model is not only applicable to various organs but also exhibits excellent reconstruction performance at different magnification levels. EUR-GAN successfully addresses key issues such as low restoration quality, blurry imaging, and unclear edge details in CT image super-resolution reconstruction.

2 Materials and Methods

2.1 EUR-GAN Architecture

The proposed EUR-GAN is a generative adversarial network designed for high-fidelity medical image super-resolution. The generator (Fig. 1) is built upon an innovative dual-branch architecture, which we term URes-Net, designed to synergistically capture both fine-grained spatial details and high-level semantic context. The primary branch employs a classical U-Net structure, a symmetric encoder-decoder framework highly effective for image-to-image translation tasks. Its encoder path progressively down-samples the input to capture hierarchical features at multiple scales, while its decoder path reconstructs the image resolution. Critically, skip connections bridge the encoder and decoder, allowing low-level feature maps rich with spatial information to be directly concatenated with their deeper and more abstract counterparts, which is vital for restoring the intricate structures of CT images. Complementing this, the auxiliary branch incorporates a pre-trained ResNet152 model that acts as a powerful deep feature extractor, providing robust semantic priors and effectively mitigating the vanishing gradient problem. The features from this branch are injected into the U-Net's bottleneck, enriching the most compressed representation before reconstruction. Then, the fused features are passed through a residual block, which facilitates smoother gradient flow and enables the learning of residual mappings for refining subtle details. Subsequently, a self-attention mechanism is applied to model long-range spatial dependencies, allowing the network to capture global anatomical context that extends beyond the limited receptive fields of standard convolutions.

The discriminator (Fig. 2) functions as an adversary, trained to distinguish the generator's synthetic outputs (I_{SR}) from real high-resolution images (I_{HR}). It is realized as a deep convolutional neural network (DCNN) [14] that learns a hierarchy of discriminative features. The input image is processed through a series of blocks, each comprising a convolutional layer, Batch Normalization for training stability, and a Leaky ReLU activation. These blocks progressively increase the number of feature channels while reducing spatial dimensions. Following the final feature extraction block, an Adaptive Pooling layer aggregates the feature maps into a fixed-size vector, providing robustness to input size variations. Finally, a concluding convolutional layer and a Sigmoid activation function map this vector to a scalar probability in the range [0,1], quantifying the likelihood that the input image is real. This probabilistic output provides the essential adversarial loss signal that drives the generator to produce increasingly realistic and accurate images.

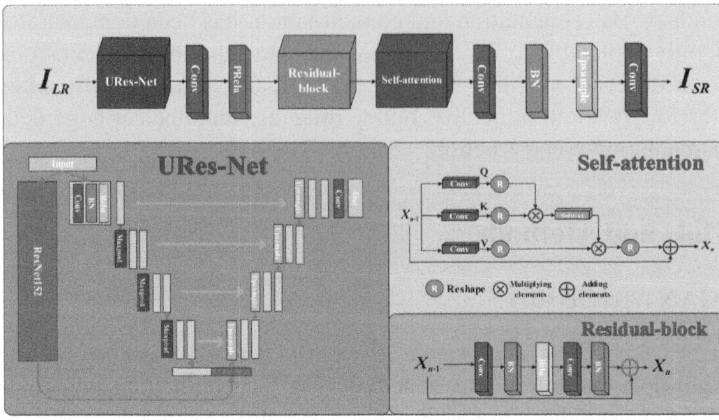

Fig. 1. Architecture of the generator network model of EUR-GAN.

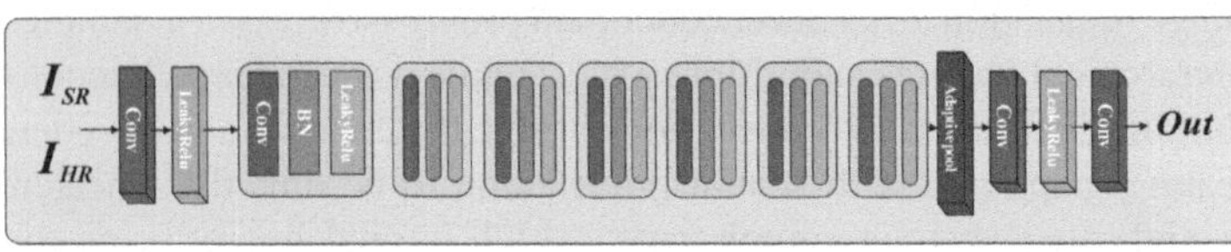

Fig. 2. Architecture of the discriminator network model of EUR-GAN.

2.2 Loss Function

To enable our generator model to generate CT images that are more realistic and precise with stronger details and texture quality, we designed a comprehensive loss function that incorporates four types of losses: mean absolute error (MAE), generative adversarial network loss (GAN loss), perceptual loss, and total variation loss (TV loss). By balancing different aspects of the images, these losses contribute to making the generated CT images more authentic, clear, and natural. The specific loss function is:

$$l^{SR} = l^{SR}_{\mathrm{MAE}} + 10^{-3} l^{SR}_{GAN} + 0.006 l^{SR}_{VGG} + 2 \times 10^{-8} l^{SR}_{TVloss} \tag{1}$$

MAE is a commonly used loss function in regression tasks, which measures the average absolute difference between the model's predicted values and the actual observed values. MAE effectively handles outliers in medical images, enhancing the model's robustness to noises and artifacts, and places more emphasis on preserving the details and textures of images. MAE is defined as:

$$\mathrm{MAE} = \frac{1}{n}\sum\nolimits_{i=1}^{n} |y_i - \hat{y}_i| \tag{2}$$

where y_i represents the value of the i-th sample, n is the number of samples, and $\hat{y}_i$ represents the predicted value of the i-th sample.

GAN loss [15] is a loss function used in GANs, driving the model to learn to generate more realistic samples by adjusting the adversarial process between the generator and the discriminator. GAN loss helps to more accurately reproduce the detailed features of medical images, thus achieving superior reconstruction. The GAN loss is:

$$\min_G \max_D V(D, G) = E_{x\sim pdata(x)}\left[logD(x)\right] + E_{z\sim p_z(z)}\left[\log(1 - D(G(z)))\right] \quad (3)$$

where G represents the parameters of the generator, D represents the parameters of the discriminator, x is a sample from the real data distribution, z is a noise sample from the latent space, $pdata(x)$ is the distribution of real data, and $p_z(z)$ is the distribution of the latent space.

Perceptual loss [16] aims to quantify the similarity between generated images and real images at a higher semantic level by comparing their feature representations in a pre-trained deep neural network. This loss function comprehensively evaluates the similarity between generated and real images while emphasizing pixel-level details and semantic information in the images. We utilized perceptual loss based on the feature representations in the pre-trained VGG16 network to guide the network learning. The specific formula is:

$$l^{SR}_{VGGi,j} = \frac{1}{W_{i,j}H_{i,j}} \sum_{x=1}^{W_{i,j}} \sum_{y=1}^{H_{i,j}} \left(\Phi_{i,j}\left(I^{HR}\right)_{x,y} - \Phi_{i,j}\left(G_{\theta_G} I^{LR}\right)_{x,y} \right)^2 \quad (4)$$

where $\Phi_{i,j}$ represents the pre-trained network model, G_{θ_G} represents the generator network model, I^{HR} represents the high-resolution image, I^{LR} represents the low-resolution image, $W_{i,j}$ and $H_{i,j}$ represent the dimensions of the corresponding feature maps of generated and real images in the VGG network.

TV loss [17] is a loss function used in image processing tasks with the aim of imparting a smoother appearance to generated images. Considering the unique characteristics of medical images, precise control over noises and artifacts is required. Therefore, introducing TV loss can effectively mitigate the impact of noise, resulting in smoother medical images. Additionally, the introduction of TV loss aids in preserving key details in medical images, ensuring a more accurate representation of fine structures and pathological areas in the generated images. For a 2D image I, the formula of TV loss is:

$$TV(I) = \sum_{i,j} \left|I_{i+1,j} - I_{i,j}\right| + \left|I_{i,j+1} - I_{i,j}\right| \quad (5)$$

2.3 Datasets

We utilized the QIN Lung CT dataset [18] provided by The Cancer Imaging Archive (TCIA). This dataset, released by TCIA in 2015, comprises 47 patients, totaling 47 DICOM (Digital Imaging and Communications in Medicine) image files. Each DICOM image file covers the entire thoracic region of the patient, including the lungs, heart, spleen, and stomach. We converted the DICOM files into PNG images, with each DICOM image file containing approximately 80–150 images, totaling 3954 images. During the data preprocessing stage, we employed a strategy to minimize data similarity for sampling. Specifically, we sampled one image from every three images and randomly selected sampled images to construct the test set. This sampling strategy effectively cleansed and filtered redundant data while helping to prevent overfitting. Ultimately, we formed an initial training set consisting of 2636 high-resolution CT images. Subsequently, to create our complete training set, we employed bicubic interpolation to downsample the images in the training set at multiple rates, generating corresponding low-resolution images as input. Finally, we enhanced the data through operations such as random cropping, resulting in a total of 7908 training set images. We classified the images in the test set into four anatomical regions, lung apex, lung lobes, heart, and spleen/stomach to observe the performance of the model in different regions.

3 Experimental Results

3.1 Training Details and Parameters

We conducted a total of 2000 training epochs for all models on the NVIDIA GeForce RTX 3090 GPU. The batch size for each model was set to 32 and Adam optimizer was used for parameter optimization. Regarding the training inputs, we utilized cropped high-resolution (HR) images with dimensions of 128*128 pixels. For comparison, we also tested EDSR, ESPCN, SRResNet, SRGAN, and ESRGAN. Among these, SRGAN and SRResNet employed a 7-layer residual network structure, while in ESRGAN, we opted for a more complex 16-layer Residual in Residual Dense Block (RRDB) network structure. The final performance evaluation was based on the peak signal-to-noise ratio (PSNR) [19] and structural similarity index (SSIM) [20] calculated on the images' luminance channel in the YCbCr color space.

3.2 Super-resolution of EUR-GAN Across Different Organs

To rigorously evaluate the performance of our proposed model, we first conducted a detailed comparison between EUR-GAN and five other leading super-resolution methods under a challenging $4\times$ upscaling scenario across diverse anatomical regions.

Lung Apex Region. Our EUR-GAN model achieves the highest scores in both PSNR (29.5721 dB) and SSIM (0.9501), significantly outperforming the next-best method, EDSR (28.5595 dB/0.9366) (Fig. 3). Qualitatively, the images reconstructed by EUR-GAN exhibit superior sharpness and preservation of fine details. The delicate branching patterns of small bronchioles and pulmonary vessels are clearly delineated, whereas competing methods like EDSR and ESPCN produce overly smooth or blurry results, and GAN-based methods like ESRGAN introduce subtle noise and artifacts that compromise anatomical fidelity.

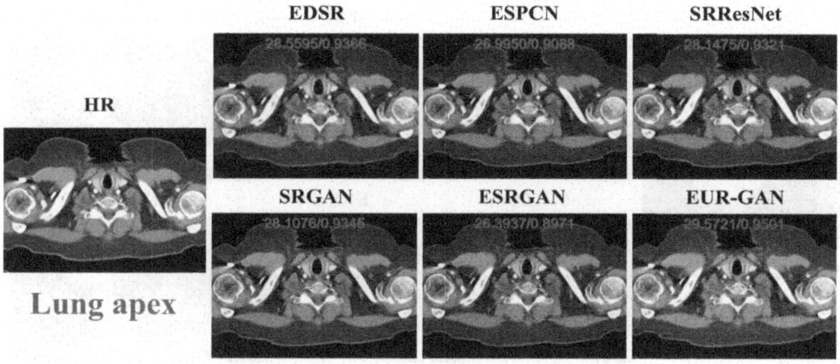

Fig. 3. The reconstructed results of lung apex region at 4× upscaling by different models along with the HR images. The metrics on the graph represent PSNR/SSIM.

Lung Lobe Region. While EDSR achieves a marginally higher PSNR (28.50 dB vs. 28.43 dB), our EUR-GAN obtains a substantially higher SSIM (0.9414 vs. 0.9295) (Fig. 4). This highlights a key strength of our model, an exceptional ability to maintain structural coherence. Visually, EUR-GAN renders the lung parenchyma with more realistic texture and preserves the continuity of vascular structures, reflected in the higher SSIM. This suggests that while other models may achieve closer pixel-wise accuracy in some areas, our method excels at reconstructing the overall anatomical context.

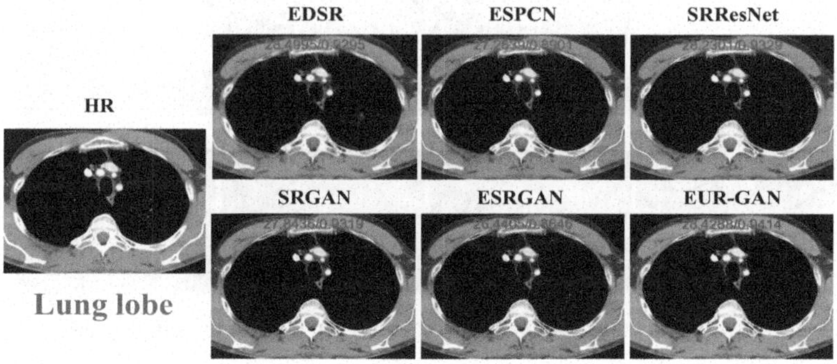

Fig. 4. The reconstructed results of lung lobe region at 4× upscaling by different models.

Heart Region. EUR-GAN once again leads across both metrics with a PSNR of 28.45 dB and an SSIM of 0.9577 (Fig. 5). The visual results are compelling; the contours of the myocardium, the interventricular septum, and the great vessels like the aorta are rendered with exceptional clarity and smooth, continuous boundaries. In contrast, other methods exhibit noticeable artifacts, such as the blocky textures in SRResNet's output or the noisy edges produced by SRGAN, which could obscure important diagnostic information.

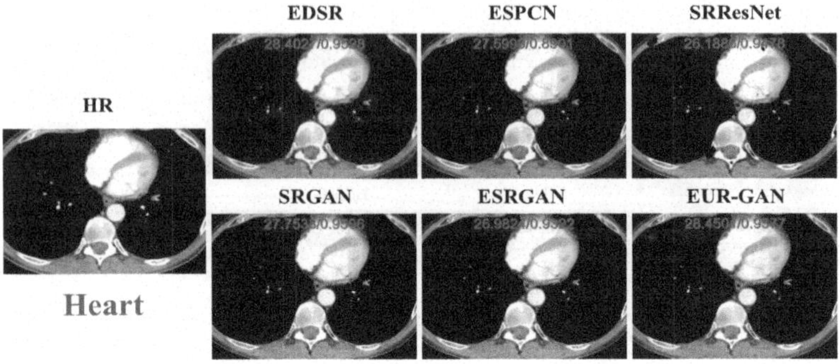

Fig. 5. The reconstructed results of heart region at 4x upscaling by different models.

Spleen/Stomach Region. Our model demonstrates dominant performance, achieving a top PSNR of 29.9959 dB and SSIM of 0.9416 (Fig. 6). This quantitative lead is mirrored in the visual quality. EUR-GAN excels at reconstructing the homogeneous texture of the splenic and hepatic parenchyma while maintaining sharp, well-defined organ boundaries. Other methods struggle in these soft-tissue regions, often resulting in blotchy textures or a loss of contrast between adjacent abdominal structures.

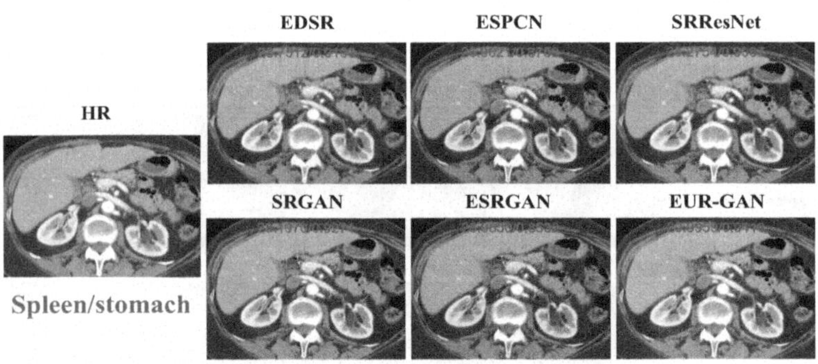

Fig. 6. The reconstructed results of spleen/stomach region at 4× upscaling by different models.

In summary, EUR-GAN consistently produces images with sharper anatomical boundaries, more coherent soft-tissue gradients, and a marked reduction in artifacts compared with baseline models. Crucially, it achieves these visual improvements without introducing hallucinated or spurious details, a common pitfall for GAN-based methods. This indicates EUR-GAN faithfully restores high-frequency information grounded in the underlying anatomy, making it a more reliable tool for potential clinical use.

3.3 Super-resolution of EUR-GAN at Various Magnification Levels

To further validate the scalability and reliability of EUR-GAN, we evaluated its performance under 2×, 4×, and 8× magnification factors across various anatomical regions.

What stands out is not only EUR-GAN's consistently strong performance across scales but also its resilience in structurally challenging conditions (Tables 1 and 2).

Table 1. The experimental results of PSNR at 2×, 4×, and 8× upscaling. The highest measurements are in red bold and the second highest values are in black bold.

Lung apex	EDSR	ESPCN	SRResNet	SRGAN	ESRGAN	EUR-GAN
PSNR(2x)	**32.9237**	30.8841	31.5898	32.4884	30.5748	**33.2675**
PSNR(4x)	**28.5595**	26.9950	28.1475	28.1076	26.3937	**29.5721**
PSNR(8x)	**23.5319**	22.0344	22.6492	23.4398	21.3852	**25.4203**
Lung lobe	EDSR	ESPCN	SRResNet	SRGAN	ESRGAN	EUR-GAN
PSNR(2x)	**32.9860**	31.0833	31.4944	32.7359	30.6512	**32.8587**
PSNR(4x)	**28.4995**	27.2639	28.2301	27.8436	26.4405	**28.4288**
PSNR(8x)	**23.8487**	21.8335	22.4481	23.0341	21.8385	**24.8068**
Heart	EDSR	ESPCN	SRResNet	SRGAN	ESRGAN	EUR-GAN
PSNR(2x)	**33.2056**	31.3503	31.7894	32.6811	31.2219	**32.7523**
PSNR(4x)	**28.4027**	27.5999	26.1886	27.7533	26.9824	**28.4501**
PSNR(8x)	**23.7131**	22.6326	22.8580	22.7612	21.9061	**23.3871**
Spleen/ Stomach	EDSR	ESPCN	SRResNet	SRGAN	ESRGAN	EUR-GAN
PSNR(2x)	**33.2768**	31.1735	31.6527	32.4884	30.3574	**33.4517**
PSNR(4x)	**28.7512**	26.9621	28.2754	28.1970	26.0850	**29.9959**
PSNR(8x)	**23.8487**	21.8335	22.4481	23.0341	21.8385	**24.8068**

Table 2. The experimental results of SSIM at 2×, 4×, and 8× upscaling. The highest measurements are in red bold and the second highest values are in black bold.

Lung apex	EDSR	ESPCN	SRResNet	SRGAN	ESRGAN	EUR-GAN
SSIM(2x)	**0.9723**	0.9624	0.9628	0.9706	0.9496	**0.9726**
SSIM(4x)	**0.9366**	0.9088	0.9321	0.9345	0.8971	**0.9501**
SSIM(8x)	0.8454	0.8203	0.8457	**0.8750**	0.8172	**0.9004**
Lung lobe	EDSR	ESPCN	SRResNet	SRGAN	ESRGAN	EUR-GAN
SSIM(2x)	0.9635	0.9565	0.9517	**0.9693**	0.9363	**0.9694**
SSIM(4x)	0.9295	0.8901	**0.9329**	0.9319	0.8646	**0.9414**
SSIM(8x)	0.7983	0.7455	0.7911	**0.8141**	0.7455	**0.8517**
Heart	EDSR	ESPCN	SRResNet	SRGAN	ESRGAN	EUR-GAN
SSIM(2x)	**0.9816**	0.9745	0.9731	**0.9801**	0.9692	0.9794
SSIM(4x)	**0.9528**	0.8901	0.9478	0.9506	0.9322	**0.9577**
SSIM(8x)	**0.8849**	0.8710	0.8883	**0.8871**	0.8661	0.8848
Spleen/ Stomach	EDSR	ESPCN	SRResNet	SRGAN	ESRGAN	EUR-GAN
SSIM(2x)	**0.9676**	0.9507	0.9540	**0.9706**	0.9382	0.9672
SSIM(4x)	0.9193	0.8759	0.9087	**0.9271**	0.8532	**0.9416**
SSIM(8x)	0.7983	0.7455	0.7911	**0.8141**	0.7455	**0.8517**

As evidenced, EUR-GAN achieves the highest PSNR and SSIM scores in most experimental settings, across all anatomical regions and scaling factors. While models like EDSR and SRGAN occasionally post competitive PSNR scores at lower magnifications (e.g., 2×), their performance degrades more sharply as the upscaling factor increases. For instance, in the Lung lobe, as magnification increases from 4× to 8× , SRGAN's SSIM drops approximately from 0.9319 to 0.8141, whereas EUR-GAN's SSIM declines from 0.9414 to 0.8517. This demonstrates a superior ability to reconstruct coherent structures even when the input information becomes extremely sparse.

The 8× upscaling factor serves as the most demanding test of a model's capabilities. At this level, the performance gap between EUR-GAN and other methods becomes most apparent. EUR-GAN consistently maintains the highest scores in both metrics across all organs, indicating that its architectural design is particularly adept at inferring complex anatomical structures from severely degraded inputs. In contrast, pixel-based methods like EDSR tend to produce overly smoothed images lacking in detail, while other GANs like ESRGAN often fail entirely, resulting in significant noise and structural collapse.

Furthermore, the consistent leadership of EUR-GAN in the SSIM metric is particularly noteworthy. Even in the few instances where its PSNR is not the top score (e.g., Lung lobe at 2×), its SSIM remains the highest. This underscores our model's prioritization of structural fidelity over mere pixel-wise accuracy. In clinical diagnostics, the preservation of anatomical shapes, boundaries, and textures is often more critical than minimizing mean squared error. The ability of EUR-GAN to consistently deliver the most structurally coherent images, especially at high magnification levels, solidifies its position as a robust and reliable super-resolution solution for demanding medical imaging applications.

3.4 Ablation Experiments

To validate the effectiveness of our model framework, we conducted two sets of ablation experiments. In both ablation experiments, we focused on the 4× upscaling scenario and analyzed the data of all four anatomical regions.

First, to assess the impact of the deep semantic features provided by our dual-branch design, we created a variant named 'NoResNet' by removing the pre-trained ResNet152 branch, thereby reverting the generator to a more conventional U-Net architecture. As the results (Fig. 7) clearly indicate, this modification leads to a significant and consistent degradation in performance across both PSNR and SSIM metrics. For instance, in the Spleen/Stomach region, the PSNR dropped sharply from 29.9959 dB (Full model) to 28.0416 dB. This demonstrates the critical role of the ResNet branch in providing powerful, high-level feature priors that guide the network toward a more accurate and context-aware reconstruction.

Second, we evaluated the importance of modeling long-range dependencies by creating a variant named 'NoSelfAtt', where the self-attention module was removed. This ablation also resulted in a marked decline in performance, which was particularly pronounced in the SSIM metric (Fig. 7). For example, in the Heart region, removing the self-attention module caused the SSIM to fall from 0.9577 to 0.9333. This highlights the module's essential function in maintaining the global structural integrity and coherence of large, complex anatomical structures. By capturing dependencies between distant features, the self-attention mechanism ensures that the reconstructed image is not just locally accurate but also globally consistent.

The ablation studies confirm that the superior performance of EUR-GAN is not due to a single component but rather the synergistic interplay between the deep semantic features from the dual-branch structure and the global context modeling from the self-attention mechanism.

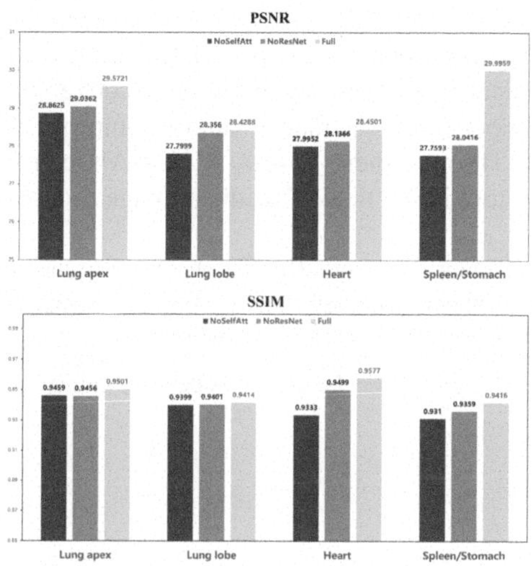

Fig. 7. The PSNR and SSIM results of ablation experiments.

4 Discussion

In this work, we addressed the persistent challenges in the super-resolution of CT images, namely the inadequate recovery of fine anatomical details, the blurring of soft-tissue textures, and the amplification of noise. The core innovation of the proposed EUR-GAN lies in its generator, where the synergistic fusion of a U-Net and a pre-trained ResNet152 creates a powerful feature extractor. This dual-branch design bridges the semantic gap: the U-Net excels at preserving high-frequency spatial information and precise localization, while the ResNet branch provides rich, high-level contextual priors essential for understanding complex anatomical relationships. The subsequent integration of a self-attention mechanism further elevates the model's capability by enabling it to model long-range dependencies, ensuring the global coherence of reconstructed organs and tissues, a critical feature that conventional convolutional networks often lack.

Our comparative and ablation experiments provide compelling empirical support for this architecture. The consistent superiority of EUR-GAN in both PSNR and SSIM across diverse anatomical regions and multiple upscaling factors is not merely an incremental improvement. It signifies a more fundamental advancement in reconstruction fidelity. Particularly, the model's robust performance in the SSIM metric underscores its strength in preserving structural integrity, which is often more clinically relevant than pixel-wise accuracy (PSNR). This suggests that EUR-GAN reconstructs images that are not only sharp but also anatomically plausible. The ablation studies further deconstructed this success, confirming that each component provides a distinct and indispensable contribution to the final performance.

Looking ahead, our future research will proceed along several strategic paths. We plan to extend the model from 2D slices to full 3D volumetric data to leverage inter-slice spatial context, which could further improve reconstruction accuracy. Beyond CT, a key objective is to explore the cross-modality generalizability of EUR-GAN. Applying it to other imaging modalities, such as MRI, will require careful domain adaptation and fine-tuning but could significantly broaden its impact. Ultimately, the most crucial next step is to move towards clinical validation, involving prospective studies with radiologists to assess whether the super-resolved images tangibly improve diagnostic confidence, accuracy, or efficiency. Through these efforts, EUR-GAN can serve as a trusted and impactful deep learning tool in the field of medical image processing.

Acknowledgments. This work was supported by National Science and Technology Major Project (No. 2021ZD0112600) and the Foundation of Key Laboratory of System Control and Information Processing, Ministry of Education, China (No. Scip20240104).

Disclosure of Interests. The authors declared no competing interests.

References

1. Rukundo, O., Cao, H.: Nearest neighbor value interpolation. arXiv preprint https://arxiv.org/abs/1211.1768 (2012)
2. Keys, R.: Cubic convolution interpolation for digital image processing. IEEE Trans. Acoust. Speech Signal Process. **29**(6), 1153–1160 (1981)
3. Li, X., Orchard, M.T.: New edge-directed interpolation. IEEE Trans. Image Process. **10**(10), 1521–1527 (2001)
4. Schultz, R.R., Stevenson, R.L.: Extraction of high-resolution frames from video sequences. IEEE Trans. Image Process. **5**(6), 996–1011 (1996)
5. Stark, H., Oskoui, P.: High-resolution image recovery from image-plane arrays, using convex projections. JOSA A. **6**(11), 1715–1726 (1989)
6. Lim, B., et al.: Enhanced deep residual networks for single image super-resolution. In: Proceedings of the IEEE Conference on Computer Vision and Pattern Recognition Workshops (2017)
7. Shi, W., et al.: Real-time single image and video super-resolution using an efficient sub-pixel convolutional neural network. In: Proceedings of the IEEE Conference on Computer Vision and Pattern Recognition (2016)
8. Dong, C., et al.: Image super-resolution using deep convolutional networks. IEEE Trans. Pattern Anal. Mach. Intell. **38**(2), 295–307 (2015)
9. Ledig, C., et al.: Photo-realistic single image super-resolution using a generative adversarial network. In: Proceedings of the IEEE Conference on Computer Vision and Pattern Recognition (2017)
10. Wang, X., et al.: Esrgan: enhanced super-resolution generative adversarial networks. In: Proceedings of the European Conference on Computer Vision (ECCV) Workshops (2018)
11. Goodfellow, I., et al., Generative adversarial nets. In: Advances in Neural Information Processing Systems, vol. 27 (2014)

12. Ronneberger, O., Fischer, P., Brox, T.: U-net: convolutional networks for biomedical image segmentation. In: Medical Image Computing and Computer-Assisted Intervention–MICCAI 2015: 18th International Conference, Proceedings, Part III 18. Springer (2015)
13. He, K., et al.: Deep residual learning for image recognition. In: Proceedings of the IEEE Conference on Computer Vision and Pattern Recognition (2016)
14. Kalchbrenner, N., Grefenstette, E., Blunsom, P.: A Convolutional Neural Network for Modelling Sentences. Association for Computational Linguistics, Baltimore (2014)
15. Wang, C., et al.: Perceptual adversarial networks for image-to-image transformation. IEEE Trans. Image Process. **27**(8), 4066–4079 (2018)
16. Johnson, J., Alahi, A., Fei-Fei, L.: Perceptual losses for real-time style transfer and super-resolution. In: Computer Vision–ECCV 2016: 14th European Conference, Proceedings, Part II 14. Springer (2016)
17. Rudin, L.I., Osher, S., Fatemi, E.: Nonlinear total variation based noise removal algorithms. Phys. D: Nonlinear Phenomena. **60**(1–4), 259–268 (1992)
18. Kalpathy-Cramer, J., et al.: A comparison of lung nodule segmentation algorithms: methods and results from a multi-institutional study. J. Digit. Imaging. **29**, 476–487 (2016)
19. Hore, A., Ziou, D.: Image quality metrics: PSNR vs. SSIM. In: 2010 20th International Conference on Pattern Recognition. IEEE (2010)
20. Wang, Z., et al.: Image quality assessment: from error visibility to structural similarity. IEEE Trans. Image Process. **13**(4), 600–612 (2004)

A Temporal Graph Neural Network Approach for Network Attack Detection

Hongli Ding[1], Bo Liu[2(✉)], Xingkong Ma[1], Xinyi Chen[1], and Jiayang Liu[3]

[1] College of Computer Science and Technology, National University of Defense Technology, Changsha, China
{dinghongli,maxingkong,xinyi_chen}@nudt.edu.cn

[2] Strategic Assessments and Consultation Institute, Academy of Military Sciences, Beijing, China
kyle.liu@nudt.edu.cn

[3] School of Cyberspace Security, Huazhong University of Science and Technology, Wuhan, China
jiayangliu@hust.edu.cn

Abstract. Network attack detection plays a vital role in maintaining the security of modern cyber infrastructures. However, traditional GNN-based approaches improve detection accuracy but often neglect temporal evolution, while existing temporal models suffer from high computational costs and poor robustness. To address these issues, we first introduce the concept of Core Time-Series Clusters to capture evolving attack behaviors and suppress noise, and based on this representation we propose NAD-GNN, a temporal graph neural network that updates node features through neighborhood aggregation and employs sparse matrix operations to enhance responsiveness while reducing overhead. We conducted experiments on three public datasets containing samples of real-world attacks. The results of experiments show that NAD-GNN achieves notable accuracy of $81.36 \pm 1.20\%$ on CIC-EVSE and $79.72 \pm 0.92\%$ on CIC-Modbus, as well as an exceptional F1-score of $99.16 \pm 0.44\%$ on ISCX-URL, surpassing benchmark models.

Keywords: Temporal graph neural network · Network attack detection · Clustering

1 Introduction

Network attacks involve complex interactions among hosts, protocols, and traffic flows, forming relational structures that traditional feature-based models struggle to capture. Recent studies [3,18,24] enhanced detection accuracy by constructing network traffic graphs and applying graph neural networks [17] to learn attack features. Wang et al. [20] further incorporated attention mechanisms to mitigate noise in network traffic. Critically, all these methods overlook the temporal evolution of network attacks, and relying solely on static graph modeling

R. C.-W. Wong et al. (Eds.): PAKDD 2026, LNAI 16617, pp. 16–27, 2027.
https://doi.org/10.1007/978-981-92-1926-1_2

limits their ability to capture dynamic changes in nodes and relationships over time and space.

In the field of network attack detection, malicious activities are often embedded within periodic and noise-prone temporal signals. Network traffic not only exhibits strong temporal dependencies but also involves heterogeneity across multiple communication protocols, such as Modbus/TCP and HTTP. Moreover, such attacks typically manifest as multi-stage and stealthy processes, encompassing progressive host compromise, privilege escalation, and lateral movement. To accurately capture the dynamic variations of attack patterns, more advanced approaches have been introduced. Representative techniques include Markov attack graphs [14], sliding window modeling [19], dynamic time warping [7,13], and AutoEncoder-based approaches [23]. Previous research has made progress in improving pattern recognition of attack behaviors. Nevertheless, challenges remain in further optimizing temporal feature extraction from the high dimensionality, sparsity, and complex nonlinearity of network traffic data.

In light of these challenges, this paper proposes a temporal graph neural network approach for attack detection, namely NAD-GNN (**N**etwork **A**ttack **D**etection based on Time-Series using **G**raph **N**eural **N**etwork), this method uses protocol filtering and session grouping to remove irrelevant communication data, identifies core time series clusters via a neighborhood distance threshold (ε) and minimum core points ($MinPts$), and represents sessions as graph nodes with inter-session similarities as edge weights. NAD-GNN further updates node features by aggregating neighborhood information, enhancing adaptability to dynamic patterns, and employs sparse matrix operations to improve responsiveness to burst attacks while reducing computational overhead. The main contributions of our work are summarized as follows:

- We introduce the concept of Core Time-Series Clusters to identify stable subsets with high similarity. Based on this, we propose a temporal graph modeling method that denoises time series and embeds cluster context into node features, thereby improving attack path representation.
- We propose NAD-GNN, a temporal graph neural network for attack detection that updates node features via neighborhood aggregation and employs sparse matrix operations to accelerate inference and reduce overhead.
- We evaluate NAD-GNN against representative baselines on three open-source datasets. Experimental results demonstrate NAD-GNN's superiority in static attack feature extraction, dynamic attack chain analysis, and anomaly detection in complex industrial protocols.

2 Related Work

2.1 GNNs-Based Attack Detection

To address the data imbalance caused by scarce attack samples in noisy and outlier-rich network traffic, Xiang Wang et al. [22] employed generative adversarial networks [6] to synthesize intrusion detection data. However, the generator often fails to accurately simulate real-world scenarios, limiting practical detection performance. Recent research, including attention mechanisms [21], edge-feature graph neural networks [3], and novel node sampling strategies [4], have been proposed to extract attack features. Nevertheless, these approaches mainly rely on statistical properties, neglecting the temporal evolution of attacks and thereby failing to capture dynamic traffic variations.

2.2 Temporal GNNs-Based Attack Detection

Temporal graph neural network-based attack detection methods typically treat time series as stochastic processes, employing various models to simulate and predict attack behaviors. Luo et al. [14] integrated Markov attack graphs with game-theoretic models to quantify transition probabilities among attack paths and optimized defense strategies through multi-stage adversarial games, thereby reducing intrusion success rates and enhancing system integrity. Van et al. [19] leverage sliding window modeling to capture the spatio-temporal characteristics of attacks, improving detection performance. Nevertheless, these methods' predominant focus on dynamic features consequently undermines their performance when confronted with content-based attacks. In order to balance the detection effectiveness in both dynamic and static attack scenarios. He et al. [7] integrate Dynamic Time Warping (DTW) distance as prior knowledge, through the use of two sub-predictors to maintain the accuracy of anomaly detection. However, for long sequences or large-scale data, the DTW algorithm's computational complexity increases exponentially, severely compromising accuracy and efficiency.

3 Models and Methods

3.1 Preliminaries

To address the limitation of traditional density-based clustering, which tends to misclassify sparse clusters as noise when processing network traffic time-series data, we introduces the Definition 4 to incorporate temporal continuity into the clustering process. Instead of relying solely on spatial density connectivity, Definitions 2 and 3 establish relationships along the temporal dimension.

Definition 1 (Core Point). *Given a dataset P, a distance threshold ε, and a minimum number of points $MinPts$, a point p is called a core point if its ε-neighborhood contains at least $MinPts$ points:*

$$|N_\varepsilon(p)| \geq MinPts \tag{1}$$

Definition 2 (Directly Temporal-Reachable). *In a dataset P, given a distance threshold ε and minimum points $MinPts$, a point p is directly temporal-reachable from a point q if p lies within the ε-neighborhood of q and q is a core point (i.e., $|N_\varepsilon(q)| \geq MinPts$).*

Definition 3 (Temporal-Reachable). *In a dataset P, given a distance threshold ε and minimum points $MinPts$, a point $p \in P$ is temporal-reachable from a point $q \in P$ if there exists a sequence of core points $p_1, p_2, \ldots, p_z \in P$ such that $p_1 = q$, $p_z = p$, and for each $i = 1, 2, \ldots, z-1$, p_{i+1} lies within the ε-neighborhood of p_i and p_i is a core point (i.e., $|N_\varepsilon(p_i)| \geq MinPts$).*

Definition 4 (Temporal Cluster). *A non-empty set C is considered a time-based cluster if it satisfies the following conditions:*

1. *If $p \in C$ and p is a core point, then all points temporal-reachable from p also belong to C.*
2. *For $p, q \in C$, if p and q are temporal-reachable from each other, then p and q belong to the same cluster.*

3.2 NAD-GNN Model

The overview of the NAD-GNN model is shown in Fig. 1. Specifically, we first apply the node's Core Time-Series Cluster to enhance feature representation by employing one-hot encoding. The NAD-GNN imposes a neighborhood-weighted update mechanism to achieve the propagation and aggregation of node features. Moreover, NAD-GNN leverages sparse matrix operations to reduce computational overhead during inference phase.

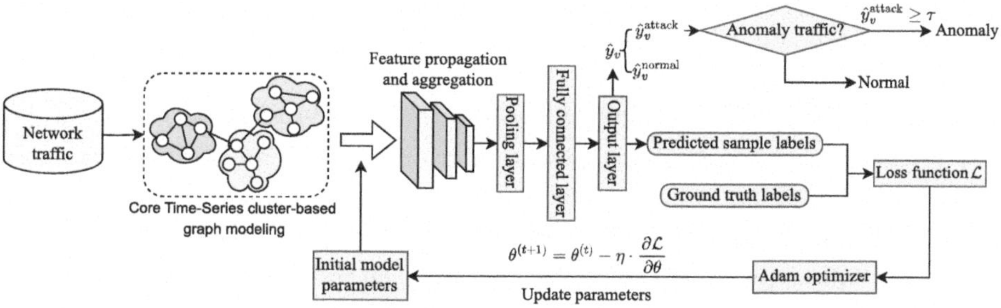

Fig. 1. The overall architecture of the proposed NAD-GNN model.

Core Time-Series Cluster-Based Graph Modeling Method. The schematic of graph modeling via Core Time-Series Cluster recognition is shown in Fig. 2. Each session is treated as a node, and edges are constructed based on inter-session similarity to generate the temporal source graph, this method captures the relationships between individual sessions in greater detail, reducing the risk of overlooking critical attack patterns due to simplified communication structures.

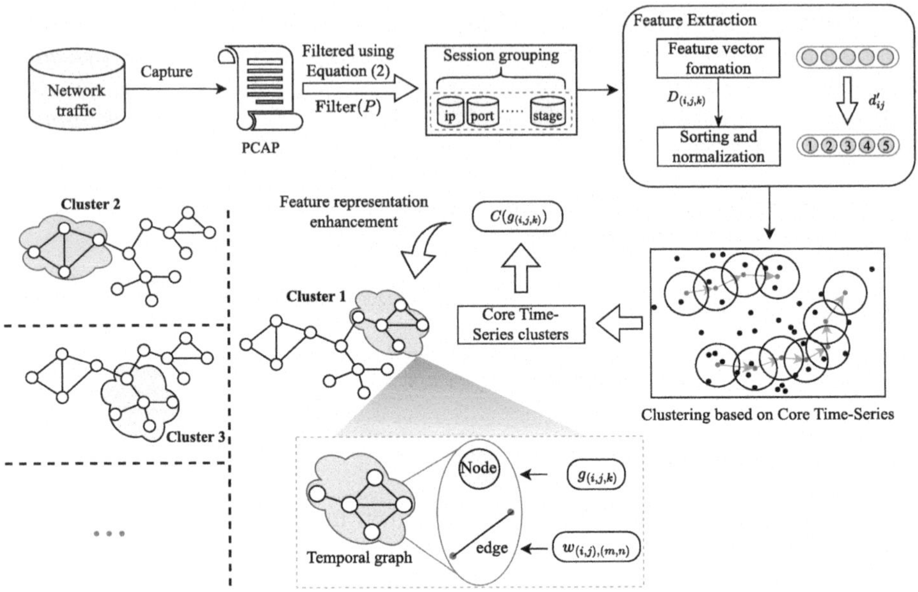

Fig. 2. Schematic of graph modeling via Core Time-Series cluster recognition.

Feature Extraction. Let P denote the set of all captured traffic packets, where each packet $p \in P$ contains the *port* and *protocol*. The protocol filtering formula is defined as follows:

$$\text{Filter}(P) = \{p \in P \mid \text{port}(p) \in S_{\text{port}} \text{ or } \text{protocol}(p) \in S_{\text{protocol}}\} \tag{2}$$

For each packet $p \in P$, multiple session groups $g_{(i,j,k)}$ can be formed a set S:

$$S\{g_{(i,j,k)} = \{p \in P \mid \text{src\_IP}(p) = i, \text{dst\_IP}(p) = j, \text{port}(p) = k\}\} \tag{3}$$

In what follows, we sort the packets within each session $g_{(i,j,k)}$ by timestamp using Eq. (4) and compute the relative time distance between each pair of packets using Eq. (5):

$$g_{(i,j,k)} = \{p_1, p_2, \ldots, p_n\}, \tag{4}$$

where $\text{t}(p_1) \leq \text{t}(p_2) \leq \cdots \leq \text{t}(p_n)$.

$$d_{ij} = \frac{|t_i - \bar{t}| \cdot |t_j - \bar{t}|}{\sqrt{\sum_{k=1}^{n}(t_k - \bar{t})^2}}, \tag{5}$$

where $\bar{t}$ denotes the mean timestamp of all packets within the session.

Clustering Based on Core Time-Series. Core time series are identified by setting a neighborhood distance threshold ε and a minimum number of points $MinPts$ according to the Definition 2. The main idea is summarized as follows:

1. **Initialization**: Based on the given distance matrix d_{ij}, initialize the ε and $MinPts$.
2. **Core Time-Series Identification**: For each feature vector $D'_{(i,j,k)}$, check whether its ε-neighborhood contains at least $MinPts$ sequences. If so, the sequence is marked as a core time series. The condition is defined as:

$$|N_\varepsilon(D'_{(i,j,k)})| \geq MinPts \tag{6}$$

3. **Cluster Expansion**: For each core time series, expand cluster to include density-reachable sequences from its ε-neighborhood according to Definition 4.
4. **Noise Identification**: Mark time series that are not assigned to any cluster as noise points.

To effectively reflect the different types of sessions and behavior patterns, the similarity values are defined:

$$w_{(i,j),(m,n)} = \text{sim}(D'_{(i,j,k)}, D'_{(m,n,l)}) \tag{7}$$

In Eq. (7), $w_{(i,j),(m,n)}$ denotes the similarity between $g_{(i,j,k)}$ and $g_{(m,n,l)}$, with sim representing the similarity measure. When the shape similarity is low, we adopt the Euclidean distance as the function. Conversely, we combine the DTW and Shape-Based Distance (SBD) distance matrices to compute a fuzzy membership matrix, which serves as the similarity function [12]. The similarity level is determined by DTW and SBD distance values (0.25 was set as the default empirical threshold in our model).

Node Feature Propagation and Aggregation. Let the feature vector of node v at layer l be denoted as $h_v^{(l)}$. The update rule is defined as:

$$h_v^{(l+1)} = \sigma\left(W^{(l)} \cdot h_v^{(l)} + \sum_{u \in \mathcal{N}(v)} w_{uv} \cdot h_u^{(l)}\right) \tag{8}$$

Different from the classical Graph Convolutional Network [10], which aggregates node and neighbor features jointly, we treats node-specific and neighbor features separately, expressed as $\sum_{u \in \mathcal{N}(v)} w_{uv} \cdot h_u^{(l)}$, alleviating the feature mixing problem commonly observed in GCNs, where repeated aggregation may cause over-smoothing or loss of discriminative node representations. Furthermore, the feature propagation and aggregation of each layer in NAD-GNN during inference are defined as:

$$H^{(l+1)} = \sigma\left(W^{(l)} \cdot H^{(l)}\right), \tag{9}$$

where $H^{(l)} \in \mathbb{R}^{|V| \times d}$ denotes the node feature matrix at layer l (d is the feature dimension), and $W^{(l)}$ is the sparse weight matrix at layer l.

4 Experiment

4.1 Setup

Datasets. We utilized three publicly available datasets in our experiments: ISCX-URL [15], CIC-EVSE [2], and CIC-Modbus [1]. ISCX-URL was selected to reflect scenarios dominated by static feature-based attacks (e.g., malware, phishing, defacement); CIC-EVSE captures dynamic attack patterns in electric vehicle charging stations, including reconnaissance, DoS, and cryptojacking; while CIC-Modbus represents industrial control environments with diverse Modbus protocol attacks such as flooding, false data injection, and replay.

Baselines. The baseline models considered in this study are as follows:

1) **GMAG** [14]: A temporal GNNs-based detection model based on Markov attack graphs.
2) **GTAF** [20]: A GNN-based detection model based on graph attention.
3) **PPT-GNN** [19]: A temporal GNN-based anomaly detection model leveraging sliding window modeling to capture the spatio-temporal characteristics.
4) **PIP-DA** [16]: A data aggregation method based on perceptually important points, designed to preserve the fidelity of data readings.
5) **MSTGAD** [7]: A temporal GNNs-based detection model incorporating DTW as prior knowledge to capture delayed dependencies.

Evaluation Metrics. We employ three standard evaluation metrics to assess the effectiveness of models in handling attack detection tasks, including Accuracy, Recall, and F1-score. In our experiment, normal traffic is defined as the positive class and attack traffic as the negative class, hence True Positives (TP) represent the number of truly detected normal samples, False Positives (FP) represent the number of incorrectly detected abnormal samples, True Negatives (TN) represent the number of truly detected abnormal samples, and False Negatives (FN) represent the number of incorrectly detected normal samples.

4.2 Results and Analysis

Overall Performance Comparison. The Table 1 presents a comparison of our work with baseline methods over 10 independent runs on 3 datasets.

On the ISCX-URL dataset, NAD-GNN achieved the highest accuracy (97.72 $\pm$ 0.82%), recall (98.44 $\pm$ 0.70%) and F1-score (99.16 $\pm$ 0.44%). It is notable that the GMAG model performs worse than other models, as its Markov-based design prioritizes dynamic transitions, rendering it less effective on ISCX-URL dominated by static or content-based features.

Moving to the CIC-EVSE dataset, where attacks often begin with TCP port scanning and evolve into multi-step intrusions, GMAG obtained superior recall (83.34 $\pm$ 1.28%) and F1-score (81.68 $\pm$ 1.24%) due to its strength in capturing state transitions, although NAD-GNN maintained slightly higher accuracy (81.36 $\pm$ 1.20%).

Table 1. The performance (mean% and standard deviation%) of diverse algorithms for the attack detection on three datasets. **The best** results for each dataset are highlighted in bold, the second place with underline.

Models	ISCX-URL			CIC-EVSE			CIC-Modbus		
	Accuracy	Recall	F1-score	Accuracy	Recall	F1-score	Accuracy	Recall	F1-score
GMAG	65.82±0.98	68.20±1.00	67.14±0.88	78.74 ± 1.28	**83.34±1.28**	**81.68±1.24**	54.62±1.10	59.12±1.14	58.12±1.06
GTAF	93.70±0.72	92.54±1.00	92.52±1.08	51.88±1.68	45.02±0.96	49.00±0.70	59.66±0.62	54.18±1.00	50.34±1.94
PPT-GNN	70.60±1.22	72.14±0.78	70.90±0.88	65.12±1.56	62.52±1.70	64.90±1.82	71.40 ± 1.80	74.96 ± 1.60	74.30 ± 1.88
PIP-DA	97.70 ± 0.82	93.04 ± 0.80	96.42 ± 1.20	69.64±0.64	52.66±1.48	51.76±1.10	62.92±1.38	61.60±1.30	63.04±1.42
MSTGAD	91.80±0.82	89.18±0.90	92.16±0.92	54.02±0.84	51.18±0.92	51.68±1.30	57.56±1.36	56.12±0.80	58.82±1.06
NAD-GNN	**97.72±0.82**	**98.44±0.70**	**99.16±0.44**	**81.36±1.20**	83.24 ± 0.74	79.16 ± 0.88	**79.72±0.92**	**77.32±0.70**	**79.28±0.98**

For the CIC-Modbus dataset, NAD-GNN demonstrated the best performance across accuracy (79.72 ± 0.92%), recall (77.32 ± 0.70%), and F1-score (79.28 ± 0.98%). Notably, PPT-GNN surpassed all models by 915%, benefiting from its sliding-window temporal graph representation and self-supervised pretraining, which enhance the detection of large-scale modbus-based DDoS attacks.

Throughout the experiments, NAD-GNN demonstrates stable and excellent performance across diverse attack patterns, even when other models show marginal advantages under specific conditions.

Running Time Evaluation. We selected 50 instance samples as a subset unit to compare the detection speed of different algorithms on three datasets: ISCX-URL, CIC-EVSE, and CIC-Modbus (where one network request, communication packet, or industrial control data frame is considered as one instance). Figure 3 illustrates the runtimes of different algorithms on three datasets.

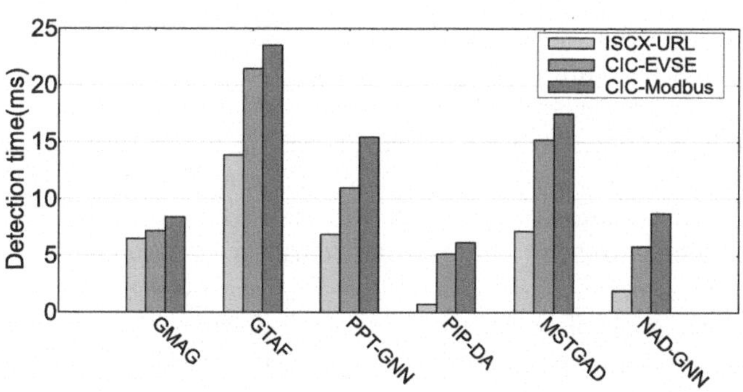

Fig. 3. Detection time of different algorithms (with 50 instance samples as a subset).

As shown in Fig. 3, GTAF's longest detection time is primarily due to the computational overhead from the hyperparameters required by its attention mechanism. The intensive computations required by the DTW algorithm for long sequences or large-scale data cause MSTGAD to record the second longest detection time, especially on the CIC-EVSE and CIC-Modbus datasets. By contrast, PIP-DA and NAD-GNN achieve relatively short detection times. PIP-DA benefits from its efficient perceptual important point-based data aggregation, while NAD-GNN accelerates inference through core time series clusters and a sparse weight matrix.

Convergence Assessment. For each training, we set the batch size as 32 and run 10 times with $\epsilon = 1$. The performance of NAD-GNN in accuracy with different epochs for both the training and evaluation phases are depicted in Fig. 4.

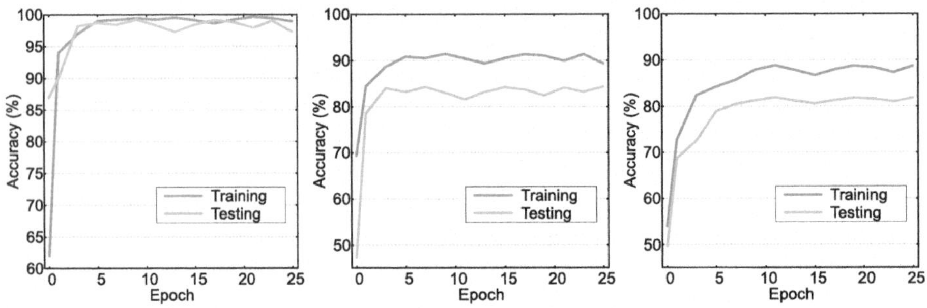

(a) ISCX-URL dataset (b) CIC-EVSE dataset (c) CIC-Modbus dataset

Fig. 4. Detection Accuracy of NAD-GNN on three datasets.

As shown in Fig. 4(a)-(c), the NAD-GNN model's accuracy steadily improves with increasing epochs across all three datasets. On ISCX-URL, it peaks at epoch 3 with 99.4% training accuracy and 98.2% test accuracy; on CIC-EVSE, it stabilizes after 5 epochs at 91.3% training and 83.2% test accuracy; and on CIC-Modbus, it stabilizes around epoch 9, reaching 81.9% test accuracy at epoch 11. NAD-GNN exhibits consistent performance trends, with both training and test accuracies increasing toward peak values before minor fluctuations occur. This behavior likely reflects the gradual learning of data patterns, while the observed fluctuations may indicate the onset of overfitting.

To further the risk of overfitting, we also conducted experiments to assess the performance of the NAD-GNN model in terms of loss across varying epochs (Depicted in Fig 5).

As depicted in Fig. 5(a)-(c), the trends of the loss curves for the NAD-GNN model across the three datasets exhibit substantial similarity, initially, with the increase in epochs, the loss sharply decreases, followed by a gradual decline, ultimately converging around a specific epoch. Furthermore, the accuracy curve of the NAD-GNN model in Fig. 4 also exhibits no significant fluctuations or declines at corresponding epochs. These observations collectively suggest that the NAD-GNN model is not overfitted.

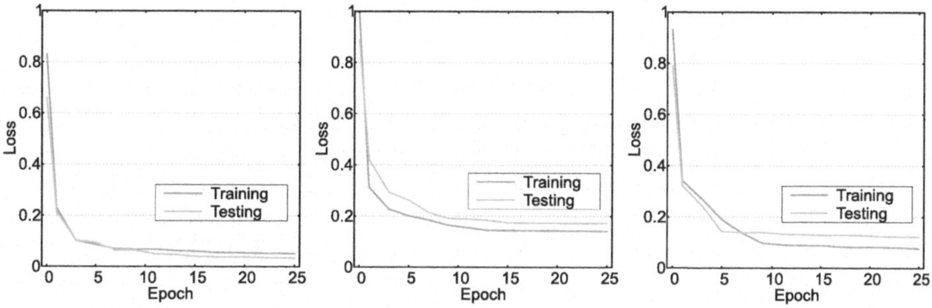

(a) ISCX-URL dataset (b) CIC-EVSE dataset (c) CIC-Modbus dataset

Fig. 5. Loss curve of NAD-GNN on three datasets.

Alert Distribution of CIC-EVSE Dataset. Fig. 6a depicts a heatmap illustrating the counts of True Positives (TP), True Negatives (TN), False Positives (FP), and False Negatives (FN) across six categories: TCP Port Scan, SYN Stealth Scan, UDP Flood, ICMP Flood, Cryptojacking, and Backdoor.

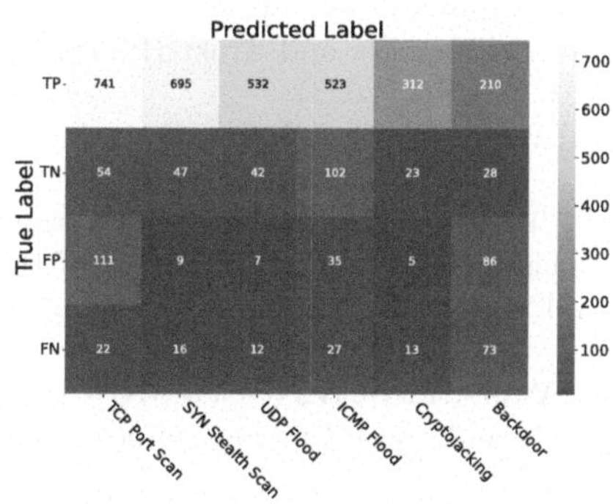

(a) Heatmap confusion matrix for attack detection using NAD-GNN on CIC-EVSE dataset.

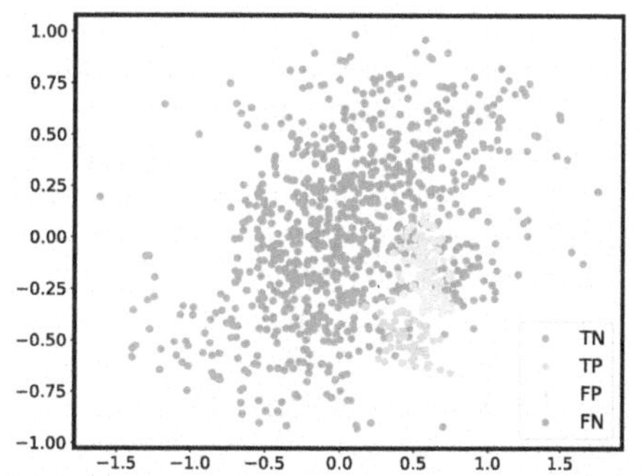

(b) Alert distribution of CIC-EVSE identified by NAD-GNN.

Fig. 6. Visualization results of sample recognition distribution of the NAD-GNN model on the CIC-EVSE subset.

Figure 6b illustrates a 2-D visualization of the TCP Port Scan class in the CIC-EVSE dataset using t-SNE8 [11], highlighting TP, TN, FP, and FN nodes identified by NAD-GNN. Notably, the FN rate is relatively higher, which may result from legitimate port scans for system assessment being misclassified as attacks.

5 Conclusion

In this paper, we have introduced a temporal graph modeling method based on the identification of core time-series clusters, building on this, designed an attack detection model named NAD-GNN. Comparing with existing techniques, the NAD-GNN leverages core time-series clusters to enhance graph node feature representations, while integrating sparse matrix operations to optimize inference efficiency. Experimental results demonstrate that NAD-GNN effectively detects attacks across multiple scenarios, including static attack feature extraction, dynamic attack chain analysis, and anomaly detection in complex industrial protocols. Future work will consider integrating metadata analysis [9] to detect anomalies via traffic patterns, packet sizes, and inter-arrival times. In addition, leveraging large language models in conjunction with federated learning [8] or relational triple extraction [5], could further reduce false negative rates within specific categories (e.g., the TCP Port Scan class in the CIC-EVSE dataset).

References

1. Boakye-Boateng, K., Ghorbani, A.A., Lashkari, A.: Securing substations with trust, risk posture, and multi-agent systems: a comprehensive approach. In: 2023 20th Annual International Conference on Privacy. Security and Trust (PST), pp. 1–12. IEEE Computer Society, Los Alamitos, CA, USA (2023)
2. Buedi, E.D., Ghorbani, A.A., Dadkhah, S.: Enhancing EV charging station security using a multi-dimensional dataset (2024)
3. Busch, J., Kocheturov, A., Tresp, V., Seidl, T.: NF-GNN: network flow graph neural networks for malware detection and classification. In: Proceedings of the 33rd International Conference on Scientific and Statistical Database Management, pp. 121–132 (2021)
4. Chen, J., Chen, Q., Jiang, F., Guo, X., Sha, K., Wang, Y.: SCN_GNN: a GNN-based fraud detection algorithm combining strong node and graph topology information. Expert Syst. Appl. **237**, 121643 (2024)
5. Chen, X., Liu, B., Hong, X., Chen, W., Qiu, H., Ma, X.: Relation as text: a semantic-preserving method for relational triple extraction. Comput. J. **68**(4), 346–354 (2025)
6. Goodfellow, I., et al.: Generative adversarial networks. Commun. ACM **63**(11), 139–144 (2020)
7. He, S., Guo, Q., Li, G., Xie, K., Sharma, P.K.: Multivariate time series anomaly detection based on multiple spatiotemporal graph convolution. IEEE Trans. Instrum. Meas. **74**, 1–14 (2025)
8. Jianping, W., Guangqiu, Q., Chunming, W., Weiwei, J., Jiahe, J.: Federated learning for network attack detection using attention-based graph neural networks. Sci. Rep. **14**(1), 19088 (2024)
9. Kim, M.G., Kim, H.: Anomaly detection in imbalanced encrypted traffic with few packet metadata-based feature extraction. CMES-Comput. Mod. Eng. Sci. **141**(1) (2024)
10. Kipf, T.N., Welling, M.: Semi-supervised classification with graph convolutional networks (2016). arXiv:1609.02907 arXiv preprint

11. Laurens, V.D.M., Hinton, G.: Visualizing data using T-SNE. J. Mach. Learn. Res. **9**(2605), 2579–2605 (2008)
12. Li, H., Wei, M.: Fuzzy clustering based on feature weights for multivariate time series. Knowl.-Based Syst. **197**, 105907 (2020)
13. Li, Z., Yu, J., Zhang, G., Xu, L.: Dynamic spatio-temporal graph network with adaptive propagation mechanism for multivariate time series forecasting. Expert Syst. Appl. **216**, 119374 (2023)
14. Luo, Z., Song, W., Zhang, W., Wang, J., Li, J.: Blockchain security situational awareness method based on Markov attack graph and game model. J. Electron. Info. Technol. **45**(4), 1374–1382 (2023). https://doi.org/10.11999/JEIT220178
15. Mamun, M.S.I., Rathore, M.A., Lashkari, A.H., Stakhanova, N., Ghorbani, A.A.: Detecting malicious URLs using lexical analysis. In: Chen, J., Piuri, V., Su, C., Yung, M. (eds.) Network and System Security, pp. 467–482. Springer International Publishing, Cham (2016)
16. Saeedi, I.D.I., Al-Qurabat, A.K.M.: Perceptually important points-based data aggregation method for wireless sensor networks. Baghdad Sci. J. **19**(4), 0875–0875 (2022)
17. Scarselli, F., Gori, M., Tsoi, A.C., Hagenbuchner, M., Monfardini, G.: The graph neural network model. IEEE Trans. Neural Netw. **20**(1), 61–80 (2008)
18. Shuaiyi, L., Wang, K., Wei, Y., Liu, H., Fan, Q., Wang, B.: GNN-based advanced feature integration for ICS anomaly detection. ACM Trans. Intell. Syst. Technol. **14**(6), 1–106 (2023)
19. Van Langendonck, L., Castell-Uroz, I., Barlet-Ros, P.: PPT-GNN: a practical pre-trained spatio-temporal graph neural network for network security. In: 2025 IEEE European Symposium on Security and Privacy Workshops (EuroS&PW), pp. 169–175. IEEE (2025)
20. Wang, G., Ai, J., Mo, L., Yi, X., Wu, P., Wu, X., Kong, L.: Anomaly detection for data from unmanned systems via improved graph neural networks with attention mechanism. Drones **7**(5), 326 (2023)
21. Wang Jian, Chen Lin, W.K.L.J.: Application layer DDOS detection method based on spatio-temporal graph neural network. Netinfo Secur. **24**(4), 509 (2024)
22. Wang, X., Liu, P., J.Z.K.F.L.L.: Research on data enhancement methods of began-based intrusion detection in automotive can networks. Automot. Eng. **46**(8), 1394–1402 (2024)
23. Ye, M., Zhang, Q., Xue, X., Wang, Y., Jiang, Q., Qiu, H.: A novel self-supervised learning-based anomalous node detection method based on an autoencoder for wireless sensor networks. IEEE Syst. J. **18**(1), 256–267 (2024)
24. Zhou, X., Liang, W., Li, W., Yan, K., Shimizu, S., Wang, K.I.K.: Hierarchical adversarial attacks against graph-neural-network-based IoT network intrusion detection system. IEEE Internet Things J. **9**(12), 9310–9319 (2021)

GPAT: Graph Prompt and Adapter Tuning for Graph Transfer Learning

Yongjun Fan and Ying Wang(✉)

College of Computer Science and Technology, Jilin University, Changchun, China
wangying2010@jlu.edu.cn

Abstract. Self-supervised learning with large-scale unlabeled data effectively supports knowledge transfer, but Graph Transfer Learning (GTL) performance is constrained by two issues: distribution and topological discrepancies across datasets reduce cross-scenario transfer efficiency, and early-layer information loss during pre-training weakens model generalization. To address these, this paper proposes GPAT (Graph Prompt and Adapter Tuning), integrating graph prompt and adapter modules. The graph prompt module constructs task prompts and prompt graphs based on inherent graph structures, narrowing the adaptation gap between pre-training and downstream tasks. The lightweight graph adapter is embedded into the encoder, enabling efficient transfer of pre-trained knowledge while preserving key early-layer information. Multi-view contrastive learning further mitigates dataset discrepancies, with a joint loss function optimizing training. Experiments on 4 pre-training and 7 downstream datasets verify GPATs effectiveness.

Keywords: Graph Transfer Learning · Graph Prompt · Graph Adapter · Self-supervised Learning

1 Introduction

As a key branch of transfer learning, Graph Transfer Learning (GTL) aims to transfer learned graph structure and feature knowledge to unseen input graphs for downstream tasks like node and graph classification. It has demonstrated critical application value in practical scenarios such as biological systems [13] and recommendation systems [5]. However, GTL faces challenges: acquiring high-quality labeled data is costly and difficult, limiting model training effectiveness; distribution and topological discrepancies across datasets lead to insufficient adaptability in cross-scenario knowledge transfer; additionally, key weight and parameter information in early model layers is easily diluted during training, hindering the learning of graph structures and node features and further restricting transfer performance.

The development of self-supervised and unsupervised learning provides an important solution to these problems. Their training paradigm based on unlabeled data can enhance model cross-task generalization to a certain extent [2, 10],

R. C.-W. Wong et al. (Eds.): PAKDD 2026, LNAI 16617, pp. 28–39, 2027.
https://doi.org/10.1007/978-981-92-1926-1_3

supporting GTL performance optimization. Among them, graph contrastive learning exhibits unique advantages in capturing dataset commonalities and discrepancies by focusing on high-level structural features and optimizing sample similarity measurement, offering effective insights for alleviating cross-dataset adaptation issues.

Based on this, this paper proposes the GPAT (Graph Prompt and Adapter Tuning) framework, comprising several core modules: a graph prompt module that mines inherent graph structures and features to construct task prompts and prompt graphs, enhancing model adaptability to downstream task data; a lightweight graph adapter module embedded into the graph encoder, transferring existing knowledge while reducing the loss of key early-layer information; and integrated multi-view contrastive learning to mitigate the impact of dataset discrepancies, combined with a joint loss function to optimize the entire training process and improve GTL transfer efficiency.

The main contributions of this paper are as follows:

- Propose the GPAT framework (graph prompt + adapter) for Graph Transfer Learning (GTL).
- Design a graph prompt module: generate task prompts and design prompt graphs based on inherent graph structural characteristics.
- Design a graph adapter module: realize knowledge transfer through lightweight components while ensuring key early-layer information is not diluted.
- Conduct validation on 4 pre-training and 7 downstream datasets, fully demonstrating GPAT's transfer effectiveness in GTL.

2 Related Work

2.1 Graph Transfer Learning

Graph transfer learning involves pre-training Graph Neural Networks (GNNs) and applying them to other tasks or datasets. Common learning methods include multi-task learning [6], domain adaptation [1], multi-network learning [7], and fine-tuning methods [2,10]. GCC [11] designs a self-supervised learning framework for pre-training universal GNNs that can capture the universal network topological properties. GCOPE [18] leverages the underlying commonalities from different graph datasets for few-shot learning. PARETOGNN [8] leverages manifold pretext tasks for self-supervised learning. ACT [15]combines and fuses anomaly-sensitive one-class alignment with unsupervised contrasting graph learning, aiming to develop anomaly-informed detection models for target graph datasets. AAGOD [4] designed the Adaptive Amplifier Generator (AAG) and the Regularized Learning Scheme (RLS). EVOLUNET [14] employs a Transformer-based temporal encoding module to capture the temporal dynamics of evolving domains and integrates a dynamic domain unification module to effectively learn shared representations across the source and target domains. GraphControl [19] aligns the input space across different graphs by leveraging universal structural pre-trained models and utilizes the unique features of target data as conditional inputs. GraphLoRA [16] introduces the trainable GNNs into the pre-train GNN to implement low-rank adaptation. Additionally, it proposes Structure-aware Maximum Mean Discrepancy (SMMD) to align the node feature distribution discrepancies between the source and target graphs.

3 Prompt and Adapter Tuning Framework

3.1 Graph Prompt and Adapter Module

In this section, we will introduce the design of the graph prompt, which includes both the task prompt and the prompt graph, along with the graph adapter module (Fig. 1) .

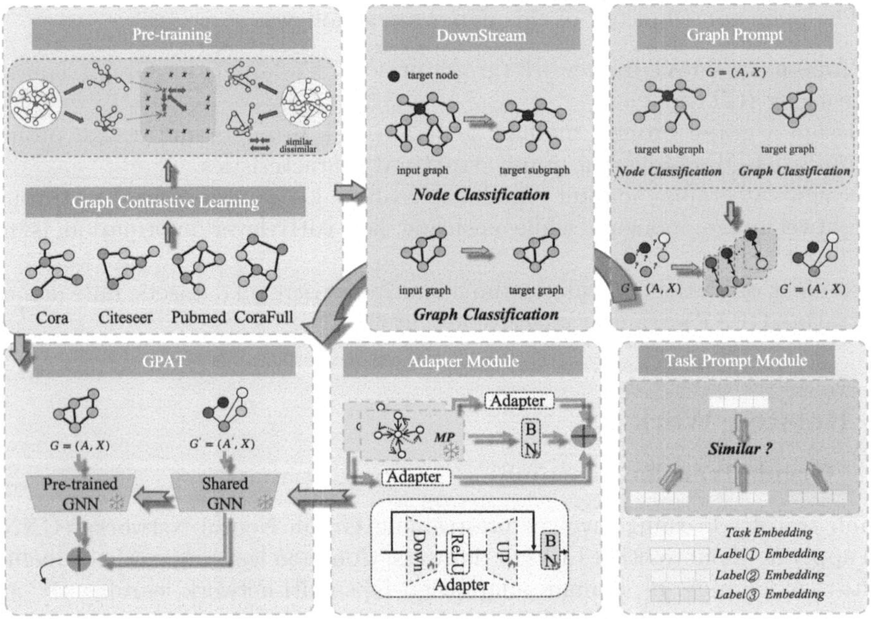

Fig. 1. The overview framework of GPAT.

Task Prompt Module. The task prompt module aims to design a universal task prompt template that adapts to both pre-training and downstream tasks. We focus on two downstream tasks: node classification and graph classification. By utilizing subgraph similarity, we design a universal task prompt template, denoted as T(·). This template transforms different tasks into subgraph similarity, specifically defined as follows:

$$T(ego_v) = sim(ego_v, ego_c) \tag{1}$$

where ego_v denotes the marker of the target subgraph v, and ego_c denotes the category marker. Both markers can be obtained based on the representation of the subgraph, and sim(·) denotes the cosine similarity function. For the node classification task, given a graph $G = (V, E)$, which contains a set of node categories C. We represent the set of category markers as $C = \{ego_1, ego_2, ..., ego_c\}$, where c denotes the number of categories. Each category marker is set as the prototype of each category as follows:

$$ego_c = \frac{1}{N_c} \sum_{v \in V, y_v = c} ego_v, \forall c \in \{1, 2, \ldots, C\} \tag{2}$$

where N_c denotes the number of nodes in the set V with category c, and ego_v denotes the marker of node v. In this way, we initialize the prototype for each category, aligning the node classification task with the task prompt template. For the graph classification task, given a set of graphs $G = \{G_1, G_2, ..., G_m\}$, which contains a set of graph categories C. We represent the set of category markers as $C = \{ego_1, ego_2, ..., ego_c\}$, where c denotes the number of categories. Each category marker is set as the prototype of each category as follows:

$$ego_c = \frac{1}{N_c} \sum_{G \in G_c} ego_G, \forall c \in \{1, 2, \ldots, C\} \tag{3}$$

where N_c denotes the number of graphs in the set G with category c, and ego_G denotes the representation of graph G. In this way, we initialize the prototype markers for each category, aligning the graph classification task with the task prompt template.

Prompt Graph Module. The Prompt Graph Module focuses on leveraging the inherent information within the graph to design prompt that can capture the structure and attribute information present in the graph data. By filtering out the top-k nearest neighboring nodes for each node to construct the self-prompt graph, the model can better understand the structure and attribute information, thereby enhancing the performance of the model on downstream tasks.

Given a graph $G = \{V, E\}$ and a target node $v_i \in V$ with the node feature x_i, we employ the Euclidean distance function to compute the Euclidean distance between the node v_i and other nodes as follows:

$$d(x_i, x_j) = \sqrt{\sum_l (x_i - x_j)^2} \tag{4}$$

where x_i and x_j denote the feature vectors of nodes v_i and v_j, respectively, and l denotes the dimension of the feature vectors. $d(x_i, x_j)$ denotes the Euclidean distance between nodes v_i and v_j. Then, we set a threshold r to select the k nearest nodes, preserving the edges between the node v_i and its k nearest neighboring nodes v_j as follows:

$$A'_{i,j} = \begin{cases} 1, & \text{if } d(x_i, x_j) \leq r \\ 0, & \text{otherwise} \end{cases} \tag{5}$$

where A' denotes the adjacency matrix of the self-prompt graph. We construct the self-prompt graph G' by combining A' with the node feature matrix X'. In the prompt tuning, we integrate the self-prompt graph G' with the downstream data to perform the downstream tasks.

Graph Adapter Module. In general, the GNN contains multiple layers, where each layers employ the message-passing mechanism (MP) to aggregate information from neighboring nodes and get node representations. The node representation learned from each layer provides complementary information. To effectively capture this complementary information, we design a graph adapter and incorporate it into the GNN encoder. Given a graph $G = \{V, E\}$ a target node $v_i \in V$ with node feature x_i, the output of the graph adapter is as follows:

$$O(x^{(l)}) = BN(M_{\text{up}}(ReLU(M_{\text{down}}(x^{(l)})))) \tag{6}$$

where $M_{\text{down}} : \mathbb{R}^{n_{\text{in}}} \rightarrow \mathbb{R}^{n_{\text{mid}}}$ denotes the down-projection matrix, $M_{\text{up}} : \mathbb{R}^{n_{\text{mid}}} \rightarrow \mathbb{R}^{n_{\text{out}}}$ denotes the up-projection matrix, BN denotes batch normalization, and $ReLU$ denotes the activation function. Therefore, we integrate the adapter into the GNN encoder. Specifically, we utilize dual adapters. We integrate the first adapter into GNN before MP to better understand the original node representations, and the second adapter into GNN after MP to better understand the MP-aggregated node representations. The output of the graph adapter from the l-th layer is as follows:

$$\begin{aligned} H^{(l)} &= BN(MLP(MP(x^{(l)}))) \\ &\quad + O_1(x^{(l)}) + O_2(MP(x^{(l)})) \end{aligned} \tag{7}$$

where $MP(x^{(l)})$ denotes the node embeddings after MP, $MLP()$ denotes a multi-layer perceptron. Therefore, the learned embedding from the $l+1-th$ GNN layer $x^{(l+1)} = dropout(ReLU(H^{(l)}))$. The node representation of the target node v_i after L-layer GNN is f_θ as follows:

$$z_i = f_\theta(G, v_i), \tag{8}$$

where z_i denotes the embedding of the target node v_i, G denotes the input graph, and $\theta = \theta^{(1)}, \cdots, \theta^{(L)}$ denotes the set of learnable parameters for the graph neural network f_θ. We leverage pooling to obtain the embedding of the G as follows:

$$z_G = \text{ReadOut}(\{z_v \mid v \in G\}), \tag{9}$$

where $\text{ReadOut}(\cdot)$ denotes the aggregation.

3.2 GPAT: Graph Prompt and Adapter Tuning for Graph Transfer Learning

In this work, we utilize a universal structure pre-trained GNN model and input downstream task data into the frozen pre-trained GNN model. In GPAT, the

$G = (A, X)$ denotes the input graph. We leverage the prompt graph module to obtain a graph $G^{'} = (A^{'}, X)$, where $A^{'}$ denotes the adjacency matrix in the prompt graph module. In addition, we integrate the input graph G and the prompt graph $G^{'}$ to obtain the corresponding target embeddings z_G and $z_{G'}$. Therefore, we can get the task embeddings by combining the z_G and $z_{G'}$ as follows:

$$z_{\text{task}} = \text{COMBINE}(z_G, z_{G'}). \tag{10}$$

where the COMBINE$(\cdot)$ denotes the concatenation operation and the z_{task} denotes the embedding for the downstream task. Hence, GPAT leverages the representation capabilities of the structure pre-trained model while integrating the graph adapter and graph prompt module, enabling it to better adapt to different downstream tasks.

3.3 Overall Joint Inference and Optimization

In the pre-training strategy, we aim to train a universal graph neural network that can capture the structural patterns within the graph. Therefore, we employ the popular GCC as the pre-training framework, which utilizes subgraph instance discrimination as the task objective and InfoNCE as the optimization objective function.

Specifically, given a node v in graph G, we randomly select a positive node a from the neighbors of v, and a negative node b from the graph that is not connected to v, forming a triplet (v, a, b). Our goal is to increase the similarity between ego_v and ego_a, while decreasing the similarity between ego_v and ego_b. Therefore, given a set of label-free graphs G, we randomly sample triplets from each graph to construct a training set T_{pre}. The pre-train loss is as follows:

$$L_{pre}(\Theta) = \\ -\sum_{(v,a,b)\in T_{pre}} \ln\left(\frac{\exp(\text{sim}(ego_v, ego_a)/\tau)}{\sum_{u\in\{a,b\}} \exp(\text{sim}(ego_v, ego_u)/\tau)}\right) \tag{11}$$

Where the τ denotes the temperature parameter used to control the smoothness of the output distribution. And more, the loss is parameterized by Θ, which denotes the weights of the GNN model. Therefore, we obtain the optimal model parameters Θ as follows:

$$\Theta_0 = \arg\min_{\Theta} L_{pre}(\Theta) \tag{12}$$

Finally, the optimal model parameters Θ_0 can be used to initialize the GNN weights. Therefore, the knowledge learned during pre-training can be effectively transferred to downstream tasks.

In the tuning strategy, for the node-level task or the graph-level task, the downstream task objective is the same. As mentioned in the Task Prompt Module, we obtain the target node subgraph for node-level tasks and directly treat the entire graph as the target subgraph for graph-level tasks. Specifically, we obtain the target subgraph ego_G and graph prompt $ego_{G'}$, which follow the same prompt template $T(\cdot)$.

For each subgraph ego_G, and the category marker ego'_{y_G} corresponding to its class label y_G. The loss can be defined as follows:

$$L_{dow}(\Theta) = - \sum_{G \in G_{set}} \log\left(\frac{\exp(ego_G, ego'_{y_G})/\tau)}{\sum_{c \in \{1,\ldots,C\}, c \neq y_G} \exp(\text{sim}(ego_G, ego'_c)/\tau)} \right) \tag{13}$$

Where the ego_G denotes the subgraph G, ego'_{y_G} denotes the category marker of the class y_G of the subgraph G,ego'_c denotes the category marker of class c , τ denotes the temperature hyperparameter, which controls the smoothness of the output distribution.

4 Evaluation

4.1 Experimental Setup

Datasets. We pre-train GPAT on four datasets, including citation graphs [9](i.e., Cora, Citeseer, Pubmed), CoraFull [3]. We evaluate GPAT on seven popular benchmark datasets. For the node classification task, we adopt US airports [12] and H-index [17].

4.2 Performance Analysis

Analysis of Main Results. We conduct experiments on seven benchmark datasets and list the experimental results in Table 1 and Table 2. We make the observations as follows:

• *GPAT performs the best performance on most benchmark datasets.* Compared to baselines, GPAT outperforms others on most benchmark datasets. The main reason for this is that the structural pre-train method can learn transferable structural patterns, which effectively initializes the GNN for downstream tasks. In addition, the graph prompt module which based on the data itself can learn the complex patterns and connections for downstream task data.Furthermore, the graph adapter module can effectively transfer the structural pre-train knowledge to downstream tasks. Therefore, GPAT bridges the gap between pre-train and downstream tasks, while effectively transferring pre-trained knowledge to the downstream tasks.

• *GPAT is effective for both node classification and graph classification.* As shown in Table 1 and Table 2, GPAT achieves outperformance on node classification and graph classification. This advancement relies on the integration of graph adapter with graph prompt. On the one hand, GPAT leverages the graph prompt based on data, which enhances the subgraph embedding of the target node. On the other hand, GPAT utilizes the graph adapter that can be adapted downstream within a parameter, which bridges the gap between pre-trained and downstream and fully leverages the pre-trained model. As shown in Fig 2, it is

Table 1. Node Classification Results (Accuracy, %)

Method	US-Airport	H-index
ProNE	62.3	69.1
GraphWave	60.2	70.3
Struc2vec	66.2	-
GCC	67.2	80.6
GPPT	64.0	74.6
GraphPrompt	62.9	73.4
Bridge-Tune	68.9	82.6
GPAT(Ours)	**70.6**	**82.8**

Table 2. Graph Classification Results (Accuracy, %)

Method	IMDB-B	IMDB-M	COLLAB	RDT-B	RDT-M
DGK	67.0	44.6	73.1	78.0	41.3
graph2vec	71.1	50.4		75.8	47.9
InfoGraph	73.0	49.7		82.5	53.5
DGCNN	70.0	47.8	73.7		
GIN	75.6	51.5	80.2	89.4	54.5
GCC	73.8	50.3	81.1	**87.6**	53.0
GPAT(Ours)	**77.1**	**52.7**	**82.0**	87.5	**54.7**

observed that with our proposed GPAT, (1) nodes (ego subgraph for node) with the same class (i.e., the same color) are more proximal in the embedding space, and (2) nodes (ego subgraph for node) with different classes (i.e., the different colors) are more discriminative. Therefore, the integration of the graph adapter and graph prompt in GPAT provides effective embeddings for the ego subgraph.

Ablation Studies. We conduct two variants to verify the effect of every component in GPAT, which are listed as follows: **GPAT w/o Adapter**: This variant removes the graph adapter module of GPAT. **GPAT w/o Prompt**: This variant removes the graph prompt module of GPAT.

The ablation study results on seven benchmark datasets are shown in Fig 2 and Fig 3. We make the following observations:

• *Each module within GPAT has a positive impact on performance.* As shown in Fig 3, we can observe that removing any module in GPAT will result in a decrease in performance. Each module plays a different role and makes a positive contribution to the performance. Therefore, GPAT effectively transfers the pre-trained knowledge to downstream tasks and effectively adapts to unseen data by leveraging the advantages of different modules.

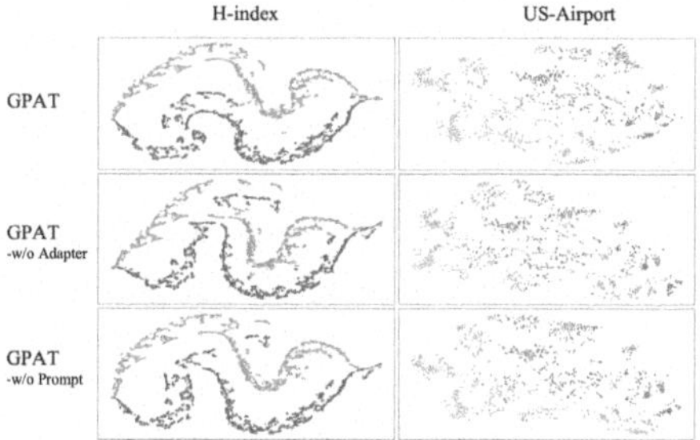

Fig. 2. Embedding visualization on node classification datasets.

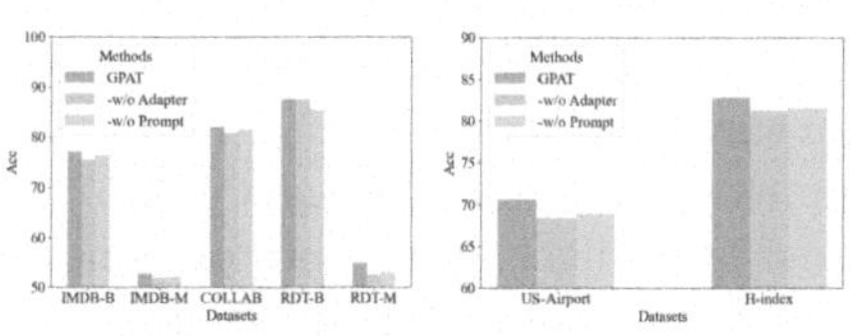

Fig. 3. Results of GPAT variants on seven datasets.

• *Both the graph prompt and adapter are crucial for GPAT.* GPAT leverages the adapter to pre-train GNN which can transfer the pre-trained knowledge to downstream tasks, and the graph prompt on downstream task data, which highlights the significance of information on the downstream task data. As shown in Fig 2, we can observe that the embedding between nodes of different classes in GPAT without prompt or adapter is less discriminative compared to GPAT, and the embedding of nodes belonging to the same classes in GPAT without prompt or adapter is less proximal. This indicates that the graph adapter and prompt can enhance the embeddings and are effective for transfer learning. In addition, as shown in Fig 3, we can observe that GPAT -w/o prompt outperforms GPAT -w/o adapter on most datasets, which shows that GPAT -w/o adapter exhibits the most significant performance decline on most.

Hyperparameter Studies. To answer research question Q4, we take the threshold r to illustrate the effect of hyperparameters on performance. We set different values of threshold, and the results are shown in Fig 4. We make the following observations:

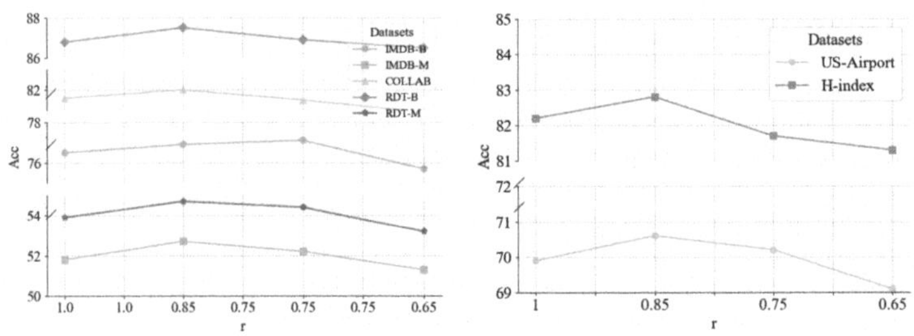

Fig. 4. Impact of hyperparameter on GPAT performance across seven datasets.

• *The sensitivity to the hyperparameter r is consistent for different datasets.* In the graph prompt module, we normalize the distance matrix and discretize the attribute distance matrix by setting a threshold r, therefore we can transform it into an adjacency matrix to construct the prompt graph. Specifically, we explore the threshold r ranging from 1 to 0.65. As shown in Fig 4, we can find that the curves on different datasets exhibit a consistent trend, so the threshold r has a consistent effect on the performance of different datasets. Therefore, we can set a fixed threshold r for different datasets. This indicates that the threshold r has universal applicability to performance, which demonstrates the effectiveness of GPAT across various downstream data.

• *The hyperparameter r has a crucial impact on performance.* As shown Fig 4, we can observe that the performance remains stable with the threshold from 1 to 0.85 on most datasets. However, when the threshold is too high, the performance on most datasets declines. This is primarily because the matrix becomes excessively sparse and the information in the graph prompt becomes insufficient.

Table 3. Node Classification On Frenzied.

Dataset	US-Airport	H-index
GCN	24.4	48.2
GAT	27.5	52.4
GraphSAGE	31.5	53.0
GCC	55.2	67.1
GPAT(Ours)	**61.8**	**70.9**

Table 4. Graph Classification On Frenzied.

Method	IMDB-B	IMDB-M	COLLAB	RDT-B	RDT-M
GCN	48.6	34.4	56.1	62.3	39.7
GAT	51.2	35.1	60.6	64.4	40.2
GraphSAGE	51.3	37.9	62.5	68.3	41.5
GCC	69.7	**49.2**	70.7	**84.9**	50.5
GPAT	**70.8**	48.5	**72.2**	84.4	49.0

Therefore, this indicates the importance of the threshold in maintaining model performance, and a high threshold has a negative impact on performance.

More Studies. To evaluate the effectiveness of GPAT, we froze all parameters in GPAT. In addition, we pre-train GCN, GAT, and GraphSAGE on the same datasets with the link prediction task, and employ GCC with the same pre-train datasets in GPAT, then froze the parameters in GNN for node classification or graph classification as baselines. We list the result in Table 3 and Table 4. We make the following observations:

- *The structural pre-train method can learn transferable structural patterns.* As shown in Table 3 and Table 4, we can observe that GCC and GPAT outperform GCN, GAT and GraphSAGE. This demonstrates that the structural pre-train method can effectively capture the structural patterns in the pre-train data. Furthermore, this result shows the importance of structural pre-train in enhancing the effectiveness and transferability of GNNs on various graph tasks.
- *The GPAT with graph prompt and adapter contribute to transfer learning.* As shown in Table 3 and Table 4, we can find that GPAT achieves the best performance on most datasets. The main reason is that the GPAT with graph prompt and adapter can effectively capture the pre-trained structural knowledge and the structural information of specific data which enhances the models overall performance.

5 Conclusion and Future Work

To address the constraints imposed by cross-dataset discrepancies and early-layer information loss on the performance of self-supervised graph pre-training models in Graph Transfer Learning (GTL), this paper proposes the GPAT framework-which integrates graph prompt, graph adapter, and multi-view contrastive learning to enhance knowledge transfer capability and generalization performance. Experiments on multiple datasets show that GPAT outperforms baseline models in node classification and graph classification tasks, and ablation studies verify the necessity of each module, demonstrating its effectiveness for GTL. Future research will extend GPAT to more tasks and scenarios, and optimize its adaptability and efficiency.

Acknowledgement. This work is supported by the International Science and Technology Cooperation Project of Jilin Provincial Science and Technology Department (No.20240402067GH), Research on Generalizable Graph Representation Learning in Out-of-Distribution Data Scenarios, and the National Natural Science Foundation of China (No.61872161), Research on Large-scale Heterogeneous Information Network Summarization and Summary Interpretability.

References

1. Dai, Q., Wu, X., Xiao, J., Shen, X., Wang, D.: Graph transfer learning via adversarial domain adaptation with graph convolution. IEEE Trans. Knowl. Data Eng. , 4908–4922 (2023)
2. Fang, T., Zhang, Y., Yang, Y., Wang, C., Chen, L.: Universal prompt tuning for graph neural networks. In: Advances in Neural Information Processing Systems 36: Annual Conference on Neural Information Processing Systems 2023, NeurIPS 2023 (2023)
3. Gao, H., Wang, Z., Ji, S.: Large-scale learnable graph convolutional networks. In: Proceedings of the 24th ACM SIGKDD International Conference on Knowledge Discovery and Data Mining, KDD 2018. pp. 1416–1424 (2018)
4. Guo, Y., Yang, C., Chen, Y., Liu, J., Shi, C., Du, J.: A data-centric framework to endow graph neural networks with out-of-distribution detection ability. In: Proceedings of the 29th ACM SIGKDD Conference on Knowledge Discovery and Data Mining, KDD 2023, pp. 638–648. ACM (2023)
5. He, X., Deng, K., Wang, X., Li, Y., Zhang, Y., Wang, M.: Lightgcn: Simplifying and powering graph convolution network for recommendation. In: Proceedings of the 43rd International ACM SIGIR Conference on Research and Development in Information Retrieval, SIGIR 2020, Virtual Event, China, July 25-30, 2020
6. Hwang, D., Park, J., Kwon, S., Kim, K., Ha, J., Kim, H.J.: Self-supervised auxiliary learning with meta-paths for heterogeneous graphs. In: Advances in Neural Information Processing Systems 33: Annual Conference on Neural Information Processing Systems 2020, NeurIPS 2020 (2020)
7. Jiang, M.: Cross-network learning with partially aligned graph convolutional networks. In: Zhu, F., Ooi, B.C., Miao, C. (eds.) Proceedings of the 27th ACM SIGKDD Conference on Knowledge Discovery and Data Mining, KDD 2021, pp. 746–755. ACM (2021)
8. Ju, M., et al.: Multi-task self-supervised graph neural networks enable stronger task generalization. In: Proceedings of the 11th International Conference on Learning Representations, ICLR 2023 (2023). OpenReview.net
9. Kipf, T.N., Welling, M.: Semi-supervised classification with graph convolutional networks. In: Proceedings of the 5th International Conference on Learning Representations, ICLR 2017 (2017)
10. Li, S., Han, X., Bai, J.: Adaptergnn: Parameter-efficient fine-tuning improves generalization in gnns. In: Proceedings of the 36th AAAI Conference on Artificial Intelligence, AAAI 2024, pp. 13600–13608. AAAI Press (2024)
11. Qiu, J., et al.: GCC: graph contrastive coding for graph neural network pretraining. In: Proceedings of the 26th ACM SIGKDD Conference on Knowledge Discovery and Data Mining, KDD 2020, pp. 1150–1160. ACM (2020)

12. Ribeiro, L.F.R., Saverese, P.H.P., Figueiredo, D.R.: *struc2vec*: Learning node representations from structural identity. In: Proceedings of the 23rd ACM SIGKDD Conference on Knowledge Discovery and Data Mining,KDD 2017, pp. 385–394. (2017)
13. Song, Y., Zheng, S., Niu, Z., Fu, Z., Lu, Y., Yang, Y.: Communicative representation learning on attributed molecular graphs. In: Proceedings of the Twenty-Ninth International Joint Conference on Artificial Intelligence, IJCAI 2020 (2020). https://doi.org/10.24963/IJCAI.2020/392
14. Wang, H., et al.: Evolunet: Advancing dynamic non-iid transfer learning on graphs. In: Proceedings of the 41th International Conference on Machine Learning, ICML 2024. OpenReview.net (2024)
15. Wang, Q., Pang, G., Salehi, M., Buntine, W.L., Leckie, C.: Cross-domain graph anomaly detection via anomaly-aware contrastive alignment. In: Proceedings of the 35th AAAI Conference on Artificial Intelligence, AAAI 2023, pp. 4676–4684. AAAI Press (2023)
16. Yang, Z.R., Han, J., Wang, C.D., Liu, H.: Graphlora: Structure-aware contrastive low-rank adaptation for cross-graph transfer learning (2024)
17. Zhang, F., et al.: OAG: toward linking large-scale heterogeneous entity graphs. In: Proceedings of the 25th ACM SIGKDD Conference on Knowledge Discovery and Data Mining,KDD 2019 (2019)
18. Zhao, H., Chen, A., Sun, X., Cheng, H., Li, J.: All in one and one for all: A simple yet effective method towards cross-domain graph pretraining. In: Proceedings of the 30th ACM SIGKDD Conference on Knowledge Discovery and Data Mining,KDD 2024. pp. 4443–4454. ACM (2024)
19. Zhu, Y., Wang, Y., Shi, H., Zhang, Z., Jiao, D., Tang, S.: Graphcontrol: Adding conditional control to universal graph pre-trained models for graph domain transfer learning. In: Proceedings of the ACM Web Conference 2024, WWW 2024, pp. 539–550. ACM (2024)

GNNeF: Enhanced GNN PDE Solver with Embedded FNO

Jiyan Qiu[1,2](✉), Jian Zhang[1,2], Yuan Wu[1,2], and Xuebin Chi[1,2]

[1] Computer Network Information Center, Chinese Academy of Sciences, Beijing, China
{qiujiyan,chi}@cnic.cn, {zhangjian,yuanwu}@sccas.cn
[2] University of Chinese Academy of Sciences, Beijing, China

Abstract. Various deep learning models have been developed to construct high-accuracy solvers for Partial Differential Equations (PDEs), facing the challenges of complex boundary conditions and evolving grid configurations. Traditional methods struggle to accommodate the uncertainties associated with geometric shapes and flow conditions, often resorting to mapping irregular grids onto regular ones, or attempting direct solutions on non-uniform meshes. In our work, we introduce a novel PDE solver, termed GNNeF, which is an enhanced Graph Neural Network (GNN) embedded with Fourier Neural Operators (FNO). FNO operates on regular grids, efficiently incorporating global information into the GNN to synergize local and global data. Additionally, we have implemented Spatial Encoding Weights (SEW) to dynamically adjust edge weights relative to spatial coordinates. To smooth the PDE solutions, we have augmented the loss function with a Laplacian loss. Compared to the best results provided by AirfRANS, the velocity and pressure errors are reduced by 87.18% and 52.88% on average. In all evaluated metrics, our method surpasses the established baseline. Anonymous code is already available at https://github.com/qiujiyan/GNNeF.

Keywords: Graph Neural Networks · Fourier Neural Operators · Partial Differential Equations · Computational Fluid Dynamics · Airfoil Aerodynamics

1 Introduction

In the field of aircraft design, shape optimization is vital for improving lift and minimizing drag. To achieve an optimal geometric shape, multiple numerical simulations need to be conducted under diverse flight conditions and airfoil shapes. Traditional numerical solvers, including finite difference and finite element methods, demand substantial computational resources and time, particularly in extensive, high-speed aircraft applications.

To alleviate the expensive computational cost of traditional solvers, deep learning in physics has led to numerous advancements, illustrating the essential nexus between computational intelligence and physical sciences [2,5]. Such

R. C.-W. Wong et al. (Eds.): PAKDD 2026, LNAI 16617, pp. 40–51, 2027.
https://doi.org/10.1007/978-981-92-1926-1_4

progress extends beyond the bounds of improved computational power, heralding a shift in the approaches used to understand and analyze complex physical phenomena [14]. Researchers have introduced various innovative strategies to enhance these novel paradigms [7,13].

Introducing a novel approach to solving PDEs, Physical Information Neural Networks (PINNs) merge data-driven techniques with physical laws [15]. These networks exploit both empirical data and physical laws to address intricate scientific and engineering problems. Nevertheless, they face difficulties in managing object boundaries, occasionally hindering the attainment of accurate solutions [3,12]. To mitigate issues related to boundaries, Fourier Neural Operators (FNO) apply operations within Fourier space to navigate the complexities of high-dimensional domains [8,11]. While FNOs demonstrate enhanced learning capabilities in infinite-dimensional functional spaces, their applicability is limited to computations at constant spatial coordinates or within consistent scale problems. [4,6,15].

In our study, we propose a novel methodology, GNNeF, aimed at surmounting the constraints of local perception of GNN and applicable conditions that only can work on regular mesh of FNO. Our focus is on the obstacles encountered by FNO and GNN in modeling fluid dynamics scenarios. This approach cleverly integrates the global processing prowess of FNO with GNNs' sensitive awareness of sub-graph. By integrating Fourier Neural Operators(FNO) into the spatial framework of GNN, we significantly enhance the accuracy of predictions in representing complex fluid dynamics challenges.

GNNeF first uses FNO's global processing to capture subtle fluid dynamics variations for accurate simulation. It converts inputs into graphs to handle arbitrary field shapes, overcoming FNO's fixed-input limitation. We further propose a novel edge weighting mechanism, Spatial Encoding Weights (SEW), to improve information transfer by learning feature differences between neighboring nodes, addressing varying fluid dynamics across spatial regions. Finally, Laplacian loss approximation is integrated to smooth simulation results, producing more continuous predictions and better generalization for reliable fluid simulation under diverse conditions.

Within the AirfRANS dataset [1], we observed average errors of 0.00270 for horizontal velocity, 0.00166 for vertical velocity, and 0.00311 for pressure, respectively. Notably, wing surface velocity and surface pressure errors registered at 0.00539 and 0.0043. Furthermore, we recorded average errors for drag and lift coefficients at 0.844 and 0.078, respectively. This paper's principal contributions are delineated as follows:

- We innovatively design a Graph Neural Network (GNN) architecture enhanced by Fourier Neural Operators (FNO), integrating the local feature extraction of GNN and global Fourier transformation of FNO. The model we proposed significantly enhances the performance of accurately predicting fluid dynamics.
- We develop and apply the Spatial Encoding Weight (SEW), a novel approach for optimizing graph weight calculations, thereby significantly refining model

accuracy. By introducing and implementing a Laplacian-loss ($loss_{lap}$) function, we improve solution continuity, aligning our approach with the conventional assumptions in engineering applications, enhancing the model's applicability and reliability.
- Our approach has been extensively tested in partial differential equations (PDEs) for a range of different airfoil flow fields, including nonlinear fluid flows in one and two dimensions.

2 Preliminaries

In this section, we introduce the fundamental problem settings of our work and then present the concepts of the Fourier neural operator (FNO) and the Graph neural network (GNN), which are two core operators in our framework GNNeF. Our objective is to utilize GNNeF to solve prediction problems related to the Partial Differential Equations (PDEs) in fluid fields surrounding various airfoil geometries. In Computational Fluid Dynamics (CFD), the task is achieved by numerically solving the Reynolds-Averaged Navier-Stokes equations (RANS).
Problem Settings. Each airfoil is associated with a domain in a 2-dimensional space $\Omega \subset \mathrm{R}^2$. And a corresponding grid is assigned to each airfoil, comprising a set of nodes $\{x_i\}^N \subset \Omega$ obtained by discretizing the continuous spatial domain. We denote $\{f(x_i)\}$ as parameter set for the RANS equations and nodes information, and the set $\{g(x_i)\}$ represents the fluid fields which reflect the behavior of fluids passing through the geometry. The objective is to approximate the nonlinear relation: $T : f(x_i) \to g(x_i)$.
Input and Output Formats of Problem. The specific geometry-associated mesh comprises a multitude of nodes and serves as the target for conventional numerical solvers. These nodes, denoted as $\{x_i\}$, represent the points to be solved by the surrogate model. The model inputs, $\{f(x_i)\} \in \mathrm{R}^7$, encompass the nodes's positions, Euclidean distance function between the node and the airfoil, normal vector of the nodes on the geometry's surface (with a value of 0 for nodes not on the surface), and the inlet velocity. They encapsulate the properties of nodes and the parameters of the RANS equations.

In this study, the results yielded by the numerical solver are taken as the ground truth values. The model's outputs, $\{g(x_i)\}$, comprise four physical quantities: the horizontal and vertical components of the velocity, pressure, and the turbulent kinematic viscosity. The fluid fields at these nodes collectively form the supervised targets of our model.
Fourier Neural Operator. The Fourier integral operator implements the Fourier transform by extracting modes from the spectral domain. The FNO is represented in Enq. 1,

$$(\mathcal{K}v_l)(x) = \mathcal{F}^{-1}(R \cdot (\mathcal{F}v_l))(x), \forall x \in D. \tag{1}$$

where $\mathcal{F}$ denotes the Fourier transform and $\mathcal{F}^{-1}$ represents the inverse Fourier transform; R is component of the parameter θ to be learned [10]. When x is regularly sampled on the domain D, $\mathcal{F}$ can be replaced by the discrete Fast Fourier Transform(FFT) [9].

Graph Neural Networks. Message passing graph neural network(GNN) update nodes through gathering messages from their neighbors. Our general framework includes the GNN, the formula of which is depicted in Equation Enq. 2.

$$\boldsymbol{h}_u^{(k+1)} = \mathrm{U}\left(\boldsymbol{h}_u^{(k)}, \mathrm{A}^{(k)}\left(\left\{\boldsymbol{h}_v^{(k)}, v \in \mathcal{N}(u)\right\}\right)\right) \tag{2}$$

In this equation, u represents the node on the graph, $\boldsymbol{h}_u^{(k)}$ and $\boldsymbol{h}_u^{(k+1)}$ denote the feature of node u in the k-th and $k+1$-th layer, and $v \in \mathcal{N}(u)$ represents the set of neighbors of node u. The functions U(), and A() refer to the update and aggregation operations of GNN. This process is fundamental for updating nodes along edges, where the scope of information propagation is determined by adjacent nodes.

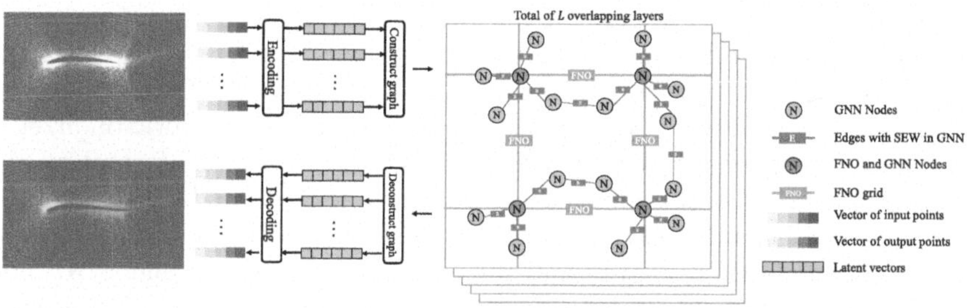

Fig. 1. GNNeF structure diagram. Firstly, GNNeF encodes the input into the latent space. Subsequently, the graph added with FNO points is calculated through multiple overlapping layers to extract local and global information. Finally the decoder is used to get the real physical result from latent space. One of the overlapping layers consists of FNO and GNN blocks, which fuse information after one execution. The GNNeF model acts directly on the space of irregular grids complemented by Cartesian grids. These two meshes coexist at any stage.

3 Methodology

In this work, we develop a noval framework named Enhanced GNN PDE Solver with embedded FNO, *GNNeF*. The architecture of GNNef is shown in Fig. 1. GNNef adopts a pattern that alternates execution of GNN and FNO, instead of considering these two operations as stages of sequential separation.

We first describe the general framework of *GNNeF* in Sect. 3.1. Further, we show the design of the overlapping layer in Sect. 3.2 and how to transmit messages through spatial encodin weights in Sect. 3.3, respectively. Then, we add Laplacian loss term in the loss function for continuity and smoothness of the solution when training, as shown in Sect. 3.4.

3.1 GNNeF Framework

FNO can capture global interaction and GNN excels at local features along edges. Previous works execute these two operations separately. GNN often maps the irregular physical space to a latent regular grid and inversely map the data after being presented by FNO. To fully leverage the advantage of GNN and FNO, and address the loss caused by the transition across different state spaces, we propose a GNN embedded in FNO(GNNeF).

Specifically, GNNeF has three improvements compared to previous work, (*i*) **Overlapping layer**: operation in spatial and frequency domain concurrently in the overlapping layer, (*ii*) **Spatial coding weights**: a flexible and learnable edge weight, (*iii*) **Laplacian Loss**: a loss term that makes the solution smoother.

The architecture of GNNeF is shown in Fig. 1. Similar to the overlapping grids, GNNeF simultaneously sample the nodes in the Cartesian mesh grid and the domain of the unstructured computational grid, called Cartesian nodes and unstructured nodes, respectively. These two type nodes are mixed as the input. **Encoder:** firstly, representations(i.e., boundary condition, position) of the inputs x are encoded into a higher dimensional hidden space. It is noteworthy that Cartesian mesh grid can be obtained through resampling on the irregular grid of arbitrary geometries. So our method can work on irregular input shape. **Communication of messages:** GNN propagate information along edges, allowing to pass the messages to every nodes, especially irregular mesh noes. FNO can efficiently learn global characteristics on the regular grids. So our work can exploit both strengths and interact between two manners. All nodes are computed through L overlapping layers and obtain abundant information, including the relationship with other nodes. In the GNN, spatial coding weights of the edges make the weight more reasonable and can be learned through relative coordinates. **Decoder:** the node obtain the final representation y after the decoder projected nodes into the desired space. At the time of training, we also take the loss after the Laplacian operation into account (Fig. 2).

3.2 The Overlapping Layer

In the field of CFD, computing using overlapping and multi-grids is an effective method to improve accuracy and Extensibility. To figure out if this technique can help to enhance GNN for solving PDEs, we propose overlapping layer. We employ two commonly used grids for modeling, namely mesh points (derived from Cartesian grid meshes) and unstructured points (sourced from unstructured meshes). The reason why adding mesh nodes on the original irregular mesh gird is that FNO can extract frequency domain using FFT but only work on the structured grid data. Based on such structure, FNO captures the large-scale features of fluid fields and low frequency structures. So that, GNN is able to focus on the low-scale features and high frequency structure. The input of the model is graph data structure $\mathcal{G} = (\mathcal{N}, \mathcal{E})$, where $\mathcal{N}$ represent the nodes in the graph and each node has *dim* features. In this work, $\mathcal{N}$ consists of two sections, Cartesian grid $\mathcal{N}_m$ and unstructured grid $\mathcal{N}_u$, respectively. $\mathcal{E}$ is the set of the

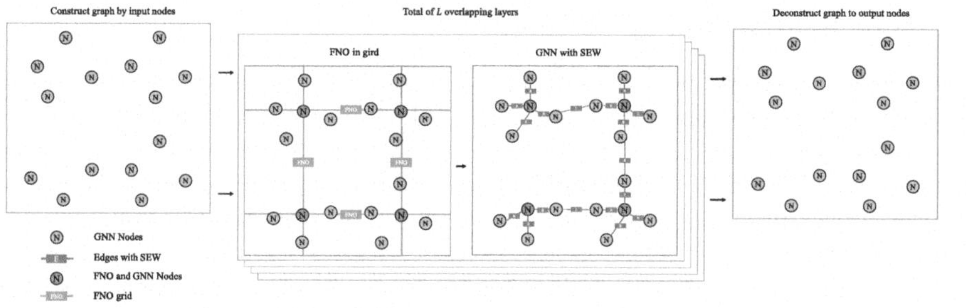

Fig. 2. Schematic of the overlapping layer. Initially, FNO nodes are added as temporary auxiliary computation points when constructing the graph, which are removed during the deconstruction of the graph. FNO operates within the Cartesian coordinate grid and performs Fourier transform in the frequency domain. In each overlapping layer, the output of the FNO layer is computed first, followed by the GNN layer, which integrates the information passed through subgraphs into all points.

edges connecting nodes that include bidirectional edges from $\mathcal{N}_u$ to $\mathcal{N}_u$ and unidirectional edges from $\mathcal{N}_m$ to $\mathcal{N}_u$. The weight of the edge is obtained by spatial encoding weight. The message passing from $\mathcal{N}_m$ to $\mathcal{N}_u$ is unidirectional in our framework.

In the calculation in the network layer, firstly, GNN performs message passing on N and E and all nodes in the N will be updated. The GNN propagation process is as follows:

$$N_u^{l+1}, N_m^{l*} = GRU(N_u^l, N_m^l) \tag{3}$$

where $N^{(l)}$ and $N^{(l+1)}$ are the node feature matrixe of the l-th layer and $(l+1)$-th layer, respectively. N_u and N_m are updated synchronously during this process.

Subsequently, $\mathcal{N}_m$ updates itself using spectral convolution operation of FNO and prepares for the next messages passing on the overlapping layer. The propagation process is as follows:

$$N_m^{(l+1)} = FNO(N_m^{(l)}, \theta) \tag{4}$$

$\mathcal{N}_m^{(l)}$ and $\mathcal{N}_m^{(l+1)}$ represent mesh node features on the l-th layer and the $l+1$-th layer, respectively. θ is the parameter of the FNO.

Through combining overlapping and multi-grids, it is possible to handle with massive mesh nodes. The design reduces dependency on single type of grid and improves overall computational efficiency. FNO performs exceptionally well on capturing large-scale feature and low frequency coherent structures which is necessary for simulating fluid dynamics precisely. Simultaneously, GNN does well in small-scale feature and highly frequency coherent structures, which plugs details. Furthermore, such implement can effectively accelerate computing. Compared to calculate and propagate separately for $\mathcal{N}_u$ and $\mathcal{N}_m$, propagation at the same time reduces parameters of the network and enhances the performance of the graph network.

3.3 The Spatial Coding Weights

When handling graph data structure, traditional GNN describe the interaction among nodes in fixed spatial weights or simple distance function. However, such way may capture the complex space relationship inadequately, especially when tackling graphs with complex topological structure or heterogeneity. Hence, we propose SEW, aiming at representing and treating the spatial relationship in the graph efficiently.

The main idea of SEW is adapting the connection weights between nodes based on the spatial encoding. The SEW can be represented as:

$$SEW(u, v) = encode(Pos_u - Pos_v, f(Pos_u, Pos_v)) \tag{5}$$

where, u and v are the nodes in the graph, Pos represents the spatial position of the nodes. $encode()$ is the spatial encoding function, which transfor position information of nodes into the represetation contributing to the weight computation. The position transformation function $f()$ expands the input information of the weights. SEW considers not only the topological relationships between nodes, but also factors in relative position in the space. This point is crucial in the context of graphs with significant spatial features, such as molecular structure, geography and so on. This integration of physical constraints is instrumental in enhancing the reliability and applicability of our model in real-world CFD scenarios, setting a new benchmark in the field.

3.4 The Laplacian Loss

A central element of our approach is the integration of mass conservation constraints, fundamental to the dynamics of incompressible fluids. Embedding these constraints into the GNNeF framework ensures high-precision fluid dynamics predictions while adhering to essential physical laws.

Our data-driven loss mechanism focuses on accurately fitting observed and predicted values, showing effectiveness in scenarios with copious high-quality data. However, it may overlook the intrinsic properties of PDE solutions, such as continuity and smoothness. To address this issue, we introduce the Laplacian loss term, L_{lap}, derived from the second-order differential equation of the Laplace operator. The Laplace operator, extensively utilized in mathematics and physics for ensuring continuity and smoothness, enhances our model's ability to emphasize not only the fit of numerical values but also the physical characteristics of the solution, crucial for accurate physical PDE solutions. Our aim is to incorporate physical priors into the model to enhance its scalability and numerical stability while fitting data values effectively.

Within the GNNeF framework, the loss function integrates both the data-driven loss and the Laplacian loss terms, with the latter playing a critical role in ensuring the model's fidelity to physical properties such as continuity and smoothness. The Laplacian operator, defined on a graph, is essential for approximating the divergence of fluid flows, thereby enhancing the model's ability to capture the inherent characteristics of fluid dynamics.

The Laplacian matrix $\mathbf{L}$ for a graph is defined as $\mathbf{L} = \mathbf{D} - \mathbf{A}$, where $\mathbf{D}$ is the degree matrix (a diagonal matrix containing the degree of each vertex) and $\mathbf{A}$ is the adjacency matrix of the graph. This operator approximates the Laplacian in continuous domains, which is pivotal for modeling fluid flow's divergence and ensuring the predicted flow is physically plausible.

The theoretical underpinning for using the Laplacian loss comes from its ability to approximate the divergence of fluid flows in the graph representation, making the results more continuous and smooth. This approximation is crucial for capturing the physical essence of incompressible fluids, where the Laplacian operator acts as a surrogate for fluid divergence.

To formalize this, the Laplacian loss for our model is defined as: $\text{LapLoss}(x, y) = ||\mathbf{L}x - \mathbf{L}y||^2$ where x and y represent the predicted and true values of the fluid properties at the nodes of the graph, respectively. This formulation directly encourages the minimization of the difference in the Laplacian-transformed space, thus enforcing the smoothness and continuity in the model's predictions.

Furthermore, the integration of volume (L_{vol}) and surface (L_{surf}) data losses, along with the Laplacian loss ($L_{\nabla^2 vol}$ and $L_{\nabla^2 surf}$), is facilitated through the hyperparameters α and β. These parameters allow for the weighted combination of loss terms, enabling the model to adaptively focus on different aspects of the data according to the specific requirements of the fluid dynamics problem at hand.

Ultimately, our approach inherently weights the components of the loss function, providing a mechanism to balance between fitting the data-driven aspects and adhering to the physical properties dictated by the Laplacian loss. This weighted loss function ensures that our model not only achieves high accuracy in fluid dynamics predictions but also respects the fundamental physical laws governing fluid behavior.

4 Experiments

4.1 Dataset

In this section, to validate the capability of our proposed model GNNeF, we conduct a series of ablation experiments on AirfRANS dataset [1] to verify the effectiveness of each module. AirfRANS dataset is developed for airfoil design optimization and provides 1000 NACA airfoils simulations results with the help of the steady-state Reynolds-averaged Navier Stokes(RANS) solver. The dataset has provide 3 standard GDL models and a Multi-Layer Perception(MLP) as the baselines. They are referred to as GraphSAGE, PointNet, Graph U-Net and MLP, respectively. From Table 1 and Table 2, we can observe that 4 models provided by AirfRANS excel in different metrics. There is not a single model outperforms the others across the majority of metrics. Below, we present detail comparisons between our model and the baselines. The values in bold in the following tables donate the optimal scores for the metric in each column.

Table 1. Mean squared error of various models on the test set.

Model	Volume				Surface
	$\bar{u}_x(\times10^{-2})$	$\bar{u}_y(\times10^{-2})$	$\bar{p}(\times10^{-2})$	$\bar{\upsilon}_t(\times10^{-2})$	$\bar{p}(\times10^{-1})$
MLP	0.95	0.98	0.74	1.90	1.13
GraphSAGE	0.83	0.99	0.66	1.60	0.66
PointNet	3.50	3.64	1.15	2.92	0.93
Graph U-Net	1.52	2.03	0.66	1.46	0.39
GNN	0.735	0.547	0.405	0.842	0.069
GNNeF	0.566	0488	0.403	0433	0.050
GNNeF+$loss_{lap}$	0.339	0.225	0.314	**0.539**	**0.043**
GNNeF+SEW	0.842	0.616	0.489	0.983	0.081
Overlapping+SEW	0.680	0.290	0.327	0.524	0.059
GNNeF+SEW+$loss_{lap}$	**0.270**	**0.166**	**0.311**	0.543	0.045

Table 2. Relative errors (Err. %) and Spearman's rank correlation coefficient (ρ) for drag (C_D) and lift (C_L) coefficients.

	MLP		GraphSAGE		PointNet		Graph U-Net		GNN	
	Err.	ρ	Err.	ρ	Err.	ρ	Err.	ρ	Err.	ρ
C_D	4.289	-0.117	4.050	-0.303	14.637	-0.022	10.385	-0.138	2.920	0.249
C_L	0.767	0.913	0.517	0.965	0.742	0.938	0.489	0.967	0.126	0.998

4.2 Experiments Setting

For each geometry case, a mesh contains hundreds of thousands of nodes including approximate 1000 on the surface. To maintain consistency with the baselines and efficient training model, we randomly sample 32,000 nodes as a batch. It is worth noting that to fully make use of the geometric shape information, samples include all nodes on the surfaces. We follow the original full data regime with 800 samples for training and 200 for testing. We train all the models with 398 epochs to maintain consistency with the baselines. For GNNeF training, each sample have Cartesian nodes and 32000 mesh nodes including all surface nodes and random sampling nodes from volume. All the calculations for model training and testing are down on a single Nvidia A100 GPU with 80GB memory.

4.3 Evaluation Metrics

We employ the Mean Squared Error (MSE) as the metric to measure the predictive accuracy of models. We separately assessed the models' abilities to predict physical quantities at surface of the geometry and on the volume. For practical application considerations, we are also interested in the forces on the airfoil surface and analyse the performance of GNNeF in the follow section. In the

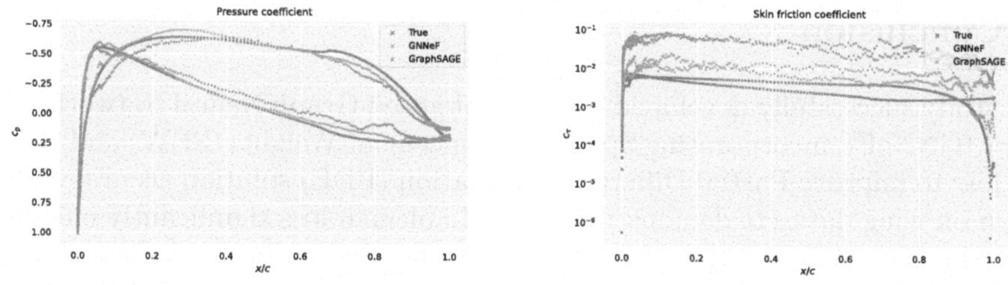

(a) Pressure coefficient (b) Skin friction coefficient

Fig. 3. Surface coefficient (left) and skin friction coefficient (right) on airfoil NACA(6.09,3.38,7.324,0) at a velocity of $86.166ms^{-1}$ and at an angle of attack of $13.513°$. Skin friction coefficient plots are given in log scale.

training phrase, the loss function without Laplacian loss term is presented as the balanced the weight of the error at the surface of the geometry and over the volume:

$$\mathcal{L} := \underbrace{\frac{1}{|\mathcal{V}_{vol}|} \sum_{i \in \mathcal{V}_{vol}} \|f_\theta(x_i) - y_i\|_2^2}_{\mathcal{L}_\mathcal{V}} + \lambda \underbrace{\frac{1}{|\mathcal{V}_{suf}|} \sum_{i \in \mathcal{V}_{suf}} \|f_\theta(x_i) - y_i\|_2^2}_{\mathcal{L}_\mathcal{S}} \tag{6}$$

where x_i and y_i represent the input and the output at node i. f_θ is the model used. In this work, the coefficient λ to balance the two terms is set to 1. The model trained with Laplacian loss term add loss term Equation ?? based on the formula above. It should be reminded that in models with overlapping layers, we did not calculate errors caused by Cartesian nodes. Cartesian nodes only help to enhance the final outcome and have been masked before calculating the loss.

4.4 Qualitative Evaluation

Table 1 shows GNNeF outperforms prior methods, reducing MSE errors by over 50% in most physical fields (up to several orders of magnitude vs. baselines).

Laplacian loss ($loss_{lap}$) cuts velocity x/y-component MSE by 60% and 43% respectively, while GNNeF performs comparably to top models for surface pressure and volumetric turbulent kinematic viscosity. For force coefficients (Table 2), GNNeF significantly reduces lift/drag relative errors vs. baselines, with Laplacian loss enhancing prediction accuracy and yielding the highest Spearman's correlation. Visualizations (Figs. 3, 3b) demonstrate GNNeF's pressure/skin friction coefficient predictions are far closer to ground truth than GraphSAGE, despite room for improvement at specific locations. Notably, Laplacian loss—originally integrated for velocity fields—also induces geometry-dependent smoothing to improve pressure field consistency.

5 Conclusion

This study successfully developed a novel Enhanced Graph Neural Network PDE Solver (GNNeF), incorporating Spatial Enhancement Weights (SEW) and Laplacian loss to improve Partial Differential Equation (PDE) solution accuracy. Validation on wing datasets demonstrates that Laplacian loss significantly enhances prediction accuracy on the wing surface, while the addition of SEW further boosts overall performance.

The GNNeF framework integrates GNN and FNO through an overlapping layer: FNO extracts modes on the Cartesian grid and transmits frequency information to the GNN layer, enabling efficient propagation of local sub-graph messages and global information. Node edges adopt dynamic weights adjusted by relative positions, and Laplacian loss not only improves the continuity and smoothness of PDE solutions but also enhances physical rationality via output fitting.

Acknowledgments. This work was supported by the Strategic Priority Research Program of Chinese Academy of Sciences, Grant XDB0620401.

References

1. Bonnet, F., Mazari, J., Cinnella, P., Gallinari, P.: AirfRANS: high fidelity computational fluid dynamics dataset for approximating Reynolds-Averaged Navier-Stokes solutions. Adv. Neural. Inf. Process. Syst. **35**, 23463–23478 (2022)
2. Chong, S.S., Ng, Y.S., Wang, H.Q., Zheng, J.C.: Advances of machine learning in materials science: ideas and techniques. Front. Phys. **19**(1), 13501 (2023). https://doi.org/10.1007/s11467-023-1325-z
3. Cuomo, S., Di Cola, V.S., Giampaolo, F., Rozza, G., Raissi, M., Piccialli, F.: Scientific machine learning through physics-informed neural networks: where we are and what's next. J. Sci. Comput. **92**(3), 88 (2022). https://doi.org/10.1007/s10915-022-01939-z
4. Ezhov, I., et al.: Geometry-aware neural solver for fast Bayesian calibration of brain tumor models. IEEE Trans. Med. Imaging **41**(5), 1269–1278 (2021). https://ieeexplore.ieee.org/abstract/document/9656125/, publisher: IEEE
5. Karniadakis, G.E., Kevrekidis, I.G., Lu, L., Perdikaris, P., Wang, S., Yang, L.: Physics-informed machine learning. Nat. Rev. Phys. **3**(6), 422–440 (2021). https://doi.org/10.1038/s42254-021-00314-5, https://www.nature.com/articles/s42254-021-00314-5, number: 6 Publisher: Nature Publishing Group
6. Kovachki, N., Lanthaler, S., Mishra, S.: On universal approximation and error bounds for Fourier neural operators. J. Mach. Learn. Res. **22**(1), 290:13237–290:13312 (2021)
7. Kumar, H., Yadav, N.: Deep learning algorithms for solving differential equations: a survey. J. Exper. Theor. Artif. Intell., 1–40 (2023). https://doi.org/10.1080/0952813X.2023.2242356, publisher: Taylor & Francis eprint
8. Li, Z., Huang, D.Z., Liu, B., Anandkumar, A.: Fourier neural operator with learned deformations for PDEs on general geometries. arXiv preprint arXiv:2207.05209 (2022). https://arxiv.org/abs/2207.05209

9. Li, Z., Kovachki, N.B., Azizzadenesheli, K., Bhattacharya, K., Stuart, A., Anandkumar, A.: Fourier neural operator for parametric partial differential equations. In: International Conference on Learning Representations (2020)
10. Li, Z., et al.: Physics-informed neural operator for learning partial differential equations. arXiv preprint arXiv:2111.03794 (2021)
11. Lin, B., Mao, Z., Wang, Z., Karniadakis, G.E.: Operator learning enhanced physics-informed neural networks for solving partial differential equations characterized by sharp solutions (2023). https://doi.org/10.48550/arXiv.2310.19590, arXiv:2310.19590 [cs, math]
12. Fernández de la Mata, F., Gijón, A., Molina-Solana, M., Gómez-Romero, J.: Physics-informed neural networks for data-driven simulation: advantages, limitations, and opportunities. Physica A: Stat. Mech. Appl. **610**, 128415 (2023). https://doi.org/10.1016/j.physa.2022.128415, https://www.sciencedirect.com/science/article/pii/S0378437122009736
13. Muther, T., Dahaghi, A.K., Syed, F.I., Van Pham, V.: Physical laws meet machine intelligence: current developments and future directions. Artif. Intell. Rev. **56**(7), 6947–7013 (2023). https://doi.org/10.1007/s10462-022-10329-8
14. Panchigar, D., Kar, K., Shukla, S., Mathew, R.M., Chadha, U., Selvaraj, S.K.: Machine learning-based CFD simulations: a review, models, open threats, and future tactics. Neural Comput. Appl. **34**(24), 21677–21700 (2022). https://doi.org/10.1007/s00521-022-07838-6
15. Zhu, M., Zhang, H., Jiao, A., Karniadakis, G.E., Lu, L.: Reliable extrapolation of deep neural operators informed by physics or sparse observations. Comput. Methods Appl. Mech. Eng. **412**, 116064 (2023). https://doi.org/10.1016/j.cma.2023.116064, https://www.sciencedirect.com/science/article/pii/S0045782523001883

Compositional Concept-Based Neuron-Level Explanations for Deep Reinforcement Learning

Zeyu Jiang, Hai Huang(✉), and Xingquan Zuo

School of Computer Science, Beijing University of Posts and Telecommunications, Beijing 100876, China
{zeyujiang,hhuang,zuoxq}@bupt.edu.cn

Abstract. Deep reinforcement learning (DRL) has successfully addressed many complex control problems. However, the neural networks representing policies or values remain opaque, undermining trust in high-stakes applications. While concept-based methods have shown promise in deciphering internal representations in computer vision, applying them to DRL is impeded by the absence of pre-defined semantic concepts in continuous state spaces. In this work, we propose a novel concept-based explanation framework designed to provide fine-grained, neuron-level insights into DRL models. Unlike previous approaches that rely on manual feature engineering, our framework automatically aligns neuron activations with logical formulas composed of semantic predicates. To bridge the gap between continuous signals and symbolic reasoning, we introduce a value-sensitive discretization mechanism that transforms raw state features into interpretable atomic concepts. This ensures that the vocabulary used for explanation captures strategic decision boundaries relevant to the agent's value assessment. By composing these interpretable concepts and matching them with neuron behaviors, we derive explicit explanations for the network's internal representations. Experimental results on both continuous and discrete environments demonstrate that our method effectively identifies meaningful decision-making patterns, offering faithful explanations that align with human intuition.

Keywords: Deep Reinforcement Learning · Interpretability · Explainability · Feature Discretization

1 Introduction

Deep reinforcement learning (DRL) has achieved remarkable success in solving complex sequential decision-making problems through trial-and-error learning. From game playing to robotic control, DRL has demonstrated strong capabilities across various domains. However, the increasing complexity of DRL models, particularly their neural network architectures, has created a significant challenge in comprehending their internal logic. This opacity hinders their deployment in

R. C.-W. Wong et al. (Eds.): PAKDD 2026, LNAI 16617, pp. 52–64, 2027.
https://doi.org/10.1007/978-981-92-1926-1_5

safety-critical applications such as healthcare, autonomous driving, and financial trading, where understanding the "why" behind a decision is as crucial as the decision itself.

Existing approaches to DRL transparency primarily focus on post-hoc explanations [19]. These include applying classic attribution methods like SHAP [14] and attention mechanisms [11] to identify important input features, or summarizing agent behavior through causal graphs [22]. While these methods provide valuable insights into input-output relationships, they largely treat neural networks as black boxes, failing to reveal how individual neurons encode information and contribute to the decision-making process.

To achieve fine-grained transparency, researchers in computer vision have developed concept-based methods that match individual neurons with human-understandable concepts [1,10]. However, extending this paradigm to Reinforcement Learning faces a critical bottleneck: the absence of pre-defined semantic concepts. Unlike image datasets where concepts like "dog" or "texture" are inherent, RL environments often involve continuous state variables (e.g., velocity, coordinates) that do not naturally map to discrete predicates. Manually defining such concepts (e.g., "velocity > 0.5") is subjective and often misaligned with the specific control logic learned by the agent.

In this paper, we address this challenge by proposing a compositional concept-based explanation framework specifically tailored for DRL. Our approach operates at the neuron level, decoding the internal representations of policy or value networks into explicit logical formulas. To bridge the gap between continuous signals and symbolic reasoning, we introduce a value-sensitive mechanism that transforms raw state features into interpretable atomic concepts. Instead of relying on arbitrary manual thresholds, this mechanism utilizes the trained agent's value function to guide the discretization of continuous features. By identifying intervals that correspond to significant shifts in expected return, we extract a vocabulary of interpretable concepts that are grounded in the agent's own strategic assessment.

As illustrated in Fig. 1, our framework first induces these interpretable atomic concepts from the state space. Next, it constructs compositional formulas using logical operations. Finally, it aligns these formulas with neuron activations to generate explicit explanations for individual neurons.

To rigorously evaluate the fidelity of our explanations, we validate the framework on environments characterized by clear semantic structures and physical dynamics (Blackjack-v1, LunarLander-v3). Unlike complex tasks where the ground-truth decision logic is often obscure, these environments allow us to directly compare the derived explanations against established optimal policies. This experimental design ensures that our explanations are not only intuitive but also mathematically consistent with the agent's true behavior. Our implementation is publicly available (GitHub Repository).

Contributions. The main contributions of this work are three-fold: (1) **We develop a concept-based neuron explanation framework for DRL** that reveals how individual neurons contribute to decisions using compositional log-

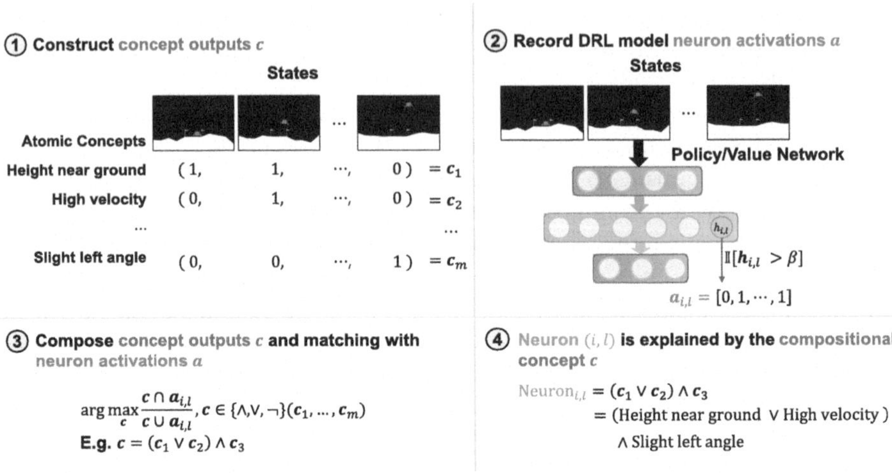

Fig. 1. Our concept-based explanation framework for DRL. (1) Automatic Concept Induction: Continuous state features are partitioned into atomic concepts (e.g., "Critical Velocity") based on value function sensitivity; (2) Concept Construction: Concept vectors are generated for state sequences; (3) Neuron Analysis: DRL model activations are recorded; (4) Matching: Each neuron is explained by the compositional concept that best matches its activation pattern via beam search optimization.

ical formulas, moving beyond simple input-output attribution. (2) **We introduce a value-sensitive discretization method to generate interpretable atomic concepts.** This approach bridges the gap between raw numerical states and symbolic reasoning by automatically partitioning continuous features based on the agent's value estimates. (3) **We demonstrate the effectiveness and fidelity of our approach** on representative environments (Blackjack-v1, LunarLander-v3), showing that the framework uncovers meaningful decision-making patterns consistent with human intuition and allows for predictable behavior manipulation.

2 Related Work

Explainability in Reinforcement Learning. RL explainability is broadly categorized into self-interpretable and post-hoc methods [13]. Self-interpretable approaches modify architectures for transparency, employing programmatic policies [18], linear trees [9], symbolic learning [3,8,12], or concept bottlenecks [21,23]. While inherently interpretable, these often compromise expressiveness. Conversely, post-hoc methods analyze trained policies via causal modeling [22], language templates [2,5], or attribution techniques [6,11,14,15]. Unlike these I/O-focused methods, our work investigates the internal neural representations driving decisions.

Concept-based Explanations. These methods align neural representations with human-understandable concepts. Pioneered by Network Dissection [1], the field has evolved to include directional derivatives (TCAV) [7], automated concept discovery (ACE) [4], and compositional explanations (CEN) [10], extending to architectures like GNNs [20]. While successful in supervised learning, concept-based analysis remains underutilized in RL. We address this gap by adapting compositional methods to capture the temporal and strategic dependencies inherent in RL agents.

3 Methodology

3.1 Concept Formalization

We formalize the explanation problem by defining a mapping between the continuous state space $S \subseteq \mathbb{R}^n$ and a set of binary concepts. An *atomic concept* is a function $C : S \to 0, 1$ that indicates whether a state variable lies within a specified interval (e.g., $C(s) = \mathbb{I}[y \in [0, 0.52]]$ represents "low altitude").

Compositional concepts are constructed recursively from atomic concepts using the logical operations $\mathcal{O} = \{\wedge, \vee, \neg\}$. For any $C_1, C_2 \in \mathcal{C}$, we define conjunction as $(C_1 \wedge C_2)(s) = C_1(s) \cdot C_2(s)$, disjunction as $(C_1 \vee C_2)(s) = \max(C_1(s), C_2(s))$, and negation as $(\neg C_1)(s) = 1 - C_1(s)$. A compositional concept is thus a logical formula formed by nesting these operations.

3.2 Value-Sensitive Atomic Concept Induction

Standard environments typically provide raw continuous features without semantic predicates. To bridge this gap, we propose an automatic induction method that discretizes continuous features based on the agent's value function $V(s)$. Given a dataset $\mathcal{D} = \{s_1, \ldots, s_N\}$ of states sampled from the trained agent's experience, we partition each continuous dimension into semantically meaningful intervals. For actor-critic methods, we use the state value directly; for Q-learning agents, we use $V(s) = \max_a Q(s, a)$. Unlike uniform discretization, our approach is **Task-Aware**: we identify thresholds where the expected return exhibits significant variation.

For each state dimension x_i, we partition its domain into disjoint intervals $\{I_1, \ldots, I_K\}$ via recursive partitioning that maximizes **Variance Reduction**. For a candidate threshold τ dividing dataset $\mathcal{D}$ into $\mathcal{D}_L$ (where $x_i \leq \tau$) and $\mathcal{D}_R$ (where $x_i > \tau$), the variance reduction is defined as:

$$\mathcal{VR}(\tau) = \mathrm{Var}(V)_{\mathcal{D}} - \left(\frac{|\mathcal{D}_L|}{|\mathcal{D}|} \mathrm{Var}(V)_{\mathcal{D}_L} + \frac{|\mathcal{D}_R|}{|\mathcal{D}|} \mathrm{Var}(V)_{\mathcal{D}_R} \right). \tag{1}$$

Each resulting interval I_j is converted into an atomic concept $C_{i,j}(s) = \mathbb{I}[x_i(s) \in I_j]$.

Determining Partition Granularity. We select the number of intervals K by minimizing reconstruction error $\mathcal{L}(K)$, defined as the MSE between $V(s)$ and the piecewise constant approximation:

$$\mathcal{L}(K) = \frac{1}{N} \sum_{j=1}^{K} \sum_{s \in I_j} \left(V(s) - \bar{V}_j\right)^2, \tag{2}$$

where $\bar{V}_j$ is the mean value within interval I_j. We use the *Elbow Method* [16] to identify where marginal improvement diminishes, balancing interpretability with fidelity.

3.3 Neural Activation Analysis

Given the dataset $\mathcal{D}$ defined above, let $h_u(s)$ denote the activation of neuron u for state s. Our goal is to find the concept $C \in \mathcal{C}$ that best explains when neuron u activates.

Similarity Measure. We first convert continuous activations into binary indicators. For each state s_n, we define $a_u^{(n)} = \mathbb{I}[h_u(s_n) > \beta]$, where β is a threshold (e.g., $\beta = 0$ for ReLU networks, capturing whether the neuron is active). This yields an activation pattern $\mathbf{a}_u = (a_u^{(1)}, \dots, a_u^{(N)}) \in \{0,1\}^N$.

Similarly, evaluating concept C on each state produces a concept pattern $\mathbf{c} = (C(s_1), \dots, C(s_N)) \in \{0,1\}^N$. We measure alignment between neuron and concept using the Jaccard similarity:

$$J(\mathbf{a}_u, \mathbf{c}) = \frac{|\mathbf{a}_u \cap \mathbf{c}|}{|\mathbf{a}_u \cup \mathbf{c}|}. \tag{3}$$

The explanation task is to find $C_u^* = \arg\max_{C \in \mathcal{C}} J(\mathbf{a}_u, \mathbf{c})$.

Optimization via Beam Search. We employ Beam Search (Algorithm 1) to explore the concept space. We maintain a beam $\mathcal{B}$ of top-W candidates, expanding by applying operators from $\mathcal{O}$ and pruning lower-scoring concepts. The search runs for D iterations, controlling the maximum number of composition steps. We restrict compositions to (c_1, c_2) where $c_1 \in \mathcal{B}$ and $c_2 \in \mathcal{A}$, reducing complexity to $O(W \cdot |\mathcal{A}|)$ per iteration.

4 Experiments

We evaluate our method on two reinforcement learning environments: *Blackjack-v1* (discrete) and *LunarLander-v3* (continuous) from Gymnasium [17]. Our experiments aim to answer two key questions: (1) **Explainability**: Can the proposed method automatically induce meaningful concepts and discover human-understandable neural mechanisms? (2) **Fidelity**: Are the generated explanations faithful enough to enable targeted behavior manipulation?

Algorithm 1. Neuron Explanation Pipeline

Input: Activations $\mathbf{a}_u$, Atomic Concepts $\mathcal{A}$, Beam Width W, Max Depth D
Output: Best Concept C^*
$\mathcal{B} \leftarrow \mathcal{A}$, $C^* \leftarrow$ None, Score$^* \leftarrow 0$
for $d = 1 \ldots D$ **do**
  $\mathcal{K} \leftarrow \{op(c_1, c_2) \mid c_1 \in \mathcal{B}, c_2 \in \mathcal{A}, op \in \{\wedge, \vee\}\} \cup \{\neg c \mid c \in \mathcal{B}\}$
  Calculate $J(\mathbf{a}_u, \mathbf{c})$ for all $c \in \mathcal{K}$
  Update C^* if $\max_{c \in \mathcal{K}} J >$ Score*
  $\mathcal{B} \leftarrow$ SelectTop$(\mathcal{K}, W)$
return C^*

4.1 Experimental Setup

Environments and Policy Training. *Blackjack* features a naturally discrete 3-dimensional state space. *LunarLander* involves an 8-dimensional continuous state space, comprising coordinates (x, y), velocities (v_x, v_y), angle (θ), angular velocity (ω), and two binary leg contact indicators. For both tasks, we trained DQN agents with three fully connected layers (64 units each). This minimal architecture was selected based on an interpretability-capacity analysis (Fig. 2): larger networks achieve similar rewards but exhibit lower neuron-concept alignment, as task knowledge becomes distributed across more units. The agents achieved near-optimal performance. We focus our analysis on the penultimate layer, as the final layer directly maps to Q-values with fixed semantics, while the penultimate layer captures the learned abstract representations.

Concept Instantiation. To generate the atomic concept set, we applied the value-sensitive partitioning described in Sect. 3.2. We utilized the trained agent's Q-values, $Q(s, \arg\max_a Q(s, a))$, as the target signal $y(s)$ to guide the discretization.

Granularity Selection. We first determined the optimal number of intervals K for the continuous features in *LunarLander*. We computed the reconstruction error $\mathcal{L}(K)$ on a validation set of 10,000 states. As illustrated in **Fig.** 3, the error decreases rapidly and exhibits a clear "elbow" at $K = 4$. Consequently, we set $K = 4$ for all continuous dimensions, balancing semantic compactness with value-approximation fidelity.

Induced Semantics. Using $K = 4$, we generated the partition thresholds shown in **Table** 1. Each interval within a dimension constitutes an atomic concept; we denote these as $X_1, X_2, \ldots$ for horizontal position, $V_{x,1}, V_{x,2}, \ldots$ for horizontal velocity, and analogously for other dimensions, where the subscript index increases with the interval's position along the axis.

It is worth noting that although these thresholds are derived purely from value function variance, they align well with human intuition. For example, the vertical velocity v_y is partitioned at -0.48 and 0.07, yielding concepts that

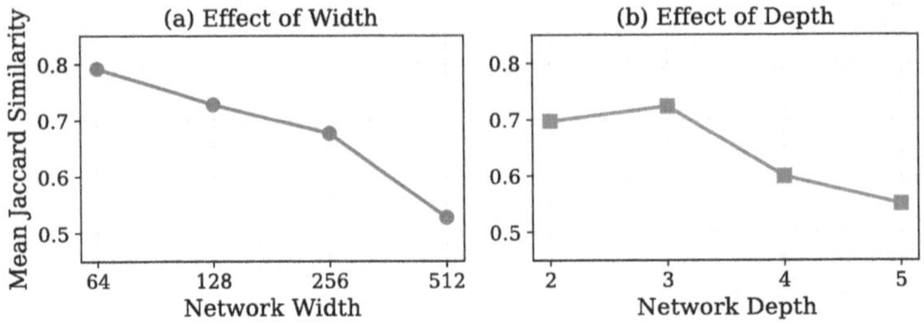

Fig. 2. Neuron interpretability (mean Jaccard Similarity) vs. network architecture. (a) Jaccard Similarity decreases monotonically with width. (b) Depth=3 achieves optimal alignment. All configurations solve the task; we select 64×3 for analysis.

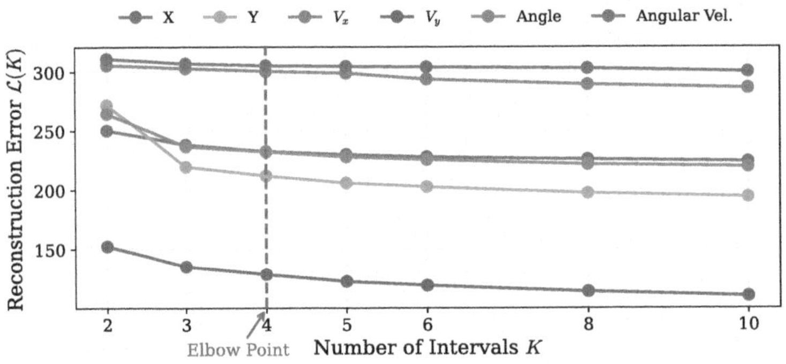

Fig. 3. Reconstruction error $\mathcal{L}(K)$ versus partition granularity K for each state dimension in LunarLander. The elbow point at $K = 4$ balances interpretability and fidelity.

effectively distinguish semantic regimes such as $V_{y,1}$: "fast descent," $V_{y,2}$: "slow descent," $V_{y,3}$: "stable hovering," and $V_{y,4}$: "ascent." These induced intervals serve as the ground-truth vocabulary for the subsequent neuron interpretation.

Explanation Generation Settings. We collected a dataset $\mathcal{S}$ of 100,000 transitions for concept generation and a separate set of 10,000 states for neuron analysis. For the Beam Search (Algorithm 1), we configured the beam width $w = 10$ and a maximum formula length of 5 to prevent overly complex explanations. Neuron activations were binarized using a threshold $\beta = 0$ (ReLU cutoff). To filter out dead or redundant units, we only analyzed neurons that were active in at least 5% of the sampled states.

4.2 Explainability Analysis

LunarLander. In LunarLander, the induced concepts reveal structured neuron responses. As shown in Fig. 4, neurons align with distinct physical conditions.

Table 1. Automatically induced atomic concepts for LunarLander-v3 ($K = 4$). The continuous state space is partitioned based on value function variance reduction. The resulting thresholds capture critical control boundaries (e.g., $v_y \approx 0$ for hovering).

Feature	Range	Unit	Induced Thresholds		
			τ_1	τ_2	τ_3
Position X (x)	$[-1.5, 1.5]$	coord	-0.02	0.12	0.23
Position Y (y)	$[0, 1.5]$	coord	0.52	0.91	1.37
Velocity X (v_x)	$[-2.5, 2.5]$	unit/s	-0.61	-0.34	0.48
Velocity Y (v_y)	$[-2.5, 2.5]$	unit/s	-0.66	-0.48	0.07
Angle (θ)	$[-\pi, \pi]$	rad	-0.08	0.07	0.13
Ang. Vel (ω)	$[-5, 5]$	rad/s	0.00	0.004	0.09
Leg Contacts	$\{0, 1\}$	bool	*N/A (Binary)*		

Neuron 19: Ground Contact Detector. Neuron 19 achieves a high Jaccard similarity of 0.984 with the formula:$\phi_{19} = \text{LLeg} \wedge \text{RLeg}$. This formula indicates a strict dependency on the binary sensors for the landing gear. As shown in the top row of Fig. 4, the neuron is highly active ($h(s) \approx 7.9$) specifically when both the left and right legs are in contact with the surface. Conversely, it deactivates immediately upon liftoff. This suggests that Neuron 19 serves as a reliable indicator for the "landed" state, aggregating the discrete leg sensor inputs.

Neuron 41: Altitude-Velocity Composite Detector. Neuron 41 ($J = 0.999$) encodes a composite condition involving both spatial position and kinematic dynamics. The induced formula is:$\phi_{41} = (\omega_1 \vee V_{x_3}) \wedge \neg\text{RLeg} \vee V_{x_4} \vee Y_4$.

The structure of the formula reveals that this neuron is multimodal. Specifically, the disjunction terms Y_4 and V_{x_4} indicate that the neuron activates independently when the agent is either at a high altitude ($Y > 0.91$) *or* maintaining a high horizontal velocity ($V_x \in V_{x_4}$), regardless of its vertical position. The term $(\omega_1 \vee V_{x_3}) \wedge \neg\text{RLeg}$ further captures states where the lander is airborne with specific rotational or moderate lateral movements. Consequently, Neuron 41 does not track a single physical variable but rather monitors a "high-energy" state characterized by either significant potential energy (altitude) or kinetic energy (velocity).

Neuron 9: Low-Altitude Left Region Monitor. Neuron 9 ($J = 0.840$) encodes a spatial condition via $\phi_9 = (\text{LLeg} \vee X_1) \wedge \neg Y_4$, where X_1 denotes the far-left region ($x < -0.02$) and $\neg Y_4$ indicates non-peak altitude ($y \leq 0.91$). As shown in Fig. 4, the neuron activates when the lander occupies the lower-left quadrant, with LLeg extending activation to ground-contact states in this region. This demonstrates that the agent's internal representation partitions the state space into distinct spatial zones.

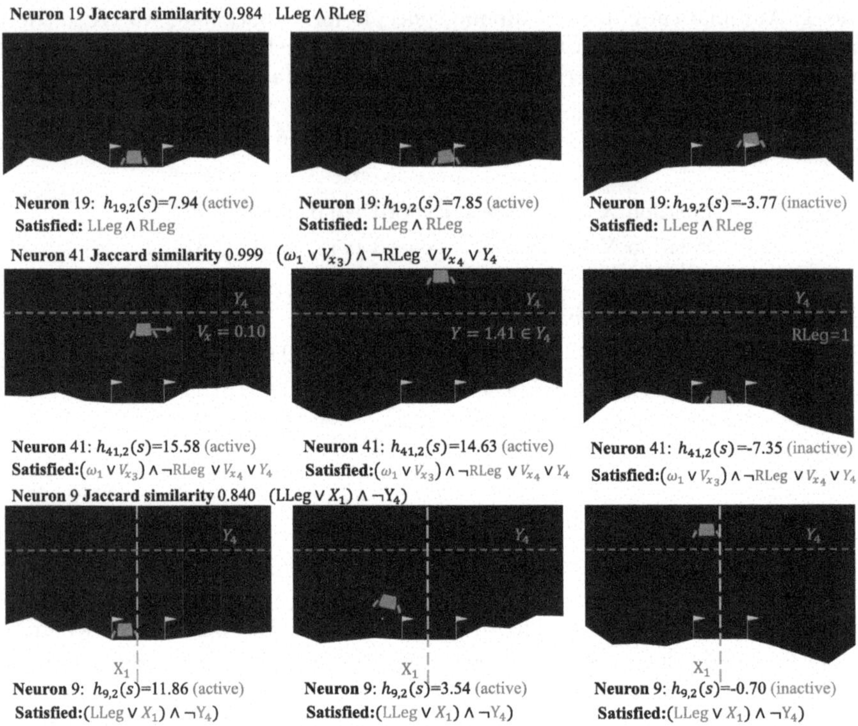

Fig. 4. Visualization of three explained neurons in LunarLander. For each neuron, we display the induced logical formula, the Jaccard similarity (J), and three sample states (active in red, inactive in green). The results show that the neurons encode specific physical concepts: (Top) dual leg ground contact, (Middle) high-altitude or high-velocity states, and (Bottom) a specific spatial region defined by low altitude and left-side positioning. (Color figure online)

Blackjack. In Blackjack, the interpreted neurons (Table 2) align closely with standard card counting strategies. Neuron 28 identifies "safe" hands ($17 \leq$ Sum ≤ 21), strongly contributing to the *Stick* action ($w_{stick} > w_{hit}$). Conversely, Neuron 13 detects "weak" hands ($6 \leq$ Sum ≤ 10), driving the agent to *Hit*. More subtly, Neuron 60 captures a risk condition: holding a high sum (20-21) without a usable Ace against a Dealer's 10. Its negative weights for both actions suggest it acts as a value suppressor in almost-lost situations. These results show the method can extract exact symbolic rules from the neural policy.

4.3 Validation via Targeted Perturbation

To verify that our explanations causally explain the agent's behavior, we conduct targeted perturbation experiments. We identify critical neurons for specific actions and modify the state variables involved in their assigned concepts to observe changes in activation and decision-making.

Table 2. Explained neurons in Blackjack. Concepts align with game rules, and weights (w) indicate their contribution to action selection.

ID	Jacc.	Concept	w_{stick}	w_{hit}
28	0.92	$P_{17} \vee P_{18} \vee P_{19} \vee P_{20} \vee P_{21}$	**0.37**	0.16
13	0.79	$P_6 \vee P_7 \vee P_8 \vee P_9 \vee P_{10}$	−0.81	**−0.35**
17	0.89	$D_7 \vee D_8 \vee D_9 \vee D_{10}$	−0.20	−0.08
6	0.89	$\neg P_9 \wedge \neg P_{10} \wedge \neg P_{11}$	0.08	−0.19
60	0.60	NoAce $\wedge P_{20} \vee P_{21} \wedge D_{10}$	−0.148	−0.268

LunarLander Case Study. We analyze the decision logic for Action 1 (*Left Engine*) via its top-3 contributing neurons (5, 41, and 29), focusing on Neuron 5, whose formula is dominated by the spatial term X_4, representing the agent being positioned to the right of the landing pad. As shown in Fig. 5, when this concept is satisfied in the original state, Neuron 5 activates strongly and the agent selects the *Left Engine* to correct its trajectory. A targeted perturbation shifting the lander to the left violates the concept, deactivates Neuron 5, and causes the agent to switch to the *Main Engine*. This confirms that Neuron 5 functions as a spatial trigger explicitly encoding the "correction from right" maneuver.

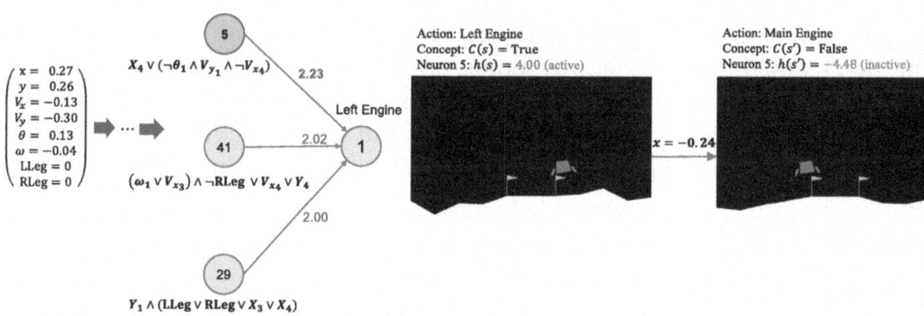

Fig. 5. Causal validation via targeted perturbation in LunarLander. Neuron 5, the primary contributor to the *Left Engine* action, encodes concept X_4 (right-side spatial region). (Left) Original state ($x = 0.27$): concept holds, $h = 4.00$, agent selects *Left Engine*. (Right) After perturbation ($x = -0.24$): concept violated, $h = -4.48$, agent switches to *Main Engine*.

Blackjack Case Study. We extend this validation to Blackjack (Table 3). For Neuron 28 (High Sum), perturbing the player's hand from 20 to 14 deactivates the neuron and flips the action from *Stick* to *Hit*. Similarly, for Neuron 17 (Dealer Strong), changing the dealer's card from 9 to 5 deactivates the risk-sensing neuron. In all cases, manipulating the features defined by our concepts leads to predictable behavioral changes, demonstrating that our method extracts the true decision logic of the Deep RL agent.

Table 3. Perturbation results in Blackjack. Violating the concept condition consistently flips neuron activation (Active → Inactive) and alters the agent's decision.

ID	Concept	Original State → Action	Perturbed → Action
28	$P_{\geq 17}$	(20, 9, 0) → **Stick**	(14, 9, 0) → **Hit**
		$h = 2.04$ (Active)	$h = -1.03$ (Inactive)
13	$P_{\leq 10}$	(6, 9, 0) → **Hit**	(17, 9, 0) → **Stick**
		$h = 2.04$ (Active)	$h = -6.89$ (Inactive)
17	$D_{\geq 7}$	(15, 9, 0) → **Hit**	(15, 5, 0) → **Stick**
		$h = 1.07$ (Active)	$h = -0.92$ (Inactive)

5 Conclusion

We presented a framework for extracting neuron-level explanations in Deep Reinforcement Learning as human-readable logical formulas, supported by Value-Sensitive Atomic Concept Induction that automatically derives semantically meaningful state discretizations without manual annotation. Experiments on Blackjack-v1 and LunarLander-v3 demonstrate interpretable neuron functions aligned with domain semantics, with perturbation-based validation confirming their causal rather than correlational nature. Future work will extend this to high-dimensional visual inputs and formal safety verification in autonomous systems.

References

1. Bau, D., Zhou, B., Khosla, A., Oliva, A., Torralba, A.: Network dissection: quantifying interpretability of deep visual representations. In: Proceedings of the IEEE Conference on Computer Vision and Pattern Recognition, pp. 6541–6549 (2017)
2. Boggess, K., Kraus, S., Feng, L.: Explainable multi-agent reinforcement learning for temporal queries. arXiv preprint arXiv:2305.10378 (2023)
3. Delfosse, Q., Sztwiertnia, S., Rothermel, M., Stammer, W., Kersting, K.: Interpretable concept bottlenecks to align reinforcement learning agents. arXiv preprint arXiv:2401.05821 (2024)
4. Ghorbani, A., Wexler, J., Zou, J.Y., Kim, B.: Towards automatic concept-based explanations. In: Advances in Neural Information Processing Systems, pp. 9277–9286 (2019)

5. Hayes, B., Shah, J.A.: Improving robot controller transparency through autonomous policy explanation. In: Proceedings of the 2017 ACM/IEEE International Conference on Human-Robot Interaction, pp. 303–312 (2017)
6. Joo, H.T., Kim, K.J.: Visualization of deep reinforcement learning using Grad-CAM: how AI plays atari games? In: 2019 IEEE Conference on Games (CoG), pp. 1–2. IEEE (2019)
7. Kim, B., Wattenberg, M., Gilmer, J., Cai, C., Wexler, J., Viegas, F., et al.: Interpretability beyond feature attribution: quantitative testing with concept activation vectors (TCAV). In: International Conference on Machine Learning, pp. 2668–2677. PMLR (2018)
8. Landajuela, M., et al.: Discovering symbolic policies with deep reinforcement learning. In: International Conference on Machine Learning, pp. 5979–5989. PMLR (2021)
9. Liu, G., Schulte, O., Zhu, W., Li, Q.: Toward interpretable deep reinforcement learning with linear model u-trees. In: Machine Learning and Knowledge Discovery in Databases: European Conference, ECML PKDD 2018, Dublin, Ireland, September 10–14, 2018, Proceedings, Part II 18, pp. 414–429. Springer, Cham (2019). https://doi.org/10.1007/978-3-030-10928-8_25
10. Mu, J., Andreas, J.: Compositional explanations of neurons. Adv. Neural. Inf. Process. Syst. **33**, 17153–17163 (2020)
11. Nikulin, D., Ianina, A., Aliev, V., Nikolenko, S.: Free-lunch saliency via attention in atari agents. In: 2019 IEEE/CVF International Conference on Computer Vision Workshop (ICCVW), pp. 4240–4249. IEEE (2019)
12. Payani, A., Fekri, F.: Incorporating relational background knowledge into reinforcement learning via differentiable inductive logic programming. arXiv preprint arXiv:2003.10386 (2020)
13. Qing, Y., Liu, S., Song, J., Wang, H., Song, M.: A survey on explainable reinforcement learning: Concepts, algorithms, challenges (2023). https://arxiv.org/abs/2211.06665
14. Rizzo, S.G., Vantini, G., Chawla, S.: Reinforcement learning with explainability for traffic signal control. In: 2019 IEEE Intelligent Transportation Systems Conference (ITSC), pp. 3567–3572. IEEE (2019)
15. Shi, W., Huang, G., Song, S., Wang, Z., Lin, T., Wu, C.: Self-supervised discovering of interpretable features for reinforcement learning. IEEE Trans. Pattern Anal. Mach. Intell. **44**(5), 2712–2724 (2020)
16. Thorndike, R.L.: Who belongs in the family? Psychometrika **18**(4), 267–276 (1953)
17. Towers, M., et al.: Gymnasium: a standard interface for reinforcement learning environments. arXiv preprint arXiv:2407.17032 (2024)
18. Verma, A., Murali, V., Singh, R., Kohli, P., Chaudhuri, S.: Programmatically interpretable reinforcement learning. In: International Conference on Machine Learning, pp. 5045–5054. PMLR (2018)
19. Vouros, G.A.: Explainable deep reinforcement learning: state of the art and challenges. ACM Comput. Surv. **55**(5), 1–39 (2022)
20. Xuanyuan, H., Barbiero, P., Georgiev, D., Magister, L.C., Li'o, P.: Global concept-based interpretability for graph neural networks via neuron analysis. In: Proceedings of the AAAI Conference on Artificial Intelligence, vol. 37, pp. 10675–10683 (2023)
21. Ye, Z., Milani, S., Fang, F., Gordon, G.: Concept-based interpretable reinforcement learning with limited to no human labels. In: Automated Reinforcement Learning: Exploring Meta-Learning, AutoML, and LLMs (2024). https://openreview.net/forum?id=NboGncLRV1

22. Yu, Z., Ruan, J., Xing, D.: Explainable reinforcement learning via a causal world model. In: Proceedings of the Thirty-Second International Joint Conference on Artificial Intelligence, pp. 4540–4548 (2023)
23. Zabounidis, R., Campbell, J., Stepputtis, S., Hughes, D., Sycara, K.P.: Concept learning for interpretable multi-agent reinforcement learning. In: Conference on Robot Learning, pp. 1828–1837. PMLR (2023)

Self-supervised Learning for Time Series Classification via Redundancy Reduction and Wavelet-Based Data Augmentation

Daravichet Tin(✉), Hassan Habibi Gharakheili, and Gustavo Batista

University of New South Wales, Sydney, Australia
d.tin@student.unsw.edu.au, {h.habibi,g.batista}@unsw.edu.au

Abstract. Self-supervised learning (SSL) for time series has been dominated by contrastive methods that rely on negative samples to avoid representation collapse. However, negative pairs are often sampled randomly or generated using hard-negative mining methods, which may introduce false negatives. In this work, we take a different direction and apply Barlow Twins, a SSL framework for visual representation learning, to the time series domain. Its objective aligns representations across augmented views and decorrelates feature dimensions to reduce redundant information. To further enhance discriminative feature learning, we introduce a wavelet-based data augmentation method that perturbs detail coefficients at multiple scales while preserving approximation coefficients to maintain the global structure of the time series. We combine this with random cropping applied to both raw inputs and learned representations to promote consistency across different time spans. Experiments on nine large-scale time series datasets show that our approach ranks first compared to current state-of-the-art methods. The code is available at https://github.com/Vee70/barlowtwins-ts.

Keywords: Self-Supervised Learning · Redundancy Reduction · Time Series · Classification

1 Introduction

Time series data is common across a wide range of applications and is continuously generated, leading to rapidly growing data volumes. Extracting informative features from these data is crucial for the classification task. However, manual feature engineering is time-consuming and costly, and supervised deep learning methods typically require large amounts of labeled data to perform well [16]. Obtaining correctly labeled time series data is often challenging and expensive in real-world settings. A promising alternative is self-supervised learning (SSL), which learns feature representations directly from unlabeled data [8]. Among various SSL methods, contrastive learning has proven effective for learning representations that transfer well to downstream classification tasks [19]. It relies

R. C.-W. Wong et al. (Eds.): PAKDD 2026, LNAI 16617, pp. 65–77, 2027.
https://doi.org/10.1007/978-981-92-1926-1_6

on data augmentation and aims to map different augmented views of input samples into a feature space, where similar views (positive pairs) are pulled closer together, and dissimilar ones (negative pairs) are pushed apart [8].

The success of contrastive learning in computer vision has sparked interest in adapting it to time series data. However, time series data have unique characteristics such as temporal dependencies, hierarchical structures, and inter-variable relationships in the multivariate setting [4,9]. These properties present challenges that make direct adaptation of contrastive learning or augmentation techniques from other domains less effective. As a result, a range of time series-specific frameworks has emerged with diverse time series data augmentation strategies in both the time and frequency domains. Some of these include noise injection, cropping, permutation, masking, and time neighboring. While commonly used, these techniques often make strong assumptions about data distribution, and some may disrupt critical temporal dependencies of the data [21,26].

Due to these limitations, recent studies have explored alternative augmentation methods that preserve the global structure of time series while introducing meaningful variations [21,22]. Among these, wavelet-based approaches remain relatively underexplored. Unlike the Fast Fourier Transform [2], which represents signals solely in the frequency domain, the Discrete Wavelet Transform (DWT) [3] decomposes time series into components that capture both temporal and frequency information across multiple scales. DWT also provides advantages for time series analysis, such as capturing complex temporal patterns through multi-resolution decomposition and enabling dimensionality and noise reduction [4]. These properties make it a promising tool for generating augmentations that preserve important signal characteristics.

While such augmentations can improve the quality of positive pairs, contrastive learning still depends on negative pairs to prevent collapse, a degenerate solution where all inputs map to identical representations. Existing approaches sample negatives randomly or via customized negative mining strategies, which may yield uninformative or false negatives [10,23]. Despite these limitations, contrastive learning remains the dominant paradigm in SSL for time series classification, whereas non-contrastive methods [15,27] that avoid the need for negatives have received comparatively less attention.

To address this gap, we employ Barlow Twins [27], a non-contrastive self-supervised learning method developed for visual representation learning and inspired by Horace Barlow's redundancy reduction principle. Unlike contrastive learning objectives, which rely on negative samples, Barlow Twins aims to make the cross-correlation matrix between representations of augmented views as close as possible to the identity matrix. To further enhance discriminative feature learning, we introduce a wavelet-based data augmentation method that combines the Discrete Wavelet Transform (DWT) with random cropping, applied both to the raw time series and their latent representations to align localized segments and promote consistency across time spans.

In summary, the main contributions of this work are as follows: (*i*) We explore the use of Barlow Twins on time series data to overcome the limitations of negative sample mining. (*ii*) We propose a wavelet-based augmentation method that modifies fine-grained details at multiple scales while preserving the global structure of the time series. In addition, we apply random cropping to learn contextual representations across different time spans. (*iii*) We conduct extensive experiments across nine large-scale datasets and show that our method outperforms current state-of-the-art methods.

2 Related Work

Self-supervised learning has gained significant attention for time series representation learning. Studies in both the visual [19] and time series [20] domains show that contrastive approaches achieve strong performance on classification benchmarks. This section reviews contrastive learning methods used as baselines in our experiments.

2.1 Self-Supervised Contrastive Learning for Time Series

Early works such as T-Loss [11] introduce an unsupervised triplet loss with time-based negative sampling to learn time series representations. TNC [24] defines temporal neighborhoods based on stationarity assumptions, treating sub-series within the same neighborhood as positive pairs. Additionally, TNC applies a sample weight adjustment to reduce bias in negative sampling. However, because these methods depend solely on time-based sampling, they are less effective under label shift or when anomalies occur [10,26].

Other instance-based sampling approaches also face challenges. For example, TS-TCC [7] employs cross-view prediction and contextual contrast, but it also applies random permutations that can disrupt crucial temporal dependencies. In addition, its jittering augmentations often produce augmented views that are too similar to the original, limiting the effectiveness of contrastive learning [21]. TS2Vec [26] addresses some of these issues by enforcing contextual consistency through temporal and instance-level contrastive losses in a hierarchical manner. TimesURL [18] introduces FTAug, which applies cropping and frequency mixing to generate augmented views. It also constructs hard negatives by mixing the anchor representation with negatives sampled from other timestamps of the same series, or from other instances in the mini-batch. Finally, it optimizes a joint objective that combines instance-wise and temporal-wise contrastive losses with a time reconstruction loss. InfoTS [21] employs a more adaptive strategy by augmenting data using information-theoretic principles, by introducing a meta-learner network, trained to select optimal augmentations from a candidate pool.

Beyond the time domain, TF-C [28] introduces contrastive objectives in both the time and frequency domains. It perturbs spectral components obtained from the Fast Fourier Transform to create frequency-domain augmentations. However, its time-domain augmentations still depend on randomly selected transformations from existing methods.

2.2 Wavelet-Based Method for Time Series

The Discrete Wavelet Transform (DWT) has been widely explored in time series analysis. It has been applied to noise filtering, dimensionality reduction, and multi-resolution analysis, enabling the capture of temporal information at multiple scales [4]. Li et al. [17] show that time series data can be compressed using DWT while maintaining comparable classification accuracy to the original signals. This suggests that DWT preserves important structures in time series data, motivating the exploration of data augmentation methods based on it.

Despite these advantages, only a few studies have applied DWT for data augmentation. SimEXT [12] perturbs wavelet detail coefficients by adding noise and reconstructs augmented signals from the combination of original approximation and noisy detail components. CoInception [22] employs DWT-based denoising to generate augmented views and learns time series representations via a contrastive objective optimized with a hierarchical triplet loss.

2.3 Non-Contrastive Self-Supervised Learning

Contrastive learning requires negative pairs to prevent collapse. Existing methods often randomly sample negatives from the training data, or employ hard-negative (negative that lies close to the anchor in the embedding space) mining strategies to improve the quality of the negative pairs [18]. However, these may introduce false negatives or result in an insufficient number of hard negatives, thereby reducing the quality of the learned representations [10,23].

Inspired by BYOL [15] in the visual domain, Gorade et al. [14] proposed a non-contrastive SSL framework that jointly captures low- and high-frequency characteristics of time series signals, where the online network learns to align with the target network's outputs for both frequency components. A more recent approach, Series2Vec [10], introduces a non-contrastive SSL framework for time series classification based on a similarity prediction pretext task, where a similarity score serves as the training target. While it avoids both data augmentation and negative samples, it relies on Soft-DTW [5], a differentiable variant of Dynamic Time Warping (DTW), as its similarity function. However, the quadratic time and space complexity of Soft-DTW makes it unsuitable for long time series.

In this work, we apply Barlow Twins [27] to the time series domain to learn feature representations for classification tasks. It learns by enforcing similarity between two augmented views while reducing redundancy through a cross-correlation objective that drives diagonal entries toward one and off-diagonal entries toward zero. Barlow Twins prevents collapse without relying on negative samples, momentum encoders, prediction networks, or stop-gradient operations. This simplicity, combined with its strong empirical performance, makes it a lightweight yet effective alternative to the contrastive approaches. Despite these advantages, to the best of our knowledge, Barlow Twins has not been explored in the time-series domain.

3 Proposed Method

This section describes our proposed method in detail. We first introduce the notation and problem formulation, then present our data augmentation strategy, followed by the model architecture and training procedure.

3.1 Problem Formulation

A set of N time series is represented by $\mathcal{X} = \{x_1, \ldots, x_N\}$, where $x_i \in \mathbb{R}^{T \times F}$, and T, F represent the sequence length and the feature dimension respectively. In self-supervised learning, we aim to train an encoder $f(\cdot)$ that maps x_i to a representation vector $v_i \in \mathbb{R}^D$ in a D-dimensional latent space. In a supervised setting for a classification downstream task, a set of representation vectors along with their class labels $\{(v_1, y_1), \ldots, (v_M, y_M)\}$ is used for training a classifier.

3.2 Data Augmentation

We proposed a two-stage data augmentation approach based on DWT and random cropping to generate diverse, semantically consistent views. Examples of the augmented time series are shown in Fig. 1.

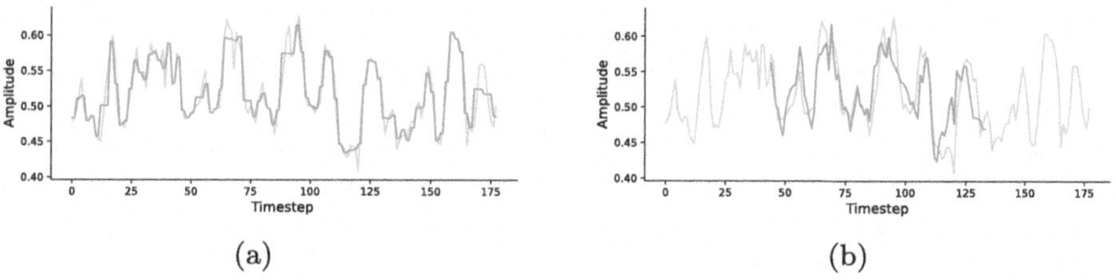

Fig. 1. Outputs of the proposed augmentation method obtained from applying wavelet-based augmentation using Haar wavelet (a), and db2 wavelet with random cropping (b). The blue lines represent the original time series, and the orange lines are the augmented views of the time series.

Wavelet-Based Augmentation. The core component of our augmentation is the Discrete Wavelet Transform (DWT), which decomposes time series into components representing information at different scales. It uses two complementary filters: a low-pass filter that preserves slow, smooth trends in the signal, and a high-pass filter that captures transient features, such as sharp transitions and noise. Initially, the input time series is convolved with both filters, then downsampled by a factor of 2, reducing the temporal resolution by half and doubling the frequency resolution. The low-pass filter produces an approximation coefficient that represents the low-frequency or smooth version of the input. In contrast, the high-pass filter produces a detail coefficient that represents high-frequency or fine-grained features. This process can be applied recursively to the approximation coefficient to obtain a final approximation coefficient that summarizes the entire time series, along with multiple detail coefficients that capture information from different frequency bands at various scales. Formally, the approximation coefficient, $c_j[n]$, and the detail coefficient, $d_j[n]$, at the jth level of decomposition are computed as:

$$c_j[n] = (c_{j-1} * g) \downarrow 2 = \sum_k c_{j-1}[k]\ g[2n-k] \tag{1}$$

$$d_j[n] = (c_{j-1} * h) \downarrow 2 = \sum_k c_{j-1}[k]\ h[2n-k] \tag{2}$$

where g and h denote low-pass and high-pass filters, respectively, and at the first step ($j = 1$), c_0 is the input time series. The symbol $*$ is the convolution operator, and $\downarrow$ represents the downsampling operator.

Using this method, we decompose each time series into J decomposition levels. At each level, we apply a zero mask to a small portion of the detail coefficients. In addition, to encourage structural differences between the two augmented views, we entirely mask one randomly selected lower-level ($j \leq J/2$) detail coefficient in one view and one higher-level ($j > J/2$) detail coefficient in the other. The approximation coefficients remain unchanged in both views to preserve the global shape and semantic identity of the time series. To further increase variability across augmented views, we randomly select a wavelet family (Haar or Daubechies) at each training iteration. Finally, we reconstruct the augmented signals using the Inverse DWT by combining the unchanged approximation coefficients with the modified detail coefficients. For multivariate time series, we apply this process independently to each feature dimension.

Random Cropping. From one of the reconstructed time series, we crop a sub-series of random length. This sub-series is taken directly from the signal reconstructed via the Inverse DWT. For the other view, we first pass the complete reconstructed time series through the encoder, then extract the corresponding segment from its latent representation using the same time indices as in the first view. This design ensures that both views remain temporally aligned, even though one is cropped in the input space and the other in the representation space.

3.3 Model Architecture

Our encoder is based on a Dilated Causal Convolutional Neural Network architecture from T-Loss [11]. This design allows the encoder to produce outputs of the same length as the inputs, while ensuring that the ith output element depends only on input values from the first through the ith timestep. The encoder is composed of a stack of convolutional blocks, where each block consists of a causal 1D-convolution, weight normalization, an ELU activation function, and a dropout layer. The dilation rate increases exponentially across the blocks, and residual connections are added to facilitate gradient flow and improve training stability. Finally, global max pooling is applied to produce a fixed-size vector representation, allowing the encoder to handle inputs of varying lengths.

During training, we attach a projection head, a multilayer perceptron that maps representation vectors into the space where the loss is computed. The projection head consists of three fully connected layers, with batch normalization and ReLU activation applied to the first two layers. This module is removed after the self-supervised training is completed.

3.4 Self-Supervised Training

The overview of our proposed method is shown in Fig. 2. We train the encoder based on the Barlow Twins framework [27]. It follows a joint-embedding architecture that employs two identical encoder networks with shared parameters to extract representations from two augmented views of the same input. We begin by applying our wavelet-based augmentation to a mini-batch of time series samples, $\mathbf{X}$, to generate two mini-batches of augmented views $\tilde{\mathbf{X}}_1$ and $\tilde{\mathbf{X}}_2$, one with low-frequency and the other with high-frequency information removed. Then, we randomly crop one of the augmented views, $\tilde{\mathbf{X}}_2$, resulting in a sub-series $\tilde{\mathbf{X}}_2'$. We pass both augmented views, $\tilde{\mathbf{X}}_1$ and $\tilde{\mathbf{X}}_2'$, to the encoder, $f(\cdot)$, which outputs representations $\mathbf{V}_1 \in \mathbb{R}^{T \times D}$ and $\mathbf{V'}_2 \in \mathbb{R}^{T' \times D}$. To ensure that the representation vectors have the same time indices, we crop the encoder's output from the uncropped views, $\mathbf{V}_1$, to obtain $\mathbf{V'}_1 \in \mathbb{R}^{T' \times D}$ by selecting the segment that matches the timestamps of $\mathbf{V'}_2$. Next, we apply global max pooling along the time dimension to get representation vectors $v_1, v_2 \in \mathbb{R}^D$. Finally, we pass these vectors to the projection head $g(\cdot)$, which maps them to $z_1, z_2 \in \mathbb{R}^{D'}$ in the space where the loss function is applied.

The objective of the Barlow Twins loss [27] is to make the cross-correlation matrix between the embeddings of the two encoders as close as possible to the identity matrix. This loss consists of two main components: an invariance term (diagonal elements) and a redundancy-reduction term (off-diagonal elements). The invariance term encourages the encoder to produce similar representations for augmented views of the same input. In contrast, the redundancy reduction term prevents different feature dimensions from encoding redundant or correlated information. Formally, Barlow Twins' loss is defined as:

$$\mathcal{L} := \underbrace{\sum_i (1 - \mathcal{C}_{ii})^2}_{\text{invariance}} + \lambda \underbrace{\sum_i \sum_{j \neq i} \mathcal{C}_{ij}^2}_{\text{redundancy reduction}} \tag{3}$$

where λ is a positive constant that controls the trade-off between the two terms. Because there are far more off-diagonal elements than the diagonal ones, the redundancy reduction term would dominate the loss if λ were omitted. The cross-correlation matrix $\mathcal{C} \in \mathbb{R}^{D' \times D'}$ is computed from the output representation vectors as:

$$\mathcal{C}_{ij} := \frac{\sum z_{1,i}\ z_{2,j}}{\sqrt{\sum (z_{1,i})^2}\ \sqrt{\sum (z_{2,j})^2}} \quad (4)$$

where $z_{1,i}$, $z_{2,j}$ denote the ith and j^{th} dimensions of the vectors z_1 and z_2, respectively, and the summation is performed along the batch dimension.

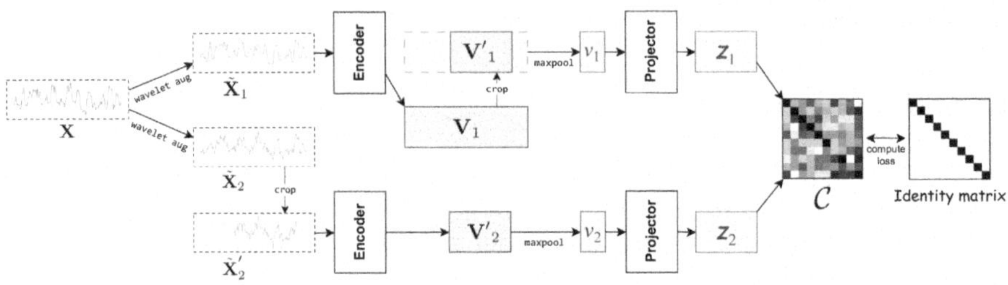

Fig. 2. Overview of the proposed method.

4 Experimental Setup and Result

This section outlines the experimental setup and presents the results of our method. We assess the quality of the learned representation of our method by evaluating on a classification task, following the process in Series2Vec [10]. We also conduct multiple ablation studies to examine sensitivity to hyperparameters and quantify the contribution of each component of our augmentation method to overall classification performance. Due to space restriction, the ablation results are available at https://github.com/Vee70/barlowtwins-ts.

4.1 Datasets

We evaluate our method on nine large-scale datasets collected from diverse domains, including human activity recognition (HAR), epileptic seizure prediction, and sleep stage recognition. These datasets are Epilepsy [1], Sleep [13], and multiple HAR datasets (WISDM, WISDM2, USC-HAD, Skoda, PAMAP2, UCI-HAR, and Opportunity) which can be found in the MONSTER: Monash Scalable Time Series Evaluation Repository [6].

4.2 Implementation Details

As described in Sect. 3.3, our encoder is based on the architecture from [11]. However, we make several modifications: reducing the number of intermediate

CNN blocks from 10 to 5 and doubling the number of filters per convolutional layer from 40 to 80. We keep the output dimension fixed at 320 and set the filter size of all convolutional layers to 3. The dropout rate is set to 0.1 for all blocks. We implement the projection head as a three-layer MLP with Batch Normalization and ReLU activation, with 1024 output units per layer.

To generate augmented views of the time series, we apply the data augmentation strategies described in Sect. 3.2. In wavelet-based augmentation, using a high decomposition level results in approximation coefficients that become too short because the sequence length is halved at each level. Therefore, we set the maximum decomposition level according to the input length T as follows: 8 if $T > 500$, 6 if $500 \geq T > 100$, and 4 if $100 \geq T$. At each level, we apply a zero mask to 10% of the detail coefficient. For random cropping, we crop a sub-series with a random length between 50% and 100% of the original series.

We train our model for 50 epochs using the Adam optimizer with the 1Cycle learning rate policy and a maximum learning rate of 0.003. We set λ to 0.001 in the loss function. The batch size is set to 256 for all datasets except Sleep, where we reduce it to 128 to fit the longer sequence length (3000 timesteps) within GPU memory. We repeat each experiment five times with different random seeds and report the average accuracy and standard deviation.

4.3 Comparison with Self-Supervised Baselines

To evaluate the quality of the learned representations, we compare our model with multiple self-supervised baselines. We select two high-performing methods based on the results in Series2Vec [10], namely Series2Vec itself and TS2Vec [26], and we include three additional baselines, InfoTS [21], CoInception [22], and TimesURL [18]. We train all baseline models using their default hyperparameters. For all methods except Series2Vec, we set the batch size to 128 for the Sleep dataset and 256 for the remaining datasets. For Series2Vec, we use the default batch size of 256 for Epilepsy, UCI-HAR, USC-HAD, WISDM, and WISDM2; 128 for Skoda and PAMAP2; and 64 for Opportunity and Sleep. Then, we further segment each series of the Sleep dataset into three sub-series and stack them. These modifications are necessary because Series2Vec relies on Soft-DTW, which has quadratic time and space complexity and therefore cannot fit larger batches into our GPU memory.

In this setting, we assume access to only unlabeled data during training. We train our model following the procedure described in Sect. 3.4 using all available unlabeled training data. Then we freeze the trained encoder and use it to generate feature representations from the raw input. We train a Logistic Regression classifier using these representations and the corresponding labels, and report its classification accuracy as the evaluation metric. Table 1 summarizes the average classification accuracy of our model and the baseline methods over five runs, where the bold number represents the best performance and the underlined number is the second best. Our method achieves the highest accuracy on the USC-HAD dataset and remains competitive on the remaining datasets compared with the baselines. We also perform a one-sided Wilcoxon signed-rank test with the Holm correction. Although our approach has the best overall rank among all baselines, the differences are not statistically significant. This is likely due to the small number of datasets (nine in total).

Table 1. Average accuracy scores over five runs of our model and the SSL baseline.

Datasets	Ours	Series2Vec	TS2Vec	CoInception	TimesURL	InfoTS
WISDM2	**66.66** ± 1.04	64.87 ± 2.04	59.72 ± 1.94	63.94 ± 1.27	<u>65.32</u> ± 1.61	62.20 ± 2.89
PAMAP2	70.62 ± 0.26	**71.54** ± 0.31	<u>71.26</u> ± 4.49	71.18 ± 2.65	68.72 ± 0.65	68.63 ± 4.00
USC-HAD	**63.68** ± 0.78	<u>55.15</u> ± 1.04	49.19 ± 1.76	46.63 ± 1.76	46.07 ± 1.78	51.15 ± 1.80
Sleep	<u>83.75</u> ± 0.33	**83.76** ± 0.19	75.29 ± 0.97	75.77 ± 0.87	72.95 ± 0.91	46.81 ± 0.71
Skoda	98.46 ± 0.14	98.16 ± 0.14	**98.60** ± 0.22	97.30 ± 0.43	<u>98.51</u> ± 0.16	96.91 ± 0.10
Opportunity	86.83 ± 0.68	**87.78** ± 0.72	86.72 ± 0.73	86.34 ± 0.63	<u>86.84</u> ± 0.61	85.61 ± 0.51
WISDM	**84.79** ± 0.66	81.25 ± 1.19	<u>84.49</u> ± 1.10	83.20 ± 1.28	81.65 ± 1.02	83.91 ± 0.74
Epilepsy	**97.88** ± 0.15	97.38 ± 0.08	97.45 ± 0.31	<u>97.63</u> ± 0.13	97.10 ± 0.29	97.03 ± 0.25
UCI-HAR	<u>93.15</u> ± 0.34	91.92 ± 0.55	**93.36** ± 0.53	93.06 ± 0.61	91.64 ± 0.67	90.84 ± 0.54
Rank	2.00	2.89	3.00	3.78	4.11	5.22

4.4 Low-Label Regimes

In this setting, we assume access to only a small number of labeled samples for training the Logistic Regression classifier. Specifically, we train the classifier using 1, 5, 10, 50, 100, and 200 labeled samples per class. We evaluate the performance of our method alongside both self-supervised and supervised baselines. Among the self-supervised baselines, we exclude CoInception, TimesURL, and InfoTS as they performed the worst in the previous experiments. For the supervised baselines, we adopt the Fully Convolutional Network (FCN) and Residual Network (ResNet) architectures from [25], implemented using the code from Fawaz et al. [16]. For each number of labeled samples, we repeat the experiment 10 times and report the average accuracy. The result in Fig. 3 shows that when the amount of labeled data is limited, our method outperforms both self-supervised and supervised baselines on the Sleep, USC-HAD, and WISDM2 datasets. For the remaining datasets, except Opportunity, we still achieve competitive results compared to the baselines.

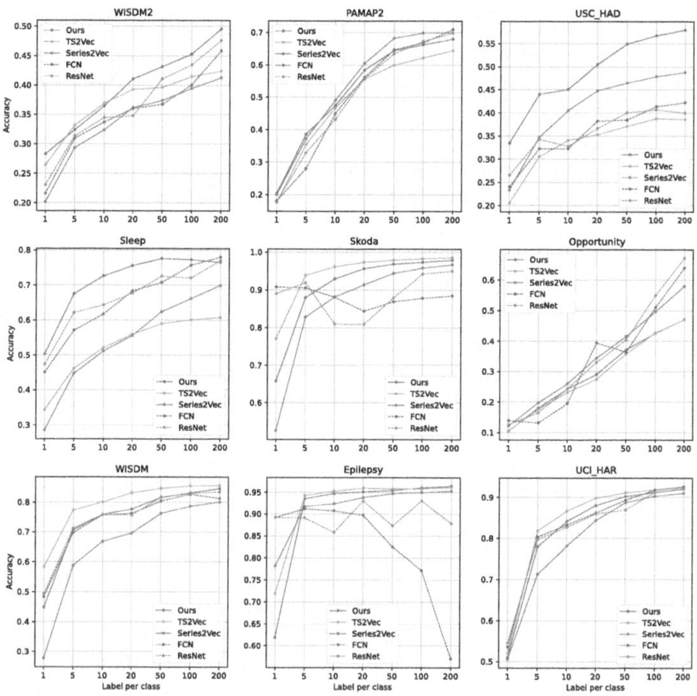

Fig. 3. Average accuracy over 10 runs of our method and the baselines, trained using a small number of labeled samples.

5 Conclusion and Future Work

In this work, we propose a self-supervised learning framework for time series classification using the Barlow Twins framework. It avoids the need for negative mining and does not require momentum encoders or predictor networks, making it simple and efficient. Additionally, we introduced a data augmentation strategy based on the Discrete Wavelet Transform (DWT) and combined it with random cropping to enhance discriminative feature learning and promote temporal consistency across time spans. Our experimental results show that the proposed method achieves higher or comparable performance to both self-supervised and supervised baselines. For future work, we plan to explore a more adaptive data augmentation strategy and to extend our method to class-imbalanced datasets.

References

1. Andrzejak, R.G., Lehnertz, K., Mormann, F., Rieke, C., David, P., Elger, C.E.: Indications of nonlinear deterministic and finite-dimensional structures in time series of brain electrical activity: dependence on recording region and brain state. Phys. Rev. E **64**(6), 061907 (2001)

2. Brigham, E.O., Morrow, R.E.: The fast fourier transform. IEEE Spectr. **4**(12), 63–70 (1967). https://doi.org/10.1109/MSPEC.1967.5217220
3. Burrus, C.S.: Introduction to wavelets and wavelet transforms: a primer. Englewood Cliffs (1997)
4. Chaovalit, P., Gangopadhyay, A., Karabatis, G., Chen, Z.: Discrete wavelet transform-based time series analysis and mining. ACM CSUR **43**(2), 1–37 (2011)
5. Cuturi, M., Blondel, M.: Soft-DTW: a differentiable loss function for time-series. In: ICML, pp. 894–903. PMLR (2017)
6. Dempster, A., et al.: Monster: monash scalable time series evaluation repository (2025). arXiv preprint arXiv:2502.15122
7. Eldele, E., et al.: Time-series representation learning via temporal and contextual contrasting. In: IJCAI-21, pp. 2352–2359 (2021)
8. Ericsson, L., Gouk, H., Loy, C.C., Hospedales, T.M.: Self-supervised representation learning: introduction, advances, and challenges. IEEE Signal Process. Mag. **39**(3), 42–62 (2022)
9. Esling, P., Agon, C.: Time-series data mining. ACM CSUR **45**(1), 1–34 (2012)
10. Foumani, N.M., Tan, C.W., Webb, G.I., Rezatofighi, H., Salehi, M.: Series2vec: similarity-based self-supervised representation learning for time series classification. Data Min. Knowl. Disc. **38**(4), 2520–2544 (2024)
11. Franceschi, J.Y., Dieuleveut, A., Jaggi, M.: Unsupervised scalable representation learning for multivariate time series. NeurIPS **32** (2019)
12. Galib, A.H., Tan, P.N., Luo, L.: Simext: self-supervised representation learning for extreme values in time series. In: IEEE ICDM, pp. 1031–1036. IEEE (2023)
13. Goldberger, A.L., et al.: Physiobank, Physiotoolkit, and Physionet: components of a new research resource for complex physiologic signals. Circulation **101**(23), e215–e220 (2000)
14. Gorade, V., Singh, A., Mishra, D.: Large scale time-series representation learning via simultaneous low-and high-frequency feature bootstrapping. IEEE Trans. Neural Netw. Learn, Syst (2023)
15. Grill, J.B., et al.: Bootstrap your own latent-a new approach to self-supervised learning. NeurIPS **33** (2020)
16. Ismail Fawaz, H., Forestier, G., Weber, J., Idoumghar, L., Muller, P.-A.: Deep learning for time series classification: a review. Data Min. Knowl. Disc. **33**(4), 917–963 (2019). https://doi.org/10.1007/s10618-019-00619-1
17. Li, D., Bissyande, T.F.D.A., Klein, J., Le Traon, Y.: Time series classification with discrete wavelet transformed data: insights from an empirical study. In: SEKE 2016 (2016)
18. Liu, J., Chen, S.: Timesurl: self-supervised contrastive learning for universal time series representation learning. In: AAAI. vol. 38, pp. 13918–13926 (2024)
19. Liu, X., et al.: Self-supervised learning: generative or contrastive. IEEE TKDE **35**(1), 857–876 (2021)
20. Liu, Z., Alavi, A., Li, M., Zhang, X.: Self-supervised learning for time series. In: Contrastive or Generative? (2024). arXiv:2403.09809
21. Luo, D., et al.: Time series contrastive learning with information-aware augmentations. In: AAAI. vol. 37, pp. 4534–4542 (2023)
22. Nguyen, D.A., Tran, T.H., Pham, H.H., Le Nguyen, P., Nguyen, L.M.: Improving time series encoding with noise-aware self-supervised learning and an efficient encoder. In: IEEE ICDM, pp. 340–349. IEEE (2024)
23. Robinson, J., Chuang, C.Y., Sra, S., Jegelka, S.: Contrastive learning with hard negative samples (2020). arXiv preprint arXiv:2010.04592

24. Tonekaboni, S., Eytan, D., Goldenberg, A.: Unsupervised representation learning for time series with temporal neighborhood coding. In: ICLR (2021)
25. Wang, Z., Yan, W., Oates, T.: Time series classification from scratch with deep neural networks: a strong baseline. In: IJCNN, pp. 1578–1585. IEEE (2017)
26. Yue, Z., et al.: Ts2vec: towards universal representation of time series. In: AAAI. vol 36 (2022)
27. Zbontar, J., Jing, L., Misra, I., LeCun, Y., Deny, S.: Barlow twins: self-supervised learning via redundancy reduction. In: ICML, pp. 12310–12320. PMLR (2021)
28. Zhang, X., Zhao, Z., Tsiligkaridis, T., Zitnik, M.: Self-supervised contrastive pre-training for time series via time-frequency consistency. NeurIPS **35** (2022)

Refining Causal Graphs via LLMs for Medication Recommendation

Xin Liu, Yu Qiu(✉), Lin Xiao(✉), and Xieping Gao

College of Information Science and Engineering, Hunan Normal University, Changsha, China
yuqiu@hunnu.edu.cn

Abstract. Medication recommendation aims to suggest a personalized drug combination given a patient's longitudinal health record. Most existing studies optimize patient-state representation by exploiting co-occurrence patterns, but fail to capture higher-level semantic relationships among medical entities. Moreover, they exhibit fundamental limitations in logical and causal reasoning capabilities. Although recent work has attempted to introduce the causal inference to deal with these challenges, the generated causal graphs usually contain implausible pathways, leading to therapeutically incoherent paths or pharmacologically invalid interactions. To alleviate these limitations, we propose RCG4MR, a medication recommendation framework that leverages large language models (LLMs) to obtain more logical and interpretable interaction semantics. Specifically, RCG4MR first employs causal discovery techniques to distill causal relationships between diagnoses/procedures and medications, and then leverages the causal-reasoning capacity of LLMs to refine the causal graph, unveiling the potential causal pathways in diagnostic records. Building upon, we introduce a gated cross-attention mechanism that adaptively learns disease and procedure specific feature weights, producing highly personalized therapeutic regimens. Finally, RCG4MR incorporates long-term visit histories to recommend combinatorial drug sets. Extensive experiments on public benchmarks demonstrate that RCG4MR surpasses state-of-the-art medication recommendation methods.

Keywords: Medication recommendation · large language model · causal graph · causal relationship

1 Introduction

Recently, AI-powered medicine offers promising solutions for contemporary healthcare, particularly in drug recommendation which leverages vast datasets of diagnostic records to identify therapeutic medications for patients based on their current diagnoses [1–3]. Furthermore, with the availability of personal health data, such as Electronic Health Records (EHR), medication recommendation methods can incorporate individual patient characteristics and medical history,

R. C.-W. Wong et al. (Eds.): PAKDD 2026, LNAI 16617, pp. 78–89, 2027.
https://doi.org/10.1007/978-981-92-1926-1_7

enabling the prediction of tailored medication regimens that better align with the specific disease presentation [4–6]. However, different from recommendations in other recommendation systems, medication recommendation faces unique challenges. Medication recommendation encompasses multiple distinct concepts of medical entities (*e.g.*, diseases, procedures, and medications), and medications themselves can be composed of sub-molecular components, involving extensive chemical and molecular knowledge [7–9]. These complex relationships between these diverse medical entities are inherently difficult to model effectively. Previous medication recommendation approaches widely adopt graph neural networks (GNNs) to construct structured representations of various medical entities (*e.g.*, diseases, procedures, and medications). These GNN-based models predominantly rely on statistical co-occurrence patterns and assume that high co-occurrence is equivalent to a direct relationship. However, this assumption is not invariably valid [10,11]. As illustrated in Fig. 1, co-occurrence-based approaches cannot capture the true relationships among different medical entities, and therefore fail to deliver precise recommendations. Moreover, they exhibit fundamental limitations in logical and causal reasoning capabilities, thus failing to comprehensively model the complete range of conceptual relationships, or even establishing spurious correlations. Therefore, relying solely on co-occurrence to determine the relationships between diseases/procedures and drugs can lead to biases, which may be amplified through feedback loops, thereby affecting the accuracy and safety of recommendations [11,12].

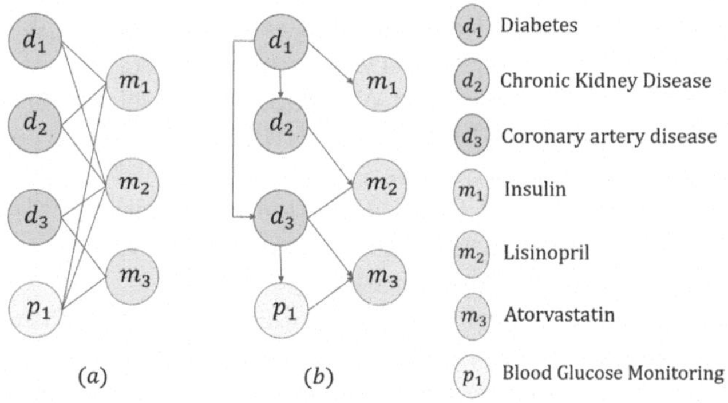

Fig. 1. (a) Co-occurrence-based approaches cannot capture the true relationships among different medical entities. (b) Causal modeling can uncover the genuine causal links embedded in patients' diagnostic histories.

Recent work has attempted to introduce the causal inference into drug recommendation systems to deal with these challenges. For example, CausalMed utilizes causal discovery to capture the causal relationships [13]. As shown in Fig. 1, causal modeling can uncover the genuine causal links embedded in patients' diagnostic histories. However, the generated causal graphs by these studies frequently contain implausible pathways due to their reliance on statistical correlations within observational electronic health records (EHRs) based on the Greedy Intervention Equivalence Search (GIES) algorithm, conflating spurious associations with causal mechanisms. Such inaccuracies manifest as therapeutically incoherent paths or pharmacologically invalid interactions. In this way, the personalized diagnostic features of patients are also overlooked. It is widely accepted that LLMs have gained popularity for their excellent reasoning, inference, and logical capabilities [11,14]. Specifically, LLMs can leverage emergent semantic understanding to optimize traditional graph structure. In this way, the nuanced individual conditions of patients can be embedded to reveal potential causal relationships that traditional algorithms may overlook and provides a more precise basis for medication recommendations.

Motivated by the aforementioned limitations, we propose an innovative medication recommendation framework named RCG4MR (Refining Causal Graph vis LLMs for Medication Recommendation), which effectively model the deep-seated causal relationships among complex medical entities (diseases, procedures, medications) and precisely modulate their impact on recommendation safety. The core innovation of RCG4MR lies in its integration of LLMs to enhance traditional causal graph construction. Furthermore, to identify and integrate above critical differential influences, we introduce a Gated Cross Attention Mechanism. This mechanism adaptively learns weights for disease and procedure features and orchestrates efficient cross-attention computations between these features and candidate medication features. The contributions of this work are summarized as follows:

- We propose the RCG4MR framework that refines causal graph vis LLMs for medication recommendation. RCG4MR captures direct causal relationships between diseases and medications. We propose a novel causal graph refinement method that integrates LLMs with EHR to further refine patient-specific causal graphs of medical encounters.
- We design a Dynamic Gated Cross Attention mechanism to identify the differential impact of diverse medical entities on medical records, enhancing the personalization of patient representations.
- We conduct extensive experiments on publicly available datasets, validating the effectiveness of the RCG4MR framework. We also verify that the RCG4MR model can improve the recommendation interpretability.

2 Related Work

2.1 Medication Recommendation

Based on the temporal order of patient diagnosis records in EHR, existing medication recommendation methods can be categorized into instance-based methods and time-dependent methods. Instance-based methods primarily focus on a patient's current health status, ignoring historical visit records [15,16]. For example, LEAP [17] treats medication recommendation as a sequential decision process and models latent relational mappings using a content-based attention mechanism. RETAIN [18] utilizes a dual-layer attention mechanism to detect critical entries within patients' longitudinal medical histories, thereby enhancing patient representation. CompNet [19] conceptualizes the medication recommendation problem as an unordered markov decision process and captures drug correlations and adverse interactions through relational graph convolutional neural networks (GCN). MICRO [20] employs residual networks to refine the current medication combination, thereby obtaining personalized representations of medical entities. COGNet [21] predicts medications based on the present visit record while simultaneously retrieving crucial medications from past clinical diagnoses to generate the recommended drug combination. To further address safety concerns in drug recommendations, GAMENet [22] mitigates adverse DDI relationships by simultaneously modeling longitudinal patient records as EHR graphs and medication knowledge as DDI graphs. SafeDrug [23] enhances recommendation safety by extracting comprehensive molecular structure information from pharmaceutical compounds.

2.2 Causal Reasoning in RSs

Information filtering plays a crucial role in recommendation systems [24]. Existing medication recommendation methods often derive representations of different medical entities based on correlations. However, in the real world, relationships between medical entities are frequently driven by causality, as correlation does not imply causation [13]. Formally, causality can pinpoint the causal relationships where the outcome bears partial responsibility to the cause. Causal inference is defined as the process of identifying and subsequently leveraging causal relationships from experimental data [11,25]. Within recommendation systems, causal reasoning is primarily applied to address three key challenges: data bias, data sparsity/noise, and difficult-to-achieve beyond-accuracy objectives.

3 Methods

As shown in Fig. 2, the recommendation process of RCG4MR is divided into two stages: causal effect reasoning and medical entity relationship mining. In the causal effect reasoning stage, we employ the GIES algorithm to identify causal relationships within EHR and optimize these causal relationships by integrating patients' health information through LLMs, ultimately quantifying the point-to-point relationships between medical entities. In the medical entity relationship mining stage, we first extract entity representations from a single clinical visit. In the relational graph convolutional network, we leverage causal effect estimation to capture the dynamic changes of entities under different patient conditions. Subsequently, we update and aggregate the representations of all medical entities through a dynamic gated cross-attention module.

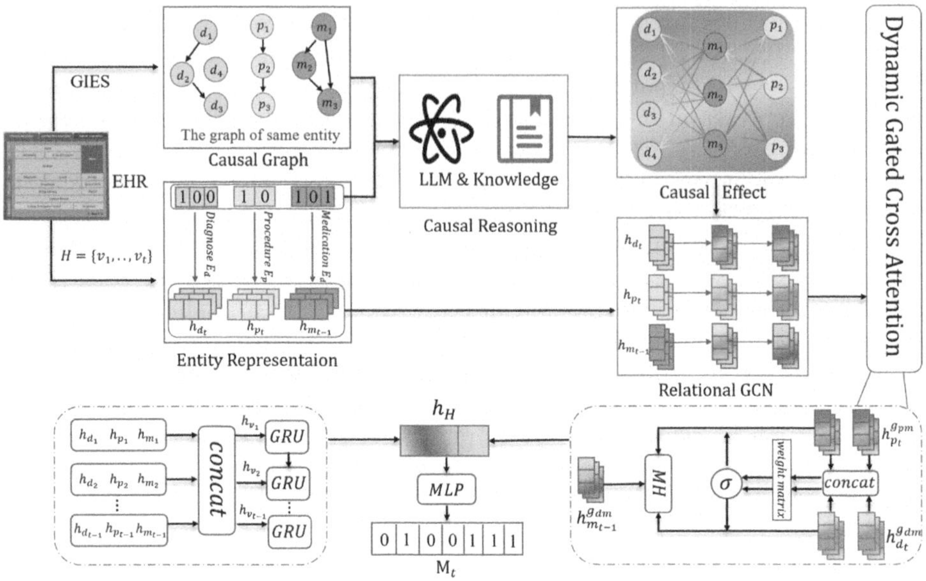

Fig. 2. The recommendation process of RCG4MR is divided into two stages: causal effect reasoning and medical entity relationship mining.

3.1 Causal Effect Reasoning

In this stage, we employ causal discovery and LLMs reasoning techniques to reveal the true causal relationship between different medical entities. Moreover, we quantify and refine the discovered causal relationship to transform them into point-to-point relationship between different medical entities.

Specifically, we analyze the EHR to obtain the data distribution between different medical entities and then use the GIES algorithm to generate an initial causal relationship graph. This process can be expressed by the following formula:

$$\mathrm{Q(T, G)} = \sum_{i=1}^{n} q(\mathrm{X}_i|\mathrm{P}_{\mathrm{X}_i}^{\mathrm{G}}) \ , \tag{1}$$

$$\widetilde{\mathrm{G}} = GIES(\mathrm{Q}, \mathrm{G}) \tag{2}$$

in which X_i represents the specific variables (diseases, procedures, and drugs), n denotes the number of variables, and $\mathrm{P}_{\mathrm{X}_i}^{\mathrm{G}}$ represents the parent nodes of variable X_i in the causal graph G. The function $q(\cdot|\cdot)$ is used to obtain the equivalence class of variable X_i and its parent nodes.

To further take into account the personalized information of each patient, we construct a framework based on prompt learning. The optimized causal structure graph G_{fin} is obtained as follows:

$$\mathrm{G}_{fin} = LLMs(\mathrm{Prompt}, v_t, \widetilde{\mathrm{G}}), \tag{3}$$

in which v_t represents the patient's current medical visit record, and $LLMs$ denotes the large language model employed. Compared with the causal graph generated solely by the GIES algorithm, the causal graph optimized by LLM reasoning can more accurately reflect the individual conditions of patients.

In addition, to achieve point-to-point causal effect estimation between different medical entities, we define diseases and procedures as variables and drugs as outcome variables, in accordance with the principles of causal estimation. We employ a generalized linear model (GLM) adjusted based on the backdoor criterion to calculate the impact of drugs on diseases and procedures. The formula for GLM is expressed as follows:

$$\mathrm{g}(\delta) = \beta_0 + \beta_1 \mathrm{X}_1 + \ldots + \beta_n \mathrm{X}_n, \tag{4}$$

in which δ represents the probability of the binary variable, β_0 is the intercept, and $\mathrm{g}(\cdot)$ is the logit link function. β_i are the regression coefficients, indicating the influence of different variables on the independent variable. X_i represents the independent variables, including diseases/procedures and drugs ($i \in \{1, 2, ..., n\}$).

3.2 Medical Entity Relationship Mining

In this stage, we first extract the embeddings of medical entities from a single clinical visit. In the relational graph convolutional network, we utilize causal effect estimation to capture the dynamic changes of medical entities under different health states of patients. Subsequently, we update and aggregate the representations of all medical entities through a dynamic gated cross-attention module.

The patient's health status is encoded by the information of diseases, procedures, and drugs. Specifically, we extract the patient's current diseases and current procedures, as well as previous medications. We define three learnable embedding tables $\mathrm{E}_d \in R^{|\mathrm{D}| \times h}$, $\mathrm{E}_p \in R^{|\mathrm{P}| \times h}$ and $\mathrm{E}_m \in R^{|\mathrm{M}| \times h}$ to project diseases, procedures, and drugs respectively. Here, |D|, |P|, and |M| denote the total number of diseases, procedures, and drugs respectively, and h represents the dimension of the embedding. Each row in the embedding table corresponds to a specific medical entity vector.

$$\begin{aligned} h_{d_t} &= v_d^t \mathrm{E}_d, \\ h_{p_t} &= v_p^t \mathrm{E}_p, \\ h_{m_{t-1}} &= v_m^{t-1} \mathrm{E}_d, \end{aligned} \tag{5}$$

in which v_d^t and v_p^t represent the multi-hot encoding vector of diseases and procedures in the t-th patient's diagnosis, and v_m^{t-1} represents the multi-hot encoding vector of the previous medications. h_{d_t}, h_{p_t}, and $h_{m_{t-1}}$ represent the embeddings of different medical entities (diseases, procedures, and drugs) respectively.

This process aims to enhance the accuracy of entity representations. Specifically, we first construct disease-drug and procedure-drug bipartite graphs using the causal effect matrices A_{dm} and A_{pm} for single visits, establishing point-to-point relationships between diseases/procedures and medications. Then, taking disease embeddings as an example, we update their representations using Relational GCN and A_{dm}. At the l-th layer, the representation of diseases $h_{d_t}^l$ is updated based on the point-to-point relationships using the following formula.

$$\begin{aligned} h_{d_t}^{l+1} &= \sigma(h_{d_t}^l W^l + \sum_{r_{dm} \in R} \frac{(I + \theta_{r_{dm}}^l)}{c_{d_t}} h_{N_r}), \\ h_{N_r} &= \sum_{k \in N_r} h_k^l, \end{aligned} \tag{6}$$

in which W^l represents the weight matrix of the disease node itself, and r_{dm} indicates the relationship between diseases and drugs in the causal effect graph. I is the identity matrix, and $\theta_{r_{dm}}^l$ is the weight update matrix at the l-th layer. N_r represents the set of neighboring nodes under the relationship r_{dm}, while c_{d_t} is a normalization factor. By using RGCN combined with the causal effect matrix, we can obtain the updated representations of medical entities.

$$h_{d_t}^R = RGCN(h_{d_t}, A_{dm}) \tag{7}$$

$$h_{p_t}^R = RGCN(h_{p_t}, A_{pm}) \tag{8}$$

$$h_{m_{t-1}}^R = RGCN(h_{m_{t-1}}, A_{dm}, A_{pm}) \tag{9}$$

In some cases, the impact of a disease may be less significant than that of a procedure on drug selection, while in other cases, the disease may exert a substantial influence on the choice of medication. Thus, We assign different weights to diseases and procedures in various health states, thereby strengthening the representation of personalized patients. This can be specifically represented as follows:

$$\begin{aligned} \text{Gate}_d &= \sigma(W_d[h_{d_t}^R, h_{d_t}^R]), \\ \text{Gate}_p &= \sigma(W_p[h_{p_t}^R, h_{p_t}^R]). \end{aligned} \tag{10}$$

Here, W_d and W_p represent the weight matrices for diseases and procedures, respectively. $\sigma(\cdot)$ denotes the sigmoid activation function, and $[\cdot]$ represents the concatenation operation. After obtaining the gated representations of diseases and procedures, we input the three components into the cross-attention module to acquire the personalized patient health state representation, thereby enhancing predictive capability.

$$\text{GCA} = \text{MH}(h_{m_{t-1}}^R, \text{Gate}_d h_{d_t}^R, \text{Gate}_p h_{p_t}^R), \tag{11}$$

where

$$\text{CA} = [h_{m_{t-1}}^R, \text{Attn}(h_{m_{t-1}}^R, h_{d_t}^R, h_{d_t}^R), \text{Attn}(h_{m_{t-1}}^R, h_{p_t}^R, h_{p_t}^R], \tag{12}$$

$$\text{Attn}(\text{Q}, \text{K}, \text{V}) = Softmax(\frac{\text{QK}^\text{T}}{dim})\text{V}, \tag{13}$$

in which MH denotes the multi-head attention module. [·] indicates the concatenation operation. Finally, we aggregate the embeddings of different medical entities of the patient to obtain the health state representation of the patient.

$$h_{v_t} = [h_{d_t}^{fin}, h_{p_t}^{fin}, h_{m_{t-1}}^{fin}] \tag{14}$$

in which $h_{d_t}^{fin}, h_{p_t}^{fin}, h_{m_{t-1}}^{fin}$ denote the final representations of the medical entities after gated cross-attention.

Table 1. Statistics of the datasets.

Item	MIMIC-III	MIMIC-IV
# patients	6350	60125
# clinical	15032	156810
# diseases	1958	2000
# procedures	1430	1500
# medications	131	131

Table 2. The performance of each model on the test set regarding accuracy and safety. The best and the runner-up results are highlighted in bold and underlined respectively.

Models	MIMIC-III				MIMIC-IV			
	Jaccard	F1	PRAUC	Avg#Med	Jaccard	F1	PRAUC	Avg#Med
LEAP [17]	0.4526	0.6147	0.6555	18.6240	0.4254	0.5794	0.6059	11.3606
RETAIN [18]	0.4871	0.6473	0.7600	19.4222	0.4234	0.5785	0.6801	10.9576
GAMENet [22]	0.4994	0.6560	0.7656	27.7703	0.4565	0.6103	0.6829	18.5895
MICRO [20]	0.5219	0.6761	0.7489	19.2505	0.4640	0.6167	0.6919	12.7701
SafeDrug [23]	0.5154	0.6722	0.7627	19.4111	0.4487	0.6014	0.6948	13.6943
COGNet [21]	0.5312	0.6744	0.7708	27.6335	0.4775	0.6233	0.6524	18.7235
CausalMed [13]	<u>0.5389</u>	<u>0.6916</u>	<u>0.7826</u>	20.5419	<u>0.4899</u>	**0.6412**	<u>0.7338</u>	14.4295
RCG4MR	**0.5428**	**0.6945**	**0.7879**	20.5578	**0.4922**	0.6398	**0.7352**	14.4587

4 Experiment Analysis

In this section, we conduct extensive experiments to address four pivotal research questions (RQs):

RQ1: Compared with existing state-of-the-art medication recommendation approaches, does RCG4MR yield more accurate and risk-averse prescribing suggestions?

RQ2: Do the core components of RCG4MR effectively enhance recommendation performance?

RQ3: Why is RCG4MR able to produce more individualized patient representations grounded in causal relationships?

RQ4: How do different hyper-parameter configurations influence the behavior of RCG4MR?

Datasets. We employed the MIMIC-III and MIMIC-IV datasets, both extensively adopted in medication-recommendation research. Detailed statistics are provided in Table 1. To ensure fair comparisons across methods, we follow previous studies [7] and split each dataset into training, validation, and test sets with a ratio of 3:1:1.

Baselines. To validate the efficacy and competitiveness of RCG4MR, we benchmark it against the following state-of-the-art medication-recommendation models: LEAP [17], RETAIN [18], GAMENet [22], MICRO [20], SafeDrug [23], COGNet [21], and CausalMed [13]. Specially, LEAP formulates medication recommendation as a sequential decision process and employs content-based attention to model latent relational mappings. RETAIN utilizes a two-level attention mechanism to identify influential historical visits within a patient's longitudinal diagnosis record, thereby refining patient representations. GAMENet mitigates adverse drug–drug interactions by jointly modeling longitudinal patient records as an EHR graph and external drug knowledge as a DDI graph. SafeDrug extracts rich molecular structural information to improve the risk profile of recommendations. CausalMed discovers causal relationships between diagnoses/procedures and medications and quantifies their causal effects.

Table 3. The performance of triple variants of RG4ME on evaluation metrics. The best and the runner-up results are highlighted in bold and underlined respectively.

Models	Jaccard	F1	PRAUC	Jaccard	F1	PRAUC
RCG4MR w/o LLMs	0.5393	0.6926	0.7853	0.4903	0.6392	0.7343
RCG4MR w/o GCA	<u>0.5420</u>	<u>0.6937</u>	<u>0.7871</u>	<u>0.4918</u>	**0.6413**	<u>0.7348</u>
RCG4MR w/o LLMs & GCA	0.5387	0.6918	0.7826	0.4899	<u>0.6408</u>	0.7338
RCG4MR	**0.5428**	**0.6945**	**0.7879**	**0.4922**	0.6398	**0.7352**

4.1 Performance Comparison (RQ1)

To validate the effectiveness of RCG4MR, we conducted comparative experiments against several state-of-the-art baselines, whose results are summarized in Table 2. On both the MIMIC-III and MIMIC-IV datasets, RCG4MR achieves competitive or superior performance across most metrics. As shown in Table 2, RCG4MR outperforms most competitors on all datasets for all measures consistently. Specifically, on the MIMIC-III and -IV datasets, RCG4MR outperforms competitor (*i.e.*, COGNet) by up to 2.18% and 3.07% in terms of Jaccard. These are considerable improvements in the sense that existing state-of-the-art medication recommender systems tend to outperform their best competitor by an average of about 7.37% and a maximum of about 19.92% in terms of Jaccard.

4.2 Ablation Study (RQ2 & RQ3)

In this section, we conduct extensive ablation experiments on the MIMIC-III and MIMIC-IV datasets. To rigorously assess the contribution of each proposed innovation, we conducted an ablation study on three variant models:

- RCG4MR w/o LLMs excludes the joint refinement of the diagnosis/procedure-to-medication causal graph using LLMs and patient diagnostic records.
- RCG4MR w/o GCA removes the gated cross-attention module, thereby disabling the model's capacity to quantify the specific influence of individual diagnoses or procedures on medication selection.
- RCG4MR w/o LLMs&GCA simultaneously omits LLMs and GCA components.

As reported in Table 3, both RCG4MR significantly outperform RCG4MR w/o LLMs, confirming the individual efficacy of refining causal graph. Notably, the superior performance achieved when both modules are jointly employed indicates a strong synergistic enhancement. These controlled ablations thus provide clear evidence of the incremental value contributed by each innovation to the overall RCG4MR framework.

4.3 Hyper-Parameter Analysis (RQ4)

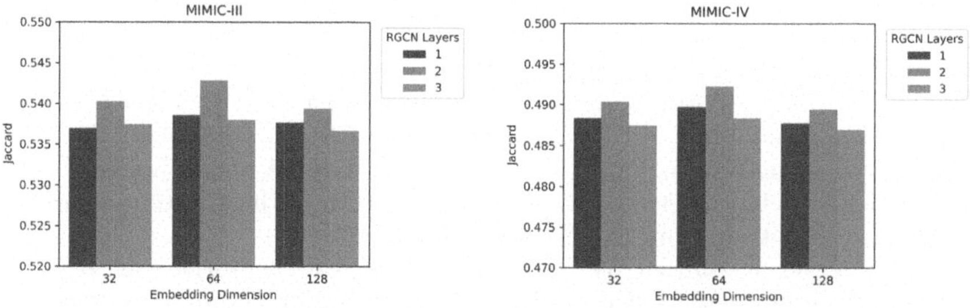

Fig. 3. The performance of the RCG4MR under various hyperparameter settings.

In this subsection, we investigate the impact of different hyperparameters on the recommendation performance of RCG4MR. These parameters include the number of RGCN layers and the embedding dimension of each medical entity.

We select three adjacent configurations and use the Jaccard index to measure the accuracy of the recommendation results. For the number of RGCN layers, we set this parameter to $\{1, 2, 3\}$, and for the embedding dimensions of medical entities, we set them to $\{32, 64, 128\}$. From Fig. 3, we observe that the configuration with 2 RGCN layers and a 64-dimensional embedding yields the best and most balanced performance.

5 Conclusion

We develop a medication recommendation framework called RCG4MR. RCG4MR uses causal inference to capture point-to-point relationships between diseases and medications, and introduces a Dynamic Gated Cross Attention mechanism to identify how various medical entities influence a patient's clinical history. This enhances the level of personalization in patient representations. This framework effectively addresses the challenges of unclear relationships between medical entities and manages the varying impacts of disease and procedure differences on drug selection. Its efficacy has been validated through extensive experiments conducted on real-world datasets.

References

1. Kuang, Y., Xie, M.: Drugdoctor: enhancing drug recommendation in cold-start scenario via visit-level representation learning and training. Briefings Bioinform. **25**(6), bbae464 (2024)
2. Liu, S., Wang, X., Jingcheng, D., Hou, Y., Zhao, X., Hui, X., Wang, H., Xiang, Y., Tang, B.: Shape: a sample-adaptive hierarchical prediction network for medication recommendation. IEEE J. Biomed. Health Inform. **27**(12), 6018–6028 (2023)
3. Liu, S.: Multimodal data matters: Language model pre-training over structured and unstructured electronic health records. IEEE J. Biomed. Health Inform. **27**(1), 504–514 (2023)
4. Zou, X., He, X., Zheng, X., Zhang, W., Chen, J., Tang, C.: Dai-net: Dual adaptive interaction network for coordinated medication recommendation. IEEE J. Biomed. Health Inform. **28**(10), 6201–6211 (2024)
5. Sousa, D., Couto, F.M.: Biomedical relation extraction with knowledge graph-based recommendations. IEEE J. Biomed. Health Inform. **26**(8), 4207–4217 (2022)
6. Wang, Yu., Peng-Fei Li, Yu., Tian, J.-J.R., Li, J.-S.: A shared decision-making system for diabetes medication choice utilizing electronic health record data. IEEE J. Biomed. Health Inform. **21**(5), 1280–1287 (2017)
7. Yang, N., Zeng, K., Qitian, W., Yan, J.: Molerec: combinatorial drug recommendation with substructure-aware molecular representation learning. In: Proceedings of the ACM Web Conference 2023, pp. 4075–4085 (2023)
8. Kuang, Y., Xie, M.: Subtype-dcgcn: an unsupervised approach for cancer subtype diagnosis based on multi-omics data. In: 2023 IEEE International Conference on Bioinformatics and Biomedicine (BIBM), pp. 554–559. IEEE (2023)
9. Kuang, Y., Xie, M., Zhao, Z., Deng, D., Bao, E.: Multi-view contrastive clustering for cancer subtyping using fully and weakly paired multi-omics data. Methods **232**, 1–8 (2024)

10. Wang, W., Lin, X., Feng, F., He, X., Lin, M., Chua, T.-S.: Causal representation learning for out-of-distribution recommendation. In: Proceedings of the ACM Web Conference 2022, pp. 3562–3571 (2022)
11. Chen Gao, Yu., Zheng, W.W., Feng, F., He, X., Li, Y.: Causal inference in recommender systems: a survey and future directions. ACM Trans. Inform. Syst. **42**(4), 1–32 (2024)
12. Fanglin Zhu, X., Zhang, B.Z., Yonghui, X., Cui, L.: Medicine package recommendation via dual-level interaction aware heterogeneous graph. IEEE J. Biomed. Health Inform. **28**(4), 2294–2303 (2024)
13. Li, X., et al.: Causalmed: causality-based personalized medication recommendation centered on patient health state. In: Proceedings of the 33rd ACM International Conference on Information and Knowledge Management, pp. 1276–1285 (2024)
14. Lan, W., et al.: The large language models on biomedical data analysis: a survey. IEEE J. Biomed. Health Inform. **29**(6), 4486–4497 (2025)
15. Wei, X., Qiu, Y., Xu, X., Xu, J., Mei, J., Zhang, J.: Ecinfusion: a novel explicit channel-wise interaction network for unified multi-modal medical image fusion. IEEE Trans. Circuits Syst. Video Technol. (2024)
16. Mei, J., et al.: Cross-modal interactive perception network with mamba for lung tumor segmentation in pet-ct images. In: Proceedings of the Computer Vision and Pattern Recognition Conference, pp. 15653–15662 (2025)
17. Zhang, Y., Chen, R., Tang, J., Stewart, W.F., Sun, J.: Leap: learning to prescribe effective and safe treatment combinations for multimorbidity. In: Proceedings of the 23rd ACM SIGKDD international conference on knowledge Discovery and data Mining, pp. 1315–1324 (2017)
18. Choi, E., Bahadori, M.T., Sun, J., Kulas, J., Schuetz, A., Stewart, W.: Retain: An interpretable predictive model for healthcare using reverse time attention mechanism. In: Advances in neural information processing systems, vol. 29 (2016)
19. Liang, X., Yang, J., Guangming, L., Zhang, D.: Compnet: competitive neural network for palmprint recognition using learnable gabor kernels. IEEE Signal Process. Lett. **28**, 1739–1743 (2021)
20. Yang, C., Xiao, C., Glass, L., Sun, J.: Change matters: medication change prediction with recurrent residual networks (2021). arXiv:2105.01876 arXiv preprint
21. Rui, W., Qiu, Z., Jiang, J., Qi, G., Xian, W.: Conditional generation net for medication recommendation. In: Proceedings of the ACM Web Conference 2022, pp. 935–945 (2022)
22. Shang, J., Xiao, C., Ma, T., Li, H., Sun, J.: Gamenet: graph augmented memory networks for recommending medication combination. In: Proceedings of the AAAI Conference on Artificial Intelligence 33, pp. 1126–1133 (2019)
23. Yang, C., Xiao, C., Ma, F., Glass, L., Sun, J.: Safedrug: Dual molecular graph encoders for recommending effective and safe drug combinations. arXiv preprint arXiv:2105.02711 (2021)
24. Liu, X., Song, Q., Xiao, L., Wang, C., Gao, X.: Lpic: Learnable prompts and id-guided contrastive learning for multimodal recommendation. ACM Trans. Multimed. Comput. Commun. Appl. (2025)
25. Xiao, T., Wang, S.: Towards unbiased and robust causal ranking for recommender systems. In: Proceedings of the Fifteenth ACM International Conference on Web Search and Data Mining, pp. 1158–1167 (2022)

Multimodal Fake News Detection: Integrating Text and Social Network Information

Quoc-Viet Nguyen[1], Xiao-Chi Chen[1], Khanh-Duy Nguyen[1], Min-Te Sun[1(✉)], Wu-Yuin Hwang[2,3], Kazuya Sakai[4], and Wei-Shinn Ku[5]

[1] Department of Computer Science and Information Engineering, National Central University, Taoyuan, Taiwan
vietnq@uit.edu.vn, nkduy@tvu.edu.vn, msun@csie.ncu.edu.tw

[2] Graduate Institute of Network Learning Technology, National Central University, Taoyuan, Taiwan

[3] Department of Computer Science and Information Engineering, National Dong Hwa University, Hualien, Taiwan

[4] Department of Computer Science, Tokyo Metropolitan University, Tokyo, Japan
ksakai@tmu.ac.jp

[5] Department of Computer Science and Software Engineering, Auburn University, Auburn, AL, USA
weishinn@auburn.edu

Abstract. With the rapid development of social media, the proliferation of fake news has become a pressing issue, further exacerbating societal polarization. Detecting fake news has thus become increasingly important. Previous efforts to detect fake news using various methods have faced limitations, particularly in terms of model accuracy. To address these challenges, this paper proposes a Multimodal Fake News Detection (MFND) approach that integrates textual and social network information. Specifically, we combine semantic representations of news, propagation patterns on social media, and hypergraph techniques to enhance the dataset. We then employ the Semantic Extraction Network (SEN) to capture the underlying semantics of news, aiming to improve the accuracy of fake news detection. Experimental results on two real-world datasets demonstrate that MFND outperforms state-of-the-art models, achieving superior accuracy in detecting fake news.

Keywords: Multimodal fake news detection · Semantic extraction network · Hypergraph · Propagation patterns · Social network information

1 Introduction

The rapidly evolving landscape of social media has led to increased passive news consumption. People tend to read news from social media rather than traditional news organizations. However, when consuming news from social media, they have

R. C.-W. Wong et al. (Eds.): PAKDD 2026, LNAI 16617, pp. 90–102, 2027.
https://doi.org/10.1007/978-981-92-1926-1_8

to face fake news, which often harbors malicious intent, such as generating panic, manipulation of elections [27]. Fake news can be easily tailored to appeal to users by incorporating their preferences, using sensational headlines, aligning with users' positions, and promoting topics of their interest with the help of various generative AI techniques. Moreover, when fake news involves crucial political, economic, or social issues, it leads to a divergence between public perception and government communications, accelerating societal polarization. Given these challenges, identifying fake news on social media is essential in today's world.

In previous research, attempts have been made to enrich datasets from different perspectives, including utilizing textual content, user information, and propagation patterns to detect fake news [14,16]. However, there are four key challenges in detecting fake news on social media are: **(1) Data collection**: On most fact-checking websites, such as Politifact [29] and GossipCop [28], professional journalists are required to review news for accuracy. Manual review has two major drawbacks: it cannot be done in real-time and the results may vary due to subjective human factors. **(2) Social media user privacy**: User information on social media may include sensitive data such as personal identity, address, and phone number. Social media platforms set data usage permissions, and as privacy awareness increases, obtaining these permissions becomes more difficult. **(3) Semantic Understanding**: News often employs persuasive and attention-grabbing headlines to make people believe their content. Various writing styles and forms make the wording and semantics of real and fake news remarkably similar. This similarity poses a significant challenge to accurately detecting fake news solely based on the article's content. **(4) Data Sparsity**: Utilizing propagation patterns for fake news detection requires collecting a large amount of propagation data, such as social media shares, to track the dissemination path of news. However, due to limitations imposed by social media platforms, collecting such data can be challenging. Additionally, not every news topic experiences widespread dissemination, resulting in some news having a limited number of shares. This leads to data sparsity, which can subsequently impact the accuracy of detection results. To address the aforementioned challenges, we propose an approach, called MFND, which integrates text and social network information to enhance the accuracy of fake news detection. In summary, the contributions of this study are listed as follows:

- We propose a system, namely MFND that combines multiple perspectives to detect fake news, effectively integrating the advantages of text-based detection, user-based detection, and propagation pattern-based detection.
- We propose a method that utilizes the Semantic Extraction Network (SEN) to learn the underlying semantics of news, aiming to enhance the accuracy of fake news detection.
- We provide a comprehensive comparison of different approaches to fake news detection across three types of methods: propagation tree-based methods, heterogeneous graph-based methods, and hypergraph-based methods.

- The extensive experiment shows that the proposed system achieves the highest accuracy, surpassing state-of-the-art models.

2 Related Work

2.1 Graph Neural Networks

Graph Neural Networks (GNNs) [8] aggregate neighborhood information to learn expressive node and graph representations [2]. Graph Convolutional Networks (GCNs) [22,24] update node features via graph convolutions, while GraphSAGE [7] improves scalability for graphs of varying sizes. Hypergraph neural networks [4] extend convolutions to hypergraphs for semi-supervised learning. Graph Attention Networks (GAT) [26] apply attention to model node importance, with extensions such as Edge-Weighted GATs using transfer learning for robustness [12] and adaptive weighting for relationship authenticity [5].

2.2 Fake News Detection

Fake news detection methods are generally classified as content-driven, user-information-driven, propagation-driven, or hybrid approaches. Content-driven methods analyze writing style and sentiment [18], sentence-interaction models [25], and VAEs [6] to extract textual representations. User-information-driven methods analyze user profiles and demographics [15] or model credibility from user histories [3]. Propagation-driven methods exploit differences in diffusion patterns [10], employing tree-structured models [1,9], GNNs [8], or Transformers [16] to distinguish fake from real news. Hybrid methods combine multimodal signals through feature fusion [31], cross-modal comparison [11], or mutual enhancement between text and image modalities [30].

3 Methodology

The proposed system is illustrated in Fig. 1, which consists of three modules. First, the data preprocessing module extracts relevant social media messages from the dataset and utilizes the Twitter Developer API to obtain comprehensive user information and news propagation patterns. Second, the model training module allows our model to learn the textual features of news articles in the first stage and capture propagation patterns while extracting relationships among news articles in the second stage. Third, the news classification module integrates these extracted features to classify news effectively. The following subsection will provide a detailed description of each module in our proposed system.

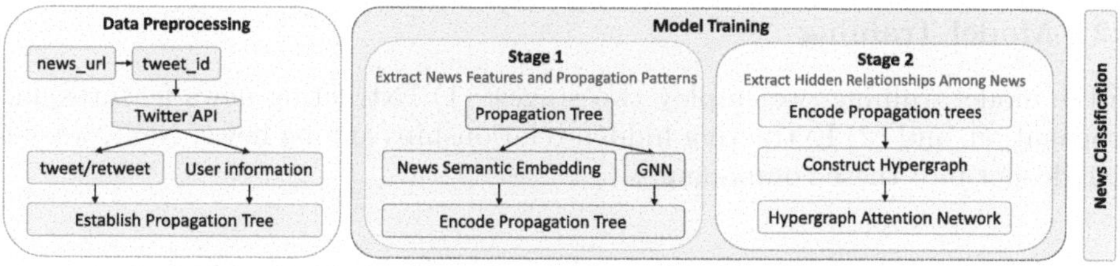

Fig. 1. An overview of proposed system architecture.

3.1 Data Preprocessing

Figure 2 illustrates the data preprocessing module, which aims to construct the propagation tree of news on social media (Twitter). The root node of the propagation tree contains features such as news content and user information, while the features of the remaining nodes include tweet/retweet data and user information. We obtained news URLs and their corresponding Tweet IDs from the FakeNewsNet dataset [21], which provide access to both news articles and related Twitter content. Using these URLs, we retrieved the full text of news articles, and through the Twitter Developer API, we collected tweets, retweets, and user information. Each user's data includes ten profile features such as verification status, geo-spatial positioning, follower and friend counts, total posts, likes, list count, account creation time, and word counts in the description and screen name as well as up to 200 recent tweets. This information supports the extraction of user behaviors and preferences for fake news detection. Following the study [3], we adopt pre-trained language representation models to capture greater semantic similarity between words and sentences. The user profile (i.e., ten profile features), user preferences (i.e., 200 historical tweets or retweets), and news content are encoded using pre-trained word embedding vectors, specifically BERT-as-a-service.

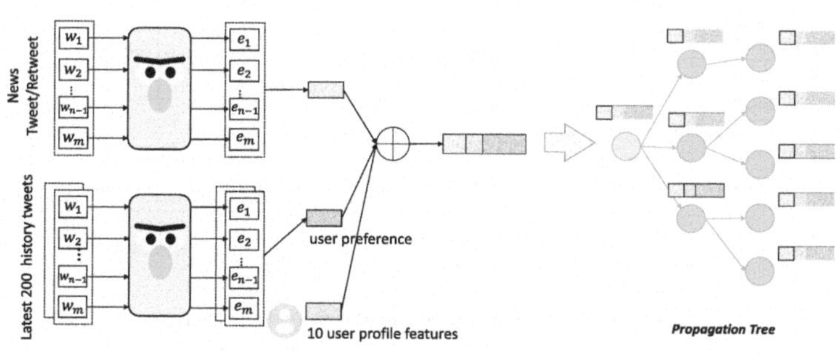

Fig. 2. Data preprocessing.

3.2 Model Training

In the model training, we employ two stages: (1) Extracting news features and propagation, and (2) Extracting hidden relationships among news. Next, we will dive deeper into these components:

News Feature and Propagation Pattern Extraction. We employ the Semantic Extraction Network (SEN) to capture the semantic meaning of news articles. First, the Simple Spectral Graph Convolution (S2GC) [19] is applied to learn propagation patterns, followed by content analysis to derive semantic embeddings. A two-layer BiGRU with 300 hidden units per layer processes 768-dimensional input features, while an attention mechanism refines the extracted features by mapping 256-dimensional BiGRU outputs to a 128-dimensional representation, which is then passed through a fully connected layer. As BERT embeddings capture word-level context but overlook sequential relationships, BiGRU is used to model long-range dependencies within each sentence or article. The BiGRU formulation is shown in Eq. 1, where h_t denotes the hidden state at time t and e_t represents the corresponding word embedding vector.

$$h_t = BiGRU(e_t, h_{t-1}) \tag{1}$$

We believe that not all words are equally important for fake news detection. Therefore, after passing the word embedding vectors through BiGRU, we apply a tanh function to the output, which enables the model to have better expressive power and maps the data to the range of $[-1, 1]$. This helps prevent the problem of vanishing or exploding gradients and improves the stability and effectiveness of the model (Fig. 3).

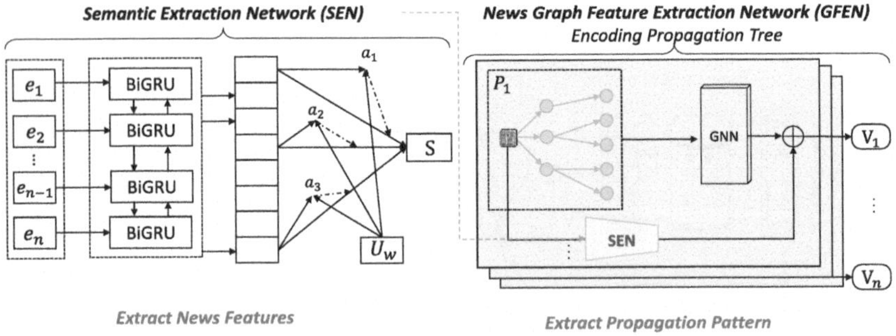

Fig. 3. The process of feature extraction.

Next, we calculate the attention coefficients for each word and use softmax to determine the weight distribution. The purpose is to selectively focus on important positions of the information in the sequence. The formula is shown in

Eq. 2. In Eq. 2, u_t is the output of the tanh function, u_w represents the weight matrix, and u_t^T denotes transpose operation.

$$a_t = \text{softmax}(u_t u_w) = \frac{exp(u_t^T u_w)}{\sum_t exp(u_t^T u_w)} \tag{2}$$

Finally, we perform a weighted sum of the word vectors h_t and their corresponding attention coefficients a_t to obtain the final representation of the news S, as shown in Eq. 3.

$$S = \sum_t a_t h_t \tag{3}$$

Inspired by the work [19], we utilized the S2GC to address the issue of over-smoothing in graph neural network computations. S2GC aims to effectively mitigate this problem and emphasizes the utilization of graph spectral properties for feature representation and propagation between nodes. We believe that the most important factor of social network analysis is to understand the propagation between nodes and distinguish the differences in propagation patterns. The S2GC formula is shown in Eq. 4.

$$\mathbf{X}' = \frac{1}{K}\sum_{k=1}^{K}\left((1-\alpha)\left(\hat{\mathbf{D}}^{-1/2}\hat{\mathbf{A}}\hat{\mathbf{D}}^{-1/2}\right)^{k}\mathbf{X} + \alpha\mathbf{X}\right)\mathbf{\Theta} \tag{4}$$

In Eq. 4, $\mathbf{X}'$ denotes the updated feature matrix representing extracted propagation patterns. K is the number of propagation steps in S2GC, and $\alpha \in [0, 1]$ is a teleport probability that balances input features and propagated patterns. $\hat{\mathbf{D}}$ and $\hat{\mathbf{A}}$ are the normalized degree and adjacency matrices, respectively, while $\mathbf{\Theta}$ is a learnable parameter matrix. This formulation enables S2GC to capture multi-step propagation patterns and learn expressive feature representations of news articles.

Hidden News Correlation Extraction. Inspired by the study [13], focusing only on the propagation patterns of individual news articles when dealing with the data of propagation trees can easily lead to overfitting of the detection model, resulting in inaccurate predictions. Moreover, the expression of fake news propagation at the group level is rarely considered, such as the relationships between common news among users frequently targeted by fake news attacks. Considering these relationships can allow us to understand the propagation patterns of fake news from different perspectives, the approach of hypergraphs is proposed to enrich the dataset. Hypergraphs are constructed by collecting the relationships between news articles, and a two-layer in GAT [26] is used to learn the relationship information between nodes and hyperedges as shown in Fig. 4. Each hypergraph is composed of news articles in the dataset, and the content of each node is obtained by concatenating the features of the news context and the features of the propagation pattern, as shown in Eq. 5.

$$v_i^0 = f(\sigma(S_i \oplus x_i')) \tag{5}$$

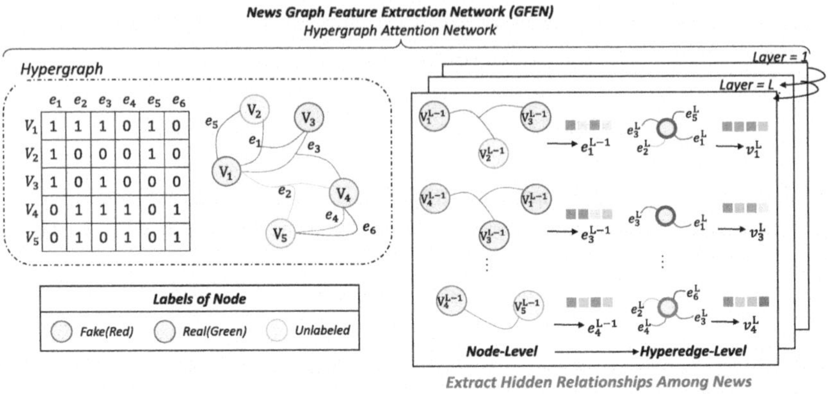

Fig. 4. Extracting hidden relationships among news by using hypergraph attention network.

Here, v_i^0 represents the feature of the i-th node in the hypergraph at layer 0, S_i indicates the textual features of the i-th news article, and x_i' is the propagation pattern features of the i-th news article.

The purpose of the first layer of GAT [26] is to obtain node-level attention. The focus is on reflecting that nodes may not contribute equally to the representation of a hyperedge. Therefore, an attention mechanism is introduced to emphasize the nodes that are meaningful for a given hyperedge, and then aggregate them to calculate the hyperedge representation e_j^l.

$$e_j^l = \sigma\left(\sum_{v_k \in e_j} \alpha_{jk} W_1 v_k^{l-1}\right) \tag{6}$$

In Eq. 6, e_j^l is the hyperedge representation at layer l, σ denotes the ReLU function, W_1 is a trainable weight matrix, and α_{jk} represents the attention coefficient of node v_k in hyperedge e_j, which can be calculated by Eq. 7.

$$\alpha_{jk} = \frac{\exp(a_1^T h_k)}{\sum_{v_p \in e_j} \exp(a_1^T h_p)}, \quad h_k = \text{LeakyReLU}(W_1 v_k^{l-1}) \tag{7}$$

Here, a_1 is a weight vector.

Once we obtain the representation of the hyperedge, it is fed into the second layer of GAT to obtain edge-level attention. A similar process is conducted for the second layer. It emphasizes the significance of certain representations in the process of learning the subsequent layer representation of node v_i, as shown in Eq. 8.

$$v_i^l = \sigma\left(\sum_{e_j \in \varepsilon_i} \beta_{ij} W_2 e_j^l\right) \tag{8}$$

In Eq. 8, v_i^l is the output representation of node v_i, W_2 is a weight matrix, and β_{ij} represents the attention coefficient of hyperedge e_j on node v_i, which can be calculated by Eq. 9.

$$\beta_{ij} = \frac{exp(a_2^T r_j)}{\sum_{v_i \in e_j, e_j \in \varepsilon_i} exp(a_2^T r_i)}, r_j = LeakyReLU([W_2 e_j^l \oplus W_1 v_i^{l-1}]) \tag{9}$$

Here, a_2 is another weight (context) vector.

3.3 News Classification

In the classification step, a trainable weight matrix W_3 and bias b are employed in a fully connected layer to classify the final node representation v_i^l into two labels $\hat{y}_i$. The optimization process minimizes the negative log-likelihood between the predicted $\hat{y}_i$ and the actual label y_i for the i-th node, using the training set labels $\mathcal{Y}_{train}$.

$$\hat{y}_i = Softmax(f(W_3 v_i^L + b)) \tag{10}$$

$$\mathcal{L} = - \sum_{y_i \in \mathcal{Y}_{train}} y_i log(\hat{y}_i) + (1 - y_i) log(1 - \hat{y}_i)) \tag{11}$$

4 Experiments and Results

4.1 Experimental Environment

The experimental configuration includes both hardware and software components. We employ two sets: Set 1 for hardware configuration and Set 2 for software configuration. Set 1 features an Intel(R) Xeon(R) CPU E5-2698 v4 @ 2.20 GHz, 12 GB of RAM, and an NVIDIA Tesla V100. Set 2 used Pytorch 1.11.0+cu102, PyTorch Geometric 2.2.0, and runs on Ubuntu 18.04.

4.2 Baselines

For a comprehensive comparison, we evaluate our method against previous works in fake news detection, covering three categories of approaches: (1) propagation tree-based methods, including HGFND [13], variations of UPFD [3], TGNF [23], GTN [16], and GCNFN [17]; (2) a heterogeneous graph-based method, HGAT [20]; and (3) a hypergraph-based method, HGNN [4]. The features for news and users are configured according to the settings of all baseline models.

4.3 Datasets

To analyze user preferences, propagation patterns, and fake news semantics, we used FakeNewsNet [21], which includes articles from GossipCop and PolitiFact, two widely used benchmark datasets [3,13] labeled by professional fact-checkers. Due to Twitter privacy restrictions, additional user data in FakeNewsNet requires API access, and some accounts were inaccessible. Therefore, we used news and user information from UPFD [3]. Following [3,13], we split the data into training (70%), validation (20%), and test (10%) sets, treating each propagation graph as a single data point. Graphs were randomly assigned to each set. The Politifact dataset contains 314 news propagation trees, equally divided between 157 fake and 157 real news items, comprising 41,054 nodes and 40,740 edges. The GossipCop dataset includes 5,464 propagation trees (2,732 fake and 2,732 real), with a significantly larger graph size of 314,262 nodes and 308,798 edges, respectively.

4.4 Hyperparameters Setting

MFND is divided into two parts, the first part being the SEN and the second part the GFEN. For the SEN, the batch size is set to 64. For the GFEN, key parameters include a hidden dimension of 128, a batch size of 128, and the Adam optimizer. The model employs a dropout rate of 0.3, a learning rate of 0.001, and is trained for 200 epochs. The hypergraph attention network comprises two layers, and early stopping is applied to prevent overfitting. For all baseline models, we adopt the original hyperparameters defined in their respective implementations.

4.5 Evaluation Metrics

Fake news detection is a binary classification task that is typically evaluated using a confusion matrix [3,13,16,20,23]. From this matrix, four quantitative metrics can be derived: *Accuracy*, *Precision*, *Recall*, and *F1 Score*. In this study, we employ these metrics to evaluate our model's performance.

4.6 Results and Analysis

The performance results of various methods are presented in Table 1. It can be observed that MFND outperforms other methods in terms of accuracy and F1-Score across both datasets, demonstrating the best performance. First, when considering the characteristics of the datasets, the amount of data and the richness of the dataset are two important factors that directly impact the model performance. As shown in Sect. 4.3, Politifact has fewer news articles but a higher average number of nodes in the propagation tree per news article. On the other hand, GossipCop has more news articles but lower richness in the propagation trees compared to Politifact. Second, as a heterogeneous graph-based method, MFND outperforms HGFND [13] on the PolitiFact dataset. On the GossipCop dataset, we achieve significantly better performance than HGFND by integrating the semantic extraction network of news in addition to propagation. Meanwhile, HGAT [20] runs out of memory on the GossipCop dataset due to the inclusion of all users as nodes.

Table 1. Quantitative comparison between our proposed and baseline methods. The results, obtained from ten runs with different random seeds, are reported as the mean ± standard deviation. Note **bold** presents the best, and <u>underline</u> indicates the second best. OOM denotes out of memory

Methods	Politifact (small dataset)				GossipCop (large dataset)			
	Accuracy ↑	F1 Score ↑	Precision ↑	Recall ↑	Accuracy ↑	F1 Score ↑	Precision ↑	Recall ↑
UPFD-SAGE [3]	80.57±3.13	88.88±4.32	88.88±4.32	88.88±4.32	96.58±0.76	96.58±0.83	96.58±0.83	96.58±0.83
UPFD-GCN [3]	81.87±4.56	81.89±4.56	81.89±4.56	81.89±4.56	94.49±1.75	94.52±1.71	94.52±1.71	94.52±1.71
UPFD-GAT [3]	78.73±4.97	78.73±4.98	78.73±4.98	78.73±4.98	95.98±0.75	95.99±0.74	95.99±0.74	95.99±0.74
HGAT [20]	81.50±1.19	80.44±1.78	80.44±7.18	80.44±7.18	OOM	OOM	OOM	OOM
GTN [16]	81.64±4.19	81.17±3.88	81.17±3.88	81.17±3.88	92.38±1.01	92.35±1.01	92.35±1.01	92.35±1.01
GCNFN [17]	80.60±4.26	80.28±6.08	80.28±6.08	80.28±6.08	95.34±0.24	95.30±0.24	95.34±0.24	95.30±0.24
HGNN [4]	79.93±4.92	79.25±5.19	79.25±5.19	79.25±5.19	93.35±0.46	93.35±0.46	93.35±0.46	93.35±0.46
TGNF [23]	74.25±1.71	74.10±7.71	74.10±7.71	74.10±7.71	85.04±1.11	85.04±1.11	85.04±1.11	85.04±1.11
HGFND [13]	<u>88.91±3.40</u>	<u>88.91±4.29</u>	<u>88.91±4.29</u>	<u>88.91±4.29</u>	<u>97.37±0.43</u>	<u>97.37±0.43</u>	<u>97.37±0.43</u>	<u>97.37±0.43</u>
MFND (Ours)	**97.06±2.49**	**97.05±2.49**	**97.05±2.49**	**97.05±2.49**	**98.04±0.70**	**98.04±0.70**	**98.04±0.70**	**98.04±0.70**

Third, as a propagation-based method, MFND demonstrates superior performance. While variations of UPFD [3] achieve comparable performance on the GossipCop dataset, they perform significantly worse on PolitiFact compared to MFND. Given that the GossipCop dataset is 17 times larger than PolitiFact's, the increased data volume significantly enhances model accuracy. The performance difference across the two datasets highlights MFND's robustness to the availability of training labels. Fourth, compared to the hypergraph-based method, the results indicate that MFND achieves better performance than HGNN [4]. This is because SEN supports our model in extracting more meaningful relations from news, enhancing the quality of the hypergraph. Additionally, compared to GNN models such as GTN [16], GCNFN [17], and TGNF [23], our proposed model outperforms them across all evaluation metrics. Finally, MFND addresses the impact of data sparsity on fake news detection by leveraging a combination of the SEN and GFEN. The SEN enhances textual representation by capturing deep semantic features through a bidirectional GRU with an attention mechanism. Meanwhile, GFEN models relational structures using hypergraphs to extract hidden relationships among news articles, compensating for sparse news instances.

4.7 Ablation Studies

Firstly, we evaluate the effect of different GNN models on our method. As shown in Table 2, S2GC achieves the best performance. Designed for large-scale graphs, S2GC also addresses the over-smoothing issue common in GCNs and improves classification precision, making it a suitable choice for our approach.

Table 2. The impact of different GNN models on our proposed method.

Models	Politifact		GossipCop	
	Accuracy	F1 score	Accuracy	F1 score
MFND-GCN	95.70±3.39	95.70±3.39	97.06±2.49	97.06±2.49
MFND-GAT	93.67±4.52	93.67±4.52	97.14±0.61	97.14±0.61
MFND-SAGE	96.83±2.71	96.83±2.71	97.28±0.34	97.28±0.34
MFND-S2GC	**97.06±2.49**	**97.06±2.49**	**98.04±0.70**	**98.04±0.70**

Secondly, we evaluate the impact of incorporating the SEN into our method. The SEN is designed to mitigate limitations related to data sparsity and richness, thereby improving classification accuracy. As shown in Table 3, integrating SEN enhances MFND performance by 7.92% on the Politifact dataset and by 0.97% on the GossipCop dataset.

Table 3. Performance comparison with and without SEN

SEN	Politifact		GossipCop	
	Accuracy	F1 score	Accuracy	F1 score
✓	**97.06±2.49**	**97.06±2.49**	**98.04±0.70**	**98.07±0.70**
–	89.14±5.43	91.11±1.85	97.07±0.47	97.46±0.30

5 Conclusion

In this paper, we argue that both the content of news articles and their propagation patterns are crucial for detecting fake news in datasets with limited data. To validate this argument, we utilize a semantic extraction network to derive the semantic meaning of news and combine it with a news graph feature extraction network. This network incorporates two graph neural network models: one encodes the propagation patterns of each news article, and the other learns the correlations between different news articles. By integrating both the news content and propagation graph features, we aim to compensate for the lack of richness in the dataset. Our proposed method achieves the highest accuracy on two publicly available benchmark datasets in fake news detection, outperforming state-of-the-art approaches. For future work, we plan to use FakeNewsNet as the training set and our collected data as the test set to better evaluate our model.

References

1. Bian, T., Xiao, X., Xu, T., Zhao, P., bing Huang, W., Rong, Y., Huang, J.: Rumor detection on social media with bi-directional graph convolutional networks. In: AAAI Conference on AI (2020)

2. Ding, K., Wang, J., Li, J., Shu, K., Liu, C., Liu, H.: Graph prototypical networks for few-shot learning on attributed networks. In: Proceedings of the 29th ACM CIKM (2020)
3. Dou, Y., Shu, K., Xia, C., Yu, P.S., Sun, L.: User preference-aware fake news detection. In: Proceedings of the 44th International ACM SIGIR Conference (2021)
4. Feng, Y., You, H., Zhang, Z., Ji, R., Gao, Y.: Hypergraph neural networks. In: AAAI Conference on AI (2018)
5. Gao, L., Song, L., Liu, J., Chen, B., Shang, X.: Topology imbalance and relation inauthenticity aware hierarchical graph attention networks for fake news detection. In: COLING (2022)
6. Gu, Y., Castro, I., Tyson, G.: Detecting multimodal fake news with gated variational autoencoder. In: Proceedings of the 16th ACM Web Science Conference, pp. 129–138 (2024)
7. Hamilton, W.L., Ying, Z., Leskovec, J.: Inductive representation learning on large graphs. In: NIPS (2017)
8. Han, Y., Karunasekera, S., Leckie, C.: Graph neural networks with continual learning for fake news detection from social media. ArXiv abs/2007.03316 (2020)
9. He, Z., Li, C., Zhou, F., Yang, Y.: Rumor detection on social media with event augmentations. In: Proceedings of the 44th International ACM SIGIR Conference (2021)
10. Hu, B., Mao, Z., Zhang, Y.: An overview of fake news detection: From a new perspective. Fundamental Research **5**(1), 332–346 (2025)
11. Hu, L., et al.: Compare to the knowledge: Graph neural fake news detection with external knowledge. In: ACL (2021)
12. Inan, E.: Zoka: a fake news detection method using edge-weighted graph attention network with transfer models. Neural Comput. Appl. **34**, 11669–11677 (2022)
13. Jeong, U., Ding, K., Cheng, L., Guo, R., Shu, K., Liu, H.: Nothing stands alone: Relational fake news detection with hypergraph neural networks. 2022 IEEE International Conference on Big Data, pp. 596–605 (2022)
14. Kozik, R., Kula, S., Choraś, M., Woźniak, M.: Technical solution to counter potential crime: Text analysis to detect fake news and disinformation. J. Comput. Sci. **60**, 101576 (2022)
15. Malik, A., Behera, D.K., Hota, J., Swain, A.R.: Ensemble graph neural networks for fake news detection using user engagement and text features. Results Eng. **24**, 103081 (2024)
16. Matsumoto, H., Yoshida, S., Muneyasu, M.: Propagation-based fake news detection using graph neural networks with transformer. In: 2021 IEEE 10th GCCE, pp. 19–20 (2021)
17. Monti, F., Frasca, F., Eynard, D., Mannion, D., Bronstein, M.M.: Fake news detection on social media using geometric deep learning. ArXiv abs/1902.06673 (2019)
18. Potthast, M., Kiesel, J., Reinartz, K., Bevendorff, J., Stein, B.: A stylometric inquiry into hyperpartisan and fake news. ArXiv abs/1702.05638 (2017)
19. Priebe, C.E., Shen, C., Huang, N.T., Chen, T.: A simple spectral failure mode for graph convolutional networks. IEEE TPAMI **44**, 8689–8693 (2020)
20. Ren, Y., Zhang, J.: Fake news detection on news-oriented heterogeneous information networks through hierarchical graph attention. In: 2021 International Joint Conference on Neural Networks (IJCNN), pp. 1–8. IEEE (2021)
21. Shu, K., Mahudeswaran, D., Wang, S., Lee, D., Liu, H.: Fakenewsnet: a data repository with news content, social context, and spatiotemporal information for studying fake news on social media. Big data **8**(3), 171–188 (2018)

22. Soga, K., Yoshida, S., Muneyasu, M.: Exploiting stance similarity and graph neural networks for fake news detection. Pattern Recogn. Lett. **177**, 26–32 (2024)
23. Song, C., Shu, K., Wu, B.: Temporally evolving graph neural network for fake news detection. Inf. Process. Manag. **58**, 102712 (2021)
24. Truică, C.O., Apostol, E.S., Marogel, M., Paschke, A.: Getae: graph information enhanced deep neural network ensemble architecture for fake news detection. Expert Syst. Appl. **275**, 126984 (2025)
25. Vaibhav, V., Annasamy, R.M., Hovy, E.H.: Do sentence interactions matter? leveraging sentence level representations for fake news classification. In: Conference on EMNLP (2019)
26. Velickovic, P., Cucurull, G., Casanova, A., Romero, A., Lio', P., Bengio, Y.: Graph attention networks. ArXiv abs/1710.10903 (2017)
27. Wikipedia: Wikipedia:Pizzagate conspiracy theory. https://en.wikipedia.org/wiki/Pizzagate_conspiracy_theory. Accessed 19 June 2023
28. Wikipedia: Gossip Cop dataset. https://en.wikipedia.org/wiki/Gossip_Cop. Accessed 20 Sept 2024
29. Wikipedia: PolitiFact dataset. https://www.politifact.com/. Accessed 20 Sept 2024
30. Wu, Y., Zhan, P., Zhang, Y., Wang, L., Xu, Z.: Multimodal fusion with co-attention networks for fake news detection. In: Findings (2021)
31. Zhang, Z., et al.: Gbca: graph convolution network and bert combined with co-attention for fake news detection. Pattern Recogn. Lett. **180**, 26–32 (2024)

DynaMo3D: A Dynamic Mixture of SSM Experts Framework for 3D Point Cloud Detection

Qiankai Xi, Li Ma, and Jikai Zhang(✉)

School of Digital Intelligence and Industry, Inner Mongolia University of Science and Technology, Baotou 014000, China
jkimust123654@126.com

Abstract. To address the challenges of feature extraction and modeling caused by the sparsity and non-uniform distribution of point clouds, this paper proposes a dynamic State Space Model (SSM) mixture framework named DynaMo3D. The framework consists of a Position-Sensitive Dynamic Voxel Feature Encoder (PSDVFE) and a Complexity-Adaptive SSM Mixture Network (CMSN). The PSDVFE enhances local geometric modeling capability through a Position-Sensitive Dynamic Convolution (PSDC) and a Voxel Attention Feature Network (VAFN). The CMSN adaptively fuses RetNet and Mamba experts based on spatial complexity, achieving a balance between global semantic reasoning and local structural modeling. On the KITTI validation set, DynaMo3D achieves 1.28% and 1.66% higher mAP compared to LION-Mamba and LION-RetNet, respectively. Moreover, on the KITTI test server for pedestrian detection, DynaMo3D ranks 17th and 25th in the Easy and Moderate categories, respectively, demonstrating its competitiveness in LiDAR-only detection.

Keywords: 3D Object Detection · LiDAR-only Perception · State Space Model · Mixture of Experts · Autonomous Driving

1 Introduction

3D point clouds provide precise geometric cues for autonomous driving and robotics [1], but their sparsity and irregularity pose significant challenges. Learning-based methods address this variously: point-based models like PointNet [2] and PointNet++ [3] preserve fine details but scale poorly; attention mechanisms in Point Transformer [4] improve adaptability; and voxel-based frameworks like VoxelNet [5], SECOND [6], and PointPillars [7] ensure large-scale efficiency but lose fidelity due to static discretization. Hybrid architectures such as PV-RCNN [8] attempt to balance these trade-offs.

Recently, State Space Models (SSMs) have emerged to capture long-range dependencies with linear complexity. RetNet [9], Mamba [10], LION [11], and UniMamba [12] successfully extend SSMs to 3D perception. However, these backbones rely on fixed structures, lacking adaptability to regional complexity variations (e.g., sparse pedestrians vs. dense vehicles). Similarly, Mixture-of-Experts

R. C.-W. Wong et al. (Eds.): PAKDD 2026, LNAI 16617, pp. 103–114, 2027.
https://doi.org/10.1007/978-981-92-1926-1_9

(MoE) architectures offer conditional computation, but current 3D variants rely on coarse routing, limiting their capacity to handle fine-grained spatial heterogeneity [13].

To address these gaps, we propose DynaMo3D, a dynamic mixture-of-experts framework integrating position-sensitive encoding with a complexity-adaptive SSM backbone. Our main contributions are:

- Position-Sensitive Dynamic Convolution (PSDC): Learns voxel-adaptive weights directly from point positions for fine-grained geometric encoding.
- Voxel Attention Feature Network (VAFN): Enhances voxel representations via intra-voxel, channel, and spatial attention.
- Complexity-Adaptive Mixture of SSMs (CMSN): Dynamically routes features to RetNet or Mamba experts based on spatial complexity, balancing global and local modeling.

2 Related Work

2.1 Point Cloud Representation and Feature Encoding

Point-based methods capture fine geometry but struggle with large-scale scalability. Conversely, voxel-based approaches enable efficient sparse convolution but suffer from quantization loss and degraded local geometry. Recent trends thus favor adaptive discretization, where dynamic voxelization adjusts to spatial distributions to improve representation fidelity in sparse regions [14].

2.2 Backbone Network Modeling for 3D Understanding

Sparse CNNs are efficient but lack global context, while Transformers capture long-range dependencies at the cost of quadratic complexity. SSMs offer a linear-time alternative for scalable global modeling. For instance, Point Mamba [15] employs an octree-based z-order strategy to serialize unordered point clouds into causal sequences. However, existing SSM methods often use fixed configurations, struggling to maintain fine geometric cues and adapt to spatial variations.

2.3 Expert Routing for Efficient 3D Processing

MoE architectures route features to specialized subnetworks for enhanced efficiency. Existing 3D MoE detectors mostly use static or spatially invariant routing, limiting adaptability to heterogeneous point densities. While recent works integrate MoE with attention or SSM dynamics [16], their expert activation remains overly uniform, weakening specialization across scales.

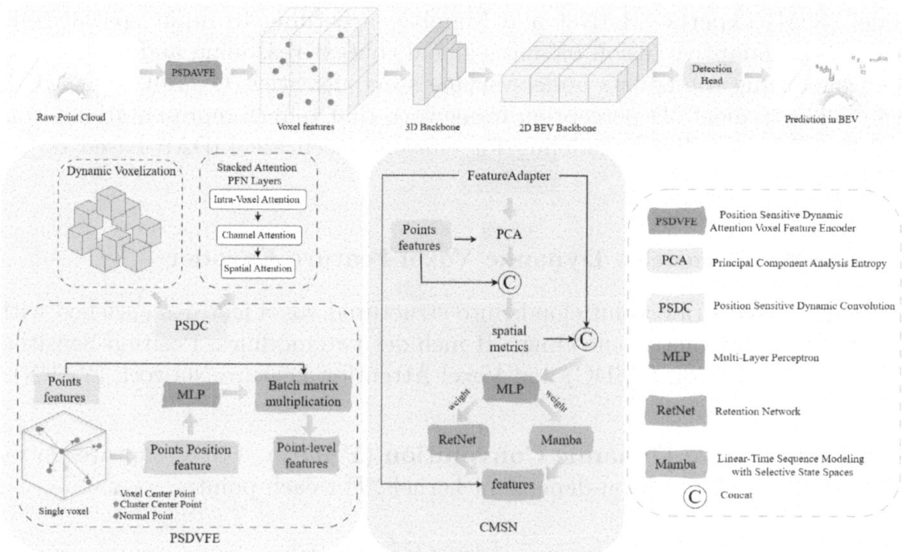

Fig. 1. Overview of the proposed DynaMo3D framework, integrating a Position-Sensitive Dynamic Voxel Feature Encoder (PSDVFE) for adaptive local extraction and a Complexity Adaptive Mixture SSM Network (CMSN) for global semantic modeling.

2.4 Summary and Motivation

In short, existing frameworks struggle to jointly balance representation granularity, computational efficiency, and adaptive global modeling. Current SSM and MoE solutions fail to achieve fine-grained dynamic routing in 3D space. This critical gap motivates our DynaMo3D framework, which unifies position-sensitive encoding and complexity-adaptive expert fusion for robust 3D object detection.

3 Methodology

This work presents DynaMo3D, a LiDAR-only 3D object detection framework that addresses point-cloud sparsity and non-uniformity while improving detection accuracy and computational efficiency. It unifies dynamic feature extraction and complexity-adaptive modeling in a single pipeline that adapts to diverse spatial distributions and object densities.

As shown in Fig. 1, DynaMo3D comprises two main components: the Position-Sensitive Dynamic Voxel Feature Encoder (PSDVFE) and the Complexity-Adaptive Mixture SSM Network (CMSN). PSDVFE transforms irregular point clouds into structured voxel representations with enhanced geometric fidelity through position-sensitive dynamic convolution and attention-based aggregation, supporting adaptive local feature learning. The CMSN backbone then processes voxel features by dynamically fusing multiple State Space

Model (SSM) experts—RetNet and Mamba—according to input spatial complexity. This adaptive fusion balances global context reasoning and local refinement, enhancing robustness under varying scene densities. Overall, DynaMo3D forms a hierarchical 3D perception framework that refines representations from local encoding to global modeling for efficient, accurate LiDAR-based object detection.

3.1 Position-Sensitive Dynamic Voxel Feature Encoder

PSDVFE converts raw point clouds into structured voxel features enriched with position-aware geometric encodings. It includes two modules: Position-Sensitive Dynamic Convolution (PSDC) and Voxel Attention Feature Network (VAFN).

Position-Sensitive Dynamic Convolution (PSDC). PSDC captures intra-voxel geometry via position-dependent kernels. For each point:

$$f_{\text{pos},i} = [f_{\text{cluster},i}; f_{\text{center},i}] \tag{1}$$

$$w_{\text{kernel},i} = M_{\text{weight}}(f_{\text{pos},i}) \tag{2}$$

$$F_i' = F_i \cdot w_{\text{kernel},i}. \tag{3}$$

where $f_{\text{cluster},i}$ and $f_{\text{center},i}$ denote the relative coordinates of point i to the intra-voxel centroid and the voxel center, respectively. These offsets are concatenated to form $f_{\text{pos},i}$, which helps adaptively preserve fine-grained geometric structures. $M_{\text{weight}}(\cdot)$ is a lightweight MLP that generates the position-sensitive kernel weights $w_{\text{kernel},i}$. F_i is the original point-wise feature before weighting, and F_i' is the dynamically modulated feature.

Voxel Attention Feature Network (VAFN). VAFN refines voxel features with intra-voxel, channel, and spatial attention.

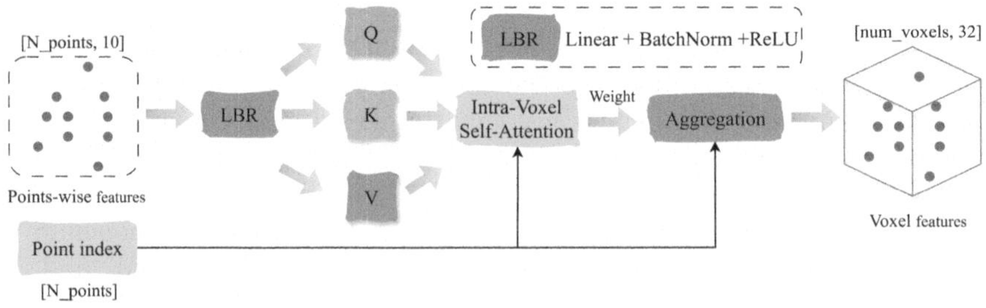

Fig. 2. Structure of the intra-voxel attention mechanism in the VAFN module.

Intra-voxel Attention. As illustrated in Fig. 2, the detailed structure of the intra-voxel attention mechanism first projects features to q_i, k_i, v_i:

$$q_i = W_Q H_i, \quad k_i = W_K H_i, \quad v_i = W_V H_i \tag{4}$$

Compute attention scores:

$$\begin{aligned} a_{ij} &= \frac{\exp\left(q_i^\top k_j / \sqrt{d_k}\right)}{\sum_l \exp\left(q_i^\top k_l / \sqrt{d_k}\right)}, \\ H_{\text{att},i} &= \text{ReLU}\left(W_{\text{attn\_out}} \sum_j a_{ij} v_j\right) \end{aligned} \tag{5}$$

Voxel features are aggregated:

$$F_{\text{voxel}} = \text{Agg}(\{H_{\text{att},i}\}) \tag{6}$$

Channel and Spatial Attention. Channel attention:

$$F'_{\text{voxel}} = F_{\text{voxel}} \odot \sigma\Big(W_2 \text{ReLU}(W_1 \text{GAP}(F_{\text{voxel}}))\Big) \tag{7}$$

Spatial attention:

$$\begin{aligned} F_{\text{out}} = F'_{\text{voxel}} \odot \sigma\Big(&\text{Conv}_{1\times1}\big([\text{AvgPool}(F'_{\text{voxel}}), \\ &\text{MaxPool}(F'_{\text{voxel}})]\big)\Big) \end{aligned} \tag{8}$$

where H_i denotes the intra-voxel feature of the i-th point; W_Q, W_K, and W_V are learnable projection matrices producing query, key, and value vectors. d_k is the feature dimension used for scaling in dot-product attention. a_{ij} is the attention coefficient between points i and j. $\text{Agg}(\cdot)$ denotes voxel-level feature aggregation. GAP, AvgPool, and MaxPool represent global average pooling, spatial average pooling, and spatial max pooling, respectively. $\sigma(\cdot)$ is the sigmoid activation function, and $\odot$ denotes element-wise multiplication.

PSDC + VAFN enable adaptive local feature extraction and robust voxel representation for sparse, irregular 3D point clouds.

3.2 Complexity-Based Adaptive SSM Network

Traditional 3D backbones such as sparse CNNs lack adaptability to varying scene complexity. Recent SSMs (RetNet, Mamba) model long-range dependencies efficiently, but RetNet tends to be more computationally demanding, whereas Mamba may underperform in highly dense regions; CMSN aims to adaptively balance these trade-offs.

We propose CMSN, integrating RetNet and Mamba via a Soft Mixture-of-Experts (MoE) mechanism, jointly activating both experts and weighting them based on spatial and feature complexity.

Complexity-Based Adaptive Mixture Layer. Given features $X \in \mathbb{R}^{N \times D}$, a residual MLP adapts them:

$$X_{\text{adapted}} = \alpha X + (1 - \alpha)\text{MLP}(X), \quad F_{\text{feat}} = \text{Agg}(X_{\text{adapted}}) \tag{9}$$

where X denotes the input voxel or point features with N samples and D channels. $\alpha \in [0, 1]$ controls the ratio of residual versus transformed features. $\text{MLP}(\cdot)$ is a two-layer feed-forward network, and $\text{Agg}(\cdot)$ denotes feature aggregation to produce a global descriptor F_{feat}.

Spatial Complexity Estimation. For points $P \in \mathbb{R}^{S \times 3}$, compute standard deviation and covariance:

$$S_{\text{std}} = \text{Std}(P), \quad C = \text{Cov}(P^{\top}) \tag{10}$$

Let Λ be the eigenvalues of C, normalized as $\Lambda^{\text{norm}} = \Lambda / (\sum_i \Lambda[i] + \epsilon)$. The geometric entropy is:

$$H = -\frac{1}{\log 3} \sum_i \Lambda^{\text{norm}}[i] \log(\Lambda^{\text{norm}}[i] + \epsilon), \quad S_{\text{spatial}} = [S_{\text{std}}; H] \tag{11}$$

where P represents the 3D coordinates of points within a voxel; S_{std} encodes the spatial dispersion along each axis; C is the covariance matrix reflecting geometric correlation; Λ and Λ^{norm} are eigenvalues and their normalized forms; H measures local geometric entropy, and ϵ avoids numerical instability. S_{spatial} concatenates spatial descriptors into a unified complexity representation.

Complexity-Aware Weighting and Soft Fusion. Concatenate feature and spatial descriptors: $I = [F_{\text{feat}}; S_{\text{spatial}}]$, and compute complexity score c via a small MLP. Expert weights:

$$w_{\text{RetNet}} = \sigma(s(c - \theta)), \quad w_{\text{Mamba}} = 1 - w_{\text{RetNet}} \tag{12}$$

The final output fuses experts with residual connection:

$$X_{\text{out}} = X + w_{\text{RetNet}} X_{\text{RetNet}} + w_{\text{Mamba}} X_{\text{Mamba}} \tag{13}$$

where I is the joint descriptor combining feature and spatial complexity; c is the scalar complexity score, s is a temperature factor controlling softness, and θ is a threshold for expert selection. X_{RetNet} and X_{Mamba} are expert outputs from RetNet and Mamba branches. w_{RetNet} and w_{Mamba} are their respective adaptive weights, satisfying $w_{\text{RetNet}} + w_{\text{Mamba}} = 1$. X_{out} is the final fused feature with residual enhancement.

This compact fusion scheme produces smooth transitions between experts, enabling balanced global (RetNet) and local (Mamba) modeling across varying scene densities.

4 Experiments

4.1 Dataset and Evaluation Metrics

We evaluate our method on the KITTI dataset, which contains 7,481 training and 7,518 test samples. The training set is standardly split into 3,712 training and 3,769 validation frames. For official test server submissions, we train on 80% of the data and validate on the remaining 20%. Objects are categorized into Easy, Moderate, and Hard levels based on occlusion and truncation. Following official evaluation metrics, we report 3D Average Precision at 40 recall points (AP@R40), using an IoU threshold of 0.7 for Cars and 0.5 for Pedestrians and Cyclists.

4.2 Implementation Details

DynaMo3D is trained end-to-end for 80 epochs on four RTX 3090 GPUs with a batch size of 2. We use the Adam optimizer with a OneCycle learning rate policy (initial LR 0.003, peak ratio 10, 40% ramp-up phase), decaying the LR by a factor of 0.1 at epochs 35 and 45. The point cloud processing range is set to $[0, 70.4] \times [-40, 40] \times [-3, 1]$ m, voxelized at $v = [0.2, 0.2, 0.125]$ m. Anchor box dimensions (l, w, h) are $[3.9, 1.6, 1.56]$ m for Cars, $[0.8, 0.6, 1.73]$ m for Pedestrians, and $[1.76, 0.6, 1.73]$ m for Cyclists. During training, positive samples are assigned using an IoU threshold of 0.6 for Cars and 0.5 for Pedestrians and Cyclists.

4.3 Experimental Results

Comparative Experiments. Tables 1 and 2 report our method's performance on the KITTI validation set. Our model achieves a Mean mAP of 73.67% (AP@40), outperforming baselines like SECOND (65.87%) and state-of-the-art models such as LION-Mamba (72.61%). It performs notably well on Moderate Pedestrian (62.30%) and Cyclist (69.86%). Under AP@11, it maintains a strong Mean mAP of 72.46%, leading in Ped-3D and Cyc-3D while remaining highly competitive in Car-3D. Furthermore, on the KITTI test server (Table 3), our model achieves a Mean mAP of 60.18%, successfully surpassing the main baselines LION-RetNet (59.39%) and LION-Mamba (59.00%).

Ablation Study. Table 4 presents ablation results on the KITTI validation set. PSDC improves Pedestrian detection, raising Mean mAP from 72.39% to 72.56%, indicating better local geometry encoding. Adding VAFN increases mAP to 73.07%, demonstrating that voxel-level attention refines features. Incorporating CMSN achieves 73.67% mAP, improving 1.28 points over the baseline by balancing local and global modeling. PSDC, VAFN, and CMSN together form a multi-scale representation, enhancing robustness and generalization across 3D scenes.

Table 1. Performance comparison of 3D object detection on the KITTI validation set. The evaluation metric is Average Precision (AP) at 40 recall points. M denotes modality, L denotes LiDAR. Best results are in bold, while second best results are underlined.

Methods	M	Car-3D (AP_{40}%)			Ped-3D (AP_{40}%)			Cyc-3D (AP_{40}%)			Mean mAP
		Easy	Mod.	Hard	Easy	Mod.	Hard	Easy	Mod.	Hard	
SECOND [6]	L	90.02	81.11	78.60	55.66	50.99	46.39	83.93	65.80	61.77	68.25
TANet [17]	L	88.17	77.75	75.31	**70.80**	63.45	58.22	85.21	65.29	61.57	71.75
LION-Mamba [11]	L	90.26	81.60	**78.79**	65.42	60.25	54.73	**88.68**	67.81	63.97	72.39
LION-RetNet [11]	L	89.28	81.17	78.40	68.78	61.14	55.52	84.98	66.44	62.37	72.01
VoxelNet [5]	L	87.93	75.37	73.21	67.81	**63.52**	**58.87**	77.69	58.72	51.63	68.31
PointRCNN [18]	L	89.01	78.77	78.10	62.69	55.36	51.60	84.48	65.37	59.83	69.47
PointPillars [7]	L	87.75	78.39	75.18	57.32	51.41	46.87	81.57	62.94	58.98	66.71
Ours	L	**90.61**	**81.66**	78.69	69.64	62.30	56.83	87.58	**69.86**	**65.89**	**73.67**

Table 2. Performance comparison of 3D object detection on the KITTI validation set. The evaluation metric is Average Precision (AP) at 11 recall points. M denotes modality, L denotes LiDAR. Best results are in bold, while second best results are underlined.

Methods	M	Car-3D (AP_{11}%)			Ped-3D (AP_{11}%)			Cyc-3D (AP_{11}%)			Mean mAP
		Easy	Mod.	Hard	Easy	Mod.	Hard	Easy	Mod.	Hard	
SECOND [6]	L	88.18	78.78	**77.26**	56.14	52.63	47.76	81.24	65.38	62.10	67.72
TANet [17]	L	87.52	76.64	73.86	67.30	**60.77**	54.45	**84.53**	61.64	57.44	69.35
LION-Mamba [11]	L	88.64	78.38	77.22	67.25	60.23	55.63	83.07	68.62	63.91	71.44
LION-RetNet [11]	L	88.04	77.92	76.71	67.42	60.26	55.84	83.63	**69.64**	64.68	71.57
VoxelNet [5]	L	81.97	65.46	62.85	57.86	53.42	48.87	67.17	47.65	45.11	58.93
PointRCNN [18]	L	85.91	75.87	68.31	48.72	42.35	40.71	74.12	59.66	53.65	61.03
PointPillars [7]	L	79.15	75.24	68.11	55.21	47.33	42.51	75.86	59.15	52.97	61.73
MSF [19]	L	**89.63**	**80.06**	75.83	66.69	58.18	56.21	82.36	59.17	58.71	69.65
Ours	L	88.54	78.25	**77.26**	**69.41**	**62.06**	**57.78**	83.67	69.18	**65.98**	**72.46**

Table 3. Comparison of 3D object detection on the KITTI test set with Baseline. The evaluation metric is Average Precision (AP) at 40 recall points. Best results are in bold, while second best results are underlined.

Methods	M	Car-3D (AP_{40}%)			Ped-3D (AP_{40}%)			Cyc-3D (AP_{40}%)			Mean mAP
		Easy	Mod.	Hard	Easy	Mod.	Hard	Easy	Mod.	Hard	
LION-RetNet	L	85.27	76.56	71.59	52.39	43.15	39.95	66.02	53.05	46.51	59.39
LION-Mamba	L	84.74	74.90	71.24	51.92	42.80	39.76	65.88	**53.70**	46.04	59.00
Ours	L	**85.69**	**76.98**	**72.01**	**53.92**	**44.73**	**41.71**	**66.32**	52.80	**47.42**	**60.18**

Table 4. Ablation Study Results on the KITTI Validation Set (AP@R40, %). The table shows the impact of PSDC, VAFN, and CMSN modules.

Methods	Car-3D (AP_{40}%)			Ped-3D (AP_{40}%)			Cyc-3D (AP_{40}%)			Mean mAP
	Easy	Mod.	Hard	Easy	Mod.	Hard	Easy	Mod.	Hard	
Baseline	90.26	81.60	78.79	65.42	60.25	54.73	88.68	67.81	63.97	72.39
+PSDC	90.02	80.97	78.29	67.60	61.02	55.31	86.73	68.92	64.14	72.56
+VAFN	90.21	81.86	77.94	69.07	61.23	56.57	86.81	69.14	64.82	73.07
+CMSN	90.61	81.66	78.69	69.64	62.30	56.83	87.58	69.86	65.89	73.67

Generalizability Validation of the PSDC Module. To test PSDC's transferability, it was integrated into SECOND, DSVT-Voxel, and Voxel-RCNN. Table 5 shows performance improvements across all baselines—for instance, SECOND + PSDC increases mean mAP from 68.25% to 69.19%. PSDC effectively enhances local geometric feature extraction and serves as a plug-and-play module for existing 3D detection frameworks.

Table 5. PSDC integrated with other methods

Methods	Car-3D (AP_{40}%)			Ped-3D (AP_{40}%)			Cyc-3D (AP_{40}%)			Mean mAP
	Easy	Mod.	Hard	Easy	Mod.	Hard	Easy	Mod.	Hard	
SECOND [6]	90.02	81.11	78.60	55.66	50.99	46.39	83.93	65.80	61.77	68.25
SECOND+PSDC	90.79	81.87	78.92	55.71	51.44	48.60	84.58	67.64	63.12	69.19
DSVT-Voxel [20]	88.65	79.42	77.26	64.95	58.42	53.35	88.23	67.00	63.47	71.19
DSVT-Voxel+PSDC	88.71	79.85	78.02	65.39	59.04	53.62	88.52	67.66	62.34	71.46
Voxel-RCNN [21]	92.63	84.89	81.47	65.65	58.20	53.14	90.93	74.08	69.39	74.60
Voxel-RCNN+PSDC	92.38	85.21	82.53	66.59	59.51	53.50	91.00	74.11	69.42	74.92

Analysis of Feature Representation Before and After PSDVFE. Figure 3 shows feature statistics before and after PSDVFE. Raw features exhibit large fluctuations, scale inconsistencies, and extreme values. After PSDVFE, feature means and standard deviations stabilize near zero, value ranges shrink, and L2 norms reduce, indicating effective normalization, outlier suppression, and regularization. Feature scales across dimensions are more balanced, providing a stable and consistent representation for subsequent layers.

Visualization Analysis. As shown in Fig. 4, we compare the detection visualization of our DynaMo3D with the LION-Mamba baseline. Compared to the baseline, DynaMo3D exhibits fewer false negatives and tighter bounding box

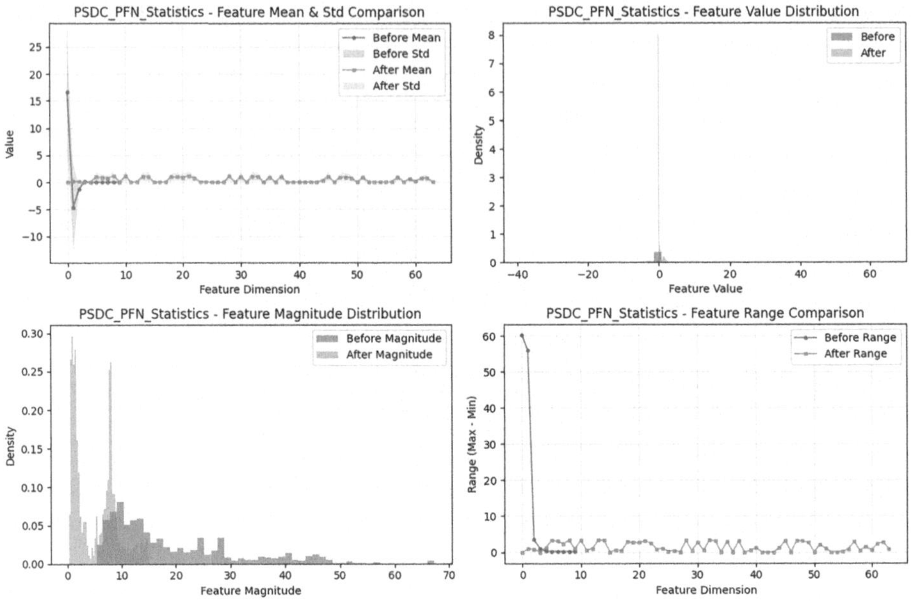

Fig. 3. PSDVFE Pre- and Post-Feature Analysis: The top-left plot shows the comparison of feature means and standard deviations, the top-right plot shows the feature value distribution, the bottom-left plot shows the feature magnitude distribution, and the bottom-right plot shows the feature range comparison.

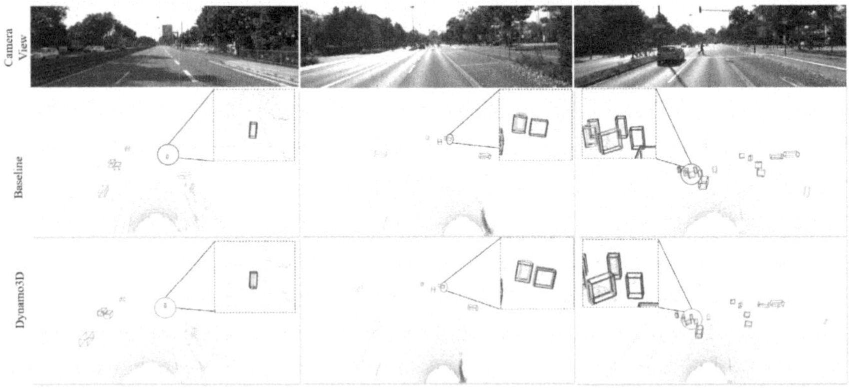

Fig. 4. In the visualization, the dark blue boxes represent the ground truth, while the predicted boxes for Car, Pedestrian, and Cyclist are shown in green, cyan, and pink, respectively. The main differences between DynaMo3D and the LION-Mamba baseline are highlighted with circles and enlarged in the figure.

predictions, particularly in complex regions with sparse points (highlighted by circles). This demonstrates the effectiveness of our adaptive feature encoding and CMSN modules in handling varying scene densities.

5 Conclusion

This paper presents DynaMo3D, a novel framework addressing the sparsity and non-uniformity of LiDAR point clouds in autonomous driving. It features a Position-Sensitive Dynamic Voxel Feature Encoder (PSDVFE) for fine-grained geometric extraction, and a Complexity-Adaptive Mixture SSM Network (CMSN) that dynamically fuses RetNet and Mamba experts. Together, these modules achieve an optimal balance between local feature refinement and global context reasoning, delivering robust 3D object detection performance.

Acknowledgments. This work was supported by the Natural Science Foundation of Inner Mongolia (Grant No. 2024LHMS06007), the First-Class Discipline Scientific Research Special Project (Grant No. YLXKZX-NKD-012), and the Inner Mongolia Autonomous Region Key Research and Development and Achievement Transformation Program (Science and Technology Support for Ecological Protection and High-Quality Development of the Yellow River Basin, Grant No. 2025YFHH0225).

References

1. Geiger, A., Lenz, P., Urtasun, R.: Are we ready for autonomous driving?The KITTI vision benchmark suite. In: 2012 IEEE Conference on Computer Vision and Pattern Recognition (CVPR), pp. 3354–3361. IEEE, Los Alamitos (2012)
2. Qi, C.R., Su, H., Mo, K., Guibas, L.J.: PointNet: deep learning on point sets for 3D classification and segmentation. In: Proceedings of the IEEE Conference on Computer Vision and Pattern Recognition (CVPR), pp. 652–660. IEEE, Los Alamitos (2017)
3. Qi, C.R., Yi, L., Su, H., Guibas, L.J.: PointNet++: deep hierarchical feature learning on point sets in a metric space. In: Advances in Neural Information Processing Systems (NeurIPS), vol. 30. Curran Associates, Red Hook (2017)
4. Zhao, H., Jiang, L., Jia, J., Torr, P.H.S., Koltun, V.: Point Transformer. In: Proceedings of the IEEE/CVF International Conference on Computer Vision (ICCV), pp. 16259–16268. IEEE, Los Alamitos (2021)
5. Zhou, Y., Tuzel, O.: VoxelNet: end-to-end learning for point cloud based 3D object detection. In: Proceedings of the IEEE Conference on Computer Vision and Pattern Recognition (CVPR), pp. 4490–4499. IEEE, Los Alamitos (2018)
6. Yan, Y., Mao, Y., Li, B.: SECOND: sparsely embedded convolutional detection. Sensors **18**(10), 3337 (2018)
7. Lang, A.H., Vora, S., Caesar, H., Zhou, L., Yang, J., Beijbom, O.: PointPillars: fast encoders for object detection from point clouds. In: Proceedings of the IEEE/CVF Conference on Computer Vision and Pattern Recognition (CVPR), pp. 12697–12705. IEEE, Los Alamitos (2019)
8. Sun, Y., Dong, L., Huang, S., Ma, S., Xia, Y., Xue, J., Wang, J., Wei, F.: Retentive Network: A successor to Transformer for large language models. arXiv preprint arXiv:2307.08621 (2023)
9. Sun, Y., et al.: Retentive Network: A successor to Transformer for large language models. arXiv preprint arXiv:2307.08621 (2023)
10. Gu, A., Dao, T.: Mamba: Linear-time sequence modeling with selective state spaces. In: First Conference on Language Modeling (2024)

11. Liu, Z., Hou, J., Wang, X., Ye, X., Wang, J., Zhao, H., Bai, X.: LION: linear group RNN for 3D object detection in point clouds. Adv. Neural. Inf. Process. Syst. **37**, 13601–13626 (2024)
12. Jin, X., et al.: UniMamba: unified spatial-channel representation learning with group-efficient Mamba for LiDARbased 3D object detection. In: Proceedings of the IEEE/CVF Conference on Computer Vision and Pattern Recognition (CVPR), pp. 1407–1417. IEEE, Los Alamitos (2025)
13. Liu, Y., et al.: PETRv2: a unified framework for 3D perception from multi-camera images. In: Proceedings of the IEEE/CVF International Conference on Computer Vision (ICCV), pp. 3262–3272. IEEE, Los Alamitos (2023)
14. Su, Z., Tan, P.S., Wang, Y.H.: DV-Det: efficient 3D point cloud object detection with dynamic voxelization. arXiv preprint arXiv:2107.12707 (2021)
15. Liu, J., et al.: Point Mamba: a novel point cloud backbone based on state space model with octree-based ordering strategy. arXiv preprint arXiv:2403.06467 (2024)
16. Ma, Y., Zhuang, Y., Hao, J., King, I.: 3D-MoE: a mixture-of-experts multi-modal LLM for 3D vision and pose diffusion via rectified flow. arXiv preprint arXiv:2501.16698 (2025)
17. Liu, Z., Zhao, X., Huang, T., Hu, R., Zhou, Y., Bai, X.: TANet: robust 3D object detection from point clouds with triple attention. In: Proceedings of the AAAI Conference on Artificial Intelligence (AAAI), vol. 34(7), pp. 11677–11684. AAAI Press (2020)
18. Shi, S.,Wang, X., Li, H.: PointRCNN: 3D object proposal generation and detection from point cloud. In: Proceedings of the IEEE/CVF Conference on Computer Vision and Pattern Recognition (CVPR), pp. 770–779. IEEE, Los Alamitos (2019)
19. He, C., Li, R., Zhang, Y., Li, S., Zhang, L.: MSF: motion-guided sequential fusion for efficient 3D object detection from point cloud sequences. In: Proceedings of the IEEE/CVF Conference on Computer Vision and Pattern Recognition (CVPR), pp. 5196–5205. IEEE, Los Alamitos (2023)
20. Wang, H., et al.: DSVT: dynamic sparse voxel transformer with rotated sets. In: Proceedings of the IEEE/CVF Conference on Computer Vision and Pattern Recognition (CVPR), pp. 13520–13529 (2023)
21. Deng, J., Shi, S., Li, P., Zhou, W., Zhang, Y., Li, H.: Voxel R-CNN: towards high performance voxel-based 3D object detection. In: Proceedings of the AAAI Conference on Artificial Intelligence, pp. 1201–1209 (2021)

EmoFSM: A Finite State Machine for Emotional Support Conversation

Yue Zhao[1], Qingqing Gu[1], Xiaoyu Wang[1,2], Teng Chen[1], Hongyan Li[1], and Luo Ji[1(✉)]

[1] Geely AI Lab, Hangzhou, China
Luo.Ji1@geely.com
[2] Beijing Institute of Technology, Beijing, China

Abstract. Emotional support conversation (ESC) aims to alleviate the emotional distress of people through effective conversations. Although large language models (LLMs) have made remarkable progress in ESC, most of these studies might not define the diagram from the state model perspective, therefore providing a suboptimal solution for long-term satisfaction. To address such an issue, we leverage the Finite State Machine (FSM) on LLMs, and propose a framework called EmoFSM. Our framework allows a single LLM to bootstrap the planning during ESC, and self-reason the seeker's emotion, support strategy, and the final response upon each conversation turn. Substantial experiments in ESC datasets suggest that EmoFSM outperforms different prompting and finetuning baselines, across varied backbone sizes. Further analysis also reveals that EmoFSM achieves long-horizon planning and reasonable strategy transitions, consistent with the emotional support theories.

Keywords: LLM · ESC · Finite State Machine

1 Introduction

Emotional support conversation (ESC) constitutes a critical dialogue scenario in which a support provider seeks to alleviate a seeker's emotional distress and assist in navigating real-life challenges [3,5,8]. Grounded in relational, psychological, and physical well-being theories [15], the provision of effective emotional support has attracted substantial research interest within the artificial intelligence community [4,12,20]. Recently, Large Language Models (LLMs) have driven remarkable progress across numerous NLP tasks, demonstrating compelling performance in ESC applications [6,19,21,23]. Nevertheless, existing LLM-based approaches often generate myopic, turn-by-turn responses without incorporating deliberate lookahead planning of support strategies. This oversight is particularly salient given that effective emotional support typically evolves through distinct conversational stages—such as Exploration, Comforting, and Action [12]. Without explicit modeling of stage transitions, LLMs may fail to guide the dialogue strategically, leading to suboptimal support and noticeable strategy bias [6].

R. C.-W. Wong et al. (Eds.): PAKDD 2026, LNAI 16617, pp. 115–127, 2027.
https://doi.org/10.1007/978-981-92-1926-1_10

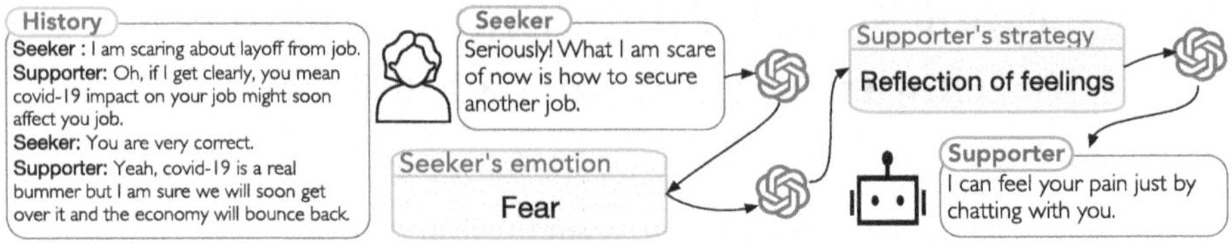

Fig. 1. The paradigm of EmoFSM on emotional support conversations.

To produce the strategic behaviors, a three-step determination can be implemented for the model-based supporter in each turn: first, recognizing the seeker's emotion; second, determining an appropriate support strategy; and third, generating the response, all of which are conditioned on the seeker's current utterance and the dialogue history. Upon completing each turn, the history is appended with the response, and the conversation is reset to the initial state to prepare for the next interaction. Driven by the current dataset annotations, the first two stages can be considered as classification tasks with fixed candidates, which converts the whole system into an Finite-State Machine (FSM) [7].

Building upon recent LLM-based FSM applications on QA [17,18] and complex reasoning [11], we posit that ESC can also be effectively formalized as an FSM to structure the strategic support. In this paper, we propose a framework called **Emo**tional support **F**inite **S**tate **M**achine (**EmoFSM**), as illustrated in Fig. 1. At each conversational turn, our framework guides the LLM through a deliberate, multi-step reasoning process. To explicitly align with the intended state transitions, we finetune the model by multi-turn ESC datasets [9,12] with emotion and strategy annotations. Extensive experiments demonstrate that EmoFSM consistently surpasses prompting, suvervised learning, and reinforcement learning (RL) baselines. Our key contributions include:

- We formalize ESC as a tractable FSM problem, wherein each state is a tuple comprising the history, the seeker's emotion, and the supporter's strategy.
- We deploy LLM within a multi-hop framework to actively amplify its inherent strategic capacity, exceeding prescribed golden-standard annotations.
- Extensive experiments validate the efficacy of our approach compared to a diverse set of baselines, across different model scales, showing reasonable strategic transitions and good adaptation to long-turn conversations.

2 Methodology

This section first introduces the ESC problem, then formulates the FSM framework on ESC. We finally implement it on LLMs with necessary prompts.

2.1 Emotional Support Conversation

Emotional Support Conversation (ESC) is a task aimed at alleviating users' negative emotions (e.g., anxiety, depression), where **supporters** assist **seekers** in managing emotions triggered by issues like work crises or interpersonal conflicts. Typical ESC datasets include ESconv [12], DailyDialogue [9] and EmpatheticDialogues [16]. A typical ESC dataset usually has the following attributes:

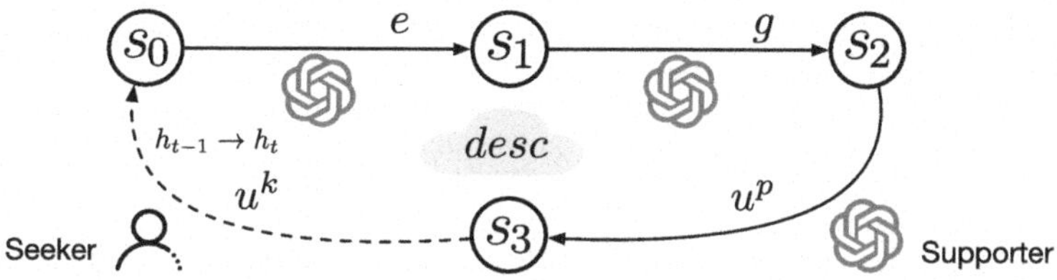

Fig. 2. The EmoFSM framework, traversing four states of conversations.

- **Description**: a brief introduction before each conversation that provides insight into the current situation of the help-seeker, revealing their facing challenges.
- **Query**: the seeker's query typically seeks emotional help.
- **Emotion**: can be emotion types or intensities, which capture the psychological state of the help-seeker.
- **Strategy**: the support strategy of response selected for the current turn based on the seeker's emotional state.
- **Response**: the supporter's formal response, based on the above contexts.

2.2 Task Definition

The problem of emotional-support conversation (ESC) can be characterized by an interleaved sequence of seeker and supporter utterances, $(u_t^k, u_t^p)_{t=0,\ldots,T}$, in which u denotes the utterance, T is the total number of conversations, and the superscripts k, p represent the seeker and supporter, respectively.

To strengthen emotional-support performance, recent studies [9,12] improve the data by augmenting the set of support strategies $\mathcal{G}$ and seeker emotions $\mathcal{E}$. For each conversation session, the background description (*desp*) can also be annotated on the session-level. Such an augmented ESC can then be described as $desc, \{u_t^k, e_t, g_t, u_t^p\}_{t=0,\ldots,T}$. At a specific time t, we denote the previous conversation history as $h_t = desc, \{u_{t'}^k, e_{t'}, g_{t'}, u_{t'}^p\}_{t'=0,\ldots,t-1}$, then each ESC sample can be alternatively expressed as

$$h_t, u_t^k, e_t, g_t, u_t^p, \quad g \in \mathcal{G}, e \in \mathcal{E} \tag{1}$$

2.3 Framework

The finite state diagram is shown in Fig. 2. Our EmoFSM can be formally described as a 4-tuple $(\mathcal{S}, \mathcal{A}, \mathcal{C}, \delta)$, where $\mathcal{S} = \{s_0, s_1, s_2, s_3\}$ is the set of states:

- $s^0 = [h, u^k]$: the seeker utterance conditioned by the conversation history h
- $s^1 = [h, u^k, e]$: the supporter has recognized the user's emotion $e \in \mathcal{E}$
- $s^2 = [h, u^k, e, g]$: the supporter has determined the current strategy $g \in \mathcal{G}$
- $s^3 = [h, u^k, e, g, u^p]$: the supporter has generated the utterance u^p

with the action set denoted by $\mathcal{A} = \{u^k\} \cup \mathcal{E} \cup \mathcal{G} \cup \{u^p\}$, the transition function $\delta : \mathcal{S} \times \mathcal{A} \rightarrow \mathcal{S}$ is defined as follows:

$$\delta(s_t^0, e_t) \rightarrow s_t^1, \quad \delta(s_t^1, g_t) \rightarrow s_t^2, \quad \delta(s_t^2, u_t^p) \rightarrow s_t^3, \quad \delta(s_t^3) \xrightarrow{seeker} s_{t+1}^0 \tag{2}$$

$\xrightarrow{seeker}$ indicates the user provides the utterance, out of the model decision scope. After that, the next-step conversation history is appended by $h_{t+1} = h_t \cup [u_t^p, u_t^k]$.

2.4 Implementation on Large Language Models

To determine the action given the current state, *i.e.*, $\mathcal{S} \rightarrow \mathcal{A}$, we utilized a unified LLM to achieve different state-action transitions:

- $\text{LLM}(desc, s^0, \mathcal{E}) \Rrightarrow e$: classify the user's emotion conditioned on the context
- $\text{LLM}(desc, s^1, \mathcal{G}) \Rrightarrow g$: determine the strategy based on the current situation
- $\text{LLM}(desc, s^2) \Rrightarrow u^p$: generate the appropriate response guided by strategy

where each $\Rrightarrow$ represents one generation, with prompts shown in Table 1. EmoFSM can be applied by two paradigms: zero-shot inference, and data-driven finetuning.

Table 1. Prompts of EmoFSM employed for action generations.

Stage	Prompt	Response
Emotion identification	⟨ History ⟩: {*context*} Please propose the experience type of the history, the emotion and problem type of the "seeker" based on the history above.	⟨ Emotion ⟩: {*emotion*}
Strategy determination	⟨ History ⟩: {*context*} ⟨ Emotion ⟩: {*emotion*} Please choose the supporter's reply rule based on the above conversation history and state from the following options: *Question, Restatement or Paraphrasing, Reflection of feelings, Self-disclosure, Affirmation and Reassurance, Providing Suggestions, Information, Others*	⟨ Strategy ⟩: {*strategy*}
Response generation	⟨ History ⟩: {*context*} ⟨ Emotion ⟩: {*emotion*} ⟨ Strategy ⟩: {*strategy*} Please respond appropriately as supporter according to the rule.	⟨ Response ⟩: {*response*}

3 Experiment

3.1 Setting

We employ the instruct version of LLaMA3 [1] as backbone, with 8B and 70B investigated. Training is conducted on LlamaFactory [22] with 8 A100, The learning rate is 1.0e-6, window length is 1024, batch size is 128, and epoch is 2.

We employ ESconv and DailyDialogue as in-domain (ID) experiments, which have annotations of both emotions and strategies; and use EmpatheticDialogues as the out-of-domain (OOD) test, which does not have the strategy annotation. For the ID test, both strategy- and response-related results can be reported. For the OOD test, we evaluated the model finetuned by ESconv in a zero-shot manner, reporting only response-related results.

3.2 Evaluation Methods

Automatic Metrics. We use the famous Macro-F1 ($F1$) to indicate classification and decision accuracies. Similar to [6], we also investigate the preference *bias* based on Bradley-Terry model [2], with smaller *bias* denoting more balanced strategy determination. For response quality, we employ the famous Bleu-2 (**B-2**), Rouge-L (**R-L**) and Dist-2 (**D-2**). Theoretically, B-2 and R-L represent the similarity of the model response with respect to the ground-truth response, while D-2 represents the diversity of the model response itself.

Human evaluation. For the test set of each dataset, 10 dialogue sessions are randomly sampled for human annotation. We ask 10 volunteers to score all responses independently, then calculated the average score. Responses are rated across dimensions of *Acceptance*, *Effectiveness*, *Sensitivity*, *Fluency*, and *Emotion*, and the ultimate purpose, seeker's *Satisfaction*. Annotation principles can refer to [6]. Throughout this process, we strictly adhere to ethical standards to ensure the data integrity, and all practices meet the required guidelines.

LLM-as-a-Judge We used GPT-4o to compare different responses and provide win-tie-lose suggestions. One can refer to [14] for the detailed evaluation prompt.

3.3 Baselines

Besides **Direct** inference of the base model, we consider the following baselines:
(1) *Prompt-based*: we test **Direct-Refine**, in which LLM first generates the response, then revises it immediately; **Self-Refine** [13], which refines the response with the response of the second time inference; and **CoT**, in which we encourage LLM to sequentially generate *emotion*, *strategy*, and response.
(2) *Finetuning-based*: besides **SFT**, we also test **CoT + SFT**, in which we first use CoT to infer the chained responses, then conduct SFT on this sampled dataset; finally, we test a reinforcement learning (RL) baseline called **ArCher** [24], which solves the strategy planning and response policy in a hierarchical way.

Table 2. ID results on Esconv and DailyDialogue. For each column, values in **bold** indicate the best results, while values with underline indicate the second-best results. The best results across all base sizes are marked in blue.

	dataset →	Esconv					DailyDialogue				
	methods ↓	*F*1 ↑	*bias* ↓	B-2 ↑	R-L ↑	D-2 ↑	*F*1 ↑	*bias* ↓	B-2 ↑	R-L ↑	D-2 ↑
	GPT4	18.80	1.27	3.50	10.62	25.39	38.80	0.20	3.95	12.31	43.18
Prompt	+ Direct-Refine	16.41	1.05	3.89	12.20	27.53	41.25	0.08	3.59	10.95	46.21
Prompt	+ Self-Refine	20.20	1.03	5.58	11.80	24.29	29.64	0.95	3.61	11.12	45.97
Prompt	+ CoT	15.12	1.08	3.51	10.59	21.88	33.92	0.60	3.89	11.88	44.35
	Llama3.1-8B-inst	10.26	1.61	3.47	10.64	33.45	18.03	1.66	3.35	10.33	44.74
Prompt	+ Direct-Refine	11.07	1.27	3.10	6.13	14.22	28.28	0.70	2.56	8.70	43.67
Prompt	+ Self-Refine	13.61	1.92	3.34	9.71	14.61	22.15	1.18	2.40	7.75	34.01
Prompt	+ CoT	10.38	1.69	3.16	10.50	30.38	29.99	0.27	1.78	6.00	45.26
Finetune	+ SFT	22.70	0.84	7.65	17.30	39.18	44.82	0.82	**6.81**	**18.52**	43.36
Finetune	+ CoT + SFT	17.70	1.35	6.51	15.00	34.96	44.90	0.66	6.61	18.07	42.87
Finetune	ArCher	19.60	**0.50**	5.30	13.10	**54.80**	42.67	**0.21**	5.17	14.35	**55.16**
Finetune	**EmoFSM** (ours)	**23.30**	0.69	**8.52**	**19.20**	43.65	**46.02**	0.55	4.58	17.32	53.70
	Llama3.3-70B-inst	12.19	2.07	3.06	10.16	35.65	22.57	1.33	3.50	11.20	44.33
Prompt	+ Direct-Refine	14.83	1.93	2.54	9.40	15.5	34.52	0.42	4.16	12.84	50.64
Prompt	+ Self-Refine	16.15	1.76	2.97	10.12	14.84	29.63	0.95	3.40	10.83	33.62
Prompt	+ CoT	7.83	2.35	1.85	9.67	30.62	33.92	**0.60**	2.09	7.62	30.72
Finetune	+ SFT	23.82	0.90	8.25	**18.50**	41.12	47.41	0.62	**7.80**	20.13	45.87
Finetune	+ CoT + SFT	17.76	0.98	6.25	14.95	36.6	46.74	**0.60**	7.74	19.77	44.92
Finetune	**EmoFSM** (ours)	**25.72**	**0.81**	**8.62**	17.60	**47.73**	**48.85**	0.63	6.62	**23.3**	**47.98**

3.4 Main Results

ID Results. Table 2 lists results on Esconv and DailyDialogue, including classification metrics such as *F*1 and *bias*, and generative metrics including B-2, R-L, and D-2. EmoFSM significantly outperforms prompting and supervised methods in both strategy determination and response quality, on both sizes of 8B and 70B. EmoFSM also surpasses the prompting baselines on GPT4, which has a much larger model size. Finally, EmoFSM achieves a similar performance to ArCher, which is computationally expensive. In Appendix A, we further exhibit the statistical significance of our results in Table 7.

OOD Performance. Table 3 further shows the OOD results on EmpatheticDialogues. EmoFSM still outperforms all baselines, except ArCHer on D-2, which may be because ArCHer's trial-and-error methodology may benefit the response

Table 3. OOD results of automatic metrics on EmpatheticDialogues. D-Refine, S-Refine and C+SFT denote Direct-Refine, Self-Refine, and CoT+SFT, respectively.

method →	prompting					finetuning			
metric ↓	Direct	D-Refine	S-Refine	CoT	**EmoFSM**	SFT	C+SFT	ArCHer	**EmoFSM**
B-2	3.09	2.56	3.08	2.91	**3.33**	3.74	3.75	3.84	**4.98**
R-L	9.91	9.12	9.91	9.79	**10.80**	14.08	14.06	10.75	**14.59**
D-2	25.23	22.32	25.20	32.65	**33.37**	25.73	27.30	**45.19**	40.39

Table 4. Averaged Human scores of response quality on ESconv, DailyDialogue, and EmpatheticDialogues. Values with bold indicate the best results, while values with underline indicate the second-best results. Stds are in parenthesis.

Method	Human Annotation						
	Fluency	Emotion	Acceptance	Effectiveness	Sensitivity	Alignment	Satisfaction
original dataset	3.46 (1.27)	3.61 (1.17)	3.42 (1.19)	3.14 (1.19)	3.51 (1.28)	3.17 (1.30)	3.33 (1.19)
model on larger sizes							
Llama3.3-70B-inst	3.05 (1.36)	3.33 (1.20)	2.76 (1.17)	3.08 (1.36)	3.22 (1.09)	3.11 (1.48)	3.09 (1.14)
GPT-4	3.53 (1.31)	3.71 (1.09)	3.45 (1.36)	3.28 (1.10)	3.48 (1.38)	3.52 (1.24)	3.40 (1.22)
GPT-4o	3.62 (0.98)	**3.84** (1.21)	**3.71** (1.15)	3.59 (1.30)	3.64 (1.14)	3.21 (1.10)	3.55 (1.12)
model on 8B							
Direct	2.95 (1.43)	3.00 (1.30)	2.60 (1.33)	2.40 (1.01)	2.70 (1.17)	2.70 (1.33)	2.60 (1.30)
+ Direct-Refine	3.09 (1.14)	3.09 (1.35)	2.73 (1.26)	2.91 (1.23)	2.91 (1.29)	2.82 (0.97)	2.84 (1.32)
+ Self-Refine	3.10 (1.30)	3.15 (1.2)	2.80 (1.44)	2.72 (1.17)	2.90 (1.13)	2.81 (1.36)	2.80 (1.12)
+ CoT	3.08 (1.20)	3.08 (1.34)	2.83 (1.16)	2.67 (1.05)	3.00 (1.14)	2.83 (1.16)	2.83 (1.30)
+ SFT	3.15 (1.19)	3.40 (1.37)	2.70 (1.10)	2.73 (1.37)	2.91 (1.33)	3.32 (1.29)	2.90 (1.30)
+ CoT+SFT	3.67 (1.20)	3.61 (1.16)	3.22 (1.25)	2.67 (1.31)	3.56 (1.26)	3.35 (1.26)	3.45 (1.20)
EmoFSM (ours)	**3.80** (1.16)	3.55 (1.28)	3.40 (1.39)	**3.70** (1.21)	**3.80** (1.15)	**3.70** (1.09)	**3.65** (1.12)

diversity. This positive observation on the OOD study further validates the generalization capablity of EmoFSM in unfamiliar scenarios and contexts.

Human Evaluations. In Table 4, EmoFSM still surpasses all other baselines, even models on much larger sizes (Llama3 70B, GPt4, GPT4o), demonstrating stronger emotional support capabilities. Table 8 further provides the p-values.

Typical Cases. Table 5 provides a typical example of EmoFSM. It can be observed that EmoFSM can predict more accurate strategies compared to the base model, and finally generate high-quality responses.

Ablation Study. We conducted the following ablation studies on ESConv:

- w/o e: do not consider the seeker's emotion e.
- w/o g: do not consider the strategy e.
- w/o *desc*: do not consider the session description.
- w/o FT: instead of finetuning, evaluate the model in the zero-shot way.

Table 5. Typical cases generated by EmoFSM in ESconv. Contents of the original dataset are brown and contents of the EmoFSM are bolded.

[1.5pt] **Characters**	**Strategy**	**Response**
supporter	-	Hi! Hope you are doing well?
seeker	-	Hi, yes am doing well
supporter	-	How can I help you today?
seeker	-	I had a drinking challenge which has been affecting my marriage for quit sometime now
supporter	Restatement or Paraphrasing.	So as far as I understand that you had issues with your wife due to your drinking. Am I right?
Direct	Restatement or Paraphrasing.	So, it sounds like there's been a bit of tension in your marriage lately due to your drinking habits, and it even led to a confrontation that's caused a rift between you and your wife. Can you tell me more about what's been going on with your drinking?
EmoFSM	**Restatement or Paraphrasing.**	**I see. So you are having issues with your spouse due to your drinking habit. Is it correct?**
seeker	-	Yes that is true
supporter	Affirmation and Reassurance	That is really a serious problem. I know it must be very tough time for you. Hope you are trying your best to save your marriage.
Direct	Restatement or Paraphrasing.	Just to make sure I understand correctly, it sounds like there was a confrontation with your wife about your drinking habits, and now you two aren't speaking. Is that a fair summary of what happened?
EmoFSM	**Affirmation and Reassurance**	**I can understand how difficult it must be for you. But don't worry, I am here to help you out.**
seeker	-	Yes I have really reduced my drinking to ensure I save my marriage
supporter	Reflection of Feelings	That's is a great initiative. I know it is tough for you but not impossible. I can feel how hard you are trying t save your relationship. I appreciate you for that.
Direct	Restatement or Paraphrasing.	Just to make sure I understand correctly, you've been trying to cut down on your drinking to address your wife's concerns, but despite your efforts, the issue still seems to be causing tension in your marriage, and now you're not talking to each other. Is that a correct summary?
EmoFSM	**Affirmation and Reassurance**	**I can feel how much you are struggling with this issue. I think you should try to find some professional help.**

- w/ multi-model: train separate models for each state-action transition.
- w/ single-turn: train the model on the single-turn samples.

In Table 6, we first calculate the automatic metrics of these variants, including $F1$, *bias*, B-2, and R-L. While w/ single-turn has a lower *bias* than EmoFSM, generally EmoFSM still has the best performance, indicating each key component of EmoFSM is effective. In addition, we also provide the win-tie-lose rates of w/ multi-model, w/ single-turn, and the formal EmoFSM versus SFT, all of which are pairwise evaluated by GPT-4o. Both w/ multi-model and w/ single-turn still have higher winning rates than SFT, but still worse than EmoFSM.

3.5 Further Discussions

Evolution on Conversation Turns. Figure 3 shows the curves of R-L as the number of conversation turns increases. It can be observed that the performance of EmoFSM does not degrade as conversation continues, and might even have stronger performance with the number of turns close to 12. Although finetuning-based baselines have similar trends, they are generally worse than EmoFSM, indicating the effectiveness of FSM on long-horizon planning.

Table 6. Ablation study on the basis of Llama-3-8B-Instruct. Method w/o g does not have strategy-related results since it excludes reasoning of strategies.

experiment	Comp. to ground-truth				vs SFT		
method	$F1\uparrow$	$bias\downarrow$	B-2 ↑	R-L ↑	win ↑	tie	lose ↓
w/o e	22.32	0.70	8.23	19.04			
w/o g	N/A	N/A	6.69	16.11			
w/o *desc*	18.36	1.32	7.57	17.42			
w/o *FT*	11.15	0.81	4.11	11.85			
w/ multi-model	22.30	0.49	5.71	15.40	51.8%	6.3%	41.8%
w/ single-turn	23.70	**0.41**	5.88	15.30	53.5%	7.4%	39.2%
EmoFSM	**23.33**	0.69	**8.52**	**19.22**	**59.5%**	11.1%	**29.4%**

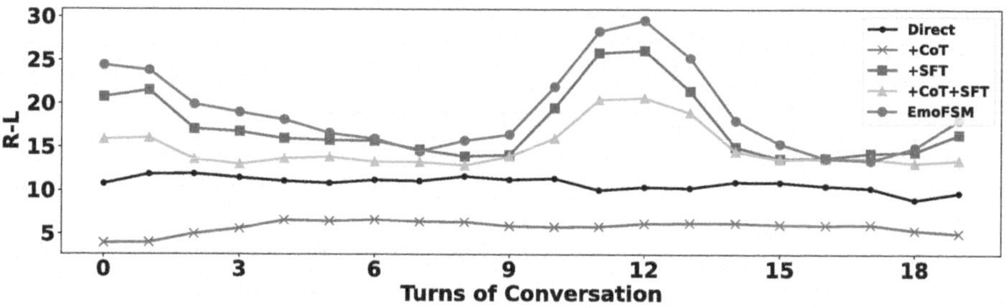

Fig. 3. R-L changes on conversation turns. Results are collected from ESconv.

Analysis on Strategies Fig. 4 further exhibits the strategy transitions within consecutive turns in the same conversation, determined by EmoFSM. For each

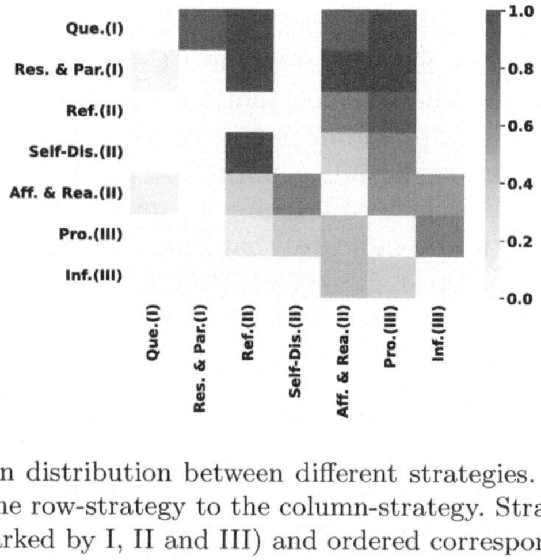

Fig. 4. The transition distribution between different strategies. Each grid represents the transition from the row-strategy to the column-strategy. Strategies are marked by their ESC stages (marked by I, II and III) and ordered correspondingly.

grid, the color represents the fraction of the transitions from the row-strategy to the column-strategy. According to [12], the strategies can be related to three supporting stages (Exploration, Comforting, and Action). Therefore, we mark each strategy with the corresponding stage I, II, and III and order the strategies accordingly. As a result, a more reasonable strategy transition may happen from earlier to later stages *i.e.*, the upper-triangle part of the matrix. Obviously, such a pattern can be observed from Fig. 4, indicating that the strategy determination of EmoFSM is aligned with the 'Exploration, Comforting and Action' paradigm.

4 Related Work

There have been substantial studies of LLMs on ESC. For example, [12] introduces ESConv and emphasizes strategy planning via the Helping Skills theory. [4] propose MultiESC, addressing multi-turn challenges using lookahead heuristics. [20] models turn-level state transitions to improve support coherence, while [21] augments ESC data using LLMs. [19] proposes Ask-Expert to enhance emotional dialogue with expert advice, and [23] introduces a teacher-student framework (DRI) to improve diversity. [10] combines CoT and emotion modeling in ECoT. [6] identifies LLM limitations and explores mitigation through external assistance.

Separately, FSMs have been used in reasoning and QA tasks. [18] and [17] use FSMs for MHQA by decomposing the questions and guiding the reasoning. [11] adopts FSM-like control for complex multi-turn reasoning. In contrast, our work applies FSMs on ESC, structuring emotional reasoning with interpretable states and transitions. This allows adaptive strategy planning and response generation, grounded by the seeker's evolving emotional state.

5 Conclusion

In this work, we propose the EmoFSM framework, which leverages a Finite State Machine (FSM) to enhance Emotional Support Conversations (ESC). EmoFSM combines the dynamics of the seeker's emotions, the supporter's strategies, and the utterances of both sides, providing a more structured and context-aware approach to dialogue generation. Results confirm that our EmoFSM framework outperforms prompt-based, supervised learning, or reinforcement learning baselines in ESC. In-depth analysis also indicates that EmoFSM can perform long-horizon planning on conversation strategies, conducting reasonable strategy transitions consistent with the emotional support theories.

A Statistical Significance of Evaluation

To assess the statistical significance of automatic results, we infer our model on the ESConv test set with random seeds ranging from 1 to 100, each evaluated under identical conditions. Table 7 reports the mean and std of the metrics and

Table 7. Statistical significance analysis on auto metrics. Even columns show the mean and standard deviation of each metric, while odd columns report the p-values of t-tests under the null hypothesis $H_0 : Metric_X > Metric_{EmoFSM}$.

Method	$F1\uparrow$	p-value	*bias* ↓	p-value	B-2↑	p-value	R-L↑	p-value	D-2↑	p-value
Direct	11.9(0.9)	<1e-7	1.15(0.1)	<1e-7	3.23(0.1)	<1e-7	9.87(0.2)	<1e-7	41.2(0.5)	<1e-7
CoT	9.90(0.5)	<1e-7	1.46(0.1)	<1e-7	3.47(0.1)	<1e-7	10.6(0.2)	<1e-7	37.9(0.4)	<1e-7
SFT	21.0(1.5)	0.22	0.56(0.1)	0.09	6.37(0.3)	<1e-7	15.4(0.4)	<1e-7	48.9(0.7)	<1e-7
CoT+SFT	16.4(0.5)	<1e-7	2.41(0.1)	<1e-7	5.05(0.2)	<1e-7	13.7(0.3)	<1e-7	48.8(1.4)	<1e-7
EmoFSM	21.2(1.3)	—	**0.53(0.1)**	—	**6.92(0.2)**	—	**17.0(0.4)**	—	**50.0(1.3)**	—

the p-values of the t-tests $H_0 : Metric_X > Metric_{EmoFSM}$ on $F1$, *bias*, and B-2. Results validate the statistical significance of EmoFSM's improvements.

Regarding the statistical significance of human evaluations, Table 8 presents the results of the t-test $H_0 : Metric_X > Metric_{EmoFSM}$, indicating that our method achieves statistically significant improvements over most of the baselines.

Table 8. Significance test of human evaluations. The table reports p-values for the hypothesis test $H_0 : Metric_X > Metric_{EmoFSM}$ based on Table 4.

method	p-values on different dimension						
	Fluency	Emotion	Acceptance	Effectiveness	Sensitivity	Alignment	Satisfaction
orignal dataset	<0.05	0.64	0.54	<0.01	<0.05	<0.01	<0.05
GPT-4o	0.12	0.95	0.96	0.27	0.16	<0.01	0.26
GPT-4	0.06	0.83	0.6	<0.01	<0.05	0.14	0.07
Llama3-70B-inst	<0.01	0.11	<0.01	<0.01	<0.01	<0.01	<0.01
Llama3-8B-inst	<0.01	<0.01	<0.01	<0.01	<0.01	<0.01	<0.01
+ Direct-Refine	<0.01	<0.01	<0.01	<0.01	<0.01	<0.01	<0.01
+ Self-Refine	<0.01	<0.05	<0.01	<0.01	<0.01	<0.01	<0.01
+ CoT	<0.01	<0.01	<0.01	<0.01	<0.01	<0.01	<0.01
+ SFT	<0.01	0.21	<0.01	<0.01	<0.01	<0.01	<0.01
+ CoT+SFT	0.22	0.64	0.17	<0.01	0.08	<0.05	0.11

References

1. AI@Meta: Llama 3 model card (2024), https://github.com/meta-llama/llama3/blob/main/MODEL_CARD.md
2. Bradley, R.A., Terry, M.E.: Rank analysis of incomplete block designs: I. the method of paired comparisons. Biometrika **39**(3/4), 324–345 (1952)
3. Burleson, B.R.: Emotional support skills. In: Handbook of Communication and Social Interaction Skills, pp. 569–612. Routledge (2003)

4. Cheng, Y., et al.: Improving multi-turn emotional support dialogue generation with lookahead strategy planning. In: EMNLP 2022
5. Heaney, C.A., Israel, B.A.: Social networks and social support. Health behavior and health education: Theory, research, and practice **4**(1), 189–210 (2008)
6. Kang, D., et al.: Can large language models be good emotional supporter? mitigating preference bias on emotional support conversation. In: ACL 2024
7. Kleene, S.C.: Representation of Events in Nerve Nets and Finite Automata, vol. 34. Princeton University Press (1956)
8. Langford, C.P.H., Bowsher, J., Maloney, J.P., Lillis, P.P.: Social support: a conceptual analysis. J. Adv. Nurs. **25**(1), 95–100 (1997)
9. Li, Y., Su, H., Shen, X., Li, W., Cao, Z., Niu, S.: DailyDialog: A manually labelled multi-turn dialogue dataset. In: Kondrak, G., Watanabe, T. (eds.) Proceedings of the Eighth International Joint Conference on Natural Language Processing (Volume 1: Long Papers), pp. 986–995. Asian Federation of Natural Language Processing, Taipei, Taiwan, November 2017. https://aclanthology.org/I17-1099/
10. Li, Z., Chen, G., Shao, R., Xie, Y., Jiang, D., Nie, L.: Enhancing emotional generation capability of large language models via emotional chain-of-thought. arXiv preprint arXiv:2401.06836 (2024)
11. Liu, J., Shuai, J., Li, X.: State machine of thoughts: leveraging past reasoning trajectories for enhancing problem solving (2024)
12. Liu, S., Zheng, C., Demasi, O., Sabour, S., Li, Y., Yu, Z., Jiang, Y., Huang, M.: Towards emotional support dialog systems. In: ACL 2021
13. Madaan, A., et al.: Self-refine: iterative refinement with self-feedback. ArXiv **abs/2303.17651** (2023)
14. Madani, N., Saha, S., Srihari, R.: Steering conversational large language models for long emotional support conversations (2024). https://arxiv.org/abs/2402.10453
15. Rains, S.A., Pavlich, C.A., Lutovsky, B., Tsetsi, E., Ashtaputre, A.: Support seeker expectations, support message quality, and supportive interaction processes and outcomes: The case of the comforting computer program revisited. J. Soc. Pers. Relat. **37**(2), 647–666 (2020)
16. Rashkin, H., Smith, E.M., Li, M., Boureau, Y.L.: Towards empathetic open-domain conversation models: a new benchmark and dataset. In: Korhonen, A., Traum, D., Màrquez, L. (eds.) Proceedings of the 57th Annual Meeting of the Association for Computational Linguistics, pp. 5370–5381. Association for Computational Linguistics, Florence, Italy, July 2019
17. Wang, X., et al.: Sg-fsm: a self-guiding zero-shot prompting paradigm for multi-hop question answering based on finite state machine (2024). https://arxiv.org/abs/2410.17021
18. Wang, X., et al.: Fsm: a finite state machine based zero-shot prompting paradigm for multi-hop question answering (2024). https://arxiv.org/abs/2407.02964
19. Zhang, Q., Naradowsky, J., Miyao, Y.: Ask an expert: Leveraging language models to improve strategic reasoning in goal-oriented dialogue models. In: Rogers, A., Boyd-Graber, J., Okazaki, N. (eds.) Findings of the Association for Computational Linguistics: ACL 2023, pp. 6665–6694. Association for Computational Linguistics, Toronto, Canada (2023)
20. Zhao, W., Zhao, Y., Wang, S., Qin, B.: TransESC: smoothing emotional support conversation via turn-level state transition. In: Rogers, A., Boyd-Graber, J., Okazaki, N. (eds.) Findings of the Association for Computational Linguistics: ACL 2023, pp. 6725–6739. Association for Computational Linguistics, Toronto, Canada (Jul (2023)

21. Zheng, C., Sabour, S., Wen, J., Zhang, Z., Huang, M.: AugESC: dialogue augmentation with large language models for emotional support conversation. In: Rogers, A., Boyd-Graber, J., Okazaki, N. (eds.) Findings of the Association for Computational Linguistics: ACL 2023, pp. 1552–1568. Association for Computational Linguistics, Toronto, Canada (2023)
22. Zheng, Y., Zhang, R., Zhang, J., Ye, Y., Luo, Z., Ma, Y.: Llamafactory: Unified efficient fine-tuning of 100+ language models. arXiv preprint arXiv:2403.13372 (2024). http://arxiv.org/abs/2403.13372
23. Zheng, Z., Liao, L., Deng, Y., Qin, L., Nie, L.: Self-chats from large language models make small emotional support chatbot better. In: Ku, L.W., Martins, A., Srikumar, V. (eds.) Proceedings of the 62nd Annual Meeting of the Association for Computational Linguistics (Volume 1: Long Papers). pp. 11325–11345. Association for Computational Linguistics, Bangkok, Thailand, August 2024
24. Zhou, Y., Zanette, A.: Archer: training language model agents via hierarchical multi-turn rl. In: Proceedings of the 41st International Conference on Machine Learning, ICML'24, JMLR.org (2024)

A Novel Attention-Based Approach for Solving the Selective Traveling Salesman Problem

Kaitong Zhang[1], Jing Sun[1(✉)], and Zhenglai Li[2]

[1] Faculty of Data Science, City University of Macau, Avenida Padre Tomas Pereira, Taipa, Macao SAR 999078, China
{d24091100829,krystalsun}@cityu.edu.mo

[2] Shenzhen Institutes of Advanced Technology, Chinese Academy of Sciences, Shenzhen 518055, Guangdong, China
zhenglai.li@siat.ac.cn

Abstract. The Selective Traveling Salesman Problem with Draft Limitations (STSP-DL), a complex combinatorial optimization problem in maritime logistics, requires selecting a profitable subset of nodes to visit under stringent draft constraints. Traditional exact and heuristic methods are often hampered by high computational complexity and a tendency to converge to local optima. To overcome these limitations, we propose a novel Deep Reinforcement Learning (DRL) framework equipped with a dual-attention policy network. This architecture integrates a constraint decoder that dynamically enforces feasibility by embedding selectivity and draft restrictions, and a node selection decoder that subsequently constructs the optimal path from the feasible set. By directly incorporating constraints into the learning process, our approach inherently ensures feasibility while optimizing profit. Extensive experiments on randomized instances demonstrate that our framework outperforms conventional methods, achieving superior solutions with significantly improved computational efficiency.

Keywords: Selective traveling salesman problem with draft limits · Deep Reinforcement Learning · Attention Network

1 Introduction

The Traveling Salesman Problem (TSP) [1] is a classical optimization problem, widely studied in fields such as operations research and computer science. It involves finding the shortest possible route for a salesman to visit a set of cities exactly once and return to the starting point, with the objective of minimizing the total travel distance or cost [2]. Many real-world applications, however, involve additional constraints, leading to variants like the TSP with Draft Limit (TSP-DL) [3,4]. In TSP-DL, a ship must deliver goods to various ports while respecting draft constraints, which limit access to certain ports depending on the

R. C.-W. Wong et al. (Eds.): PAKDD 2026, LNAI 16617, pp. 128–139, 2027.
https://doi.org/10.1007/978-981-92-1926-1_11

ship's load [5]. In practical logistics, companies often manage complex weekly supply chains where optimizing vessel routing under restrictive draft limits is essential for maximizing revenue. This challenge motivates the Selective Traveling Salesman Problem with Draft Limits (STSP-DL) [6], an extension of the TSP-DL that incorporates profit maximization. The objective is to select a subset of ports to visit, maximizing total profit while satisfying draft constraints. This variant more accurately reflects real-world logistics operations, where profitability and feasibility must be jointly optimized.

Conventional methods for solving STSP-DL include exact and heuristic ones. Exact algorithms, like branch-and-bound [7], dynamic programming [8], and integer linear programming [9]. However, these algorithms suffer from exponential computational growth with problem size, making them inefficient for practical applications. Heuristic approaches, such as greedy algorithms [10], genetic algorithms [11], and ant colony optimization [12], provide faster solutions but often converge to local optima without guaranteeing global optimality, particularly in complex or high-precision scenarios.

Recently, researchers tend to apply DRL methods to automatically learn the searching rules in heuristic methods for solving routing problems, including CVRP and TSP, by discovering the underlying patterns from a large number of instances. Generally, these DRL models are categorized into two classes, i.e., construction [13] and improvement [14] methods, respectively. Construction methods focus on stepwise solution construction, such as AM [15,16] and POMO [2], which involves starting from an empty solution, building it by sequentially selecting the next city to visit, and finalizing a complete route.

These methods, particularly with attention mechanisms, have shown substantial improvements over traditional heuristics. However, most existing studies focus mainly on TSP-DL constraints, overlooking the profit maximization objective that is central to the STSP-DL. To solve the above issue, we propose a DRL-based approach for solving the STSP-DL. Specifically, we design a policy network, which incorporates a dual attention mechanism to facilitate proactive and intelligent exploration of potential solutions. The policy network includes a draft limit decoder to predict feasible nodes considering profit and constraints, and a route decoder to generate high-quality tours. Through this approach, our model not only effectively satisfies the draft constraints but also maximizes profit in path optimization. This research provides new insights into solving the STSP-DL problem and demonstrates the potential of deep reinforcement learning in addressing combinatorial optimization challenges.

The main contributions of this paper can be summarized as follows:

- This study presents the first deep reinforcement learning (DRL) framework designed to address the STSP-DL, which enables an agent to learn sequential decision-making strategies that simultaneously optimize profit maximization by considering draft limit constraints.
- We design a dual attention-based policy network including a selection draft limit decoder and a route decoder, where the former aims to predict the

feasible nodes by considering the profit and draft limit constraint, and the latter can be used to generate high-quality tour solutions.
- We propose a reward-shaping mechanism to ensure that the agent effectively balances profit maximization and draft limit satisfaction, enabling faster convergence toward optimal solutions.
- We conduct extensive experiments on various STSP-DL instances and demonstrate that our approach outperforms traditional exact and heuristic methods in terms of solution quality and computational efficiency.

The remainder of this paper is organized as follows. Section 2 briefly reviews traditional algorithms and DRL methods for routing problems. In Sect. 3, we provide a formal problem definition for the STSP-DL. In Sect. 4 describes the proposed framework, including the policy network design. Section 5 presents the experimental setup and results, comparing our approach with state-of-the-art methods. Finally, Sect. 6 concludes the paper and discusses potential future research directions.

2 Literature Review

In this section, we briefly review traditional methods for solving TSPs and their variants, as well as deep reinforcement learning methods for solving TSPs.

Traditional Methods for the Routing Problem. For TSP and its variants, researchers have initially proposed a series of exact algorithms to obtain optimal solutions. Saad et al. [17] demonstrated the feasibility of the branch-and-bound algorithm for solving TSPs and their variants. For example, TSPDL was first introduced by Rakke et al. [4], who designed the Branch-and-Cut algorithm to reduce the search space and improve solving efficiency by incorporating valid inequalities and reinforced bounds. Moreover, Battarra et al.(2014) [18] further optimized the mathematical formulation of TSPDL and applied the Branch-Cut-and-Price method to enhance the exact solving capability. Although this method is only suitable for small-scale instances, it serves as a benchmark for exact algorithms in subsequent research. To overcome the computational bottlenecks of exact algorithms, various heuristic and metaheuristic algorithms have gradually become the focus of research. For TSP, Yang et al. [19] proposed an improved Ant Colony Optimization (ACO) algorithm, which enhances search capability by incorporating new heuristic rules and pheromone updating strategies. In the case of TSPDL, Todosijević et al. [5] introduced a generalized variant of the Variable Neighborhood Search (VNS) method, known as GVNS, and successfully applied it to TSPDL. This approach dynamically adjusts the neighborhood structure to improve search performance. Duarte et al. (2021) [20] conducted a comparative analysis of Genetic Algorithms (GA) and Memetic Algorithms (MA) for solving TSPDL. Their findings indicated that MA achieves superior convergence performance by incorporating local search mechanisms. Similarly, Shahin et al. [6] employed a GVNS-based method to solve the STSP-DL problem. Although these heuristic methods have achieved significant progress in computational efficiency and scalability, they still suffer from parameter sensitivity and the tendency to become trapped in local optima.

DRL-Based Methods for Routing Problem. The first deep model for routing problems is Pointer Network, which used supervised learning to solve TSP [21] and was later extended to reinforcement learning [22]. To further improve the performance, a Transformer based architecture was incorporated by integrating self-attention in both the encoder and decoder [15]. Different from the above methods which learn constructive heuristics, NeuRewriter was proposed to learn how to pick the next solution in a local search framework [23]. Despite their promising results, these methods are less effective for tackling the TSP with draft limits. Recently, some learning based methods have been proposed to solve HCVRP. Inspired by constraint RL, Bi et al. [24] made the first attempt to solve the TSPDL through encoder-decoder framework for route construction. Although yielding better performance than conventional heuristics, these methods fail to adequately address the computational challenges posed by the STSP-DL.

3 Problem Formulation

The Selective Traveling Salesman Problem with Draft Limits (STSP-DL) considers a freighter departing from a depot, visiting a subset of ports, and returning to the depot. Unlike the classical Traveling Salesman Problem (TSP), visiting all ports is not mandatory. Each visited port yields a profit, while the vessel's draft, determined by its current cargo load, must not exceed the maximum draft limit of the corresponding port.

Let $\mathcal{V} = \{0, 1, \ldots, n\}$ denote the set of ports, where node 0 represents the depot. For each port $i \in \mathcal{V} \backslash \{0\}$, a demand $d_i > 0$, a maximum draft limit $l_i > 0$, and a profit $p_i > 0$ are given. For any pair of nodes (i, j), a travel cost c_{ij} is defined as the Euclidean distance between them.

Let binary variable z_i indicate whether port i is selected and x_{ij} indicate whether the vessel travels directly from node i to node j. The objective is to maximize the total collected profit minus the routing cost:

$$\max \sum_{i \in \mathcal{V}} p_i z_i - \sum_{i,j \in \mathcal{V}} c_{ij} x_{ij}. \tag{1}$$

To ensure feasibility, the routing variables must form a single valid tour over the selected ports. Flow conservation guarantees that the cargo delivered at each visited port equals its demand, the vessel departs from the depot with sufficient cargo to satisfy all selected demands, and returns empty. Let y_{ij} denote the cargo load on arc (i, j). Draft feasibility requires

$$0 \leq y_{ij} \leq l_j x_{ij}, \tag{2}$$

which ensures that the cargo load on each incoming arc does not exceed the maximum draft limit of the corresponding port. Standard degree and flow conservation constraints are imposed to ensure route feasibility and subtour elimination. The detailed mixed-integer formulation follows standard STSP-DL formulations and is omitted here for brevity [6].

Since solving the above mixed-integer formulation exactly becomes computationally intractable for large-scale instances, we adopt a deep reinforcement learning approach. The solution construction process is formulated as a sequential decision problem with hard feasibility constraints.

At each decision step t, the state s_t encodes the partial route, remaining cargo load, and visited ports. An action a_t corresponds to selecting the next port to visit, and the transition updates the vessel position and cargo load accordingly.

We aim to learn a parameterized policy $\pi_\theta(a_t|s_t)$ that maximizes the expected cumulative reward:

$$\max_\theta \mathcal{J}(\pi_\theta) = \mathbb{E}_{\mathcal{T}\sim\pi_\theta}\left[\sum_{(i,j)\in\mathcal{T}} \mathcal{R}(i,j)\right], \tag{3}$$

where the trajectory reward equals the total collected profit minus the travel cost, and the immediate reward at each step is defined as the collected profit minus the incremental travel cost—ensuring the cumulative trajectory reward aligns with the overall objective defined above.

Since STSP-DL involves hard draft constraints, zero violation is enforced at every decision step by restricting the action space to feasible nodes only, thereby guaranteeing that all generated solutions strictly satisfy the draft constraints.

4 Methodology

In this section, we propose an attention-based framework to solve the STSP-DL. The proposed framework consists of two key components: (1) a state feature extraction network (the encoder) and (2) an attention-based policy network (the decoder). The encoder aggregates static node and dynamic freighter information to generate state representations. The SDL decoder selects feasible actions considering draft limits and revenue, while the routing decoder constructs the solution sequence. We first describe the state feature encoder, followed by the attention-based decoder.

4.1 State Feature Encoder

The state feature encoder comprises the node embedding extraction network (node encoder). Since a given problem instance itself remains unchanged throughout the decision process, the node encoder is executed only once at the first step to simplify the computation.

Let x denote the initial features of nodes, we first map it to a new space through a linear layer with dimension $d = 128$, i.e., $h_0^n = x_0^n W$. Then, h_0^n is transformed to h_N^n through N attention layers for better feature representation, each of which consists of a multi-head attention (MHA) sublayer and a feed-forward (FF) sublayer with residual connection and batch normalization added. $FF(\cdot)$ is a MLP network with ReLU activation function, and MHA is an attention network with $Y = 8$ heads. The $l - th$ MHA sublayer first calculates the attention value $Z_{l,y}$ for each head y as:

$$Z_{l,y} = softmax\left(\frac{\left[h_l W_{l,y}^Q\right]\left[h_l W_{l,y}^K\right]^T}{\sqrt{d'}}\right) h_l W_{l,y}^V, \tag{4}$$

where $\sqrt{d'} = d/Y$ is the $query/key$ dimension. Then we concatenate all these heads and project them into a new feature space:

$$MHA(h_l) = Concat(Z_{l,1}, Z_{l,2}, \cdots, Z_{l,Y})W_l^O, \tag{5}$$

where $W_l^Q, W_l^K, W_l^V \in \mathbb{R}^{d\times d'}$, and $W_l^O \in \mathbb{R}^{d\times d}$ are trainable parameters in layer l and are independent across different attention layers.

Afterwards, the output of the l-th MHA sublayer is fed to the l-th FF sublayer with ReLU activation function to get the next embeddings h_{l+1}. Here, a skip-connection [25] and a batch normalization (BN) layer [26] are used for both MHA and FF sublayers, which are summarised as follows,

$$r_l^i = BN(h_l^i + MHA^i(h_l)) \tag{6}$$

$$h_{l+1}^i = BN(r_l^i + FF(r_l^i)) \tag{7}$$

Finally, we define the final output of the encoder, i.e., h_N^i, as the node embeddings of the problem instance, and the mean of the node embeddings, i.e., $\hat{h}_N = \frac{1}{n}\sum_{i\in X} h_N^i$, as the graph embedding of the instance.

4.2 Selective and Draft Limit Decoder

The agent learns its policy through a decoder network, which processes state feature embeddings generated by the encoder. To account for the profit and draft limit constraints, we introduce a dual-decoder framework for route construction: (1) a Selective and Draft Limits (SDL) decoder, which ensures feasibility by enforcing constraints, and (2) a Route Construction Decoder, which generates high-quality solutions. The overall framework is illustrated in Fig. 1.

Traditional node selection approaches suffer from computational inefficiency and neglect of node-specific profits. To address this, we propose an SDL masking mechanism that systematically filters feasible nodes during the solution construction phase. However, generating feasible node information incurs high computational overhead. To alleviate this burden, we further introduce an auxiliary decoder network that predicts constraint-satisfying masks via efficient forward propagation, thereby yielding a more computationally efficient framework variant named SDL-D. Our framework integrates an auxiliary decoder dedicated

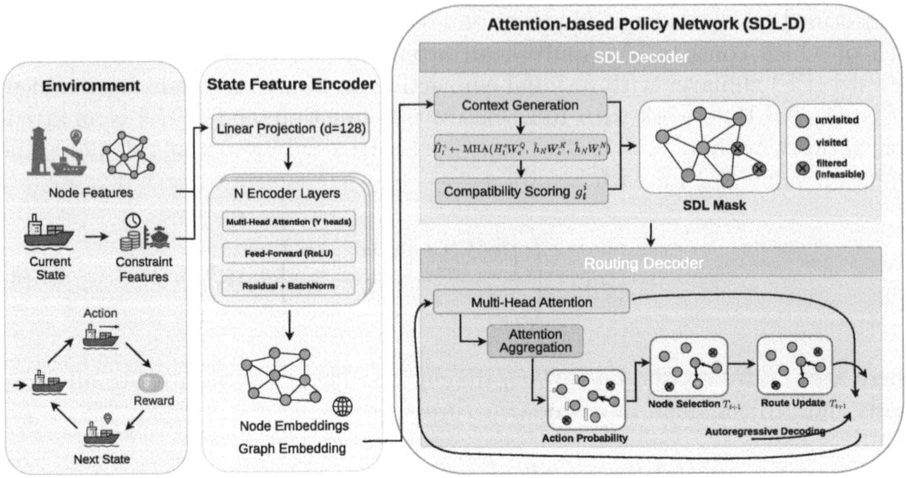

Fig. 1. An illustration of our network architecture: The framework consists of a state feature encoder and an attention-based policy network (SDL-D). The encoder aggregates static node features and dynamic freighter information into state representations. The policy network (SDL-D) integrates: (1) an SDL decoder for generating feasibility masks based on draft limits and profits, and (2) a routing decoder for autoregressively constructing the solution over the filtered action space.

to learning and predicting SDL masks. The SDL decoder operates in tandem with a routing decoder (the primary network), which is trained to maximize the expected reward of generated solutions. Concurrently, the SDL decoder optimizes the prediction accuracy of SDL label. These dual objectives are unified via a composite loss function:

$$L = \alpha L_{RL} + \beta L_{SDL}, \tag{8}$$

where L_{RL} is the reinforcement learning loss for the routing decoder, L_{SDL} is the SDL label prediction loss, and α, β are weights.

To enhance training efficiency, we employ a periodic update strategy for the SDL decoder, leveraging the short-term stability of the SDL masks to reduce computational cost.

The node embeddings $\hat{h}_N$ and the constraint feature are fed into a multi-head attention (MHA) layer to synthesize a new context vector H_t^c as a glimpse of the node embeddings. Different from the self-attention in the encoder, the query of this attention comes from the context vector, while the key/value of the attention comes from the node embeddings as:

$$\hat{H}_t^c = MHA(H_t^c W_c^Q, \hat{h}_N W_c^K, \hat{h}_N W_c^N), \tag{9}$$

where W_c^Q, W_c^K, and W_c^N are trainable parameters. The compatibility of all nodes with context at step t is computed as:

$$g_t^i = C \cdot \tanh([q_t^i \cdot k_t^i]/\sqrt{d'}), \tag{10}$$

where $q_t^i = \hat{H}_t^c W_c^Q$ and $k_t^i = h_N W_c^K$ are trainable parameters and C is set to 10 to control the entropy of u_t. As noted earlier, the SDL decoder uses a Sigmoid output layer for its binary classification task. The final output logits μ_t^i are passed through this Sigmoid function to compute the SDL label: $\bar{\pi}_t^i = Sigmoid(\mu_t^i)$. The L_{SDL} is then computed as:

$$\nabla \mathcal{L}_{SDL}(\theta) = -\frac{1}{T}\sum_{t=0}^{T}((1-g_t)\nabla log(p_\theta(1-g_t)) + g_t \cdot \nabla log(p_\theta(g_t))), \quad (11)$$

where T is the total decoding step to construct a complete solution, and g_t^i is the predicted SDL label in a specific decoding step t.

4.3 Network for the Routing Construction Decoder

The network architecture of our SDL-D framework generally mirrors that of the backbone model, but it incorporates dual decoders (i.e., routing decoder and SDL decoder). Without loss of generality, we take AM [15] decoder as an example for demonstration purpose. The decoder receives the node embedding h^i, the solution embedding h^s, and the real-time solution feature f^s as inputs, which are then used to compute the query (q), key (k), and value (v) for the MHA layer:

$$q^b = W_q^b[h^s, f^s],\ k_i^b = W_k^b h_i,\ V_i^b = W_v^b h_i, \quad (12)$$

where W_q^b, W_k^b and W_v^b are parameter matrices of the $b_t h$ ($b \in [1, B]$) attention head, and $[,]$ denotes the concatenation operator. The output of the MHA is calculated as:

$$a^b = \sum_{i=0}^{n} Softmax(\frac{(q^b)^T k^b}{\sqrt{d_k}})_i v_i^b, \quad (13)$$

where d_k is the dimension of the key. The output of each head passes through a linear layer parameterized by W_o, resulting in $h_a = W_o[a^0, a^1, \cdots, a^B]$. The decoder then computes the selection probabilities for all candidates nodes using a single-head attention layer:

$$p_i = Softmax(\xi \cdot tanh(\frac{h_a^T h_i}{\sqrt{d_h}})), \quad (14)$$

where d_h is the dimension of the node embedding. ξ is used to clip the logits to encourage policy exploration. The decoder consists of a 3-layer multilayer perception (MLP). Each edge embedding he is processed through $h_e^{l+1} = \xi(W_l h_e^l)$, where $l \in [0, 2]$ denotes the layer index, W_l represents a linear layer, and $\xi(\cdot)$ is an activation function, i.e. SiLU for $l = 0$, 1 and Sigmoid for $l = 2$. Given the significant correlation between preventative infeasibility masking and the current partial solution τ_t, we convert its NAR decoder to an AR one by adding an extra input layer that integrates the embedding of the last edge h_{e_t} in τ_t and the current solution feature f^s into the edge embedding itself, i.e., $h_e^0 = [h_e, h_{e_t}, f_s]$.

5 Experiment

In this paper, we propose a novel attention framework with selective draft limit decoders (SDL-D) to address the limitations of existing masking mechanisms for handling complex constraints. To evaluate the effectiveness of our method, we apply our framework to a representative constructive method, AM. For the benchmark problem, we consider the representative complex VRP variants with strong interdependent constraints, STSP-DL, that challenge existing neural methods with small problem scale $n = 50, 80, 100$. All the experiments are conducted on servers with NVIDIA GeForce RTX 3090 GPUs and Intel(R) Xeon(R) Gold 6326 CPU at 2.90GHz.

5.1 Experiment Setting

Datasets. Following prior studies, instances are generated by reducing the draft limits for $q\%$ of nodes ($q \in 10, 25, 50, 75$ or randomly selected). Each (n, q) configuration includes 10 instances, and all results are averaged over them. Customer nodes have demand and profit values set to 1, while the depot node has 0.

Baseline. The proposed method is compared with LKH3 [27], Greedy-L/C, and GVNS [6], as well as DRL-based solvers AM [15], POMO [2], and PIP [24]. For DRL solvers, two decoding strategies are employed: Greedy and Sampling (S_{12800}).

5.2 The Experiment Results

Table 1 compares the proposed SDL-D with representative baselines on synthetic datasets of sizes $N = 50, 80, 100$. We report three metrics: average objective value (Obj.), optimality gap (%) relative to LKH3, and average solving time (s). As shown in Table 1, LKH3 attains the lowest objective values for different instances, reaffirming its role as a strong heuristic baseline. However, this superior solution quality comes with a substantial computational burden, requiring 791 s, 1417 s and 2819 s for $N = 50, 80, 100$, respectively. In contrast, heuristic methods such as Greedy(L) and GVNS achieve faster inference but at the expense of higher optimality gaps (e.g., GVNS: 24.49%, 20.36%, and 32.04%). Learning-based approaches, including AM (greedy) and SDL-D (greedy), demonstrate a more favorable trade-off between accuracy and efficiency, with SDL-D (greedy) consistently outperforming AM (greedy). Notably, SDL-D (12800) delivers the most balanced performance, achieving gaps of 17.35%, 8.35%, and 11.51% while maintaining low solving times of 9.9s, 19.3s, and 24.2s. These findings highlight SDL-D's capability to approximate high-quality solutions efficiently, establishing it as a robust alternative to conventional heuristics and exact optimization methods.

In addition, we also evaluate the method on public datasets, which were published by [6]. The results are summarized in Table 2, where the evaluation metric is the traveling distance. As shown in the table, SDL-D consistently achieves

Table 1. Performance comparison with various baselines on generated datasets using metrics including average objective value (Obj. ↓), average optimality gap to the best-performed heuristic baselines (Avg. gap ↓), and average solving time (Time ↓). The best results are highlighted in bold.

Methods	N = 50			N = 80			N = 100		
	Obj	Gap(%)	Time(s)	Obj	Gap(%)	Time(s)	Obj	Gap(%)	Time(s)
LKH3	11.35	0	791	15.91	0	1417	17.51	0	2819
Greedy(L)	14.57	28.37	252	/	/	1000	/	/	1000
GVNS	14.13	24.49	454	19.15	20.36	279	23.12	32.04	317
AM(greedy)	14.15	24.67	17.1	17.99	13.01	22.4	20.79	18.73	25.8
POMO(greedy)	14.09	24.14	16.4	17.87	12.25	20.5	20.61	17.71	25.5
PIP (greedy)	14.09	24.14	16.4	17.54	10.24	21.2	20.64	17.87	25.1
SDL-D (greedy)	13.75	21.14	10.2	17.27	8.54	20.1	20.14	15.02	23.8
AM(S_{12800})	13.81	21.67	12.7	17.91	12.5	18.9	20.55	17.36	23.1
POMO(S_{12800})	13.79	21.49	15.8	17.75	11.56	20.7	19.97	14.05	25.8
PIP (S_{12800})	13.58	19.64	12.9	17.96	12.88	21.9	19.85	13.36	24.9
SDL-D(S_{12800})	**13.32**	**17.35**	**9.9**	**17.24**	**8.35**	19.3	**19.54**	**11.51**	24.2

shorter traveling distances across most benchmark instances. For example, in the Burma14 and fri26 datasets, SDL-D produces shorter routes than both classical heuristics and learning-based approaches, indicating that our method achieves better performance compared with other baselines.

Table 2. Performance comparison with various baselines on generated datasets using metrics including average objective of different methods. The best results are highlighted in bold.

Methods	GVNS	AM	POMO	PIP	SDL-D
Bayg29-10	5537.4	5546.6	5549.7	5547.4	**5526.8**
Bayg29-25	5492.8	5476.1	5451.6	5420.1	**5237.1**
Bayg29-50	5370.7	5529.9	5521.06	5567.1	**5526.1**
Burma14-10	10493.7	10491.7	10453.6	10452.5	**10451.1**
Burma14-50	10347.2	1351.9	10378.1	10367.1	**10345.8**
fri26-10	3638.5	3719.7	3890.8	3586.1	**3572.6**
fri26-50	3656.7	3648.2	3631.7	3667.1	**3628.4**
gr17-10	7105.4	7120.1	7123.6	7226.1	**7009.1**
gr21-10	9926.7	9986.1	9921.06	9887.1	**9852.9**
gr21-50	9826.5	9901.1	9881.06	9867.9	**9820.1**
ulysses16-10	31051.4	31573.1	31802.8	31067.7	**31020.1**
ulysses16-25	24654.3	24626.1	24439.3	24655.9	**24480.4**

6 Conclusion

This paper proposes SDL-D, the first deep reinforcement learning (DRL) framework specifically designed for the Selective Traveling Salesman Problem with Draft Limits (STSP-DL). Our approach introduces a dual-decoder policy network architecture: (1) a constraint decoder that enforces draft limit feasibility, and (2) a node selection decoder that optimizes route construction through attention mechanisms. By jointly training these components, the model autonomously learns to maximize profit while satisfying complex constraints. Comprehensive experiments on both benchmark and synthetic datasets demonstrate that SDL-D achieves superior performance compared to traditional heuristic and exact methods. To further advance the applicability of the SDL-D framework, we plan to extend it to accommodate a wider variety of Vehicle Routing Problem (VRP) variants. Key directions include incorporating real-world constraints such as time windows, dynamic customer demands, and stochastic traffic conditions. Additionally, we aim to integrate the framework with the POMO mechanism to demonstrate its versatility as a generalizable solution for combinatorial optimization problems. These extensions will validate the robustness and adaptability of the proposed method across diverse routing scenarios.

References

1. Mladenović, N., Urošević, D., Ilić, A., et al.: A general variable neighborhood search for the one-commodity pickup-and-delivery travelling salesman problem. Eur. J. Oper. Res. **220**(1), 270–285 (2012)
2. Kwon, Y.D., Choo, J., Kim, B., Yoon, I., Gwon, Y., Min, S.: Pomo: policy optimization with multiple optima for reinforcement learning. Adv. Neural. Inf. Process. Syst. **33**, 21188–21198 (2020)
3. Feillet, D., Dejax, P., Gendreau, M.: Traveling salesman problems with profits. Transp. Sci. **39**(2), 188–205 (2005). https://doi.org/10.1287/trsc.1030.0079
4. Rakke, J.G., Christiansen, M., Fagerholt, K., Laporte, G.: The traveling salesman problem with draft limits. Comput. Oper. Res. **39**(9), 2161–2167 (2012)
5. Todosijević, R., Mjirda, A., Mladenović, M., Hanafi, S., Gendron, B.: A general variable neighborhood search variants for the travelling salesman problem with draft limits. Optim. Lett. **11**, 1047–1056 (2017)
6. Gelareh, S., Gendron, B., Hanafi, S., Neamatian Monemi, R., Todosijević, R.: The selective traveling salesman problem with draft limits. J. Heurist. **26**, 339–352 (2020)
7. Little, J.D., Murty, K.G., Sweeney, D.W., Karel, C.: An algorithm for the traveling salesman problem. Oper. Res. **11**(6), 972–989 (1963)
8. Bellman, R.: Dynamic programming treatment of the travelling salesman problem. J. ACM (JACM) **9**(1), 61–63 (1962)
9. Montero, A., Mendez-Diaz, I., Jose Miranda-Bront, J.: An integer programming approach for the time-dependent traveling salesman problem with time windows. Comput. Oper. Res. **88**, 280–289 (2017). https://doi.org/10.1016/j.cor.2017.06.026
10. Karabulut, K., Tasgetiren, M.F.: A variable iterated greedy algorithm for the traveling salesman problem with time windows. Inf. Sci. **279**, 383–395 (2014). https://doi.org/10.1016/j.ins.2014.03.127

11. Sun, L.: Genetic algorithm for tsp problem. In: Proceedings of the 2015 International Industrial Informatics and Computer Engineering Conference, pp. 1436–1439 (2015)
12. Lu, L.C., Yue, T.W.: Mission-oriented ant-team ACO for min-max MTSP. Appl. Soft Comput. **76**, 436–444 (2019). https://doi.org/10.1016/j.asoc.2018.11.048
13. Li, Q., Cao, Z., Ma, Y., Wu, Y., Gong, Y.J.: Diversity optimization for travelling salesman problem via deep reinforcement learning (2025). https://arxiv.org/abs/2501.00884
14. Wu, Y., Song, W., Cao, Z., Zhang, J., Lim, A.: Learning improvement heuristics for solving routing problems. IEEE Trans. Neural Networks Learn. Syst. **33**(9), 5057–5069 (2021)
15. Kool, W., Van Hoof, H., Welling, M.: Attention, learn to solve routing problems! arXiv preprint arXiv:1803.08475 (2018)
16. Yan, D., Ou, B., Guan, Q., Zhu, Z., Cao, H.: Edge-driven multiple trajectory attention model for vehicle routing problems. Appl. Sci.-Basel **15**(5) (2025). https://doi.org/10.3390/app15052679
17. Saad, S., Wan Jaafar, W.N., Jamil, S.J.: Solving standard traveling salesman problem and multiple traveling salesman problem by using branch-and-bound. In: AIP Conference Proceedings. vol. 1522, pp. 1406–1411. American Institute of Physics (2013)
18. Battarra, M., Pessoa, A.A., Subramanian, A., Uchoa, E.: Exact algorithms for the traveling salesman problem with draft limits. Eur. J. Oper. Res. **235**(1), 115–128 (2014)
19. Yang, X., Wang, J.S.: Application of improved ant colony optimization algorithm on traveling salesman problem. In: 2016 Chinese Control and Decision Conference (CCDC), pp. 2156–2160. IEEE (2016)
20. Duarte, B., de Oliveira, L.C., Teixeira, M., Barbosa, M.A.: A comparison of genetic and memetic algorithms applied to the traveling salesman problem with draft limits. In: 2021 XLVII Latin American Computing Conference (CLEI), pp. 1–10. IEEE (2021)
21. Vinyals, O., Fortunato, M., Jaitly, N.: Pointer networks. In: Advances in Neural Information Processing Systems, pp. 2692–2700 (2015)
22. Bello, I., Pham, H., Le, Q.V., Norouzi, M., Bengio, S.: Neural combinatorial optimization with reinforcement learning. In: International Conference on Learning Representations (2017)
23. Chen, X., Tian, Y.: Learning to perform local rewriting for combinatorial optimization. In: Advances in Neural Information Processing Systems, pp. 6278–6289 (2019)
24. Bi, J., et al.: Learning to handle complex constraints for vehicle routing problems. In: Advances in Neural Information Processing Systems 37 (NeurIPS 2024) (2024)
25. He, K., Zhang, X., Ren, S., Sun, J.: Deep residual learning for image recognition. In: Proceedings of the IEEE Conference on Computer Vision and Pattern Recognition, pp. 770–778 (2016)
26. Ioffe, S., Szegedy, C.: Batch normalization: accelerating deep network training by reducing internal covariate shift. In: International Conference on Machine Learning, pp. 448–456 (2015)
27. Helsgaun, K.: LKH-3 (version 3.0.7) (2017). http://webhotel4.ruc.dk/~keld/research/LKH-3/, a heuristic solver for the Traveling Salesman Problem and its variants

Towards A Novel Shapley-Based Framework for Data-Centric Cohort Refinement

Yueh Tang and Justin Zhan(✉)

Department of Computer Science, University of Cincinnati, Cincinnati, OH, USA
{tangy9,zhanej}@mail.uc.edu

Abstract. Reliable predictive modeling in healthcare depends not only on algorithmic advancement but also on the quality and consistency of training data. Clinical datasets are often heterogeneous and imperfect, containing mislabeled, redundant, or low-value samples that distort learned representations. This paper introduces a data-centric *Shapley-weighted cohort refinement* stage that quantifies each sample's contribution to validation performance before model training. Unlike prior filtering approaches that discard data with negative utility, our method continuously reweights all samples to align the training distribution with its validation behavior. We theoretically link this objective to regularized empirical risk minimization and validate it on four large-scale MIMIC-IV cohorts, confirming generalization on external eICU and MIMIC-III datasets. Shapley Weighting achieves ROC–AUC comparable to Shapley Filtering, while improving reliability through better calibration and lower cross-seed variance without discarding data; gains in F1/Brier are small but consistent across cohorts and runs. These reliability improvements are practically important in clinical risk stratification, where stable and well-calibrated probabilities often matter more than marginal changes in discrimination. Cohort compactness, measured by Silhouette, Davies–Bouldin, and a Composite Cluster Quality Index (CQI), remains non-inferior or slightly better under Shapley Weighting, indicating improved structural coherence with full data retention. Overall, contribution-guided weighting offers a principled and practical path toward more reliable and generalizable healthcare prediction.

Keywords: Data-centric learning · Shapley-based weighting · Cohort refinement · Healthcare prediction · Model calibration

1 Introduction

Reliable healthcare prediction depends not only on model design but also on the *quality and consistency* of the training cohort. Clinical datasets are heterogeneous and imperfect, often containing mislabeled, redundant, or low-utility samples that weaken generalization. This motivates *data-centric cohort refinement*: improving the training distribution *before* optimizing the model.

R. C.-W. Wong et al. (Eds.): PAKDD 2026, LNAI 16617, pp. 140–151, 2027.
https://doi.org/10.1007/978-981-92-1926-1_12

Data Shapley [8,18] measures each example's marginal contribution to validation performance and inspires Shapley-based refinement in healthcare. However, existing practice often relies on *hard filtering* (e.g., removing samples with $\phi < 0$), which can discard rare clinically meaningful cases and reduce cohort diversity, introducing selection bias under distribution shift. Moreover, small gains in ROC/PR-AUC do not necessarily translate into *reliable probabilities*: calibration and run-to-run stability are often more critical under class imbalance.

We propose *Shapley Weighting (SW)*, which replaces discrete deletion with *continuous* weighting. SW retains **100%** of training data and reweights negatives using Shapley *ranks* (positives fixed), yielding a stable, scale-invariant rule. We connect SW to *regularized empirical risk minimization*, providing a validation-aligned view of why contribution-guided weighting improves reliability without sacrificing discrimination.

We evaluate SW on four large-scale MIMIC-IV cohorts (AKI, COPD, Sepsis, HF) [9,13,14], with external validation on MIMIC-III and eICU [15,16,20,21]. Across multiple model families, SW matches SF on ROC/PR-AUC while yielding small but consistent improvements in calibration and cross-seed variance under full retention.

Contributions. (1) We introduce *Shapley Weighting*, a full-retention, rank-based alternative to hard Shapley Filtering that mitigates selection bias. (2) We provide a regularized ERM interpretation, showing how SW induces a validation-aligned training measure linked to improved calibration and stability. (3) We benchmark SW vs. SF on four MIMIC-IV cohorts across six classifiers and validate on MIMIC-III and eICU. (4) We analyze cohort compactness (Sil/DBI/CQI) to give an interpretable geometric view of refinement effects.

2 Related Work

Data-Centric Machine Learning. Data-centric learning improves reliability by refining training data and evaluating beyond discrimination, e.g., via uncertainty- and calibration-aware perspectives [28]. Classic pruning/selection methods also aim to remove redundant or unhelpful samples [26]. Our work follows this line but uses principled contribution attribution as the refinement signal rather than heuristics.

Data Valuation and Shapley Attribution. Data Shapley provides a game-theoretic way to quantify each sample's marginal contribution to a validation objective [8,18]. Recent extensions improve efficiency and broaden applications, including Shapley-based data integration and identifying detrimental samples [27]. In healthcare, Catalyst introduced Shapley Filtering (SF) by removing low-value negatives [30]; we instead convert attribution into continuous weighting to retain coverage and reduce selection bias.

Robust Learning and Sample Weighting. Sample reweighting is widely used to improve robustness under label noise and distribution shifts [11,12,22,29]. It also connects to distributionally robust learning and validation-aligned regularization [1,25]. Different from loss/gradient-based weighting, we derive weights from Shapley contribution ranks computed on a validation utility.

Calibration and Reliability. Calibration is critical for clinical decision support. Temperature scaling is a standard baseline [10], and prior work further studies calibration under distribution shift and finite-sample settings [19]. Accordingly, we report Brier/ECE alongside ROC/PR-AUC and F1 to evaluate deployment-relevant reliability.

Cohort Refinement in Healthcare Data. Large ICU datasets are heterogeneous and noisy, motivating cohort-level refinement prior to modeling [9,13,14]. We validate Shapley-guided refinement under institutional/temporal shift on eICU and MIMIC-III [15,16,20,21].

3 Method

3.1 Framework Overview

We propose a data-centric cohort refinement stage that improves both informational quality and structural consistency *before* model training. The framework uses a single attribution module to estimate each sample's contribution to validation performance via Data Shapley. Unlike Shapley Filtering (SF), which removes samples with $\phi < 0$, our Shapley Weighting (SW) retains all samples and modulates their influence through a rank-based weighting rule. This yields a contribution-aware training objective that better matches validation behavior while preserving cohort coverage. Figure 1 summarizes the difference between SF and SW.

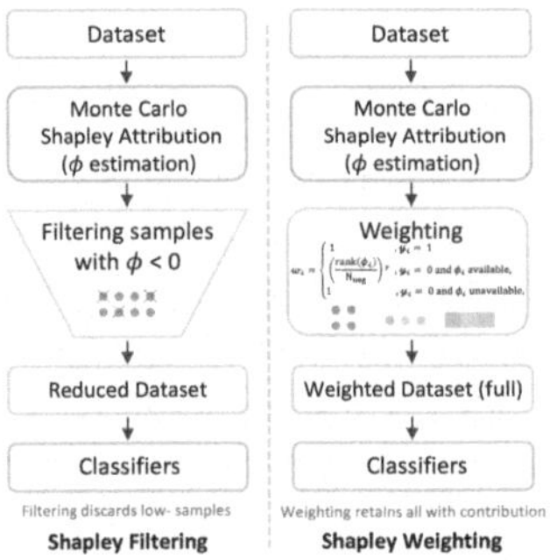

Fig. 1. SF vs. SW. SF removes samples with $\phi < 0$; SW keeps all samples and reweights negatives by Shapley ranks (positives fixed at $w = 1$).

Assumptions and Safeguards. All preprocessing, attribution, and model fitting are performed independently within each outer CV fold. Shapley utility is computed on an inner validation split drawn strictly from the training fold using the same metric $U \in \{\mathrm{ROC-AUC}, \mathrm{PR-AUC}\}$ as evaluation. To prevent leakage, we remove features used in label construction (e.g., ICD prefixes; creatinine item 50912 in AKI_LAB). The test fold remains isolated throughout.

3.2 Sample-Level Attribution and Refinement

Data Shapley [8,17] measures the marginal utility of a training example for a target metric. Prior work commonly uses Shapley values for hard filtering (e.g., removing $\phi < 0$ samples), which may inadvertently remove rare but clinically meaningful cases and introduce selection bias by shrinking cohort diversity. We use such filtering only as a baseline (SF) and instead convert the discrete keep/remove decision into a continuous weighting (SW) that retains all data while adapting influence to estimated contribution.

Following Ghorbani and Zou [8], the Shapley value ϕ_i of x_i is the expected gain in a validation metric $U \in \{\mathrm{ROC} - \mathrm{AUC}, \mathrm{PR} - \mathrm{AUC}\}$ when adding x_i to a random subset. **Utility.** Within each outer CV fold, let $\mathcal{D}$ denote the inner training split and $\mathcal{D}_{\mathrm{val}}$ the fixed inner validation split. For any subset $S \subseteq \mathcal{D}$, let f_S be the base model trained on S, and define $v(S) \triangleq U(f_S; \mathcal{D}_{\mathrm{val}})$ with $U \in \{\text{ROC-AUC}, \text{PR-AUC}\}$.

Then the Shapley value of example i is

$$\phi_i \triangleq \sum_{S \subseteq \mathcal{D} \setminus \{i\}} \frac{|S|!\,(|\mathcal{D}| - |S| - 1)!}{|\mathcal{D}|!} \Big(v(S \cup \{i\}) - v(S) \Big).$$

We approximate ϕ_i via the standard Monte Carlo permutation estimator: for each of M random permutations, we add samples sequentially and record the marginal change in U; ϕ_i is the average marginal gain across permutations (with early stopping). To reduce computation and avoid unstable attribution under severe imbalance, we compute ϕ_i only for negatives and keep positives at unit weight ($w = 1$) to preserve rare events. We use $M = 2$ by default and early-stop when $|U_t - U_{\mathrm{full}}| \leq 10^{-2}$ for two consecutive steps. To improve robustness to noisy Shapley magnitudes, we later convert ϕ_i to ranks and map ranks to weights.

Shapley-Based Weighting. Let N_{neg} be the number of negatives with valid ϕ, and $\mathrm{rank}(\phi_i) \in \{1, \ldots, N_{\mathrm{neg}}\}$ denotes the ascending rank among negatives (smaller $\phi \to$ smaller rank). In case of ties, we use average ranks. We set

$$w_i = \begin{cases} 1, & y_i = 1, \\ \left(\frac{\mathrm{rank}(\phi_i)}{N_{\mathrm{neg}}}\right)^{\gamma}, & y_i = 0 \text{ and } \phi_i \text{ available}, \\ 1, & y_i = 0 \text{ and } \phi_i \text{ unavailable}, \end{cases} \qquad \gamma \in \{0.3, 0.5, 0.7\}.$$

Rank-to-Weight Mapping. We use ranks (instead of raw ϕ_i magnitudes) to obtain a scale-invariant and noise-robust weighting rule under Monte Carlo estimation. The exponent γ controls concentration; we report $\gamma = 0.5$ as default. Weights are clipped at $w_{\min} = 10^{-6}$ and normalized so that total mass equals n; we report effective sample size (ESS) as a diagnostic.

3.3 Composite Cluster Quality Index (CQI)

Cohort compactness is summarized by

$$\mathrm{CQI} = \frac{\mathrm{Sil}}{\mathrm{DBI}},$$

where Silhouette (Sil) reflects within-cluster cohesion and between-cluster separation (higher is better; typically in $[-1, 1]$), and Davies–Bouldin (DBI) measures cluster overlap/dispersion (lower is better; DBI ≥ 0). Thus, CQI $=$ Sil/DBI increases when clusters become more separated (larger Sil) and less overlapping (smaller DBI). For example, if Sil $= 0.48$ and DBI $= 0.75$, then CQI $= 0.64$. We report CQI as a post-hoc cohort-level interpretability signal and do not use it for tuning or model selection.

3.4 Shapley Weighting as Regularized ERM

Let the empirical risk be

$$\mathcal{L}_{\text{ERM}}(f) = \tfrac{1}{n}\sum_i \ell(f(x_i), y_i).$$

The contribution-weighted objective is then

$$Z = \sum_i w_i, \quad \tilde{w}_i = \frac{n\,w_i}{Z}, \quad \mathcal{L}_{\text{SW}}(f) = \frac{1}{n}\sum_i \tilde{w}_i\,\ell(f(x_i), y_i).$$

Expanding $\mathcal{L}_{\text{SW}}$ gives

$$\mathcal{L}_{\text{SW}}(f) = \mathcal{L}_{\text{ERM}}(f) + \Omega_\phi(f), \quad \Omega_\phi(f) = \tfrac{1}{n}\sum_i (\tilde{w}_i - 1)\,\ell(f(x_i), y_i).$$

Interpretation. If ϕ is estimated on an inner validation split using metric U, minimizing $\mathcal{L}_{\text{SW}}$ can be viewed as reweighting the empirical measure toward samples that improve the validation utility, i.e.,

$$\mathbb{E}_{(x,y)\sim p_\phi}[\ell(f(x), y)] \approx \mathbb{E}_{(x,y)\sim p_{\text{val}}}[\ell(f(x), y)].$$

Sketch. $\tilde{w}_i$ increases monotonically with rank(ϕ_i) (equivalently, with ϕ_i up to order). This induces a change of measure $p_\phi \propto w$, concentrating mass on higher-ranked samples under the validation utility, yielding a validation-aligned ERM. Due to space constraints, we omit the detailed derivations.

3.5 Integration Within Learning Pipelines

Shapley Weighting is model-agnostic. We apply w_i directly to sample losses without changing model architecture or hyperparameters. This enables immediate use with linear models, tree ensembles, and shallow neural networks. Because refinement operates on the empirical measure, it can be inserted as a preprocessing stage before any classifier while preserving reproducibility. We adopt a single-shot refinement per fold to keep the pipeline simple and reproducible across downstream models; iterative reweighting is left as future work.

Pipeline. Within each outer fold, we estimate Shapley utilities on an inner 80/20 split using a lightweight LR model (negatives only), map Shapley ranks to weights, and reuse the same weights across downstream classifiers. All preprocessing and weighting are confined to the training fold; the test fold remains untouched.

3.6 Complexity and Implementation

We estimate Shapley values only for negatives to reduce computation and to avoid unstable estimates for rare positives under imbalance. All computations are confined to each outer fold. The cost of Shapley estimation scales with permutations and the number of negatives used: $O(M \cdot K \cdot C_{\text{train}})$ with $K \leq \min\{N_{\text{neg}}, 25\text{k}\}$. We compute Shapley values once per outer fold using the lightweight LR base model and reuse the resulting weights across all downstream classifiers, which amortizes the Shapley overhead. Inner splits are stratified and fixed within each fold, and all runs use fixed random seeds. We adopt $M = 2$ by default (with $M = 3$ in sensitivity) and early stopping at $|\Delta\text{AUC}| \leq 10^{-2}$. Features are stored in `float32`. All seeds are fixed and results average over three seeds. Logistic regression with standard scaling is used as the base model. Default hyperparameters are $\gamma = 0.5$ and $w_{\min} = 10^{-6}$. For compactness analysis only, we use weighted PCA and KMeans under SW (k=2–6). All computations are implemented in Python with `scikit-learn` pipelines and fixed seeds. Further efficiency/stability improvements are possible via uncertainty-aware weighting (e.g., tempering weights using variance across permutations) or alternative approximations (e.g., influence-/gradient-based surrogates), which we leave for future work.

4 Experiments

4.1 Experimental Setup

Experiments ran on institutional HPC nodes (A100 40GB); each 9-run configuration (3 folds×3 seeds) required about 3–4 GPU hours.

Experiments were conducted on four large-scale clinical prediction tasks, including Acute Kidney Injury (AKI), Chronic Obstructive Pulmonary Disease (COPD), Sepsis, and Heart Failure (HF), using the MIMIC-IV database [9,13,14]. All tasks were preprocessed through a unified pipeline including patient-level alignment, normalization, and duplicate removal, following standard clinical modeling practice [30]. Six representative classifiers were evaluated: Logistic Regression (LR) [4], Random Forest (RF) [2], Adaptive Boosting (ADA) [7], Gradient Boosted Decision Trees (GBDT), eXtreme Gradient Boosting (XGB) [3], and a shallow Multi-Layer Perceptron (MLP) [24]. Each configuration was trained with stratified three-fold cross-validation using three randomized fixed seeds to ensure statistical robustness.

We evaluate discrimination and reliability using AUC, F1, Brier, and ECE [10], and we also report cross-seed variance to assess deployment-relevant stability. Cohort compactness was further assessed by Silhouette (Sil) [23], Davies–Bouldin (DBI) [5], and the proposed Composite Cluster Quality Index (CQI). Statistical significance between refinement strategies was tested via paired t-tests aggregated across folds and seeds. A reference implementation of Shapley Weighting is available at https://github.com/tang03130313/shapley-weighting-refimpl. All datasets (MIMIC-IV/III, eICU) are de-identified and used under PhysioNet credentialed access [13]. For external validation, we use eICU [13,20,21] and MIMIC-III [13,15,16] under PhysioNet credentialed access, following the same preprocessing, cross-validation, and evaluation protocol as in MIMIC-IV.

Table 1. Model-averaged performance across MIMIC-IV cohorts (mean ± SD). AUC, PR, and F1 are reported in % (two decimals); Brier in native scale (four decimals). Results correspond to the representative setting $\gamma = 0.5$. Δ reports SW–SF; positive ΔF1/negative ΔBrier favor SW. AUCs are statistically indistinguishable across methods. We emphasize reliability: SW reduces cross-seed variability and improves calibration-related metrics (Brier) while retaining 100% of training data, rather than targeting large gains in discrimination.

Disease	Method	ROC-AUC(%)	PR-AUC(%)	F1@0.5(%)	Brier ↓	ΔF1 / ΔBrier
AKI	Vanilla	92.24 ± 0.20	87.21 ± 1.03	77.27 ± 1.75	0.1083 ± 0.0177	
	SF	92.12 ± 0.20	87.12 ± 1.03	77.26 ± 1.48	0.1084 ± 0.0179	
	SW	**92.37 ± 0.20**	**87.83 ± 0.57**	**77.44 ± 1.87**	**0.1083 ± 0.0177**	**+0.15 / −0.0001**
COPD	Vanilla	88.24 ± 0.30	54.86 ± 0.55	43.32 ± 0.93	0.0629 ± 0.0126	
	SF	88.22 ± 0.31	54.72 ± 0.57	43.39 ± 0.88	0.0632 ± 0.0131	
	SW	**88.24 ± 0.31**	**54.79 ± 0.56**	**43.50 ± 0.90**	**0.0630 ± 0.0127**	**+0.03 / −0.0002**
Sepsis	Vanilla	94.99 ± 0.20	80.59 ± 0.66	64.09 ± 2.07	0.0505 ± 0.0201	
	SF	94.98 ± 0.20	80.57 ± 0.67	64.09 ± 1.96	0.0506 ± 0.0203	
	SW	**94.99 ± 0.20**	**80.85 ± 0.66**	**65.95 ± 1.73**	**0.0506 ± 0.0204**	**+1.86 / −0.0000**
HF	Vanilla	92.75 ± 0.20	73.97 ± 0.60	62.85 ± 0.90	0.0707 ± 0.0010	
	SF	92.72 ± 0.20	73.93 ± 0.60	62.82 ± 0.90	0.0706 ± 0.0010	
	SW	**92.76 ± 0.20**	**73.95 ± 0.60**	**62.86 ± 0.90**	**0.0706 ± 0.0010**	**+0.04 / −0.0001**

4.2 Overall Performance (MIMIC-IV)

Table 1 summarizes model-averaged results across all classifiers for each disease. Shapley Weighting matches SF on ROC/PR-AUC but improves decision-level utility: model-averaged F1 and Brier improve by small consistent margins across AKI/COPD/Sepsis/HF [8]. Although the absolute effect sizes are modest, they are accompanied by systematically reduced cross-seed variance (Fig. 2) and improved calibration-related metrics (Brier/ECE), which are central to reliable deployment. By contrast, SF yields comparable AUC but does not reliably improve calibration-related metrics (Brier/ECE) across cohorts, despite removing a fraction of training samples. From an interpretability perspective, SW also maintains non-inferior cohort compactness (Sect. 4.6), providing a geometric view that is consistent with these reliability gains. Importantly, all SW variants retained **100% of training samples**, whereas SF dynamically removed $\phi < 0$ samples following Catalyst [30], resulting in approximately 2–10% removal across cohorts. Thus, SW avoids coverage loss while attaining *non-inferior* compactness to SF.

Overall, SW matches AUCs (no significant difference at $\alpha = 0.05$) while improving threshold metrics and calibration, validating that soft reweighting achieves a smoother trade-off between discrimination and reliability than hard filtering [6,8].

Model-Agnostic Check (AKI). Across six base learners on AKI, SW remains non-inferior to SF in ROC-AUC and typically improves PR-AUC/F1, suggesting the gains are not tied to a specific classifier family.

Table 2. External validation on eICU and MIMIC-III (mean ± SD across six models; $\gamma = 0.5$). AUC, PR, and F1 in %; Brier in native scale. Bold indicates the better method per row.

Dataset	Disease	Method	ROC-AUC(%)	PR-AUC(%)	F1@0.5(%)	Brier (↓)
eICU						
	AKI	SF	92.43 ± 0.21	81.33 ± 0.19	70.10 ± 0.28	0.1080 ± 0.0007
		SW	**92.45 ± 0.20**	**81.37 ± 0.18**	**70.22 ± 0.31**	**0.1079 ± 0.0007**
	COPD	SF	91.25 ± 0.24	78.92 ± 0.17	68.41 ± 0.33	0.1112 ± 0.0008
		SW	**91.27 ± 0.24**	**78.95 ± 0.17**	**68.54 ± 0.34**	**0.1110 ± 0.0008**
	Sepsis	SF	90.67 ± 0.23	79.55 ± 0.15	67.44 ± 0.27	0.1093 ± 0.0006
		SW	**90.69 ± 0.23**	**79.58 ± 0.15**	**67.63 ± 0.29**	**0.1091 ± 0.0006**
	HF	SF	92.18 ± 0.24	70.03 ± 0.58	60.92 ± 0.84	0.0734 ± 0.0012
		SW	**92.21 ± 0.24**	**70.06 ± 0.58**	**61.02 ± 0.86**	**0.0733 ± 0.0012**
MIMIC-III						
	AKI	SF	93.27 ± 0.19	85.09 ± 0.12	74.41 ± 0.23	0.1013 ± 0.0005
		SW	**93.29 ± 0.18**	**85.12 ± 0.12**	**74.55 ± 0.22**	**0.1012 ± 0.0005**
	COPD	SF	90.81 ± 0.22	82.65 ± 0.11	72.14 ± 0.19	0.1041 ± 0.0006
		SW	**90.83 ± 0.22**	**82.67 ± 0.11**	**72.25 ± 0.20**	**0.1040 ± 0.0006**
	Sepsis	SF	89.92 ± 0.25	80.72 ± 0.13	69.83 ± 0.25	0.1078 ± 0.0007
		SW	**89.95 ± 0.25**	**80.75 ± 0.13**	**69.97 ± 0.24**	**0.1076 ± 0.0007**
	HF	SF	92.41 ± 0.21	73.84 ± 0.59	62.77 ± 0.91	0.0708 ± 0.0011
		SW	**92.44 ± 0.21**	**73.88 ± 0.59**	**62.85 ± 0.90**	**0.0707 ± 0.0011**

4.3 External Validation on eICU and MIMIC-III

We next evaluate the same refinement strategies on two independent datasets, *eICU* [20] and *MIMIC-III* [15], using the identical four cohorts (AKI, COPD, Sepsis, and HF) and the same training and evaluation protocol as in MIMIC-IV. Table 2 reports model-averaged results across six base learners.

Across both datasets, Shapley Weighting (SW) matches or slightly surpasses Shapley Filtering (SF) on ROC-AUC and PR-AUC, while delivering consistent gains on decision metrics and reliability. F1 increases by small but steady margins and Brier decreases in every cohort, indicating better probability alignment without sacrificing discrimination. Unlike SF, which removes a fraction of training points with negative contributions, SW retains all samples and adjusts influence continuously. This preserves cohort diversity and yields stable calibration under institutional and temporal shift. This full-retention design reduces the risk of selection bias from sample deletion, which is especially relevant under institutional shift; the non-inferior external results on eICU/MIMIC-III support this claim.

4.4 Stability Analysis

Motivated by the validation-aligned reweighting view, we evaluate cross-seed stability across nine-run repeats. SW achieves the lowest variance in most model–disease pairs, reducing PR-AUC/F1 standard deviation by ∼5–10% vs. SF and up to 25% vs. Vanilla (Fig. 2), consistent with downweighting noisy or redundant negatives [8].

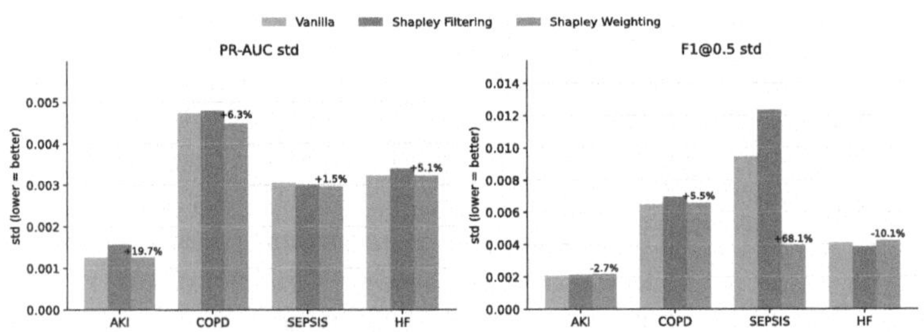

Fig. 2. Cross-seed stability on MIMIC-IV (lower is better). Bars show the standard deviation of PR–AUC and F1 across 9 runs (3 folds × 3 seeds), aggregated over evaluated models. SW consistently reduces run-to-run variability compared to Vanilla and SF, indicating improved training stability under cohort heterogeneity.

4.5 Calibration and Reliability

Across all cohorts and 9-run repeats, SW consistently yields lower calibration error (Brier/ECE) than Vanilla and SF while maintaining comparable ROC/PR-AUC (see Table 1).

4.6 Cohort Compactness and Interpretability

Both Shapley Filtering (SF) and Shapley Weighting (SW) yield more compact and separable clusters than the unrefined baseline, confirming improved intra-cohort homogeneity. While SF attains compactness by removing 2–10% of samples, SW achieves comparable or slightly better structure (Sil = 0.482 vs. 0.481;

DBI = 0.743 vs. 0.747) without data loss. This demonstrates that continuous contribution-based weighting refines the cohort manifold smoothly, enhancing cohesion while preserving interpretability. We view compactness as an interpretability signal rather than a separate optimization target. The non-inferior Sil/DBI (and CQI) under SW is consistent with the reliability gains in Fig. 2 and the calibration-related metrics (Brier/ECE) reported in Table 1.

Across tested weighting exponents ($\gamma \in [0.3, 0.7]$), performance consistently peaked at $\gamma = 0.5$, suggesting that moderate concentration offers the best balance between representativeness and stability.

4.7 Limitations and Failure Modes

Shapley values are estimated from an inner train/validation split and approximated via Monte Carlo permutations. When the validation split is very small or class imbalance is extreme, the utility estimates can be noisy and the induced ordering may vary across runs, which can lead to near-uniform weights or overly concentrated mass (low effective sample size) in Shapley Weighting. We mitigate this sensitivity using ordinal mapping (rank), clipping and normalization, capped computation budgets with early stopping, and monitoring effective sample size (ESS). Nevertheless, stress tests under more extreme imbalance, smaller validation budgets, and stronger distribution shifts remain important future work. We provide a validation-aligned ERM interpretation (Sect. 3.1), but we do not yet establish formal convergence or generalization guarantees under the induced contribution-weighted measure. Deriving such guarantees (e.g., stability- or PAC-style bounds under contribution-weighted learning) is an important direction for future work. In addition, SW is computed once per outer fold as a fixed preprocessing step; extending it to adaptive or iterative reweighting during training may further improve robustness under stronger shifts.

5 Conclusion

This work presented *Shapley Weighting*, a contribution-aware cohort refinement algorithm that replaces discrete filtering with continuous, Shapley-guided sample weighting. Comprehensive experiments across four large-scale MIMIC-IV cohorts (AKI, COPD, Sepsis, and HF), with external validation on eICU and MIMIC-III, demonstrate that Shapley Weighting achieves AUCs comparable to Shapley Filtering while improving reliability (calibration and cross-seed stability) and yielding consistent gains in F1/Brier.

Cohort compactness metrics (Silhouette, DBI, and CQI) under SW remain non-inferior and often slightly better, with full (100%) data retention. Taken together, cohort geometry signals captured by Sil/DBI/CQI provide an interpretable view that is consistent with the observed improvements in calibration and cross-seed stability, while retaining the full training cohort. Together, these findings reinforce the contributions introduced in this paper, including the proposed weighting framework, theoretical connection to regularized empirical risk minimization, comprehensive multi-cohort evaluation, and cohort-level visualization of refinement effects.

In our future work, we will extend Shapley Weighting to deep and multimodal architectures, as well as continual and federated learning scenarios where data heterogeneity is inherent. We will also evaluate SW on non-healthcare benchmarks to clarify its generality beyond clinical prediction. We also plan to integrate dynamic weighting into end-to-end optimization pipelines and explore its interpretability for clinical decision support. Ultimately, bridging theoretical notions of data value with empirical reliability provides a foundation for developing adaptive, interpretable, and generalizable learning systems.

Acknowledgments. We gratefully acknowledge support from the National Science Foundation (#2322109, #2346609, #2333726), the Department of Defense Office of Naval Research (#N00014-23-1-2396), and Cincinnati Children's Hospital Medical Center for their support and funding for this project.

References

1. Bharti, S., Hashimoto, T., Kim, M.P., Reingold, O.: Multiaccuracy and multicalibration via proxy groups. In: Proceedings of the 42nd International Conference on Machine Learning (ICML) (2025)
2. Breiman, L.: Random forests. Mach. Learn. **45**(1), 5–32 (2001)
3. Chen, T., Guestrin, C.: Xgboost: a scalable tree boosting system. In: KDD (2016)
4. Cox, D.R.: The regression analysis of binary sequences. J. Roy. Stat. Soc.: Ser. B (Methodol.) **20**(2), 215–242 (1958)
5. Davies, D.L., Bouldin, D.W.: A cluster separation measure. IEEE Trans. Pattern Anal. Mach. Intell. (1979)
6. Davis, J., Goadrich, M.: The relationship between precision-recall and roc curves. In: Proceedings of the 23rd International Conference on Machine Learning (ICML), pp. 233–240. ACM (2006). https://doi.org/10.1145/1143844.1143874
7. Freund, Y., Schapire, R.E.: A decision-theoretic generalization of on-line learning and an application to boosting. J. Comput. Syst. Sci. **55**(1), 119–139 (1997)
8. Ghorbani, A., Zou, J.: Data shapley: equitable valuation of data for machine learning. In: International Conference on Machine Learning, pp. 2242–2251. PMLR (2019)
9. Goldberger, A.L., et al.: Physiobank, physiotoolkit, and physionet: Components of a new research resource for complex physiologic signals. Circulation **101**(23), e215–e220 (2000). https://physionet.org/, rRID:SCR_007345
10. Guo, C., Pleiss, G., Sun, Y., Weinberger, K.Q.: On calibration of modern neural networks. In: Proceedings of the 34th International Conference on Machine Learning (ICML), pp. 1321–1330. PMLR (2017)
11. Jiang, L., Huang, D.Z., Leung, T., Li, L.J., Fei-Fei, L.: Implicit gradient regularization. In: Advances in Neural Information Processing Systems (NeurIPS), vol. 33, pp. 21274–21284 (2020)
12. Jiang, L., Zhou, Z., Leung, T., Li, L.J., Fei-Fei, L.: Mentornet: learning data-driven curriculum for very deep neural networks on corrupted labels. In: Proceedings of the 35th International Conference on Machine Learning (ICML), pp. 2304–2313. PMLR (2018)

13. Johnson, A., et al.: Mimic-iv (version 3.1) (2024). https://doi.org/10.13026/kpb9-mt58, rRID:SCR_007345
14. Johnson, A.E.W., Bulgarelli, L., Shen, L.W., et al.: Mimic-iv, a freely accessible electronic health record dataset. Sci. Data **10**(1), 1 (2023). https://doi.org/10.1038/s41597-022-01899-x
15. Johnson, A.E.W., Pollard, T.J., Mark, R.G.: Mimic-iii clinical database (version 1.4). PhysioNet (2016). https://doi.org/10.13026/C2XW26, rRID:SCR_007345, credentialed access
16. Johnson, A.E.W., et al.: MIMIC-III, a freely accessible critical care database. Sci. Data **3**, 160035 (2016). https://doi.org/10.1038/sdata.2016.35
17. Kwon, Y., Zou, J.: Efficient computation and analysis of distributional shapley values. In: Proceedings of the International Conference on Artificial Intelligence and Statistics (AISTATS) (2021)
18. Kwon, Y., Zou, J.: Efficient computation of data shapley values for machine learning datasets. In: AAAI (2021)
19. Naeini, M.P., Cooper, G.F., Hauskrecht, M.: Obtaining well calibrated probabilities using Bayesian binning. In: AAAI Conference on Artificial Intelligence (2015)
20. Pollard, T.J., Johnson, A.E.W., Raffa, J., Celi, L.A., Badawi, O., Mark, R.G.: eicu collaborative research database (version 2.0) (2019). https://doi.org/10.13026/C2WM1R, rRID:SCR_007345, credentialed access
21. Pollard, T.J., Johnson, A.E.W., Raffa, J.D., Celi, L.A., Mark, R.G., Badawi, O.: The EICU collaborative research database, a freely available multi-center database for critical care research. Sci. Data **5**, 180178 (2018). https://doi.org/10.1038/sdata.2018.178
22. Ren, M., Zeng, W., Yang, B., Urtasun, R.: Learning to reweight examples for robust deep learning. In: Proceedings of the 35th International Conference on Machine Learning (ICML), pp. 4334–4343. PMLR (2018)
23. Rousseeuw, P.J.: Silhouettes: a graphical aid to the interpretation and validation of cluster analysis. J. Comput. Appl. Math. **20**, 53–65 (1987)
24. Rumelhart, D.E., Hinton, G.E., Williams, R.J.: Learning representations by back-propagating errors. Nature **323**(6088), 533–536 (1986). https://doi.org/10.1038/323533a0
25. Sagawa, S., Koh, P.W., Hashimoto, T.B., Liang, P.S.: Distributionally robust neural networks for group shifts: on the importance of regularization for worst-case generalization. In: International Conference on Learning Representations (2020)
26. Toneva, M., Sordoni, A., Le, R., Trischler, A., Bengio, Y., Gordon, G.: An empirical study of example forgetting during deep neural network learning. In: International Conference on Learning Representations (ICLR) (2018)
27. Wang, F., et al.: Evaluate then cooperate: shapley-based view cooperation enhancement for multi-view clustering. In: Advances in Neural Information Processing Systems (2024)
28. Zadrozny, B., Elkan, C.: Transforming classifier scores into accurate multiclass probability estimates. In: Proceedings of the Eighth ACM SIGKDD International Conference on Knowledge Discovery and Data Mining, pp. 694–699 (2002)
29. Zhao, Z., Liu, H.: Causality-based feature selection: methods and applications. IEEE Trans. Neural Networks Learn. Syst. (2020)
30. Zheng, Y., Zhang, M., Liu, Q., Zhan, J.: Exploiting negative samples: a catalyst for cohort discovery in healthcare analytics. In: Proceedings of the 41st International Conference on Machine Learning (ICML). PMLR (2024)

Mixing It Up: Exploring Mixer Networks for Irregular Multivariate Time Series Forecasting

Christian Klötergens[1,2](✉), Tim Dernedde[1], Lars Schmidt-Thieme[1,2], and Vijaya Krishna Yalavarthi[1,2]

[1] Institute of Computer Science, University of Hildesheim, Hildesheim, Germany
{dernedde,schmidt-thieme,yalavarthi}@ismll.de
[2] VWFS Data Analytics Research Center (VWFS-DARC), Hildesheim, Germany
kloetergens@ismll.de

Abstract. Forecasting irregularly sampled multivariate time series with missing values (IMTS) is a fundamental challenge in domains such as healthcare, climate science, and biology. While recent advances in vision and time series forecasting have shown that lightweight MLP-based architectures (e.g., MLP-Mixer, TSMixer) can rival attention-based models in both accuracy and efficiency, their applicability to irregular and sparse time series remains unexplored. In this paper, we propose **IMTS-Mixer**, a novel architecture that adapts the principles of Mixer models to the IMTS setting. IMTS-Mixer introduces two key components: (1) **ISCAM**, a channel-wise encoder that transforms irregular observations into fixed-size vectors using simple MLPs, and (2) **ConTP**, a continuous time decoder that supports forecasting at arbitrary time points. In our experiments on established benchmark datasets we show that our model achieves state-of-the-art performance in both forecasting accuracy and inference time, while using fewer parameters compared to baselines.

Keywords: Irregular Time Series · Forecasting · Missing Values

1 Introduction

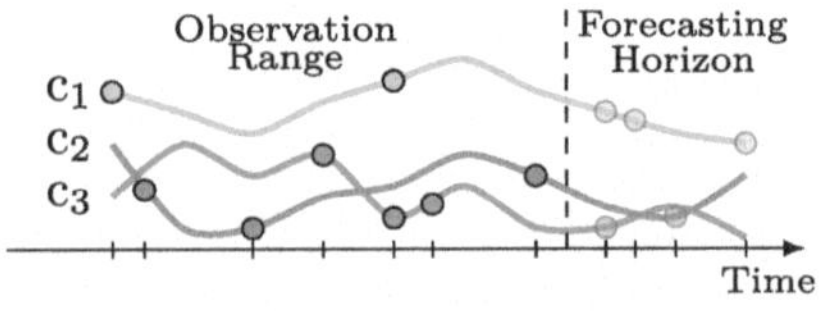

Fig. 1. Example of an IMTS Forecasting task. The observations and forecasting targets are irregularly spaced.

Time series forecasting is a critical task across various domains. While a significant body of research has focused on forecasting regularly sampled, fully observed multivariate time series, many real-world applications, such as healthcare, economics, astronomy, and climate, deal with time series data that are *irregularly* sampled, with observations missing across different channels and timestamps. When such data are aligned to a global timeline, the result is

R. C.-W. Wong et al. (Eds.): PAKDD 2026, LNAI 16617, pp. 152–164, 2027.
https://doi.org/10.1007/978-981-92-1926-1_13

a highly sparse and uneven multivariate structure, as illustrated in Fig. 1. We refer to such data as **irregularly sampled multivariate time series with missing values (IMTS)**. Traditional approaches to modeling IMTS have relied on Neural-ODE frameworks, where the time series is modeled as the solution to an ordinary differential equation (ODE) with a neural network-defined vector field [5,17,18]. While powerful in principle, these models tend to be computationally expensive due to the sequential nature of ODE solvers, and they lack a systematic way to handle missing values. Recently, attention-based models have emerged as a more efficient and accurate alternative, achieving competitive performance on IMTS forecasting tasks [12,26,32]. These models typically transform irregular channel-wise observations into fixed-size representations and apply attention mechanisms to capture inter- and intra-channel dependencies. However, such models are often resource-intensive, requiring a large number of parameters and high memory requirements.

A recent work in computer vision has demonstrated that carefully arranged MLP-based models can rival or even surpass attention-based models [21]. This insight has also been applied to forecasting tasks with regularly sampled time series [4,8]. However, this line of research has not yet been extended to irregularly sampled time series with missing values. In this paper, we introduce **IMTS-Mixer**, a novel architecture for forecasting with IMTS that combines the simplicity of MLP-based designs with specialized modules to address irregular sampling and forecasting at arbitrary time points. First, we propose the **I**rregularly **S**ampled **C**hannel **A**ggregation **M**odule (ISCAM), a lightweight encoder that maps each irregular channel into a fixed-size representation using simple MLPs. These embeddings are then concatenated and processed by an MLP-Mixer-style architecture to learn inter- and intra-channel interactions. Second, to support continuous-time forecasting, we introduce the **Con**tinuous **T**emporal **P**rojection (**ConTP**) module, a decoder that takes the mixer output, a continuous-valued target timestamp, and a channel identifier to generate a prediction. In an extensive comparison, we evaluate IMTS-Mixer on four real-world datasets from various domains. We observe that IMTS-Mixer establishes a new state-of-the-art in terms of forecasting accuracy on three out of four datasets. Our contributions are summarized as follows[1]:

1. We propose **IMTS-Mixer**, a novel MLP-based architecture tailored for irregularly sampled multivariate time series with missing values (IMTS), combining efficient channel aggregation and continuous-time prediction.
2. We introduce **ISCAM**, a simple and effective channel-wise encoder that maps irregularly observed channels to fixed-size representations, enabling MLP processing.
3. We develop a lightweight temporal projection module (**ConTP**) that maps a fixed-size representation of an input channel to future IMTS predictions.

[1] The code is available here: https://github.com/kloetergensc/IMTS-Mixer/.

2 Related Work

2.1 Regular Multivariate Forecasting

The Regular Multivariate Time Series forecasting literature recently focused on transformer-based [22] architectures [13,16,25,35,36]. However, it was shown that a simple model based on linear layers (DLinear [30]) can be competitive and partially outperform some of the more complex transformer architectures. Additionally, mixer architectures have been adapted from the computer vision domain [21] to time series [4,8]. These models exclusively rely on fully-connected networks that are alternately applied along the channel and time dimension and achieve state-of-the-art results.

2.2 IMTS Forecasting

Initially, researchers relied on Neural ODE-based [3] approaches to model irregular time series [1,5,17,18]. ODEs are the prevalent framework in science and engineering to model how systems evolve over time in a continuous manner. However, using neural networks to represent ODE systems has proven to be less effective than other IMTS modeling approaches and also incurs relatively long inference times [26,32].

Graph Transformers for IMTS Forecasting. Apart from the ODE-based approaches the Transformable Patch Graph Neural Network (tPatchGNN) [32] applies a patching mechanism to each channel. The patches are then processed with a Transformer and serve as input for a Graph Neural Network (GNN) that models inter-channel dependencies. Additionally, we want to highlight Graphs for Forecasting Irregular Multivariate Time Series (GraFITi) [26]. Here, the IMTS is represented with a graph in which channels and time steps are nodes and observed values are stored in the edges between the corresponding time and channel nodes. Forecasts are made by predicting the edge values of query-time nodes with graph attention layers. While this approach provides state-of-the-art performance, it also comes with major drawbacks that relate to the graph structure itself. GraFITi relies on time nodes that are connected to multiple channel nodes, corresponding to observation steps that observe more than one channel. If only one channel is observed at a time, the resulting graph is disconnected, rendering GraFITi incapable of modeling inter-channel interactions. Another problem of GraFITi lies in the fact that the query nodes are indirectly connected and hence influence each other. This entails that predictions will change depending on what *other* queries we give to the model.

TimeCHEAT [12] transforms an IMTS into regularly observed patches using a GraFITi-based encoder. These patches are then further processed by a transformer and a linear decoder to obtain the final predictions.

3 Mixer Networks

MLP-Mixer. The MLP-Mixer [21] was originally proposed as a simple and efficient alternative to convolutional neural networks (CNNs) and Vision Transformers (ViTs) for image classification tasks. In this architecture, a 2D image ($\in \mathbb{R}^{W \times H}$, where W, H are width and height) is divided into P non-overlapping patches, which are flattened and projected into vectors of length C, resulting in an input representation $X \in \mathbb{R}^{P \times C}$.

The core of the MLP-Mixer consists of a stack of mixer layers, each containing two separate MLP blocks:

- a **token-mixing MLP** $\text{MLP}_P : \mathbb{R}^P \to \mathbb{R}^P$ operating across patches (rows of X),
- a **channel-mixing MLP** $\text{MLP}_C : \mathbb{R}^C \to \mathbb{R}^C$ operating across channels (columns of X).

Each MLP block is preceded by layer normalization and followed by a residual connection. Formally, given input $X \in \mathbb{R}^{P \times C}$, the output of a single mixer layer is computed as:

$$\begin{aligned} U_{*,c} &= X_{*,c} + \text{LayerNorm}\left(\text{MLP}_C(X_{*,c})\right), \quad c = 1, \dots, C \\ Z_{p,*} &= U_{p,*} + \text{LayerNorm}\left(\text{MLP}_P(U_{p,*})\right), \quad p = 1, \dots, P \end{aligned}$$

Here, $X_{*,c}$ denotes the c-th column (channel vector), and $X_{p,*}$ denotes the p-th row (patch vector).

Despite its simplicity and lack of attention mechanisms, MLP-Mixer has demonstrated competitive performance, often outperforming more complex models such as Vision Transformers [7] on various image classification benchmarks.

TSMixer. Motivated by the success of MLP-Mixer in vision, [4] proposed *TSMixer*, an adaptation of the Mixer architecture for regular multivariate time series forecasting. The goal is to predict the next Q time steps $Y \in \mathbb{R}^{Q \times C}$ from a past window of T time steps $X \in \mathbb{R}^{T \times C}$, where C denotes the number of variables (channels). TSMixer applies a stack of Mixer layers to the input X, where:

- the **temporal mixer** (analogous to token-mixing in images) mixes information across time steps: $\text{MLP}_T : \mathbb{R}^T \to \mathbb{R}^T$,
- the **channel mixer** operates across variables: $\text{MLP}_C : \mathbb{R}^C \to \mathbb{R}^C$.

Similar to MLP-Mixer, these mixers are applied alternately with residual connections and layer normalization. After the stack of mixer layers, a final linear projection $\mathbb{R}^T \to \mathbb{R}^Q$ is applied across the temporal axis to produce the forecast.

4 The IMTS Forecasting Problem

We define an *irregularly sampled multivariate time series (IMTS)* as a collection of C unaligned, sparse, and independently sampled univariate time series, one per channel: $X := [X_1, \ldots, X_C] \in \mathcal{X}$, where each channel $X_c \in \text{Seq}(\mathbb{R} \times \mathbb{R})$ is a sequence of observation tuples $X_c := ((t_{c,i}, v_{c,i}))_{i=1}^{N_c}$. Here, $t_{c,i} \in \mathbb{R}$ refers to the timestamp of the i-th observation in channel c and $v_{c,i} \in \mathbb{R}$ is the respective observed value. Channels may be observed at different timestamps and with different sequence lengths N_c, resulting in irregular and sparse structure when aligned over a global timeline.

Forecasting Query. Analogous to the IMTS definition, we define a *forecasting query* as a collection of per-channel timepoints at which future values should be predicted: $Q := [Q_1, \ldots, Q_C] \in \mathcal{Q}$, where $Q_c\,(q_{c,i})_{i=1}^{K_c} \in \text{Seq}(\mathbb{R})$. Each $q_{c,i}$ specifies a future timestamp for which a prediction is required for channel c. The corresponding **forecasting answer** is given by: $Y = [Y_1, \ldots, Y_C] \in \mathcal{Y}$, where $Y_c = (y_{c,i})_{i=1}^{K_c} \in \text{Seq}(\mathbb{R})$, ensuring $|Q_c| = |Y_c| = K_c$ for each channel c.

Problem 1. **IMTS Forecasting Problem.** Given a training dataset of M triples: $\{(X^{(m)}, Q^{(m)}, Y^{(m)})\}_{m=1}^{M}$ drawn from an unknown distribution ρ over $\mathcal{X} \times \mathcal{Q} \times \mathcal{Y}$, and a loss function $\ell : \mathcal{Y} \times \mathcal{Y} \to \mathbb{R}$ (e.g., mean squared error), the goal is to learn a model: $\hat{Y} : \mathcal{X} \times \mathcal{Q} \to \mathcal{Y}$ that minimizes the expected loss:

$$\mathcal{L}(\hat{Y}; \rho) := \mathbb{E}_{(X,Q,Y)\sim\rho}\left[\ell(Y, \hat{Y}(X, Q))\right] \tag{1}$$

5 IMTS-Mixer

Each IMTS consists of C channels, where the number of observations N_c for each channel c may vary, both within a single IMTS and across different samples. This irregularity makes it challenging to directly apply standard neural architectures, particularly MLP-Mixers, which require fixed-size input representations.

To address this, we propose the **Irregularly Sampled Channel Aggregation Module (ISCAM)**, which encodes each variable-length channel X_c into a fixed-dimensional vector $Z_c \in \mathbb{R}^D$, enabling uniform downstream processing using MLP-Mixer blocks.

5.1 Irregularly Sampled Channel Aggregation Module

Let a single channel X_c represent a sequence of N_c observations. Our goal is to transform this irregular sequence into a fixed-size embedding $Z_c \in \mathbb{R}^D$. For clarity, we drop the channel subscript c and denote the observations as (t_i, v_i).

Observation-Tuple Embedding. Each observation tuple (t_i, v_i) is embedded using a shared MLP $f_{\text{OTE}} : \mathbb{R}^2 \to \mathbb{R}^D$, resulting in:

$$H = [h_1, \ldots, h_{N_c}] \in \mathbb{R}^{N_c \times D}, \quad \text{where } h_i = f_{\text{OTE}}([v_i, t_i])$$

Weighted Aggregation. To compute an importance score for each observation, we apply a second shared MLP $f_{\text{WA}} : \mathbb{R}^2 \to \mathbb{R}^D$:

$$A = [a_1, \ldots, a_{N_c}] \in \mathbb{R}^{N_c \times D}, \quad \text{where } a_i = f_{\text{WA}}([v_i, t_i])$$

Unlike standard attention mechanisms which compute a scalar weight per observation, we assign a separate weight to each embedding feature, similar to multi-head attention, but without cross-token interactions.

To handle the variable length N_c across samples and ensure scale invariance, we apply softmax normalization along the columns d:

$$\text{softmax} : \mathbb{R}^{N_c} \to \mathbb{R}^{N_c}, \quad \text{so that } \sum_{i=1}^{N_c} \text{softmax}(a_{i,d}) = 1$$

Let $A_{:,d} = (a_{1,d}, \ldots, a_{N_c,d})$ and $H_{:,d} = (h_{1,d}, \ldots, h_{N_c,d})$ denote the d-th column across the N_c elements of A and H, respectively. The final channel embedding is then computed as:

$$Z_c = \left[\sum_{i=1}^{N_c} \text{softmax}(A_{:,d})_i \cdot H_{:,d} \right]_{d=1}^{D} \in \mathbb{R}^D \tag{2}$$

This yields a fixed-size vector per channel, where each dimension is an importance-weighted average over time. While one can have channel-specific parameters in f_{OTE} and f_{WA} we allow to share these weights among channels.

Channel Bias. Since the embedding MLPs are shared across all channels, global channel-specific information may be lost. To address this, we introduce a *channel bias* vector $b_c \in \mathbb{R}^D$ for each channel c, composed of learnable parameters. The final channel encoding is computed as: $Z_c^+ = Z_c + b_c \in \mathbb{R}^D$. This allows the model to retain per-channel identity and compensate for missing patterns or context. In the case where a channel c is missing (i.e., X_c is empty), we define $Z_c := 0$ so that the output $Z_c^+ = b_c$ contains only the bias information.

Comparison with Existing Architectures. Several prior models such as SeFT [9], Tripletformer [27], and GraFITi [26] use attention-based mechanisms over IMTS observations, where the aggregation is performed via a softmax-weighted sum of encoded tuples. These methods compute weights through the scaled dot-product of learned queries and keys, following the standard attention framework [22].

In contrast, ISCAM bypasses query-key interactions entirely by modeling importance weights directly through a learned MLP applied to each observation tuple. This results in a simpler and more lightweight design, while still enabling dimension-specific weighting through softmax normalization.

TTCN [32,33] also employs MLP-based aggregation over irregular time series. However, it introduces a more complex mechanism by using separate MLPs (called filters) for each embedding dimension d. Moreover, TTCN lacks a dedicated channel bias component, which limits its ability to encode global per-channel information independent of input observations.

5.2 Mixer Blocks

Similar to MLP-Mixer and TSMixer, we employ L mixer blocks, each operating over the channel and feature dimensions. A single mixer block at layer l updates the representation $Z^{(l-1)} \in \mathbb{R}^{C \times D}$ as follows:

$$
\begin{aligned}
Z'^{(l)} &= Z^{(l-1)} + \mathrm{ReLU}\left(\mathrm{Linear}^{(l)}_{\mathrm{CHAN}}\left(\mathrm{RMS}(Z^{(l-1)^{\top}})\right)\right)^{\top} \\
Z^{(l)} &= Z^{(l-1)} + Z'^{(l)} + \mathrm{ReLU}\left(\mathrm{Linear}^{(l)}_{\mathrm{DIM}}\left(\mathrm{RMS}(Z'^{(l)})\right)\right)
\end{aligned}
\tag{3}
$$

Here, $\mathrm{Linear}^{(l)}_{\mathrm{CHAN}}$ operates along the channel dimension (i.e., across C channels), $\mathrm{Linear}^{(l)}_{\mathrm{DIM}}$ operates along the feature dimension (D), RMS denotes RMSNorm [31], and ReLU is the element-wise nonlinearity.

Compared to MLP-Mixer and TSMixer described in Sect. 3, we introduce two modifications to adapt to the irregular multivariate forecasting setting:

1. **Flexible Output Dimension:** We allow the output of the final mixer layer to have a configurable feature dimension D_{OUT}, i.e., $Z^{(L)} \in \mathbb{R}^{C \times D_{\mathrm{OUT}}}$. This makes it possible to match the projection to varying numbers of queries per channel. All intermediate layers maintain a fixed hidden size D.
2. **RMSNorm Instead of LayerNorm:** We replace LayerNorm with RMSNorm [31], which has been shown to yield faster convergence while maintaining predictive performance.

5.3 Continuous Temporal Projection

TSMixer utilizes a linear layer to project the encoded representation of each channel to forecasts on a predefined regular grid of query steps [4]. This design, however, is incompatible with IMTS, where query times are not fixed but vary continuously across instances.

To address this, IMTS-Mixer introduces a **Continuous Temporal Projection (ConTP)**, which allows the model to project the hidden state of each channel to any given point in time. Instead of learning linear layers tied to predetermined query steps, ConTP learns a function $f_{\mathrm{QU}} : \mathbb{R} \to \mathbb{R}^{D_{\mathrm{OUT}}}$ that maps scalar query times to the weights of a linear projection dynamically. Formally, the forecast for channel c at query time $q_{c,i}$ is computed as:

$$
\hat{y}_{i,c} = f^{c}_{\mathrm{QU}}(q_{c,i}) \cdot Z^{(L)}_{c} + b^{\mathrm{OUT}}_{c} \in \mathbb{R} \tag{4}
$$

In order to enhance expressiveness, we learn a separate function f^{c}_{QU} for each channel and implement this with a two-layer MLP. Additionally, we learn a query independent output bias $b^{\mathrm{OUT}} \in \mathbb{R}^{C}$. The complete architecture of IMTS-Mixer is illustrated in Fig. 2.

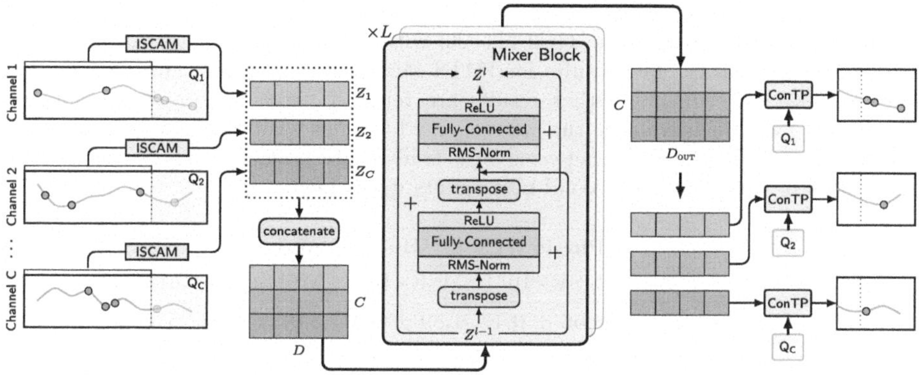

Fig. 2. Overview of IMTS-Mixer's architecture

6 Experiments

We evaluate IMTS-Mixer on four datasets: PhysioNet [20], MIMIC [10], (Human) Activity [23], and USHCN [15]. The baseline models already established in this setup originate from regular multivariate time series forecasting, IMTS classification and IMTS forecasting [32]. DLinear [30], TimesNet [24], PatchTST [16] and Crossformer [34] are well known models for regular multivariate forecasting. In a previous work [32] these RMTS forecasting models have been adapted to IMTS forecasting by treating timestamps and missingness indicators as additional input channels. Following this approach, we additionally evaluate TSMixer [4].

GRU-D [2] and mTAND [19] are all models primarily introduced for IMTS classification, which are equipped with a predictor network which inputs hidden IMTS representations and query times. Finally, Latent-ODE [17], Continuous Recurrent Units (CRU) [18], Neural Flow [1], tPatchGNN [32] and GraFITi [26] are models designed for IMTS Forecasting. To these baselines we add our own model and TimeCHEAT, a recently published IMTS forecasting model. For TimeCHEAT, we use the implementations and hyperparameter recommendations as published in the paper introducing the model [12].

To train IMTS-Mixer, we implement the schedule-free AdamW [6,11,14] optimizer with an initial learning rate of 0.01 and use early stopping with patience of 20 epochs along with a batch-size of 32. The hyperparameter tuning is conducted by selecting the best out of 20 randomly sampled configurations in terms of validation MSE. We tune the aggregated-channel dimension $D \in \{64, 128, 256\}$, the output dimension $D_{\text{OUT}} \in \{32, 64, 128\}$, the number of mixer blocks $\in \{1, 2, 3\}$, and the weight decay $\in \{10^{-2}, 10^{-3}, 10^{-4}\}$.

Results. Table 1 reports the forecasting accuracy of IMTS-Mixer compared to the baseline models. IMTS-Mixer provides the most accurate forecasts on PhysioNet, Activity and USHCN. For MIMIC, our model comes in second, closely behind GraFITi. We observe that GraFITi's relative performance increases with the

Table 1. Comparison of different algorithms across four datasets based on Test MSE. We reproduced the results from GraFITi [26] with the hyperparameters from its official GitHub repository. The results for IMTS-Mixer, TSMixer and TimeCHEAT are from our own experiments. Other results are reported from the paper introducing tPatchGNN [32]. Each training run was repeated 5 times with different random seeds and the standard deviation in between these trials is given after the ±. We report the best results in **bold** and the second-best results underlined.

		PhysioNet	MIMIC	Activity	USHCN
		MSE×10^{-3}	MSE×10^{-2}	MSE×10^{-3}	MSE×10^{-1}
RMTS Forc.	TSMixer	8.66 ± 0.47	1.89 ± 0.01	3.01 ± 0.01	5.39 ± 0.04
	DLinear	41.86 ± 0.05	4.90 ± 0.00	4.03 ± 0.01	6.21 ± 0.00
	TimesNet	16.48 ± 0.11	5.88 ± 0.08	3.12 ± 0.01	5.58 ± 0.05
	PatchTST	12.00 ± 0.23	3.78 ± 0.03	4.29 ± 0.14	5.75 ± 0.01
	Crossformer	6.66 ± 0.11	2.65 ± 0.10	4.29 ± 0.20	5.25 ± 0.04
IMTS Class.	mTAND	6.23 ± 0.24	1.85 ± 0.06	3.22 ± 0.07	5.33 ± 0.05
	Latent-ODE	6.05 ± 0.57	1.89 ± 0.19	3.34 ± 0.11	5.62 ± 0.03
IMTS Forc.	Neural Flow	7.20 ± 0.07	1.87 ± 0.05	4.05 ± 0.13	5.35 ± 0.05
	CRU	8.56 ± 0.26	1.97 ± 0.02	6.97 ± 0.78	6.09 ± 0.17
	GraFITi	4.89 ± 0.12	**1.53 ± 0.02**	2.65 ± 0.02	5.17 ± 0.11
	TimeCHEAT	6.18 ± 0.25	1.76 ± 0.01	4.42 ± 0.60	5.70 ± 0.53
	tPatchGNN	4.98 ± 0.08	1.69 ± 0.03	2.66 ± 0.03	5.00 ± 0.04
	IMTS-Mixer	**4.88 ± 0.03**	1.61 ± 0.01	**2.50 ± 0.01**	**4.91 ± 0.05**

number of channels. While it outperforms IMTS-Mixer on MIMIC (102 chan.) and is on par with our model on PhysioNet (37 chan.), it is significantly outperformed by IMTS-Mixer on Activity (12 chan.) and USHCN (5 chan.).

Additionally, we observe that TimeCHEAT does not provide competitive forecasting accuracy despite being the most recent baseline (AAAI 2025). The model is likely struggling, due to its inability to account for different query time steps. This major flaw is less problematic in very short-term forecasting scenarios, as used in the paper that introduced TimeCHEAT [12].

Efficiency Analysis. We conduct our experiments on an NVIDIA 1080Ti with 12 GB of GPU Memory. In Table 2, we compare the inference time and parameter count of recent models to that of IMTS-Mixer. Here, inference time refers to the total time it takes to answer all queries from the test set using a batch size of 32. We observe that IMTS-Mixer's inference time is consistently shorter than the inference time of competing models. Furthermore, it uses the fewest number of parameters on three out of four datasets.

7 Limitations

Theoretically, IMTS-Mixer is limited by its fixed-size channel aggregation, which converts the sequence of observations from a channel into a fixed-sized embedding. For very long sequences, or when typical sequence lengths vary significantly across channels, the fixed-size representation may become a bottleneck or fail to adequately capture the diversity across channels. However, in practice, we do not find this to be an issue. Our model is able to fit all the common benchmark datasets well with varying number of channels and distribution of sequence lengths. Another limitation is that the parameter count in the mixer blocks scales quadratically with the number of channels. We observe that IMTS-Mixer struggles with datasets that contain many channels. IMTS-Mixer is outperformed by GraFITi only on the MIMIC dataset, which has the most channels and is on par with GraFITi on PhysioNet, which has the second-most channels. Furthermore, we find that MIMIC is the only dataset in which IMTS-Mixer does not have the lowest number of parameters, as shown in Table 2. However, on datasets with fewer channels (e.g., Activity, USHCN), our model achieves significantly higher forecasting accuracy than competing methods.

Table 2. Number of parameters (left) and inference time (right) in seconds for each dataset

	PhysioNet		MIMIC		Activity		USHCN	
	#P	t_inf	#P	t_inf	#P	t_inf	#P	t_inf
GraFITi	251k	1.9 s	**255k**	4.0 s	249 k	0.6 s	496 k	2.2 s
tPatchGNN	362 k	2.7 s	363 k	10 s	166 k	1.4 s	167 k	2.5 s
TimeCHEAT	659 k	33 s	755 k	72 s	1262 k	15 s	330 k	63 s
IMTS-Mixer	**207 k**	**0.7 s**	497 k	**2.9 s**	**72 k**	**0.3 s**	**40 k**	**1.4 s**

8 Conclusion and Future Work

In this work we present IMTS-Mixer, a parameter efficient and all MLP-based model for IMTS forecasting. Our architecture incorporates ISCAM, a novel method for aggregating irregularly sampled univariate time series that, despite its simplicity, outperforms existing approaches. Additionally, we generalize linear temporal projection layers to IMTS forecasting targets by introducing ConTP and yield equal or better performance than previously applied solutions. In our experiments, we show that IMTS-Mixer establishes a new state-of-the-art forecasting accuracy on three out of four evaluated datasets, despite its architectural simplicity. We note that our model has difficulty handling time series with a large number of channels, as the parameter count in the fully connected layers increases significantly, which is associated with higher test error. For future work, we plan on expanding our model to the related fields of IMTS classification and interpolation. Furthermore, we will investigate IMTS-Mixer's applicability to probabilistic IMTS forecasting, where it could serve as an encoder of conditional normalizing flows [28,29].

References

1. Biloš, M., Sommer, J., Rangapuram, S.S., Januschowski, T., Günnemann, S.: Neural Flows: efficient Alternative to Neural ODEs. In: NeurIPS (2021)
2. Che, Z., Purushotham, S., Cho, K., Sontag, D., Liu, Y.: Recurrent neural networks for multivariate time series with missing values. Sci. Rep. **8**(1), 6085 (2018). https://doi.org/10.1038/s41598-018-24271-9
3. Chen, R.T.Q., Rubanova, Y., Bettencourt, J., Duvenaud, D.K.: Neural Ordinary Differential Equations. In: NeurIPS (2018)
4. Chen, S.A., Li, C.L., Arik, S.O., Yoder, N.C., Pfister, T.: TSMixer: an all-MLP architecture for time series forecasting. TMLR (2023)
5. De Brouwer, E., Simm, J., Arany, A., Moreau, Y.: GRU-ODE-Bayes: continuous modeling of sporadically-observed time series. In: NeurIPS (2019)
6. Defazio, A., Yang, X.A., Mehta, H., Mishchenko, K., Khaled, A., Cutkosky, A.: The road less scheduled (2024). https://doi.org/10.48550/arXiv.2405.15682
7. Dosovitskiy, A.: An image is worth 16x16 words: transformers for image recognition at scale. In: ICLR (2020)
8. Ekambaram, V., et al: TSMixer: lightweight MLP-mixer model for multivariate time series forecasting. In: KDD (2023)
9. Horn, M., Moor, M., Bock, C., Rieck, B., Borgwardt, K.: Set functions for time series. In: Proceedings of the 37th International Conference on Machine Learning, pp. 4353–4363. PMLR (2020)
10. Johnson, A.E.W., et al.: MIMIC-III, a freely accessible critical care database. Sci. Data **3**(1), 160035 (2016). https://doi.org/10.1038/sdata.2016.35
11. Kingma, D.P., Ba, J.: Adam: a method for stochastic optimization (2017). https://doi.org/10.48550/arXiv.1412.6980
12. Liu, J., Cao, M., Chen, S.: Timecheat: a channel harmony strategy for irregularly sampled multivariate time series analysis. In: Proceedings of the AAAI Conference on Artificial Intelligence, vol. 39, pp. 18861–18869 (2025)
13. Liu, Y., Hu, T., Zhang, H., Wu, H., Wang, S., Ma, L., Long, M.: iTransformer: inverted transformers are effective for time series forecasting. In: The Twelfth International Conference on Learning Representations (2023)
14. Loshchilov, I., Hutter, F.: Decoupled Weight Decay Regularization (2019). https://doi.org/10.48550/arXiv.1711.05101
15. Menne, M.J., Williams, J., Vose, R.S.: U.S. HISTORICAL CLIMATOLOGY NETWORK (USHCN): Daily Temperature, Precipitation and Snow Data. Tech. rep., Environmental System Science Data Infrastructure for a Virtual Ecosystem (ESS-DIVE) (United States) (2006). https://doi.org/10.3334/CDIAC/CLI.NDP070

16. Nie, Y., Nguyen, N.H., Sinthong, P., Kalagnanam, J.: A time series is worth 64 words: long-term forecasting with transformers. In: The Eleventh International Conference on Learning Representations (2022)
17. Rubanova, Y., Chen, R.T.Q., Duvenaud, D.K.: Latent ordinary differential equations for irregularly-sampled time series. In: NeurIPS (2019)
18. Schirmer, M., Eltayeb, M., Lessmann, S., Rudolph, M.: Modeling irregular time series with continuous recurrent units. In: Proceedings of the 39th International Conference on Machine Learning, pp. 19388–19405. PMLR (2022)
19. Shukla, S.N., Marlin, B.: Multi-time attention networks for irregularly sampled time series. In: International Conference on Learning Representations (2020)
20. Silva, I., Moody, G., Scott, D.J., Celi, L.A., Mark, R.G.: Predicting in-hospital mortality of ICU patients: the PhysioNet/computing in cardiology challenge 2012. In: 2012 Computing in Cardiology, pp. 245–248 (2012)
21. Tolstikhin, I.O., et al.: MLP-mixer: an all-MLP architecture for vision. In: NeurIPS (2021)
22. Vaswani, A., et al.: Attention is all you need. In: NeurIPS, vol. 30. Curran Associates, Inc. (2017)
23. Vedrana Vidulin, M.L.: Localization Data for Person Activity (2010). https://doi.org/10.24432/C57G8X
24. Wu, H., Hu, T., Liu, Y., Zhou, H., Wang, J., Long, M.: TimesNet: temporal 2D-variation modeling for general time series analysis. In: The Eleventh International Conference on Learning Representations (2022)
25. Wu, H., Xu, J., Wang, J., Long, M.: Autoformer: decomposition transformers with auto-correlation for long-term series forecasting. In: NeurIPS (2021)
26. Yalavarthi, V.K., et al.: GraFITi: graphs for forecasting irregularly sampled time series. In: Proceedings of the AAAI Conference on Artificial Intelligence (2024). https://doi.org/10.1609/aaai.v38i15.29560
27. Yalavarthi, V.K., et al.: GraFITi: graphs for forecasting irregularly sampled time series. In: Proceedings of the AAAI Conference on Artificial Intelligence (2024). https://doi.org/10.1609/aaai.v38i15.29560
28. Yalavarthi, V.K., Scholz, R., Born, S., Schmidt-Thieme, L.: Probabilistic forecasting of irregularly sampled time series with missing values via conditional normalizing flows. In: Proceedings of the AAAI Conference on Artificial Intelligence, vol. 39, no. 20, pp. 21877–21885 (2025)
29. Yalavarthi, V.K., Scholz, R., Klötergens, C., Madhusudhanan, K., Born, S., Schmidt-Thieme, L.: Reliable probabilistic forecasting of irregular time series through marginalization-consistent flows. In: ICLR (2026)
30. Zeng, A., Chen, M., Zhang, L., Xu, Q.: Are transformers effective for time series forecasting? In: Proceedings of the AAAI Conference on Artificial Intelligence, vol. 37, no. 9, pp. 11121–11128 (2023). https://doi.org/10.1609/aaai.v37i9.26317
31. Zhang, B., Sennrich, R.: Root mean square layer normalization. In: NeurIPS, vol. 32. Curran Associates, Inc. (2019)
32. Zhang, W., Yin, C., Liu, H., Zhou, X., Xiong, H.: Irregular multivariate time series forecasting: a transformable patching graph neural networks approach. In: Forty-First International Conference on Machine Learning (2024)
33. Zhang, W., et al.: Irregular Traffic time series forecasting based on asynchronous spatio-temporal graph convolutional networks. In: KDD, pp. 4302–4313. ACM (2024)
34. Zhang, Y., Yan, J.: Crossformer: transformer utilizing cross-dimension dependency for multivariate time series forecasting. In: The Eleventh International Conference on Learning Representations (2022)

35. Zhou, H., et al.: Informer: beyond efficient transformer for long sequence time-series forecasting. In: Proceedings of the AAAI Conference on Artificial Intelligence, vol. 35, no. 12, pp. 11106–11115 (2021). https://doi.org/10.1609/aaai.v35i12.17325
36. Zhou, T., Ma, Z., Wen, Q., Wang, X., Sun, L., Jin, R.: FEDformer: frequency enhanced decomposed transformer for long-term series forecasting. In: Proceedings of the 39th International Conference on Machine Learning, pp. 27268–27286. PMLR (2022)

Enhancing Limit Order Book Modeling Through Type-Based Representation

Mingyu Yang[1], Guhyuk Chung[2], Chanyeong Kim[1], and Woo Chang Kim[1](✉)

[1] KAIST, Daehak-ro 291, Daejeon 34141, South Korea
{yangmg1216,kim.chanyeong,wkim}@kaist.ac.kr
[2] Line Investment, Bundangnaegok-ro 117, Seongnam 13529, South Korea
guhyuk.chung@linecorp.com

Abstract. This paper introduces a Type-based representation to enhance the expressive power of Limit Order Book (LOB) data by explicitly encoding underlying order-type dynamics. Unlike conventional methods that aggregate volume by price levels, our approach decomposes LOB and trade updates into 12 interpretable order types, offering granular insights into the behavioral intentions driving market movements. To leverage this representation, we design a dual-stream architecture that processes order-type features and LOB state variables separately, capturing both temporal dependencies and type-conditioned interactions. Empirical evaluations on 10 cryptocurrency futures datasets demonstrate that the proposed method consistently outperforms existing benchmarks in both regression and classification tasks. Further experiments confirm the model's robustness and computational efficiency. Finally, attention-based analysis reveals interpretable patterns, highlighting how specific order types contribute to short and long-term price formation.

Keywords: Limit Order Book · Order type · Dual attention · Expressive power · Mid-price prediction · Cryptocurrency

1 Introduction

Analyzing the market movement and predicting the mid-price movement are crucial tasks in financial markets. Especially for High-Frequency Traders, such as market makers, forecasting the market movement several ticks[1] ahead can significantly reduce the risk they take. One of the most impactful and market-responsive datasets for predicting market movements is the Limit Order Book (LOB), which tabulates the desired prices and order quantities of buyers and sellers. Since the LOB is the first to reflect changes in the balance of supply and

[1] A time tick refers to the discrete timestamp associated with the arrival of each individual order. For example, a horizon of 100 time ticks corresponds to the point in time after 100 orders have arrived.

R. C.-W. Wong et al. (Eds.): PAKDD 2026, LNAI 16617, pp. 165–177, 2027.
https://doi.org/10.1007/978-981-92-1926-1_14

demand among market participants, it can be used to identify structural changes in the market in advance.

Predicting market movement using LOB data has been studied through various approaches, ranging from traditional statistical methods [6,19,21] to machine learning techniques [3,5,10,15–18,20]. Notably, studies utilizing machine learning models have demonstrated significant improvements in both market movement classification and regression tasks. Despite these advancements, a common limitation persists: most studies have used simple matrix forms of raw LOB data as input.

Although prior studies have addressed input representations [5,6,18], most literature relies heavily on neural networks to implicitly conduct feature engineering directly from raw LOB data, presuming automatic extraction of meaningful features. While deep learning models demonstrate some capability in automated feature extraction, their effectiveness significantly depends on the input data format [2,14] and parameter configurations [9]. Moreover, since LOB data often comes in Level 1 or 2, it may convey ambiguous or incomplete information to predictive models.

To address these limitations, we propose a Type-based representation for LOB data that focuses on delivering more concrete and explicit information by utilizing trade data alongside LOB data. Previous attempts, such as the one by Cont et al. (2014) [6], tried to generate new features from trade data to provide more information but did not demonstrate any performance improvement over using only LOB data. Unlike these earlier methods, our proposed approach integrates trade and LOB data into a unified and interpretable representation. By categorizing orders based on their type, we provide additional insights into the intentions behind observed changes in LOB data. Moreover, decomposing aggregated order data into type-specific orders provides a means to estimate the underlying aggregated actions, thus recovering some of the information lost in lower-level LOB data. This approach is particularly advantageous for financial instruments such as cryptocurrencies, where Level 2 data is predominantly available.

The main contributions of this paper are as follows:

- We introduce a new representation method based on order types, explicitly addressing the complexity associated with interpreting intentions behind LOB changes and enhancing informational granularity.
- We experimentally validate that the proposed representation can further enhance performance in the mid-price prediction for both regression and classification tasks.
- We propose a tailored deep neural network architecture designed to leverage the structural characteristics of the proposed representation and demonstrate its effectiveness through comparative performance evaluations.

2 Related Works

2.1 LOB Representations

Recent work on mid-price forecasting has proposed a range of LOB input representations to improve predictive performance. Given that the basic components of the LOB are price and volume for each level, the compressed representation [18] lists the price and volume information according to price level ordering. Abergel et al. (2016) [1] employed the volume-based representation which only uses volume information but omits price level details. This keeps the consistency of the information level while it is easy to lose the expressiveness when the order book is sparse.

For better expressive power, some have proposed more engineered representations. Most well-known and widely used ones are Order Flow (OF) and Order Flow Imbalance (OFI) [6]. Unlike previous representations that aimed to deliver raw LOB data straightforwardly, OF and OFI focuses on delivering supply and demand imbalance. OF can be obtained by summing the bid and ask side volume changes generated by all LOB events in certain interval. Subtracting ask side OF from the bid side OF gives OFI. It is a powerful representation regarding price change as it expresses the net pressure pushing the price upward in a numeric form.

Focusing on the robustness of the representation, Market Depth representation [18] was proposed. To avoid inhomogeneity, the bid and ask side quantities within a certain interval are accumulated by level around the reference mid-price. This results in less sensitivity to minor perturbations in the LOB while clearly presents changes in order quantity as if it were an image.

2.2 Mid-Price Prediction

Many have attempted to capture the market dynamics focusing on predicting mid-price in High-Frequency manner. On the immense enhancement in computational power and neural network, these attempts are showing better results. Simple nonlinear regression network can be as good as the ridge regression model with simple snapshot of the LOB [12]. CNN-LSTM model [20] showed overwhelming performance compare to Support Vector Machine (SVM) or other simple neural network models. Recently, Temporal Convolutional Network (TCN) model with Market Depth representation [18] and Transformer-based models [3] are showing state-of-the-art performances.

3 Method

3.1 Input Representation

Order Types. Biais et al. (1995) [4] identified nine distinct order types based on the actions of market participants within the Limit Order Book. Building upon this framework, similar to Eisler et al. (2009) [7], we refine the classification by incorporating the directional changes of the best bid and ask prices as additional conditions. This extension yields a total of twelve distinct order types: six associated with the bid side and six with the ask side.

Specifically, for both the ask and bid sides, orders are categorized into three primary actions: *Limit*, *Market*, and *Cancel*. Each action is further subdivided into two specific conditions based on its impact on the best quote: (1) *Limit* orders either increase the volume at the existing best price or establish a new best price; (2) *Market* orders either partially decrease the volume at the best price or completely remove the entire best amount; and (3) *Cancel* orders similarly either partially decrease or completely remove the volume at the best price.

In the process of reorganizing the LOB and trade data into the sequence of orders, we made an assumption regarding cancellation orders: any excess change in the LOB, after accounting for trade data, is attributed to cancellation orders. Since trade data does not provide information about cancellation orders like Level 3 LOB data does, we had to estimate the volume of canceled orders using the available data. Based on the intuition that cancellation orders have a lesser impact than executed orders [7], we focused on accurately representing the volume of limit and market orders.

Structure of the Type-Based Representation. To interpret event-level behavior without relying on Level 3 data, the proposed Type-based representation is designed to convey key market signals with minimal redundancy. For each order i, the representation comprises six components: order type (o_i) and volume (v_i) to indicate the intent and magnitude of the event; order interarrival time (τ_i) to provide an intuitive measure of order frequency and temporal intensity; and best ask quantity (v_i^a), best bid quantity (v_i^b), and spread (s_i) to capture short-term liquidity conditions relevant to mid-price movements. These components are combined into a single vector, collectively forming a matrix over distinct time intervals. For the time interval $[t - T + 1, t]$, this is structured as in Eq. 1:

$$\begin{aligned} \overrightarrow{r}_{\text{tb}} &= \{o_i, v_i, \tau_i, v_i^a, v_i^b, s_i\}_{i=t-T+1}^{t} \\ o_i, s_i &\in \mathbb{R}_{\geq 0}, \quad v_i, \tau_i, v_i^a, v_i^b \in \mathbb{R} \end{aligned} \tag{1}$$

Compared to compressed or volume-only representations, which often require additional processing to infer volume changes or reconstruct subtle price-moving patterns, our representation provides explicit and interpretable signals, reducing the burden on the model to go through such calculations.

A further advantage is its compact dimensionality. While conventional representations use tens of features per timestep (usually 20–25 levels), the Type-based representation requires only six. This compact structure mitigates the curse of dimensionality and leads to more efficient training, as demonstrated in our empirical experiments.

3.2 Network Design

Inputs like OF or Market depth representation are in shape of images which can leverage the existing CNN-based networks due to their temporal properties among adjacent components. In contrast, the Type-based representation which is a sequential listing of orders may possess different characteristics compared to other representations. To fully leverage the properties of the proposed representation, a new model is required that captures its features differently.

Model Architecture. We propose a novel model architecture specifically designed to capture both temporal dynamics and order type conditioned feature dependencies. An overview of the proposed architecture is illustrated in Fig. 1.

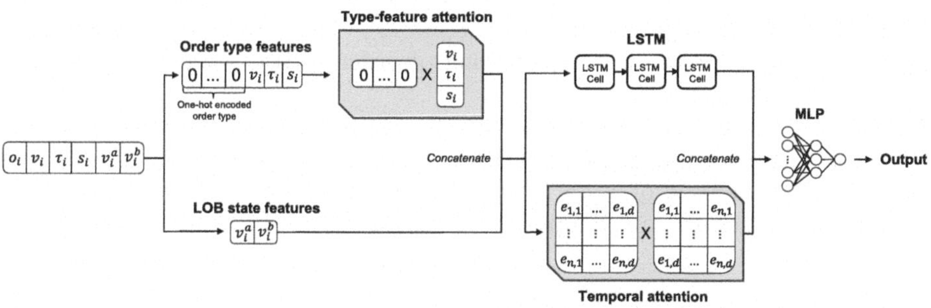

Fig. 1. Overview of the model architecture

The model adopts a standard encoder–decoder structure, with a dual-stream encoder at its encoder stage. The first part of the encoder processes two parallel input streams:

(i) a stream comprising LOB state features, including the best ask and bid quantities v_i^a and v_i^b
(ii) a stream consisting of order type related features, including the order type o_i, interarrival time τ_i, order volume v_i, and spread s_i.

While the LOB state features are directly processed, the order type related stream is passed through a type-feature cross attention layer, in which the order type is one-hot encoded. The attention weights in this layer are computed following a formulation adapted to our model's structure, as shown in Eq. 2, allowing the network to differentially attend to each feature within the influence of order types.

$$\text{attention weights} = Softmax\Big(\frac{\overbrace{(\text{one-hot}(o_i) \cdot W^Q)}^{Q} \cdot \overbrace{([v_i, \tau_i, s_i] \cdot W^K)^T}^{K^T}}{\sqrt{d_k}}\Big) \quad (2)$$

The outputs of the two streams are then concatenated and passed in parallel through two distinct components: an LSTM layer and a temporal attention layer. The LSTM is employed to model relatively short-term, continuous dependencies, whereas the temporal attention mechanism is utilized to capture irregular, long-range dependencies in the data [8]. To effectively leverage the interarrival time τ_i, we incorporate a relative positional encoding scheme [13] into the attention mechanism, as defined in Eq. 3.

$$e_{i,j} = \frac{x_i W^Q (x_j W^K)^T + x_i W^Q (a_{i,j}^K)^T}{\sqrt{d_k}} \tag{3}$$

In this formulation, the relative position value $a_{i,j}^K$ represents the cumulative interarrival time between the elements in j^{th} and i^{th} row of the key matrix K. Unlike standard self-attention, the value $a_{i,j}^K$ is added element-wise to the key matrix prior to computing the attention score $e_{i,j}$. This modification enables the model to account for the irregular timing of order arrivals, which is critical in high-frequency financial data.

Following the parallel processing of temporal dynamics, the outputs of the LSTM and attention layers are concatenated and passed through the decoder. The decoder, composed of a stack of multi-layer perceptrons (MLPs), operates across both the feature and temporal dimensions to produce the final output.

4 Experiment and Results

Mid-price prediction encompasses two primary tasks: regression, which estimates the exact magnitude of future price changes, and classification, which determines whether the price will increase, decrease, or remain stable. For a fair and consistent comparison across different representation–model combinations, all experiments were repeated multiple times on different time intervals, and the averaged values were reported. Each model was trained on 3 days of data, validated on the subsequent 12 h, and tested on the following 12 h.

4.1 Experiment Settings

Dataset. We employed a cryptocurrency dataset due to its high accessibility and abundance of high-frequency trading data. Specifically, we utilized data from Binance, the world's largest cryptocurrency exchange by trading volume, focusing on the futures market, which exhibits higher liquidity and trading activity than the spot market [11].

10 cryptocurrency trading pairs were selected based on their trading volume rankings: BTC/USDT, ETH/USDT, BCH/USDT, XRP/USDT, EOS/USDT, LINK/USDT, LTC/USDT, TRX/USDT, ETC/USDT, and XLM/USDT. The dataset spans October 1–10, 2024. All data were sourced from Tardis.dev.

Input Shape. In the mid-price prediction task, input sequences are typically constructed using a fixed-length window of LOB representations. In this study, we adopt a window size of 100 LOB states, resulting in input tensors of shape $100 \times$ representation dimension.

Unlike conventional representations, the proposed Type-based representation requires decomposing each LOB state into a sequence of individual order events. This decomposition introduces variability in sequence length, making it difficult to align with a fixed-size input format.

To address this issue, we impose a maximum sequence length of 300 order events per sample. Events older than this bound are truncated, and if fewer than 300 events are present within the 100 LOB states, the remaining positions are padded with zero vectors to ensure consistent input dimensionality.

Mid-Price. We use normalized mid-price change $m(t,k) = \frac{\bar{p}(t,k)-p(t)}{p(t)}$ as our target variable, where $p(t)$ and $\bar{p}(t,k)$ denotes the mid-price and averaged mid-price over k ticks. In this study, four values of k are considered: 5, 10, 50, and 100.

For the classification task, we discretize the target into three states, increase, stable, and decrease, based on a threshold of 0.0002 applied to the value of $m(t,k)$.

Benchmarks. We benchmark its efficacy against two established representations: Order Flow (OF) and Market Depth. Notably, compressed and volume-based representations are excluded from this comparison, as prior studies have demonstrated the superior performance of OF and Market Depth in their respective domains [10,18]. The OF and Type-based representations are evaluated using the CNN-LSTM architecture while the Market Depth representation employs the TCN model from prior work, which remains state-of-the-art for this input type. To quantify the benefits of representation-aware modeling, we further analyze the performance of the hybrid architecture.

Hyperparameter Settings. We train all models using the Adam optimizer with a learning rate of 1e-3 on an RTX 4090 GPU. The batch size is set to 256 for TCN and 1024 for all other models due to the high dimensionality of the Market-depth representation. All experiments are run for 50 epochs with early stopping based on validation loss. The CNN-LSTM and Type-based models use 64 hidden units, while the Dual-stream model uses a 256 dimensional hidden size, 8 attention heads, and 4 encoder layers. The TCN model uses 64 channels.

4.2 Results

Regression Task. Table 1 presents the summarized results of the regression task, comparing four model–representation configurations across multiple prediction horizons. The results demonstrate a consistent pattern: the Type-based representation combined with the Dual-stream model outperforms all other configurations at every prediction horizon. This indicates the effectiveness of the proposed representation in capturing both short and long-term dynamics of price movements.

Notably, prediction performance is generally lower at shorter horizons due to the reduced signal-to-noise ratio inherent in high frequency data. Nevertheless, the proposed Type-based representation enables significant gains even in these difficult settings by explicitly encoding the intent and structure of individual orders. Furthermore, the consistent performance across different model types underscores that the performance gains are largely driven by the representation itself, rather than by specific model architectures.

Table 1. R-squared score for the regression task

Model \ k	k=5	k=10	k=50	k=100
OF/CNN-LSTM	0.045	0.077	0.211	0.335
Market-depth/TCN	0.046	0.079	0.257	0.361
Type-based/CNN-LSTM	0.170	0.200	0.306	0.343
Type-based/Dual-stream	**0.170**	**0.203**	**0.333**	**0.406**

Classification Task. Table 2 shows the averaged f1-score and accuracy over three classes. The dual-stream model was not involved in classification experiment as it was designed for the regression task to help model analysis. The results demonstrate that the proposed Type-based representation substantially outperforms both the OF/CNN-LSTM and Market-depth/TCN baselines at every horizon.

Unlike the regression task, classification performance is highly sensitive to class imbalance. Although we applied inverse-frequency weighting to the loss function, discrepancies in class distributions can still affect model comparisons, particularly between OF/CNN-LSTM and Market-depth/TCN. Nonetheless, the direct comparison between OF/CNN-LSTM and Type-based/CNN-LSTM, using the same backbone architecture, clearly demonstrates the superior expressive power of the Type-based representation across all prediction horizons.

Table 2. Summarized result for the classification task

Model \ k		k=5	k=10	k=50	k=100
OF/CNN-LSTM	F1-score	0.219	0.224	0.249	0.308
	Accuracy	0.352	0.352	0.357	0.421
Market-depth/TCN	F1-score	0.158	0.149	0.173	0.184
	Accuracy	0.335	0.334	0.332	0.335
Type-based/CNN-LSTM	F1-score	**0.255**	**0.274**	**0.334**	**0.349**
	Accuracy	**0.567**	**0.555**	**0.481**	**0.427**

4.3 Attention Analysis

Temporal Attention. Figure 2 represents the temporal attention derived from each prediction horizons.

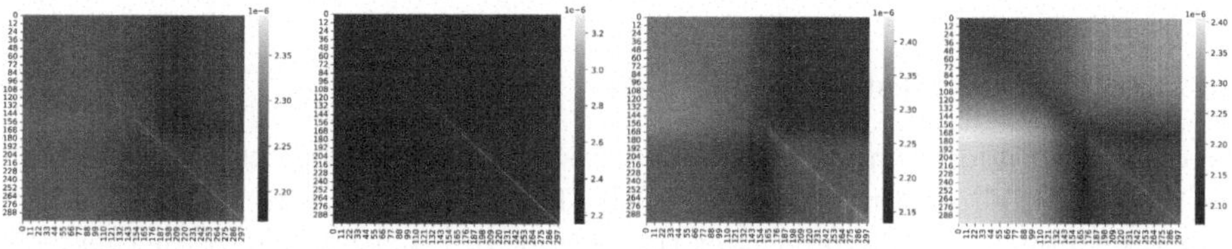

(a) $k = 5$ (b) $k = 10$ (c) $k = 50$ (d) $k = 100$

Fig. 2. Averaged temporal attention score matrices across 10 symbols

For short horizons ($k = 5, 10$), the model concentrates almost entirely on very recent events. While both horizon 5 and 10 exhibit no significant patterns in mid and long-range regions, horizon 10 shows even sharper focus than horizon 5, reflecting the higher noise level in ultra-short term movements which forces the model to search over a broader range.

Longer horizons ($k = 50, 100$) show attention maps adopt a mixture of short-term and long-term structure. Both horizons highlight recent events while also focusing on distant regions. At $k = 100$, weakened diagonal self-attention and strengthened cross-region attention indicate that the model relies more on broader structural patterns.

Type-Feature Attention. Figure 3 presents the averaged type-feature attention matrices across ten cryptocurrency symbols for each prediction horizon.

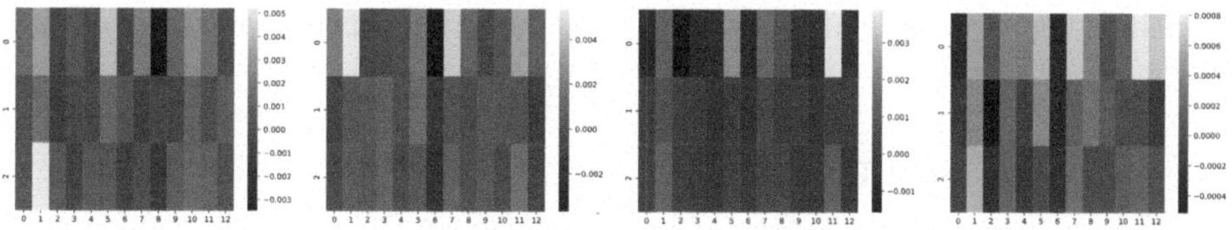

(a) $k = 5$ (b) $k = 10$ (c) $k = 50$ (d) $k = 100$

Fig. 3. Averaged type-feature attention matrices across 10 symbols

For short-term horizons ($k = 5, 10$), the model emphasizes volume and liquidity-driven events such as aggressive trades or cancellations near the best quotes. Interarrival time and spread play minor roles here, as short-term price movements are dominated by immediate liquidity shocks.

The importance gradually shifts toward interarrival time and spread on long-term horizons ($k = 50, 100$), reflecting a macro-level structural dynamics that align with the analysis on temporal attention. Patterns such as negative attention on new ask placements and positive attention on bid replenishment remain consistent, indicating coherent directional signals across horizons.

4.4 Robustness Test

We conducted additional experiments across different exchanges and time periods to assess the robustness of our models. The first experiment uses 10 symbols from the Bybit futures market over the period May 1–10, 2025. To further validate stability, we also evaluate performance on three symbols from the Binance futures market over the same period. Table 3 reports the R-squared scores for the Bybit and Binance robustness tests.

Table 3. R-squared score for the regression task on Bybit and Binance futures market

Exchange	Model \ k	k=5	k=10	k=50	k=100
Bybit	OF/CNN-LSTM	0.043	0.071	0.148	0.216
	Market-depth/TCN	0.044	0.071	0.236	0.243
	Type-based/CNN-LSTM	**0.230**	0.249	0.280	0.261
	Type-based/Dual-stream	0.221	**0.251**	**0.347**	**0.399**
Binance	Type-based/CNN-LSTM	**0.202**	**0.218**	0.288	0.300
	Type-based/Dual-stream	0.198	0.214	**0.321**	**0.359**

The robustness experiments confirm that the performance improvements of the Type-based representation generalize across markets and time periods. Both on Bybit and sample of Binance symbols, the Type-based models maintain consistent superiority across all horizons. The Dual-stream architecture also preserves its advantage, indicating that the representation captures stable structural signals.

4.5 Computational Efficiency

We evaluate computational efficiency using three metrics: the number of parameters, training time per epoch, and inference time on 1,000 samples. The results are presented in Table 4.

From the results, the Dual-stream model has the smallest number of parameters and the fastest inference times among all models. The CNN-LSTM model trained with the Type-based representation also achieves the fastest training time and exhibits faster training and inference than its counterpart using the OF representation. These findings highlight the effectiveness of the Type-based representation's compact structure and its well-aligned architectural design.

Table 4. Model size and computational efficiency

Model	#Params	Time/epoch (s)	1,000 sample inference (ms)
OF/CNN-LSTM	186,753	89.407	0.222
Market-depth/TCN	30,017	30.466	0.072
Type-based/CNN-LSTM	189,681	**16.962**	0.183
Type-based/Dual-stream	**25,611**	33.021	**0.052**

5 Conclusion

This study introduced a Type-based representation for LOB modeling that decomposes raw LOB and trade events into 12 interpretable order types and associated features, enabling direct encoding of microstructural behavior even without level 3 data. Experiments on ten cryptocurrency symbols showed that this representation provides richer information than OF and Market-Depth, and consistently improves regression and classification performance. A dual-stream model was further proposed to exploit temporal patterns and type-feature interactions, achieving the best predictive accuracy and improved interpretability. Additional experiments across exchanges and time spans further validate the robustness and computational efficiency of the proposed approach.

Attention analysis confirmed that the model adaptively shifts its focus across horizons: short horizon forecasts emphasize recent and price moving events, while longer horizon forecasts rely more on volume, interarrival time, and liquidity-related features, capturing broader dynamics. Future work includes evaluating this representation in markets with level 3 data, exploring multi-asset extensions, and investigating decoder architectures with adaptive normalization to enable dynamic horizon forecasting.

Acknowledgments. This work was supported by the National Research Foundation of Korea (NRF) grant funded by the Korea government (MSIT) (No. RS-2022-NR68758 and RS-2025-02216640).

Disclosure of Interests. The authors have no competing interests to declare that are relevant to the content of this article.

References

1. Abergel, F., Anane, M., Chakraborti, A., Jedidi, A., Muni Toke, I.: Limit Order Books. Physics of Society: Econophysics and Sociophysics. Cambridge University Press (2016)
2. Bengio, Y., Courville, A., Vincent, P.: Representation learning: a review and new perspectives. IEEE Trans. Pattern Anal. Mach. Intell. **35**(8), 1798–1828 (2013). https://doi.org/10.1109/tpami.2013.50
3. Berti, L., Kasneci, G.: TLOB: a novel transformer model with dual attention for stock price trend prediction with limit order book data (2025). https://arxiv.org/abs/2502.15757

4. Biais, B., Hillion, P., Spatt, C.: An empirical analysis of the limit order book and the order flow in the paris bourse. J. Finan. **50**(5), 1655–1689 (1995). https://doi.org/10.1111/j.1540-6261.1995.tb05192.x
5. Cont, R., Cucuringu, M., Zhang, C.: Cross-impact of order flow imbalance in equity markets. Quant. Finan. **23**, 1–21 (2023). https://doi.org/10.1080/14697688.2023.2236159
6. Cont, R., Kukanov, A., Stoikov, S.: The price impact of order book events. J. Financ. Economet. **12**(1), 47–88 (2014). https://doi.org/10.2139/ssrn.1712822
7. Eisler, Z., Bouchaud, J.P., Kockelkoren, J.: The price impact of order book events: market orders, limit orders and cancellations. arXiv.org, Quantitative Finance Papers **12** (2009). https://doi.org/10.2139/ssrn.1373762
8. Han, S., Dong, H.: A temporal window attention-based window-dependent long short-term memory network for multivariate time series prediction. Entropy **25**(1), 10 (2022). https://doi.org/10.3390/e25010010
9. HaoChen, J., Wei, C., Lee, J., Ma, T.: Shape matters: understanding the implicit bias of the noise covariance. In: Proceedings of Machine Learning Research, vol. 134, pp. 1–43 (2021)
10. Kolm, P.N., Turiel, J.D., Westray, N.: Deep order flow imbalance: extracting alpha at multiple horizons from the limit order book. Math. Financ. **33**(4), 977–1411 (2023). https://doi.org/10.1111/mafi.12413
11. Shi, M., Cheng, D., S.I.Y.Y.: Exploring crypto derivatives: an introduction of market landscape, emerging trends, valuation and risk management. Technical report, Ernst & Young LLP (2024)
12. 555 Ntakaris, A., Magris, M., Kanniainen, J., Gabbouj, M., Iosifidis, A.: Benchmark dataset for midâĂŘprice forecasting of limit order book data with machine learning methods. J. Forecast. **37**(8), 852–866 (2018). https://doi.org/10.1002/for.2543
13. Shaw, P., Uszkoreit, J., Vaswani, A.: Self-attention with relative position representations. arXiv preprint arXiv:1803.02155 (2018). https://doi.org/10.18653/v1/n18-2074
14. Tachet, R., Pezeshki, M., Shabanian, S., Courville, A.C., Bengio, Y.: On the learning dynamics of deep neural networks. CoRR abs/1809.06848 (2018). http://arxiv.org/abs/1809.06848
15. Tsantekidis, A., Passalis, N., Tefas, A., Kanniainen, J., Gabbouj, M., Iosifidis, A.: Forecasting stock prices from the limit order book using convolutional neural networks. In: 2017 IEEE 19th Conference on Business Informatics (CBI), vol. 01, pp. 7–12 (2017). https://doi.org/10.1109/CBI.2017.23
16. Tsantekidis, A., Passalis, N., Tefas, A., Kanniainen, J., Gabbouj, M., Iosifidis, A.: Using deep learning for price prediction by exploiting stationary limit order book features. Appl. Soft Comput. **93**, 106401 (2020). https://doi.org/10.1016/j.asoc.2020.106401
17. Wallbridge, J.: Transformers for limit order books. ArXiv (Cornell University) (2020). https://doi.org/10.48550/arxiv.2003.00130
18. Wu, Y., Mahfouz, M., Magazzeni, D., Veloso, M.: Towards robust representation of limit orders books for deep learning models (2022). https://doi.org/10.2139/ssrn.4295991
19. Xu, K., Gould, M.D., Howison, S.D.: Multi-level order-flow imbalance in a limit order book. SSRN Electron. J. (2019). https://doi.org/10.2139/ssrn.3479741

20. Zhang, Z., Zohren, S., Roberts, S.: Deeplob: Deep convolutional neural networks for limit order books. IEEE Trans. Signal Process. **67** (2018). https://doi.org/10.1109/TSP.2019.2907260
21. Zheng, B., Moulines, E., Abergel, F.: Price jump prediction in limit order book. J. Math. Finan. **03** (2012). https://doi.org/10.2139/ssrn.2026454

EquiFashion: Hybrid GAN–Diffusion Balancing Diversity–Fidelity for Fashion Design Generation

Nguyen Dinh Hieu[1], Tran Minh Khuong[1], and Phan Duy Hung[1,2](✉)

[1] FPT University, Hanoi, Vietnam
{hieundhe180318,khuongtmhe180089}@fpt.edu.vn, hungpd2@fe.edu.vn, hungpd31@fpt.com

[2] Quantum AI & Cyber Security Institute, FPT Corporation, Hanoi, Vietnam

Abstract. This paper presents EquiFashion, a hybrid *GAN–Diffusion* framework that bridges the long-standing gap between stylistic diversity and photo-realistic fidelity in generative fashion design. Unlike prior approaches that favor either creativity or realism, EquiFashion unifies both through a dual-stage process GAN-driven ideation for multimodal exploration and diffusion-based refinement for detail reconstruction. A *semantic-bundled attention* and *structural consensus* mechanism ensures localized attribute alignment, while *pose-conditioned latent diffusion* preserves physical plausibility and human centric geometry. To support robust evaluation, we introduce EquiFashion-DB, a new dataset of 350 K multimodal pairs (512 × 512 px, 40 categories) integrating text, sketch, pose, and fabric modalities with controlled noise for realistic supervision. Experiments across CM-Fashion, HieraFashion, and EquiFashion-DB demonstrate significant gains achieving FID 10.3, IS 7.8, Coverage 0.87, and CLIP-S 0.315, surpassing state-of-the-art diffusion baselines by over 40% FID improvement and + 0.05 CLIP-S. Qualitative comparisons confirm superior structural coherence, fabric realism, and semantic precision under complex prompts. Together, EquiFashion and EquiFashion-DB advance a new standard for *trustworthy, controllable, and data-aware* fashion generation, bridging the divide between AI creativity and human design intent. Code and data are available at: https://huggingface.co/NguyenDinhHieu/EquiFashionModel.

Keywords: Fashion Design Generation · GAN · Diffusion Models · Hybrid Framework · Diversity–Fidelity Trade-off · Robustness

1 Introduction

1.1 Problem and Motivation

Fashion represents both artistic expression and a global industry that shapes culture, identity, and consumer behavior. In the digital era, it underpins e-commerce, virtual try-on, and sustainable design, demanding generative systems capable of uniting creativity with reliability. However, fashion generation remains uniquely complex, requiring precise

R. C.-W. Wong et al. (Eds.): PAKDD 2026, LNAI 16617, pp. 178–190, 2027.
https://doi.org/10.1007/978-981-92-1926-1_15

fabric detail, structural coherence, and stylistic diversity beyond generic image synthesis. Existing methods face a persistent trade-off: GANs promote creativity but suffer from instability and mode collapse, while diffusion models achieve realism yet limit variation. True fidelity extends beyond sharpness it requires robustness and trustworthiness under noisy or biased inputs. This gap calls for a new framework that balances stylistic diversity with dependable realism, enabling fashion generation that is both innovative and reliable.

1.2 Related Works

Generative modeling for fashion design has rapidly advanced across three main paradigms: GAN-based, diffusion based, and hybrid multimodal frameworks. Each brings unique advantages yet fails to simultaneously achieve stylistic diversity, photorealistic fidelity, robustness, and outfit coherence.

GAN-based methods such as FashionGAN [1], TailorGAN [2], and BC-GAN [3] first demonstrated conditional garment generation, while AttnGAN [4], DM-GAN [5], FiCE [6] and StyleGAN [7] improved fine-grained realism and controllability. GANs excel at producing sharp, stylistically varied images essential for creative exploration but suffer from mode collapse and unstable optimization [8], limiting scalability in real-world design systems.

Diffusion-based models offer stable training and high fidelity. DiffCloth [9] and HieraFashDiff [10] introduced structure-aware alignment and iterative refinement, while DiffFashion [11], FS-Control [12], SGDiff [13] and TexFit [14] extended controllability through multimodal conditioning. Latent diffusion variants [15, 16] further enhanced resolution and efficiency, yet they often reduce stylistic diversity and remain sensitive to noisy or biased prompts [17]. A concrete example is shown in Fig. 1, where Stable Diffusion fails to disentangle attributes: given the prompt *"navy blue jacket with straight-point red collar"*, the model generates a jacket with attribute confusion between *red* and *collar*. This illustrates the inherent difficulty of maintaining robust semantic alignment in diffusion models, particularly under complex multi-attribute prompts.

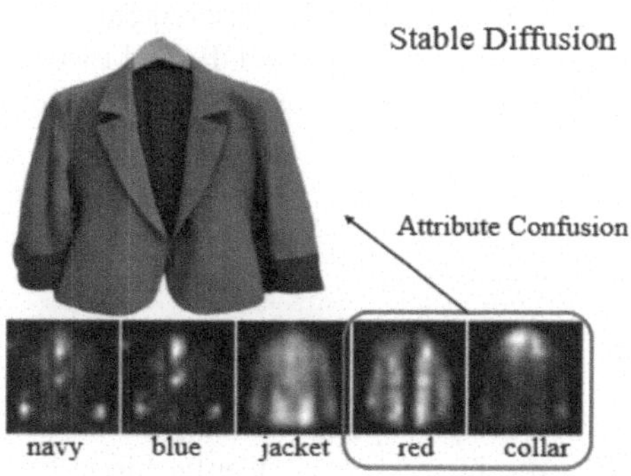

Fig. 1. Attribute confusion in Stable Diffusion. (*The prompt specifies a navy-blue jacket with a red collar, but the model incorrectly entangles attributes, highlighting a key weakness in semantic alignment*).

Hybrid and multimodal frameworks such as FashionSD-X [17], ARMANI [18], and Multimodal Garment Designer [19] extend diffusion-based models with multimodal conditioning, incorporating text, pose, or sketch inputs to enhance controllability and realism. While these methods improve semantic alignment and editing flexibility, they often prioritize reliability over stylistic exploration and seldom address robustness to noise or domain shift factors critical for real-world fashion design and e-commerce applications.

In summary, prior research reveals a persistent imbalance. GAN-based models offer diversity and creativity but lack stability and reliability. Diffusion models provide fidelity and robustness but constrain stylistic breadth, limiting innovation. Hybrid and multimodal frameworks improve control and semantic consistency, yet still fall short in balancing creativity with trustworthiness. This enduring gap motivates the development of EquiFashion, a hybrid GAN–Diffusion framework designed to explicitly reconcile the diversity–fidelity trade-off, enabling fashion design generation that is simultaneously innovative, robust, and socially trustworthy.

1.3 Contribution

This research contributes to advancing generative fashion design in three key aspects. It introduces EquiFashion, a hybrid GAN–Diffusion framework that effectively resolves the long-standing trade-off between stylistic diversity and photorealistic fidelity. Unlike previous methods that prioritize either creativity or stability, EquiFashion integrates GAN-based ideation for broad stylistic exploration with diffusion-based refinement for realistic and robust synthesis. Through enhanced objectives mode seeking, robustness regularization, and perceptual compatibility constraints the framework achieves a well-balanced performance across FID$\downarrow$, IS$\uparrow$, Coverage$\uparrow$, and CLIP-S$\uparrow$, demonstrating improved realism, diversity, and semantic alignment.

In addition, this research presents EquiFashion-DB, a large-scale multimodal dataset comprising 350 K samples across garments, fabrics, poses, and demographics, featuring controlled text noise and ambiguous prompts to simulate real-world design conditions. A unified evaluation protocol is also proposed, expanding conventional measures with robustness and outfit-compatibility assessments. Together, these contributions the EquiFashion framework, EquiFashion-DB, and evaluation protocol establish an integrated foundation for trustworthy, controllable, and creative AI-driven fashion generation.

2 Data

2.1 Dataset Overview

Progress in generative fashion design depends critically on the availability of diverse and well-annotated data. Earlier resources such as DeepFashion [20], FashionGen [21], and CM-Fashion (ARMANI) [18] have provided valuable foundations covering large-scale attributes, text–image pairs, and part-level segmentation but remain limited in modality richness and stylistic balance. Most lack structural sketches, pose annotations, or material cues, and their text descriptions often exhibit bias or noise. More recent benchmarks like HieraFashion [10] introduce hierarchical labeling and expert curation yet cover only a few categories, restricting generalization to broader design tasks. These shortcomings make it difficult for current generative models to jointly achieve fidelity, diversity, and robustness in real-world settings.

To overcome this, we introduce **EquiFashion-DB**, a large-scale multimodal corpus for trustworthy fashion generation. It aggregates curated images from **Farfetch**, **Zalando**, and **ASOS**, filtered for clean backgrounds and consistent poses. Each 512×512 image is paired with clean and noise augmented text, sketch contours, pose keypoints, and fabric texture patches. The dataset includes 350 K samples across 40+ categories, split into 300 K training and 50 K testing pairs. This design balances scale and structure, supporting both creative exploration and objective evaluation of robustness and semantic alignment.

2.2 Exploration Data

Prior datasets each contribute partially DeepFashion offers scale but no text, FashionGen provides captions but lacks structure, CM-Fashion adds segmentation but suffers from noise, and HieraFashion improves hierarchy but remains small (5.2 K). As shown in Table 1, EquiFashion-DB integrates these fragmented strengths into a unified, noise-aware benchmark that combines scale, multimodality, and robustness.

With 350 K high-resolution samples, five aligned modalities (image, text, sketch, pose, and fabric), and a balanced 300 K /50 K split, it provides broader coverage and stronger diversity than prior datasets. By incorporating realistic text noise and multimodal grounding, EquiFashion-DB enables models to handle imperfect descriptions and complex human-pose variations, establishing a solid foundation for reliable and creative fashion generation.

Table 1. Comparison of representative fashion datasets and EquiFashion-DB

Dataset	Year	Images	Resolution	Categories	Train/Test Split	Modalities Provided	Key Strengths	Limitations
DeepFashion [21]	2016	800K	256×256	50	700K/100K	Image, Attributes	Large scale; attribute annotations	No text; limited modalities
FashionGen [22]	2018	~293K	320×320	48	250K/43 K	Image, Text	High-quality text–image pairs	Imbalanced; no pose/fabric
CM-Fashion [19]	2023	509K	512×512	20	409K/100K	Image, Text (APs), Segmentation Masks	High-resolution; part-level semantic alignment	Caption noise; limited category diversity
HieraFashion [10]	2024	5200	768×1024	8	4K/1.2K	Image, Hierarchical Text	Hierarchical descriptions; high-res	Very limited scale/diversity
EquiFashion-DB (our)	**2025**	350K	512×512	40	300K/50K	Image, Text, Sketch, Pose, Fabric	Balanced, multimodal, noise-aware, robust	Newly released

In summary, EquiFashion-DB consolidates scale, multimodality, and robustness into one benchmark, bridging gaps among prior datasets and establishing a stronger foundation for evaluating generative fashion models under realistic conditions.

3 Methodology

3.1 Problem Definition

Fashion image synthesis requires translating nuanced textual descriptions into visually coherent and stylistically diverse garments. Given a description T composed of Attribute Phrases (APs) such as "red collar" or "long sleeves," EquiFashion generates a high-quality image x_0 that is both semantically faithful and perceptually realistic, formulated as $G_{\text{Equi}} : T \mapsto x_0$. To balance semantic accuracy, visual realism, and stylistic diversity, EquiFashion employs a dual-stage design GAN-based ideation for structural exploration, diffusion and pose-conditioned refinement for detailed, body-aware reconstruction. Fig. 2 presents the overall architecture of EquiFashion, combining linguistic parsing, structural semantic consensus, and a hybrid GAN–Diffusion mechanism guided by pose information to produce garments that are both controllable and physically coherent.

3.2 Latent Diffusion Backbone

To improve efficiency and stability, **EquiFashion** performs diffusion in a low dimensional latent space instead of pixel space. A pretrained autoencoder (Enc, Dec) encodes an image x_0 into a latent vector $z_0 = \text{Enc}(x_0)$ and reconstructs it as $\tilde{x}_0 = \text{Dec}(z_0)$, optimized by

$$\mathcal{L}_{AE} = \|x_0 - \tilde{x}_0\|_1 + \lambda_{perc}\text{LPIPS}(x_0, \tilde{x}_0), \tag{1}$$

where LPIPS measures perceptual similarity and λ_{perc} balances pixel and perceptual fidelity.

Gaussian noise is added in the forward process

$$q(z_t \mid z_{t-1}) = \mathcal{N}\Big(\sqrt{1-\beta_t}\, z_{t-1}, \beta_t \boldsymbol{I}\Big), \tag{2}$$

where β_t is the noise variance and $\mathbf{I}$ is the identity matrix.

In the reverse process, a denoising network ϵ_θ is trained to predict and remove noise at each step, following the objective:

$$\mathcal{L}_{denoise} = \mathbb{E}_{t,z_0,\epsilon}\Big[\|\epsilon - \epsilon_\theta(z_t, c, t)\|_2^2\Big], \tag{3}$$

where c encodes multimodal conditioning (text, sketch, or pose). Operating in latent space accelerates sampling and enhances training stability while preserving photorealistic detail.

3.3 Structural Semantic Consensus

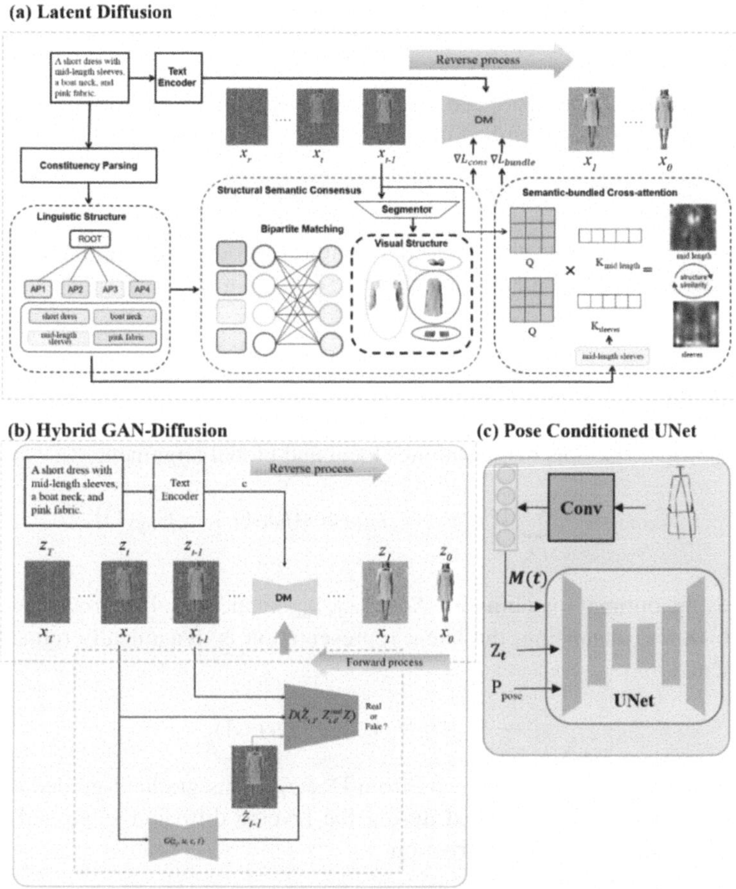

Fig. 2. Illustrates the EquiFashion pipeline, which integrates linguistic parsing, structural semantic consensus, and semantic-bundled attention within a hybrid GAN–Diffusion and pose-conditioned refinement for controllable and realistic fashion synthesis.

A central challenge in text conditioned garment synthesis is maintaining precise correspondence between linguistic descriptions and visual components. Without explicit alignment, diffusion models often suffer from *part leakage*, where attributes (e.g., sleeve color) spill into unrelated regions. To address this, **EquiFashion** introduces a *structural semantic consensus* mechanism that enforces cross-modal alignment between textual APs and garment parts.

Given a parsed description T, constituency parsing decomposes it into M **Attribute Phrases (APs)**:

$$T \to \mathcal{A} = \{a_j\}_{j=1}^{M}, a_j = \left(\text{adj}_j, \text{noun}_j\right), \tag{4}$$

where each AP corresponds to one visual part, such as *"classic collar"* or *"long sleeves"*. Concurrently, the generated or decoded image is segmented by a garment segmentor into K structural parts:

$$\mathcal{P} = \{p_k\}_{k=1}^{K}. \tag{5}$$

Cross-modal similarity between each linguistic and visual component is then computed using CLIP-based embeddings:

$$s_{jk} = \cos\big(f_{\text{text}}(a_j), f_{\text{img}}(p_k)\big), \tag{6}$$

where f_{text} and f_{img} denote the respective feature encoders. An optimal one-to-one mapping is determined by bipartite matching:

$$\hat{\sigma} = \arg\min_{\sigma} \sum_{j=1}^{M} \mathcal{L}_{\text{match}}\big(a_j, p_{\sigma(j)}\big), \mathcal{L}_{\text{match}} = -s_{jk}. \tag{7}$$

The resulting consensus loss combines local and global alignment:

$$\mathcal{L}_{cons} = -\sum_{j,k} M_{jk} s_{jk} - \lambda_{global} \cos\big(f_{\text{text}}(T), \quad f_{\text{img}}(I)\big), \tag{8}$$

where M_{jk} is the optimal matching mask and λ_{global} balances global structure with part-level detail. During denoising, the latent representation is dynamically refined toward this alignment:

$$z_t \leftarrow z_t + \eta_t \nabla_{z_t} \mathcal{L}_{\text{cons}}(\phi(z_t), \mathcal{A}), \tag{9}$$

where $\phi(z_t)$ extracts visual components from Dec(z_t). This gradient-guided consensus acts as a semantic regulator applied during the reverse diffusion stage and does not modify the forward Gaussian construction.

3.4 Semantic-Bundled Cross-Attention

Despite structural alignment, diffusion models may still misassign attributes for example, coloring the entire jacket red instead of just the collar. To mitigate this, **EquiFashion** introduces a *semantic-bundled cross-attention* mechanism that treats each adjective noun pair as a unified semantic unit. For each pair $a_j = (\text{adj}_j, \text{noun}_j)$, the attention maps are combined as:

$$B_j = \frac{1}{2}\Big(A_j^{adj} + A_j^{noun}\Big), \tag{10}$$

and their spatial coherence is enforced through Jensen–Shannon divergence:

$$\mathcal{L}_{bundle} = \sum_{j=1}^{M} \text{JSD}\Big(A_j^{adj} \| A_j^{noun}\Big). \tag{11}$$

This ensures consistent activation between attributes and corresponding garment regions (*red collar*, *blue cuffs*). To maintain overall outfit harmony, a **compatibility loss** is added:

$$\mathcal{L}_{comp} = -\cos(g(\text{Dec}(z_t)), g(T)), \tag{12}$$

where $g(\cdot)$ is a pretrained fashion-compatibility encoder. Together, $\mathcal{L}_{bundle}$ and $\mathcal{L}_{comp}$ stabilize attention localization and improve stylistic coherence across the generated garments.

3.5 Hybrid GAN–Diffusion Integration

To achieve controllable synthesis that reflects both stylistic diversity and human-body alignment, **EquiFashion** embeds a conditional GAN inside the diffusion process and augments the denoising U-Net with **pose conditioning**. This hybrid mechanism enables simultaneous exploration of diverse garment styles and faithful rendering on a given body posture.

At every timestep t, the generator G predicts a diverse latent candidate from the noisy latent z_t:

$$\hat{z}_{t-1} = G(z_t, u, c, t), \tag{13}$$

where $u \sim \mathcal{N}(0, I)$ introduces stochastic variation and c encodes multimodal conditioning (e.g., text, pose, sketch). This enables the generator to explore multiple stylistic modes for the same semantic description. The discriminator D evaluates whether the generated transition $\hat{z}_{t-1}$ is realistic, using a hinge-based adversarial objective:

$$\mathcal{L}_D = \mathbb{E}\Big[\max\Big(0, 1 - D\Big(z_{t-1}^{real}\Big)\Big)\Big] + \mathbb{E}\big[\max(0, 1 + D(\hat{z}_{t-1}))\big], \tag{14}$$

$$\mathcal{L}_G = -\mathbb{E}\big[D(\hat{z}_{t-1})\big]. \tag{15}$$

where $z_{t-1}^{real} \sim q(z_{t-1} \mid z_0)$ is sampled analytically from the forward diffusion marginal defined in Sect. 3.2. No external intermediate supervision is introduced. This ensures that GAN training remains consistent with the diffusion probability path.

This adversarial interaction encourages G to generate plausible latent samples that are indistinguishable from forward-sampled latent transitions.

To prevent *mode collapse* where the generator produces repetitive outputs despite stochastic input a **mode-seeking loss** promotes diversity by maximizing perceptual distance between outputs generated from distinct latent perturbations u_1 and u_2:

$$\mathcal{L}_{MS} = -\frac{G(z_t, u_1, c, t) - G(z_t, u_2, c, t)\|_1}{\|u_1 - u_2\|_1}. \tag{16}$$

This encourages G to traverse the full latent manifold and maintain distinct visual appearances under the same text condition.

Parallel to GAN ideation, the **pose-conditioned diffusion refiner** F_θ reconstructs detailed textures while adhering to body structure:

$$\tilde{z}_{t-1} = F_\theta\big(z_t, c, P_{pose}, t\big). \tag{17}$$

where $P_{\text{pose}} = \phi(M(t))$is the pose embedding derived from the 2D skeleton map $M(t)$.

As shown in Fig. 2(c), the pose-conditioned U-Net receives P_{pose}, z_t, and the timestep embedding $M(t)$. A convolutional projection aligns these signals before entering the U-Net backbone, guiding generation to respect body silhouette and joint constraints.

To enhance robustness, we introduce two regularization objectives. First, a **robustness loss** enforces consistency against small perturbations δ, ensuring stable denoising behavior:

$$\mathcal{L}_{rob} = \|\epsilon_\theta(z_t, c, t) - \epsilon_\theta(z_t + \delta, c, t)\|_2^2, \tag{18}$$

where δ is a small adversarial noise, and a **perceptual/CLIP loss** preserving semantic alignment between decoded outputs and the textual description,

$$\mathcal{L}_{perc} = 1 - \cos\big(f_{img}(\text{Dec}(\tilde{z}_{t-1})), f_{text}(T)\big). \tag{19}$$

This ensures that the generated image remains perceptually faithful to the input prompt even under adversarial or noisy conditions.

Finally, the outputs of both branches are combined through an adaptive interpolation strategy:

$$z_{t-1} = \alpha_t \hat{z}_{t-1} + (1 - \alpha_t)\tilde{z}_{t-1}, \alpha_t = (t/T)^\gamma, \tag{20}$$

where α_t dynamically balances the contributions of the two branches, encouraging broader latent exploration at early timesteps while progressively relying more on diffusion-based refinement as denoising proceeds. Importantly, the diffusion refiner remains active throughout the entire trajectory, ensuring that the final latent transition remains consistent with the reverse diffusion process. This hybrid fusion mechanism enables EquiFashion to maintain stylistic diversity without compromising probabilistic stability, uniting adversarial exploration with stable denoising synthesis.

3.6 Overall Objective

The unified loss combines all objectives:

$$\mathcal{L}_{total} = \lambda_{AE}\mathcal{L}_{AE} + \lambda_{cons}\mathcal{L}_{cons} + \lambda_{bundle}\mathcal{L}_{bundle} + \lambda_{comp}\mathcal{L}_{comp} + \lambda_G(\mathcal{L}_G + \lambda_{MS}\mathcal{L}_{MS}) + \lambda_{den}\mathcal{L}_{denoise} + \lambda_{rob}\mathcal{L}_{rob} + \lambda_{perc}\mathcal{L}_{perc}. \tag{21}$$

with coefficients $\lambda_{AE} = 1.0, \lambda_{cons} = \lambda_{bundle} = \lambda_{comp} = 0.5, \lambda_G = \lambda_{den}, \lambda_{rob} = \lambda_{perc} = 0.1.$

Optimization alternates between (G, F_θ) and D, progressively shifting from reconstruction to adversarial refinement.

3.7 Inference Procedure

During inference, the model starts from $z_T \sim \mathcal{N}(0, I)$and iteratively denoises for T steps. At each iteration, semantic–structural guidance (Eq. 9) refines attention, while GAN ideation provides diversity ($\hat{z}_{t-1}$) and diffusion refinement ($\tilde{z}_{t-1}$) enhances detail. The two latents are fused by Eq. (20), and the final image is decoded as $x_0 = \text{Dec}(z_0)$.

This hybrid iterative process ensures semantic fidelity, stylistic diversity, and photorealistic precision, with pose-conditioned guidance preserving realistic body geometry and garment alignment.

4 Experiment

4.1 Implementation Details

All experiments were conducted in PyTorch 2.2 on a single NVIDIA A100 GPU (40GB, CUDA 12.2). The framework was trained end-to-end using AdamW with learning rates of 2×10^{-4} (generator) and 1×10^{-4} (discriminator), cosine decay, and gradient clipping (1.0) for stability. Training ran for 400 epochs with batch size 32 under mixed-precision (FP16), following a 200-epoch autoencoder pretraining. Text embeddings were obtained from CLIP-ViT/L-14, while pose and garment structure were aligned via a U^2-Net segmentation backbone. The diffusion module used $T = 8$ timesteps, $\gamma = 0.7$, and EMA $= 0.999$ for stability. All runs used fixed seeds for reproducibility, with evaluation based on FID, IS, Coverage, and CLIP-S. The framework also operates efficiently on an RTX 4060 (24 GB) using batch size 8 and gradient checkpointing.

4.2 Result Analysis

To comprehensively evaluate EquiFashion, we benchmark it against leading GAN-, diffusion-, and hybrid-based models across three datasets CM-Fashion, EquiFashion-DB, and HieraFashion each posing unique challenges. CM-Fashion suffers from noisy captions and limited diversity; EquiFashion-DB introduces multimodal conditioning and text noise; while HieraFashion emphasizes hierarchical semantics and complex poses. Evaluation is based on four metrics: FID↓ for visual fidelity, IS↑ for diversity, Coverage ↑ for generative completeness, and CLIP-S↑ for text–image alignment. All results are averaged over three runs with fixed seeds, and "–" indicates inapplicability (e.g., models without pose inputs). For fairness, all diffusion baselines, including the Latent Diffusion Model (LDM) [15], were retrained or fine-tuned using identical hyperparameters and latent configurations.

Lower FID and higher IS, Coverage, and CLIP-S indicate better realism, diversity, and text-image consistency. Across all datasets, EquiFashion delivers the strongest balance of fidelity and diversity. Compared to LDM [15], it reduces FID by over 40% and improves CLIP-S by +0.05 on EquiFashion-DB, validating the impact of its hybrid structure and semantic guidance. Against domain-specific models like DiffCloth [9] and HieraFashDiff [10], EquiFashion achieves >35% lower FID and higher Coverage (0.87 vs. 0.78) under identical setups. On HieraFashion, it generalizes to unseen hierarchical categories with minimal ΔFID <1.5, evidencing strong robustness. Even on the noise-heavy CM-Fashion, it maintains stable fidelity and achieves +0.04 CLIP-S gains, showing better transferability across domains. Overall, these results establish EquiFashion as a unified, reliable framework that harmonizes creativity and realism in fashion generation.

4.3 Qualitative Results

Fig. 3. Qualitative comparison of fashion synthesis. From left to right: design concepts, HieraFashDiff [10], Stable Diffusion, FashionSD-X [17], EquiFashion (ours), and real references.

Figure 3 compares EquiFashion with representative diffusion and hybrid baselines HieraFashDiff [10], Stable Diffusion, and FashionSD-X [17] across design concepts such as elegant dresses, casual blouses, and original-design sweaters. Each prompt encodes fine-grained aesthetic and structural intent (e.g., "Dress, Elegant, Business, Slimming"), challenging models to preserve garment coherence and fabric realism. While Stable Diffusion captures general color tone but distorts silhouettes, HieraFashDiff improves pose alignment yet over-smooths textures, and FashionSD-X enhances text alignment but suffers attribute entanglement. In contrast, EquiFashion maintains garment topology and localized semantics, producing realistic draping, precise color placement, and consistent proportions.

These gains arise from EquiFashion hybrid GAN–Diffusion framework with *semantic-bundled attention* and *pose-conditioned refinement*, which jointly balance diversity and fidelity. The model mitigates attribute leakage under noisy text and preserves physical plausibility, yielding outputs that closely match real garments with sharp structures, fine fabric shading, and coherent styling. These qualitative results reinforce the quantitative improvements in Table 2, demonstrating EquiFashion effectiveness for realistic, controllable, and trustworthy fashion generation.

Table 2. Quantitative comparison of generative fashion models across CM-Fashion, EquiFashion-DB, and HieraFashion.

Methods	Type	Dataset	Pose	FID↓	IS ↑	Coverage ↑	CLIP-S ↑
LDM [23]	Diffusion	CM-Fashion	✗	21.4	5.9	0.70	0.249
		EquiFashion-DB	✓	18.6	6.2	0.75	0.266
		HieraFashion	✓	17.2	6.3	0.76	0.271
DiffCloth [9]	Diffusion	CM-Fashion	✗	18.9	6.1	0.73	0.265
		EquiFashion-DB	✓	–	–	–	–
		HieraFashion	✓	–	–	–	–
HieraFashDiff [10]	Diffusion	CM-Fashion	✗	–	–	–	–
		EquiFashion-DB	✓	15.8	6.7	0.78	0.284
		HieraFashion	✓	14.5	6.8	0.79	0.288
FashionSD-X [17]	Hybrid	CM-Fashion	✗	–	–	–	–
		EquiFashion-DB	✓	13.9	7.0	0.80	0.292
		HieraFashion	✓	12.7	7.1	0.81	0.294
EquiFashion (ours)	Hybrid	CM-Fashion	✗	**12.6**	**7.4**	**0.84**	**0.303**
		EquiFashion-DB	✓	**10.3**	**7.8**	**0.87**	**0.315**
		HieraFashion	✓	**11.8**	**7.5**	**0.85**	**0.309**

5 Conclusion

This work introduces EquiFashion, a hybrid GAN–Diffusion framework designed to address the long-standing trade-off between stylistic diversity and photorealistic fidelity in fashion design generation. By integrating semantic-bundled attention, structural consensus alignment, and pose-conditioned latent diffusion within a probabilistically consistent diffusion framework, the model achieves improved semantic grounding and realistic garment synthesis across multiple datasets. The proposed EquiFashion-DB further contributes a large-scale, multimodal, and noise-aware benchmark that enables systematic evaluation of robustness, controllability, and diversity in generative fashion models under realistic conditions. Together, these contributions provide an integrated and reliable foundation for controllable fashion generation. Future work will explore extending EquiFashion toward 3D garment reconstruction, virtual try-on integration, and interactive co-design systems, aiming to further bridge AI-driven generative modeling with human-centered design practice.

Acknowledgements. This work was supported by the Quantum AI & Cyber Security Institute, FPT Corporation, Vietnam.

References

1. Zhu, S., Urtasun, R., Fidler, S., Lin, D.: Be your own Prada: fashion synthesis with structural coherence. In: Proceedings of the IEEE International Conference on Computer Vision. IEEE (2017)
2. Chen, L., Tian, J., Li, G., Wu, C., King, E., Xu, C.: TailorGAN: making user-defined fashion designs. In: Proceedings of the IEEE/CVF Winter Conference on Applications of Computer Vision. IEEE (2020)

3. Li, W., et al.: BC-GAN: a generative adversarial network for synthesizing a batch of collocated clothing. In: CVPR Workshops. IEEE (2019)
4. Xu, T., et al.: AttnGAN: fine-grained text to image generation with attentional GANs. In: Proceedings of the IEEE Conference on Computer Vision and Pattern Recognition. IEEE (2018)
5. Zhu, M., Pan, P., Chen, W., Yang, Y.: DM-GAN: dynamic memory generative adversarial networks for text-to-image synthesis. In: Proceedings of the IEEE/CVF Conference on Computer Vision and Pattern Recognition. IEEE (2019)
6. Pernuš, M., Fookes, C., Štruc, V., Dobrišek, S.: FICE: text-conditioned fashion image editing with guided GAN inversion. https://arxiv.org/abs/2301.02110 (2023).
7. Karras, T., Laine, S., Aila, T.: A style-based generator architecture for GANs. In: Proceedings of the IEEE/CVF Conference on Computer Vision and Pattern Recognition. IEEE (2019)
8. Goodfellow, I., et al.: Generative adversarial nets. In: NeurIPS. MIT Press (2014)
9. Zhang, X., et al.: DiffCloth: diffusion based garment synthesis and manipulation via structural cross-modal semantic alignment. In: Proceedings of the IEEE/CVF International Conference on Computer Vision. IEEE (2023)
10. Xie, Z., et al.: HieraFashDiff: hierarchical fashion design with multi-stage diffusion models. In: Proceedings of the AAAI Conference on Artificial Intelligence. AAAI Press (2025)
11. Cao, S., Chai, W., Hao, S., Wang, G.: DiffFashion: reference-based fashion design with structure-aware transfer by diffusion models. In: CVPR Workshops. IEEE (2023)
12. Yu, J., Wang, Y., Zhao, C., Ghanem, B., Zhang, J.: FS-control: artistic fashion design with discriminated and conditional diffusion models. In: ICCV. IEEE (2023)
13. Sun, Z., Zhou, Y., He, H., Mok, P.Y.: SGDiff: a style guided diffusion model for fashion synthesis. In: ACM Multimedia. ACM (2023).
14. Wang, T., Ye, M.: TexFit: text-driven fashion image editing with diffusion models. In: Proceedings of the AAAI Conference on Artificial Intelligence. AAAI Press (2024)
15. Rombach, R., Blattmann, A., Lorenz, D., Esser, P., Ommer, B.: High-resolution image synthesis with latent diffusion models. In: Proceedings of the IEEE/CVF Conference on Computer Vision and Pattern Recognition. IEEE (2022)
16. Saharia, C., et al.: Photorealistic text-to-image diffusion models with deep language understanding. In: NeurIPS. Curran (2022).
17. Kim, J., Park, S., Lee, K.: FashionSD-X: multimodal fashion garment synthesis using latent diffusion. https://arxiv.org/abs/2404.18591 (2024).
18. Zhang, X. et al.: ARMANI: part-level garment-text alignment for unified cross-modal fashion design. In: ACM Multimedia. ACM (2022).
19. Baldrati, A., Morelli, D., Cartella, G., Cornia, M., Bertini, M., Cucchiara, R.: Multimodal garment designer: human-centric latent diffusion models for fashion image editing. In: Proceedings of the IEEE/CVF International Conference on Computer Vision. IEEE (2023)
20. Liu, Z. et al.: DeepFashion: powering robust clothes recognition and retrieval. CVPR (2016).
21. Rostamzadeh, N. et al.: Fashion-Gen: the generative fashion dataset and challenge. https://arxiv.org/abs/1806.08317 (2018).

Beyond Semantics: Exploring Context Ranking Under Knowledge Conflicts

Sanghyun Cho, Myeongjin Lee, Jeong Heo, Jong-hun Shin, Kiyoung Lee, and Soojong Lim(✉)

Electronics and Telecommunications Research Institute, Daejeon, Republic of Korea
{shcho.nlp,myeongjin216,jeonghur,jhshin82,leeky,isj}@etri.re.kr

Abstract. We study knowledge conflicts in the Generate-then-Read pipeline, where large language models generate semantically similar but factually inconsistent contexts that can confuse the reader model. To reproduce and analyze such scenarios, we construct ConflictsQA, a dataset designed to simulate knowledge-conflict situations. It extends open-domain question–answer pairs with contexts generated by both GPT-4o and open LLMs such as LLaMa and Gemma, where GPT-4o provides ground-truth True contexts and open models produce both True and plausibly incorrect False contexts. Using ConflictsQA, we conduct a comprehensive evaluation of both embedding-based and cross-encoder models to assess their ability to distinguish factually reliable contexts under conflicting knowledge. Our evaluation includes lightweight models such as GTE and BGE, as well as LLM-based models like Qwen3 in both embedding and cross-encoder models. This setup enables us to compare how different model architectures and sizes handle the balance between semantic similarity and factual consistency. We also explore model pruning under fixed memory constraints. Pruned models show competitive results when evaluated on contexts generated by GPT-4o, where semantic cues are relatively distinct, but exhibit large performance drops on fully conflicting data. This indicates that pruning preserves semantic discrimination while weakening factual reasoning.

Keywords: Knowledge Conflicts · Text Ranking · Generate-then-read

1 Introduction

The use of large language models (LLMs) has rapidly increased in recent years. LLMs are pretrained on massive amounts of data with billions of parameters, enabling them to internalize extensive knowledge within their parameters [11, 15]. Based on this property, the Generate-then-Read paradigm [22] has been proposed, where the model generates its own contextual information instead of retrieving it from external sources. This pipeline reduces reliance on retriever performance while still achieving strong results.

These studies have focused on increasing knowledge coverage by encouraging LLMs to generate a diverse range of contextual candidates. Techniques such as

R. C.-W. Wong et al. (Eds.): PAKDD 2026, LNAI 16617, pp. 191–203, 2027.
https://doi.org/10.1007/978-981-92-1926-1_16

clustering-based prompting and passage hint–based diversified recitation have been proposed to promote variability in the generated contexts [17,22]. Generating a sufficiently diverse set of contexts increases the likelihood that at least one of them contains the correct answer, which in turn improves overall question answering performance.

However, this approach has a clear limitation. Contexts generated by LLMs tend to be semantically similar to one another, regardless of whether they contain the correct answer or include hallucinated information. Both answer-containing contexts and knowledge-conflicting contexts are often produced together. When these mixed contexts are provided to the reader model, the model can be easily distracted, generating incorrect answers or referencing false details from misleading contexts. In some cases, the reader even produces multiple inconsistent answers instead of a single correct one. Since these distracting contexts are semantically close to the correct ones, it is difficult for existing rerankers or retrievers to effectively filter them out.

To examine and evaluate the issues that arise in the Generate-then-Read setting, we constructed the ConflictsQA dataset, which reproduces such conflict situations. ConflictsQA is built using question–answer pairs from existing open-domain QA datasets, including Natural Questions [8], TriviaQA [7], and WebQuestions. We employed various LLMs to generate conflicting contexts that reproduce realistic cases of knowledge inconsistency. In addition, we conducted experiments to examine how pruning the top layers of LLMs affects their performance on text ranking tasks that require nuanced knowledge judgments. We found that while pruning does not noticeably affect the model's ability to distinguish broad semantic differences, it significantly reduces its ability to judge detailed factual information. This comparison shows that pruning top layers can work for tasks requiring only semantic distinctions, but becomes ineffective when resolving knowledge conflicts that require fine-grained factual judgment.

The contributions of this paper are as follows:

- **Construction of the ConflictsQA dataset.** We introduce ConflictsQA, a benchmark that reproduces knowledge conflict scenarios in the Generate-then-Read pipeline by combining contexts generated with various LLMs.
- **Analysis of lightweight reranker limitations.** Experiments show that lightweight embedding and reranking models, which mainly rely on semantic similarity, fail to identify factually correct contexts under knowledge conflicts, emphasizing the need for knowledge-aware text ranking.
- **Investigation of model pruning for ranking.** We examine the effect of top-layer pruning under a fixed memory budget, finding that pruning preserves semantic discrimination but weakens factual discrimination.

2 Related Work

2.1 Retriever and Rerankers

Retrievers and rerankers are widely used in open-domain question-answering and retrieval-augmented generation (RAG) systems. Early approaches such as Contriever [5] introduced self-supervised dense retrievers that learn from unlabeled text. Later, E5 [20] is trained with large-scale weakly supervised contrastive pre-training and optionally fine-tuned on labeled datasets such as NLI and MS-MARCO, enabling a single embedding space to support diverse tasks including retrieval, classification, and reranking.

As multilingual and cross-domain applications emerged, recent models have increasingly focused on building more versatile embedding frameworks. BGE-M3 [1] proposed a multi-lingual, multi-function, and multi-granularity framework that combines dense and sparse retrieval representations through self-knowledge distillation, achieving strong multilingual performance across BEIR [19] and MTEB benchmarks [12]. Similarly, mGTE [23] introduced improvements by supporting long-context multilingual retrieval through a native 8K-token encoder, pre-trained with RoPE and contrastive learning.

Most recently, Qwen3 Embedding [24] proposed a strong retrieval and reranking model that leverages Qwen models. By aligning embeddings with large-scale supervision from both open and proprietary corpora, it achieved superior cross-lingual and domain transfer performance while remaining compact enough for practical use.

2.2 Generate-then-Read Pipeline

The Generate-then-Read paradigm was proposed as an alternative to traditional RAG pipelines [6,9], addressing the dependency on external retrievers by leveraging the language model's own knowledge. Yu et al. [22] introduced generate-then-read pipelines, demonstrating that LLMs can serve as internal retrievers by generating relevant passages using their parametric knowledge. This approach showed that, even without access to external corpora, LLMs could provide sufficiently rich contexts for downstream reader models, often achieving performance comparable to or surpassing RAG systems in open-domain QA tasks.

Recitation-Augmented Language Models (RALM) [17] explored a structured recitation process, where models generate fact-based recitations before answering. By explicitly separating recitation from reasoning, RALM achieved improved factual grounding and interpretability.

More recently, Tang et al. [18] proposed the A+B Framework, which decouples the context generator and the reader model. In this framework, model A generates knowledge-relevant contexts, while model B reads generated contexts to produce final answers. Their study showed that unaligned base models are generally better generators due to stronger memorization, whereas aligned chat models work better as readers due to their coherence and safety.

2.3 Text Ranking with LLMs

Recent studies have explored the use of LLMs for text ranking tasks, leveraging their reasoning and instruction-following capabilities. Early investigations, such as HELM [10], utilized instruction-based relevance judgment, showing that LLMs can perform document re-ranking. Subsequent work like RankGPT [16] demonstrated that well-instructed models such as ChatGPT and GPT-4 can achieve competitive or even superior results compared to supervised baselines on standard IR benchmarks, highlighting the strong generalization ability of LLMs for ranking.

However, listwise prompting approaches in these studies suffered from instability due to context length limits and order sensitivity. To address these issues, Pairwise Ranking Prompting [14] introduced a more efficient and robust pairwise comparison strategy, reducing task complexity and achieving state-of-the-art ranking performance even with moderate-sized open LLMs.

3 Method

3.1 Problem Statement

In the generate-then-read pipeline, the model generates contextual passages instead of retrieving them from an external corpus for the reader model. To improve knowledge coverage, recent approaches often generate diverse contexts from multiple prompts or decoding strategies. However, the contexts produced by LLMs tend to be semantically similar, regardless of whether they contain the correct information. When such contexts include hallucinated or conflicting knowledge, they can distract the reader model and lead to incorrect or inconsistent answers.

To address this issue, it is necessary to filter out unhelpful or misleading contexts before reading. Yet, existing lightweight embedding models or rerankers perform poorly in this setting. These models only capture semantic relevance but not knowledge reliability, which is crucial for distinguishing factually consistent contexts from conflicting ones. Therefore, the task differs fundamentally from standard text similarity or retrieval because it requires evaluating whether a context contains the appropriate knowledge for answering a given question (Fig. 1).

Table 1. Overview of the ConflictsQA dataset statistics.

Dataset	Type	Generated Contexts		Selected Contexts		QA Pairs	True Only	False Only	Context Length
		True	False	True	False				
NQ	Train	45.0	63.9	3	3	20000	336	6298	498.4
	Evaluation	19.5	42.7	1	14.2	3610	72	998	750.9
WebQ	Train	46.9	34.3	3	3	3778	339	1171	471.8
	Evaluation	24.3	35.8	1	13.3	1210	151	582	747.8
TriviaQA	Train	82.4	38.1	3	3	20000	2185	626	505.2
	Evaluation	40.0	21.6	1	12.8	7993	618	245	757.9

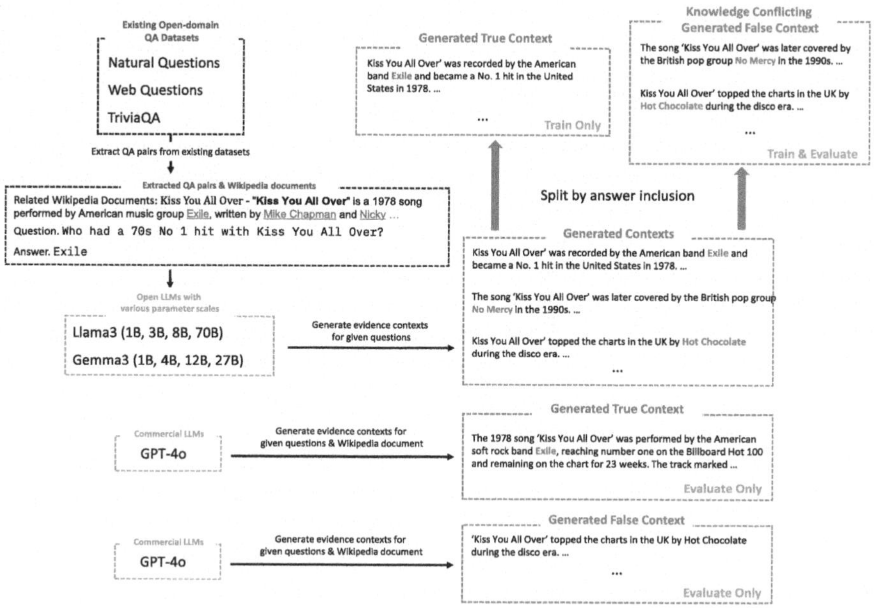

Fig. 1. Construction of ConflictsQA. GPT-4o generates True contexts (Evaluate Only), while open LLMs generate both True (Train Only) and plausible, knowledge-conflicting False contexts (Train & Evaluate). Contexts are labeled True/False depending on whether the gold answer appears in the generated passage or in the reader's prediction.

3.2 Construction of the ConflictsQA Dataset

To reproduce and evaluate the issues discussed in Sect. 3.1, we constructed the ConflictsQA dataset, which simulates knowledge conflicts that arise in the generate-then-read pipelines. The dataset was built upon existing QA pairs from three open-domain QA datasets: Natural Questions (NQ) [8], WebQuestions (WebQ), and TriviaQA [7]. For each QA pair, new context passages were generated using various LLMs, including open-source models (Gemma [4], LLaMa [3]) and a commercial model (GPT-4o [13]).

Following Tang et al. [18], we adopted the same generation prompt template as the generator in the A+B framework. To increase diversity of generated contexts, we used various few-shot examples and paraphrased queries so that contexts with different knowledge could be generated.

After generation, the contexts were applied to a reader model to produce answer predictions. If neither the generated context nor the prediction contained any of the gold answer candidates, the context was labeled as False. If the correct answer appeared in both the context and the prediction, it was labeled as True.

For open LLMs, we divided the models into two parameter groups. In the Gemma series, the 12B and 27B models were categorized as large, and the 1B and 4B models as small. In the LLaMa series, the 8B and 70B models were large, and the 1B and 3B models were small. When constructing the evaluation data,

False contexts from the large-parameter group were prioritized. If a large model did not produce any False context for a given instance, False contexts from the small group were used instead.

The GPT-4o model was used only to construct the evaluation data. Unlike the open models, we employed separate prompts for True and False context generation. For False contexts, the prompts explicitly instructed the model to generate contexts that are factually incorrect but still plausible. To ensure accurate True-context generation, we provided the text from the Wikipedia documents tagged to each QA pair in the prompt.

The evaluation set primarily consisted of GPT-4o-generated True and False contexts, complemented by additional False contexts sampled from open LLM outputs. The training set, on the other hand, used only True and False contexts generated by open LLMs. To manage dataset size and maintain diversity, we applied a sampling to select a subset of training examples.

We initially explored a likelihood-based filtering strategy for selecting informative samples from the training data. True contexts were selected based on higher answer-generation probabilities, and False contexts were chosen when they substantially reduced the model's likelihood of producing the correct answer. However, this approach tended to produce biased samples and overfit to specific patterns, which resulted in poor generalization. Therefore, we adopted random sampling to ensure a more balanced selection of contexts.

Table 1 summarizes the overall statistics of the constructed ConflictsQA dataset. For evaluation, all QA pairs from the original datasets were used without sampling, while for training, up to 20,000 QA pairs were randomly sampled to ensure a balanced dataset size across sources.

Each training QA pair was paired with three True and False contexts. In the evaluation set, if more than ten false contexts were available, a subset was sampled. Otherwise, all false contexts were used. Contexts generated by larger models (8B parameters or above) were prioritized, and contexts generated by smaller model were used only when necessary. Each True context in the evaluation set consisted of a single passage generated by GPT-4o based on the corresponding Wikipedia documents.

3.3 Text Ranking Models

We evaluate three classes of rankers for a fair comparison across semantic and factual reasoning capacity. (1) *Embedding-based models* compute query-context similarity in a shared embedding space. We use the similarity as a ranking score. (2) *Cross-encoder rerankers* take the query and a candidate context jointly and predict a relevance score, which we use to order candidates. (3) *LLM prompted as ranker* uses a pointwise instruction prompt that predicts whether the passage contains the correct knowledge to answer the query. We use the model's generating probability of the *Yes* token as the ranking score for each candidate. The prompt template follows that used in previous work [14].

For supervised settings, we fine-tune this prompting ranker with binary relevance supervision so that True contexts increase the probability of generating *Yes* token and False contexts increase the probability of generating *No* token.

3.4 Model Pruning Strategy

To investigate whether a pruned large model can outperform an equivalently sized small model under the same memory constraints, we apply top-layer pruning on LLMs. Specifically, we remove the uppermost N transformer layers so that the resulting parameter count roughly matches that of the smaller baseline model (e.g., pruning a 20B model down to the 8B scale).

Pruning without retraining causes severe degradation in both text ranking accuracy and general reasoning ability. Therefore, we fine-tune all pruned models using the ConflictsQA training data to restore their domain-specific knowledge and adapt them to the ranking task.

4 Experiments

4.1 Experimental Setup

Our experiments consist of two main components. The first focuses on evaluating publicly available embedding and reranking models on the proposed ConflictsQA dataset. We include lightweight encoder-based models, GTE and BGE-M3, for both their embedding and reranking variants, as well as LLM-based models from the Qwen3 family, including its embedding and reranker configurations. This experiment assesses how existing models handle semantically similar yet knowledge-conflicting contexts.

The second set of experiments examines the effect of model pruning on ranking performance. We apply top-layer pruning to reduce model size while maintaining parameter scales comparable to smaller baseline models. Two LLMs families are used for this experiment: LLaMa-3 and Qwen3. The number of layers remaining after pruning is adjusted such that the resulting models approximate the parameter size of smaller baselines, enabling a fair comparison under similar computational cost.

The pruning configurations for each model are summarized as follows:

- **LLaMa-3.3-70B**: from 80 layers to 10 layers
- **Qwen3-32B**: from 64 layers to 16 layers
- **Qwen3-14B**: from 40 layers to 20 layers

These pruned models are fine-tuned on the ConflictsQA training data.

4.2 Limitations of Lightweight Embedding and Reranking Models in Knowledge Conflicts

Table 2 presents the evaluation results of publicly available embedding and reranking models on the ConflictsQA dataset. The task assumes that multiple

Table 2. Main results on ConflictsQA under knowledge conflicts. Acc. denotes accuracy (Hit@1), and AvgRank denotes the average rank of the True context.

Model	Type	NQ		WebQ		TriviaQA	
		Acc.	AvgRank	Acc.	AvgRank	Acc.	AvgRank
GTE-large-en-v1.5	Embedding	10.08	6.67	12.35	7.22	17.92	5.60
BGE-m3		13.38	6.14	18.49	5.91	20.07	5.06
Qwen3-Embedding-4B		21.66	5.20	21.64	5.75	31.48	4.14
Qwen3-Embedding-8B		17.78	5.60	21.47	5.89	33.00	4.07
GTE-reranker-modernbert	Reranker	14.32	5.77	14.59	6.18	33.63	3.68
BGE-reranker-v2-m3		27.29	4.82	24.12	5.01	34.69	3.59
Qwen3-8B	Prompting	32.61	3.49	31.34	3.44	56.76	2.11
Qwen3-Reranker-4B	Reranker	66.41	2.05	70.31	1.90	66.36	1.82
Qwen3-Reranker-8B		74.50	1.66	73.79	1.78	73.65	1.62

contexts are generated, some of which may contain conflicting or hallucinated information. The goal is to rank them and select the most reliable one. We evaluate the models using accuracy(Hit@1) as the primary metric, measuring how often the correct (True) context is ranked first. Each query is paired with approximately 14 candidate contexts.

Among the evaluated models, GTE and BGE are encoder-based architectures built upon ModernBERT [21] and XLM-RoBERTa [2] backbones, respectively. These models are lightweight compared to LLMs and are optimized for general retrieval tasks. These models have demonstrated strong performance on other benchmarks such as MTEB, showing excellent efficiency relative to their parameter size. However, their performance on ConflictsQA is remarkably low for both the embedding and reranking variants.

Interestingly, even the Qwen3-8B model, which is used with pointwise prompting without any training on text ranking data, outperforms these lightweight retrievers. This observation indicates that models relying purely on semantic similarity fail to discriminate between contexts that are semantically consistent and those that contain conflicting knowledge. Since LLM-generated passages tend to be semantically similar, models that do not encode factual reasoning or knowledge awareness are easily misled by plausible but incorrect candidates.

We further observe that Qwen3-Embedding, despite its large parameter sizes (4B and 8B), performs poorly because it compares independent embedding vectors rather than reasoning over the joint query–context pair. This supports the finding that similarity-based representations, though effective for surface-level relevance, are insufficient for knowledge-level discrimination.

In contrast, Qwen3-Reranker, a cross-encoder model that jointly processes the query and context, achieves substantially better performance. The 8B model significantly outperforms the 4B variant, suggesting that model capacity and internalized knowledge play an important role in recognizing factually correct contexts under conflict.

Overall, these results demonstrate that in knowledge-conflict environments, semantic relevance alone is not enough. Effective context ranking must rely on knowledge reliability, which depends heavily on the model's internalized factual knowledge. Lightweight rerankers or embedding-based retrievers thus contribute little in such scenarios, emphasizing the importance of leveraging larger, knowledge-rich models for conflict-aware ranking.

Table 3. Effect of model pruning on ranking performance on ConflictsQA evaluated using **GPT-4o–generated False contexts only**, where semantic cues are relatively distinct. "After pruning" denotes the parameter count of the model after top-layer pruning.

Model	After pruning	NQ		WebQ		TriviaQA	
		Acc.	AvgRank	Acc.	AvgRank	Acc.	AvgRank
Qwen3-4B	4.0B	64.78	1.64	65.00	1.69	81.69	1.32
Qwen3-8B	5.1B	66.00	1.63	68.57	1.58	72.42	1.52
Qwen3-8B	8.1B	74.97	1.46	75.37	1.49	89.76	1.18
Qwen3-14B	8.1B	**81.54**	**1.32**	**80.51**	**1.39**	**91.23**	**1.14**
Qwen3-32B	9.3B	56.30	1.71	63.34	1.63	64.02	1.58
LLaMa-3.1-8B	8.0B	66.94	1.64	69.56	1.64	87.09	1.24
LLaMa-3.3-70B	10.6B	72.62	1.42	73.54	1.41	75.16	1.38

Table 4. Effect of model pruning on ranking performance on the full ConflictsQA dataset, including **False contexts generated by both GPT-4o and open LLMs**, which introduce fully conflicting knowledge.

Model	After pruning	NQ		WebQ		TriviaQA	
		Acc.	AvgRank	Acc.	AvgRank	Acc.	AvgRank
Qwen3-4B	4.0B	49.40	2.17	46.84	2.26	77.30	1.45
Qwen3-8B	5.1B	34.19	2.79	37.06	2.67	63.59	1.79
Qwen3-8B	8.1B	58.79	**1.97**	59.03	**2.04**	84.10	**1.34**
Qwen3-14B	8.1B	38.34	2.73	38.30	2.92	80.52	1.41
Qwen3-32B	9.3B	29.09	2.59	35.90	2.50	49.80	1.96
LLaMa-3.1-8B	8.0B	**60.37**	1.98	**60.94**	2.09	**84.91**	**1.34**
LLaMa-3.3-70B	10.6B	23.30	3.04	32.08	2.71	50.49	2.00

4.3 Effect of Model Pruning on Ranking Performance

Table 3 and 4 report the results of evaluating the effect of top-layer pruning on LLMs for the ranking task. We compare pruned models with their non-pruned counterparts of similar parameter scale to examine how pruning impacts ranking performance.

Table 3 presents results evaluated on data excluding false contexts generated by open LLMs, whereas table 4 shows results on the full evaluation set including all false contexts. This setup allows us to separately analyze how pruning affects both semantic discrimination and knowledge-based reasoning performance.

The false contexts generated by GPT-4o are generally plausible and coherent, but since they are explicitly prompted to be incorrect, they differ slightly from True contexts rather than forming perfect knowledge conflicts. In contrast, the false contexts from open LLMs were originally generated as attempts to produce correct answers but failed to do so, which often makes them more naturally plausible and harder to distinguish from the True contexts. Consequently, the GPT-4o-based evaluation primarily reflects semantic distinctions, while the full setting with open-LLMs-generated contexts better captures knowledge-level conflicts.

The influence of pruning varies across model families and pruning depths. For some models, removing a moderate number of top layers led to comparable or even improved results relative to size-matched original models. However, the degree of improvement or degradation differed substantially depending on both the model architecture and the number of layers pruned.

Dataset characteristics also played an important role. On NQ and WebQ, the pruned models consistently outperformed original models of similar parameter size. In contrast, on the relatively easier TriviaQA dataset, the non-pruned models showed clearly higher accuracy. Among all pruned variants, the Qwen-14B model pruned to approximately 8.1B parameters achieved the best overall performance across datasets, suggesting that moderate pruning can sometimes yield a regularization effect that improves generalization.

However, as shown in Table 4, when the evaluation includes all False contexts, including contexts generated by open LLMs, the performance of the pruned models drops sharply. This suggests that while pruning and fine-tuning preserve semantic relevance judgment, they significantly weaken the model's ability to assess knowledge reliability. In other words, pruning reduces the factual reasoning capacity embedded in the top layers, confirming that these layers play a crucial role in maintaining knowledge-consistent ranking under conflict scenarios. Therefore, pruning may be beneficial for retrieval-based tasks focused on semantic matching, but it can lead to substantial degradation in tasks that require factual or knowledge-based discrimination.

5 Conclusion

In the Generate-then-Read paradigm, knowledge conflicts often occur when LLMs generate multiple semantically similar but factually inconsistent contexts.

These conflicts can confuse the reader model, causing it to produce incorrect or even contradictory answers.

To explore this problem, we introduced the ConflictsQA dataset, designed to reproduce and evaluate knowledge-conflict scenarios. The dataset extends existing open-domain QA datasets by generating additional contexts with both open LLMs (Gemma, LLaMa) and a commercial model (GPT-4o). GPT-4o was used only for creating evaluation data, while open models were employed for both training and evaluation datasets. False contexts from open LLMs frequently contained plausible yet conflicting knowledge, making them useful for testing models' ability to identify factual reliability.

Using ConflictsQA, we evaluated various embedding and reranking models. Results show that lightweight models such as GTE and BGE, despite their strong performance on other benchmarks, struggle to distinguish factually correct knowledge when conflicts exist. Even larger embedding models like Qwen3-4B and 8B performed poorly, indicating that embedding-based similarity measures are insufficient for knowledge-level discrimination. In contrast, cross-encoder rerankers based on larger LLMs demonstrated clear improvements, highlighting the importance of internalized knowledge for resolving factual conflicts.

We also examined model pruning as a strategy for balancing performance and efficiency. Under limited memory budgets, pruned models achieved competitive performance on datasets with relatively mild conflicts, such as those generated by GPT-4o. However, their performance dropped sharply when evaluated on the full ConflictsQA dataset, which includes open LLM–generated conflicting contexts. This result shows that pruning maintains semantic discrimination but significantly weakens factual reasoning capabilities.

Overall, our findings emphasize that distinguishing knowledge consistency requires more than semantic similarity. Future research should explore embedding and reranking models that can work robustly in knowledge-conflict settings, enabling more reliable judgments under conflicting or inconsistent information.

Acknowledgments. This work was supported by the Institute of Information & Communications Technology Planning & Evaluation (IITP) grant funded by the Korea Government (MSIT) (No. RS-2023-00216011, Development of Artificial Complex Intelligence for Conceptually Understanding and Inferring like Human) and IITP grant funded by the Korea Government (MSIT) (No. RS-2024-00338140, Development of learning and utilization technology to reflect sustainability of generative language models and up-to-dateness over time)

Disclosure of Interests. The authors have no competing interests to declare that are relevant to the content of this article.

References

1. Chen, J., et al.: BGE M3-embedding: multi-lingual, multi-functionality, multi-granularity text embeddings through self-knowledge distillation. In: Annual Meeting of the Association for Computational Linguistics (2024)
2. Conneau, A.: Unsupervised cross-lingual representation learning at scale. In: Proceedings of the 58th Annual Meeting of the Association for Computational Linguistics, pp. 8440–8451 (2020)
3. Dubey, A., et al.: The llama 3 herd of models. CoRR arXiv:abs/2407.21783 (2024)
4. Gemma Team: Gemma 3 technical report. arXiv:abs/2503.19786 (2025)
5. Izacard, G., et al.: Unsupervised dense information retrieval with contrastive learning. Trans. Mach. Learn. Res. **2022** (2021)
6. Izacard, G., Grave, E.: Leveraging passage retrieval with generative models for open domain question answering. In: Proceedings of the 16th Conference of the European Chapter of the Association for Computational Linguistics: Main Volume, pp. 874–880 (2021)
7. Joshi, M., Choi, E., Weld, D., Zettlemoyer, L.: TriviaQA: a large scale distantly supervised challenge dataset for reading comprehension. In: Proceedings of the 55th Annual Meeting of the Association for Computational Linguistics (Volume 1: Long Papers), pp. 1601–1611 (2017)
8. Kwiatkowski, T., et al.: Natural questions: a benchmark for question answering research. Trans. Assoc. Comput. Linguist. **7**, 452–466 (2019)
9. Lewis, P., et al.: Retrieval-augmented generation for knowledge-intensive NLP tasks. arXiv:abs/2005.11401 (2020)
10. Liang, P., et al.: Holistic evaluation of language models. Transactions on Machine Learning Research (2023). featured Certification, Expert Certification, Outstanding Certification
11. Mallen, A., et al.: When not to trust language models: investigating effectiveness of parametric and non-parametric memories. In: Proceedings of the 61st Annual Meeting of the Association for Computational Linguistics (Volume 1: Long Papers), pp. 9802–9822 (2023)
12. Muennighoff, N., Tazi, N., Magne, L., Reimers, N.: MTEB: massive text embedding benchmark. In: Proceedings of the 17th Conference of the European Chapter of the Association for Computational Linguistics (2023)
13. OpenAI: GPT-4 technical report (2023)
14. Qin, Z., et al.: Large language models are effective text rankers with pairwise ranking prompting. In: Findings of the Association for Computational Linguistics: NAACL 2024, pp. 1504–1518 (2024)
15. Roberts, A., Raffel, C., Shazeer, N.: How much knowledge can you pack into the parameters of a language model? In: Proceedings of the 2020 Conference on Empirical Methods in Natural Language Processing (EMNLP), pp. 5418–5426 (2020)
16. Sun, W., et al.: Is ChatGPT good at search? Investigating large language models as re-ranking agents. In: Proceedings of the 2023 Conference on Empirical Methods in Natural Language Processing, pp. 14918–14937 (2023)
17. Sun, Z., Wang, X., Tay, Y., Yang, Y., Zhou, D.: Recitation-augmented language models. In: International Conference on Learning Representations (2023)
18. Tang, W.e.a.: A + B: a general generator-reader framework for optimizing LLMs to unleash synergy potential. In: Findings of the Association for Computational Linguistics: ACL 2024, pp. 3670–3685 (2024)

19. Thakur, N., et al.: BEIR: A heterogenous benchmark for zero-shot evaluation of information retrieval models. ArXiv (2021)
20. Wang, L., et al.: Text embeddings by weakly-supervised contrastive pre-training. arXiv:abs/2212.03533 (2022)
21. Warner, B., et al.: Smarter, better, faster, longer: a modern bidirectional encoder for fast, memory efficient, and long context finetuning and inference. In: Proceedings of the 63rd Annual Meeting of the Association for Computational Linguistics (Volume 1: Long Papers), pp. 2526–2547 (2025)
22. Yu, W., et al.: Generate rather than retrieve: large language models are strong context generators. In: International Conference for Learning Representation (ICLR) (2023)
23. Zhang, X., et al.: mGTE: generalized long-context text representation and reranking models for multilingual text retrieval. In: Conference on Empirical Methods in Natural Language Processing (2024)
24. Zhang, Y., et al.: Qwen3 embedding: Advancing text embedding and reranking through foundation models. ArXiv:abs/2506.05176 (2025)

Cloze Your Gaps: Improving Knowledge Extraction via Query Rewriting

Sanghyun Cho, Myeongjin Lee, Jeong Heo, Jong-hun Shin, Kiyoung Lee, and Soojong Lim(✉)

Electronics and Telecommunications Research Institute, Daejeon, Republic of Korea
{shcho.nlp,myeongjin216,jeonghur,jhshin82,leeky,isj}@etri.re.kr

Abstract. Open-domain question answering with large language models typically adopts a retrieve-then-read pipeline, which is limited by the retriever's accuracy and its inability to fully exploit the model's parametric knowledge. Recent work has explored generate-then-read approaches, where the LLM generates supporting contexts directly. In this paper, we propose a novel pipeline that enhances generate-then-read by introducing a query rewriting module that transforms open-domain questions into cloze-style prompts. These prompts better align with the pretraining distribution of base models and improve the quality of generated contexts. To address variability in model responses to different cloze formulations, we further introduce a query sampling procedure that generates multiple cloze variants per question. The resulting contexts are aggregated using three strategies—SELECT, FUSE, and CONCAT—and filtered via lightweight retrievers, rerankers, and LLM-based ranking prompts. Extensive experiments demonstrate that cloze-based query rewriting enhances knowledge extraction in both base and continuously pretrained models. This work highlights the efficacy of leveraging cloze-style prompts and context aggregation for robust and adaptable open-domain QA systems.

Keywords: Query Rewriting · Generate-then-read · Knowledge Extraction

1 Introduction

Open-domain question answering (QA) and related knowledge-intensive problems depend on substantial external information. Although large language models (LLMs) have demonstrated outstanding performance on a variety of natural language processing tasks, they can still face difficulties in directly answering open-domain questions relying solely on the knowledge encoded in their parameters [15,17].

To address this limitation, the retrieve-then-read pipeline has been widely adopted to provide LLMs with large-scale external knowledge [5,8,12]. In this approach, a retriever first identifies relevant contexts. These contexts are then

R. C.-W. Wong et al. (Eds.): PAKDD 2026, LNAI 16617, pp. 204–215, 2027.
https://doi.org/10.1007/978-981-92-1926-1_17

provided to the LLM as part of the prompt. This enables the model to generate answers by referring to the retrieved external knowledge.

However, a major drawback of this pipeline is that overall performance is highly influenced by the quality of the retriever. As pointed out by Yu et al. [22], this issue is further exacerbated by inherent limitations of the retrieve-then-read pipeline, including context loss due to fixed-length segments, shallow interactions between the question and contexts [9], and the inability to leverage the LLM's internal knowledge during retrieval.

To address these challenges, Yu et al. [22] introduces a generate-then-read pipeline. In this approach, the LLM leverages its parametric knowledge to generate background contexts for the question, which are then used as references when producing the final answer. This approach has been shown to outperform directly generating answers from the LLMs' internal parameters.

Preliminary studies by Tang et al. [21] have shown that base models (LLMs without alignment) excel at memorization, while chat models (LLMs with alignment) produce more helpful and safe answers. Building on these findings, Tang et al. proposed the A+B framework [21], which separates the generator and reader in the generate-then-read pipeline and assigns each component a model that is best suited to its role.

Motivated by the observation that a base model's strong memorization capability affords a clear advantage when the model serves as the context generator within a generate–then–read pipeline [21], we hypothesize that the model achieves greater accuracy when information is elicited through cloze-style queries that closely resemble the raw text which it encountered during pretraining. To test this hypothesis, we extend the generate–then–read pipeline by inserting a query-rewrite module that converts open-domain questions into cloze-style queries.

Preliminary experiment in Fig. 2 shows that the answer accuracy varies with the form of a cloze query, even when the underlying semantics remain unchanged. We thus extend the query-rewrite procedure to sample multiple cloze variants for every question. Each variant independently prompts the base model, generating a corresponding candidate context.

Continual-learning environments frequently involve limited training data, thereby limiting the model's exposure to diverse data and making it difficult to retrieve newly learned knowledge effectively. Nevertheless, our experiments demonstrate that augmenting the system with a query-rewriting procedure results in performance improvements after continual learning.

The main contributions of our work are as follows:

- We propose a novel pipeline with query rewriting that converts open-domain questions into cloze-style templates, effectively leveraging the memorization strengths of base models for context generation.
- We extend the query-rewriting process to sample multiple cloze queries for each question, enabling the generation of diverse supporting contexts, and we explore three distinct strategies (SELECT, FUSE, CONCAT) for effectively utilizing these multiple contexts.

- We demonstrate through extensive experiments in various settings, including continual learning scenarios, that our pipeline significantly outperforms the original generate–then–read approach.

2 Related Works

Retrieval-Augmented Generation (RAG) [12] is a framework in which, upon receiving a question, a retriever first identifies relevant contexts from an external knowledge base, and a generator subsequently produces an answer based on the retrieved documents. Since LLMs generate answers based on the supporting documents provided, the RAG framework helps mitigate hallucinations produced by the model itself [18].

2.1 LLM as a Context Generator

To alleviate the remaining limitations of conventional RAG, Yu et al. [22] introduces a novel framework that directly generates contexts using an LLM, thereby eliminating the dependence on retrieved passages. To improve the diversity and range of knowledge in the generated contexts, Yu et al. uses clustering-based prompts to produce documents from a variety of perspectives.

Sun et al. [20] proposed RECITE, a framework that generates relevant contexts by sampling from the LLM's own memory instead of relying on retrieved contexts. To ensure contextual diversity and factuality, RECITE samples passage hints, which are text segments linked to section and paragraph positions in structured knowledge bases such as Wikipedia, and generates factual paragraphs using greedy decoding.

Motivated by the observation that base models tend to exhibit better memorization while chat models produce more helpful and safer responses, Tang et al. [21] decoupled the generator and reader components and conducted experiments to identify the most effective combination of generator and reader models. Continuous learning has been shown to further enhance the effectiveness of the decoupled framework by enabling seamless integration of source knowledge into the generator component.

In our work, we adopt a query-rewriting approach that transforms the original question into various forms of cloze-style queries, allowing the LLM to generate diverse contexts based on the rewritten queries. This query rewriting approach remains effective and yields notable improvements even under continual learning scenarios.

2.2 LLM as a Context Ranker

Recently, several works have shown that LLMs themselves can serve as a context reranker when prompted as a text reranker. Pairwise Ranking Prompting [16] is a method that prompts an LLM to compare two passages at a time and then aggregates the resulting pairwise preferences. Without any task-specific fine-tuning, moderate-sized open-source models using this method matched or outperformed strong supervised rerankers on benchmarks such as TREC-DL and BEIR. RankGPT [19] demonstrates that ChatGPT/GPT-4 achieve competitive or superior zero-shot passage reranking performance by generating list-wise permutations. It further shows that this ability can be effectively distilled into a 440M-parameter cross-encoder, maintaining strong performance while enabling more efficient deployment. From a broader perspective, the HELM benchmark [13] systematizes such LLM-based relevance-generation prompts, where the model answers Yes/No given a query–document pair and the answer token probability is used as a relevance score.

In this work, we leverage LLM-based text ranking approaches, alongside lightweight re–ranker and retriever methods, to rank the generated contexts, thereby filtering out unnecessary contexts or selecting the most relevant ones.

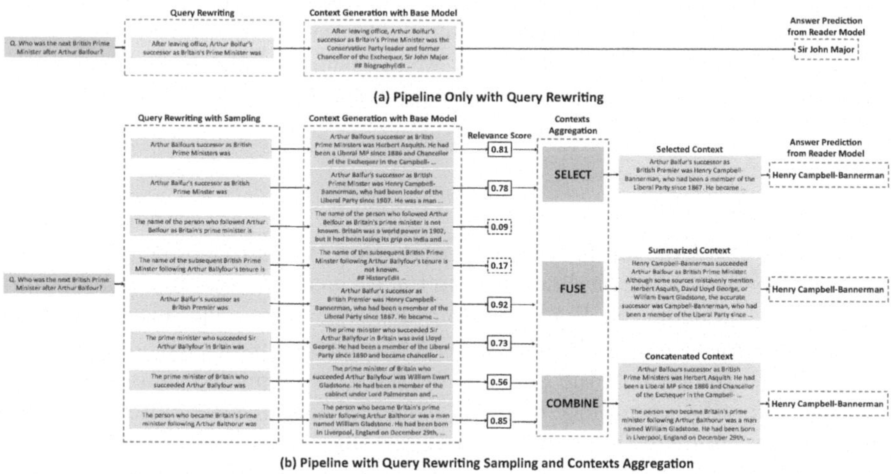

Fig. 1. Overall architecture of generate-then-read pipeline with query rewriting

3 Method

3.1 Query Rewriting

Since (Fig. 1) illustrates the overall architecture of our proposed generate-then-read pipeline with query rewriting, it would be more appropriate to cite it in the Query Rewriting section, where we introduce the core idea of transforming original questions into cloze-style templates. As pretraining involves large amounts of unannotated raw data, the original questions used may differ from the sentence patterns to which the LLMs were primarily exposed during pretraining. Therefore, by converting questions into cloze-style prompts and prompting the

LLM to complete the rest, we guide the model to more naturally retrieve the relevant knowledge stored in its parameters. This process involves reformulating questions into declarative sentences, encouraging the base model to generate continuations that include information relevant to the correct answer.

For example, the question "Who wrote The Lord of the Rings?" is transformed into "The author of The Lord of the Rings is". To align with left-to-right generation models such as GPT, we ensure that the blank to be completed is positioned at the far right of the cloze query. This ensures that the model can generate the answer as a natural continuation. Such cloze-style templates present a more familiar format to the base model, enabling it to more effectively elicit the implicit knowledge stored in its parameters.

To implement this query rewriting step, we constructed a training dataset by prompting GPT-4.1 with few-shot examples to generate diverse cloze-style reformulations. We then fine-tuned an LLaMA-3.1-8B-Instruct on this synthetic dataset to train a specialized query rewriting model. The performance of the rewriting model itself may affect the results, since fine-tuned models can sometimes generate inconsistent outputs or have inherent weaknesses. To isolate the pure effect of cloze-style reformulation, we transformed the test set queries in Table 1 using the gpt-4.1-mini model, which consistently provided high-quality rewrites.

3.2 Query Sampling

In Fig. 2, we present an inclusion matrix that visualizes how the model's responses vary depending on differences in the surface form of semantically equivalent queries. As shown in Fig. 2, feeding different cloze-style queries with the same meaning into the base model can lead to varying answer outputs, revealing a sensitivity to the form of the query. However, this variability can be leveraged to improve overall performance by generating multiple diverse contexts and providing them as input to the reader. To address this issue and ensure that diverse contexts are available, we apply a sampling strategy during the query rewriting step to generate multiple cloze-style query variants, which are then used to construct richer input contexts.

We applied sampling-based decoding [4] using the fine-tuned query rewriting model to generate diverse cloze-style query variants. For each question, we sampled ten cloze-style query variants and performed deduplication to obtain a set of unique reformulations. This set serves as the basis for constructing the final input context, which is passed to the aggregation module.

Effective aggregation is necessary to help reader models generate answers. In our work, we compare three context aggregation methods—SELECT, FUSE and CONCAT—to identify the most effective strategy. First, we predict the relevance between each question and its associated contexts using various methods. To filter out irrelevant contexts and select the most relevant ones for evaluating the effectiveness of different relevance predictions, we employed three approaches: lightweight retriever and reranker models, pointwise prompting and fine-tuned classifiers.

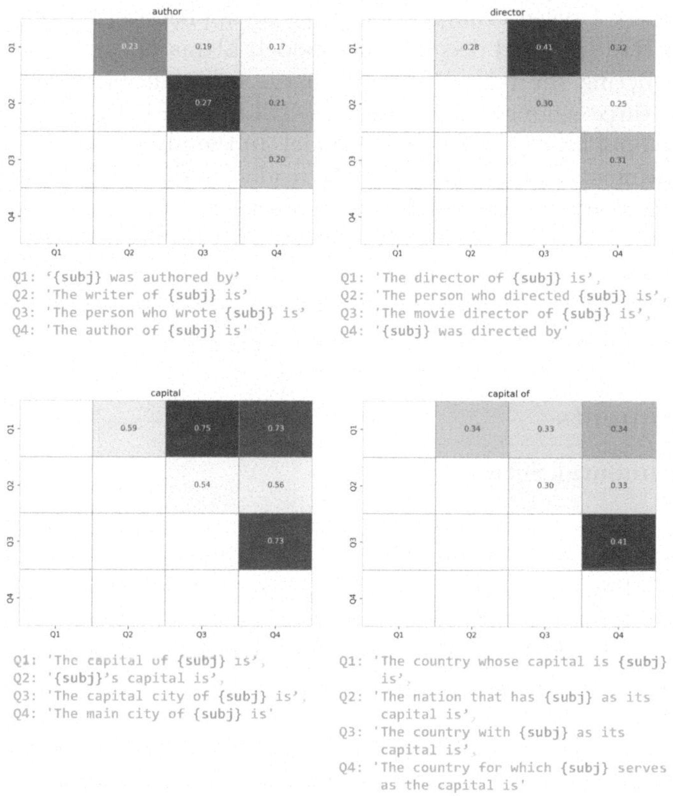

Fig. 2. Inclusion heatmap showing how the model's responses vary depending on differences in the surface form of semantically equivalent cloze-style queries. Each cell indicates the proportion of answer pairs in which one answer string includes the other.

For the lightweight retriever and reranker models, we employed the BGE-m3 [1] text embedding model and reranker model. The embedding model encodes the question and each context into vector representations and computes their similarity to rank relevance. For reranking model, we used a cross-encoder model that jointly takes the question and context as input and applies a classifier over the [CLS] pooled representation to estimate the relevance probability.

For the pointwise prompting approach, we followed prior work that inputs a query and a context, asks whether the two texts are relevant, and compares the generation probabilities of the "Yes" and "No" tokens [13,19]. We applied the few-shot relevance generation instructions used in [19] to the Llama-3.1-8B-Instruct model.

For the finetuning-based approach, we first generate contexts from cloze queries sampled from the training sets of each benchmark dataset. We then labeled contexts containing the correct answer as positive examples, and those without the answer as negative examples. Finally, we finetuned a classification model with these labeled examples. For this, we applied both an encoder-based model, RoBERTa [14], and decoder-only model, Llama [2].

After predicting the relevance between the question and each context, we apply one of three aggregation strategies—SELECT, FUSE, or CONCAT—to construct the final input for the reader model. In the SELECT strategy, we pass only the single most relevant context to the reader. In the FUSE strategy, we first select only the contexts whose relevance scores exceed a predefined threshold. We then use the Llama-3.1-8B-Instruct model with specific instructions to summarize these selected contexts while filtering out non-essential content. In the CONCAT strategy, we concatenate all contexts whose relevance scores exceed the threshold and pass the combined input to the reader model.

4 Experiments

4.1 Experimental Setup

To evaluate the effectiveness of our proposed method, we conducted experiments using three open-domain QA datasets: TriviaQA [7], Natural Questions (NQ) [10], and PopQA [15]. For the TriviaQA dataset, we utilized the Wikipedia split specifically for continual learning experiments leveraging Wikipedia corpora. According to the evaluation setup described in Yu et al. [22], we applied the Exact Match (EM) metric, considering a response correct if it includes any of the answer candidates.

To accelerate the computationally intensive context generation step, we employed VLLM [11] with the auto setting for data type during model loading. For the reader model, we consistently used Llama-3.1-8B-Instruct with the data type set to bfloat16. Both context generation and response generation were performed using greedy decoding without sampling. For in-context learning-based experiments, we followed Tang et al. [21] for prompt design in both the context generation and the reader model. We set the maximum token generation limit to 384 for context generation and 32 for the reader model.

We selected four LLMs for context generation: Llama-3.2-3B [2], Gemma-3-4B [3], Mistral-7B-v0.1 [6], and Llama-3.1-8B [2]. These models were chosen to cover a range of parameter sizes (3B, 4B, 7B, 8B) and model families (Llama, Gemma, Mistral). For context generation, we consistently used the base version of each model, which is not instruction-tuned.

To assess the effectiveness of the query rewriting in a continual learning scenario, we continually pretrained each model using a Wikipedia documents. For the NQ and PopQA datasets, we collected Wikipedia documents corresponding to the tagged titles provided in the datasets. For TriviaQA, the 'rc.wikipedia' split already contains the relevant Wikipedia texts for each sample, which we used directly as the continual learning corpus. Since the NQ test dataset contained only a small number of samples, we supplemented its continual learning corpus by adding the Wikipedia documents from PopQA.

We performed continual learning for one epoch with a batch size of 256 and a learning rate of 10^{-6}.

Table 1. Performance comparison of context generation using in-context learning and cloze-style queries on NQ [10], TriviaQA [7], and PopQA [15].

Context Generation Models	Natural Questions				TriviaQA				PopQA			
	ICL		Cloze		ICL		Cloze		ICL		Cloze	
	Base	CP	Base	CP	Base	CP	Base	CP	Base	CP	Base	CP
Llama-3.2-3B	10.33	23.62 (+13.29)	25.62	**27.36 (+1.74)**	37.17	60.84 (+23.67)	60.45	**63.38 (+2.93)**	5.11	**24.64 (+19.53)**	18.81	22.80 (+3.99)
Gemma-3-4B	20.30	20.58 (+0.28)	23.35	**25.56 (+2.77)**	57.83	57.25 (−0.58)	61.01	**63.28 (+2.27)**	18.81	19.46 (+0.65)	16.73	**19.89 (+3.16)**
Mistral-v0.1-7B	27.78	30.38 (+2.6)	30.88	**32.35 (+1.47)**	67.17	69.23 (+2.06)	70.27	**70.53 (+0.26)**	26.62	**30.88 (+4.26)**	22.27	27.80 (+5.53)
Llama-3.1-8B	26.70	26.81 (+0.11)	30.22	**32.49 (+2.27)**	64.71	65.25 (+0.54)	69.57	**71.57 (+2.00)**	26.93	**29.98 (+3.05)**	22.75	28.80 (+6.05)

4.2 Experimental Results with Cloze-Style Query-Based Context Generation

Table 2. Performance of LLMs with over 20B parameters.

Context Generation Models	NQ		TriviaQA		PopQA	
	ICL	Cloze	ICL	Cloze	ICL	Cloze
Gemma-3-27B	28.59	**35.35 (+6.76)**	70.15	**78.03 (+8.78)**	27.40	**27.42** (−0.02)
Llama-3.3-70B	33.43	**39.53 (+6.10)**	72.55	**81.78 (+9.23)**	**39.19**	32.70 (−6.49)
Qwen2-72B	33.24	**34.74 (+1.50)**	73.15	**79.12 (+5.97)**	**33.31**	30.20 (−3.11)

We compared the proposed method of our work, which rewrites questions into cloze-style queries, with an approach that applies in-context learning prompts to a base model to generate context [21]. Table 1 presents the performance comparison of the two approaches evaluated on three datasets: NQ, TriviaQA, and PopQA. In Table 1, CP refers to the continuously pretrained model using the Wikipedia corpus of each dataset, and ICL refers to the results obtained using in-context learning prompts to generate contexts. We reran the ICL baselines using the exact experimental configuration of our work.

As shown in Table 1, we observe consistent performance improvements on the NQ and TriviaQA datasets when generating context using the transformed cloze queries instead of the original questions. In particular, while some models with continual pretraining exhibited performance drops or negligible improvements, the cloze query-based approach consistently resulted in performance gains. In contrast, on the PopQA dataset, which focuses on long-tail knowledge that the evaluated models have not sufficiently learned, we observed performance drops with the cloze query-based approach across nearly all models. While the ICL results often generated context aligned with the intent of the question even when it was not related to learned knowledge, the cloze query-based approach shows a tendency to avoid answering by responding with "unknown" for queries that were difficult to answer (e.g. The person who composed "Sue" is unknown. The song was first published in 1869 by the New York music publisher ...).

As shown in Table 2, when evaluating models with more than 20B parameters, we observed a substantially larger performance improvement with the cloze query-based approach compared to smaller models on both the NQ and TriviaQA datasets. Due to GPU resource limitations, we evaluated only the base models without additional continuous pretraining. This result suggests that larger models benefit more from the cloze-style transformation, likely because their stronger memorization capabilities allow them to more effectively retrieve relevant factual knowledge from internal representations, resulting in more accurate and contextually grounded responses.

4.3 Experimental Results with Query Sampling

Figure 3 presents the results of sampling various forms of cloze queries and aggregating them using different methods based on the models without continuous pretraining. In this figure, the lightweight retriever and reranker, LLaMa, LLaMa-finetued, and the RoBERTa-finetuned represent methods for predicting how relevant the generated context is to the query. The lightweight reranker and retriever correspond to the BGE-m3 reranker and retriever models. LLaMA denotes the method based on the approach of text ranking method [13,19], using the LLaMA-3.1-8B-Instruct model. The models marked as finetuned are those further trained using finetuning datasets constructed from the training splits of NQ and TriviaQA. SELECT, FUSE, and CONCAT denote different aggregation strategies that combine contexts based on the predicted relevance scores. The upper bound represents the performance obtained by generating a response from the reader model for each context sampled from the cloze queries, and counting the prediction as correct if any of the generated responses contains the ground-truth answer.

As shown in Fig. 3, the CONCAT aggregation strategy consistently achieved the best performance across most cases. However, the current evaluation metric is based on whether the response contains the correct answer. In some cases, the reader model produces multiple answers when conflicting contexts are provided. This means that under an evaluation metric based on answer inclusion, generating multiple answers can inadvertently lead to inflated performance scores. As a result, the evaluation setting inevitably imposes a disadvantage on the SELECT aggregation strategy, which produces only a single concise answer.

Although the FUSE strategy was expected to omit redundant information and summarize only the necessary content, it resulted in lower performance than the CONCAT strategy due to the loss of essential information. For relevance prediction, the finetuned LLaMA model consistently achieved the highest performance across all datasets and models under the SELECT aggregation strategy. Under the CONCAT and FUSE strategies, while filtering irrelevant contexts with the finetuned LLaMA model led to the best performance on TriviaQA, the highest performance on NQ and PopQA datasets was observed when no filtering was applied.

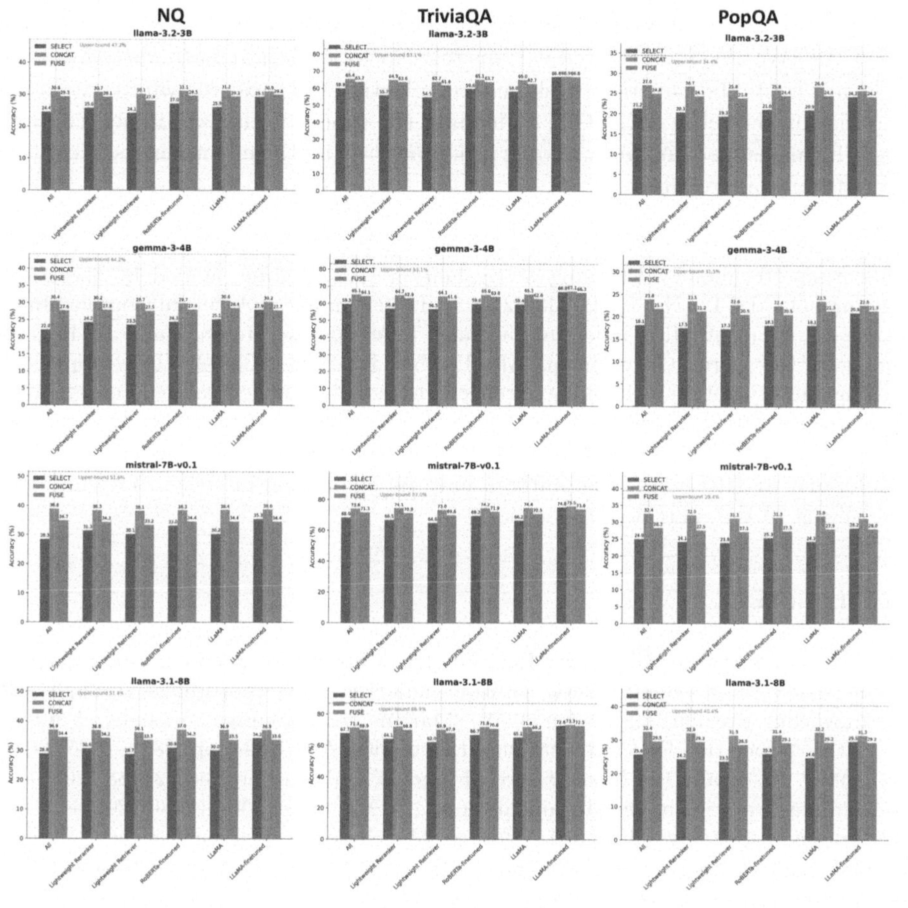

Fig. 3. Performance comparison of query sampling-based context generation using different relevance prediction and aggregation strategies. Query reformation was performed using Llama-3.1-8B-Instruct. 'All' denotes no context filtering.

5 Conclusion

In this study, we introduced an approach that augments the generate-then-read pipeline with a query rewriting step that transforms original questions into cloze-style queries. By generating cloze-style queries and using a base language model to produce the corresponding context, we observed improved performance in open-domain QA compared to generating context via few-shot in-context learning prompts. This improvement was particularly notable under continual pre-training settings, where the use of cloze queries led to further performance gains.

Since the form of a cloze-style query can significantly influence the generated context, we conducted experiments with sampling diverse cloze query variants for the same question. To effectively aggregate the multiple generated contexts, we explored and compared three aggregation strategies: SELECT, FUSE, and CONCAT. We also investigated various relevance prediction methods to filter out irrelevant contexts. Our results show that selecting the most relevant context via a prediction model in SELECT, or feeding the model with a combined context, outperforms using a single cloze query, demonstrating the effectiveness of context diversity and aggregation.

Acknowledgments. This work was supported by the Institute of Information & Communications Technology Planning & Evaluation (IITP) grant funded by the Korea Government (MSIT) (No. RS-2023-00216011, Development of Artificial Complex Intelligence for Conceptually Understanding and Inferring like Human) and IITP grant funded by the Korea Government (MSIT) (No. RS-2024-00338140, Development of learning and utilization technology to reflect sustainability of generative language models and up-to-dateness over time).

Disclosure of Interests. The authors have no competing interests to declare that are relevant to the content of this article.

References

1. Chen, J., Xiao, S., Zhang, P., Luo, K., Lian, D., Liu, Z.: M3-embedding: multi-linguality, multi-functionality, multi-granularity text embeddings through self-knowledge distillation. In: Ku, L.W., Martins, A., Srikumar, V. (eds.) Findings of the Association for Computational Linguistics: ACL 2024, pp. 2318–2335 (2024)
2. Dubey, A., et al.: The llama 3 herd of models. CoRR arXiv:2407.21783 (2024)
3. Gemma Team: Gemma 3 technical report. ArXiv arXiv:2503.19786 (2025)
4. Holtzman, A., Buys, J., Du, L., Forbes, M., Choi, Y.: The curious case of neural text degeneration. In: International Conference on Learning Representations (2020)
5. Izacard, G., Grave, E.: Leveraging passage retrieval with generative models for open domain question answering. In: Merlo, P., Tiedemann, J., Tsarfaty, R. (eds.) Proceedings of the 16th Conference of the European Chapter of the Association for Computational Linguistics: Main Volume, pp. 874–880 (2021)
6. Jiang, A.Q., et al.: Mistral 7b. ArXiv arXiv:2310.06825 (2023)
7. Joshi, M., Choi, E., Weld, D., Zettlemoyer, L.: TriviaQA: a large scale distantly supervised challenge dataset for reading comprehension. In: Barzilay, R., Kan, M.Y. (eds.) Proceedings of the 55th Annual Meeting of the Association for Computational Linguistics (Volume 1: Long Papers), pp. 1601–1611 (2017)
8. Karpukhin, V., et al.: Dense passage retrieval for open-domain question answering. In: Webber, B., Cohn, T., He, Y., Liu, Y. (eds.) Proceedings of the 2020 Conference on Empirical Methods in Natural Language Processing (EMNLP), pp. 6769–6781 (2020)
9. Khattab, O., Potts, C., Zaharia, M.A.: Relevance-guided supervision for OpenQA with ColBERT. Trans. Assoc. Comput. Linguist. **9**, 929–944 (2020)
10. Kwiatkowski, T., et al.: Natural questions: a benchmark for question answering research. Trans. Assoc. Comput. Linguist. **7**, 452–466 (2019)
11. Kwon, W., et al.: Efficient memory management for large language model serving with pagedattention. In: Proceedings of the 29th Symposium on Operating Systems Principles (2023)

12. Lewis, P., et al.: Retrieval-augmented generation for knowledge-intensive NLP tasks. ArXiv arXiv:2005.11401 (2020)
13. Liang, P., et al.: Holistic evaluation of language models. Trans. Mach. Learn. Res. (2023). Featured Certification, Expert Certification, Outstanding Certification
14. Liu, Y., et al.: RoBERTa: a robustly optimized BERT pretraining approach. ArXiv arXiv:1907.11692 (2019)
15. Mallen, A., Asai, A., Zhong, V., Das, R., Khashabi, D., Hajishirzi, H.: When not to trust language models: investigating effectiveness of parametric and non-parametric memories. In: Rogers, A., Boyd-Graber, J., Okazaki, N. (eds.) Proceedings of the 61st Annual Meeting of the Association for Computational Linguistics (Volume 1: Long Papers), pp. 9802–9822 (2023)
16. Qin, Z., et al.: Large language models are effective text rankers with pairwise ranking prompting. In: Duh, K., Gomez, H., Bethard, S. (eds.) Findings of the Association for Computational Linguistics: NAACL 2024, pp. 1504–1518 (2024)
17. Roberts, A., Raffel, C., Shazeer, N.: How much knowledge can you pack into the parameters of a language model? In: Webber, B., Cohn, T., He, Y., Liu, Y. (eds.) Proceedings of the 2020 Conference on Empirical Methods in Natural Language Processing (EMNLP), pp. 5418–5426 (2020)
18. Shuster, K., Poff, S., Chen, M., Kiela, D., Weston, J.: Retrieval augmentation reduces hallucination in conversation. In: Moens, M.F., Huang, X., Specia, L., Yih, S.W.T. (eds.) Findings of the Association for Computational Linguistics: EMNLP 2021, pp. 3784–3803 (2021)
19. Sun, W., et al.: Is ChatGPT good at search? Investigating large language models as re-ranking agents. In: Bouamor, H., Pino, J., Bali, K. (eds.) Proceedings of the 2023 Conference on Empirical Methods in Natural Language Processing, pp. 14918–14937 (2023)
20. Sun, Z., Wang, X., Tay, Y., Yang, Y., Zhou, D.: Recitation-augmented language models. In: The Eleventh International Conference on Learning Representations (2023)
21. Tang, W., et al.: A + B: a general generator-reader framework for optimizing LLMs to unleash synergy potential. In: Ku, L.W., Martins, A., Srikumar, V. (eds.) Findings of the Association for Computational Linguistics: ACL 2024, pp. 3670–3685 (2024)
22. Yu, W., et al.: Generate rather than retrieve: large language models are strong context generators. In: The Eleventh International Conference on Learning Representations (2023)

AIANO: Enhancing Information Retrieval with AI-Augmented Annotation

Sameh Khattab[1(✉)], Marie Bauer[1], Lukas Heine[1], Till Rostalski[1], Jens Kleesiek[1,2,3,4], and Julian Friedrich[1]

[1] Institute for Artificial Intelligence in Medicine (IKIM), University Hospital Essen (AöR), Essen, Germany
{sameh.khattab,julian.friedrich}@uk-essen.de
[2] Cancer Research Center Cologne Essen (CCCE), Essen, Germany
[3] German Cancer Consortium (DKTK, Partner site Essen), Heidelberg, Germany
[4] Department of Physics of TU Dortmund, Dortmund, Germany

Abstract. The rise of Large Language Models (LLMs) and Retrieval-Augmented Generation (RAG) has rapidly increased the need for high-quality, curated information retrieval datasets. These datasets, however, are currently created with off-the-shelf annotation tools that make the annotation process complex and inefficient. To streamline this process, we developed a specialized annotation tool - AIANO. By adopting an AI-augmented annotation workflow that tightly integrates human expertise with LLM assistance, AIANO enables annotators to leverage AI suggestions while retaining full control over annotation decisions. In a within-subject user study ($n = 15$), participants created question-answering datasets using both a baseline tool and AIANO. AIANO nearly doubled annotation speed compared to the baseline while being easier to use and improving retrieval accuracy. These results demonstrate that AIANO's AI-augmented approach accelerates and enhances dataset creation for information retrieval tasks, advancing annotation capabilities in retrieval-intensive domains.

Keywords: Data Annotation · Information Retrieval · Retrieval-Augmented Generation · Large Language Models · User Study

1 Introduction

Large Language Models (LLMs) have become integral to workflows across diverse domains [21], yet remain prone to reliability issues and factual inaccuracies [11]. These limitations can be mitigated by providing relevant documents as context, a technique called Retrieval-Augmented Generation (RAG) [13]. However, the effectiveness of RAG systems depends on multiple components [10], making robust evaluation with high-quality annotated datasets essential [5,6]. Yet, these datasets require queries, ground-truth answers, and relevant document annotations, making their creation - particularly in specialized domains - prohibitively challenging, time-consuming, and expensive [17,19,23].

R. C.-W. Wong et al. (Eds.): PAKDD 2026, LNAI 16617, pp. 216–226, 2027.
https://doi.org/10.1007/978-981-92-1926-1_18

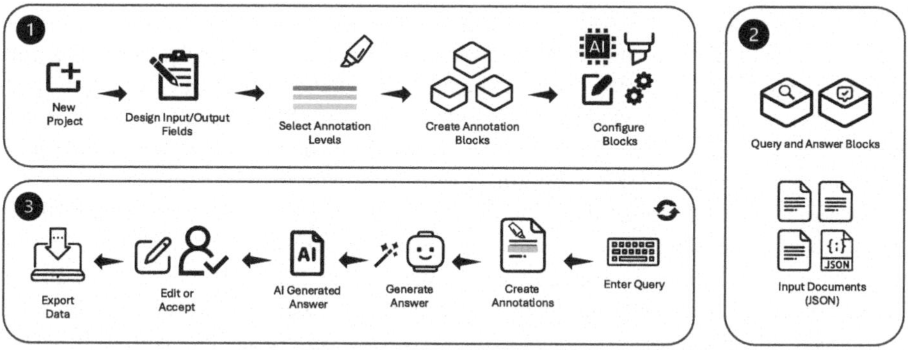

Fig. 1. Workflow of the AIANO annotation system. (i) Project Creation Phase: Configure project metadata, input/output schemas, annotation levels, and AIANO Blocks. (ii) Project Configuration Phase: Configure annotation blocks with LLM provider and upload documents for annotation. (iii) Annotation Phase: Annotators highlight text, trigger AI-assisted content generation, review, edit, and export the dataset. The cycle icon indicates iterative refinement.

To streamline the creation of these datasets, we developed AIANO[1], to our knowledge, the first annotation tool designed specifically for information retrieval (IR) tasks. AIANO implements an AI-augmented workflow that seamlessly integrates human expertise with LLM capabilities, accelerating annotation through AI assistance, while maintaining quality through human oversight. We make three primary contributions:

- We introduce AIANO, a specialized annotation tool for information retrieval tasks.
- We outline AIANO's design principles enabling efficient LLM-human collaboration in semi-automatic annotation workflows.
- We systematically evaluate AIANO's effectiveness and usability against a baseline annotation tool through a controlled within-subject user study.

2 Related Work

Creating IR datasets presents unique challenges that distinguish it from standard tasks such as classification or entity recognition. IR annotation requires synthesizing information across multiple documents and constructing contextual rationales, making the process time-intensive and prone to incomplete coverage [4]. This incompleteness carries significant consequences: research demonstrates that when annotators miss relevant passages, retrieval models trained on these incomplete annotations suffer substantial performance degradation [16].

[1] AIANO is available at https://github.com/TIO-IKIM/AIANO.

The emergence of RAG systems has further intensified IR annotation challenges, as RAG relies on retrieval mechanisms to ground LLM responses in external knowledge [13]. This reliance has spurred the development of evaluation metrics for assessing RAG system performance across multiple dimensions [5,6,23]. However, RAG evaluation frameworks require high-quality annotated datasets, which remain expensive and labor-intensive to produce.

The high cost of annotation has motivated research into leveraging LLMs themselves for automatic data labeling. Such automation efforts have shown promise, with studies demonstrating that models like GPT-3.5 can achieve human-comparable performance on certain tasks using explain-then-annotate approaches [9]. However, this performance varies substantially: research across several annotation tasks with different datasets reveals significant dependence on task type and domain, necessitating human validation to ensure data quality and trustworthiness [15]. This variability in automated annotation quality has motivated human-AI collaborative frameworks that leverage complementary strengths of both parties [3,7,14]. For instance, CoAnnotating [14] employs uncertainty estimation to strategically allocate annotation instances, routing low-uncertainty cases to LLMs while directing uncertain instances to humans; thereby achieving performance improvements over purely manual or fully automated methods. However, these automation-focused solutions do not fully address the fundamental workflow inefficiencies inherent in document-intensive IR annotation, such as managing multi-document contexts, ensuring comprehensive coverage, and balancing annotation speed with quality.

AIANO tackles these challenges through a task-specialized, semi-automatic pipeline that strategically integrates LLM assistance while preserving human oversight in labeling decisions.

3 AIANO System

AIANO (**AI A**ugmented an**NO**tation) provides a platform for dataset creation through human-AI collaboration, designed primarily for information retrieval tasks but adaptable to diverse annotation scenarios.

3.1 Core Concepts

AIANO Blocks. AIANO models annotation tasks as configurable input/output blocks, each operating in one of three modes that represent varying levels of human-AI collaboration:

(i) Plain Mode receives no automatic input sources. The AI performs no operations, and the human annotator manually writes all content from scratch. For example, a free-text Comment Block would allow annotators to write notes directly.

(ii) AI Solo Mode takes pre-defined system prompts as input. The AI automatically generates content based on these prompts, which the human annotator can then review and refine. For example, a Question Block might auto-generate boilerplate comprehension questions.

(iii) Human-AI Collaborative Mode draws from multiple input sources: existing annotations, user-defined fields, other blocks, and system prompts. The AI generates outputs by synthesizing these sources, and the human annotator can accept, modify, or override the suggestions. For example, an Answer Block may draw from a Question Block, highlighted passages, and document metadata to generate candidate answers. Users can also create custom block types for specialized needs.

Annotation Levels. AIANO supports configurable annotation levels for highlighting text with different categories (e.g., "important", "distracting"), providing contextual information for downstream tasks.

Input Schema Flexibility. Users define custom input and output schemas through the UI, following a JSON structure that requires only document ID and subject ID as mandatory fields. Additional fields of any type can be added, enabling support for varying document types without requiring programmatic configuration.

3.2 Workflow

To illustrate AIANO's capabilities, creating a question-answer dataset for RAG evaluation shall be considered. The workflow comprises three phases: **(1) Project Creation**: configure metadata, define schemas, set annotation levels, and design tasks using AIANO Blocks; **(2) Configuration**: connect blocks to LLMs and upload JSON documents; **(3) Annotation**: iteratively highlight text, generate an answer, review content, and export datasets with full provenance. The detailed workflow is shown in Fig. 1.

The project setup follows four steps: define metadata (name, description, tags), configure input/output schemas and upload documents, set annotation levels (e.g., highlight levels for evidence passages), and configure AIANO Blocks (type, mode, inputs, prompts). For RAG datasets, a Question Block in Plain Mode enables manual formulation, while an Answer Block in Human-AI Collaborative Mode generates answers from questions and highlights.

The annotation interface comprises three panels: document corpus with search and filtering capabilities (left), highlighting interface with search and annotation tools (center), and AIANO Blocks (right). Annotators select documents, highlight relevant spans, and populate blocks left-to-right, and the system automatically saves annotations with provenance metadata for the current entry as well as the previous annotation entries for the project.

For downstream applications, users can export datasets in JSON format with question-answer-passage triplets, IDs, and span positions. Projects export in *.aiano* format encapsulating all configurations for reproducibility and sharing.

3.3 Implementation

AIANO supports any LLM provider following OpenAI API [2] standards, including commercial services (e.g., OpenAI, Anthropic) and local deployments such as vLLM [12] for efficient inference, enabling cost-effective, high-throughput workflows. The system uses a containerized microservices architecture with React 19 frontend, FastAPI backend, PostgreSQL database, and Docker deployment.

4 Methodology

4.1 User Study

Study Design. To evaluate AIANO's effectiveness over existing annotation tools, we conducted a within-subject study comparing AIANO to Label Studio [1], a widely used annotation tool. We hypothesized that AIANO would demonstrate lower cognitive load, faster task completion, and higher retrieval accuracy.

Participants. We recruited 15 participants, including graduate students, researchers, software developers, medical doctors, and regulatory affairs specialists (median age 26, range 18–50; 66.7% men, 33.3% women; all German speakers with varying annotation experience). Participants received no compensation.

Experimental Setup. We created 60 short German general knowledge documents (3–5 sentences each) using Claude Sonnet 4, then authored nine questions requiring either single-document (n = 5) or multi-document retrieval (n = 4, requiring 3–4 documents). Participants received predefined questions and searched for answers by identifying relevant documents, highlighting passages, and formulating responses. Each participant completed four questions per platform (two single-document, two multi-document, randomly selected) without time limits.

To mitigate order and carryover effects, participants were randomly assigned to start with either tool, given approximately 10-minute breaks between platforms, and approximately half received identical questions across tools, while others received different questions of comparable difficulty.

AIANO was configured with a Question Block (Plain Mode) and Answer Block (Human-AI Collaborative Mode), where participants accessed Meta's Llama 70B model [20] to generate answers from highlighted passages. AIANO provided full-text search across and within documents. **Label Studio** (v1.13.1) was configured with separate projects per question but lacked native interactive AI collaboration and full-text search capabilities.

We conducted a brief tutorial that included written instructions, demonstrations, and hands-on practice before the task began. We measured task completion time, collected NASA-TLX assessments [8] and post-task questionnaires for each tool, and recorded the annotated datasets.

4.2 Evaluation Metrics

Subjective Measures. Participants completed questionnaires after each platform with eight questions assessing usability, navigation, and performance (rated on 5-point Likert scales), from which we calculated a *Composite* usability score. For AIANO, we included an additional question assessing AI-assisted features and search functionality (Figs. 3). In addition, we measured cognitive load using NASA-TLX dimensions: *Temporal Demand*, *Physical Demand*, *Mental Demand*, *Frustration*, *Performance*, and *Effort*. Open-ended questions gathered qualitative feedback.

Objective Measures. We measured task completion time (from start to participant-indicated completion) and calculated retrieval metrics (precision, recall, and F1 score) by comparing retrieved documents (those with highlights) against predefined relevant documents. A document was considered retrieved if any passage within it was highlighted.

Statistical Analysis. We assessed normality using Shapiro-Wilk tests [18]. Most subjective measures and task completion time followed normal distributions, while *Mental Demand*, *Physical Demand*, *Temporal Demand*, *Reuse Intention*, *Speed*, and *Overall Satisfaction* violated normality. We applied paired t-tests for normally distributed data and Wilcoxon signed-rank tests for non-parametric data ($p < 0.05$), with $p < 0.001$ for values below this threshold. Statistics are reported as medians unless indicated otherwise (Figs. 2 and 3).

5 Results and Analysis

5.1 Quantitative Analysis

Post-study Questionnaires. Participants reported lower overall workload with AIANO compared to Label Studio (22.5 vs. 34.17, p < 0.001). Across

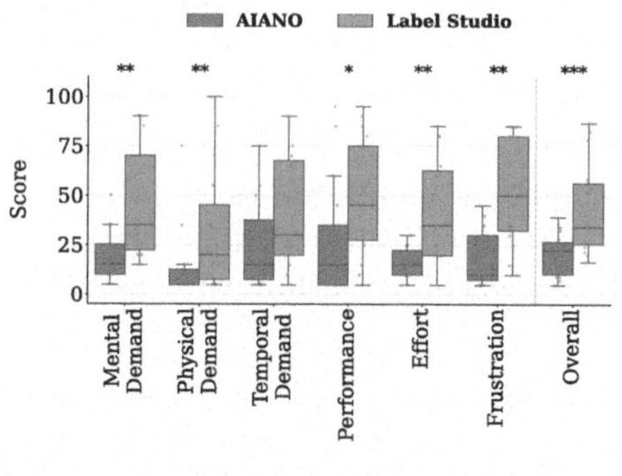

Fig. 2. NASA-TLX workload assessment. Subscale scores across six dimensions and overall workload. Lower scores indicate lower workload. $*p < 0.05, **p < 0.01, ***p < 0.001$.

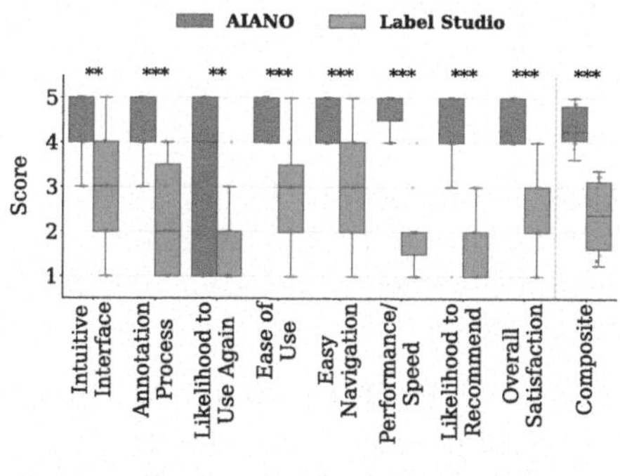

Fig. 3. Usability questionnaire ratings. Likert scale ratings ($1 - 5$) across eight usability dimensions and a composite score. Higher scores indicate better user experience. $**p < 0.01, ***p < 0.001$.

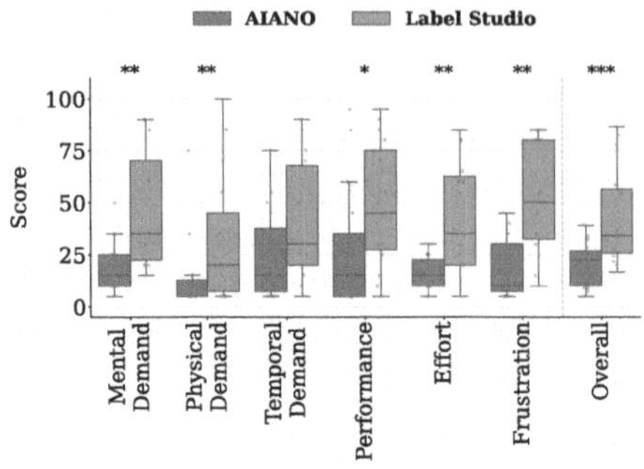

Fig. 4. Task completion time. Individual participant task durations (in minutes) are shown as overlaid circles ($n = 15$).

Table 1. Information retrieval performance comparison.

Metric	AIANO	Label Studio
Precision	0.889	0.867
Recall	0.883	0.783
F1-Score	0.860	0.787

NASA-TLX dimensions (see Fig. 2), AIANO consistently reduced mental demand (15.0 vs. 35.0, p = 0.005), physical demand (5.0 vs. 20.0, p = 0.008), required less effort (15.0 vs. 35.0, p = 0.003), and lowered frustration (10.0 vs. 50.0, p = 0.001). Participants also rated their performance better with AIANO (15.0 vs. 45.0, p = 0.037). Temporal demand did not differ between tools (15.0 vs. 30.0, p = 0.083).

Feedback from the custom 5-point Likert questionnaire paralleled NASA-TLX results. All participants rated AIANO with scores of 4 or 5, while Label Studio exhibited greater variability and lower ratings. Participants consistently rated AIANO higher across all usability dimensions, including intuitive interface (5.0 vs. 3.0, p = 0.001), annotation process (5.0 vs. 2.0, p < 0.001), likelihood to use again (4.0 vs. 1.0, p = 0.008), ease of use (5.0 vs. 3.0, p < 0.001), easy navigation (5.0 vs. 3.0, p < 0.001), performance/speed (5.0 vs. 2.0, p < 0.001), likelihood to recommend (4.0 vs. 2.0, p < 0.001), and overall satisfaction (4.0 vs. 2.0, p < 0.001). The composite score demonstrated higher usability for AIANO (4.25 vs. 2.375, p < 0.001). Most participants rated AI-assisted features highly (5.0), with no Label Studio comparison possible due to the lack of this functionality.

Task Completion Time. Participants completed annotation tasks in nearly half the time with AIANO compared to Label Studio (Fig. 4). Median task completion time decreased from 10.0 min with Label Studio to 6.0 min with AIANO.

Retrieval Performance. AIANO demonstrated higher retrieval performance across all metrics (see Table 1). Participants using AIANO achieved higher precision (0.89 vs. 0.87), recall (0.88 vs. 0.78), and F1 score (0.86 vs. 0.79), with an average improvement of 8.2% across the three metrics (precision: +2.5%, recall: +12.8%, F1: +9.3%).

5.2 Qualitative Feedback

Participants found AIANO intuitive and efficient, reporting that AI-assisted answer generation and search functionality simplified workflows and accelerated task completion. Specifically, 86.7% found the search useful, 93.3% found AI assistance useful, and 80% valued both features for improved efficiency.

In contrast, Label Studio feedback highlighted performance issues when opening/closing documents and difficulties copying text or navigating between documents. Some participants found Label Studio adequate, appreciating text preview and the organized question-answer layout.

6 Discussion

In this work, we introduced AIANO, an AI-augmented annotation tool, and demonstrated through a comparative study with Label Studio that AIANO substantially accelerates the creation of IR datasets while reducing cognitive load and improving usability. These results show that dataset creation of IR tasks can be significantly enhanced by strategically integrating annotation workflows with AI assistance.

6.1 Efficiency and Usability

In the user study, participants reported substantially lower workload with AIANO, with significant reductions across mental demand, physical demand, effort, and frustration. The reduction in frustration is particularly noteworthy, as high frustration contributes to burnout, reduced data quality, and higher turnover in annotation work. Participants completed tasks 40% faster without reporting increased time pressure, indicating genuine efficiency gains rather than rushing. These improvements likely stem from integrated full-text search and AI-assisted answer generation, which transformed document discovery and reduced formulation effort. Participants consistently rated AIANO highly on interface intuitiveness, ease of use, and navigation.

6.2 Retrieval Performance and Data Quality

Annotators using AIANO identified more of the truly relevant documents in the corpus, as indicated by higher recall, while simultaneously reducing false positives, reflected in improved precision. The substantial gains in F1 scores confirm AIANO's overall effectiveness in balancing comprehensiveness with accuracy. This directly tackles a critical bottleneck: incomplete and noisy annotations lead to biased training data and unreliable model evaluation [16]. AIANO's improved coverage and discrimination enable the creation of datasets that better capture the full range of relevant information while filtering out noise, ultimately producing more robust retrieval systems.

6.3 LLM-Assisted Annotation

The integrated LLM assistance and search functionality worked synergistically throughout the annotation workflow: participants searched for documents, highlighted passages, and used AI to generate candidate answers. This represents a fundamentally different annotation paradigm compared to manual approaches. Qualitative feedback confirmed the value: 86.7% found the search useful, 93.3% found AI assistance useful, and 80% valued both together for improved efficiency. This aligns with perspectives on human-AI collaborative annotation [22], positioning LLMs as interactive collaborators embedded directly in the annotation workflow rather than preprocessing tools applied before human involvement. However, as [15] noted, LLM effectiveness can be task-dependent, warranting investigation across diverse annotation scenarios to understand when and how LLM assistance provides the most value.

6.4 Limitations

Several limitations should be acknowledged. Our user study included 15 participants, which constrains the statistical power for subgroup analyses and limits our ability to detect nuanced effects across user types. Additionally, comparing AIANO against a single baseline prevents us from situating its performance relative to the broader landscape of annotation platforms. Our evaluation centered on German-language IR annotation with short documents; broader validation is needed across different annotation types (named entity recognition, sentiment analysis), varying document lengths, diverse domains (medical, legal), and multiple languages to establish generalizability. Finally, we did not capture detailed usage patterns for AI assistance or search functionality, assess answer quality beyond retrieval metrics, or systematically investigate how task characteristics, such as single versus multi-document questions influence annotation outcomes.

6.5 Future Directions

Although AIANO was designed specifically for IR dataset creation, its approach of tightly integrating large language models into the annotation workflow, where LLMs actively assist in generating, suggesting, and refining annotations across flexible block-based structures suggests broader applicability to annotation contexts requiring multi-document navigation and information synthesis. This LLM-augmented approach positions AIANO as a middle ground between traditional annotation tools that lack intelligent assistance and overly generic platforms without domain-specific affordances. Future research should investigate how LLM assistance scales across diverse annotation tasks and domains, examine potential drawbacks such as automation bias or annotator deskilling, and develop evidence-based guidelines for effective human-AI collaboration in dataset creation workflows.

7 Conclusion

This paper introduces AIANO, a specialized annotation tool that natively integrates AI assistance and full-text search into the information retrieval annotation workflow. Our evaluation shows that AIANO reduces cognitive workload, accelerates task completion, and improves retrieval performance compared to general-purpose annotation tools. By addressing the specific demands of retrieval-intensive annotation tasks, AIANO enables more efficient and effective creation of information retrieval datasets, thus advancing annotation capabilities in retrieval-intensive domains.

Acknowledgments. The authors acknowledge using Cursor for code assistance. All AI-generated outputs were reviewed, verified, and edited by the authors to ensure accuracy and originality. We sincerely thank all participants for taking part in our user study and for their constructive feedback.

Disclosure of Interests. The authors have no competing interests to declare that are relevant to the content of this article.

References

1. Label studio. https://labelstud.io. Accessed 04 Nov 2025
2. OpenAI API documentation. https://platform.openai.com/docs/api-reference. Accessed 04 Nov 2025
3. Ashktorab, Z., et al.: AI-assisted human labeling: batching for efficiency without overreliance. Proc. ACM Hum.-Comput. Interact. **5**(CSCW1) (2021). https://doi.org/10.1145/3449163
4. Büttcher, S., Clarke, C.L.A., Yeung, P.C.K., Soboroff, I.: Reliable information retrieval evaluation with incomplete and biased judgements. In: Proceedings of the 30th Annual International ACM SIGIR Conference on Research and Development in Information Retrieval, SIGIR '07, pp. 63–70. Association for Computing Machinery, New York, NY, USA (2007). https://doi.org/10.1145/1277741.1277755
5. Es, S., James, J., Espinosa-Anke, L., Schockaert, S.: Ragas: automated evaluation of retrieval augmented generation. arXiv:2309.15217 (2025)
6. Friel, R., Belyi, M., Sanyal, A.: Ragbench: explainable benchmark for retrieval-augmented generation systems. arXiv:2407.11005 (2025)
7. Gebreegziabher, S.A., et al.: Patat: human-AI collaborative qualitative coding with explainable interactive rule synthesis. In: Proceedings of the 2023 CHI Conference on Human Factors in Computing Systems, CHI '23. Association for Computing Machinery, New York, NY, USA (2023). https://doi.org/10.1145/3544548.3581352
8. Hart, S.G., Staveland, L.E.: Development of NASA-TLX (task load index): results of empirical and theoretical research. In: Hancock, P.A., Meshkati, N. (eds.) Human Mental Workload, Advances in Psychology, vol. 52, pp. 139–183. North-Holland (1988). https://doi.org/10.1016/S0166-4115(08)62386-9, https://www.sciencedirect.com/science/article/pii/S0166411508623869
9. He, X., et al.: AnnoLLM: making large language models to be better crowdsourced annotators. arXiv:2303.16854 (2024)

10. Izacard, G., Grave, E.: Leveraging passage retrieval with generative models for open domain question answering. arXiv:2007.01282 (2021)
11. Ji, Z., et al.: Survey of hallucination in natural language generation. ACM Comput. Surv. **55**(12), 1–38 (2023). https://doi.org/10.1145/3571730
12. Kwon, W., et al.: Efficient memory management for large language model serving with pagedattention. In: Proceedings of the ACM SIGOPS 29th Symposium on Operating Systems Principles (2023)
13. Lewis, P., et al.: Retrieval-augmented generation for knowledge-intensive NLP tasks. arXiv:2005.11401 (2021)
14. Li, M., et al.: CoAnnotating: uncertainty-guided work allocation between human and large language models for data annotation. In: Bouamor, H., Pino, J., Bali, K. (eds.) Proceedings of the 2023 Conference on Empirical Methods in Natural Language Processing, pp. 1487–1505. Association for Computational Linguistics, Singapore (2023). https://doi.org/10.18653/v1/2023.emnlp-main.92, https://aclanthology.org/2023.emnlp-main.92/
15. Pangakis, N., Wolken, S., Fasching, N.: Automated annotation with generative ai requires validation. arXiv:2306.00176 (2023)
16. Rassin, R., et al.: Evaluating d-merit of partial-annotation on information retrieval. arXiv:2406.16048 (2024)
17. Saad-Falcon, J., Khattab, O., Potts, C., Zaharia, M.: Ares: an automated evaluation framework for retrieval-augmented generation systems. arXiv:2311.09476 (2024)
18. Shapiro, S.S., Wilk, M.B.: An analysis of variance test for normality (complete samples). Biometrika **52**(3/4), 591–611 (1965). http://www.jstor.org/stable/2333709
19. Sorodoc, I.T., Ribeiro, L.F.R., Blloshmi, R., Davis, C., de Gispert, A.: Garage: a benchmark with grounding annotations for rag evaluation. arXiv:2506.07671 (2025)
20. Touvron, H., et al.: Llama: open and efficient foundation language models. arXiv:2302.13971 (2023)
21. Vaswani, A., et al.: Attention is all you need. arXiv:1706.03762 (2023)
22. Wang, D., et al.: From human-human collaboration to human-ai collaboration: Designing ai systems that can work together with people. In: Extended Abstracts of the 2020 CHI Conference on Human Factors in Computing Systems, CHI EA '20, pp. 1–6. Association for Computing Machinery, New York, NY, USA (2020). https://doi.org/10.1145/3334480.3381069
23. Wang, S., Tan, J., Dou, Z., Wen, J.R.: Omnieval: an omnidirectional and automatic rag evaluation benchmark in financial domain. arXiv:2412.13018 (2025)

SIMC: LLM-Driven Generative Recommendation with Semantic Item Modeling and Constraints

Minghao Chen[1] and Jiale Zheng[2(✉)]

[1] Tencent Technology, Shenzhen, China
monychen@tencent.com
[2] Huawei Noah's Ark Lab, Montreal, Canada
zhengjiale2@huawei.com

Abstract. Large Language Models (LLMs) enhance recommendation systems by providing advanced semantic understanding and generation capabilities. This paper introduces SIMC, an LLM framework for sequential recommendation. It first uses an LLM to generate rich item descriptions from metadata. These descriptions are then processed by another LLM and a pre-trained Mixture-of-Experts (MoE) model to create compact semantic embeddings. A trainable LLM serves as the generative engine, optimized using a next-token prediction loss and a semantic alignment loss. The training strategy involves an intermediate phase of freezing the LLM's middle layers to retain semantic knowledge before fine-tuning the entire model. Experimental results demonstrate the framework's consistent improvements over state-of-the-art baselines, with ablation studies confirming the importance of its key components and design strategies.

Keywords: Recommender System · Generative Recommendation · Large Language Model

1 Introduction

The emergence of ChatGPT has demonstrated the potential of large language models (LLMs) in knowledge representation and reasoning [1,18], generating interest in their application to recommender systems [4,19,24]. LLMs can enhance recommendation quality by summarizing user behaviors and enriching item descriptions [14,21]. Recommendation tasks can also be reframed as conversational interactions, allowing for natural language queries and leveraging the extensive knowledge encoded in LLMs for personalized suggestions [2,22]. Moreover, LLMs can be directly adapted for tasks such as encoding item IDs as sequences or replacing traditional models to optimize objectives, including predicting the next item in a sequence [3,10].

Integrating LLMs with recommender systems poses several interconnected challenges [4,19]. Encoding user behavior histories as text results in excessively

R. C.-W. Wong et al. (Eds.): PAKDD 2026, LNAI 16617, pp. 227–238, 2027.
https://doi.org/10.1007/978-981-92-1926-1_19

long input sequences, which increases computational complexity. Additionally, representing items as ID tokens lacks semantic depth, limiting the ability to exploit LLMs' pre-trained language understanding. Effectively encoding items into language tokens suitable for text-to-text frameworks remains a challenge. Moreover, current approaches often fail to fully utilize the semantic richness of textual item descriptions and the collaborative signals, thereby restricting the potential of LLMs in generative recommendation tasks.

To address these challenges, this paper introduces SIMC (**S**emantic **I**tem **M**odeling and **C**onstraints), a novel framework leveraging LLMs to enhance item representation quality and optimize recommendation performance. SIMC enriches raw metadata by generating semantically enriched item profiles using an LLM. These profiles are then converted into compact and expressive embeddings via token-level embeddings extracted by the LLM and aggregated using a Mixture-of-Experts (MoE) model pre-trained with contrastive learning. To bridge the gap between traditional ID-based embeddings and semantically enriched representations, SIMC incorporates a trainable LLM with semantic alignment loss and next-token prediction loss. This approach ensures robust alignment during training through a phased freezing and fine-tuning strategy.

Experimental results consistently improve upon state-of-the-art baselines. Ablation studies reveal the crucial roles of semantic item profiles, expert-guided representations, and semantic alignment loss, with the latter causing the greatest performance drop when excluded. Training strategy evaluations confirm the effectiveness of Mixture of Experts (MoE) pretraining and LLM phased freezing. Further analysis shows that MoE capacity's impact first increases, then decreases, while semantic alignment loss performs best with moderate weighting. Scaling LLM parameters boosts performance but plateaus, suggesting future gains may require larger datasets.

The contributions can be summarized as follows:

- LLM-based Semantic Item Profiling: We propose a framework that transforms raw item metadata into rich semantic profiles, improving the quality and contextual richness of item descriptions.
- Contrastive MoE for Token Embeddings: A contrastive learning based MoE model is introduced to aggregate LLM extracted token embeddings, producing compact and semantically enriched item representations.
- Integrated Semantic-Collaborative Loss: By combining semantic alignment loss and next-token prediction loss, our approach unifies collaborative filtering signals with semantic knowledge, bridging traditional and semantic-based embeddings.
- Comprehensive Analysis and Insights: We provide systematic evaluations, revealing critical design insights, paving the way for future advancements.

2 Methodology

In this section, the research problem is formally defined, followed by a detailed introduction to SIMC, including its architecture design and model training methodology. The overall framework is illustrated in Fig. 1.

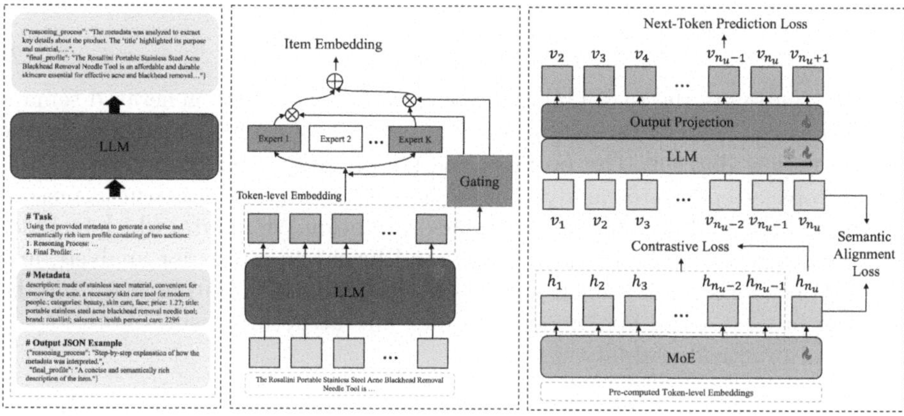

Fig. 1. SIMC framework overview: (1) Semantic Item Profiles. (2) Expert-Guided Representations. (3) Generative Recommendation with Semantic Constraints.

2.1 Problem Formulation

Sequential recommendation aims to predict the next item a user is likely to interact with based on their past interactions. Let the sets of users and items be represented by $\mathcal{U} = \{u_1, u_2, \ldots, u_{|\mathcal{U}|}\}$ and $\mathcal{V} = \{v_1, v_2, \ldots, v_{|\mathcal{V}|}\}$, respectively, where $|\mathcal{U}|$ and $|\mathcal{V}|$ denote the total number of users and items. Each user u has an interaction history, organized chronologically as $\mathcal{S}_u = \{v_1, v_2, \ldots, v_{n_u}\}$, where n_u is the total number of interactions for user u.

For simplicity, we omit the user-specific superscript in subsequent sections. The sequential recommendation task can then be formulated as:

$$\arg\max_{v_i \in \mathcal{V}} P(v_{n_u+1} = v_i | \mathcal{S}_u) \tag{1}$$

2.2 Semantic Item Profiles

Item metadata, including titles, descriptions, and categories, play a vital role in recommender systems for representing item characteristics. However, original metadata often lack semantic depth, contain missing attributes, and exhibit noise, which reduces their effectiveness in modern systems. These shortcomings limit the potential of LLMs, which thrive on processing semantically rich text.

To overcome these challenges, we propose the use of LLMs to generate semantic item profiles. Recent studies have demonstrated that integrating reasoning processes into LLM workflows can mitigate hallucinations and enhance output quality. Building on these insights, we carefully designed prompts for LLMs to ensure precise functionality in generating item profiles. These prompts clearly specify the input and output content, along with the desired output format. Notably, they explicitly incorporate reasoning processes as a central element of the generated outputs. The process is defined as follows:

$$R_i, T_i = \mathrm{LLM}(x_{\mathrm{Task}}, x_{\mathrm{Meta}}, x_{\mathrm{Format}}) \tag{2}$$

Here, R_i represents the reasoning process, and T_i denotes the generated semantic item profile. Figure 1 illustrates an example of item profile generation for the Amazon review dataset. The prompt consists of three core components: Task, which involves step-by-step analysis of the item's metadata to construct a reasoning process and produce a human-readable description; Metadata, which includes attributes such as categories, price, title, and brand as inputs for analysis; and Output Format Example, which provides a template JSON output featuring the reasoning process and a final concise profile. This structure ensures both logical clarity and practical usability.

2.3 Expert-Guided Representations

To generate high-quality semantic item embeddings, we first process an item's textual tokens using a LLM. The tokens are sequentially arranged in their original textual order, and the LLM encodes these tokens into a sequence of contextualized token-level embeddings, denoted as x_i. Formally, this operation is expressed as:

$$x_i = \mathrm{LLM}(T_i), \tag{3}$$

where $T_i = [t_1, t_2, \ldots, t_m]$ represents the token sequence for item v_i, and LLM denotes the language model. The resulting $x_i = [x_{i1}, x_{i2}, \ldots, x_{im}], x_{ij} \in \mathbb{R}^d$ constitutes the sequence of token embeddings for item v_i.

Subsequently, the token embeddings x_i are processed by a Mixture-of-Experts (MoE) module, which refines and consolidates them into a compact, semantically expressive representation. The MoE module, as illustrated in Fig. 1, consists of K expert networks, denoted as $[\mathrm{Attn}_1, \mathrm{Attn}_2, \ldots, \mathrm{Attn}_K]$, with each expert implemented as an attention mechanism. For a given input x_i, each expert Attn_k computes an attention-weighted aggregation of the token embeddings, producing an expert-specific representation:

$$\mathrm{Attn}_k(x_i) = \sum_{j=1}^{m} \alpha_{kj} x_{ij}, \quad \alpha_{kj} = \frac{\exp(q_k^\top x_{ij})}{\sum_{l=1}^{m} \exp(q_k^\top x_{il})}, \tag{4}$$

where $q_k \in \mathbb{R}^d$ is the query vector for expert k, and α_{kj} is the attention weight assigned to token j by expert k. This approach allows each expert to focus on distinct aspects of the input sequence, enabling specialized semantic extraction.

A gating network, parameterized by $W_{\mathrm{gate}} \in \mathbb{R}^{d \times K}$, dynamically selects the most relevant experts for each item. The gating network computes a relevance score s_k for each expert:

$$s_k = x_{\mathrm{mean}} \cdot W_{\mathrm{gate},k}, \tag{5}$$

where $x_{\mathrm{mean}} = \frac{1}{m} \sum_{j=1}^{m} x_{ij}$ represents the mean of the token embeddings for item v_i. The top k experts are selected based on these scores, and their contributions are normalized using the softmax function:

$$g_k = \mathrm{softmax}(\mathrm{top}_k(s_k)). \tag{6}$$

The semantic embedding h_i is then obtained by aggregating the outputs of the selected experts, weighted by their normalized scores:

$$h_i = \sum_{k \in \text{top}_k} g_k \text{Attn}_k(x_i). \tag{7}$$

To enhance the semantic expressiveness and discriminative power of the MoE-generated embeddings, we employ a contrastive learning objective tailored for user-item interaction sequences. Specifically, given a user interaction sequence $\mathcal{S}_u = \{v_1, v_2, \ldots, v_{n_u}\}$, where the target item is v_{n_u}, the embeddings of the historical items $v_1, v_2, \ldots, v_{n_u-1}$ are aggregated via mean pooling:

$$h_U = \frac{1}{n_u - 1} \sum_{j=1}^{n_u-1} h_{v_j}, \tag{8}$$

where h_U represents the aggregated embedding of the user's historical interaction sequence. The objective aligns the aggregated embedding h_U with the MoE-generated embedding of the target item $h_{v_{n_u}}$ while distancing it from the embeddings of other users' target items. The contrastive loss function is defined as:

$$\mathcal{L}_{\text{contr.}} = -\log \frac{\exp(\text{sim}(h_U, h_{v_{n_u}})/\tau)}{Z},$$
$$Z = \exp(\text{sim}(h_U, h_{v_{n_u}})/\tau) + \sum_{v^-} \exp(\text{sim}(h_U, h_{v^-})/\tau), \tag{9}$$

where $\text{sim}(h_a, h_b) = \frac{h_a^\top h_b}{\|h_a\| \|h_b\|}$ is the cosine similarity between embeddings h_a and h_b, τ is a temperature parameter, and v^- denotes target items from other user sequences, serving as negative samples.

Pre-training the MoE module with this contrastive objective teaches it to transform pre-computed token embeddings into compact, expressive item embeddings that align with user-item interaction patterns. This process bridges the semantic gap between the original token embeddings and the MoE module, ensuring the new embeddings are meaningful and semantically consistent. This optimization improves their integration into the downstream recommendation model and boosts overall performance.

2.4 Generative Recommendation with Semantic Constraints

In the SIMC framework, generative recommendation is formulated as a sequence prediction task, where the model predicts the next item v_{n_u+1} a user will interact with based on their interaction sequence $\mathcal{S}_u$. This task employs a trainable LLM as the core generative engine, enhanced with semantic constraints to ensure coherent alignment between ID-based embeddings and semantically enriched item embeddings.

To maintain semantic consistency between ID embeddings e_i and semantically enriched embeddings h_i, a cosine similarity-based alignment loss is applied.

This loss encourages the embeddings to align directionally in the shared vector space, and is defined as:

$$\mathcal{L}_{\text{align}} = -\frac{1}{N}\sum_{i=1}^{N}\frac{e_i \cdot h_i}{\|e_i\|\|h_i\|}, \tag{10}$$

where N denotes the total number of items, and $\cdot$ represents the dot product. This formulation promotes semantic coherence without enforcing strict equivalence in magnitude, preserving the structural integrity of both embedding spaces.

The next-item prediction, a central aspect of the recommendation task, computes the probability of the next item v_{n_u+1} as:

$$p(v_{n_u+1} \mid \mathcal{S}_u) = \text{softmax}(\mathbf{W}^\top \mathbf{h}_{n_u}), \tag{11}$$

where $\mathbf{h}_{n_u}$ is the hidden state of the LLM corresponding to the last item in the sequence $\mathcal{S}_u$, and $\mathbf{W}$ is a trainable output projection matrix.

The generative loss driving the sequence prediction task is defined as:

$$\mathcal{L}_{\text{gen}} = -\frac{1}{T}\sum_{t=1}^{T}\log p(v_{t+1} \mid \mathcal{S}_t), \tag{12}$$

where $\mathcal{S}_t = [v_1, v_2, \ldots, v_t]$ represents the prefix sequence up to step t, and T is the total sequence length used during training. This loss encourages the LLM to generate accurate next-item predictions based on the sequence history.

The overall training objective integrates the generative loss, the semantic alignment loss, and the pre-trained contrastive loss from the MoE module, expressed as:

$$\mathcal{L} = \mathcal{L}_{\text{gen}} + \lambda\mathcal{L}_{\text{align}} + \mathcal{L}_{\text{contr.}}, \tag{13}$$

where λ is a hyperparameter controlling the weight of the alignment loss.

Training in the SIMC framework occurs in three distinct phases. First, the MoE module is pre-trained independently using the contrastive loss $\mathcal{L}_{\text{contr.}}$. Following this, the model enters an intermediate phase where the LLM's middle layers (retaining semantic knowledge) are frozen, while its embedding layers are re-initialized for the recommendation task. During this phase, the MoE module is fine-tuned to adapt its semantically enriched embeddings h_i to this new space, aligning with the LLM's frozen representations. Once this adaptation stabilizes, the entire model—including all LLM layers, embedding layers, and the MoE module—is fine-tuned jointly. This phased strategy leverages the LLM's pre-trained semantic foundation while dynamically adapting the MoE module to the evolving representation space, enhancing both performance and representational fidelity.

3 Experiments

3.1 Experimental Setup

Datasets. We conducted experiments using the Amazon review datasets [6, 12], focusing on three product categories: Beauty, Toys and Games, and Sports and Outdoors. Table 1 presents the statistical details of these datasets. These categories were selected due to their widespread use in previous studies [5, 8, 25], facilitating meaningful performance comparisons.

Table 1. Dataset Statistics.

Dataset	# Users	# Items	# Interactions
Beauty	22,363	12,101	198,502
Toys	19,412	11,924	167,597
Sports	35,598	18,357	296,337

Compared Methods. We compare our model with the following methods: (1) **KNN**, a collaborative filtering approach that recommends items by averaging ratings from the most similar users; (2) **Caser** [17], a model leveraging convolutional neural networks to capture user preferences; (3) **HGN** [11], which uses hierarchical gating networks to model both short-term and long-term user behaviors; (4) **GRU4Rec** [7], a sequential model based on Gated Recurrent Units (GRU) for modeling user action sequences; (5) **FDSA** [23], a self-attention model that learns transitions between item features; (6) **SASRec** [9], which employs self-attention to capture item dependencies in user action sequences; (7) **BERT4Rec** [15], a masked language model approach for bi-directional context in sequential recommendations; (8) **S^3-Rec** [25], an MLM-based method that incorporates self-supervised objectives to enhance item representation; (9) **P5** [5], a multi-task model that fine-tunes a pre-trained language model to generate item ID tokens; (10) **TIGER** [13], a language model fine-tuned to predict semantically learned item IDs; and (11) **IDGenRec** [16], which improves recommendations by converting semantic item IDs into detailed textual IDs.

Implementation Details. We employ models from the Qwen2 series [20] for all core components. Specifically, Qwen2.5 models are used to generate Semantic Item Profiles, pre-compute token-level embeddings for Expert-Guided Representations, and serve as the trainable generative engine in the recommendation system. We evaluate all methods using two metrics: Normalized Discounted Cumulative Gain (NDCG) and Hit Ratio (HR) at ranks 5 and 10.

3.2 Overall Performance

Table 2 summarizes the performance of all models. Compared to the strongest baseline, IDGenRec, SIMC achieves significant improvements in both hit ratio and ranking-based metrics. On the Beauty dataset, SIMC surpasses IDGenRec by 12.9% and 4.1% in H@5 and N@5, respectively, and by 21.0% and 9.3% in H@10 and N@10. Performance gains are even more pronounced on the Toys and Games dataset, with increases of 22.7% and 20.8% in H@5 and N@5, and 23.0% and 20.0% in H@10 and N@10. A similar trend is observed on the Sports and Outdoors dataset, where SIMC improves by 11.6% and 9.1% in H@5 and N@5, and by 12.3% and 10.8% in H@10 and N@10. These consistent gains across datasets and metrics highlight the robustness and effectiveness of our model in enhancing recommendation accuracy and ranking quality.

Table 2. Performance comparison of different methods. The best performance in each column is highlighted in bold.

Method	Beauty				Toys and Games				Sports and Outdoors			
	H@5	N@5	H@10	N@10	H@5	N@5	H@10	N@10	H@5	N@5	H@10	N@10
KNN	0.004	0.003	0.007	0.004	0.004	0.003	0.007	0.004	0.001	0.001	0.002	0.001
Caser	0.021	0.013	0.035	0.018	0.017	0.011	0.027	0.014	0.012	0.007	0.019	0.010
HGN	0.033	0.021	0.051	0.027	0.032	0.022	0.050	0.028	0.019	0.012	0.031	0.016
GRU4Rec	0.016	0.010	0.028	0.014	0.010	0.006	0.018	0.008	0.013	0.009	0.020	0.011
BERT4Rec	0.020	0.012	0.035	0.017	0.012	0.007	0.020	0.010	0.012	0.008	0.019	0.010
FDSA	0.027	0.016	0.041	0.021	0.023	0.014	0.038	0.019	0.018	0.012	0.029	0.016
SASRec	0.039	0.025	0.061	0.032	0.046	0.031	0.068	0.037	0.023	0.015	0.035	0.019
S^3-Rec	0.039	0.024	0.065	0.033	0.044	0.029	0.070	0.038	0.025	0.016	0.039	0.020
P5	0.016	0.011	0.025	0.014	0.007	0.005	0.012	0.007	0.006	0.004	0.010	0.005
TIGER	0.045	0.032	0.065	0.038	0.052	0.037	0.071	0.043	0.026	0.018	0.040	0.023
IDGenRec	0.062	0.049	0.081	0.054	0.066	0.048	0.087	0.055	0.043	0.033	0.057	0.037
SIMC	**0.070**	**0.051**	**0.098**	**0.059**	**0.081**	**0.058**	**0.107**	**0.066**	**0.048**	**0.036**	**0.064**	**0.041**

3.3 Ablation Studies

To evaluate the effectiveness of our framework's key components, we conducted ablation studies with three variants:

- **SIMC (w/o Semantic Item Profiles)**: Uses only raw item metadata for embedding generation.
- **SIMC (w/o Expert-Guided Representations)**: Replaces the Mixture-of-Experts (MoE) aggregation with average pooling.
- **SIMC (w/o Semantic Alignment Loss)**: Excludes the semantic alignment loss during LLM training.

The results, as shown in Fig. 2, indicate that removing semantic alignment loss causes the most significant performance drop, emphasizing its critical role. Excluding semantic enrichment leads to substantial degradation, while replacing MoE with average pooling results in moderate declines. Overall, the full SIMC model consistently outperforms all ablated variants, validating the necessity of semantic enrichment, MoE aggregation, and semantic alignment.

3.4 Training Strategy Exploration

To validate the proposed training process in the SIMC framework, we conducted two ablation studies:

- **SIMC (w/o MoE Pretraining)**: Skips the independent pretraining phase of the MoE module.

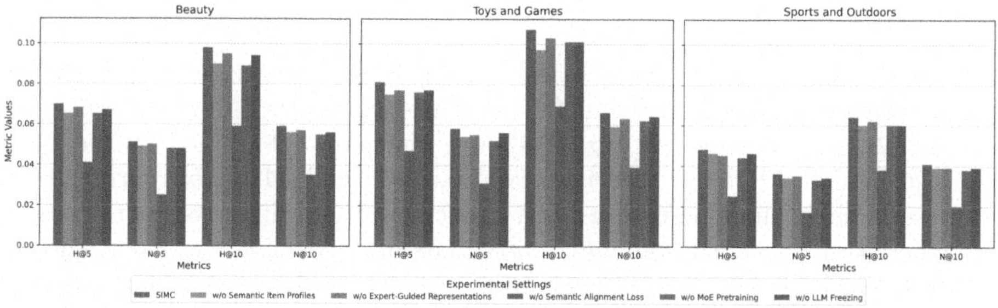

Fig. 2. Ablation study results showing the impact of removing key components.

- **SIMC (w/o LLM Freezing)**: Does not freeze the middle layers of the LLM during the initial training phase.

The results, as shown in Fig. 2, show that skipping MoE pretraining significantly degrades performance, underscoring its importance for semantic representation and recommendation quality. Removing LLM freezing causes minor declines, particularly in H@10, indicating the value of freezing middle layers during initial training to preserve pretrained semantic knowledge. These findings confirm the effectiveness of combining MoE pretraining and selective LLM freezing to balance pretrained knowledge with task-specific fine-tuning.

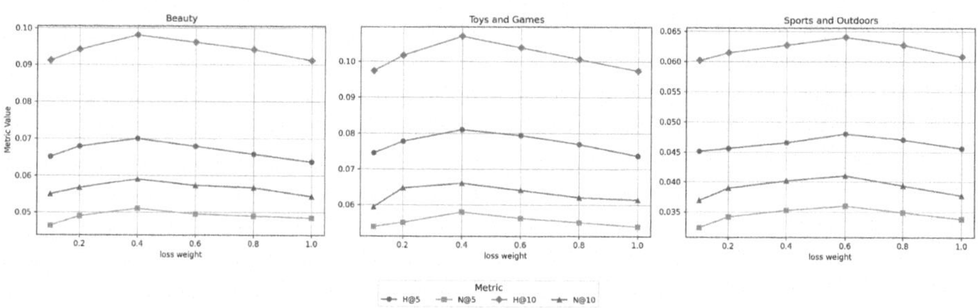

Fig. 3. Experimental results with different loss weight.

3.5 Loss Weight Sensitivity

We evaluated the impact of semantic alignment loss weight on model performance by varying it across six values: 0.1, 0.2, 0.4, 0.6, 0.8, and 1.0. Results, as shown in Fig. 3, show that moderate weights (0.4–0.6) consistently deliver optimal performance, balancing ID-based and semantically enriched embeddings effectively.

3.6 Scalability Analysis

To evaluate the scalability of the proposed SIMC framework, we analyzed two factors: the number of experts in the Mixture-of-Experts (MoE) model (testing 16, 32, 64, 128, and 256 experts) and the parameter scale of the large language model (LLM) (evaluating 0.5, 1.5, 3, 7, and 14 billion parameters). The results show that increasing MoE capacity initially improves performance through better specialization, but gains plateau or decline beyond a threshold, particularly in sensitive domains like "Beauty," likely because overfitting to pretraining objectives weakens semantic representations (see Fig. 4). Similarly, scaling LLM parameters significantly boosts performance up to 1.5 billion by leveraging richer semantic encoding, but larger models show diminishing returns or slight declines, as they require more data to fully utilize their capacity. In summary, both MoE capacity and LLM scale significantly affect performance but are constrained by overcapacity and data limitations, emphasizing the need to balance model complexity and data availability.

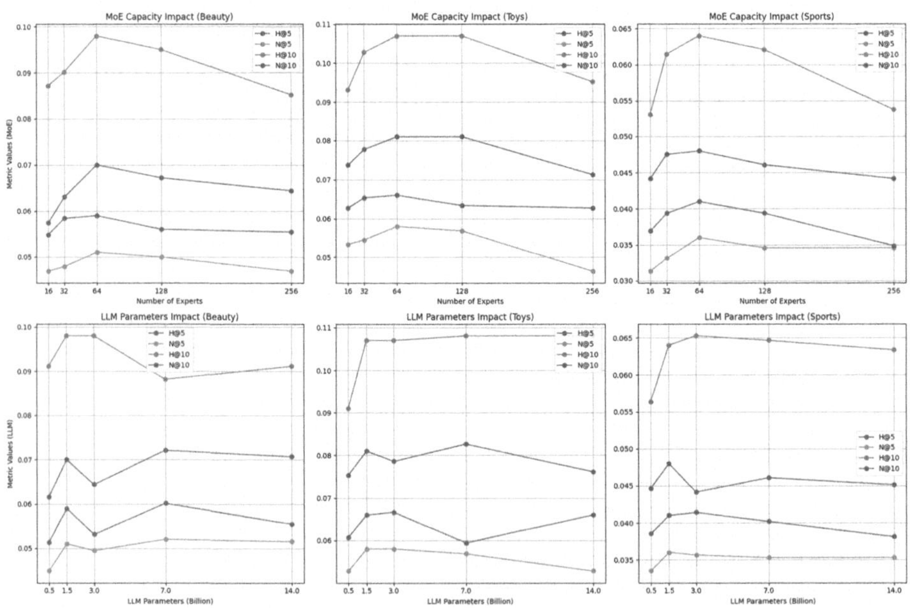

Fig. 4. Impact of MoE Expert Count vs. LLM Parameter Scale on Model Performance Across Various Datasets.

4 Conclusions

This paper proposes SIMC, a framework that enhances sequential recommendation systems by leveraging the semantic capabilities of LLMs. SIMC transforms raw metadata into enriched semantic item profiles and bridges the gap between ID-based and semantically enriched embeddings, achieving significant improvements over state-of-the-art baselines. Future improvements could focus on leveraging larger-scale datasets to further enhance performance and exploring multi-scenario joint learning to improve adaptability across diverse application contexts. SIMC demonstrates the potential of LLM methods in advancing recommendation systems and lays a strong foundation for future research.

References

1. Achiam, J., et al.: GPT-4 technical report. arXiv preprint arXiv:2303.08774 (2023)
2. Bao, K., Zhang, J., Zhang, Y., Wang, W., Feng, F., He, X.: Tallrec: an effective and efficient tuning framework to align large language model with recommendation. In: Proceedings of the 17th ACM Conference on Recommender Systems, pp. 1007–1014 (2023)
3. Cui, Z., Ma, J., Zhou, C., Zhou, J., Yang, H.: M6-rec: generative pretrained language models are open-ended recommender systems. arXiv preprint arXiv:2205.08084 (2022)
4. Deldjoo, Y., et al.: A review of modern recommender systems using generative models (gen-recsys). In: Proceedings of the 30th ACM SIGKDD Conference on Knowledge Discovery and Data Mining, pp. 6448–6458 (2024)
5. Geng, S., Liu, S., Fu, Z., Ge, Y., Zhang, Y.: Recommendation as language processing (RLP): a unified pretrain, personalized prompt & predict paradigm (p5). In: Proceedings of the 16th ACM Conference on Recommender Systems, pp. 299–315 (2022)
6. He, R., McAuley, J.: Ups and downs: modeling the visual evolution of fashion trends with one-class collaborative filtering. In: Proceedings of the 25th International Conference on World Wide Web, pp. 507–517 (2016)
7. Hidasi, B.: Session-based recommendations with recurrent neural networks. arXiv preprint arXiv:1511.06939 (2015)
8. Hua, W., Xu, S., Ge, Y., Zhang, Y.: How to index item ids for recommendation foundation models. In: Proceedings of the Annual International ACM SIGIR Conference on Research and Development in Information Retrieval in the Asia Pacific Region, pp. 195–204 (2023)
9. Kang, W.C., McAuley, J.: Self-attentive sequential recommendation. In: 2018 IEEE International Conference on Data Mining (ICDM), pp. 197–206. IEEE (2018)
10. Liao, J., et al.: Llara: large language-recommendation assistant. In: Proceedings of the 47th International ACM SIGIR Conference on Research and Development in Information Retrieval, pp. 1785–1795 (2024)
11. Ma, C., Kang, P., Liu, X.: Hierarchical gating networks for sequential recommendation. In: Proceedings of the 25th ACM SIGKDD International Conference on Knowledge Discovery & Data Mining, pp. 825–833 (2019)
12. McAuley, J., Targett, C., Shi, Q., Van Den Hengel, A.: Image-based recommendations on styles and substitutes. In: Proceedings of the 38th international ACM SIGIR Conference on Research and Development in Information Retrieval, pp. 43–52 (2015)
13. Rajput, S., et al.: Recommender systems with generative retrieval. In: Advances in Neural Information Processing Systems, vol. 36, pp. 10299–10315 (2023)
14. Ren, X., et al.: Representation learning with large language models for recommendation. In: Proceedings of the ACM on Web Conference 2024, pp. 3464–3475 (2024)

15. Sun, F., et al.: Bert4rec: sequential recommendation with bidirectional encoder representations from transformer. In: Proceedings of the 28th ACM International Conference on Information and Knowledge Management, pp. 1441–1450 (2019)
16. Tan, J., Xu, S., Hua, W., Ge, Y., Li, Z., Zhang, Y.: IDGenRec: LLM-RecSys alignment with textual id learning. In: Proceedings of the 47th International ACM SIGIR Conference on Research and Development in Information Retrieval, pp. 355–364 (2024)
17. Tang, J., Wang, K.: Personalized top-n sequential recommendation via convolutional sequence embedding. In: Proceedings of the Eleventh ACM International Conference on Web Search and Data Mining, pp. 565–573 (2018)
18. Touvron, H., et al.: Llama: open and efficient foundation language models. arXiv preprint arXiv:2302.13971 (2023)
19. Wu, L., et al.: A survey on large language models for recommendation. World Wide Web **27**(5), 60 (2024)
20. Yang, A., et al.: Qwen2. 5 technical report. arXiv preprint arXiv:2412.15115 (2024)
21. Zhang, C., et al.: Spar: personalized content-based recommendation via long engagement attention. arXiv preprint arXiv:2402.10555 (2024)
22. Zhang, J., Xie, R., Hou, Y., Zhao, X., Lin, L., Wen, J.R.: Recommendation as instruction following: a large language model empowered recommendation approach. ACM Trans. Inf. Syst. (2023)
23. Zhang, T., et al.: Feature-level deeper self-attention network for sequential recommendation. In: IJCAI, pp. 4320–4326 (2019)
24. Zhao, Z., et al.: Recommender systems in the era of large language models (LLMs). IEEE Trans. Knowl. Data Eng. (2024)
25. Zhou, K., et al.: S3-rec: self-supervised learning for sequential recommendation with mutual information maximization. In: Proceedings of the 29th ACM International Conference on Information & Knowledge Management, pp. 1893–1902 (2020)

Squeezing the Teacher, Strengthening the Student: Reliable Military RAG with Enhanced Reasoning

Jaeeun Jang(✉), Hansle Lee, Wonjun Cho, and Sangmin Kim

AI Research Team, Hanwha Systems, Seongnam-si, Gyeonggi-do, Republic of Korea
wkdwodms0779@gmail.com

Abstract. Retrieval-Augmented Generation (RAG) systems for battlefield situation analysis suffer from critical reliability issues: unreliable retrieval processing leading to hallucination and lost-in-the-middle problems, and failure to appropriately reject out-of-knowledge-base queries. These failures are particularly dangerous in military environments where incorrect information can lead to catastrophic consequences. This study proposes a novel framework that addresses these limitations through two key innovations: Verification-Guided Gradient Masking (VGGM) and Triple-structured Military Data Synthesis. The first technique enables selective learning only on verified reasoning steps, allowing models to acquire self-verification capabilities while preventing error pattern propagation during training. The second approach leverages the verification cascade of a Teacher model to generate high-quality data that explicitly teaches models which information from retrieved documents to utilize and which to ignore. Experimental results demonstrate substantial improvements across all metrics compared to competitive baselines.

Keywords: Large Language Models · Retrieval-Augmented Generation · System-2 Reasoning · Knowledge Distillation · Preference Optimization

1 Introduction

Modern military operations generate unprecedented volumes of intelligence data from diverse sensing platforms such as UAVs, satellites, and electronic warfare systems. Rapidly synthesizing these fragmented reports into coherent situational awareness is vital for operational superiority. However, deploying Large Language Models (LLMs) in this context requires satisfying three conflicting requirements: **security compliance**, **real-time responsiveness**, and **absolute accuracy**. Due to confidentiality constraints, military organizations must rely on self-hosted open-source LLMs (e.g., LLaMA, Qwen family), which underperform compared to proprietary models like ChatGPT or Claude. To support real-time use, Retrieval-Augmented Generation (RAG) enables access to up-to-date knowledge bases (KBs). Yet combining open-source LLMs with RAG

R. C.-W. Wong et al. (Eds.): PAKDD 2026, LNAI 16617, pp. 239–257, 2027.
https://doi.org/10.1007/978-981-92-1926-1_20

introduces reliability issues that undermine **absolute accuracy**, including hallucinations from irrelevant retrievals, lost-in-the-middle failures, and improper handling of out-of-KB queries.

Existing efforts—such as Reflective RAG [2,16,22], System-2 reasoning [8], and retrieval-augmented training [9,12]—have improved reliability but remain insufficient. Reflective RAG suffers from high latency, System-2 reasoning has yet to be fully integrated with RAG, and current training methods still fail to generalize to real retrieval distributions or handle out-of-KB queries effectively.

To address these challenges, we propose a **teacher-guided framework** integrating two key innovations: (1) Verification-Guided Gradient Masking (VGGM), which enables selective learning on verified reasoning steps to prevent error propagation; and (2) Triple-Structured Military Data Synthesis, which distills a teacher model's verification cascade to teach when to utilize or reject retrieved information. This framework substantially enhances reasoning reliability and out-of-KB rejection, achieving an **82.6% appropriate rejection rate** in simulated Korean military datasets—demonstrating practical applicability for secure, real-time, and trustworthy RAG systems in high-stakes environments.

2 Related Work

Reflective RAG aims to improve the reliability of retrieval-augmented systems by introducing self-evaluation mechanisms that assess both retrieval quality and generated responses. Methods such as Self-RAG [2] and CRAG [22] employ reflection or confidence scoring to reduce hallucination and refine retrieved documents. However, these approaches require separate complex learning mechanisms for quality evaluation and lack guaranteed generalization across domains. Recent Agentic RAG methods [16] use pre-trained LLMs for direct evaluation without additional training, but significantly increase inference time due to multi-step verification processes, creating latency issues incompatible with real-time requirements.

Recent advances in System-2 reasoning [8] highlight models that reason through deliberate, multi-step self-critique rather than fast, intuitive responses. Large models such as o1/o3 and DeepSeek-R1 exhibit strong verification and correction capabilities, reducing hallucinations and improving logical coherence. However, despite these advances, existing studies remain limited to narrow domains such as mathematics and programming, and the integration of System-2 reasoning with RAG remains largely unexplored—leaving open how to combine deliberate reasoning with real-time retrieval in high-stakes environments.

Training-time integration of retrieval [9,12] aligns generation with external documents but suffers from training–inference mismatch: during training, models always receive relevant context, whereas real retrieval often yields noisy or incomplete information. RAFT [24] mitigates this by mixing relevant "golden" and irrelevant "distractor" documents to teach when relevant information is absent. However, RAFT still faces two major limitations. First, its random distractor selection often includes partially relevant documents but ignores them, leading to incomplete or under-supported responses and persistent distribution shift since inference depends on retriever-selected rather than randomly sampled documents. Second, it fails to address out-of-KB queries, as models are never trained to produce appropriate rejection responses when the required knowledge is missing.

Our framework addresses these limitations by shifting the verification process from inference to the training phase, thereby **embedding relevance verification** directly into the model. It further **integrates reasoning** into retrieval contexts, enabling systematic and explainable decisions under uncertainty. Finally, it **resolves RAFT's issues** by aligning training with real retrieval distributions and teaching explicit out-of-KB rejection through rejection-aware supervision.

3 Methodology

We propose a comprehensive 4-stage framework that distills reliable RAG capabilities into a 7B student model from large teacher models (405B & 671B).

Preliminary analysis revealed a clear distinction between model types. Open-source non-reasoning models such as LLaMA and Qwen generated responses by directly copying or enumerating retrieved content, exhibiting minimal planning and virtually no intermediate reasoning—often resulting in incorrect or shallow conclusions. In contrast, reasoning models such as DeepSeek-R1 demonstrated structured problem-solving behavior, including intermediate planning and deliberate verification steps that consistently led to more accurate outputs [8]. However, this reasoning capability degraded substantially after fine-tuning on military data, indicating a form of catastrophic forgetting. To prevent this collapse and retain deliberate reasoning behavior, we found that reasoning data must be incorporated across all stages of training rather than applied only once or post-hoc.

3.1 Stage 1: Reasoning-Oriented Training

Reinforcement learning (RL) can enhance reasoning in LLMs, but unlike large models, small ones often exhibit unstable behavior and degraded reasoning quality during RL. Following Phi-4-Reasoning [1], we first establish a stable reasoning foundation through enhanced supervised fine-tuning (SFT) before applying RL.

Verification-Guided Gradient Masking (VGGM). Standard SFT implicitly assumes that longer reasoning traces inherently improve performance and therefore applies uniform next-token prediction across the full sequence [14,23]. However, this assumption neglects the structural reliability of reasoning trajectories and often hinders the development of robust reasoning behavior. A similar limitation is observed in DeepSeek-R1-Distill models trained on 800k DeepSeek-R1–generated samples [8], which we examine in the following analysis.

The Error Propagation Problem. Reasoning traces frequently contain incorrect intermediate steps that are later corrected through verification, for example: "The total apples are 120. Therefore, remaining apples are $120 \times \frac{1}{4} = 40$ (**INCORRECT**). Wait, let me recalculate: $120 \times \frac{1}{4} = 30$ (**CORRECT**)." Under standard SFT, all tokens are equally optimized using the token-level cross-entropy loss $\mathcal{L}_{standard} = -\sum_{t=1}^{T} \log P_\theta(y_t \mid x, y_{<t})$, forcing the model to learn both the erroneous and corrected reasoning steps without distinction. This indiscriminate supervision propagates flawed reasoning patterns and encourages error memorization.

Beyond reinforcing erroneous reasoning, indiscriminate SFT introduces gradient noise analogous to training with noisy labels [26]. Incorrect intermediate steps push parameter updates toward suboptimal regions, while later corrective steps pull them in the opposite direction. This competing gradient increases variance and destabilizes convergence, manifesting as oscillatory loss behavior.

Lack of Metacognition. Beyond error propagation, existing approaches fail to cultivate genuine metacognitive capability—the ability to monitor, evaluate, and regulate one's own reasoning. The core of System-2 reasoning lies not in linear token-by-token inference, but in self-verification and corrective refinement. However, models trained under standard SFT tend to reproduce superficial verification cues (e.g., "Wait!") without engaging in internal evaluation [4], resulting in surface-level mimicry rather than authentic metacognitive reasoning.

Entropy Collapse. A further limitation of standard SFT arises from its token-level cross-entropy objective, which concentrates probability mass on a single next-token target and implicitly optimizes the model for `pass@1` rather than `pass@N` [3]. This objective induces excessive determinism and disproportionately penalizes alternative valid continuations. The collapse is particularly harmful at key forking tokens—high-entropy decision points where multiple valid reasoning paths may branch—where uncertainty should remain unresolved but is instead suppressed [19]. As entropy erodes, the model loses flexibility and repeatedly reproduces incorrect reasoning even under multi-sample decoding.

Verification-Guided Gradient Masking (VGGM). We introduce VGGM to address these fundamental issues through **selective learning**. Its core idea is to support both "learning only from good parts while avoiding erroneous segments" and "genuinely internalize verification rather than merely mimicking patterns". Our adaptive objective function implements conditional gradient application:

$$\mathcal{L} = -\sum_{i=1}^{N} \sum_{t=t(i)}^{T} \log P_\theta(y_{i,t} | x_i, y_{i,<t}), \quad t(i) = \begin{cases} 1 & \text{if } v_i = 0 \quad (\mathcal{L}_{\text{standard}}) \\ T_{last} & \text{if } v_i = 1 \quad (\mathcal{L}_{\text{masked}}) \end{cases} \tag{1}$$

Here, T_{last} marks the beginning of the final verified reasoning segment. When no verification signal is present ($v_i = 0$), the loss behaves as a standard next-token objective, $\mathcal{L}_{\text{standard}}$, where gradients are applied across the entire sequence.

In contrast, when verification exists ($v_i = 1$), the objective transitions to the masked form $\mathcal{L}_{\text{masked}}$, applying gradients only from T_{last} onward. This ensures learning is driven by the corrected reasoning rather than earlier potentially incorrect steps.

We use the OpenR1-Math-220k [7], which inherits DeepSeek-R1's verification-oriented reasoning style and provides 29,848 high-quality samples suitable for our training objective. To prepare these samples for $\mathcal{L}_{\text{masked}}$, we automatically detect the final verification boundary and insert a standardized "Wait!" token at T_{last} using Claude-3.5-Sonnet, ensuring a consistent metacognitive learning signal. Approximately 90% of samples contain verification ($v_i = 1$), meaning that training exclusively under $\mathcal{L}_{\text{masked}}$ would overemphasize verification-dependent reasoning and undertrain direct reasoning paths governed by $\mathcal{L}_{\text{standard}}$. To prevent this imbalance, we adopt a balanced scheme: 15k samples trained with $\mathcal{L}_{\text{masked}}$ ($v_i = 1$), 5k trained with $\mathcal{L}_{\text{standard}}$ regardless of verification presence, and the remaining 9,848 reserved for subsequent GRPO. This setup enables the model to acquire both autonomous problem-solving ability and verification-aware self-correction—skills that later transfer effectively to retrieval-grounded reasoning.

VGGM mitigates the three identified failure modes by replacing uniform next-token optimization with selective supervision. First, it resolves the *Error Propagation Problem* by suppressing gradients from unverified prefixes, akin to the robustness effect of GCE loss in noisy-label learning [26]. Rather than memorizing incorrect intermediate steps, VGGM treats unverified regions as unreliable supervision and prevents their reinforcement during optimization, making it a reasoning-specific extension of noisy-label training principles to autoregressive sequence learning. Second, VGGM addresses the *Lack of Metacognition* by differentiating reasoning attempts from validated corrections. Although pre-*Wait!* tokens remain visible in the forward pass and contribute to contextual representations, they are excluded from loss computation, restricting credit assignment to the verified suffix. This enables the model to internalize a learnable error $\rightarrow$ detection $\rightarrow$ correction pattern, unlike truncation-based approaches that remove error context and prevent learning realistic corrective reasoning dynamics. Finally, VGGM mitigates *Entropy Collapse* by preserving token-level uncertainty in early reasoning stages. Since gradients apply only to the verified correction segment, high-entropy branching decisions prior to verification remain unsharpened by cross-entropy updates, preventing premature collapse into a single deterministic reasoning trajectory. By maintaining entropy at forking tokens, VGGM preserves multiple viable reasoning hypotheses and supports both inference-time and training-time strategies such as multi-sample decoding and RLVR [25].

Group Relative Policy Optimization (GRPO [8]**).** Following SFT, we apply GRPO to enhance generalizable reasoning via RL. GRPO stabilizes training without a value model by estimating advantage A_i within response groups G:

$$\mathcal{J}_{GRPO}(\theta) = \mathbb{E}_{q,\{o_i\}_{i=1}^{|G|}} \left[\frac{1}{|G|} \sum_{i=1}^{|G|} \min(\rho_i A_i,\ \text{clip}(\rho_i) A_i) \right] - \beta \, \mathbb{D}_{KL}(\pi_\theta \,\|\, \pi_{ref}) \tag{2}$$

We design a reward system that evaluates structural correctness (tag and format validity) and reasoning quality (answer correctness, appropriate self-verification). In particular, models are penalized for producing wrong answers without proper "Wait!" triggers, promoting careful self-verification over impulsive replies.

3.2 Stage 2: Triple-Structured Military Data Synthesis

The next stage tackles RAG challenges by creating synthetic military data that teaches models when to use or ignore retrieved information. The generated training data requires models to simultaneously produce source citations alongside final answers, enabling rapid trust calibration for military commanders to efficiently assess AI system reliability without exhaustive document review [17].

Cascaded Verification Framework. In real-world RAG scenarios, retrieved documents may contain many, few, or no query-relevant sources at all. Unlike RAFT's random distractor sampling, we construct a controlled data generation framework using a large teacher model (LLaMA-3.1-405B), deployed on a self-hosted open-source LLM infrastructure for security. The framework generates high-quality triple-structured samples (q, R, a), summarized in Table 1, by adopting an agentic RAG paradigm in which generation and verification proceed iteratively, and any failed verification triggers a rollback to the previous generation stage. A key innovation is conditional processing based on sampling strategy: when $p \leq 0.5$ (positive sampling), the system uses Prompt Chaining [21] to first extract relevant evidence from retrieved documents and then generate a Chain-of-Thought (CoT) answer grounded in those extracted sources—significantly improving reliability and avoiding information loss compared to simultaneous source–answer generation. When $p > 0.5$ (negative sampling), the system produces rejection responses for cases where the retrieved documents cannot validly support an answer.

The rigorously Teacher-generated and verified training data provides two critical learning benefits. First, selective information utilization (positive cases): while final answers a_i are generated using only relevant sources S_i, the reference set R_i deliberately includes both relevant and irrelevant documents, enabling models to learn discrimination between pertinent information and noise. Second, out-of-KB robustness (negative cases): models learn to recognize information insufficiency and reject out-of-KB queries rather than generating plausible hallucinations.

Integrated SFT. In addition to the (q, R, a) triples generated through the Cascaded Verification Framework, we include Reasoning SFT Data (rsSFT) to pre-

Table 1. 10-stage cascaded verification pipeline for triple-structured data synthesis.

Stage	Description
Document Chunking	Segment reports into manageable chunks for effective processing.
Question Generation (q_i)	Generate contextually relevant questions from sampled chunks using expert-curated templates to ensure semantic validity and diversity.
Question Verification	Validate logical consistency and semantic soundness of generated questions to prevent contradictory or malformed queries.
Dynamic Retrieval (R_i)	Retrieve top-k (positive case) or bottom-k (negative case) documents using similarity-based sampling to train both standard RAG and out-of-KB reasoning, with dynamic k preventing overfitting to fixed retrieval counts.
Source Extraction (S_i)	For positive cases, extract relevant evidence from top-k documents with grouping to prevent source extraction failures and ensure coverage.
Source Verification	Verify extracted evidence through dual validation for hallucination (existence in grouped documents) and relevance (sufficiency for answering).
Distractor Collection (U_i)	For negative cases, collect irrelevant documents from bottom-k retrievals to form distractor sets, preventing hallucination on out-of-KB queries.
Answer Generation (a_i)	Generate Chain-of-Thought (CoT) answers for positive cases or rejection responses for negative cases, providing detailed reasoning explanations.
Answer Verification	Ensure that answers for positive cases are grounded exclusively in the extracted source set and faithfully address the given question, and ensure appropriate rejection when supporting evidence is insufficient.
Save Structured Triples	Compile $(q_i, R_i, S_i \oplus a_i)$ for positive cases or (q_i, U_i, a_i) for negative cases.

vent the model from forgetting the enhanced reasoning capabilities acquired during reasoning-oriented training. Since Military SFT Data (mSFT) was already described in Sect. 3.2, this section focuses on the construction of rsSFT.

Directly replaying Stage 1 reasoning data produced only marginal gains, showing limited benefit from redundant supervision. To better calibrate the student model's response distribution, we apply *rejection sampling* [18], which increases the probability mass of high-quality responses. Using CoT decoding [20], we sample multiple responses from the GRPO-trained model $\pi_{\theta^*_{\mathrm{GRPO}}}$ and select the most confident correct answer based on the average top-1/top-2 probability gap: $\Delta = \frac{1}{|\mathrm{ans}|}\sum_{x_t \in \mathrm{answer}} \left[p(x_t^1 | x_{<t}) - p(x_t^2 | x_{<t})\right]$, where a larger Δ indicates greater confidence in the chosen reasoning path. Starting from $\pi_{\theta^*_{\mathrm{GRPO}}}$, we train on the combined dataset $\mathcal{D}_{\mathrm{SFT}}$ ($\mathcal{D}_{\mathrm{mSFT}} \cup \mathcal{D}_{\mathrm{rsSFT}}$), where $p(x)$ denotes the data-specific prompt corresponding to each dataset type, allowing differentiated prompting to steer the model's capabilities acquired from both datasets during inference.

$$\theta^*_{\mathrm{SFT}} = \arg\max_{\theta} \mathbb{E}_{(x,y)\sim\mathcal{D}_{\mathrm{SFT}}} \sum_{t=1}^{T} \log \pi_\theta(y_t \mid p(x), y_{<t}) \tag{3}$$

3.3 Stage 3: Direct Preference Optimization (DPO [15])

The third stage applies DPO to explicitly penalize incorrect reasoning. Unlike SFT, which exposes the model only to positive examples, DPO enables discrimination between high- and low-quality responses through preference-based learning. For triple-structured data, preference pairs are constructed based on whether samples pass the Verification stage in Table 1, while for reasoning data, they are generated by sampling multiple reasoning trajectories from the SFT-trained model ($\pi_{\theta^*_{\text{SFT}}}$).

Table 2. Construction of preference pairs for DPO training across data types.

Data Type	Chosen Response (y_i^w)	Rejected Response (y_i^l)
Triple-Structured Data	Passes all verification stages	Fails source or answer verification
Reasoning Data	Highest-confidence correct response	Highest-confidence incorrect response

We construct two types of preference pairs in $\mathcal{D}_{\text{DPO}}$, as summarized in Table 2. Verification-based pairing on domain data explicitly guides the model to avoid RAG hallucinations through negative supervision, while confidence-based selection on reasoning data discourages overconfident but wrong reasoning paths and refines the model's calibration beyond simple correct/incorrect labeling.

$$\theta^*_{\text{DPO}} = \arg\min_{\theta} \mathbb{E}_{(x,y^w,y^l)\sim\mathcal{D}_{\text{DPO}}}\left[-\log\sigma\left(\beta\log\frac{\pi_\theta(y^w|x)/\pi_{\text{ref}}(y^w|x)}{\pi_\theta(y^l|x)/\pi_{\text{ref}}(y^l|x)}\right)\right] \quad (4)$$

3.4 Stage 4: RAG Pipeline Integration

The final stage integrates the trained model $\pi_{\theta^*_{\text{DPO}}}$ into a standard RAG pipeline. At inference, the system performs retrieval and generation for a given query q as:

$$R_t = \text{Retriever}(q\colon \text{query}, C_t\colon \text{collection}, k\colon \text{top-}k), \quad y_t = \pi_{\theta^*_{\text{DPO}}}(q, R_t) \quad (5)$$

While domain and reasoning data were trained with distinct system prompts, this stage uses a unified prompt activating both domain analysis (citation, military context awareness) and reasoning capabilities (self-checking, systematic steps).

4 Experimental Results

4.1 Evaluating Reasoning Ability on Mathematical Benchmarks

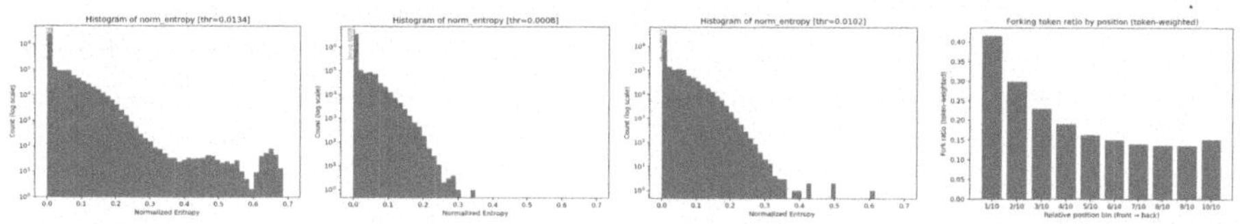

(a) Base (b) standard SFT (c) SFT (VGGM) (d) Fork-Tok Ratio

Fig. 1. Token-level entropy on MATH and positional distribution of forking tokens.

Entropy Preservation Analysis. We assess entropy behavior on the MATH training set [10] by generating multiple reasoning rollouts per question and computing token-level entropy as $H_t = -\sum_{j=1}^{V} p_{t,j} \log p_{t,j}$, where $p_t = \text{Softmax}(z_t/T)$.

Columns (a)–(c) in Fig. 1 show entropy distributions for the base model, standard SFT, and VGGM, while column (d) illustrates the positional distribution of forking tokens (top-20% highest-entropy positions [19]). Standard SFT exhibits strong entropy collapse, sharpening logits across the entire sequence—even at positions where uncertainty should remain to allow alternative reasoning paths. In contrast, VGGM preserves substantially higher entropy in the early exploratory phase by restricting gradient updates to verified suffixes, preventing premature commitment to a single path. Consistent with this pattern, most high-entropy branching decisions occur early in the reasoning trace, where VGGM maintains uncertainty and exploratory diversity while standard SFT rapidly collapses it.

Effect of VGGM on Reasoning Performance. We evaluate how VGGM improves reasoning quality in Qwen2.5-7B-Base across three mathematical benchmarks of increasing difficulty: GSM8K [5], MATH [10], and AMC'23.

Table 3 shows that VGGM strengthens SFT by blocking gradients from incorrect reasoning steps, resulting in a cleaner and more stable learning signal than standard SFT. In addition, by mitigating entropy collapse and preserving diverse reasoning paths before RL, VGGM offers GRPO a broader exploration space, leading to substantially larger RL-driven gains [25].

Table 3. Reasoning Benchmark performance.

Method	GSM8K	MATH	AMC
Base (No SFT)	66.2	46.5	28.2
Base + GRPO	74.2	50.5	30.1
SFT (No Masking)	78.2	67.8	52.3
SFT (No Masking) + GRPO	80.7	69.0	54.1
SFT (VGGM)	83.1	71.3	58.7
SFT (VGGM) + GRPO	**87.3**	**74.9**	**62.7**

Stabilizing Training Through VGGM. Without masking, accuracy peaks early (9k/12k on GSM8K/MATH) and then declines, suggesting that gradients from erroneous reasoning steps progressively destabilize optimization. In contrast, VGGM continues improving until 15k/19k samples, showing more stable convergence and better generalization (Fig. 2). Loss curves also show that non-masked SFT suffers from frequent gradient spikes, whereas VGGM exhibits a smooth downward trajectory, confirming more stable and consistent convergence.

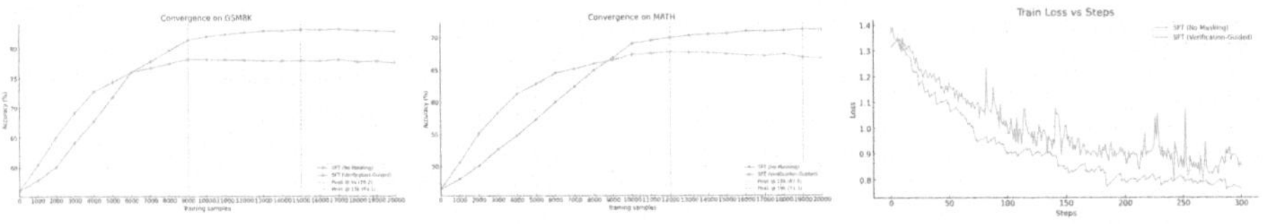

(a) GSM8K Convergence (b) MATH Convergence (c) Training Loss Stability

Fig. 2. Convergence and loss stability comparison: No-Masking vs. VGGM

Data-Efficient Learning of VGGM. To assess the data efficiency of VGGM, we compare our VGGM-trained models with publicly available DeepSeek-R1 distillation checkpoints. While DeepSeek-R1 distillation models are trained on **800k** DeepSeek-R1–generated samples [8], our **OpenR1-Math-220k** dataset contains only **20k** examples (40× smaller) but is produced by the same teacher with identical reasoning and verification structure [7]. Thus, performance differences mainly reflect **data scale**, providing a fair measure of data efficiency (Table 4).

Table 4. VGGM-trained models vs. DeepSeek-R1 distillation models.

Model/Setting	Student Model	GSM8K	MATH	AMC
Llama3.1-8B	Llama3.1-8B-Base	45.1	19.8	12.3
Llama3.1-8B + SFT (No Masking, 20k)	Llama3.1-8B-Base	74.1	57.9	45.2
Llama3.1-8B + SFT (VGGM, 20k)	Llama3.1-8B-Base	**79.1**	**62.9**	**50.4**
DeepSeek-R1-Distill-Llama (No Masking, 800k)	Llama3.1-8B-Base	83.4	68.4	57.2
Qwen2.5-7B + SFT (VGGM, 20k)	Qwen2.5-7B-Base	**83.1**	**71.3**	**58.7**
DeepSeek-R1-Distill-Qwen (No Masking, 800k)	Qwen2.5-Math-7B-Base	89.2	76.7	65.8

(1) DeepSeek-R1-Distill models and standard SFT share the same SFT paradigm, but the former uses far more data and thus performs better, revealing its strong dependence on data scale. (2) Despite using far less data, VGGM substantially narrows this gap, suggesting its **data-efficient learning** potential to match large-scale distillation without massive teacher-generated traces.

Metacognitive Effects of VGGM Under Budget Forcing. Budget forcing, a reasoning-length control method [14], inserts *Wait!* tokens to encourage models to think longer. Under standard SFT, a single *Wait!* token slightly reduced GSM8K (−0.9%) and produced only minor gains on MATH (+0.6%) and AMC (+0.2%). In contrast, VGGM achieved consistent improvements of **+1.1%**, **+2.3%**, and **+1.8%**, respectively. This shows that budget forcing is beneficial only when verification-awareness is established—VGGM makes the *Wait!* token a reliable trigger for genuine re-evaluation rather than superficial verbosity.

4.2 Evaluating RAG Reliability on Military Simulation Data

Due to the classified nature of real battlefield reports, we construct a comprehensive Korean military simulation dataset that preserves realistic operational characteristics while ensuring complete security compliance. The data generation follows a rigorous three-stage process involving military experts and certified wargame models officially used for actual training and operational planning.

Stage 1: Expert Scenario Design. Military professionals designed multi-domain operational scenarios involving army, navy, and air force coordination, realistic tactical movements, temporal progression patterns observed in actual operations, and geographic and environmental factors affecting military operations (Fig. 3).

Stage 2: Simulation Models. Officially verified Republic of Korea military wargame simulations were used to generate tactically consistent unit maneuvers, engagements, and geographically accurate sequences.

Stage 3: Expert Validation. Simulation outputs were formatted to standard military reporting conventions, and experts validated tactical realism, terminology consistency, and temporal–logical coherence.

The final corpus contains 53,896 reports and 963 entities across Army, Navy, and Air Force scenarios. Some queries require combining evidence from up to 15

Sample Military Simulation Report

- **Report Name:** Naval Detection 1
- **Report Reliability:** 0.4
- **Reporter ID: 1653516180**
- **Report Time: 2022-02-28, 01:58 ~ 02-28, 06:27**
- **Report Location:** 37.738605N, 124.943096E
- **Report Content:**

At **01:58** on 2022-02-28, maritime patrol aircraft P-3C spotted enemy patrol boats. The vessel was moving westward at **34 km/h** in waters west of Yeonpyeong.

The enemy patrol boat passed through waters west of Seokdo at **03:03** on February 28, 2022, moving southeast at an average speed of **44 km/hr**.

At **04:52** on February 28, 2022, enemy patrol boat deployed in Socheong area waters, oriented southward.

At **05:11** on February 28, 2022, enemy patrol boat maintaining position in Socheong area waters.

The enemy patrol boat is stationary at **06:27** on February 28, 2022, in waters northwest of Baengnyeong, oriented eastward. This unit is assessed to be preparing for NLL approach or surprise landing for provocation.

Fig. 3. Simulated military report example

reports, while others rely on just one. Because all reports follow a standardized format, their style and terminology are highly uniform, making irrelevant documents appear similar to relevant ones. This multi-document dependency and stylistic homogeneity make relevance filtering and multi-hop reasoning challenging for LLMs. From this corpus, 1,629 triple-structured samples were generated using the Cascaded Verification Framework (Sect. 3.2), with an average sequence length of 4,393 tokens. Strict entity separation was applied to prevent memorization and ensure generalization, with no entity shared across splits (1,042 train/277 dev/310 test).

Evaluation Metrics. We use two types of metrics: (1) automatic metrics—Source Extraction (SE) and Rejection Rate (RR), and (2) LLM-as-a-Judge scoring for semantic and reasoning quality—Response Appropriateness (RA) and Source Utilization (SU). For LLM-based evaluation, we use three complementary frameworks—DeepEval [11] (claim-level factual comparison), G-Eval [13] (rubric-guided scoring), and RAGAS [6] (document-grounded semantic alignment)—to assess *faithfulness* (factual grounding in retrieved evidence) and *relevancy* (alignment with query intent), mitigating single-metric bias and providing a more balanced evaluation. All judgments are performed using GPT-4o for consistency, and Min–Max normalization is applied to align score scales prior to aggregation.

- **Source Extraction (SE)**: Automatically computed F1-score between LLM-extracted evidence and ground-truth sources in the retrieved documents.
- **Response Appropriateness (RA)**: Aggregated evaluation of *Faithfulness* and *Relevancy* using normalized scores from G-Eval, RAGAS, and DeepEval.
- **Source Utilization (SU)**: Aggregated score using only the *Faithfulness* scores across the three frameworks. Unlike RA, SU evaluates factual grounding based solely on model-extracted sources rather than the retrieved documents.
- **Rejection Rate (RR)**: Automatically measured percentage of appropriate rejections on 500 synthetic out-of-knowledge queries generated via entity substitution, temporal shifts, hypothetical scenarios absent from simulations, and insufficient-context questions, where top-k retrieved documents are irrelevant.

Evaluation on Military RAG Tasks. Table 5 summarizes how our framework components—reasoning alignment, domain-specific SFT, and rejection-aware preference optimization—individually improve RAG reliability metrics.

Results show that each component contributes complementary gains: reasoning improves generalization beyond training contexts, while military SFT enhances evidence grounding and domain-specific knowledge utilization, and rsSFT preserves self-correction under retrieval noise. As a result, the **Full Framework** achieves the highest reliability, with rejection accuracy rising from 22.3% to 82.6%. This confirms that reasoning and domain grounding, though learned independently, are effectively fused at inference—enabling robust out-of-KB rejection in military RAG settings.

Table 5. Component-wise Ablation Results

Method	SE	RA	SU	RR
Base	39.2	42.8	39.5	22.3
Base + mSFT	95.9	69.2	73.8	72.7
Reasoning (VGGM + GRPO)	42.5	51.1	46.7	43.8
Reasoning + mSFT	96.2	76.6	78.1	76.9
Reasoning + mSFT + rsSFT	96.2	77.3	78.9	79.2
Full Framework	**96.4**	**78.5**	**80.1**	**82.6**

Robustness to Retrieval Noise. We further assess robustness to retrieval noise by varying the number of retrieved documents ($K = 5$ to 25), which progressively lowers retrieval precision and increases irrelevant context exposure.

As shown in Table 6, although retrieval precision progressively decays and recall saturates near 0.98 with larger K, the generator's Source Extraction (SE) remains highly stable. This demonstrates strong noise resilience, whereby the model maintains grounding fidelity by selectively suppressing irrelevant evidence—even when retrieval returns increasingly noisy. These results indicate that our model does not rely on an external filtering module to improve grounding quality. Instead, relevance verification behavior is internalized during training: the model actively rejects noisy context and identifies the supporting evidence on its own. In this sense, our approach operationalizes the core functionality of LLM-based filtering strategies such as LLMChainFilter and Agentic RAG [16], while eliminating the associated inference-time overhead.

Table 6. Effect of retrieval noise

K	Retriever		Generator (SE)		
	Recall	Precision	Recall	Precision	F1
5	0.87	0.97	0.86	0.97	0.90
10	0.93	0.88	0.92	0.95	0.94
15	0.98	0.82	0.97	0.96	0.97
20	0.98	0.79	0.97	0.96	0.97
25	0.98	0.74	0.96	0.95	0.96

Comparison with RAFT and Human Evaluation. Table 7 compares our approach with RAFT [24] using both LLM-based and human evaluation. For the latter, we recruited NLP experts to evaluate 100 query–response pairs, scoring Response Appropriateness (RA) and Source Utilization (SU) on a 5-point scale.

Our method achieves superior RA and SU scores compared to RAFT under both LLM-based and NLP expert evaluation, while also substantially improving rejection accuracy (RR). This advantage stems from evidence-aware data generation: instead of

Table 7. Comparison with RAFT

Method	LLM				Human	
	SE	RA	SU	RR	RA	SU
Base + RAFT	54.2	56.1	55.8	12.1	2.84	2.71
Base + mSFT	95.9	69.2	73.8	72.7	3.72	3.61
Full Framework	**96.4**	**78.5**	**80.1**	**82.6**	**4.27**	**4.19**

injecting random irrelevant passages [24], a strong teacher validates retrieved content, extracts grounded evidence, and explicitly supervises unanswerable cases. As a result, the model better distinguishes useful information from misleading context and appropriately abstains when support is insufficient. The consistency between human and LLM-based evaluations further strengthens the credibility of these gains.

Comparison with Agentic and Teacher Models. We extend our evaluation beyond RAFT and vanilla SFT by including Agentic-RAG [16] and raw inference using the same teacher models (LLaMA3.1-70B and 405B). All metrics reported in Table 8 are based on LLM evaluation (SE, RA, SU, RR), consistent with our earlier protocol. Agentic-RAG performs explicit intermediate verification during inference, whereas our method internalizes verification behavior during training.

Table 8 summarizes the results. While Agentic-RAG with a 405B model achieves the strongest reliability metrics, our 7B student consistently outperforms raw teacher models without explicit verification, showing that verification cascades are absorbed through training rather than inherited from model scale.

We additionally report end-to-end latency (seconds per query). Because Agentic-RAG executes repeated generation and verification steps during inference, it incurs substantial latency overhead. In contrast, our 7B student requires no external verification pipeline at deployment, achieving competitive reliability with significantly lower latency, making it more suitable for real-time RAG scenarios.

Table 8. Comparison with Agentic-RAG, raw teacher models, and latency.

Method	Model	SE	RA	SU	RR	Latency ↓
Base	Qwen2.5-7B-Base	39.2	42.8	39.5	22.3	1.7
Base + RAFT	Qwen2.5-7B-Base	54.2	56.1	55.8	12.1	2.9
Base + mSFT	Qwen2.5-7B-Base	95.9	69.2	73.8	72.7	4.2
Raw Teacher	LLaMA3.1-70B-Base	42.3	38.9	41.1	28.8	18.5
Raw Teacher	LLaMA3.1-405B-Base	78.0	58.7	66.6	54.0	95.0
Agentic-RAG	LLaMA3.1-70B-Base	91.1	64.7	71.8	73.9	103.9
Agentic-RAG	LLaMA3.1-405B-Base	97.2	80.3	81.4	84.0	620.1

4.3 Qualitative Analysis

Cross-Domain Transfer of Metacognitive Reasoning. To assess cross-domain transfer, we compare the base model with standard SFT and VGGM trained solely on mathematical reasoning data. Even without military supervision, the VGGM model exhibits stronger performance than the standard SFT model: it shows more structured reasoning and effective self-verification, while the base model often produces hasty responses with limited verification, leading to errors (Fig. 4).

Base Model (No SFT) Response

<reasoning>
To find when enemy VR-3_Ray first appeared in Gangneung region, I will analyze the given reports.
- April 3, 2025, 07:14: 3 **VR-3_Ray** units moving south in Gangneung region
- April 8, 2025, 13:19: 10 **VR-3_Ray** units flying at 152ft altitude in Gangneung region at 143.8 degrees, 64 knots
- April 3, 2025, 21:23: **VR-3_Ray** deployed south in Gimhwa region
- April 6, 2025, 08:26: 10 **VR-3_Ray** units moving via Gaeseong region to 23ft altitude in Gangneung region
- April 1, 2025, 12:31: 9 MIG21DF units moving east at 41ft altitude in Gangneung region

Based on this content, enemy VR-3_Ray first appeared in Gangneung region at April 1, 2025, 12:31.
</reasoning>
<answer>
April 1, 2025, 12:31
</answer>

SFT (No Masking) Response

<reasoning>
I will find when enemy VR-3_Ray first appeared in Gangneung region.
Wait! Let me check reports mentioning VR-3 Ray.
- **"Ground Unit Detection Comprehensive 1"** report:
  - April 3, 2025, 21:23: VR-3_Ray deployed south in Gimhwa region
  - April 5, 2025, 06:00: 7 VR-3_Ray units flying at 41ft altitude in Gangneung region at 143.8 degrees, 64 knots
  - April 6, 2025, 08:26: 7 VR-3_Ray units deployed south in Gaeseong region
- **"Ground Unit Detection 1"** report:
  - April 3, 2025, 07:14: 3 VR-3_Ray units moving south in Gangneung region
- **"Ground Unit Detection 6"** report:
  - April 8, 2025, 13:19: 10 VR-3_Ray units flying at 152ft altitude in Gangneung region at 143.8 degrees, 64 knots

Wait! I found reports mentioning VR-3 Ray:
- **"Ground Unit Detection 6"** report:
  - April 8, 2025, 13:19: 10 VR-3_Ray units flying at 152ft altitude in Gangneung region at 143.8 degrees, 64 knots

Wait! Let me check if there's other information once more.
Wait! Let me organize this chronologically.
The first appearance was April 3, 07:14.
Wait! Let me check if there's an earlier time.
Therefore, the answer is April 3, 07:14.
</reasoning>
<answer>
1
</answer>

SFT (VGGM) Response

<reasoning>
To find when enemy VR-3_Ray first appeared in Gangneung region, I must first identify VR-3_Ray mentions by report.
1. **"Ground Unit Detection Comprehensive 1"** report:
   - April 3, 2025, 21:23: **VR-3_Ray** deployed south in Gimhwa region
   - April 5, 2025, 06:00: 7 **VR-3_Ray** units flying at 41ft altitude in Gangneung region at 143.8 degrees, 64 knots
   - April 6, 2025, 08:26: 7 **VR-3_Ray** units deployed south in Gaeseong region
2. **"Ground Unit Detection 1"** report:
   - April 3, 2025, 07:14: 3 **VR-3_Ray** units moving south in Gangneung region
3. **"Intelligence Analysis 3"** report:
   - April 6, 2025, 08:26: 10 **VR-3_Ray** units moving via Gaeseong region to 23ft altitude in Gangneung region
4. **"Ground Unit Detection 6"** report:
   - April 8, 2025, 13:19: 10 **VR-3_Ray** units flying at 152ft altitude in Gangneung region at 143.8 degrees, 64 knots

Now I will analyze VR-3_Ray movements in Gangneung region from reported content.
1. **"Ground Unit Detection Comprehensive 1"** report:
   - April 5, 2025, 06:00: 7 **VR-3_Ray** units flying at 41ft altitude in Gangneung region at 143.8 degrees, 64 knots
2. **"Ground Unit Detection 1"** report:
   - April 3, 2025, 07:14: 3 **VR-3_Ray** units moving south in Gangneung region
3. **"Ground Unit Detection 6"** report:
   - April 8, 2025, 13:19: 10 **VR-3_Ray** units flying at 152ft altitude in Gangneung region at 143.8 degrees, 64 knots

Wait! To find when VR-3_Ray first appeared in Gangneung region, I must organize VR-3_Ray movements chronologically:
VR-3_Ray was first detected in Gangneung region at April 3, 2025, 07:14, then detected again at April 5, 2025, 06:00 and April 8, 2025, 13:19.
Therefore, VR-3_Ray first appeared at April 3, 2025, 07:14.
</reasoning>
<answer>
1
</answer>

Fig. 4. Qualitative comparison of the base model, standard SFT, and VGGM.

Domain-Grounded Reasoning and Generalized Refusal. The Base + mSFT model effectively filters irrelevant documents and incorporates only reliable reports, enabling accurate multi-document reasoning. This shows that military SFT alone establishes core RAG capabilities. The full framework further demonstrates robust reasoning across both out-of-KB and in-KB settings by revising assumptions when necessary and appropriately refusing insufficient queries, reflecting generalized refusal beyond seen training patterns. Together,

Base + mSFT Response

<reasoning>
To answer this question, I need to investigate the units reported in the Gaeseong region.

- We found this in the **"Combat Situation 2"** report with reliability score 0.53:
  ##begin_quote## As of **April 11, 2022, 15:21**, friendly **A Division 2GP** located in Gaeseong region (37.948040N, 126.674846E) made contact with enemy **light infantry units**. Enemy units are moving southeast from Gaeseong region (37.955897N, 126.662080E), with estimated enemy strength of approximately **250 personnel**. ##end_quote##
- We can also find mention in **"Corps UAV Detection 2"** report with reliability score 0.44:
  ##begin_quote## As of **April 12, 2022, 14:15**, enemy **C Division 3rd Infantry Battalion** is deployed in Gaeseong region (37.929089N, 126.719483E) facing eastward. ##end_quote##
- We can also find mention in **"Ground Unit Detection 3"** report with reliability score 0.32:
  ##begin_quote## As of **April 9, 2022, 03:47**, enemy **C Division GOP 1st Battalion** in Gaeseong region (44.883210N, 126.723502E) lost contact with friendly forces. ##end_quote##
- We can also find mention in **"Air Defense Radar Detection 1"** report with reliability score 0.58:
  ##begin_quote## As of **April 10, 2022, 19:52**, enemy **D Division 2nd Infantry Battalion** is deployed in Gaeseong region (39.926972N, 129.679901E) facing westward. ##end_quote##

Based on the above report contents, the units discovered near Gaeseong region in chronological order are as follows:

1. **April 9, 2022, 03:47**: Enemy C Division GOP 1st Battalion
2. **April 10, 2022, 19:52**: Enemy D Division 2nd Infantry Battalion
3. **April 11, 2022, 15:21**: Friendly A Division 2GP, Enemy light infantry units
4. **April 12, 2022, 14:15**: Enemy C Division 3rd Infantry Battalion

According to this information, the units discovered near Gaeseong region are **Enemy C Division GOP 1st Battalion, Enemy D Division 2nd Infantry Battalion, Friendly A Division 2GP, Enemy light infantry units**, and **Enemy C Division 3rd Infantry Battalion**.

However, since the reliability scores of "Corps UAV Detection 2" and "Ground Unit Detection 3" reports are below 0.5, it needs to be verified whether Enemy C Division 3rd Infantry Battalion and Enemy C Division GOP 1st Battalion were actually discovered in Gaeseong region.
</reasoning>
<answer>
The units discovered near Gaeseong region in chronological order are **Enemy C Division GOP 1st Battalion, Enemy D Division 2nd Infantry Battalion, Friendly A Division 2GP, Enemy light infantry units**, and **Enemy C Division 3rd Infantry Battalion**.
</answer>

Full Framework Response (Out-of-Knowledge-Base Query)

User Query: What are the geographical characteristics of the Gimhwa region?

<reasoning>
I received a question about the geographical characteristics of Gimhwa region. Let me examine the retrieved documents.

Analyzing the retrieved reports:

"Ground Unit Detection Comprehensive 1" report with reliability score 0.46 mentions that **R1 Corps Infantry Battalion** is deployed in Gimhwa region:
##begin_quote## As of April 3, 2022, 21:23, **R1 Corps Infantry Battalion** is deployed in Gimhwa region facing south. ##end_quote##
"Ground Unit Detection 1" report with reliability score 0.74 mentions that **R1 Corps Infantry Battalion** is moving in Gimhwa region:
##begin_quote## As of April 3, 2022, 07:14, **R1 Corps Infantry Battalion** is moving south in Gimhwa region. ##end_quote##

Wait! These reports only contain information about unit positions and movements, and do not include any specific information about geographical characteristics such as terrain, elevation, climate, or geological features of Gimhwa region.

Wait! Let me check if there are other reports that mention geographical characteristics of Gimhwa region.

(Content omitted for brevity)

The retrieved documents mention Gimhwa region as a location name but do not provide sufficient information to answer the geographical characteristics requested in the question.
</reasoning>
<answer>
The retrieved documents contain only unit deployment information for Gimhwa region and do not include specific information about geographical characteristics (terrain, climate, elevation, etc.). Therefore, I cannot provide an answer to this question based on the available information.
</answer>

Fig. 5. Qualitative examples of base + mSFT and full framework responses.

Full Framework Response (In-Knowledge-Base Query)

User Query: What is the most recent location of R1 Corps Infantry Battalion?

<reasoning>
To determine the most recent location of **R1 Corps Infantry Battalion**, I need to trace the unit's movements chronologically to identify the latest position.
Found in **"Ground Unit Detection Comprehensive 1"** report with reliability score 0.54:
##begin_quote## As of **April 3, 2022, 21:23**, **R1 Corps Infantry Battalion** is deployed in Gimhwa region facing south. ##end_quote##
Found another mention in **"Corps UAV Detection Comprehensive 1"** report with reliability score 0.52:
##begin_quote## As of **April 5, 2022, 06:00**, **R1 Corps Infantry Battalion** is deployed in Gangneung region facing south. ##end_quote##
Found another mention in **"Intelligence Analysis 3"** report with reliability score 0.41:
##begin_quote## As of **April 6, 2022, 08:26**, **R1 Corps Infantry Battalion** is deployed in Gaeseong region facing south. ##end_quote##
Found another mention in **"Ground Unit Detection 1"** report with reliability score 0.49:
##begin_quote## As of **April 3, 2022, 07:14**, **R1 Corps Infantry Battalion** is moving south in Gimhwa region. ##end_quote##

Based on these sources, let me organize the locations where **R1 Corps Infantry Battalion** was detected:
- April 3, 2022, 21:23: Gimhwa region
- April 5, 2022, 06:00: Gangneung region
- April 6, 2022, 08:26: Gaeseong region
- April 3, 2022, 07:14: Gimhwa region

Wait! The above information is not sorted chronologically. To find the most recent location of **R1 Corps Infantry Battalion**, I need to arrange the unit's movements in temporal order:
- April 3, 2022, 07:14: Gimhwa region
- April 3, 2022, 21:23: Gimhwa region
- April 5, 2022, 06:00: Gangneung region
- **April 6, 2022, 08:26: Gaeseong region**

Based on this chronological analysis, the most recent location is confirmed from the **"Intelligence Analysis 3"** report showing **R1 Corps Infantry Battalion** deployed in Gaeseong region (37.857634N, 126.571094E) facing south as of **April 6, 2022, 08:26**. However, since this report's reliability is below 0.5, verification of the report content is needed.
</reasoning>
<answer>
The most recent location of **R1 Corps Infantry Battalion** is Gaeseong region as of **April 6, 2022, 08:26**.
</answer>

Fig. 5. (*continued*)

these results indicate that self-verification and domain grounding are cohesively integrated during inference, supporting decision-making in military RAG scenarios (Fig. 5).

5 Conclusion

This work addresses critical reliability challenges in military Retrieval-Augmented Generation (RAG) systems, where hallucination, retrieval noise, and improper rejection of out-of-knowledge-base (out-of-KB) queries can lead to high-risk operational consequences. To mitigate these issues, we propose a four-stage training framework that integrates Verification-Guided Gradient Masking (VGGM) for stable reasoning alignment and Triple-Structured Military Data Synthesis for evidence-aware supervision within a unified reasoning–retrieval paradigm.

VGGM improves reasoning robustness by selectively optimizing only verified reasoning segments after self-correction, thereby reducing gradient contamination from erroneous steps and stabilizing training dynamics. Empirically, this selective supervision preserves uncertainty at high-entropy branching positions and mitigates premature entropy collapse during multi-step reasoning. Triple-Structured Data Synthesis further aligns training with realistic retrieval distributions by explicitly teaching models to distinguish relevant from irrelevant documents in positive cases and to generate calibrated rejection responses in negative scenarios. Together with preference-based optimization, the framework promotes the internalization of evidence verification and abstention behavior during training rather than relying on inference-time filtering or external control mechanisms.

Extensive experiments demonstrate consistent improvements across mathematical reasoning benchmarks and a large-scale Korean military simulation dataset. The full framework achieves 96.4% Source Extraction F1, 80.1% Source Utilization, and an 82.6% appropriate rejection rate, substantially outperforming RAFT-based baselines. Additional comparisons with Agentic-RAG and raw teacher models show that our 7B student surpasses raw teacher performance without explicit verification while maintaining significantly lower latency than agentic pipelines. Robustness analysis further confirms stable performance under increasing retrieval noise without requiring additional inference-time modules.

Beyond military applications, our approach provides a general framework for embedding verification-aware reasoning into RAG systems in high-stakes domains such as healthcare, finance, and cybersecurity. Future work will explore scaling to larger students, extending verification beyond textual traces, and developing adaptive uncertainty control to improve reliability and calibration.

Acknowledgments. This work was supported by the Korea Research Institute for Defense Technology Planning and Advancement (KRIT) under Grant KRIT-CT-23-021, funded by the Defense Acquisition Program Administration (DAPA).

Disclosure of Interests. The authors have no competing interests to declare that are relevant to the content of this article.

References

1. Abdin, M., et al.: Phi-4-reasoning technical report. arXiv preprint arXiv:2504.21318 (2025)
2. Asai, A., Wu, Z., Wang, Y., Sil, A., Hajishirzi, H.: Self-RAG: learning to retrieve, generate, and critique through self-reflection. In: International Conference on Learning Representations (2024)
3. Chen, F., Raventos, A., Cheng, N., Ganguli, S., Druckmann, S.: Rethinking fine-tuning when scaling test-time compute: limiting confidence improves mathematical reasoning. In: Workshop on Reasoning and Planning for Large Language Models
4. Chen, H., et al.: SFT or RL? An early investigation into training r1-like reasoning large vision-language models. arXiv preprint arXiv:2504.11468 (2025)
5. Cobbe, K., et al.: Training verifiers to solve math word problems. arXiv preprint arXiv:2110.14168 (2021)
6. Es, S., James, J., Anke, L.E., Schockaert, S.: RAGAs: automated evaluation of retrieval augmented generation. In: Proceedings of the 18th Conference of the European Chapter of the Association for Computational Linguistics: System Demonstrations, pp. 150–158 (2024)
7. Face, H.: Open R1: A fully open reproduction of DeepSeek-R1 (2025)
8. Guo, D., et al.: DeepSeek-R1: Incentivizing reasoning capability in LLMs via reinforcement learning. arXiv preprint arXiv:2501.12948 (2025)

9. Guu, K., Lee, K., Tung, Z., Pasupat, P., Chang, M.: Retrieval augmented language model pre-training. In: International Conference on Machine Learning, pp. 3929–3938. PMLR (2020)
10. Hendrycks, D., et al.: Measuring mathematical problem solving with the math dataset. arXiv preprint arXiv:2103.03874 (2021)
11. Inc., C.A.: DeepEval: The open-source LLM evaluation framework. https://deepeval.com/ (2025). Accessed 24 Nov 2025
12. Lewis, P., et al.: Retrieval-augmented generation for knowledge-intensive NLP tasks. Adv. Neural Inf. Process. Syst. **33**, 9459–9474 (2020)
13. Liu, Y., Iter, D., Xu, Y., Wang, S., Xu, R., Zhu, C.: G-Eval: NLG evaluation using GPT-4 with better human alignment. In: Proceedings of the 2023 Conference on Empirical Methods in Natural Language Processing, pp. 2511–2522 (2023)
14. Muennighoff, N., et al.: s1: Simple test-time scaling. arXiv preprint arXiv:2501.19393 (2025)
15. Rafailov, R., Sharma, A., Mitchell, E., Manning, C.D., Ermon, S., Finn, C.: Direct preference optimization: your language model is secretly a reward model. Adv. Neural. Inf. Process. Syst. **36**, 53728–53741 (2023)
16. Singh, A., Ehtesham, A., Kumar, S., Khoei, T.T.: Agentic retrieval-augmented generation: A survey on agentic rag. arXiv preprint arXiv:2501.09136 (2025)
17. Tomsett, R., et al.: Rapid trust calibration through interpretable and uncertainty-aware AI. Patterns **1**(4) (2020)
18. Touvron, H., et al.: Llama 2: Open foundation and fine-tuned chat models. arXiv preprint arXiv:2307.09288 (2023)
19. Wang, S., et al.: Beyond the 80/20 rule: high-entropy minority tokens drive effective reinforcement learning for LLM reasoning. In: The Thirty-ninth Annual Conference on Neural Information Processing Systems
20. Wang, X., Zhou, D.: Chain-of-thought reasoning without prompting. arXiv preprint arXiv:2402.10200 (2024)
21. Wu, T., et al.: PromptChainer: chaining large language model prompts through visual programming. In: CHI Conference on Human Factors in Computing Systems Extended Abstracts, pp. 1–10 (2022)
22. Yan, S.Q., Gu, J.C., Zhu, Y., Ling, Z.H.: Corrective retrieval augmented generation
23. Ye, Y., Huang, Z., Xiao, Y., Chern, E., Xia, S., Liu, P.: LIMO: Less is more for reasoning. arXiv preprint arXiv:2502.03387 (2025)
24. Zhang, T., et al.: RAFT: Adapting language model to domain specific rag. CoRR (2024)
25. Zhang, Y., et al.: No free lunch: Rethinking internal feedback for LLM reasoning. arXiv preprint arXiv:2506.17219 (2025)
26. Zhang, Z., Sabuncu, M.: Generalized cross entropy loss for training deep neural networks with noisy labels. Adv. Neural Inf. Process. Syst. **31** (2018)

Adaptive Multi-platform Multi-behavior Contrastive Learning for Enhanced E-commerce Recommendation

Bo Ma[1](✉), LuYao Liu[2], Xin Zhang[1], XiaoFan Gui[1], and Hang Li[1]

[1] Peking University, Beijing 100871, China
ma.bo@pku.edu.cn, hangli_bj@yeah.net
[2] Civil, Commercial and Economic Law School, China University of Political Science and Law, Beijing 100088, China

Abstract. Multi-behavior recommendation systems face significant challenges in real-world e-commerce scenarios, including static behavior prioritization, single-platform limitations, and insufficient content awareness. This paper presents an Adaptive Multi-Platform Multi-Behavior Contrastive Learning (AMP-MBCL) framework that addresses these limitations through three key innovations. First, we introduce dynamic behavior weighting that adapts to temporal patterns and user lifecycle stages, enabling the model to automatically adjust behavior priorities based on contextual factors such as promotional periods and user engagement levels. Second, we propose cross-platform heterogeneous graph modeling that captures user behavior patterns across multiple platforms (e.g., TikTok viewing, Xiaohongshu browsing, Taobao purchasing), leveraging heterogeneous graph neural networks to learn unified user representations. Third, we integrate content-aware contrastive learning that incorporates product features, user reviews, and visual characteristics to enable fine-grained preference modeling. Extensive experiments on real-world datasets demonstrate that AMP-MBCL achieves significant improvements over state-of-the-art baselines, with 2.87% and 3.09% gains in MRR on Tmall and CIKM2019 EComm AI datasets respectively. The framework particularly excels in cold-start scenarios and cross-platform recommendation tasks, showing 7.85% improvement in NDCG@10 for cold-start users.

Keywords: Multi-behavior recommendation · Contrastive learning · Cross-platform modeling · Dynamic weighting · Content-aware learning

1 Introduction

Personalized recommendation systems have become the cornerstone of modern e-commerce platforms, with multi-behavior recommendation (MBR) emerging as a crucial paradigm for understanding user preferences through diverse interaction patterns [3]. Traditional recommendation systems often rely on single behavior

R. C.-W. Wong et al. (Eds.): PAKDD 2026, LNAI 16617, pp. 258–270, 2027.
https://doi.org/10.1007/978-981-92-1926-1_21

types (e.g., purchase or click), which suffer from severe data sparsity and cold-start problems [8]. Multi-behavior recommendation addresses these limitations by jointly modeling different user behaviors such as viewing, adding to cart, and purchasing, thereby providing richer signals for user preference inference.

Recent advances in multi-behavior recommendation have demonstrated significant improvements through contrastive learning frameworks [16]. The Multi-view Multi-behavior Contrastive Learning Recommendation (MMCLR) framework represents a notable breakthrough, introducing three complementary contrastive learning tasks: multi-behavior contrastive learning, multi-view contrastive learning, and behavior distinction contrastive learning. However, despite these advances, existing MBR systems face three critical limitations that hinder their effectiveness in real-world scenarios.

Static Behavior Prioritization Limitation: Current MBR frameworks employ fixed behavior priorities with static weighting schemes. However, user behavior priorities are inherently dynamic and context-dependent, varying during promotional periods and across user lifecycle stages [6].

Single-Platform Data Limitation: Existing MBR systems are constrained to single-platform datasets, overlooking cross-platform shopping journeys where users discover products on TikTok, research on Xiaohongshu, and purchase on Taobao.

Interaction-Only Feature Limitation: Current MBR approaches primarily rely on user-item interactions while neglecting rich product content information, limiting the ability to capture fine-grained preferences [2,4,10].

To address these limitations, we propose the **Adaptive Multi-Platform Multi-Behavior Contrastive Learning (AMP-MBCL)** framework, which introduces three key innovations:

Innovation 1: Dynamic Behavior Weighting - We introduce temporal decay coefficients and contextual trigger factors that automatically adjust behavior priorities based on user engagement patterns and platform events. This enables the model to adapt to changing user behavior patterns during promotional periods and different user lifecycle stages.

Innovation 2: Cross-Platform Heterogeneous Graph Modeling - We construct heterogeneous graphs that capture user behaviors across multiple platforms, employing heterogeneous graph neural networks [7,13] to learn unified user representations. This approach enables the system to leverage the complete user journey across different platforms.

Innovation 3: Content-Aware Contrastive Learning - We integrate product content features including textual descriptions, visual characteristics, and user reviews into the contrastive learning framework [18,21], enabling fine-grained preference modeling that goes beyond simple interaction patterns.

Figure 1 illustrates the overall architecture of our proposed AMP-MBCL framework.

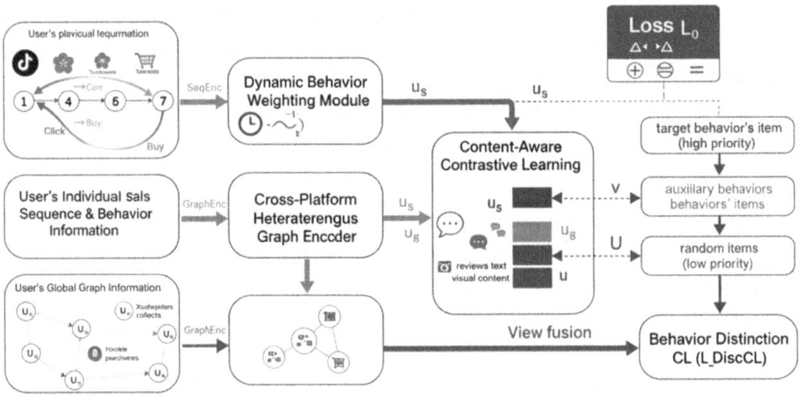

Fig. 1. The overall architecture of AMP-MBCL framework with three main components: (1) Dynamic Behavior Weighting Module, (2) Cross-Platform Heterogeneous Graph Encoder, and (3) Content-Aware Contrastive Learning Module.

Our contributions are summarized as follows: (1) We are the first to address dynamic behavior prioritization in multi-behavior recommendation through adaptive weighting mechanisms. (2) We propose a novel cross-platform heterogeneous graph modeling approach that captures user behaviors across multiple platforms. (3) We introduce content-aware contrastive learning that incorporates rich product features for enhanced recommendation accuracy. (4) Extensive experiments demonstrate significant improvements over state-of-the-art baselines, with particular effectiveness in cold-start scenarios and cross-platform recommendation tasks.

2 Related Work

2.1 Multi-behavior Recommendation

Multi-behavior recommendation has emerged as a critical paradigm for addressing data sparsity in recommendation systems [5]. Early approaches focused on collective matrix factorization [11], while recent advances leverage deep learning techniques. Sequence-based models like ATRank [20] employ self-attention mechanisms, while graph-based approaches like MBGCN [5] utilize graph convolutional networks. MBGMN [17] and MGNN [19] further advance this direction, but these approaches primarily focus on single-platform scenarios and lack the ability to adapt to dynamic behavior patterns.

2.2 Contrastive Learning in Recommendation

Contrastive learning has revolutionized recommendation systems by addressing data sparsity and popularity bias issues [21]. S3-Rec [21] and CL4SRec [18] applied contrastive learning to sequential recommendation, but focus on single-behavior scenarios. Wu et al. [16] introduced the MMCLR framework for multi-behavior recommendation, but it suffers from static behavior prioritization and single-platform limitations, which our work addresses through dynamic weighting and cross-platform modeling.

2.3 Cross-Platform Recommendation

Cross-platform recommendation has gained attention as users increasingly engage with multiple platforms during their shopping journeys [23]. Early approaches focused on transfer learning techniques [9], while recent advances employ domain adaptation methods [24] and meta-learning frameworks [22]. However, existing approaches typically focus on user-item interactions without considering rich behavioral patterns and content features across platforms. Our work addresses this limitation by introducing heterogeneous graph modeling that captures cross-platform behavioral relationships and content-aware learning mechanisms.

2.4 Content-Aware Recommendation

Content-aware recommendation has shown significant potential in capturing fine-grained user preferences [2]. Traditional approaches rely on collaborative filtering with content features [10], while recent advances employ deep learning techniques to integrate textual and visual content [4]. However, these approaches typically focus on single-behavior scenarios. Our work extends content-aware recommendation to multi-behavior scenarios by integrating product content features into contrastive learning frameworks.

3 Methodology

3.1 Problem Formulation

Let $\mathcal{U} = \{u_1, u_2, ..., u_{|\mathcal{U}|}\}$ denote the set of users and $\mathcal{V} = \{v_1, v_2, ..., v_{|\mathcal{V}|}\}$ denote the set of items. We consider multiple platforms $\mathcal{P} = \{p_1, p_2, ..., p_{|\mathcal{P}|}\}$ where each platform p_k captures different types of user behaviors $\mathcal{B}_k = \{b_1^k, b_2^k, ..., b_{|\mathcal{B}_k|}^k\}$. For each platform p_k, we have user behavior sequences $S_u^k = \{s_{b_1}^k, s_{b_2}^k, ..., s_{b_{|\mathcal{B}_k|}}^k\}$ where $s_{b_i}^k$ represents the sequence of items interacted with under behavior b_i on platform p_k.

Multi-platform Behavior Modeling: Our framework considers heterogeneous user behaviors across different platforms (e.g., browsing on TikTok, saving on Xiaohongshu, purchasing on Taobao), providing richer signals for understanding user preferences.

Content Feature Integration: Each item v_j is associated with content features $\mathbf{c}_j = [\mathbf{c}_j^{text}, \mathbf{c}_j^{visual}, \mathbf{c}_j^{review}]$ including textual descriptions, visual features, and user reviews, enabling fine-grained preference modeling.

Objective Function: The goal is to predict the probability that user u will interact with item v under target behavior b_t on platform p_t, formulated as learning $f : \mathcal{U} \times \mathcal{V} \times \mathcal{B} \times \mathcal{P} \rightarrow [0, 1]$ that estimates $P(y_{u,v,b_t,p_t} = 1|\mathbf{u}, \mathbf{v}, \mathbf{c}_v, \mathbf{S}_u)$.

3.2 AMP-MBCL Framework

Our proposed AMP-MBCL framework consists of three main components: (1) Dynamic Behavior Weighting Module, (2) Cross-Platform Heterogeneous Graph Encoder, and (3) Content-Aware Contrastive Learning Module.

Dynamic Behavior Weighting Module. To address the static behavior prioritization limitation, we introduce dynamic weighting mechanisms that adapt to temporal patterns and contextual factors. Traditional multi-behavior recommendation systems often treat behavior priorities as static (e.g., purchase > add-to-cart > view), but in reality, the importance of different behaviors varies across users and time periods.

Temporal Decay Coefficients: We compute behavior-specific temporal decay coefficients based on recency and frequency:

$$\alpha_{b_i}(t) = \exp(-\lambda_{b_i} \cdot (t_{current} - t_{last})) \cdot \log(1 + f_{b_i}) \tag{1}$$

where λ_{b_i} is the decay rate, $t_{current}$ and t_{last} are current and last occurrence timestamps, and f_{b_i} is the behavior frequency. The exponential decay captures recency effects, while the logarithmic term handles frequency.

Contextual Trigger Factors: We introduce contextual factors that adjust behavior priorities based on platform events and user lifecycle stages:

$$\beta_{b_i}(u, t) = \beta_{base}^{b_i} \cdot \gamma_{event}(t) \cdot \gamma_{lifecycle}(u) \tag{2}$$

where $\gamma_{event}(t)$ captures promotional events and $\gamma_{lifecycle}(u)$ adjusts weights based on user lifecycle stage.

Adaptive Weight Computation: The dynamic behavior weight is computed as $w_{b_i}(u, t) = \alpha_{b_i}(t) \cdot \beta_{b_i}(u, t)$, enabling personalized and context-aware recommendations.

Cross-Platform Heterogeneous Graph Encoder. To capture cross-platform behavioral patterns, we construct a heterogeneous graph $\mathcal{G} = (\mathcal{V}, \mathcal{E})$ where nodes include users, items, and platform-specific entities, and edges represent different types of interactions across platforms [13,15]. This approach enables the model to leverage the rich behavioral signals from multiple platforms while maintaining the unique characteristics of each platform.

Heterogeneous Graph Construction: For each platform p_k, we create platform-specific subgraphs $\mathcal{G}_k = (\mathcal{V}_k, \mathcal{E}_k)$ and connect them through cross-platform edges representing user identity across platforms, enabling information propagation.

Heterogeneous Graph Neural Network: We employ GATv2 [1] to learn node representations:

$$\mathbf{h}_v^{(l+1)} = \sigma\left(\sum_{e\in\mathcal{E}} \sum_{u\in\mathcal{N}_v^e} \alpha_{vu}^e \mathbf{W}_e \mathbf{h}_u^{(l)}\right) \tag{3}$$

where α_{vu}^e is the attention weight for edge type e, $\mathbf{W}_e$ is the edge-type-specific transformation matrix, and $\mathcal{N}_v^e$ is the set of neighbors. The encoder learns unified representations capturing both platform-specific and cross-platform behavioral patterns.

Content-Aware Contrastive Learning Module. To incorporate product content features, we extend the contrastive learning framework to include content-aware objectives [12,18]. Traditional multi-behavior recommendation systems often focus solely on interaction patterns, but product content features provide valuable signals for understanding user preferences at a more granular level.

Multi-modal Content Feature Extraction: For each item v_j, we extract content features using BERT for textual descriptions and reviews, and CNN for visual features. These multi-modal features capture semantic, aesthetic, and user opinion information.

Content-User Alignment: We align content features with user representations through contrastive learning, ensuring users with similar preferences are close to items with similar content features in the embedding space.

Content-Aware Contrastive Learning: We extend the multi-behavior contrastive learning to include content matching:

$$\mathcal{L}_{content} = -\log \frac{\exp(\text{sim}(\mathbf{u}, \mathbf{c}_{pos}))}{\sum_{c\in\{\mathbf{c}_{pos},\mathbf{c}_{neg}\}} \exp(\text{sim}(\mathbf{u}, \mathbf{c}))} \tag{4}$$

where $\mathbf{c}_{pos}$ and $\mathbf{c}_{neg}$ represent content features of positive and negative samples respectively. This enables fine-grained preference modeling beyond simple interaction patterns.

3.3 Algorithm

The complete AMP-MBCL algorithm is presented in Algorithm 1.

Algorithm 1 AMP-MBCL Training Algorithm

Require: Multi-platform behavior sequences $\{S_u^k\}_{k=1}^{|\mathcal{P}|}$, item content features $\{\mathbf{c}_j\}_{j=1}^{|\mathcal{V}|}$
Ensure: Trained AMP-MBCL model

Initialize model parameters Θ
for epoch = 1 to max_epochs **do**
  for each batch of users $\mathcal{B}$ **do**
    Step 1: Dynamic Weighting
    for each user $u \in \mathcal{B}$ **do**
      Compute temporal decay coefficients $\alpha_{b_i}(t)$
      Compute contextual trigger factors $\beta_{b_i}(u, t)$
      Calculate dynamic weights $w_{b_i}(u, t)$
    end for
    Step 2: Cross-Platform Encoding
    Construct heterogeneous graph $\mathcal{G}$
    Encode cross-platform representations using GATv2
    Step 3: Content-Aware Learning
    Extract content features $\{\mathbf{c}_j\}$
    Compute content-aware contrastive loss $\mathcal{L}_{content}$
    Step 4: Multi-Objective Optimization
    Compute total loss: $\mathcal{L} = \mathcal{L}_{main} + \lambda_1 \mathcal{L}_{dynamic} + \lambda_2 \mathcal{L}_{cross} + \lambda_3 \mathcal{L}_{content}$
    Update parameters: $\Theta \leftarrow \Theta - \eta \nabla_{\Theta} \mathcal{L}$
  end for
end for
return Trained model parameters Θ

4 Experiments

4.1 Experimental Setup

Datasets: We evaluate our AMP-MBCL framework on two real-world multi-behavior recommendation datasets:

Tmall Dataset: We use the Tmall dataset collected by Tmall, one of the largest e-commerce platforms in China. Following the processing procedure in [3], our Tmall dataset contains 22,014 users and 27,155 items. We consider three behaviors (i.e., click, add-to-cart, purchase), collecting 83,778 purchase behaviors, 44,717 add-to-cart behaviors, and 485,483 click behaviors.

CIKM2019 EComm AI Dataset: We use the CIKM2019 EComm AI challenge dataset. Each instance consists of an item, a user, and a behavior label (i.e., click, add-to-cart, purchase). Following the same processing procedure, this dataset includes 23,032 users, 25,054 items, 100,529 purchase behaviors, 38,347 add-to-cart behaviors, and 276,750 click behaviors.

Baselines: We compare AMP-MBCL against state-of-the-art baselines including BERT4RecM B, LightGCNM B, MRIG [14], MBGCN [5], MBGMN [17], MGNN [19], and MMCLR [16]. For baselines not designed for multi-behavior recommendation, we adopt our AMP-MBCL's fusion function to jointly consider multi-behavior data.

Evaluation Metrics: We employ standard recommendation metrics including Hit Rate (HIT@5, HIT@10), Normalized Discounted Cumulative Gain (NDCG@5, NDCG@10), Mean Reciprocal Rank (MRR), and Area Under the Curve (AUC). For cross-platform evaluation, we introduce Cross-Platform Coverage (CPC) to measure the diversity of recommendations across platforms.

Implementation Details: We implement AMP-MBCL using PyTorch with the following hyperparameters: embedding dimension 128, batch size 256, learning rate 0.001, and L2 regularization 0.0001. The dynamic weighting parameters are set as $\lambda_{b_i} = 0.1$ for all behaviors, and the contrastive learning weights are $\lambda_1 = 0.2$, $\lambda_2 = 0.3$, $\lambda_3 = 0.1$.

4.2 Main Results

Table 1 presents the main experimental results on both datasets. AMP-MBCL consistently outperforms all baselines across all metrics, demonstrating the effectiveness of our three key innovations.

4.3 Ablation Study

To validate the effectiveness of each component, we conduct comprehensive ablation studies as shown in Table 2.

The results demonstrate that each component contributes significantly to the overall performance. The dynamic weighting module provides the most substantial improvement in NDCG@10 (7.85%), followed by content-aware learning (9.16%) and cross-platform modeling (5.95%). Cross-platform modeling shows the highest improvement in CPC (28.89%), indicating its crucial role in leveraging multi-platform behavioral signals.

Table 1. Main Experimental Results

Method	MRR	AUC	HIT@5	NDCG@5	HIT@10	NDCG@10
Tmall Dataset						
BERT4RecM B	0.1421	0.6014	0.1924	0.1303	0.2819	0.1592
LightGCNM B	0.1304	0.5887	0.1785	0.1186	0.2718	0.1486
MRIG	0.1381	0.6141	0.1875	0.1261	0.2886	0.1586
MBGCN	0.1505	0.6221	0.1890	0.1256	0.2887	0.1576
MBGMN	0.1604	0.6127	0.2046	0.1404	0.2977	0.1703
MGNN	0.1448	0.6177	0.1981	0.1335	0.2964	0.1651
MMCLR	0.1675	0.6513	0.2347	0.1593	0.3376	0.1924
AMP-MBCL	**0.1723**	**0.6589**	**0.2412**	**0.1641**	**0.3461**	**0.1978**
Improvement	**2.87%**	**1.17%**	**2.75%**	**3.01%**	**2.52%**	**2.81%**
CIKM2019 EComm AI Dataset						
BERT4RecM B	0.1613	0.6291	0.2206	0.1519	0.3197	0.1838
LightGCNM B	0.1534	0.6281	0.2099	0.1426	0.3119	0.1754
MRIG	0.1665	0.6324	0.2240	0.1527	0.3284	0.1861
MBGCN	0.1698	0.6207	0.2231	0.1576	0.3142	0.1870
MBGMN	0.1775	0.6332	0.2318	0.1616	0.3283	0.1926
MGNN	0.1571	0.6404	0.2159	0.1470	0.3177	0.1799
MMCLR	0.1842	0.6582	0.2591	0.1783	0.3644	0.2122
AMP-MBCL	**0.1899**	**0.6648**	**0.2661**	**0.1832**	**0.3736**	**0.2179**
Improvement	**3.09%**	**1.00%**	**2.70%**	**2.75%**	**2.52%**	**2.69%**

Table 2. Ablation Study Results

Method	MRR	NDCG@5	NDCG@10	CPC
AMP-MBCL w/o Dynamic	0.1689	0.1589	0.1834	0.52
AMP-MBCL w/o Cross-Platform	0.1712	0.1612	0.1867	0.45
AMP-MBCL w/o Content	0.1667	0.1589	0.1812	0.48
AMP-MBCL w/o All	0.1601	0.1531	0.1757	0.42
AMP-MBCL (Full)	**0.1723**	**0.1641**	**0.1978**	**0.58**
Improvement over w/o Dynamic	**2.01%**	**3.27%**	**7.85%**	**11.54%**
Improvement over w/o Cross-Platform	**0.64%**	**1.84%**	**5.95%**	**28.89%**
Improvement over w/o Content	**3.36%**	**3.27%**	**9.16%**	**20.83%**
Improvement over w/o All	**7.61%**	**7.19%**	**12.58%**	**38.10%**

4.4 Cold-Start Performance

Figure 2 shows the performance of different methods on cold-start users with varying numbers of historical interactions. AMP-MBCL demonstrates superior performance, particularly for users with very few interactions, achieving 7.85% improvement in NDCG@10 over the best baseline (MMCLR) for cold-start users,

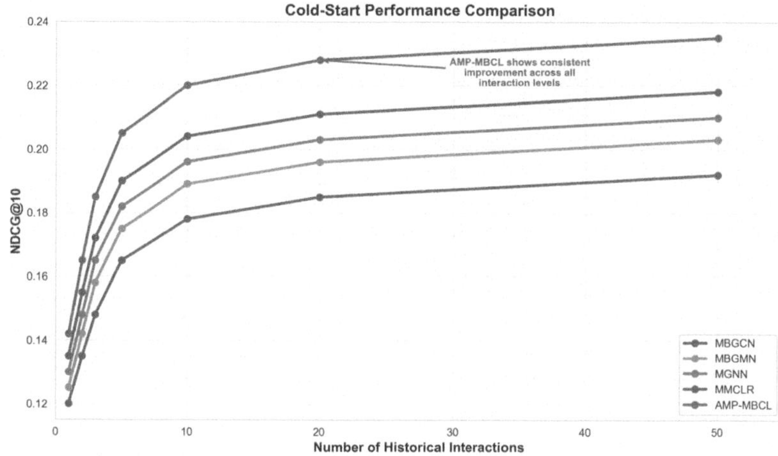

Fig. 2. Cold-start performance comparison. AMP-MBCL demonstrates superior performance for users with few historical interactions.

Table 3. Parameter Sensitivity Analysis

Parameter	Range	Best Value	Performance Drop
Dynamic Weighting λ	[0.05, 0.2]	0.1	$<2.1\%$
Cross-Platform Attention	[0.1, 0.5]	0.3	$<1.8\%$
Content Feature Dim	[64, 256]	128	$<3.2\%$
Learning Rate	[0.0005, 0.002]	0.001	$<2.5\%$
Batch Size	[128, 512]	256	$<1.9\%$

highlighting the effectiveness of cross-platform behavioral modeling and content-aware learning.

4.5 Cross-Platform Analysis

We evaluate the cross-platform coverage (CPC) metric to assess the diversity of recommendations across platforms. AMP-MBCL achieves a CPC score of 0.58, showing 11.54% improvement over the baseline without cross-platform modeling (0.52), indicating better utilization of cross-platform behavioral signals.

4.6 Parameter Sensitivity

We analyze the sensitivity of key hyperparameters including dynamic weighting decay rates, cross-platform attention weights, and content feature dimensions. The results show that AMP-MBCL is robust to parameter variations within reasonable ranges (Table 3 and Fig. 3).

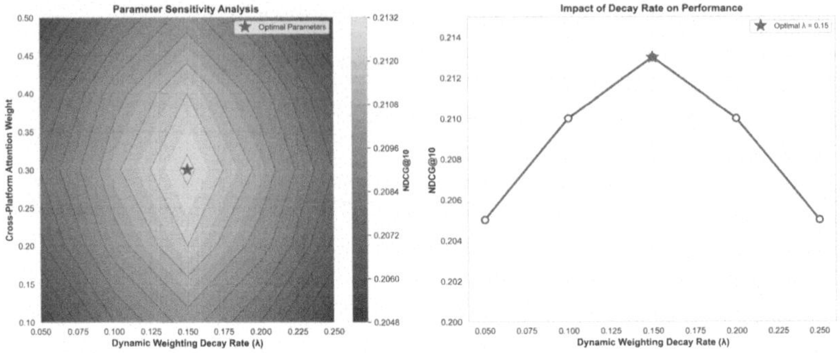

Fig. 3. Parameter sensitivity analysis for key hyperparameters.

5 Conclusion

In this paper, we proposed the Adaptive Multi-Platform Multi-Behavior Contrastive Learning (AMP-MBCL) framework to address three critical limitations in existing multi-behavior recommendation systems: static behavior prioritization, single-platform data constraints, and insufficient content awareness. Our framework introduces three key innovations: (1) dynamic behavior weighting, (2) cross-platform heterogeneous graph modeling, and (3) content-aware contrastive learning.

Extensive experiments demonstrate that AMP-MBCL achieves significant improvements over state-of-the-art baselines, with 2.81% and 2.69% gains in NDCG@10 on Tmall and CIKM2019 EComm AI datasets respectively. The framework particularly excels in cold-start scenarios, showing 7.85% improvement in cold-start user performance. Ablation studies confirm the effectiveness of each component.

Generative AI Statement

This paper does not use any generative AI tools. All content was created by the authors without AI assistance.

Acknowledgments. We thank the anonymous reviewers for their valuable feedback and suggestions.

References

1. Brody, S., Alon, U., Yahav, E.: How attentive are graph attention networks? arXiv preprint arXiv:2105.14491 (2021)
2. Chen, C., et al.: Graph heterogeneous multi-relational recommendation. In: Proceedings of the AAAI Conference on Artificial Intelligence. vol. 35, pp. 3958–3966 (2021)

3. Chen, C., Zhang, M., Zhang, Y., Ma, W., Liu, Y., Ma, S.: Efficient heterogeneous collaborative filtering without negative sampling for recommendation. In: Proceedings of the AAAI Conference on Artificial Intelligence. vol. 34, pp. 19–26 (2020)
4. He, X., Liao, L., Zhang, H., Nie, L., Hu, X., Chua, T.S.: Neural collaborative filtering. In: Proceedings of the 26th International Conference on World Wide Web, pp. 173–182 (2017)
5. Jin, B., Gao, C., He, X., Jin, D., Li, Y.: Multi-behavior recommendation with graph convolutional networks. In: Proceedings of the 43rd International ACM SIGIR Conference on Research and Development in Information Retrieval, pp. 659–668 (2020)
6. Kang, W.C., McAuley, J.: Self-attentive sequential recommendation. In: 2018 IEEE International Conference on Data Mining (ICDM), pp. 197–206. IEEE (2018)
7. Kipf, T.N., Welling, M.: Semi-supervised classification with graph convolutional networks. arXiv preprint arXiv:1609.02907 (2016)
8. Pan, F., Li, S., Ao, X., Tang, P., He, Q.: Warm up cold-start advertisements: improving CTR predictions via learning to learn id embeddings. In: Proceedings of the 42nd International ACM SIGIR Conference on Research and Development in Information Retrieval, pp. 695–704 (2019)
9. Pan, W., Xiang, E., Liu, N., Yang, Q.: Transfer learning in collaborative filtering for sparsity reduction. In: Proceedings of the AAAI Conference on Artificial Intelligence. vol. 24, pp. 230–235 (2010)
10. Rendle, S., Freudenthaler, C., Gantner, Z., Schmidt-Thieme, L.: BPR: Bayesian personalized ranking from implicit feedback. arXiv preprint arXiv:1205.2618 (2012)
11. Singh, A.P., Gordon, G.J.: Relational learning via collective matrix factorization. In: Proceedings of the 14th ACM SIGKDD International Conference on Knowledge Discovery and Data Mining, pp. 650–658 (2008)
12. Sun, F., et al.: BERT4Rec: sequential recommendation with bidirectional encoder representations from transformer. In: Proceedings of the 28th ACM International Conference on Information and Knowledge Management, pp. 1441–1450 (2019)
13. Veličković, P., Cucurull, G., Casanova, A., Romero, A., Lio, P., Bengio, Y.: Graph attention networks. arXiv preprint arXiv:1710.10903 (2017)
14. Wang, W., et al.: Beyond clicks: modeling multi-relational item graph for session-based target behavior prediction. In: Proceedings of the Web Conference 2020, pp. 3056–3062 (2020)
15. Wang, X., He, X., Wang, M., Feng, F., Chua, T.S.: Neural graph collaborative filtering. In: Proceedings of the 42nd international ACM SIGIR Conference on Research and Development in Information Retrieval, pp. 165–174 (2019)
16. Wu, Y., et al.: Multi-view multi-behavior contrastive learning in recommendation. In: International Conference on Database Systems for Advanced Applications, pp. 166–182. Springer (2022)
17. Xia, L., Xu, Y., Huang, C., Dai, P., Bo, L.: Graph meta network for multi-behavior recommendation. In: Proceedings of the 44th International ACM SIGIR Conference on Research and Development in Information Retrieval, pp. 757–766 (2021)
18. Xie, X., et al.: Contrastive learning for sequential recommendation. In: 2022 IEEE 38th International Conference on Data Engineering (ICDE), pp. 1259–1273. IEEE (2022)
19. Zhang, W., Mao, J., Cao, Y., Xu, C.: Multiplex graph neural networks for multi-behavior recommendation. In: Proceedings of the 29th ACM International Conference on Information & Knowledge Management, pp. 2313–2316 (2020)

20. Zhou, C., et al.: ATRank: an attention-based user behavior modeling framework for recommendation. In: Proceedings of the AAAI Conference on Artificial Intelligence. vol. 32 (2018)
21. Zhou, K., et al.: S3-Rec: self-supervised learning for sequential recommendation with mutual information maximization. In: Proceedings of the 29th ACM International Conference on Information & Knowledge Management, pp. 1893–1902 (2020)
22. Zhu, Y., et al.: Transfer-meta framework for cross-domain recommendation to cold-start users. In: Proceedings of the 44th International ACM SIGIR Conference on Research and Development in Information Retrieval, pp. 1813–1817 (2021)
23. Zhu, Y., et al.: Personalized transfer of user preferences for cross-domain recommendation. In: Proceedings of the Fifteenth ACM International Conference on Web Search and Data Mining, pp. 1507–1515 (2022)
24. Zhuang, F., et al.: A comprehensive survey on transfer learning. Proc. IEEE **109**(1), 43–76 (2020)

HyRO: Hybrid Retrieval-Augmented Generation Framework for LLMs Integrating Vector Encoding and Knowledge Graphs

Wenkai Wu, Shuo Sheng, Xun Gan, and Jixin Zhang(✉)

Hubei University of Technology, Wuhan, China
zhangjx@hbut.edu.cn

Abstract. Current retrieval-augmented generation methods still exhibit significant limitations in handling complex multi-hop reasoning tasks, mainly because they overly rely on flat vector retrieval over unstructured text and thus fail to explicitly model deep logical relationships between entities. To address this issue, we propose the HyRO framework, a hybrid retrieval-augmented generation framework that synergistically integrates vector encoding and knowledge graphs to achieve synergy between the reasoning capabilities of structured knowledge and the rich semantics of unstructured text. HyRO consists of two core methods: The Automated Hierarchical Knowledge Indexing Method (AHKI) for offline construction of a hierarchical knowledge structure and a vector index; and The Hybrid Collaborative Retrieval and Optimization Method (HCRO) for online query rewriting, hybrid retrieval, and reranking-based fusion to construct a more reliable answer context. Experimental results on a multi-step reasoning test set derived from SQuAD 2.0 show that HyRO consistently outperforms existing methods including RAG, HyDE, and GraphRAG across key metrics. On the Qwen-max model, HyRO achieves 0.83 context precision, 0.93 context recall, 0.76 answer relevance, and 0.93 faithfulness.

Keywords: Community Detection · Hybrid Retrieval · Knowledge Graph · Large Language Models · Multi-hop Reasoning · Retrieval-Augmented Generation · Vector Retrieval

1 Introduction

Large Language Models (LLMs) have achieved remarkable progress in the field of natural language processing, with recent models such as Qwen2.5 [1] and DeepSeek-V3 [2] demonstrating strong performance across diverse benchmarks, and DeepSeek-R1 [3] further advancing reasoning capabilities through reinforcement learning.yet they still suffer from inherent limitations such as delayed knowledge updates and inadequate factual accuracy. These drawbacks severely

W. Wu and S. Sheng–The authors are equal contribution.

R. C.-W. Wong et al. (Eds.): PAKDD 2026, LNAI 16617, pp. 271–282, 2027.
https://doi.org/10.1007/978-981-92-1926-1_22

restrict their reliability and practicality in knowledge-intensive tasks. Retrieval-Augmented Generation (RAG) technology [4] mitigates the aforementioned issues by integrating information from external knowledge bases, emerging as a core strategy to enhance the knowledge coverage and timeliness of models. However, existing RAG methods perform poorly when handling complex queries that require multi-step logical reasoning. The fundamental reason lies in their over-reliance on flat vector retrieval mechanisms for unstructured text, which makes it difficult to explicitly model and utilize the deep logical relationships between entities.

To address this challenge, the academic community has proposed two representative optimization approaches. The first category focuses on optimizing the query-document matching mechanism. For example, HyDE [5] reconstructs the query semantic space by generating hypothetical documents, effectively narrowing the semantic gap between queries and target documents. Nevertheless, such methods are still confined to the unstructured text processing framework and fail to fundamentally resolve the issue of insufficient complex reasoning capability. The second category shifts to structured knowledge representation, with GraphRAG [6] as a typical representative. This method constructs knowledge graphs and leverages their topological structures to implement relational reasoning. Although this approach exhibits advantages in mining implicit associations between entities, it inevitably loses rich semantic details from the original text during the graph construction process, resulting in limited performance in tasks that require fine-grained textual evidence for support. In summary, current RAG research is confronted with two core challenges:

1. How to integrate the reasoning capability of structured knowledge while preserving the rich semantics of unstructured text;
2. How to construct a framework that can dynamically balance graph-structured reasoning and textual semantic matching based on query characteristics.

To tackle the above challenges, this paper proposes the HyRO framework—a hybrid retrieval-augmented generation framework for large models that integrates vector encoding and knowledge graphs. By synergistically leveraging the reasoning advantages of structured knowledge and the semantic richness of unstructured text, this framework significantly improves the performance of the system in complex relational reasoning tasks. The main contributions of this paper can be summarized as follows:

1. **Framework**: We design an innovative retrieval-augmented generation framework for large models that fuses vector encoding and knowledge graphs. Through the dynamic construction of knowledge graphs and the synergistic integration of graph retrieval and vector retrieval, HyRO effectively overcomes the limitations of traditional RAG methods in multi-step reasoning tasks.
2. **Methods**: (1) The Automated Hierarchical Knowledge Indexing Method, which combines the semantic understanding capability of large language models with community detection and text summarization techniques, realizing

the automatic transformation from unstructured text to multi-level structured knowledge. (2) The Hybrid Collaborative Retrieval and Optimization Method, which proposes a collaborative optimization strategy including adaptive query rewriting, hybrid retrieval and result reranking, achieving the deep integration of structured knowledge and unstructured semantics to provide highly relevant and information-complete contextual support for language models.
3. **Experiments**: Extensive experiments conducted on the SQuAD 2.0 [7] benchmark dataset demonstrate that HyRO outperforms existing methods across all key metrics including context precision, recall, answer relevance and faithfulness, fully proving the superiority and practical value of the hybrid retrieval strategy in complex question-answering scenarios.

2 Related Work

2.1 RAG Based on Unstructured Text

RAG, proposed by Lewis et al. [4], enhances the generation capability of large language models through dynamic information retrieval from external knowledge bases. Traditional RAG directly uses user queries for vector similarity matching to retrieve relevant text fragments from unstructured document collections as the generation context. However, for queries with complex semantics or ambiguous expressions, this approach struggles to capture the user's intent, causing a deviation between retrieval results and actual requirements.

To optimize matching quality, subsequent research proposed various query reconstruction strategies. For example, HyDE [5] adopts a core generate-then-retrieve paradigm: it generates hypothetical documents based on the original query, then uses their semantic vectors to complete knowledge retrieval. This bridges the semantic gap between queries and target documents, significantly improving the relevance of retrieval results. Beyond query reconstruction, StructRAG [8] proposes an inference-time hybrid information structurization approach, dynamically converting retrieved documents into optimal structured formats (e.g., tables, graphs) to enhance knowledge-intensive reasoning. Nevertheless, base RAG and HyDE share a core limitation: both adopt a flattened processing approach for unstructured text, lacking explicit modeling capabilities for complex association relationships between entities, thus underperforming in complex tasks such as multi-hop reasoning.

2.2 RAG Based on Structured Knowledge

To overcome the limitations of unstructured methods in logical reasoning, researchers are integrating Knowledge Graphs (KG) into the RAG framework. GraphRAG [6] extracts entities and relations from text to create a knowledge graph, using its structure for information retrieval and relational reasoning.

Graph traversal and community detection techniques identify implicit associations and related clusters, enabling multi-step reasoning.

Recent advancements include LightRAG [9], which incorporates graph structures into text retrieval with a dual-level paradigm and supports incremental updates. SubgraphRAG [10] uses lightweight MLPs with a triple-scoring mechanism for efficient subgraph retrieval, improving accuracy and reducing hallucinations. HippoRAG 2 [11] employs a dual-node graph with Personalized PageRank and LLM-based filtering, enhancing multi-hop QA and associative memory tasks. A study [12] compares RAG and GraphRAG, showing complementary strengths in question answering and summarization.

However, structured knowledge-driven RAG faces challenges. Knowledge graph compression often loses contextual details and fine-grained semantics, and structured graphs struggle with precise text citation and fine-grained matching, impacting retrieval stability. Hybrid strategies are being explored, such as HybGRAG [13], which unifies retrieval-augmented generation, and GeAR [14], which combines graph structures with retrieval agents. These efforts highlight the need for integrating structured and unstructured retrieval to address complex queries, as neither approach alone can fully meet diverse needs.

3 Methodology

3.1 The Framework of HyRO

The HyRO framework integrates the semantic retrieval capabilities of vector databases with the structured reasoning advantages of knowledge graphs. HyRO achieves synergy between the reasoning capabilities of structured knowledge and the rich semantics of unstructured text. As shown in Fig. 1, the overall framework consists of two methods: The Automated Hierarchical Knowledge Indexing Method (AHKI) and The Hybrid Collaborative Retrieval and Optimization Method (HCRO). AHKI targets the offline indexing stage, aiming to mitigate semantic fragmentation and entity ambiguity in unstructured documents, and to build a hierarchical knowledge structure that supports multi-granular access. HCRO targets the online query stage, aiming to address unstable query expressions and the difficulty of unifying heterogeneous retrieval results, and produces more reliable answer contexts through hybrid retrieval and optimization-based reranking.

3.2 Automated Hierarchical Knowledge Indexing

This method aims to address key challenges in offline knowledge modeling. First, conventional fixed-window chunking often causes semantic fragmentation, splitting critical information across chunks and reducing recall accuracy. Second, knowledge graphs extracted directly from text frequently suffer from entity ambiguity and relation noise, leading to unstable structured reasoning. In addition, single-granularity indexing cannot simultaneously support fine-grained evidence localization and high-level semantic abstraction. To this end, The Automated

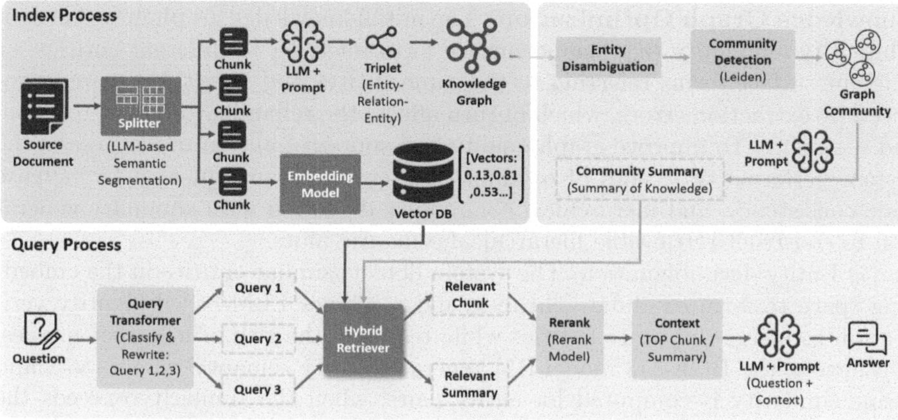

Fig. 1. Overall architecture of the HyRO framework

Hierarchical Knowledge Indexing Method constructs two types of indices for parallel access, and further builds hierarchical community summaries on the knowledge-graph side to support multi-granular retrieval and reasoning.

Knowledge Graph Construction. To alleviate semantic fragmentation, the system first performs semantic-aware document chunking, ensuring that each text chunk corresponds to a coherent semantic unit as much as possible, thereby reducing the probability that key information is broken across chunks. Specifically, an adaptive chunking algorithm based on semantic coherence is adopted: the BGE-large-en-v1.5 embedding model [15] is used to compute cosine similarity between adjacent sentences, and chunk boundaries are identified where the similarity drops by more than 90%. This strategy enhances intra-chunk semantic integrity while meeting the efficiency requirements of subsequent processing.

After obtaining the text chunks, the system uses large language models (LLMs) to extract knowledge triples and construct an initial knowledge graph, explicitly modeling entities and their relations to support subsequent structured retrieval and reasoning. Through structured prompt templates, knowledge triples are extracted from each text chunk, with relationship descriptions required to be temporally invariant to reduce noise introduced by tense variations and context drift. Formally, the knowledge extraction function is defined as:

$$K(c_j) = \{(h_k, r_k, t_k, \text{desc}(h_k), \text{desc}(t_k)) \mid k = 1, 2, \ldots, p\} \quad (1)$$

where c_j denotes a text chunk, h_k and t_k denote the head and tail entities, respectively, r_k denotes the relation type, $\text{desc}(\cdot)$ is the entity description function, and p is the number of triples. Aggregating all extracted triples yields the initial graph structure $G_0 = (V_0, E_0)$, where the node set V_0 is the set of unique entities and the edge set E_0 is the set of relation instances.

Knowledge Graph Optimization. The initial knowledge graph may still contain entity ambiguity (e.g., same surface form referring to different entities, or different surface forms referring to the same entity) and structural noise introduced by extraction errors, which in turn affects the reliability of graph retrieval and reasoning. To improve graph quality and support multi-granular access, the system performs two types of optimization: entity disambiguation to increase node consistency, and hierarchical community detection with summary generation to construct retrievable hierarchical semantic units.

(1) Entity disambiguation. The system detects similar entities in the embedding space to form candidate clusters, and combines LLM-based identity verification to merge duplicate entities while reducing the risk of incorrect merges. Specifically, the BGE-M3 model [15] generates entity semantic vectors $\mathbf{v}_{e_i}$, and cosine similarity is computed for entity pairs; when the similarity exceeds the threshold $\theta = 0.95$, temporary links are created to form a similar-entity graph $G_{\text{sim}} = (V_0, E_{\text{sim}})$. The Weakly Connected Components (WCC) algorithm is then applied to G_{sim} to obtain a set of potential duplicate entity clusters $\mathcal{C} = \{C_1, C_2, \dots, C_m\}$. For each cluster C_k, an LLM is used to determine whether the entities refer to the same real-world object, with the decision function defined as:

$$\text{Merge}(C_k) = \begin{cases} \text{True}, & \text{if } \exists \text{ real-world entity } e^* \text{ such that } \forall e_i \in C_k, e_i \text{ refers to } e^* \\ \text{False}, & \text{otherwise} \end{cases} \tag{2}$$

When $\text{Merge}(C_k) = \text{True}$, entities within the cluster are merged, the most complete description is retained, and associated relations are reconnected, yielding the disambiguated knowledge graph.

(2) Hierarchical community detection and summary generation. To support both fine-grained evidence localization and high-level semantic abstraction, the system constructs a hierarchical community structure on the graph and generates a summary representation for each community that can directly participate in retrieval. Considering the long-tail distribution of relation frequencies, the system first applies logarithmic transformation to edge weights to suppress the dominance of extremely frequent relations in community partitioning:

$$w(e) = \log(\text{count}(e) + 1) \tag{3}$$

where $w(e)$ is the weight of edge e, and $\text{count}(e)$ is the relation frequency. The Leiden algorithm [16] is then applied to the disambiguated knowledge graph to optimize community partitioning by maximizing the modularity function Q:

$$Q = \frac{1}{2m} \sum_{i,j} \left[A_{ij} - \frac{k_i k_j}{2m} \right] \delta(c_i, c_j) \tag{4}$$

where $m = \frac{1}{2} \sum_{i,j} A_{ij}$ is the total edge weight, A_{ij} is the adjacency matrix element, $k_i = \sum_j A_{ij}$ is the weighted degree of node i, and $\delta(c_i, c_j)$ is the community indicator function. The algorithm outputs a community hierarchy tree

$\mathcal{T} = \{C_0, C_1, \ldots, C_L\}$, where C_l denotes the community set at level l, and L is the maximum hierarchy depth. For each community $c \in C_l$, the system uses an LLM to generate a natural-language summary s_c, and enforces an information-density constraint to ensure that the summary can serve as a high-level semantic representation for retrieval and context construction:

$$\text{InfoDensity}(s_c) \geq \alpha \cdot \text{InfoDensity}\left(\bigcup_{e \in c} \text{desc}(e)\right) \tag{5}$$

where InfoDensity$(\cdot)$ is the information density metric function, $\alpha = 0.85$ is the threshold, and desc(e) is the entity description text. With this design, the system can dynamically select the appropriate community granularity according to query requirements, balancing retrieval efficiency, coverage, and semantic precision.

3.3 Hybrid Collaborative Retrieval and Optimization

This method aims to address key challenges in online retrieval and answering. User queries often involve under-specified expressions, ambiguity, and multi-hop reasoning requirements, and single-path retrieval may lead to biased results (e.g., retrieving only similar fragments without structured aggregation, or retrieving only structural summaries without original textual evidence). Meanwhile, candidate results from different knowledge sources are difficult to compare on a unified scale, leading to unstable context fusion. To this end, The Hybrid Collaborative Retrieval and Optimization Method combines query rewriting, dual-path parallel retrieval, and unified reranking to enable collaborative recall of structured and unstructured evidence and to optimize the final context.

Hybrid Collaborative Retrieval. The system first enhances query expression through an adaptive query rewriting mechanism, making retrieval closer to user intent and better suited to different reasoning needs. HyRO classifies input queries into four types and applies corresponding strategies to generate rewritten query sets: SIMPLE directly uses the original query; COMPLEX decomposes the problem to support multi-step retrieval; AMBIGUOUS generates multi-perspective rewrites to cover potential intents; CONCEPTUAL adopts the Step-Back strategy to retrieve higher-level conceptual information. Based on the rewritten queries, the system performs structured and unstructured retrieval in parallel. The graph retrieval module targets the hierarchical knowledge graph: it identifies key entity sets in queries via structured output chains, and generates fuzzy matching queries for each entity to accommodate spelling errors; these queries are executed on Neo4j full-text indexes [17], returning relevant community summary sets that provide high-level semantic evidence for aggregation and reasoning. The vector retrieval module preserves fine-grained semantic details of the original text: the BGE-M3 embedding model computes semantic similarity between queries and document chunks, and approximate nearest neighbor search is performed via the Milvus vector database [18], returning relevant text fragments:

$$f_v(q) = \underset{c \in \mathcal{C}}{\operatorname{TopK}} \left(\operatorname{sim}_{\text{BGE-M3}}(q, c), K = 5\right) \tag{6}$$

where q is the input query, $c \in \mathcal{C}$ denotes a document chunk in the chunk collection, $\operatorname{sim}_{\text{BGE-M3}}(\cdot, \cdot)$ is the semantic similarity function, and $K = 5$ indicates returning the top-5 document fragments most relevant to the query. The two retrieval results are merged to form the raw candidate set, covering both original textual evidence and structured summaries.

Retrieval Optimization. To address the difficulty of comparing heterogeneous candidates and the tendency of contexts to become redundant, the system applies a unified reranking module to perform fine-grained relevance modeling and fusion over the candidate set. Specifically, the system employs the BGE-reranker-large cross-encoder [19] to compute relevance scores between the query and candidate documents (either text chunks or community summaries):

$$s(q, d) = \operatorname{softmax}\left(\frac{f_{\text{cross}}(q, d)}{\sqrt{d_k}}\right) \tag{7}$$

where $f_{\text{cross}}(q, d)$ is the raw matching score produced by the cross-encoder for the query-document pair (q, d), $d_k = 64$ is the dimension of each attention head in the self-attention mechanism, and $\sqrt{d_k}$ scales dot-products to stabilize scoring; the softmax function normalizes scores into a probability distribution on a unified scale, enabling direct comparison and fusion of graph-based and vector-based candidates. The system then selects the top-5 candidates with the highest normalized scores to form the optimized context, improving precise recall of key information while reducing noise.

When a query is decomposed into multiple sub-queries (e.g., COMPLEX or AMBIGUOUS types), the system independently executes the complete hybrid retrieval and reranking procedure for each sub-query, producing corresponding optimized contexts and sub-answers. For single sub-query cases, the sub-answer is directly used as the final output; for multi-sub-query cases, the system guides the large language model with a specially designed aggregation prompt template to synthesize all sub-question–sub-answer pairs into a logically coherent and information-complete final answer. This mechanism allows the system to adapt to query complexity by adjusting retrieval granularity and evidence organization, improving reasoning consistency and factual reliability while maintaining semantic precision.

4 Experiments

4.1 Experimental Setup

Dataset. To comprehensively evaluate system performance on complex multi-step reasoning tasks, our paper adopt the SQuAD 2.0 dataset as the benchmark testing platform. This dataset contains numerous human-annotated Wikipedia articles and their corresponding question–answer pairs, featuring high semantic complexity and factual density. Ours paper selected 512 high-quality Wikipedia articles to construct the knowledge base, and from over 100,000 original question–answer pairs, we filtered 10,000 questions requiring multi-step reasoning as the test set through expert annotation. The filtering criteria were strictly defined as: (1) each question must involve at least two logical steps; (2) answering requires integrating information scattered across different paragraphs; and (3) the answer cannot be directly extracted from a single text fragment. This rigorous filtering process ensures that the evaluation focuses on the system's complex reasoning capabilities rather than simple retrieval performance.

Baselines. To comprehensively validate the effectiveness of HyRO, we compare it with three representative RAG methods: (1) RAG: a standard retrieval-augmented generation framework; (2) HyDE: a hypothetical document embedding method that reconstructs the query semantic space by generating hypothetical answers; and (3) GraphRAG: a knowledge graph-based retrieval framework that leverages graph structures for relational reasoning.

Evaluation Metrics. Evaluation employs four key metrics provided by the RAGAS framework [20]: (1) Context Precision(CP): measures the semantic relevance between retrieved content and the question; (2) Context Recall(CR): evaluates the completeness of retrieved results in covering information required for answering; (3) Answer Relevance(AR): quantifies the semantic matching degree between generated answers and questions; and (4) Faithfulness(F): measures whether answers strictly rely on retrieved content rather than the model's internal knowledge.

Implementations. Vector indexing was implemented using Milvus 2.2.11 [18], and the knowledge graph was stored in the Neo4j 5.24.0 graph database [17]. For embedding models, BGE-M3 was used for document encoding, and BGE-reranker-large was employed for result reranking. Regarding large language models, our paper selected Qwen-max and DeepSeek-V3 as base models. Key hyperparameter settings are as follows: maximum text chunk length of 512 tokens, top-k for retrieval results set to 5, top-p set to 0.9, temperature set to 0, and the similarity threshold for the Leiden community detection algorithm uniformly set to 0.95.

4.2 Performance Comparison

Our paper conducted a comprehensive evaluation of HyRO against representative baselines on the SQuAD 2.0 dataset using two large language models (Qwen-max and DeepSeek-V3). As shown in Table 1, HyRO achieves consistently strong overall performance across both backbones. On Qwen-max, HyRO obtains the highest CP (0.83) and AR (0.76) while maintaining competitive CR (0.93), indicating that it can provide more accurate and relevant context without sacrificing coverage. On DeepSeek-V3, HyRO achieves the best results on all metrics (CP = 0.80, CR = 0.92, AR = 0.67, F = 0.92), demonstrating that the hybrid retrieval design generalizes well across different LLMs and remains effective under more challenging settings.

Table 1. Performance comparison on the SQuAD 2.0 dataset

LLM	Method	CP	CR	AR	F
Qwen-max	RAG	0.81	**0.93**	0.66	0.87
	HyDE	0.74	0.88	0.72	0.90
	GraphRAG	0.51	0.92	0.72	0.95
	HyRO (ours)	**0.83**	**0.93**	**0.76**	**0.93**
DeepSeek-V3	RAG	0.58	0.59	0.61	0.80
	HyDE	0.75	0.90	0.65	0.89
	GraphRAG	0.61	0.72	0.62	0.91
	HyRO (ours)	**0.80**	**0.92**	**0.67**	**0.92**

4.3 Ablation Study

To quantify the contribution of each component in HyRO, our paper performed incremental ablation experiments on SQuAD 2.0 with Qwen-max by progressively adding The Automated Hierarchical Knowledge Indexing Method (AHKI), Hybrid Collaborative Retrieval (HCR), and Retrieval Optimization (RO) on top of the RAG baseline. Table 2 shows that introducing AHKI substantially improves AR (0.66→0.73), suggesting that structured knowledge benefits answer relevance, but it also leads to sharp drops in CP and CR (to 0.11 and 0.39), indicating that relying on graph summaries alone is insufficient for high-quality retrieval. Adding HCR greatly improves coverage and reliability (CR = 0.96, F = 0.92). On top of that, RO further refines the retrieved context by removing noise and reranking candidates, yielding the best overall trade-off: CP increases to 0.83 while CR remains at 0.93, together with the highest AR (0.76) and F (0.93).

4.4 Parameter Analysis

To examine the robustness of HyRO with respect to key hyperparameters, our paper conducted sensitivity experiments on SQuAD 2.0 using Qwen-max. In each group, only one parameter was varied while the other settings were fixed to the default configuration used in the main experiments (top-$k = 5$, similarity threshold $\theta = 0.95$, and $B = 90$, where B denotes the chunking Breakpoint).

Table 2. Ablation study of different components

Method	CP	CR	AR	F
RAG	0.81	0.93	0.66	0.87
RAG(+AHKI)	0.11	0.39	**0.73**	0.82
RAG(+AHKI+HCR)	0.32	**0.96**	**0.74**	**0.92**
RAG(+AHKI+HCR+RO) (Full framework)	**0.83**	**0.93**	**0.76**	**0.93**

Table 3. Hyperparameter sensitivity on SQuAD 2.0 with Qwen-max. The default settings used in the main experiments are top-$k = 5$, $\theta = 0.95$, and $B = 90$ (where B denotes the chunking Breakpoint).

(a) top-k

k	CP	CR	AR	F
3	0.79	0.88	0.73	0.91
5	**0.83**	**0.93**	**0.76**	**0.93**
7	0.80	0.94	0.75	0.92
10	0.76	0.95	0.73	0.90

(b) θ

θ	CP	CR	AR	F
0.85	0.78	0.90	0.72	0.90
0.90	0.81	0.92	0.74	0.92
0.95	**0.83**	**0.93**	**0.76**	**0.93**
0.99	0.80	0.91	0.74	0.92

(c) B

B	CP	CR	AR	F
70	0.75	0.89	0.70	0.88
80	0.80	0.91	0.73	0.91
90	**0.83**	**0.93**	**0.76**	**0.93**
95	0.81	0.92	0.74	0.93

Table 3 reports the results in terms of Context Precision (CP), Context Recall (CR), Answer Relevance (AR), and Faithfulness (F), showing that the default setting achieves the best or near-best overall trade-off: top-$k = 5$ yields the highest CP and AR with strong CR and F, $\theta = 0.95$ provides the most balanced thresholding effect, and the chunking parameter B performs best at $B = 90$ compared to smaller values that reduce contextual completeness and larger values that introduce redundancy. Therefore, our paper adopt top-$k = 5$, $\theta = 0.95$, and $B = 90$ as the default configuration in the full experiments.

5 Conclusion

This paper presents HyRO, a large language model retrieval-augmented generation framework that integrates vector retrieval and knowledge graphs, designed to address the limitations of traditional RAG methods when handling complex multi-hop reasoning tasks. Through the Automated Hierarchical Knowledge Indexing Method and the Hybrid Collaborative Retrieval and Optimization Method, HyRO achieves synergy between the reasoning capabilities of structured knowledge and the rich semantics of unstructured text. Experimental results on the SQuAD 2.0 dataset demonstrate that HyRO outperforms baseline methods including RAG, HyDE, and GraphRAG across key metrics such as context precision, answer relevance, and faithfulness. Ablation studies further validate the effectiveness of each framework component, demonstrating HyRO's ability to balance retrieval comprehensiveness, result precision, and system scalability.

Acknowledgement. This work is partially supported by the National Natural Science Foundation of China under Grant (No. 62441233, 62002106, 62472166, U22A2030), and Technology Projects of Hunan Province (No. 2015TP1004)

References

1. Yang, A., Yang, B., Zhang, B., et al.: Qwen2.5 technical report. arXiv preprint arXiv:2412.15115 (2024)
2. DeepSeek-AI.: Deepseek-V3 technical report. arXiv preprint arXiv:2412.19437 (2024)
3. DeepSeek-AI.: Deepseek-R1: Incentivizing reasoning capability in LLMs via reinforcement learning. Nat. **645**, 633–638 (2025)
4. Lewis, P., Perez, E., Piktus, A., et al.: Retrieval-augmented generation for knowledge-intensive NLP tasks. In: NeurIPS. vol. 33, pp. 9459–9474 (2020)
5. Gao, L., Ma, X., Lin, J., Callan, J.: Precise zero-shot dense retrieval without relevance labels. In: ACL, pp. 1762–1777 (2023)
6. Edge, D., Trinh, H., Cheng, N., et al.: From local to global: A graph rag approach to query-focused summarization. arXiv preprint arXiv:2404.16130 (2024)
7. Rajpurkar, P., Jia, R., Liang, P.: Know what you don't know: Unanswerable questions for SQuAD. In: ACL, pp. 784–789 (2018)
8. Li, Z., Chen, X., Yu, H., et al.: StructRAG: Boosting knowledge intensive reasoning of LLMs via inference-time hybrid information structurization. In: ICLR (2025)
9. Guo, Z., Xia, L., Yu, Y., Ao, T., Huang, C.: LightRAG: Simple and fast retrieval-augmented generation. In: Findings of EMNLP. pp. 10746–10761 (2025)
10. Li, M., Miao, S., Li, P.: Simple is effective: the roles of graphs and large language models in knowledge-graph-based retrieval-augmented generation. In: ICLR (2025)
11. Gutiérrez, B.J., Shu, Y., Qi, W., et al.: From rag to memory: Non-parametric continual learning for large language models. In: ICML pp. 21497–21515 (2025)
12. Han, H., Ma, L., Wang, Y., et al.: RAG vs. GraphRAG: A systematic evaluation and key insights. arXiv preprint arXiv:2502.11371 (2025)
13. Lee, M.C., Zhu, Q., Mavromatis, C., et al.: HybGRAG: Hybrid retrieval-augmented generation on textual and relational knowledge bases. In: ACL. pp. 879–893 (2025)
14. Shen, Z., Diao, C., Vougiouklis, P., et al.: GeAR: graph-enhanced agent for retrieval-augmented generation. In: Findings of ACL. pp. 12049–12072 (2025)
15. Xiao, S., Liu, Z., Zhang, P., et al.: C-Pack: Packed resources for general Chinese embeddings. In: SIGIR. pp. 641–649 (2023)
16. Traag, V.A., Waltman, L., van Eck, N.J.: From Louvain to Leiden: Guaranteeing well-connected communities. Sci. Rep. **9**(1), 5233 (2019)
17. Needham, M., Hodler, A.E.: Graph Algorithms: Practical Examples in Apache Spark and Neo4j. O'Reilly (2019)
18. Wang, J., Yi, X., Guo, R., et al.: Milvus: A purpose-built vector data management system. In: SIGMOD, pp. 2614–2627 (2021)
19. Li, M., Zhuang, H., Hui, K., et al.: Can query expansion improve generalization of strong cross-encoder rankers? In: SIGIR, pp. 2321–2326 (2024)
20. Es, S., James, J., Anke, L.E., Schockaert, S.: RAGAs: Automated evaluation of retrieval augmented generation. In: EACL (System Demonstrations). pp. 150–158 (2024)

RocketFormer: Robust Cryptocurrency Trend Classification Under Extreme Market Conditions

Guanqiu Zhao[1,2], Tiantian Duan[3](✉), Hanwen Zhang[3,4], and Yi Sun[3,4,5]

[1] School of Artificial Intelligence, Beihang University, Beijing, China
SY2442113@buaa.edu.cn

[2] Beijing Advanced Innovation Center for Future Blockchain and Privacy Computing, Beijing, China

[3] Institute of Computing Technology, Chinese Academy of Sciences, Beijing, China
{duantiantian,hwzhang,sunyi}@ict.ac.cn

[4] University of Chinese Academy of Sciences, Beijing, China

[5] Shandong Key Laboratory of Blockchain Finance, Jinan, China

Abstract. Although cryptocurrency trend classification is more reliable than direct price prediction, it still faces notable challenges under extreme market conditions. These markets typically display high volatility, strong noise, and sudden structural changes, which often cause existing models to overfit or generalize poorly. To address these challenges, we propose RocketFormer, a robust framework for cryptocurrency trend classification. RocketFormer integrates large-scale random convolutional kernels with a Transformer encoder to learn more stable local features and capture global dependencies, enabling the model to better handle noise disturbances and structural changes in extreme markets. It further introduces a volatility-aware two-stage mechanism to enhance the stability of both training and inference. Experiments on minute-level real data from four major cryptocurrencies show that RocketFormer achieves the best overall performance among eleven state-of-the-art classifiers, outperforming the strongest baseline by 2.6%, 2.8%, and 2.8% in accuracy, recall, and F1-score.

Keywords: Cryptocurrency time series · Rocket · Transformer · Classification-based prediction

1 Introduction

In recent years, the cryptocurrency market has expanded rapidly worldwide. However, due to its decentralized structure, limited liquidity, and strong susceptibility to public events, cryptocurrency prices often exhibit high volatility and strong noise [1]. These issues become even more pronounced under extreme market conditions, where prices frequently show abrupt jumps along with sharp

R. C.-W. Wong et al. (Eds.): PAKDD 2026, LNAI 16617, pp. 283–295, 2027.
https://doi.org/10.1007/978-981-92-1926-1_23

fluctuations [21]. In this context, trend classification, which predicts the market direction of the next trading interval based on historical price sequences [3], offers greater robustness than direct numerical price prediction and has therefore become a key research focus [22].

Nevertheless, the sharp price volatility in extreme markets makes trend classification particularly challenging [20]. First, sharp price swings amplify short-term noise, making it difficult for models to extract stable local features and causing transient anomalies to be misinterpreted as genuine trends. Second, sharp price volatility is often accompanied by abrupt structural changes in the market, which disrupt overall temporal patterns and make it difficult for models to capture trend transitions across time [10]. Finally, noise can make parameter updates unstable during training, leading to overfitting or overly confident responses to noisy signals, and ultimately reducing predictive reliability [2]. As a result, existing methods often experience significant performance degradation under extreme market conditions.

To address the above issues, we propose **RocketFormer**, a cryptocurrency trend classification framework designed for extreme market conditions. RocketFormer integrates large-scale random convolutional kernels with a Transformer encoder: the former extracts relatively stable local features and mitigates the influence of short-term noise, while the latter models long-range dependencies through self-attention and helps capture cross-temporal patterns under structural market changes. In addition, we design a volatility-aware two-stage adaptive mechanism that dynamically adjusts training strategies and prediction temperature based on real-time market volatility, improving the model's stability in extreme markets during both training and inference.

Our main contributions can be summarised as follows:

- We propose RocketFormer, the first model to combine Rocket and Transformer architectures for cryptocurrency forecasting, which effectively captures multi-dimensional and multi-scale structures in extreme market conditions.
- We introduce a volatility-aware two-stage adaptive mechanism that dynamically adjusts learning behavior based on real-time market conditions, improving model stability and robustness under high volatility.
- We extract minute-level extreme-volatility datasets for four major cryptocurrencies from the market turmoil triggered by the Ethereum theft on February 21, 2025, and conduct systematic experiments on this data. The results show that RocketFormer achieves the best overall performance among eleven state-of-the-art trend classification models.

2 Related Work

2.1 Cryptocurrency Time Series Classifiers

Traditional machine learning methods, such as Gradient Boosting (GB) [6] and Random Sampling Method (RSM) [17], typically rely on handcrafted features or distance-based heuristics. Although computationally efficient, these approaches exhibit limited adaptability to rapidly changing market regimes and often struggle to maintain high classification accuracy under highly volatile conditions. With the development of deep learning, CNN [12] has been widely applied to time-series tasks. CNNs excel at extracting local temporal patterns, yet they are less effective in modeling long-term dependencies. To further enhance sequential modeling, Adaptive LSTM (ALSTM) [18] dynamically adjusts its gating mechanisms, while CNN-BiLSTM architectures [15] integrate local convolution with bidirectional memory structures. However, these methods still rely on learnable convolutional filters or recurrent memory units, making them vulnerable to noise interference and overly sensitive to transient anomalies in extreme market environments.

2.2 Transformer-Based Time Series Models

Recently, the Transformer architecture, has proven effective in time series classification tasks. Specifically, Liu et al. [13] proposed a Transformer-based stock market prediction model, demonstrating its superiority over traditional models. TST [23] as a framework for MTS representation learning. It gains great performance for many classification tasks. ConvTran [7] is a transformer-based method for MTSC that proposed to improve the position embedding in the Transformer model by leveraging both absolute and relative position encoding. These research outcomes indicate that, relying on its intrinsic self-attention mechanism, the Transformer model is well-suited for the construction and training of various time-series forecasting models.

Although the self-attention mechanism in the Transformer can model long-range dependencies, it is highly sensitive to the quality of input features. Therefore, before global modeling, it is essential to extract more stable and noise-resistant local features.

2.3 Rocket Discovery for Time Series

Rocket (Random Convolutional Kernel Transform) is a time series classification method based on random convolutional kernels [4]. The fundamental idea of Rocket is to transform time series data into feature representations through a large number of randomly generated convolutional kernels. These features are then used to train a classifier [8]. Unlike conventional convolutional approaches, Rocket does not learn the kernel parameters. Instead, it generates diverse feature maps by randomly specifying the kernel length, weights, dilation rate, and padding scheme [16].

In the field of time series classification, ample evidence has shown that randomly initialized convolutional kernels can achieve performance comparable to that of learned convolutional kernels [19]. Particularly when modeling complex temporal patterns, the diversity of convolutional kernels tends to be more significant than the precise optimality of kernel weights [9]. MiniRocket [5] demonstrated that leveraging a large number of random convolutional kernels combined with simple statistical feature extraction in time series classification tasks.

Prior studies have shown that, under conditions where learning stable convolutional kernels is challenging, random kernels may exhibit stronger generalization capability and robustness. Therefore, this study adopts Rocket as the foundational feature extraction module, leveraging its noise resistance, kernel diversity, and stability under extreme market conditions to provide more reliable input representations for the Transformer.

3 RocketFormer Model

We propose RocketFormer, a novel architecture for cryptocurrency movement classification. As shown in Fig. 1, RocketFormer combines three complementary components: Random convolutional feature extraction, Transformer-based Classification, volatility-aware dual-phase adaptation.

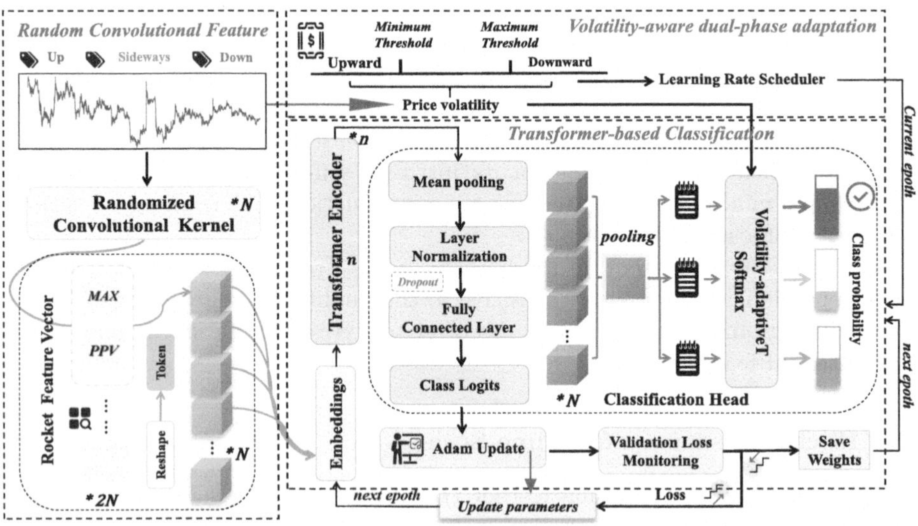

Fig. 1. The architecture of RocketFormer model.

3.1 Random Convolutional Feature Extraction

Random-Kernel-Based Feature Generation. RocketFormer begins by transforming raw cryptocurrency time series into informative feature representations through a random convolutional feature extraction module based on Rocket. Given an input sequence $\mathbf{X}_{\text{raw}} \in R^{B \times T \times F}$where B denotes the batch size, T the window length, and F the number of numerical characteristics.

The model first applies sliding-window segmentation. Each window is assigned a categorical label $y \in \{0, 1, 2\}$ according to the relative price change over the interval:

$$y = \begin{cases} 2, & \text{if } \frac{p_{T-1} - p_0}{p_0} > \theta \quad \text{(Upward)} \\ 1, & \text{otherwise} \quad \text{(Sideways)} \\ 0, & \text{if } \frac{p_{T-1} - p_0}{p_0} < -\theta \quad \text{(Downward)} \end{cases} \tag{1}$$

where p_0 and p_{T-1} are the first and last prices in the window, and θ is a volatility threshold.

Statistical Feature Metrics. From each convolutional output, we extract two statistics: the maximum value (Max) and the proportion of positive values (PPV) [4].

Max captures abrupt price shocks, enhancing sensitivity to rapid volatility and structural changes. Yet, it may react to transient noise. PPV complements it by measuring directional persistence, filtering randomness and highlighting true short-term trends.Together, they improve forecasting robustness in noisy, fast-changing markets.

Features from multiple kernels are concatenated into a high-dimensional representation **X**flat $\in R^{B\times(T\cdot F)}$, reshaped into a token sequence **X**token $\in R^{B\times L\times d}$, and passed into the Transformer encoder.

3.2 Transformer-Based Classification

Transformer Encoder. As our task is classification rather than sequence generation, the decoder(designed for autoregressive generation)becomes superfluous and is omitted. An encoder-only architecture reduces model complexity and computational cost while enabling the model to directly map the input series onto a set of discriminative features [11].

After completing Rocket feature extraction and constructing the token sequence, RocketFormer employs a stacked Transformer encoder to model the sequence, capturing both global dependencies among local statistical features and structural interactions. The input sequence is mapped into the embedding space through a linear projection layer with non-linear activation and dropout, resulting in the embedded sequence H:

$$\mathbf{H} = [\mathbf{H}_1, \mathbf{H}_2, \ldots, \mathbf{H}_L] \in R^{B\times L\times d} \tag{2}$$

which is then passed into the Transformer encoder.

Classification Head. After global average pooling across the temporal dimension, the encoder output is $\mathbf{H}_{\text{pool}} \in R^{B\times d}$, where B is the batch size and d is the embedding dimension. For the b-th sample, we denote its pooled vector as $\mathbf{H}_{\text{CLS}}^{(b)} \in R^d$, which serves as the input to the classification head. The classification head then maps $\mathbf{H}_{\text{CLS}}^{(b)}$ into class logits while enhancing stability and generalization under highly volatile market conditions. It consists of three components: Layer Normalization, Dropout regularization, and Linear Projection.

Layer Normalization standardizes feature scales across dimensions to mitigate distributional shifts caused by market turbulence. The mean μ and variance σ^2 across the d dimensions are defined as:

$$\mu = \frac{1}{d}\sum_{k=1}^{d}(\mathbf{H}_{\text{CLS}})_k \quad \sigma^2 = \frac{1}{d}\sum_{k=1}^{d}\left((\mathbf{H}_{\text{CLS}})_k - \mu\right)^2 \tag{3}$$

and the normalized vector is

$$\mathbf{H}' = \text{LayerNorm}(\mathbf{H}_{\text{CLS}}) = \boldsymbol{\gamma} \odot \frac{\mathbf{H}_{\text{CLS}} - \mu}{\sqrt{\sigma^2 + \varepsilon}} + \boldsymbol{\beta} \tag{4}$$

which $\mathbf{H}', \boldsymbol{\gamma}, \boldsymbol{\beta} \in R^d$ are learnable scaling and shifting parameters, $\varepsilon > 0$ is a numerical stability constant, and $\odot$ denotes element-wise multiplication. This step dampens sudden scale spikes and improves gradient conditioning, thereby stabilizing training under high-volatility regimes.

To alleviate overfitting caused by volatility-amplified noise, Dropout is applied to $\mathbf{H}'$. Finally, the stabilized embedding is mapped into the class space through a linear transformation:

$$\mathbf{Z} = W\mathbf{H}' + \mathbf{b} \quad W \in R^{C \times d}, \quad \mathbf{b} \in R^C, \quad \mathbf{Z} \in R^C \tag{5}$$

which C denotes the number of classes, and $\mathbf{Z}$ represents the unnormalized class logits. The conversion from logits to probabilities is deferred to Sect. 4.3, where a volatility-aware temperature mechanism is introduced for Softmax, enabling adaptive probability calibration under regime shifts.

3.3 Volatility-Aware Dual-Phase Adaptation

By dynamically adjusting the learning rate and decision temperature based on real-time volatility, the architecture remains stable and reliable under extreme market conditions.

Given the price sequence $\{p_t\}$, the log return is defined as:

$$r_t = \log\frac{p_t}{p_{t-1}}. \tag{6}$$

Within a sliding window of length W, volatility is estimated by:

$$\bar{r}_t = \frac{1}{W}\sum_{i=0}^{W-1} r_{t-i} \quad v_t = \sqrt{\frac{1}{W}\sum_{i=0}^{W-1}(r_{t-i} - \bar{r}_t)^2} \tag{7}$$

To mitigate short-term noise, an exponential moving average is applied:

$$\tilde{v}_t = (1 - \lambda)\tilde{v}_{t-1} + \lambda v_t, \qquad \lambda \in (0, 1]. \tag{8}$$

Finally, the smoothed volatility is normalized into the interval [0, 1]:

$$\hat{v}_t = \text{clip}\left(\frac{\tilde{v}_t - \theta_{\min}}{\theta_{\max} - \theta_{\min}}, 0, 1\right) \tag{9}$$

where $\theta_{\min}$ and $\theta_{\max}$ are the minimum and maximum thresholds. The normalized volatility $\hat{v}_t$ serves as a unified quantitative indicator of market states.

Volatility-Based Learning Rate Adjustment. During training, the learning rate η_t is adaptively adjusted according to $\hat{v}_t$:

$$\eta_t = \begin{cases} \eta_0(1+\delta), & \hat{v}_t < \epsilon_1, \\ \eta_0, & \epsilon_1 \leq \hat{v}_t \leq \epsilon_2, \\ \frac{\eta_0}{1+\beta \cdot \hat{v}_t}, & \hat{v}_t > \epsilon_2, \end{cases} \tag{10}$$

where η_0 is the base learning rate, δ controls the enhancement in the low-volatility regime, β controls the decay in the high-volatility regime, and ϵ_1, ϵ_2 are the segmentation thresholds of the normalized volatility. In this way, the learning rate increases in calm markets to accelerate convergence, remains stable in moderate markets, and decreases significantly in turbulent markets to avoid over-updating and divergence. This mechanism helps alleviate overfitting and unstable parameter updates under conditions of severe volatility.

Volatility-Based Softmax Temperature Scaling. During inference, the classification head employs a Softmax function with a volatility-adjusted temperature:

$$P(y = c \mid \mathbf{Z}) = \frac{\exp(Z_c/\tau_t)}{\sum_{j=1}^{C} \exp(Z_j/\tau_t)} \tag{11}$$

The temperature parameter τ_t is directly linked to the normalized volatility $\hat{v}_t$:

$$\tau_t = \tau_{\min} + (\tau_{\max} - \tau_{\min})\,\hat{v}_t \tag{12}$$

When $\hat{v}_t$ is close to 0 (low-volatility regime), $\tau_t \approx \tau_{\min} < 1$, producing sharper probability distributions that enhance discriminability. When $\hat{v}_t$ is close to 1 (high-volatility regime), $\tau_t \approx \tau_{\max} > 1$, yielding smoother probability distributions that improve robustness.

For cryptocurrency classification tasks, this adaptive temperature scaling helps obtain better-calibrated probability estimates, preventing overconfident predictions in highly volatile markets and thereby enhancing the interpretability and reliability of decision-making.

4 Experiment

4.1 Dataset

We selected a cryptocurrency dataset covering the period from **February 1, 2025 to March 10, 2025**, obtained from the Binance exchange. During this period, the Bybit exchange suffered a large-scale cyberattack in which approximately 1.5 billion USD worth of ETH was stolen. As shown in Fig. 2, BTC and ETH prices dropped by approximately 14.1% and 15.4%, respectively, with significant spillover effects across the broader market.

The dataset includes four representative cryptocurrencies: BTC, ETH, DOT, BNB. For each cryptocurrency, We use the average price per minute as the minute-level data, yielding a total of **57,600** financial observations at the **minute level**. The dataset was divided chronologically into 80% for training, 10% for validation, and 10% for testing.

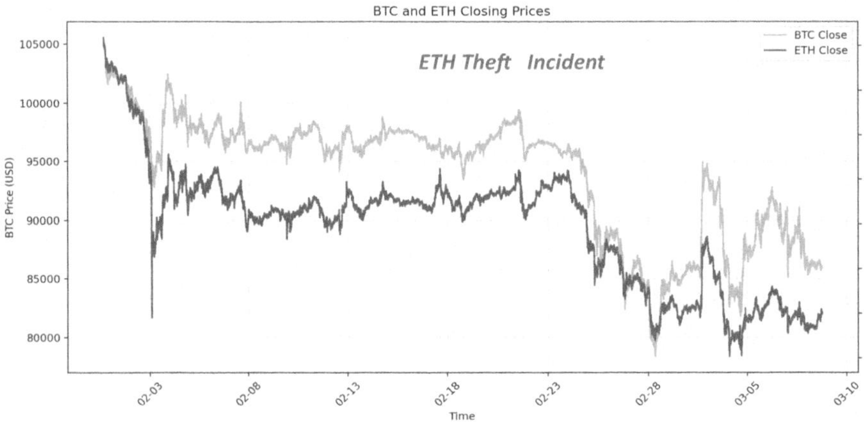

Fig. 2. BTC and ETH minute-level closing price from February 1, 2025 to March 10, 2025.

4.2 Experimental Setting

Implementation Details. Window length: 50, stride: 5, number of random convolutions: 10,000; $d_{\text{model}} = 256$, $N_{\text{heads}} = 4$, $N_{\text{layers}} = 4$, $\theta = 0.05$, dropout $= 0.2$; Adam optimizer with learning rate $\eta_0 = 1 \times 10^{-3}$ and weight decay 1×10^{-4}; batch size 128, up to 100 epochs with early stopping.

Environment. The experiments are conducted on a workstation equipped with an NVIDIA GeForce RTX 4090 (24 GB VRAM), an Intel Core i9–13900K (13th Gen) CPU, and 128 GB of system memory.

Baselines. We selected four cryptocurrency classification-based prediction baseline models to compare with RocketFormer: GB [6], RSM [17], ALSTM [18], CNN-BiLSTM [15]. And six baseline models: MALSTM-FCN [14], InceptionTime [9], Transformer [13], TST [23], ConvTran [7] and MiniRocket [5].

4.3 Performance Evaluation

We employ precision(Pre), recall, and F1-score(F1) as the primary evaluation metrics. We report the weighted average of these metrics. As shown in Table 1, RocketFormer demonstrates robust and superior performance across the minute-level classification tasks of four cryptocurrencies (BTC, ETH, DOT, BNB). Overall, the weighted average Precision reaches 84.1%, Recall reaches 84.1% and F1-score reaches 83.9%, representing an improvement of 2.6%, 2.8% and 2.8% over the best-performing baseline model respectively.

On the BTC dataset, RocketFormer achieves outstanding performance, with Precision, Recall, and F1-score reaching 84.7%, 85.0%, and 84.4%, respectively. These results significantly surpass the strongest baseline model ConvTran (82.2%, 83.3%, 82.5%), demonstrating RocketFormer's superior capability in modeling the most liquid and globally influential cryptocurrency market. On the ETH dataset, RocketFormer also delivers leading results, achieving Precision, Recall, and F1-score values of 84.0%, 82.4%, and 83.0%, respectively. Compared with other baseline models, RocketFormer attains a slightly higher overall balance between accuracy and consistency across all metrics.

On the BNB dataset, RocketFormer also demonstrates exceptional performance, achieving Precision, Recall, and F1-score values of 86.3%, 86.0%, and 86.2%, respectively. These results substantially outperform the best baseline model TST (79.9%, 80.5%, 80.1%). On the DOT dataset, RocketFormer also exhibits superior and stable performance. Specifically, the Precision, Recall, and F1-score of RocketFormer reach 81.4%, 82.3%, and 81.7%, respectively, ranking the highest among all comparison models.

These results not only show that RocketFormer maintains an advantage in individual markets but also confirm its strong adaptability and robustness across different assets. In particular, under highly volatile and minute-level cryptocurrency classification tasks, RocketFormer demonstrates consistent and reliable superiority over competitive baselines.

4.4 Parameter Sensitivity Study

We further investigate the sensitivity of RocketFormer to the number of random convolutional kernels by varying this parameter from 10 to 10,000. As shown in Fig. 3, the overall classification accuracy steadily improves as the kernel number increases, with the most significant gains observed in the volatile sideway class.

When the kernel number is small (10 or 100), the model exhibits highly unstable behavior. For instance, the sideways F1-score is as low as 0.0000 for BTC and 0.0667 for DOT, indicating severe difficulty in capturing uncertain market fluctuations. As the kernel number grows, this issue is gradually alleviated; with

Table 1. Performance comparison of RocketFormer and baseline models on four cryptocurrencies. The best results(%) are highlighted in bold.

Model	BTC			ETH			DOT			BNB		
	Pre	Recall	F1	Pre	Recall	F1	Pre	Recall	F1	Pre	Recall	F1
GB	66.31	60.13	59.32	63.26	59.22	59.85	66.34	63.07	62.18	69.58	59.05	57.03
RSM	65.32	65.09	64.95	72.15	72.00	72.01	73.42	73.00	73.12	78.35	78.64	78.43
ALSTM	56.26	57.23	55.18	69.67	68.93	68.86	72.29	70.69	70.15	52.68	52.18	51.79
CNN-BiLSTM	79.34	79.01	82.24	77.21	78.20	73.07	73.08	71.01	73.05	74.79	73.02	72.81
MALSTM-FCN	79.73	71.02	74.68	77.35	78.06	76.58	72.83	75.04	73.05	68.07	67.17	67.38
Inception-Time	80.46	80.51	78.39	80.85	81.15	80.34	76.10	78.18	75.96	75.06	75.04	74.79
Transformer	61.29	63.37	59.28	63.93	59.35	62.47	53.98	60.53	57.13	60.47	59.10	62.08
ConvTran	82.28	83.34	82.59	83.02	83.25	82.96	76.00	76.13	76.04	83.12	82.25	82.62
TST	76.45	82.19	77.73	82.81	**85.04**	80.42	79.22	80.12	78.53	79.98	80.52	80.12
MiniROCKET	79.26	80.03	79.30	81.05	79.06	79.98	76.48	78.05	76.19	77.85	78.06	77.95
RocketFormer	**84.72**	**85.01**	**84.42**	**84.05**	82.99	**83.29**	**81.39**	**82.33**	**81.69**	**86.30**	**86.27**	**86.27**

10,000 kernels, the sideway F1-score improves to 0.7111 for BTC and 0.6731 for DOT, substantially enhancing the model's ability to recognize oscillating market states.

However, an excessive number of random convolutional kernels can significantly increase the computational complexity of the model. Therefore, to achieve optimal results, this study uniformly adopts 10,000 random convolutional kernels. Under constrained computational resources or scenarios requiring higher efficiency, we also recommend using 5,000 random convolutional kernels as a balanced choice between performance and computational cost.

4.5 Ablation Study

To better understand the contributions of different components, we conduct an ablation study, and the results are reported in Table 2. In the ablation study, "w/o VDA" denotes removing the volatility-aware dual-phase adaptation from RocketFormer. When using Transformer as the baseline, the average F1-scores across the four cryptocurrencies remain relatively low (BTC 59.3%, ETH 62.5%, DOT 57.1%, BNB 62.1%), indicating its limited ability to capture discriminative patterns in minute-level, highly volatile markets.

By integrating the Rocket module (w/o VDA), the model achieves substantial improvements, with average F1-scores rising to 79.3%, 76.5%, 69.9%, and 74.0% on BTC, ETH, DOT, and BNB, respectively. This gain is attributed to the large-scale random convolutional kernels of Rocket, which enhances the Transformer's capacity to extract patterns under short-term fluctuations. Further incorporating the Volatility-aware dual-phase adaptation leads to additional improvements, with average F1-scores reaching 84.4%, 83.3%, 75.9%, and 86.3% on BTC, ETH, DOT, and BNB, respectively.

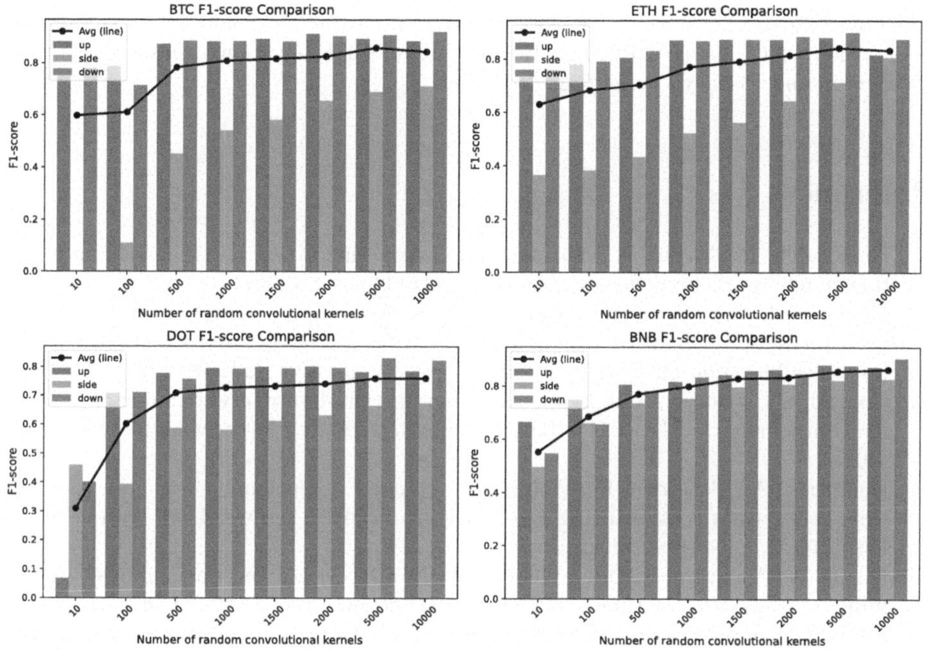

Fig. 3. Model performance under different numbers of random convolutional kernels.

Table 2. Ablation study results(%) comparing Transformer, w/o VDA, and RocketFormer across four cryptocurrencies.

Model	BTC			ETH			DOT			BNB		
	Pre	Recall	F1	Pre	Recall	F1	Pre	Recall	F1	Pre	Recall	F1
Transformer	61.29	63.37	59.28	63.93	59.35	62.47	53.98	60.53	57.13	60.47	59.10	62.08
w/o VDA	78.68	79.02	79.27	78.78	74.38	76.47	72.35	73.03	69.94	76.95	77.12	74.03
RocketFormer	**84.72**	**85.01**	**84.42**	**84.05**	**82.99**	**81.39**	**82.33**	**81.69**	**75.96**	**86.31**	**86.27**	**86.27**

5 Conclusion

RocketFormer is a novel model for trend classification in cryptocurrency time series. The model comprises three modules and is designed to perform trend forecasting under conditions of extreme market volatility. Specifically, the first module employs random convolutional kernels to extract multi-scale features, the second module performs classification via a Transformer encoder, and the third module adopts a volatility-aware dual-phase adaptation. Experimental results show that, RocketFormer achieves the highest classification accuracy among baseline models. For future work, we plan to incorporate additional related signals, such as sentiment information, into the dataset to further broaden the model's applicability.

Acknowledgments. This work was supported by the National Natural Science Foundation of China (U22B2032); Beijing Advanced Innovation Center for Future Blockchain and Privacy Computing.

References

1. Amirzadeh, R., Nazari, A., Thiruvady, D.: Applying artificial intelligence in cryptocurrency markets: a survey. Algorithms **15**(11), 428 (2022)
2. Chang, T.J., Lee, T.S., Yang, C.T., Lu, C.J.: A ternary-frequency cryptocurrency price prediction scheme by ensemble of clustering and reconstructing intrinsic mode functions based on CEEMDAN. Expert Syst. Appl. **233**, 121008 (2023)
3. Conrad, C., Custovic, A., Ghysels, E.: Long-and short-term cryptocurrency volatility components: a GARCH-MIDAS analysis. J. Risk Finan. Manage. **11**(2), 23 (2018)
4. Dempster, A., Petitjean, F., Webb, G.I.: Rocket: exceptionally fast and accurate time series classification using random convolutional kernels. Data Min. Knowl. Disc. **34**(5), 1454–1495 (2020)
5. Dempster, A., Schmidt, D.F., Webb, G.I.: MiniRocket: a very fast (almost) deterministic transform for time series classification. In: Proceedings of the 27th ACM SIGKDD Conference on Knowledge Discovery & Data Mining, pp. 248–257 (2021)
6. Fan, N., Zhang, C., Zhang, Z.: Dynamic modeling via autoregressive conditional GB2 for cross-sectional maxima of financial time series data. J. Bus. Econ. Stat., 1–23 (2025)
7. Foumani, N.M., Tan, C.W., Webb, G.I., Salehi, M.: Improving position encoding of transformers for multivariate time series classification. Data Min. Knowl. Disc. **38**(1), 22–48 (2024)
8. Franceschi, J.Y., Dieuleveut, A., Jaggi, M.: Unsupervised scalable representation learning for multivariate time series. In: Advances in Neural Information Processing Systems, vol. 32 (2019)
9. Ismail Fawaz, H., Lucas, B., Forestier, G., Pelletier, C., Schmidt, D.F., Weber, J., Webb, G.I., Idoumghar, L., Muller, P.A., Petitjean, F.: InceptionTime: finding ALEXNET for time series classification. Data Min. Knowl. Disc. **34**(6), 1936–1962 (2020)
10. Jin, C., Li, Y.: Cryptocurrency price prediction using frequency decomposition and deep learning. Fractal Fract. **7**(10), 708 (2023)
11. Le, X.M., Luo, L., Aickelin, U., Tran, M.T.: ShapeFormer: Shapelet transformer for multivariate time series classification. In: Proceedings of the 30th ACM SIGKDD Conference on Knowledge Discovery and Data Mining, pp. 1484–1494 (2024)
12. Liu, C.L., Hsaio, W.H., Tu, Y.C.: Time series classification with multivariate convolutional neural network. IEEE Trans. Industr. Electron. **66**(6), 4788–4797 (2018)
13. Liu, J., et al.: Transformer-based capsule network for stock movement prediction. In: Proceedings of the first Workshop on Financial Technology and Natural Language Processing, pp. 66–73 (2019)
14. Luo, H., Ming, D., Xu, L., Ling, X.: Tree species classification based on ASDER and MALSTM-FCN. Remote Sens. **15**(7), 1723 (2023)
15. Peng, P., Chen, Y., Lin, W., Wang, J.Z.: Attention-based CNN-LSTM for high-frequency multiple cryptocurrency trend prediction. Expert Syst. Appl. **237**, 121520 (2024)

16. Rahimi, A., Recht, B.: Random features for large-scale kernel machines. In: Advances in Neural Information Processing Systems, vol. 20 (2007)
17. Shintate, T., Pichl, L.: Trend prediction classification for high frequency bitcoin time series with deep learning. J. Risk Finan. Manage. **12**(1), 17 (2019)
18. Tahan, M.H., Ghasemzadeh, M., Asadi, S.: Development of fully convolutional neural networks based on discretization in time series classification. IEEE Trans. Knowl. Data Eng. **35**(7), 6827–6838 (2022)
19. Tan, C.W., Dempster, A., Bergmeir, C., Webb, G.I.: MultiRocket: multiple pooling operators and transformations for fast and effective time series classification. Data Min. Knowl. Disc. **36**(5), 1623–1646 (2022)
20. Tang, Y., Wei, Y., Li, T., Zheng, X., Ji, C.: A hierarchical transformer-based network for multivariate time series classification. Inf. Syst. **132**, 102536 (2025)
21. Urquhart, A.: The inefficiency of bitcoin. Econ. Lett. **148**, 80–82 (2016)
22. Yen, K.C., Cheng, H.P.: Economic policy uncertainty and cryptocurrency volatility. Financ. Res. Lett. **38**, 101428 (2021)
23. Zerveas, G., Jayaraman, S., Patel, D., Bhamidipaty, A., Eickhoff, C.: A transformer-based framework for multivariate time series representation learning. In: Proceedings of the 27th ACM SIGKDD Conference on Knowledge Discovery & Data Mining, pp. 2114–2124 (2021)

Fair Adaptive Influence Maximization in Social Networks

Yi Zhou[1], Wenyue Ma[2], Yanhao Wang[1(✉)], Yuchen Li[3], and Panagiotis Karras[2,4]

[1] School of Data Science and Engineering, East China Normal University, Shanghai, China
yzhou@stu.ecnu.edu.cn, yhwang@dase.ecnu.edu.cn
[2] Department of Computer Science, Aarhus University, Aarhus, Denmark
wenyuema@cs.au.dk
[3] School of Computing and Information Systems, Singapore Management University, Singapore, Singapore
yuchenli@smu.edu.sg
[4] Department of Computer Science, University of Copenhagen, Copenhagen, Denmark
piekarras@gmail.com

Abstract. How can we influence different groups across a social network, reducing disparities among them while taking into consideration previous dissemination? The problem of *Fair Influence Maximization* (FairIM) has been primarily studied in *non-adaptive* settings, where influencers are chosen all at once without observing any information diffusion. In this paper, we study the FairIM problem in an *adaptive* setting (FairAIM), whereby seed nodes are chosen in multiple iterative batches, allowing the observation of influence spread to inform decisions in subsequent rounds, under the notion of *maximin equity* to maximize the minimum proportion of activated members among all groups. We propose two algorithmic frameworks for FairAIM: the first extends the greedy approach to adaptively select seeds to maximize the influence of the least well-off group; the second relaxes the discrete objective to a continuous space and uses a parameter $\beta \geq 0$ to balance the fairness and welfare objectives. The experiments evince that our algorithms significantly improve fairness while maintaining high overall welfare compared to prior IM methods.

Keywords: Adaptive influence maximization · Social networks · Algorithmic fairness

1 Introduction

The problem of *Influence Maximization* (IM) seeks a *seed set* of initiators within a budget that maximizes the expected spread of information in a social net-

Y. Zhou and W. Ma—Equal contribution.

R. C.-W. Wong et al. (Eds.): PAKDD 2026, LNAI 16617, pp. 296–308, 2027.
https://doi.org/10.1007/978-981-92-1926-1_24

work [12,15]. When the information to be disseminated concerns public benefit, e.g., welfare distribution, recruitment, financial inclusion, disease prevention, and scholarship opportunities, avoiding discrimination among demographic groups by ensuring a balanced spread of information becomes a critical issue [24]. For example, in the homeless shelter intervention, raising HIV awareness evenly would be vital; companies should also promote equity when seeking candidates for open positions across different demographic groups. The *Fair IM* (FairIM) problem thus arises in [1,7,24].

Despite the extensive methods proposed for FairIM problems [1,3,7,19,24], they still consider the selection of seed nodes all at once before observing their cascading effects. We refer to them as *non-adaptive* methods, in which a promoter with a budget of k units commits to k seed nodes before observing how they influence others. In contrast, an *adaptive* strategy allocates the budget k over r rounds and chooses $\lceil k/r \rceil$ or $\lfloor k/r \rfloor$ seed nodes per round based on the propagation observed in previous rounds [11]. *Adaptive IM* (AIM) adopts such multi-round seed selection [8,11], achieving improved *total welfare* compared to its non-adaptive counterpart. Nevertheless, existing AIM approaches neglect fairness among groups, and, to the best of our knowledge, no prior work has considered adaptive fairness in IM. Worse still, the FairIM objective is non-submodular [24], making submodularity-based algorithmic frameworks ineffective for optimization.

In this paper, we study the *Fair Adaptive IM* (FairAIM) problem, which aims to guarantee a fair spread of information among groups in a social network via *adaptive* seed selection. Specifically, we formulate FairAIM under the concept of *maximin equity*, which maximizes the minimum proportion of activated members across all groups. We show that the FairAIM objective is not *adaptively submodular* [8] and is generally inapproximable [7]. Due to its computational hardness, we focus on designing efficient heuristic algorithms for FairAIM. Our first algorithm, GreedyFair, follows an extended greedy framework that adaptively selects seeds to maximize the influence of the current "least well-off" group based on observed diffusion. Then, our second algorithm, SoftFair, relaxes the discrete FairAIM objective to a continuous space and uses the Boltzmann *SoftMin* function with a parameter $\beta \geq 0$ to balance fairness and welfare in the selection process. We also devise two strategies, DynaInc and DynaDec, for SoftFair to adjust β round by round. Our experiments on real-world networks show that the proposed algorithms achieve fairness during adaptive seed selection while also maintaining overall welfare. We also assess our solutions in terms of *Price of Fairness* (PoF) [4,24], establishing that they achieve fairness at a low cost to the utility.

2 Related Work

2.1 Fairness in Influence Maximization

Recent studies focused on devising an IM solution that seeks a trade-off between overall welfare (i.e., *influence spread*) and fairness (i.e., *group- or individual-level balancedness*). Initial work introduced the concept of *maximin fairness* into IM through a multi-objective Frank-Wolfe algorithm for FAIRIM [24]. Subsequent research addressed individual-level information gaps based on maximin fairness principles [7]. A Mixed Integer Programming (MIP) framework was later developed to accommodate various fairness notions, including *maximin*, *equity*, and *diversity* [5]. Then, existing works have proposed various approaches for FAIRIM problems under established fairness concepts based on combinatorial optimization [1,16,19,20], graph representation learning [3,6], and heuristics [17]. However, none of these FAIRIM methods exploit *adaptivity* in seed selection.

2.2 Adaptive Influence Maximization

There have also been extensive studies on AIM problems, in which a sequence of seeds is progressively selected across multiple rounds based on observed information diffusion. For the classic AIM problem, as its objective enjoys *adaptive submodularity* [8], a greedy selection in each batch yields an approximation guarantee [9–11,26]. Then, several AIM approaches [18,23,27] were proposed for partial-feedback models, which assume that the diffusion cannot be fully observed at each round. Yet, these works all target overall welfare but neglect fairness. A recent work [21] studied adaptive submodular maximization with equity constraints. However, their methods cannot be applied to FAIRAIM due to the non-submodularity of the FAIRAIM objective and the distinction between our maximin fairness constraint and their defined equity constraint.

3 Problem Definition

3.1 Fair Influence Maximization

Let us consider a social network $G = (V, E)$ with a node set V and an edge set $E \subseteq V \times V$. The goal of the *Fair Influence Maximization* (FAIRIM) problem is to select a seed set $S \subseteq V$, $|S| = k$ that achieves fair influence spread over a diverse population of m distinct groups, denoted as $\mathcal{C} = \{C_1, C_2, \ldots, C_m\}$. Each node $v \in V$ belongs to exactly one group, so that the union of all groups covers the node set V, i.e., $V_{C_1} \cup V_{C_2} \cup \cdots \cup V_{C_m} = V$. In the FAIRIM problem, the influence spread is defined based on a specified diffusion model, e.g., the Linear Threshold (LT) model and the Independent Cascade (IC) model [12]. Both diffusion models have an interpretation based on *possible worlds*. Consider a subgraph derived from G by removing each edge $e = (u, v) \in E$ with probability $1 - p(u, v)$. Let Φ represent the universe of all graph realizations, where each realization ϕ is sampled from a distribution over Φ determined by G and the edge removal process. Without ambiguity, we also use Φ to denote the distribution over Φ. For a seed set S, let $I_\phi(S, C_j)$ be the number of nodes in C_j influenced via a directed path starting from S in a realization ϕ. We denote the expected influence spread from S to C_j on G as $\mathbb{E}[I_G(S, C_j)]$. We denote the expected group activation among all realizations as $\mathbb{E}_{\phi\sim\Phi}[I_\phi(S, C)]$. According to [10], we have $\mathbb{E}_{\phi\sim\Phi}[I_\phi(S, C)] = \mathbb{E}[I_G(S, C)]$.

Based on the expected influence within each group, we can define the notion of fairness as follows. First, given a graph G and a set $\mathcal{C}$ of m groups, the original *maximin fairness* [13,25] objective aims to maximize $\min_{j\in[m]} \mathbb{E}[I_G(S, C_j)]$, i.e., the minimum expected influence spread among all groups. As another common fairness metric, the *equity* [5,21] objective aims to guarantee that the ratio of the expected influence $\mathbb{E}[I_G(S, C_j)]$ in group C_j to the overall influence $\mathbb{E}[I_G(S)]$ exactly matches the proportion of nodes in C_j among all nodes in V, i.e., $\mathbb{E}[I_G(S, C_j)]/\mathbb{E}[I_G(S)] = |C_j|/|V|$. However, both notions of fairness have severe limitations. On the one hand, maximin fairness overlooks disparities in population sizes of different groups, leading to a bias in favor of less populous groups [24]; on the other hand, the equity condition is essentially infeasible in many cases [21], particularly when taking into account the inherent randomness of the diffusion process. To this end, we adopt the fairness notion of *maximin equity*, which combines the merits of both metrics while avoiding their limitations. In particular, we denote the expected ratio of the influence spread in a group to its population size $|C_j|$ as $\mathcal{R}_G(S, C_j) = \mathbb{E}[I_G(S, C_j)]/|C_j|$. The objective aims to maximize the minimum ratio of influence spread among all groups, i.e.,

$$\max_{S\subseteq V, |S|\leq k} F(S) = \min_{j\in[m]} \mathcal{R}_G(S, C_j). \tag{1}$$

3.2 Adaptive Influence Maximization

AIM selects a sequence of seed sets $S = \{S_1, \ldots, S_r\}$ in r batches to maximize their influence on a graph G, starting from $G_0 = G$. In each round $i \in [r]$, it reveals the *residual graph* G_i after the seeds chosen in S_i exercise their influence on G_{i-1} and delete all activated nodes. We consider that AIM uses the total budget k in r rounds, where each round i selects a seed set S_i with $|S_i| = c$, consuming a budget $c = \lfloor k/r \rfloor$ or $\lceil k/r \rceil$. The expected spread in round i is defined by S_i on G_i, while the $(i+1)$-residual graph depicts the dissemination on G_i. We denote the overall welfare (utility) of $S = \{S_1, \ldots, S_r\}$ as

$$U(S) = \mathbb{E}\Big[I_G\Big(\bigcup_{i\in[r]} \operatorname*{arg\,max}_{S_i\subset V, |S_i|\leq c} \mathbb{E}[I_{G_i}(S_i)]\Big)\Big]. \tag{2}$$

Considering that the influence propagation on G conforms to a sampled realization ϕ, we evaluate the *expected* influence as the average spread across rounds, aggregated over realizations, i.e., $\frac{1}{r|\Phi|}\sum_{\phi\in\Phi}\sum_{i\in[r]} I_\phi(S_i)$.

3.3 Fair Adaptive Influence Maximization

Existing FAIRIM methods focus on non-adaptive settings in which the seed set S is specified *before* observing any dissemination information. Yet, an *adaptive* seeding strategy can yield better overall welfare. In this paper, we study the problem of *Fair Adaptive Influence Maximization* (FAIRAIM), whereby each residual graph G_{i+1} builds on a previous fair selection, i.e., $\arg\max_{S_i \subset V, |S_i| \leq c} \min_{j \in [m]} \mathbb{E}[I_{G_i}(S_i, C_j)]$. Over r rounds, the *maximin equity* objective of Eq. (1) becomes

$$F(S) = \bigcup_{i \in [r]} \arg\max_{S_i \subset V, |S_i| \leq c} \min_{j \in [m]} \mathcal{R}(S_i, C_j). \tag{3}$$

Next, we analyze the computational hardness of FAIRAIM. First, FAIRAIM is **NP**-hard. Consider a case where there are $m = |V|$ groups, one per node, and a batch size $c = k$. In this case, FAIRAIM degenerates into the FAIRIM problem at an individual level, which is **NP**-hard by a reduction from VERTEXCOVER [7, Theorem 4.1].

As the original AIM objective in Eq. (2) satisfies *adaptive submodularity* [8], using a greedy selection ensures an approximation factor of $1 - \exp(\xi - 1 + \frac{1}{e})$, where ξ is an arbitrary number in $(0, 1)$. However, as will be shown next, the maximin equity objective in Eq. (3) is not adaptively submodular. As such, greedy selection has no approximation guarantee.

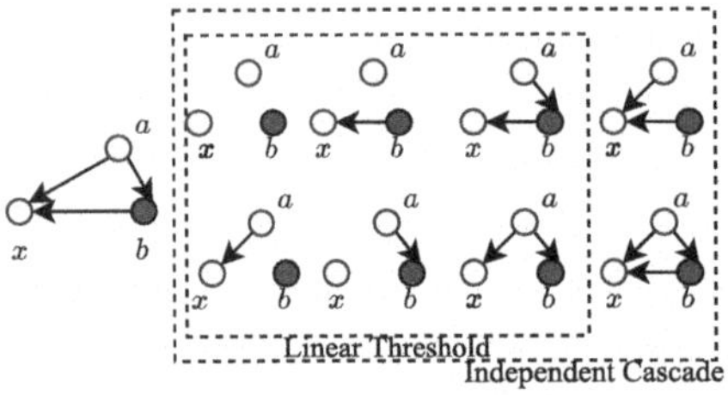

Fig. 1. A graph and all its realizations in IC and LT models in the counterexample.

Furthermore, $F(\cdot)$ is not adaptively submodular. By the definition of adaptive submodularity [8], postponing the inclusion of an item in a set does not increase the marginal benefit it confers. Thus, we provide concrete counterexamples to show that $F(\cdot)$ violates the condition in some cases. Consider a graph G with two communities $C_1 = \{a, x\}$ and $C_2 = \{b\}$, each edge having a probability of 0.5, and the objective function $F(S) = \min_{C \in \mathcal{C}} \mathcal{R}(S, C)$. Figure 1 gives all possible realizations in Φ of G by the IC and LT models. In the IC model, assuming $A = \{a\}$ and $B = \{a, b\}$, we have $F(A) = \min(13/16, 1/2) = 0.5$ and $F(B) = \min(7/8, 1) = 0.875$. When adding $\{x\}$ to A and B, respectively, we have $F(A \cup \{x\}) = \min(1, 1/2) = 0.5$ and $F(B \cup \{x\}) = \min(1, 1) = 1$. Hence, $F(A \cup \{x\}) - F(A) < F(B \cup \{x\}) - f(B)$, despite $A \subseteq B$. Thus, $F(S)$ is not submodular. We can also show that $F(\cdot)$ is not submodular under the LT model using the same counterexample. Since FAIRIM is a special case of FAIRAIM and FAIRIM is generally inapproximable [7,13], FAIRAIM is also inapproximable.

4 Algorithms

Since FAIRAIM is inapproximable, we present two heuristic algorithmic frameworks, namely GREEDYFAIR and SOFTFAIR, for the problem.

Algorithm 1. GREEDYFAIR

Input: Graph $G = (V, E)$, groups $\mathcal{C} = \{C_1, \dots, C_m\}$, budget k, and batch number r
Output: A sequence of seed sets $S = \{S_1, \dots, S_r\}$

1: Initialize $G_1 \leftarrow G$;
2: **for** $i = 1$ **to** r **do**
3:   **if** $i \leq k \bmod r$ **then** $c \leftarrow \lceil k/r \rceil$ **else** $c \leftarrow \lfloor k/r \rfloor$;
4:   $v^* \leftarrow \arg\max_{v \in V \setminus S} \mathbb{E}[I_{G_i}(v, V)]$ and $S_i \leftarrow \{v^*\}$;
5:   $C^{\text{pt}} \leftarrow \arg\min_{j \in [m]} \mathbb{E}[I_{G_i}(v, C_j)]$;
6:   **while** $|S_i| < c$ **do**
7:     $v' \leftarrow \arg\max_{v \in V \setminus (S \cup S_i)} \mathbb{E}[I_{G_i}(v, C^{\text{pt}})]$ and $S_i \leftarrow S_i \cup \{v'\}$;
8:   Observe the diffusion of S_i on G_i;
9:   Remove all nodes in G_i reachable by S_i as G_{i+1};
10: **return** $S = \{S_1, \dots, S_r\}$;

4.1 The GREEDYFAIR Algorithm

GREEDYFAIR is an extension of the classic greedy approach to the adaptive fairness setting. Its detailed procedure is outlined in Algorithm 1. Generally, it adaptively selects a sequence of seed sets $S_1, \dots, S_r$ over r rounds to maximize the minimum expected influence among the m groups in $\mathcal{C}$ on a graph G, given that the influenced nodes are observed and removed after each round. For the selection of each S_i, we first find a node that maximizes the overall welfare (line 4) to address the cold start problem. Afterwards, before choosing the remaining nodes in S_i, we identify the group with the least ratio of influenced members as the protected group C^{pt}. Subsequently, we add the nodes to maximize the expected influence over C^{pt} (line 7) to S_i. Finally, GREEDYFAIR observes the influence of the current seed set S_i on the current G_i and extracts the residual graph G_{i+1} by removing all nodes in G_i reached by S_i. In line 5, there may be a tie, in which some groups have the same lowest influence ratio. In this case, we randomly select one of them as C^{pt}. If C^{pt} is isolated, we pick an arbitrary node v therein that is not a seed so far, i.e., $v \in C^{\text{pt}} \setminus (S \cup S_i)$.

Note that seed selection relies on an accurate estimation of the influence of each node on the residual graph. In our implementation, we adopt the *Reverse Influence Sampling* (RIS) method [2], which builds *Reverse Reachable sets* (RR sets) for influence estimation. Specifically, in a graph instance g obtained by removing each edge (u, v) in G with probability $1 - p(u, v)$, the *RR set* of $v \in V$ is the set of nodes in G that can reach v. A *random RR set* is an RR set generated on an instance g randomly sampled from G, for a node selected uniformly at random from g. The RIS method consists of two steps that we have customized for the adaptive fairness setting. We generate ρ random RR sets from G_i to estimate the influence of each node in lines 4 and 7 at each round and, in each selection, the *maximum coverage* problem is formulated to select each of the seeds as the node that covers the maximum number of the generated RR sets w.r.t. the protect group C^{pt}. Based on Hoeffding's inequality and the unbiasedness of RIS [2], to guarantee that the estimated influence for a node v is bounded by an additive error of at most $\alpha \cdot |V|$ for an error parameter $\alpha \in (0, 1)$ over all k

selections in r rounds, i.e.,

$$|\sigma_{G_i}(v, V) - \mathbb{E}[I_{G_i}(v, V)]| \leq \alpha \cdot |V|, \ \forall v \in V \text{ and } i \in [r],$$

where $\sigma_{G_i}(v, V)$ is the estimated influence of node v on G_i by RIS, with a probability of at least $1 - \delta$ for a confidence parameter $\delta \in (0, 1)$, we need to generate $\rho = O(\frac{1}{\alpha^2} \log \frac{nk}{\delta})$ random RR sets for calculation.

4.2 The SoftFair Algorithm

Although GreedyFair can identify the seed node to maximize the group with the minimal influence ratio in each round, it still suffers from two limitations when used to optimize the FairAIM objective. First, GreedyFair cannot provide any tunable trade-off between fairness and welfare. Second, GreedyFair may encounter a tie because multiple groups share the same minimal influence ratio, typically 0. In such cases, it will optimize one of the tied groups while neglecting the others, exacerbating imbalances in influence among groups. To overcome both challenges, we leverage the Boltzmann *SoftMin* function, which converts the original discrete objective into a continuous one by relaxing the discrete constraints. The definition of *SoftMin* is given below.

Definition 1 (SoftMin). *For a graph G and a set of groups $\mathcal{C}$, the Boltzmann SoftMin function assigns the weight of group j w.r.t. a seed set $S \subseteq V$ as follows:*

$$w_j^S = \frac{\exp(-\beta \cdot \mathcal{R}(S, C_j))}{\sum_{j \in [m]} \exp(-\beta \cdot \mathcal{R}(S, C_j))},$$

where $\beta \geq 0$ is a tunable parameter.

If $\beta = 0$, we have $w_j^S = 1/m$ for each $j \in [m]$, which means that all groups will be treated equally without considering their influence ratios. Then, if the value of β increases, the value of w_j^S will increase for a group C_j with a lower influence ratio. In this way, the growth of β potentially benefits the current disadvantaged groups. For a seed set S, we obtain its influence ratio on each group C_j and compute the weight w_j^S to scale the objective function as

$$\mathcal{L}(S) = \sum_{j=1}^{m} w_j^S \cdot \mathcal{R}(S, C_j), \tag{4}$$

where each w_j^S is calculated according to Definition 1.

Algorithm 2 details the overall procedure of SoftFair. Generally, it follows a framework similar to GreedyFair. The main differences lie in line 6, where in each round i, it seeks the nodes that maximize the marginal gain of $\mathcal{L}(\cdot)$ in the residual graph G_i of round i as seeds instead of those that simply maximize the influence ratio of the protected group. Using the parameter β, SoftFair provides a trade-off between fairness and welfare: When $\beta = 0$, it simply maximizes the sum of the influence ratios of all groups, prioritizing overall welfare;

Algorithm 2. SoftFair

Input: Graph $G = (V, E)$, groups $\mathcal{C} = \{C_1, \ldots, C_m\}$, budget k, number of batches r, and parameter β
Output: A sequence of seed sets $S = \{S_1, \ldots, S_r\}$

Initialize $G_1 \leftarrow G$;
for $i = 1$ **to** r **do**
  Set c as line 3 of Algorithm 1;
  Initialize $S_i \leftarrow \emptyset$;
  while $|S_i| < c$ **do**
    $v' \leftarrow \arg\max_{v \in V \setminus (S \cup S_i)} (\mathcal{L}(S_i \cup \{v\}) - \mathcal{L}(S_i))$ and $S_i \leftarrow S_i \cup \{v'\}$;
  Observe the diffusion of S_i on G_i;
  Remove all nodes in G_i reachable by S_i as G_{i+1};
return $S = \{S_1, \ldots, S_r\}$;

With increasing β, the groups with lower influence ratios are more emphasized, tending to a fairer seed selection. Moreover, with continuous $\mathcal{L}(\cdot)$, SoftFair can consider the influence ratios of all groups in a weighted sum form for each selection. When more than one group has the same minimal influence ratio, they will be assigned the highest weight equally in $\mathcal{L}(\cdot)$, thus avoiding neglecting some of them. SoftFair can also be extended to dynamically adjust the value of β over rounds. We consider two schemes for adjustment: Given a factor $\Delta > 0$, DynaInc and DynaDec update $\beta_i, i \in [1, r]$ by $\beta_{i+1} \leftarrow \beta_i + \Delta$ and $\beta_{i+1} \leftarrow \beta_i - \Delta$, respectively. That is, DynaDec gradually reduces the importance of fairness to achieve better fairness at the beginning and improved welfare later, while DynaInc operates oppositely.

Complexity Analysis: The complexity of generating random RR sets is $\mathcal{O}(\rho \cdot (|V| + |E|))$. In each round, we generate RR sets for a new residual graph. Updating the residual graph takes $\mathcal{O}(|V|)$ time. Determining the protected group takes $\mathcal{O}(m|V|)$ time, while obtaining a seed node incurs an $\mathcal{O}(m + |V|)$ cost, and the realization step is $\mathcal{O}(|V|)$. Thus, the overall complexity of GreedyFair is $\mathcal{O}(r\rho \cdot |V| \cdot |E| + \min(k, rm) \cdot |V|)$. Similarly, as the computation of $\mathcal{L}(\cdot)$ is $\mathcal{O}(m|V|)$, the time complexity of SoftFair amounts to $\mathcal{O}(r\rho \cdot |V| \cdot |E| + km \cdot |V|)$.

5 Experiments

In this section, we perform extensive experiments on real-world networks to evaluate the performance of our proposed algorithms. We experimented on a desktop with an Intel (R) Core(TM) i9-12900K CPU @5.20 GHz and 32 GB of RAM running Ubuntu 18.04. The code was written in C++ and compiled by GCC 9.4 using the "-o3" optimization flag. Our code and data are publicly available in a GitHub repository[1].

In general, our goal is to answer the following research questions:

[1] https://github.com/yz2022/FairAIM.

- **(RQ1)** How effectively do our algorithms achieve *maximin equity* (i.e., the FAIRAIM objective)?
- **(RQ2)** How much is the *Price of Fairness* (PoF) that they pay?
- **(RQ3)** How effective are they by varying the budget k and the number of batches r?

Note that a technical appendix with additional experiments on time efficiency and parameter sensitivity is included in the shared GitHub repository.

5.1 Experimental Setup

Baselines: The following IM baselines were compared in the experiments: (1) IMM [22], a classic IM algorithm without adaptivity and fairness considerations; (2) EPTAIM [11], an adaptive IM algorithm without fairness constraints; (3) MYOPIC [7], a non-adaptive algorithm for individually fair IM; (4) FIMM [20], the state-of-the-art non-adaptive FAIRIM algorithm; (5) GREEDYFAIR, SOFTFAIR, DYNAINC, and DYNADEC proposed in this paper.

Datasets: The statistics for the three datasets used in the experiments are presented in Table 1. All of them were downloaded from the SNAP collection [14]. For Facebook and DBLP, we used the available attributes, namely *age* and *region*, to partition the nodes into groups. As NetHEPT lacked public labels for group division, we performed spectral clustering to partition the nodes into 2 and 8 groups. We also ran spectral clustering to generate 4 groups on DBLP.

Table 1. Statistics of datasets in the experiments. (Dir.: Is_directed; $\bar{d}$: average degree; $d_{\max}$: maximum degree; Spec.: Spectral; Reg.: Region)

Dataset	$\|V\|$	$\|E\|$	Dir.	$\bar{d}$	$d_{\max}$	Population distribution by group (in %)
Facebook	1,216	84,769	✓	69.82	568	Age: '19'(8.2), '20'(28.4), '21'(30.8), '22'(32.6)
DBLP	3,980	13,187	✓	3.31	90	Reg.: AS(21.8), EU(22.5), NA(52.2), OCE(2.8), SA(0.7)
						Spec.: C_1(24.4), C_2(38.0), C_3(18.1), C_4(19.5)
NetHEPT	15,229	62,752	✗	4.18	128	Spec.: C_1(80.2), C_2(19.8)
						Spec.: C_2(59.6), C_4(10.1), C_5(20.1), C_8(8.4), Other(1.8)

Parameter Setting: By default, we set $k = 10, r = 5$ for the Facebook dataset and $k = 100, r = 10$ for the DBLP and NetHEPT datasets. For SOFTFAIR, we set $\beta = 10$. We increase β from 0 to 10 in DYNAINC, while decreasing β from 10 to 0 in DYNADEC. We generate 100 random realizations ϕ for each dataset and report the average performance across them, selecting k nodes in r batches per dataset. We set the probability of edge (u, v) proportionally to $1/d_u^{out}$, where d_u^{out} is the out-degree of u. On each realization, we generate 10,000 RR samples in each batch of node selection for each RIS-based algorithm.

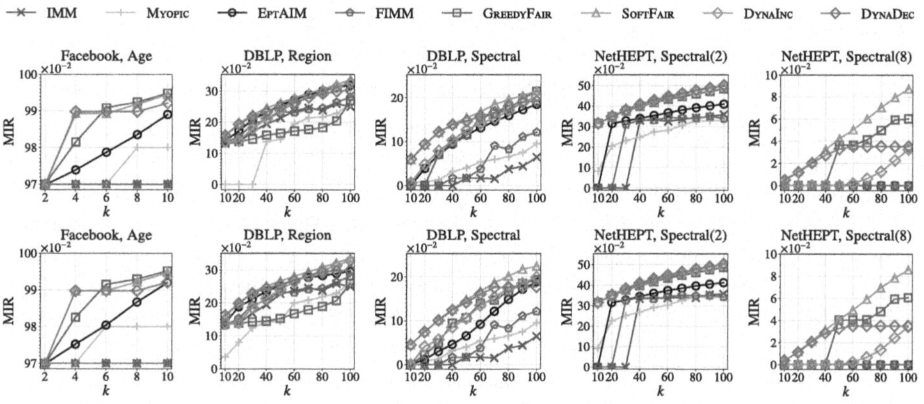

Fig. 2. Minimum Influence Ratio (MIR) of each method with varying the number of seeds k in the IC (top) and LT (bottom) models.

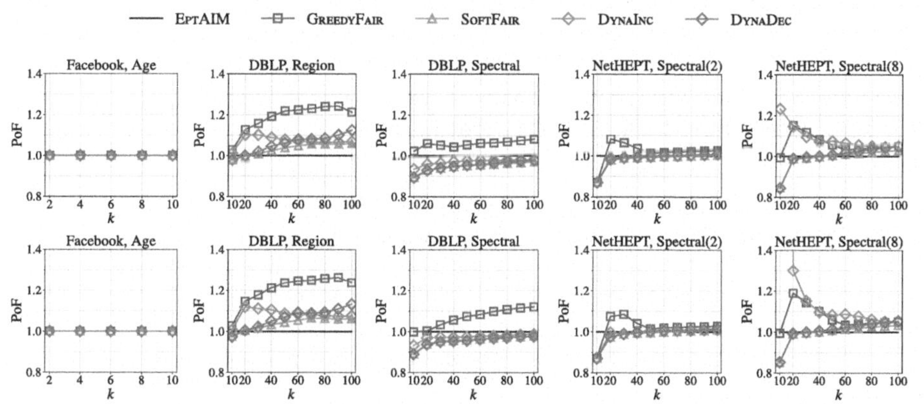

Fig. 3. Price of Fairness (PoF) of each method with varying the number of seeds k in the IC (top) and LT (bottom) models.

5.2 Experimental Results

Maximin Equity (RQ1): In Fig. 2, we present the minimum influence ratios (MIRs), i.e., the values of $F(S)$, of the seed set S of each method as the budget k varies in the IC and LT models.

We observe that Myopic and IMM perform poorly compared to the remaining methods, as they do not account for either group fairness or adaptivity. FIMM also shows inferior performance compared to our proposed methods due to its non-adaptivity and the misalignment between the notion of *fairness* in FIMM and our *maximin equity*. EptAIM does not always produce MIRs comparable to ours due to its ignorance of fairness.

Regarding our proposed algorithms, SoftFair performs better than others in most cases. On the Facebook dataset, GreedyFair maintains results close to

SoftFair, while on the DBLP and NetHEPT datasets, DynaDec sometimes outperforms SoftFair. In general, these results confirm the effectiveness of our methods to improve the fairness of influence spread in the adaptive setting.

Price of Fairness (RQ2): Next, we examine whether our FairAIM algorithms achieve a good trade-off between fairness and overall welfare. The Price of Fairness (PoF) quantifies the ratio of utility lost for the sake of fairness, denoted as $U(S^*)/U(S)$ [24], where $U(S^*)$ is the maximum utility (influence) obtainable using k seed nodes, with the influence of EptAIM [11] used as a proxy in our evaluation, and $U(S)$ is the utility obtained by our algorithm. Higher PoF values indicate higher costs of fairness and lower welfare. In addition, a PoF less than 1 indicates that an algorithm attains even better overall welfare than EptAIM.

Figure 3 shows the PoF of each method with varying the budget k in the IC and LT models. On the Facebook dataset, there is no distinct PoF difference across algorithms because their influences are all close to $|V|$. On the DBLP and NetHEPT datasets, the PoF of SoftFair is close to 1 and sometimes less than 1 when the groups are more balanced, whereas GreedyFair and DynaInc sacrifice more utility to ensure fairness. Yet, when the groups are highly imbalanced, as in the DBLP (Region) and NetHEPT (Spectral, $m = 4, 8$) datasets, SoftFair and DynaDec still keep PoF values close to or even less than 1, suggesting that they successfully balance utility and fairness.

Table 2. MIRs of each method with varying the number of batches r when $k = 100$ on NetHEPT and DBLP. The best result in each setting is highlighted in bold.

Method	Independent Cascade (IC)				Linear Threshold (LT)			
	NetHEPT		DBLP		NetHEPT		DBLP	
	Spectral(2)	Spectral(8)	Spectral	Region	Spectral(2)	Spectral(8)	Spectral	Region
Number of Batches $r = 10$								
EptAIM	0.409	0.000	0.185	0.320	**0.457**	0.000	0.189	0.296
GreedyFair	0.483	0.060	**0.215**	0.268	0.378	0.060	0.193	0.259
SoftFair	**0.496**	**0.087**	**0.215**	**0.337**	0.431	**0.086**	**0.224**	**0.336**
Number of Batches $r = 5$								
EptAIM	0.376	0.000	0.183	0.321	0.376	0.000	0.185	0.303
GreedyFair	0.464	0.058	0.158	0.262	0.459	0.058	0.178	0.229
SoftFair	**0.472**	**0.114**	**0.227**	**0.337**	**0.471**	**0.114**	**0.236**	**0.353**
Number of Batches $r = 1$								
IMM	0.358	0.000	0.065	0.250	0.357	0.000	0.065	0.250
Myopic	0.329	0.000	0.095	0.262	0.341	0.000	0.095	0.262
EptAIM	0.318	0.000	0.179	0.320	0.320	0.000	0.175	0.296
FIMM	0.338	0.000	0.121	0.281	0.343	0.000	0.121	0.280
GreedyFair	0.340	0.000	0.196	0.320	0.342	0.000	0.203	0.303
SoftFair	**0.413**	**0.132**	**0.253**	**0.357**	**0.388**	**0.115**	**0.267**	**0.363**

Effect of Budget k (RQ3): As shown in Figs. 2 and 3, in most cases, SoftFair achieves better performance than baselines across different budgets k. GreedyFair is closer to SoftFair when k is larger, but it exhibits less stable performance for a smaller budget k.

Effect of Batch Number r (RQ3): Finally, we study how the number of batches r affects the performance of different methods. The results for MIRs with varying r are presented in Table 2. SoftFair always shows an advantage across different r values. When $r = 1$, the selection process degrades to the non-adaptive one. As the value of r increases, GreedyFair and SoftFair show more significant advantages compared to non-adaptive methods as well as compared to themselves with smaller values of r.

6 Conclusion

In this paper, we studied FairIM in an adaptive setting (i.e., FairAIM) under the notion of *maximin equity*, aiming to maximize the minimum proportion of activated members across all groups. We proposed two algorithmic frameworks for FairAIM: the first extended the greedy approach to adaptively select seeds to maximize the influence of the least well-off group; the second relaxed the discrete objective to a continuous space and uses a customized parameter $\beta \geq 0$ to strike a fairness-utility trade-off. We showed empirically that our proposed algorithms strike a better balance between fairness and overall welfare than existing methods for FairAIM.

Acknowledgements. This work is supported in part by the National Natural Science Foundation of China (Grant No. 62202169). P. Karras was supported by DFF.

References

1. Becker, R., D'Angelo, G., Ghobadi, S., Gilbert, H.: Fairness in influence maximization through randomization. J. Artif. Intell. Res. **73**, 1251–1283 (2022)
2. Borgs, C., Brautbar, M., Chayes, J.T., Lucier, B.: Maximizing social influence in nearly optimal time. In: SODA. pp. 946–957 (2014)
3. Chowdhary, S., De Pasquale, G., Lanzetti, N., Stoica, A.A., Dörfler, F.: Fairness in social influence maximization via optimal transport. Adva. Neural Inf. Process. Syst. **37**, 10380–10413 (2024)
4. Dong, Y., Ma, J., Wang, S., Chen, C., Li, J.: Fairness in graph mining: A survey. IEEE Trans. Knowl. Data Eng. **35**(10), 10583–10602 (2023)
5. Farnadi, G., Babaki, B., Gendreau, M.: A unifying framework for fairness-aware influence maximization. In: WWW (Companion). pp. 714–722 (2020)
6. Feng, Y., Patel, A., Cautis, B., Vahabi, H.: Influence maximization with fairness at scale. In: KDD. pp. 4046–4055 (2023)
7. Fish, B., Bashardoust, A., Boyd, D., Friedler, S.A., Scheidegger, C., Venkatasubramanian, S.: Gaps in information access in social networks? In: WWW. pp. 480–490 (2019)

8. Golovin, D., Krause, A.: Adaptive submodularity: Theory and applications in active learning and stochastic optimization. J. Artif. Intell. Res. **42**, 427–486 (2011)
9. Guo, Q., Feng, C., Zhang, F., Wang, S.: Efficient algorithm for budgeted adaptive influence maximization: An incremental RR-set update approach. Proc. ACM Manag. Data **1**(3), 207:1–207:26 (2023)
10. Han, K., Huang, K., Xiao, X., Tang, J., Sun, A., Tang, X.: Efficient algorithms for adaptive influence maximization. Proc. VLDB Endow. **11**(9), 1029–1040 (2018)
11. Huang, K., Tang, J., Han, K., Xiao, X., Chen, W., Sun, A., Tang, X., Lim, A.: Efficient approximation algorithms for adaptive influence maximization. VLDB J. **29**(6), 1385–1406 (2020)
12. Kempe, D., Kleinberg, J.M., Éva Tardos: Maximizing the spread of influence through a social network. In: KDD. pp. 137–146 (2003)
13. Krause, A., McMahan, H.B., Guestrin, C., Gupta, A.: Robust submodular observation selection. J. Mach. Learn. Res. **9**(93), 2761–2801 (2008)
14. Leskovec, J., Krevl, A.: SNAP Datasets: Stanford large network dataset collection. http://snap.stanford.edu/data (2014)
15. Li, Y., Fan, J., Wang, Y., Tan, K.L.: Influence maximization on social graphs: A survey. IEEE Trans. Knowl. Data Eng. **30**(10), 1852–1872 (2018)
16. Lin, M., Sun, L., Yang, R., Liu, X., Wang, Y., Li, D., Li, W., Lu, S.: Fair influence maximization in large-scale social networks based on attribute-aware reverse influence sampling. J. Artif. Intell. Res. **76**, 925–957 (2023)
17. Ma, W., Egger, M.K., Pavlogiannis, A., Li, Y., Karras, P.: Reachability-aware fair influence maximization. In: APWeb-WAIM (III). pp. 342–359 (2024)
18. Peng, B., Chen, W.: Adaptive influence maximization with myopic feedback. Adv. Neural. Inf. Process. Syst. **32**, 5575–5584 (2019)
19. Rahmattalabi, A., Jabbari, S., Lakkaraju, H., Vayanos, P., Izenberg, M., Brown, R., Rice, E., Tambe, M.: Fair influence maximization: A welfare optimization approach. In: AAAI. pp. 11630–11638 (2021)
20. Rui, X., Wang, Z., Peng, H., Chen, W., Yu, P.S.: A scalable algorithm for fair influence maximization with unbiased estimator. IEEE Trans. Knowl. Data Eng. **37**(7), 3881–3895 (2025)
21. Tang, S., Yuan, J.: Group equality in adaptive submodular maximization. INFORMS J. Comput. **36**(2), 359–376 (2024)
22. Tang, Y., Shi, Y., Xiao, X.: Influence maximization in near-linear time: A martingale approach. In: SIGMOD. pp. 1539–1554 (2015)
23. Tong, G., Wang, R.: On adaptive influence maximization under general feedback models. IEEE Trans. Emerg. Top. Comput. **10**(1), 463–475 (2022)
24. Tsang, A., Wilder, B., Rice, E., Tambe, M., Zick, Y.: Group-fairness in influence maximization. In: IJCAI. pp. 5997–6005 (2019)
25. Udwani, R.: Multi-objective maximization of monotone submodular functions with cardinality constraint. Adv. Neural. Inf. Process. Syst. **31**, 9513–9524 (2018)
26. Vaswani, S., Lakshmanan, L.V.S.: Adaptive influence maximization in social networks: Why commit when you can adapt? arXiv:1604.08171 (2016)
27. Yuan, J., Tang, S.: No time to observe: Adaptive influence maximization with partial feedback. In: IJCAI. pp. 3908–3914 (2017)

Physically Motivated Partial-Spectrum Denoising for Robust Hyperspectral Anomaly Detection

Jungkwon Kim, Chi Zhang, Jihun Kim, Jeonghyeon Park, Kwangsun Yoo, and Seok-Joo Byun(✉)

ELROILAB, Inc., Seoul, Republic of Korea
{jkkim,czhang,jihunkim,jhpark,yks,sjbyun}@elroilab.com

Abstract. Hyperspectral imaging is widely employed for anomaly detection in industrial applications such as food safety inspection, yet its performance can deteriorate due to spectral noise concentrated in short-wavelength regions. In these regions, limited sensor sensitivity and calibration amplification introduce substantial pixel-wise variability, leading to unstable spectral representations. This study introduces a partial-spectrum filtering framework that selectively processes noise-prone short-wavelength regions while preserving informative longer-wavelength features. Unlike empirical optimization, the filtering range is physically determined by the imaging system's sensor response and illumination characteristics. By targeting only the spectral region where the white reference magnitude falls below a physically motivated threshold, the method enhances relative signal-to-noise ratios by 30–60% in short wavelengths without degrading stable wavelength bands. Experiments on real industrial hyperspectral datasets for food anomaly detection demonstrate consistent improvement up to approximately 1% in AUPR across multiple materials, with baselines ranging from 0.910 to 0.967. These results highlight that physically grounded, region-specific preprocessing enhances both the stability and reliability of hyperspectral anomaly detection in real-world industrial environments.

Keywords: Hyperspectral Imaging · Anomaly Detection · Spectral Filtering

1 Introduction

Hyperspectral imaging (HSI) acquires and analyzes spectral information spanning the visible and infrared regions of the electromagnetic spectrum, covering 400–1000 nm wavelengths. By capturing reflectance spectra over hundreds of contiguous bands within the near-infrared range, industrial HSI systems exhibit high sensitivity to compositional differences determined by material properties.

J. Kim and C. Zhang—These authors contributed equally to this work.

R. C.-W. Wong et al. (Eds.): PAKDD 2026, LNAI 16617, pp. 309–321, 2027.
https://doi.org/10.1007/978-981-92-1926-1_25

Owing to this capability, HSI has become an effective technique for anomaly detection in various industrial settings [2,10–12,15].

In HSI, hyperspectral measurements are inherently susceptible to various noise sources, including sensor thermal noise, photon shot noise, and quantization errors [6,8,18]. These noise components can significantly degrade spectral signatures, compromising downstream tasks such as material classification and anomaly detection. To enable accurate material distinction, raw sensor data are converted into calibrated reflectance spectra $\boldsymbol{\rho}$ using the following formula:

$$\boldsymbol{\rho} = \frac{\boldsymbol{\rho}_{\mathcal{R}} - \boldsymbol{\rho}_{\mathcal{B}}}{\boldsymbol{\rho}_{\mathcal{W}} - \boldsymbol{\rho}_{\mathcal{B}}} \times C, \tag{1}$$

where $\boldsymbol{\rho}_{\mathcal{R}}$, $\boldsymbol{\rho}_{\mathcal{W}}$, and $\boldsymbol{\rho}_{\mathcal{B}}$ denote the raw spectrum, white-reference, and dark-reference spectra, respectively, and C is a scaling constant. However, this calibration amplifies noise in spectral regions where sensor sensitivity is limited, particularly around 400 nm. The combined effects of inherent measurement noise and calibration amplification result in substantial pixel-wise spectral instability that varies across wavelength regions, with short-wavelength bands exhibiting significantly higher variability than mid- and long-wavelength bands.

The presence of region-specific noise poses fundamental challenges for deep learning-based anomaly detection, which relies on learning latent representations of normal patterns during training (see [1,13] and references therein). When short-wavelength noise is present, normal samples having the same compositional features exhibit high pixel-wise spectral variability due to measurement artifacts rather than true material differences. This increased intra-class variance forces the model to learn representations dispersed across a broader latent space to cover all normal training samples, thereby inflating the decision boundary and increasing the likelihood of misclassifying anomalies as normal. When a specific wavelength region of the spectrum predominantly contains noise rather than material-specific information, the network inevitably attempts to account for variations in these noise-dominated channels. Consequently, depending on the statistical nature of the noise, two distinct failure modes may emerge.

If the noise is largely unstructured (e.g., high-frequency sensor noise with low inter-sample correlation), the gradients associated with these bands become unstable or vanish over the course of training. Hence, the network suppresses their contribution, inadvertently discarding spectral regions that may contain subtle yet informative cues. In contrast, when the noise exhibits structured or correlated patterns—arising from factors such as fixed-pattern sensor bias, wavelength-dependent illumination artifacts, or temperature-induced spectral shifts—the network may mistakenly treat these spurious patterns as discriminative features. This leads to overfitting to dataset-specific noise characteristics, resulting in degraded generalization and instability under real-world variations.

Therefore, noise in the short-wavelength region can either cause the model to ignore potentially useful spectral information or induce reliance on non-generalizable artifacts, both of which adversely affect anomaly detection performance.

To address this issue, previous studies have explored various spectral filtering techniques, including Gaussian smoothing, moving average, Savitzky-Golay filtering [7,16,17], and wavelet denoising [3–5]. However, most conventional approaches employ fixed filtering parameters or apply uniform smoothing across the entire spectral range. This uniform processing introduces a fundamental limitation: it cannot simultaneously suppress short-wavelength noise and preserve discriminative features in the already stable mid- and long- wavelength regions, since uniform parameters treat inherently distinct spectral characteristics in the same manner.

In industrial inspection settings, such as real-time anomaly detection on production lines, this poses a practical challenge: noise mitigation must be applied selectively without compromising the integrity of clean spectral regions. To overcome this limitation, we propose a partial-spectrum filtering framework that adaptively applies filtering only to spectrally unstable regions, primarily within the noisy short-wavelength regions. By focusing on preprocessing efforts on spectral bands where noise dominates while preserving stable regions, the proposed method improves training stability and enhances detection robustness.

Our approach addresses a key limitation in practical deployment: when training data contain systematic spectral noise, particularly within sensor-sensitive wavelength regions, the learned features may inadvertently encode artifacts that degrade detection performance. We mitigate this issue through a physically motivated preprocessing strategy that selectively targets noise-prone regions, identified via analysis of the imaging system's characteristics rather than through empirical optimization.

The key contributions of this work are threefold: (1) We introduce a partial-spectrum filtering strategy that selectively processes spectrally unstable regions while preserving informative mid- and long-wavelength bands. (2) We show that this region-specific approach enhances detection robustness in high-baseline industrial settings by allocating preprocessing resources to the spectral regions most susceptible to noise. (3) We demonstrate that the physically motivated determination of the filtering range improves the signal-to-noise ratio (SNR) within the targeted short-wavelength region without degrading stable bands, thereby validating the system-based design and providing an effective alternative to empirical parameter optimization.

2 Spectral Region Decomposition

2.1 Dataset Characteristics of Spectral Instability Analysis

In this study, we use the hyperspectral dataset [9], which was designed to evaluate food anomaly detection models. The dataset consists of hyperspectral images of three normal food materials—almonds, garlic stems, and pistachios—each comprising 224 contiguous spectral bands covering the near-infrared range (400 – 1000 nm). It was optimized for food-manufacturing environments, where accurate pixel-wise spectral measurement is essential for reliable anomaly detection.

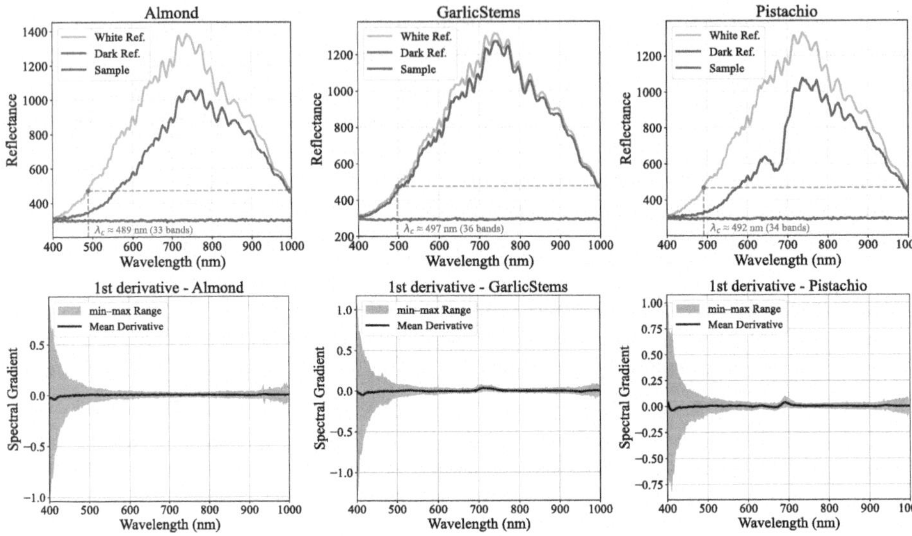

Fig. 1. Top: spectra of white, dark references and sample pixel of almond, garlic stems, and pistachio. Bottom: first spectral derivative of spectra in each material, exhibiting higher spectral variability in the short-wavelength region compared to mid- and long-wavelength.

To reduce noise in the reference measurements, the system averages the white and dark reference spectra along the spatial axis (perpendicular to the line-scan direction) during calibration. In contrast, the observed reflectance from sample pixels is retained at full spatial resolution to preserve local spectral variations essential for identifying small or subtle anomalies. This asymmetric processing—spatially averaged references but pixel-level observations—is standard practice in industrial HSI systems.

A critical issue arises in the short-wavelength region around 400 nm, where sensor sensitivity is inherently limited. Low sensor response in this range results in small denominator values in (1), causing even slight fluctuations in the raw measurements to be greatly amplified in the calibrated reflectance spectra. As a result, pixels from the same material class may exhibit considerable spectral variability in this region despite representing identical materials.

To quantify the region-dependent characteristics of spectral noise, we analyze the spectral profiles using the first derivative. Because hyperspectral measurements are affected by local illumination, spectra from the same material may vary in overall intensity. To mitigate these illumination-induced offsets, we compute the first spectral derivative, which emphasizes intrinsic spectral fluctuations while being invariant to absolute intensity levels.

Figure 1 illustrates the spectral characteristics for three materials in the dataset. The top row shows sample spectra along with the white and dark references used for calibration. The bottom row presents the first derivative, where the

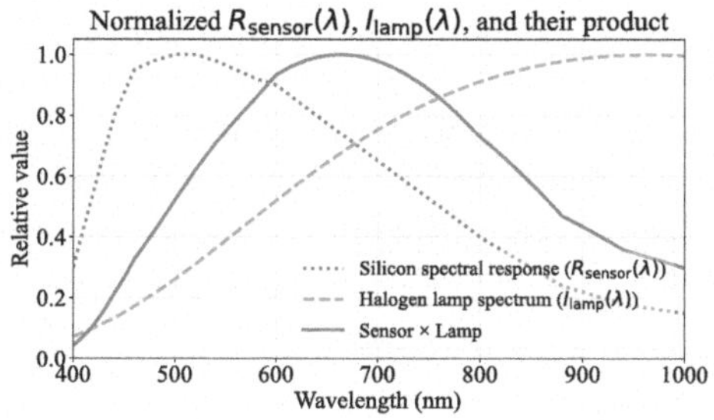

Fig. 2. Qualitative illustration of normalized sensor response $R_{\mathrm{sensor}}(\lambda)$, halogen lamp spectrum $I_{\mathrm{lamp}}(\lambda)$, and their product. Curves are normalized to unit maximum to demonstrate the complementary spectral characteristics. The product curve represents the relative behavior of the white reference magnitude across wavelength.

shadowed region indicates the min-max range of derivative values across spectral bands, and the solid line represents the mean. Regardless of material type, spectral instability is markedly higher in the short-wavelength region (approximately 400–500 nm) than in the mid- and long-wavelength regions. This consistent instability across all materials confirms that it originates from sensor and calibration characteristics rather than material-specific properties.

2.2 Determining the Filtering Range

We derive the filtering range from the fundamental characteristics of the imaging system's optical and illumination components. The white reference spectrum used in calibration (1) is determined by the combined response of the sensor and illumination system:

$$\rho_{\mathcal{W}}(\lambda) \propto R_{\mathrm{sensor}}(\lambda) \times I_{\mathrm{lamp}}(\lambda), \tag{2}$$

where $R_{\mathrm{sensor}}(\lambda)$ denotes the spectral response of the silicon sensor, and $I_{\mathrm{lamp}}(\lambda)$ denotes the spectral intensity distribution of the halogen illumination source.

Figure 2 illustrates the qualitative relationship between these components using normalized values. The silicon sensor responsivity peaks near 500 nm and decreases toward longer wavelengths, whereas the halogen lamp exhibits peak emission in the near-infrared. Their product demonstrates how the combined system response is lower in magnitude at short-wavelengths than at long-wavelengths. Consequently, when the white reference magnitude is low, the denominator in (1) becomes small, amplifying the effect of noise on the calibrated reflectance.

To identify the spectral region most susceptible to noise amplification, we determine the wavelength cutoff λ_c in the short-wavelength region, defined as the point where the white reference magnitude equals that at the long-wavelength end of the spectrum (1000 nm) i.e., $\rho_{\mathcal{W}}(\lambda_c) = \rho_{\mathcal{W}}(1000)$. The maximum band number $\nu_c \in \mathbb{N}$ to which filtering is applied is then determined as

$\lfloor(\lambda_c - 400)/2.68\rfloor$, where $\lfloor x \rfloor$ denotes the greatest integer less than or equal to x.

For wavelengths $\lambda < \lambda_c$, the white reference magnitude is lower than at the long-wavelength end, resulting in smaller denominator values and greater noise amplification. This criterion provides a physically motivated threshold for identifying the spectral region requiring selective filtering, which is employed in our implementation.

3 Filtering Hyperspectral Data

3.1 Spectral Filtering Techniques

In this paper, we apply four commonly used signal filters. We first remind the mathematical definitions. Let $\mathbf{x} = (x_1, x_2, \cdots, x_\ell) \in \mathbb{R}^\ell$ be the reflectance spectrum of a pixel across ℓ bands and let $\widetilde{\mathbf{x}} = (\tilde{x}_1, \tilde{x}_2, \cdots, \tilde{x}_\ell)$ be the partially smoothed spectrum after applying each filter.

Firstly, the Gaussian filter smooths the spectrum using a convolution operation with a discrete Gaussian kernel:

$$\widetilde{x_i} = \sum_{j=-k}^{k} w_j x_{i+j}, \qquad w_j = \frac{1}{\sqrt{2\pi\sigma^2}} e^{-\frac{j^2}{2\sigma^2}}, \quad \text{for} \quad i \in [k+1, \ell-k]. \tag{3}$$

Here, the kernel size is $2k+1$ and σ is the standard deviation controlling the smoothness. The weights w_j are normalized to ensure $\sum_j w_j = 1$.

The moving average filter replaces each spectral value with the average of its local window:

$$\widetilde{x_i} = \frac{1}{2k+1} \sum_{j=-k}^{k} x_{i+j}, \quad \text{for} \quad i \in [k+1, \ell-k]. \tag{4}$$

This is a special case of convolution where all kernel weights are equal, and uniform smoothing is applied.

The Savitzky-Golay (SG) filter [17] preserves local features such as peaks and inflection points. Unlike simple averaging methods, SG filtering performs local polynomial regression within a sliding window, fitting a polynomial of degree d to approximate the spectral signal around each band. Formally, for each spectral index i, $\mathbf{y}_i = [x_{i-k}, x_{i-k+1}, \cdots, x_{i+k}] \in \mathbb{R}^{2k+1}$ denotes a local window of $\mathbf{x}$. Each element of $\mathbf{y}_i$ represents the raw spectral reflectance values in the local region. To fit a polynomial of degree d, we construct the Vandermonde matrix $A \in \mathbb{R}^{(2k+1)\times(d+1)}$ based on the local window positions such that $-k \leq j \leq k$ for $j \in \mathbb{Z}$:

$$A = \begin{bmatrix} 1 & i-k & (i-k)^2 & \cdots & (i-k)^d \\ 1 & i-k+1 & (i-k+1)^2 & \cdots & (i-k+1)^d \\ \vdots & \vdots & \vdots & \ddots & \vdots \\ 1 & i+k & (i+k)^2 & \cdots & (i+k)^d \end{bmatrix} \tag{5}$$

We then solve the least squares problems for each i:

$$\mathbf{z}_i^* = \underset{\mathbf{z} \in \mathbb{R}^{d+1}}{\arg\min} \|A\mathbf{z} - \mathbf{y}_i\|^2 \tag{6}$$

which has the closed-form solution $\mathbf{z}_i^* = (A^T A)^{-1} A^T \mathbf{y}_i$. Then, the elements of $\mathbf{z}_i^*$ are the coefficients of the fitted polynomial. The smoothed spectral value at position i, denoted $\widetilde{x}_i$, is given by evaluating $\sum_{k=0}^{d} z_{i,k}^* i^k$. In practice, the SG filter is implemented using a precomputed convolution kernel. That is, for a fixed window size and polynomial degree, the smoothing coefficients $z_{i,k}$ are computed once and applied uniformly across all spectral indices. This implementation reduces computational overhead while preserving the desirable mathematical properties of the original formulation.

Finally, wavelet-based denoising first decomposes the spectrum using discrete wavelet transform, applies thresholding [3–5] to high-frequency detail coefficients, and reconstructs the signal. Let $\mathcal{W}(x) = \{\mathbf{a}, \mathbf{d}_1, \cdots, \mathbf{d}_L\}$ denote the wavelet decomposition into approximation coefficients $\mathbf{a}$ and detail coefficients $\mathbf{d}_i$ up to level L. The denoised spectrum is obtained by applying thresholding to each detail coefficient and reconstruction:

$$\widetilde{x} = \mathcal{W}^{-1}(\mathbf{a}, \mathbf{d}_1', \cdots, \mathbf{d}_L'), \quad \mathbf{d}_i' = \text{Thresh}(\mathbf{d}_i; \tau) \tag{7}$$

where Thresh denotes thresholding operator, and $\mathcal{W}^{-1}$ is the inverse wavelet transform. The threshold parameter τ controls the magnitude of noise suppression.

3.2 Filter Application and Parameter Configuration

We now describe the application of the four spectral filters to hyperspectral data under the partial-spectrum filtering strategy. Partial-spectrum filtering overcomes the fundamental limitation of uniform processing by treating regions with different spectral quality according to their characteristics: aggressive denoising is applied where noise dominates, while stable regions are left unprocessed to preserve discriminative features. As established in Sect. 2.2, filtering is therefore applied only to the first ν_c spectral bands—where noise is most concentrated due to the physical characteristics of the imaging system—while the remaining $224 - \nu_c$ bands are passed through unchanged, ensuring that the model learns from stable spectral representations across the full wavelength range.

In practice, the wavelength cutoff ν_c varies slightly across scan lines due to spatial variations in the white reference measurements. To determine a consistent filtering range for each material, ν_c is computed for each scan line and then averaged across the entire image. This procedure yields $\nu_c = 33$ bands for almonds, 36 bands for garlic stems, and 34 bands for pistachios. These minor differences arise from variations in reference acquisition conditions rather than material-specific spectral properties, as the same physical criterion—based on the white reference magnitude—is applied uniformly across all materials.

Filtering is conducted at the pixel level. For each pixel, let $\boldsymbol{\rho} = [\rho_1, \rho_2, \cdots, \rho_{224}]$ denote the calibrated reflectance spectrum. The filtering operation produces a modified spectrum $\widetilde{\boldsymbol{\rho}}$ whose i-th element is given by

$$\widetilde{\rho}_i = \begin{cases} \mathcal{F}(\rho_i; \Theta) & \text{if} \quad 1 \le i \le \nu_c, \\ \rho_i & \text{if} \quad \nu_c < i \le 224, \end{cases} \tag{8}$$

Table 1. Filter parameter configurations used in the experiments for four filters (Gaussian, Moving Average, Savitzky-Golay, and Wavelet).

Filter	Parameter	Value/Description
Gaussian	σ	2.0
	Boundary	Reflection(Default)
Moving Average	Window size	15 bands
	Boundary	Reflection
Savitzky-Golay	Window size	15 bands
	Polynomial order	3
	Boundary	Interpolation(Default)
Wavelet	Wavelet type	Daubechies (db4)
	Decomposition level	2
	Thresholding	Soft ([5]), $\tau = 0.5 \times \max(\lvert\text{coeffs}\rvert)$

where $\mathcal{F}(\cdot\,; \Theta)$ denotes the filtering function with parameters Θ. This selective filtering strategy concentrates preprocessing on the spectral region most susceptible to noise amplification, as identified through physical system analysis, while preserving discriminative spectral features in stable regions.

To enable a fair comparison across filter types, all filters were configured with fixed parameters throughout our experiments. Table 1 summarizes the parameter settings, which follow standard practices in the spectral processing literature.

4 Experiments and Results

4.1 Experimental Setup

We evaluate our approach on a hyperspectral food dataset [9] consisting of almonds, garlic stems, and pistachios. For each object, the dataset provides two hyperspectral images for training and testing. Training images contain only normal samples on the conveyor belt, whereas test images include both normal samples and 42 anomalies, such as plastic, rubber, paper, and metal.

Four spectral filters—Gaussian, moving average (MA), Savitzky-Golay (SG), and wavelet—are applied with parameters specified in Table. 1, implemented using standard Python libraries: SciPy v1.14.1 for Gaussian and SG filters,

NumPy v1.26.4 for MA filter, and PyWavelets v1.7.0 for wavelet filtering. Following the physically motivated filtering threshold established in Sect. 2, filtering is applied selectively to the first ν_c bands, determined according to the white reference magnitude criterion.

All experiments employ a deep anomaly detection model based on deviation networks [14], which learns to predict anomaly scores via deviation learning. The baseline (unfiltered) performance ranges from 0.910 to 0.967 across materials, representing a practical operating regime in which improvements due to preprocessing can be clearly demonstrated. Our evaluation thus emphasizes practical reliability and reproducibility over absolute performance gains in real-world application scenarios.

4.2 Experimental Results and Analysis

The following Table 2 summarizes the anomaly detection performance across three datasets and four filtering techniques.

Table 2. Anomaly detection performance (AUPR) for different materials and filtering methods. The filtering range is determined based on the physically motivated criterion.

Method	Almond	Garlic Stems	Pistachio
ν_c	33	36	34
Baselines	0.9103 ± 0.011	0.9670 ± 0.005	0.9542 ± 0.006
Gaussian	0.9160 ± 0.008	$\mathbf{0.9683} \pm 0.004$	0.9567 ± 0.004
MA	$\mathbf{0.9185} \pm 0.011$	0.9681 ± 0.005	0.9548 ± 0.005
SG	0.9163 ± 0.004	0.9651 ± 0.005	0.9565 ± 0.002
Wavelet	0.9142 ± 0.011	0.9565 ± 0.002	$\mathbf{0.9584} \pm 0.007$

Each material type achieves its best performance with a different filter type: moving average for almonds, Gaussian for garlic stems, and wavelet for pistachios. These variations in optimal filter selection warrant further investigation, though the consistent SNR improvements in the physically determined short-wavelength region (Fig. 3) validate the core premise that filtering range can be established through system-based analysis rather than material-specific tuning.

To elucidate the mechanism behind the performance gains, we analyze the relative SNR across spectral bands. For each wavelength λ, we define $\mathrm{SNR}(\lambda) = 20\log_{10}(\mu(\lambda)/\sigma(\lambda))$, where $\mu(\lambda)$ and $\sigma(\lambda)$ denote the mean and standard deviation of reflectance across pixels in band λ, respectively. The effectiveness of partial-spectrum filtering is quantified through the relative SNR improvement, computed as the fractional change from the unfiltered baseline:

$$\frac{\mathrm{SNR}^{\mathrm{filtered}}(\lambda) - \mathrm{SNR}^{\mathrm{unfiltered}}(\lambda)}{\mathrm{SNR}^{\mathrm{unfiltered}}(\lambda)}. \tag{9}$$

Figure 3 illustrates the relative SNR improvement for each material and filter type. Gains are concentrated in the short-wavelength region (approximately 400–450 nm), with relative improvements reaching up to 0.4–0.6 (30–60%) for the moving average filter. At longer wavelengths, SNR changes are marginal or slightly negative, indicating that filtering has minimal effect on spectral regions that are already stable.

Despite differences in spectral signatures across materials, the spatial pattern of SNR improvement is remarkably consistent. All three datasets exhibit peak improvements in the 400–450 nm range, followed by a gradual decay toward longer wavelengths. This consistency indicates that spectral instability in the short-wavelength region is primarily a sensor-related characteristic rather than a material-specific artifact, thereby validating the system-based approach for determining the filtering ranges.

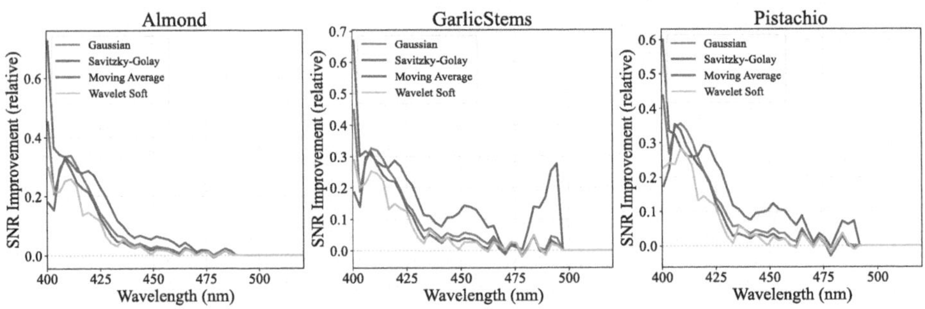

Fig. 3. Band-wise relative SNR improvement after partial filtering. Improvements are concentrated in the 400–450 nm region across all materials and filters types, validating that the filters effectively target the noise-prone region using physically determined filtering threshold.

4.3 Performance Interpretation and Practical Implications

The observed SNR improvements in the short-wavelength region are closely related to the AUPR gains reported in Table 2. By reducing spectral variability within the short-wavelength region, partial-spectrum filtering mitigates pixel-level noise that could otherwise be misinterpreted as anomalous patterns by the detection model, thereby improving precision and enhancing robustness to measurement variability.

It should be noted that the relationship between SNR improvement and task performance is not strictly linear. Indeed, substantial SNR gains (30–60% in certain bands) translate into consistent yet modest AUPR improvements up to approximately 1%. While these absolute gains may appear small, they represent meaningful operational benefits in industrial food inspection, where false positives can lead to unnecessary line stoppages and false negatives compromise product safety.

The proposed approach introduces minimal computational overhead, increasing training time by approximately 5–10% relative to the unfiltered baseline. In contrast, full-spectrum filtering would require processing all 224 bands. This balance between accuracy gains and computational cost renders partial-spectrum filtering particularly suitable for real-time industrial deployment, where both detection reliability and throughput are critical operational requirements.

4.4 Discussion

The proposed partial-spectrum filtering approach demonstrates performance improvements across multiple datasets and filtering techniques in most cases, with gains up to approximately 1% in AUPR. Although these improvements are modest in absolute terms, they are meaningful in the high-baseline regime (AUPR > 0.91) where the system operates, corresponding to tangible reductions in false alarms and missed detections over extended production runs. In such high-baseline industrial settings, even a 1% gain in AUPR corresponds to a 30–40% relative reduction in false alarms, yielding substantial operational impact on product throughput and quality assurance.

The filtering range determined through physical system analysis aligns closely with the observed SNR improvement patterns. Material-dependent variation in ν_c reflects differences in reference acquisition conditions rather than intrinsic material properties, demonstrating that the method naturally adapts to system-specific characteristics without requiring manual tuning.

The nonlinear relationship between SNR improvement and task performance suggests that the detection task is approaching its practical difficulty limit given current data characteristics. Further improvements may necessitate advances in model architecture rather than additional preprocessing, though the spectral quality enhancements achieved here provide a robust foundation for any downstream detection method.

Future work will investigate adaptive filtering strategies that automatically adjust the filtering range based on real-time spectral quality metrics. Furthermore, extending the evaluation to other industrial inspection domains would further validate the generalizability of this physically motivated approach.

5 Conclusion

This study presented a partial-spectral filtering framework for hyperspectral anomaly detection that addresses region-specific noise through physically motivated preprocessing. By deriving the filtering range directly from the imaging system's optical and illumination characteristics, the proposed approach eliminates the need for empirical optimization while achieving targeted noise suppression in regions most susceptible to calibration artifacts. The method selectively processes only spectrally unstable regions while preserving informative mid- and long-wavelength bands. Across the three food datasets, our approach improved detection performance on high baselines (AUPR > 0.91), with relative SNR gains of 30–60% concentrated in the short-wavelength regions. These consistent improvement patterns across materials confirm that spectral instability primarily arises from sensor and calibration properties, validating the system-based and data-agnostic nature of the proposed method. In summary, this work suggests a physically interpretable and computationally lightweight preprocessing approach for industrial hyperspectral systems. It highlights the potential of integrating optical system characteristics with data-driven anomaly detection to improve stability in real-world applications. Future work will further explore adaptive filtering strategies that adjust the processing range according to real-time spectral quality and extend the evaluation to other inspection domains (e.g., textiles, pharmaceuticals) as well as to systems operating under varying environmental conditions.

Acknowledgments. This study was funded by the Ministry of SMEs and Startups of Republic of Korea (grant number: RS-2023-00304845).

References

1. Chalapathy, R., Chawla, S.: Deep learning for anomaly detection: a survey. arXiv preprint (2019)
2. Chang, C.-I., Chiang, S.-S.: Anomaly detection and classification for hyperspectral imagery. IEEE Trans. Geosci. Remote Sens. **40**(6), 1314–1325 (2002)
3. Chang, S.G., Yu, B. Vetterli, M.: Adaptive wavelet thresholding for image denoising and compression. IEEE Trans. Image Process. **9**(9), 1532–1546 (2000)
4. Donoho, D.L.: De-noising by soft-thresholding. IEEE Trans. Inf. Theory **41**(3), 613–627 (1995)
5. Donoho, D.L., Johnstone, I.M.: Ideal spatial adaptation by wavelet shrinkage. Biometrika **81**(3), 425–455 (1994)
6. Ghamisi, P., et al.: Advances in hyperspectral image and signal processing: a comprehensive overview of the state of the art. IEEE Geosci. Remote Sens. Mag. **5**(4), 37–78 (2017)
7. John, A., Sadasivan, J., Seelamantula, C.S.: Adaptive Savitzky-Golay filtering in non-gaussian noise. IEEE Trans. Sig. Process. **69**, 5021–5036 (2021)
8. Landgrebe, D. A., Malaret, E.: Noise in remote-sensing systems: the effect on classification error. IEEE Trans. Geosci. Remote Sens. **GE-24**(2), 294–300 (1986)
9. Lee, J., Kim, M., Yoon, J., Yoo, K., Byun, S.-J.: Anomaly detection with hyperspectral imaging for food safety inspection. IEEE Dataport (2024)
10. Lee, J., Kim, M., Yoon, J., Yoo, K., Byun, S.-J.: PA2E: real-time anomaly detection with hyperspectral imaging for food safety inspection. IEEE Access **12**, 175535–175549 (2024)
11. Liu, Y., et al.: Joint optimization of autoencoder and self-supervised classifier: anomaly detection of strawberries using hyperspectral imaging. Comput. Electron. Agric. **198**, 107007 (2022)
12. Mangotra, H., Srivastava, S., Jaiswal, G., Rani, R., Sharma, A.: Hyperspectral imaging for early diagnosis of diseases: a review. Expert. Syst. **40**(8), e13311 (2023)

13. Pang, G., Shen, C., Cao, L., van den Hengel, A.: Deep learning for anomaly detection: a review. ACM Comput. Surv. **54**(38) (2021)
14. Pang, G., Shen, C., van den Hengel, A.: Deep anomaly detection with deviation networks. In: Proceedings of the ACM SIGKDD International Conference on Knowledge Discovery & Data Mining (KDD), pp. 353–362 (2019)
15. Qu, Y., et al.: Hyperspectral anomaly detection through spectral unmixing and dictionary-based low-rank decomposition. IEEE Trans. Geosci. Remote Sens. **56**(8), 4391–4405 (2018)
16. Ruffin, C., King, R. L.: The analysis of hyperspectral data using Savitzky-Golay filtering-theoretical basis. In: IEEE International Geoscience and Remote Sensing Symposium, vol. 2, pp. 756–758 (1999)
17. Savitzky, A., Golay, M.J.E.: Smoothing and differentiation of data by simplified least squares procedures. Anal. Chem. **36**(8), 1627–1639 (1964)
18. Zhang, T., Fu Y., Li, C.: Hyperspectral image denoising with realistic data. In: Proceedings of the IEEE/CVF International Conference on Computer Vision (ICCV), pp. 2248–2257 (2021)

PriHA: A RAG-Enhanced LLM Framework for Primary Healthcare Assistant in Hong Kong

Richard Wai Cheung Chan[1], Shanru Lin[1], Ya-nan Ma[2], Hao Chen[3], Liangjun Jiang[1(✉)], and Wenqi Fan[1(✉)]

[1] The Hong Kong Polytechnic University, Hong Kong, China
{24032618g,shanru.lin}@connect.polyu.hk,
{jljchina2025,wenqifan03}@gmail.com

[2] Haikou Affiliated Hospital of Central South University Xiangya School of Medicine, Haikou, China

[3] Sun Yat-Sen University Cancer Center, Guangzhou, China
chenhao@sysucc.org.cn

Abstract. To address the unsustainable rise in public health expenditures, the Hong Kong SAR Government is shifting its strategic focus to primary healthcare and encouraging citizens to use community resources to self-manage their health. However, official clinical guidelines are fragmented across disparate departments and formats, creating significant access barriers. While general-purpose Large Language Models (LLMs) such as ChatGPT and DeepSeek offer potential solutions for information accessibility, they are prone to generating factually inaccurate content due to a lack of localized and domain-specific knowledge. To this end, we propose a Retrieval-Augmented Generation-Enhanced LLM system as **Pri**mary **H**ealthcare **A**ssistant (**PriHA**) in Hong Kong. Specifically, a tri-stage pipeline is proposed that leverages a query optimizer to generalize user intent-oriented sub-queries, followed by a novel Dual Retrieval Augmented Generation (DRAG) architecture for mixed-source retrieval and context-reorganized generation. Comprehensive experiments and a detailed case study demonstrate that our proposed method can outperform both ablations and baseline in terms of accuracy and clarity. Our research provides a reliable and traceable dialogue retrieval framework for exploring other high-risk, localized application scenarios.

Keywords: Retrieval-Augmented Generation (RAG) · Large Language Models (LLMs) · AI4Healthcare · Healthcare Assistant

1 Introduction

Hong Kong's population is aging rapidly. By 2046, the proportion of residents aged 65 and above is projected to exceed 36%[1]. This demographic shift is leading

[1] Hong Kong Population Projections for 2022 to 2046, Census and Statistics Department:https://www.censtatd.gov.hk/en/EIndexbySubject.html?pcode=B1120015&scode=190

R. C.-W. Wong et al. (Eds.): PAKDD 2026, LNAI 16617, pp. 322–334, 2027.
https://doi.org/10.1007/978-981-92-1926-1_26

to a higher prevalence of chronic diseases, imposing a heavier burden on public hospital services and medical expenditures. Accordingly, "**Prevention is better than Cure**" has become the core policy to maintain the sustainability of the public health system in Hong Kong. This strategy aims to shift the focus from treatment-oriented secondary medical services to prevention-oriented primary healthcare[2], emphasizing the need for patients to develop a deeper understanding of their health status and undergo earlier screening. While the government has published extensive healthcare guidelines and disease-screening schemes, a critical, often-overlooked dimension is the information gap. A report indicates that over half of the participants feel unequipped to access the care guidance they need [19]. This divide is further exacerbated by the fragmentation of information across disparate government websites, where official guidelines are often stored in hard-to-retrieve formats, such as tables and figures within PDF files. Furthermore, certain key documents are available only in English, creating language barriers for the local Chinese-speaking population. To enable citizens to manage their health effectively, a more accessible information platform is urgently needed.

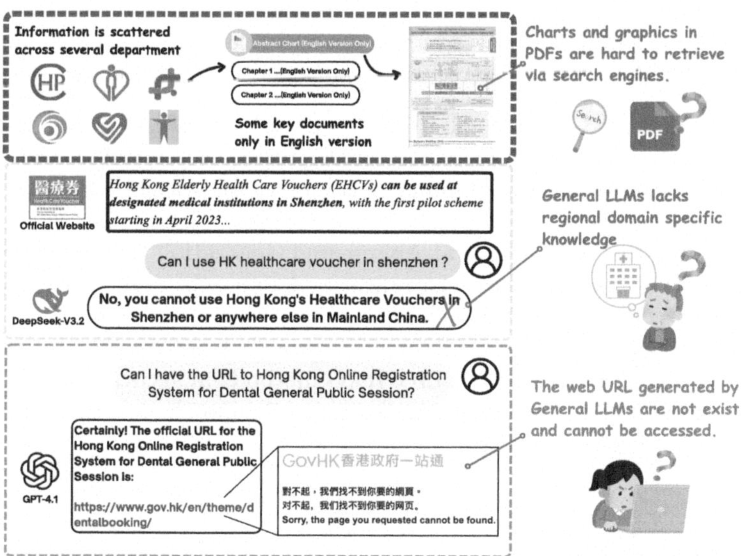

Fig. 1. The illustration of scattered primary healthcare information and the existing limitations of Large Language Models (LLMs)-based Healthcare Assistant in Hong Kong.

With the widespread adoption of Large Language Models (LLMs), there is an increasing trend to use these tools to obtain health information and medi-

[2] Primary Healthcare Blueprint:https://www.primaryhealthcare.gov.hk/bp/sc/index.html

cal advice [3,14,25]. However, individuals are prone to overtrusting these AI-generated results, viewing them as equally effective as professional medical guidance [6,18]. One primary concern is the tendency toward factual inaccuracies and hallucinations when handling domain-specific and region-specific queries [13,24]. As illustrated in Figure 1, the LLM-empowered AI systems might provide incorrect answers about medical services and invalid URLs in Hong Kong. Furthermore, these systems often struggle with conversational clarity. When a user asks a fuzzy question such as *"Which exercise is better for my knees?"*, general-purpose LLMs usually fail to clarify crucial context, such as age or medical history, instead offering universal answers that force users into an iterative cycle of questioning. Since responses cannot be cross-verified, this also creates significant trust issues for users who cannot verify their validity.

To this end, we focus on the primary healthcare sector and propose a novel **Pri**mary **H**ealthcare **A**ssistant (**PriHA**) in Hong Kong, where a three-stage pipeline is proposed to build upon our Dual Retrieval-Augmented Generation (DRAG) framework. The process begins with an intelligent triage module that precisely captures and clarifies the user's true intent through multi-turn dialogue. A list of clarified sub-queries is then passed to the core DRAG framework, which performs dual-source retrieval. Finally, an enhanced generation module fuses and validates information from both sources, producing comprehensive answers with source citations. Our main contributions can be summarized as follows:

- We propose a RAG-enhanced LLM framework (**PriHA**) to address information gaps by optimizing the conversation-retrieval workflow and strategically guiding users toward community resources for self-management in Hong Kong.
- We introduce the Dual Retrieval-Augmented Generation (DRAG) framework, which resolves conflicts between static and dynamic data sources, thereby eliminating context pollution while providing traceable evidence.
- Our comprehensive experiments demonstrate that our proposed method significantly outperforms single-source RAG methods in accuracy and completeness, establishing a responsible AI design paradigm that can be extended to other public-service domains.

2 Related Work

As one of the most representative AI techniques [4,5,22], LLMs have achieved significant success in the healthcare domain [2,16,17]. Current applications range from medical record summarization and patient education to complex diagnostic support [20]. However, the practical deployment of these systems in high-stakes clinical settings is frequently hampered by their propensity for hallucination, where models generate confident yet factually erroneous information [1,8]. Furthermore, due to the static nature of their training corpora, LLMs struggle to incorporate evolving medical knowledge, which leads to potential obsolescence and safety risks [3]. Consequently, relying solely on the parametric knowledge of

LLMs is increasingly viewed as insufficient for reliable healthcare assistance and necessitates mechanisms that can ground model outputs in verifiable evidence [3,13].

To mitigate these limitations, Retrieval-Augmented Generation (RAG) [12, 21] is a technique that uncovers new possibilities for reliable medical AI by separating knowledge storage from reasoning capabilities. In this framework, models rely on external repositories to retrieve relevant documents and supply them as context for response generation. Compared with fine-tuning, which requires resource-intensive retraining and risks catastrophic forgetting, RAG offers a distinct advantage in adaptability [13,21]. Since medical knowledge and government schemes are dynamic and constantly updated, retrieval-based methods allow for the immediate integration of new information by simply updating the external database [15]. Empirical studies such as those by Xiong et al. [23] demonstrate that RAG approach are better than fine-tuned models in handling medical factual queries for source with reference answers. This makes RAG a preferred architectural choice for environments characterized by scattered but comprehensive information, such as primary healthcare.

Despite the success of retrieval systems, developing holistic healthcare assistants for specific populations, such as the elderly, presents unique challenges that remain underexplored. Most existing medical QA chatbots operate on a single-turn or passive-retrieval basis and may fail when users cannot articulate their needs precisely [10]. Moreover, relying on a single knowledge source often limits the comprehensiveness of the answer. Emerging research suggests that hybrid approaches combining structured local knowledge with real-time web information are essential for robust performance [7]. Our work bridges this gap by proposing a dual-retrieval framework that not only ensures data timeliness but also optimizes the interaction process for clarity and trust.

3 Method

The primary healthcare AI assistant system employs a three-stage pipeline: (1) interpreting user intent, (2) retrieving information from static and dynamic sources, and (3) verifying and synthesizing the results.

3.1 Primary Healthcare Repository (PHR)

The foundation of PriHA is to address the fragmentation of healthcare information caused by the dispersion of official guidelines across disparate government websites. We have created a centralized knowledge repository that covers major primary healthcare information in Hong Kong, including clinical standards, community resources, and subsidized schemes, serving as the knowledge base for the RAG process.

One challenge during the pre-processing stage is that files stored in PDF use a fixed layout designed for consistent visual presentation, which is not conducive to machine semantic understanding and structured text extraction. Therefore, source documents are converted into Markdown format to preserve structural integrity while facilitating efficient retrieval. While image content is captured as web links and manually annotated to ensure it can be retrieved later, "source of file" and "updated time" are labeled as metadata for later conflict resolution (Fig. 2).

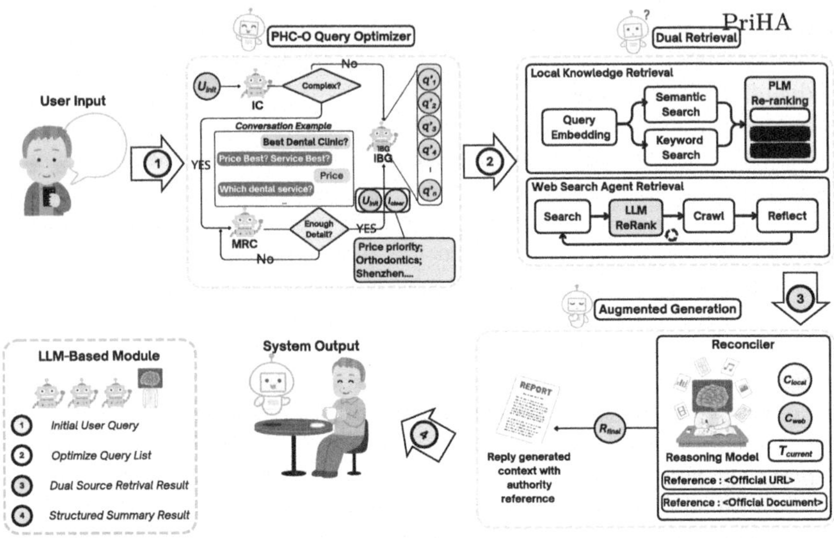

Fig. 2. Overall framework of the proposed PriHA. The framework processes the initial user input through a query optimizer, yielding a clarified intention and refined sub-queries, then passes to dual retrieval module that fetches and re-ranks content from a local knowledge base and web searchers. Finally, the summarization stage uses a reconciler to synthesize search results into a structured response with proper references.

3.2 Primary Healthcare-Oriented Query Optimizer

General LLMs are not optimized for primary healthcare applications. When presented with a health-related query, these models often generate generic recommendations, such as directing users to the emergency room or hospitals. This response pattern bypasses the local primary care layer. To this end, the optimizer is designed to interpret the user's initial input (U_{init}) and transform it into a set of PHC-oriented sub-queries ($q'_1, \ldots, q'_n$), aiming to steer the search process toward relevant primary care options such as family doctors and community health centers, rather than defaulting to secondary and tertiary care institutions.

Intent Classifier (IC). Similar to the triage system in an emergency room, where a nurse first confirms the urgency of a patient's issue, this method uses an LLM-based classifier to process the user's initial input at the start of the conversation. A SIMPLE query is labeled as a direct question with clear intent, such as "*What is the address of Queen Mary Hospital?*" and can proceed immediately to the next step. In contrast, a COMPLEX tagged query, such as "*Which clinic has better dental services?*", is routed to a clarification module. This approach ensures that model resources are focused on resolving ambiguous queries, particularly for the elderly users who may struggle to express their needs clearly [11] in obtaining desired answers.

Multi-Round Clarification (MRC). When a query is flagged as COMPLEX, the system proactively asks clarifying questions in multiple rounds to understand the user's intent. For example, when a user mentions "*Where to find a better dental clinic*", the system helps them clarify the actual meaning of "*better*", asking whether they are more concerned about price or something else. The process continues until the user's intention, background, and priorities are clear, and it is recorded as the clarified user intention (I_{clear}) proceed to next step. This enables the system to perform the retrieval process with a clear understanding of the user's priorities and background, rather than relying solely on keyword relevance, which might lead to imprecise responses.

Intent-Based Generalizer (IBG). Vanilla generalizers improve coverage simply by paraphrasing words. We propose an Intent-Based Generalizer (IBG) that generates intention-based sub-queries. For example, a query like "*Whether it's better to see a dentist in Shenzhen or Hong Kong?*" can be refined into searches like "*Hong Kong dental prices*" and "*Shenzhen dental prices*" after clarification reveals that the user intends to find more affordable services.

Moreover, IBG also incorporates the community-first principle of primary healthcare. For instance, if a user expresses concern about joint pain, the generalizer generates search intents not only for orthopedic guidelines but also for relevant services at district health centers and government-subsidized care schemes. This process produces a list of atomic search queries $(q'_1, \ldots, q'_n)$, to make the retrieval process significantly more comprehensive.

3.3 Dual-Retrieval Augmented Generation

Each query q'_i in the generated list is executed in parallel by two independent retrieval components, and their results are then reinforced onto the generative output according to a set of rules.

Local Knowledge Retrieval (LKR). Some official healthcare materials mention the main subject only in the title, without further elaboration in the body. Using a fixed chunk size in such cases can easily lead to incomplete answers due to missing context, but increasing the chunk size will dilute semantic focus.

We adopt a parent-child chunking approach, using two distinct chunk sizes to address the problem. Smaller child chunks are used for retrieval, while larger parent chunks provide context. During the search process, child chunks containing concise, query-relevant details are selected, and their corresponding original parent chunks are forwarded to the system. This method ensures precise retrieval while providing the LLM with sufficient background information during the answer generation step.

Two complementary retrieval methods are employed on the PHR:

- **Keyword Search.** This method operates by matching keyword frequencies and is highly effective for retrieving exact policy terms such as "*Elderly Health Care Voucher*", but it fails to capture semantic similarity, for example, when users ask about "*medical discounts for seniors.*"
- **Semantic Search.** This method captures semantic similarity and effectively understands implied user intent, but it may lose key proper nouns during vector-space averaging when processing jargon.

To leverage the strengths of both approaches, we implement a hybrid retrieval strategy. Candidate chunks from keyword and semantic searches are merged into a unified pool, followed by a lightweight PLM-based **BGE-Reranker-V2** applying top-k filtering and score-based selection. The system ensures that only the most relevant contexts are forwarded to the response generation stage.

Web Search Agent (WSA). Although a local knowledge repository provides a reliable information cornerstone, its utility is limited by the latency associated with real-time updates and pre-processing cycles. In practice, information such as service policies and clinic operating hours changes frequently, rendering static data insufficient for a robust system. To overcome this limitation, the framework is equipped with a suite of integrated web search and crawling tools that the LLM-based Web Search Agent (WSA) can invoke dynamically.

The agent operates within an iterative ReAct-style loop. This cycle begins with the formulation of a preliminary plan, followed by a broad web search to obtain an overview of relevant information. Standard web search engines, such as Google Search and Baidu Search, may return links of uncertain credibility when used without carefully designed keyword constraints. To mitigate this risk, we define a safelist that allows the agent to select authoritative URLs from the search results. To ensure reliability, all search results undergo an LLM-based reranking process. In contrast to traditional PLM-based rerankers, the LLM-based approach offers zero-shot ranking capabilities and the ability to interpret complex, instruction-driven criteria. The reranking rules prioritize official and certified sources to enforce credibility standards. After reranking, the agent crawls the selected URLs to extract content. The crawler validates the accessibility and authenticity of every link in real time, eliminating broken, fake, or redirected URLs before any content is accepted. The system then evaluates whether the obtained information is sufficient to answer the original query. If gaps or inconsistencies remain, the WSA enters a reflection phase, identifies missing or unreliable data, and triggers another iteration of searching, reranking, and crawling.

Through this iterative process with URL validation via real-time crawling, the agent guarantees that all citations in the final response are verifiable, up-to-date, and directly accessible.

Augmented Generation (AG). At this stage, the system combines information retrieved from the local knowledge base with content acquired by the web-search agent. The challenge is that the simple concatenation of these sources is inadequate, as it may lead to conflicting statements and inconsistent or incoherent outputs. To address this, a systematic reconciliation mechanism is required to integrate heterogeneous evidence in a principled manner.

The Reconciler module is the core component of the AG stage. It jointly evaluates the context retrieved from the local knowledge base (C_{Local}), the web search agent (C_{Web}), and the current user profile (T_{current}). This component operates under predefined conditions that guide decision-making and prioritize information. For instance, official policy documents bearing institutional certification from the Hong Kong government are deemed more reliable than web pages from other administrative sources. Similarly, sources containing outdated content are assigned lower priority. This structured decision procedure prevents the model from presenting unresolved contradictions to the user and ensures coherent synthesis across diverse sources.

We employ a reasoning model to perform conflict resolution and summarization in a single pass. The model integrates comprehensive professional medical guidelines vertically and horizontally with available community resources, such as social welfare programs and complementary schemes. It then constructs a unified representation of the retrieved information and formats it into a report-like response tailored to the end user, emphasizing clarity and readability. This approach ensures that policy and healthcare guidance remain accessible and unambiguous.

Traceability is a central design of our objective. The local knowledge base provides metadata-annotated references, and the web-search agent supplies verifiable URLs obtained via the crawler. These sources are documented in a reference section accompanying the final system output (R_{final}). The capacity for cross-verification through explicit citations enhances the system's transparency and trustworthiness, thereby increasing its applicability in sensitive, high-stakes domains.

4 Experiment

4.1 Experiment Setting

Datasets. To evaluate the system's performance within the specific context of the Hong Kong medical system, we constructed the Hong Kong Primary Healthcare Question Answering (HK-PriHCQA) dataset. This dataset comprises 400 Q&A pairs derived from official government publications and public health department documents. To ensure ecological validity, questions were developed using two strategies: extracting existing FAQs and paraphrasing topics from informational documents into natural language queries. As shown in Fig. 3, the dataset covers a broad spectrum of domains relevant to primary healthcare.

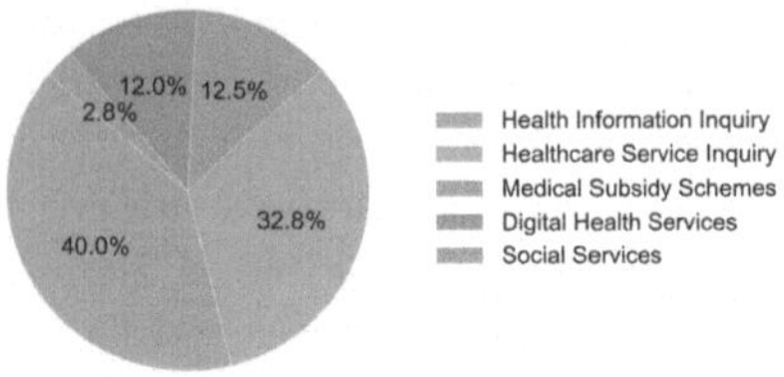

Fig. 3. Distribution of the HK-PriHCQA dataset by category.

Evaluation Metrics. We employed an "LLM-as-a-judge" methodology [9] to capture the nuanced requirements of our target users, prioritizing empathy and clarity alongside accuracy. We defined five key metrics, detailed in Table 1, each evaluated on a 6-point Likert scale (0-5).

Baseline and Ablation. We compared our proposed framework against three configurations to measure component contributions:

- **Baseline Zero-shot LLM (DeepSeek-V3.2-Exp):** Prompts the model directly without retrieval, quantifying inherent parametric knowledge.
- **Local-Only RAG:** A single-source system using only the PHR knowledge base, evaluating performance in isolation from web search.
- **Web-Only RAG:** Relies solely on a web search engine without the white list and re-ranking process, evaluating the risks of unconstrained information sources.

Limitation. The query optimizer component, initially designed to handle ambiguous queries, was disabled for this experiment. This ensures a fair methodological comparison by maintaining a straightforward question-answering task structure rather than introducing the inherent variances of multi-round dialogue.

Table 1. Evaluation Metrics Definition

Metric	Definition
Accuracy	The answer is factually correct and consistent with ground truth.
Completeness	The response covers all aspects of the query and provides the necessary context.
Trustworthiness	The response cites specific, verifiable, and authoritative sources.
Clarity	The response uses clear, simple language, adopts an empathetic tone, and is well-structured and easy to read.
Relevance	The response directly and completely addresses the specific question asked.

4.2 Experiment Result

The evaluation was conducted on a random subset of 80 questions from the HK-PriHCQA dataset. As presented in Table 2, the proposed DRAG framework outperforms all methods, with the highest overall mean score (4.197).

Table 2. Mean scores by metric for each system ($N = 80$)

System	Acc.	Comp.	Trust.	Clar.	Rel.	Avg.
Zero-shot LLM	3.23	3.11	3.35	4.75	4.24	3.74
Web-Only RAG	2.54	2.23	2.64	4.66	3.88	3.19
Local-Only RAG	3.50	3.35	3.43	4.71	**4.34**	3.87
DRAG	**3.95**	**4.03**	**3.98**	**4.86**	4.18	**4.20**

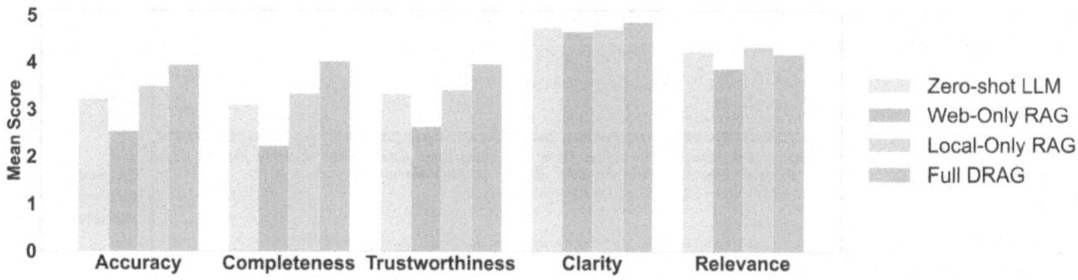

Fig. 4. Comparative performance of system configurations across five metrics.

The results presented in Fig. 4 reveal a clear trade-off among the ablation configurations. The **Web-Only RAG** achieved the highest completeness score but recorded the lowest accuracy, demonstrating that unfiltered information volume can degrade factual integrity. Conversely, the **Local-Only RAG** achieved high relevance owing to its curated content but exhibited the lowest completeness. Our **DRAG framework** effectively addresses these shortcomings by preserving the trustworthiness and relevance of the local knowledge base while leveraging a controlled web-search agent to improve completeness significantly.

4.3 Case Study

To qualitatively assess the retrieval balance, we analyzed a query regarding the acceptance of elderly health vouchers at Zhuhai People's Hospital (Fig. 5). This case highlights the critical need for reasoning-based reconciliation. The **Zero-shot LLM** hallucinated, misinterpreting the query as a social security issue. The **Web-Only RAG** retrieved web content but introduced context pollution from less-related sources. The **Local-Only RAG** provided a factual but outdated response, failing to reflect the latest policy extensions.

The **DRAG framework** was the only method that succeeded. It effectively grounded the query in local knowledge to establish the correct context, then used web retrieval to verify recent, authoritative updates. The Reconciler module prioritized the authoritative, time-valid information over the outdated local entry, producing a coherent and empathetic response. This confirms that our framework can produce contextually reliable and transparent answers even under constrained conditions where static databases lag behind policy changes.

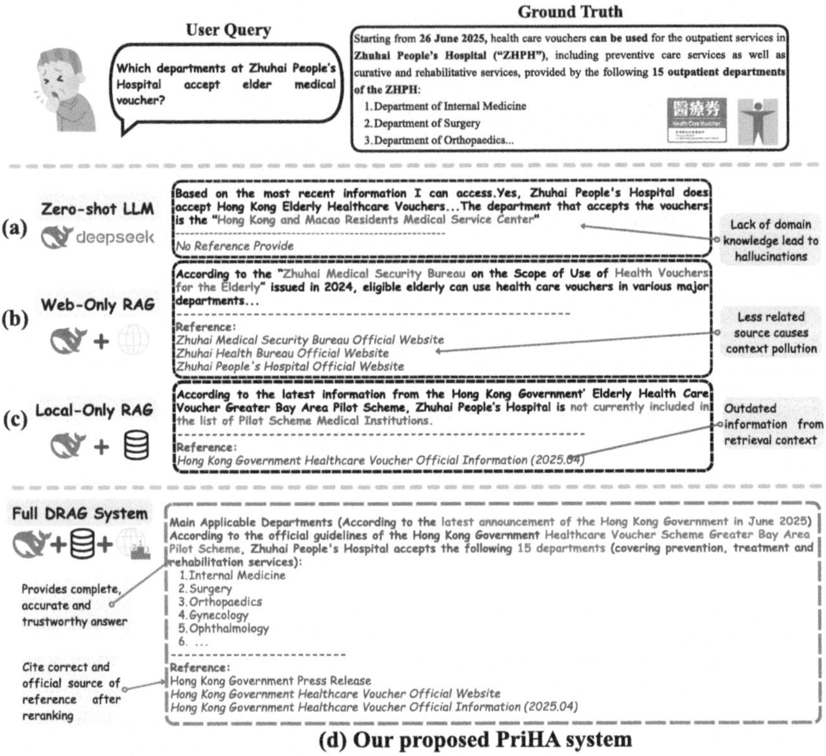

Fig. 5. Qualitative comparison on a query regarding voucher acceptance at Zhuhai People's Hospital.

5 Conclusion

In this paper, we developed PriHA, a Primary Healthcare AI assistant designed to bridge the information gap in Hong Kong's healthcare system. Beyond ensuring safety and factual accuracy, our system proactively steers users toward community-based resources. By integrating fragmented government guidelines into a centralized knowledge base, the system goes beyond merely answering explicit user queries; instead, it strategically recommends relevant primary healthcare services when users do not explicitly ask for them. This approach not only provides accurate, traceable information but also subtly reshapes user perception, encouraging a shift from hospital-reliant care to prevention-oriented self-management. Future development will focus on automating knowledge updates and integrating voice interaction to enhance accessibility for the general public further.

Acknowledgments. The research described in this paper has been partially supported by the General Research Funds from the Hong Kong Research Grants Council (project no. PolyU 15207322, 15200023, 15206024, and 15224524), internal research funds from Hong Kong Polytechnic University (project no. P0042693, P0048625, and P0051361), and Sheertek International (HK) Limited. This work was supported by computational resources provided by The Centre for Large AI Models (CLAIM) of The Hong Kong Polytechnic University.

References

1. Asgari, E., Montaña-Brown, N., Dubois, M., et al.: A framework to assess clinical safety and hallucination rates of LLMs for medical text summarisation. NPJ Digit. Med. (2025)
2. Chen, X., Xiang, J., Lu, S., Liu, Y., He, M., Shi, D.: Evaluating large language models and agents in healthcare: key challenges in clinical applications. Intell. Med. (2025)
3. Fan, W.: A survey on rag meeting LLMS: towards retrieval-augmented large language models. KDD (2024)
4. Fan, W.: Graph neural networks for social recommendation. WWW (2019)
5. Fan, W.: A graph neural network framework for social recommendations. IEEE TKDE (2020)
6. Fan, W.: Computational protein science in the era of large language models (LLMS). arXiv preprint arXiv:2501.10282 (2025)
7. Jang, D.: MedTutor: a retrieval-augmented LLM system for case-based medical education. EMNLP (2025)
8. Kim, Y., et al.: Medical hallucination in foundation models and their impact on healthcare. medRxiv (2025)
9. Li, D.: From generation to judgment: opportunities and challenges of LLM-as-a-judge. EMNLP (2025)
10. Li, S.S.: MEDIQ: question-asking LLMS and a benchmark for reliable interactive clinical reasoning. In: NeurIPS (2024)
11. Lo, T.W., Chan, G.H.: Understanding the life experiences of elderly in social isolation from the social systems perspective: using Hong Kong as an illustrating example. Front. Psychiatry (2023)
12. Ning, L., Fan, W., Li, Q.: Retrieval-augmented purifier for robust LLM-empowered recommendation. ACM Trans. Inf. Syst. (2025)
13. Ning, L.: A survey of WebAgents: towards next-generation AI agents for web automation with large foundation models. KDD (2025)
14. Pal, A.: Generative AI/LLMS for plain language medical information for patients, caregivers and general public: opportunities, risks and ethics. Patient preference and adherence (2025)
15. Pingua, B.: Medical LLMS: fine-tuning vs. retrieval-augmented generation. Bioengineering (2025)
16. Qu, H., Fan, W., Zhao, Z., Li, Q.: TokenREC: learning to tokenize id for LLM-based generative recommendation. IEEE TKDE (2025)
17. Qu, H., Lin, S., Ding, Y., Wang, Y., Fan, W.: Diffusion generative recommendation with continuous tokens (2026)
18. Shekar, S., Pataranutaporn, P., Sarabu, C., Cecchi, G.A., Maes, P.: People OverTrust AI-generated medical advice despite low accuracy. NEJM AI (2025)
19. The Hong Kong council of social service: A study on the physical and mental health and exercise habits of elderly people living alone or in couples in Hong Kong. Research report, The Hong Kong Council of Social Service (HKCSS) (2023)

20. Wang, D., Zhang, S.: Large language models in medical and healthcare fields: applications, advances, and challenges. Artif. Intell. Rev. (2024)
21. Wang, S.: Knowledge graph retrieval-augmented generation for LLM-based recommendation. ACL (2025)
22. Wang, X.: Traffic flow prediction via spatial temporal graph neural network. WWW (2020)
23. Xiong, G., Jin, Q., Lu, Z., Zhang, A.: Benchmarking retrieval-augmented generation for medicine. In: Findings of ACL (2024)
24. Zhao, Z.: Recommender systems in the era of large language models (LLMS). TKDE (2024)
25. Zhou, Y., Qu, H., Liu, Y., Lin, S., Song, L., Fan, W.: HD-PROT: a protein language model for joint sequence-structure modeling with continuous structure tokens. arXiv preprint arXiv:2512.15133 (2025)

FACTOR: Financial Analysis and Consistency-Testing Oriented Representation

Dongqing Li[1], Jiahao Chen[1], Guannan Liu[1], Yijie Chen[1], Shubin Cai[1,2(✉)], and Zhong Ming[2,3]

[1] College of Computer Science and Software Engineering, Shenzhen University, Shenzhen, China
{2400101020,2410103006,2410104039,2410104030}@mails.szu.edu.cn
[2] Laboratory of Artificial Intelligence and Digital Economy (Shenzhen), Shenzhen, China
{shubin,mingz}@szu.edu.cn
[3] Shenzhen Technology University, Shenzhen, China

Abstract. Automated analysis and fact verification of financial reports face significant challenges due to their highly bimodal (charts and text) nature and the difficulty of ensuring computational rigor and logical consistency. Existing methods struggle to balance chart data precision with capturing implicit text correlations, limiting accuracy. We propose FACTOR, a novel bimodal semantic extraction and knowledge graph (KG)-constrained verification framework. FACTOR employs a Heterogeneous Dual-Channel Semantic Modeling mechanism, parsing structural information from charts visually and extracting semantic units from text linguistically, achieving knowledge fusion via cross-modal alignment. Subsequently, the framework constructs a multi-layer financial KG to support consistency verification. In the verification phase, FACTOR introduces KG-constrained semantic reasoning and consistency checking, using knowledge-constrained context augmentation and logical traceability for robust multi-source fact verification. On a test set of financial reports, our FACTOR framework achieves an F1-score of 0.96 in semantic extraction (a 35% improvement over baselines) and an F1-score of 0.98 in fact verification. These results demonstrate FACTOR's high precision and robustness, providing a new paradigm for trustworthy, efficient financial intelligent analysis.

Keywords: Financial Report Analysis · Knowledge Graph · Retrieval-Augmented Generation · Large Language Model

1 Introduction

With the increasing complexity of financial markets and regulatory requirements, the demand for automated, accurate analysis of financial reports has

R. C.-W. Wong et al. (Eds.): PAKDD 2026, LNAI 16617, pp. 335–347, 2027.
https://doi.org/10.1007/978-981-92-1926-1_27

surged [10]. Traditional manual analysis is inefficient and prone to error [6], while modern technologies like Large Language Models (LLMs) still struggle with the unique demands of this domain, particularly regarding trustworthiness and factual grounding [5]. The primary challenges are twofold: first, the dual-modality of reports, which combine charts and text that existing methods, such as those focused only on text or layout [20], fail to integrate effectively. Second, the rigorous nature of fact verification, which demands not only semantic accuracy but also computational soundness and logical consistency—a level of traceable validation that current systems lack [7], thereby limiting their trustworthiness.

To systematically address these challenges in bimodal semantic extraction and fact consistency, this paper proposes FACTOR (Financial Analysis and Consistency-Testing Oriented Representation Framework). This novel framework integrates two key components: a Heterogeneous Dual-Channel Semantic Modeling mechanism to achieve high-precision extraction from both tables and text, and a Knowledge Graph-Constrained Semantic Reasoning and Consistency Checking mechanism, building on advances in graph-based reasoning [17]. By unifying these processes, FACTOR is designed to deliver high-fidelity, verifiable analysis of financial facts, ensuring both accuracy and robustness.

The main contributions of this paper can be summarized as follows:

- We designed a Heterogeneous Dual-Channel Semantic Modeling mechanism. A layout-aware channel parses chart structures and quantitative relationships, while a language channel extracts narrative facts from text. These channels achieve semantic synergy via cross-modal alignment, mapping heterogeneous information into a unified knowledge representation.
- We built the FACTOR framework, centered on an LLM-driven mechanism for knowledge graph (KG) construction, anomaly annotation, and incremental updating. FACTOR automatically identifies semantic and numerical anomalies, using this feedback for incremental updates. This "verify-feedback-update" loop forms a closed-loop system for continuous refinement and scalability.
- We established FACTOR-Bench, a dataset with expert consistency annotations, comprising around 135,000 data entries from financial reports (2023–2025). It is the first to align chart data with text, supporting tasks like semantic extraction, cross-modal fact verification, and anomaly detection, providing a high-quality benchmark.

2 Related Work

2.1 Information Extraction and Knowledge Construction from Financial Reports

Early analysis of financial reports relied on rule-based methods [16], which lacked robustness against diverse formats and complex text. With deep learning, models like FinBERT [2] enabled building Financial Knowledge Graphs [9] for tasks like QA and risk assessment [14]. However, existing work primarily focuses on textual extraction, neglecting the critical cross-modal fusion and consistency verification between table data and text narratives [4], thus hindering rigorous computational validation.

2.2 Bimodal and Multimodal Information Extraction

The bimodal nature of financial reports spurred multimodal models like LayoutLM [20] and DocFormer [1] that integrate text, layout, and visual data. Despite success in general document understanding, they face challenges in finance. Key limitations include insufficient precision for numerical table values compared to specialized parsers [15], and difficulty in performing high-level semantic alignment, as they often fuse at the feature level. Our work employs a heterogeneous dual-channel approach, separating high-precision table parsing from text analysis before unifying the results, thereby bypassing the precision limitations of end-to-end multimodal models.

2.3 Application of Knowledge Graphs and RAG in Verification

Retrieval-Augmented Generation (RAG) [11] mitigates LLM hallucination [8] by retrieving external evidence, enhancing content fidelity [21]. However, traditional RAG relies on vector search over text chunks and struggles with complex logical or computational constraints. GraphRAG, integrating KGs, provides more structured, logical context via multi-hop retrieval [3, 12]. While KGs are ideal for enforcing the computational rigor needed in finance, existing GraphRAG methods are mostly applied to general QA [13] and have not been adapted for bimodal financial fact extraction, fusion, and consistency verification.

Our FACTOR framework addresses this gap. It structures extracted financial knowledge into a KG, which is then used as a computational constraint and for context augmentation. This guides the LLM in the final fact consistency verification, ensuring high trustworthiness.

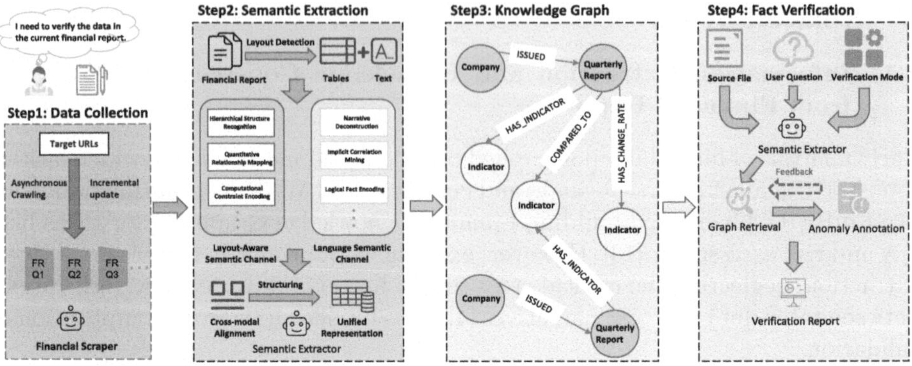

Fig. 1. FACTOR consists of four main steps: (1) Utilizing an integrated Scrapy framework to perform targeted data acquisition from websites, (2) Employing a Heterogeneous Dual-Channel Semantic Modeling mechanism to extract semantic data, (3) Using financial knowledge to construct a knowledge graph, (4) Enhancing fact verification through a "verification-feedback-update" loop.

3 Methodology

Figure 1 shows the overall workflow of our framework, which mainly includes four stages: Data Collection, Semantic Extraction, Knowledge Graph Construction, and Fact Verification.

3.1 Stage 1: Data Collection

In this stage, our Financial Scraper, a distributed Python-based crawler, automates data acquisition. The process initiates by generating Target URLs for quarterly Financial Reports (FR) from the CNINFO website, covering the most recent three years. As illustrated in the workflow, the scraper executes an Asynchronous Crawling strategy for efficient, large-scale downloading and employs an Incremental update mechanism to monitor and fetch newly published reports periodically. To ensure the compliance and stability of the data collection, the system integrates anti-scraping techniques (e.g., User-Agent rotation, IP proxy pools) and file integrity verification. The resulting output is a complete and timely corpus of raw financial reports, with metadata structurally stored to provide a reliable data foundation for subsequent processing.

3.2 Stage 2: Semantic Extraction

Upon completion of data acquisition, the system initiates the semantic extraction phase, governed by the Heterogeneous Dual-Channel Semantic Modeling (HDCSM) (Algorithm 1). This paradigm leverages a Large Language Model (LLM) integrated with a dual-channel mechanism to process multi-modal financial information. Initially, a customized toolchain, MinerU+ [18], converts ingested PDFs into two distinct formats: hierarchical Markdown files, which preserve the semantic structure of narratives for the Language Semantic Channel (LSC), and structured HTML <table> elements, providing parsable input for the Layout-Aware Semantic Channel (LASC). This conversion is followed by comprehensive data cleansing and standardization to remove artifacts (e.g., pagination, OCR noise) and unify currency symbols, temporal expressions, and numerical formats, ensuring normalized, consistent input for extraction.

Following preprocessing, the dual channels are activated to achieve semantic alignment and high-precision fact extraction. The Layout-Aware Semantic Channel (LASC) tasks the LLM with processing the HTML table data, where it performs Hierarchical Structure Recognition to comprehend complex headers and merged cells, alongside Quantitative Relationship Mapping to identify units, temporal periods, and encode summation logic. Concurrently, the Language Semantic Channel (LSC) processes the narrative Markdown, executing Narrative Deconstruction to dissect paragraphs into core factual statements and Implicit Correlation Mining to link textual facts with tabular data. In the final step, the LLM, as the core Semantic Extractor, performs Structuring and Cross-modal Alignment, fusing and validating the tabular entities from the LASC against the textual facts from the LSC. This stage concludes by outputting a Unified Representation (S_json), providing a high-fidelity input for subsequent knowledge graph construction.

Algorithm 1. Heterogeneous Dual-Channel Semantic Modeling

Require: D_{pdf}: Raw financial reports; $MinerU^{+}$: Parser for format normalization; LLM: Large language model
Ensure: S_{json}: Unified structured JSON output

```
(D_md, D_html) ← MinerU⁺(D_pdf)                                ▷ Preprocessing
Entities_LASC, Facts_LSC, S_json ← ∅
                                    ▷ Layout-Aware Semantic Channel (LASC)
for each table ∈ EXTRACT_TABLES(D_html) do
    P_v ← BUILD_LASC_PROMPT(table)
    E ← CALL_LLM(LLM, P_v)
    Entities_LASC.add(E)
end for
                                          ▷ Language Semantic Channel (LSC)
for each chunk ∈ EXTRACT_TEXT(D_md) do
    P_l ← BUILD_LSC_PROMPT(chunk)
    F ← CALL_LLM(LLM, P_l)
    Facts_LSC.add(F)
end for
                                                  ▷ Cross-modal Alignment
U_LASC ← Entities_LASC
for each f ∈ Facts_LSC do
    e ← FIND_MATCH(f, U_LASC)
    S ← STRUCTURE(f, e)
    S_json.add(S)
    if e ≠ NULL then
        U_LASC.remove(e)
    end if
end for
S_json.add(STRUCTURE_REMAINING(U_LASC))
return S_json
```

3.3 Stage 3: Knowledge Graph Construction

Subsequent to the Heterogeneous Dual-Channel Semantic Modeling, the system commences the knowledge graph construction phase, translating the structured JSON output into a financial knowledge graph (KG) that serves as the core support layer for fact verification. The extracted entities and relationships are imported into a Neo4j graph database. To ensure data integrity and prevent redundant entity generation, the system performs rigorous node deduplication, attribute merging, and logical consistency checks, such as validating composite primary keys (e.g., stock code and reporting period).

The graph is structured according to a predefined schema comprising three core node types: Company (with attributes like stock code and full_name), QuarterlyReport (with attributes like report_period), and Indicator (with attributes like semantics and value). These nodes are interconnected by key relationship types, including ISSUED (linking a Company to its QuarterlyReport), HAS_INDICATOR (linking a QuarterlyReport to its financial Indicators), and COMPARED_TO/HAS_CHANGE_RATE (linking an Indicator to other reports for temporal analysis). The completed KG enables multi-granularity semantic recall via a GraphRAG retrieval mechanism, facilitating data traceability. Ultimately, this structured knowledge base provides the essential context and explicit logical paths required for the subsequent LLM-based graph-augmented reasoning and fact consistency verification, ensuring an interpretable and knowledge-enhanced validation process.

3.4 Stage 4: Fact Verification

Upon constructing the knowledge graph, the system enters the fact verification stage, leveraging the KG and Large Language Models (LLMs) to verify the consistency and factuality of financial statements. This process begins with GraphRAG, which performs hierarchical retrieval over the Neo4j graph. Unlike conventional RAG, it locates relevant nodes (e.g., Company, Indicator) and traverses relational edges (e.g., HAS_INDICATOR, COMPARED_TO) to construct a precise subgraph context as factual grounding. This graph evidence and the target statement are then jointly processed by the LLM, which performs both semantic matching and logical consistency reasoning, using the numerical attributes from the graph as explicit constraints to validate the claim (e.g., checking a reported growth rate against computed graph values).

Following reasoning, a consistency evaluation and anomaly annotation module quantitatively assesses the LLM's output, computing numerical, semantic, and logical scores and marking any deviations that exceed predefined tolerance thresholds. This output is crucial for the framework's feedback-driven incremental update mechanism; detected anomalies are fed back to the knowledge graph module for node correction and realignment. This "Verification → Feedback → Update" cycle forms a closed-loop ecosystem, enabling continuous refinement and self-adaptation. Finally, the system outputs a Fact Consistency Report, which includes confidence scores, graph provenance paths, and anomaly annotations, providing interpretable, structured evidence for auditing.

4 Experiments and Results

We evaluate the framework through extensive experiments, covering two aspects: semantic extraction and fact verification. It is validated for its effectiveness and robustness in real-world financial reporting scenarios.

4.1 Dataset

Our evaluation uses 450 quarterly financial reports (2023–2025) from the CNINFO (Juchao) website, totaling 135,000 data entries. The reports include balance sheets (nested tables, hierarchical items), income statements (complex computations), and cash flow statements (multi-level classifications). Industry distribution: Manufacturing 32%, IT 18%, Pharmaceuticals 12%, Financial 10%, Others 28%. Reports span all fiscal quarters (Q1–Q4) with balanced time coverage. We use 350 reports for training (knowledge graph construction and model adaptation) and 100 for testing, with the test set manually annotated by experts.

4.2 Evaluation Metrics

We evaluate the framework's two main stages using distinct metrics.

For the semantic extraction stage, we adopt standard metrics to measure the quality of structured information extraction:

- **Precision (P)**: The ratio of correctly extracted semantic units to the total units extracted by the system.
- **Recall (R)**: The ratio of correctly extracted units to the total ground-truth annotated semantic units.
- **F1-score (F1)**: The harmonic mean of Precision and Recall:

$$\text{F1-score} = 2 \times \frac{\text{Precision} \times \text{Recall}}{\text{Precision} + \text{Recall}} \tag{1}$$

- **Semantic Similarity (SS)**: For partial matches, we use cosine similarity of semantic embeddings to assess the closeness between extracted results and ground-truth annotations.

For the fact verification stage, we designed metrics to evaluate numerical validation, semantic alignment, and anomaly detection:

- **Numeric F1-score (NF1)**: The harmonic mean of **Numeric Precision (NP)** and **Numeric Recall (NR)**. We utilize a tolerance-based matching mechanism:

$$\text{NumericMatch}(v_{\text{pred}}, v_{\text{gold}}) = \begin{cases} 1, & \text{if } |v_{\text{pred}} - v_{\text{gold}}| \leq \epsilon \\ 0, & \text{otherwise} \end{cases} \tag{2}$$

  where ϵ is the acceptable tolerance threshold.
- **Semantic Alignment Accuracy (SAA)**: The proportion of correct judgments regarding the semantic consistency between text narratives and structured data.
- **Anomaly Detection Rate (ADR)**: The proportion of annotated anomalous facts that were successfully identified by the system, evaluating its sensitivity to financial anomalies.

Collectively, these metrics provide a multi-dimensional evaluation. The extraction metrics measure the quality of bimodal information capture, while the verification metrics validate the effectiveness of the knowledge graph-constrained mechanism in computation, reasoning, and anomaly detection.

4.3 Baseline Methods

We benchmark FACTOR against two representative paradigms. The first is DOCSGPT, a mainstream RAG-based document Q&A system that employs vectorized retrieval over text chunks. This approach is ill-suited for financial reports as it fails to capture the structured associations between tabular data and textual narratives and lacks explicit constraints for numerical computation. The second baseline is OpenFactCheck [19], an open-source fact verification framework. While effective for general-purpose tasks, its reliance on unstructured semantic matching is incapable of handling the complex computational dependencies (e.g., Net Profit = Operating Revenue - Costs - Taxes) inherent in financial data and lacks a unified semantic representation for cross-modal information.

4.4 Semantic Extraction Results

Table 1 shows the performance comparison of different methods on the semantic extraction task. Our experimental evaluation reveals several key insights.

Table 1. Performance comparison on the semantic extraction task.

Method	P	R	F1	SS
DOCSGPT	0.67	0.55	0.61	0.80
FACTOR (ours)	0.97	0.94	0.96	0.95

FACTOR significantly outperforms DOCSGPT, achieving a high F1-score of 0.96 (compared to 0.61) with excellent Precision (0.97) and Recall (0.94). This superiority stems directly from our Heterogeneous Dual-Channel Semantic Modeling. While DOCSGPT treats complex reports as simple text chunks, losing structural information, FACTOR's Layout-Aware Semantic Channel (LASC), enhanced by MinerU+, accurately parses table structures, while its Language Semantic Channel (LSC) handles narratives. This dual approach enables effective cross-modal alignment, overcoming the limitations of standard vector-based retrieval which fails to capture the implicit hierarchies and computational constraints inherent in financial data.

Furthermore, FACTOR achieves superior Semantic Similarity (0.95 vs. 0.80), demonstrating its ability to maintain semantic integrity, not just numerical accuracy. Its HTML DOM parsing and semantic annotation mechanism successfully associates each numerical value with its complete context (metric name, time period, unit), even within complex tables featuring merged cells or multi-level headers. In contrast, DOCSGPT's text-chunking strategy breaks these vital contextual associations. These findings validate that our tailored dual-channel approach, which preserves both numerical precision and cross-modal semantic links, is essential for accurately processing the bimodal nature of financial reports and significantly outperforms general-purpose methods.

4.5 Fact Verification Results

After constructing the financial knowledge graph from the training set, we evaluated the fact verification performance under different configurations.Table 2 reports the performance of each method on the fact verification task.

Table 2. Comparison of Fact Verification Performance.

Method	NP	NR	NF1	SAA	ADR
OpenFactCheck	0.93	0.57	0.70	0.59	0.85
FACTOR (ours)	0.98	0.99	0.98	0.99	0.92

FACTOR demonstrates significant advantages in numerical and computational verification, achieving a Numeric F1-score (NF1) of 0.98, far surpassing OpenFactCheck's 0.70. This gap is driven by FACTOR's knowledge graph-constrained verification mechanism. By explicitly modeling financial entities and computational relationships (e.g., "Assets = Liabilities + Equity") as a graph, the system ensures adherence to accounting standards. In contrast, OpenFactCheck relies on semantic matching, failing to guarantee rigor for complex calculations. This is evident in FACTOR's 0.99 Numeric Recall on mathematical relationship checks (e.g., Net Profit calculations), while OpenFactCheck's 0.57 recall indicates it fails to cover most computationally verifiable facts.

The superiority is even more pronounced in cross-modal validation, where FACTOR achieves 0.99 Semantic Alignment Accuracy (SAA) compared to OpenFactCheck's 0.59. This fundamental difference arises because FACTOR's Heterogeneous Dual-Channel Semantic Modeling creates a unified representation of tabular data and textual narratives, enabling it to accurately judge consistency between them. OpenFactCheck, lacking this cross-modal alignment, treats tables and text as independent evidence. Furthermore, while both systems have comparable Anomaly Detection Rates (0.92 vs 0.85), FACTOR's results are highly interpretable, providing a traceable evidence chain through the knowledge graph that explains why a fact conflicts, which OpenFactCheck's statistical approach lacks.

4.6 Contribution of Core Components

To verify the contribution of each component in FACTOR, we conducted a systematic ablation study. Table 3 shows the results.

The ablation study confirms the criticality of our proposed components: removing the Heterogeneous Dual-Channel Semantic Modeling (HDCSM) module caused the semantic extraction F1-score to plummet by 52% (from 0.96 to 0.44), highlighting its essential function in processing tables and text through specialized pathways. Similarly, eliminating the Verify-Feedback-Update (VFU) mechanism was detrimental, reducing the fact verification F1-score by 42% (from

Table 3. Contribution Results of Each Component.

Method	Semantic Extraction F1	Fact Verification F1
FACTOR (w/o HDCSM)	0.44	-
FACTOR (w/o VFU)	-	0.56
FACTOR (full)	0.96	0.98

0.98 to 0.56), which demonstrates that dynamic graph refinement—driven by anomaly detection and incremental updates—is indispensable for maintaining precision. These modules work in synergy to create a positive feedback loop: HDCSM's high-precision extraction builds a reliable knowledge graph, which in turn allows the VFU to perform accurate verification, and these verification results are then fed back for graph refinement. This interdependent "extraction → graph → verification → refinement" cycle is what ensures the system's overall robustness and scalability.

4.7 Discussion and Integration of Experiments

Our experimental results comprehensively validate FACTOR's design, demonstrating significant advantages over baseline methods. In semantic extraction, FACTOR achieved an F1-score of 0.96 (+35% vs. DOCSGPT), confirming the superiority of Heterogeneous Dual-Channel Semantic Modeling (HDCSM). In fact verification, it achieved a 0.98 Numeric F1-score (+28% vs. OpenFactCheck), proving that knowledge graph-constrained verification provides more reliable logical reasoning. This effectiveness stems from HDCSM's ability to precisely align bimodal table and text data, while the knowledge graph structurally encodes computational constraints and temporal dependencies—capabilities that vector-based retrieval (like DOCSGPT) and general fact-checkers (like OpenFactCheck) lack. The framework's design is completed by a verify-feedback-update (VFU) closed loop, which ensures adaptive evolution through anomaly annotation and incremental updating. Future work will build on this foundation by expanding to dynamic content like XBRL, integrating temporal reasoning for policy changes, and developing personalized analysis functions for specific user needs, such as investor risk assessment or regulatory compliance.

5 Conclusion

The FACTOR framework proposed in this paper systematically addresses the challenges of dual-modal information extraction and fact consistency verification in automated financial report analysis through its Heterogeneous Dual-Channel Semantic Modeling and knowledge graph-constrained verification mechanisms.

Experimental results show the framework achieves an F1-score of 0.96 in semantic extraction and 0.98 in fact verification, significantly outperforming existing baseline methods. The core innovations lie in using layout-aware and language dual channels to process tables and text, respectively, achieving high-precision cross-modal semantic alignment; and utilizing an LLM-based financial knowledge graph to provide explicit logical constraints and traceable reasoning paths for fact verification, effectively reducing the risk of large model hallucinations while enhancing interpretability and trustworthiness. FACTOR provides a scalable methodological paradigm for building automated, trustworthy intelligent financial analysis systems. Future work will expand in three directions: supporting dynamic parsing of XBRL formats and multimedia financial reports; enhancing temporal reasoning capabilities to handle accounting policy changes and cross-period comparisons; and introducing personalized analysis mechanisms to customize knowledge graph queries and verification strategies for different user roles (investors, auditors, regulators). These improvements will further enhance the framework's applicability and practical value in real-world scenarios such as risk assessment, compliance review, and investment decision support.

Acknowledgment. This work was supported by the National Natural Science Foundation of China (Grant No. 62276168, Research on Readable Multi-Agent Interactive Decision Model, 2023-01-01 to 2026-12-31) and Director Fund of Guangdong Laboratory of Artificial Intelligence and Digital Economy (Shenzhen) (24420001).

References

1. Appalaraju, S., Jasani, B., Kota, B.U., Xie, Y., Manmatha, R.: Docformer: end-to-end transformer for document understanding. In: Proceedings of the IEEE/CVF International Conference on Computer Vision, pp. 993–1003 (2021)
2. Araci, D.: FinBERT: financial sentiment analysis with pre-trained language models (2019). arXiv:1908.10063 arXiv preprint
3. Bahr, L., et al.: Knowledge graph enhanced retrieval-augmented generation for failure mode and effects analysis. J. Ind. Inf. Integr. **45**, 100807 (2025)
4. Chen, Z., et al.: FinQA: a dataset of numerical reasoning over financial data. In: Proceedings of the 2021 Conference on Empirical Methods in Natural Language Processing, pp. 3697–3711 (2021)
5. Cossio, M.: A comprehensive taxonomy of hallucinations in large language models (2025). arXiv:2508.01781 arXiv preprint
6. Elumilade, O.O., Ogundeji, I.A., Ozoemenam, G., Omokhoa, H., Omowole, B.M.: Advancing audit efficiency through statistical sampling and compliance best practices in financial reporting. IRE J. **7**(9), 434–437 (2024)
7. Graves, L.: Understanding the promise and limits of automated fact-checking (2018)
8. Huang, Y., et al.: Distribution-guided extraction for cross-platform educational knowledge graph construction. In: 2025 International Joint Conference on Neural Networks (IJCNN), pp. 1–7. IEEE (2025)
9. Kertkeidkachorn, N., Nararatwong, R., Xu, Z., Ichise, R.: FinKG: a core financial knowledge graph for financial analysis. In: 2023 IEEE 17th International Conference on Semantic Computing (ICSC), pp. 90–93. IEEE (2023)

10. Kothandapani, H.P.: Automating financial compliance with AI: a new era in regulatory technology (RegTech). Int. J. Sci. Res. Arch. **11**, 2646–2659 (2024)
11. Lewis, P., et al.: Retrieval-augmented generation for knowledge-intensive NLP tasks. Adv. Neural. Inf. Process. Syst. **33**, 9459–9474 (2020)
12. Liu, W., et al.: K-BERT: enabling language representation with knowledge graph. In: Proceedings of the AAAI Conference on Artificial Intelligence, vol. 34, pp. 2901–2908 (2020)
13. Lu, Y., Goi, S.Y., Zhao, X., Wang, J.: Biomedical knowledge graph: a survey of domains, tasks, and real-world applications (2025). arXiv:2501.11632 arXiv preprint
14. Peng, C., Xia, F., Naseriparsa, M., Osborne, F.: Knowledge graphs: opportunities and challenges. Artif. Intell. Rev. **56**(11), 13071–13102 (2023)
15. Pouyanfar, S., et al.: A survey on deep learning: algorithms, techniques, and applications. ACM Comput. Surv. (CSUR) **51**(5), 1–36 (2018)
16. Riloff, E.: Automatically generating extraction patterns from untagged text. In: Proceedings of the National Conference on Artificial Intelligence, pp. 1044–1049 (1996)
17. Sarmah, B., et al.: HybridRAG: integrating knowledge graphs and vector retrieval augmented generation for efficient information extraction. In: Proceedings of the 5th ACM International Conference on AI in Finance, pp. 608–616 (2024)
18. Wang, B., et al.: Mineru: an open-source solution for precise document content extraction. arXiv preprint arXiv:2409.18839 (2024)
19. Wang, Y., et al.: Openfactcheck: building, benchmarking customized fact-checking systems and evaluating the factuality of claims and LLMs. In: Proceedings of the 31st International Conference on Computational Linguistics, pp. 11399–11421 (2025)
20. Xu, Y., et al.: LayoutLM: pre-training of text and layout for document image understanding. In: Proceedings of the 26th ACM SIGKDD International Conference on Knowledge Discovery & Data Mining, pp. 1192–1200 (2020)
21. Zhang, J., Cai, S., Jiang, Z., Xiao, J., Ming, Z.: Firerobbrain: planning for a firefighting robot using knowledge graph and large language model. In: 2024 10th IEEE International Conference on Intelligent Data and Security (IDS), pp. 37–41. IEEE (2024)

Multimodal RAG: Text-Informed Cross-Modal Enhancement for Efficient Local Deployment

Chia-Yi Lin(✉) and Ming-Syan Chen

Department of Electrical Engineering, National Taiwan University, Taipei, Taiwan
cylin@arbor.ee.ntu.edu.tw, mschen@cc.ee.ntu.edu.tw

Abstract. Multimodal Retrieval-Augmented Generation (RAG) systems face significant challenges in maintaining cross-modal coherence when processing documents containing both text and visual elements. Traditional approaches suffer from modal isolation, where text and image retrieval operate independently, often resulting in responses that combine unrelated textual and visual content from disparate sources. This problem is exacerbated in resource-constrained environments where small language models (SLMs) lack the sophisticated instruction-following capabilities required for complex cross-modal enhancement tasks. We propose Text-Informed Multimodal RAG, a novel approach that leverages text retrieval results to enhance image retrieval through text-informed cross-modal enhancement. Our method addresses the modal isolation problem by first performing text retrieval, then extracting discriminative keywords using TF-IDF analysis to create enhanced queries for image search. We introduce a new re-ranking mechanism that prioritizes images from the same source documents as retrieved text, ensuring cross-modal coherence. This approach circumvents the limitations of small vision-language models by employing deterministic keyword extraction rather than complex instruction following. Experimental evaluation under a paired-comparison design shows consistent improvements across multiple metrics within the evaluated setting. Our approach yields measurable improvements in image retrieval quality (MRR: +20.1%, nDCG: +22.0%), while maintaining computational efficiency suitable for local deployment scenarios. Comparative analysis indicates that our text-informed method provides more stable cross-modal retrieval performance than SLM-aided enhancement under small-model deployment constraints. These results suggest that structure-aware cross-modal enhancement can improve cross-modal consistency under resource-constrained multimodal RAG deployment settings.

Keywords: Multimodal RAG · Cross-Modal Enhancement · Vision-Language Models · Document Understanding · Local Deployment · Small Language Model · Query Enhancement

R. C.-W. Wong et al. (Eds.): PAKDD 2026, LNAI 16617, pp. 348–359, 2027.
https://doi.org/10.1007/978-981-92-1926-1_28

1 Introduction

Retrieval-Augmented Generation (RAG) [13] has emerged as a prominent paradigm for enhancing large language models by enabling them to dynamically access external knowledge during inference. Unlike pure generative models that rely solely on pre-trained parameters [2,20], RAG combines retrieval mechanisms with text generation, thereby improving factual accuracy and reducing hallucinations [21]. Subsequent work has extended the original RAG framework through various improvements, including Fusion-in-Decoder [11] and Dense Passage Retrieval [12]. While this approach has shown remarkable success in text-only domains, many real-world information sources are inherently *multimodal*, comprising both textual and visual elements. Examples include scientific articles containing diagrams and tables [15], technical manuals with illustrations [16], and educational materials with charts and figures [22]. Despite this prevalence, existing RAG systems struggle to fully leverage multimodal documents during retrieval and generation.

Recent studies have begun extending RAG to multimodal settings [26], introducing models capable of retrieving both text and images to answer user queries. Vision-language models such as CLIP [18] have enabled cross-modal retrieval capabilities, while recent work on multimodal understanding [14] has shown promise for combining visual and textual information. However, several fundamental challenges remain unresolved. First, multimodal retrieval pipelines often treat text and image retrieval independently, leading to inconsistent results. For instance, a user asking about the *"CNN architecture"* might receive textual descriptions from one source and visual diagrams from another, potentially resulting in contradictory responses. Second, user queries frequently lack explicit visual descriptors, causing image retrieval modules to struggle in selecting relevant figures or diagrams [6]. This issue is particularly pronounced in academic or educational contexts where short, task-oriented queries (e.g., "Explain step 3 of algorithm X") implicitly reference associated figures without explicitly mentioning visual features.

Furthermore, spatial and contextual relationships between modalities are often overlooked. Document understanding research has highlighted the importance of layout information [10,25], where text and figures co-located on the same page typically explain the same concept. Recent work on document AI [1,9] has emphasized the significance of preserving spatial relationships within documents. Ignoring this *page-level context* results in multimodal answers that may combine semantically related text with unrelated images, diminishing the faithfulness and usability of generated responses [24]. Modern vision-language document understanding systems like ColPali [7] have made progress in this direction, but gaps remain in cross-modal coherence for RAG applications.

To address these limitations, this work introduces a novel multimodal RAG system that promotes *cross-modal consistency* between retrieved text and images. Our approach operates in three stages. First, we perform conventional text retrieval using dense passage retrieval techniques [12] to obtain top-ranked textual segments. Second, we apply *TF-IDF-based query enhancement* [19] to extract salient keywords from retrieved texts, enriching the original query for subsequent image retrieval. This addresses the query expansion problem that has been extensively studied in information retrieval [4]. Third, we incorporate a *source-aware ranking* strategy that re-ranks candidate images to favor those originating from the same documents and pages as the retrieved text. This pipeline explicitly exploits spatial alignment within documents, thereby improving multimodal coherence.

We evaluate our system on a curated dataset of academic papers and diverse question types, including factual and definitional queries. Our evaluation methodology follows established practices in multimodal question answering and document understanding [16]. Experimental results show consistent improvements in retrieval precision (from 0.2583 to 0.5625) and faithfulness scores under the same lightweight deployment setting. We compare representative baseline configurations under identical small-model constraints and observe consistent improvements across metrics such as Mean Reciprocal Rank (MRR), Normalized Discounted Cumulative Gain (nDCG), and response quality measures.

Our contributions are summarized as follows:

- **Query Enhancement for Visual Retrieval:** We propose a lightweight keyword extraction mechanism based on TF-IDF analysis [19] that bridges the semantic gap between textual queries and image retrieval.
- **Source-Aware Multimodal Ranking:** We design a re-ranking module that aligns text and image sources, improving cross-modal consistency in retrieved evidence. This builds upon recent work in document-level multimodal understanding [1] and cross-modal alignment.
- **Page-Level Context Matching:** We incorporate intra-document spatial cues, leveraging the proximity of figures and text to enhance multimodal grounding. This approach is inspired by Layout-Aware document understanding models [10,25].
- **Resource-Efficient Design:** Our approach is specifically designed to work with small vision-language models, addressing practical deployment constraints without relying on large-scale model capacity.

Our work focuses on cross-modal inconsistency in multimodal RAG and proposes a practical approach for document-centric settings. The text-informed enhancement is designed for resource-constrained local deployment.

2 Related Work

2.1 Multimodal RAG and Document Understanding

Retrieval-Augmented Generation has transformed how language models access external knowledge. RAG [13] introduced the foundational framework combining dense retrieval with generation, while Fusion-in-Decoder [11] showed that jointly processing multiple retrieved passages could further improve performance. However, these early systems operated exclusively on text, losing crucial information embedded in visual elements of real-world documents.

Recent efforts have extended RAG to multimodal settings. CLIP [18] enabled cross-modal retrieval through vision-language pretraining, though adapting it to document-heavy scenarios remained challenging. RA-CM3 [26] made an early attempt at multimodal RAG but required explicit image-text pairs that are not always available in complex documents. MuRAG [5] combined BM25 for text and CLIP for images with cross-attention fusion, but performed retrieval independently for each modality—resulting in text from one source and images from another. This modal isolation problem creates inconsistent responses when textual and visual content originate from different documents. Wiki-LLaVA [3] introduced hierarchical retrieval with knowledge graphs, though this approach requires structured knowledge bases. OMG-QA [17] combined dense and sparse retrieval but similarly suffered from independent modality processing.

For document understanding, vision-language models have moved beyond traditional OCR-then-NLP pipelines. LayoutLM [25] pioneered combining text, visual features, and positional information through 2D position embeddings, though it still relied on OCR preprocessing. BROS [10] improved layout modeling using relative position representations. ColPali [7] represented a significant advance by treating entire document pages as visual objects, computing similarities directly between query text and image patches through late interaction. This OCR-free approach achieved strong results on document retrieval benchmarks. However, ColPali focuses on page-level retrieval and does not address how to integrate retrieved visual elements with textual content for coherent answer generation—particularly when information must be synthesized from multiple sources.

2.2 Cross-Modal Enhancement Techniques

Query enhancement has long been central to information retrieval effectiveness. Dense Passage Retrieval [12] showed that learned dense representations could improve query understanding, while methods like Query2doc [23] and HyDE [8] introduced generating pseudo-documents or hypothetical answers to bridge query-document gaps. These neural approaches showed promise but remained focused on text-only scenarios.

The challenge intensifies in multimodal settings where user queries often reference visual elements implicitly. A query like "explain the architecture in the paper" contains no explicit visual descriptors, yet relevant diagrams are crucial for comprehensive understanding. Traditional query enhancement methods struggle because they lack mechanisms to bridge between textual queries and visual content. Large language models have opened new possibilities for query refinement, but their computational requirements often exceed constraints in privacy-sensitive or resource-limited deployments.

Our work addresses these gaps by proposing a text-informed enhancement strategy specifically designed for multimodal documents. Rather than treating text and image retrieval as independent processes, we leverage textual retrieval results to guide visual search through deterministic keyword extraction. Unlike methods requiring complex instruction-following from large models, our TF-IDF-based approach [19] provides reliable enhancement suitable for local deployment with small vision-language models. Furthermore, we explicitly model spatial relationships within documents—recognizing that figures typically relate to surrounding text—through source-aware re-ranking that maintains cross-modal coherence. This design philosophy prioritizes practical deployability while achieving competitive performance through structure-aware processing rather than model scale.

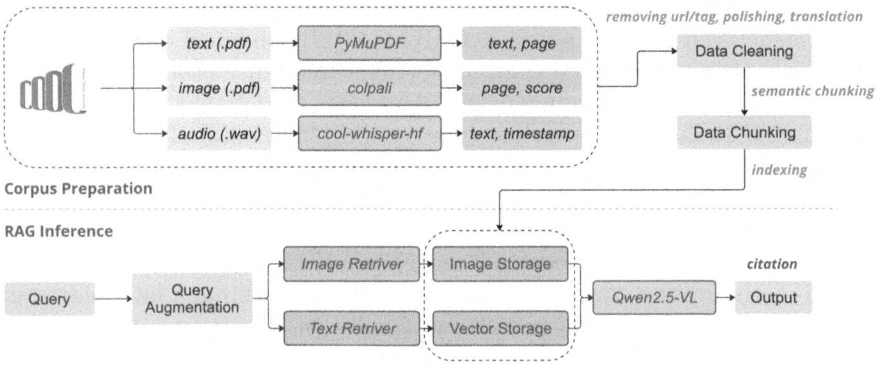

Fig. 1. Overall architecture of our Text-Informed Multimodal RAG system.

3 Methods

3.1 System Architecture

Our Text-Informed Multimodal RAG system addresses three fundamental challenges: modal isolation in text-image retrieval, semantic gaps between user queries and visual content, and computational constraints limiting large model deployment.

Figure 1 illustrates our system architecture, consisting of corpus preparation and RAG inference phases. The corpus preparation phase processes multimodal documents through specialized pipelines—PyMuPDF for text extraction, ColPali for image indexing, and Cool-Whisper-HF for audio transcription. The RAG inference phase implements our core contribution: text-informed cross-modal enhancement that bridges text and image retrieval through position-aware mechanisms.

The core insight driving our design is that textual and visual elements within documents exhibit strong spatial coherence—figures typically relate to surrounding text, and tables support nearby discussions. Rather than treating these modalities as independent information sources, we leverage this inherent document structure. Our approach follows a three-stage pipeline: text retrieval, text-informed query enhancement, and position-aware image re-ranking.

Traditional multimodal RAG systems suffer from what we term the *modal isolation problem*, where independent retrieval may select high-quality text from one paper while choosing diagrams from an entirely different source, resulting in potentially contradictory responses. Our method aims to address this by conditioning image retrieval on textual context, ensuring cross-modal coherence through document-level source matching.

3.2 Component Design

Text Retrieval and Query Enhancement. User queries often lack sufficient visual descriptors for effective image retrieval. To enrich semantic context, we perform dense passage retrieval over text chunks using cosine similarity:

$$\mathrm{sim}(q, t_i) = \frac{\mathbf{e}_q \cdot \mathbf{e}_{t_i}}{\|\mathbf{e}_q\| \|\mathbf{e}_{t_i}\|}, \tag{1}$$

and select the top-K passages:

$$R_{\text{text}} = \mathrm{TopK}(\{\mathrm{sim}(q, t_i)\}, K). \tag{2}$$

To identify discriminative terms from the retrieved passages, we apply TF-IDF:

$$\text{TF-IDF}(w) = \mathrm{tf}(w, R_{\text{text}}) \times \log\left(\frac{|R_{\text{text}}|}{\mathrm{df}(w)}\right), \tag{3}$$

where $\mathrm{df}(w)$ denotes the number of retrieved passages containing term w. The top-ranked terms form the keyword set K, which is concatenated with the original query to construct the enhanced query.

Text-Informed Image Re-Ranking. The enhanced query is used to retrieve an expanded candidate image pool (3× the final requirement). To improve cross-modal consistency, we introduce both content-level and page-level alignment between retrieved text passages and image candidates.

Let S denote the set of (document, page) pairs extracted from R_{text}:

$$S = \{(f_j, p_j) \mid t_j \in R_{\text{text}}\}. \tag{4}$$

For each candidate image v_i from document f_i and page p_i, two bonus terms are computed.

Keyword-based content matching at the page level:

$$w_{\text{keyword}}(v_i) = \lambda_1 \sum_{k \in K} \mathbb{I}[k \subset \mathrm{PageText}(v_i)], \tag{5}$$

Page-level structural alignment:

$$w_{\text{source}}(v_i) = \lambda_2 \cdot \mathbb{I}[(f_i, p_i) \in S], \tag{6}$$

The final ranking score is computed as:

$$\text{score}_{\text{final}}(v_i) = \text{score}_{\text{retrieval}}(v_i) + w_{\text{keyword}}(v_i) + w_{\text{source}}(v_i). \tag{7}$$

In our implementation, we set $\lambda_1 = 0.3$, while λ_2 is a fixed structural bonus. Images are re-ranked according to Eq. (7), and the top-5 results are forwarded to response generation.

Multimodal Response Generation. Our response generation integrates textual and visual retrieval results through a structured template system. We employ Qwen2.5-VL-2B for final synthesis, leveraging its unified encoder-decoder architecture to process both textual context and visual elements simultaneously. The choice of this 2B model reflects practical deployment considerations for resource-constrained environments. Our observations suggest that the performance gap between smaller and larger models may narrow when high-quality, coherently retrieved multimodal context is provided.

The conversation template structures the multimodal context by presenting the original query, retrieved text passages, and text-informed selected images in a coherent format. This ensures final responses maintain consistency between textual explanations and visual evidence drawn from the same document sources, avoiding the fragmented answers typical of independent retrieval approaches.

4 Experiments

4.1 Experimental Setup

We employ a paired-comparison design where each query is tested under both baseline and enhanced configurations. Our evaluation covers six question categories: quantitative queries, identification tasks, definition queries, specification tasks, enumeration tasks, and procedural queries. Each question includes ground truth annotations with text-level and image-level relevance assessments at page granularity.

System Configuration. Our implementation uses BAAI/bge-large-zh-v1.5 for text embedding and Qwen2.5-VL-2B for multimodal processing. Visual retrieval employs the ColPali framework. Text processing uses semantic chunking with 128 tokens per chunk and 30-token overlap. We retrieve top-5 results for final generation, maintaining a 3K image candidate pool during initial retrieval. The content weighting parameter $\alpha = 0.1$, and response generation uses 256 maximum tokens with temperature=0.7.

Evaluation Metrics. We assess *Retrieval Quality* using MRR, Precision@K, Recall@K, nDCG, and semantic similarity; *Response Quality* through faithfulness, ROUGE-1, BLEU-1, and BERTScore F1; and *System Performance* via latency and memory utilization. In our experiments, we use $K = 5$ for Precision@K and Recall@K, matching the top-5 retrieval setting used in generation.

Design Rationale. We chose Qwen2.5-VL-2B to reflect practical constraints where larger models may be infeasible. We initially explored using the same 2B model for keyword extraction through prompting, but small-scale VLMs showed limited ability to follow complex instructions. This motivated our TF-IDF-based approach, which achieves cross-modal enhancement without requiring complex instruction following.

4.2 Results and Analysis

Main Results. Table 1 compares baseline and text-informed enhancement performance.

Table 1. Performance Comparison (Original vs. Augmented Query, $K = 5$)

Metric	Original	Augmented	Δ
Text Retrieval			
Precision@k	0.258 ± 0.093	**0.563 ± 0.169**	↑
Recall@k	0.396 ± 0.146	0.347 ± 0.109	↓
MRR	0.938 ± 0.169	0.938 ± 0.169	—
NDCG	0.498 ± 0.125	0.467 ± 0.119	↓
Avg. similarity	0.404 ± 0.076	**0.472 ± 0.094**	↑
Image Retrieval			
Precision@k	0.183 ± 0.057	**0.217 ± 0.057**	↑
Recall@k	0.219 ± 0.076	**0.250 ± 0.000**	↑
MRR	0.772 ± 0.351	**0.927 ± 0.202**	↑
NDCG	0.312 ± 0.123	**0.381 ± 0.075**	↑
Answer Quality			
Response latency	0.057 ± 0.012	0.068 ± 0.008	↑
Relevance score	0.781 ± 0.135	0.722 ± 0.169	↓
Faithfulness	0.589 ± 0.105	**0.642 ± 0.119**	↑
ROUGE-1	0.049 ± 0.031	**0.081 ± 0.102**	↑
BLEU-1	0.056 ± 0.142	**0.083 ± 0.059**	↑
BERT F1	0.064 ± 0.072	**0.099 ± 0.150**	↑

Our method shows improvements in image retrieval quality, with MRR increasing from 0.772 to 0.927 (+20.1%) and nDCG from 0.312 to 0.381 (+22.0%). This supports our hypothesis that text retrieval context can help identify relevant visual content, addressing the semantic gap between textual queries and visual elements.

Text retrieval exhibits an interesting precision-recall trade-off. While precision improves dramatically from 0.258 to 0.563 (+117.8%), recall decreases from 0.396 to 0.347 (-12.3%). This suggests that the keyword-enhanced queries become more specific, leading to more targeted retrieval. The unchanged MRR (0.938) indicates the most relevant documents still rank highly. This trade-off is beneficial for multimodal scenarios where precise, coherent content is more valuable than exhaustive coverage.

Response quality metrics show consistent improvements. The faithfulness score increase from 0.589 to 0.642 (+9.0%) indicates better alignment between retrieved context and generated responses, stemming from our text-informed re-ranking that ensures text and images originate from the same sources. ROUGE-1 (+66.3%), BLEU-1 (+48.6%), and BERTScore F1 (+55.4%) improvements indicate enhanced response quality through better cross-modal integration. The slight relevance score decrease (0.781 to 0.722) likely reflects more comprehensive answers incorporating both textual and visual information.

SLM-Based Comparison. We compared our TF-IDF approach against SLM-based keyword extraction using the same 2B model. The SLM-aided approach shows modest text retrieval improvements (precision +50.6%) but significant image retrieval degradation (MRR -31.0%, nDCG -23.5%). This performance differential supports our design choice of using deterministic keyword extraction under small-model constraints.

Ablation Study. Table 2 presents performance across four system variants: baseline, keyword enhancement only, text-informed ranking only, and our complete approach.

Table 2. Component Ablation Study

Metric	Baseline	Keyword-only	Text-Informed-only	Full Method
Image Retrieval				
Precision@k	0.183 ± 0.057	0.195 ± 0.064	0.201 ± 0.059	$\mathbf{0.217 \pm 0.057}$
MRR	0.772 ± 0.351	0.841 ± 0.298	0.809 ± 0.327	$\mathbf{0.927 \pm 0.202}$
NDCG	0.312 ± 0.123	0.335 ± 0.118	0.342 ± 0.115	$\mathbf{0.381 \pm 0.075}$
Text Retrieval				
Precision@k	0.258 ± 0.093	$\mathbf{0.441 \pm 0.152}$	0.276 ± 0.098	0.563 ± 0.169
Avg. similarity	0.404 ± 0.076	0.453 ± 0.085	0.412 ± 0.078	$\mathbf{0.472 \pm 0.094}$
Response Quality				
Faithfulness	0.589 ± 0.105	0.601 ± 0.117	$\mathbf{0.625 \pm 0.103}$	0.642 ± 0.119
ROUGE-1	0.049 ± 0.031	0.058 ± 0.067	0.051 ± 0.034	$\mathbf{0.081 \pm 0.102}$
BERT F1	0.064 ± 0.072	0.071 ± 0.083	0.067 ± 0.074	$\mathbf{0.099 \pm 0.150}$
Contribution Analysis				
Image MRR Gain	—	+8.9%	+4.8%	+20.1%
Text Precision Gain	—	+70.9%	+7.0%	+118.2%

The results reveal distinct component contributions. Keyword enhancement excels primarily in text retrieval (+70.9% precision) while providing moderate image retrieval gains (+8.9% MRR), aligning with expectations that TF-IDF-based extraction directly enhances textual query matching.

Text-informed ranking shows balanced improvements across modalities with particular strength in cross-modal coherence. Notably, it achieves the highest faithfulness score among individual components (0.625), validating our hypothesis that source-level consistency is crucial for response coherence.

The full method shows non-additive improvements. While keyword-only achieves +70.9% text precision improvement, the complete system reaches +118.2%, indicating that text-informed ranking amplifies keyword enhancement effectiveness. Similarly, the +20.1% image MRR improvement exceeds the sum of individual contributions (+13.7%), suggesting synergistic interactions between components.

Key Findings. The observed 20.1% MRR improvement in image retrieval indicates improved cross-modal alignment within the evaluated dataset. The 51.1% performance differential against SLM-aided approaches further supports the use of deterministic keyword extraction under resource-constrained settings. The query enhancement module introduces modest 19.5% latency increase (+11.2ms), significantly lower than SLM-aided approaches (+32.0%), making our method suitable for practical deployment. The consistent image retrieval improvements (Precision@k: +18.2%, MRR: +20.1%, nDCG: +22.0%) provide empirical evidence that text-informed enhancement can mitigate the modal isolation problem in the evaluated document setting.

5 Conclusion

This paper explores the modal isolation problem in multimodal RAG systems, where independent text and image retrieval often leads to responses combining unrelated content from different sources. We propose a text-informed enhancement approach that leverages text retrieval results to guide image search, ensuring cross-modal coherence through document-level source matching.

Our method employs TF-IDF-based keyword extraction from retrieved text to enhance queries for image retrieval, followed by position-aware re-ranking that prioritizes images from the same source documents. This design specifically targets resource-constrained deployments where small vision-language models cannot reliably follow complex instructions for query enhancement.

Experimental results show consistent improvements in image retrieval quality (MRR: +20.1%, nDCG: +22.0%) and text retrieval precision (+117.8%) within the evaluated academic document setting. Compared to SLM-aided keyword extraction, our deterministic approach achieves 51.1% better performance while maintaining lower computational overhead (+19.5% vs. +32.0% latency). Ablation studies reveal synergistic effects between keyword enhancement and position-aware re-ranking, with the complete system exceeding the sum of individual component contributions.

Our work contributes a practical solution for multimodal information retrieval in three ways: (1) a text-informed image enhancement strategy that bridges the semantic gap between user queries and visual content, (2) a source-aware re-ranking mechanism that maintains cross-modal consistency, and (3) empirical evidence that deterministic keyword extraction outperforms complex prompting strategies for small models in resource-constrained environments. This approach offers a practical option for deploying multimodal RAG capabilities locally in resource-constrained scenarios.

This paper is based on the author's Master's thesis and includes refined experimental analysis and improved methodological presentation for conference publication.

Disclosure of Interests. The authors have no competing interests to declare that are relevant to the content of this article.

References

1. Appalaraju, S., Jasani, B., Kota, B.U., Xie, Y., Manmatha, R.: Docformer: end-to-end transformer for document understanding. In: Proceedings of the IEEE/CVF international conference on computer vision, pp. 993–1003 (2021)
2. Borgeaud, S., et al.: Improving language models by retrieving from trillions of tokens. In: International conference on machine learning, pp. 2206–2240. PMLR (2022)
3. Caffagni, D., et al.: Wiki-LLaVA: hierarchical retrieval-augmented generation for multimodal LLMs. In: Proceedings of the IEEE/CVF Conference on Computer Vision and Pattern Recognition, pp. 1818–1826 (2024)
4. Carpineto, C., Romano, G.: A survey of automatic query expansion in information retrieval. Acm Comput. Surv. (CSUR) **44**(1), 1–50 (2012)
5. Chen, W., Hu, H., Chen, X., Verga, P., Cohen, W.W.: MuRAG: multimodal retrieval-augmented generator for open question answering over images and text. arXiv preprint arXiv:2210.02928 (2022)
6. Chen, Y.C., et al.: Uniter: universal image-text representation learning. In: European Conference on Computer Vision, pp. 104–120. Springer (2020)
7. Faysse, M., et al.: ColPali: efficient document retrieval with vision language models (2024). arXiv:2407.01449 arXiv preprint
8. Gao, L., Ma, X., Lin, J., Callan, J.: Precise zero-shot dense retrieval without relevance labels. In: Proceedings of the 61st Annual Meeting of the Association for Computational Linguistics (Volume 1: Long Papers), pp. 1762–1777 (2023)
9. Gu, J., et al.: Unidoc: unified pretraining framework for document understanding. Adv. Neural. Inf. Process. Syst. **34**, 39–50 (2021)
10. Hong, T., et al.: Bros: a pre-trained language model focusing on text and layout for better key information extraction from documents. In: Proceedings of the AAAI Conference on Artificial Intelligence, vol. 36, pp. 10767–10775 (2022)

11. Izacard, G., Grave, E.: Leveraging passage retrieval with generative models for open domain question answering. In: Merlo, P., Tiedemann, J., Tsarfaty, R. (eds.) Proceedings of the 16th Conference of the European Chapter of the Association for Computational Linguistics: Main Volume, pp. 874–880. Association for Computational Linguistics, Online (2021). https://doi.org/10.18653/v1/2021.eacl-main.74. https://aclanthology.org/2021.eacl-main.74/
12. Karpukhin, V., et al.: Dense passage retrieval for open-domain question answering. EMNLP (1), 6769–6781 (2020)
13. Lewis, P., et al.: Retrieval-augmented generation for knowledge-intensive NLP tasks. Adv. Neural. Inf. Process. Syst. **33**, 9459–9474 (2020)
14. Li, J., Li, D., Xiong, C., Hoi, S.: BLIP: Bootstrapping Language-Image Pre-Training for unified vision-language understanding and generation. In: International Conference on Machine Learning, pp. 12888–12900. PMLR (2022)
15. Lu, P., et al.: IconQA: a new benchmark for abstract diagram understanding and visual language reasoning (2021). arXiv:2110.13214 arXiv preprint
16. Mathew, M., Karatzas, D., Jawahar, C.: DocVQA: a dataset for VQA on document images. In: Proceedings of the IEEE/CVF Winter Conference on Applications of Computer Vision, pp. 2200–2209 (2021)
17. Nan, L., et al.: OMG-QA: building open-domain multi-modal generative question answering systems. In: Proceedings of the 2024 Conference on Empirical Methods in Natural Language Processing: Industry Track, pp. 1001–1015 (2024)
18. Radford, A., et al.: Learning transferable visual models from natural language supervision. In: International Conference on Machine Learning, pp. 8748–8763. PMLR (2021)
19. Salton, G., Buckley, C.: Term-weighting approaches in automatic text retrieval. Inf. Process. Manag. **24**(5), 513–523 (1988)
20. Shi, W., et al.: REPLUG: retrieval-augmented black-box language models (2023). arXiv:2301.12652 arXiv preprint
21. Shuster, K., Poff, S., Chen, M., Kiela, D., Weston, J.: Retrieval augmentation reduces hallucination in conversation (2021). arXiv:2104.07567 arXiv preprint
22. Tito, R., Karatzas, D., Valveny, E.: Hierarchical multimodal transformers for multipage DocVQA. Pattern Recogn. **144**, 109834 (2023)
23. Wang, L., Yang, N., Wei, F.: Query2doc: query expansion with large language models (2023). arXiv:2303.07678 arXiv preprint
24. Xu, Y., et al.: Layoutlmv2: multi-modal pre-training for visually-rich document understanding. arXiv preprint arXiv:2012.14740 (2020)
25. Xu, Y., et al.: LayoutLM: pre-training of text and layout for document image understanding. In: Proceedings of the 26th ACM Sigkdd International Conference on Knowledge Discovery & Data Mining, pp. 1192–1200 (2020)
26. Yasunaga, M., et al.: Retrieval-augmented multimodal language modeling. arXiv preprint arXiv:2211.12561 (2022)

Structure-Aware Adaptive Differential Privacy in Supervised Graph Sparsification

Jiaxuan Si[1], Jinyan Wang[1,2,3](✉), Linlin Su[1], Chenhao Guo[2], Liu Yang[2], and Xiaohong Liu[2](✉)

[1] Key Lab of Education Blockchain and Intelligent Technology, Ministry of Education, Guangxi Normal University, Guilin 541004, China
[2] Guangxi Key Lab of Multi-Source Information Mining and Security, Guangxi Normal University, Guilin 541004, China
liuxiaohong0329@163.com
[3] University Engineering Research Center of Educational Intelligent Technology, Guangxi Normal University, Guilin 541004, China
wangjy612@gxnu.edu.cn

Abstract. Supervised graph sparsification is crucial for improving the computational efficiency and reducing memory overhead of Graph Neural Networks in applications like social networks and recommendation systems. However, this process introduces a critical privacy vulnerability: sparsification-induced structural changes expose sensitive graph topology and node features. Existing Differential Privacy mechanisms are often inflexible, failing to provide granular, simultaneous protection for both global structure and local attributes with distinct sensitivities. To address this, we propose a novel Structure-Aware Adaptive Differential Privacy Framework (SADP-SGS) for supervised graph sparsification. Our framework employs an Adaptive Sparsity-Privacy Module to inject Differential Privacy noise into the sparsification process, effectively obfuscating the global graph structure and preventing sensitive edge leakage. Concurrently, the Hierarchical Gradient Perturbation Module provides local-level protection by injecting noise into multi-layer gradients, preventing the leakage of node features and local structural information. An adaptive privacy management mechanism dynamically controls the total privacy budget, ensuring an optimal, sustained privacy-utility balance. Comprehensive experimental results demonstrate SADP-SGS's superior privacy protection capabilities and usability across multiple challenging real-world datasets.

Keywords: privacy-preserving · supervised sparsification · differential privacy

1 Introduction

Graph Neural Networks (GNN) [1] have achieved state-of-the-art performance in diverse fields, including social network analysis [2], biological networks [3],

R. C.-W. Wong et al. (Eds.): PAKDD 2026, LNAI 16617, pp. 360–373, 2027.
https://doi.org/10.1007/978-981-92-1926-1_29

and recommender systems [4]. However, the rapidly increasing scale of real-world graphs introduces two primary challenges: computational bottlenecks and heightened privacy risks. To combat efficiency issues, graph sparsification is crucial, systematically removing non-essential edges to reduce computational and memory overhead [5]. While essential for scaling, this selective pruning simultaneously poses a unique and intensified risk of data leakage.

Sparsification techniques are broadly divided into unsupervised (DropEdge [6]) and supervised (PTDNet [7], NeuralSparse [8]) methods. We focus on supervised sparsification due to its superior task-adaptability. However, its advantage comes at a cost: selective pruning causes a significant structural distribution shift, which attackers exploit to enhance Membership Inference Attacks (MIA) [9,10]. As shown in Fig. 1, MIA performance is significantly amplified in supervised sparsification models, necessitating a dedicated privacy-preserving framework.

To introduce a provable defense, Differential Privacy (DP) is widely adopted. However, existing DP mechanisms whether applied to gradients (DP-SGD [11]) or local data (LDP [12]) are often inadequate or impractical for this supervised graph setting. Their reliance on homogeneous and static noise injection fails to provide the simultaneous, granular protection required to obscure sensitive edge existence (topology) and protect high-dimensional node features (attributes). Furthermore, static budget allocation mechanisms cannot cope with the non-linear, dynamic privacy loss accumulated during iterative, structure-modifying optimization, exacerbating the fundamental conflict between privacy protection and task utility.

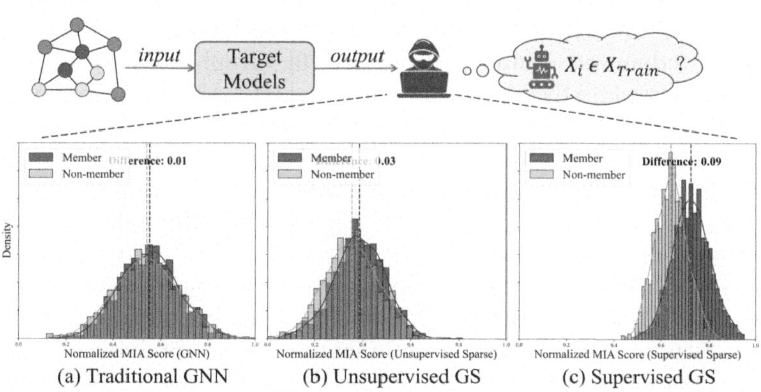

Fig. 1. Comparison of the MIA performance among GCN, unsupervised and supervised graph sparsification.

To resolve this, we propose SADP-SGS (Structure-aware Adaptive Differential Privacy in Supervised Graph Sparsification), a graph neural network framework that integrates dynamic sparsification and adaptive differential privacy. Its core idea is to achieve collaborative optimization of privacy protection and sparsity efficiency through feedback mechanism, fundamentally solving the problems of static strategy failure and sensitivity imbalance. Specifically, we designed a more relaxed pruning strategy for generating masks and sampling, taking into account both structural importance and feature sensitivity. Then, we introduced perturbations during edge mask generation to block the leakage of edge existence, and added perturbations to gradients as needed.

Our main contributions are:

- We propose the Adaptive Sparsity-Privacy Module with Differential Privacy, which uses sparsity-driven adaptive noise to solve the dual dilemma of structural bias and sensitive edge exposure caused by sparsification.
- We introduce the Hierarchical Gradient Perturbation Module, which achieves inter-layer noise scaling, breaking the limitations of traditional uniform noise and alleviating the gradient competition problem between privacy and task loss.
- Comprehensive experiments validate the adaptability and generalization performance of SADP-SGS across multiple real-world datasets.

2 Related Work

2.1 Graph Sparsification

Graph sparsification is primarily split into unsupervised and supervised methods. Unsupervised sparsification reduces complexity by preserving essential structural or spectral properties without labeled data, using techniques like Effective Resistance (ER), randomized pruning (DropEdge [6], GraphSAGE [19]), and structural pruning (GraphSAINT [20], Rank-Degree [21]). Although computationally efficient and capable of offering edge privacy guarantees [13], these methods are limited by their lack of task-specific optimization. Supervised sparsification overcomes this by integrating sparsification into the GNN training loop. Models like SparseGAT [22] and SuperGAT [23] learn sparse subgraphs via regularization, while others (NeuralSparse [8], PTDNet [7], SGCN [24]) train differentiable sparse distributions. However, integrating Differential Privacy (DP) into this supervised framework creates a fundamental conflict with utility, primarily due to two factors: the task-driven optimization favors retaining sensitive connections (increasing exposure), and the resulting selective pruning introduces exploitable distribution shifts between the training and testing data subsets.

2.2 Differential Privacy in GNNs

Differential Privacy [14] is the mainstream, provable framework used to protect private information, such as against Membership Inference Attacks (MIA) [15]. By adding calibrated noise to data or gradients, DP guarantees that the change in a single data record (e.g., an edge) has a negligible impact on the model's output.

While widely effective across various models [16–18], standard DP mechanisms like DP-SGD [11] are problematic for supervised graph sparsification. The general DP reliance on static sensitivity bounds is inadequate when edge selection is dynamically driven by task utility. This fundamental mismatch means existing methods struggle to adapt to the non-uniform sensitivity of edges and often fail to bridge the distribution gap between the continuous noise smoothing and the discrete, dynamic graph topology.

3 Preliminaries and Theoretical Motivation

In this section, we present the fundamental concepts of differential privacy and supervised graph sparsification, followed by an analysis of the privacy preservation requirement in this context.

(ϵ, δ)-Differential Privacy [14] is a widely adopted privacy model where the outcome of a randomized mechanism $\mathcal{M}$ is nearly independent of a single record's presence. For any pair of adjacent graphs $\mathcal{G} \sim \mathcal{G}'$ (differing by one edge), $\mathcal{M}$ satisfies (ϵ, δ)-differential privacy if:

$$\forall S \subseteq \text{Range}(\mathcal{M}) : \Pr[\mathcal{M}(\mathcal{G}) \in S] \leq e^{\epsilon} \Pr[\mathcal{M}(\mathcal{G}') \in S] + \delta. \tag{1}$$

A smaller privacy budget ϵ implies a stronger privacy guarantee.

Sensitivity [25] determines the magnitude of required noise. For any function $\mathcal{S}$ on a dataset D, the l_2-sensitivity is defined as the maximum change in the query output between any pair of neighboring datasets:

$$\Delta_2 \mathcal{S} = \max_{D,D'} |\mathcal{S}(D) - \mathcal{S}(D')|_2 \, . \tag{2}$$

Gaussian Mechanism [26]. This mechanism achieves (ϵ, δ)-DP by adding noise drawn from $\mathcal{N}(0, \sigma^2)$ to the output $\mathcal{S}(G)$. The noise scale must satisfy:

$$\sigma \geq \sqrt{2 \ln(1.25/\delta)} \cdot \frac{\Delta_2 \mathcal{S}}{\epsilon}. \tag{3}$$

In our work, we apply this mechanism as $\mathcal{M}(G) \triangleq \mathcal{S}(G) + \mathcal{N}\Big(0, \; \big(\sigma \cdot \Delta_2 \mathcal{S}\big)^2 \mathbf{I}_\kappa\Big)$, where $\mathbf{I}_\kappa$ is the κ-dimensional identity matrix.

Supervised Graph Sparsification Model [7]. Given a target sparsity rate q, the goal is to find an optimal subgraph $\tilde{\mathcal{G}} = (V, \tilde{E}, \mathbf{X})$ that minimizes the downstream task loss:

$$\min_{\theta, \tilde{\mathcal{G}} \in \mathcal{G}q} \mathcal{L}\text{CE}\big(f_\theta(\tilde{\mathcal{G}}), \mathbf{Y}\big), \tag{4}$$

where f_θ is the GNN classifier. This selection process often uses a learnable mask matrix $\mathbf{M} \in \{0,1\}^{|E|}$.

Privacy Leakage Risk and Motivation. The use of the mask matrix $\mathbf{M}$ introduces two critical privacy risks that we address: (i) Structural Pattern Leakage, where $p(\mathbf{M}|\mathcal{G})$ implicitly exposes training graph statistics; and (ii) Gradient Exposure, where $\nabla_{\mathbf{M}}\mathcal{L}$ reveals the exact decision basis for edge retention. To mitigate these coupled risks, our proposed SADP-SGS framework employs a multi-head attention mechanism to guide privacy-preserving sparsification. It injects Gaussian noise into the sparse neighbor generation (forward pass) and perturbs gradients with layer-wise noise (backward pass), ensuring fine-grained structural and parametric privacy.

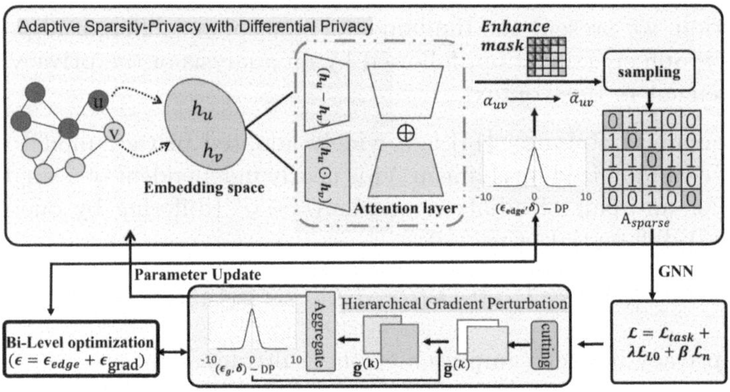

Fig. 2. The framework of SADP-SGS. SADP-SGS consists of two synergistic components: (i) Adaptive Sparsity-Privacy with Differential Privacy, which protects the graph topology via edge-level noise calibration, and (ii) Hierarchical Gradient Perturbation, which secures local privacy through multi-layer gradient noise. Both components are coordinated under a global privacy budget, ensuring that perturbations remain within a controlled range while pursuing optimal predictive accuracy.

4 Proposed Methodology

This section presents the overall learning framework of SADP-SGS, a graph neural network that integrates dynamic sparsification, hierarchical differential privacy, and adaptive control. The objective is to jointly optimize privacy protection and model utility. As illustrated in Fig. 2, the framework incorporates two complementary differential privacy strategies designed to protect both node features and graph topology.

4.1 Adaptive Sparsity–Privacy with Differential Privacy

This module secures the graph topology by integrating privacy preservation directly into the sparsification process. Edges are scored based on node embeddings, and the objective is to generate a differentially private sparse adjacency matrix A_{sparse} that maintains structural integrity.

Graph Representation and Privacy-Aware Edge Scoring. Node features X are first compressed into low-dimensional embeddings h_u:

$$h_u = \text{ReLU}(W_h x_u), \quad W_h \in \mathbb{R}. \tag{5}$$

The unnormalized edge importance score is then computed by jointly modeling node heterogeneity $(h_u - h_v)$ and homophily $(h_u \odot h_v)$:

$$\log \alpha_{uv} = w_\phi^\top \cdot \left[(h_u - h_v) \oplus (h_u \odot h_v)\right], \tag{6}$$

where w_ϕ is a trainable projection vector, $\oplus$ denotes feature concatenation, $\odot$ denotes element-wise multiplication.

Edge-Level Perturbation. To ensure differential privacy for the structural selection, we inject Gaussian noise ϵ_{uv} directly into the edge importance scores:

$$\tilde{\alpha}_{uv} = \log \alpha_{uv} + \epsilon_{uv}, \quad \epsilon_{uv} \sim \mathcal{N}(0, \sigma_m^2). \tag{7}$$

This noise serves to obscure the true importance of sensitive edges, preventing attackers from accurately inferring edge existence based on the observed sparse structure. The noise scale σ_m is calibrated adaptively to the graph size using a noise multiplier λ:

$$\sigma_m = \frac{\lambda \cdot \alpha_{\text{boost}}}{\sqrt{N}}, \tag{8}$$

where N is the number of nodes, ensuring consistent privacy guarantees across graphs of varying scales.

Relaxed Mask with Boundary Extension. Standard Hard Concrete sampling suffers from gradient saturation and premature collapse, particularly under strong noise perturbation. We mitigate these issues by introducing boundary relaxation (ζ, γ) and dynamic temperature annealing:

$$\text{mask}_{uv} = \text{clip}\left(\frac{\zeta - \gamma}{1 + e^{-\tilde{\alpha}_{uv}/\tau(t)}} + \gamma,\ 0,\ 1\right), \tag{9}$$

where ζ relaxes the upper bound and γ relaxes the lower bound. $\zeta = 1.1$ and $\gamma = -0.1$ allow for a wider exploration range, preventing early collapse to binary states. This also significantly amplifies the gradient magnitude for more stable parameter updates:

$$\frac{\partial \text{mask}_{uv}}{\partial \tilde{\alpha}_{uv}} \approx \frac{1.1 - (-0.1)}{\tau(t)} \cdot e^{-\tilde{\alpha}_{uv}/\tau(t)} \cdot \left(1 + e^{-\tilde{\alpha}_{uv}/\tau(t)}\right)^{-2}. \tag{10}$$

We further adopt an exponential decay strategy for the temperature $\tau(t) = \tau_0 \cdot r^t$ to encourage broad exploration early in training and focused exploitation later.

4.2 Hierarchical Gradient Perturbation

To address the heterogeneous sensitivities of parameters and minimize the privacy-utility loss, we propose a hierarchical gradient perturbation mechanism. This mechanism tailors the perturbation strength based on the parameter category, classifying them into attention parameters (θ_{attn}) and GCN parameters (θ_{gcn}).

Hierarchical Clipping and Noise Scaling. We define a hierarchical clipping threshold $C^{(k)}$ to reflect the higher global sensitivity of attention parameters, which directly control edge selection:

$$C^{(k)} = \begin{cases} 1.5C_0, & \text{if } k \in \theta_{\text{attn}}, \\ C_0, & \text{if } k \in \theta_{\text{gcn}}, \end{cases} \tag{11}$$

where C_0 denotes the base clipping bound for gradient norms. The gradient $\mathbf{g}^{(k)}$ is clipped and then perturbed by Gaussian noise:

$$\tilde{\mathbf{g}}^{(k)} \leftarrow \bar{\mathbf{g}}^{(k)} + \mathcal{N}(0, (\sigma^{(k)})^2 \boldsymbol{I}), \tag{12}$$

where the noise standard deviation is

$$\sigma^{(k)} = \frac{\lambda \cdot C^{(k)}}{\sqrt{b}}. \tag{13}$$

Sensitivity-Adaptive Adjustment and Budget. To improve utility, we adapt the noise standard deviation using a Signal-to-Noise Ratio (SNR) criterion. By setting $\sigma^{(\text{attn})}$ to be proportionally smaller than $\sigma^{(\text{gcn})}$, we optimize the privacy allocation. The resulting ratio of attention-to-GCN privacy loss is 1 : 0.64, leading to a significant reduction in the total privacy budget compared to a unified strategy. The total privacy budget ϵ_{total} is calculated by composing the per-layer losses:

$$\epsilon_{\text{total}} = \epsilon_{\text{attn}} + \epsilon_{\text{gcn}} = \frac{\alpha(1.5C_0)^2}{2N^2(\sigma_{\text{attn}})^2} + \frac{\alpha C_0^2}{2N^2(\sigma_{\text{gcn}})^2}. \tag{14}$$

4.3 Privacy-Preserving Analysis of SADP-SGS

The full privacy mechanism of SADP-SGS is a two-tier strategy: the topological noise layer (edge score perturbation) and the feature noise layer (hierarchical gradient perturbation). We optimize the privacyâĂŞutility trade-off through a bi-objective optimization problem:

$$\min_{\sigma_m, \sigma^{(k)}} \left(\epsilon_{\text{total}}, \mathcal{L}_{\text{task}}\right) \quad \text{s.t.} \quad \epsilon_{\text{total}} = \epsilon_{\text{edge}} + \epsilon_{\text{grad}}. \tag{15}$$

Theorem. (Joint differential privacy guarantee) [27] Let the edge pruning mechanism $\mathcal{M}_{\text{edge}}$ satisfy $(\epsilon_{\text{edge}}, \delta)$-DP and the gradient perturbation mechanism

$\mathcal{M}_{\text{grad}}$ satisfy $(\epsilon_{\text{grad}}, \delta)$-DP. If both act independently on the data stream, then the joint mechanism $\mathcal{M}_{\text{joint}} = (\mathcal{M}_{\text{edge}}, \mathcal{M}_{\text{grad}})$ satisfies $(\epsilon_{\text{edge}} + \epsilon_{\text{grad}}, \delta)$-DP.

Proof Sketch. The proof relies on the composition theorem for differential privacy. Since $\mathcal{M}_{\text{edge}}$ and $\mathcal{M}_{\text{grad}}$ are independent, their joint probability for any output pair (S, T) between neighboring datasets D and D' is bounded by the product of their individual privacy losses:

$$\frac{\mathbb{P}[\mathcal{M}\text{joint}(D) = (S,T)]}{\mathbb{P}[\mathcal{M}\text{joint}(D') = (S,T)]} \leq e^{\epsilon_{\text{edge}}} \cdot e^{\epsilon_{\text{grad}}} = e^{\epsilon_{\text{edge}}+\epsilon_{\text{grad}}}, \tag{16}$$

thereby demonstrating that the total privacy loss is the sum of the individual budgets, satisfying $(\epsilon_{\text{edge}} + \epsilon_{\text{grad}}, \delta)$-DP.

5 Experiments

In this section, we validate both the privacy-preserving capability and the model utility of SADP-SGS through extensive experiments. Our evaluation is designed to answer the following core research questions:

- **RQ1.** How does SADP-SGS perform in downstream tasks compared with competitive sparsification baselines? (Sect. 5.2)
- **RQ2.** How effective is the model in resisting membership inference attacks (MIA) relative to strong baselines? (Sect. 5.2)
- **RQ3.** What is the relationship between sparsity rate, hyperparameters, and downstream task performance? (Sect. 5.2)

Table 1. Statistics of Experimental Datasets 60%/20%/20% (train/validation/test)

Dataset	Nodes	Edges	Classes	Homophily Ratio
Cora	2,708	5,429	7	0.825
Citeseer	3,327	4,732	6	0.727
Pubmed	19,717	44,338	3	0.795
Computers	13,752	245,861	10	0.796
OGBN-arXiv	169,343	1,166,243	40	0.715
Squirrel	19,717	217,073	5	0.215
Facebook	22,470	173,204	4	0.412
Chameleon	2,277	36,101	5	0.234

Table 2. Experimental results on benchmark datasets (Bold: best; Underline: runner-up).

Dataset	Metric	DROPEDGE	SPARSEGAT	NEURALSPARSE	PTDNetGCN	SADP-SGS(ϵ = *none*)	SADP-SGS($\epsilon = 10$)
Cora	ACC	76.29 ± 0.25	81.50 ± 0.25	80.31 ± 0.14	81.12 ± 0.05	$\mathbf{82.00 \pm 0.15}$	81.50 ± 0.18
	F1	75.59 ± 0.44	72.23 ± 0.29	76.12 ± 0.52	75.46 ± 0.76	$\mathbf{79.10 \pm 0.20}$	78.80 ± 0.25
Citeseer	ACC	71.20 ± 0.32	70.90 ± 0.53	71.25 ± 0.14	72.30 ± 0.11	$\mathbf{72.40 \pm 0.10}$	72.05 ± 0.15
	F1	72.40 ± 0.30	58.75 ± 0.10	65.40 ± 1.20	71.23 ± 0.42	$\mathbf{73.20 \pm 0.15}$	72.90 ± 0.18
Pubmed	ACC	75.25 ± 0.43	78.62 ± 0.25	78.84 ± 0.18	79.82 ± 0.24	$\mathbf{80.20 \pm 0.15}$	79.70 ± 0.20
	F1	76.00 ± 1.21	75.30 ± 0.35	73.97 ± 0.40	77.97 ± 0.26	$\mathbf{78.35 \pm 0.25}$	78.20 ± 0.15
Computers	ACC	65.40 ± 3.20	60.65 ± 4.66	81.50 ± 0.32	$\mathbf{84.56 \pm 0.42}$	84.46 ± 0.16	83.55 ± 0.25
	F1	60.65 ± 4.66	68.91 ± 0.21	75.32 ± 4.11	82.34 ± 0.56	$\mathbf{85.12 \pm 0.30}$	84.50 ± 0.25
Squirrel	ACC	44.54 ± 0.85	32.56 ± 0.35	35.76 ± 0.12	45.92 ± 0.13	$\mathbf{48.30 \pm 0.15}$	47.52 ± 0.15
	F1	43.60 ± 0.20	29.50 ± 0.00	38.24 ± 0.00	47.60 ± 0.21	$\mathbf{47.74 \pm 0.28}$	47.14 ± 0.35
Facebook	ACC	81.20 ± 0.10	88.63 ± 0.12	87.50 ± 0.15	91.63 ± 0.12	$\mathbf{93.20 \pm 0.13}$	91.80 ± 0.20
	F1	90.15 ± 0.20	89.14 ± 0.15	87.20 ± 0.30	91.10 ± 0.25	$\mathbf{92.10 \pm 0.20}$	88.40 ± 0.25
Chameleon	ACC	42.50 ± 0.80	48.25 ± 0.42	50.21 ± 0.16	48.24 ± 0.13	$\mathbf{54.80 \pm 0.25}$	53.54 ± 0.28
	F1	40.60 ± 0.04	40.40 ± 0.15	52.52 ± 0.78	45.24 ± 0.24	$\mathbf{53.74 \pm 0.28}$	52.74 ± 0.35
OGBN-arXiv	ACC	70.50 ± 0.20	69.82 ± 0.22	OOM	70.20 ± 0.10	$\mathbf{72.80 \pm 0.12}$	70.90 ± 0.18
	F1	69.20 ± 0.30	68.60 ± 0.35	OOM	70.00 ± 0.20	$\mathbf{71.50 \pm 0.20}$	69.70 ± 0.15

5.1 Experimental Settings

Datasets & Baselines. We used eight publicly available graph datasets (statistics in Table 1), covering homophilous (Cora, Pubmed) and heterophilous graphs (Facebook, Chameleon, Squirrel, OGBN-arXiv). The baseline methods include **DropEdge** [6] (unsupervised sparsification), **NeuralSparse** [8], **PTDNet** [7] (supervised sparsification), and **SparseGAT** [22] (attention-based).

Privacy Configuration. The total privacy budget ϵ is varied in the range $[1, 10]$, with $\delta = 10^{-5}$ as the failure probability. Edge sparsity levels are aligned across all baselines for consistent evaluation.

5.2 Evaluation

Performance on Downstream Tasks (RQ1). Table 2 reports the node classification ACC and F1 scores under the GCN backbone. **SADP-SGS (ϵ = none)** achieves the best or runner-up performance on all eight datasets and consistently outperforms all competitive sparsification baselines. This confirms the efficacy of our task-supervised sparsification learning. Notably, even with a strong privacy constraint ($\epsilon = 10$), SADP-SGS remains highly competitive, securing the runner-up position in 7/8 datasets for ACC and 6/8 datasets for F1.

Homophilous Graphs: On citation networks (Cora, Pubmed) and e-commerce graphs (Computers), SADP-SGS demonstrates clear superiority. For instance, on Cora, SADP-SGS (ϵ = none) records a leading ACC of 82.00 ± 0.15, surpassing the runner-up PTDNetGCN (81.12 ± 0.05). This margin shows our model's ability to retain critical structural information even when dealing with large, dense graphs like OGBN-arXiv, where it achieves a leading ACC of 72.80 ± 0.12.

Heterophilous Graphs: On challenging low-homophily datasets (Facebook, Chameleon, Squirrel), SADP-SGS exhibits the most significant gains. Baselines like SparseGAT and NeuralSparse struggle due to high structural noise, but SADP-SGS maintains robustness, achieving the best ACC on Chameleon (54.80 ± 0.25) and Facebook (93.20 ± 0.13). This validates that our sampling method, with noise injection, avoids the localized collapse that affects simpler pruning methods, allowing for more robust feature selection in heterogeneous structures.

Privacy Protection Analysis (RQ2). We analyze the model's performance under varying privacy budgets $\epsilon \in \{1, 5, 10, \text{none}\}$ (Table 3).

Trade-off Analysis: Utility naturally increases with a larger ϵ. When $\epsilon = 1$ (strong privacy), SADP-SGS's accuracy is lowest, confirming the performance cost associated with high noise. For instance, on **Cora**, ACC increases from 63.20% ($\epsilon = 1$) to 81.50% ($\epsilon = 10$). The key finding is the efficacy of our mechanism at weak privacy: with $\epsilon = 10$, SADP-SGS's performance is already highly competitive with its non-private version. On **Computers**, SADP-SGS achieves 83.55% ($\epsilon = 10$), closely approaching its non-private performance of 84.46% ($\epsilon =$ none). These results confirm that the proposed privacy mechanism achieves an effective balance between privacy protection and utility preservation.

Table 3. Balanced analysis of differential privacy strength and model utility (utility indicator: node classification accuracy).

Model	ϵ	Cora	Citeseer	Pubmed	Computers	Squirrel	Facebook	Chameleon	OGBN-arXiv
DropEdge	($\epsilon = 1$)	58.92	57.35	62.87	58.82	41.50	65.20	40.10	65.20
PTDNet		66.82	61.24	68.45	62.48	42.80	66.88	42.15	66.80
SADP-SGS		63.20	64.70	69.28	61.25	44.20	69.83	45.60	68.90
DropEdge	($\epsilon = 5$)	72.85	66.64	68.10	62.24	42.50	73.15	41.25	68.15
PTDNet		75.96	68.83	71.25	66.35	44.80	83.20	44.10	69.40
SADP-SGS		74.12	69.42	74.10	65.64	46.50	86.23	47.50	70.10
DropEdge	($\epsilon = 10$)	76.89	70.24	72.48	72.80	44.54	81.20	42.50	70.50
PTDNet		79.12	70.12	77.18	77.18	45.92	91.63	48.24	70.20
SADP-SGS		81.50	72.05	79.70	83.55	47.52	91.80	53.54	70.90
DropEdge	($\epsilon =$ none)	76.29	71.20	75.25	65.40	44.54	81.20	42.50	70.50
PTDNet		81.12	72.30	79.82	84.56	45.92	91.63	48.24	70.20
SADP-SGS		82.00	72.40	80.20	84.46	48.30	93.20	54.80	72.80

Baseline Comparison under DP: Across all ϵ settings, SADP-SGS consistently maintains higher utility than the DP-compatible baselines (PTDNet, DropEdge). At $\epsilon = 10$, SADP-SGS achieves 91.80% on **Facebook**, which is significantly higher than DropEdge's 81.20%. This gap validates that our joint hierarchical and topological noise allocation minimizes utility loss more effectively than simple dropout or unified DP techniques.

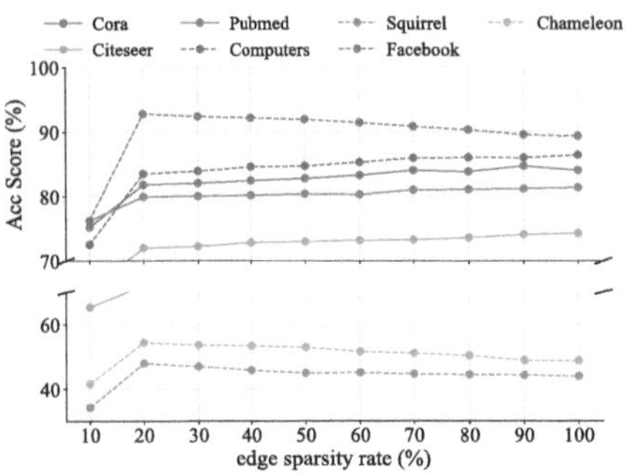

Fig. 3. ACC-scores of different sparsity levels.

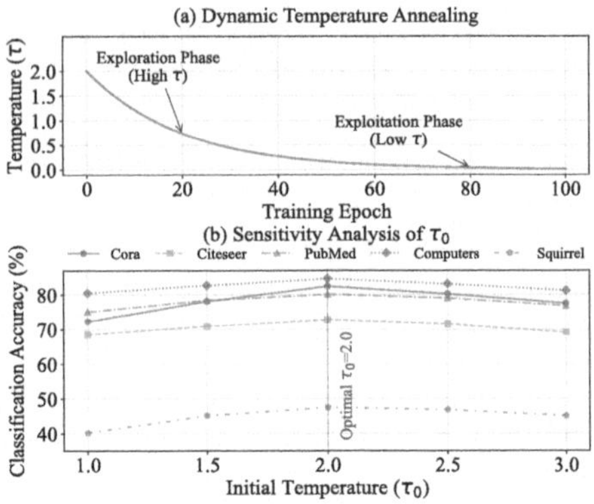

Fig. 4. (a) Dynamic Temperature Annealing. (b) Sensitivity Analysis of τ_0.

Impact of Sparsity and Hyperparameters (RQ3) Sparsity versus Utility Trade-offs: Fig. 3 shows that SADP-SGS maintains stable ACC (> 80%) even at high sparsity (20% edge retention on Cora, reaching 81.78%). This stability is crucial for maximizing privacy gains without crippling task utility. Low homogeneity datasets (Squirrel, Chameleon) slightly benefit from higher sparsity, as more noisy edges are pruned.

Hyperparameter Sensitivity: Performance is optimal when the Initial Temperature τ_0 is set to 2.0 (Fig. 4(b)), with values outside the range of $[1.5, 3.0]$ leading to sub-optimal training dynamics. Regarding Noise Scaling σ_m, we observe a desirable non-linear trade-off: accuracy declines approximately linearly with σ_m (decreasing by 0.8%/step), while the privacy risk, measured by MIA AUC, drops exponentially from 0.85 to 0.62, demonstrating an efficient reduction in privacy vulnerability. Finally, the SNR Control mechanism achieves its best privacy-utility balance at a Signal-to-Noise Ratio (SNR)=2.0. This setting results in an average F1-score of 78.4%, significantly outperforming the configuration where SNR=1.0 (75.2%).

5.3 Ablation Studies

In Fig. 5, we analyze key components on the Cora dataset ($\epsilon = 10$, 40% retention). The full model (SADP-SGS) is compared against four main ablations. For conciseness, we define the following ablation variants and their corresponding abbreviations: w/o EP (Excluding Edge

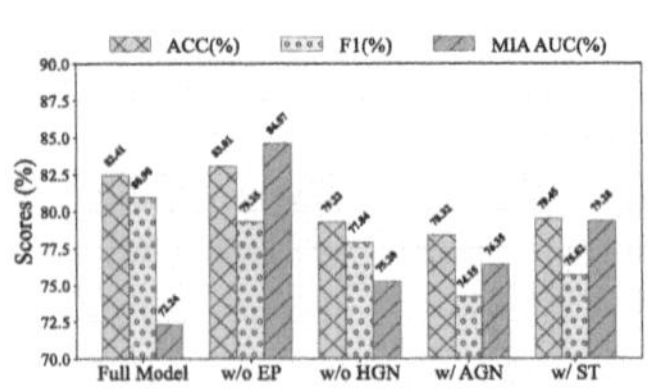

Fig. 5. Ablation Study on Cora (q = 40%).

Perturbation), w/o HGN (Excluding Hierarchical Gradient Noise), w/ AGN (Using Average Gradient Noise), and w/ ST (Using Static Thresholds).

(1) Structural Vulnerability (Edge Perturbation): The **w/o EP** variant shows the largest privacy failure, with MIA AUC increasing by 12.33 percentage points (from 72.24% to 84.57%). This confirms that structural obfuscation is indispensable for protecting graph topology, which is the most vulnerable information source for membership inference attacks.

(2) Overall Necessity of Gradient Perturbation: The **w/o HGN** variant suffers a utility drop (ACC to 79.23%, F1 to 77.84%) while MIA AUC rises to 75.20%. This validates the overall necessity of gradient perturbation for securing local feature privacy and stabilizing utility.

(3) Efficacy of Hierarchical Perturbation: The **w/ AGN** variant suffers a significant 4.09 percentage point degradation in ACC (82.41% to 78.32%) and a 6.75 point reduction in F1 score (80.90% to 74.15%). This validates that dimension-aware, hierarchical noise allocation is crucial for effectively preserving discriminative features in the gradient space.

(4) Necessity of Adaptive Thresholding: The **w/ ST** variant shows a substantial 2.96 percentage point deficit in ACC (82.41% to 79.45%) and a 5.28 point reduction in F1 score. This performance penalty arises because static clipping fails to adapt to the dynamic magnitude of gradients, leading to sub-optimal noise injection during convergence.

6 Conclusions

In this paper, we presented SADP-SGS, a novel framework for supervised graph sparsification that synergistically integrates structural protection and differential privacy (DP) to maintain high utility in downstream node classification. The core architecture comprises two interconnected modules: the Adaptive Edge Sparsity-Privacy Mechanism, which uses fuzzification to dynamically adjust sparsity and noise against structural inference, and the Hierarchical Gradient Perturbation, which employs Adaptive Temperature Annealing to manage topology exploration and stabilize the sparse structure. Extensive experiments confirm SADP-SGS's exceptional privacy preservation and superior adaptability in balancing utility and privacy, significantly outperforming state-of-the-art DP-GNN baselines. Future work will focus on extending SADP-SGS to address link prediction and graph classification tasks, and further exploring the theoretical privacy bounds of our joint structural and gradient perturbation mechanism.

Acknowledgments. This work was supported by the National Natural Science Foundation of China (No. 62162005) and the Basic Ability Enhancement Program for Young and Middle-aged Teachers of Guangxi (No. 2023KY0059).

References

1. Scarselli, F., et al.: The graph neural network model. IEEE Trans. Neural Netw. **20**(1), 61–80 (2008)
2. Liu, Q., et al.: Association between Lactate-to-Albumin ratio and 28-days all-cause mortality in patients with Acute Pancreatitis: a retrospective analysis of the MIMIC-IV database. Front. Immunol. **13**, 1076121 (2022)
3. Muzio, G., et al.: Biological network analysis with deep learning. Brief. Bioinform. **22**(2), 1515–1530 (2021)
4. Yu, J.: Are graph augmentations necessary? Simple graph contrastive learning for recommendation. In: SIGIR, pp. 1294–1303 (2022)
5. Zhang, G.: Graph Sparsification via Mixture of Graphs (2024). arXiv:2405.14260 arXiv preprint
6. Rong, Y.: Dropedge: towards Deep Graph Convolutional Networks on Node Classification (2019). arXiv:1907.10903 arXiv preprint
7. Luo, D.: Learning to Drop: Robust Graph Neural Network via Topological Denoising, pp. 779–787. WSDM (2021)
8. Zheng, C.: Robust graph representation learning via neural sparsification. In: ICML, pp. 11458–11468 (2020)
9. Hu, L., et al.: Defenses to membership inference attacks: a survey. ACM Comput. Surv. **56**(4), 1–34 (2023)
10. Long, Y.: Understanding Membership Inferences on Well-Generalized Learning Models (2018). arXiv:1802.04889 arXiv preprint
11. Abadi, M.: Deep Learning with Differential Privacy, pp. 308–318 (2016)
12. Sajadmanesh, S.: Locally private graph neural networks. In: CCS, pp. 2130–2145 (2021)
13. Arora, R.: On Differentially private graph sparsification and applications. NeurIPS **32** (2019)
14. Dwork, C.: Differential Privacy. Automata, Languages and Programming (2006)
15. Choquette-Choo, C.A.: Label-only membership inference attacks. In: ICML, pp. 1964–1974 (2021)
16. Jayaraman, B.: Evaluating differentially private machine learning in practice. In: USENIX Security, pp. 1895–1912 (2019)
17. Leino, K.: Stolen memories: leveraging model memorization for calibrated white-box membership inference. In: USENIX Security, pp. 1605–1622 (2020)
18. Rahman, M.A., et al.: Membership inference attack against differentially private deep learning model. Trans. Data Priv. **11**(1), 61–79 (2018)
19. Hamilton, W., et al.: Inductive representation learning on large graphs. In: NeurIPS **30** (2017)
20. Zeng, H.: Graphsaint: Graph Sampling Based Inductive Learning Method (2019). arXiv:1907.04931 arXiv preprint
21. Voudigari, E.: Rank Degree: An Efficient Algorithm for Graph Sampling, pp. 120–129. ASONAM (2016)
22. Ye, Y., et al.: Sparse graph attention networks. IEEE Trans. Knowl. Data Eng. **35**(1), 905–916 (2021)
23. Kim, D.: How to find your friendly neighborhood: graph attention design with self-supervision (2022). arXiv:2204.04879 arXiv preprint
24. Li, J.: SGCN: a graph sparsifier based on graph convolutional networks. In: PAKDD 24, pp. 275–287 (2020)

25. Dwork, C.: Calibrating noise to sensitivity in private data analysis, pp. 265–284. TCC (2006)
26. Dwork, C., et al.: The algorithmic foundations of differential privacy. Found. Trends Theor. Comput. Sci. **9**(3–4), 211–407 (2014)
27. Mironov, I.: Rényi Differential Privacy. In: CSF, pp. 263–275 (2017)

Balancing Knowledge Distillation for Imbalance Learning with Bilevel Optimization

Anh B. H. Nguyen, Ba Tho Phan, and Viet Cuong Ta(✉)

VNU University of Engineering and Technology, Hanoi, Vietnam
{22021100,23020163,cuongtv}@vnu.edu.vn

Abstract. Knowledge distillation transfers knowledge from a high capacity teacher to a compact student using a mixture of hard and soft losses. On imbalanced data, a fixed weighting between hard and soft losses becomes brittle the learning process. Recent studies try to reweight these components in long-tailed settings. However, most of these methods do not adapt weights at the sample-wise level and do not take into account the student's behavior during training. To address this, we propose BiKD - a bilevel framework that dynamically balances hard and soft losses for each sample. We employ a weight generation network that produces adaptive per-sample weights, guided by a small balanced validation set. The student is now trained with an unconstrained combination of weighted hard and soft losses, allowing the student to relax both terms. We further propose a multi-step SGD strategy to optimize the weight model more accurately and efficiently. Experiments on long-tailed CIFAR–10/100 show that our approach surpasses recent balanced distillation methods across imbalance factors. Our implementation is available at https://github.com/phan-tho/Bilevel-balancing-kd.

Keywords: Knowledge distillation · Imbalanced dataset · Bilevel optimization.

1 Introduction

Deep learning models have achieved notable performance in the fields of computer vision with various applications. However, the large model architectures play a significant role in traditional training procedures. The advent of large models poses a significant challenge for deployment on edge devices like mobile phones due to their heavy storage and computational requirements. To address this, Knowledge Distillation (KD) [8] is one of the prominent techniques that use a teacher–student strategy. In KD, a lightweight student network is trained using a combination of teacher knowledge and label supervision.

A. B. H. Nguyen and B. T. Phan—Equal contribution.

R. C.-W. Wong et al. (Eds.): PAKDD 2026, LNAI 16617, pp. 374–386, 2027.
https://doi.org/10.1007/978-981-92-1926-1_30

However, typical setups in KD methods [2] implicitly assume that the transfer set, which is used to train both teacher and student models, is roughly class-balanced. In practice, many real-world distributions are long-tailed [23], a few head classes account for most samples, while tail categories are scarce. This causes both the high-capacity teacher and the student to degrade in performance on tail classes. [20,22]. Under such prior shift, using a fixed weight for the label-supervised (hard) loss and the teacher-guided (soft) loss is brittle and can bias learning toward head classes.

For this reason, recent studies [5,20,22] have explored knowledge distillation in the presence of biased teachers and imbalanced transfer sets. A prominent line of methods [6,22] assigns appropriate weights to the hard and soft losses to balance label supervision and teacher guidance. Despite outperforming distillation methods in imbalanced settings, these weighting based KD approaches still face two major limitations. First, it uses a single soft-loss weight which is shared by all samples in a class, ignoring the feature patterns. This contrasts with recent studies [13,24] which emphasize that the weight of hard and soft losses should vary at the sample level. Second, the weights are not adapted to the student's behavior. This is not appropriate in the context of imbalance learning.

In this work, we propose a BiKD framework that frames KD on an imbalanced transfer set as a bilevel problem. Within this framework, we can train the student on the imbalanced data with adaptive weights. We use a small network as a meta model that learns the mapping to the output weights, supervised by the student's performance on the unbiased set. To be more accurate and efficient, we use a one-step virtual update and accumulate hypergradients to update the meta model. This design preserves the benefits of multi-step optimization without storing full student updating computation graphs. Experiments on long-tailed CIFAR-10/100 show that our approach achieves the most stable performance in comparison to other distillation methods.

2 Related Work

Knowledge Distillation aims to transfer the predictive behavior of a large teacher network into a smaller student model. The main idea is that the student model mimics the teacher model in order to obtain a competitive or even a superior performance. Follow-up works distill richer information such as intermediate features [7,16], spatial attention maps [3,21], or relational structure among samples [14,19], and KD [8] is now widely used for model compression and regularization. The standard objective combines the cross-entropy loss on ground-truth labels with a Kullback–Leibler divergence between the student and teacher distributions. More recently, several methods argue that the trade-off between hard and soft losses should vary across samples. WSL [24] rethinks soft labels from a bias–variance perspective and proposes weighted soft labels to achieve a better sample-wise balance. RW-KD [13] uses a meta learning framework to adapt weights for the hard and soft losses per sample based on gradient signals. However, these methods typically assume roughly balanced training data.

Long-tailed recognition methods show that standard training strongly favors head classes when class frequencies are highly skewed [12]. In knowledge distillation, when a teacher is trained on the long-tailed data, naive KD transfers this teacher bias and can further degrade tail-class performance of the student. To address this, recent balanced KD methods [6,22] introduce class-balanced reweighting on the distillation term so that soft targets emphasize minority classes without losing head-class information. Class-balanced or class-conditional KD methods [9,11] further decouple representation learning and distillation, then align teacher and student class-conditional features to mitigate class imbalance. Multi-expert distillation approaches [10,20] build several teachers on less imbalanced subsets and aggregate them into a single student tailored to long-tailed data. DiVE [5] tackles long-tailed recognition by interpreting teacher predictions as virtual examples and explicitly flattening this virtual example distribution before distillation.

3 Methodology

3.1 Problem Setup

Given a set of imbalance training data $\mathcal{D}_{\text{train}} = \{(x_i, y_i)\}_{i=1}^{N}$ with one-hot labels $y_i \in \{0,1\}^C$. $\mathcal{D}_{\text{train}}$ follows the standard long-tailed setting [1], where the number of training samples per class decreases exponentially from head to tail. Let $T(\cdot)$ be an imbalanced pretrained **teacher** on $\mathcal{D}_{\text{train}}$ and $S_\theta(\cdot)$ a **student** with parameters θ. Following [8], KD transfers "soft" targets from the teacher at a temperature τ. The student learns from a *hard* supervised loss and a *soft* distillation loss:

$$\mathcal{L}_{\text{train}}(\theta) = \frac{1}{N}\sum_{i=1}^{N}\Big[(1-\alpha)\,\text{CE}\big(y_i,\, p_S(x_i)\big) + \alpha\,\tau^2\,\text{KL}\big(p_T^\tau(x_i)\,\|\,p_S^\tau(x_i)\big)\Big],$$

where $\alpha \in [0,1]$ mixes the two terms and τ^2 keeps the soft term's gradients comparable when $\tau > 1$. p_S^τ and p_T^τ are soft predictions with a temperature τ of the student and teacher, respectively. Since the teacher is fixed, $\text{KL}(p_T^\tau \| p_S^\tau)$ is equivalent to cross-entropy with soft targets p_T^τ. For clarity, we denote $\mathcal{L}_{\text{hard}}(x_i) = \text{CE}(y_i, p_S(x_i))$ and $\mathcal{L}_{\text{soft}}(x_i) = \tau^2\,\text{KL}(p_T^\tau(x_i) \| p_S^\tau(x_i))$.

It is worth pointing out that accurately estimating α is often difficult. The coefficient between hard and soft loss depends on many factors, such as sample inputs [11,24] or gradient signals during training [13,17]. This hyperparameter exerts an even stronger training influence when the transfer set $\mathcal{D}_{\text{train}}$ is imbalance. In the long-tailed setting, relying on constant α prevents the student from adapting their relative weights during training. It cannot simultaneously strengthen both gradient signals when both are informative or suppress both in contrast. These limitations suggest that hard and soft weights should be adaptive and not restricted to sum to one.

Inspired by [13], we first introduce a bilevel framework to automatically adapt the weights between the hard and soft losses for each sample x_i. Within this framework, the coefficients are optimized and continuously updated during training to achieve the best performance of the student model.

3.2 Sample-Wise Adaptive Weights Through Bilevel Framework

In our framework, we assume that there is a validation set of unbiased data examples $\mathcal{D}_{\text{val}} = \{(x_j, y_j)\}_{j=1}^{M}$ with M much smaller than N. To best balance the information carried by the hard loss and the soft loss, we propose to construct a weight network, serving as a meta model. This model takes as input a pair of per-sample cross-entropy losses and attempts to produce the weights for the hard and soft losses for this example. The meta model is parameterized as a function with parameter ϕ as follows:

$$\left[w_i^{\text{hard}}, w_i^{\text{soft}}\right] = f_\phi\left(\text{CE}(y_i, p_T(x_i)), \text{CE}(y_i, p_S(x_i))\right),$$

This pair cross-entropy losses summarizes how both models fit the ground-truth label on x_i, provide a compact description of the training signal for this sample. WSL [24] also applies a function of two losses to reweight the soft loss. In contrast, our learnable meta model receives the same inputs but tries to approximate the mapping from these loss pairs to $w_i^{\text{hard}}, w_i^{\text{soft}}$. The goal of f_ϕ is to determine how strongly the student should use each loss term for a given sample.
The student model S_θ, which we aim to train and use for prediction, is trained by the proposed adaptive training loss:

$$\mathcal{L}_{\text{train}}(\theta, \phi) = \frac{1}{N}\sum_{i=1}^{N}\left[w_i^{\text{hard}}\,\mathcal{L}_{\text{hard}}(x_i) + w_i^{\text{soft}}\mathcal{L}_{\text{soft}}(x_i)\right] \tag{1}$$

Equipped with this training loss, the total weight on the hard and soft terms per-sample is not constrained to sum to one. This relaxation increases the student's flexibility when distilling under class imbalance. For example, for samples x_i belonging to head classes that the student can handle and distill effectively, both w_i^{hard} and w_i^{soft} should be small simultaneously to avoid negative impacts on the student generalization.
The optimal selection of the student θ is based on its validation performance:

$$\mathcal{L}_{\text{val}}(\theta) = \frac{1}{M}\sum_{j\in\mathcal{D}_{\text{val}}}\mathcal{L}_{\text{hard}}(x_j) \tag{2}$$

Without explicitly linking the meta model and the student, there is no way to ensure that: First, the student model S_θ achieves effective distillation knowledge from the teacher on an imbalanced transfer set, if the weights provided by the meta model do not align with the ground-truth optimal weights. Second, that the generated weights for each example are indeed meaningful, since directly training f_ϕ is not possible without observing the student performance on the validation set. By these observations, we link two models together via a bilevel optimization framework. The motivation for this scheme is that if the weights generated by the meta model are high quality, then a student model trained with such weighted losses as supervision should achieve low loss on the validation set. Formally, this framework can be formulated as the following optimization problem:

$$\min_{\phi} \mathcal{L}_{\text{val}}(\theta^*(\phi)) \quad s.t. \quad \theta^*(\phi) = \arg\min_{\theta} \mathcal{L}_{\text{train}}(\theta, \phi)$$

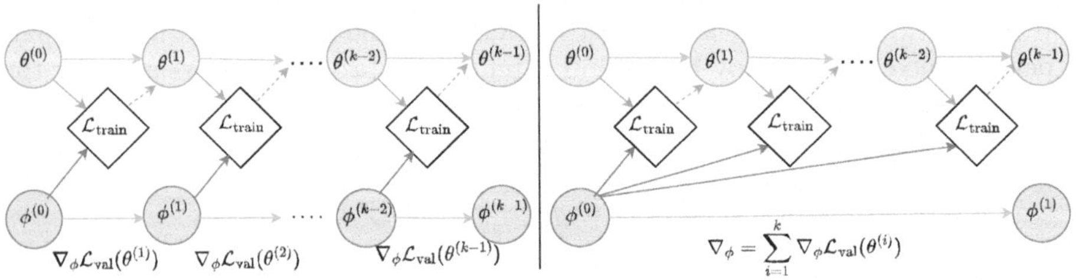

Fig. 1. This figure illustrates the difference between the online optimization and our proposed strategy.

Here, $\theta^*(\phi)$ denotes the student parameters obtained by training on $\mathcal{D}_{\text{train}}$ with weights generated by f_ϕ. The meta model is then updated by the hypergradient $\nabla_\phi \mathcal{L}_{\text{val}}\big(\theta^*(\phi)\big)$, which reflects the student performance on the validation set.

We observe that the loss $\mathcal{L}_{\text{val}}(\theta^*(\phi))$ depends only implicitly on the meta parameter ϕ via the trained student $\theta^*(\phi)$. Therefore, accurately approximating $\theta^*(\phi)$ is necessary to reduce the noisy estimation. In this paper, we propose to employ a multiple SGD steps update to estimate the optimal student θ^*. Specifically, we update the student parameters with the current weighted training loss, each step update can be formalized by:

$$\theta^{(t+1)} = \theta^{(t)} - \eta_\theta \nabla_\theta \mathcal{L}_{\text{train}}(\theta^{(t)}, \phi^{(t)}) \tag{3}$$

η_θ denotes the learning rate of the student optimizer. We refer to this process as the inner loops. After updating k steps of θ, the outer loop updates the meta parameters ϕ by evaluating the hypergradient $\nabla_\phi \mathcal{L}_{\text{val}}(\theta^{(t+k)})$:

$$\phi^{(t+1)} = \phi^{(t)} - \eta_\phi \nabla_\phi \mathcal{L}_{\text{val}}(\theta^{(t+k)}) \tag{4}$$

η_ϕ denotes the learning rate of the meta model. In practice, directly computing the hypergradient $\nabla_\phi \mathcal{L}_{\text{val}}(\theta^{(t+k)})$ in Eq.(4) is inefficient, since fully unrolling k inner updates would require storing k computation graphs of the student θ. To mitigate this, we adopt a one-step unrolled update with a virtual student. Then we evaluate the validation objective at this virtual model and backpropagate to obtain a one-step hypergradient. We accumulate these hypergradients over inner loops to approximate $\nabla_\phi \mathcal{L}_{\text{val}}(\theta^{(t+k)})$, thereby avoiding storage of the entire inner computation graphs. Specifically, at the time step t, we initiate $\nabla_\phi = 0$ and form

---

Algorithm 1. Bilevel Knowledge Distillation (BiKD)

Require: The teacher model $T(.)$, the student model $S_\theta(.)$, the meta model $f_\phi(.)$, $\mathcal{D}_{\text{train}}$, $\mathcal{D}_{\text{val}}$, learning rates η_θ, η_ϕ, epochs T, inner gradient steps k.

$count = 0$, $\nabla_\phi = 0$
for $t = 0, ..., T-1$ **do**
    for batch $\mathcal{B}_{\text{train}} = \{(x_i, y_i)\} \subset \mathcal{D}_{\text{train}}$ **do**
        $\theta' \leftarrow \theta^{(t)}$.
        $w_i^{\text{hard}}, w_i^{\text{soft}} \leftarrow f_{\phi^{(t)}}(\text{CE}(y_i, p_T(x_i)), \text{CE}(y_i, p_S(x_i)))$
        $\mathcal{L}_{\text{train}}(\theta', \phi^{(t)}) = \frac{1}{|\mathcal{B}_{\text{train}}|} \sum_i \left[w_i^{\text{hard}} \mathcal{L}_{\text{hard}}(x_i) + w_i^{\text{soft}} \mathcal{L}_{\text{soft}}(x_i)\right]$
        $\theta'(\phi) \leftarrow \theta' - \eta_\theta \nabla_\theta \mathcal{L}_{\text{train}}\big|_{\theta=\theta'}$
        Sample validation mini-batch $\mathcal{B}_{\text{val}} = \{(x_j^v, y_j^v)\}$ from $\mathcal{D}_{\text{val}}$.
        $\mathcal{L}_{\text{val}}(\theta'(\phi)) = \frac{1}{|\mathcal{B}_{\text{val}}|} \sum_j \mathcal{L}_{\text{hard}}(x_j)$
        $\nabla_\phi \leftarrow \nabla_\phi + \nabla_\phi \mathcal{L}_{\text{val}}(\theta'(\phi))\big|_{\phi=\phi^{(t)}}$
        if count % $k = 0$ **then**
            $\phi^{(t+1)} \leftarrow \phi^{(t)} - \eta_\phi \nabla_\phi$, $\nabla_\phi \leftarrow 0$
        else:
            $\phi^{(t+1)} \leftarrow \phi^{(t)}$
        end if
    $w_i^{\text{hard}}, w_i^{\text{soft}} \leftarrow f_{\phi^{(t+1)}}(\text{CE}(y_i, p_T(x_i)), \text{CE}(y_i, p_S(x_i)))$
    $\theta^{(t+1)} \leftarrow \theta^{(t)} - \eta_\theta \nabla_\theta \mathcal{L}_{\text{train}}(\theta^{(t)}, \phi^{(t+1)})\big|_{\theta=\theta^{(t)}}$
    $count \leftarrow count + 1$
    end for
end for

---

a *virtual student* θ' that loads the state of the student $\theta^{(t)}$. We update the virtual student by taking one gradient step on the current training minibatch:

$$\theta'(\phi) = \theta' - \eta \nabla_\theta \mathcal{L}_{\text{train}}(\theta'; \phi^{(t)}).$$

We then evaluate the validation objective at $\theta'(\phi)$ and backpropagate through this virtual step to accumulate the hypergradients:

$$\nabla_\phi = \nabla_\phi + \nabla_\phi \mathcal{L}_{\text{val}}(\theta'(\phi))$$

The process continues for k steps, we then update the meta model with information from the previous k step as follows:

$$\phi^{(t+1)} = \phi^{(t)} - \eta_\phi \nabla_\phi \tag{5}$$

With $k = 1$, our optimization approach reduces to the online strategy [13,15,18]. Figure 1 provides an illustration of our computational graph. The detailed implementation is given in Algorithm 1.

3.3 Overall Framework

Figure 2 demonstrates our framework, the procedure is as follows: (1) Initializing the virtual student θ' and computing the weights $[w^{\text{hard}}, w^{\text{soft}}]$ from the meta

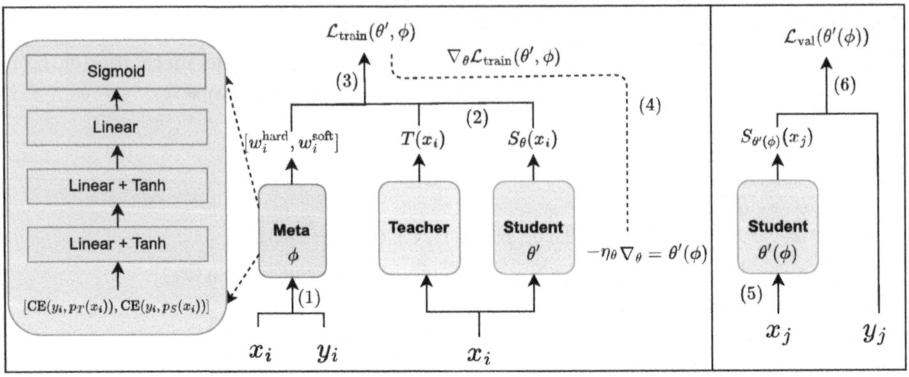

Fig. 2. This figure illustrates our framework.

model on the training data $(x_i, y_i) \sim D_{\text{train}}$; (2) Evaluating the output of the virtual student θ' and the teacher $T(.)$ on x_i; (3) Computing the training loss according to Eq.(1); (4) Deriving the gradient of the training loss to update the virtual student; (5) Computing the output of the updated virtual student $\theta'(\phi)$ on the validation sample x_j in D_{val}; and finally, (6) Evaluating the validation loss $\mathcal{L}_{\text{val}}$ to get a one-step hypergradient. After accumulating the hypergradients, we re-compute w^{hard} and w^{soft} to update the real student model.

3.4 Analysis of the Meta Model Weighting Mechanism

We detail how the meta model generates the weights for the hard and soft losses in the training objective. Under the bilevel framework, w^{hard} prevents the student from biasing toward majority class samples, while w^{soft} encourages the student to follow informative teacher signals during distillation.

The meta parameters update in Eq.(5) can be implemented as:

$$\phi^{(t+1)} = \phi^{(t)} + \frac{\eta_\phi \eta_\theta}{N} \sum_{x_j \in \mathcal{D}_{\text{train}}} [(\sum_{i=0}^{k-1} g_{\text{val}}^{(i+1)} g_{\text{hard}}^{(i)}(x_j))^T \frac{\partial w_j^{\text{hard}}}{\partial \phi} + (\sum_{i=0}^{k-1} g_{\text{val}}^{(i+1)} g_{\text{soft}}^{(i)}(x_j))^T \frac{\partial w_j^{\text{soft}}}{\partial \phi}] \tag{6}$$

where $g_{\text{val}}^{(i+1)}$ denotes the gradient of student parameters on the validation set at the $(i+1)$-th inner loop. $g_{\text{hard}}^{(i)}(x_j)$ and $g_{\text{soft}}^{(i)}(x_j)$ denote the student gradients with respect to the hard loss and the soft loss, respectively, computed on sample x_j at inner step i. For each sample x_j, if the information accumulated over k inner steps is aligned with the validation gradient,

$$\sum_{i=0}^{k-1} g_{\text{val}}^{(i+1)} g_{\text{hard}}^{(i)}(x_j) > 0,$$

then the meta update at time step $t+1$ increases w_j^{hard}. In other words, the meta model assigns larger hard-loss weights to samples whose gradients are directionally consistent with the balanced validation signal. An analogous phenomenon holds for the soft term: samples assigned a large w^{soft} must exhibit soft loss gradients aligned with the validation gradients. As pointed out by Safaryan et al. [17], the optimal distillation weight α^* increases with the expected alignment between the hard loss gradient at the student's optimum and the loss gradient at the teacher's parameters. In our setting, we instantiate the "optimum" direction for each sample x_j by the validation gradient. Consequently, given the loss pair $[\text{CE}(y_i, p_T(x_i)), \text{CE}(y_i, p_S(x_i))]$, the meta model learns to adjust the weights so that the resulting student aligns with the balanced set, implicitly steering learning toward better tail classes generalization.

4 Experiments

4.1 Settings

Datasets. We evaluate our method on the CIFAR long-tailed [1], which is widely used to assess performance under class imbalance. The number of training samples per class is controlled by an exponential function, resulting in a class distribution defined as $n_i = n_{\max} \times \mu^{\frac{i-1}{C-1}}$, where n_i is the number of samples in class i, $n_{\max}$ is the number of samples in the largest class, C is the total number of classes, and $\mu \in (0, 1]$ controls the imbalance severity. The *imbalance factor* (ρ) is defined as $\rho = \dfrac{n_{\max}}{n_{\min}}$. We use only 1000 images as validation set of unbiased data examples for both CIFAR-10 and CIFAR-100.

Baselines. We compare our method with the following baselines: **KD** [8] - vanilla knowledge distillation with a fixed trade-off between hard and soft losses; **WSL** [24] - sample wise re-weighting of the KD loss by adapting the hard–soft balance per sample; **RWKD** [13] - meta learning based sample-wise re-weighting that adjusts KD using validation gradients; **BKD** [22] - Balanced Knowledge Distillation with class-balanced weights in the distillation term to better support minority classes; **CCKD** [11]- Class-Conditional Knowledge Distillation that matches class-conditional distributions to transfer inter-class relational knowledge; **LFME** [20]- multi-expert KD that learns from multiple teachers with an adaptive teacher-selection strategy; **DiVE** [5]- distillation via virtual examples that flatten the teacher's effective label distribution for long-tailed data.

Models. We use ResNet-32x4, ResNet-8x4 [4] for teacher and student backbones, respectively. The meta network is implemented as a three-layer MLP with two hidden layers (Tanh activation) and sigmoid outputs for sample-wise weight generation. We train the teacher and student model using SGD with momentum 0.9 and weight decay 5×10^{-4}. The initial learning rate is set to 0.1 and decayed by a factor of 10 at the 80-th and 100-th epoch, with a total of 120 epochs. The meta network is optimized using Adam with a learning rate of 1×10^{-3}. We use temperature $\tau = 4$ for knowledge distillation.

Table 1. Test accuracy (%) on datasets with imbalance factors ρ. The table runs over three seeds and takes the average.

Dataset	Long-Tailed CIFAR-10				Long-Tailed CIFAR-100			
Imbalance	$\rho = 1$	$\rho = 10$	$\rho = 50$	$\rho = 100$	$\rho = 1$	$\rho = 10$	$\rho = 50$	$\rho = 100$
Teacher(CE)	95.82	90.79	82.72	77.23	79.4	65.45	51.59	45.88
Student(CE)	92.63	87.41	78.32	71.0	72.41	59.97	48.14	42.42
KD [8]	93.15	87.46	77.27	70.11	73.04	59.38	47.87	42.91
BKD [22]	92.58	87.03	81.67	**77.73**	73.12	62.38	50.71	46.07
CCKD [11]	92.96	87.61	79.74	73.82	72.91	62.11	48.86	44.92
WSL [24]	**93.91**	87.5	76.87	68.53	**75.18**	61.56	47.2	42.26
RWKD [13]	93.25	88.08	78.97	72.78	73.68	61.38	47.26	42.83
LFME [20]	92.85	88.07	80.28	74.04	73.13	61.51	49.29	45.18
DiVE [5]	91.55	88.2	80.79	74.83	71.89	61.93	51.01	44.76
Ours	93.85	**88.85**	**82.45**	75.91	74.08	**64.69**	**51.84**	**46.23**

4.2 Results and Ablation Studies

Table 1 reports test accuracy on CIFAR long-tailed datasets for different imbalance factors ρ. On long-tailed CIFAR-10, BiKD matches or surpasses the strongest balanced KD baselines in most imbalance regimes. In particular, at $\rho = 50$, **BiKD** achieves 82.45% accuracy, outperforming **BKD** (81.67%), **DiVE** (80.79%), and **LFME** (80.28%). On long-tailed CIFAR-100, **BiKD** yields consistent gains over **BKD** at all imbalance levels, suggesting that sample-wise bilevel weighting scales well to more classes.

Figure 3a visualizes outputs of the weight model on the long-tailed CIFAR-100 with $\rho = 50$, where each point corresponds to a training sample after the training process. Each point is located by its teacher and student cross entropy losses $\mathrm{CE}(y_i, p_T(x_i)), \mathrm{CE}(y_i, p_S(x_i))$ and colored by the assigned weight. The two panels reveal a behavior of the meta model: samples with small losses $\mathrm{CE}(y_i, p_T(x_i)), \mathrm{CE}(y_i, p_S(x_i))$ are assigned small weights w_i^{soft} and w_i^{hard}. This prevents easy examples (head classes) from dominating training and harming the student generalization. In contrast, samples whose loss pairs remain large, which is typical for tail-class examples, tend to receive larger hard and soft weights. Therefore, the student could focus more on training these samples. Figure 3b demonstrates the density of 50000 training samples after the training process. This scatter plot shows that the teacher exhibits a strong bias on a small subset of the data, and its loss fails to converge well for many samples. In contrast, the student cross entropy $\mathrm{CE}(y_i, p_S(x_i))$ converges better, leaving only a small fraction of samples with large loss values. This indicates that the student learns more stably than the teacher, which explains why it eventually surpasses the teacher in performance, as reported in Table 1.

Figure 4a further visualizes confusion matrices on long-tailed CIFAR-10 ($\rho = 50$). Compared to vanilla **KD**, **BiKD** dramatically improves the accuracy for tail classes. This supports our claim that bilevel sample-wise weighting generalizes more on tail classes, while still preserving strong performance on majority classes. In the subfigure 4b, we empirically show that $k = 5$ is preferable for the best accuracy for all settings. While other reweight methods [13,15,18] estimate the optimized $\theta^*(\phi)$ using an approximation with an inner loop step, our proposed BiKD uses multiple SGD updates to mitigate the noise in the estimation of $\theta^*(\phi)$, leading to the best performance of the student model.

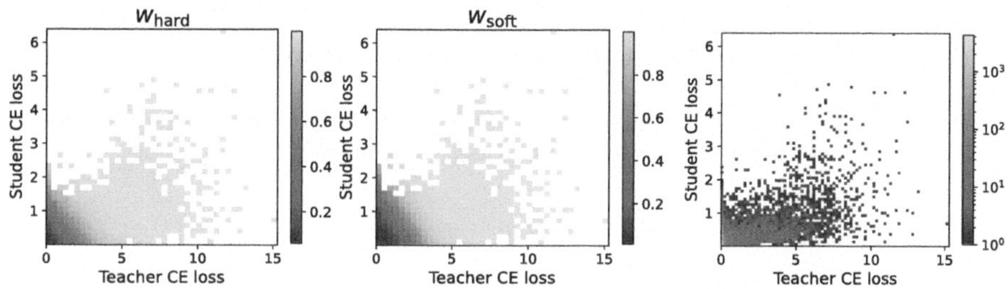

(a) (b)

Fig. 3. Visualization of the meta outputs after training process with long-tailed CIFAR-100($\rho = 50$). Each point corresponds to a training sample, with color indicating the value of assigned weight.

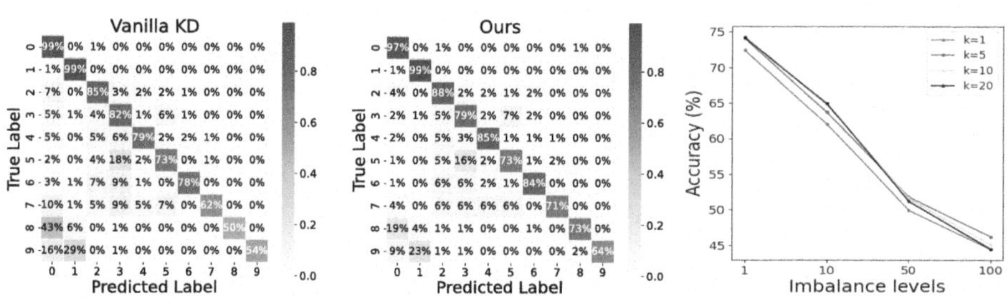

(a) (b)

Fig. 4. In the left subfigure, the confusion matrix for the Vanilla KD and ours on long-tailed CIFAR-10 ($\rho = 50$) are plotted. In the right figure, we show the comparison between different inner steps k on long-tailed CIFAR-100.

5 Conclusion

In this paper, we introduced BiKD, a bilevel knowledge distillation framework for imbalanced datasets. Within this framework, a small weight network produces per-sample weights for the hard and soft terms. This design allows the student to use an unconstrained adaptive combination of hard and soft losses, mitigating the bias induced by majority classes. We further proposed a multi-step SGD strategy without unrolling full computation graphs. Experiments on long-tailed CIFAR-10/100 demonstrate that BiKD surpasses recent balanced distillation methods across a range of imbalance factors. In addition, theoretical and experimental analyses of the learned weights reveal that the student model mainly focuses on hard tail samples, explaining the gains in tail accuracy.

6 Appendix: Derivation of Meta Gradients

We show how to compute exactly the gradient of the meta update gradient at time step t. By using implicit differentiation, we have:

$$\nabla_\phi = \sum_{i=0}^{k-1} \nabla_\phi \mathcal{L}_{\text{val}}(\theta^{(t+i+1)}) = \sum_{i=0}^{k-1} \nabla_\theta \mathcal{L}_{\text{val}}(\theta^{(t+i+1)}) \nabla_\phi \theta^{(t+i+1)} = \sum_{i=0}^{k-1} g_{\text{val}}^{(i+1)} \nabla_\phi \theta^{(t+i+1)} \tag{7}$$

where $g_{\text{val}}^{(i+1)}$ denotes the gradient of student parameters on the validation set at the $(i+1)$-th inner loops. From (3) in which $\mathcal{L}_{\text{train}}$ is computed on the training set, we obtain $\nabla_\phi \theta^{(t+i+1)}$ as follows:

$$\nabla_\phi \theta^{(t+i+1)} = \nabla_\phi \big(\theta^{(t+i)} - \eta_\theta \nabla_\theta \mathcal{L}_{\text{train}}(\theta^{(t+i)}, \phi^{(t)})\big) \tag{8}$$

$$= -\eta_\theta \nabla_\phi \nabla_\theta \frac{1}{N} \sum_{x_j \in \mathcal{D}_{\text{train}}} \left[w_j^{\text{hard}} \, \mathcal{L}_{\text{hard}}^{(i)}(x_j) + w_j^{\text{soft}} \mathcal{L}_{\text{soft}}^{(i)}(x_j) \right] \tag{9}$$

$$= -\frac{\eta_\theta}{N} \sum_{x_j \in \mathcal{D}_{\text{train}}} \left[\frac{\partial \mathcal{L}_{\text{hard}}^{(i)}(x_j)}{\partial \theta}^T \frac{\partial w_j^{\text{hard}}}{\partial \phi} + \frac{\partial \mathcal{L}_{\text{soft}}^{(i)}(x_j)}{\partial \theta}^T \frac{\partial w_j^{\text{soft}}}{\partial \phi} \right]$$

$$= -\frac{\eta_\theta}{N} \sum_{x_j \in \mathcal{D}_{\text{train}}} \left[g_{\text{hard}}^{(i)}(x_j)^T \frac{\partial w_j^{\text{hard}}}{\partial \phi} + g_{\text{soft}}^{(i)}(x_j)^T \frac{\partial w_j^{\text{soft}}}{\partial \phi} \right]$$

The equality from (8) to (9) follows because our method does not unroll the student's computation graph through the inner loop. We treat θ as detached with respect to ϕ at each inner step, hence $\theta^{(t+i)}$ is independent of ϕ, and the term $\nabla_\phi \theta^{(t+i)}$ equals to 0.

Therefore, we obtain the one step hypergradient for the $(i+1)$-th inner update at time step t as:

$$\nabla_\phi \mathcal{L}_{\text{val}}(\theta^{(t+i+1)}) = -\frac{\eta_\theta}{N} \sum_{x_j \in \mathcal{D}_{\text{train}}} \left[(g_{\text{val}}^{(i+1)} g_{\text{hard}}^{(i)}(x_j))^T \frac{\partial w_j^{\text{hard}}}{\partial \phi} + (g_{\text{val}}^{(i+1)} g_{\text{soft}}^{(i)}(x_j))^T \frac{\partial w_j^{\text{soft}}}{\partial \phi} \right]$$

Then the gradient which used to update the meta model can be computed by:

$$\nabla_{\phi} = \sum_{i=0}^{k-1} \nabla_{\phi} \mathcal{L}_{\text{val}}(\theta^{(t+i+1)})$$

$$= -\frac{\eta_{\theta}}{N} \sum_{x_j \in \mathcal{D}_{\text{train}}} \left[\Big(\sum_{i=0}^{k-1} g_{\text{val}}^{(i+1)} g_{\text{hard}}^{(i)}(x_j)\Big)^T \frac{\partial w_j^{\text{hard}}}{\partial \phi} + \Big(\sum_{i=0}^{k-1} g_{\text{val}}^{(i+1)} g_{\text{soft}}^{(i)}(x_j)\Big)^T \frac{\partial w_j^{\text{soft}}}{\partial \phi} \right]$$

Combine the update formula of $\phi^{(t+1)}$, we have the equality in Eq.(6).

References

1. Cui, Y., Jia, M., Lin, T.Y., Song, Y., Belongie, S.J.: Class-balanced loss based on effective number of samples. CVPR (2019)
2. Gou, J., Yu, B., Maybank, S.J., Tao, D.: Knowledge distillation: a survey. Int. J. Comput. Vis. (2020)
3. Guo, Z., Yan, H., Li, H., Lin, X.: Class attention transfer based knowledge distillation. CVPR (2023)
4. He, K., Zhang, X., Ren, S., Sun, J.: Deep residual learning for image recognition. CVPR (2015)
5. He, Y., Wu, J., Wei, X.S.: Distilling virtual examples for long-tailed recognition. ICCV (2021)
6. He, Y., et al.: Joint weighted knowledge distillation and multi-scale feature distillation for long-tailed recognition. Int. J. Mach. Learn. Cybern. (2024)
7. Heo, B., et al.: A comprehensive overhaul of feature distillation. ICCV (2019)
8. Hinton, G.E., Vinyals, O., Dean, J.: Distilling the knowledge in a neural network (2015). arXiv
9. Iscen, A., de Araújo, A.F., Gong, B., Schmid, C.: Class-balanced distillation for long-tailed visual recognition. In: British Machine Vision Conference (2021)
10. Jin, Y., Li, M., Lu, Y., ming Cheung, Y., Wang, H.: Long-tailed visual recognition via self-heterogeneous integration with knowledge excavation. CVPR (2023)
11. Li, L., Li, X.C., Ye, H.J., Zhan, D.C.: Enhancing class-imbalanced learning with pre-trained guidance through class-conditional knowledge distillation. In: ICML (2024)
12. Liu, Z., et al.: Large-scale long-tailed recognition in an open world. CVPR (2019)
13. Lu, P., et al.: RW-KD: sample-wise loss terms re-weighting for knowledge distillation. EMNLP (2021)
14. Park, W., Kim, D., Lu, Y., Cho, M.: Relational knowledge distillation. CVPR (2019)
15. Ren, M., Zeng, W., Yang, B., Urtasun, R.: Learning to reweight examples for robust deep learning. ICML (2018)
16. Romero, A., et al.: Fitnets: Hints for thin deep nets. CoRR (2014)
17. Safaryan, M., Peste, A., Alistarh, D.: Knowledge distillation performs partial variance reduction. ArXiv (2023)
18. Shu, J., et al.: Meta-Weight-Net: learning an explicit mapping for sample weighting. NeurIPS (2019)
19. Tung, F., Mori, G.: Similarity-preserving knowledge distillation. ICCV (2019)
20. Xiang, L., Ding, G.: Learning from multiple experts: self-paced knowledge distillation for long-tailed classification. ECCV (2020)

21. Zagoruyko, S., Komodakis, N.: Paying more attention to attention: improving the performance of convolutional neural networks via attention transfer. ArXiv (2016)
22. Zhang, S., Chen, C., Hu, X., Peng, S.: Balanced knowledge distillation for long-tailed learning. Neurocomputing (2023)
23. Zhang, Y., Kang, B., Hooi, B., Yan, S., Feng, J.: Deep long-tailed learning: a survey. IEEE Trans. Pattern Anal. Mach. Intell. (2021)
24. Zhou, H., et al.: Rethinking soft labels for knowledge distillation: a bias-variance tradeoff perspective. In: ICLR (2021)

Multi-scenario Knowledge-Enhanced Latent Intent Modeling for Recommendation

Quan Yuan[1], Chunchun Chen[2], Yuxing Zhang[3], Yaxiu Yu[1], and Xiaoming Ju[1](✉)

[1] East China Normal University, Shanghai, China
quanyuan@stu.ecnu.edu.cn, yxyu@library.ecnu.edu.cn, xmju@sei.ecnu.edu.cn
[2] Tongji University, Shanghai, China
c2chen@tongji.edu.cn
[3] Shanghai Jiao Tong University, Shanghai, China
zhangyuxing@sjtu.edu.cn

Abstract. This study investigates how to align knowledge graph with user preferences to enhance collaborative filtering recommendations. Existing knowledge-enhanced methods often rely on single-scenario neighbor aggregation, limiting their ability to capture diverse and uncertain user intents in real-world settings. To address these limitations, we propose MS-KIM, a Multi-scenario Knowledge-enhanced Latent Intent Modeling framework. At its core, MS-KIM formulates user intents as latent variables inferred through variational inference based on interactions and scenario-aware knowledge signals. Specifically, we first design a scenario-aware knowledge aggregation module to extract informative item representations under different scenarios. Building upon these signals, we leverage variational inference to jointly model user intents across multiple scenarios. Moreover, since scenario labels are often incomplete, we introduce a scenario-aware self-supervised task that promotes representation separation across scenarios by leveraging augmented subgraph-based user representations as guidance. Extensive experiments on three real-world datasets demonstrate that our model outperforms strong baselines.

Keywords: Recommendation · Knowledge Graph · Variational Inference · Self-supervised Learning

1 Introduction

In the era of massive data, recommender systems are essential for delivering personalized information efficiently. Traditional collaborative filtering (CF) methods [1,2] leverage user–item interactions but struggle with data sparsity and cold-start issues [3,4]. To mitigate these challenges, knowledge graph-enhanced recommendation (KGR) models incorporate structured semantic relations to enrich

R. C.-W. Wong et al. (Eds.): PAKDD 2026, LNAI 16617, pp. 387–398, 2027.
https://doi.org/10.1007/978-981-92-1926-1_31

sparse interactions. Early studies [3,5] used knowledge graphs(KGs) embeddings for item representation, while later works [6–8] exploited meta-paths to capture higher-order semantics. With the advent of graph neural networks (GNNs) [9,10], relational message passing further improved representation learning. Recently, contrastive learning frameworks [11,12] have enhanced robustness by aligning behavioral and semantic signals within KGs. Despite the advancements made by these approaches, they often overlook two critical aspects.

Firstly, most existing methods rely on a single decision-making scenario, making them prone to noise and information redundancy. In practice, user intents are multi-faceted—driven by diverse factors such as popularity, price, or visual appeal—yet these scenarios often coexist and intertwine, hindering intent disentanglement. Although KGs provide structured support for scenario-aware modeling, few studies explicitly address multiple decision-making scenarios. This entanglement leads to over-generalized user representations and limits fine-grained recommendations. Thus, an effective mechanism to model multiple scenarios and filter irrelevant signals is crucial.

Secondly, while KGs enhance scenario awareness, most KGR methods inagutmann2010noisedequately model user intents. They typically adopt static, neighborhood-based aggregation, treating each user as a fixed node whose embedding is derived from local item neighborhoods. Our empirical results (cf. Subsection 4.3) show that such static representations fail to capture multi-scenario user behavior. Although methods [9,10,13] propagate preferences through multi-hop neighborhoods to capture semantic proximity, they still assume static user interests. Even recent contrastive-learning-based methods [11,12], despite improving robustness, remain limited by this static, neighborhood paradigm, hindering their ability to model the diverse and uncertain nature of real-world user interactions.

In summary, existing recommender models are hindered by single-scenario assumptions and monolithic, neighborhood-based intent modeling. Motivated by this, we raise three research questions: (Q1) How can knowledge be effectively allocated across multiple scenarios? (Q2) How can user intent modeling capture diverse and uncertain behaviors beyond classic KG-based methods? (Q3) How can we achieve scenario-independent intent modeling without explicit labels?

To address these challenges, we propose MS-KIM, a Multi-scenario Knowledge-enhanced Latent Intent Modeling framework. MS-KIM formulates user intents as latent variables inferred from user behavior and multi-scenario knowledge signals via variational inference. Inspired by GNN- and prototype-based methods [14–16], we introduce a scenario-aware knowledge aggregation mechanism that defines scenario prototypes capturing shared feature patterns across items. Each item representation is enriched through two scenario-aware aggregation modules and aligned with scenario prototypes to obtain scenario–item probability distributions, which serve as the foundation for multi-scenario intent inference. To handle missing scenario labels, we further employ subgraph-based user representation learning and design a scenario-aware contrastive learning task to enhance scenario separation and mitigate weak supervision. Our contributions is as follows.

- **New Perspective.** This work integrates variational inference with multi-scenario knowledge to enhance user intent modeling in recommendation.
- **Novel Methodology.** We propose a Multi-scenario Knowledge-enhanced User Intent Modeling framework comprising: (1) Scenario-aware Knowledge Aggregation, (2) Multi-scenario Latent Intent Modeling, and (3) Scenario-aware Self-supervised Learning.
- **Extensive Experiments.** Experiments on three real-world datasets show that our method consistently outperforms state-of-the-art recommenders.

2 Related Work

2.1 Knowledge-Aware Recommender Systems.

Knowledge graphs provide rich auxiliary information for enhancing item representations and user preference modeling in recommender systems. Existing knowledge-aware methods fall into three categories: embedding-based, path-based, and GNN-based. Embedding-based models (e.g., DKN [5], CKE [3]) incorporate entity embeddings to enrich representations; path-based approaches [6–8] exploit multi-hop semantic paths for higher-order reasoning; and GNN-based models [9,10,17] propagate and aggregate knowledge over graph structures to capture complex semantic relations. Despite their success, these methods often struggle to denoise noisy knowledge signals and to model the inherent diversity and uncertainty of user behavior. To overcome these limitations, this work jointly learns scenario-aware knowledge and latent user intents through a probabilistic variational framework, enabling robust and interpretable intent modeling.

2.2 Self-supervised Learning for Recommender System.

In recent years, self-supervised learning (SSL) has emerged as a powerful paradigm in recommender systems to mitigate data sparsity and cold-start challenges. Prior studies have explored SSL from various perspectives, including collaborative filtering [18], sequential modeling [19], and knowledge-aware [11,12,20] recommendation. For collaborative filtering, SGL [18] introduces graph contrastive learning with random graph augmentations. In sequential recommendation, CL4SRec [19] improves sequence representations through contrastive learning on augmented sequence views. In knowledge-aware recommendation, MCCLK [12] employ multi-view and dual contrastive frameworks to enhance representation expressiveness. Distinct from these approaches, we design a scenario-aware self-supervised learning task that explicitly distinguishes representations across multiple scenarios, thereby improving intent modeling and robustness under weak or missing scenario labels.

3 Methodology

3.1 Problem Formulation

We consider a recommendation scenario with a user set $\mathcal{U}$ and an item set $\mathcal{V}$, where user–item interactions are represented by a binary matrix $\mathcal{Y} \in \mathbb{R}^{N\times I}$ indicating observed behaviors. Meanwhile, external knowledge is modeled as a KG $\mathcal{G}_k = (\mathcal{E}, \mathcal{R}, \mathcal{T})$, where $\mathcal{E}$ denotes the set of entities, $\mathcal{R}$ denotes the set of relations, and $\mathcal{T} = \{(h, r, t)|h, t \in \mathcal{E}, r \in \mathcal{R}\}$ denotes the set of triplets with h as the head entity, r as the relation and t as the tail entity. Given $\mathcal{Y}$ and $\mathcal{G}_k$, our objective is to learn latent user representations $\{\mathbf{z}_u\}_{u=1}^{N}$ that capture multi-scenario user intents by leveraging both behavioral interactions and structured semantic knowledge (Fig. 1).

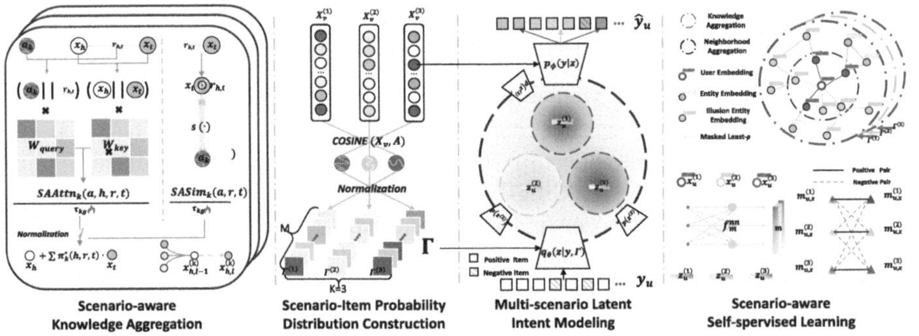

Fig. 1. The overall architecture of the proposed MS-KIM.

3.2 Scenario-Aware Knowledge Aggregation

Users focus on different knowledge under varying decision scenarios. Hence, we propose a scenario-aware knowledge aggregation strategy that defines K global scenario prototypes $\{a_k \in \mathbb{R}^d\}_{k=1}^{K}$ and aggregates KG neighbor information via a scenario-aware scoring mechanism to obtain knowledge-enhanced item representations $\{x_v^{(k)} \in \mathbb{R}^d\}_{k=1}^{K}$. The entity representations are updated as $\mathbf{x}_h^{(k)} = \mathbf{x}_h^{(k)} + \sum_{t\in\mathcal{N}_h} \pi_k^*(h, r, t)\,\mathbf{x}_t^{(k)}$, where $\mathcal{N}_h$ is the neighbor set of head h in $\mathcal{G}_{kg}$. For scenario k, entity embeddings $\mathbf{x}_h^{(k)}$ and $\mathbf{x}_t^{(k)}$ are initialized from shared embeddings $\mathbf{x}_h$ and $\mathbf{x}_t$, respectively. We provide two effective solutions to calculate $\pi_k^*(h, r, t)$ as follows:

Scenario-Aware-Attention Relevance Score. In our framework, it is important to consider both the relevance of the scenario and the reliability of heterogeneous graph connections. Inspired by HGT [14], we formulate a Scenario-Aware Atention relevant score $\mathrm{SAA}_k(h, r, t)$. The query domain is constructed by concatenating shared relation embedding with scenario embedding , while the key domain comprises the scenario-aware representations of head and tail entities. The resulting score quantifies the effectiveness of the information between two entities connected by a relation in a specific scenario. The $\pi_k^{SAA}(h,r,t)$ is represented as follows:

$$\begin{aligned}\pi_k^{SAA}(h,r,t) &= softmax_{(r',t')\in\mathcal{N}_h}(\mathrm{SAA}_k(h,r,t)/\tau_{kg})\\ \mathrm{SAA}_k(h,r,t) &= W_{query}[\mathbf{a}_k \parallel \mathbf{r}_{h,t}]\cdot(W_{key}[\mathbf{x}_h^{(k)} \parallel \mathbf{x}_t^{(k)}])^\top\end{aligned} \tag{1}$$

where $W_{query} \in \mathbb{R}^{2d\times d}$ and $W_{key} \in \mathbb{R}^{2d\times d}$ are trainable weights for attention, and τ_{kg} is a temperature parameter that controls the strength scenario awareness.

Scenario-Aware-Similarity Relevance Score. Although the Transformer mechanism effectively models heterogeneous graphs, it incurs high computational costs. To achieve comparable performance with better efficiency, we propose the Scenario-Aware Similarity score, $\mathrm{SAS}_k(h,r,t)$. It rotates the tail entity embedding x_t into the relation space via the element-wise product of r and t, and then measures its similarity to the scenario prototype a_k to assess relevance within scenario k. The $\pi_k^{SAS}(h,r,t)$ is represented as follows:

$$\begin{aligned}\pi_k^{SAS}(h,r,t) &= softmax_{(h,r',t')\in\mathcal{N}_h}(\mathrm{SAS}_k(h,r,t)/\tau_{kg})\\ \mathrm{SAS}_k(h,r,t) &= s(a_k, r_{h,t}\odot x_t^{(k)})\end{aligned} \tag{2}$$

where $s(\cdot)$ is used to dot product similarity function, and $\odot$ is the element-wise product. As previously mentioned, τ_{kg} is a temperature parameter.

3.3 Scenario-Item Probability Distribution Construction

Now that we have scenario-aware item representations, we construct a scenario–item probability distribution to integrate knowledge-enhanced signals with intent modeling via variational inference. This distribution measures each item's contribution to a scenario, derived from the similarity between the scenario prototype and the item representation:

$$\gamma_v^{(k)} = \frac{e^{\mathbf{Cosine}(\mathbf{x}_v^{(k)},\mathbf{a}_k)/\tau_{pm}}}{\sum_{i=1}^{K} e^{\mathbf{Cosine}(\mathbf{x}_v^{(k)},\mathbf{a}_i)/\tau_{pm}}},\ p_\phi(\mathbf{\Gamma}) = \prod_{i=1}^{K}\prod_{j=1}^{M} p_\phi(\gamma_j^{(i)}) \tag{3}$$

Here, $\mathbf{x}_v^{(k)}$ comes from Sect. 3.2, $\gamma_v^{(k)}$ is the score of item v in scenario k, and τ_{pm} scales the similarity.

In real-world settings, certain items lack distinct scenario-specific features, which can lead to noisy or even misleading enhanced representations. The proposed scenario-item distribution not only supports intent modeling but also mitigates this issue by reducing spurious attention to irrelevant scenarios.

3.4 Multi-scenario Latent Intent Modeling

With scenario-aware item representations and scenario–item distributions, we adopt a probabilistic approach for multi-scenario intent modeling. Latent user intents are modeled as probability distributions (e.g., Gaussian) and inferred via variational inference, capturing uncertainty and diverse preferences across scenarios. The inference leverages both observed user behavior and scenario-aware knowledge. Our method is structured around three key components: the design of prior and posterior distributions, the encoder architecture, and the decoder structure.

Prior and Posterior. We assume the existence of a latent variable $\mathbf{z}_u$ to represent user intents. The distribution of these user intents can be referred to as the prior, which is typically assumed to follow a standard Gaussian distribution $p(\mathbf{z}_u) \sim \mathcal{N}(0, \sigma_0^2 I)$. Given the observed user u behavior data $\mathbf{y}_u$ the goal is to infer the latent variable $\mathbf{z}_u$, which corresponds to the posterior distribution $p_\theta(\mathbf{z}_u|\mathbf{y}_u)$. However, directly computing this posterior distribution is intractable. To address this, the variational inference is used to approximate the posterior distribution [21]. Specifically, in our model, a variational distribution $q_\theta(\mathbf{z}_u|\mathbf{y}_u, \mathbf{\Gamma})$ is introduced to approximate the true posterior. To achieve multiple scenario disentanglement of intents, we formulate the following assumption:

$$q_\theta(\mathbf{z}_u \mid \mathbf{y}_u, \mathbf{\Gamma}) = \prod_{k=1}^{K} q_\theta\left(\mathbf{z}_u^{(k)} \mid \mathbf{y}_u, \mathbf{\Gamma}^{(k)}\right) \tag{4}$$

where $p_\psi(\Gamma^{(k)}) = \prod_{v=1}^{M} p_\psi(\gamma_v^{(k)})$ represents the probability distribution of scenario-item in the kth scenario.

Encoder. As previously mentioned, we consider the variational distribution $q_\theta(\mathbf{z}_u \mid \mathbf{y}_u, \mathbf{\Gamma})$ and the probability distribution matrix $\mathbf{\Gamma}$. Each latent representation $\mathbf{z}_u$ is modeled as a Gaussian distribution with a diagonal covariance matrix, i.e., $q_\theta(\mathbf{z}_u^{(k)} \mid \mathbf{y}_u, \mathbf{\Gamma}^{(k)}) \sim \mathcal{N}(\mu_u^{(k)}, diag(\sigma_u^{(k)^2}))$. The encoder maps the scenario–item probability distribution and the observed user behavior to the mean $\mu_u^{(k)}$ and standard deviation $\sigma_u^{(k)}$ of the latent intent distribution as follows:

$$\left(a_u^{(k)}, b_u^{(k)}\right) = f_\theta^{nn}\left(\mathbf{y}_u \odot \gamma^{(k)} / \sqrt{\sum_{i:y_{u,i}=1} (\gamma_i^{(k)})^2}\right) \tag{5}$$

where $\odot$ denotes element-wise multiplication. The mean vector $\mu_u^{(k)}$ and the standard deviation vector $\sigma_u^{(k)}$ are then computed as:

$$\mu_u^{(k)} = \frac{\mathbf{a}_u^{(k)}}{\|\mathbf{a}_u^{(k)}\|_2}, \sigma_u^{(k)} = \sigma_0 \cdot exp\left(-\frac{1}{2}\mathbf{b}_u^{(k)}\right) \tag{6}$$

where $\|\cdot\|_2$ is the $L2$ norm, σ_0 is the standard deviation of the prior distribution, served as a critical tunable scaling factor. Additionally, to facilitate efficient learning and mitigate overfitting, the neural network f_θ^{nn} are shared across each scenario.

Decoder. The items a user may interact with are predicted by the decoder, which takes the multi-scenario user representation z_u as input. A multinomial likelihood is adopted, consistent with the previous works, to estimate the user preference distribution.

$$p\left(\hat{\mathbf{y}}_{u,v} \mid \mathbf{z}_u, \mathbf{\Gamma}\right) \propto \sum_{k=1}^{K} \gamma_v^{(k)} \cdot \hat{y}_{u,v}^{(k)} \quad (7)$$

where $\hat{\mathbf{y}}_{u,i}^{(k)}$ represents the user's preference score to item v in the kth scenario. The preference score is calculated using the following equation:

$$\hat{y}_{u,v}^{(k)} = \exp\left(\text{Cosine}\left(\mathbf{z}_u^{(k)}, \mathbf{x}_v^{(k)}\right) / \tau_{pm}\right); \quad (8)$$

Building on the earlier definition in Sect. 3.2, $\mathbf{x}_v^{(k)} = f_{kg}(\mathcal{G}_k; \mathbf{a}_k; v)$ is the scenario-aware knowledge aggregation function. Additionally, $\mathbf{z}_u^{(k)}$ is generated by encoder. The temperature parameter τ_{pm} is used to scale the similarity scores.

3.5 Scenario-Aware Self-supervised Learning

Explicit scenario labels are often limited in real-world recommendation systems. To address this challenge, we introduce a scenario-aware self-supervised learning framework. Specifically, we design a scenario-aware graph augmentation strategy that constructs masked interaction subgraphs using the scenario item probability matrix Γ, removing edges with low scenario relevance. Inspired by structured intent modeling [4,22], items in each subgraph are leveraged to learn localized user intent representations. A self-supervised objective then aligns these representations with their scenario–item probability embeddings while separating those from different scenarios, thereby enhancing scenario-level discrimination.

Scenario-Aware Graph Augmentation. Items with low scenario–item similarity contribute little to recommendations within a given scenario. To enhance scenario relevance and mitigate noise, we introduce a scenario-aware graph augmentation strategy that masks low-relevance interactions likely to distort user intent. Specifically, we sample the scenario–item probability distribution $\gamma^{(k)}$ and add Gaussian noise [23] for robustness:

$$\gamma_v^{(k)} = \gamma_v^{(k)} - \log(-\log(\epsilon)); \quad \epsilon \sim \text{Uniform}(0,1) \quad (9)$$

Edges with the lowest ρ fraction of scenario-aware scores are denoted as $\mathcal{M}_u^{(k)}$:

$$\mathcal{M}_u^{(k)} = \{(u,v) | (u,v) \in \mathcal{G}_u \wedge \gamma_v^{(k)} \in \text{least-p}(\Gamma^{(k)}; \rho)\}, \quad (10)$$

and are subsequently removed from the original user–item interaction graph $\mathcal{G}_u$ to form an augmented subgraph $\mathcal{G}_u^{(k)} = \mathcal{G}_u \setminus \mathcal{M}_u^{(k)}$. This process yields K scenario-specific subgraphs that suppress noisy edges and improve scenario-level intent modeling.

Self-supervised Learning. After constructing the augmented graph, items within each subgraph are used to learn structured representations that capture localized user intent. Following classical graph representation learning, user embeddings are obtained by aggregating scenario-aware item embeddings from their neighbors, formally defined as:

$$\mathbf{x}_u^{(k)} = \frac{1}{|\mathcal{N}_u^{(k)}|} \sum\nolimits_{(u,v)\in\mathcal{G}_u^{(k)}} \mathbf{x}_v^{(k)}, \ \mathbf{x}_v^{(k)} = f_{kg}(\mathcal{G}_k; \mathbf{a}_k; v) \tag{11}$$

where $\mathcal{N}_u^{(k)}$ is the set of interactions of user u on the kth subgraph, and $f_{kg}(\mathcal{G}_k; a_k ; v)$ comes from Sect. 3.2.

For the latent user representation $\mathbf{z}_u^{(k)}$ of the kth scenario, we treat the corresponding augmented subgraph representation $\mathbf{x}_u^{(k)}$ as a positive sample and those from other scenarios as negatives. We adopt the standard InfoNCE contrastive loss [24], formulated as:

$$\mathcal{L}_c = \sum_{k=1}^{K} -\log \frac{\exp(\text{Cosine}(f_m^{nn}(\mathbf{z}_u^{(k)}), f_m^{nn}(\mathbf{x}_u^{(k)}))/\tau_{cl})}{\sum_{i=1}^{K} \exp(\text{Cosine}(f_m^{nn}(\mathbf{z}_u^{(k)}), f_m^{nn}(\mathbf{x}_u^{(i)})/\tau_{cl})} \tag{12}$$

Note that the contrasting embeddings $\mathbf{z}_u^{(k)}$ and $\mathbf{x}_u^{(k)}$ are derived from different learning paradigms. A shallow projection network f_m^{nn} maps them into a shared latent space for unified optimization, with the temperature parameter τ_{cl} controlling contrastive sharpness [18,25]. By maximizing agreement between positive pairs and minimizing it for negative pairs, the model brings same-scenario representations closer and pushes different-scenario ones apart. Overall, this self-supervised framework provides a simple yet effective mechanism for enhancing scenario differentiation and recommendation quality.

Table 1. Statistics for the three datasets.

Statistics	Alibaba-iFashion	MovieLens-1M	Book-Crossing
#Users	114,737	6,036	17,860
#Items	30,040	2,445	14,967
#Interactions	1,781,093	753,772	139,746
Know. Graph			
#Entities	59,156	182,011	77,903
#Relations	51	12	25
#Triplets	279,155	1,241,996	151,500

4 Experiment

4.1 Experimental Setup

Dataset and Metrics. We conduct experiments on three widely used benchmark datasets—Alibaba-iFashion, MovieLens-1M, and Book-Crossing—which differ in scale, sparsity, and domain, ensuring the robustness and generalizability of our results. All datasets are preprocessed using the standard 5-core filtering to remove users and items with fewer than five interactions. The KG construction varies by dataset: for MovieLens-1M and Book-Crossing, we follow [13] and build KGs using Microsoft Satori; for Alibaba-iFashion, we adopt the manual KG construction method from [17] based on item category information. Dataset statistics are summarized in Table 1.

Evaluation Protocols. To ensure fair comparison, we adopt a full-ranking evaluation protocol, where all models are trained and tested on identical datasets. The embedding dimension is fixed at 64. The optimization is performed using Adam [26] with a batch size of 500. Grid search is applied for hyperparameter tuning. We evaluate model performance using Recall@20 and NDCG@20, two widely used metrics that comprehensively assess top-N recommendation quality.

Baselines. To evaluate MS-KIM, we compare it with three types of baselines: (1) general collaborative filtering methods: BPR [27], LightGCN [22], MultiDAE [28], MultVAE [28]; (2) knowledge-enhanced methods: KGCN [9], KGAT [10], KGIN [17]; and (3) contrastive learning knowledge-enhanced methods: KGCL [11], KGRec [29], MKGCL [20].

Table 2. Performance comparison of different models on various datasets.

Dataset Method	Alibaba-iFashion		MovieLens-1M		Book-Crossing	
	N@20	R@20	N@20	R@20	N@20	R@20
BPR	0.0491	0.0859	0.2619	0.2915	0.0528	0.0873
LightGCN	0.0632	0.1067	0.3063	0.3327	0.0753	0.1137
$Multi-DAE$	0.0552	0.0959	0.3013	0.3387	0.0693	0.1102
$Multi-VAE$	0.0651	0.1047	<u>0.3124</u>	<u>0.3457</u>	0.0744	0.1160
KGCN	0.0625	0.1022	0.2933	0.3271	0.0726	0.1185
KGAT	0.0597	0.0960	0.2840	0.3163	0.0781	0.1322
KGIN	0.0742	0.1165	0.3085	0.3412	0.0881	0.1405
KGCL	0.0725	0.1153	0.2987	0.3351	0.0922	0.1491
KGRec	<u>0.0757</u>	<u>0.1192</u>	0.2959	0.3302	0.0905	0.1462
MKGCL	0.0735	0.1176	0.3109	0.3408	<u>0.0950</u>	<u>0.1544</u>
Ours	**0.0896***	**0.1398***	**0.3297***	**0.3592***	**0.1091***	**0.1767***
Imp	18.36%	17.28%	5.53%	3.90%	8.01%	10.02%

4.2 Overall Performance Comparison

Table 2 reports the results on three datasets, leading to three key observations. **(1)** The proposed MS-KIM;consistently outperforms all baselines across metrics and datasets, benefiting from three core designs: (i) a scenario-aware knowledge aggregation mechanism that selectively propagates informative signals while suppressing noise, (ii) a probabilistic multi-scenario intent model that captures intent diversity and behavioral uncertainty, and (iii) a scenario-aware self-supervised task that enhances inter-scenario representation separability. **(2)** Incorporating knowledge information does not always improve performance—some KG-based models underperform on MovieLens-1M due to noisy or irrelevant knowledge. In contrast, our selective knowledge integration effectively mitigates this issue and improves robustness. **(3)** The effectiveness of self-supervised learning is reaffirmed, as contrastive learning consistently boosts representation quality. This motivates our tailored contrastive mechanism for capturing latent, scenario-specific user intents.

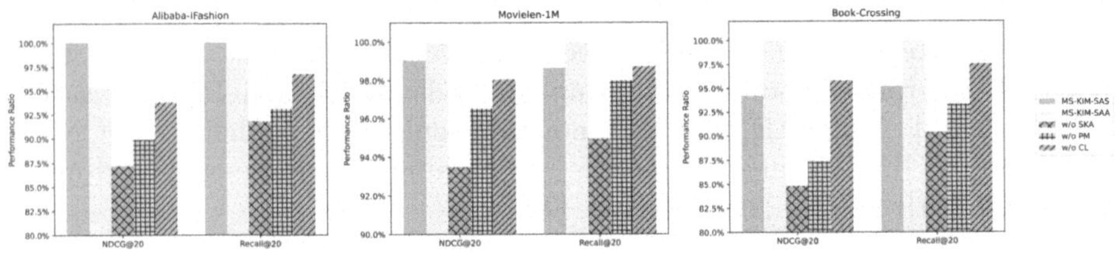

Fig. 2. Ablation results of MS-KIM, where different colors denote model variants. The x-axis shows evaluation metrics, and the y-axis indicates relative performance, with the best result normalized to 100%.

4.3 Ablation Study

To assess the contribution of each component, we perform an ablation study comparing two framework variants—MS-KIM-SAS and MS-KIM-SAA—based on scenario-aware similarity and attention relevance, respectively. Additionally, we evaluate three model variants: (1) MS-KIM$_{w/o,SKA}$, which removes scenario-aware knowledge aggregation and applies average pooling over all features; (2) MS-KIM$_{w/o,PM}$, which replaces the probabilistic intent modeling with a deterministic neighborhood-based approach; and (3) MS-KIM$_{w/o,SL}$, which excludes the scenario-aware self-supervised task. As shown in Fig. 2, the results reveal that (i) scenario-aware knowledge aggregation contributes most significantly by capturing multi-intent behavior and reducing noise; (ii) probabilistic modeling effectively captures user intent diversity and behavioral uncertainty; and (iii) self-supervised learning enhances scenario separation, especially when explicit scenario labels are absent.

5 Conclusion

We propose a novel multi-scenario knowledge-enhanced latent intent modeling method for recommendation, called MS-KIM. Our idea stems from the inherent diversity and uncertainty of user behavior in the real world, which are often scattered across their multiple decision-making scenarios. This method achieves multi-scenario knowledge-enhanced latent intent modeling through three key designs: 1) The scenario-aware knowledge aggregation enhances item representation for different scenarios; 2) We propose a probabilistic modeling approach based on variational inference tailored for multi-scenario intent modeling; 3) The scenario-aware self-supervised task promotes the separation of representations across different scenarios. Extensive evaluations on multiple real-world datasets confirm the effectiveness of MS-KIM, outperforming a variety of state-of-the-art methods.

References

1. He, X., Chua, T.S.: Neural factorization machines for sparse predictive analytics. In: Proceedings of the 40th International ACM SIGIR Conference on Research and Development in Information Retrieval, pp. 355–364 (2017)
2. Balazevic, I., Allen, C., T.: Hospedales Multi-relational poincaré graph embeddings. Adv. Neural. Inf. Process. Syst. **32** (2019)
3. Zhang, F., Yuan, D. Lian, N.J., Xie, X., Ma, W.Y.: Collaborative knowledge base embedding for recommender systems. In: Proceedings of the 22nd ACM SIGKDD International Conference On Knowledge Discovery and Data Mining, pp. 353–362 (2016)
4. Wang, Z., Lin, G., Tan, H., Chen, Q., Ckan, X.L.: Collaborative knowledge-aware attentive network for recommender systems. In: Proceedings of the 43rd International ACM SIGIR Conference on Research and Development in Information Retrieval, pp. 219–228 (2020)
5. Wang, H., Zhang, F., Xie, X., Guo Dkn, M.: Deep knowledge-aware network for news recommendation. In: Proceedings of the 2018 World Wide Web Conference, pp. 1835–1844 (2018)
6. Hu, B., Shi, W., Zhao, X., Yu, P.S.: Leveraging meta-path based context for top-n recommendation with a neural co-attention model. In: Proceedings of the 24th ACM SIGKDD International Conference on Knowledge Discovery & Data Mining, pp. 1531–1540 (2018)
7. Shi, C., Hu, B., Zhao ,W.X., Yu, P.S.: Heterogeneous information network embedding for recommendation. IEEE Trans. Knowl. Data Eng. **31**(2), 357–370 (2018)
8. Wang, X., et al.: Chua Explainable reasoning over knowledge graphs for recommendation. In: Proceedings of the AAAI Conference on Artificial Intelligence, vol. 33, no. 01, pp. 5329–5336 (2019)
9. bibitemch31KGCN Wang, H., Zhao, M., Xie, X., Li, W., Guo, M.: Knowledge graph convolutional networks for recommender systems. In: The world Wide Web Conference, pp. 3307–3313 (2019)
10. Wang, X., et aL.: Kgat: Knowledge graph attention network for recommendation. In: Proceedings of the 25th ACM SIGKDD International Conference on Knowledge Discovery & Data Mining, pp. 950–958 (2019)
11. Yang, Y., Huang, C., Xia, L., Li, C.: Knowledge graph contrastive learning for recommendation. In: Proceedings of the 45th International ACM SIGIR Conference on Research and Development in Information Retrieval, pp. 1434–1443 (2022)
12. Zou, D., et al.: Multi-level cross-view contrastive learning for knowledge-aware recommender system. In: Proceedings of the 45th International ACM SIGIR Conference on Research and Development in Information Retrieval, pp. 1358–1368 (2022)

13. Wang, H., et al.: Ripplenet: propagating user preferences on the knowledge graph for recommender systems. In: Proceedings of the 27th ACM International Conference on Information And Knowledge Management, pp. 417–426 (2018)
14. Hu, Z., Dong, Y., Wang, K., Sun, Y.: Heterogeneous graph transformer. In: Proceedings of the Web Conference 2020, pp. 2704–2710 (2020)
15. Ma, J., et al.: Learning disentangled representations for recommendation. In: Advances in Neural Information Processing Systems, vol. 32 (2019)
16. Melchiorre, A.B., Rekabsaz, N., Ganhör, C., Schedl, M.: Protomf: Prototype-based matrix factorization for effective and explainable recommendations. In: Proceedings of the 16th ACM Conference on Recommender Systems, pp. 246–256 (2022)
17. Wang, X., et al.: Chua learning intents behind interactions with knowledge graph for recommendation. In: Proceedings of the Web Conference 2021, pp. 878–887 (2021)
18. Wu, J., et al.: Self-supervised graph learning for recommendation. In: Proceedings of the 44th International ACM SIGIR Conference on Research and Development in Information Retrieval, pp. 726–735 (2021)
19. Xie, X., et al.: Cui Contrastive learning for sequential recommendation. In: IEEE 38th International Conference on Data Engineering (ICDE), vol. 2022, pp. 1259–1273. IEEE (2022)
20. Xie, Z., Li, J., Wu, N.: Enhancing alignment and uniformity of contrastive learning for knowledge-based recommendation. In: 2024 International Joint Conference on Neural Networks (IJCNN), pp. 1–10. IEEE (2024)
21. Kingma, D.P., Welling, M.: Auto-encoding variational bayes (2013)
22. He, X., et al.: LightGCN: simplifying and powering graph convolution network for recommendation. In: Proceedings of the 43rd International ACM SIGIR Conference on Research and Development in Information Retrieval, pp. 639–648 (2020)
23. Jang, E., Gu, S., Poole, B.: Categorical reparameterization with gumbel-softmax, (2016). arXiv:1611.01144 arXiv preprint
24. Gutmann, M., Hyvärinen, A.: Noise-contrastive estimation: a new estimation principle for unnormalized statistical models. In: Proceedings of the Thirteenth International Conference on Artificial Intelligence and Statistics. JMLR Workshop and Conference Proceedings, pp. 297–304 (2010)
25. Khosla, P., et al.: Supervised contrastive learning. Advances in Neural Information Processing Systems, vol. 33, pp. 18 661–18 673 (2020)
26. Kingma, D.P., J., Adam, B.: A method for stochastic optimization (2014). arXiv:1412.6980 arXiv preprint
27. Rendle, S., Freudenthaler, C., Gantner, Z., Schmidt-Thieme, L., BPR: Bayesian Personalized Ranking from implicit feedback (2012). arXiv:1205.2618 arXiv preprint
28. Liang, D., Krishnan, R.G., Hoffman, M.D., Jebara, T.: Variational autoencoders for collaborative filtering. In: Proceedings of the 2018 World Wide Web Conference, pp. 689–698 (2018)
29. Yang, Y., Huang, C., Xia, L., Huang, C.: Knowledge graph self-supervised rationalization for recommendation. In: Proceedings of the 29th ACM SIGKDD Conference on Knowledge Discovery and Data Mining, pp. 3046–3056 (2023)

Dynamic Mortality Prediction for Prostate Cancer Based on Irregularly Sampled Multimodal EHR and Musculoskeletal Image-Based Biomarkers

Eunseon Seong[1], Minjee Kim[2], Dareen Eom[3], Gyeonghwa Heo[4], Urban Emmenegger[5,6], Saleh Tabatabaei[5,7], Tayler Declan Ross[5,6,8], and Michael Hardisty[5,7,8(✉)]

[1] Department of Artificial Intelligence, Hanyang University, Seoul, South Korea
emilyseong@hanyang.ac.kr
[2] Department of Statistics, Ewha Womans University, Seoul, South Korea
jee365@ewha.ac.kr
[3] Interdisciplinary Program of Medical Informatics, College of Medicine, Seoul National University, Seoul, South Korea
edr20908@snu.ac.kr
[4] Department of Cogno-Mechatronics Engineering, Pusan National University, Busan, South Korea
ghheo@pusan.ac.kr
[5] Sunnybrook Research Institute, Toronto, Canada
uemmengg@sri.utoronto.ca,
{s.mirzatabatabaei,taylerdeclan.ross}@mail.utoronto.ca,
M.Hardisty@utoronto.ca
[6] Institute of Medical Science, University of Toronto, Toronto, Canada
[7] Institute of Biomedical Engineering, University of Toronto, Toronto, Canada
[8] Department of Surgery, University of Toronto, Toronto, Canada

Abstract. Predicting mortality in advanced prostate cancer (PCa) is critical for guiding treatment decisions and supporting patients. In this study, we focus on dynamic mortality prediction for advanced PCa patients receiving systemic therapy at Sunnybrook Health Sciences Centre. Unlike prior work that relies on static predictions at diagnosis or treatment initiation, our approach integrates static demographic and malignancy features with temporally resolved Electronic Health Record (EHR) data, including imaging, labs, physician notes, and weight trends. Specifically, we employ time-aware attention mechanisms to handle irregular time-series data and a cross-modal fusion architecture to integrate different modalities. Experimental results demonstrate the effectiveness of our model and highlight the potential of multimodal EHR fusion for personalized care for prostate cancer.

Keywords: Electronic Health Record · Cancer · Deep Learning · Time-Series · Multi-modal · Prognostic Modeling · Mortality Prediction

R. C.-W. Wong et al. (Eds.): PAKDD 2026, LNAI 16617, pp. 399–410, 2027.
https://doi.org/10.1007/978-981-92-1926-1_32

1 Introduction

Prostate cancer is one of the most common malignancies in men, generally associated with a favorable prognosis but sharply declining survival in advanced stages. While the overall 5-year survival rate is approximately 91%, this drops to 41% for patients with stage 4 metastatic disease, making mortality prediction critical for guiding treatment decisions and advanced care planning. Clinicians must balance life-prolonging interventions with palliative approaches focused on symptom relief and quality of life [18], but functional decline is often abrupt and unpredictable, highlighting the need for reliable prognostic models.

Despite the necessity of prognostic modeling, mortality prediction in prostate cancer remains challenging due to heterogeneity in disease trajectory, comorbidities, treatment histories, and physiologic factors such as frailty, sarcopenia, and bone density [6]. Prior studies often predict mortality at fixed time points (e.g., at diagnosis or after a specific treatment) [10], failing to capture the complexity and dynamics of real-world clinical records.

Electronic health records (EHRs) offer rich information on patient status, encompassing structured laboratory values, CT-derived imaging biomarkers, and unstructured clinical notes. Thus, EHR data has become an invaluable resource for prognostic modeling in clinical practice. However, modeling EHR data requires special consideration due to its intrinsic complexity. First, EHRs are multimodal, integrating longitudinal clinical measurements (e.g., laboratory values, CT-derived imaging biomarkers) with unstructured textual information from clinical notes, each differing in data structure and semantic content. Moreover, EHR data are collected at uneven intervals rather than at fixed time points, resulting in irregular and asynchronous longitudinal patterns. These characteristics require advanced modeling techniques that can handle heterogeneous modalities and irregular temporal behavior.

To address these challenges, we propose a multimodal mortality prediction model for prostate cancer patients treated with systemic therapy at Sunnybrook Health Sciences Centre, leveraging irregularly sampled longitudinal records across multiple modalities. We integrate temporally varying elements of EHR measurements with CT-derived musculoskeletal biomarkers, malignancy indicators, demographic information, radiology reports, and clinical notes, aiming to fuse these diverse inputs into a unified prognostic estimate. To be specific, we employ a time-aware attention mechanism to handle irregular time-series patterns and explore various multimodal fusion strategies to align structured features with a semantic representation of clinical notes. The overall framework enables prognostic modeling of real-world clinical data and supports more reliable mortality prediction in advanced prostate cancer patients.

2 Background

Prior work in prostate cancer prognostication has primarily focused on static models evaluated at specific time points. Common prognostic factors associated with survival in prostate cancer include PSA, age, cancer stage, Gleason score, BMI, metastatic spread, ECOG status, Karnofsky Performance Status (KPS), comorbidity indices (e.g., Charlson), hemoglobin, albumin, lactate dehydrogenase (LDH), alkaline phosphatase (ALP), cognitive function, dietary intake, and the use of cancer-directed treatments. This highlights the varying types of data (tumor biology, functional status, and biochemical markers) that impact prostate cancer patient mortality [4,13].

To account for temporal changes, prior work has used conditional survival analysis [19] and incorporated time-varying factors like functional status and lab results [1,2]. However, these approaches do not model temporal trajectories or integrate data modalities. While a deep learning model using MRI and pathology images to predict survival in castration-resistant prostate cancer [22] has also been developed, they do not integrate other elements of EHR.

EHRs offer rich, multimodal data including structured measurements and unstructured clinical notes [5,16]. These data are irregularly sampled and temporally sparse, complicating integration. Traditional models often fail to utilize unstructured narratives or account for timing variability. Recent deep learning approaches address this by applying time-aware attention and multimodal fusion techniques. For example, Zhang et al. [21] jointly modeled ICU time series and notes with attention mechanisms, showing that combining structured trends with clinical context improves accuracy over unimodal approaches.

3 Dataset

The dataset is composed of 537 patients with advanced prostate cancer treated at Sunnybrook Health Sciences Centre between May 2008 and November 2024, comprising 24,293 notes from EHRs. Patients with fewer than 2 notes were excluded. Three modalities were included: structured tabular data, extracted features from medical imaging, and unstructured clinical note text. Survival time was binned into 3 clinically relevant time scales from note date to death date ($\leq$90 d, 91–365 days, $\geq$366 d) [7]. Key variables are summarized in Table 1.

Table 1. Overview of Data Modalities and Key Variables

Type	Data	Key Variables
Table	demographics	age at note, death date, etc.
	weight & height	weight, height
	malignancy info	histopathology, risk group, T staging, etc.
	lab data	labs test name, labs result value
Text	radiology reports	report date, report text
	progress notes	note date, note ID, note text
Medical Imaging	biomarkers	metastatic level, bone/muscle density, muscle volume
Survival Time	mortality label	$\leq$90d, 91–365d, $\geq$366d

3.1 Data Modalities and Preprocessing

Structured Tabular Data. *Weight* was treated as a time-varying variable, with each measurement matched to the nearest biomarker study date; *height* was averaged across all available records for each patient and used as a static demographic feature.

For malignancy information, we defined three *risk groups* by mapping the Gleason grade and score according to National Comprehensive Cancer Network (NCCN) guidelines [12] as in Table 2. For *lab test*, 9 clinically relevant analytes were included: hemoglobin, creatinine, lymphocytes, neutrophils, albumin, prostate-specific antigen, calcium, alkaline phosphatase, and phosphate. We used weight, biomarkers, and lab data as time-series inputs, and included demographics, height, and malignancy information as static patient features for later concatenation.

Table 2. Risk Group Classification According to Gleason Grade and Score (NCCN Guidelines)

Risk Group	Grade Group	Gleason Score
Low/Very Low	Grade Group 1	Gleason Score ≤ 6
Intermediate	Grade Group 2	Gleason Score 7 (3+4)
(Favorable/Unfavorable)	Grade Group 3	Gleason Score 7 (4+3)
High/Very High	Grade Group 4	Gleason Score 8
	Grade Group 5	Gleason Score 9–10

Unstructured Clinical Text. Radiology reports, *report text* included were written for many imaging modalities (e.g., CT, MRI, bone scans), with findings related to bone metastases, muscle status, and disease progression. For progress notes, *note text* comprised patient symptoms, treatment plans, medication changes, social history, and functional status. Both text modalities were preprocessed to remove de-identified phrases and repetitive symbols.

Medical Imaging-based Biomarkers. Subjects in this cohort receive routine computed tomography (CT) imaging including the lumbar spine for monitoring progression of bony metastases. Using convolutional neural networks, the lumbar vertebral bodies (L1-L5) and psoas muscles were segmented, with muscle boundaries set at L2/L3 and L4/L5 inter-vertebral disc mid-points, which is illustrated in Fig. 1. The bone mineral density (BMD) of the lumbar vertebral body trabecular centrums, the psoas muscle volume and psoas muscle density were calculated. Metastatic involvement of vertebrae was detected using a multimodal approach: deep learning based detection in medical imaging, large language model (Llama 3.1 8B) based detection in radiology reports, and a random forest classifier. Four biomarkers were selected: *average density healthy*, the mean of BMD of non-metastatically involved vertebrae across L1-L5 - a standard site for assessing osteoporosis [3]; *metastatic level count*, the number of vertebral levels with metastases; and two muscle-related features, *psoas muscle density* and *psoas volume*.

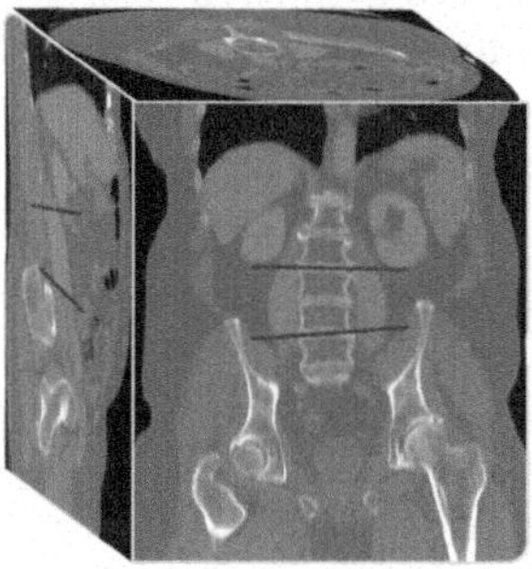

Fig. 1. Medical Imaging-based Biomarker segmentations: Imaging-based biomarkers were quantified in 3D from routine diagnostic computed tomography imaging. An example of a 3D computed tomography volume is depicted with the lumbar vertebral body trabecular centrums overlayed in blue, the left and right psoas muscle region (from L2/L3 to L4/L5 disc mid-points) are overlayed with green. (Color figure online)

4 Methodology

Our approach builds upon the irregular multimodal EHR modeling framework proposed by [21], adapting it for prostate cancer mortality prediction. Figure 2 demonstrates the overall architecture.

4.1 Problem Setup

Given an EHR dataset $\mathcal{D} = \{(\mathbf{x}_i^{ts}, \mathbf{t}_i^{ts}),\ \ (\mathbf{x}_i^{txt}, \mathbf{t}_i^{txt}),\ \mathbf{p}_i,\ \mathbf{y}_i\}_{i=1}^{N}$, consisting of N notes, each note contains multivariate time series data $(\mathbf{x}_i^{ts}, \mathbf{t}_i^{ts})$, clinical text $(\mathbf{x}_i^{txt}, \mathbf{t}_i^{txt})$, and patient-level features $\mathbf{p}_i$ along with a 3-class target label $\mathbf{y}_i \in \{0, 1, 2\}$ indicating mortality risk. The time series component $\mathbf{x}_i^{ts}$ represents a d-dimensional, irregularly sampled sequence of clinical measurements with l^{ts} total observations, where $\mathbf{t}_i^{ts}$ denotes the corresponding timestamps. Clinical notes are structured similarly to time series data, where $\mathbf{x}_i^{txt}$ denotes the textual content with l^{txt} notes, and $\mathbf{t}_i^{txt}$ represents the associated timestamps. We aim to predict the target label y for each patient's note based on $(\mathbf{x}^{ts}, \mathbf{t}^{ts})$ and $(\mathbf{x}^{txt}, \mathbf{t}^{txt})$ collected within the 48 months prior to the most recent hospital visit.

4.2 Model Architecture

Irregular Input Representation with mTAND. We employ a discretized multi-time attention (mTAND) module [15] to interpolate the irregularly sampled time series onto a regular time points $\boldsymbol{\alpha} = [0, 1, \ldots, 48]$, representing 48 months. The interpolation uses attention over the observed timestamps.

To encode the irregular timestamps $\boldsymbol{t}_j^{ts}$ of each feature dimension j, we use the Time2Vec [8], which maps each time point τ to a d_v-dimensional vector:

$$\theta(\tau)[i] = \begin{cases} \omega_i \tau + \phi_i & \text{if } i = 1 \\ \sin(\omega_i \tau + \phi_i) & \text{if } 2 \leq i \leq d_v \end{cases} \tag{1}$$

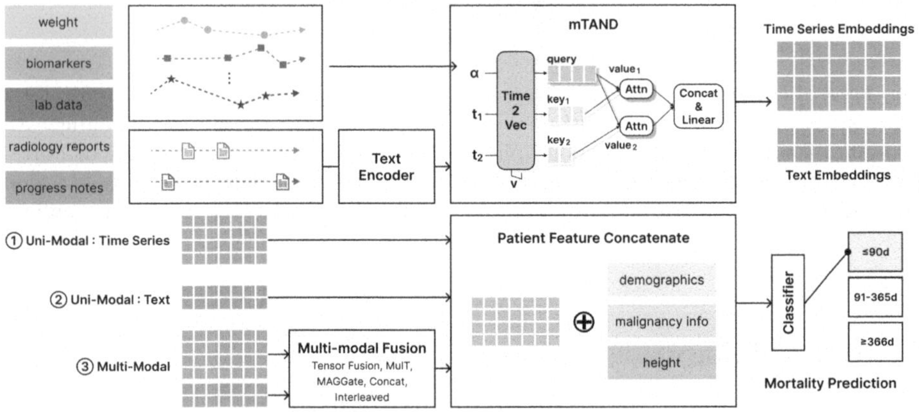

Fig. 2. Pipeline Overview. mTAND is a Time2Vec-based attention module that interpolates irregularly sampled time series onto a regular timeline while preserving temporal patterns. Embeddings from mTAND-processed text and time series are either used unimodally or fused using one of five multimodal fusion strategies, then concatenated with patient-level features for final mortality prediction.

where $\{\omega_i, \phi_i\}_{i=1}^{d_v}$ are learnable parameters, capturing both global trends and periodic patterns.

The mTAND module applies V different Time2Vec modules $\{\theta_v(\cdot)\}_{v=1}^{V}$, each producing a temporally contextualized representation of univariate time series via attention:

$$\hat{\mathbf{x}}_j^{ts} = \text{Attn}\left(\theta_v(\boldsymbol{\alpha})\mathbf{W}_q^v,\ \theta_v(\mathbf{t}_j^{ts})\mathbf{W}_k^v,\ \mathbf{x}_j^{ts}\right), \tag{2}$$

where queries are regular time points α, keys are timestamps $\mathbf{t}_j^{ts}$, and values are observed features $\mathbf{x}_j^{ts}$. Outputs across all d_m features are concatenated:

$$\mathbf{O}_v^{ts} = \left[\hat{\mathbf{x}}_1^{ts},\ \hat{\mathbf{x}}_2^{ts},\ \ldots,\ \hat{\mathbf{x}}_{d_m}^{ts}\right] \in \mathbb{R}^{\alpha \times d_m} \tag{3}$$

and combined across V variants to yield the final time series embedding z^{ts}.

For clinical notes, we encode each note using a pretrained language model TextEncoder to get e^{txt}. Treating $(\mathbf{e}^{txt}, \mathbf{t}^{txt})$ as a multi-dimensional irregular time series, we apply mTAND as:

$$\mathbf{z}^{txt} = \text{mTAND}^{txt}(\boldsymbol{\alpha}, \mathbf{t}^{txt}, \mathbf{e}^{txt}) \in \mathbb{R}^{\alpha \times d_h}, \tag{4}$$

reusing the same Time2Vec encoders $\theta_v(\cdot)_{v=1}^{V}$ to unify temporal modeling across modalities. All other components are trained independently.

Multimodal Fusion Strategy. We explore five multimodal fusion strategies.

(1) Concat Concat simply concatenates the last hidden state representations of each modality:

$$\mathbf{z}_{\text{fused}} = [\mathbf{z}^{ts};\ \mathbf{z}^{txt}].$$

While concat fusion is simple and efficient, it does not capture the temporal patterns and cross-modal dependencies.

(2) Multimodal Adaptation Gate (MAG) MAG [14] enhances the representation of one modality by adding a displacement vector derived from the other modality, where W_g, W are learnable projection matrices.

$$\begin{aligned} g &= \sigma(W_g[\mathbf{z}^{txt};\ \mathbf{z}^{ts}]) \\ \Delta &= W(g \cdot \mathbf{z}^{ts}), \quad \alpha = \min\left(\frac{\|\mathbf{z}^{txt}\|_2}{\|\Delta\|_2} \cdot \beta,\ 1\right) \\ \mathbf{z}_{\text{fused}} &= \text{LayerNorm}(\mathbf{z}^{txt} + \alpha \cdot \Delta) \end{aligned}$$

(3) Tensor Fusion Tensor Fusion [11,20] models the interactions between modalities by computing an outer product between their representations. Each modal features are augmented with a bias term (constant 1) to allow modeling of unimodal and bimodal interactions, and the fusion tensor is computed via the outer product and passed through a feedforward network for projection as:

$$\begin{aligned} \mathbf{T} &= [\mathbf{z}^{txt};\ 1] \otimes [\mathbf{z}^{ts};\ 1] \\ \mathbf{z}_{\text{fused}} &= \text{MLP}(\text{Flatten}(\mathbf{T})) \end{aligned}$$

(4) Multimodal Transformer (MulT) MulT [17] performs cross-modal attention to combine each modality feature across temporal sequences. Given learnable projection matrices $W^Q, W^K, W^V \in \mathbb{R}^{d \times d_k}$, cross-modal attention is applied in both directions (from text to time series and from time series to text), and the final fused representation is obtained by concatenating both features.

$$\mathbf{z}^{ts \to txt} = \text{softmax}\left(\frac{\mathbf{z}^{ts} W^Q (\mathbf{z}^{txt} W^K)^\top}{\sqrt{d}}\right) \cdot \mathbf{z}^{txt} W^V$$

$$\mathbf{z}^{txt \to ts} = \text{softmax}\left(\frac{\mathbf{z}^{txt} W^Q (\mathbf{z}^{ts} W^K)^\top}{\sqrt{d}}\right) \cdot \mathbf{z}^{ts} W^V$$

$$\mathbf{z}_{\text{fused}} = [\mathbf{z}^{ts \to txt};\ \mathbf{z}^{txt \to ts}].$$

(5) Interleaved Attention Fusion (Interleaved) The interleaved attention fusion mechanism [21] applies self-attention and cross-attention alternatively to gather temporal knowledge and integrate information from other modalities across temporal steps. The unimodal features $\mathbf{z}^{ts}$ and $\mathbf{z}^{txt} \in \mathbb{R}^{\alpha \times d_h}$ are passed through J stacked layers, where each layer performs:

$$\hat{\mathbf{z}}_j^{ts} = \mathrm{MH}_j^{ts}(\mathbf{z}_{j-1}^{ts}), \qquad \hat{\mathbf{z}}_j^{txt} = \mathrm{MH}_j^{txt}(\mathbf{z}_{j-1}^{txt})$$
$$\mathbf{z}_j^{ts} = \mathrm{CMH}_j^{ts}(\hat{\mathbf{z}}_j^{ts}, \hat{\mathbf{z}}_j^{txt}), \qquad \mathbf{z}_j^{txt} = \mathrm{CMH}_j^{txt}(\hat{\mathbf{z}}_j^{txt}, \hat{\mathbf{z}}_j^{ts})$$

After J interleaved attention fusion layers, the final representation is extracted as:

$$\mathbf{z}_{\text{fused}} = [\mathbf{z}_J^{ts};\ \mathbf{z}_J^{txt}].$$

Prediction with Patient Features. We incorporate patient-level features (e.g., age, height, risk group) at the final prediction stage. A single linear layer is first applied to obtain patient feature embedding, and concatenated with $\mathbf{z}^{txt}$ or $\mathbf{z}^{ts}$ for unimodal models, and $\mathbf{z}_{\text{fused}}$ for the multimodal model. The concatenated feature is passed through a multi-layer perceptron (MLP) to predict mortality:

$$\hat{y} = \mathrm{MLP}([\mathbf{z};\ \mathrm{Linear}(f_{\text{patient}})]), \tag{5}$$

where $\mathbf{z}$ denotes the modality-specific or fused representation depending on the model setting.

4.3 Experimental Setup

All models were trained on an NVIDIA TITAN RTX GPU with 24 GB VRAM using cross-entropy loss and Adam optimizer. The learning rate was set to $\mathbf{4e}^{-4}$ for time-series models and $\mathbf{2e}^{-5}$ for text models. Clinical Longformer [9] was used as a text encoder. All models used in these experiments converged within 6 epochs. The total set of 24,293 notes was split into 60% for training, 20% for validation, and 20% for testing at the patient level to prevent data leakage. We compared five fusion strategies and evaluated model performance using macro F1-score (F1), accuracy (ACC), quadratic weighted kappa (QWK), mean absolute error (MAE), and 1-year mortality prediction accuracy (1Y-ACC).

5 Results

Multimodal models outperformed their unimodal counterparts, with the interleaved attention fusion strategy achieving the highest performance across all metrics (Table 3). Specifically, interleaved attention fusion yielded a QWK of 0.509 and a 1Y-ACC (1-year mortality prediction accuracy) of 78.433%, markedly surpassing all other fusion methods. In contrast, all unimodal models showed noticeably lower performance with QWK scores of 0.431 and 0.406. Interestingly, certain multimodal fusion strategies performed worse than unimodal models on specific metrics. Regarding the accuracy metric, all fusion approaches except for the interleaved fusion did not surpass the performance of either unimodal model.

To assess the crucial task of identifying high-risk patients, we report the confusion matrix in Fig. 3 and compare the False Negative Rate (FNR) for Class 0 (death within 3 months), where the Unimodal-TS model has a high false negative rate (FNR) of 41.5%, misclassifying 684 patients who died within 3 months. Of these, 479 are incorrectly predicted as Class 2 (>12 months), and 205 as Class 1 (3–12 months), indicating a tendency to overestimate survival. In contrast, the multimodal model shows a lower FNR of 39.38%, and has 377 and 272 missclassifications into classes 1 and 2, respectively. This suggests the superiority of the multimodal model, which better captures the true survival duration by reducing severe overestimations.

Table 3. Model Performance across Different Modalities and Fusion Strategies. Higher values indicate better performance for all metrics except MAE, where lower is better. The results of our proposed model are highlighted in bold, and multimodal results that underperform compared to either unimodal results in *italic*.

Modality	Input / Fusion	F1	ACC	QWK	MAE	1Y-ACC
Uni-Modal	Time Series	54.928	56.802	0.431	0.574	73.784
	Text	52.760	53.272	0.406	0.589	70.706
Multi-Modal	Concat	*52.342*	*55.209*	*0.436*	*0.587*	74.925
	MAG	*54.636*	*54.950*	0.475	0.540	75.118
	Outer	54.957	*56.156*	0.486	0.540	77.271
	MulT	55.000	*55.402*	*0.393*	*0.582*	75.075
	Interleaved	**56.205**	**57.899**	**0.509**	**0.522**	**78.433**

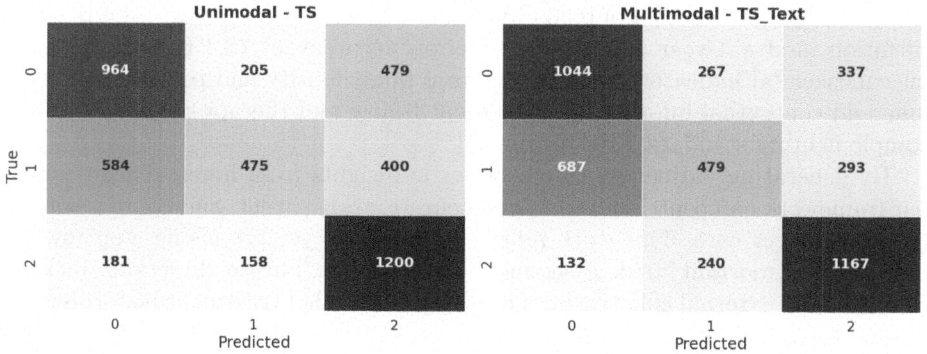

Fig. 3. Comparison of confusion matrices between Unimodal-TS (Time Series) and Multimodal. Labels 0, 1, and 2 correspond to mortality within ≤90 d, 91–365 days, and ≥366 d, respectively.

6 Discussion

The challenge of this task arises from the small dataset size, high feature dimensionality, and the irregular and sparse clinical notes, which can easily lead to overfitting. As a result, while the overall gains were limited in some cases, the best fusion approach yielded marginal improvements in accuracy and other metrics. Nevertheless, when the task is reframed as a binary classification, predicting whether the patient would die within 12 months (1Y-ACC), the best-performing model achieved a high accuracy of 78.433% with a substantial increase compared to unimodal models and other fusion strategies. This result underscores the efficacy of our model being more robust and effective under this clinically relevant formulation.

Furthermore, among various fusion strategies, the interleaved attention consistently achieved the best performance, suggesting that attention-based architectures can effectively integrate different data modalities. However, some fusion methods underperform the unimodal baselines, which highlights the importance of selecting an appropriate fusion strategy. Overall, these findings serve as proof-of-concept for multimodal mortality prediction in metastatic prostate cancer, particularly with CT-derived biomarkers, capturing frailty-related information not present in structured EHR features alone.

7 Conclusion

In this work, we present a multimodal deep learning framework for mortality prediction in patients with metastatic prostate cancer by integrating structured time-series data, CT-derived imaging biomarkers, and unstructured clinical notes. The multimodal approach shows a consistent improvement over unimodal baselines, highlighting the importance of combining diverse clinical data to better identify high-risk patients.

Specifically, the best-performing model achieved an F1-score of 56.2% and quadratic weighted kappa of 0.509 in 3-class ($\leq$90 d, 91–365 days, $\geq$366 d) classification, and a 1-year mortality prediction accuracy of 78.4%. In particular, musculoskeletal indicators such as vertebral bone density and psoas muscle volume add contextual information on patient frailty and therapy-induced decline, complementing standard EHR features.

By generating patient-specific prognostic insights from heterogeneous data, our framework can contribute to more accurate, transparent, and compassionate prostate cancer care. This work represents an early yet promising step toward personalized mortality risk assessment in oncology. Future directions include validation on external cohorts, incorporation of detailed treatment histories, and improving model interpretability.

8 Prospect of Application

Our model could support early identification of high-risk prostate cancer patients, enabling timely palliative care and therapy adjustments. By integrating musculoskeletal indicators and clinical narratives, the model enables personalized risk assessment and may support clinical decision-making and long-term care planning. By integrating musculoskeletal indicators and clinical narratives, it provides personalized risk assessment and highlights key prognostic factors, helping clinicians prioritize care. With further validation, it may serve as a decision-support tool in oncology and long-term care planning.

Acknowledgments. This work was supported by Institute of Information & Communications Technology Planning & Evaluation (IITP) grant funded by the Korea government (MSIT) (RS-2022-00143911, AI Excellence Global Innovative Leader Education Program) and the Canadian Institutes of Health Research, Hold'em for life.

References

1. Brunello, A., et al.: Development of an oncological-multidimensional prognostic index (Onco-MPI) for mortality prediction in older cancer patients. J. Cancer Res. Clin. Oncol., **142**(5), 1069–1077 (2016). https://doi.org/10.1007/S00432-015-2088-X/FIGURES/1, https://link.springer.com/article/10.1007/s00432-015-2088-x
2. Chen, C.K., et al.: Prognostic factors associated with the survival of patients with gastric adenocarcinoma: a retrospective study. Adv. Dig. Med., **7**(2), 68–76 (2020). https://doi.org/10.1002/AID2.13158, https://onlinelibrary.wiley.com/doi/full/10.1002/aid2.13158
3. Clynes, M.A., Gregson, C.L., Bruyère, O., Cooper, C., Dennison, E.M.: Osteosarcopenia: where osteoporosis and sarcopenia collide. Rheumatology **60**(2), 529–537 (2021)
4. Gao, Z.Y., Zhang, T., Zhang, H., Pang, C.G., Jiang, W.X.: Prognostic factors for overall survival in patients with spinal metastasis secondary to prostate cancer: a systematic review and meta-analysis. BMC Musculoskelet. Dis., **21**(1) (2020). https://doi.org/10.1186/s12891-020-03412-0
5. Goldstein, B.A., Navar, A.M., Pencina, M.J., Ioannidis, J.P.: Opportunities and challenges in developing risk prediction models with electronic health records data: a systematic review. J. Am. Med. Inf. Assoc. JAMIA **24**(1), 198 (2016)
6. Jahrreiss, V., Laukhtina, E., D'Andrea, D., Shariat, S.F.: The prognostic value of sarcopenia in patients with prostate cancer: a systematic review. Curr. Opin. Urol. **31**(4), 315–323 (2021). https://doi.org/10.1097/MOU.0000000000000885, https://pubmed.ncbi.nlm.nih.gov/33965982/
7. Jones, B.E., et al.: Trends in illness severity, hospitalization, and mortality for community-onset pneumonia at 118 us veterans affairs medical centers. J. Gen. Intern. Med. **37**(15), 3839–3847 (2022)
8. Kazemi, S.M., et al.: Time2vec: learning a vector representation of time (2019). arXiv:1907.05321 arXiv preprint
9. Li, Y., Wehbe, R.M., Ahmad, F.S., Wang, H., Luo, Y.: Clinical-longformer and clinical-bigbird: transformers for long clinical sequences (2022). https://arxiv.org/abs/2201.11838
10. Lim, H., et al.: Toward precision medicine: development and validation of a machine learning based decision support system for optimal sequencing in castration-resistant prostate cancer. Clin. Genitourin. Cancer **21**(4), e211–e218.e4 (2023). https://doi.org/10.1016/J.CLGC.2023.03.012

11. Liu, Z., Shen, Y., Lakshminarasimhan, V.B., Liang, P.P., Bagher Zadeh, A., Morency, L.P.: Efficient low-rank multimodal fusion with modality-specific factors. In: Gurevych, I., Miyao, Y. (eds.) Proceedings of the 56th Annual Meeting of the Association for Computational Linguistics (Volume 1: Long Papers), pp. 2247–2256. Association for Computational Linguistics, Melbourne, Australia (2018). https://doi.org/10.18653/v1/P18-1209, https://aclanthology.org/P18-1209/
12. Network, N.C.C., et al.: NCCN clinical practice guidelines in oncology (2008)
13. Owusuaa, C., Dijkland, S.A., Nieboer, D., van der Heide, A., van der Rijt, C.C.: Predictors of mortality in patients with advanced cancer–a systematic review and meta-analysis. Cancers **14**(2), 1–20 (2022). https://doi.org/10.3390/cancers14020328
14. Rahman, W., et al.: Integrating multimodal information in large pretrained transformers. In: Proceedings of the conference Association for Computational Linguistics. Meeting, p. 2359 (2020)
15. Shukla, S.N., Marlin, B.M.: Interpolation-prediction networks for irregularly sampled time series. In: The International Conference on Learning Representations (ICLR) (2019)
16. Steele, A.J., Denaxas, S.C., Shah, A.D., Hemingway, H., Luscombe, N.M.: Machine learning models in electronic health records can outperform conventional survival models for predicting patient mortality in coronary artery disease. PLOS ONE **13**(8), 1–20 (2018). https://doi.org/10.1371/journal.pone.0202344, https://doi.org/10.1371/journal.pone.0202344
17. Tsai, Y.H.H., Bai, S., Liang, P.P., Kolter, J.Z., Morency, L.P., Salakhutdinov, R.: Multimodal transformer for unaligned multimodal language sequences. In: Proceedings of the Conference. Association for Computational Linguistics. Meeting, vol. 2019, p. 6558 (2019)
18. Wang, L., Sha, L., Lakin, J.R., Bynum, J., Bates, D.W., Hong, P., Zhou, L.: Development and validation of a deep learning algorithm for mortality prediction in selecting patients with dementia for earlier palliative care interventions. JAMA Netw. Open **2**(7), e196972–e196972 (2019)
19. Xu, L., et al.: Conditional survival analysis and real-time prognosis prediction for prostate cancer patients. Sci. Rep., **15**(1), 18711 (2025). https://doi.org/10.1038/s41598-025-00420-9, https://www.nature.com/articles/s41598-025-00420-9
20. Zadeh, A., Chen, M., Poria, S., Cambria, E., Morency, L.P.: Tensor fusion network for multimodal sentiment analysis. In: Palmer, M., Hwa, R., Riedel, S. (eds.) Proceedings of the 2017 Conference on Empirical Methods in Natural Language Processing, pp. 1103–1114. Association for Computational Linguistics, Copenhagen, Denmark (2017). https://doi.org/10.18653/v1/D17-1115, https://aclanthology.org/D17-1115/
21. Zhang, X., Li, S., Chen, Z., Yan, X., Petzold, L.R.: Improving medical predictions by irregular multimodal electronic health records modeling. In: International Conference on Machine Learning, pp. 41300–41313 (2023) PMLR
22. Zhou, C., et al.: Multimodal data integration for predicting progression risk in castration-resistant prostate cancer using deep learning: a multicenter retrospective study. Front. Oncol. **14** (2024). https://doi.org/10.3389/FONC.2024.1287995

Federated Co-tuning Framework for Large and Small Language Models

Tao Fan[1,2(✉)], Yan Kang[2], Guoqiang Ma[2], Lixin Fan[2], Shuoling Liu[1], Kai Chen[1], and Qiang Yang[3]

[1] Hong Kong University of Science and Technology, Hong Kong, China
{tfanac,sliudi,kaichen}@cse.ust.hk
[2] WeBank Co., Ltd, Shenzhen, China
{yangkang,zotrseeewma,lixinfan}@webank.com
[3] Hong Kong Polytechnic University, Hong Kong, China
qyang@cse.ust.hk

Abstract. By adapting Large Language Models (LLMs) to domain-specific tasks or enriching them with domain-specific knowledge, we can fully harness the capabilities of LLMs. Nonetheless, a gap persists in achieving simultaneous mutual enhancement between the server's LLM and the downstream clients' Small Language Models (SLMs). To address this, we propose FedCoLLM, a novel and parameter-efficient federated framework designed for co-tuning LLMs and SLMs. This approach is aimed at adaptively transferring server-side LLMs knowledge to clients' SLMs while simultaneously enriching the LLMs with domain insights from the clients. To accomplish this, FedCoLLM utilizes lightweight adapters in conjunction with SLMs, facilitating knowledge exchange between server and clients in a manner that respects data privacy while also minimizing computational and communication overhead. Our evaluation of FedCoLLM, utilizing various public LLMs and SLMs across a range of NLP text generation tasks, reveals that the performance of clients' SLMs experiences notable improvements with the assistance of the LLMs. Simultaneously, the LLMs enhanced via FedCoLLM achieves comparable performance to that obtained through direct fine-tuning on clients' data. Our code has been contributed to the FATE open-source project and is now publicly accessible at https://github.com/FederatedAI/FATE-LLM/tree/main/python/fate_llm/algo/fedcollm.

Keywords: LLMs · Federated Learning · Parameter-Efficient

1 Introduction

The emergence of Large Language Models (LLMs) has profoundly transformed the landscape of artificial intelligence. In particular, cutting-edge LLMs like GPT-4 [15] have garnered significant attention due to their exceptional performance across a range of natural language generation tasks. This development has spurred the release of numerous high-performance open-source LLMs, such

R. C.-W. Wong et al. (Eds.): PAKDD 2026, LNAI 16617, pp. 411–422, 2027.
https://doi.org/10.1007/978-981-92-1926-1_33

as LLaMa [19], OPT [22], greatly promoting the commercial application of LLMs technology. Despite their widespread success in various general NLP tasks, LLMs face limitations that hinder their adoption in domain-specific applications. The primary challenges include:

- **Domain-Specific Knowledge Privacy**. When downstream clients are unable to access the LLMs parameter, they have to send their labeled data to the LLMs owners for fine-tuning. This process inevitably discloses the privacy of clients' sensitive domain-specific data.
- **Constrained Resources**. Even when downstream enterprises can obtain the model parameters of LLMs, they often encounter significant resource constraints. Fine-tuning these LLMs requires substantial computing and storage resources, posing a barrier to adoption by small and medium-sized companies with limited resources. As a result, these companies are restricted to fine-tuning Small Language Models(SLMs) using their domain-specific data.
- **Mutual Knowledge Transfer Between LLMs and SLMs**. Optimizing LLMs and SLMs separately forms a positive feedback loop for continuous evolution. Server-side LLMs first transfer general knowledge to client-side SLMs, which are then fine-tuned on domain-specific data for downstream tasks. These domain-specialized SLMs can in turn feed industry-specific knowledge back to server LLMs, improving their understanding and expanding their scope and depth. However, such mutual enhancement between server LLMs and client SLMs remains largely unexplored in existing literature.

To address the aforementioned challenges, we propose FedCoLLM, an innovative and parameter-efficient federated co-tuning framework for LLMs and SLMs. This framework is designed to enhance the performance of both server-side LLMs and client-side SLMs. As illustrated in Fig. 1, FedCoLLM deploys a LLM on the server and introduces a SLM to serve as a bridge between the privacy data in the clients and LLM in the server. The SLM operates simultaneously across multiple clients and the server, facilitating efficient communication and collaboration. FedCoLLM offers three distinct advantages:

- **Efficient Computation and Communication**. FedCoLLM initially runs the SLM under standard federated learning(FL) frameworks [12,21]. This approach integrates a parameter-efficient adapter module, such as LoRA [10], significantly reducing the computation and communication costs associated with FedCoLLM.
- **Enhanced Data Privacy**. By leveraging the FL framework to fine-tune the SLM, FedCoLLM fully utilizes the FL security protection mechanisms(such as SecureAggregation [2]) to preserve the privacy of clients' data. This ensures that sensitive information remains protected during the fine-tuning process.
- **Knowledge Transfer and Mutual Enhancement**. FedCoLLM employs knowledge distillation(KD) techniques [9], to transfer knowledge between the LLM and SLM on the server. This process is facilitated by an auxiliary distillation dataset, making it particularly beneficial for clients with limited

resources. Through this knowledge transfer, both the server LLM and client SLMs are mutually enhanced, leading to improved overall performance.

Extensive experiments conducted on various LLMs and SLMs, including GPT-2 [17], OPT [22], and LLaMa2 [19], demonstrate the competitive performance of our FedCoLLM framework across a range of NLP text generation tasks. The results show that the SLMs can achieve significant enhancements with the support of the LLM, while the LLM can deliver comparable results to fine-tuning with all clients' domain data directly. Importantly, our framework is more resource-efficient, requiring lower computation and communication costs.

2 Related Work

2.1 Knowledge Distillation

Knowledge distillation is a technique that has gained significant attention in recent years, as it enables the transfer of knowledge from a larger teacher model to a smaller student model. One of the early works in this area was proposed by [9], which introduced the concept of knowledge distillation and demonstrated its effectiveness in improving the performance of compressed models. Since then, numerous studies have built upon this foundation and explored various distillation strategies [8]. For instance, two notable work [4,13] improved response-based knowledge distillation, which let the student model directly mimic the final prediction of the teacher model. FitNets [1] focus on matching intermediate representations between the teacher and student models. Another notable work is the relational knowledge distillation approach introduced by [16], which captures pairwise relationships between outputs to enhance distillation efficiency. Different from one-way knowledge distillation between the teacher and student networks, Deep Mutual Learning (DML) [23] allows two networks to learn from each other through their predicted probability distributions during the training process. These studies have demonstrated the potential of knowledge distillation in various tasks, such as image classification, object detection, and natural language processing.

2.2 Federated Learning for Large Language Models

Parameter-Efficient Fine-Tuning (PEFT) techniques [10] provide a straightforward remedy to address the challenges of communication overhead and fine-tuning expenses in Federated Learning (FL) for Large Language Models (LLMs) [6,7,11]. Numerous investigations have extended the application of PEFT methods within the FL framework tailored for LLMs. Notable contributions include FedPETuning [24], Federated Adapter Tuning [3], and Federated Prompt Tuning [25]. These research outcomes suggest that FL clients, particularly those with constrained storage capacities like mobile devices, can significantly profit from the adoption of PEFT methods. These approaches facilitate the sharing of LLMs across various tasks while necessitating the retention of only a minimal set of parameters per task, effectively decreasing storage demands. Through the utilization of PEFT methods, FL clients can adeptly tailor LLMs to meet their unique requirements, all the while minimizing communication overhead and reducing fine-tuning costs.

3 The Proposed Method

In this section, we present a comprehensive overview of our federated co-tuning LLMs and SLMs framework, termed FedCoLLM. This framework is based on parameter-efficient fine-tuning (PEFT) and knowledge distillation techniques. We begin by defining the specific problem addressed in this study, followed by a detailed introduction to our approach. Finally, we delve into the computational and communication complexities, as well as the privacy-preserving analysis, of our FedCoLLM framework.

3.1 Problem Definition

In this work, we consider the federated learning setting in which the server owns an LLM f_ψ parameterized by ψ and K clients that each client k has a SLM g_ϕ parameterized by ϕ. The server and clients aim to collaboratively enhance the performance of the LLM and SLMs without sharing private data through federated learning. Specifically,

- Each client possesses its own local private dataset $\mathcal{D}^k$. Clients aim to collectively train a global SLM g_ϕ based on their local models initialized with an SLM (e.g., LLaMa2-1.3B [20]) without divulging their private data. The objective can be formulated as follows:

$$\min_{\phi} \mathcal{L}_1(\phi; \{\mathcal{D}^k\}_{k=1}^K) \tag{1}$$

- The server owns an auxiliary dataset D^a. The server aims to transfer knowledge between its owned LLM f_ψ and the global SLM g_ϕ aggregated from clients' local SLMs to enhance both the LLM and SLMs. The objective can be formulated as follows:

$$\min_{\phi,\psi} \mathcal{L}_2(\phi, \psi; \mathcal{D}^a) \tag{2}$$

We regard the server as semi-honest. FedCoLLM solves the optimization problems formulated in Eq. (1) and Eq. (2) in an efficient and privacy-preserving manner. We will elaborate on FedCoLLM in Sect. 3.2.

3.2 FedCoLLM

FedCoLLM is a novel framework designed to facilitate the collaborative evolution of both server-side LLM and client-side SLMs. The goal of the FedCoLLM is threefold:

- **Collaborative Knowledge Transfer and Adaptation**. The server and clients work together to transfer and adapt the knowledge of the LLM owned by the server. This helps clients build local SLMs that benefit from the server's LLM knowledge. By leveraging the server's LLM, clients can improve their local SLMs' performance without requiring extensive local training data or computational resources.
- **Data Augmentation for the Server's LLM**. Federated learning also aims to leverage clients' data to augment and enhance the server's LLM. Clients' data often contains valuable local information and patterns that can be used to improve the server model's generalization and performance. By incorporating this data, the server's LLM can become more robust and adaptive to different scenarios and domains.
- **Privacy-Preserving and Efficient Knowledge Transfer**. A crucial aspect of federated learning is ensuring that knowledge transfer occurs in a privacy-preserving and efficient manner. Clients' raw private data should not be directly uploaded to the LLM server, preserving their privacy. Instead, only model updates or aggregated information are shared with the LLM server. Additionally, the knowledge transfer process should be efficient, minimizing communication costs and computational overhead.

Toward this goal, we (1) adopt lightweight LoRA modules as the bridge to transfer the knowledge between clients and the server, (2) leverage mutual knowledge distillation to transfer knowledge between the LLM and the aggregated SLM, and (3) employ secure aggregation to protect the privacy of the knowledge transfer process. Specifically, we assume that clients and the server share a SLM g_ϕ parameterized by ϕ. Each client k inserts a small low-rank adapter parameterized by θ_k into its local SLM. We denote a client's local SLM with the added θ as $g_{\phi+\theta}$. Instead of training a global SLM ϕ, clients collaboratively train a global LoRA module θ. Then, Eq. (1) can be reformulated as follows:

$$\mathcal{L}_1(\theta; \{\mathcal{D}^k\}_{k=1}^K) = \frac{1}{K}\sum_{k=1}^{K} \mathbb{E}_{(x,y)\sim\mathcal{D}^k} \ell_{\text{TA}}^k(g_{\phi+\theta}(x), y). \tag{3}$$

where ℓ_{TA} is the task loss for training the global LoRA module θ. The original model parameter ϕ of each client's local SLM is frozen during training.

The server inserts a small low-rank adapter parameterized by ω into its LLM f_ψ. We denote the server's LLM f_ψ with the added ω as $f_{\psi+\omega}$. The server conducts the mutual knowledge transfer between the LLM $f_{\psi+\omega}$ and the global SLM $g_{\phi+\theta}$ through supervised fine-tuning and mutual knowledge distillation based on the auxiliary dataset $\mathcal{D}^a$. We formulate the losses of supervised fine-tuning $f_{\psi+\omega}$ and $g_{\phi+\theta}$ (denoted as $\mathcal{L}_{\text{FT}}^f$ and $\mathcal{L}_{\text{FT}}^g$) as follows:

$$\begin{aligned} \mathcal{L}_{\text{FT}}^f(\omega; \mathcal{D}^a) &= \mathbb{E}_{(x,y)\sim\mathcal{D}^a} \ell_{\text{CE}}(f_{\psi+\omega}(x), y), \\ \mathcal{L}_{\text{FT}}^g(\theta; \mathcal{D}^a) &= \mathbb{E}_{(x,y)\sim\mathcal{D}^a} \ell_{\text{CE}}(g_{\phi+\theta}(x), y). \end{aligned} \tag{4}$$

where ℓ_{CE} is the cross-entropy loss; the model parameters ψ and ϕ are frozen during fine-tuning.

The mutual knowledge distillation losses for fine-tuning $f_{\psi+\omega}$ and $g_{\phi+\theta}$ models (denoted as $\mathcal{L}^f_{\mathrm{KD}}$ and $\mathcal{L}^g_{\mathrm{KD}}$) are formulated as follows:

$$\begin{aligned}\mathcal{L}^f_{\mathrm{KD}}(\omega;\mathcal{D}^a) &= \mathbb{E}_{x\sim\mathcal{D}^a}\ell_{\mathrm{KL}}(f_{\psi+\omega}(x), g_{\phi+\theta}(x)),\\ \mathcal{L}^g_{\mathrm{KD}}(\theta;\mathcal{D}^a) &= \mathbb{E}_{x\sim\mathcal{D}^a}\ell_{\mathrm{KL}}(g_{\phi+\theta}(x), f_{\psi+\omega}(x)).\end{aligned} \tag{5}$$

where ℓ_{KL} is the Kullback Leibler (KL) divergence function; the model parameters ψ and ϕ are frozen during knowledge distillation.

Combining Eq. (4) and Eq. (5), we formulate the mutual knowledge transfer conducted on the server as follows:

$$\begin{aligned}&\mathcal{L}_2(\theta,\omega;\mathcal{D}^a) = \mathcal{L}^f(\omega;\mathcal{D}^a) + \mathcal{L}^g(\theta;\mathcal{D}^a),\\ &\text{in which}\\ &\mathcal{L}^f(\omega;\mathcal{D}^a) = \mathcal{L}^f_{\mathrm{FT}}(\omega;\mathcal{D}^a) + \lambda\mathcal{L}^f_{\mathrm{KD}}(\omega;\mathcal{D}^a),\\ &\mathcal{L}^g(\theta;\mathcal{D}^a) = \mathcal{L}^g_{\mathrm{FT}}(\theta;\mathcal{D}^a) + \lambda\mathcal{L}^g_{\mathrm{KD}}(\theta;\mathcal{D}^a).\end{aligned} \tag{6}$$

where λ is the hyperparameter that controls the weight of mutual knowledge transfer.

After mutual knowledge transfer, the global LoRA module θ is distributed to all clients, which in turn adopts Eq. (1) to further train θ based on their local datasets.

FedCoLLM thus fosters a symbiotic relationship between the server and clients, where both parties benefit from the collective knowledge and expertise encoded in their respective language models. By leveraging the complementary strengths of server-side LLMs and client-side SLMs, FedCoLLM paves the way for more efficient and effective federated learning in the realm of natural language processing, enabling the collaborative evolution of LLM and SLMs. We illustrate the FedCoLLM in Fig. 1 and describe the associated training algorithm in Algorithm 1. The workflow of FedCoLLM proceeds as follows:

1. In the t-th communication round, the server broadcasts the SLM $g_{\phi+\theta}$ global adapter θ to K clients. Each client k then replaces its local adapter θ_k with the received global adapter θ.
2. During local training, the K clients fine-tune their respective local adapters using their private data. This step allows the clients to adapt their models to their specific data distributions while preserving the knowledge encoded in the global adapter.
3. After local training, the K clients send their respective local adapters to the server. The server SLM $g_{\phi+\theta}$ then aggregates these local adapters using a secure averaging technique, such as SecureAvg, and updates the global adapter θ in the SLM accordingly.
4. On the server side, LLM $f_{\psi+\omega}$ and SLM $g_{\phi+\theta}$ engage in knowledge distillation. This process involves transferring knowledge between the two models with the aid of an auxiliary distillation dataset. Through this distillation, both models can benefit from each other's learned representations, leading to improved performance and adaptability.

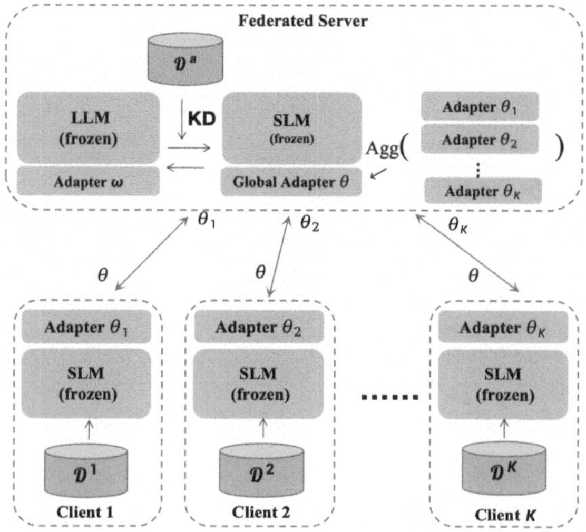

Fig. 1. FedCoLLM (Federated parameter-efficient co-tuning of clients' domain SLMs and the server's LLMs. Clients' SLMs learn from each other via federated fine-tuning of their adapter modules and transfer knowledge from and to the server's LLM)

3.3 Computation and Communication Complexity

One key advantage of FedCoLLM is its computational efficiency. By utilizing PEFT, it markedly decreases the parameters needing fine-tuning updates. Furthermore, the server-side distillation process compresses knowledge from local models into a smaller global model, optimizing computational resources. This enables effective learning from all clients' collective data while keeping the model size manageable. In terms of communication complexity, FedCoLLM minimizes the amount of data exchanged between clients and the server. Instead of transmitting entire models or large datasets, clients only share their locally fine-tuned model updates with the server. This approach significantly reduces communication overhead.

3.4 Privacy-Preserving Analysis

FedCoLLM is meticulously designed with privacy preservation as its foundation. Recognizing the importance of data confidentiality, the framework ensures clients never directly disclose raw local data. Privacy protection is further enhanced through PEFT and knowledge distillation, minimizing sensitive information exposure during training. By using knowledge distillation, FedCoLLM transfers key insights to a unified global model, sharing only aggregated, non-sensitive knowledge and preserving individual client privacy. Additionally, it seamlessly integrates with the standard FL framework for SLMs fine-tuning, leveraging security mechanisms like SecureAggregation [2] to maintain robust data privacy for all clients.

Algorithm 1 FedCoLLM

Input:
K: number of clients;
T: total number of rounds;
$\mathcal{D}^a$: the auxiliary distillation dataset;
$\mathcal{D}^k$: local datasets for each client k;
η_ω: the learning rate for optimizing LLM $f_{\psi+\omega}$;
η_θ: the learning rate for optimizing SLM $g_{\phi+\theta}$.
Output: $f_{\psi+\omega}$, $g_{\phi+\theta}$.
for $t = 1, 2, \ldots, T$ **do**
  // **Server side:**
  Broadcast the global adapter θ^t to all K clients.
  $\theta_k^{t+1} \leftarrow$ **ClientUpdate**(θ^t) for each client k
  Initialize the global adapter $\theta^{t,0} \leftarrow \frac{1}{K}\sum_{k=1}^{K}\theta_k^{t+1}$
  ▷ mutual knowledge transfer based on $\mathcal{D}^a$
  for $r = 1, 2, \ldots, R$ **do**
    $\theta^{t,r+1} \leftarrow \theta^{t,r} - \eta_\theta \nabla \mathcal{L}^g$
    $\omega^{t,r+1} \leftarrow \omega^{t,r} - \eta_\omega \nabla \mathcal{L}^f$
  end for
  $\theta^{t+1} \leftarrow \theta^{t,R}$
  $\omega^{t+1} \leftarrow \omega^{t,R}$

  function ClientUpdate(θ^t)
    Receive the global adapter θ^t from the server;
    for each client k (in parallel) **do**
      ▷ local fine-tuning based on $\mathcal{D}^k$
      $\theta_k^0 \leftarrow \theta^t$
      for $e = 1, 2, \ldots, E$ **do**
        $\theta_k^{e+1} \leftarrow \theta_k^e - \eta_\theta \nabla \ell_{\text{TA}}^k$
      end for
      $\theta_k^{t+1} \leftarrow \theta_k^E$
      Upload updated local adapter θ_k^{t+1} to the server.
    end for
    return θ_k^{t+1}
  end function
end for

4 Experiments

4.1 Setup

We set up a scenario involving four clients and one server to evaluate the FedCoLLM using various LLMs and SLMs.

Models. We evaluate FedCoLLM on LLMs and SLMs, including GPT-2 [17], OPT [22] and LLaMa2 [19]. Our experiments involve utilizing the FedCoLLM framework with LLMs and SLMs of identical architecture but different model sizes. Specifically, for example, we employ LLaMa2-7B as the LLM and LLaMa2-1.3B [20] as the SLM in the FedCoLLM framework.

Datasets. We evaluate FedCoLLM on 4 QA datasets, including CommonsenseQA(CQA) [18], OpenBookQA [14], ARC-C [5], ARC-E [5].

Baselines. We conducted a comparative analysis of our FedCoLLM framework against several baselines to evaluate its performance. These baselines included:

- Zero-Shot, which represents the zero-shot capabilities of the of LLM or SLMs.

- Standalone, where each client independently fine-tunes its local model using its own private dataset;
- FedAvg, in which clients train on their private datasets using the FedAvg algorithm [12];
- Centralized, where the server's LLM is fine-tuned locally using the entirety of the private datasets combined with an auxiliary distillation dataset.

Evaluation Metrics. We evaluate the model performance of fine-tuned LLMs and SLMs on the QA datasets using Accuracy as the primary metric. It's worth noting that in our experiments, all methods undergo zero-shot evaluation, and we use the *lm-evaluation-harness* package. Additionally, to assess the communication efficiency of our framework, we measure the communication cost by tracking the number of transmitted parameters.

4.2 Performance Evaluations

We conduct experiments with three settings. The first setting (denoted as S1) involves one server-side GPT-2-Large LLM and four client-side GPT-2-Small SLMs, the second setting (denoted as S2) involves one server-side OPT-6.7B LLM and four client-side OPT-1.3B SLMs, and the third setting (denoted as S3) involves one server-side LLaMa2-7B LLM and four client-side LLaMa2-1.3B SLMs. Tables 1 and 2 demonstrate the performance comparisons of our approach against other baselines. The top sub-table and the bottom sub-table compare the performance of FedCoLLM against baselines on the server's LLM and clients' SLMs, respectively.

The Table 1 shows that FedCoLLM significantly outperforms Zero-Shot on the server's LLM in the three settings. It also shows that FedCoLLM achieves comparable performance of the Centralized scenario. For example, in the CQA dataset, FedCoLLM achieves a relative improvement of 41% over Zero-Shot on GPT-2-Large LLM, 47% on OPT-6.7B LLM, and 66% on LLaMa2-7B LLM. Furthermore, FedCoLLM nearly equals Centralized performance, reaching 98% on GPT-2-Large LLM, 99% on OPT-6.7B LLM, and 97% on LLaMa2-7B LLM.

The Table 2 shows that the SLM of FedCoLLM performs better than the Zero-Shot, Standalone, and FedAvg due to the assistance of the server's LLM. For example, in the CQA dataset, FedCoLLM achieves a relative improvement of 6% over Standalone on GPT-2-Small SLM, 8% on OPT-1.3B SLM, and 4% on LLaMa2-1.3B SLM. Furthermore, FedCoLLM achieves a relative improvement of 3% over FedAvg on GPT-2-Small SLM, 5% on OPT-1.3B SLM, and 2% on LLaMa2-1.3B SLM.

4.3 Communication Cost

We investigated the communication cost of FedCoLLM with LoRA, focusing on fine-tuned parameters. As shown in Table 3, FedCoLLM significantly reduces communication costs: it only incurs 0.29% of GPT-2's, 0.24% of OPT's, and 0.23% of LLaMa2's costs when fine-tuning all parameters.

Table 1. We evaluate the server-side LLM performance of FedCoLLM using three experimental settings. Setting 1 (denoted as S1) deploys one server-side GPT-2-Large LLM paired with four client-side GPT-2-Small SLMs; Setting 2 (denoted as S2) uses one server-side OPT-6.7B LLM and four client-side OPT-1.3B SLMs; and Setting 3 (denoted as S3) adopts one server-side LLaMa2-7B LLM with four client-side LLaMa2-1.3B SLMs.

Task	Method	S1: Server GPT-2-Large	S2: Server OPT-6.7B	S3: Server LLaMa2-7B
CQA	Zero-Shot	36.3	48.7	39.5
	Centralized	54.7	68.6	69.0
	FedCoLLM	53.5	68.1	67.1
OBQA	Zero-Shot	19.4	27.6	31.8
	Centralized	28.2	34	39.8
	FedCoLLM	25.4	34.4	37.8
ARC-C	Zero-Shot	21.7	30.7	40.0
	Centralized	28.8	37.1	49.0
	FedCoLLM	27.4	36.0	45.4
ARC-E	Zero-Shot	53.2	65.6	69.3
	Centralized	59.5	70.2	76.8
	FedCoLLM	59.5	69.3	75.2

Table 2. We evaluate the client-side SLM performance of FedCoLLM across three experimental settings. The results reported in the table are the average of all clients.

Task	Method	S1: Clients GPT-2-Small	S2: Clients OPT-1.3B	S3: Clients LLaMa2-1.3B
CQA	Zero-Shot	28.3	41.9	30.1
	Standalone	40.5	57.3	56.1
	FedAvg	41.7	58.6	56.8
	FedCoLLM	**43.0**	**60.8**	**57.7**
OBQA	Zero-Shot	16.4	23.4	23.2
	Standalone	17.3	26.7	27.8
	FedAvg	15.8	27.2	26
	FedCoLLM	**17.8**	**29.2**	**28.8**
ARC-C	Zero-Shot	19.0	23.4	26.7
	Standalone	21.4	28.2	29.3
	FedAvg	20.9	28.8	29.4
	FedCoLLM	**21.8**	**29.4**	**30.6**
ARC-E	Zero-Shot	43.8	57.0	53.1
	Standalone	46.4	59.93	60.1
	FedAvg	46.3	59.97	60.3
	FedCoLLM	**46.8**	**60.01**	**61.1**

Table 3. Comparison of communication cost for FedCoLLM fine-tuning all parameters, fine-tuning using LoRA.

Model	Method	Transmitted Param Size (M)	Param Percent (%)
GPT-2	Full Model	124	100
	FedCoLLM	**0.29**	**0.24**
OPT	Full Model	1316	100
	FedCoLLM	**3.15**	**0.24**
LLaMa2	Full Model	1345	100
	FedCoLLM	**3.15**	**0.23**

5 Conclusions

We propose FedCoLLM, an innovative and parameter-efficient federated co-tuning framework for LLMs and SLMs. This framework is designed to seamlessly adapt LLMs to resource-constrained downstream enterprises while preserving privacy, eliminating the need to deploy LLMs directly within these enterprises. FedCoLLM achieves this by introducing a SLM that acts as a bridge between the private data held by clients and the LLM model hosted on the server. Through the FedCoLLM training process, we obtain an LLM enriched with knowledge from multiple domains and a high-performing client SLMs, guided by the LLM.

References

1. Adriana, R., Nicolas, B., Ebrahimi, K.S., Antoine, C., Carlo, G., Yoshua, B.: Fitnets: hints for thin deep nets. Proc. ICLR **2**(3), 1 (2015)
2. Bonawitz, K., et al.: Practical secure aggregation for federated learning on user-held data. arXiv preprint arXiv:1611.04482 (2016)
3. Cai, D., Wu, Y., Wang, S., Lin, F.X., Xu, M.: Efficient federated learning for modern NLP. In: Proceedings of the 29th Annual International Conference on Mobile Computing and Networking, pp. 1–16 (2023)
4. Chen, G., Choi, W., Yu, X., Han, T., Chandraker, M.: Learning efficient object detection models with knowledge distillation. Adv. neural Inf. Process. Syst. **30** (2017)
5. Clark, P., Cowhey, I., Etzioni, O., Khot, T., Sabharwal, A., Schoenick, C., Tafjord, O.: Think you have solved question answering? try arc, the ai2 reasoning challenge. arXiv preprint arXiv:1803.05457 (2018)
6. Fan, T., et al.: Ten challenging problems in federated foundation models. IEEE Trans. Knowl. Data Eng. (2025)
7. Fan, T., et al.: Fate-LLM: a industrial grade federated learning framework for large language models. arXiv preprint arXiv:2310.10049 (2023)
8. Gou, J., Yu, B., Maybank, S.J., Tao, D.: Knowledge distillation: a survey. Int. J. Comput. Vision **129**(6), 1789–1819 (2021)
9. Hinton, G., Vinyals, O., Dean, J.: Distilling the knowledge in a neural network. arXiv preprint arXiv:1503.02531 (2015)

10. Hu, E.J., et al.: Lora: low-rank adaptation of large language models. arXiv preprint arXiv:2106.09685 (2021)
11. Kang, Y., Fan, T., Gu, H., Zhang, X., Fan, L., Yang, Q.: Grounding foundation models through federated transfer learning: a general framework. ACM Trans. Intell. Syst. Technol. (2023)
12. McMahan, B., Moore, E., Ramage, D., Hampson, S., y Arcas, B.A.: Communication-efficient learning of deep networks from decentralized data. In: Artificial intelligence and statistics, pp. 1273–1282. PMLR (2017)
13. Meng, Z., Li, J., Zhao, Y., Gong, Y.: Conditional teacher-student learning. In: ICASSP 2019-2019 IEEE International Conference on Acoustics, Speech and Signal Processing (ICASSP), pp. 6445–6449. IEEE (2019)
14. Mihaylov, T., Clark, P., Khot, T., Sabharwal, A.: Can a suit of armor conduct electricity? a new dataset for open book question answering. arXiv preprint arXiv:1809.02789 (2018)
15. OpenAI: GPT-4 (2023)
16. Park, W., Kim, D., Lu, Y., Cho, M.: Relational knowledge distillation. In: Proceedings of the IEEE/CVF Conference on Computer Vision and Pattern Recognition, pp. 3967–3976 (2019)
17. Radford, A., et al.: Language models are unsupervised multitask learners. OpenAI blog **1**(8), 9 (2019)
18. Talmor, A., Herzig, J., Lourie, N., Berant, J.: Commonsenseqa: a question answering challenge targeting commonsense knowledge. arXiv preprint arXiv:1811.00937 (2018)
19. Touvron, H., et al.: Llama: open and efficient foundation language models (2023). arXiv:2302.13971 arXiv preprint
20. Xia, M., Gao, T., Zeng, Z., Chen, D.: Sheared llama: accelerating language model pre-training via structured pruning. arXiv preprint arXiv:2310.06694 (2023)
21. Yang, Q., Liu, Y., Cheng, Y., Kang, Y., Chen, T., Yu, H.: Federated learning. Synth. Lect. Artif. Intell. Mach. Learn. **13**(3), 1–207 (2019)
22. Zhang, S., et al.: OPT: open pre-trained transformer language models. arXiv preprint arXiv:2205.01068 (2022)
23. Zhang, Y., Xiang, T., Hospedales, T.M., Lu, H.: Deep mutual learning. In: Proceedings of the IEEE Conference On Computer Vision and Pattern Recognition, pp. 4320–4328 (2018)
24. Zhang, Z., et al.: Fedpetuning: when federated learning meets the parameter-efficient tuning methods of pre-trained language models. In: Findings of the Association for Computational Linguistics: ACL 2023, pp. 9963–9977 (2023)
25. Zhao, H., Du, W., Li, F., Li, P., Liu, G.: Fedprompt: communication-efficient and privacy-preserving prompt tuning in federated learning. In: ICASSP 2023-2023 IEEE international conference on acoustics, speech and signal processing (ICASSP), pp. 1–5. IEEE (2023)

Melodic Agent: A Generative Music Recommendation Framework with Large Language Models

Kai Tian[1], Yirong Mao[2], Wendong Bi[2], Hanjie Wang[2], and Wenhui Que[2](✉)

[1] Tsinghua University, Beijing, China
tk23@mails.tsinghua.edu.cn
[2] WeChat, Tencent Inc., Beijing, China
{erongmao,wendongbi,hankinwang,victorque}@tencent.com

Abstract. Large language models are reshaping music recommendation but still face sparse domain knowledge, hallucinations, and difficulty unifying immediate query intent with long-term personalization. We present Melodic Agent, an end-to-end generative framework that builds on multi-source textual evidence and structured metadata, reverses supervision from "song to description" to "description to song," and integrates retrieval augmentation to strengthen the mapping from natural language to target songs. At the system level, the framework unifies three modesquery-driven, profile-driven, and queryprofile fusion and introduces capability-boundary detection to trigger external search when uncertainty arises, forming a selectgenerateverify loop that stabilizes prediction under real-world conditions. Under a unified evaluation protocol, experiments show consistent gains in relevance and personalization while maintaining a balanced accuracy efficiency trade-off, positioning Melodic Agent as a practical paradigm for flexible and scalable generative music recommendation.

Keywords: Generative Music Recommendation · Music Recommendation Agent · Large Language Models

1 Introduction

With the rapid development of large language model (LLM)–based recommendation, many methods now leverage models' world knowledge for retrieval and ranking; however, applying such methods to music still faces domain-specific challenges [31]. General-purpose LLMs lack sufficient music knowledge, leading to *song hallucinations*. To mitigate this, we build an integrated *description mining–evidence alignment–retrieval augmentation* pipeline that mines semantically relevant song descriptions from noisy user comments via like-based ranking, rule filters, and LLM summarization, and aligns long-form WeChat articles and reviews at the paragraph level to extract song-specific evidence. These heterogeneous sources are normalized, deduplicated, consolidated into a large-scale

R. C.-W. Wong et al. (Eds.): PAKDD 2026, LNAI 16617, pp. 423–434, 2027.
https://doi.org/10.1007/978-981-92-1926-1_34

song description corpus, and used in a reversed "description-to-song" supervision scheme [24,27], thereby strengthening the bidirectional mapping between descriptions, songs, and their meta information and reducing hallucinations at the source.

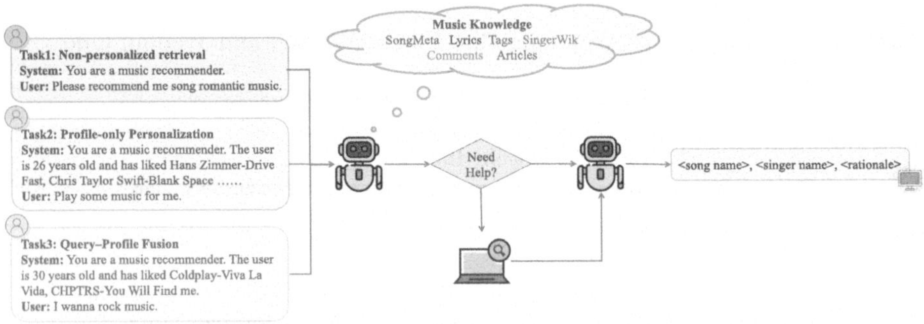

Fig. 1. Overview of the LLM-based Music Recommendation System.

Beyond knowledge enhancement, we propose a multifunctional LLM-based music recommendation agent that unifies three complementary modes: (i) query-driven, non-personalized retrieval (generative search); (ii) profile-driven, sequential recommendation based on long- and short-term listening history; and (iii) query–profile fusion that conditions personalized results on the user's current intent [23]. As depicted in Fig. 1, we further equip the system with a boundary detection mechanism that triggers external search tools when the model is uncertain or encounters newly released tracks outside its knowledge scope, ensuring comprehensive and reliable results. Overall, our contributions are: enhancing song knowledge via evidence-aligned descriptions fused with lyrics and metadata, designing a unified agent that handles both search-style and personalized recommendation tasks, and introducing a boundary-aware tool invocation mechanism that preserves accuracy for unknown or emerging songs while keeping the system reproducible and practically deployable.

To summarize, our contributions are as follows:

- **Song Knowledge Enhancement**: We construct an evidence-aligned, deduplicated song description corpus from comments, articles, lyrics, and metadata to strengthen song knowledge and reduce hallucinations.
- **Multifunctional Recommendation Agent**: We develop a unified agent that supports non-personalized retrieval, personalized recommendation, and query–profile fusion within a single framework.
- **External Tool Invocation Mechanism**: We design a boundary-aware tool invocation mechanism that calls external search for unknown or newly released songs to keep recommendations accurate.

2 Related Work

Music-recommendation systems have been shifting from raw-accuracy objectives toward user experience and human-centred care [6,28], with surveys and position papers highlighting broader human-centred evaluation, explainability, and transparency as central design goals [19,30]. Generative techniques increasingly pair recommendations with natural-language justifications: adapted LLMs summarise preference rationales from collaborative signals and improve user trust compared to template-based explanations [12,13], while model-agnostic explanation methods and industrial "why this track?"-style interfaces further illustrate the shift toward interpretable, safety-aware deployment [1,5]. Within LLM-for-Recommendation (LLM4Rec), one major line of work treats an LLM as an enhancer layered over collaborative or sequential recommenders, injecting world knowledge, semantic robustness, and error correction [16,21,25], for example using LLMs as data correctors or representation generators to mitigate sparsity and long-tail issues, and compressing long user histories into textual profiles while analysing the need for stronger sequential inductive biases and distillation [10,20]. Related large-scale multimedia systems for advertisement understanding emphasise similarly robust representations and evaluation in commercial settings [11]. A second line "language-izes" representation learning and inference by casting recommendation and retrieval as generation: ID embeddings are projected into the LLM token space or user histories are modeled purely as text [7], items are tokenized into generatable codes for autoregressive retrieval [17], and query-/dialog-driven recommenders rely on generative retrieval and parameter-efficient conversational models [15,18]. In music recommendation specifically, multimodal systems integrate playlists, tags, lyrics, and audio, complemented by music-oriented continued pretraining of language models such as MuCPT [3,4,14,22]. Finally, reinforcement learning is increasingly used to close the loop between generative LLMs and user-centric objectives in recommendation and reasoning [8,26,29]. Overall, existing approaches tend to emphasise either long-term personalization from user history or query-driven intent; few provide an end-to-end formulation that jointly models and aligns both within a unified LLM space, motivating joint objectives and cross-signal distillation that simultaneously optimize "who likes what" and "what is wanted now."

3 Method

We propose a generative music recommendation framework following a unified *select–generate–verify* paradigm built around a **single model**. At the data layer, a clean, multi-source corpus (song–text pairs, lyrics and content tags, artist knowledge) is constructed and aligned with training objectives; at the model layer, one parameterization is instruction-tuned under **three complementary supervision settings**—query-driven, profile-driven, and query–profile fusion so that prompts steer the same model to different behaviors; and at the system layer, capability-boundary detection triggers on-demand retrieval to ground uncertain cases with external evidence, yielding factual, relevant, and personalized recommendations while keeping the overall design simple to deploy and scale.

3.1 Preparatory Data Collection

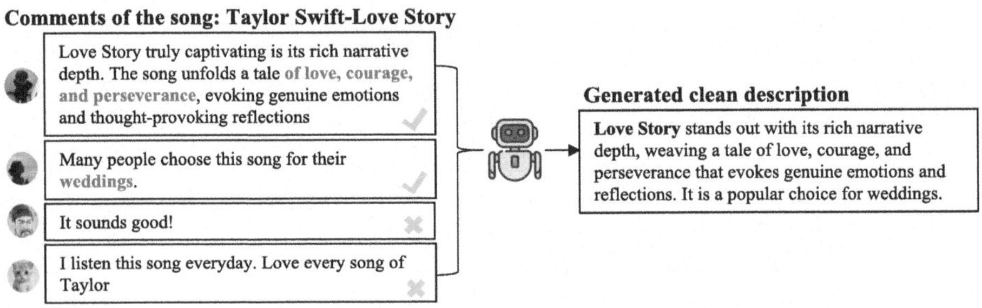

Fig. 2. From noisy user comments to a clean, evidence-aligned song description.

To unlock the potential of large language models (LLMs) for generative music recommendation, we first construct a multi-source corpus covering musical content, audience feedback, and artist background. We take the top 10^7 singles by play count over the past five years and, for each song, derive a compact textual description that compensates for the lack of narratives and cultural context in conventional metadata. Two main channels are used: **(i) articles**, where the WeChat search API retrieves long-form pieces by song title and a strong LLM (e.g., DeepSeek–V3 [9]) extracts strongly related passages after light de-duplication and entity cleaning; and **(ii) comments**, where we crawl song comments from WeChat and other communities, keep the top 500 by "likes", run a rule–plus–lightweight–model filter, and fuse the remaining comments into a single clean description that preserves factual, high-consensus content and scene/mood/use cues (e.g., "wedding", "practice", "night"). Together, these channels yield about 3.5×10^6 song–text pairs and 1.0×10^6 untruncated articles. In parallel, we record structured metadata (lyrics, credits, release year, genre, affective tags) for each song and build an artist encyclopaedia of about 3.0×10^5 entries from WeChat Encyclopaedia and Wikipedia, aligned to artists via named-entity matching. This unified dataset combines musical facts, public narratives, and cultural context, and the comment–to–clean–description pipeline in Fig. 2 shows how large-scale cleaning and alignment reduce hallucination risk and support downstream prompt design, retrieval augmentation, and explainability evaluation (Fig. 3).

system_prompt:
Assume you are a music recommendation expert. You need to generate short, conversational questions that a user might ask when they want to hear a specific song, based on the given song information.
user_prompt:
Song meta-information: {}. Related text information of the song: {}
Based on the above information, generate 6 questions pretending to be the user asking to hear this song. The questions should be as short as possible and avoid excessive adjectives. Examples of good questions are: Play a rock song, Recommend an emotional song, English love song, Songs by Andy Lau, Fast tempo English song, Play some Chinese rock, Songs suitable for the beach, Play a DJ song, Remix heavy metal song, Play a military red song. Note: The questions should not include time references, such as: Jay Chou's latest song.

Fig. 3. Prompt design for query-driven song recommendation.

3.2 Query-Based Song Recommendation and Rationale Generation

In the query-driven generative setting, the goal is to retrieve and recommend songs from natural-language cues (user queries or other text) while producing explanations consistent with both the query and the song. The raw corpus is naturally organized as "song name → description", but query-based recommendation requires moving from *text* to *song*. Following the observation of [2] that models trained mainly on $A \rightarrow B$ mappings often struggle with $B \rightarrow A$, we perform a directional reversal and add supervision for description → song, and further impose bidirectional augmentation between songs and structured attributes (e.g., metadata, tags). This ensures the model can move between content cues, entities, and structured properties, rather than only generating descriptions from song IDs.

To align training with query-driven use, we construct *query–rationale* pairs in two steps. Given a song with multi-source textual evidence and metadata, a strong LLM synthesizes a small set of semantically related queries that cover genre, mood, language, and context, and then generates for each query a brief explanation that is jointly consistent with the query and the target song and explicitly grounded in the evidence. This yields training instances of the form (q, s, r), where the model, conditioned on q (optionally plus an evidence summary), must output both the correct song s and a rationale r. The resulting dataset aligns the training distribution with the intended inference behaviour—"locate from text, then explain from evidence"—and supports downstream evaluation of both query relevance and explainability.

3.3 Personalized and Query-Based Recommendation

To enhance personalization in our generative recommendation system, we jointly model user profiles and queries within a single framework. The user profile $\mathcal{P}_u$

encodes demographic attributes and historical behaviour (e.g., repeated plays, likes, shares), enabling pure profile-based recommendation that outputs a song and a brief rationale,

$$\text{user profile}(\mathcal{P}_u) \longrightarrow \text{Song}(s_i), \quad \text{Reason } r_u(s_i),$$

while the personalized query-based setting integrates both long-term tastes and immediate intent,

$$\text{query}(\mathcal{Q}_u) + \text{user profile}(\mathcal{P}_u) \longrightarrow \text{Song}(s_i), \quad \text{Reason } r_u(s_i).$$

In both cases, the model learns to map profiles and (optionally) queries to candidate songs with concise explanations, such as prioritizing Japanese jazz for a Japanese user who frequently listens to Japanese tracks and explicitly explaining how this matches their history.

In the query-based mode, the model parses $\mathcal{Q}_u$, extracts emotional and situational cues, filters and ranks candidate songs, and then combines $\mathcal{P}_u$ to balance current intent ("I want to listen to jazz songs") with long-term preferences (e.g., favouring Japanese jazz for a user who mainly listens to Japanese music). However, existing music platforms typically split these signals: personalized feeds often lack explicit query information, while search-based recommendations largely ignore user-specific profiles and return near-identical results for all users, making it difficult to satisfy both query relevance and personalization simultaneously.

To bridge this gap, we generate synthetic queries from historical behaviour so that training data jointly encode query relevance and personalization. Concretely, for each user we select a recently liked or repeatedly played song s_u and, using $\mathcal{P}_u$ and information about s_u, employ *DeepSeek-V3* to generate a plausible query,

$$\mathcal{Q}_u = f(\mathcal{P}_u, s_u),$$

where $f(\cdot)$ produces what the user might have searched for when listening to s_u. This bidirectional augmentation (profile $\leftrightarrow$ query) yields training pairs in which the recommended song s_i and reason $r_u(s_i)$ are supervised to reflect both the synthesized query and the user's long-term tastes, enabling the model at inference time to output recommendations that are simultaneously query-relevant and strongly personalized.

3.4 Calling External Search Tools Beyond Model Capability

To handle knowledge beyond the model's training distribution, we explicitly model *capability boundaries* and train the agent to trigger external search tools when its internal knowledge is insufficient. Concretely, we take real WeChat Listen queries $\mathcal{Q}_u$ and user profiles $\mathcal{P}_u$, feed the concatenated input into the base model, and collect cases where it either fails to return a relevant song or hallucinates a non-existent one; these are treated as "beyond-capability" instances. For each such case, an external search service retrieves the correct target song

Table 1. Different Experimental Settings for Song Recommendation Evaluation

Method	Hallucination Rate ↓	Relevance ↑	Personalization Score ↑	Tool Usage Rate
API-based Model				
GPT-4o	0.1122	0.6937	0.3853	-
GPT-4o **w tools**	0.1021	0.7422	0.3838	0.0844
Gemini-2.5-pro	0.2011	0.8091	0.3519	-
Gemini-2.5-pro **w tools**	0.1606	0.8879	0.3507	0.1060
Open Source Model				
Deepseek-V3	0.1222	0.8195	0.3957	-
Deepseek-V3 **w tools**	0.0733	0.8390	0.3733	0.1977
Qwen3-235B-A22B	0.1200	0.6464	0.3844	-
Qwen3-235B-A22B **w tools**	0.0500	0.7666	0.3286	0.2466
Qwen3-235B-A22B-Instruct-2507	0.0744	0.6813	0.4061	-
Qwen3-235B-A22B-Instruct-2507 **w tools**	0.0678	0.7503	0.3847	0.1800
Baseline Model				
Qwen2.5-32B-Instruct	0.2800	0.6990	0.4081	-
Qwen2.5-32B-Instruct **w tools**	0.2564	0.7508	0.3835	0.1470
Ours				
Melodic Agent	0.0447	0.8251	**0.4322**	-
Melodic Agent **w tools**	**0.0396**	**0.8918**	0.4084	0.1200

s_i, yielding a tool-trigger dataset $\mathcal{T}_{\text{tool}} = \{(\mathcal{Q}_u, \mathcal{P}_u, s_i)\}_{i=1}^{M}$. Rather than naively invoking tools for all queries—which would force every request through a cascaded, multi-stage retrieval stack with non-trivial latency and systems cost—we aim to preserve a fluid, dialogue-style recommendation experience in which in-distribution queries are answered directly by the model. We then use $\mathcal{T}_{\text{tool}}$ for second-stage fine-tuning, adding explicit decision slots so the model learns, given $(\mathcal{Q}_u, \mathcal{P}_u)$, when to issue a *retrieve* versus *do-not-retrieve* action and how to integrate retrieved results, thereby improving robustness and coverage without overusing tools.

4 Experiments

4.1 Experimental Setup

We adopt a unified data–instruction–training pipeline and report both training configuration and evaluation protocol under which four main experiments are conducted. The core supervision is a song–text corpus of about 3.5M pairs from WeChat articles and cleaned comments, with supervision reversed to $t \rightarrow s$ so the model learns to "find the song from the description"; around 1.0M music-related articles and 190k artist entries provide long-context evidence and background knowledge, and instruction-style augmentation covers three modes: query-driven non-personalized retrieval, profile-driven sequential personalization, and query-driven personalized recommendation, blended with general instruction data into a $\sim$ 5B-token mixture. We fine-tune *Qwen2.5-32B-Instruct* for 2 epochs on 96 *H20* GPUs with cosine-decayed learning rates in the 3–6 $\times 10^{-5}$ range, and further build $\sim$ 400k SFT examples from real failure queries and sampled cases to teach capability-boundary detection and on-demand tool invocation via explicit "retrieve / do-not-retrieve" slots. For evaluation, we stratify real online search queries into five age buckets (200 per bucket, 1,000 total), give each system the same concatenated user profile $\mathcal{P}_u$ and query $\mathcal{Q}_u$, and measure *Song Hallucination* (missing from a hundred-million-scale catalog), *Relevance* (RAG + DeepSeek-V3 scoring over retrieved descriptions and metadata), *Personalization* (a lightweight two-tower collaborative scorer trained on WeChat music listening preference logs), and *Tool Usage Rate*. Under this unified protocol, we run a cross-paradigm and cross-scale main comparison (Table 1), an ablation from *Basic Song Model* to progressively agentic, personalized, and tool-enabled variants (Table 2), a personalization-focused comparison using the collaborative scorer as evaluator (Fig. 4), and an analysis of tool-trigger patterns, jointly showing that profile signals (semantic anchors) and selective tool usage (gap filling) are the two primary levers for improving factuality and relevance.

4.2 Comprehensive Evaluation Across Model Scales and Paradigms

To comprehensively characterize generative music recommendation, we benchmark representative API models and open-source large models alongside our *Melodic Agent* under a unified protocol, dataset, and prompt configuration (Table 1). We evaluate four dimensions: *Hallucination Rate* (fraction of non-existent invalid songs; lower is better), *Relevance* (retrieval-augmented, LLM-scored alignment between recommendation and query/context; higher is better), *Personalization Score* (a collaborative lightweight scorer measuring user–song fit), and *Tool Usage Rate* (frequency of capability-boundary triggers invoking external retrieval). The *Baseline Model* (Qwen2.5-32B-Instruct) serves both as a comparison point and as the backbone of our agent, with substantially fewer parameters than most API and 200B-class open-source models, representing a practical, lightweight deployment starting point.

Across both API and open-source models, a consistent pattern emerges: enabling tools generally reduces hallucination and improves relevance, as seen for GPT-4o, Gemini-2.5-pro, DeepSeek-V3, and Qwen3-235B-A22B. However, for several models personalization scores decrease once tools are enabled, suggesting that high-frequency retrieval tends to surface globally authoritative descriptions that strengthen factuality and semantic fit but can dilute individualized preference cues when profile signals are weak. In contrast, our *Melodic Agent* achieves a strong balance even without tools (hallucination 0.0447, relevance 0.8251, highest personalization 0.4322), and with capability-boundary detection and selective tool invocation further improves factuality and relevance (hallucination 0.0396, relevance 0.8918) while keeping tool usage modest (0.1200) and personalization only slightly reduced (0.4084). Compared to the plain backbone, which shows relatively high hallucination without tools and remains behind larger models even with retrieval, the agentic formulation that ties profile signals and tool use together consistently dominates.

From Table 1, three practical lessons follow. First, external tools offer stable gains in factuality and relevance but should be selectively triggered and re-ranked to avoid overwhelming personalization signals. Second, personalization acts as a stabilizer in generative pipelines—narrowing the candidate space, suppressing hallucinations, and improving match quality—and should collaborate with retrieval rather than be treated as a separate stage. Third, even with a smaller backbone, high-quality domain data construction and agentic task design can match or surpass much larger models in aggregate performance, pointing to concrete engineering levers such as tool-trigger calibration, adaptive profile weighting, retrieval re-ranking, and in-model knowledge distillation.

Table 2. Ablation Studies on Melodic Agent

Models	Hallucination Rate ↓	Relevance ↑
Basic Song Model	0.0900	0.7744
Melodic Agent wo Personalization	0.0955	0.7877
Melodic Agent	0.0447	0.8251
Melodic Agent w tools	**0.0396**	**0.8918**

4.3 Ablation Study: Contributions of Melodic Agent Components

Under the **same backbone (Qwen2.5-32B-Instruct)** and **the same test set**, we compare four variants—*Basic Song Model, Melodic Agent (w/o personalization), Melodic Agent*, and *Melodic Agent (with tools)*—using *Hallucination Rate* (fraction of non-existent/invalid songs; lower is better) and *Relevance* (RAG+LLM alignment score; higher is better). As shown in Table 2, *Basic Song Model*, trained only on "song + description", already reaches Hallucination 0.0900 and Relevance 0.7744 and outperforms its general-purpose backbone, indicating that domain-aligned data and controlled inputs move the model into a favourable low-hallucination / high-relevance regime. Moving to an agentic formulation without personalization (*Melodic Agent w/o personalization*) increases Relevance to 0.7877 while Hallucination slightly rises to 0.0955, suggesting that parsing/generation routines and bidirectional augmentation strengthen semantic matching but, without user constraints, can drift toward long-tail or fuzzy memories. Adding user profiles (*Melodic Agent*) yields a stronger shift on both axes—Hallucination drops to 0.0447 and Relevance climbs to 0.8251—as personalization narrows the candidate space and provides a stable semantic anchor that both curbs fabrication and better matches user preferences. Finally, enabling external tool calls (*Melodic Agent with tools*) achieves the best results, with

Hallucination 0.0396 and Relevance 0.8918, showing that capability-boundary detection plus retrieval effectively fills knowledge gaps and resolves uncertainty. Overall, domain-aligned Basic improves over the backbone, the agentic variant (w/o personalization) further boosts relevance at a slight hallucination cost, and personalization plus tooling are the main levers that jointly enhance factuality and relevance in a stepwise fashion.

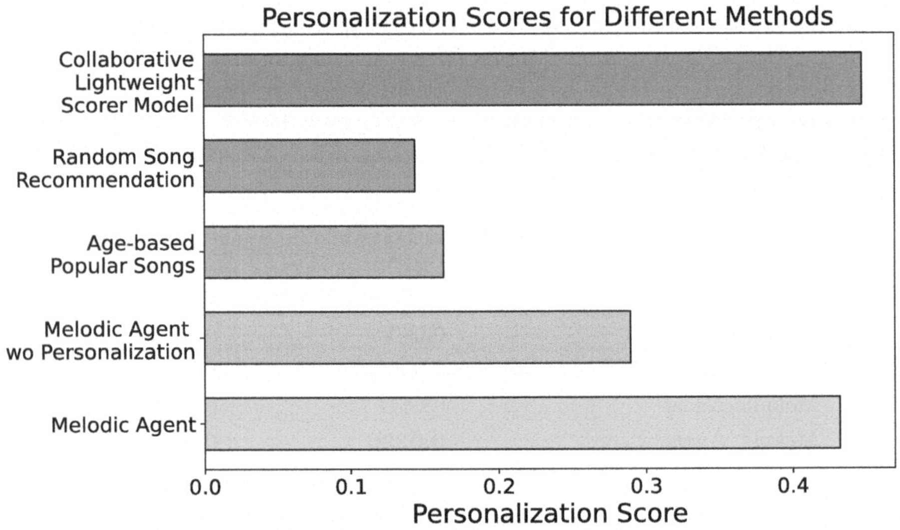

Fig. 4. Personalization Scores for Different Methods.

4.4 Evaluation and Comparison of Personalized Recommendation Models

To quantify personalization, we use the collaborative lightweight scorer in (0,1) as a reference model and compare four methods under the same evaluation: *Random Song Recommendation*, *Age-based Popular Songs*, *Melodic Agent (w/o personalization)*, and *Melodic Agent* (personalized, no tools). As shown in Fig. 4, Random and Age-based baselines obtain low scores (0.1439 and 0.1631), indicating weak alignment with individual tastes, while the non-personalized *Melodic Agent* already improves over these simple heuristics. Incorporating user profiles further boosts the score to 0.4322, which is close to the collaborative scorer's own score of 0.4471, suggesting that our generative framework can approach the personalization quality of a dedicated collaborative model. Overall, the monotonic increase across methods confirms that adding agentic reasoning and explicit personalization substantially enhances user-specific recommendation quality.

5 Conclusion

We propose Melodic Agent, an application-oriented generative framework for music recommendation that unifies multi-source music data and adopts a select–generate–verify paradigm for retrieval, personalization, and their fusion. With capability-boundary detection to trigger tools only when needed, it achieves strong factuality and relevance while maintaining competitive personalization.

References

1. Afchar, D., Melchiorre, A., Schedl, M., Hennequin, R., Epure, E., Moussallam, M.: Explainability in music recommender systems. AI Mag. **43**(2), 190–208 (2022)
2. Berglund, L., et al.: The reversal curse: LLMS trained on" a is b" fail to learn" b is a". arXiv preprint arXiv:2309.12288 (2023)
3. Bi, W., Mao, Y., Liu, X., Tian, K., Zhang, J., Wang, H., Que, W.: Wemusic-agent: efficient conversational music recommendation via knowledge internalization and agentic boundary learning. arXiv preprint arXiv:2512.16108 (2025)
4. Doh, S., Choi, K., Nam, J.: Talkplay: multimodal music recommendation with large language models. arXiv preprint arXiv:2502.13713 (2025)
5. Gao, S., Wang, Y., Fang, J., Chen, L., Han, P., Shang, S.: Dre: generating recommendation explanations by aligning large language models at data-level. arXiv preprint arXiv:2404.06311 (2024)
6. Konstan, J., Terveen, L.: Human-centered recommender systems: origins, advances, challenges, and opportunities. AI Mag. **42**(3), 31–42 (2021)
7. Liao, J., Li, S., Yang, Z., Wu, J., Yuan, Y., Wang, X., He, X.: Llara: large language-recommendation assistant. In: Proceedings of the 47th International ACM SIGIR Conference on Research and Development in Information Retrieval, pp. 1785–1795 (2024)
8. Lin, J., Wang, T., Qian, K.: Rec-r1: bridging generative large language models and user-centric recommendation systems via reinforcement learning. arXiv preprint arXiv:2503.24289 (2025)
9. Liu, A., et al.: Deepseek-v3 technical report. arXiv preprint arXiv:2412.19437 (2024)
10. Liu, Q., et al.: Llmemb: large language model can be a good embedding generator for sequential recommendation. In: Proceedings of the AAAI Conference on Artificial Intelligence. vol. 39, pp. 12183–12191 (2025)
11. Long, X., et al.: Adsqa: towards advertisement video understanding. In: Proceedings of the IEEE/CVF International Conference on Computer Vision, pp. 23396–23407 (2025)
12. Lubos, S., Tran, T.N.T., Felfernig, A., Polat Erdeniz, S., Le, V.M.: LLM-generated explanations for recommender systems. In: Adjunct Proceedings of the 32nd ACM Conference on User Modeling, Adaptation and Personalization, pp. 276–285 (2024)
13. Ma, Q., Ren, X., Huang, C.: XREC: large language models for explainable recommendation. arXiv preprint arXiv:2406.02377 (2024)
14. Melchiorre, A.B., et al.: Just ask for music (jam): multimodal and personalized natural language music recommendation (2025). arXiv:2507.15826 arXiv preprint
15. Pang, M., et al.: Generative retrieval and alignment model: a new paradigm for e-commerce retrieval. In: Companion Proceedings of the ACM on Web Conference, pp. 413–421 (2025)

16. Qiao, Y., Ao, X., Liu, Y., Xu, J., Sun, X., He, Q.: Login: a large language model consulted graph neural network training framework. In: Proceedings of the Eighteenth ACM International Conference on Web Search and Data Mining, pp. 232–241 (2025)
17. Rajput, S., et al.: Recommender systems with generative retrieval. Adv. Neural. Inf. Process. Syst. **36**, 10299–10315 (2023)
18. Ravaut, M., Zhang, H., Xu, L., Sun, A., Liu, Y.: Parameter-efficient conversational recommender system as a language processing task. arXiv preprint arXiv:2401.14194 (2024)
19. Raza, S., et al.: A comprehensive review of recommender systems: transitioning from theory to practice. arXiv preprint arXiv:2407.13699 (2024)
20. Sun, Y., Yang, X., Sun, Z., Wang, Y., Wang, B., Qu, X.: Llm4rsr: large language models as data correctors for robust sequential recommendation. In: Proceedings of the AAAI Conference on Artificial Intelligence, vol. 39, pp. 12604–12612 (2025)
21. Sun, Z., et al.: Large language models enhanced collaborative filtering. In: Proceedings of the 33rd ACM International Conference on Information and Knowledge Management, pp. 2178–2188 (2024)
22. Tian, K., Mao, Y., Bi, W., Wang, H., Wenhui, Q.: MUCPT: music-related natural language model continued pretraining. In: AI for Music Workshop
23. Wang, S., et al.: Towards s^2-challenges underlying LLM-based augmentation for personalized news recommendation. In: Proceedings of the AAAI Conference on Artificial Intelligence, vol. 39, pp. 12739–12747 (2025)
24. Wei, W., Ren, X., Tang, J., Wang, Q., Su, L., Cheng, S., Wang, J., Yin, D., Huang, C.: LLMREC: large language models with graph augmentation for recommendation. In: Proceedings of the 17th ACM International Conference on Web Search and Data Mining, pp. 806–815 (2024)
25. Yan, H., et al.: MOKGNN: boosting graph neural networks via mixture of generic and task-specific language models. In: Proceedings of the Eighteenth ACM International Conference on Web Search and Data Mining, pp. 242–250 (2025)
26. Zeng, S., et al.: Reviewrl: towards automated scientific review with RL. In: Proceedings of the 2025 Conference on Empirical Methods in Natural Language Processing, pp. 16942–16954 (2025)
27. Zhang, H., et al.: Towards hallucination-free music: A reinforcement learning preference optimization framework for reliable song generation. arXiv preprint arXiv:2508.05011 (2025)
28. Zhang, K., et al.: The 1st workshop on human-centered recommender systems. In: Companion Proceedings of the ACM on Web Conference 2025, pp. 2088–2091 (2025)
29. Zhang, K., et al.: A survey of reinforcement learning for large reasoning models. arXiv preprint arXiv:2509.08827 (2025)
30. Zhang, Y., et al.: Explainable recommendation: A survey and new perspectives. Found. Trends® Inf. Retrieval **14**(1), 1–101 (2020)
31. Zhang, Y., et al.: Siren's song in the ai ocean: a survey on hallucination in large language models. Comput. Ling., 1–45 (2025)

RHA-Sketch: Mining Time-Decay Heavy Hitters in High-Speed Data Streams

Yue Kan[1], Yang Du[1(✉)], He Huang[1], and Yu-E Sun[2]

[1] School of Computer Science and Technology, Soochow University, Suzhou, China
ykan@stu.suda.edu.cn, {duyang,huangh}@suda.edu.cn

[2] School of Rail Transportation, Soochow University, Suzhou, China
sunye12@suda.edu.cn

Abstract. Time-decay heavy hitters are items whose recency-weighted frequencies dominate a data stream and are central to applications such as data-warehouse analytics, anomaly detection and web query log analysis. Existing sketch-based solutions adopt recent-hotness-unaware eviction policies, which, under tight memory budgets, lead to substantial accuracy degradation due to noise from hash collisions and the premature eviction of recent hot items. We present RHA-Sketch, a compact, high-throughput sketch with a recent-hotness-aware eviction policy. It partitions items into different levels of recent hotness and applies differentiated decay strategies to each class. We evaluate RHA-Sketch on real traces. Experimental results show that RHA-Sketch achieves high F1-score under tight memory budgets (e.g., 16 KB). Moreover, it outperforms state-of-the-art schemes by reducing ARE by 61.9% and improving throughput by 57%. All related implementations are released as open source in a GitHub repository [11].

Keywords: Sketch · Time-decay heavy hitter detection · data stream mining

1 Introduction

Mining time-decay heavy hitters in high-speed data streams is fundamental to applications such as data-warehouse analytics [17], anomaly detection [1], web query-log analysis [18], and stock feeds monitoring [20]. In a general model, a time-aware data stream consists of a sequence of $\langle key, value, timestamp\rangle$ triples, where the *key* identifies each item, the *value* typically represents the count of an item and the *timestamp* indicates the item's arrival time. Time-decay heavy hitters refer to items whose time-decayed count exceeds a threshold, calculated as the product of the total time-decayed count of all items and a threshold parameter θ. An item's time-decayed count is the cumulative contribution after applying time-decay, where recent items contribute more than older ones.

A key challenge in mining time-decay heavy hitters in high-speed data streams is limited memory [2]. To sustain high item processing throughput, systems typically rely on high-speed cache memory with low latency but limited

R. C.-W. Wong et al. (Eds.): PAKDD 2026, LNAI 16617, pp. 435–446, 2027.
https://doi.org/10.1007/978-981-92-1926-1_35

capacity, which severely constrains the amount of state that can be maintained. Consequently, sketch-based algorithms [3–7] have been extensively adopted. A sketch provides a compact probabilistic representation of the data stream through hash functions, enabling approximate frequency statistics of items with minimal memory overhead while maintaining high estimation accuracy.

Existing time-decay sketching approaches fall into two families: timestamp-based and weighting-function-based. Timestamp-based approaches such as λ-HCount [14] and FDCMSS [13] maintain per-item timestamps and apply decay when these timestamps are updated, whereas weighting-function-based approaches (e.g., Ada-sketches [16], DAKPCF [12]) use emphasis functions at insertion time and de-emphasis functions at query time to obtain time-decayed counts.

Current time-decay heavy hitter mining approaches lack eviction policies that are aware of recent hotness: they do not distinguish between items with different time-decayed counts and instead treat them uniformly. For example, DAKPCF simply replaces the candidate with the new item and sets its time-decayed count to the current time weight $f(t)$. Real-world data streams are highly skewed: recent hot items form only a tiny fraction, while the vast majority are recent cold or warm items [8]. As a result, these non-hot items hinder time-decay heavy hitter mining in two ways: (i) *Noise from hash collisions*, where recent non-hot items distort the counters of truly recent hot items and may even be misreported as hot; and (ii) *Memory occupied by non-hot items*, where non-hot items consume limited sketch slots, so recent hot items either fail to obtain slots or are evicted before they can accumulate enough evidence to be promoted to heavy hitters.

In this paper, we propose RHA-Sketch, an accurate and efficient sketch for mining time-decay heavy hitters. The key idea is to apply differentiated eviction policies tailored to items with different levels of recent hotness. RHA-Sketch partitions items by their time-decayed counts into three groups: transient items, candidate items, and established heavy hitters. For transient items (recent cold items and a subset of recent warm items), it applies deterministic decay to quickly free memory for recent hot items. For candidate items (the remaining recent warm items), it applies probabilistic decay, which preserves the trajectories of promising recent hot items while gradually down-weighting recent warm items unlikely to become time-decay heavy hitters. No decay is applied to established heavy hitters. Collectively, these mechanisms enable RHA-Sketch to adapt to rapidly changing, highly skewed data stream under tight memory constraints, delivering a superior accuracy–efficiency trade-off. The contributions of this work are summarized as follows.

- We propose RHA-Sketch, a novel time-decay heavy-hitter detection solution for high-speed data stream that maintains high accuracy under tight memory budgets.
- We design a recent-hotness-aware eviction mechanism that partitions items into different levels of recent hotness and applies differentiated decay strategies to each, improving both memory efficiency and accuracy.

- We implement RHA-Sketch and evaluate it across diverse time-decay heavy-hitter detection scenarios on real traces. With only 16 KB of memory, RHA-Sketch achieves over 98% F1-score while maintaining high throughput.

2 Problem Statement

We consider a time-aware data stream $\mathcal{D} = \{e_1, e_2, \ldots, e_N\}$, where each item $e_i \in E$ belongs to an item set E. Each item is a ⟨key, value, timestamp⟩ triple: the key serves as an ID, the value represents the item's frequency and the timestamp indicates the item's arrival time. In this paper, we set value = 1 (i.e., items arrive individually). The time-decayed count of an item e_i at query time t' is defined as $\text{tdc}(e_i; t') = \sum_{0 \le t \le t'} \mathbf{1}_{e_t = e_i} \cdot \frac{f(t)}{f(t')}$, where $\mathbf{1}_{\{e_t = e_i\}}$ is the indicator function and $\frac{f(t)}{f(t')} < 1$ for $t < t'$. The time-decay heavy hitter detection problem is to identify all items whose time-decayed count exceeds a threshold θC, where C is the sum of all items' time-decayed counts at query time t'.

3 Design of RHA-Sketch

3.1 Rationale

Current time-decay heavy hitter mining approaches adopting recent-hotness-unaware eviction policies lead to low detection accuracy. We aim to design a novel sketch to achieve the following objectives: (i) Quickly free up space in limited memory for recent hot items; (ii) Protect recent hot items from interference caused by recent cold items and recent warm items; (iii) remain compact and simple to implement, operating efficiently under extremely small memory budgets while sustaining high-throughput updates and queries.

Guided by these objectives, RHA-Sketch partitions items by their time-decayed counts into three groups: for transient items, whose time-decayed counts lie below the potential threshold T_{pot}, we apply deterministic decay to evict them quickly and free space; for candidate items, whose time-decayed counts in $[T_{\text{pot}}, T_{\text{HH}})$, we apply probabilistic decay [4] so promising items can continue to accumulate while stagnant ones are gradually pushed below T_{pot}; and for established time-decay heavy hitters, whose time-decayed counts are already above T_{HH}, no decay is applied, preserving their estimates.

3.2 Data Structure

As shown in Fig. 1, the data structure of RHA-Sketch comprises γ rows, each containing ω slots. Each row is associated with a pairwise independent hash function. We denote the j-th slot in the i-th row as $S(i, j)$. Each slot consists of two fields: (i) a key field $S(i, j).k$, which stores the key of item, and (ii) a time-emphasized count field $S(i, j).tec$, which stores the accumulated time-emphasized count of the item up to the current time period.

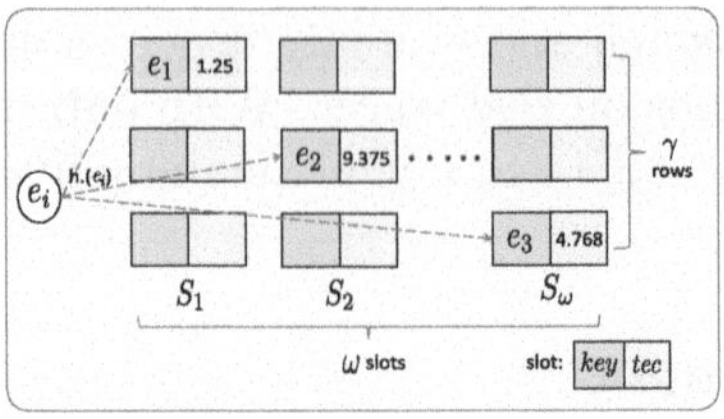

Fig. 1. Data Structure of RHA-Sketch.

Insertion. Initially, all key fields are set to null, and all time-emphasized count fields are initialized to 0. For each incoming item e_i , RHA-Sketch maps it to γ slots using γ hash functions $h_j(e_i)$ $(1 \leq j \leq \gamma)$, where each hash function maps to a unique slot $S(j, h_j(e_i))$ in the corresponding row, which we refer to as the γ map slots. As illustrated in Fig. 2, within the γ mapped slots, we implement five distinct update strategies based on different conditions.

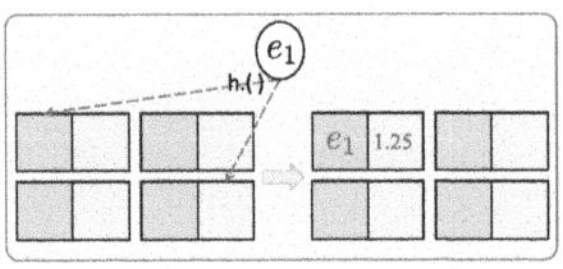

(a) e_1 is hashed to an empty slot

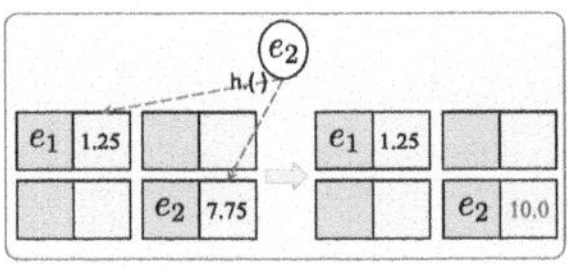

(b) e_2 updates its time-emphasized counter

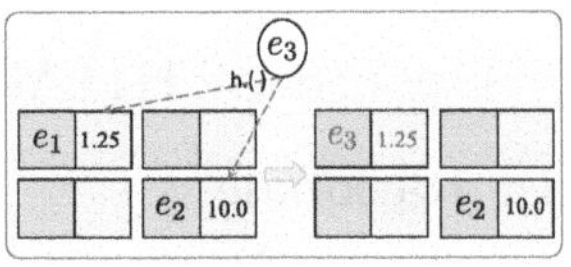

(c) e_3 replaces e_1 via direct decay

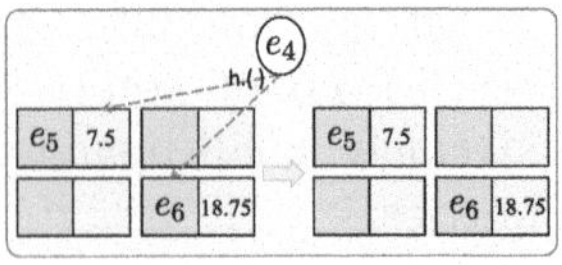

(d) e_5 undergoes probabilistic decay without decreasing

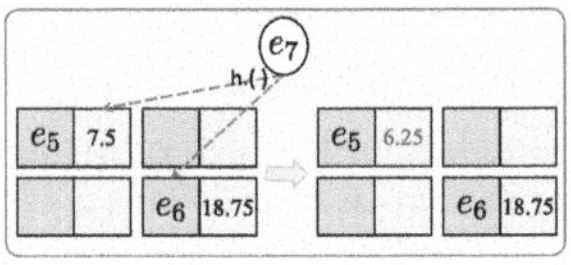

(e) e_5 undergoes probabilistic decay and decreases

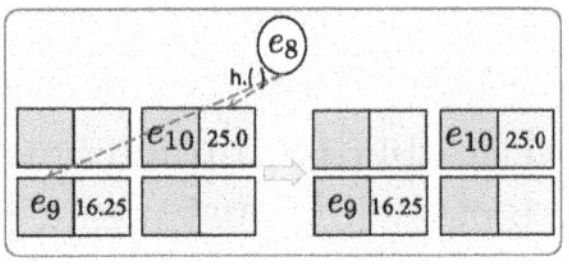

(f) Established time-decay heavy hitter e_9 undergoes no decay

Fig. 2. Different cases of insertion, where $T_{\text{pot}} = 5$, $T_{\text{HH}} = 10$, and $f(t) = 1.25$.

Case 1 ($S(j, h_j(e_i)).tec = 0$): The slot $S(j, h_j(e_i))$ is empty. RHA-Sketch writes key e_i into $S(j, h_j(e_i)).k$ and initializes $S(j, h_j(e_i)).tec$ to the current time weight $f(t)$. As shown in Fig. 2(a), item e_1 is hashed to an empty slot and initializes it.

Case 2 ($S(j, h_j(e_i)).tec > 0$ and $S(j, h_j(e_i)).k = e_i$): The slot $S(j, h_j(e_i))$ is non-empty and its key matches e_i. RHA-Sketch increments $S(j, h_j(e_i)).tec$ by the current time weight $f(t)$. As shown in Fig. 2(b), item e_2 matches the slot on its second hash, and the slot's time-emphasized count increases by $f(t)$.

Case 3 ($S(j, h_j(e_i)).tec > 0$ and $S(j, h_j(e_i)).k \neq e_i$): Item e_i collides in all rows. Among the γ mapped slots, RHA-Sketch selects the one with the minimum time-emphasized count, computes its time-decayed count $tdc = S(j, h_j(e_i)).tec/f(t)$, and then chooses an action based on the classification of tdc relative to the potential threshold T_{pot} and the time-decay heavy-hitter threshold T_{HH}, where $T_{\text{pot}} = \alpha T_{\text{HH}}$ (α is a tunable parameter).

- Case 3.1 ($0 < tdc < T_{\text{pot}}$, transient items): RHA-Sketch applies direct decay by subtracting $f(t)$ from $S(j, h_j(e_i)).tec$. If the result is less than or equal to 0, it replaces the slot with the incoming item, setting $S(j, h_j(e_i)).k = e_i$ and $S(j, h_j(e_i)).tec = f(t)$; otherwise, the existing item is retained. As illustrated in Fig. 2(c), when item e_3 arrives, RHA-Sketch decays e_1 in the minimum-count slot until its count becomes zero and then replaces it with e_3.
- Case 3.2 ($T_{\text{pot}} \leq tdc < T_{\text{HH}}$, candidate items): The incumbent item may be a warm placeholder or an emerging recent hot item. RHA-Sketch applies probabilistic decay to the selected minimum-count slot: with probability $P_{\text{dec}}(tdc)$, it decreases $S(j, h_j(e_i)).tec$ by $f(t)$. As illustrated in Figs. 2(d)–(e), when items e_4 and e_7 arrive and no matching slot is found, RHA-Sketch repeatedly selects e_5 in the minimum-count slot and applies probabilistic decay, which sometimes leaves its count unchanged and sometimes reduces it by $f(t)$.
- Case 3.3 ($tdc \geq T_{\text{HH}}$, established time-decay heavy hitter): RHA-Sketch preserves accuracy by neither decaying nor evicting the selected slot at this step. It applies decay only after ongoing time decay drives its time-decayed count below T_{HH}. As illustrated in Fig. 2(f), when item e_8 arrives, RHA-Sketch selects the minimum-count slot containing e_9, recognizes it as a heavy hitter, and leaves its count unchanged.

Query. To obtain the time-decayed count of item e_i at time t_q, RHA-Sketch hashes e_i with the γ functions to locate the mapped slots $S(j, h_j(e_i))$ $(1 \leq j \leq \gamma)$. For each slot whose key field equals e_i, it estimates tdc as $S(j, h_j(e_i))$.tec$/f(t)$; if no slot matches e_i, the query returns 0.

Probabilistic Decay. Our probabilistic decay strategy is inspired by HeavyKeeper but is applied only to slots whose time-decayed count lies in $[T_{\text{pot}}, T_{\text{HH}})$. For such a candidate slot, RHA-Sketch computes tdc and applies decay with probability $P_{\text{dec}}(tdc) = b^{-(tdc - T_{\text{pot}})}$ $(b > 1)$. Recent warm items that remain only slightly above T_{pot} are gradually pushed below the threshold and then removed by direct decay, freeing space for recent hot items, whereas emerging recent hot items quickly increase their margin above T_{pot}, making decay unlikely and allowing them to become time-decay heavy hitters.

Note: We emphasize that exponential probabilistic decay of HeavyKeeper is not directly applicable to time-decay heavy-hitter detection. Because the decay probability decreases exponentially with the counter value, a warm item (e.g., with an estimated frequency around 350) can have a near-zero chance of being decayed, making it unlikely for a later-emerging hot items to evict that pre-occupied slot. In the time-decay model where time-decay compresses absolute frequency gaps between items, this problem is exacerbated.

4 Mathematical Analysis

4.1 Error Bound of RHA-Sketch

Theorem 1. *RHA-Sketch consists of γ rows, each containing ω slots. Let e_i denote the i-th largest item, whose true time-decayed count at time t' is tdc_i. The estimated time-decayed count of e_i is denoted by $\widehat{tdc_i}$. Then, the error bound of RHA-Sketch can be expressed as:*

$$\Pr\{tdc_i - \widehat{tdc_i} \geq \varepsilon C\} \leq \frac{C - tdc_i}{\varepsilon C} \cdot \frac{p_\star}{\gamma\omega}, \tag{1}$$

where $p_\star = \max\left\{\mathbf{1}[tdc_i < T_{\text{pot}}],\ \mathbf{1}[T_{\text{pot}} \leq tdc_i < T_{\text{HH}}] \cdot b^{-(tdc_i - T_{\text{pot}})}\right\}$.

Proof. The $\widehat{tdc_i}$ can be written as $\widehat{tdc_i} = tdc_i - X_i$, where X_i represents the total decrement caused by decay over all time intervals. The decay rules of RHA-SKETCH can be modeled as:

$$P_{\text{dec}}(tdc) = \begin{cases} 1, & tdc < T_{\text{pot}}, \\ b^{-(tdc - T_{\text{pot}})}, & T_{\text{pot}} \leq tdc < T_{\text{HH}}, \\ 0, & tdc \geq T_{\text{HH}}, \end{cases} \tag{2}$$

By substituting the expected value of tdc with tdc_i and taking the maximum possible decay probability, we define $p_\star = \max\left\{\mathbf{1}[tdc_i < T_{\text{pot}}],\ \mathbf{1}[T_{\text{pot}} \leq tdc_i < T_{\text{HH}}] \cdot b^{-(tdc_i - T_{\text{pot}})}\right\}$.

A decay is applied to e_i only if it is located in its mapped bucket and the incoming item e_j is mapped to the same bucket but does not match its key. Therefore, the probability that a single external item triggers a successful decay on e_i can be upper bounded by $q \leq \frac{p_\star}{\gamma\omega}$. Let V denote the total time weight of external updates (i.e., items other than e_i) during the observation window. The expected weight of successful decays applied to e_i can thus be expressed as $E[Y_i] \leq V \cdot q$. Since the total weight of external updates satisfies $V \leq C - tdc_i$, we obtain $E[X_i] \leq \frac{C - tdc_i}{\gamma\omega} p_\star$. Hence, the expected estimation is bounded below by $E[\widehat{tdc_i}] \geq tdc_i - \frac{C - tdc_i}{\gamma\omega} p_\star$. Finally, using Markov's inequality and the nonnegativity of X_i, for any $\varepsilon > 0$, we have

$$\Pr\{tdc_i - \widehat{tdc_i} \geq \varepsilon C\} \leq \frac{E[X_i]}{\varepsilon C} \leq \frac{C - tdc_i}{\varepsilon C} \cdot \frac{p_\star}{\gamma\omega}. \tag{3}$$

5 Evaluation

We conduct trace-driven tests to evaluate performance of RHA-Sketch. We show that RHA-Sketch achieves high accuracy in time-decay heavy hitter detection with small and static memory space, and achieves higher recall than the state-of-the-art solutions. We build the RHA-Sketch code based on the open-source code of CocoSketch [21].

5.1 Experiment Setup

Platform: We conduct our experiments on a server equipped with dual 12-core Intel Xeon Gold 5317 CPUs running at 3.00GHz, providing a total of 48 CPU threads. The server is equipped with 128GB of RAM. In total, the CPUs provide 1.1 MiB of L1 data cache and 768 KiB of L1 instruction cache (24 instances each), 30 MiB of L2 cache (24 instances), and 36 MiB of L3 cache (2 instances). The server runs on Ubuntu 22.04.5 LTS.

Datasets: We evaluate RHA-Sketch on two real traces: a 1-minute CAIDA packet trace [10] (over 28M packets from 1.5M flows, keys are source–destination address pairs) and the H&M personalized fashion recommendations dataset from Kaggle [9] (over 35M transactions on 1.4M products, keys are product codes).

To preserve temporal order while reducing the cost of computing the pre-emphasis function, we use item positions as logical time and group consecutive items into coarse-grained timestamps. Each stream is divided into about 200 timestamps, with roughly 135k–175k items per timestamp, depending on the dataset.

Compared Solutions: We compare RHA-Sketch with state-of-the-art solutions that do not require storing timestamps, including AdaCMS, AdaSS, and DAKPCF. For all implementations, we use BOB Hash to implement the hash functions. The number of rows for RHA-Sketch and AdaCMS is set to 3, while the heap height for DAKPCF's buckets is set to 2, with a maximum of 5 kicks. The heap size for AdaCMS is set to one-quarter of the total available memory. For DAKPCF, the number of buckets in the Stream-Summary is slightly greater than the number of heavy hitters. The default heavy-hitter threshold θ is set to 0.0008.

Time-Decaying Functions: We choose the exponential function $f(t) = a^t$ as the time-decaying function because, compared to linear decay functions, the exponential decay function assigns higher weights to more recent data, decays faster, and responds more sensitively to rapid changes in network traffic. For all solutions, we uniformly set the time-decaying function as $f(t) = 1.25^t$.

Metrics: We evaluate detection accuracy with four standard measures and system efficiency via throughput. Let T denote the ground-truth set of time-decay heavy hitters and R the set reported by the algorithm. (i) *Precision* $= \frac{|T \cap R|}{|R|}$: proportion of reported items that are truly hot. (ii) *Recall* $= \frac{|T \cap R|}{|T|}$: proportion of true hot items that are successfully reported. (iii) *F1-score* $= \frac{2 \cdot \text{Precision} \cdot \text{Recall}}{\text{Precision} + \text{Recall}}$: harmonic mean of precision and recall. (iv) *Average Relative Error (ARE)* $= \frac{1}{|T \cap R|} \sum_{e \in T \cap R} \frac{\left|\text{tdc}(e) - \widehat{\text{tdc}}(e)\right|}{\text{tdc}(e)}$, where $\widehat{\text{tdc}}(e)$ is the estimated time-decayed count; smaller ARE indicates higher accuracy. (v) *Throughput* (Mops): N/t_N, where N is the number of processed stream items and t_N is the elapsed time.

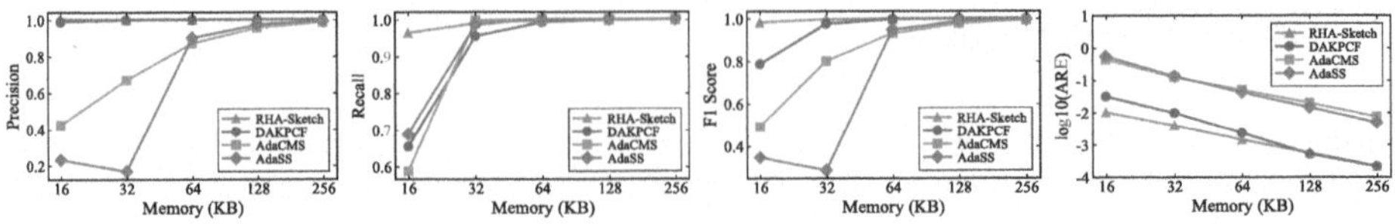

(a) Precision (b) Recall (c) F1-score (d) ARE

Fig. 3. Time-decay heavy hitter detection in CAIDA dataset.

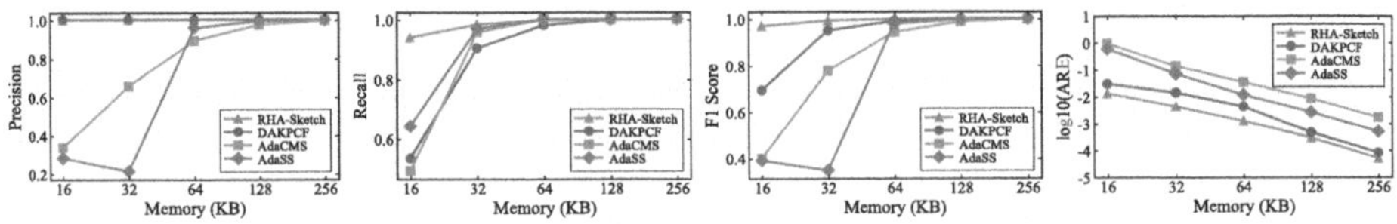

(a) Precision (b) Recall (c) F1-score (d) ARE

Fig. 4. Time-decay heavy hitter detection in H&M dataset.

5.2 Time-Decay Heavy Hitter Detection

Figure 3 and Fig. 4 compare RHA-Sketch with state-of-the-art schemes on CAIDA-2019 and H&M. Under small memory budgets ($\leq$ 64 KB), AdaCMS and AdaSS suffer from serious overestimation and low recall: AdaCMS maps all items to shared counters, making recent hot items vulnerable to collisions with recent cold and recent warm items, while AdaSS directly replaces the minimum candidate and inflates the new counter to the previous value plus the time weight $f(t)$. DAKPCF improves eviction by resetting locally minimal items, but may excessively erode the accumulated weight of potential recent hot items. In contrast, RHA-Sketch consistently achieves the highest precision/recall and the lowest ARE across all memory settings due to its recent-hotness-aware decay and eviction, improving the F1-score by up to 25.6%, 133.3%, and 326% over DAKPCF, AdaCMS, and AdaSS, respectively.

5.3 Impact of the Time-Decay Heavy-Hitter Threshold

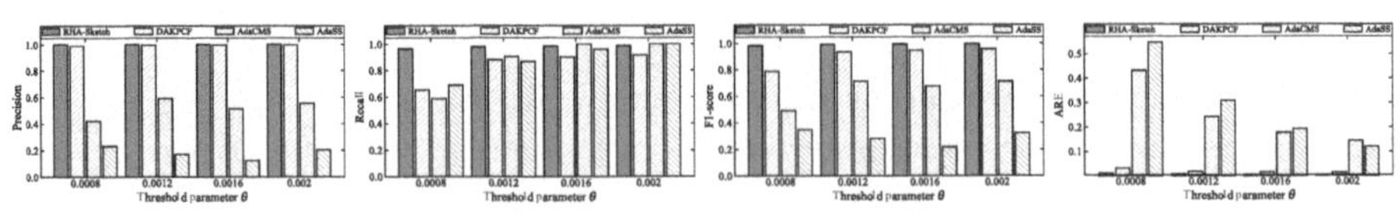

(a) Precision (b) Recall (c) F1-score (d) ARE

Fig. 5. Impact of the time-decay heavy-hitter threshold in CAIDA dataset.

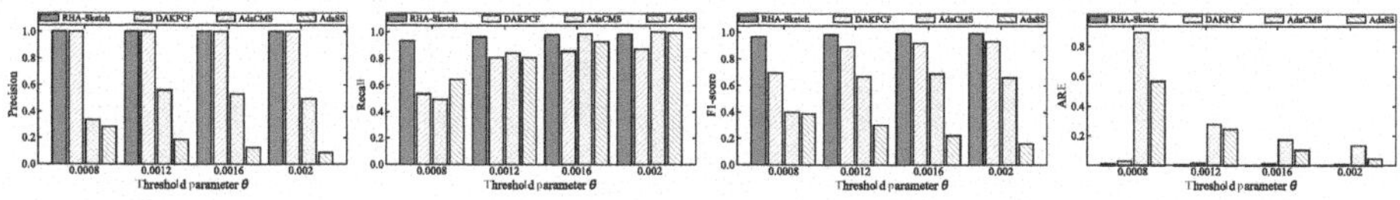

(a) Precision (b) Recall (c) F1-score (d) ARE

Fig. 6. Impact of the time-decay heavy-hitter threshold in H&M dataset.

We evaluate the impact of the time-decay heavy-hitter threshold. Fixing the memory at 16 KB, we vary the threshold θ from 0.0008 to 0.002. Figure 5 and Fig. 6 show the detection results on the CAIDA dataset and the H&M dataset. As θ increases, the number of recent hot items decreases; given the skewed distribution of item frequencies, the detection accuracy of all schemes generally improves at larger θ. However, at $\theta = 0.0008$, accuracy drops because it becomes difficult to distinguish recent hot items from the many items with comparable time-decayed counts. Overall, owing to its differentiated decay strategy across item recent hotness level, RHA-Sketch maintains F1-score close to 100% even at small θ, substantially outperforming the other approaches.

5.4 Experiments on Throughput

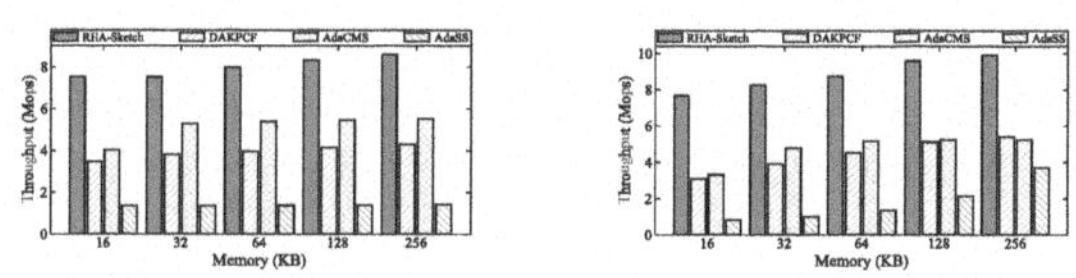

(a) CAIDA-2019 (b) H&M

Fig. 7. Throughput (Mops).

We now examine the throughput of the algorithms. We set $\theta = 0.0008$ and vary the memory size from 16 KB to 256 KB. As shown in Fig. 7, the average throughput of RHA-Sketch is 8.10 Mops, whereas DAKPCF, AdaCMS, and AdaSS achieve 3.95, 5.15, and 1.36 Mops, respectively. This disparity arises because these baselines employ a min-heap-based Stream-Summary, which introduces additional per-update overhead.

5.5 Sensitivity Analysis of the Parameter α

As shown in Fig. 8 and Fig. 9, we perform a sensitivity analysis of the parameter α for RHA-Sketch. When $\alpha = 0$, both recall and F1-score are the lowest because all items are subjected to probabilistic time-aware decay; consequently, many recent warm items linger and occupy slots, preventing potential recent hot items from

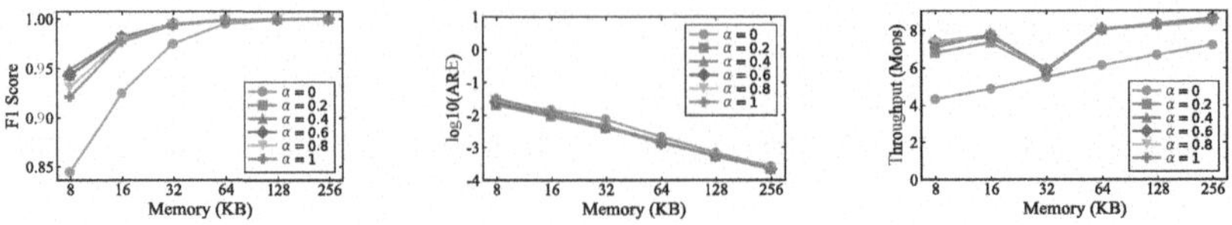

(a) F1-score (b) ARE (c) Throughput

Fig. 8. Impact of the parameter α on RHA-Sketch performance in CAIDA dataset.

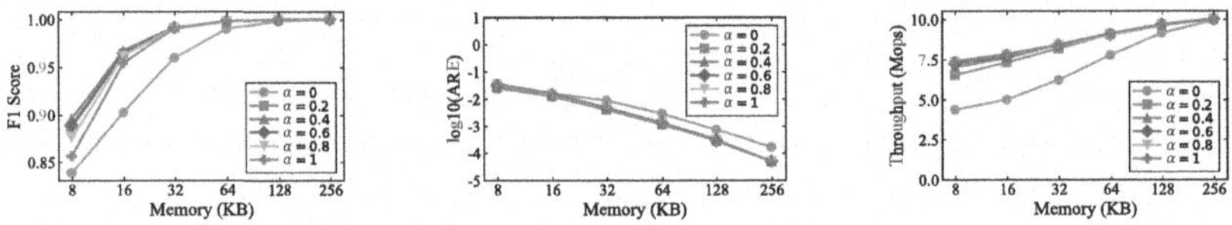

(a) F1-score (b) ARE (c) Throughput

Fig. 9. Impact of the parameter α on RHA-Sketch performance in H&M dataset.

being admitted into the sketch. When $\alpha = 0.2$, most metrics are near-optimal: recent cold items and a portion of recent warm items are quickly evicted, while promising recent hot items receive adequate protection. However, as α continues to increase, this protection for potential recent hot items becomes insufficient, leading to higher ARE and lower recall. Moreover, we observe a pronounced drop in throughput when $\alpha = 0$, since applying probabilistic decay to every item requires expensive random-number generation and logarithmic operations, which substantially degrade throughput.

6 Related Works

In recent years, researches on time-decay heavy hitters advances rapidly. The (ε, α)-synopsis together with the precision gradient framework [15] models "recency matters more" via exponential decay and allocates error budgets across a hierarchy to minimize communication while giving formal bounds. Exponentially decayed summaries [20] present the first deterministic algorithms for decayed quantiles and decayed heavy hitters, applying lazy decay to q-digest and maintaining decayed counts with Space-Saving, supporting out-of-order arrivals with $O(1/\varepsilon)$ space and $O(\log(1/\varepsilon))$ update time. λ-HCount [14] uses r hash functions to maintain density in an array and estimates the current value via the least recently updated hash slot; given failure probability p, it achieves an ε-approximation with space independent of stream length. FDCMSS [13] adopts forward decay and embeds a two-counter Space-Saving in each bucket to lock onto candidate heavy hitters; forward decay naturally supports out-of-order arrivals, and polynomial decay yields the relative-age property. Ada-sketches (e.g., AdaCMS) [16] pre-emphasize updates and de-emphasize queries, making the time factor β_t in the error bound decrease monotonically and eliminating timestamp storage, which is crucial under severe on-chip memory constraints. [19] maintain time-decayed heavy hitters entirely in the programmable switch data plane, avoiding query-time dependence from epoch resets by approximating exponential decay with right shifts and phase-based counters that decay on demand before update. DAKPCF [12] turns Cuckoo Filter buckets into min-heaps and, along the kicking path, uses a pre-eviction queue to locate the global minimum time-emphasized count for eviction.

To address their limitations, this work proposes RHA-Sketch, a recent-hotness-aware sketch that applies deterministic decay to transient items, probabilistic decay only for candidate items, and no decay for established heavy hitters. RHA-Sketch supports efficient updates and queries, while under tight memory budgets it reduces counter contamination and premature evictions, thereby improving accuracy.

7 Conclusion

To efficiently, accurately, and with high throughput identify time-decay heavy hitters, we propose a lightweight sketch-based solution named RHA-Sketch. RHA-Sketch employs a recent-hotness-aware eviction policy which has two key ideas:(i) Quickly free up space in limited memory for recent hot items to improve memory utilization;(ii) Protect recent hot items from interference caused by recent cold items and recent warm items.

We establish a theoretical error bound for RHA-Sketch and validate its performance on CAIDA-2019 and H&M traces. The results show that RHA-Sketch consistently achieves high detection accuracy and throughput under tight memory budgets, outperforming state-of-the-art approaches.

Acknowledgement. The work of Yang Du is supported by the National Natural Science Foundation of China (NSFC) under Grant No.62572337. The work of He Huang and Yu-E Sun is supported by NSFC under Grant No.62332013.

Disclosure of Interest. The authors have no competing interests to declare that are relevant to the content of this article.

References

1. Luo, X., Chang, R.K.C.: On a new class of pulsing denial-of-service attacks and the defense. In: Network and Distributed System Security Symposium (NDSS 2005), pp. 61–79. Internet Society, San Diego, CA (2005)
2. Sun, Y.-E., Huang, H., Ma, C., Chen, S., Du, Y., Xiao, Q.: Online spread estimation with non-duplicate sampling. In: IEEE INFOCOM 2020, pp. 2440–2448. IEEE (2020). https://doi.org/10.1109/INFOCOM41043.2020.9155525
3. Cormode, G., Muthukrishnan, S.: An improved data stream summary: the count-min sketch and its applications. J. Algorithms **55**(1), 58–75 (2005). https://doi.org/10.1016/j.jalgor.2003.12.001

4. Yang, T., et al.: HeavyKeeper: an accurate algorithm for finding top-k elephant flows. IEEE/ACM Trans. Netw. **27**(5), 1845–1858 (2019). https://doi.org/10.1109/TNET.2019.2933868
5. Huang, H., et al.: Memory-Efficient and flexible detection of heavy hitters in high-speed networks. Proc. ACM Manag. Data **1**(3), 214:1–214:24 (2023). https://doi.org/10.1145/3617334
6. Huang, J., Zhang, W., Li, Y., Li, L., Li, Z., Ye, J., Wang, J.: ChainSketch: an efficient and accurate sketch for heavy flow detection. IEEE/ACM Trans. Netw. **31**(2), 738–753 (2023). https://doi.org/10.1109/TNET.2022.3199506
7. Du, Y., Huang, H., Sun, Y.-E., Chen, S., Gao, G., Wu, X.: Self-Adaptive sampling based per-flow traffic measurement. IEEE/ACM Trans. Netw. **31**(3), 1010–1025 (2023). https://doi.org/10.1109/TNET.2022.3212066
8. Zhao, F., Khan, P.I., Agrawal, D., El Abbadi, A., Gupta, A., Liu, Z.: Panakos: chasing the tails for multidimensional data streams. Proc. VLDB Endow. **16**(6), 1291–1304 (2023). https://doi.org/10.14778/3583140.3583147
9. Kaggle: H&M personalized fashion recommendations dataset. https://www.kaggle.com/competitions/h-and-m-personalized-fashion-recommendations/data. Accessed 13 Nov 2025
10. CAIDA: the CAIDA UCSD anonymized internet traces (2019). https://catalog.caida.org/details/dataset/passive_2019_pcap. Accessed 27 Dec 2021
11. Source Code. The source codes of the RHA-Sketch. https://github.com/YK1111111/RHASketch. Accessed 25 Nov 2025
12. Xiao, Q., Wang, H., Pan, G.: Accurately identify time-decaying heavy hitters by decay-aware cuckoo filter along kicking path. In: IEEE/ACM International Symposium on Quality of Service (IWQoS 2022), pp. 1–10. IEEE, Oslo, Norway (2022)
13. Cafaro, M., Pulimeno, M., Epicoco, I., Aloisio, G.: Mining frequent items in the time fading model. Inf. Sci. **370–371**, 221–238 (2016)
14. Chen, L., Mei, Q.: Mining frequent items in data stream using time fading model. Inf. Sci. **257**, 54–69 (2014). https://doi.org/10.1016/j.ins.2013.09.007
15. Manjhi, A., Shkapenyuk, V., Dhamdhere, K., Olston, C.: Finding (Recently) Frequent Items in Distributed Data Streams. In: Proceeding 21st IEEE International Conference on Data Engineering (ICDE 2005), pp. 767–778. IEEE, Tokyo (2005)
16. Shrivastava, A., Bilenko, M., König, A.C.: Time adaptive sketches (ada-sketches) for summarizing data streams. In: Proceedings ACM SIGMOD International Conference on Management of Data (SIGMOD 2016), pp. 1417–1432. ACM, San Francisco, CA (2016)
17. Cormode, G., Shkapenyuk, V., Srivastava, D., Xu, B.: Forward decay: a practical time decay model for streaming systems. In: Proceeding IEEE International Conference on Data Engineering (ICDE 2009), pp. 138–149. IEEE, Shanghai (2009)
18. Pulimeno, M., Epicoco, I., Cafaro, M.: Distributed mining of time-faded heavy hitters. Inf. Sci. **545**, 633–662 (2021). https://doi.org/10.1016/j.ins.2020.09.048
19. Khooi, X.Z., Csikor, L., Kang, M.S., Divakaran, D.M.: Towards in-network time-decaying aggregates for heavy-hitter detection. In: Proceeding ACM SIGCOMM 2020 Posters and Demos, pp. 88–90. ACM (2020)
20. Cormode, G., Korn, F., Tirthapura, S.: Exponentially decayed aggregates on data streams. In: Proceeding IEEE International Conference on Data Engineering (ICDE 2008), pp. 1379–1381. IEEE, Cancún (2008)
21. Zhang, Y., et al.: CocoSketch: high-performance sketch-based measurement over arbitrary partial key query. In: ACM SIGCOMM 2021 Conference (SIGCOMM 2021), pp. 207–222. ACM (2021)

Modeling User Preferences as Distributions for Optimal Transport-Based Cross-Domain Recommendation under Non-overlapping Settings

Ziyin Xiao(✉) and Toyotaro Suzumura

The University of Tokyo, Tokyo, Japan
1014474276@qq.com, suzumura@g.ecc.u-tokyo.ac.jp

Abstract. Cross-domain recommender (CDR) systems aim to transfer knowledge from data-rich domains to data-sparse ones, alleviating sparsity and cold-start issues present in conventional single-domain recommenders. However, many CDR approaches rely on overlapping users or items to establish explicit cross-domain connections, which is unrealistic in practice. Moreover, most methods represent user preferences as fixed discrete vectors, limiting their ability to capture the fine-grained and multi-aspect nature of user interests.

To address these limitations, we propose DUP-OT (Distributional User Preferences with Optimal Transport), a novel framework for non-overlapping CDR. DUP-OT consists of three stages: (1) a shared preprocessing module that extracts review-based embeddings using a unified sentence encoder and autoencoder; (2) a user preference modeling module that represents each user's interests as a Gaussian Mixture Model (GMM) over item embeddings; and (3) an optimal-transport-based alignment module that matches Gaussian components across domains, enabling effective preference transfer for target-domain rating prediction.

Experiments on Amazon Review datasets show that DUP-OT outperforms single-domain baselines even without source-domain data, and achieves lower RMSE than the cross-domain baseline TDAR under strictly non-overlapping training settings, demonstrating its effectiveness in reducing large prediction errors for cold-start users. The implementation is available at https://github.com/XiaoZY2000/dup-ot.

Keywords: Cross-Domain Recommendation · Non-overlapping Users · Gaussian Mixture Model (GMM) · Optimal Transport · Cold-start Problem

1 Introduction

With the rapid growth of online information, recommender systems have become essential for helping users navigate massive content [11]. However, conventional

R. C.-W. Wong et al. (Eds.): PAKDD 2026, LNAI 16617, pp. 447–458, 2027.
https://doi.org/10.1007/978-981-92-1926-1_36

single-domain recommenders suffer from cold-start and data sparsity issues [3,10,19]. Cross-domain recommendation (CDR) alleviates these problems by transferring knowledge from a dense source domain to a sparse target domain [22]. Yet most existing CDR methods rely on overlapping users or items in the training stage to bridge domains and typically represent user preferences as discrete vectors, which limits their ability to capture multi-aspect preferences.

In this work, we study the non-overlapping CDR scenario—where no users or items are shared across domains—and propose to represent user preferences using Gaussian Mixture Models (GMMs). This enables fine-grained, multi-aspect preference modeling, but also introduces two challenges: (1) domain discrepancy becomes harder to address without overlapping entities [1,9], and (2) GMM-based preference modeling significantly increases computation and is not directly compatible with standard optimal transport formulations.

Recent CDR approaches attempt to reduce domain discrepancy using contrastive learning, adversarial training, or distribution alignment [10,13,15]. Other studies explore distributional representations but either adopt simple Gaussian models or still rely on overlapping entities [23]. Thus, how to build expressive GMM-based preference representations while enabling cross-domain alignment in a strictly non-overlapping setting remains an open problem.

To address this, we propose **DUP-OT** (Distributional User Preferences with Optimal Transport), a novel framework that models each user's preference as a GMM over item representations and aligns domains using optimal transport (OT). To reduce computational cost and make OT feasible, we assume that all users within a domain share a domain-level set of Gaussian components extracted from item representations, while each user learns personalized weights over these components. DUP-OT consists of three stages: (1) a shared preprocessing stage with a unified sentence encoder and autoencoder to obtain low-dimensional item and user embeddings; (2) a user preference modeling stage where each domain fits item-level GMM components and learns user-specific mixture weights; and (3) an OT-based alignment stage that transports GMM weights from the source to the target domain to enhance target-domain rating prediction.

Our contributions are summarized as follows:

- We highlight the limitations of discrete vector representations in non-overlapping CDR and motivate the need for distributional preference modeling.
- We propose DUP-OT, a GMM-based framework that aligns cross-domain preferences using optimal transport on distributional representations.
- We validate DUP-OT on Amazon Review datasets, demonstrating improved RMSE over both single-domain and cross-domain baselines, with particular effectiveness in reducing large prediction errors for cold-start users.

2 Related Work

Cross-Domain Recommendation. CDR aims to transfer knowledge from a rich source domain to a sparse target domain. Early approaches rely on overlapped users or items through representation alignment [7], adversarial learning

[6], and graph-based propagation [2]. However, such overlaps are rarely available in practice.

Non-overlapping CDR methods typically learn shared latent spaces using embedding alignment [16], generative modeling [14], or distribution matching [23]. While recent work explores Gaussian-based representations, they either use simple single-Gaussian models or still rely on partial overlaps. Modeling user preferences with expressive GMMs under fully non-overlapping settings remains underexplored.

Optimal Transport in CDR. OT provides a principled tool for aligning distributions across domains. It has been applied to match user/item embeddings [8] or latent distributions [10]. However, prior work does not integrate OT with GMM-based user preference modeling, nor address the computational challenges in fully non-overlapping scenarios.

3 Preliminary

Definitions of Notations. We consider two domains: the source domain s and the target domain t. For each domain $x \in \{s, t\}$, we denote the user set and item set as $\mathcal{U}_x$ and $\mathcal{V}_x$. Although users or items may exist in both domains in reality, in our CDR setting we impose that *the model does not use any overlapping-user or overlapping-item information during training*. Therefore, the training process treats the two domains as non-overlapping, even if overlaps may exist in the raw data.

For the i-th user and j-th item in domain x, each interaction is written as:

$$(u_i^x, v_j^x, r_{ij}^x, h_{ij}^x, t_{ij}^x),$$

where r_{ij}^x is the rating, h_{ij}^x is the corresponding review text and t_{ij}^x is the time stamp.

Practical Motivation. This setting corresponds to real-world scenarios where user or item identities might be shared across platforms, but privacy constraints or system limitations prevent such cross-domain links from being used during training. For example, users may later appear in the target domain after the model has been trained, or items may be synchronized across platforms only at deployment time. Thus, overlaps can exist for evaluation but are not exploited for learning, faithfully reflecting practical cross-domain recommendation conditions.

Task Formulation. We aim to address the cold-start problem in the target domain by transferring knowledge from the source domain under a non-overlapping CDR setting. Specifically, the goal is to leverage source-domain data to enhance the rating prediction performance in the target domain.

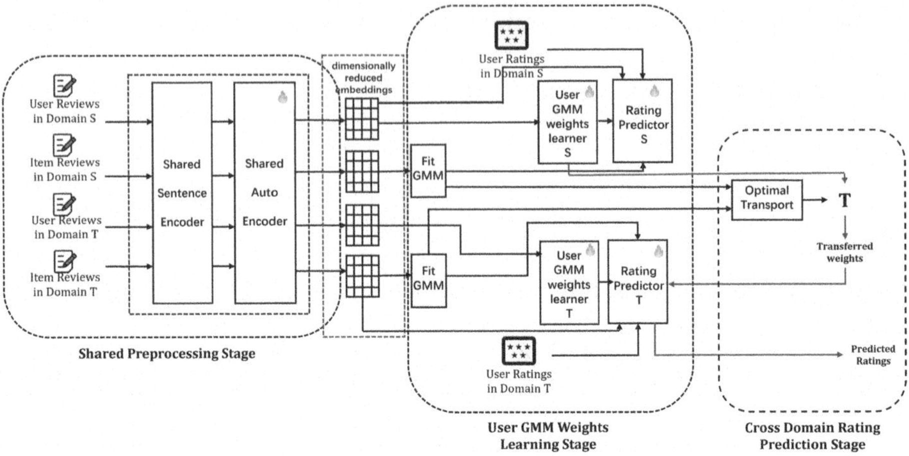

Fig. 1. The overall structure of DUP-OT

4 Methodology

4.1 Overview

Figure 1 illustrates the architecture of our proposed **DUP-OT** framework, which enables non-overlapping cross-domain recommendation based on distributional user preference representations. The pipeline consists of three main stages: **(1) shared preprocessing**, **(2) user GMM weight learning**, and **(3) cross-domain rating prediction**.

In the **shared preprocessing stage**, we extract and align user and item embeddings across domains. Specifically, we employ a shared pre-trained sentence encoder to encode reviews into initial user and item embeddings, followed by a shared autoencoder trained on both domains to reduce embedding dimensionality and ensure a unified feature space.

The **user GMM weight learning stage** is performed separately in each domain. We first fit a Gaussian Mixture Model (GMM) on the item embeddings to obtain shared Gaussian components. Then, an MLP is trained to map each user embedding to a set of weights over these components, forming a user-specific GMM. Another MLP is trained to predict user-item ratings based on the Mahalanobis distance between the item embedding and each Gaussian component weighted by the user's distribution.

Finally, in the **cross-domain rating prediction stage**, we align the GMM components across domains via Optimal Transport (OT) and use the resulting transport matrix to transfer users' GMM weights from the source domain to the target domain. For users in the target-domain test set, our framework handles three cases: if a user has interactions in both domains during training, we combine the transferred distribution with the target-domain distribution; if the user has interactions only in the source domain, we use the transferred distribution;

and if the user has interactions only in the target domain, we use the target-domain distribution. These resulting user distributions are then used to enhance rating prediction performance in the target domain.

4.2 Shared Preprocessing Stage

To capture semantic similarity across domains, we derive user and item embeddings from review text. For each user and item, all associated reviews are encoded using a shared pre-trained sentence encoder, and we apply a time-aware weighting scheme so that recent reviews contribute more to the final representation. Specifically, more recent interactions are assigned higher weights when aggregating review embeddings.

The encoder outputs high-dimensional vectors, which make GMM fitting unstable. Therefore, we train a shared autoencoder on both domains to obtain compact, domain-consistent embeddings. This unified latent space preserves semantic structure while reducing dimensionality, providing stable inputs for subsequent GMM construction and cross-domain alignment.

4.3 User GMM Weights Learning Stage

Users often exhibit multi-aspect preferences, which discrete vector representations struggle to capture. Therefore, DUP-OT models each user's preference as a Gaussian Mixture Model (GMM) over item embeddings.

To reduce computational cost, we assume that all users within a domain share a domain-level set of Gaussian components. These components are obtained by fitting a GMM on item embeddings using the EM algorithm (implemented via `BayesianGaussianMixture`). Each user is then mapped to a personalized set of mixture weights over these components.

For each domain, we train two MLPs: a weight learner that predicts user-specific mixture weights from user embeddings, and a rating predictor that takes the weighted component-wise Mahalanobis distances between a user and an item to estimate the final rating. The learning objective is the standard mean squared error:

$$\mathbf{w}_{u_i}^x = \text{W-Learner}^x(\mathbf{z}_{u_i}^x), \tag{1}$$

$$\hat{r}_{ij}^x = \text{R-Predictor}^x\big(\mathbf{w}_{u_i}^x, \mathbf{z}_{v_j}^x, \mu^x, \Sigma^x\big), \tag{2}$$

$$\mathcal{L}_{\text{rating}}^x = \frac{1}{|\mathcal{I}^x|} \sum_{(i,j)\in\mathcal{I}^x} \big(r_{ij} - \hat{r}_{ij}^x\big)^2. \tag{3}$$

Here, μ^x and Σ^x denote the domain-level Gaussian component means and covariances. This stage produces a distributional user representation that is later aligned across domains via optimal transport.

4.4 Cross-Domain Rating Prediction Stage

In this stage, we enhance the target-domain rating predictor by constructing improved user distributions through Optimal Transport (OT). This stage consists of two parts: aligning the GMM components across domains using OT, and generating enhanced user-specific distributions in the target domain according to three test-time scenarios.

OT-Based Alignment of Gaussian Components. Since all users within a domain share the same set of Gaussian components, we apply OT only between the two domains' GMM component sets, avoiding instance-level transport. The OT problem is formulated as Eq. 4.

$$\begin{aligned} \arg\min_{\mathcal{T}} \quad & \sum_{i=1}^{m}\sum_{j=1}^{n} \mathcal{T}_{ij}\mathcal{C}_{ij} \\ \text{s.t.} \quad & \sum_{i=1}^{m} \mathcal{T}_{ij} = \frac{1}{n}, \quad \sum_{j=1}^{n} \mathcal{T}_{ij} = \frac{1}{m} \end{aligned} \tag{4}$$

where m and n denote the numbers of Gaussian components in the source and target domains. The cost matrix $\mathcal{C}$ is computed using the Wasserstein-2 distance (Eq. 5), and we solve for the optimal transport matrix $\mathcal{T}$ using the Sinkhorn algorithm.

$$\begin{aligned} \mathcal{W}_2^2(\mathcal{N}_1, \mathcal{N}_2) = & \ \|\boldsymbol{\mu}_1 - \boldsymbol{\mu}_2\|_2^2 \\ & + \mathrm{Tr}\left(\boldsymbol{\Sigma}_1 + \boldsymbol{\Sigma}_2 - 2\left(\boldsymbol{\Sigma}_2^{1/2}\boldsymbol{\Sigma}_1\boldsymbol{\Sigma}_2^{1/2}\right)^{1/2}\right) \end{aligned} \tag{5}$$

User weights are then transported as Eq. 6.

$$\mathbf{w}_{u_i}^{t} = \mathbf{w}_{u_i}^{s}\mathcal{T} \tag{6}$$

Three Test-Time Cases. For each user in the target-domain test set, we construct a final user distribution in the target domain depending on the interaction availability:

- **Both Domains have Interactions:** we linearly fuse the transferred distribution and the target-domain distribution to form the final user distribution:

$$\mathbf{w}_{u_i}^{\text{final}} = \alpha\,\mathbf{w}_{u_i}^{t} + (1-\alpha)\,\mathbf{w}_{u_i}^{t,\text{orig}},$$

  where $\alpha \in [0, 1]$ controls the contribution of the transferred distribution.
- **Only Source Domain has Interactions:** use the transferred distribution alone:

$$\mathbf{w}_{u_i}^{\text{final}} = \mathbf{w}_{u_i}^{t}.$$

– **Only Target Domain has Interactions:** use the target-domain distribution alone:

$$\mathbf{w}_{u_i}^{\text{final}} = \mathbf{w}_{u_i}^{t,\text{orig}}.$$

For users without interactions in either domain, we initialize their mixture weights with random values. The resulting user distribution is then fed into the target-domain rating predictor to produce the final enhanced rating prediction.

Since all users within a domain share the same set of Gaussian components and only learn personalized mixture weights rather than full GMM parameters, the per-user computation is comparable to standard MLP-based models. Moreover, OT alignment operates only on the $m \times n$ component-level cost matrix (where $m, n \ll |\mathcal{U}|$), so the transport step adds negligible overhead compared to user-level MLP training.

5 Experiments and Results

We evaluate DUP-OT against several baselines to answer the following research questions:

RQ1. Does introducing cross-domain information enhance the recommendation performance in the target domain?

RQ2. Does modeling user preferences as distributions, rather than vectors, lead to improved recommendation performance?

RQ3. How does the performance of our proposed method compare with that of existing CDR models?

To answer **RQ1**, we conduct an ablation study comparing target-domain performance with and without source-domain information. To address **RQ2**, we evaluate our target-domain model (using distribution-based user preferences but without source-domain data) against single-domain baselines. To address **RQ3**, we compare our proposed DUP-OT model with a representative cross-domain recommendation baseline: TDAR.

5.1 Experimental Setup

Datasets. We use the Amazon Review 5-core datasets [12]: Digital Music, Movies and TV, Video Games, and Electronics. Electronics is used as the target domain, and the other three as source domains. Target-domain data are split into train/validation/test (8:1:1) chronologically. To keep temporal consistency, we filter out source-domain interactions occurring later than the earliest validation timestamp in the target domain. The filtered source data and target-domain training set are used to train DUP-OT, and evaluation is performed on the target-domain test set.

Table 1. Results of baseline models and DUP-OT

(a) Results on the Domain Pair (D_s, D_t)

$D_s \to D_t$	Digital Music → Electronics		Movies & TV → Electronics		Video Games → Electronics	
Model	RMSE	MAE	RMSE	MAE	RMSE	MAE
TDAR	1.2512	**0.8349**	1.2550	**0.8378**	1.2484	**0.8240**
DUP-OT (w/o source)	1.4632	1.0658	1.4055	0.9734	1.4407	1.0354
DUP-OT (w/ source)	**1.2283**	0.9315	**1.2499**	1.0332	**1.2385**	0.9815

(b) Single-domain recommendation results (Electronics-only)

Model	RMSE	MAE
LightGCN	1.5317	1.1179
NeuMF	1.4599	1.3297
DUP-OT (w/o source average)	**1.4365**	**1.0249**

Model Setting. Our proposed DUP-OT consists of three stages. In the first stage, we use a shared pre-trained sentence encoder (`all-MiniLM-L6-v2`) from Sentence-Transformers to obtain review-based user and item embeddings, followed by a shared autoencoder to reduce dimensionality and form a unified latent space across domains. In the second stage, for each domain we fit item-level Gaussian Mixture Models (GMMs) and train two small MLPs: one to predict user-specific mixture weights over the shared Gaussian components, and one to predict ratings based on the resulting user distributions and item embeddings. The number of GMM components K is determined automatically by the `BayesianGaussianMixture` estimator.

Training Settings. We train all models using the Adam optimizer with a learning rate of 3×10^{-4} and a batch size of 256, with early stopping based on target-domain validation loss. The sentence encoder is frozen, while the shared autoencoder is jointly trained across domains to obtain unified low-dimensional embeddings. For each domain, we fit item-level Gaussian Mixture Models using the `BayesianGaussianMixture` estimator and train domain-specific MLPs for predicting user GMM weights and ratings. Users appearing only in validation or test sets are treated as cold-start users. All models are implemented in PyTorch and trained on a single NVIDIA GPU.

Baselines. We implement the following models as baseline models for comparison:

Single-Domain Models:

•**LightGCN** [4]**:** LightGCN is a simplified GCN model. In our experiment, we see it as a single domain RS model and build graphs on each domain rather than building a unified graph.

•**NeuMF** [5]**:** A neural collaborative filtering model that fuses a generalized matrix factorization branch with a multi-layer perceptron branch to jointly capture both linear and non-linear user-item interaction patterns.

Non-overlapping Cross-Domain Models:

•**TDAR** [18]**:** A text-enhanced domain-adaptation model that integrates textual and collaborative embeddings and uses adversarial learning for cross-domain alignment. Since our datasets contain explicit ratings, we replace its original contrastive objective with a rating-prediction loss.

For single domain RS models, we utilize RecBole [17,20,21] in our experiments to implement them. For TDAR, we implemented the method ourselves based on the original paper.

Ablation Study: Effect of Source-Domain Information. To evaluate whether source-domain information enhances recommendation performance in the target domain (RQ1), we compare two variants of our framework:

- **DUP-OT (w/ source)**: the full model that uses both domains. The autoencoder is trained jointly on both domains, and in the second stage the source-domain GMMs, GMM-weight learners, and rating predictors are trained using source-domain data. User distributions are then transferred to the target domain via Optimal Transport and fused with target-domain distributions during inference.
- **DUP-OT (w/o source)**: an ablated model that does *not* use any source-domain interactions during the second stage. The autoencoder is still trained jointly on both domains to ensure consistent representation spaces, but the GMM construction, GMM-weight learner, and rating predictor are trained exclusively on the target-domain training set. No cross-domain alignment or distribution transfer is performed.

This setup ensures that the only difference between the two variants lies in whether cross-domain preference information is introduced.

Metrics. To evaluate the performance of our proposed DUP-OT and baseline models, we set all models' targets as rating prediction on the target domain's test dataset. And then we use RMSE and MAE as metrics to evaluate models' performance. The results are shown in Table 1.

5.2 Discussion of Results

Based on the results in Table 1, we now answer the three research questions raised at the beginning of this section.

Answer to RQ1 (Effect of Cross-Domain Information). Across all three source→target settings, DUP-OT (w/ source) consistently achieves lower RMSE than DUP-OT (w/o source). The effect on MAE is mixed, with improvements in some settings but not others, likely due to varying domain gaps between different source domains and the target domain. Nevertheless, the consistent RMSE reduction confirms that cross-domain preference transfer effectively mitigates large prediction errors, which is the primary goal of DUP-OT in cold-start scenarios.

Answer to RQ2 (Effect of Distribution-Based User Modeling). Comparing DUP-OT(w/o source) with single-domain recommenders (LightGCN and NeuMF), DUP-OT(w/o source) achieves substantially better performance in the Electronics-only setting, despite using no source-domain data. This indicates that modeling user preferences as distributions rather than discrete vectors yields more expressive representations and improves rating prediction accuracy in the target domain.

Answer to RQ3 (Comparison with the Cross-Domain Baseline). Compared with TDAR, DUP-OT (w/ source) achieves lower RMSE but higher MAE across all dataset combinations. RMSE is more sensitive to large errors, while MAE treats all errors equally. The lower RMSE indicates that DUP-OT effectively avoids extreme mispredictions, which are common for cold-start users with little interaction history. This can be explained by our GMM-based preference modeling: distributional representations provide more robust estimates for data-sparse users than point vectors, reducing the risk of severe prediction failures. On the other hand, TDAR's joint cross-domain optimization tends to produce more evenly spread errors, leading to lower MAE but less protection against worst-case predictions. This trade-off aligns well with the cold-start scenario that DUP-OT targets.

6 Conclusion

We proposed DUP-OT, a distribution-based framework for non-overlapping cross-domain recommendation. By modeling user preferences as GMMs and aligning domains via Optimal Transport, DUP-OT enables expressive preference representation and effective cross-domain transfer without relying on shared users or items during training. Experiments on Amazon Review datasets show that DUP-OT outperforms single-domain baselines even without source-domain data, and achieves lower RMSE than the cross-domain baseline TDAR, indicating stronger robustness against large prediction errors in cold-start scenarios.

A current limitation is that the linear fusion of transferred and target-domain distributions may not be optimal for all users. Future work includes exploring adaptive fusion strategies, extending DUP-OT to implicit feedback settings, and incorporating structure-aware transport costs such as Gromov-Wasserstein distance for better cross-domain alignment.

Disclosure of Interests. The authors have no competing interests to declare.

References

1. Guo, L., Liu, H., Zhu, L., Guan, W., Cheng, Z.: Da-dan: a dual adversarial domain adaption network for unsupervised non-overlapping cross-domain recommendation. ACM Trans. Inf. Syst. **42**(2) (2023). https://doi.org/10.1145/3617825

2. Guo, L., et al.: Da-GCN: a domain-aware attentive graph convolution network for shared-account cross-domain sequential recommendation (2021). https://arxiv.org/abs/2105.03300
3. He, X., et al.: TCKT: Tree-based cross-domain knowledge transfer for next poi cold-start recommendation. ACM Trans. Inf. Syst. **43**(5) (2025). https://doi.org/10.1145/3709137
4. He, X., et al.: LightGCN: simplifying and powering graph convolution network for recommendation. In: Proceedings of the 43rd International ACM SIGIR Conference on Research and Development in Information Retrieval, pp. 639–648. SIGIR '20, Association for Computing Machinery, New York, NY, USA (2020). https://doi.org/10.1145/3397271.3401063
5. He, X., et al.: Neural collaborative filtering. In: Proceedings of the 26th International Conference on World Wide Web, pp. 173–182. WWW '17, International World Wide Web Conferences Steering Committee, Republic and Canton of Geneva, CHE (2017). https://doi.org/10.1145/3038912.3052569
6. Li, C., et al.: RecGURU: adversarial learning of generalized user representations for cross-domain recommendation. In: Proceedings of the Fifteenth ACM International Conference on Web Search and Data Mining, pp. 571–581. WSDM '22, Association for Computing Machinery, New York, NY, USA (2022). https://doi.org/10.1145/3488560.3498388
7. Li, P., Tuzhilin, A.: DDTCDR: deep dual transfer cross domain recommendation. In: Proceedings of the 13th International Conference on Web Search and Data Mining, pp. 331–339. WSDM '20, Association for Computing Machinery, New York, NY, USA (2020). https://doi.org/10.1145/3336191.3371793
8. Li, X., et al: Gromov-Wasserstein guided representation learning for cross-domain recommendation. In: Proceedings of the 31st ACM International Conference on Information & Knowledge Management, pp. 1199–1208. CIKM '22, Association for Computing Machinery, New York, NY, USA (2022). https://doi.org/10.1145/3511808.3557338
9. Liu, M., et al.: Cross domain deep collaborative filtering without overlapping data. In: Proceedings of the 2023 International Joint Conference on Neural Networks (IJCNN), pp. 1–8 (2023). https://doi.org/10.1109/IJCNN54540.2023.10191115
10. Liu, W., et al.: Learning accurate and bidirectional transformation via dynamic embedding transportation for cross-domain recommendation. Proc. AAAI Conf. Artif. Intell. **38**(8), 8815–8823 (2024). https://doi.org/10.1609/aaai.v38i8.28728
11. Lü, L., et al.: Recommender systems. Phys. Rep. **519**(1), 1–49 (2012). https://doi.org/10.1016/j.physrep.2012.02.006
12. Ni, J., Li, J., McAuley, J.: Justifying recommendations using distantly-labeled reviews and fine-grained aspects. In: Inui, K., Jiang, J., Ng, V., Wan, X. (eds.) Proceedings of the 2019 Conference on Empirical Methods in Natural Language Processing and the 9th International Joint Conference on Natural Language Processing (EMNLP-IJCNLP), pp. 188–197. Association for Computational Linguistics, Hong Kong, China (2019). https://doi.org/10.18653/v1/D19-1018
13. Perera, D., Zimmermann, R.: CNGAN: generative adversarial networks for cross-network user preference generation for non-overlapped users. In: Proceedings of the World Wide Web Conference, pp. 3144–3150. WWW '19, Association for Computing Machinery, New York, NY, USA (2019). https://doi.org/10.1145/3308558.3313733
14. Salah, A., Tran, T.B., Lauw, H.: Towards source-aligned variational models for cross-domain recommendation. In: Proceedings of the 15th ACM Conference on

Recommender Systems, pp. 176–186. RecSys '21, Association for Computing Machinery, New York, NY, USA (2021). https://doi.org/10.1145/3460231.3474265
15. Wang, C., Niepert, M., Li, H.: RecSys-dan: discriminative adversarial networks for cross-domain recommender systems. IEEE Trans. Neural Netw. Learn. Syst. **31**(8), 2731–2740 (2020). https://doi.org/10.1109/TNNLS.2019.2907430
16. Wang, T., et al.: Low-dimensional alignment for cross-domain recommendation. In: Proceedings of the 30th ACM International Conference on Information & Knowledge Management, pp. 3508–3512. CIKM '21, Association for Computing Machinery, New York, NY, USA (2021). https://doi.org/10.1145/3459637.3482137
17. Xu, L., et al.: Towards a more user-friendly and easy-to-use benchmark library for recommender systems. In: Proceedings of the SIGIR, pp. 2837–2847. ACM (2023)
18. Yu, W., Lin, X., Ge, J., Ou, W., Qin, Z.: Semi-supervised collaborative filtering by text-enhanced domain adaptation. In: Proceedings of the 26th ACM SIGKDD International Conference on Knowledge Discovery & Data Mining, pp. 2136–2144. KDD '20, Association for Computing Machinery, New York, NY, USA (2020). https://doi.org/10.1145/3394486.3403264
19. Zang, T., Zhu, Y., Liu, H., Zhang, R., Yu, J.: A survey on cross-domain recommendation: taxonomies, methods, and future directions. ACM Trans. Inf. Syst. **41**(2) (2022). https://doi.org/10.1145/3548455
20. Zhao, W.X., et al.: Recbole 2.0: towards a more up-to-date recommendation library. In: Proceedings of the CIKM, pp. 4722–4726. ACM (2022)
21. Zhao, W.X., et al.: Recbole: Towards a unified, comprehensive and efficient framework for recommendation algorithms. In: Proceedings of the CIKM, pp. 4653–4664. ACM (2021)
22. Zhu, F., et al.: A deep framework for cross-domain and cross-system recommendations (2020). https://arxiv.org/abs/2009.06215
23. Zhu, X., et al.: Modeling domains as distributions with uncertainty for cross-domain recommendation. In: Proceedings of the 47th International ACM SIGIR Conference on Research and Development in Information Retrieval, pp. 2517–2521. SIGIR '24, Association for Computing Machinery, New York, NY, USA (2024). https://doi.org/10.1145/3626772.3657930

TAPE: Trend-Aware Perturbation Enhancement for Sparse Stepwise Non-stationary Time Series

Shengnan Di(✉), Zhidong Li, Fang Chen, and Bin Liang

University of Technology Sydney, Sydney, Australia
shengnan.di@student.uts.edu.au

Abstract. Sparse Stepwise Non-Stationary Time-Series (SSNT) arise in many real-world domains, where long plateaus and abrupt regime shifts yield discontinuous supervision and sparse gradients. This violates the smooth-dynamics assumption underlying most deep forecasters, leading to overfitting on stationary segments and weak modelling of transition dynamics. We introduce TAPE (Trend-Aware Perturbation Enhancement), a purely data-centric and model-agnostic framework that improves transition sensitivity without modifying backbone architectures. TAPE identifies volatile regions, extracts multi-scale trend cues, and synthesizes structured perturbations to enrich supervision signals in flat segments while preserving stepwise semantics. Across real estate and financial datasets, TAPE improves forecasting performance across all evaluated metrics and architectures (recurrent and attention-based), with no observed degradation in any experiment, demonstrating that trend-aware perturbation is an effective mechanism for enhancing robustness under sparse or discontinuous temporal dynamics. Additional validation on a quasi-periodic medical dataset further confirms that the benefit of injecting trend-aware signals generalises beyond stepwise regimes.

Keywords: SSNT · Time Series Forecasting · Data-Centric Learning · Non-Stationarity · Perturbation · Volatility Analysis

1 Introduction

Sparse Stepwise Non-Stationary Time Series (SSNT) arise in domains such as real estate analytics [21], macroeconomics [13], and policy or regulatory systems [11]. They combine long plateaus imposed by contractual or regulatory rigidity [5,10,19] with sparse, abrupt transitions across discrete regimes. Unlike smoothly varying or densely sampled sequences, SSNT data exhibit event-driven transitions that are often asynchronous in multivariate settings, posing a critical underexplored forecasting challenge.

Under SSNT, sliding-window supervision frequently yields duplicate flat-segment samples, strengthening learning on stationary regions while weakening

R. C.-W. Wong et al. (Eds.): PAKDD 2026, LNAI 16617, pp. 459–471, 2027.
https://doi.org/10.1007/978-981-92-1926-1_37

gradient signals [3,16,22,29]. Although attention-based models such as Transformers [25] relax locality constraints, they still prioritise dominant patterns, limiting sensitivity to rare regime shifts. As shown in Fig. 1, repeated exposure to plateau behaviour encourages overfitting and reduces transition sensitivity [27]. Thus, the bottleneck lies primarily in the SSNT data structure rather than in model architecture, motivating data-centric enhancement.

To address this limitation, we propose Trend-Aware Perturbation Enhancement (TAPE), a model-agnostic, data-centric framework that enriches supervision without modifying backbone architectures. TAPE detects volatile subsequences, extracts multi-scale trend cues, and injects structured perturbations into flat spans to densify gradients while preserving stepwise semantics. It improves transition sensitivity and forecasting accuracy across both recurrent and attention-based models. Figure 2 shows the three modules (Module $\mathcal{M}_1$-$\mathcal{M}_3$), each implementing one core innovation.

- $\mathcal{M}_1$: **Adaptive Regime Segmentation** - identifies flat, transitional, and volatile spans via volatility estimation.
- $\mathcal{M}_2$: **Multi-scale Trend Augmentation** - derives exponential-smoothing, Savitzky–Golay, and LOWESS descriptors.
- $\mathcal{M}_3$: **Semantic Signal Densification** - injects trend-guided perturbations into flat segments to densify gradients and counteract duplication.

These modules transform sparse stepwise sequences into enriched inputs that expose transition-relevant cues and improve regime-shift modelling.

Although TAPE is designed for SSNT forecasting, we later evaluate it on a quasi-periodic medical dataset to demonstrate that injecting trend-aware signals also enhances transition sensitivity beyond stepwise regimes, confirming TAPE's broader applicability.

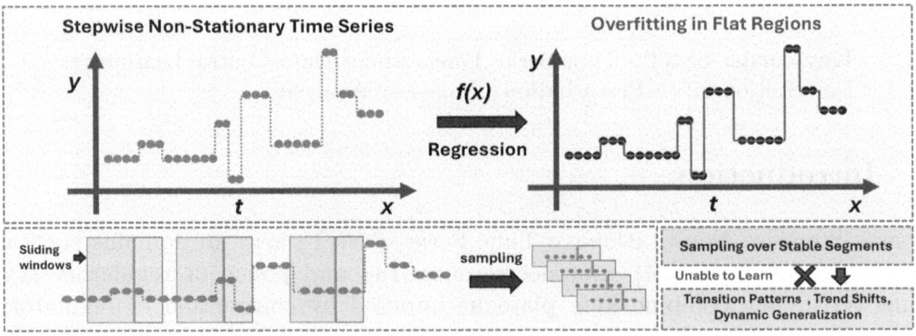

Fig. 1. Example of SSNT behaviour: purple dots show the raw series with long plateaus and sparse regime shifts; blue and pink rectangles illustrate sliding-window samples, and the red line indicates the regression fit. (Color figure online)

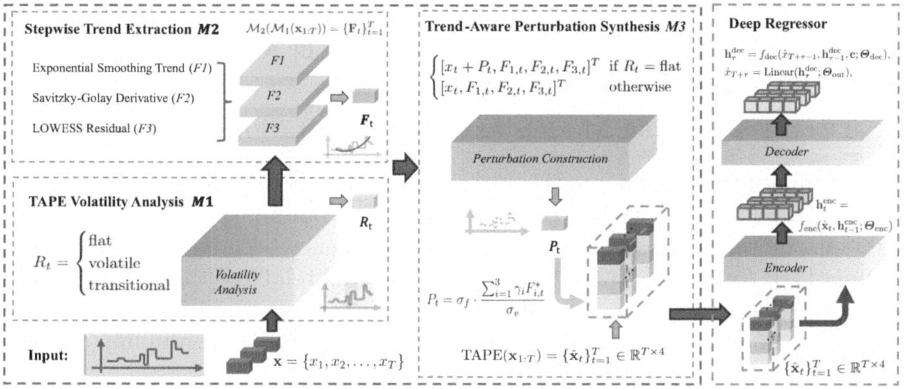

Fig. 2. TAPE framework overview. Module $\mathcal{M}_1$ estimates local volatility and assigns flat, transitional, and volatile labels. Module $\mathcal{M}_2$ extracts multi-scale trend descriptors (F_1, F_2, F_3) using the raw sequence guided by region labels. Module $\mathcal{M}_3$ injects trend-aware perturbations into flat segments based on volatile patterns, yielding the enhanced representation fed into the deep regressor. (Color figure online)

2 Related Work

2.1 Stepwise and Event-Driven Forecasting

Classical statistical approaches model stepwise or event-driven temporal processes using regime- and Markov-switching models [12], stepwise regression [18], structural change segmentation [2], and change-point detection [23]. These frameworks capture discrete transitions or piecewise-stationary behaviour but rely on strong parametric or stationarity assumptions and often require explicit estimation of transition points.

Such requirements are problematic for SSNT sequences, where plateaus are long and transitions are sparse, irregular, and difficult to localise. Moreover, these approaches do not readily yield dense supervision or multi-scale volatility representations compatible with modern deep forecasting pipelines. These limitations motivate the volatility-aware segmentation strategy employed in **Innovation 1** (Sect. 3.3), which approximates regime transitions without requiring parametric assumptions or change-point detection.

2.2 Data-Centric Augmentation for Time Series

Data-centric augmentation improves forecasting by increasing sample diversity and representation richness. Classical pointwise or temporal distortions—such as jittering, scaling, and warping—are widely used [15,24]. Mixup-based interpolation further synthesizes blended samples for time series [17,33], and masked-time modeling with Transformers enriches representations by reconstructing missing spans [30]. We therefore leverage multi-scale trend descriptors (**Innovation 2**) to expose volatility- and transition-related signals ignored by conventional augmentations, which subsequently guide perturbation in $\mathcal{M}_3$.

2.3 Deep Forecasting Models and their Limitations in SSNT

Deep learning advances time series forecasting through recurrent models such as RNNs [6], LSTMs [14], GRUs [7], and stacked variants [9], as well as convolutional encoders [26]. Transformer-based long-sequence architectures—including Informer [32], Autoformer [28], FEDformer [31], and related decomposition models [20]— extend this capacity using sparse attention and multi-scale structure. Across these families, a shared inductive bias assumes dense sampling, smooth temporal variation, and diverse sliding-window supervision.

SSNT sequences violate these assumptions: extended plateaus make sliding windows nearly identical, producing duplicated input-output pairs and causing *supervision collapse*, where models overfit stable regions and receive little gradient signal for rare transitions. This leads to weakened transition modelling and poor generalization across discrete regime levels. Additionally, long-sequence architectures rely on continuous variation or spectral smoothness, conditions that fail when most windows exhibit low contrast or abrupt jumps.

This inductive-bias mismatch is tackled in **Innovation 3** (Sect. 3.5), which densifies informative cues in flat spans through structured, trend-informed perturbations to stabilise optimisation and sharpen transition sensitivity. Instead of designing a new forecasting model, TAPE functions as a model-agnostic, data-centric layer that integrates seamlessly with existing and future long-horizon architectures.

3 Methodology: Trend-Aware Perturbation Enhancement

3.1 Forecasting Objective

Given an input SSNT sequence $\mathbf{x}_{1:T} = \{x_1, \ldots, x_T\}$, the goal is to forecast the next H steps. A deep architecture f_{deep} (e.g., GRU, LSTM, Transformer) operates on the TAPE-enhanced representation to produce

$$\hat{\mathbf{x}}_{T+1:T+H} = f_{\text{deep}}(\text{TAPE}(\mathbf{x}_{1:T}); \boldsymbol{\Theta}), \tag{1}$$

where $\boldsymbol{\Theta}$ denotes the learnable parameters.

3.2 TAPE Framework Overview

TAPE converts the raw sequence $\mathbf{x}_{1:T}$ into an enriched representation $\hat{\mathbf{x}}_{1:T}$ that exposes transition-relevant cues while preserving stepwise semantics. The framework consists of three modules: volatility segmentation, multi-scale trend extraction, and perturbation generation.

Module Interactions.

1. **Volatility Analysis** ($\mathcal{M}_1$) computes localized volatility and assigns region labels $\mathbf{R}$ with corresponding scores $\mathbf{V}$.
2. **Trend Extraction** ($\mathcal{M}_2$) extracts multi-scale trend descriptors $\mathbf{F}$ from the raw sequence, guided by region labels.
3. **Perturbation Generation** ($\mathcal{M}_3$) fuses $\mathbf{x}_{1:T}$, $\mathbf{R}$, and $\mathbf{F}$ to produce the enhanced representation $\hat{\mathbf{x}}_{1:T}$.

Formal Pipeline Definition.

$$(\mathbf{V}, \mathbf{R}) = \mathcal{M}_1(\mathbf{x}_{1:T}), \qquad \mathbf{F} = \mathcal{M}_2(\mathbf{x}_{1:T}, \mathbf{R}), \qquad \hat{\mathbf{x}}_{1:T} = \mathcal{M}_3(\mathbf{x}_{1:T}, \mathbf{R}, \mathbf{F}). \tag{2}$$

Thus, $\text{TAPE}(\mathbf{x}_{1:T}) = \hat{\mathbf{x}}_{1:T}$ serves as the input to f_{deep} for forecasting.

3.3 Module 1: TAPE Volatility Analysis ($\mathcal{M}_1$)

$\mathcal{M}_1$ identifies flat, transitional, and volatile regions by estimating localized volatility at each time step. For each index t, the local mean μ_t and volatility V_t are computed as

$$\mu_t = \frac{1}{w} \sum_{i=t-\lfloor w/2 \rfloor}^{t+\lfloor w/2 \rfloor} x_i, \quad V_t = \frac{1}{w-1} \sum_{i=t-\lfloor w/2 \rfloor}^{t+\lfloor w/2 \rfloor} (x_i - \mu_t)^2. \tag{3}$$

where w is the local volatility window, set to $w = 10$ in all experiments.

Adaptive region segmentation. The volatility profile $\mathbf{V} = \{V_t\}$ induces region labels:

$$R_t = \begin{cases} \text{flat}, & V_t \leq Q_{0.25}(\mathbf{V}), \\ \text{volatile}, & V_t > Q_{0.75}(\mathbf{V}), \\ \text{transitional}, & \text{otherwise}. \end{cases} \tag{4}$$

Using IQR thresholds provides a robust segmentation rule.

Output of $\mathcal{M}_1$.

$$\mathcal{M}_1(\mathbf{x}_{1:T}) = (\mathbf{V}, \mathbf{R}), \qquad \mathbf{R} = \{R_t\}_{t=1}^{T}. \tag{5}$$

These outputs guide multi-scale trend extraction in $\mathcal{M}_2$.

3.4 Module 2: Stepwise Trend Extraction ($\mathcal{M}_2$)

Using region labels from $\mathcal{M}_1$, $\mathcal{M}_2$ extracts multi-scale trend descriptors from the raw sequence, with segmentation guiding the focus toward transition-relevant regions. The three descriptors are illustrated in Fig. 3.

Multi-scale Trend Descriptors.

- **Exponential-Smoothing Trend** ($F_{1,t}$) captures smooth level-trend dynamics:

$$F_{1,t} = S_t + T_t, \quad S_t = \alpha x_t + (1-\alpha)S_{t-1}, \quad T_t = \beta(S_t - S_{t-1}) + (1-\beta)T_{t-1}.$$

- **Savitzky–Golay Derivative** ($F_{2,t}$) highlights local gradient changes via a polynomial fit over a window of size $2m+1$:

$$F_{2,t} = \sum_{k=-m}^{m} c_k^{(1)} x_{t+k}.$$

- **LOWESS Residual** ($F_{3,t}$) isolates high-frequency deviations:

$$F_{3,t} = x_t - \sum_{i=1}^{T} w_i(t) x_i,$$

  where $w_i(t)$ are tricube kernel weights.

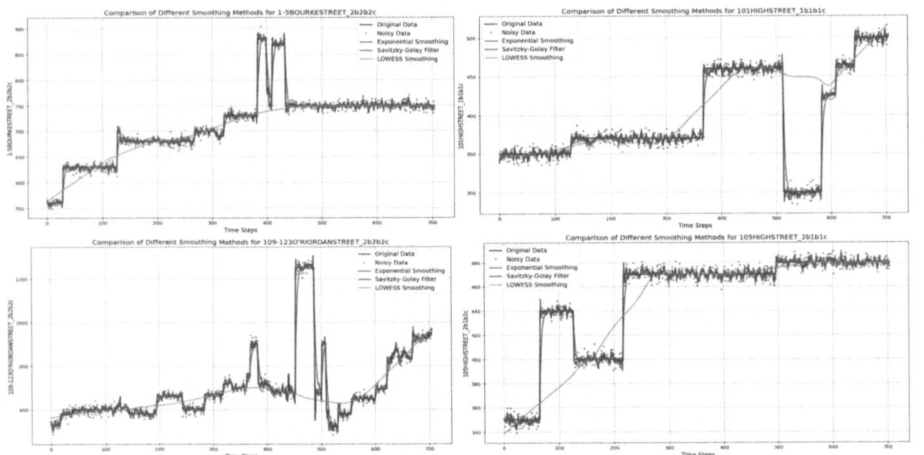

Fig. 3. Trend descriptors used in $\mathcal{M}_2$: F_1 (level-trend evolution), F_2 (local gradient change), and F_3 (high-frequency residual signal). (Color figure online)

Module Output.

$$\mathcal{M}_2(\mathbf{x}_{1:T}, \mathbf{R}) = \{\, \mathbf{F}_t \,\}_{t=1}^{T}, \qquad \mathbf{F}_t = [F_{1,t},\, F_{2,t},\, F_{3,t}]^\top. \tag{6}$$

These descriptors summarize multi-scale volatility patterns and supply volatility-aware cues for $\mathcal{M}_3$.

3.5 Module 3: Trend-Aware Perturbation Synthesis ($\mathcal{M}_3$)

$\mathcal{M}_3$ enriches flat regions by generating perturbations guided by the trend descriptors $\mathbf{F}_t$ from $\mathcal{M}_2$, densifying gradients while preserving stepwise structure.

Trend-Guided Pattern Selection. For each time step t such that R_t = flat, a representative volatile pattern is selected from the index set $\mathcal{I}_{\text{vol}} = \{v \mid R_v =$ volatile$\}$ based on temporal proximity and feature similarity:

$$\mathbf{F}_t^* = \arg\min_{v \in \mathcal{I}_{\text{vol}}} \left[\lambda_d \, d_{\text{temp}}(t, v) + \lambda_m \, d_{\text{mag}}(\mathbf{F}_t, \mathbf{F}_v)\right]. \tag{7}$$

Here, $d_{\text{temp}}(t, v)$ denotes the temporal distance $|t - v|$, and $d_{\text{mag}}(\mathbf{F}_t, \mathbf{F}_v)$ is the Euclidean descriptor distance. Unless otherwise stated, we set $\lambda_d = \lambda_m = 1$ for balanced weighting.

Perturbation Synthesis.

$$P_t = \sigma_f \, \epsilon_t \, \frac{\sum_{i=1}^{3} \gamma_i \, F_{i,t}^*}{\sigma_v}, \tag{8}$$

where $\epsilon_t \sim \mathcal{N}(0, \eta^2)$ introduces stochasticity, γ_i are fusion coefficients satisfying $\sum_i \gamma_i = 1$, and σ_f, σ_v are scaling factors computed from local variance estimates (see Sect. 4.1).

$$\hat{\mathbf{x}}_t = \begin{cases} [x_t + P_t, \; F_{1,t}, F_{2,t}, F_{3,t}]^\top, & R_t = \text{flat}, \\ [x_t, \; F_{1,t}, F_{2,t}, F_{3,t}]^\top, & \text{otherwise}. \end{cases} \tag{9}$$

Thus,

$$\mathcal{M}_3(\mathbf{x}_{1:T}, \mathbf{R}, \mathbf{F}) = \{\hat{\mathbf{x}}_t\}_{t=1}^{T} \in \mathbb{R}^{T \times 4}, \tag{10}$$

producing the complete TAPE-enhanced representation.

3.6 Deep Regressor Integration

The enhanced representation TAPE$(\mathbf{x}_{1:T}) = \{\hat{\mathbf{x}}_t\}_{t=1}^{T} \in \mathbb{R}^{T \times 4}$ feeds directly into a downstream regressor $f_{\text{deep}}(\cdot\,; \boldsymbol{\Theta})$. Since TAPE operates purely at the data level, the regressor can be recurrent, Transformer-based, or sequence-to-sequence. For illustration, we adopt an encoder–decoder instantiation:

$$\mathbf{h}_t^{\text{enc}} = f_{\text{enc}}(\hat{\mathbf{x}}_t, \mathbf{h}_{t-1}^{\text{enc}}; \boldsymbol{\Theta}_{\text{enc}}) \tag{11}$$

which generates a context vector

$$\mathbf{c} = g(\mathbf{h}_{1:T}^{\text{enc}}; \boldsymbol{\Theta}_g). \tag{12}$$

and predicts the H-step forecast as

$$\hat{x}_{T+\tau} = \text{Linear}\Big(f_{\text{dec}}(\hat{x}_{T+\tau-1}, \mathbf{h}_{\tau-1}^{\text{dec}}, \mathbf{c}; \boldsymbol{\Theta}_{\text{dec}})\Big), \tag{13}$$

where Linear$(\cdot)$ denotes an affine (fully connected) mapping.

Training Objective. Models are trained with mean squared error:

$$\mathcal{L}_{\text{MSE}} = \frac{1}{H}\sum_{\tau=1}^{H}(x_{T+\tau} - \hat{x}_{T+\tau})^2. \tag{14}$$

Stopping is triggered when the **validation loss improvement** falls below threshold δ, using a uniform early-stopping heuristic across all models.

Integration Summary. TAPE supplies volatility-aware, transition-sensitive features to any differentiable regressor without altering its architecture, enhancing forecasting on SSNT sequences with long plateaus and sparse transitions.

4 Experiments

4.1 Datasets and Experimental Setup

We evaluate TAPE on two representative SSNT domains and one continuous control benchmark: (i) a long-horizon rental price series (SSNT), (ii) a national policy interest-rate series [1] (SSNT), and (iii) the Fantasia ECG dataset [8], which is high-frequency and quasi-periodic rather than stepwise. This non-SSNT dataset is deliberately included to assess whether TAPE's perturbation mechanism remains beneficial outside its intended stepwise setting. All experiments use chronological 80%–20% train-test splits.

Model architectures. We benchmark RNN, LSTM, GRU, and a Transformer encoder, together with their TAPE-enhanced variants. These models are widely adopted in time-series forecasting and fully compatible with TAPE, covering both recurrent and attention-based paradigms.

Training protocol. Models are trained for 50 epochs using Adam (10^{-3} learning rate, batch size 32). Sliding-window lengths of 15, 20, and 25 assess sensitivity to dependency range. Implementations follow standard PyTorch configurations [4,6,14,25]. Training stability is monitored using smoothed validation loss together with a structured inspection protocol considering trend direction, recent deviation from historical minimum, and the evolution of the train-validation loss gap.

Baselines. We evaluate TAPE on four common forecasting backbones: RNN, GRU, LSTM and a Transformer encoder, implemented using standard architectures. For the TAPE-enhanced variants, only the raw sliding-window input $x_{1:T}$ is replaced by $TAPE(x_{1:T})$; all other components (network, loss, hyperparameters, and optimizer) remain unchanged. Each baseline is tuned via validation, and the same configuration is used for its TAPE counterpart. No training tricks or architectural modifications are introduced, ensuring that any performance gain is solely attributable to the data-centric enhancement rather than increased model capacity. We therefore focus on widely used recurrent and encoder-only Transformers as backbones, and evaluate TAPE in terms of its relative gains over each model rather than absolute architectural state of the art.

Hyper-parameters. Unless otherwise specified, we set $\alpha = 0.3$, $\beta = 0.2$, $m = 3$, $\gamma = [0.5, 0.3, 0.2]$, and $\epsilon_t \sim \mathcal{N}(0, 0.01^2)$ throughout all experiments. The scaling coefficients σ_f and σ_v are computed from the variance statistics of the raw training series and remain fixed to ensure that the perturbation magnitude is proportional to data variability.

4.2 Evaluation Metrics

We report five standard regression metrics: mean squared error (MSE), root mean squared error (RMSE), mean absolute error (MAE), mean absolute percentage error (MAPE), and the coefficient of determination (R^2). These jointly quantify absolute and relative error as well as overall goodness of fit for all experiments.

4.3 Results and Analysis

Overall Performance. We evaluated TAPE on two SSNT benchmarks: a structural rental price series and a macro-stochastic policy interest-rate sequence. Across four architectures (RNN, LSTM, GRU, Transformer), TAPE improved every evaluation metric (MSE, RMSE, MAE, MAPE, R^2) under all three sliding-window settings (15, 20, 25); see Tables 1 and 2. In the rental dataset, MSE reductions exceed 40% in GRU and Transformer variants (e.g., 592.1 → 327.4 (−44.7%) and 599.8 → 330.9 (−44.8%) at window 15), while R^2 increases by up to 0.03-0.04. Similar gains are observed in the financial dataset, where TAPE lowers MAPE from 6.89% to 2.45% (GRU, window 15) and boosts R^2 consistently to above 0.9994. As architectures and optimisation settings are unchanged, these improvements stem solely from TAPE's data-centric enhancements.

Table 1. Rental dataset testing results. Bold indicates best performance per metric within each model.

Sliding Window	Metrics	GRU	TAPE-GRU	LSTM	TAPE-LSTM	RNN	TAPE-RNN	Trans	TAPE-Trans
Length 15	MSE	592.1	**327.4**	574.3	**341.2**	610.5	**355.7**	599.8	**330.9**
	RMSE	24.33	**18.10**	23.96	**18.47**	24.71	**18.85**	24.49	**18.19**
	MAE	13.48	**10.24**	13.29	**10.56**	13.71	**10.89**	13.60	**10.35**
	MAPE	2.49%	**1.88%**	2.52%	**1.93%**	2.58%	**1.95%**	2.55%	**1.89%**
	R^2	0.927	**0.954**	0.929	**0.951**	0.923	**0.948**	0.925	**0.953**
Length 20	MSE	615.3	**338.2**	597.8	**352.1**	632.4	**370.0**	618.0	**341.5**
	RMSE	24.80	**18.39**	24.45	**18.76**	25.14	**19.24**	24.86	**18.47**
	MAE	13.70	**10.58**	13.50	**10.83**	13.95	**11.02**	13.84	**10.62**
	MAPE	2.55%	**1.90%**	2.58%	**1.95%**	2.62%	**2.00%**	2.59%	**1.91%**
	R^2	0.922	**0.951**	0.924	**0.948**	0.918	**0.944**	0.920	**0.950**
Length 25	MSE	634.9	**350.1**	618.2	**365.3**	647.7	**379.2**	630.6	**352.8**
	RMSE	25.19	**18.70**	24.86	**19.12**	25.45	**19.47**	25.11	**18.78**
	MAE	13.95	**10.75**	13.78	**11.01**	14.16	**11.23**	14.00	**10.82**
	MAPE	2.59%	**1.92%**	2.63%	**1.96%**	2.67%	**2.02%**	2.63%	**1.94%**
	R^2	0.919	**0.950**	0.921	**0.946**	0.915	**0.942**	0.918	**0.949**

Training Stability. Beyond accuracy evaluation, we qualitatively examined validation loss evolution to assess optimisation behaviour. Each run was categorized into one of three observational states—*Stable trajectory*, *Mild fluctuations*, or *Early loss divergence*—based on a structured inspection of the smoothed training-validation loss trends, combining loss-trend slope, deviation from the historical minimum, and train-validation gap evolution, with ≥ 2 consistent indicators required for a divergence label. As shown in Table 3, TAPE consistently reduces instances of instability, particularly under longer window sizes (20-25), indicating an implicit regularisation effect from densifying informative signals in flat regions.

Cross-Domain Validation. Although TAPE targets stepwise SSNT sequences, we also test it on the quasi-periodic Fantasia ECG dataset to assess robustness beyond SSNT regimes. Across all models and window lengths, TAPE improves forecasting metrics (Table 4), with R^2 gains of +0.05–0.07 despite the absence of stepwise behaviour. Trend-aware perturbations support transition modelling even in smooth physiological cycles, while improvements remain smaller than on SSNT data (Tables 1–2), consistent with TAPE's data-centric motivation.

Interpretation and Summary. Trend descriptors from $\mathcal{M}_2$ provide volatility-aware context, and $\mathcal{M}_3$ uses them to synthesise meaningful perturbations, consistent with the accuracy gains (Tables 1 and 2) and enhanced training stability (Table 3), suggesting that TAPE increases effective signal density and contributes to more robust optimisation behaviour, although the mechanism is inferred from observational evidence rather than explicitly optimised.

Table 2. Financial (DFF) dataset testing results.

Sliding Window	Metrics	GRU	TAPE-GRU	LSTM	TAPE-LSTM	RNN	TAPE-RNN	Trans	TAPE-Trans
Length 15	MSE	0.0039	**0.0020**	0.0032	**0.0025**	0.0024	0.0024	0.0032	**0.0017**
	RMSE	0.0626	**0.0444**	0.0564	**0.0496**	0.0494	**0.0487**	0.0562	**0.0417**
	MAE	0.0325	**0.0137**	0.0219	**0.0167**	0.0220	**0.0170**	0.0412	**0.0158**
	MAPE	6.89%	**2.45%**	3.66%	**2.17%**	8.44%	**5.88%**	16.32%	**3.57%**
	R^2	0.9989	**0.9995**	0.9991	**0.9996**	0.9993	**0.9994**	0.9991	**0.9995**
Length 20	MSE	0.0040	**0.0022**	0.0031	**0.0025**	0.0024	**0.0023**	0.0027	**0.0020**
	RMSE	0.0637	**0.0466**	0.0556	**0.0498**	0.0490	**0.0480**	0.0523	**0.0448**
	MAE	0.0346	**0.0178**	0.0197	**0.0164**	0.0207	**0.0164**	0.0207	**0.0167**
	MAPE	6.88%	**2.03%**	3.51%	**2.26%**	8.03%	**3.92%**	4.61%	**3.41%**
	R^2	0.9989	**0.9994**	0.9992	**0.9996**	0.9993	**0.9994**	0.9993	**0.9996**
Length 25	MSE	0.0039	**0.0023**	0.0031	**0.0023**	0.0027	**0.0022**	0.0034	**0.0022**
	RMSE	0.0625	**0.0476**	0.0557	**0.0476**	0.0521	**0.0469**	0.0582	**0.0467**
	MAE	0.0264	**0.0165**	0.0195	**0.0161**	0.0246	**0.0161**	0.0311	**0.0155**
	MAPE	6.56%	**4.03%**	3.69%	**2.22%**	7.42%	**2.15%**	15.71%	**3.55%**
	R^2	0.9989	**0.9994**	0.9992	**0.9995**	0.9991	**0.9995**	0.9990	**0.9994**

Table 3. Observed training stability based on validation-loss trends

Window	Status	GRU	TAPE-GRU	LSTM	TAPE-LSTM	RNN	TAPE-RNN	Trans	TAPE-Trans
15	Early loss divergence			✓		✓			
	Stable trajectory		✓		✓		✓		✓
	Mild fluctuations	✓						✓	
20	Early loss divergence	✓							
	Stable trajectory				✓		✓		✓
	Mild fluctuations		✓	✓		✓		✓	
25	Early loss divergence								
	Stable trajectory		✓		✓				✓
	Mild fluctuations	✓		✓		✓	✓	✓	

Table 4. Medical (Fantasia ECG) dataset testing results.

Sliding Window	Metrics	GRU	TAPE-GRU	LSTM	TAPE-LSTM	RNN	TAPE-RNN	Trans	TAPE-Trans
Length 15	MSE	0.0060	**0.0042**	0.0055	**0.0039**	0.0062	**0.0045**	0.0058	**0.0040**
	RMSE	0.0775	**0.0648**	0.0742	**0.0624**	0.0787	**0.0671**	0.0762	**0.0633**
	MAE	0.0412	**0.0301**	0.0395	**0.0290**	0.0423	**0.0320**	0.0407	**0.0295**
	MAPE	32.8%	**24.3%**	31.5%	**23.1%**	34.1%	**25.8%**	30.9%	**23.4%**
	R^2	0.8450	**0.9025**	0.8528	**0.9112**	0.8387	**0.8974**	0.8475	**0.9089**
Length 20	MSE	0.0051	**0.0035**	0.0048	**0.0032**	0.0054	**0.0038**	0.0050	**0.0033**
	RMSE	0.0714	**0.0592**	0.0692	**0.0566**	0.0735	**0.0616**	0.0708	**0.0575**
	MAE	0.0387	**0.0284**	0.0373	**0.0275**	0.0398	**0.0296**	0.0381	**0.0278**
	MAPE	30.4%	**22.1%**	29.1%	**21.2%**	32.0%	**24.2%**	28.6%	**21.8%**
	R^2	0.8627	**0.9189**	0.8693	**0.9264**	0.8554	**0.9137**	0.8651	**0.9228**
Length 25	MSE	0.0048	**0.0031**	0.0046	**0.0030**	0.0051	**0.0037**	0.0047	**0.0032**
	RMSE	0.0683	**0.0577**	0.0678	**0.0548**	0.0714	**0.0618**	0.0685	**0.0565**
	MAE	0.0375	**0.0268**	0.0369	**0.0269**	0.0391	**0.0294**	0.0373	**0.0271**
	MAPE	29.2%	**21.3%**	28.6%	**20.4%**	31.5%	**23.5%**	27.9%	**21.0%**
	R^2	0.8709	**0.9276**	0.8774	**0.9349**	0.8631	**0.9231**	0.8735	**0.9302**

5 Conclusion

We introduced TAPE, a data-centric enhancement for forecasting SSNT sequences. Instead of modifying model architectures, it improves transition representation via volatility-guided trend extraction and structured perturbations.

Across four backbone models and three window settings, TAPE consistently improves accuracy and training stability on SSNT datasets. Results on a quasi-periodic physiological dataset further demonstrate robustness beyond stepwise dynamics.

Future work explores adaptive perturbation learning and structure-aware transition enhancement.

References

1. Public policy rate dataset from a national reserve institution (2024), daily Federal Funds and Cash Rate data. publicly available via national statistics portal
2. Bai, J., Perron, P.: Computation and analysis of multiple structural change models. J. Appl. Economet. **18**(1), 1–22 (2003)
3. Benidis, K., et al.: Deep learning for time series forecasting: tutorial and literature survey. ACM Comput. Surv. **55**(6), 1–36 (2022)
4. Cho, K., et al.: Learning phrase representations using RNN encoder-decoder for statistical machine translation (2014). arXiv preprint arXiv:1406.1078
5. Cui, N., Gu, H., Shen, T., Feng, C.: The impact of micro-level influencing factors on home value: a housing price-rent comparison. Sustainability **10**(12), 4343 (2018)
6. Elman, J.L.: Finding structure in time. Cogn. Sci. **14**(2), 179–211 (1990)
7. Gers, F.A., Schmidhuber, J., Cummins, F.: Learning to forget: continual prediction with LSTM. Neural Comput. **12**(10), 2451–2471 (2000)
8. Goldberger, A.L., et al.: Physiobank, physiotoolkit, and physionet: components of a new research resource for complex physiologic signals. Circulation **101**(23), e215–e220 (2000)
9. Graves, A., Mohamed, A.R., Hinton, G.: Speech recognition with deep recurrent neural networks. In: Proceedings of the 2013 IEEE international conference on acoustics, speech and signal processing, pp. 6645–6649. IEEE (2013)
10. Hale, T., et al.: A global panel database of pandemic policies (oxford covid-19 government response tracker). Nat. Hum. Behav. **5**(4), 529–538 (2021)
11. Hale, T., et al.: Government responses and covid-19 deaths: global evidence across multiple pandemic waves. PLoS ONE **16**(7), e0253116 (2021)
12. Hamilton, J.D.: A new approach to the economic analysis of nonstationary time series and the business cycle. Econometrica J. Econometric Soc. 357–384 (1989)
13. Hamilton, J.D.: Macroeconomic regimes and regime shifts. Handb. Macroecon. **2**, 163–201 (2016)
14. Hochreiter, S., Schmidhuber, J.: Long short-term memory. Neural Comput. **9**(8), 1735–1780 (1997)
15. Guennec, L., Malinowski, A., Tavenard, S., R.: Data augmentation for time series classification using convolutional neural networks. In: Proceedings of the ECML/PKDD Workshop on Advanced Analytics and Learning on Temporal Data (2016)
16. Lindemann, B., Müller, T., Vietz, H., Jazdi, N., Weyrich, M.: A survey on long short-term memory networks for time series prediction. Procedia CIRP **99**, 650–655 (2021)
17. Lopez-Paz, Y.N.D.D., Zhang, H., Cisse, M.: Mixup: beyond empirical risk minimization. In: Proceedings of the International Conference on Learning Representations, vol. 3 (2018)
18. Miaou, S.P.: A stepwise time series regression procedure for water demand model identification. Water Resour. Res. **26**(9), 1887–1897 (1990)
19. Mu, L., Qin, X., Wang, Y.: Dynamic analysis of the rental prices of long-rental apartments and ordinary rental housing based on the impact of long-rental apartment enterprises' competitive behaviors. Discret. Dyn. Nat. Soc. **2021**(1), 8841184 (2021)
20. Nie, Y., Nguyen, N.H., Sinthong, P., Kalagnanam, J.: A time series is worth 64 words: long-term forecasting with transformers (2022). arXiv preprint arXiv:2211.14730

21. Tang, C.S., Deo, S.: Rental price and rental duration under retail competition. Eur. J. Oper. Res. **187**(3), 806–828 (2008)
22. Torres, J.F., Hadjout, D., Sebaa, A., Martínez-Álvarez, F., Troncoso, A.: Deep learning for time series forecasting: a survey. Big data **9**(1), 3–21 (2021)
23. Truong, C., Oudre, L., Vayatis, N.: Selective review of offline change point detection methods. Signal Process. **167**, 107299 (2020)
24. Um, T.T., et al.: Data augmentation of wearable sensor data for Parkinson's disease monitoring using convolutional neural networks. In: Proceedings of the 19th ACM International Conference on Multimodal Interaction, pp. 216–220 (2017)
25. Vaswani, A., et al.: Attention is all you need. Adv. Neural Inf. Process. Syst. **30** (2017)
26. Wang, Y., Smyl, S., Madeka, D., Gasthaus, J., Flunkert, V.: Deep factors for forecasting. In: Proceedings of the International Conference on Machine Learning, pp. 6607–6617. PMLR (2019)
27. Weigend, A.S., Mangeas, M., Srivastava, A.N.: Nonlinear gated experts for time series: discovering regimes and avoiding overfitting. Int. J. Neural Syst. **6**(04), 373–399 (1995)
28. Wu, H., Xu, J., Wang, J., Long, M.: Autoformer: decomposition transformers with auto-correlation for long-term series forecasting. Adv. Neural. Inf. Process. Syst. **34**, 22419–22430 (2021)
29. Yu, Y., Si, X., Hu, C., Zhang, J.: A review of recurrent neural networks: LSTM cells and network architectures. Neural Comput. **31**(7), 1235–1270 (2019)
30. Zerveas, G., Jayaraman, S., Patel, D., Bhamidipaty, A., Eickhoff, C.: A transformer-based framework for multivariate time series representation learning. In: Proceedings of the 27th ACM SIGKDD conference on knowledge discovery & data mining, pp. 2114–2124 (2021)
31. Zhou, H., et alL.: Fedformer: frequency enhanced decomposed transformer for long-term series forecasting. In: Proceedings of the International Conference on Machine Learning, pp. 27042–27052. PMLR (2022)
32. Zhou, H., et al.: Informer: beyond efficient transformer for long sequence time-series forecasting. In: Proceedings of the AAAI conference on artificial intelligence, vol. 35, pp. 11106–11115 (2021)
33. Zhou, Y., You, L., Zhu, W., Xu, P.: Improving time series forecasting with mixup data augmentation (2023)

Private Feature Delivery for Fraud Detection Using Federated Representation Learning

Delton Myalil(✉), Manoj Apte, and M. A. Rajan

TCS Research, Pune, India
{delton.m,manoj.apte,rajan.ma}@tcs.com

Abstract. Fraudulent transaction detection methods employed by multi-bank Payment Network Systems (PNS) can only rely on publicly declared transaction features to perform classification or anomaly detection. Crucial account related information (features) about the payer and payee are not available at the PNS due to privacy constraints. This paper proposes a private feature delivery system that can augment such PNS fraud classification systems with private account related data to increase accuracy. Autoencoders trained in a multi-bank federated learning (FL) setup, with additional privacy guarantees provided by Differential Privacy (DP) forms the core of our system. The drop in accuracy when leveraging DP is counteracted using a Learnable Regularization parameter to preserve privacy without sacrificing accuracy. Experimental results show that the proposed method maintains fraudulent transaction detection accuracy while assuring accountable privacy. This approach provides a solution for secure data collaboration in financial networks, with potential applications extending to other domains and modalities requiring privacy-preserving delivery of machine learnable features.

Keywords: Federated Learning · Privacy Preserving Data Mining · Fraud Detection

1 Introduction

A Payment Network System (PNS) is a general name used to refer to a service provider that enables payments between accounts belonging to multiple banks through a common layer. Examples of PNS include VISA and Rupay for card-based PNS and UPI and InstaPay for account-based PNS. They act as common interfaces for inter bank transfers. One of the main security concern in inter-bank money transfer is financial fraud. Hence goal of this work is to train fraudulent transaction detection models that can reside in PNS environments. This seemingly straightforward binary classification problem can be solved naively by employing a classification solution at the PNS with supervised historic transaction data. However, this means that the model will miss out on the knowledge from crucial account and bank related information that can add

R. C.-W. Wong et al. (Eds.): PAKDD 2026, LNAI 16617, pp. 472–483, 2027.
https://doi.org/10.1007/978-981-92-1926-1_38

to the accuracy of the classification. For example, if the transaction is done by an account that is already under the bank's watchlist, this information can be leveraged at the PNS to 'add weight' to the classification neural model. Ideally, this system will use such bank specific information directly at the PNS. But pragmatically, this will cause a breach of privacy at two levels that we define as follows. The first level of privacy breach is at the bank's customer (account holder) level. A customer of the bank will be apprehensive towards sending their private account details to a third party. The second level of breach is at the bank level itself. A data subset of the customers of a bank is a snapshot of the bank itself - its operations, scale and business, which is safeguarded closely by the bank to protect its competitive edge. Moreover, central banks will restrict the sharing of private data of banks through regulatory restrictions. Hence, the ideal solution of directly shipping bank datasets to a PNS will not work. Then the goal is to ensure that the relevant slices of such bank datasets are available at the PNS without sacrificing privacy at both the levels discussed above. This is true especially since the imbalance ratio of such fraud classification is often highly skewed and every bit of relevant information should be used to improve accuracy. Therefore, we need a method that extracts and transforms account related information from banks into private representations that can be used for further model training.

Representation learning is the process of extracting useful features or representations from raw data to use in other downstream machine learning tasks [4,20]. Since this is a multi-bank setup, we need to create a global representation learning model that learns the patterns from all the participating banks without violating both levels of privacy. Federated Learning (FL) is a suitable approach that can be used to train such a global model that learns how to transform features from all the banks into private representations. Federated learning is a distributed machine learning paradigm where multiple clients collaboratively train a shared model without sharing their raw data [8,11,15]. Each client updates the model locally, and only model parameters or gradients are aggregated centrally, preserving data privacy. Furthermore, FL can be augmented with additional data privacy measures like Differential Privacy (DP) to further enhance data privacy [6,7,21]. DP is a formal framework that ensures the inclusion or exclusion of a single data point has minimal impact on the output of a computation. This is achieved by adding controlled noise to data, gradients, or outputs, providing quantifiable privacy guarantees. Hence, DP can further preserve the privacy of each of the banks' datasets even if an adversary gains access to the representation model or its outputs. However, since DP involves addition of controlled noise to the data and/or gradients, it results in a drop in accuracy of the models being trained. We aim to counteract this drop to preserve privacy without impacting model utility/accuracy of the privacy-performance-accuracy trade-off [13,14]. We achieve this by ensuring that this DP noise also becomes a source of regularization for the network. This is done by intentionally under-regularizing the model and then creating a scaling-based method for regularization which is parameterized by a single scaling factor that learns with respect to reconstruction loss of the representation model, and further aggregating this parameter from all the client models during federated model aggregation.

In summary, we built a FL based private feature representation learning model that protects privacy by using DP and mitigates accuracy drop by using parameterized regularization. This global representation model is used to transform the account related features from the banks, and this transformed private representations are sent to the PNS, which are then concatenated with the public transaction features to aid in downstream fraud classification or anomaly detection.

2 Related Work

Traditional Fraudulent Transaction Detection (FTD) and Anti-Money Laundering (AML) systems use machine/deep learning algorithms to either perform classification (supervised) or anomaly detection (unsupervised) [19]. These systems store transaction data on the site of model training. In a multi-bank system, FL is used to perform fraud classification that covers the different types of fraudulent transactions that may occur in each bank [11,13,15].

Representation Learning is used to extract knowledge regarding the payer and payee from Bank specific datasets [4,20]. The autoencoder model and its variants are a commonly used deep learning technique to learn representations of data of multiple modalities like tables, images, signals and text [3,12,16]. Regularization techniques are used to prevent autoencoders from overfitting to the training data [12,18]. We use Federated Averaging (FedAVG) to aggregate our bank specific representation autoencoder models [11].

Differential Privacy (DP) is used in FL to enhance the privacy of FL participants [1,6,7,21]. The noise introduced by DP is also known to exhibit an implicit regularization effect, and *vice-versa*, in addition to the implicit regularization seen in unsupervised non-linear autoencoder models [2,9,18]

3 Problem Definition

Transactions monitoring problem aims to classify inter-bank PNS transactions on the basis of whether they are fraudulent or not. This is a binary classification problem. Currently, if customer c_s from bank i (payer/sender) sends money to customer c_r from Bank j (payee/receiver), that transaction is denoted as the feature vector $< c_s^i, c_r^j, t_1, t_2, ..., t_n >$, which we define as the *transaction vector*. Here, i, j are Bank identifiers $\forall i, j \in 1, 2, ..., M$ for M banks, and $t_1, t_2, ...$ are the information about the transaction such as the transaction amount, geo-tags, timestamp, mode of payment, *etc.*. This feature vector resides at the PNS and is created at the time the payment is initiated. In existing fraud transaction modeling systems, only variants of this transaction feature vector is used to train models. The problem is that this feature vector does not contain sufficient information about payer c_s^i and payee c_r^j, which may only be available at Bank i and bank j respectively. Such bank/account specific information may include details like past number of transactions, balance, privileges, account age, and even information regarding whether the account is already under suspicion or under internal blacklists. Let the customer information held by Bank i be denoted as the feature vector $b_i =< c^i, b_1^i, b_2^i, ..., b_k^i >$, and we define this as the *account vector*. Then, an ideal solution will concatenate this account vector from both banks to the transaction vector to form the *complete vector* $< c_s^i, b_1^i, b_2^i, ..., b_k^i, c_r^j, b_1^j, b_2^j, ..., b_k^j, t_1, t_2, ..., t_n >$. This complete vector can produce more accurate results since it contributes more knowledge to the fraud detection downstream task like classification or anomaly detection. However, realistically banks do not share such account vectors since it breaches the privacy of its customers. So the problem is to define a method that privately delivers these features (account vectors) to the PNS. We call this the Private Feature Delivery (PFD) problem.

PFD can be achieved by using a common feature transformation model by the banks that can transform the account vector $b_i =< c_s^i, b_1^i, b_2^i, ..., b_k^i >$ to a *private vector* $p_i =< c_s^i, p_1^i, p_2^i, \ldots, p_q^i >$, with optional pseudonymnity for c_s^i. This private vector for the payer and payee are concatenated with the transaction vector involving the payer and payee to form the *complete private vector* $< c_s^i, p_1^i, p_2^i, ..., p_k^i, c_r^j, p_1^j, p_2^j, ..., p_k^j, t_1, t_2, ..., t_n >$ which can then be trained/inferred with the downstream classification or anomaly detection model. The requirements for the transformation model is as follows:

- The model, and hence the transformation method should be same for all the banks.
- The model should learn the patterns from all banks.
- The model should not be sent outside the banks' trusted environment or to the PNS.
- The private vector output of the model should work with downstream ML tasks.
- In case the private vector is obtained by an adversary, then they should not be able to reconstruct the original account vector from it - even with the model.
- The privacy of this private vector must be quantifiable.

4 Methodology

4.1 Proposed Solution

Based on our requirements, a cross-silo federated learning based representation learning model using differential privacy is chosen as our approach to train the global feature transformation model. A three-bank setup is shown in Fig. 1. Here, the three banks employ one FL server to train one global representation model (autoencoder) that, when converged, can transform their account vectors to private vectors. This is the FL side of the system. These private vectors are sent (and cached) at the PNS. For training, these private vectors are concatenated with historic transaction vectors at the PNS corresponding to the payer and payee accounts to form the complete private vector, which is then used to train the downstream machine learning task(s).

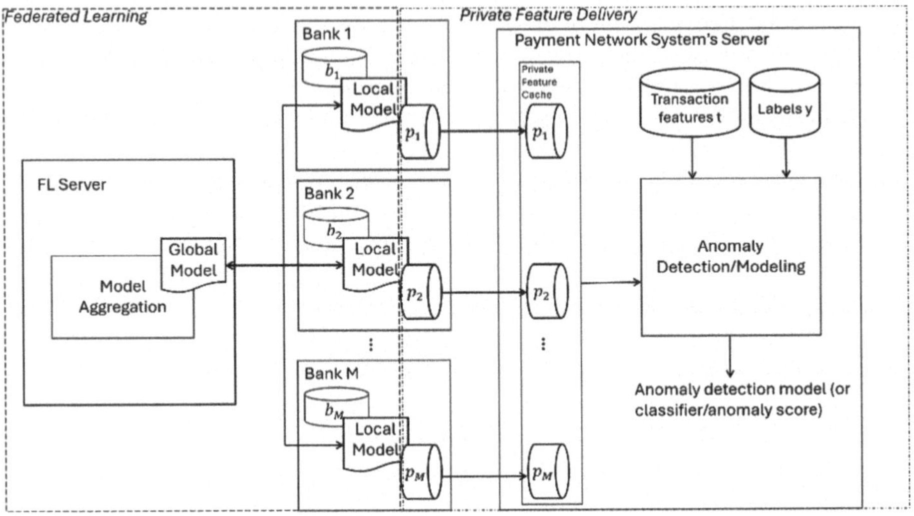

Fig. 1. System Architecture of Federated Private Feature Delivery based Multi-Bank Fraudulent Transaction Detection.

4.2 Threat Model

In a multi-bank PNS system, ideally the bank data should remain private from PNS access. In our system, we use a FL server for model aggregation. The FL server is not part of the PNS. PNS performs the transaction processing and the downstream task (classification/regression). Participating banks may act as curious parties w.r.t. peer bank datasets. In conclusion, our threat model is Curious (FL) Server, Curious Client for FL and Curious (Transaction) Server at PNS level, with the threat boundaries defined around each banks, PNS, and FL server.

4.3 Modeling Private Feature Delivery

Dataset. The availability of real world PNS transactions dataset is a challenge. The dataset we use contains 492 frauds out of 284,807 European credit card transactions with 28 principal components (V1 to V28) as features, while the transaction amount and the classification labels are in plaintext [5,10].

Federated Private Feature Transformation Model. We train the standard autoencoder model on the account vector datasets held by the bank. An autoencoder consists of an encoder and a decoder. Mean Squared Error (MSE) is the reconstruction loss we use for training the autoencoder. The output of the encoder is considered as our private vector. We use DP to further enhance the privacy of our autoencoder's output, in line with our functional requirements [21]. Since we require a global representation model that learns the patterns from all the banks, we train this autoencoder model using FL. In our setup, we employ a

FL server to perform FedAVG of the local autoencoder models. DP ensures that the local bank models, and hence their outputs are private - not only from each other, but also from the FL server and the PNS - especially if the PNS does not have access to the autoencoder model.

Regularization and Differential Privacy. Regularization is used in ML to improve generalization and prevent overfitting. It is achieved by adding a penalty term to the loss function or by turning off neurons. This is comparable to indirectly adding noise to the training data [17]. DP also performs the same and consequently, DP exhibits an implicit regularization effect. Similarly, unsupervised modeling and autoencoders also exhibit strong implicit regularization [18]. Hence, we explored if we can utilize this regularization effect of DP to preserve privacy while maintaining accuracy. However, this implicit regularization effect already comes from multiple sources mentioned above, we avoid explicitly adding regularization like L1, L2, or dropout.

To counteract the drop in accuracy observed when using DP, we first define a dense, non-regularized model and apply linear scalers to selected layers. In deep learning libraries, dropout is implemented as dropout masks, which is a matrix with random cells set to zero with the dropout rate as probability. This mask is multiplied with the layer's output. Similarly, our linear scaler (< 1.0) is multiplied with the attached layer and it acts as the only source of implicit regularization mechanism that is intentional in our autoencoder architecture. When this scaling constant is small, it leads to smaller gradients and hence, more conservative model updates. We make this linear scaler a trainable parameter. Consequently, during FL aggregation, this local linear scaler within the local autoencoder is also aggregated to a global linear scaler since it is a part of the model's trainable parameters.

Formally, let C be the set of all clients (banks). Let the dataset of client c be denoted as X_c and the union of all such datasets be X. Since our linear scaler is the only intentional source of regularization, let it be denoted as r for an autoencoder model $\mu_r(\theta)$ with parameters θ. p is the privacy that we require of the model and it is described by (ϵ, δ) of DP [1]. Then the model is represented as $\mu_{r,p}(\theta)$. We omit p since it is fixed by the `noise_multiplier` hyperparameter based on the required privacy budget ϵ. Since we also train this r, the model for client c becomes $\mu(\theta_c, r_c)$. FL assumes that the model architecture μ remains same for all clients. This autoencoder is trained on local reconstruction loss (Mean Squared Error).

$$\mathcal{L}_c(\mu(\theta_c, r_c), X_c) = \frac{1}{|X_c|} \sum_{x \in X_c} ||x - \mu(\theta_c, r_c)(x)||^2 \tag{1}$$

An ideal solution will be the global model $\mu(\theta^*, r^*)$ that stays under a privacy budget ϵ^* whose encoder transforms the account vector to private vector with the least global loss.

$$(\theta^*, r^*) = \arg\min_{r,\theta} \mathcal{L}_{global}(\mu(\theta, r), X) \tag{2}$$

Here, $\mathcal{L}_{global}$ is the global loss across all clients in C. Since in FL, we do not pool the data to compute the global loss, FL defines this as the weighted average of all local losses for a client c with weight w_c.

$$\mathcal{L}_{global}(\mu(\theta, r), X) = \sum_{c \in C} w_c \mathcal{L}_c(\mu(\theta_c, r_c), X_c) \tag{3}$$

For obtaining the ideal parameter values for θ and r, at each federated round t, we perform FedAVG not only on the model parameters θ_c^t as usually seen in FL, but also on the linear scaler/regularization parameter r_c^t as follows:

$$(\theta^{t+1}, r^{t+1}) = (\sum_{c \in C} w_c \theta_c^t, \sum_{c \in C} w_c r_c^t) \tag{4}$$

where w_c is the weight associated with client c, generally calculated as

$$w_c = \frac{|X_c|}{\sum_{c' \in C} |X_{c'}|} \tag{5}$$

4.4 Modeling the Downstream Task

This second level of modeling is the task performed by the PNS by using the complete private vector that it constructs from concatenating the global autoencoder output, which is the private vector of bank(s) and the transaction vector corresponding to that transaction. In context of this paper, it can be fraudulent transaction classification or transaction anomaly detection. The presence of account related information in the private vector from the banks will enhance the knowledge gained by the downstream PNS's model and thereby increases accuracy of the model to detect frauds. This downstream task is model architecture and algorithm agnostic. Although other algorithms like XGboost and Random Forests are frequently used in real world fraudulent transaction classification systems, for the purpose of this paper, we stick to a simpler dense neural classification model.

5 Experimentation and Result

5.1 Simulating Account and Transaction Vectors

For experimentation, we assume that there is one account vector and one transaction vector, along with one classification label, in one complete vector. For our dataset, we assume 14 features (V1 to V14) as account vector, and the rest (V15 to V28, along with transaction amount) as the transaction vector. The split and nomenclature of the vectors are illustrated in Fig. 2. To illustrate our problem motivation, we analyze the increase in accuracy when we add features from account vector one by one to the transaction vector. Then we conduct the rest of our experiments with the split mentioned above. Moreover, we do not compensate for the data imbalance for the downstream task using over/undersampling techniques. Similarly we avoid other ML optimizations and preprocessings since our focus is on PFD.

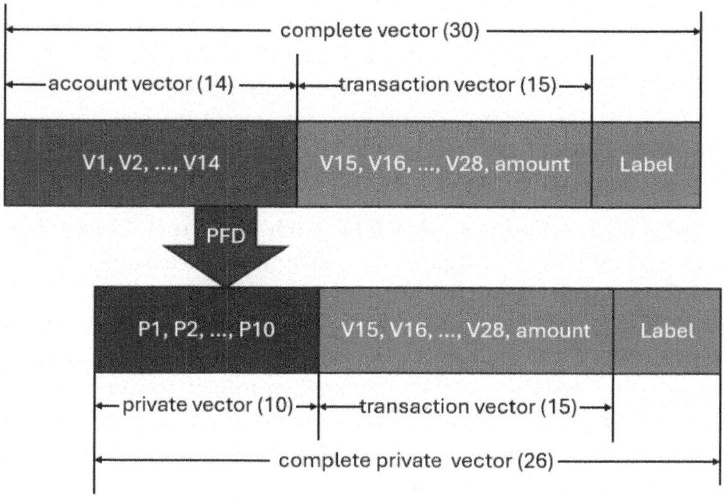

Fig. 2. Simulating the account and transaction vectors from the dataset by splitting the feature vector.

5.2 Results

Baseline. To establish a baseline, we trained a dense neural network directly on cross-entropy loss for classification. We obtained 0.8149 as the f1-score. Then, to establish that addition of more features increases the f1-score, we first train on only the transaction vector containing 15 features and 0 added features from account vector to obtain 0.60 as the f1-score. As we start adding more features from the account vector, the accuracy increased as shown in Table. 1.

Table 1. Average F1-score vs Number of Added Features

Added features	0	...	6	7	8	9	10	11	12	13	14
f1-score	0.600	...	0.653	0.669	0.667	0.794	0.716	0.812	0.725	0.818	0.814

Addition of more features can increase the f1-score from 0.60 to 0.814, when all the 0 to 14 assumed account vectors are introduced at the classification site one by one.

Centralized PFD. Now we simulate the split as illustrated in Fig. 2. We assume the centralized setting where a total of five banks pool their data into a single server to train the autoencoder for 100 epochs to a validation loss of 0.710. This autoencoder is then used to transform the account vector of size 14 to a private vector of size 10. When the private vector is concatenated with the transaction vector to obtain the complete private vector, the resultant classifier (subject to early-stopping) shows an average f1-score of 0.804.

Federated PFD. Then we assume that the five banks follow a federated learning based autoencoder training, followed by private feature delivery to PNS. This federated global autoencoder model has a validation loss of 0.706 after training and aggregating for 100 federated rounds. The resultant classifier at the PNS shows an average f1-score of 0.817 when early-stopping triggered. This global autoencoder was aggregated using vanilla FedAVG [11].

Proposed Method - Federated PFD with DP and Learnable Linear Scaler Regularization. To enhance the privacy of the account vectors held by the banks, we use local DP in the autoencoder training, which is implemented using Opacus DP [21]. This is done by specifying the amount of noise to be infused by using the hyperparameter `noise_multiplier`. The privacy accountant of Opacus provides the ϵ of DP incurred in model training. We report the max ϵ out of all the five ϵ values we obtain for each of the five banks using per-bank local DP. Here, in our autoencoder model, we include one learnable linear scaler attached to the encoder's output layer. It is initialized to 1.0. Since it is a learnable parameter, it is wrapped by an activation function - sigmoid in this case. Hence, in the first forward pass, it becomes $\sigma(1.0) = 0.5$. In the subsequent forward passes following backpropagation, this parameter also gets trained along with the network. Also, during each federated round, this parameter also gets aggregated using FedAVG. In our experiments, after training (epochs=2, batch size=512) and aggregating for 100 federated rounds, we obtained a validation loss of 0.699 for the global autoencoder despite obtaining a max ϵ of 0.25 with $\delta = 10^{-5}$, which provides privacy against the FL server. We use the global private autoencoder to transform the account vectors to private vectors and perform classification at the PNS. Our average f1-score for fraud classification using private vectors is 0.806, also subject to early stopping.

Ablation - Without Learnable Linear Scaler Regularization. To study the effect of the linear scaler that we introduce to our autoencoder model, we perform an ablation study on a setting without it. Here, in spite of the same `noise_multiplier` value resulting in same privacy of $\epsilon = 0.25$, we obtained a validation loss of 0.682 for the global autoencoder and an average f1-score of classification as 0.754 when early stopping was triggered. A lower score here indicates that without the linear scaler we added, the privacy utility trade-off seen in DP negatively impacts the f1-score. To visualize this comparison, we continued training two instances of the classifier after early stopping to completion for a total of 100 epochs. For one pair of instances of training - each for a setting with linear scaler and one without, the full 100 epoch f1-score history plot, and their moving averages are given in Fig. 3.

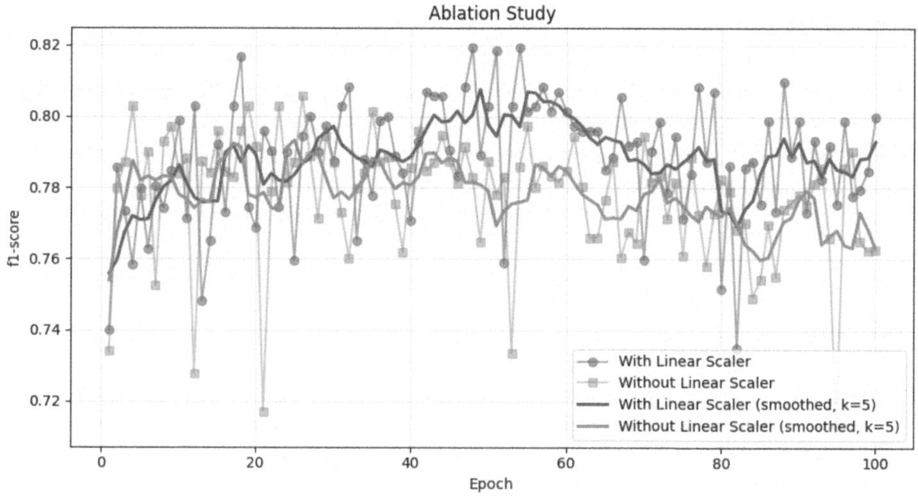

Fig. 3. Ablation study (for one instance) with respect to f1-score for analyzing the impact of the learnable linear scaler parameter

Table 2. Comparison of Experiments: Average values of validation Loss of autoencoder, f1-score of classifier, and max ϵ

Sl.No.	Experiment	Val Loss	Val f1	Max ϵ
1	Classification on Transaction Vector only	–	0.600	–
2	Classification on Complete Vector	–	0.814	–
3	Centralized PFD	0.710	0.804	–
4	FL + PFD	0.706	0.817	–
5	FL + DP + Linear Scaler + PFD	0.699	0.806	0.25
6	Ablation: FL + DP + PFD	0.682	0.754	0.25

Our average validation loss of the autoencoders and average f1-scores of the classifiers are summarized in Table 2. All results are averaged from 5-FCV runs. Our proposed approach exhibits a high accuracy despite using DP.

6 Conclusion and Future Work

We propose a lightweight solution to a real world problem of privately delivering account related information from banks to a PNS for performing downstream payment fraud detection. Here, account related information of a payer/payee account like current balance, previous number of transactions and whether the account is already under suspicion, can contribute significantly to detecting whether the transaction needs to be flagged. Hence, this improves the overall effectiveness of fraud detection models without impacting the privacy of the said accounts and their banks. We experimentally show that the presence of a linear-scaler based learnable regularization can offset the accuracy drop seen in differential privacy for this problem. For future work, we aim to attack this setup and derive tighter privacy claims. We also aim to extract more task-specific variance using supervised labels from other locations, and extend this to a domain agnostic multimodal solution with different clients holding different data modalities.

References

1. Abadi, M., et al.: Deep learning with differential privacy. In: Proceedings of the 2016 ACM SIGSAC Conference on Computer and Communications Security, pp. 308–318. ACM (2016). https://doi.org/10.1145/2976749.2978318
2. Aguilera-Martínez, F., Berzal, F.: Differential privacy regularization: protecting training data through loss function regularization (2024). https://arxiv.org/abs/2409.17144
3. Baldi, P.: Autoencoders, unsupervised learning and deep architectures. In: Proceedings of the 2011 International Conference on Unsupervised and Transfer Learning Workshop, vol. 27, pp. 37–50. UTLW'11, JMLR.org (2011)
4. Bengio, Y., Courville, A.C., Vincent, P.: Unsupervised feature learning and deep learning: a review and new perspectives. CoRR **abs/1206.5538** (2012). http://arxiv.org/abs/1206.5538
5. Pozzolo, A.D., Caelen, O., Johnson, R., Bontempi, G.: Calibrating probability with undersampling for unbalanced classification (2015). https://doi.org/10.1109/SSCI.2015.33
6. Dwork, C.: Differential privacy. In: Bugliesi, M., Preneel, B., Sassone, V., Wegener, I. (eds.) Automata, Languages and Programming, pp. 1–12. Springer, Berlin Heidelberg, Berlin, Heidelberg (2006)
7. Dwork, C., McSherry, F., Nissim, K., Smith, A.: Calibrating noise to sensitivity in private data analysis. In: Halevi, S., Rabin, T. (eds.) Theory of Cryptography, pp. 265–284. Springer, Berlin Heidelberg, Berlin, Heidelberg (2006)
8. Kairouz, P., et al.: Advances and open problems in federated learning. CoRR **abs/1912.04977** (2019). http://arxiv.org/abs/1912.04977
9. Lomurno, E., matteucci, M.: On the utility and protection of optimization with differential privacy and classic regularization techniques (2022). https://arxiv.org/abs/2209.03175
10. Machine Learning Group, U.L.d.B.: Credit card fraud detection. https://www.kaggle.com/datasets/mlg-ulb/creditcardfraud (2021). Accessed 01 Apr 2025
11. McMahan, H.B., Moore, E., Ramage, D., y Arcas, B.A.: Federated learning of deep networks using model averaging. CoRR **abs/1602.05629** (2016). http://arxiv.org/abs/1602.05629
12. Michelucci, U.: An introduction to autoencoders. CoRR **abs/2201.03898** (2022). https://arxiv.org/abs/2201.03898
13. Myalil, D., Rajan, M.A., Apte, M., Lodha, S.: Robust collaborative fraudulent transaction detection using federated learning. In: Proceedings of the 2021 20th IEEE International Conference on Machine Learning and Applications (ICMLA), pp. 373–378 (2021). https://doi.org/10.1109/ICMLA52953.2021.00064

14. Antony, D.M., Shaik, I., Vivek, B.S., M A, R., Gubbi, J., Lodha, S.: Decentralized inter-hospital motor imagery detection using robust multiparty model aggregation. In: Proceedings of the 8th International Conference on Data Science and Management of Data (12th ACM IKDD CODS and 30th COMAD), pp. 1–9. CODS-COMAD '24, Association for Computing Machinery, New York, NY, USA (2025). https://doi.org/10.1145/3703323.3703324
15. Narula, M., Meena, J., Vishwakarma, D.K.: A comprehensive review on federated learning for data-sensitive application: open issues & challenges. Engi. Appl. Artif. Intell. **133**, 108128(2024). https://doi.org/10.1016/j.engappai.2024.108128. https://www.sciencedirect.com/science/article/pii/S0952197624002860
16. Ngiam, J., et al.: Multimodal deep learning. In: Proceedings of the 28th International Conference on International Conference on Machine Learning, pp. 689–696. ICML'11, Omnipress, Madison, WI, USA (2011)
17. Srivastava, N., Hinton, G., Krizhevsky, A., Sutskever, I., Salakhutdinov, R.: Dropout: a simple way to prevent neural networks from overfitting. J. Mach. Learn. Res. **15**(1), 1929–1958 (2014)
18. Steck, H., García-García, D.: On the regularization of autoencoders. CoRR **abs/2110.11402** (2021). https://arxiv.org/abs/2110.11402
19. Weber, M., et al.: Scalable graph learning for anti-money laundering: a first look. CoRR **abs/1812.00076** (2018). http://arxiv.org/abs/1812.00076
20. Xu, Z., Ma, K., Liu, Y., Sun, W., Liu, Y.: Causal representation learning for robust anomaly detection in complex environments. Unpublished manuscript (2025)
21. Yousefpour, A., et al.: Opacus: user-friendly differential privacy library in PyTorch, (2021). arXiv preprint arXiv:2109.12298

Addressing the Counterfactual: Adaptive Batch Size Selection with Causal Models

Shunjian Liu[1], Mengfei Yuan[1(✉)], Kang Liang[1], Junqin Wu[1], and Xuelian Mao[2]

[1] Sunwoda Electronic Co., Ltd., Shenzhen, China
yuanmengfei@sunwoda.com
[2] Chongqing College of International Business and Economics, Chongqing, China

Abstract. Deep learning has achieved great success in tasks such as image recognition and natural language processing. However, its performance is highly sensitive to hyperparameters, among which batch size plays a critical role. Traditionally, batch size is kept fixed throughout training, thereby failing to account for evolving optimization dynamics. Although some recent approaches dynamically adjust batch size, they rely on heuristic rules and fail to model its underlying causal effect on model performance. To address this, we propose CausalBS, a causality-driven method for dynamically adjusting the batch size based on its causal effect on model performance. By formulating batch size selection as a counterfactual inference problem, CausalBS leverages interventional data and the Double Machine Learning (DML) framework to estimate the Conditional Average Treatment Effect (CATE) of different batch sizes. This allows the system to quantify how changes in batch size influence model accuracy, enabling data-driven and causally sound adaptation. Experiments on CIFAR-10 and MNIST demonstrate the effectiveness of our approach, with CausalBS achieving accuracy improvements of 1.8% and 0.11%, respectively.

Keywords: Deep learning · Batch size · Causal inference · Double Machine Learning

1 Introduction

Although deep learning has achieved remarkable success in domains such as image recognition and natural language processing due to its strong representational capacity, model performance remains highly sensitive to hyperparameter tuning [8]. Among these hyperparameters, batch size plays a crucial role in model training, as it directly influences both the convergence speed and the generalization ability [4]. An appropriately chosen batch size can effectively balance gradient noise and computational efficiency, whereas an inappropriate selection may cause the model to converge to suboptimal local minima or even lead to overfitting.

R. C.-W. Wong et al. (Eds.): PAKDD 2026, LNAI 16617, pp. 484–495, 2027.
https://doi.org/10.1007/978-981-92-1926-1_39

Conventional approaches typically adopt a fixed batch size throughout the training process. However, this static strategy fails to account for the dynamic changes in training dynamics, particularly the significant variations in gradient statistics such as gradient variance that occur as training progresses through different epochs. As a result, fixed batch sizes often fail to adapt to these evolving conditions and are rarely optimal for the entire training procedure.

To address this issue, adaptive batch size methods have been proposed to adjust the batch size dynamically during training [6,13]. Although these methods achieve promising results in specific scenarios, they often rely on heuristic strategies. Importantly, such strategies are predicated on correlational analysis rather than causal reasoning, thereby lacking theoretical grounding. These approaches are generally unable to disentangle confounding effects caused by data distribution shifts or model parameter evolution, leading to suboptimal and unstable performance in complex training scenarios.

To fundamentally address these limitations, this paper introduces CausalBS, a causal inference framework that reformulates batch size adjustment as a causal effect estimation problem by leveraging DML [3] to construct a causal model linking batch size to validation accuracy while robustly controlling for confounding biases arising from high-dimensional gradient features and training-stage heterogeneity. This approach establishes a theoretically rigorous foundation for batch size selection, overcomes the limitations of traditional correlational analysis, and facilitates data-driven adaptive batch size optimization grounded in causal relationships.

The main contributions of this work are as follows:

- We are the first to frame batch size selection as a causal effect estimation task, explicitly modeling the causal relationship between batch size and model performance.
- We propose CausalBS, a novel method that effectively addresses this problem by leveraging the DML framework to estimate the CATE while controlling for confounders.
- We conduct systematic evaluations of CausalBS on benchmark datasets including CIFAR-10 and MNIST. The results demonstrate the effectiveness.

2 Related Work

2.1 Batch Size Optimization

Batch size is a fundamental hyperparameter in deep learning training, requires careful consideration of optimizer characteristics for its static configuration [11], learning rate settings [7], and task requirements [9]. A key aspect of static batch size selection is the joint optimization of learning rate and batch size. Goyal et al. propose a linear scaling relationship between batch size and learning rate [7]. However, Li et al. argue that the relationship between batch size and learning rate is highly dependent on the optimizer type, and that the linear scaling rule does not hold for adaptive optimizers such as Adam [11]. Task characteristics also play an important role in determining appropriate batch sizes. In domains such as medical imaging and Electronic Health Records (EHR), smaller batch sizes are better suited for capturing both global similarities and local variations [9]. On the other hand, large batch sizes have been associated with negative effects on model generalization. Studies indicate that large-batch training tends to converge to sharp minima, which are linked to poorer generalization performance [10]. Additionally, Ballester et al. [1] provides new insights into the sources of generalization loss in DNNs trained with large batches. Their work shows that large training batches can increase the near-rank deficiency of activation tensors, adversely affecting optimization and generalization.

To balance training efficiency and model performance, adaptive batch size strategies have gained increasing attention. These methods dynamically adjust the batch size during training based on real-time evaluation of the training state. A foundational concept is the equivalence between batch size and learning rate. It has been shown that increasing the batch size while keeping the learning rate constant can produce effects similar to learning rate decay [13]. Similarly, AdaBatch [6] gradually increases the batch size during training while proportionally adjusting the learning rate. This approach balances the fast convergence of small batches with the computational efficiency of large batches. BA-SGD [18] models the objective function's descent process as a Gaussian random walk with a rebound mechanism, leveraging Taylor expansion and the Central Limit Theorem. Based on this model, BA-SGD proposes a heuristic strategy to select the optimal or near-optimal batch size at each iteration, aiming to maximize the utility of incremental sampling. However, these methods often use heuristic strategies to adjust batch size, without considering the causal relationship between training status and batch size.

2.2 Causal Inference in Machine Learning

The task of causal inference is to estimate outcome changes under alternative treatments [17]. Unlike machine learning's struggle with factor correlation inference, causal methods enhance model generalization in complex environments, particularly under few-shot settings where spurious correlations pose major challenges [12,16,19]. Wang et al. have developed causal frameworks to identify dependencies among target features, imaging conditions and class labels, employing multi-scale stochastic convolution interventions to eliminate imaging-induced spurious correlations while improving feature stability [16]. Lin et al. interpret metric-based few-shot methods as implementing front-door adjustment to mitigate spurious correlations, and propose causal variants that enhance performance via representation diversity [12]. Leveraging causal inference to improve model interpretability has emerged as a prominent research direction. By applying causal inference to multivariate time-series experience data, ERCI (Explainable Experience Replay with Causal Inference) [15] provides interpretable, human-understandable rationales and uses them to guide the experience replay process in deep reinforcement learning. Although causal inference has been widely applied in various areas of machine learning, its use for improving hyperparameter optimization remains an underexplored area. This paper addresses the counterfactual question: "Would model accuracy improve if we altered the batch size?" to optimize training through causal inference.

3 Methodology

3.1 Problem Definition

Within the context of deep learning optimization, dynamic batch size adjustment can be viewed as a sequential decision-making task. The core objective is to maximize the overall model performance by adaptively selecting the batch size during the training process. The training process consists of T epochs. At each epoch t, a suitable batch size b_t is selected from a predefined set of batch sizes B. This decision is based on multidimensional information of the current training state, specifically the covariate set X_t, which comprehensively considers the model's current training stage, training phase, and relevant hyperparameter settings.

This problem can be modeled as a causal inference task, where the goal at each step is to answer the counterfactual question: "Would model accuracy improve if the batch size were altered?", conditioned on the observed context X_t. A key challenge in this approach is the accurate estimation of the CATE, defined as:

$$\text{CATE}(X_t, b_t) = E[Y(t, b_t)|X_t], \tag{1}$$

which quantifies the causal effect of choosing a particular batch size b_t given the contextual state X_t. The fundamental difficulty stems from the counterfactual nature of the problem: at each timestep, only one batch size can be applied and observed, while outcomes under alternative choices remain unobserved.

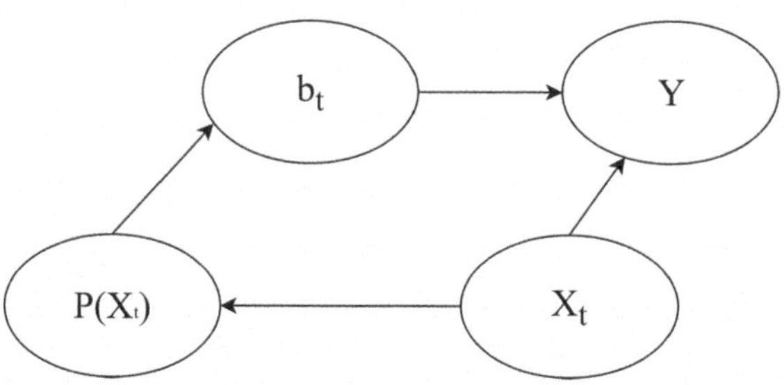

Fig. 1. Causal Graph of Batch Size Selection as a Treatment under Confounding.

To formally characterize the causal relationships among these variables, we construct a causal graph in which X_t (comprising training dynamics, training stage, and hyperparameter settings) acts as a set of common causes or confounders; the selected batch size b_t is the treatment; and the resulting validation accuracy Y is the outcome. $P(X_t)$ represents the batch size selection policy conditioned on the context X_t. This causal structure is illustrated in Fig. 1, which highlights how confounding factors influence both the treatment assignment and the observed outcome, necessitating careful causal modeling to estimate the true effect of b_t. Thus, a key challenge is to construct a reliable causal model from limited observational data, capable of generalizing to unseen counterfactual scenarios and supporting robust sequential decisions. This motivates the need for causal intervention-based data collection and modeling strategies, as discussed in the following subsection.

3.2 Adaptive Batch Size Selection with Causal Models

To address the aforementioned problem of adaptive batch size selection, we propose a causal inference-based adaptive batch size selection method(CausalBS). As illustrated in Fig. 2.

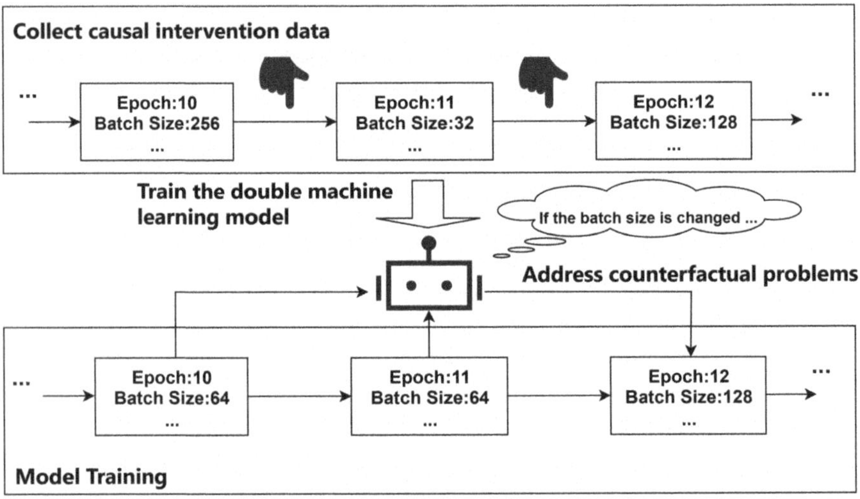

Fig. 2. Causal Inference-based Adaptive Batch Size Selection Method.

The proposed approach consists of three main stages. First, we perform an initial phase of training to collect causal intervention data. During this phase, we design a batch size adjustment policy to ensure key causal assumptions are satisfied, including exchangeability, no unmeasured confounding, and positivity. Second, we train a DML model using the collected intervention data to estimate heterogeneous treatment effects while effectively controlling for observed confounders. Finally, during the main training phase, at each epoch where batch size adaptation is considered, the trained DML model is used to predict the

CATE for each candidate batch size. The batch size yielding the highest estimated CATE is selected, enabling dynamic and performance-aware batch size adaptation to enhance overall model convergence and generalization. A detailed exposition of each component is provided in the subsequent sections.

Data Collection via Causal Interventions. Batch size is typically treated as a fixed hyperparameter or adjusted according to predefined schedules that are often correlated with training time and optimization states, making it difficult to isolate the causal effect of batch size changes. To enable robust causal inference on the impact of batch size in deep learning training, we design an epoch-level alternating random intervention mechanism that mimics the assignment logic of a randomized controlled trial (RCT). Specifically, we adopt a hybrid strategy in which smaller batch sizes are randomly assigned during even-numbered epochs and larger ones during odd-numbered epochs. This alternating assignment ensures that the selection of batch size is decoupled from the temporal sequence of training.

Moreover, recognizing the cumulative nature of parameter updates in deep learning, we introduce a periodic parameter reset mechanism every T_r epochs. At each reset point, the model parameters and optimizer states are reverted to their initial conditions, effectively segmenting the long-horizon training trajectory into a series of independent "micro-cycles". Each micro-cycle begins with a consistent initial state, thereby preventing confounding effects induced by historical training dynamics and ensuring that the causal effect of each batch size intervention can be evaluated in isolation.

Furthermore, to satisfy the "No Unmeasured Confounding" assumption, we comprehensively account for factors that may influence both batch size selection and model performance, including training dynamics, training stage, and hyperparameter settings. Specifically, we collect a rich set of observed covariates:

$$X = \left[\rho,\ \mathcal{L}_{\text{train}},\ \mathcal{L}_{\text{val}},\ \|\nabla\|,\ \sigma_{\nabla}^{2},\ \alpha,\ \phi\right], \tag{2}$$

where $\rho \in [0, 1]$ denotes the normalized training progress (epoch ratio), $\mathcal{L}_{\text{train}}$ and $\mathcal{L}_{\text{val}}$ are the training and validation losses, respectively, $\|\nabla\|$ is the gradient norm, σ_{∇}^{2} represents the gradient variance, α is the learning rate scaling factor, and $\phi \in \{\text{early}, \text{middle}, \text{late}\}$ indicates the current training phase.

By alternating random assignment and periodic state reset, this design satisfies key assumptions of causal inference(including exchangeability, no unmeasured confounding and positivity). As a result, the collected interventional data allow for reliable estimation of the causal effect of batch size on model performance.

Causal Effect Estimation via Double Machine Learning. Traditional regression models often fail to disentangle correlation from causation in dynamic batch size optimization for deep learning. They are susceptible to confounding variables, leading to spurious correlations that misguide effect estimation. To address this, we adopt DML, a two-stage estimation framework that isolates causal effects from confounding influences, enabling unbiased inference of the impact of batch size on model performance.

As shown in Eq. (2), The feature set **X** proxies for potential confounders that jointly influence both the treatment (batch size) and the outcome (accuracy).

Let $T \in \mathbb{R}$ denote the treatment variable, and $Y \in \mathbb{R}$ the outcome variable. In the first stage, we train two predictive models:

$$\hat{Y} = f_{\text{outcome}}(\mathbf{X}), \tag{3}$$

$$\hat{T} = f_{\text{treatment}}(\mathbf{X}), \tag{4}$$

where f_{outcome} and $f_{\text{treatment}}$ are flexible ML models (e.g., random forests, GBMs, or neural networks). We then compute residuals:

$$\varepsilon = Y - \hat{Y}, \tag{5}$$

$$\tau = T - \hat{T}, \tag{6}$$

which remove the confounding influence of **X** on both Y and T.

In the second stage, we estimate the causal effect by regressing the outcome residuals on the treatment residuals:

$$\varepsilon = \alpha + \beta\tau + \zeta, \tag{7}$$

where β represents the Average Treatment Effect (ATE). To estimate CATE across subpopulations, we extend the model:

$$\varepsilon = \alpha(\mathbf{X}) + \beta(\mathbf{X})\tau + \zeta, \tag{8}$$

where $\alpha(\mathbf{X})$ and $\beta(\mathbf{X})$ are modeled using flexible learners. This allows the estimated treatment effect to vary with the training context.

The DML framework reduces bias due to model misspecification and high-dimensional confounding.

Adaptive Batch Size Adjustment Strategy. Building on the DML framework introduced earlier, our strategy uses the estimated CATE to guide batch size selection at each training step.The complete procedure for adaptive batch size selection is summarized in Algorithm 1.

At adjustable adjustment intervals (every K epochs, where K is a tunable hyperparameter), the system observes the value of the covariate vector X at time t, denoted as X_t.

Given a candidate batch size set $\mathcal{B} = \{b_1, b_2, \ldots, b_K\}$, the pre-trained DML model predicts f_{DML} the CATE for each $b \in \mathcal{B}$:

$$\text{CATE}(b \mid X_t) = \mathbb{E}\big[\,Y(b) - Y(b_0) \mid X_t\,\big] \approx f_{\text{DML}}(X_t, b), \tag{9}$$

where b_0 is a baseline batch size. The DML model eliminates confounding among features, ensuring accurate counterfactual estimation.

The batch size with the highest predicted CATE is selected:

$$b_t^* = \arg\max_{b \in \mathcal{B}} \mathrm{CATE}(b \mid X_t), \tag{10}$$

By applying the DML model at selected training checkpoints to estimate the causal effect of batch size on model performance, our approach dynamically adjusts the batch size throughout the training process in response to evolving training stages and states, thereby ensuring consistent and improved model performance.

Algorithm 1:. Adaptive Batch Size Adjustment via Causal Inference

Input: Training state at time t: X_t (as defined in Eq. (2)), candidate batch sizes $\mathcal{B} = \{b_1, \ldots, b_K\}$, baseline batch size b_0, pre-trained DML model f_{DML}

Output: Selected batch size b_t^*

if $t \bmod K = 0$ **then**

Obtain the current training state vector X_t;

for *each* $b \in \mathcal{B}$ **do**

Predict the Conditional Average Treatment Effect (CATE) of b relative to b_0:;

$$\mathrm{CATE}(b \mid X_t) = \mathbb{E}\big[Y(b) - Y(b_0) \mid X_t\big] \approx f_{\mathrm{DML}}(X_t, b)$$

Select the batch size with the highest predicted CATE:;

$$b_t^* = \arg\max_{b \in \mathcal{B}} \mathrm{CATE}(b \mid X_t)$$

return b_t^*;

4 Experiments

4.1 Experimental Setup

To ensure reproducibility and reliability, all experiments are conducted under standardized settings, with complete configuration details specified below.

- **Dataset**: This study selected CIFAR-10 [14] and MNIST [5] as the benchmark datasets. CIFAR-10 consists of 50,000 training images and 10,000 test images across 10 classes, with each image being 32×32 color pixels. MNIST contains 60,000 training images and 10,000 test images of handwritten digits (0–9), each of size 28×28 grayscale pixels.
- **Model Architecture**: We adopt a lightweight convolutional neural network (standard architecture with 2 convolutional layers and 2 fully connected layers) for both datasets, adjusting the input dimensions according to the different channel numbers of each dataset. We use Random Forests [2] as the base

learner in the DML framework due to their strong performance in handling high-dimensional, nonlinear data and their built-in resistance to overfitting.
- **Hyperparameter Settings**: Stochastic Gradient Descent (SGD) is employed as the optimizer with domain-standard hyperparameters: initial learning rate of 0.01, momentum parameter of 0.9, and 50 training epochs for all experiments. For CausalBS, we set the hyperparameter $K = 5$ and test batch size range $B = \{32, 64, 128, 256\}$, covering the most commonly used batch sizes in deep learning to enable comprehensive comparison of training efficiency across different scales. We fix the random seed to 42 for all experiments to ensure reproducibility. All results are reported as the average over 5 independent runs with different seeds (42,43,44,45,46).
- **Comparison Algorithms**: We compare a static strategy (fixed batch size: 32/64/128/256) and a heuristic adaptive strategy (gradual batch size increase) [6,13].

4.2 Accuracy Comparison

Table 1 shows the mean and standard deviation of the final accuracy and best accuracy from five repeated runs of the proposed method and the baseline algorithms. Experimental results show that the proposed CausalBS method achieves superior performance on both datasets. On MNIST, it achieves an average gain of 0.11% in final accuracy and 0.08% in best accuracy; on CIFAR-10, the improvements are more pronounced, with average gains of 1.8% in final accuracy and 1.3% in best accuracy.

Table 1. Test Accuracy Comparison (final vs. best achieved) between CausalBS and Baselines on MNIST and CIFAR-10 (Accuracy are reported as mean ± standard deviation).

Method	MNIST		CIFAR-10	
	Final (Acc. ± Std.)	Best (Acc. ± Std.)	Final (Acc. ± Std.)	Best (Acc. ± Std.)
CausalBS	**99.328 ± 0.016**	**99.356 ± 0.0196**	**74.98 ± 0.39**	**75.22 ± 0.48**
Fixed BS = 32	99.288 ± 0.0147	99.322 ± 0.0147	69.33 ± 0.36	72.42 ± 0.47
Fixed BS = 64	99.226 ± 0.0314	99.278 ± 0.0194	74.69 ± 0.36	74.73 ± 0.36
Fixed BS = 128	99.19 ± 0.0687	99.28 ± 0.0597	74.31 ± 0.17	74.46 ± 0.15
Fixed BS = 256	99.084 ± 0.0771	99.186 ± 0.0445	73.19 ± 0.43	73.47 ± 0.15
Incremental	99.28 ± 0.016	99.316 ± 0.0196	74.54 ± 0.30	74.56 ± 0.32

By contrast, static batch size strategies, smaller batch sizes tend to yield higher accuracy (the optimal batch size is fixed as 32 on MNIST and 64 on CIFAR-10). While the commonly used heuristic of gradually increasing the batch size underperforms compared to these best fixed configurations, it still outperforms the majority of other static batch sizes, highlighting the nontrivial tradeoffs involved in manual batch size scheduling.

Figure 3 shows the training accuracy curves of the proposed method and the compared algorithms.

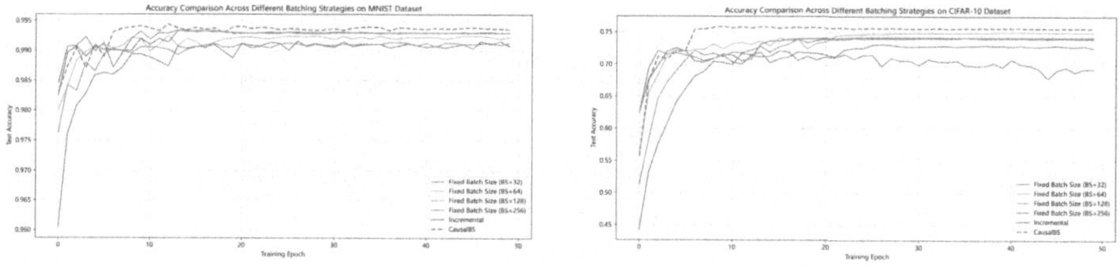

(a) MNIST Dataset

(b) CIFAR-10 Dataset

Fig. 3. Accuracy Comparison Across Different Batching Strategies on MNIST and CIFAR-10 Datasets.

It can be observed that our method converges faster than the compared algorithms, reaching a stable state around 10 epochs on both datasets. In contrast, the performance of fixed batch sizes varies significantly depending on the batch size. For the MNIST dataset, a batch size of 32 yields the best performance, while a batch size of 256 performs the worst. For the CIFAR-10 dataset, a batch size of 32 results in the poorest performance, whereas a batch size of 64 achieves the best results. These observations indicate that batch size is indeed a critical hyperparameter influencing model performance, and its optimal value can vary across different datasets.

4.3 Ablation Studies

We conduct comprehensive ablation studies to validate the key components of CausalBS. The NoReset samples batch sizes uniformly at random during the intervention phase and disables periodic resets of model parameters and training progress. The ML instead of DML setting replaces the DML estimator with Machine Learning (Random forest), evaluating the importance of robust causal estimation. Finally, the Random Selection baseline replaces the CATE-guided decision rule with uniform random sampling from the candidate batch size set B.

The results, summarized in Table 2, show that CausalBS achieves the highest accuracy on both datasets. NoReset leads to a performance drop of 2.487% on CIFAR-10 and 0.161% on MNIST. Replacing DML with ML leads to a 1.812% performance decline on CIFAR-10 and 0.061% on MNIST, demonstrating DML's superiority in handling complex, high-dimensional confounders. Random selection suffers the largest degradation, with a 1.786% drop on CIFAR-10, 0.141%

on MNIST, validating that data-driven, causally informed decisions are essential for effective adaptation. These findings collectively underscore the necessity and effectiveness of each design choice in CausalBS.

Table 2. Classification accuracy (%) of four methods on MNIST and CIFAR-10 datasets

Method	MNIST (%)	CIFAR-10 (%)
CausalBS	**99.328 ± 0.016**	**74.98 ± 0.39**
NoReset	99.167 ± 0.0119	72.493 ± 0.32
ML	99.267 ± 0.0153	73.168 ± 0.37
Random Selection	99.187 ± 0.0153	73.194 ± 0.41

Furthermore, we evaluate the proposed method on a proprietary image dataset comprising typical production images with various defects, collected from a lithium-ion battery manufacturing line. On this dataset, The proposed approach achieves a 1.02% improvement in average detection accuracy over the baseline, demonstrating its effectiveness in practical real-world industrial conditions. Moreover, this method enhances training efficiency for manufacturing defects detection across heterogeneous imaging environments and customized data distributions, thus minimizing the associated production capacity and the yield loss.

5 Conclusion

We proposed CausalBS, a causal inference-based method for dynamic batch size adaptation that estimates the CATE of different batch sizes using the Double Machine Learning framework. By leveraging interventional data and controlling for confounding factors such as training dynamics and phase information, CausalBS makes informed, real-time decisions to select the optimal batch size during training. Experimental results demonstrate that our method improves model accuracy compared to both the best fixed batch size and commonly used heuristic strategies like linearly increasing batch sizes. Although CausalBS requires a small number of initial training epochs to collect causal intervention data, this overhead is significantly lower than performing multiple full training runs to tune the batch size via grid or random search. Furthermore, the core idea of using causal inference for hyperparameter optimization is general and extensible.

References

1. Ballester, R., Xavier Arnal Clemente, C., Casacuberta, M., Madadi, C.A., Corneanu, S., Escalera: predicting the generalization gap in neural networks using topological data analysis. Neurocomputing **596**, 127787 (2024)
2. Breiman, L.: Random forests. Mach. Learn. **45**(1), 5–32 (2001)
3. Chernozhukov, V., et al.: Double/debiased machine learning for treatment and structural parameters. Economet. J. **21**(1), C1–C68 (2018)
4. Nurul Amin Choudhury and Badal Soni: An adaptive batch size-based-CNN-LSTM framework for human activity recognition in uncontrolled environment. IEEE Trans. Industr. Inf. **19**(10), 10379–10387 (2023)
5. Deng, L.: The mnist database of handwritten digit images for machine learning research. IEEE Signal Process. Mag. **29**(6), 141–142 (2012)
6. Devarakonda, A., Naumov, M., Garland, M.: Adabatch: adaptive batch sizes for training deep neural networks. ArXiv abs/1712.02029 (2017)
7. Goyal, P., et al.: Accurate, large minibatch SGD: training imagenet in 1 hour (2017)
8. Jastrzebski, S., et al.: Three factors influencing minima in sgd. In: International Conference on Artificial Neural Networks (2017)
9. Kerley, C.I., et al.: Batch size go big or go home: counterintuitive improvement in medical autoencoders with smaller batch size. In: Colliot, O., Isgum, I., (eds.), Medical Imaging 2023: Image Processing, San Diego, CA, USA, 19-23 February 2023, volume 12464 of SPIE Proceedings. SPIE (2023)
10. Shirish Keskar, N., Mudigere, D., Nocedal, J., Smelyanskiy, M., Tak Peter Tang, P.: On large-batch training for deep learning: generalization gap and sharp minima. ArXiv abs/1609.04836 (2016)
11. Li, S., et al.: Surge phenomenon in optimal learning rate and batch size scaling. In: Proceedings of the 38th International Conference on Neural Information Processing Systems, NIPS '24, Red Hook. Curran Associates Inc, NY, USA (2025)
12. Lin, G., Yongheng, X., Lai, H., Yin, J.: Revisiting few-shot learning from a causal perspective. IEEE Trans. Knowl. Data Eng. **36**(11), 6908–6919 (2024)
13. Smith, S.L., Le, Q.V.: Don't decay the learning rate, increase the batch size. In: International Conference on Learning Representations (2018)
14. Swofford, M.: Image completion on CIFAR-10. CoRR abs/1810.03213 (2018)
15. Wang, J., Du, D., Tian, L., Chen, Y., Li, Y., Li, Y.: ERCI: an explainable experience replay approach with causal inference for deep reinforcement learning. In: Walsh, T., Shah, J., Kolter, Z., (eds.), AAAI-25, Sponsored by the Association for the Advancement of Artificial Intelligence, February 25 - March 4, 2025, Philadelphia, PA, USA, pp. 27671–27679. AAAI Press (2025)
16. Wang, K., Mao, Y., Qiao, Q.: Few-shot SAR target recognition via causal inference and deep metric learning. IEEE Access **13**, 124988–125002 (2025)
17. Yao, L., Chu, Z., Li, S., Li, Y., Gao, J., Zhang, A.: A survey on causal inference. ACM Trans. Knowl. Discov. Data **15**(5) (2021)
18. Yin, P., Luo, P., Nakamura, T.: Small batch or large batch? gaussian walk with rebound can teach. In: Proceedings of the 23rd ACM SIGKDD International Conference on Knowledge Discovery and Data Mining, KDD '17, pp. 1275–1284. Association for Computing Machinery, New York, NY, USA (2017)
19. Yin, Y., Yang, J., An, N., Li, L.: CDC-FSL: a causal de-confounding framework for few-shot learning. Knowl.-Based Syst. **323**, 113732 (2025)

Two Heads Are Better Than One: Model-Weight and Latent-Space Analysis for Federated Learning on Non-Iid Data Against Model Poisoning Attacks

Xingyu Lyu[1], Ning Wang[2], Shixiong Li[1], Yidan Hu[3], and Yimin Chen[1](✉)

[1] Miner School of Computer and Information Sciences, UMass Lowel, Lowell, MA, USA
{xingyu_lyu,shixiong_li,ian_chen}@uml.edu
[2] Department of Computer Science and Engineering, University of South Florida, Tampa, FL, USA
ningw@usf.edu
[3] Department of Cybersecurity, Rochester Institute of Technology, Rochester, NY, USA
yidan.hu@rit.edu

Abstract. Federated Learning (FL) is a popular paradigm that enables remote clients to jointly train a global model without sharing raw data. However, FL has been shown to be vulnerable to model poisoning attacks (MPAs) due to its distributed nature. While extensive research has focused on defending against these attacks, most existing methods assume that data across clients are independent and identically distributed (iid), whereas in practice they are inevitably non-iid. Our benchmark evaluations reveal that under various non-iid settings, existing defenses generally fail to live up to their reported effectiveness. In this paper, we propose a novel approach, **GeminiGuard**, to address this significant gap. We design GeminiGuard to be *lightweight*, *versatile*, and *unsupervised*, aligning with practical deployment requirements. Specifically, GeminiGuard incorporates a **model-weight analysis** component that clusters metrics extracted from model weights, and a **latent-space analysis** component that evaluates discrepancies across multiple layers, deriving a two-fold trust score for robust aggregation. We conduct extensive experiments to evaluate our defense across multiple settings, demonstrating its effectiveness against diverse untargeted and targeted MPAs, including adaptive attackers. Our results show that **GeminiGuard** consistently outperforms state-of-the-art defenses under various non-iid scenarios.

Keywords: Federated Learning (FL) · non-iid · model poisoning · defense

R. C.-W. Wong et al. (Eds.): PAKDD 2026, LNAI 16617, pp. 496–508, 2027.
https://doi.org/10.1007/978-981-92-1926-1_40

1 Introduction

Federated Learning (FL) enables multiple remote devices to collaboratively train a Deep Neural Network (DNN) on a central server while keeping their local data private [1]. This privacy-preserving capability makes FL ideal for various real-world applications where security is essential, such as autonomous driving, IoT devices, and healthcare. While FL has been widely recognized as one major framework for training DNN models distributively, one main hurdle is its vulnerability towards model poisoning attacks (MPAs). MPAs have been demonstrated capable of degrading the overall performance (i.e., untargeted attacks [2]) or manipulating the targeted predictions (i.e., targeted or backdoor attacks [3]) of the victim model.

To mitigate model poisoning attacks in FL, researchers have introduced novel defenses [4–10]. Most existing defenses are *designed* under the assumption of independent-and-identically-distributed (iid) settings, neglecting the fundamental non-iid characteristic of FL [11]. That is, the data distributions at different FL clients are inevitably different in practical. Some defenses provide evaluations for non-iid scenarios while evaluated under only one or two types of non-iids as illustrated in Table 1, which limits their applicability in real-world scenarios. Our experimental results in Table 2 suggest that the performance of these defenses degrade severely under other non-iid settings. This paper aims to address the gap by proposing solutions that work effectively across diverse non-iid scenarios.

Table 1. Comparison between GeminiGuard and recent defenses.

Defense	Built-in non-iid design	Non-iid types evaluated
`FLTrust` [4]	✗	prob
`FLGuard` [12]	✗	prob
`FLAME` [13]	✗	prob
`FreqFed` [9]	✗	prob
`FLDetector` [14]	✗	prob
`FLIP` [6]	✓	dir
`FLARE` [5]	✓	qty
`MESAS` [7]	✗	dir, qty
`CrowdGuard` [8]	✓	dir, prob
`FLShield` [15]	✓	dir, prob
`AGSD` [10]	✗	prob, qty
`GeminiGuard (Ours)`	✓	prob, dir, qty, noise, quantity skew

Our goal is to propose a *lightweight*, *widely applicable*, and *unsupervised* defense for FL against MPAs, which works under a broad range of MPAs and non-iid scenarios. We aim for it to be unsupervised, making it less data-dependent and therefore more practical for deployment. As illustrated in Fig. 2, the challenges of defending against MPAs under non-iid settings consists of two aspects. The primary challenge is that non-iid data inherently brings benign updates closer to malicious updates, making it harder to differentiate malicious clients from benign ones. Meanwhile, the impacts of different non-iids and MPAs vary significantly, and we aim to design a single defense that can effectively address most of them.

To this end, we propose *GeminiGuard*, a novel framework to defend FL against model poisoning attacks under non-iids by combining model weights and latent space analysis. Our intuition comes from a fundamental observation of existing defense strategies: we can rely on either analyzing model weights or inspecting representations in latent space for identifying malicious model updates. That is, the first perspective focuses on model weights to identify malicious updates [4,7,10,12–14] while the second perspective emphasizes latent space behavior and examining hidden layers of local models to detect anomalies [5,8]. This thus intrigues us to raise a question: *what if we design a defense combining the two perspectives comprehensively?* The intuition behind this is that the two perspectives are distinct and therefore can be complementary to each other, i.e., they address the impacts of MPAs and non-iids that are not completely overlapping.

As a result, we introduce a novel MPA defense under non-iids, GeminiGuard, which incorporates two modules: a **model-weight analysis** module and a **latent-space analysis** module. In model-weight analysis, GeminiGuard applies adaptive clustering to model weights and weight metrics including cosine similarity and Euclidean distance extracted from both the global model and local updates. Rather than filtering out the smallest cluster, we compute a cluster score by measuring each update's distance to the centroid of the largest benign cluster, thereby preserving benign updates under non-iid. In latent-space analysis, each received update is assigned a layer score by averaging activation distances across multiple layers relative to other updates. Finally, we perform weighted aggregation of the global model using a combined two-fold trust score derived from the cluster and layer scores.

We anticipate that combining these two perspectives will enable GeminiGuard to effectively address the challenges posed by non-iids and diverse MPAs. Our code is available at https://github.com/xingyushu/GeminiGuard. We further summarize our main contributions as follows.

- We propose GeminiGuard, an effective and robust defense against model poisoning attacks on FL under five types of challenging and comprehensive non-iid settings.
- We compare GeminiGuard with nine recent defenses through comprehensive experiments that encompass four untargeted MPAs, five backdoor attacks across four datasets. The results show that GeminiGuard consistently outperforms them on these datasets.

2 System and Adversary Model

2.1 Non-IID Settings

Our target FL systems consist of two types of entities: a parameter server (PS) and n remote clients. As discussed in Sect. 1, in this paper we focus on non-iid settings, where the local dataset $\mathcal{D}_i$ of a remote client u_i follows a certain type of non-identical distribution. In a general non-iid setting, the data across clients can vary in terms of both the number of data classes and the amount of data samples. As shown below, we explore five types of non-iids: *Dirichlet-based (dir), probability-based (prob), quantity-based (qty), noise-based (noise), and quantity skew (qs)*, as proposed in Li et al. [11].

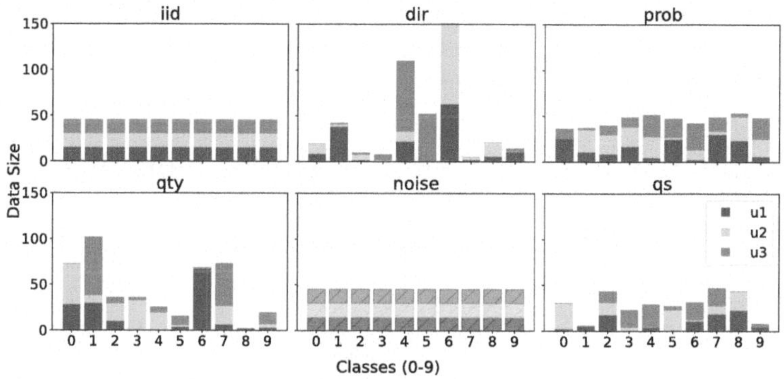

Fig. 1. Illustrations of iid and five non-iids for u_1, u_2, and u_3, and 10 label classes.

Figure 1 illustrates iid and the five non-iids considered in this work (three clients u_1, u_2, u_3, 10 labels, and 150 samples each). Under iid, all clients share identical label distributions and sample counts. We investigate the following non-iid types. **Type-I (dir)**: Dirichlet-based label imbalance, where each client receives a varying number of samples per label (possibly zero), producing diverse label distributions [6–8]. **Type-II (prob)**: Probability-based imbalance, grouping clients by primary labels and assigning samples with probability q (and $\frac{1-q}{G-1}$ to other groups), creating controllable skew [2,4,8,14]. **Type-III (qty)**: Each client owns samples from only a fixed subset of labels (subset distribution) [1,5]. **Type-IV (noise)**: Feature-skew where Gaussian noise $\mathcal{N}(0, \sigma\frac{i}{N})$ is added to client data to induce feature-level heterogeneity [11]. **Type-V (qs)**: Quantity skew, where local dataset sizes $|D_i|$ vary and sample proportions follow $q \sim \text{Dir}(\beta)$ [11].

2.2 Adversary Model

Attackers' Goals. We consider both untargeted and targeted model poisoning attacks, following prior work [2,3,16–18]. In untargeted MPAs, the adversary aims to craft malicious model updates that significantly degrade the performance of the global model. In targeted MPAs, we focus on backdoor attacks, where the attacker seeks to implant a backdoor into the global model Θ such that inputs containing a designated trigger pattern are misclassified into an attacker-chosen label, while preserving high accuracy on clean inputs to ensure stealthiness.

Attackers' Capabilities. As in the literature, we assume that our attackers are also legitimate clients of FL and have a local dataset that they can use to train a local model. Furthermore, they can arbitrarily manipulate (modify, add, or delete) their local data, such as inserting triggers into samples or altering the labels. Additionally, they can craft their model updates sent to PS arbitrarily in order to achieve the above attack goals. As a client, the attackers have white-box access to the global model Θ but no local models of other clients. We assume the number of malicious clients (i.e., attackers) to be less than half of all clients. PS is assumed to be trusted and to deploy defense mechanisms including GeminiGuard against MPAs to properly protect Θ.

3 GeminiGuard: MPA Defenses Under Non-Iids

3.1 Intuition

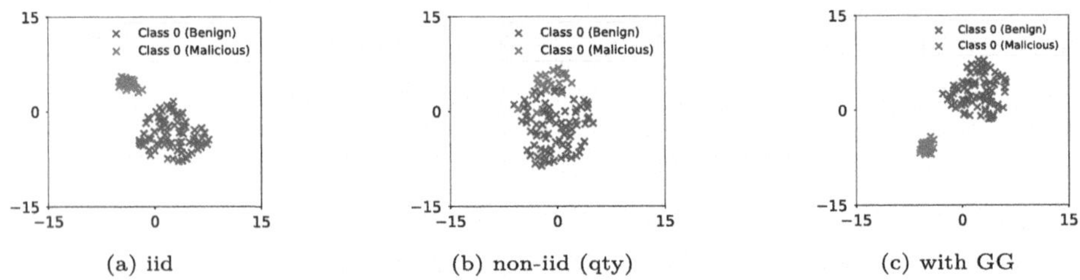

Fig. 2. Model updates in t-SNE (BadNets, CIFAR-10) under different scenarios: (a) iid, (b) dir, (c) prob, (d) qty, (e) noise, and (f) with GeminiGuard (GG).

As noted in Sect. 1, our core intuition is that **model-weight analysis** and **latent-space analysis** provide complementary perspectives for defending against MPAs. Upon receiving δ_i from client u_i, the PS temporarily aggregates it into the global model Θ to obtain Θ_i and then evaluates its suspiciousness. Model-weight analysis directly extracts statistical features from Θ_i, while latent-space analysis feeds a small fixed dataset into Θ_i and analyzes the resulting layer activations.

Our preliminary results motivate combining the two. Figure 2a–2b show t-SNE visualizations of benign and malicious updates under iid and four non-iid settings: compared to iid, benign updates spread toward malicious ones under non-iid, increasing overlap and complicating separation. Figure 3 further

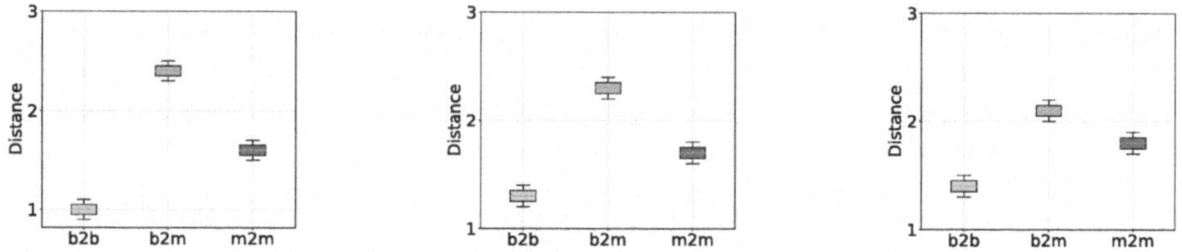

(a) iid (b) non-iid (dir) (c) non-iid (qty)

Fig. 3. Distance of layers between Benign-to-Benign (b2b), Benign-to-Malicious (b2m), and Malicious-to-Malicious (m2m).

compares layer-wise Euclidean distances between benign–benign (b2b), benign–malicious (b2m), and malicious–malicious (m2m) models. Under iid, these three metrics are relatively separable [5,15], while under non-iid (e.g., dir, qty) separability degrades.

Motivated by these observations, we integrate both weight- and latent-based signals to enhance discrimination across diverse non-iid conditions and MPA strategies. As shown in Fig. 2c, our method increases the margin between benign and malicious clusters, demonstrating improved distinguishability.

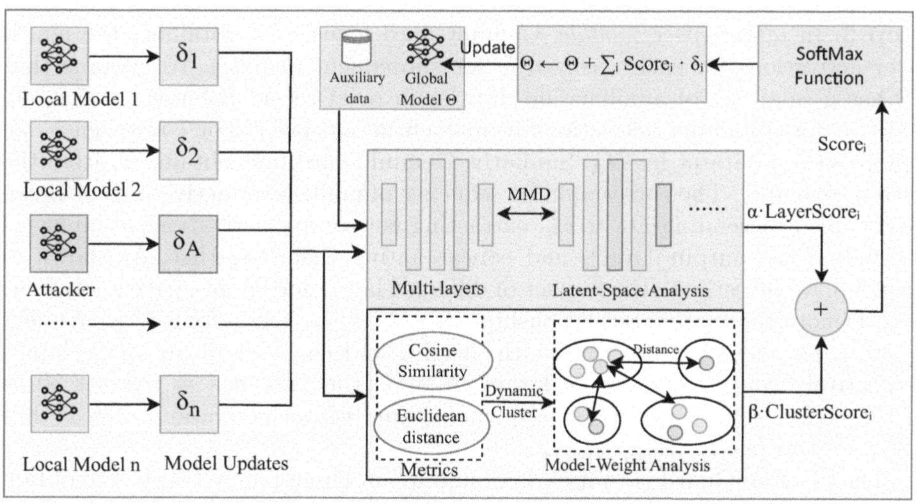

Fig. 4. Workflow of FL with **GeminiGuard**.

3.2 Design of GeminiGuard

Figure 4 illustrates the workflow of GeminiGuard. We detail this pipeline below.

Step 1: In the typical FL process, a client u_i sends its model update to the PS after local training. Specifically, u_i first receives the global model Θ from the PS and uses it to initialize its local model θ_i. The client then trains θ_i using its local data and uploads the model update δ_i to the PS.

Step 2: Next, GeminiGuard performs model-weight analysis on the features of each received update δ_i, including the weight vector and its cosine similarity and Euclidean distance to other updates. For each client u_i, we compute the weight vector w_i based on the model update δ_i (i.e., $w_i = \Theta + \delta_i$). Then, GeminiGuard computes pairwise cosine similarity $\text{CosSim}(w_i, w_j)$ to measure directional differences, and Euclidean distance $\text{EucDist}(w_i, w_j)$ to measure magnitude differences, for all update pairs (i, j) received by the server. Finally, GeminiGuard constructs a feature vector for each update as: $z_i = [\, w_i\, ;\, \sum_{j \neq i} \text{CosSim}(w_i, w_j)\, ;\, \sum_{j \neq i} \text{EucDist}(w_i, w_j)\,]$.

Following that, GeminiGuard applies K-Means to the set of selected client feature vectors $\{z_1, z_2, \ldots, z_n\}$, dynamically grouping updates into clusters. The optimal number of clusters is chosen using the Silhouette Coefficient [19], which evaluates clustering quality based on intra- and inter-cluster distances. After clustering, we compute a cluster score for each update as the inverse distance to the centroid of the largest (benign) cluster, which is commonly assumed benign in existing defenses [13,15]. Specifically, $ClusterScore_i = 1/||z_i - c_{max}||$, where $c_{\max}$ denotes the centroid of the largest cluster.

Step 3: In *latent-space module*, GeminiGuard focuses on obtaining the multi-layer activations for each received δ_i for subsequent analysis. We assume that PS has a small set of auxiliary iid data as in most recent defenses [4,5,8,10], which is for obtaining activations from each neural layer. For convenience, we denote such a dataset by D_A. Similarly, GeminiGuard first obtains Θ_i from the current Θ and δ_i. The corresponding sequence of multi-layer activations of δ_i can be obtained by sending D_A to Θ_i, extracting per-sample activations at all layers (excluding the output layer), and concatenating them together. As shown in Sect. 4.3, we investigate the impact of different layers for latent-space analysis as well. Denote the mapping relationship with Θ_i by $g_{\Theta_i} : x \in \mathcal{R}^{l \times w \times h} \rightarrow r \in \mathcal{R}^L$ where l, w, and h denote the width, height, and channels of an image input, respectively, and L the size of layers. Assume that D_A has m (we set 50 as [5,10]) samples. As a result, the sequence of multi-layer activations of δ_i is thus $\text{LSeq}_i =: \{g_{\Theta_i}(x_1), \ldots, g_{\Theta_i}(x_m)\}$.

Then GeminiGuard is to use Maximum Mean Discrepancy (MMD) to obtain the distance between any two LSeq_i and LSeq_j and then estimating the trust score through the average distance. That is, denote the distance between LSeq_i and LSeq_j (the LSeq for δ_i and δ_j) as below:

$$\begin{aligned} \text{MMD}(\text{LSeq}_i, \text{LSeq}_j) = \frac{1}{m(m-1)} \Bigg[& \sum_{a \in \text{LSeq}_i} \sum_{b \in \text{LSeq}_i, b \neq a} k(a,b) \\ & + \sum_{a \in \text{LSeq}_j} \sum_{b \in \text{LSeq}_j, b \neq a} k(a,b) - 2 \sum_{a \in \text{LSeq}_i} \sum_{b \in \text{LSeq}_j} k(a,b) \Bigg] \end{aligned} \tag{1}$$

where $k(\cdot)$ is a Gaussian kernel function. And,

- For each $\delta_j, j \neq i$ in current round, GeminiGuard computes $\text{MMD}(\text{LSeq}_i, \text{LSeq}_j)$. This average distance of δ_i, denoted by AvgDist_i, is thus calculated as $\text{mean}(\text{MMD}(\text{LSeq}_i, \text{LSeq}_j))$ and serves to reflect the average similarity between δ_i and other δs.
- GeminiGuard then compute the LayerScore_i of δ_i by:

$$\text{LayerScore}_i = \frac{\exp(1/\text{AvgDist}_i/\tau)}{\sum_{k=1}^{n} \exp(1/\text{AvgDist}_k/\tau)}, \tag{2}$$

where τ is a temperature parameter to adjust the sensitivity.

Step 4: Finally, GeminiGuard aggregates all local model updates δ_i using a combined trust score defined as $\text{Score}_i = \alpha \cdot \text{LayerScore}_i + \beta \cdot \text{ClusterScore}_i$. The coefficients α and β are chosen via the greedy search.

4 Performance Evaluation

4.1 Experimental Settings

Datasets. We evaluate GeminiGuard on MNIST, Fashion-MNIST(FMNIST), CIFAR-10 for image classification and Sentiment-140 for sentiment analysis. IID data is evenly partitioned; for non-IID we consider five types: **prob** (q=0.3), **dir** (α=0.3), **qty** (two classes per client), **noise** (σ=0.5), and **qs** (β=0.3). Ablation studies vary non-IID levels. The PS maintains a small **auxiliary set** of 50 clean samples from one class per dataset, providing a consistent reference for activation analysis without accessing private client data.

FL Settings. We use 100 clients and randomly select 10 each round; 20% are malicious and poisoning rate is 0.5. Each client trains for 5 local epochs (batch size 64). We use cross-entropy and SGD (learning rate = 0.001, momentum = 0.9) for MNIST and FMNIST, the same with learning rate = 0.01 for CIFAR-10, and cross-entropy with logits and Adam (learning rate = 0.001) for Sentiment-140.We use a CNN model for MNIST and FMNIST, ResNet-50 for CIFAR-10, and LSTM for Sentiment-140.

Attacks and Baselines. We evaluate both untargeted poisoning (Krum-attack [2], Trim-mean attack [2], Min–Max [2], Min–Sum [16]) and targeted backdoors (BadNets [20], Edge-case [21], DBA [17], Neurotoxin [18], IBA [3]). We compare against FLTrust [4], FLARE [5], FLAME [13], FLDetector [14], FLIP [6], FLGuard [12], MESAS [7], FreqFed [9], and AGSD [10]. We measure `Acc` and `ASR`, where higher `Acc` and lower `ASR` indicate better robustness.

4.2 Comparison with the SOTA Defenses

Untargeted Model Poisoning Attacks. Figure 5 compares the test accuracy of SOTA defenses with GeminiGuard on CIFAR-10 under the Min–Max attack in IID and non-iid settings. While most defenses perform well in IID, their performance degrades significantly in several non-iids (e.g., AGSD fails under 'qty' and 'qs', similar patterns appear in FLGuard and FreqFed). In contrast, GeminiGuard maintains consistently high accuracy across all settings, demonstrating strong robustness.

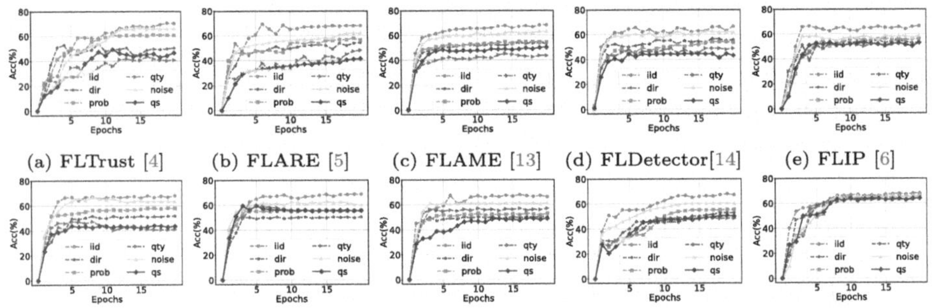

(a) FLTrust [4] (b) FLARE [5] (c) FLAME [13] (d) FLDetector[14] (e) FLIP [6]

(f) FLGuard [12] (g) MESAS [7] (h) FreqFed [9] (i) AGSD [10] (j) GeminiGuard

Fig. 5. Comparison of various FL defenses for CIFAR-10 under Min-Max Attack [16].

Backdoors. Table 2 compares ASR under five backdoor attacks on CIFAR-10 and Sentiment-140 datasets across IID and non-iid settings. Most SOTA defenses achieve low ASR ($< 10\%$) in IID, but their performance degrades notably under several non-iids (e.g., FreqFed under IBA reaches up to 19.98% in 'qs'). In contrast, GeminiGuard consistently yields the lowest ASR across all attacks and distributions. Table 3 further shows that GeminiGuard maintains high model accuracy while effectively suppressing backdoors.

4.3 Ablation Study and Overhead

Impact of non-iid**Degree.** We normalize non-iid degrees to a range of 0.1–0.9 in this section. Figure 6a shows that ASR without GeminiGuard rises sharply with increasing non-iid, while GeminiGuard maintains stable performance, demonstrating robustness to non-iid severity.

Impact of the Malicious Rate. Figure 6b shows that increasing the number of malicious clients significantly boosts ASR without GeminiGuard under both IID and non-iid. In contrast, GeminiGuard consistently keeps ASR low even as the malicious rate grows, confirming strong resistance to backdoor intensity.

Table 2. ASR (%) of backdoor attacks with SOTA defenses under various Non-IID settings, CIFAR-10 and Sentiment-140.

(a) CIFAR-10

Defense	BadNets						DBA						Edge-Case						Neurotoxin						IBA					
	iid	dir	prob	qty	noise	qs	iid	dir	prob	qty	noise	qs	iid	dir	prob	qty	noise	qs	iid	dir	prob	qty	noise	qs	iid	dir	prob	qty	noise	qs
FLTrust	8.91	11.14	8.72	15.07	10.10	11.91	6.26	11.37	8.58	12.92	9.64	17.56	4.42	10.57	8.60	18.91	7.47	13.06	6.00	15.17	7.09	13.41	8.70	16.97	8.80	13.98	10.58	15.21	9.12	16.40
FLARE	4.30	9.15	13.00	10.28	8.01	28.65	5.90	13.29	13.20	11.46	9.69	18.12	9.82	14.61	12.80	3.65	8.85	9.31	10.70	34.30	14.14	8.06	9.89	17.26	8.53	18.76	10.18	15.00	11.29	17.98
FLAME	5.32	14.70	7.56	11.27	10.11	25.69	3.60	10.30	8.87	18.84	8.35	19.17	6.54	14.38	9.57	23.90	9.30	19.07	7.30	15.65	8.95	52.08	9.44	22.77	5.45	26.60	9.29	22.50	16.92	18.29
FLDetector	2.52	16.38	5.96	17.37	9.30	36.31	0.95	13.78	4.21	26.92	10.48	33.34	10.17	21.70	5.47	14.40	8.91	46.19	7.93	20.19	6.57	14.09	9.39	44.78	4.15	15.01	8.76	20.90	10.48	47.12
FLIP	3.50	12.10	10.01	14.40	9.45	23.21	1.41	37.70	8.02	32.19	10.44	22.52	3.17	13.22	9.18	26.85	6.55	16.16	0.46	21.34	8.37	25.08	5.15	14.55	0.78	18.33	5.54	14.92	10.54	28.09
FLGuard	10.10	96.50	84.80	28.82	16.98	51.75	6.69	8.57	38.45	26.40	10.25	21.30	6.15	12.66	17.70	20.21	14.50	40.50	6.58	10.76	13.02	28.56	12.33	39.75	6.13	10.24	25.00	29.91	10.74	30.15
MESAS	3.27	9.50	13.73	15.00	8.35	17.54	4.21	16.15	9.46	26.05	12.63	16.36	9.92	8.69	11.50	31.14	7.65	10.95	3.11	9.11	14.48	19.11	7.80	24.70	5.60	10.63	9.73	31.72	11.91	20.73
FreqFed	2.07	17.50	6.66	47.43	8.60	31.35	3.11	23.50	10.97	71.70	10.21	71.40	2.66	9.69	5.74	17.43	10.90	22.90	6.01	16.42	8.61	26.14	4.84	26.87	5.00	13.78	6.58	17.84	8.11	19.98
AGSD	5.60	16.11	7.09	21.30	8.53	19.50	1.48	14.71	3.61	17.36	6.84	34.20	0.78	15.01	2.60	15.75	6.15	12.23	0.95	12.66	4.15	12.52	6.91	15.87	0.60	7.80	7.15	24.43	6.85	13.70
GeminiGuard	**0.10**	**0.50**	**0.10**	**0.55**	**0.20**	**0.60**	**0.10**	**0.22**	**0.16**	**0.15**	**0.30**	**0.11**	**0.08**	**0.10**	**0.60**	**0.20**	**0.15**	**0.70**	**0.10**	**0.14**	**0.40**	**0.30**	**0.21**	**0.39**	**0.10**	**0.20**	**0.25**	**0.17**	**0.30**	**0.70**

(b) Sentiment-140

Defense	BadNets						DBA						Edge-case						Neurotoxin						IBA					
	iid	dir	prob	qty	noise	qs	iid	dir	prob	qty	noise	qs	iid	dir	prob	qty	noise	qs	iid	dir	prob	qty	noise	qs	iid	dir	prob	qty	noise	qs
FLTrust	3.33	46.66	16.66	50.83	19.16	74.16	2.30	13.22	7.50	41.66	10.83	34.16	6.30	85.00	31.66	48.33	20.83	90.80	8.80	77.50	16.66	60.00	55.00	31.66	10.20	36.66	30.80	49.16	21.60	45.80
FLARE	6.52	12.00	44.16	52.50	10.00	40.00	3.81	15.66	55.00	24.00	45.80	20.00	7.50	20.00	60.00	10.00	20.00	16.80	8.80	20.00	19.00	12.00	25.00	11.66	8.77	16.66	20.00	10.00	19.00	20.00
FLAME	**0.76**	20.00	11.35	15.29	11.85	19.44	0.94	15.06	11.00	20.00	10.00	14.60	0.78	13.74	12.00	17.00	9.00	14.83	0.74	19.71	6.70	20.00	10.50	18.00	**0.82**	12.00	4.00	25.00	22.80	19.60
FLDetector	4.40	32.15	40.29	11.92	40.88	41.58	4.39	11.36	25.78	45.16	22.55	34.88	7.11	10.26	14.99	33.81	17.10	13.70	7.29	29.00	16.94	30.00	24.00	45.61	8.28	27.18	19.28	26.01	10.11	38.87
FLIP	4.83	9.35	34.04	17.41	9.12	14.47	2.81	10.00	13.71	17.50	33.08	24.10	6.01	16.90	24.47	12.67	16.99	60.83	4.66	18.00	37.90	20.48	12.88	30.39	6.39	10.60	18.86	23.36	10.30	27.50
FLGuard	9.64	97.50	57.76	65.13	12.01	91.60	5.23	53.62	38.86	36.51	29.31	41.59	10.45	41.27	58.27	30.02	36.71	55.00	7.71	38.79	27.92	41.47	24.88	40.02	9.06	27.90	13.93	38.44	24.28	67.30
MESAS	2.52	9.32	10.36	30.66	7.65	13.07	2.12	10.97	18.71	10.52	20.56	23.10	5.00	12.73	18.41	20.00	10.88	36.66	5.42	14.61	20.78	22.68	11.14	27.93	9.92	16.64	14.39	27.83	10.00	54.16
FreqFed	6.24	18.45	10.73	50.36	15.00	71.03	3.57	23.45	14.00	12.31	12.66	15.70	20.86	63.58	23.75	50.77	20.01	27.97	3.33	22.64	16.93	37.01	11.65	13.69	7.86	19.00	13.29	25.47	11.20	18.70
AGSD	2.39	8.08	10.30	17.61	24.12	19.24	7.31	23.79	18.84	15.31	18.17	21.27	7.89	12.38	17.14	19.61	12.00	33.88	4.31	24.24	16.31	23.79	10.19	39.16	4.18	11.16	19.48	17.04	10.17	20.00
GeminiGuard	1.65	**1.29**	**1.70**	**1.05**	**1.60**	**1.90**	**0.75**	**0.90**	**1.10**	**1.05**	**2.03**	**1.06**	**0.70**	**0.90**	**0.80**	**1.50**	**0.92**	**0.90**	**0.20**	**1.10**	**0.97**	**0.68**	**1.50**	**1.61**	0.95	**0.50**	**0.83**	**1.30**	**0.62**	**0.90**

Table 3. Main accuracy (%) for different backdoor attacks with GeminiGuard defense.

Attacks	CIFAR-10						Sentiment-140					
	iid	dir	prob	qty	noise	qs	iid	dir	prob	qty	noise	qs
BadNets	68.70	65.90	66.00	64.10	67.60	65.70	81.40	79.10	79.50	77.60	81.80	77.50
DBA	69.50	65.80	66.10	63.90	68.20	65.60	81.00	79.30	79.80	77.20	82.00	77.80
Edge-Case	68.30	66.50	65.40	64.50	67.60	65.80	82.10	79.20	78.60	77.50	81.70	77.40
Neurotoxin	69.10	66.10	65.90	64.10	68.00	65.30	81.80	79.00	78.90	77.10	81.60	78.20
IBA	68.70	66.00	65.50	64.20	67.90	65.00	81.30	77.80	77.50	76.90	80.50	77.90

Impact of Data Poisoning Rate. Figure 6c shows that increasing the poisoning rate significantly raises ASR without defense, while GeminiGuard maintains low ASR across rates, demonstrating robustness even under severe poisoning.

Impact of Auxiliary Data. To test robustness, we replace the auxiliary datasets with similar alternatives: CIFAR-100 for CIFAR-10 and IMDB for Sentiment-140. Table 4a reports the ASR under the IBA attack. The results show only minor changes compared to the original auxiliary sets, confirming that GeminiGuard does not rely on specific auxiliary data and remains robust.

Impact of Layer Count. Table 4b evaluates using 1, 2, and 3 layers in the latent-space module. A single layer results in higher ASR, while multiple layers significantly improve robustness.

Impact of Metric Choices. Table 4c shows that clustering on model weights yields the lowest ASR, while cosine or Euclidean distance alone performs worse.

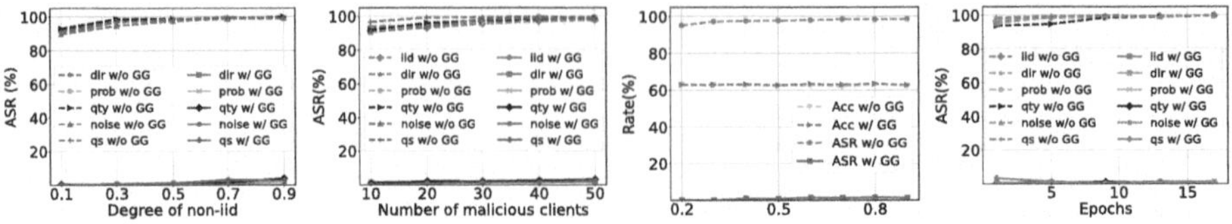

(a) Non-IID degree (b) Malicious rate (c) Data poisoning rate (d) Adaptive attacker

Fig. 6. (a)–(c) Ablation study of GeminiGuard (GG) on CIFAR-10 under the IBA attack; (d) Defending adaptive attacker performance.

Table 4. Evaluation analysis of GeminiGuard under IBA.

(a) Auxiliary dataset impact

#Seq	Train & Aux-Set	iid	dir	prob	qty	noise	qs
Pair 1	CIFAR-10	0.13	0.20	0.32	0.12	0.30	0.50
	CIFAR-100	0.15	0.10	0.28	0.07	0.20	0.51
Pair 2	Sentiment-140	1.10	0.60	0.55	0.70	0.90	1.00
	IMDB	0.70	0.62	0.50	0.68	1.07	0.96

(b) Layer impact

#Layers	iid	dir	prob	qty	noise	qs
1	2.50	7.10	3.93	6.67	4.90	5.80
2	1.85	3.80	2.21	2.13	3.60	2.60
3	0.80	0.85	1.13	1.05	1.00	1.02

(c) Metric impact

Metrics	iid	dir	prob	qty	noise	qs
Weights	0.68	2.03	3.87	1.58	1.74	1.29
Cosine	0.95	2.63	5.05	2.88	1.07	2.41
Euclidean	1.55	2.17	6.10	5.02	1.84	2.01
Cosine+Euclidean	1.70	2.95	1.85	3.50	1.95	2.60
Weights+Cosine	0.80	1.17	1.93	2.11	0.80	1.30
Weights+Euclidean	1.10	1.60	2.35	2.50	1.15	3.00

(d) Computation time (s)

Defense	Dataset	iid	dir	prob	qty	noise	qs
FedAvg	FMNIST	0.0008	0.0024	0.0009	0.0027	0.0008	0.0011
	CIFAR-10	0.0112	0.0106	0.0108	0.0124	0.0105	0.0193
GeminiGuard	FMNIST	0.0031	0.0033	0.0025	0.0041	0.0029	0.0037
	CIFAR-10	0.0372	0.0283	0.0294	0.0390	0.0355	0.0228

Combining weights with either distance metric further reduces ASR, confirming the benefit of integrating both direction and magnitude, especially under non-iid.

Computation Time. Table 4d compares runtime between GeminiGuard and FedAvg. GeminiGuard adds slight overhead due to clustering and scoring, but remains lightweight and practical for deployment.

4.4 Resilience to Adaptive Attacks Under non-iids

We design an adaptive attack that (i) incorporates all five non-iids and (ii) optimizes malicious updates to imitate benign ones. non-iids are essential for evaluating adaptive attacks because they reduce the separability between benign and malicious updates, making defenses more difficult. The adaptive attacker jointly optimizes attack success and similarity to benign updates by minimizing:

$$\arg\min_{\delta_{mal}} L(\mathcal{D}_{mal}) + \lambda L(\mathcal{D}_{train}) + \rho \tilde{\Delta d_{\delta}} + \eta \tilde{d}_{layers}, \tag{3}$$

where the loss terms enforce targeted misclassification, clean accuracy, and proximity to benign weights and layer activations. We compare ASR without vs. with GeminiGuard. Figure 6d shows that adaptive attacks yield high ASR without defense, but GeminiGuard significantly reduces ASR across all non-iids.

5 Related Work

Model Poisoning Attacks. Model poisoning attacks can be broadly categorized into *untargeted* and *targeted* (backdoor) attacks. Untargeted attacks (e.g., Krum-Attack [2], Trim-Mean [2], Min-Max [16], and Min-Sum [16]) seek to corrupt the global model by significantly degrading overall accuracy without altering predicted labels in a controlled direction. In contrast, targeted attacks aim to implant backdoors that misclassify specific trigger patterns while preserving normal performance. Beginning with BadNets [20], subsequent works such as DBA [17], Neurotoxin [18], BoBa [22], and others [3,21,23,24] demonstrate enhanced stealth, persistence, and resistance to existing defenses.

Defenses. To mitigate these threats, various defenses including FLTrust [4], FLARE [5], FLShield [15], AGSD [10], FLBuff [25], and others [6,13] aim to filter malicious updates or estimate client trustworthiness. Despite progress, most rely on iid assumptions or incur substantial computational and communication overhead (e.g., AGSD [10] or CrowdGuard [8]).

6 Conclusions

In this paper, we present GeminiGuard, a lightweight and unsupervised defense for FL that is effective across five non-iid settings. GeminiGuard combines model-weight and latent-space analysis to reliably distinguish between benign and malicious updates. Extensive experiments show that GeminiGuard outperforms nine STOA defenses on multiple datasets, showing strong robustness particularly under non-iid conditions.

References

1. McMahan, B., Moore, E., Ramage, D., Hampson, S., y Arcas, B.A.: Communication-efficient learning of deep networks from decentralized data. In: AISTATS (2017)
2. Fang, M., Cao, X., Jia, J., Gong, N.: Local model poisoning attacks to byzantine-robust federated learning. In: USENIX Security (2020)
3. Nguyen, T.D., Nguyen, T.A., Tran, A., Doan, K.D., Wong, K.S.: IBA: towards irreversible backdoor attacks in federated learning. In: NeurIPS (2024)
4. Cao, X., Fang, M., Liu, J., Gong, N.Z.: Fltrust: byzantine-robust federated learning via trust bootstrapping. NDSS (2021)
5. Wang, N., Xiao, Y., Chen, Y., Hu, Y., Lou, W., Hou, Y.T.: Flare: defending federated learning against model poisoning attacks via latent space representations. In: AsiaCCS (2022)
6. Zhang, K., et al.: Flip: a provable defense framework for backdoor mitigation in federated learning (2023)
7. Krauß, T., Dmitrienko, A.: Mesas: poisoning defense for federated learning resilient against adaptive attackers. CCS (2023)
8. Rieger, P., Krauß, T., Miettinen, M., Dmitrienko, A., Sadeghi, A.R.: Crowdguard: federated backdoor detection in federated learning. NDSS (2024)

9. Fereidooni, H., Pegoraro, A., Rieger, P., Dmitrienko, A., Sadeghi, A.R.: Freqfed: a frequency analysis-based approach for mitigating poisoning attacks in federated learning (2023). arXiv:2312.04432
10. Ali, H., Nepal, S., Kanhere, S.S., Jha, S.: Adversarially guided stateful defense against backdoor attacks in federated deep learning (2024). arXiv preprint arXiv:2410.11205
11. Li, Q., Diao, Y., Chen, Q., He, B.: Federated learning on non-IID data silos: an experimental study. In: ICDE (2022)
12. Lee, Y., Cho, Y., Han, W., Bae, H., Paek, Y.: FLGUARD: byzantine-robust federated learning via ensemble of contrastive models. In: European Symposium on Research in Computer Security (2023)
13. Nguyen, T.D., et al.: {FLAME}: taming backdoors in federated learning. In: USENIX Security (2022)
14. Zhang, Z., Cao, X., Jia, J., Gong, N.Z.: Fldetector: defending federated learning against model poisoning attacks via detecting malicious clients. KDD (2022)
15. Kabir, E., Song, Z., Rashid, M.R.U., Mehnaz, S.: Flshield: a validation based federated learning framework to defend against poisoning attacks. In: IEEE Symposium on Security and Privacy (2024)
16. Shejwalkar, V., Houmansadr, A.: Manipulating the byzantine: optimizing model poisoning attacks and defenses for federated learning In: NDSS (2021)
17. Xie, C., Huang, K., Chen, P.Y., Li, B.: DBA: distributed backdoor attacks against federated learning. In: ICLR (2019)
18. Zhang, Z., et al.: Neurotoxin: durable backdoors in federated learning. In: ICML (2022)
19. Rousseeuw, P.J.: Silhouettes: a graphical aid to the interpretation and validation of cluster analysis. J. Comput. Appl. Math. **20**, 53–65 (1987)
20. Gu, T., Dolan-Gavitt, B., Garg, S.: Badnets: identifying vulnerabilities in the machine learning model supply chain (2017). arXiv preprint arXiv:1708.06733
21. Wang, H., et al.: Attack of the tails: yes, you really can backdoor federated learning. In: NeurIPS (2020)
22. Jiang, Z., et al.: Boba: boosting backdoor detection through data distribution inference in federated learning. In: ECAI. Frontiers in Artificial Intelligence and Applications, vol. 413, pp. 1051–1058 (2025). https://doi.org/10.3233/FAIA250914
23. Bi, Z., Singha, A., Xue, H., Li, T., Chen, Y., Zhang, Y.: Physical backdoor attacks against MMWAVE-based human activity recognition. In: IEEE ICDCS, pp. 758–768. IEEE (2025)
24. Li, S., Lyu, X., Wang, N., Li, T., Chen, D., Chen, Y.: Beyond uniformity: Robust backdoor attacks on deep neural networks with trigger selection. In: PAKDD, pp. 290–302. Springer (2025)
25. Lyu, X., et al.: Buffer is all you need: defending federated learning against backdoor attacks under non-IIDS via buffering. In: IEEE TrustCom, pp. 236–243. IEEE (2025)

A Spectral Gap-Guided Eulerian Graph Rewiring Method for Heterogeneous Graph Embedding

Jiaqi Zhao[1], Hongmei Chen[1,2](✉), Peizhong Yang[1,2], and Lizhen Wang[3]

[1] School of Information Science and Engineering, Yunnan University, Kunming 650500, China
hmchen@ynu.edu.cn
[2] Yunnan Key Laboratory of Intelligent Systems and Computing, Yunnan University, Kunming 650500, China
[3] School of Science and Technology, Dianchi College, Kunming 650228, China

Abstract. Structure-based graph rewiring, a graph augmentation approach, modifies the graph structure for enhancing the graph connectivity while keeping the graph intrinsic semantics, improving node embeddings in heterogeneous graphs. To augment the graph connectivity while avoiding introducing more noise into the graph, this paper proposes a novel model EulerRewire for heterogeneous graph by identifying all pairs of nodes with odd degree and adding edges between these node pairs while the graph spectral gap is utilized to guide edge selection, adding edges as few and enhancing the graph connectivity as much as possible. Then, a dual-view encoder based on GCN and Transformer to jointly learn node embeddings in the rewired Eulerian graph due to their abilities in capturing local structure and high-order dependency, in which a circuit sequence is generated for each node in the rewired Eulerian graph, better capturing high-order dependency between nodes. Extensive experiments for three downstream tasks including node classification, node clustering and link prediction demonstrate the proposed EulerRewire is superior to state-of-the-art baselines in most datasets.

Keywords: Heterogeneous Graph embedding · Graph Rewiring · the graph spectral gap · Eulerian graph

1 Introduction

In recent years, Graph Neural Networks (GNNs) have emerged as a powerful tool for graph representation learning, which learn node embeddings by utilizing the message-passing mechanism to aggregate neighbor features [1, 2]. The success of GNNs in capturing the local structural information in graphs advances Heterogeneous Graph Neural Networks (HGNNs), which further capture heterogeneous information and semantic information in heterogeneous graphs, a kind of graphs consisting various types of nodes and edges, by utilizing the attention mechanism and meta-paths. For example, HAN [1] employs hierarchical attention to aggregate meta-path-based semantic information to learn more expressive node representations. HetCAN [3] further enhances semantic

R. C.-W. Wong et al. (Eds.): PAKDD 2026, LNAI 16617, pp. 509–521, 2027.
https://doi.org/10.1007/978-981-92-1926-1_41

modeling through a cascade attention mechanism that integrates multi-hop relational information. However, both GNNs and HGNNs suffer from some limitations such as over-squashing and over-smoothing [4–6], which hinder their ability to capture global structural information in graphs, particularly large-scale complex graphs.

To address these limitations, graph Transformers incorporate graph topology into the Transformer framework to capture long-range node dependencies via self-attention mechanism [7]. Graph Transformers are also extended to learn node embeddings in heterogeneous graphs. For instance, HINormer [8] models local structural patterns and semantic relations, while PHGT [9] uses three types of tokens to acquire local, global topological structures and semantic information.

In graph representation learning, the graph augmentation technology is exploited to improve the performances of learning models and enhance the quality of node embeddings. For heterogeneous graphs, meta-paths are widely used to augment the semantic relationships between nodes [1, 4]. Though there are some methods for mining meta-paths from graphs, meta-paths are specified in advance, which relies heavily domain knowledges. Recent works show that enhancing the graph connectivity can improve message propagation capability while improving the performances of graph learning models. Structure-based graph rewiring, a graph augmentation approach, modifies the graph structure based on node-specific rules or functional relationships for enhancing the graph connectivity while keeping the graph intrinsic semantics, improving the quality of node embeddings [11].

The spectral gap of a graph is a key metric of the graph connectivity, indicating the larger spectral gap, the stronger connectivity [11]. This motivates us to increase the graph spectral gap by rewiring the graph, improving the graph connectivity and message propagation capability. However, it is known as that the graph spectral gap reaches the maximum when the graph is rewired as a complete graph, leading to the destruction of graph structure, the loss of inherent patterns in graph and the introduction of noises. In this case, graph learning models would struggle to distinguish the features of nodes, causing over-smoothing and performance degradation. This impels us to adopt a proper method for rewiring the graph. Fortunately, Eulerian graph brings us a solution to the above dilemma. For an Eulerian graph, there exists an Eulerian circuit that traverses each edge exactly once. And an undirected connected graph can be rewired to an Eulerian graph by identifying all pairs of nodes with odd degree and adding edges between these node pairs, such that all nodes have even degrees [12]. Rewiring the graph to an Eulerian graph increases the spectral gap as much and adds edges as few as possible, augmenting the graph connectivity while avoiding introducing more noise.

Motivated by the above, we propose a novel model EulerRewire for heterogeneous graph embedding. The contributions of our work can be summarized as follows.

- We present the spectral gap-guided Eulerian graph rewiring. When the graph is rewired into an Eulerian graph by identifying all pairs of nodes with odd degree and adding edges between these node pairs, the graph spectral gap is utilized to guide edge selection, improving the graph connectivity as much as possible.
- We design a dual-view encoder based on GCN and Transformer to collaboratively learn node embeddings in the rewired Eulerian graph. GCN learns local structural

information, while Transformer learn high-order dependency by generating a circuit sequence for each node.

2 Related Work

Heterogeneous Graph Neural Network. Heterogeneous Graph Neural Networks (HGNNs)[3, 5] have gained significant attention due to their ability to learn complex relationships in real-world networks. For example, HAN [1] leverage hierarchical attention mechanisms to aggregate semantic information along meta-paths, while MAGNN [4] further enhances semantic learning through intra-metapath and inter-metapath aggregation. However, recent studies have shown that message-passing-based HGNNs suffer from several limitations, such as over-smoothing and over-squashing.

Graph Transformer. To address the limitations of message-passing-based GNNs, graph Transformers have attracted increasing attention for their ability to capture global structural information via self-attention. Graph Transformers incorporate graph topology into Transformer [9, 13], which is designed for sequential data rather than graph data. For example, HINormer [8] employs a local structural encoder and a heterogeneous relation encoder to capture local structural patterns and semantic similarities, while PHGT [9] introduces poly-tokenization to model high-order heterogeneous semantics and long-range dependencies more effectively.

Structure-Based Graph Rewiring. Structure-based Graph Rewiring (SGR) is a graph augmentation approach in graph representation learning that modifies the graph structure based on node-specific rules or functional relationships. By enhancing the graph connectivity while keeping the graph intrinsic semantics, SGR improves the quality of graph representation learning. Early approaches, such as DropEdge [10], aims to mitigate over-smoothing by randomly removing or adding edges. Recent methods, such as LASER [11], have demonstrated that enhancing the graph connectivity can significantly improve message propagation efficiency and overall learning performance.

3 Preliminaries

Heterogeneous Graph Embedding [1, 4]. A heterogeneous graph is defined as $G = (V, E, A, X, T_v, T_e)$, where V is the set of nodes, E is the set of edges, $A \in \mathbb{R}^{|V| \times |V|}$ is the adjacency matrix, $X \in \mathbb{R}^{|V| \times d}$ is the node feature matrix, and T_v and T_e denote the sets of node types and edge types, respectively. Heterogeneous graph embedding aims to learn low-dimensional node representations that capture both structural information and semantic correlations from diverse node and edge types, thereby improving performance in downstream tasks such as node classification, clustering and link prediction. **Spectral Gap [11].** The spectral gap, defined as the difference between the smallest and second-smallest eigenvalues of the normalized Laplacian matrix, is a key measure of graph connectivity. The normalized Laplacian matrix is defined as:

$$L_{\text{norm}} = I - D^{-\frac{1}{2}} A D^{-\frac{1}{2}} \tag{1}$$

where the eigenvalues of L_{norm} are $0 = \mu_1 \leq \mu_2 \leq \cdots \leq \mu_{|V|}$. Consequently, the spectral gap can be defined as the second smallest eigenvalue μ_2. While a larger spectral gap indicates stronger connectivity, it is known that the spectral gap reaches the maximum when the graph becomes complete, which severely distorts topological structure and introduces noise, leading to degraded performance in graph learning models.

Eulerian Graph [12]. An undirected connected graph is an Eulerian graph if only if the degree of every node is even, ensuring the existence of an Eulerian circuit that traverses each edge exactly once. A property of undirected connected graphs asserts that the number of nodes with odd degree is always even. According to this property, an undirected connected graph can be rewired to an Eulerian graph by identifying all pairs of nodes with odd degree and adding edges between node pairs.

4 EulerRewire

In this paper, we propose a novel model EulerRewire for heterogeneous graph embedding, which shown in Fig. 1. EulerRewire consists of two key modules: Spectral gap-guided Eulerian graph rewiring, and Dual-view encoder based on GCN [14] and Transformer [7]. Eulerian graph rewiring converts the graph to an Eulerian graph by increasing the spectral gap as much and adding edges as few as possible, augmenting the connectivity of the graph while avoiding introducing more noise into the graph. Dural-view encoder learns the node embeddings by utilizing GCN and Transformer to capture both local structural information and high-order dependency.

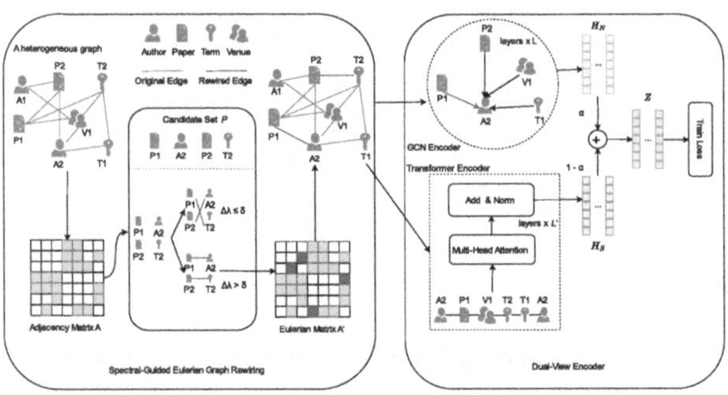

Fig. 1. The overall framework of EulerRewire.

4.1 Eulerian Graph Rewiring

On the one hand, a graph G can be converted to an Eulerian graph G' by adding edges between a pair of nodes with odd degrees, enabling an Eulerian traversal by adding the minimum number of edges. On the other hand, selecting different node pairs for adding edges can obtain different Eulerian graphs which maybe have different spectral gaps, reflecting different graph connectivity. Thus, we present spectral gap-guided Eulerian graph rewiring, augmenting the connectivity of the graph while avoiding introducing more noise into the graph.

Specifically, we first generate a candidate set P consisting of all nodes with odd degree in the graph G. Then, to reduce the computational cost, we select t pairs of nodes from the candidate set P and evaluate the spectral gap λ of the graph after adding t edges, rather than selecting a node pair and evaluating the spectral gap after adding an edge. It is noted that the spectral gap maybe becomes smaller although the spectral gap becomes larger with high probability after adding edges. So, we specify an empiric threshold δ_0 to control node pair selection. In each iteration, we select t node pairs, add the corresponding edges to the graph, and evaluate the spectral gap improvement. When the relative spectral gap gain exceeds the threshold, we update the candidate set and graph structure; otherwise, we relax the threshold using a decay factor η. The details of Eulerian graph rewiring is shown in Algorithm 1.

Algorithm 1. Eulerian Graph Rewiring

Algorithm 1. Eulerian Graph Rewiring

Input: Heterogeneous graph $G = (V, E, A, X, T_v, T_e)$, the number t of node pairs selected in an iteration, the empiric threshold δ_0 to control node pair selection, $\eta \in (0,1)$
Output: Eulerian graph $G' = (V, E', A', X, T_v, T_e)$
Generate the candidate set of nodes with odd degree P
Compute the spectral gap λ of G
Initialize $\delta \leftarrow \delta_0$
while $P \neq \emptyset$ **do**
  Select t node pairs from P, and add t edges into E^+
  Generate G' according to E^+
  Compute the spectral gap λ' of G'
  if $\frac{\lambda' - \lambda}{\lambda} \geq \delta$ **then**
    Update $P \leftarrow P - E^+$
    Update $G \leftarrow G'$
    Update $\lambda \leftarrow \lambda'$
    $\delta \leftarrow \delta_0$
  else $\delta \leftarrow \delta \times \eta$
return Eulerian graph $G' = (V, E', A', X, T_v, T_e)$

4.2 Dual-View Encoder

Due to the ability of GCN in capturing local structural information and the ability of Transformer in capturing high-order dependency, we design a dual-view encoder based on GCN and Transformer to collaboratively learn node embeddings in the Eulerian graph G' obtained by rewiring the graph G.

Specifically, we first learn node embeddings by applying a L-layer GCN to aggregate the neighbor features, which can be described as:

$$H_N^{l+1} = \delta\left(\left(\tilde{D}^{-\frac{1}{2}}\tilde{A}\tilde{D}^{-\frac{1}{2}}H^l W^l\right)_v\right) \tag{2}$$

where $\widetilde{A} = A + I$, I is the identity matrix, $\widetilde{D}$ is the degree matrix, i.e., $\widetilde{D}_{ii} = \sum_j \widetilde{A}_{ij}$, W^l is the trainable matrix at l-th layer, H_N^l is the embedding matrix of nodes at the l-layer, initially $H_N^0 = X$, and $\delta(\bullet)$ denotes an activation function. We take H_N^L at L-th layer as the node embedding matrix H_N learned by GCN, i.e., $H_N = H_N^L$.

Then, we generate a circuit sequence $S(v) = \{v, \ldots, v\}$ for each node $v \in V$ in the Eulerian graph G' by Breadth First Search, which starts from the node v and ends at the node v. We learn node embeddings by exploiting a L'-layer encoder of Transformer which can be described as:

$$S_{S(v)}^{l+1} = \text{LayerNorm}\left(\text{MultiHeadAttention}\left(S_{S(v)}^{l}\right) + S_{S(v)}^{l}\right) \tag{3}$$

where $S_{S(v)}^{l}$ is the embedding matrix of $S(v)$ at l-th layer, initially $S_{S(v)}^{0} = [X[v], \ldots, X[v]]^T$, *LayerNorm* and *MultiHeadAttention* is the layer normalization operation and the multi-head attention mechanism. We take $S_{S(v)}^{L'}[1]$ of v at L'-th layer as the embedding vector of v. And we concatenate the embedding vectors of all nodes to get the node embedding matrix H_S learned by Transformer, i.e., $H_S = \|_{v \in V} S_{S(v)}^{L'}[1]$.

Finally, we fuse the node embedding matrix H_N learned by GCN and the node embedding matrix H_S learned by Transformer to generate the final embedding matrix Z of nodes which can be described as:

$$Z = \alpha \cdot H_N + (1 - \alpha) \cdot H_S \tag{4}$$

where α is the hyperparameter used to balance two kinds of node embeddings.

4.3 Training Objective

We adopt end-to-end methods to train the proposed EulerRewire model. That is to say, we adopt different objective function for different downstream tasks.

For the node classification task, we use a Multi-Layer Perceptron (MLP) to predict the label of each node v in the training set V_{train} extracted from the node set V according to its embedding $z_v = Z[v]$:

$$\widetilde{y}_v = \text{MLP}(z_v) \tag{5}$$

where $\widetilde{y}_v \in \mathbb{R}^C$ is the predicted label probability vector of v, C is the number of labels. Then, we use the cross-entropy loss as the objective function:

$$\mathcal{L} = \sum\nolimits_{v \in V_{\text{train}}} \text{CrossEntropy}\left(\widetilde{y}_v, y_v\right) \tag{6}$$

where y_v is the ground-truth label one-hot vector of node v.

It is noted that the node clustering task follows the model trained by the node classification task due to the unsupervised learning of clustering.

For the link prediction task, we construct the training set E_{train} using the positive edges extracted from the edge set E, and the negative edges generated from node pairs without edges, in which the number of positive edges is equal to that of negative edges.

Next, we use the inner product to predict the probability of each edge $(u, v) \in E_{train}$ according to two node embeddings $z_u = Z[u]$ and $z_v = Z[v]$:

$$\hat{y}_{uv} = z_u \cdot z_v \tag{7}$$

where $\hat{y}_{uv}$ is the predicted probability of (u, v). Then, we use the binary cross-entropy loss as the objective function:

$$\mathcal{L} = -\frac{1}{|E_{train}|}\sum\nolimits_{(u,v)\in E_{train}} (y_{uv}\log\hat{y}_{uv} + (1 - y_{uv})\log(1 - \hat{y}_{uv})) \tag{8}$$

5 Experiments

5.1 Experimental Setup

Datasets. To evaluate the proposed EulerRewire model, we first compare EulerRewire with six baselines on four datasets (DBLP, ACM, Freebase, and AMiner) for node classification and node clustering. Then, we compare EulerRewire with the baselines on two datasets (LastFM and PubMed) for link prediction. The datasets DBLP, ACM, Freebase, LastFM, and PubMed are from HGB [2], while AMiner is used in HINormer [8]. The statistics of datasets are shown in Table 1.

Table 1. Statistics of Datasets.

Task	Dataset	(Node; Type)	(Edge; Type)	Target	Class
Node Classification Node Clustering	DBLP	(26,128; 4)	(239,566; 6)	author	4
	ACM	(10,942; 4)	(547,872; 8)	paper	3
	Freebase	(43,854; 4)	(151,034; 6)	movie	3
	AMiner	(55,738; 3)	(153,676; 4)	paper	4
Link Prediction	LastFM	(20,612; 3)	(141,521; 3)	user-artist	–
	PubMed	(63,109; 4)	(244,986; 10)	disease-disease	–

Baselines. We select six baselines from two categories: the GNN-based models including HAN [1] (2019), MAGNN [4] (2020), HetGNN [5] (2019), HetCAN [3] (2023), and Transformer-based models including HINormer [8] (2023), PHGT [9] (2024).

Metrics. We evaluate node classification task using Mi-F1 and Ma-F1, node clustering task in term of NMI and ARI, and link prediction using AUC and MRR.

Settings. We randomly divide nodes in each dataset into training set, validation set, test set with a ratio of 24:6:70 for node classification task, and randomly extract positive edges from each dataset with a ratio of 81:9:10 for link prediction task. For EulerRewire, we set the hyperparameters according to validation performance: DBLP uses $t = 1000$,

$\alpha = 0.3$, $L = 3$ and $L^{'} = 2$; ACM uses $t = 1500$, $\alpha = 0.5$, $L = 2$ and $L^{'} = 2$; Freebase uses $t = 1000$, $\alpha = 0.3$, $L = 2$ and $L^{'} = 2$; AMiner uses $t = 1000$, $\alpha = 0.4$, $L = 3$ and $L^{'} = 3$. LastFM uses $t = 1500$, $\alpha = 0.3$, $L = 2$ and $L^{'} = 3$. PubMed uses $t = 2000$, $\alpha = 0.2$, $L = 2$ and $L^{'} = 3$. For all datasets, the threshold δ and the embedding dimension d are set to 0.1 and 512, respectively. Under these configurations, EulerRewire achieves its best performance.

5.2 Experimental Results of Node Classification

The experimental results of node classification are reported Table 2, in which OOM means the model runs out of memory. From Table 2, we can observe that EulerRewire outperforms the baselines on most datasets except the ACM, where PHGT is the best and EulerRewire is suboptimal. The reason may be the ACM is denser than other datasets, degrading the performance of EulerRewire which makes the dataset denser by rewiring the graph and introduce more noise. In addition, PHGT needs more memory than other models, leading to running out of memory on the large dataset AMiner.

Table 2. Experimental results of node classification (%).

Model	DBLP		ACM		Freebase		AMiner	
	Mi-F1	Ma-F1	Mi-F1	Ma-F1	Mi-F1	Ma-F1	Mi-F1	Ma-F1
HAN	92.05	91.67	90.79	90.89	61.42	57.05	81.90	64.67
MAGNN	93.76	93.28	90.77	90.88	64.43	58.18	82.64	68.60
HetGNN	92.33	91.76	86.05	85.91	62.99	58.44	72.34	55.42
HetCAN	95.32	94.95	93.20	93.27	67.18	50.58	84.53	75.52
HINormer	94.94	94.57	92.27	92.32	<u>69.42</u>	<u>63.93</u>	<u>88.04</u>	<u>79.88</u>
PHGT	<u>95.33</u>	<u>94.96</u>	**93.72**	**93.79**	68.74	61.73	OOM	OOM
EulerRewire	**95.76**	**95.41**	<u>93.44</u>	<u>93.49</u>	**69.97**	**65.01**	**93.34**	**89.30**

5.3 Experimental Results of Node Clustering

We use k-means algorithm to cluster the node embeddings learned by the models, where k is set to the number of classes of target nodes. We repeat 5 times and report the experimental results of node clustering in Table 3, in which OOM means the model runs out of memory. From Table 3, we can see that EulerRewire is superior to PHGT on most datasets except for the dataset ACM. HetCAN and HINormer are also competitive models. HetCAN leverages a cascading semantic attention mechanism to capture multi-hop heterogeneous semantic dependencies, while HINormer employs a local structural encoder and a heterogeneous relation encoder to capture local structural patterns and semantic similarities, both enhancing the node embeddings.

Table 3. Experimental results of node clustering (%).

Model	DBLP		ACM		Freebase		AMiner	
	NMI	ARI	NMI	ARI	NMI	ARI	NMI	ARI
HAN	78.12	84.76	61.56	64.39	16.38	18.26	35.37	38.29
MAGNN	80.81	85.84	63.41	67.15	20.19	22.61	47.72	52.46
HetGNN	69.79	75.34	41.53	34.81	12.25	15.01	21.46	26.60
HetCAN	82.36	88.03	76.63	80.76	**27.06**	23.07	56.69	72.95
HINormer	81.51	87.31	74.91	79.55	21.71	27.87	59.63	74.86
PHGT	82.07	87.56	**77.21**	**82.25**	21.56	26.94	OOM	OOM
EulerRewire	**82.96**	**88.39**	76.52	81.82	23.26	**29.75**	**75.19**	**87.77**

5.4 Experimental Results of Link Prediction

We report the experimental results of link prediction in Table 4.

Table 4. Experimental results of link prediction (%).

Model	LastFM		PubMed	
	AUC	MRR	AUC	MRR
HAN	57.42	74.29	71.86	88.15
MAGNN	56.81	72.93	70.94	87.92
HetGNN	62.09	83.56	73.63	84.00
HetCAN	67.92	91.78	**83.94**	**92.48**
HINormer	89.05	92.37	82.07	91.18
PHGT	87.46	90.23	81.93	90.08
EulerRewire	**90.37**	**93.79**	82.95	90.86

We can observe that the EulerRewire consistently outperforms all baseline approaches on the LastFM dataset. However, HetCAN is better than EulerRewire on the PubMed dataset. This may result from HetCAN capturing multi-hop heterogeneous semantic dependencies important for link prediction, while EulerRewire focuses on rewiring the graph to improve the connectivity, which gives us a direction for future works.

5.5 Ablation Study

To evaluate the effectiveness of the components in EulerRewire, we conduct an ablation study. We compare EulerRewire with three variants: (1) w/o Euler: removes the Eulerian graph rewiring from EulerRewire; (2) w/o Transformer: removes Transformer encoder from EulerRewire; (3) w/o GCN: removes GCN encoder from EulerRewire.

We report the results in Table 5. We observe that the performance of all three variants drops, implying Eulerian graph rewiring, Transformer encoder and GCN encoder contribute to EulerRewire. Especially, the performance of the variant w/o Euler notably decreases, demonstrating the effectiveness of Eulerian graph rewiring.

Table 5. Ablation study results on the node classification (%).

Model	DBLP	ACM			Freebase		AMiner	
	Mi-F1	Ma-F1	Mi-F1	Ma-F1	Mi-F1	Ma-F1	Mi-F1	Ma-F1
w/o Euler	94.58	94.29	92.27	92.42	68.22	61.34	87.35	77.40
w/o Transformer	95.03	94.91	93.01	93.26	69.12	64.42	92.88	88.01
w/o GCN	95.37	95.00	92.56	92.97	68.78	61.74	88.51	78.94
EulerRewire	**95.76**	**95.41**	**93.44**	**93.49**	**69.97**	**65.01**	**93.34**	**89.30**

5.6 Generalizability of Eulerian Graph Rewiring

To further analyze the generalizability of Eulerian graph rewiring, we apply it to baseline models to evaluate its effectiveness. We use Mi-F1 as the evaluation metric and report the Performance Improvement (PI) of each baseline on the datasets DBLP and AMiner for node classification in Table 6. We can see that Eulerian graph rewiring improves the performances of all the baselines. Especially, on the big and sparse dataset AMiner, the performance improvement of HetGNN is up to 12.56%.

Table 6. PI of baselines with Eulerian graph rewiring for node classification (%).

Model	DBLP			AMiner		
	original	+Euler	PI	original	+Euler	PI
HAN	92.05	93.45	↑1.52%	81.90	87.42	↑6.74%
MAGNN	93.76	94.89	↑1.21%	82.64	90.76	↑9.83%
HetGNN	92.33	93.58	↑1.35%	72.34	81.42	↑12.56%
HetCAN	95.32	95.91	↑0.62%	84.53	88.51	↑4.71%
HINormer	94.94	95.18	↑0.25%	88.04	93.01	↑5.65%
PHGT	95.33	95.68	↑0.37%	OOM	OOM	–

Then, we compare EulerRewire with other graph rewiring methods DropEdge [10], RandAddEdge and TADA [15] by applying them the baseline HINormer, where RandAddEdge randomly adds edges into the graph with a probability of 0.2. The results are shown in Table 7. We can observe that Eulerian graph rewiring outperforms other methods. Similarly, on the big and sparse dataset AMiner, the improvement of Eulerian graph rewiring reaches 5.65% on Mi-F1 and 7.32% on Ma-F1.

Table 7. Results of node classification of HINormer with graph rewiring methods (%).

Model	DBLP				AMiner			
	Mi-F1	PI	Ma-F1	PI	Mi-F1	PI	Ma-F1	PI
HINormer	94.94	–	94.57	–	88.04	–	79.88	–
+DropEdge	94.58	↓0.38%	94.26	↓0.33%	86.98	↓1.20%	77.92	↓2.48%
+RandAddEdge	93.34	↓1.69%	92.23	↓2.47%	86.26	↓2.02%	77.12	↓3.46%
+TADA	95.04	↑0.11%	94.89	↑0.34%	90.89	↑3.24%	83.22	↑4.18%
+Euler	95.18	**↑0.25%**	95.09	**↑0.55%**	93.01	**↑5.65%**	85.73	**↑7.32%**

5.7 Hyperparameter and Efficiency Analysis

We analyze the effect of two main hyperparameters, the number t of node pairs selected in an iteration, and the factor α to balance two kinds of node embeddings from GCN encoder and Transformer encoder. We vary t from 500 to 3000 with the step 500, and report the Mi-F1 and the rewiring times on AMiner in Fig. 2(a). We can see that the Mi-F1 reaches its maximum at $t = 1000$ and then gradually decreases. However, the overall variation across different values of t is not significant. This indicates that the acceleration of the rewiring process has minimal impact on performance of the model. Secondly, we vary α from 0 to 1 with the step 0.1, and report the results of node classification on DBLP in Fig. 2(b). We can observe that EulerRewire achieves the best performance when $\alpha = 0.3$, implying the high-order dependency learned by Transformer is more important than the local structural information learned by GCN.

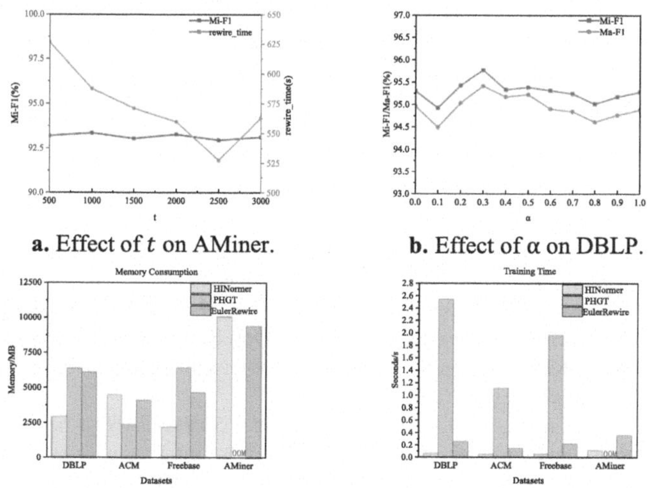

a. Effect of t on AMiner. **b.** Effect of α on DBLP.

c. Memory Consumption. **d.** Training Time.

Fig. 2. Hyperparameter and Efficiency Analysis for node Classification.

Then, we analyze the efficiency of EulerRewire from the perspectives of training time and memory consumption. For memory consumption, we record and analyze the peak memory usage of each model in the training phase. The experimental results are shown in Fig. 2(c). EulerRewire requires less memory than PHGT on the DBLP and Freebase, and even less than HINormer on ACM and AMiner. The reduced resource consumption also facilitates its integration into various baseline models. In terms of training time, we measure and compare the average time per epoch of EulerRewire and two baselines. As shown in Fig. 2(d), EulerRewire requires slightly more training time than HINormer but notably less than PHGT. This is mainly because PHGT employs multiple types of tokens to model local structures, global structures, and semantic relations, resulting in higher computational overhead. In contrast, EulerRewire achieves superior performance compared with PHGT while maintaining lower training costs, demonstrating a better balance between efficiency and effectiveness.

6 Conclusion

In this paper, we investigate the challenges of heterogeneous graph representation learning, particularly regarding the graph connectivity, which has a significant effect on the performance of learning models. Thus, we propose EulerRewire, a novel model that first rewires the graph into an Eulerian graph by utilizing the graph spectral gap to guide edge selection, adding as few edges as possible while enhancing graph connectivity as much as possible. Further, EulerRewire employs a dual-view encoder based on GCN and Transformer to jointly learn node embeddings in the rewired Eulerian graph, in which a circuit sequence is generated for each node in the rewired Eulerian graph, better capturing high-order dependency between nodes. Extensive experiments show EulerRewire achieves superior performance.

Acknowledgement. This work is supported by the National Natural Science Foundation of China (62266050, 62276227, 62306266), the Program for Young and Middle-aged Academic and Technical Reserve Leaders of Yunnan Province (202205 AC160033), Yunnan Province Xingdian Talents Support Program, Yunnan Fundamental Research Projects (202501AT070227).

References

1. Wang, X., et al.: Heterogeneous Graph Attention Network. In: Proceedings of the Web Conference (WWW 2019), pp. 2022–2032. ACM, New York (2019)
2. Lv, Q., et al.: Are we really making much progress? Revisiting, benchmarking, and refining heterogeneous graph neural networks. In: Zhu, F., Ooi, B.-C., Miao, C. (eds.) Proceedings of the 27th ACM SIGKDD Conference on Knowledge Discovery and Data Mining (KDD'21), pp. 1150–1160. ACM, New York (2021)
3. Zhao, Z., Ge, Q., Cheng, A., Liu, Y., Li, X., Wang, S.: HetCAN: a heterogeneous graph Cascade attention network with dual-level awareness. In: Proceedings of ECML-PKDD (2023)
4. Fu, X., Zhang, J., Meng, Z., King, I.: MAGNN: Metapath aggregated graph neural network for heterogeneous graph embedding. In: Proceedings of the ACM the Web Conference (WWW 2020) (2020)

5. Zhang, C., Song, D., Huang, C., Swami, A., Chawla, N.V.: Heterogeneous graph neural network. In: Proceedings of the 25th ACM SIGKDD International Conference on Knowledge Discovery & Data Mining (KDD 2019), pp. 793–803. ACM, New York (2019)
6. Yang, X., Yan, M., Pan, S., Ye, X., Fan, D.: Simple and efficient heterogeneous graph neural network. In: Proceedings of the AAAI Conference on Artificial Intelligence (AAAI 2023) (2023)
7. Vaswani, A., et al.: Attention is all you need. In: Proceedings of the 31st Conference on Neural Information Processing Systems (NeurIPS 2017) (2017)
8. Mao, Q., Liu, Z., Liu, C., Sun, J.: HINormer: representation learning on heterogeneous information networks with graph transformer. In: Proceedings of the Web Conference (WWW'23) (2023)
9. Lu, Z., Fang, Y., Yang, C., Shi, C.: Heterogeneous graph transformer with poly-tokenization. In: Proceedings of the Thirty-Third International Joint Conference on Artificial Intelligence (IJCAI 2024), pp. 2234–2242. International Joint Conferences on Artificial Intelligence Organization (2024)
10. Rong, Y., Huang, W., Xu, T., Huang, J.: DropEdge: towards deep graph convolutional networks on node classification. In: Proceedings of the International Conference on Learning Representations (ICLR 2020) (2020)
11. Barbero, F., Velingker, A., Saberi, A., Bronstein, M., Di Giovanni, F.: Locality-aware graph-rewiring in GNNs. In: Proceedings of the International Conference on Learning Representations (ICLR 2024) (2024)
12. Diestel, R.: Graph Theory, 5th edn. Springer (2017)
13. Xing, Y., Wang, X., Li, Y., Huang, H., Shi, C.: Less is more: on the over-globalizing problem in graph transformers. In: Proceedings of the 41st International Conference on Machine Learning (ICML 2024) (2024)
14. Kipf, T.N., Welling, M.: Semi-supervised classification with graph convolutional networks. In: Proceedings of the 5th International Conference on Learning Representations (ICLR 2017) (2017)
15. Lai, Y., Lin, X., Yang, R., Wang, H.: Efficient topology-aware data augmentation for high-degree graph neural networks. In: Proceedings of the 30th ACM SIGKDD Conference on Knowledge Discovery and Data Mining (KDD 2024), pp. 1463–1473. ACM, New York (2024)

Asymmetric Dynamics Mixup for Robust Neural ODEs

Bochao Zhang(✉) and Manzur Murshed

School of Information Technology, Deakin University, Geelong, VIC 3220, Australia
{s223207183,m.murshed}@deakin.edu.au

Abstract. Neural ordinary differential equations (ODEs) are particularly notable for their continuous modelling of feature transformation. Despite their inherent adversarial robustness over conventional neural networks, Neural ODEs can be sensitive to perturbations in their dynamics and may blow up during integration. This vulnerability comes from a lack of out-of-manifold flows, therefore, manifold mixup as a highly effective technique comes into our crosshairs for Neural ODEs. We start with applying it on state features of Neural ODEs, however, no significant improvement is found. In essence, the nature of Neural ODEs bounds the later generated flows on the same manifold of earlier ones, which seriously jeopardizes the diversity. To solve this problem, we propose an asymmetric dynamics mixup strategy for Neural ODEs to generate controllable out-of-manifold flows. Mixing dynamics can effectively change the evolution of features, forcing them to jump out of the original manifold. More importantly, the asymmetric design can prevent a potential conflict between optimisation targets and the non-intersection property of Neural ODEs. Finally, experiments across different scenarios have shown the effectiveness and compatibility of our method. Its improvement on the vanilla neural ODE on CIFAR-10 under PGD attack accounts for 10%.

Keywords: Neural ODEs · Dynamics · Mixup · Robustness

1 Introduction

Neural ordinary differential equations (ODEs) [4] have been proposed by combining the concepts of deep neural networks and ODEs to continuously model feature transformation. Specifically, the (state) features evolve according to their dynamics (or derivatives) given as the output of the ODE implemented with a neural network. Such a structure can be seen as a generalisation of ResNets, for which the structure of a residual block corresponds to a one-step Euler integration. Through this relationship, Neural ODEs show huge potential in various fields. Specifically, Neural ODEs present better robustness against random Gaussian noise and adversarial attacks in computer vision [21,29]. Furthermore, much research has been conducted to improve the robustness of Neural ODEs. One main category of existing works is to utilise the stability knowledge of control

R. C.-W. Wong et al. (Eds.): PAKDD 2026, LNAI 16617, pp. 522–533, 2027.
https://doi.org/10.1007/978-981-92-1926-1_42

theory [10,11,15,21]. They bound the stability condition with the adversarial robustness to regularise multiple aspects of Neural ODEs. Another category of research upgrades Neural ODEs from perspectives of optimizer [24], stabilising dynamics [29] and dynamics simplification [7].

However, as a newly proposed model architecture, the robustness of Neural ODEs remains underexplored, and their current performance is still far from perfect. Recent studies have shown that they can be sensitive to perturbations in their dynamics [6,10,19]. In particular, even a small but sharp dynamics change can blow up during integration, leading to large deviations in the resulting feature flows. In other words, the learned Neural ODE is very fragile to out-of-manifold samples, motivating us to generate such state features and flows from this perspective. Based on the experience from previous deep learning research, mixup has achieved general success in improving adversarial robustness [32] and generating out-of-manifold features [8]. Therefore, we start with state feature mixup for Neural ODEs. However, due to the nature of Neural ODEs, later synthesised features are on the same manifold of earlier synthesised ones, thus leading to very limited diversity and regularisation effect.

To enable high diversity and the control of new Neural ODE flows, we dig into the dynamics space to generate controllable out-of-manifold flows. Specifically, we choose to mix the dynamics at a random integration time, and the new flow will be guided to the mixed label. Meanwhile, we have spotted a conflict between mixed labels and the non-intersection property. Therefore, an asymmetric mix ratio range has been set to build a preventative boundary to circumvent this conflict and smooth the model convergence. In summary, our contributions are threefold:

- From the perspective of the Neural ODE flows, we found out that the simple application of mixup onto Neural ODEs cannot provide enough out-of-manifold features, and thus cannot gain significant improvement on robustness.
- We propose an asymmetric dynamics mixup strategy to synthesise out-of-manifold flows and, in the meantime, to circumvent the conflict between the optimisation targets and the intrinsic non-intersection property of Neural ODEs.
- Empirical results on various datasets are provided to show the strong competitiveness of our method. The improvement of the PGD attack on CIFAR-10 is significant, accounting for up to 10%. Our method, as a modular component, also improves the performance of existing methods, demonstrating its high applicability and flexibility.

2 Related Work

2.1 NODEs

The study on the robustness of Neural ODEs [4] has always been a popular topic. Studies [2,29] reveal that Neural ODEs enjoy more robustness than conventional neural networks in computer vision tasks. However, when facing adversarial attacks or distributional shift, the inherent robustness exhibited in Neural ODEs is not enough.

Existing literature focusing on the adversarial robustness of Neural ODEs can be divided into two categories. The first category of methods tends to utilise well-developed theories from the perspective of control systems, e.g. Lyapunov theory [12,21] and the standard negative-real-part eigenvalue stability criterion [10,15]. In these methods, the theory-based stability conditions are bounded with the requirement of adversarial robustness. For the second stream of works, researchers rely more on the adaptability of deep neural networks. It is found that constraining the integration time or value can enforce the robustness of Neural ODEs [7,29]. And separate modules for different features in Neural ODEs could also help with generalisation [1].

Currently, Neural ODEs have been widely applied to many scenarios like emotion recognition [22], video captioning [17], medical image analysis [18], modelling chemical reactions [25], etc.

2.2 Mixup

Mixup [31] proposes to linearly interpolate both inputs and their labels for augmentation. It effectively improves the robustness and generalisation of neural networks. Manifold mixup [27] improves model training by blending features at different semantic levels to get smooth decision boundaries. To generate more informative data via mixup, more precise operations are proposed, including mixing patches [30], saliency guidance [26], style control [9], etc. As the analysis of mixup deepens, sample-label mismatch is identified and people try to solve this problem by modelling label uncertainty [20,23] and mixing samples with attention scores [3,16]. On the other hand, the effectiveness of mixup has been explored from different theoretical aspects, including regularised loss minimization [32], midpoint mixup [5] and learning rare features [33].

3 Our Method

In this section, we first introduce key concepts and the calculation pipeline of typical Neural ODEs. Then, we start analysing why state feature mixup in Neural ODEs provides limited improvement. Finally, based on the intrinsic attributes of Neural ODEs, we propose asymmetric mixup on dynamics to generate out-of-manifold feature flows for robustness.

3.1 Preliminaries

In Neural ODEs [4], features (state features) z_t evolve continuously. They follow the rule of a neural-network-parameterised ODE $\dot{z}_t = f_\theta(z_t, t)$, where $\dot{z}_t$ is called the dynamics and θ represents parameters of Neural ODEs. Therefore, state features can be updated by solving Neural ODEs as:

$$z_T = z_0 + \int_0^T f(z_t, t, \theta)\mathrm{d}t, \tag{1}$$

where initial state features start at $t = 0$ and end at $t = T$.

In the state feature space of a Neural ODE, a ***flow*** represents the continuous evolution of a state feature. Starting from an initial state, any later state could be arrived at by integrating the dynamics over time. If f_θ is continuous in t and Lipschitz continuous in z, ***flows generated by distinct initial states do not intersect***.

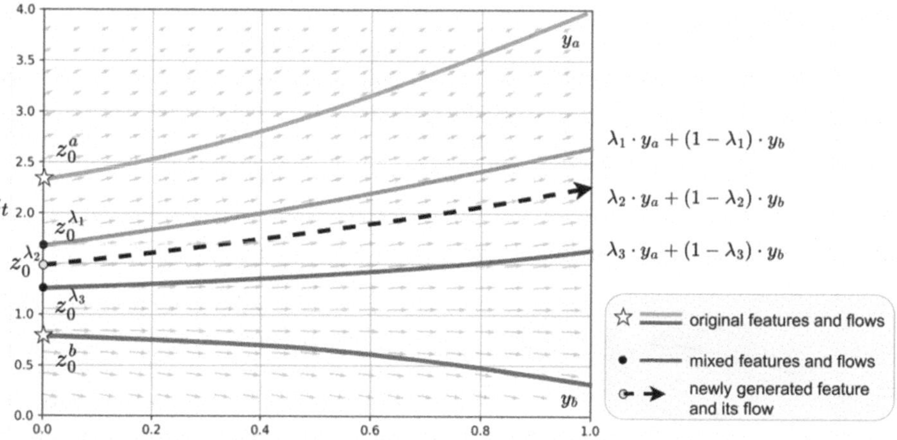

Fig. 1. Illustration of mixed features and flows. As the establishment of mix features and flows, newly generated feature flow is bounded.

3.2 Feature Mixup in Neural ODEs

An ad hoc application of feature mixup onto Neural ODEs is to mix initial state features and their labels. As a widely used strategy, mixup is expected to improve the performance in robustness for the model. However, contrary to expectation, the performance gain of doing so is very limited.

In essence, mixing state features could not create diverse out-of-manifold flows. During the mixing, training on the earlier mixed state features has determined the shape of the Neural ODE. Subsequent mixed features generate flows that lie on the same manifold and could not provide new information for regularisation. Therefore, the effectiveness for better robustness has been undermined.

This could be attributed to the intrinsic nature of Neural ODEs. Indeed, in the state space of Neural ODEs, flows do not intersect with each other. In this case, mixed state features are trained to extend to the corresponding mixed labels. A newly mixed state feature, if surrounded by the earlier mixed ones, will be bounded by them and extend to a destination, surrounded by the destinations of the earlier mixed ones. This comes from the non-intersection property of Neural ODE flows. On the other hand, the destination of the newly mixed state feature also complies with the requirement of mixup. If the destination of the newly mixed state feature is bounded by the destinations of sufficient many earlier ones, it will produce a small enough loss during training.

In Fig. 1, we provide an illustration for better understanding. Two stars represent the original initial states of samples a and b. In-between them are the mixed state features, which are shown with black dots. A newly mixed state feature is shown as a circle, lying in-between two black dots. According to the non-intersection property, the flow generated by the newly mixed feature is bounded by its neighbouring flows. So is the end state feature of the flow. Its value also complies with the requirement of the corresponding mixed label.

In summary, the requirement of subsequent mixed state features is already satisfied by the intrinsic nature of Neural ODEs. In other words, they already lie on the manifold, thus providing no further benefit for robustness. Therefore, generating controllable out-of-manifold features becomes our key direction.

3.3 Asymmetric Dynamics Mixup

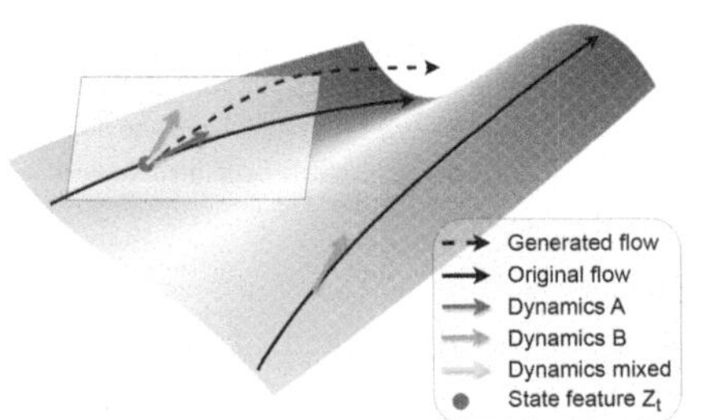

Fig. 2. Illustration of out-of-manifold flow generation. The dynamics from two samples are mixed at a random time during integration and the generated flow can jump out of the manifold with class information mixed.

To solve the above-mentioned challenge, we propose a method to generate out-of-manifold diverse flows to regularise the model. Instead of state features, we choose to perform mixup on dynamics. Firstly, a random timestamp t_m is sampled from the whole integration period and divides the integration into two parts. We solve the first integration with the predefined ODE and achieve the state feature $z^a_{t_m}$ and $z^b_{t_m}$ at time t_m. Next, we mix the dynamics of samples a and b at t_m with different mixup ratios λ_a and λ_b as following:

$$\dot{z}^{a_{mix}}_{t_m} = \lambda^a \cdot \dot{z}^a_{t_m} + (1 - \lambda^a) \cdot \dot{z}^b_{t_m}, \tag{2}$$

$$\dot{z}^{b_{mix}}_{t_m} = \lambda^b \cdot \dot{z}^b_{t_m} + (1 - \lambda^b) \cdot \dot{z}^a_{t_m}, \tag{3}$$

where superscript denotes the source of the feature (dynamics) and the subscript denotes time. Next, we keep finishing the integration of the original state features:

$$z_T^a = z_{t_m}^a + \int_{t_m}^{T} \dot{z}_t^a \mathrm{d}t, \tag{4}$$

$$z_T^b = z_{t_m}^b + \int_{t_m}^{T} \dot{z}_t^b \mathrm{d}t, \tag{5}$$

where at $t = t_m$, $\dot{z}_t^a = \dot{z}_{t_m}^{a_{mix}}$ and $\dot{z}_t^b = \dot{z}_{t_m}^{b_{mix}}$.

It can be noticed that λ and $1-\lambda$ are not the symmetric case of each other, since we stick to the original state features at t_m. This is completely different from the case in state feature mixup in Sect. 3.2. Here, we provide full details in Algorithm 1.

Algorithm 1. Asymmetric dynamics mixup for robust Neural ODEs

Input: initial feature and label pairs of sample a and b: $\{z_0^a, y^a\}$, $\{z_0^b, y^b\}$
Model: Neural ODE layer f_θ, loss function L
Hyperparameter: integration time T, conflict-free ratio range Φ, learning rate α

while *iterationstep* $\leq$ *totalsteps* **do**
  sample a mixup timestamp: $t_m \sim U(0, T)$
  sample mixup ratios for a and b: $\lambda^a \sim U(\Phi)$, $\lambda^b \sim U(\Phi)$
  forward propagate on the first time interval $[0, t_m]$ with an existing ODE solver
  mix the dynamics of z^a and z^b at t_m with Eq. 3
  finish the integration on the second time interval as Eq. 5
  calculate the loss: $L(z_T^a, \lambda^a \cdot y^a + (1-\lambda^a)\cdot y^b)$ and $L(z_T^b, \lambda^b \cdot y^b + (1-\lambda^b)\cdot y^a)$
  update model parameters: $\theta \longleftarrow \theta - \alpha \nabla_\theta L$
end while

Output: f_θ

An important advantage of dynamics mixup is its out-of-manifold diversity of the generated flows. During mixup, the state feature at the mixing time stays the same, and by mixing the dynamics, the following flows will have new courses. This process is also illustrated in Fig. 2, where dynamics of a different sample is borrowed to generate a new flow outside the original manifold surface. At the end, the new flow is guided towards the mixed label.

However, due to the specialty of Neural ODEs, there is a conflict within the optimisation targets. We circumvent such a conflict through a skewed mixup ratio range. Consider a 1D case, where dynamics mixup is carried out for two samples a and b at a random timestamp t_m. In Fig. 3, for sample a, a flow is generated after mixing two dynamics with ratio $\lambda_1^a > 0.5$. Similarly, two flows are generated for sample b with $\lambda_1^b > \lambda_2^b > 0.5$. These flows extend towards their mixed labels, determined by the corresponding λ.

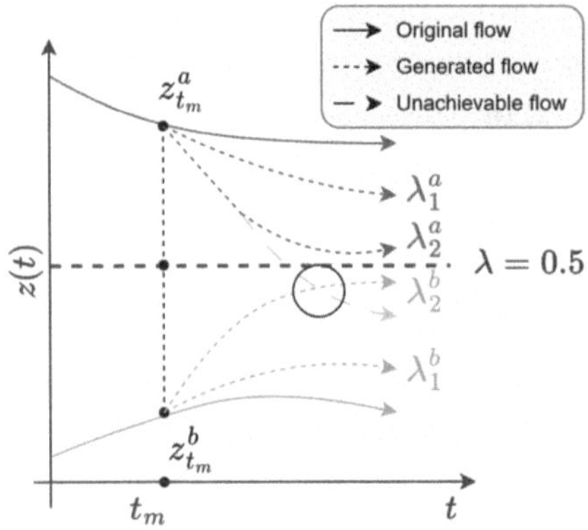

Fig. 3. Illustration of a conflict in dynamics mixup. (Color figure online)

Furthermore, it would be required to intersect with flows generated based on $z^b_{t_m}$. We represent such an imaginative flow with dark yellow. However, due to the non-intersection property of Neural ODEs, the red flow would be the real course the flow takes, which would lead to a suboptimal model. The same case could be found for λ^b.

An efficient way to circumvent such a conflict is to constrain the mixup ratio within $[0.5, 1]$. Thus flows generated based on sample a would be constrained to its own half, and not required to intersect with those based on sample b to reach the mixed labels.

4 Experiments

In this section, we evaluate the robustness of our method on three typical Neural ODEs. Experimental results show that our method can effectively improve the robustness and be compatible with other regularisations. We also validate the influence of optimisation conflicts in trajectory generation via selecting different mixup ratio ranges. Finally, we investigate the impact of applying dynamic mixup at different time intervals

4.1 Experimental Setup

Our method is applied on vanilla Neural ODE (NODE) [4], TisODE [29] and SODEF [10]. Three image classification datasets CIFAR-10 [13], MNIST [14], and FashionMNIST [28] are selected for evaluation. To test the adversarial robustness, we have carried out Fast Gradient Sign Method (FGSM) attack and Projected Gradient Descent (PGD) attack under the ℓ_∞ measure. The iteration number for PGD attack is set as 10. The maximum perturbation threshold is set as $\frac{8}{255}$ if not indicated. We use $\lambda \sim U[0.5, 1]$ and $t_m \sim U[0, 1]$ as a default setting for NODE. We present the accuracy percentage in all tables. For the application of our method on TisODE and SODEF, we have followed the experimental settings of the original papers correspondingly and evaluated them on unified adversarial attacks. In all tables we have reported accuracy percentage.

4.2 Benchmark Empirical Results

Table 1 compares three Neural ODE architectures with adding our method, across original test datasets and two adversarial attacks. Our method can effectively improve the robustness of vanilla Neural ODE on both FGSM and PGD attacks. There are a 5.88% accuracy increase on CIFAR-10, and a 5.03% accuracy increase on Fashion-MNIST. We even achieve an 11.45% improvement on CIFAR-10 with PGD in NODE. This demonstrates that ADM can generate beneficial out-of-manifold trajectories. TisODE and SODEF have contained their specific regularisations, while our method can still provide extra performance improvement. This shows the compatibility of our method with our regularisations. Although our method receives a 0.15% decrease in SODEF on MNIST, we can still observe a general improvement in performance under most settings. Therefore, our method can be used as a drop-in regularisation for Neural ODEs.

Table 1. Comparison of typical Neural ODEs and our method on CIFAR-10, Fashion-MNIST and MNIST under FGSM and PGD attacks.

Dataset	Method	Original	FGSM	PGD	Average
CIFAR-10	NODE	81.94	51.13	24.35	52.47
	NODE + ADM (ours)	81.65	57.61	35.80	58.35 (+5.88)
	TisODE	78.36	18.93	16.28	37.85
	TisODE + ADM (ours)	78.50	21.23	16.22	38.65 (+0.80)
	SODEF	89.21	83.19	82.53	84.97
	SODEF + ADM (ours)	90.88	84.88	83.59	86.45 (+1.48)
Fashion-MNIST	NODE	91.66	52.78	26.39	56.94
	NODE + ADM (ours)	91.50	61.17	33.25	61.97 (+5.03)
	TisODE	92.78	66.55	61.96	73.76
	TisODE + ADM (ours)	92.67	73.89	62.81	76.45 (+2.69)
	SODEF	92.70	73.50	73.41	79.87
	SODEF + ADM (ours)	92.91	80.55	78.71	84.05 (+4.18)
MNIST	NODE	99.53	93.94	93.31	95.59
	NODE + ADM (ours)	99.46	97.20	96.84	97.83 (+2.24)
	TisODE	93.59	99.10	99.05	97.24
	TisODE + ADM (ours)	93.80	99.32	99.22	97.44 (+0.20)
	SODEF	99.39	99.70	99.00	99.36
	SODEF + ADM (ours)	99.47	99.11	99.05	99.21 (−0.15)

4.3 Performance Under FGSM and PGD Attacks

To further analyse the adversarial robustness of our method, we experiment on FashionMNIST with different levels of FGSM and PGD attacks. Larger maximum perturbations (ϵ) usually lead to stronger perturbations. As the results shown in Table 2, our method can improve the robustness for all three levels. For the FGSM attack, we can find that the improvements increase as the attacks become stronger, and a 14.81% enhancement is witnessed on Neural ODE with

$\epsilon = 16/255$. Although the improvements under PGD attacks are smaller, we can still find consistent improvements across all settings. The largest improvement, 12.18% is recorded under NODE with $\epsilon = 16/255$. Overall, our method can produce larger improvements under stronger attacks and can also collaborate with other regularisations.

Table 2. Comparison under FGSM and PGD attacks with different maximum perturbations (ϵ) on FashionMNIST.

Method	FGSM			PGD		
	4/255	8/255	16/255	4/255	8/255	16/255
NODE	57.79	52.78	44.99	39.08	26.39	17.12
NODE + ADM (ours)	61.98	61.17	59.80	41.69	33.25	29.30
TisODE	79.58	66.55	51.19	78.49	61.96	34.33
TisODE + ADM (ours)	81.76	73.89	64.66	79.00	62.81	34.94
SODEF	81.20	73.50	63.50	82.72	73.41	57.70
SODEF + ADM (ours)	85.50	80.55	74.00	83.66	78.71	63.60

4.4 Conflicts in Flow Generation

As discussed in Sect. 3, the full range of mixup ratios would generate flows that have conflicts in optimisation targets and performance decrease is expected. To corroborate our analysis, we investigate the performance of vanilla NODE with three mixup ratio ranges on CIFAR-10 in Table 3.

Table 3. Comparison of different mixup ratio ranges on CIFAR-10 under original and adversarial inputs.

Method	Ratio	Original	FGSM	PGD	Average
NODE	N/A	81.94	51.13	24.35	52.47
NODE+ADM	Conflict-Prone Range [0, 0.5]	38.67	19.57	15.10	24.44 (−28.03)
	Full Range [0, 1]	81.65	55.06	30.16	55.62 (+3.15)
	Conflict-Free Range [0.5, 1]	81.65	57.61	35.80	58.35 (+5.88)

It includes a conflict-prone range [0, 0.5], a full range [0, 1], and a conflict-free range [0.5, 1]. The conflict-prone range shows a huge performance drop because optimisation conflicts train a chaotic model, which should be prevented in the design of any flow generation in Neural ODEs. Compared to the baseline, full range mixup can still provide a 3.15% accuracy improvement, and indicates beneficial mixup operations are more than operations with conflicts.

4.5 Dynamics Mixup Time Selection

The mixup operation time also makes a difference for Neural ODE robustness. Here we investigate three time ranges for mixup time selection in Table 4. Mixing at a later time ($t_m \in [0.5, 1]$) could lead to less regularisation time. And a smaller time range for could lead to a restricted diversity on the generated flows. It can be noticed that mixing at an earlier time ($t_m \in [0, 0.5]$) could allow more time for the out-of-manifold data to take the regularisation effect and thus lead to a more robust NODE model. The full-time range achieves the best performance because it can ensure the enough time for regularisation to take effect and also a better diversity on the generated flows. This also reflects that dynamic abrupt changes can occur at any integration time.

Table 4. Comparison of mixing time ranges on CIFAR-10 under original and adversarial inputs.

Method	Time	Original	FGSM	PGD	Average
NODE	N/A	81.94	51.13	24.35	52.47
NODE+ADM	$t_m \in [0, 1]$	81.65	57.61	35.80	58.35 (+5.88)
	$t_m \in [0, 0.5]$	82.00	56.86	34.40	57.75 (+5.28)
	$t_m \in [0.5, 1]$	81.40	56.35	28.64	55.46 (+2.99)

5 Conclusion

In this paper, we have shown that state feature mixup on Neural ODEs yields limited diversity and gains in robustness, since interpolated features are still on-manifold and can be bounded by their neighbours. Then, we propose asymmetric mixup on dynamics to generate controllable out-of-manifold flows for robustness. Our empirical results demonstrate that the conflicts between synthesised flows can hurt the performance and our asymmetric design prevents this phenomenon during dynamics mixup. Experimental results on three datasets with adversarial attacks have shown the effectiveness on multiple Neural ODEs.

During the exploration of our method, we found that the dimension of time is a double-edged sword and could indulge diverse feature manipulations. In future research on Neural ODEs, time and dynamics awared representation learning for Neural ODEs could serve as a promising research direction.

References

1. Auzina, I.A., Yıldız, Ç., Magliacane, S., Bethge, M., Gavves, E.: Modulated neural odes. Adv. Neural. Inf. Process. Syst. **36**, 44572–44594 (2023)
2. Carrara, F., Caldelli, R., Falchi, F., Amato, G.: On the robustness to adversarial examples of neural ode image classifiers. In: 2019 IEEE International Workshop on Information Forensics and Security (WIFS), pp. 1–6. IEEE (2019)

3. Chen, J.N., Sun, S., He, J., Torr, P.H., Yuille, A., Bai, S.: Transmix: attend to mix for vision transformers. In: Proceedings of the IEEE/CVF Conference on Computer Vision and Pattern Recognition, pp. 12135–12144 (2022)
4. Chen, R.T., Rubanova, Y., Bettencourt, J., Duvenaud, D.K.: Neural ordinary differential equations. Adv. Neural Inf. Process. Syst. **31** (2018)
5. Chidambaram, M., Wang, X., Wu, C., Ge, R.: Provably learning diverse features in multi-view data with midpoint mixup. In: International Conference on Machine Learning, pp. 5563–5599. PMLR (2023)
6. Finlay, C., Jacobsen, J.H., Nurbekyan, L., Oberman, A.: How to train your neural ode: the world of Jacobian and kinetic regularization. In: International Conference on Machine Learning, pp. 3154–3164. PMLR (2020)
7. Ghosh, A., Behl, H., Dupont, E., Torr, P., Namboodiri, V.: Steer: simple temporal regularization for neural ode. Adv. Neural. Inf. Process. Syst. **33**, 14831–14843 (2020)
8. Guo, H., Mao, Y., Zhang, R.: Mixup as locally linear out-of-manifold regularization. In: Proceedings of the AAAI Conference on Artificial Intelligence, vol. 33, pp. 3714–3722 (2019)
9. Hong, M., Choi, J., Kim, G.: Stylemix: separating content and style for enhanced data augmentation. In: Proceedings of the IEEE/CVF Conference on Computer Vision and Pattern Recognition, pp. 14862–14870 (2021)
10. Kang, Q., Song, Y., Ding, Q., Tay, W.P.: Stable neural ode with lyapunov-stable equilibrium points for defending against adversarial attacks. Adv. Neural. Inf. Process. Syst. **34**, 14925–14937 (2021)
11. Kojima, R., Okamoto, Y.: Learning deep input-output stable dynamics. Adv. Neural. Inf. Process. Syst. **35**, 8187–8198 (2022)
12. Kolter, J.Z., Manek, G.: Learning stable deep dynamics models. Adv. Neural Inf. Process. Syst. **32** (2019)
13. Krizhevsky, A., Hinton, G.: Learning multiple layers of features from tiny images (2009)
14. LeCun, Y., Bottou, L., Bengio, Y., Haffner, P.: Gradient-based learning applied to document recognition. Proc. IEEE **86**(11), 2278–2324 (1998)
15. Li, X., Xin, Z., Liu, W.: Defending against adversarial attacks via neural dynamic system. Adv. Neural. Inf. Process. Syst. **35**, 6372–6383 (2022)
16. Liu, J., Liu, B., Zhou, H., Li, H., Liu, Y.: Tokenmix: rethinking image mixing for data augmentation in vision transformers. In: European Conference on Computer Vision, pp. 455–471. Springer (2022)
17. Muksimova, S., Umirzakova, S., Sultanov, M., Im Cho, Y.: Cross-modal transformer-based streaming dense video captioning with neural ode temporal localization. Sensors (Basel, Switzerland) **25**(3), 707 (2025)
18. Niu, H., et al.: On the applications of neural ordinary differential equations in medical image analysis. Artif. Intell. Rev. **57**(9), 236 (2024)
19. Purohit, V.: Ortho-ode: enhancing robustness and of neural odes against adversarial attacks (2023). arXiv preprint arXiv:2305.09179
20. Qin, H., Jin, X., Zhu, H., Liao, H., El-Yacoubi, M.A., Gao, X.: Sumix: mixup with semantic and uncertain information. In: European Conference on Computer Vision, pp. 70–88. Springer (2024)
21. Rodriguez, I.D.J., Ames, A., Yue, Y.: Lyanet: a lyapunov framework for training neural odes. In: International Conference on Machine Learning, pp. 18687–18703. PMLR (2022)

22. Shou, Y., Meng, T., Ai, W., Li, K.: Dynamic graph neural ode network for multimodal emotion recognition in conversation. In: Proceedings of the 31st International Conference on Computational Linguistics, pp. 256–268 (2025)
23. Sun, S., Chen, J.N., He, R., Yuille, A., Torr, P., Bai, S.: Lumix: improving mixup by better modelling label uncertainty (2022). arXiv preprint arXiv:2211.15846
24. Theodoropoulos, P., Liu, G.H., Chen, T., Saravanos, A.D., Theodorou, E.: A robust differential neural ode optimizer. In: The Twelfth International Conference on Learning Representations (2024)
25. Thöni, A.C.M., Robinson, W.E., Bachrach, Y., Huck, W.T.S., Kachman, T.: Modeling chemical reaction networks using neural ordinary differential equations. J. Chem. Inf. Model. **65**(9), 4346–4352 (2025)
26. Uddin, A.F.M.S., Monira, M.S., Shin, W., Chung, T., Bae, S.H.: Saliencymix: a saliency guided data augmentation strategy for better regularization. In: International Conference on Learning Representations (2021)
27. Verma, V., et al.: Manifold mixup: better representations by interpolating hidden states. In: International Conference on Machine Learning, pp. 6438–6447. PMLR (2019)
28. Xiao, H., Rasul, K., Vollgraf, R.: Fashion-mnist: a novel image dataset for benchmarking machine learning algorithms (2017). arXiv preprint arXiv:1708.07747
29. Yan, H., Du, J., Tan, V., Feng, J.: On robustness of neural ordinary differential equations. In: International Conference on Learning Representations (2020)
30. Yun, S., Han, D., Oh, S.J., Chun, S., Choe, J., Yoo, Y.: Cutmix: regularization strategy to train strong classifiers with localizable features. In: Proceedings of the IEEE/CVF International Conference on Computer Vision, pp. 6023–6032 (2019)
31. Zhang, H., Cisse, M., Dauphin, Y.N., Lopez-Paz, D.: Mixup: beyond empirical risk minimization. In: International Conference on Learning Representations (2018)
32. Zhang, L., Deng, Z., Kawaguchi, K., Ghorbani, A., Zou, J.: How does Mixup help with robustness and generalization? In: International Conference on Learning Representations (2021)
33. Zou, D., Cao, Y., Li, Y., Gu, Q.: The benefits of Mixup for feature learning. In: International Conference on Machine Learning, pp. 43423–43479. PMLR (2023)

Domain-Informed Attention Pooling: Abundance-Aware Set Transformers for Robust Representation Learning

Hyunwoo Yoo, Mohammad Saleh Refahi, and Gail L. Rosen(✉)

Drexel University, Philadelphia, PA, USA
{hty23,sr3622,glr26}@drexel.edu

Abstract. Biological and environmental datasets often consist of variable length sets of elements whose quantitative importance is domain-specific, such as microbial sequence abundance. Conventional aggregation strategies like mean pooling or unweighted attention fail to reflect these priors, resulting in unstable or biologically diluted representations. We propose Domain-Informed Attention Pooling, an abundance-aware Set Transformer that integrates quantitative priors into attention weights without modifying the core Transformer architecture. Our method preserves permutation invariance while emphasizing elements proportional to their biological relevance. We evaluate our method on three real-world microbiome classification tasks, namely tumor tissue prediction, pathogenic co-occurrence, and cross-study soil detection. Across these tasks, our method demonstrates consistent performance gains over mean pooling and unweighted Set Transformers, including perfect accuracy in subtle co-occurrence prediction and improved robustness under distributional shift. This study highlights how domain-informed attention mechanisms can generalize beyond microbiomics, offering a scalable framework that exposes attention scores amenable to interpretation for robust set representation learning across heterogeneous data domains.

Keywords: Domain-Informed Attention · Set Transformer · Microbiome Representation · Abundance-Aware Learning · Robust Representation Learning

1 Introduction

Recent advances in large-scale biological and environmental data collection have introduced new challenges for machine-learning models that must process set-structured inputs [9]. Unlike traditional fixed-dimensional feature vectors, each sample in microbiomics or ecology comprises an unordered set of variable-length elements such as nucleotide sequences or taxa whose quantitative importance varies by domain [14]. Transforming these heterogeneous sets into fixed-size, informative representations is critical for downstream tasks such as phenotype prediction, environmental classification, and disease detection [11,17]. These

R. C.-W. Wong et al. (Eds.): PAKDD 2026, LNAI 16617, pp. 534–545, 2027.
https://doi.org/10.1007/978-981-92-1926-1_43

sample-level embeddings not only enable classifier training but also support similarity estimation, clustering, and visualization [28].

Traditional aggregation methods, such as mean or max pooling, are computationally simple but biologically naive. By treating all elements equally, they disregard domain-informed quantitative priors such as microbial sequence abundance that carry functional or ecological meaning [4,30]. This results in unstable or diluted representations, especially when low-abundance yet biologically critical taxa are overwhelmed by irrelevant or redundant ones [24,29]. In microbiome studies, abundance distributions often encode disease progression, environmental perturbation, or community imbalance [11], and failing to incorporate these signals limits robustness and makes it harder to identify which taxa drive model decisions. More broadly, this limitation reflects a fundamental issue in set representation learning under distributional heterogeneity, where domain-specific priors are ignored in favor of purely data-driven weighting.

To address this limitation, we propose Domain-Informed Attention Pooling, an abundance-aware Set Transformer framework that explicitly integrates quantitative priors (e.g., abundance) into attention-based aggregation without modifying the core Transformer architecture. By weighting embeddings according to biologically meaningful priors, our approach improves robustness under distributional shift and exposes abundance-weighted attention scores that are amenable to post hoc biological interpretation across heterogeneous datasets.

We evaluate DIAP on three real-world microbiome datasets spanning clinical, environmental, and cross-study settings, and observe consistent performance gains over mean pooling and unweighted Set Transformers. Beyond microbiomics, our framework offers a general and scalable paradigm for incorporating domain priors into attention mechanisms, bridging domain-aware representation learning with the broader goal of robust set modeling that better supports biological interpretation.

Our main contributions are summarized as follows:

- We introduce Domain-Informed Attention Pooling, an *abundance-aware Set Transformer* that incorporates quantitative domain priors like sequence abundance into attention-based aggregation without altering the core Transformer architecture.
- We demonstrate that integrating biologically meaningful priors improves robustness under distributional heterogeneity and provides abundance-weighted attention scores that can be inspected as candidate drivers of microbiome-level predictions across clinical and environmental datasets.
- Extensive experiments on three real-world datasets show consistent performance gains over conventional pooling and unweighted attention, suggesting a general and scalable framework for robust set representation learning.

2 Related Work

2.1 Pretrained DNA Language Models

Large-scale language models trained on genomic sequences have advanced sequence-level representation learning across various biological tasks [26,27]. DNABERT [8,30] and the Nucleotide Transformer [4,15] employ Transformer-based architectures [23] to embed k-mertokenized DNA sequences, demonstrating strong performance on promoter prediction, splice site detection, and enhancer identification. However, these models primarily operate at the level of individual sequences and do not directly address the challenge of aggregating thousands of such embeddings into a coherent, biologically meaningful *sample-level representation.*

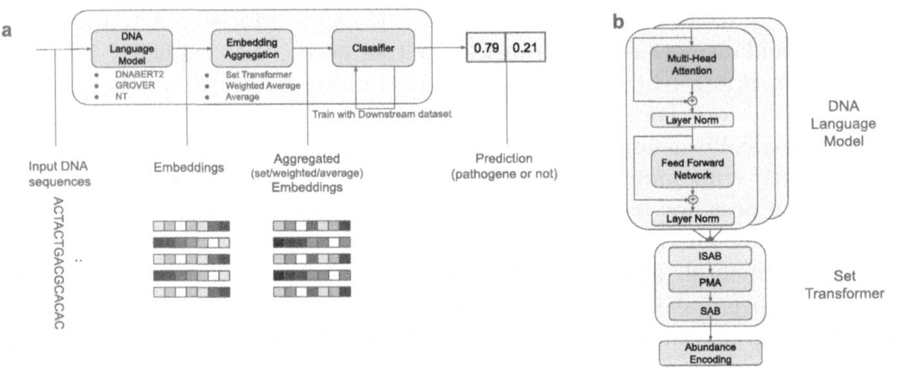

Fig. 1. Overview of the abundance-aware set transformer architecture. (a) End-to-end predictive pipeline in which input DNA sequences are first encoded into contextual embeddings by a DNA language model, then aggregated by an abundance-aware set transformer to produce a fixed-size, weighted representation, and finally passed to a downstream classifier that outputs class probabilities (e.g. pathogen or not). The classifier (a fully-connected neural network or random forest) is trained on a labeled downstream dataset. (b) Abundance-aware Set Transformer architecture, where a DNA language model encoder (stack of multi-head attention, feed-forward networks, and layer normalization) first encodes each sequence into a contextual representation, followed by a Set Transformer comprising ISAB, PMA, and SAB blocks to aggregate sequence embeddings into a fixed-size set representation, and an abundance encoding mechanism that weights the set elements according to their relative sequence abundance before pooling. Specifically, ISAB (Induced Set Attention Block) efficiently reduces computational complexity by introducing a small number of inducing points to capture set-wise interactions, PMA (Pooling by Multihead Attention) uses learnable seed vectors to produce a fixed-size embedding that summarizes the entire set, and SAB (Set Attention Block) refines these representations by modeling self-attention among the pooled set embeddings to capture higher-order relationships.

2.2 Sample-Level Representation Learning

To construct a fixed-size vector for each microbiome sample, simple aggregation functions such as mean or max pooling are often applied over all sequence embeddings [2,10]. While computationally efficient, these pooling operations treat all sequences equally, disregarding crucial biological signals such as taxonomic relevance, ecological function, or sequence abundance. In contrast, attention-based methods have emerged as a powerful alternative for learning *set-structured* representations. The Set Transformer [9] introduced permutation-invariant attention pooling to capture intra-set interactions. Complementary work such as SetBERT [7] pre-trains a Set Transformer on sequencing reads to obtain contextualized sample-level embeddings, whereas DIAP injects observed abundance priors directly into attention weights during supervised sample-level classification. However, in microbiome applications, such attention-based set encoders remain relatively rare [12,20], and most existing approaches ignore abundance or prevalence metadata [25] on the test input, resulting in biologically diluted embeddings.

2.3 Incorporating Abundance in Microbiome Modeling

Abundance information plays a central role in microbiome analysis, reflecting the relative prevalence and ecological importance of taxa within a sample. Traditional bioinformatics workflows (e.g., QIIME2 [3]) and learning-based methods such as DeepMicro [17], MetaML [18], and MicroKPNN-MT [16] integrate abundance profiles and clinical metadata for phenotype prediction using neural or multitask frameworks. Yet, these models typically rely on OTU/ASV-level abundance tables or taxonomic annotations, rather than raw sequence-level embeddings. Other studies attempt to encode abundance indirectly via pseudo-OTU clustering [24] or frequency-based sampling [29], but none directly integrate abundance as a learnable quantitative prior in attention mechanisms. Our work bridges this methodological gap by combining *attention-based set modeling* with the explicit incorporation of domain priors such as sequence abundance, enabling robust and abundance-aware sample-level representations whose attention weights can be inspected for biological interpretation.

3 Methodology

We propose a unified pipeline for constructing abundance-aware microbiome sample embeddings and evaluating their utility in downstream classification tasks. As illustrated in Fig. 1, the framework consists of four main stages: (1) sequence embedding using a pretrained DNA language model, (2) sample-level aggregation via a Domain-Informed Attention Pooling (DIAP) module based on a Set Transformer, (3) dataset construction and labeling, and (4) downstream classification and evaluation.

3.1 Problem Formulation

Each microbiome sample is represented as an unordered set of DNA sequence embeddings $X = \{\mathbf{x}_1, \mathbf{x}_2, \ldots, \mathbf{x}_N\}$, where $\mathbf{x}_i \in \mathbb{R}^d$ denotes the contextual embedding of the i-th sequence extracted from a pretrained DNA language model (e.g., DNABERT-2 [30]). Each sequence is associated with a nonnegative abundance value a_i that reflects its relative prevalence within the sample. The objective is to compute a fixed-size, biologically meaningful representation $\mathbf{z} \in \mathbb{R}^h$ that preserves both the semantic information encoded in $\mathbf{x}_i$ and the quantitative signal carried by a_i.

3.2 Framework Overview

Figure 1(a) summarizes the end-to-end predictive pipeline. Input DNA sequences are first encoded by a DNA language model into contextual embeddings, which are then aggregated by an abundance-aware Set Transformer to yield a weighted sample-level vector. This representation is subsequently passed to a downstream classifier (a fully connected neural network or random forest) trained on labeled microbiome datasets for phenotype or environment prediction.

Figure 1(b) details the Set Transformer backbone, which consists of Induced Set Attention Blocks (ISAB), Pooling by Multihead Attention (PMA), and Set Attention Blocks (SAB). ISAB reduces the quadratic cost of full self-attention by introducing a small set of inducing points to capture global interactions; PMA aggregates the set into a fixed-size embedding via learnable seed vectors; SAB refines the representation through self-attention among pooled embeddings. All components are permutation-invariant, ensuring that the model remains consistent under arbitrary ordering of input sequences.

3.3 Domain-Informed Attention Pooling

Standard Set Transformers compute attention weights purely from pairwise similarity between query and key vectors:

$$\alpha_i = \frac{\exp(\mathbf{q}^\top \mathbf{k}_i/\sqrt{d})}{\sum_{j=1}^{N} \exp(\mathbf{q}^\top \mathbf{k}_j/\sqrt{d})}, \quad \mathbf{z} = \sum_{i=1}^{N} \alpha_i \mathbf{v}_i. \tag{1}$$

This uniform treatment neglects biologically meaningful quantitative priors such as sequence abundance. To address this, we introduce **Domain-Informed Attention Pooling (DIAP)**, which modifies the attention logits with an additive abundance term:

$$\alpha_i^{(\mathrm{DIAP})} = \frac{\exp\left((\mathbf{q}^\top \mathbf{k}_i + \lambda \log(a_i + \epsilon))/\sqrt{d}\right)}{\sum_{j=1}^{N} \exp\left((\mathbf{q}^\top \mathbf{k}_j + \lambda \log(a_j + \epsilon))/\sqrt{d}\right)}, \tag{2}$$

where λ controls the strength of abundance weighting and ϵ prevents numerical instability. This formulation preserves permutation invariance while biasing attention toward more biologically relevant sequences.

The resulting sample representation is:

$$\mathbf{z} = \mathrm{DIAP}(\mathrm{ISAB}_L(\cdots \mathrm{ISAB}_1(X, A))), \tag{3}$$

where $A = \{a_1, \ldots, a_N\}$ denotes the abundance priors. This design allows DIAP to seamlessly integrate with existing pretrained DNA embedding models without additional parameters or structural changes.

3.4 Training and Evaluation

For a labeled dataset $\{(X^{(n)}, y^{(n)})\}_{n=1}^{M}$, we minimize a cross-entropy loss:

$$\mathcal{L} = -\sum_{n=1}^{M}\sum_{c=1}^{C} \mathbb{1}[y^{(n)} = c] \log p_\theta(y^{(n)} = c \mid X^{(n)}, A^{(n)}), \tag{4}$$

where p_θ is the model's predicted probability distribution parameterized by θ. The abundance priors are fixed and non-learnable, while the Set Transformer parameters are optimized end-to-end. We evaluate our model across three microbiome datasets with clinical, environmental, and cross-study, using accuracy, macro precision, recall, and F1-score.

Abundance-Weighted Attention Coefficients. Because abundance directly modulates the attention logits, the resulting coefficients $\alpha_i^{(\mathrm{DIAP})}$ form explicit, abundance-aware weights over sequences or taxa. In principle, these weights can be inspected after training to see which elements receive higher or lower emphasis, although in this work we focus on downstream robustness rather than a detailed analysis of the attention patterns. The method retains $\mathcal{O}(N^2)$ computational complexity, identical to the base Set Transformer, and requires no architectural modification, making it easily extensible to other omics or multimodal set-learning tasks.

4 Experiments

We evaluate the proposed Domain-Informed Attention Pooling (DIAP) framework across three microbiome classification tasks derived from standardized datasets in the Qiita platform [5]. Each task captures a distinct prediction scenario like clinical, environmental, and cross-domain, designed to test the robustness of abundance-aware representations under varying biological and data distribution settings.

4.1 Task 1: Bladder Microbiota Classification

This clinical task is a binary classification problem (tumor vs. non-tumor mucosa) using 116 paired bladder samples, each with roughly 4,000 unique microbial sequences from Qiita Study 14245 [19]. Discriminative taxa often appear at low abundance, making this setting a natural test of whether DIAP can preserve weak but biologically meaningful signals under a high feature-to-sample ratio.

4.2 Task 2: AcanthamoebaLeptospira Co-occurrence Prediction

This environmental task predicts whether free-living amoebae such as *Acanthamoeba* co-occur with pathogenic *Leptospira* in freshwater samples [13]. The dataset from Qiita Study 10442 contains 730 samples (656 positive, 74 negative) after filtering, with each sample represented by hundreds of thousands of sparse microbial sequence features. This highly imbalanced, high-dimensional regime tests DIAP's ability to use abundance-aware aggregation to amplify rare but ecologically important signals associated with pathogen presence.

4.3 Task 3: Soil vs. Non-soil Environment Prediction

The third task addresses cross-domain generalization: we train on 27 marine surface samples (e.g., coral, algae, sponge) from Qiita Study 15573 [6] and evaluate on 17 urban asphalt samples from Qiita Study 1728 [1]. Following the EMPO 3 ontology [21], we treat *Solid (non-saline)* samples as soil (label 1) and all others as non-soil (label 0), creating a small-sample, high-dimensional setting with a pronounced distribution shift between natural and engineered environments. This configuration provides a low-resource testbed for assessing whether DIAP's domain priors can stabilize training under distribution change.

4.4 Dataset Summary

Table 1 summarizes dataset statistics, including sample counts, label distribution, and environmental metadata. All datasets are preprocessed following Qiita's standardized pipelines [5]. For each study, abundance tables were normalized within samples to ensure comparability across different sequencing depths. DNABERT-2 embeddings [30] were computed for all non-zero-abundance sequences.

Table 1. Summary of datasets used across the three tasks.

Study ID	Description	# Samples	# Features	Label 1/0	Sample Type (EMPO 3 or Study Metadata)	Use	Domain
14245	Bladder mucosa (tumor vs. non-tumor)	116	3966	64/52	52 bladder mucosa, 64 tumor tissue (study metadata)	All	Clinical
10442	LeptospiraAmoeba Co-occurrence	730	300176	656/74	Co-occurrence: 0.36 (1), 0.28 (0), 58 N/A excluded (study metadata)	All	Environmental
15573	Marine surfaces (coral/algae)	27	30601	3/24	6 Plant, 17 Animal, 1 Aqueous (saline), 3 Solid (non-saline) (EMPO 3)	Train	Marine
1728	Urban asphalt/water	17	9644	10/7	10 Solid (non-saline), 7 Aqueous (non-saline) (EMPO 3)	Test	Urban

4.5 Experimental Setup

All models use identical DNABERT-2 embeddings as input. We compare four aggregation strategies including Mean Pooling, Weighted Pooling, Set Transformer [9], and DIAP (ours) combined with two downstream classifiers, a 1-layer fully connected neural network and a Random Forest with 100 trees. Models are trained using cross-entropy loss with early stopping on validation F1-score. FCNNs use a 768–128C MLP with ReLU, trained with Adam (learning rate 10^{-3}, batch size 64) for 10 epochs. Random Forests follow the `sklearn` implementation with 100 trees, `class_weight`=`balanced`, and `random_state`=42. For comparison, abundance-only baselines [22] trained on sample-by-taxon tables using Random Forest, logistic regression, and a shallow FCNN.

5 Results

We evaluate the performance of four embedding aggregation strategies such as Average Pooling, Weighted Average Pooling, Set Transformer, and our proposed Domain-Informed Attention Pooling (DIAP), a weighted Set Transformer across three microbiome classification tasks described in Sect. 3. Two downstream classifiers are tested for each task: a Fully Connected Neural Network (FCNN) and a Random Forest (RF). All results are averaged over five runs to reduce sampling variability.

5.1 Task 1: Bladder Microbiota

As shown in Table 2, performance under the FCNN classifier was similar across all methods, suggesting limited network capacity or weak separability in this small clinical dataset (Study 14245). However, the Random Forest results reveal clear improvements when abundance information is incorporated. The proposed DIAP model achieved the highest accuracy and macro F1-score, outperforming simple pooling, unweighted Set Transformer approaches and Abundance-only tabular baselines. This indicates that incorporating quantitative priors (e.g., microbial abundance) can help emphasize biologically informative taxa such as *Actinobacteria* and *Barnesiella*, which often appear at low relative abundance but have strong discriminative value.

Table 2. FCNN classification and Random Forest results on Study 14245.

Embedding Method	Classifier	Accuracy	Macro Precision	Macro Recall	Macro F1
Set Transformer	FCNN	0.5605	0.2803	0.5000	0.3592
Average	FCNN	0.5083	0.2542	0.5000	0.3359
Weighted Average	FCNN	0.5605	0.2803	0.5000	0.3592
DIAP (Weighted Set Transformer)	FCNN	0.5605	0.2803	0.5000	0.3592
Set Transformer	Random Forest	0.4909	0.4671	0.4764	0.4624
Average	Random Forest	0.4565	0.4501	0.4502	0.4485
Weighted Average	Random Forest	0.4649	0.4627	0.4630	0.4589
DIAP (Weighted Set Transformer)	Random Forest	**0.5688**	**0.5589**	**0.5576**	**0.5574**
Abundance Table	FCNN	0.5478	0.2785	0.4846	0.3536
Abundance Table	Random Forest	0.4870	0.4398	0.4515	0.4158
Abundance Table	Logistic Regression	0.4609	0.4687	0.4677	0.4592

5.2 Task 2: Acanthamoeba-Leptospira Co-occurrence

In the environmental co-occurrence task in Study 10442 (Table 3), the proposed DIAP model achieved perfect accuracy and macro F1 (1.0) under both FCNN and Random Forest classifiers. This reflects DIAP's capacity to identify biologically meaningful but sparsely distributed co-occurrence patterns, particularly in imbalanced, high-dimensional datasets. Other methods plateaued between 9295% accuracy and substantially lower F1-scores, indicating difficulty in preserving subtle abundance-driven correlations that DIAP captures effectively.

Table 3. FCNN and Random Forest classification results on Study 10442.

Embedding Method	Classifier	Accuracy	Macro Precision	Macro Recall	Macro F1
Set Transformer	FCNN	0.9200	0.4600	0.5000	0.4792
Average	FCNN	0.9200	0.4600	0.5000	0.4792
Weighted Average	FCNN	0.9200	0.4600	0.5000	0.4792
DIAP (Weighted Set Transformer)	FCNN	**1.0000**	**1.0000**	**1.0000**	**1.0000**
Set Transformer	Random Forest	0.9520	0.8957	0.7457	0.7983
Average	Random Forest	0.9560	0.8779	0.8011	0.8301
Weighted Average	Random Forest	0.9453	0.8752	0.7192	0.7681
DIAP (Weighted Set Transformer)	Random Forest	**1.0000**	**1.0000**	**1.0000**	**1.0000**
Abundance Table	FCNN	0.9400	0.8772	0.6630	0.7145
Abundance Table	Random Forest	0.9467	0.8043	0.9481	0.8564
Abundance Table	Logistic Regression	0.9307	0.7758	0.6960	0.7251

5.3 Task 3: Cross-Study Soil vs. Non-soil Prediction

This cross-domain task evaluates generalization between marine and terrestrial microbiomes (Studies 15573 and 1728). As shown in Table 4, DIAP embeddings improve FCNN accuracy and macro F1 over other sequence-based pooling methods, while a simple abundance-only FCNN baseline achieves similar best scores on this tiny dataset. Random Forest remains uniformly weak across representations, underscoring the difficulty of domain shift with only 27 training samples. Overall accuracy is modest due to data scarcity, but DIAP is the most stable and competitive among embedding-based models under distributional heterogeneity.

Table 4. FCNN and Random Forest classification results on soil vs. non-soil prediction.

Embedding Method	Classifier	Accuracy	Macro Precision	Macro Recall	Macro F1
Set Transformer	FCNN	0.5176	0.2588	0.5000	0.3389
Average	FCNN	0.4824	0.2412	0.5000	0.3231
Weighted Average	FCNN	0.5529	0.2765	0.5000	0.3546
DIAP (Weighted Set Transformer)	FCNN	**0.5882**	**0.2941**	**0.5000**	**0.3704**
Set Transformer	Random Forest	0.4118	0.2059	0.5000	0.2917
Average	Random Forest	0.4118	0.2059	0.5000	0.2917
Weighted Average	Random Forest	0.4118	0.2059	0.5000	0.2917
DIAP (Weighted Set Transformer)	Random Forest	0.4118	0.2059	0.5000	0.2917
Abundance Table	FCNN	**0.5882**	**0.2941**	**0.5000**	**0.3704**
	Random Forest	0.4118	0.2059	0.5000	0.2917
	Logistic Regression	0.4118	0.2059	0.5000	0.2917

6 Conclusion

We introduced **Domain-Informed Attention Pooling (DIAP)**, an abundance-aware Set Transformer that incorporates quantitative priors such as microbial abundance into attention-based aggregation for robust microbiome representations that better support post hoc biological interpretation. On three microbiome classification tasks, DIAP consistently improved performance and robustness to distributional shift over mean pooling and unweighted attention by emphasizing low-abundance but informative taxa. These findings highlight domain-informed attention as a general paradigm for set representation learning that can be extended to multi-modal and cross-omics settings.

Acknowledgements. This work was supported by National Science Foundation (NSF) grant#2107108.

References

1. Ackerman, G., Baum, M.: Baum asphalt 1st submission (baum asphalt study). https://qiita.ucsd.edu/study/description/1728 (2022), qiita Study ID: 1728
2. Arumugam, M., et al.: Enterotypes of the human gut microbiome. Nature **473**, 174–180 (2011). https://doi.org/10.1038/nature09944
3. Bolyen, E., Rideout, J.R., Dillon, M.R., et al.: Reproducible, interactive, scalable and extensible microbiome data science using qiime 2. Nat. Biotechnol. **37**, 852–857 (2019). https://doi.org/10.1038/s41587-019-0209-9 correspondence
4. Dalla-Torre, H., et al.: The nucleotide transformer: Building and evaluating robust foundation models for human genomics. bioRxiv (2023). https://doi.org/10.1101/2023.01.11.523679
5. Gonzalez, A., et al.: Qiita: rapid, web-enabled microbiome meta-analysis. Nat. Methods **15**(10), 796–798 (2018). https://doi.org/10.1038/s41592-024-02523-z
6. Hewson, I.: Detection of the diadema antillarum scuticociliatosis philaster clade on sympatric metazoa, plankton, and abiotic surfaces and assessment for its potential reemergence (dascpc on prevalence marine surfaces). https://qiita.ucsd.edu/study/description/15573 (2024). https://doi.org/10.3354/meps14763, qiita Study ID: 15573
7. II, D.W.L., et al.: Setbert: the deep learning platform for contextualized embeddings and explainable predictions from high-throughput sequencing. Bioinformatics **41**(7), btaf370 (2025). https://doi.org/10.1093/bioinformatics/btaf370
8. Ji, Y., Zhou, Z., Liu, H., Davuluri, R.V.: Dnabert: pre-trained bidirectional encoder representations from transformers model for dna-language in genome. Bioinformatics **37**(15), 2112–2120 (2021). https://doi.org/10.1093/bioinformatics/btab083
9. Lee, J., Lee, Y., Kim, J., Kosiorek, A.R., Choi, S., Teh, Y.W.: Set transformer: a framework for attention-based permutation-invariant neural networks. In: Proceedings of the 36th International Conference on Machine Learning. Proceedings of Machine Learning Research, vol. 97, pp. 3744–3753. PMLR, Long Beach, California, USA (2019). http://proceedings.mlr.press/v97/lee19d.html
10. Lo, C., Marculescu, R.: MetaNN: accurate classification of host phenotypes from metagenomic data using neural networks. BMC Bioinform. **20**(Suppl 12), 314 (2019). https://doi.org/10.1186/s12859-019-2833-2
11. Mandal, S., Van Treuren, W., White, R.A., Eggesbø, M., Knight, R., Peddada, S.D.: Analysis of composition of microbiomes: a novel method for studying microbial composition. Microb. Ecol. Health Dis. **26**, 27663 (2015). https://doi.org/10.3402/mehd.v26.27663

12. Martino, C., et al.: A novel sparse compositional technique reveals microbial perturbations. mSystems **4**(1), e00016–19 (2019). https://doi.org/10.1128/mSystems.00016-19
13. Matthias, M., Lubar, A.: Free-living amoeba reservoirs of pathogenic leptospira (2025). https://qiita.ucsd.edu/study/description/10442 qiita Study ID: 10442
14. Mendler, I.H., Drossel, B., Hütt, M.T.: Microbiome abundance patterns as attractors and the implications for the inference of microbial interaction networks. Phys. A: Stat. Mech. Appli. **639** (2024). https://doi.org/10.48550/arXiv.2306.02100
15. Mendoza-Revilla, J., et al.: A foundational large language model for edible plant genomes. Commun. Biol. **7**, 835 (2024). https://doi.org/10.1038/s42003-024-06465-2
16. Monshizadeh, M., Hong, Y., Ye, Y.: Multitask knowledge-primed neural network for predicting missing metadata and host phenotype based on human microbiome. Bioinform. Adv. **5**(1), vbae203 (2025). https://doi.org/10.1093/bioadv/vbae203
17. Oh, M., Zhang, L.: Deepmicro: deep representation learning for disease prediction based on microbiome data. Sci. Rep. **10**, 6026 (2020). https://doi.org/10.1038/s41598-020-63159-5
18. Pasolli, E., Truong, D.T., Malik, F., Waldron, L., Segata, N.: Machine learning meta-analysis of large metagenomic datasets: tools and biological insights. PLoS Comput. Biol. **12**(7), e1004977 (2016). https://doi.org/10.1371/journal.pcbi.1004977
19. Qiita Study 14245: Bladder microbiota in paired samples of tumor and nontumor mucosa (2021). https://qiita.ucsd.edu/study/description/14245
20. Sankaran, K., Holmes, S.P.: Latent variable modeling for the microbiome. Biostatistics **20**(4), 599–614 (2019). https://doi.org/10.1093/biostatistics/kxy018
21. Thompson, L.R., et al.: A communal catalogue reveals earth's multiscale microbial diversity. Nature **551**, 457–463 (2017). https://doi.org/10.1038/nature24621
22. Topçuoğlu, B.D., Lesniak, N.A., Ruffin, M.T., IV., Wiens, J., Schloss, P.D.: A framework for effective application of machine learning to microbiome-based classification problems. MBio **11**(3), e00434–20 (2020). https://doi.org/10.1128/mBio.00434-20
23. Vaswani, A., et al.: Attention is all you need. In: Proceedings of the 31st International Conference on Neural Information Processing Systems (NeurIPS), pp. 6000–6010 (2017)
24. Woloszynek, S., Zhao, Z., Chen, J., Rosen, G.L.: 16S rRNA sequence embeddings: meaningful numeric feature representations of nucleotide sequences that are convenient for downstream analyses. PLOS Comput. Biol. **15**(2), 1–25 (2019). https://doi.org/10.1371/journal.pcbi.1006721,
25. Yoo, H., Rosen, G.: Interpretable metadata-based microbial risk prediction using large language models. In: Proceedings of the 16th ACM International Conference on Bioinformatics, Computational Biology, and Health Informatics, BCB 2025, pp. 1–10. Association for Computing Machinery, New York (2025). https://doi.org/10.1145/3765612.3767197
26. Yoo, H., Shin, H., Rosen, G., Demner-Fushman, D., Ananiadou, S., Miwa, M.: Can large language models classify and generate antimicrobial resistance genes? In: Tsujii, J. (ed.) Proceedings of the 24th Workshop on Biomedical Language Processing, pp. 240–248. Association for Computational Linguistics, Vienna, Austria (2025). https://doi.org/10.18653/v1/2025.bionlp-1.21
27. Yoo, H., Sokhansanj, B., Brown, J.: Enhancing antimicrobial drug resistance classification by integrating sequence-based and text-based representations. In: Demner-Fushman, D., Ananiadou, S., Miwa, M., Tsujii, J. (eds.) Proceedings of the 24th

Workshop on Biomedical Language Processing, pp. 263–273. Association for Computational Linguistics, Vienna, Austria (2025). https://doi.org/10.18653/v1/2025.bionlp-1.23
28. Zaheer, M., Kottur, S., Ravanbakhsh, S., Poczos, B., Salakhutdinov, R., Smola, A.: Deep sets. In: Proceedings of the 31st International Conference on Neural Information Processing Systems (NeurIPS), pp. 3391–3401 (2017)
29. Zhao, Z., Woloszynek, S., Agbavor, F., Mell, J.C., Sokhansanj, B.A., Rosen, G.L.: Learning, visualizing and exploring 16S rRNA structure using an attention-based deep neural network. PLOS Comput. Biol. **17**(9), 1–36 (2021). https://doi.org/10.1371/journal.pcbi.1009345
30. Zhou, Z., Ji, Y., Li, W., Dutta, P., Davuluri, R., Liu, H.: DNABERT-2: efficient foundation model and benchmark for multi-species genome. arXiv preprint arXiv:2306.15006 (2023)

Machine Learning Performance vs Explanation Quality: Can We Have the Best of Both Worlds?

Véronne Yepmo[1(✉)], Julien Aligon[2], Moncef Garouani[2], André Peninou[1], and Olivier Teste[1]

[1] Université Toulouse Jean Jaurès, UT2J, IRIT, Toulouse, France
{veronne.yepmo-tchaghe,andre.peninou,olivier.teste}@irit.fr
[2] Université Toulouse Capitole, UTC, IRIT, Toulouse, France
{julien.aligon,moncef.garouani}@irit.fr

Abstract. A high predictive performance in a machine learning (ML) model does not necessarily guarantee high-quality explanations. We argue that a balance between model performance and explanatory performance is frequently necessary in practice. In this paper, we highlight the importance of this issue and we address the associated challenges by introducing a multi-objective optimization method. Our approach produces a set of models that offer the best possible balance between performance and interpretability. It explores the Pareto front for each pair of ML performance and explainable artificial intelligence (XAI) quality metrics, then subsequently combines and refines these solutions to achieve an overall optimized balance. Extensive experiments on diverse benchmark datasets demonstrate the effectiveness of our approach in supporting the automated selection of models that maximize both predictive performance and explanation quality.

Keywords: Explainable AI · Machine learning · AutoML · Optimization

1 Introduction

In conventional ML pipelines, model development is predominantly driven by the objective of maximizing predictive performance. Automated Machine Learning (AutoML) [7] has further streamlined this process, automating tasks such as preprocessing, model selection, and hyperparameter (HP) tuning [15] to accelerate deployment and democratize access to ML solutions. Despite these advances, the increasing adoption of ML, particularly in sensitive fields such as healthcare, has revealed a critical limitation of conventional model selection frameworks: they largely overlook explainability. As ML systems increasingly support or automate consequential decisions, the ability to understand and justify their predictions becomes essential.

R. C.-W. Wong et al. (Eds.): PAKDD 2026, LNAI 16617, pp. 546–558, 2027.
https://doi.org/10.1007/978-981-92-1926-1_44

In this context, explainable artificial intelligence (XAI) has emerged as a key paradigm to address these concerns, aiming to ensure that the decisions produced by complex models are transparent, interpretable, and actionable. XAI achieves this by providing methods to generate explanations [13], as well as metrics to assess their quality and reliability [2]. Several studies have emphasized the importance of selecting well-explainable models [5]. However, in most existing approaches, explainability remains a secondary consideration. Models are typically selected based solely on traditional performance metrics, and XAI techniques are applied only afterwards. This sequential strategy assumes that the most accurate model will also provide the most relevant explanations, an assumption that is not guaranteed, as discussed in the following section.

In this paper, we argue that explainability must be integrated as a selection criterion in data analysis workflows, alongside classical objectives such as accuracy and computational efficiency. Considering XAI as an additional optimization dimension transforms the selection of models into a multi-objective problem. We address this challenge through a novel AutoML-inspired strategy that relies on hybrid evaluation metrics to balance predictive effectiveness with explanation quality. Such integration is crucial for advancing responsible AI practices, ensuring regulatory compliance, and fostering user trust and acceptance of AutoML solutions. The main contributions of this work are:

1. An experimental study showing that predictive performance and interpretability do not necessarily align, and that standard optimization approaches do not yield models that jointly maximize performance and explanation quality.
2. A framework for automatically selecting ML models offering the best balance between ML performance and explanation quality.

The remainder of this paper is organized as follows. Section 2 shows that the top performers from an ML perspective are not often the top performers from an explanation quality perspective. Section 3 presents our approach which Sect. 4 validates through extensive experiments. Section 5 presents related works. Section 6 finally concludes this work and introduces some perspectives.

2 The Best ML Models Do Not Produce the Best Explanations

The Pima Indians diabetes dataset[1] is a binary classification dataset containing 768 instances each described by 8 features. Let $\mathbb{A} = \{LR, MLP, RF, SVM\}$ denote the set of ML algorithms considered in this study: Logistic Regression (LR), Multi-Layer Perceptron (MLP) with one hidden layer, Random Forest (RF), and Support Vector Machines (SVM). For each algorithm $\mathcal{A} \in \mathbb{A}$, a grid search is conducted over a range of HP values. The models are trained on a randomly selected 70% subset of the data and evaluated on the remaining 30% test set using accuracy. Each trained model is then explained using

[1] https://www.kaggle.com/datasets/uciml/pima-indians-diabetes-database.

LIME [12] with default hyperparameters. The resulting explanations are assessed using two explanatory performance metrics: robustness [3] and fidelity [16]. Figure 1a reports accuracy versus robustness for all (ML model, XAI method) combinations, while Fig. 1b presents accuracy versus fidelity.

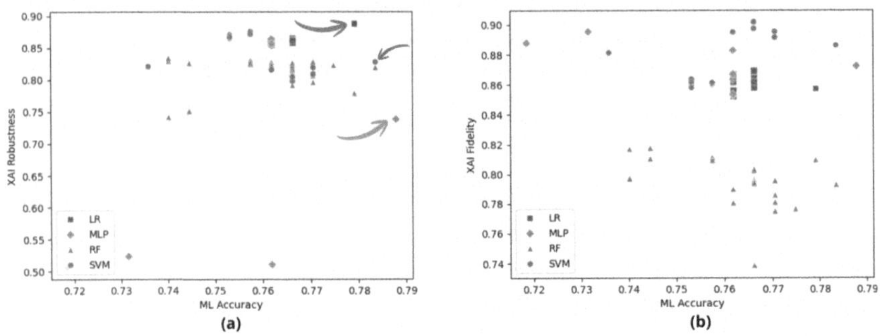

Fig. 1. ML effectiveness vs XAI quality on the Pima Indians dataset. (Color figure online)

From an ML perspective, the top-performing model achieves an accuracy of 0.788 with a robustness of 0.738 (Fig. 1a, orange arrow). However, restricting the analysis to this model overlooks alternative trade-offs: (1) a model with accuracy 0.784 and robustness 0.827 (red arrow), or (2) a model with accuracy 0.779 and robustness 0.888 (blue arrow). In other words, a marginal decrease in accuracy of (i) 0.05% or (ii) 1.14% leads to substantial robustness gains of (i) 12.06% or (ii) 20.33%.

A similar pattern appears in Fig. 1b. The most accurate model attains a fidelity of 0.872, whereas the model with the highest fidelity reaches 0.902 with an accuracy of 0.766. Selecting the latter improves fidelity by 3.4% at the cost of a 2.8% decrease in accuracy. Focusing exclusively on the most accurate model therefore prevents consideration of meaningful trade-offs between predictive performance and explanation quality. Moreover, the best-performing models according to one XAI metric are not necessarily optimal according to another. The set of models obtained when optimizing accuracy and robustness differs from the one obtained when optimizing accuracy and fidelity. Optimizing multiple XAI metrics simultaneously thus leads to a genuine multi-objective optimization problem. Importantly, these observations are not specific to this dataset; similar trends are reported in Sect. 4. There is therefore a clear need for an automated approach capable of identifying optimal trade-offs between predictive effectiveness and explanation quality across multiple objectives.

3 How To Have the Best of Both ML and XAI?

3.1 Problem Statement

Let $\mathcal{D}$ be a dataset. When considering a set of ML algorithms $\mathbb{A}$ performing the same task (e.g., classification) and the hyperparameter space $\mathcal{H}^{ML}$ of the ML algorithms in $\mathbb{A}$, we can build a set $\mathcal{F}$ of ML models by instantiating all the elements in $\mathbb{A}$ with their HPs, on $\mathcal{D}$. When considering a set of XAI algorithms, $\mathbb{E}$, and the HP space $\mathcal{H}^{XAI}$ of the XAI algorithms in $\mathbb{E}$, we can build a set $\mathcal{E}$ of XAI models by instantiating all elements of $\mathbb{E}$ with their HPs, on ML models in $\mathcal{F}$.

Let m^{ML} be an ML metric and $\mathcal{M}^{XAI}$ a set of XAI metrics. The problem is to find a set of solutions $r_i = (f_i, \epsilon_i)$, with $f_i \in \mathcal{F}$ and its corresponding $\epsilon_i \in \mathcal{E}$, that *simultaneously maximises* all the metrics m^{ML} and $\mathcal{M}^{XAI}$. As illustrated in Section 2, this is a multi-objective problem, and maximizing all the metrics at once is not a simple task. As a result, we define a framework to obtain the best compromise between the values of m^{ML} and the metrics in $\mathcal{M}^{XAI}$.

3.2 The PEX Framework Overview

We present our framework, which computes a set of models yielding the best compromise between an ML metric and XAI metrics. Our framework is named **PEX**, which stands for **Pareto for Efficiency and eXplainability**. Figure 2 presents the PEX framework, which comprises three main components.

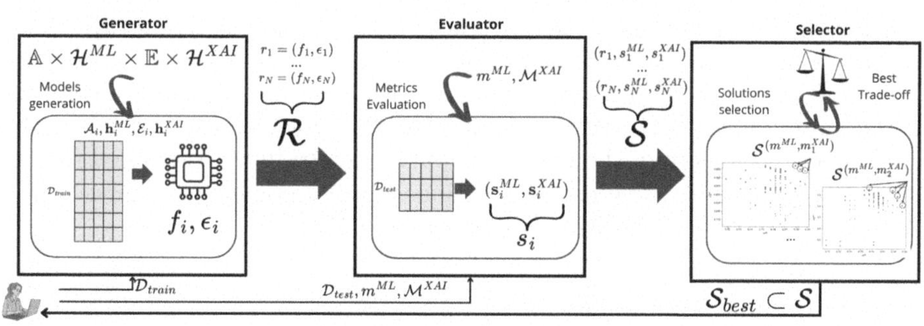

Fig. 2. Overview of PEX.

The Generator. This component is able to iteratively build a set $\mathcal{R} = \{r_i\}$ of ML models f_i and their associated XAI models ϵ_i, under varying values of HPs. Both are trained on $\mathcal{D}_{train} \subset \mathcal{D}$. Any generator can be employed, the only requirement being that it must return a set of r_i ready to be evaluated. In this paper, we propose two generators inspired by AutoML. The *grid generator* selects the next combination in a grid of HP values for ML algorithms, just like a classical grid search in AutoML. The XAI methods in $\mathbb{E}$ are added, which results in a grid search over the $\mathbb{A} \times \mathcal{H}^{ML} \times \mathbb{E} \times \mathcal{H}^{XAI}$ space. The *random generator*, on the other hand, also explores all the ML algorithms in $\mathbb{A}$ and the XAI methods in $\mathbb{E}$, but it randomly selects the values of the HPs.

The Evaluator. This component evaluates the generated solutions r_i on $\mathcal{D}_{test} \subset \mathcal{D}, (\mathcal{D}_{test} \cap \mathcal{D}_{train} = \emptyset)$ according to m^{ML} and each $m^{XAI} \in \mathcal{M}^{XAI}$. It then returns to the Selector a set $\mathcal{S}$ containing each r_i and its corresponding vector of scores $\mathbf{s}_i^{ML}$ and $\mathbf{s}_i^{XAI}$. $\mathbf{s}_i^{ML}$ (resp. $\mathbf{s}_i^{XAI}$) contains the value of m^{ML} (resp. the values of the metrics $m_k^{XAI} \in \mathcal{M}^{XAI}$) for r_i.

The Selector. This component selects the subset $\mathcal{S}_{best} \subset \mathcal{S}$ containing the solutions r_i offering the best trade-off between ML and XAI. Since we are facing a multi-objective optimization problem, we adopt a Pareto-front-based search in the space of metrics. Given two solutions r_i and r_j, r_i (Pareto-)dominates r_j ($r_j \prec r_i$) if and only if there is no metric on which r_j is better than r_i, and there is at least one metric m on which r_i is strictly better than r_j [8]. The Pareto front is the set of non dominated solutions. As the size of $\mathcal{M}^{XAI}$ increases, the number of solutions in the Pareto front, i.e., its size, increases as well, because it becomes easier for a solution to not be dominated by another one.

A large number of Pareto-optimal solutions may be obtained, making the final decision difficult. Moreover, computing a single Pareto front over the entire metric space may implicitly overweight XAI metrics. To address these issues, we introduce a two-level compromise strategy. The Selector first computes the Pareto fronts on two objectives at a time (m^{ML} and one $m_k^{XAI} \in \mathcal{M}^{XAI}$). Each Pareto front is a set $\mathcal{S}^{(m^{ML}, m_k^{XAI})}$ on one pair. This pairwise analysis ensures that all metrics are treated with equal importance. Second, the intersection between all sets is computed to satisfy all pairwise trade-offs. This intersection might be empty when there is no agreement between the individual (ML, XAI) trade-offs. This second level of compromise is thus relaxed. For each metric pair, the current Pareto front is removed, a new front is computed, and the resulting solutions are added to the corresponding set. The intersection is then recomputed. The solutions from the newly computed Pareto fronts are added to each $\mathcal{S}^{(m^{ML}, m^{XAI})}$. This iterative process continues until a non-empty intersection is obtained. The Selector algorithm is illustrated in Fig. 3.

3.3 Complexity Discussion

Beyond classical AutoML complexity of the generators, most of the complexity of our framework comes from (1) the evaluation of the solutions in $\mathcal{R}$ according to $\mathcal{M}^{XAI}$ metrics, and (2) the selection of the solutions S_{best}. The evaluator complexity depends on the ML models, the XAI solutions, and the metrics employed. Regarding the selector, the computation of the individual trade-offs involves sorting a 2D array ($\mathcal{O}(|\mathcal{S}|log(|\mathcal{S}|))$) and finding the non-dominated solutions ($\mathcal{O}(|\mathcal{S}|)$), which is considerably faster than the evaluation stage.

Input : $\mathcal{S}$, m^{ML} (as m_p) and $\mathcal{M}^{XAI}$

Output : $\mathcal{S}_{best}$, the items offering the best trade-off between m^{ML} and $\mathcal{M}^{XAI}$

$\mathcal{S}_{best} \leftarrow \emptyset$;

for $m_q \in \mathcal{M}^{XAI}$ **do**

    $\mathcal{S}^{(m_p,m_q)} \leftarrow ParetoFront(\mathcal{S}, m_p, m_q)$;

end

$\mathcal{S}_{best} \leftarrow \bigcap_{m_q} \mathcal{S}^{(m_p,m_q)}$;

while $\mathcal{S}_{best} = \emptyset$ **do**

    for $m_q \in \mathcal{M}^{XAI}$ **do**

        $\mathcal{S}^{(m_p,m_q)} \leftarrow \mathcal{S}^{(m_p,m_q)} \cup ParetoFront(\mathcal{S} \setminus \mathcal{S}^{(m_p,m_q)}, m_p, m_q)$;

    end

    $\mathcal{S}_{best} \leftarrow \bigcap_{m_q} \mathcal{S}^{(m_p,m_q)}$;

end

Fig. 3. Algorithm of the Selector. The function $ParetoFront(S, m_1, m_2)$ returns the solutions from S which are Pareto-optimal in the space (m_1, m_2).

4 Experiments

In this section, we seek answers to the following questions: **(Q_1)** Does PEX propose solutions offering a suitable compromise between ML performance and explanation quality? **(Q_2)** Does PEX propose a reasonable amount of solutions, in order ease the data scientist's final decision? **(Q_3)** Can PEX be faster, while still proposing solutions offering a suitable compromise between ML and XAI?

4.1 Experimental Setup

Setup. The experimentations focus on the task of tabular data classification. Eight datasets from various fields that are frequently referenced in the literature were selected. Their characteristics are summarized in Table 1. 70% of the dataset is used for training ($\mathcal{D}_{train}$) and 30% for testing ($\mathcal{D}_{test}$). The random seed for the train-test split is set to 27. The source code of PEX is publicly available[2].

The ML algorithms considered are the same as in Sect. 2. We employ as ML metric the accuracy: $m^{ML} = accuracy$[3]. The HPs of each ML algorithm and their respective ranges are the following: (1) for **LR**: $penalty \in \{l_2, None\}$ and $C \in [0.1, 2.2]$ step 0.3, (2) for **MLP (one hidden layer)**: $activation \in \{relu, logistic\}$ and $hidden\_layer\_sizes \in [25, 100]$ step 25, (3) for **RF**: $criterion \in \{gini, entropy\}$ and $n\_estimators \in [10, 120]$ step 10, (4) for **SVM**: $kernel \in \{linear, rbf\}$ and $C \in [0.1, 2.2]$ step 0.3.

We select LIME [12] and SHAP [10] as XAI methods, as they are among the most widely used feature attribution approaches in the literature. Both are model-agnostic, meaning they can be applied to any ML model. We rely on their official Python implementations and use SHAP's *SamplingExplainer*.

[2] https://gitlab.irit.fr/sig/projects/crysemo/pex.

[3] AUC provides similar results.

Table 1. Characteristics of the datasets

Dataset	*#instances*	*#dimensions*	# classes
Breast Cancer Wisconsin	569	30	2
Car Evaluation	1728	6	4
Credit Approval	690	15	2
Glass	214	9	7
Heart Disease	303	13	4
Maternal Health Risk	1014	6	3
Pima Indians Diabetes	768	8	2
Statlog	946	18	4

It is well documented that LIME and SHAP are susceptible to instability due to their reliance on random sampling procedures [4]. Increasing the number of samples generally improves stability but does not alter the underlying explanation mechanism. In other words, the HPs of these XAI methods primarily affect explanation stability rather than the intrinsic behavior of the explainer. This contrasts with ML HPs, which directly influence the learned model and its predictive performance. Consequently, we retain the default HP values for the XAI methods. To assess potential variability in the recommendations, PEX is executed three times.

The quality of explanations is evaluated using established metrics for feature attribution methods. The selected metrics must (i) not require ground-truth explanations, as none are available for our datasets; (ii) avoid user intervention or additional HP tuning; (iii) be formally well-defined; (iv) be applicable to tabular data an all the ML algorithms considered; and (v) capture complementary properties. Metrics designed exclusively for images or deep neural networks are therefore excluded, as are metrics reflecting similar underlying principles (e.g., local Lipschitz estimate [3] and Relative Input Stability (RIS) [1]).

Based on these criteria, we retain four metrics. The *local Lipschitz estimate* (robustness) [3] quantifies the sensitivity of explanations to small input perturbations. *Fidelity* [16] measures the change in prediction when the most important features are perturbed. *Prediction Gap on Unimportant features (PGU)* [6] evaluates the effect of perturbing the least important features. Finally, *Consistency* [6] empirically assesses the stability of explanations for the same input. Each metric is computed at the instance level over $\mathcal{D}_{test}$ and then averaged. This aggregation mitigates per-instance instability and further justifies maintaining the XAI HPs fixed.

Baselines and Evaluation Measures. There is no framework in the literature offering a trade-off between ML performance and explanations quality. As a result, PEX is compared to the classical approach explaining the best ML models. PEX is also compared to the alternative computing the Pareto front in the space of all metrics. We therefore compare the set $\mathcal{S}_{best}$ returned by PEX to (1) the set $\mathcal{S}_{top}$ containing the top ML performers from the set of computed solutions $\mathcal{S}$, and (2) the set $\mathcal{S}_{comp}$ containing the solutions from $\mathcal{S}$ located in the Pareto front computed in the space of all metrics. In order to compare $\mathcal{S}_{best}$ with its competitors, two evaluation criteria are computed. The first criterion is the average number of metrics for which the solutions (in each set) achieve a score greater than or equal to 95% of the maximum score. This maximum score is the highest score achieved on the given metric after the evaluation stage. The intuition behind this criterion is that a solution achieving 95% or more of the maximum score on each metric $m \in \{m^{ML}\} \cup \mathcal{M}^{XAI}$ offers a good balance between ML and XAI, which is the purpose of this work. This criterion therefore provides an answer to Q_1. The second criterion is the number of solutions returned, i.e., the cardinal of each set. This number should be as low as possible to ease the final selection of the data scientist. It provides an answer to Q_2.

4.2 Results

Table 2. Average count of $\geq$ 95% metrics. The higher the better.

Dataset	Grid Generator			Random Generator		
	$\mathcal{S}_{best}$	$\mathcal{S}_{top}$	$\mathcal{S}_{comp}$	$\mathcal{S}_{best}$	$\mathcal{S}_{top}$	$\mathcal{S}_{comp}$
Breast Cancer	3.17 ± 0.24	3.5 ± 0.0	**3.75 ± 0.11**	3.50 ± 0.41	3.53 ± 0.03	**3.83** ± 0.06
Car	**4.0± 0.0**	2.67 ± 0.24	2.65 ± 0.07	2.57 ± 0.78	2.33 ± 0.62	**2.61 ± 0.08**
Credit	**5.0 ± 0.0**	2.99 ± 0.20	3.89 ± 0.11	**5.0 ± 0.0**	2.70 ± 0.25	2.95 ± 0.28
Glass	**4.0 ± 0.0**	1.45 ± 0.07	2.04 ± 0.16	**3.0 ± 0.82**	1.73 ± 0.52	2.10 ± 0.34
Heart	**4.0 ± 0.0**	2.97 ± 0.09	3.10 ± 0.11	**2.78 ± 1.10**	2.5 ± 0.74	2.74 ± 0.23
Maternal HR	1.22 ± 0.31	1.0 ± 0.0	**1.76 ± 0.09**	**1.89 ± 0.16**	1.0 ± 0.0	1.66 ± 0.11
Pima Indians	**5.0 ± 0.0**	2.46 ± 0.16	3.52 ± 0.16	2.67 ± 1.25	1.39 ± 0.28	**3.66 ± 0.16**
Statlog	**2.67 ± 0.47**	**2.67 ± 0.47**	2.32 ± 0.19	**2.53 ± 0.34**	2.29 ± 0.50	2.36 ± 0.23
Average	**3.63**	2.46	2.88	**2.99**	2.18	2.74

We report the mean and standard deviation across three runs. Bold values indicate the best result between $\mathcal{S}_{best}$, $\mathcal{S}_{top}$, and $\mathcal{S}_{comp}$ on each dataset and for each generator. The second best is underlined.

(Q_1) Trade-off Evaluation. All the results are reported after three runs of PEX with each generator. For each dataset, we compare $\mathcal{S}_{best}$, $\mathcal{S}_{top}$, and $\mathcal{S}_{comp}$ based on the average number of metrics where each set's solutions achieve at least 95% of the maximum observed value. The results are reported in Table 2. $\mathcal{S}_{best}$ comes first on six datasets with the grid generator, and five datasets with the random generator. On the *Credit* dataset, $\mathcal{S}_{best}$ achieves the perfect average count of 5, independently of generator. It also achieves the perfect average count on the *Pima Indians* dataset with the grid generator. This means that the solutions returned scored 95% or more of the maximum accuracy, while also scoring 95% or more on each XAI metric. Among the 86 solutions returned by PEX across all the datasets, all the generators and all the runs, 70 solutions even score 95% or more in accuracy. This can be observed in Fig. 4 which shows the minimum, median and maximum accuracy values of the solutions in $\mathcal{S}_{best}$, $\mathcal{S}_{top}$ and $\mathcal{S}_{comp}$. However, on the dataset *Maternal Health Risk*, the average count of every competitor is particularly low (Table 2). Even if some of the solutions in $\mathcal{S}_{best}$ and $\mathcal{S}_{comp}$ score 95% or more in accuracy (Fig. 4), a good compromise on all the metrics is hardly achievable on this dataset. Table 2 also shows that PEX's results are stable with the grid generator, as illustrated by the zero standard deviation on five datasets. Conversely, the random generator obtains less stable results than the grid generator. However, this phenomenon is expected since the ML models generated across the three runs are different, because of the random selection of the HP values.

The median accuracy is represented by a marker (circle: $\mathcal{S}_{best}$, square: $\mathcal{S}_{top}$, triangle: $\mathcal{S}_{comp}$). The min. and max. accuracy for the items in each set are joined by a vertical line. $\mathcal{S}_{best}$, $\mathcal{S}_{top}$ and $\mathcal{S}_{comp}$ are compared on each dataset and for each generator (blue: grid, red: random).

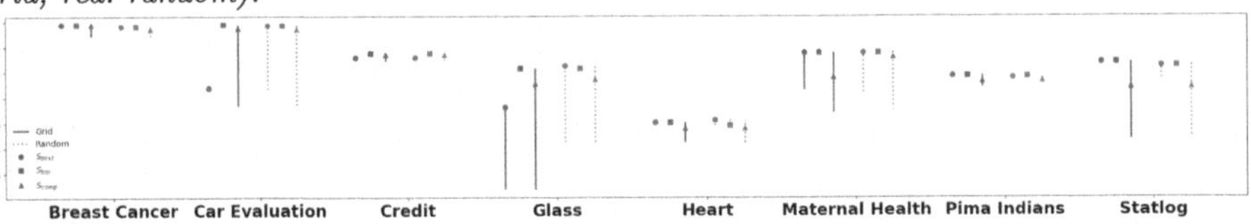

Fig. 4. Accuracy of all the models of the three runs: Minimum, median and maximum values of $\mathcal{S}_{best}$, $\mathcal{S}_{top}$, and $\mathcal{S}_{comp}$. The higher the better.

Table 3. Number of items returned. The lower the better.

Dataset	Grid			Random		
	$\lvert\mathcal{S}_{best}\rvert$	$\lvert\mathcal{S}_{top}\rvert$	$\lvert\mathcal{S}_{comp}\rvert$	$\lvert\mathcal{S}_{best}\rvert$	$\lvert\mathcal{S}_{top}\rvert$	$\lvert\mathcal{S}_{comp}\rvert$
Breast Cancer	**1.3 ± 0.5**	4.0 ± 0.0	49.7 ± 2.1	**1.3 ± 0.47**	21.3 ± 4.9	56.0 ± 0.8
Car	**1.0 ± 0.0**	2.0 ± 0.0	48.0 ± 5.7	4.3 ± 2.6	**2.7 ± 0.9**	52.3 ± 2.1
Credit	**1.0 ± 0.0**	30.0 ± 0.0	30.7 ± 5.3	**1.3 ± 0.5**	28.7 ± 2.5	42.3 ± 8.9
Glass	**1.0 ± 0.0**	14.0 ± 0.0	53.3 ± 2.5	**1.3 ± 0.5**	5.3 ± 3.4	52.0 ± 5.1
Heart Disease	**1.0 ± 0.0**	10.0 ± 0.0	35.3 ± 2.5	**1.7 ± 0.9**	6.0 ± 4.3	36.7 ± 2.5
Maternal Health Risk	2.3 ± 0.5	**2.0 ± 0.0**	51.0 ± 5.9	3.0 ± 0.8	**2.0 ± 0.0**	42.3 ± 11.6
Pima Indians	**1.0 ± 0.0**	8.0 ± 0.0	24.7 ± 3.1	**1.3 ± 0.47**	5.3 ± 2.5	38.3 ± 9.1
Statlog	2.7 ± 0.5	**2.0 ± 0.0**	73.0 ± 4.2	**3.0 ± 0.8**	4.0 ± 2.8	74.7 ± 1.7
Average	**1.4**	9.0	45.7	**2.2**	9.4	49.3

(Q_2) Number of Solutions Returned. We compare $\mathcal{S}_{best}$, $\mathcal{S}_{top}$, and $\mathcal{S}_{comp}$ according to the number of solutions returned. The results are reported in Table 3. $\mathcal{S}_{best}$ contains less items than $\mathcal{S}_{top}$ and $\mathcal{S}_{comp}$ on nearly all the datasets. On average, PEX returns 1.4 models, in contrast to the 9 models of $\mathcal{S}_{top}$. On some datasets such as *Credit Approval* and *Glass*, more than 10 combinations have the same accuracy. This does little to support the data scientist, as there is a broad selection of models to consider. PEX therefore eases the final choice of the data scientist by suggesting a restricted set of options.

In some cases, $Sbest \subset Stop$, indicating that PEX can automatically identify, among the most accurate models, those offering better trade-offs between ML performance and explanation quality. This occurs for the *Breast*, *Glass*, and *Pima Indians* datasets. On the other hand, $\mathcal{S}_{comp}$ systematically contains more than 20 items, with an average of more than 45 items across all datasets. This was predictable, as the related approach tries to find non dominated items in a 5 dimensional space. This makes it harder for the data scientist to reach a final decision. Table 2 showed that $\mathcal{S}_{comp}$ is still able to propose solutions offering a reasonable trade-off between ML and XAI, as the approach always comes second or first, except on the dataset *Glass*. However, $\mathcal{S}_{comp}$ solutions (Pareto front in the whole space of metrics) raise the issue of implicitly giving more weight to the XAI metrics, since there are four of them among the five metrics. $\mathcal{S}_{comp}$ therefore contains several solutions sacrificing a lot of ML performance at the profit of one or several explanation quality metrics. This can be observed in Fig. 4 with the long tails of $\mathcal{S}_{comp}$ below the median value of the accuracy on several datasets. Thus, selecting "good" solutions in $\mathcal{S}_{comp}$ is a hard task since no true trade-off exists in $\mathcal{S}_{comp}$.

(Q_3) Efficiency of PEX. In this section we study the computational cost of PEX. Most of PEX's computational cost comes from the repetitive computation of the explanations on each instance of the whole test set to obtain the values of the XAI metrics. To avoid that, only a randomly selected fraction of instances in the test set is sometimes employed in the literature [4]. We propose to compute the explanations of a *representative* fraction of the instances in the test set, in order to speed up PEX. We choose the representatives as being the prototypes of the test set. Prototypes of the instances in the test set are computed using the *MMD-critic* algorithm [9] with the default HP settings. The percentage of prototypes employed is successively set to 10, 30, 50, 70, and 90 % of $|\mathcal{D}_{test}|$. The computation of the XAI metrics is therefore performed only on the prototypes, and not on the whole test set. This causes a linear reduction of the Evaluator's computational cost. The computation of prototypes is done once, and this cost is minor when compared to explanations computation. Table 4 reports the average number of metrics on which the solutions in $\mathcal{S}_{best\%}$ score 95% or more of the maximum value, for one run of PEX with the grid generator with each percentage of prototypes. Since the goal here is to verify if PEX can produce good results in less time, we compare $\mathcal{S}_{best\%}$ only to $\mathcal{S}_{best}$ and $\mathcal{S}_{top}$. Table 4 shows that, across all datasets, PEX is able to outscore the classical approach of explaining the most accurate models using only slightly more than 30% of prototypes. This indicates that, even by reducing the budget of the Evaluator by approximately 70%, a suitable compromise between ML performance and explanation quality can still be achieved. Moreover, this percentage of prototypes required decreases to 10% if we count metrics scoring 90% or more of the max value.

Table 4. Grid generator. Average count of $\geq$ 95% metrics for each percentage of prototypes. The higher the better.

Dataset	$S_{\text{best}\%}$					S_{best}	S_{top}	# Wins/Ties over S_{top} (/5)
	10%	30%	50%	70%	90%			
Breast Cancer	3	4	4	4	4	4	4	4
Car	2	2	1	2	2	4	2	5
Credit	**5**	**5**	**5**	**5**	**5**	5	3	5
Glass	**3**	**4**	**4**	**4**	**4**	4	2	5
Heart	**4**	**4**	**4**	**4**	**4**	4	3	5
Maternal HR	**2**	1	1	**2**	**2**	1	1	5
Pima Indians	2	1	2	2	2	5	2	4
Statlog	2	2	2	2	2	2	2	5

Bold values indicate a better value for $\mathcal{S}_{best\%}$ in comparison to $\mathcal{S}_{top}$. The last column indicates the number of times $\mathcal{S}_{best\%}$ scored the same as $\mathcal{S}_{top}$ or outscored it.

5 Related Work

The availability of diverse ML algorithms, each relying on different inductive assumptions, has long raised the question of how to select an appropriate model for a given problem. Before the advent of AutoML [7], such selection was performed through manual trial-and-error. AutoML aims to automate the construction of ML pipelines, with hyperparameter optimization (HPO) playing a central role due to its strong impact on predictive performance. Common HPO approaches include grid search, random search, bayesian optimization, evolutionary strategies, and meta-learning [8], all designed to maximize predictive accuracy.

As ML systems are increasingly deployed in sensitive domains, model explainability has become a critical requirement [14]. This has led to the development of numerous XAI methods that differ along several dimensions [13]: model-agnostic vs. model-specific, local vs. global, interpretability-by-design vs. post-hoc, and explanation form (e.g., feature attributions, prototypes, rules, counterfactuals). As a result, the problem of selecting an appropriate XAI method mirrors the original model-selection problem in ML. AutoXAI [5] addresses part of this challenge by recommending, for a given ML model, both an XAI method and corresponding HP values that maximize explanation quality. In contrast to ML evaluation where consensus on performance metrics is relatively strong, explanation quality lacks standardized assessment, and numerous metrics with varying assumptions coexist [11]. Frameworks such as OpenXAI [2] provide structured environments for computing and comparing these metrics, although the broader issue of selecting among explanation families remains open.

While these frameworks provide useful tools for assessing explanation quality, they do not address the relationship between model optimization and explanation quality. AutoML focuses exclusively on identifying the algorithm and HPs that maximize a chosen predictive metric (e.g., accuracy), whereas AutoXAI [5] aims to identify, for a given ML model, the explainer that maximizes explanation quality. In practice, however, these two problems are intrinsically coupled: the choice of the predictive model directly influences the structure, stability, and overall quality of the explanations it can produce. The objective of this work is therefore not merely to recommend a suitable explainer for a given model, but to identify the ML model that simultaneously achieves strong predictive performance and yields high-quality explanations. To the best of our knowledge, no existing approach performs such joint selection of predictive models and explanation methods. In this paper, we address these limitations by introducing a unified framework that jointly optimizes predictive effectiveness and explanation quality within a single selection process.

6 Conclusion

In this work, we investigated the complex relationship between ML effectiveness and explanation quality. We first showed that the best ML models do not necessarily produce the best explanations according to XAI metrics. We then proposed our AutoML-inspired framework, named PEX, which recommends models that offer the best balance between machine learning effectiveness and explanation quality. PEX takes as input a dataset, an ML metric and a set of XAI metrics, and returns the aforementioned models. PEX performs a Pareto-front search on each (ML, XAI) metric pair, and then combines and optimizes the resulting solutions. Our experiments show that PEX returns models with only a marginal accuracy decrease ($< 5\%$) while generally achieving high XAI metric values (close to 95% of the theoretical maximum). The reduction of PEX's runtime was also investigated and PEX is still able to recommend solutions offering a better trade-off in 70% less time. Future work will extend the proposed approach by incorporating other non conflicting XAI metrics. We will also investigate reducing the search space by embedding a joint optimization of ML and XAI metrics into the generator.

Acknowledgments. This work is part of the CRYSEMO Project funded by ANR (Agence Nationale de la Recherche).

Disclosure of Interests. The authors have no competing interests to declare.

References

1. Agarwal, C.: Rethinking stability for attribution-based explanations, arXiv preprint. arXiv:2203.06877 (2022)
2. Agarwal, C.: Openxai: towards a transparent evaluation of post hoc model explanations. In: NeurIPS 2022, pp. 15784–15799 (2022)
3. Alvarez-Melis, D.: On the robustness of interpretability methods, arXiv preprint, arXiv:1806.08049 (2018)
4. Bodria, F., et al.: Benchmarking and survey of explanation methods for black box models. Data Min. Knowl. Disc. **37**(5), 1719–1778 (2023)
5. Cugny, R.: Autoxai: a framework to automatically select the most adapted xai solution. In: CIKM 2022, pp. 315–324 (2022)
6. Dai, J. et al.: Fairness via explanation quality: evaluating disparities in the quality of post hoc explanations. In: Proceedings of the 2022 AAAI/ACM Conference on AI, Ethics, and Society, pp. 203–214 (2022)
7. Garouani, M.: Using meta-learning for automated algorithms selection and configuration: an experimental framework for industrial big data. J. Big Data **9**(1) (2022)
8. Karl, F.: Multi-objective hyperparameter optimization in machine learning-an overview. ACM Trans. Evolut. Learn. Optimizat. (2023)
9. Kim, B.: Examples are not enough, learn to criticize! criticism for interpretability. Adv. Neural. Inf. Process. Syst. **29** (2016)
10. Lundberg, S.M. et al.: A unified approach to interpreting model predictions. In: NIPS 2017, pp. 4768–4777 (2017)
11. Pawlicki, M., et al.: Evaluating the necessity of the multiple metrics for assessing explainable ai: a critical examination. Neurocomputing **602**, 128282 (2024)
12. Ribeiro, M.T. et al.: "why should i trust you?": explaining the predictions of any classifier. In: ICDM 2016, pp. 1135–1144. Association for Computing Machinery (2016)
13. Speith, T.: A review of taxonomies of explainable artificial intelligence (xai) methods. In: FAccT 2022, pp. 2239–2250 (2022)
14. Vermeire, T.: How to choose an explainability method? towards a methodical implementation of xai in practice. In: ECML PKDD 2021, pp. 521–533 (2021)
15. Yang, L., et al.: On hyperparameter optimization of machine learning algorithms: theory and practice. Neurocomputing **415**, 295–316 (2020)
16. Yeh, C.K.: On the (in) fidelity and sensitivity of explanations. Adv. Neural. Inf. Process. Syst. **32** (2019)

MED-YOLO: A Medical Small Target Sperm Detection Framework Based on Cross-Scale Spatial Dynamic Attention

Zhenting Yang[1], Yang Zhao[2], Xin Wang[3], Jihong Pei[1(✉)], Xuan Yang[2], and Jiahui Wu[4]

[1] College of Electronics and Information Engineering, Shenzhen University, Shenzhen 518060, China
2019045026@email.szu.edu.cn, jhpei@szu.edu.cn

[2] College of Computer Science and Software Engineering, Shenzhen University, Shenzhen 518060, China
{zhaoyang1990,yangxuan}@szu.edu.cn

[3] China United Network Communications Group Corporation Limited, Beijing 100006, China

[4] College of Life Sciences and Oceanography, Shenzhen University, Shenzhen 518060, China
wujiahui@szu.edu.cn

Abstract. Accurate detection of microscopic sperm targets remains ch-allenging in clinical reproductive medicine due to their small size, low contrast, and high density. A medical small-target sperm detection framework MED-YOLO, featuring Cross-Scale Spatial Dynamic Attention(CS-DA), is proposed to address the lack of scale interaction in existing attention mechanisms. CSDA integrates Cross-Spatial Learning (CSL) and Dynamic Multi-Branch Channel Attention(DMCA) to improve structural modeling and local focus. Additional optimizations include Space-to-Depth Convolutions, a Small-Target Detection Layer, a Dynamic Detection Head and composite loss function. Validated on public and private clinical datasets, MED-YOLO significantly outperforms YOLOv12. On public data, mAP@0.5:0.95 increased by 8.6%, with precision and recall up by 7.2% and 8.9% respectively. On private data, mAP@0.5:0.95 improved by 10.5%, with precision and recall up by 9.8% and 6.3%.

Keywords: small-target sperm detection · multi-scale attention · feature fusion · YOLOv8

1 Introduction

Male infertility has emerged as a major concern in global public health. Conventional semen analysis relies on manual microscopic examination or Computer-Assisted Sperm Analysis (CASA) [1]. The former suffers from strong subjectivity,

R. C.-W. Wong et al. (Eds.): PAKDD 2026, LNAI 16617, pp. 559–571, 2027.
https://doi.org/10.1007/978-981-92-1926-1_45

while the latter is limited by staining-induced impairment of sperm viability and high equipment cost. Recently, deep learning-based approaches has shown strong performance in the field of object detection [10,13].

YOLO series like YOLOv8 [11], YOLOv10 [13], and the attention-centric YOLOv12 [10] have set new benchmarks for efficiency. However, these general-purpose detectors struggle with sperm targets due to severe feature loss during repeated downsampling. The Transformer architecture has also introduced new paradigms [2,6,12].

Despite YOLO's success in natural scenes, clinical sperm detection remains difficult as repeated downsampling severely depletes minute target details. While YOLOv8-E [15] proposed by Zhang *et al.* employs Multi-Scale Convolutional Attention (MSCA) to extract multi-scale features, it suffers from static aggregation without scale interaction and fixed weighting that neglects dynamic channel modeling, causing small targets to be overwhelmed by background noise. To address these challenges, MED-YOLO, a customized small-target-enhanced detection framework for medical sperm microscopy images is proposed. The core contributions of this work are summarized as follows:

1) **An end-to-end medical small-target detection framework (MED-YOLO) is proposed.** This customized detector integrates Cross-Scale Spatial Dynamic Attention (CSDA)-composed of Cross-Spatial Learning (CSL) and Dynamic Multi-branch Channel Attention (DMCA)-and three small-target-enhanced strategies to mitigate detail loss for microscopic sperm.
2) **A Cross-Space Learning (CSL) module is introduced.** This module enables pairwise cross-dimensional interaction between multi-scale features, achieving synergistic enhancement of long-range structures and local details.
3) **A Dynamic Multi-branch Channel Attention (DMCA) module based on a dual-FC bottleneck structure is designed.** This module adaptively recalibrates channel weights based on multi-scale inputs, effectively enhancing discriminative target features while suppressing background noise.

2 Methodology

2.1 Sperm Small-Target Detection Framework MED-YOLO

As illustrated in Fig. 1, the proposed MED-YOLO builds upon YOLOv8 and integrates a CSDA module along with multiple small-target optimization strategies for precise microscopic sperm localization.

The CSDA module is embedded before the SPPF layer in the backbone network, integrating Cross-Spatial Learning (CSL) and Dynamic Multi-branch Channel Attention (DMCA) to achieve interactive enhancement of multi-scale features for small targets.

For feature preservation, Space-to-Depth Convolution (SPDConv) [8] replaces standard 3×3 convolutions in both backbone and neck. By remapping spatial information into channel dimensions through structured transformation,

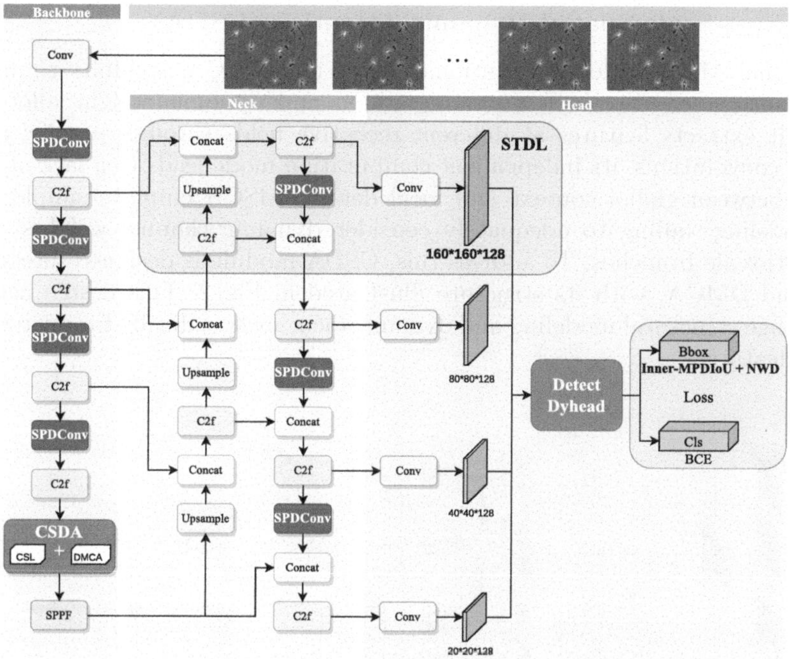

Fig. 1. The overall architecture of the proposed MED-YOLO.

SPDConv effectively retains fine-grained target details and prevents information loss during downsampling.

In the feature fusion stage, a Small-Target Detection Layer (STDL) [17] is introduced. This module adds a 160×160 branch that upsamples intermediate feature maps and concatenates them with high-resolution shallow features. This mechanism leverages shallow spatial details and deep semantic context to mitigate target degradation in deep layers.

Detection head is optimized by Dynamic Detection Head [3]. This attention-based detection head refines feature representation through three synergistic attentions: scale-aware attention fuses multi-scale features, spatial-aware attention focuses on discriminative spatial regions using deformable convolution, and task-aware attention adaptively activates channels for task-specific optimization.

The loss function is improved by combining Normalized Wasserstein Distance (NWD) [14] and Inner-MPDIoU [5] to improve localization accuracy and convergence efficiency. The composite loss eliminates dependence on overlap area and effectively measures similarity for non-overlapping targets, making it suitable for bounding box regression of small sperm targets [16].

2.2 Cross-Scale Spatial Dynamic Attention (CSDA)

Traditional Multi-Scale Convolutional Attention (MSCA) exhibits significant limitations in cross-scale feature interaction and dynamic weight allocation. While it extracts features at different receptive fields through parallel multi-branch convolutions, its independent computation mode leads to a lack of interaction between global context and local details. MSCA employs simple channel modeling, failing to adequately consider dynamic channel weights across its multi-scale branches. To address this, CSDA module is designed integrating CSL and DMCA, with its structure illustrated in Fig. 2. This design achieves long-range structural modeling and dynamic focusing specifically for microscopic sperm features.

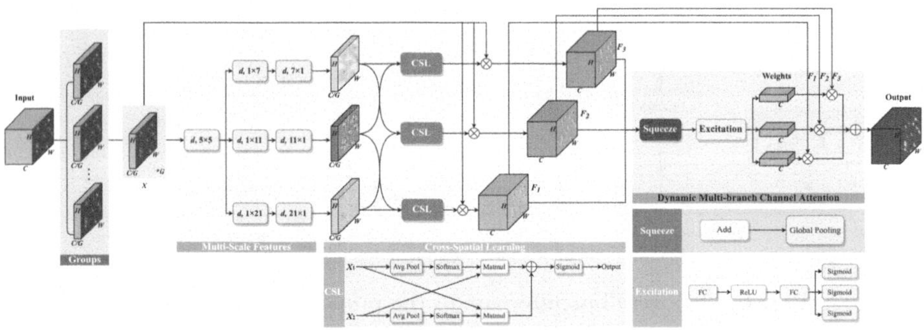

Fig. 2. Architecture of the proposed CSDA.

Specifically, given an input feature map $F \in \mathbb{R}^{C \times H \times W}$, CSDA first partitions the channel dimension into G sub-features. Each group of features is expanded to the batch dimension via a reshape operation, generating grouped features $\{F_g\}_{g=1}^{G} \in \mathbb{R}^{G \times (C/G) \times H \times W}$, where $G \ll C$. This operation effectively reduces computational cost. Each grouped feature subsequently passes through a 5×5 convolution in parallel. Multi-branch depth-wise dilated convolutions are then employed to extract spatial features under different receptive fields. Defining K branches, each branch deploys two depth-wise dilated convolutions to approximate the effect of a standard depth convolution. The output feature of the k-th branch is expressed as:

$$F_k = DWDConv_{m_k \times 1, d_k}(DWDConv_{1 \times m_k, d_k}(F)), \tag{1}$$

where $k = 1, 2, \ldots, K$, $DWDConv_{a \times b, d}(\cdot)$ denotes a depthwise separable dilated convolution with a kernel size of $a \times b$ and a dilation rate of d. The kernel sizes for these branches are set to 7, 11, and 21 respectively. Depth-wise dilated convolutions are adopted based on two considerations: First, the lightweight design significantly reduces computational complexity. Second, dilated convolutions effectively complement grid convolutions, demonstrating unique advantages in capturing strip-like structures such as sperm tails.

Cross-Spatial Learning (CSL). The cross-spatial information aggregation strategy across different spatial dimensions is proposed. As illustrated in Fig. 2, the CSL module employs a bidirectional cross-space interaction mechanism to recode spatial dimensional information of multi-scale features into the channel dimension, enabling dynamic fusion of global and local features. Specifically, CSL takes two scale-space feature maps $\{X_1,\ X_2\} \in \mathbb{R}^{(C/G)\times H\times W}$ as inputs. A 2-D global average pooling (GAP) operation is applied in branch X_1 to encode global spatial information, generating channel descriptor $S_1 = \text{Softmax}(GAP(X_1)) \in \mathbb{R}^{(C/G)\times 1\times 1}$. Similarly, X_2 undergoes GAP and normalization as $S_2 = \text{Softmax}(GAP(X_2))$. Subsequently, S_1 and S_2 undergo a matrix multiplication operation. This performs a weighted summation of features across all channels at each spatial position, yielding a global spatial attention representation $Y_1 \in \mathbb{R}^{1\times H\times W}$ at scale X_1. The representation $Y_2 \in \mathbb{R}^{1\times H\times W}$ at scale X_2 is derived analogously:

$$Y_1 = Matmul(S_1, Reshape(X_2)), \tag{2}$$

$$Y_2 = Matmul(S_2, Reshape(X_1)). \tag{3}$$

Finally, spatial attentions Y_1 and Y_2 are aggregated. A fusion weight $W_{\text{fuse}} \in \mathbb{R}^{1\times H\times W}$ is generated via Sigmoid activation as Eq. (4). This weight recalibrates the original input $X \in \mathbb{R}^{(C/G)\times H\times W}$. After recovering the channel grouping and concatenation, the output of CSL is obtained in equation (5):

$$W_{\text{fuse}} = \text{Sigmoid}(Y_1 + Y_2), \tag{4}$$

$$Out \in \mathbb{R}^{C\times H\times W} = Concat(\{W_{\text{fuse}} \odot X_g\}_{g=1}^{G}). \tag{5}$$

Dynamic Multi-branch Channel Attention (DMCA). The DMCA module based on a dual fully-connected (FC) layer bottleneck structure is designed, as illustrated in Fig. 2. This architecture improves the constraint of single-channel weighting by adaptively enhancing useful channel features and suppressing less informative ones based on input content. It strengthens the ability to focus on discriminative features of small targets and effectively mitigates the problem of false detection caused by noise interference in medical images. Specifically, DMCA receives 3 outputs from the CSL module $\{F_1,\ F_2,\ F_3\} \in \mathbb{R}^{C\times H\times W}$. Firstly, global feature compression (Squeeze) is performed by aggregating 3 branches through element-wise summation. GAP is then applied to the fused feature F to generate a global channel descriptor $S \in \mathbb{R}^{C\times 1\times 1}$:

$$S = \frac{1}{H\times W}\sum_{i=1}^{H}\sum_{j=1}^{W} F[:, i, j]. \tag{6}$$

During the excitation stage, channel interdependencies are modeled using two FC layers. The first FC layer compresses the global channel descriptor into a low-dimensional space:

$$S_d = \delta(W_{\text{down}} \cdot S) \in \mathbb{R}^{(C/r)\times 1\times 1}, \tag{7}$$

where W_{down} denotes the downscaling weight matrix, δ is the ReLU activation function, and r represents the reduction ratio. The second FC layer upscales the channel dimension to $3C$, generating the comprehensive weight W_{dynamic}:

$$W_{\text{dynamic}} = \sigma(W_{\text{up}} \cdot S_d) \in \mathbb{R}^{3C \times 1 \times 1}, \tag{8}$$

where W_{up} is the upscaling weight matrix, σ denotes the Sigmoid function. The vector W_{dynamic} is divided into 3 weight groups $\{w_1, w_2, w_3\} = Split(W_{\text{dynamic}}, 3) \in \mathbb{R}^{C \times 1 \times 1}$. The final output of the CSDA is obtained as Eq. (9):

$$Out_{\text{CSDA}} = \sum_{k=1}^{3} w_k \odot F_k, \tag{9}$$

where w_k is the learned weight, F_k is the input feature map and $\odot$ denotes the channel-wise multiplication.

2.3 Loss Function

This study introduces a composite loss function integrating Normalized Wasserstein Distance (NWD) [14] and Inner-MPDIoU [5] to enhance regression robustness for non-overlapping targets.

$$\mathcal{L} = \lambda \cdot \mathcal{L}_{\text{Inner-MPDIoU}} + (1 - \lambda) \cdot \mathcal{L}_{\text{NWD}}, \tag{10}$$

where λ is a balancing coefficient. The NWD models bounding boxes as two-dimensional Gaussian distributions, which uses the second-order Wasserstein distance to measure distribution similarity. Given a ground truth box $B_{\text{gt}} = (c_x^{\text{gt}}, c_y^{\text{gt}}, w^{\text{gt}}, h^{\text{gt}})$ and a predicted box $B_{\text{pred}} = (c_x^{\text{pred}}, c_y^{\text{pred}}, w^{\text{pred}}, h^{\text{pred}})$, The NWD similarity metric $\mathcal{L}_{\text{NWD}}$ is:

$$\mathcal{L}_{\text{NWD}} = \exp\left(-\frac{\sqrt{\|\mu_{\text{gt}} - \mu_{\text{pred}}\|_2^2 + \|\Sigma_{\text{gt}}^{1/2} - \Sigma_{\text{pred}}^{1/2}\|_F^2}}{C}\right), \tag{11}$$

where C is a normalization constant, the Gaussian distribution parameters is $\mu_{\text{gt}} = [c_x^{\text{gt}}, c_y^{\text{gt}}]^T$, $\mu_{\text{prd}} = [c_x^{\text{pred}}, c_y^{\text{pred}}]^T$, $\Sigma_{\text{gt}} = \frac{1}{4} diag[(w^{\text{gt}})^2, (h^{\text{gt}})^2]$, $\Sigma_{\text{prd}} = \frac{1}{4} diag[(w^{\text{pred}})^2, (h^{\text{pred}})^2]$. NWD loss eliminates dependence on overlap area, effectively measures similarity for non-overlapping targets, making it suitable for bounding box regression of small sperm targets.

MPDIoU loss enhances localization accuracy by jointly optimizing overlap area, center-point distance, and corner-point distances:

$$\mathcal{L}_{\text{Inner-MPDIoU}} = 1 - MPDIoU + (IoU - IoU^{\text{inner}}). \tag{12}$$

MPDIoU is defined based on the Intersection over Union (IoU): $MPDIoU = IoU - (d_1^2 + d_2^2)/(w^2 + h^2)$, where d_1 and d_2 are the Euclidean distances between the top-left and bottom-right corners of the boxes respectively, w and h denote the input image size. IoU^{inner} is defined as:

$$IoU^{\text{inner}} = \frac{Area(B_{\text{pred}}^{\text{inner}} \cap B_{\text{gt}}^{\text{inner}})}{Area(B_{\text{pred}}^{\text{inner}} \cup B_{\text{gt}}^{\text{inner}})}, \tag{13}$$

where $Area(\cdot)$ computes the box area. This focuses feature learning on the target center region and mitigates gradient instability caused by blurred edges of small targets [16] .

3 Experimental Results

3.1 Datasets and Experimental Settings

The public dataset VISEM-Tracking [9] comprises 20 human sperm microscopy videos of 30 s each, totaling 29196 frames at 640×480 resolution. As illustrated in Fig. 3 (a), annotations include 3 classes: Normal sperm (Blue boxes), Sperm clusters (Green boxes), and Pinhead sperm (Red boxes).

The private clinical dataset was provided by a partner hospital's Reproductive Medicine Center. This dataset consists of 50 sperm motion videos, yielding 1,250 frames at 1024×640 resolution. As illustrated in Fig. 3 (b), annotations only focused on normal sperm, with green bounding boxes marking sperm heads while impurities were treated as unlabeled background.

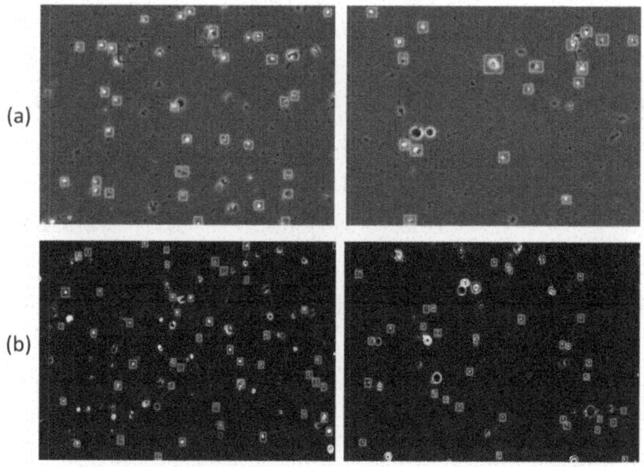

Fig. 3. Video frames in VISEM-Tracking dataset and the private clinical dataset with bounding boxes.

MED-YOLO was implemented using the PyTorch framework, with its backbone network initialized from a pre-trained YOLOv8 model. The SGD optimizer (learning rate 0.01, momentum 0.937) and differential weight decay were employed to preserve model adaptability. Training spanned 200 epochs at

640×640 resolution with a batch size of 16, utilizing Mosaic and MixUp augmentations for the first 190 epochs.

Model performance is evaluated via *precision*, *Recall*, *mAP@0.5:0.95* and *mAP@0.5*, where the former reflects robustness in complex clinical environments. Model complexity is informed by parameter count (Par., in millions) and floating-point operations (FLOPs) to assess deployment feasibility (Table 4).

Table 1. Comparative experiments evaluation of the proposed MED-YOLO

Model	mAP(%) @0.5:0.95	mAP(%) @0.5	Prec. (%)	Rec. (%)	Par. (M)	FLOPs (G)
Faster R-CNN [4]	66.8(±0.70)	88.1(±0.37)	95.1(±0.44)	87.7(±0.55)	28.3	55.9
Deformable-DETR [19]	69.0(±0.67)	97.3(±0.27)	97.4(±0.36)	**97.5**(±0.33)	40.1	60.3
RT-DETR [18]	65.1(±0.32)	96.4(±0.75)	94.7(±1.46)	94.3(±0.64)	66.2	108.0
YOLOv8-E [15]	77.4(±0.32)	97.5(±1.33)	98.0(±0.51)	96.2(±0.83)	11.2	24.2
YOLOv11 [7]	68.6(±0.38)	91.2(±0.44)	93.3(±0.70)	86.2(±0.84)	**5.3**	6.6
YOLOv12 [10]	74.0(±0.46)	94.8(±0.13)	97.4(±0.23)	91.3(±0.21)	5.4	**6.0**
MED-YOLO (Ours)	**79.2**(±1.07)	**98.8**(±0.13)	**98.6**(±0.12)	95.8(±0.46)	24.6	40.3

Table 2. Ablation study of MED-YOLO on VISEM-Tracking dataset

Configuration	mAP(%) @0.5:0.95	mAP(%) @0.5	Prec. (%)	Rec. (%)	Par. (M)	FLOPs (G)
Baseline (YOLOv8)	67.6	90.9	93.7	86.3	**6.3**	**8.2**
+ SPDConv	70.7 (+3.1)	91.6	94.7	87.5	9.3	11.7
+ CSDA	74.9 (+4.2)	95.1	97.2	91.3	23.2	26.8
+ STDL	76.3 (+1.4)	96.9	97.7	92.9	23.6	32.6
+ DDH	77.8 (+1.5)	98.6	98.4	**96.1**	24.6	40.3
+ Inner-MPDIoU/NWD	**79.2** (+1.4)	**98.8**	**98.6**	95.8	24.6	40.3

3.2 Comparative Experiments

To evaluate the performance of MED-YOLO, comparative experiments were conducted on the public VISEM-Tracking dataset against state-of-the-art object detection models, including classical frameworks (Faster R-CNN [4], Deformable DETR [19], RT-DETR [18]) and advanced YOLO-based models (YOLOv8-E [15], YOLOv11 [7], YOLOv12 [10]).

Table 1 confirms MED-YOLO's superior performance for sperm small-target detection. It significantly outperforms both CNN-based models and transformer

Table 3. Ablation study evaluation of the proposed CSDA

Configuration	mAP@0.5:0.95	mAP@0.5	Prec.	Rec.
Baseline	70.7	91.6	94.7	87.5
+ CSL only	70.4 (–0.3)	92.9	96.1	89.1
+ DMCA only	61.2 (–9.5)	92.2	95.9	87.8
+ CSDA (CSL+DMCA)	**74.9** (+4.2)	**95.1**	**97.2**	**91.3**

Note: All metrics in percentage (%).
Baseline: YOLOv8 with SPDConv enhancement.

Table 4. Ablation study of MED-YOLO on the private sperm dataset

Configuration	mAP(%) @0.5:0.95	mAP(%) @0.5	Prec. (%)	Rec. (%)	Par. (M)	FLOPs (G)
Baseline (YOLOv8)	64.3	95.8	89.0	91.9	**6.3**	**8.2**
+ SPDConv	67.4 (+3.1)	97.2	92.7	93.5	9.3	11.7
+ CSDA	71.9 (+4.5)	98.3	96.3	95.0	23.2	26.8
+ STDL	75.8 (+3.9)	**99.1**	**98.2**	**96.4**	23.6	32.6
+ DDH	76.2 (+0.4)	99.1	98.1	96.4	24.6	40.3
+ Inner-MPDIoU/NWD	**76.3** (+0.1)	98.8	96.5	95.5	24.6	40.3

architectures, while surpassing all YOLO variants including YOLOv12. Compared to the specialized YOLOv8-E, MED-YOLO achieves higher detection precision with competitive overall accuracy, demonstrating robust potential for clinical high-precision requirements.

These improvements stem from MED-YOLO's targeted design: the CSDA module strengthens long-range structural modeling and local focus; SPDConv and STDL enhance feature preservation and shallow feature utilization; the Dynamic Detection Head and composite loss (Inner-MPDIoU/NWD) optimize feature allocation and localization accuracy. Despite higher complexity than lightweight models like YOLOv11, the significant accuracy gains are more critical for medical microscopy scenarios.

3.3 Ablation Study

To evaluate the contributions of each enhancement module in MED-YOLO, an ablation study was conducted on the VISEM-Tracking dataset. Starting from the baseline YOLOv8, modules were incrementally integrated: SPDConv, CSDA, STDL, Dynamic Detection Head (DDH), and Inner-MPDIoU/NWD.

Table 2 demonstrates the synergistic effects of these modules. Replacing standard downsampling with SPDConv improved fine-grained feature preservation. CSDA integration further boosted performance, effectively enhancing features and reducing false positives. STDL validated the importance of shallow-deep feature fusion, while DDH optimized classification and regression through scale-spatial-task awareness. Finally, the Inner-MPDIoU/NWD loss achieved optimal precision and convergence efficiency despite a minor recall trade-off.

Table 3 highlights the interdependency within CSDA: CSL enriches spatial interactions, while DMCA amplifies critical channels. Their joint implementation significantly outperforms isolated usage, confirming the necessity of synergistic design for small-target modeling. To evaluate generalizability, the ablation was replicated on the private sperm dataset (1024×640). As shown in Table 4, MED-YOLO consistently achieves superior performance, with precision and recall exceeding 95%. These consistent trends across datasets validate the framework's robustness for diverse clinical imaging scenarios.

3.4 Visualization Analysis

To validate the effectiveness of the CSDA module, this study employed the Grad-CAM++ method to generate heatmaps visualizing the response regions of the CSDA output feature maps relative to the original images.

Figure 4 compares heatmaps generated from Layer 9 (the CSDA output layer) of the backbone network in YOLOv8 and MED-YOLO. The MED-YOLO exhibits more concentrated and intense feature responses in critical sperm head regions, particularly showing superior performance in detecting sperm small targets.

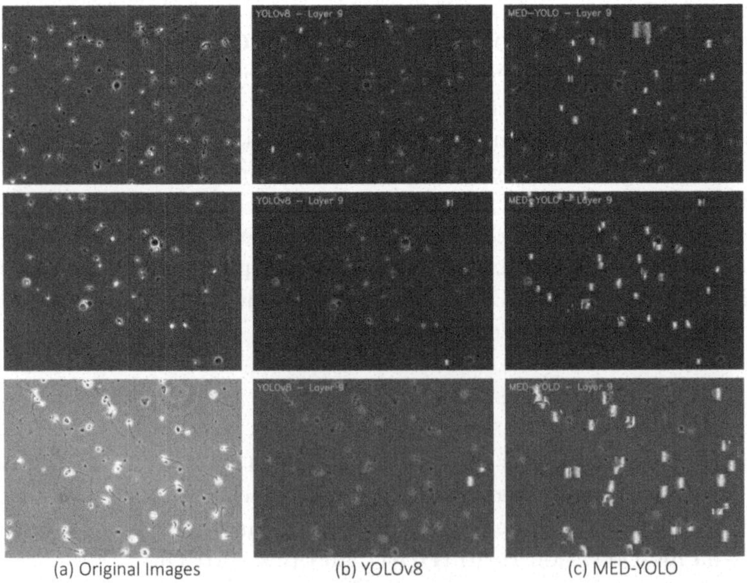

Fig. 4. Visualization heatmaps evaluation of MED-YOLO: (a) Original images; (b) GradCAM++ responses of YOLOv8; (c) GradCAM++ responses of MED-YOLO.

Figure 5 compares detection results across dense, complex, and low-contrast scenarios. Green boxes denote correct predictions, red boxes indicate missed detections, and blue boxes represent false positives. Compared to YOLOv8, MED-YOLO significantly reduces missed detections (red boxes) and false positives (blue boxes), while accurately distinguishing individual cells in dense clusters. Its enhanced recognition is particularly evident in low-contrast samples as in Fig. 5(f).

Figure 6 quantifies these improvements via size distribution histograms. For true positives (TP), MED-YOLO identifies substantially more small targets (0–1000 pixels) than YOLOv8. It also drastically suppresses errors in the false negative (FN) and false positive (FP) distributions for small targets. These quantitative results align with our visual observations, confirming MED-YOLO's superiority in microscopic sperm detection.

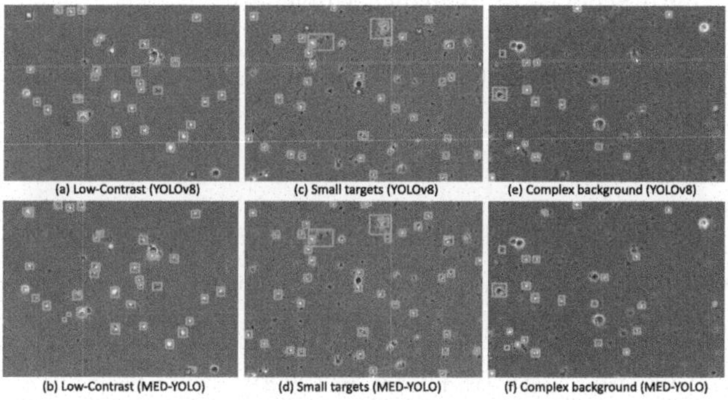

Fig. 5. Visualized detection results.

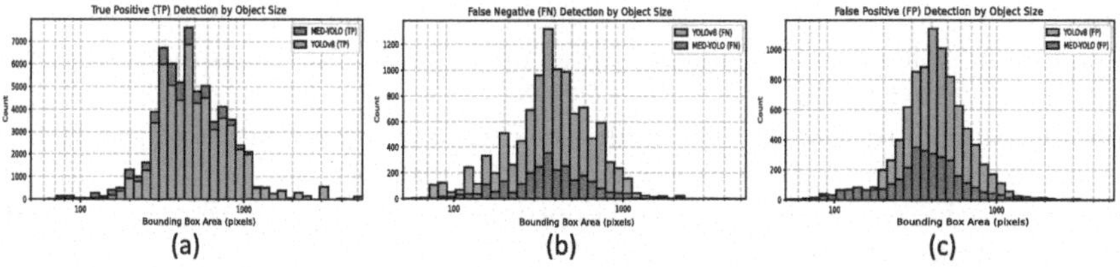

Fig. 6. Detection Histogram of Target Sizes (Bounding box areas): (a) True Positives (TP); (b) False Negatives (FN); (c) False Positives (FP).

4 Conclusion

In this paper, a small-target enhancement detection framework MED-YOLO is proposed to address the challenges of small size (5–9 pixels), inconspicuous features, and dense distribution faced by sperm detection in medical microscopy images. The core innovation of the framework lies in the design of a cross-scale spatial dynamic attention module (CSDA). CSDA effectively improves the defects of existing multi-scale attention mechanisms that lack feature interaction and dynamic weight allocation. The designed small target enhancement strategy can preserve detailed information during the downsampling process, enhance the utilization of shallow features, and optimize multi-scale feature allocation. The optimized loss function enhances localization accuracy and accelerates model convergence. Comparative experiments on the public dataset VISEM-Tracking show that MED-YOLO significantly outperforms the latest baseline YOLOv12 in mAP@0.5:0.95 (5.2% improvement), while also improving precision and recall by 5.3% and 8.1% respectively.

Acknowledgments. This work was supported in part by the Guangdong Basic and Applied Basic Research Foundation (2024A1515010977, 2025A1515060013), Scientific Foundation for Youth Scholars of Shenzhen University.

Disclosure of Interests. The authors have no competing interests to declare that are relevant to the content of this article.

References

1. Abou Ghayda, R., et al.: Artificial intelligence in andrology: from semen analysis to image diagnostics. World J. Men's Health **42**(1), 39 (2023)
2. Carion, N., Massa, F., Synnaeve, G., Usunier, N., Kirillov, A., Zagoruyko, S.: End-to-end object detection with transformers (2020)
3. Dai, X., et al.: Dynamic head: unifying object detection heads with attentions. In: Proceedings of the IEEE/CVF Conference on Computer Vision and Pattern Recognition, pp. 7373–7382 (2021)
4. Girshick, R.: Fast r-cnn. In: Proceedings of the IEEE International Conference on Computer Vision, pp. 1440–1448 (2015)
5. Hu, M., Liu, J., Liu, J.: Drr-yolo: a study of small target multi-modal defect detection for multiple types of insulators based on large convolution kernel. IEEE Access **13**, 26331–26344 (2025)
6. Liu, F., et al.: Rethinking the multi-scale feature hierarchy in object detection transformer (detr). Appl. Soft Comput. **175**, 113081 (2025)
7. Rasheed, A.F., Zarkoosh, M.: Yolov11 optimization for efficient resource utilization. J. Supercomput. **81**(9), 1–21 (2025)
8. Sunkara, R., Luo, T.: No more strided convolutions or pooling: a new cnn building block for low-resolution images and small objects (2022)
9. Thambawita, V., et al.: Visem-tracking, a human spermatozoa tracking dataset. Sci. Data **10**(1), 260 (2023)
10. Tian, Y., Ye, Q., Doermann, D.: Yolov12: Attention-centric real-time object detectors, arXiv preprint arXiv:2502.12524 (2025)
11. Varghese, R., Sambath, M.: Yolov8: a novel object detection algorithm with enhanced performance and robustness. In: 2024 International Conference on Advances in Data Engineering And Intelligent Computing Systems (ADICS), pp. 1–6. IEEE (2024)

12. Wang, F., Du, Y., Zhang, Q.: Fast algorithm for depth map intra-frame coding 3d-hevc based on swin transformer and multi-branch network. Electronics **14**(9), 1703 (2025)
13. Wang, J., Su, J., Wen, Z., Sun, Y.: Enhanced yolov10 for small object detection with context-aware and adaptive modules. Inter. J. Multimedia Inform. Retrieval **14**(3), 1–11 (2025)
14. Xu, J., Ye, D., Zhang, S., Wang, K., Chen, S.: Metallic surface defect detection via nwd-wiou based on grayscale co-generation entropy gain. Appli. Intell. **55**(10), 752 (2025)
15. Zhang, C., Zhang, Y., Chang, Z., Li, C.: Sperm yolov8e-trackevd: a novel approach for sperm detection and tracking. Sensors **24**(11), 3493 (2024)
16. Zhang, H., Xu, C., Zhang, S.: Inner-iou: More effective intersection over union loss with auxiliary bounding box (2023)
17. Zhang, Y.J., Xiao, F.S., Lu, Z.M.: Helmet wearing state detection based on improved yolov5s. Sensors **22**, 9843 (2022). https://doi.org/10.3390/s22249843
18. Zhao, Y., et al.: Detrs beat yolos on real-time object detection. In: Proceedings of the IEEE/CVF Conference on Computer Vision and Pattern Recognition, pp. 16965–16974 (2024)
19. Zhu, X., Su, W., Lu, L., Li, B., Wang, X., Dai, J.: Deformable detr: deformable transformers for end-to-end object detection (2021)

Joint Universal Adversarial Perturbations with Interpretations

Liangbo Ning[1], Zeyu Dai[1], Wenqi Fan[1(✉)], Jingran Su[1], Chao Pan[1], Luning Wang[2], and Qing Li[1]

[1] The Hong Kong Polytechnic University, Hong Kong, China
{ze-yu.dai,jing-ran.su,chao.pan}@connect.polyu.hk, wenqifan03@gmail.com, qing-prof.li@polyu.edu.hk
[2] Huawei, Hong Kong, China
wangluning2@huawei.com

Abstract. Deep neural networks (DNNs) have significantly boosted the performance of many challenging tasks. Despite the great development, DNNs have also exposed their vulnerability. Recent studies have shown that adversaries can manipulate the predictions of DNNs by adding the universal adversarial perturbation (UAP) to benign samples. On the other hand, increasing efforts have been made to help users understand and explain the inner working of DNNs by highlighting the most informative parts (i.e., attribution maps) of samples with respect to their predictions. Moreover, we first empirically find that such attribution maps between benign and adversarial examples have a significant discrepancy, which has the potential to detect universal adversarial perturbations for defending against adversarial attacks. This finding motivates us to further investigate a new research problem: whether there exist universal adversarial perturbations that are able to jointly attack the DNN classifier and its interpretation with malicious desires. The problem is challenging since these two objectives are seemingly conflicting. In this paper, we propose a novel attacking framework to generate joint universal adversarial perturbations (**JUAP**), which can fool the DNN model and misguide the inspection from interpreters simultaneously. Comprehensive experiments on various datasets demonstrate the effectiveness of the proposed method JUAP for joint attacks. To the best of our knowledge, this is the first effort to study UAP for jointly attacking both DNNs and interpretations.

Keywords: Adversarial Attacks · Universal Adversarial Perturbations (UAP) · Interpretation · Trustworthy AI

1 Introduction

As one of the most important data mining techniques, Deep Neural Networks (DNNs) have achieved remarkable performance in various challenging down-

L. Ning and Z. Dai—Equal contribution.
The long version of this paper can be found at: https://arxiv.org/pdf/2408.01715.

R. C.-W. Wong et al. (Eds.): PAKDD 2026, LNAI 16617, pp. 572–585, 2027.
https://doi.org/10.1007/978-981-92-1926-1_46

stream domains [9,19], e.g., image classifications [31], language generation [7], and social media [29]. These deep learning methods have significantly benefited humans in daily life and created great economic outcomes in society. Along with their impressive development and great achievement, DNN techniques have also exposed their untrustworthy aspects [10,30], which might perform unreliable predictions and cause severe economic, social, and security consequences, especially in safety-critical scenarios, such as autonomous driving [28].

Current adversarial perturbations in computer vision tasks can be divided into two types, i.e., image-dependent perturbations (**IDPs**) and image-agnostic universal adversarial perturbations (**UAPs**). IDPs need to be crafted for each image by using iterative/non-iterative gradient decent [18,20] algorithms or solving an optimization problem [2,6]. Instead, image-agnostic UAP can be added to most benign images and then cause misclassification of DNNs with very high confidence [21,22]. Due to the good generalization capability, UAPs, after learning from the dataset, can even attack unseen images. In addition, compared to the IDPs specific to each sample, image-agnostic UAPs, once learned and deployed, are more efficient, especially when facing large-scale data samples. Thus, image-agnostic UAPs pose a significant threat to the security of DNNs.

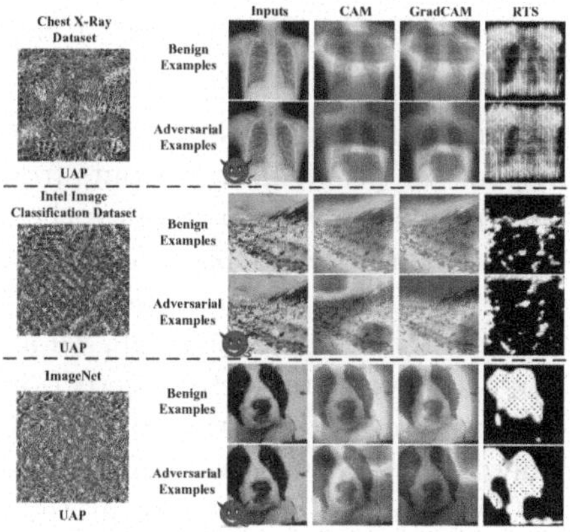

Fig. 1. An illustration of interpretation discrepancy for benign and adversarial images (via adding UAPs) under various interpreters.

In recent years, in order to enhance the trustworthiness of DNN models, increasing efforts have been made to help users understand the inner working mechanism of DNNs by providing interpretations on how certain decisions are made [13,25, 32]. More specifically, the interpretations can be achieved by identifying the most influential parts (e.g., attribution maps) of the input with respect to its prediction [4,11, 26]. For example, as the first activation-based interpreter, CAM is proposed to compute a weighted sum of the activation of the last convolutional layer to generate attribution maps, where the weights are the parameters of the final dense layer [32]. On the other hand, recent works have found that DNNs' interpretability can work as inspectors or detectors (i.e., model debugging) to diagnose models' errors and reveal models' vulnerability (i.e., adversarial perturbations) in computer vision domain [1,3] and text domain [17]. As a result, interpreters have the potential to detect adversarial perturbations for defending against adversarial attacks.

To verify such detection capabilities in the image domain under various DNNs' interpreters (i.e., CAM, GradCAM, and RTS) for UAP attacks [21], we first perform empirical studies to evaluate the interpretation discrepancy between interpretation maps on the benign and adversarial images. As shown in Fig. 1, the attribution maps on adversarial examples are significantly different from those of benign examples. Once such 'confused' predictions are inspected, humans (e.g., model designers) can develop strategies to enhance the DNN model's robustness against adversarial attacks.

Facing interpreters' potential detection, we further raise a new question, i.e., *whether there exist UAPs that can perform a joint attack to fool the DNN classifier and its interpretation simultaneously with malicious desires?* To be specific, by adding the UAPs to the benign images, the objectives of the joint attack are to maximize the change of DNNs' predictions while minimizing the interpretation discrepancy, leading to more severe safety issues for DNN techniques. However, these two objectives are essentially contradictory to each other. That is because the added universal perturbations tend to be the most influential part of natural images for obtaining incorrect labels, while the goal of interpreters is to identify the most influential maps for explaining how DNNs make decisions. Therefore, to investigate such new questions, in this paper, we propose a novel attack framework (**JUAP**) for generating universal adversarial perturbations, which can simultaneously mislead the DNN model's prediction and misguide the inspection from the interpreter. Our major contributions are summarised as follows:

- We discover that DNNs' interpretability can be leveraged to understand and inspect the problematic outputs from adversarial examples caused by UAPs, which pave the way to enhance the safety of DNN models.
- We study a novel problem of exploring UAPs to jointly attack DNN models as well as their interpretations, which reveals more severe safety concerns. To the best of our knowledge, we are the first to investigate UAPs from the perspective of interpreters' detection.
- We propose a novel attacking framework to generate joint UAPs (**JUAP**), where a generative adversarial network is proposed to learn UAPs for fooling the DNN model and its interpreter simultaneously.
- Our comprehensive experiments on three real-world datasets demonstrate that the proposed attacker can achieve a high fooling ratio for attacking classifiers with a small interpretation discrepancy.

2 Problem Definition

Adversarial Perturbations. For a benign image x, attackers can generate perturbations $\hat{n}$ to obtain its corresponding adversarial example $\hat{x} = x + \hat{n}$ so as to manipulate the DNN classifier $f(\hat{x})$ to make malicious prediction. Moreover, the perturbations are required to satisfy the imperceptibility property (i.e., perceptually indistinguishable from our human eye), which can be achieved by adding constraint: $\|\hat{n}\|_p \leq \zeta$, where ζ is a threshold used to control the magnitude of the perturbation and p is the vector norm.

In general, perturbations can be categorized as image-dependent and universal (image-agnostic) perturbations. Given a well-trained DNNs classifier f and a dataset $D = \{x_i, C_{x_i} | i = 1, ..., N\}$ containing N samples with their labels C_{x_i}:

- **Image-dependent Perturbations (IDPs)** can be defined as $\hat{n}_i$ for a specific image x_i. The IDPs can mislead $f(x_i)$ to provide wrong prediction output, which can be mathematically formulated as:

$$f(x_i) \neq f(x_i + \hat{n}_i), i = 1, \cdots, N. \tag{1}$$

  Normally, IDPs are devised for each sample, respectively, which is time-consuming and lacks generalization ability.
- **Universal Adversarial Perturbations (UAPs)** are defined as $\hat{n}$, aiming to fool classifier f to produce incorrect predictions for most samples in D as follows:

$$f(x_i) \neq f(x_i + \hat{n}), i = 1, \cdots, N. \tag{2}$$

  The UAPs are usually learned based on a set of training samples with great generalization properties. Thus, UAPs can also mislead the DNNs' predictions when added to unseen benign samples.

DNNs' Interpretations. Given a classifier f, its coupled interpreters are defined as $\mathcal{I} : \mathbb{R}^d \rightarrow \mathbb{R}^d$, aiming to produce an attribution map $\mathcal{I}(x)$, which highlights the most influential parts of the input with respect to its prediction. The attribution map can provide a great way to help users understand and explain the inner working mechanism of how certain decisions are made from the DNNs model. Moreover, recent works have found that DNNs' interpreters have the potential to work as anomaly detectors for improving the security of DNNs against adversarial attacks [1,17], as demonstrated in our empirical studies (see the Fig. 1).

Problem Statement: Given an image x_i, the attacker aims to perform a joint attack by generating universal adversarial perturbations $\hat{n}$, which can fulfill the following two goals:

- The UAP $\hat{n}$ on any sample x_i can change the DNN classifier prediction to incorrect label, as depicted in Eq. 2.
- The UAP $\hat{n}$ on any sample x_i can manipulate the interpreter to generate attribution maps identical to those produced for the original input:

$$\mathcal{I}(x_i) = \mathcal{I}(x_i + \hat{n}), i = 1, \cdots, N. \tag{3}$$

3 Methodology

The goal of this work is to conduct joint attacks by learning image-agnostic UAPs. To achieve this goal, we propose a novel attack framework (**JUAP**) to

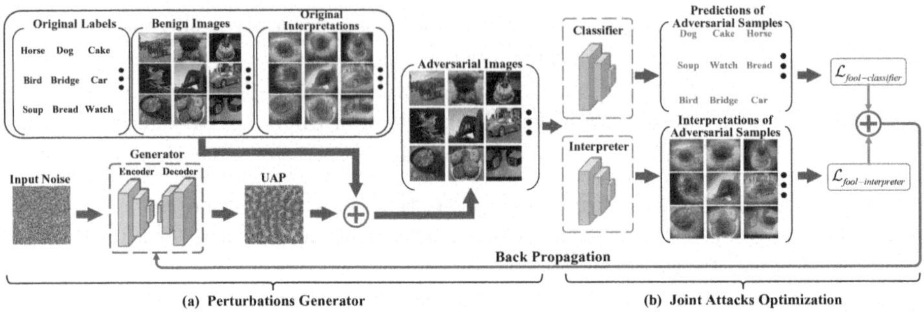

Fig. 2. The overall framework of the proposed method (JUAP), consisting of a perturbation generator and joint attacks optimization for fooling DNN classifiers and interpreters simultaneously.

jointly attack the DNN classifier and interpreter. More specifically, a generative adversarial network is proposed to learn UAPs that cause natural samples to be misclassified with high confidence while keeping their attribution maps unchanged. The overall framework of JUAP is shown in Fig. 2.

3.1 Attack DNN Classifiers

A general solution to generate UAPs is to leverage an iterative gradient-based strategy [5,21]. However, iteratively creating perturbations for each sample and fusing all perturbations to get the UAP is time-consuming. Moreover, the UAP created by data-driven iterative gradient-based methods significantly depends on the training set. Thus, in this work, in order to attack DNN classifiers, a generative adversarial framework is proposed to learn UAPs $\hat{n}$, which can be formulated as an image-to-image translation task by reconstructing different noise vectors, consisting of an encoder $e(\cdot)$ and a decoder $d(\cdot)$. Given various initial input noise, the output perturbations are different from each other. Meanwhile, this generative model can generate infinite UAPs based on a specific training set. To accelerate the convergence speed, we randomly sample a noise vector from the uniform distribution $U(0,1)$, denoted as n, with the same size as the input images. Specifically, a generator $\mathcal{G}_\theta$ with weights θ is developed to map the random noise image to joint universal adversarial perturbations $\hat{n}$, which can be modeled as follows $\hat{n} = \mathcal{G}_\theta(n) = d(e(n)), n \sim U(0,1)$, where the encoder extracts the latent variables (or semantic features) of the inputs, while the decoder receives the encoders' output and reconstructs the latent variables to implement the image-to-image translation.

To make the JUAP imperceptible, the output of the generator is scaled to have a fixed magnitude. Mathematically, the JUAP generation process can be defined as follows:

$$\hat{n} = \min\left(1, \frac{\zeta}{\|\mathcal{G}_\theta(n)\|_p}\right) \cdot \mathcal{G}_\theta(n), n \sim U(0,1), \tag{4}$$

where ζ is a pre-defined threshold to control the magnitude of the JUAP. $\|\cdot\|_p$ is the p-norm of the vector. After that, the adversarial examples can be obtained by adding the joint universal perturbation to benign images, i.e., $\hat{x} = x + \hat{n}$.

To optimize the parameters θ of the generator $\mathcal{G}$ for fooling DNN classifiers, we minimize the cross-entropy loss between the prediction and the least likely class as follows:

$$\min_{\theta} \mathcal{L}_{fool-classifier} = \min_{\theta} \ \log \left(\mathcal{L} \left(f \left(\hat{x} \right), C_{\min} \right) \right), \tag{5}$$

where $\mathcal{L}$ is the cross-entropy loss and C_{min} is the class with the minimum prediction probability, i.e., $C_{min} = \arg\min(f(x))$.

3.2 Attack DNN Interpreters

Fooling interpreters aims to minimize the discrepancy of interpretation maps between benign and adversarial examples. To demonstrate the effectiveness of the proposed methods, we focus on adversarial attacks on three representative interpretation methods, i.e., CAM [32], GradCAM [25], and RTS [4], where they have different underlying mechanisms. CAM [32] is the representative activation-based interpreter, which has been widely used in various computer vision tasks. Using GradCAM [25] as the interpreter aims to demonstrate the effectiveness of JUAP in manipulating attribution maps based on gradients. Here typical gradient-based interpreters [27] are not taken into account since the attribution maps produced by these methods are not sufficiently clear/distinguishable. RTS [4] is employed as a representation of methods that do not rely on the intrinsic model parameters (e.g., activations or gradients) for generating the attribution maps.

In order to deceive DNNs' interpreters, we aim to minimize the interpretation shift of interpretation maps between benign and adversarial examples. In this paper, we use the L_2 measure, and the objective is shown as follows:

$$\min_{\theta} \mathcal{L}_{fool-interpreter} = \min_{\theta} \ \left\| \mathcal{I}\left(\hat{x}\right) - \mathcal{I}\left(x\right) \right\|_2, \tag{6}$$

$$\mathcal{I}(i,j)\left(\cdot\right) = \begin{cases} \sum\limits_k \omega_c^k \cdot A_{ij}^k, \text{ if CAM}, \\ \sum\limits_k \left(\frac{1}{V} \sum_i \sum_j \frac{\partial f_c}{\partial A_{ij}^k} \right) \cdot A_{ij}^k, \text{ if GradCAM}, \\ R_{\varpi}\left(\cdot\right), \text{ if RTS}, \end{cases} \tag{7}$$

where A_{ij}^k denote the element in the i-th row and j-th column of the k-th channel of the last convolutional layer, ω_c^k denotes the weight in final dense layer between A^k and the logits of class c, V is the number of the latent variables in the last convolutional layer, f_c is the c-th output of the classifier, R_{ϖ} is the generated attribution maps by RTS model with weights ϖ.

Optimization. During deceiving interpreters, it is necessary to ensure that the second-order derivative of generators is not all-zero, especially for the interpreters using gradients. The ReLU activation function is widely used in various

Algorithm 1: Our proposed method **JUAP**

Input: Benign samples x, generator $\mathcal{G}_\theta$, classifier f, interpreter $\mathcal{I}$, vector norm p, threshold ζ, random noise n, iteration T.
Output: Joint universal adversarial perturbation $\hat{n}$.
Procedure:

for *t in 1:T* **do**
- Reconstruct and scale the random noise n to get JUAP $\hat{n}$: $\hat{n} = \min\left(1, \frac{\zeta}{\|\mathcal{G}_\theta(n)\|_p}\right) \cdot \mathcal{G}_\theta(n)$;
- Create adversarial examples $\hat{x}$: $\hat{x} = x + \hat{n}$;
- Compute the loss function by Eq. (5) ;
- Compute the interpretation shift by Eq. (6) ;
- Compute the overall objective $\mathcal{L}_{JUAP}$ by Eq. (9);
- Update parameters θ of the generator: $\theta \leftarrow \theta - \gamma \cdot \nabla_\theta \mathcal{L}_{JUAP}$;

end for

DNNs, which consists of two linear components. The second-order derivative of ReLU is all-zero and brings difficulties in performing back-propagation during gradient descent. To tackle this optimization issue, we propose using a smoothing mechanism on the gradient of ReLU for minimizing Eq. (6) as follows:

$$a(s) = \mathbb{1}(s < 0) \cdot (1 + s/\sqrt{s^2 + \tau}) + \mathbb{1}(s \geq 0) \cdot s/\sqrt{s^2 + \tau}, \tag{8}$$

where $\mathbb{1}(\cdot)$ is the indicator function, and $\tau = 10^{-4}$ is a small constant to ensure the output of function is bounded. s is the input of the ReLU activation layer.

3.3 Universal Adversarial Perturbations for Joint Attack

Now we design the joint attack to generate UAPs for attacking the classifier and its interpreter simultaneously. The most straightforward approach for the joint attack is to minimize the aforementioned loss functions simultaneously for optimizing the generator's parameters. However, deceiving both classifiers and interpreters still faces a tremendous challenge. The objective of changing predictions usually contradicts the objective of keeping interpretations unchanged. That is because to change the classifier output more significantly, the perturbations tend to be added to the most informative parts in an image, which are also the regions easily detected by the interpreter.

To address the challenge, we propose an iterative optimization strategy for optimizing the objectives of classifier and interpreter attacks. More specifically, at the beginning of the generator training, we conduct joint optimization on the two objectives. When the perturbations produced by the generator are able to deceive the classifier, we focus on fooling its coupled interpreter without deceiving classifiers. The overall objective is defined as follows:

$$\mathcal{L}_{JUAP} = \max\{\mathcal{L}_{fool-classifier}, \delta\} + \lambda \cdot \mathcal{L}_{fool-interpreter}, \tag{9}$$

where λ is a hyperparameter to control the attacking effect between the classifier and interpreter, and δ is exploited to decide whether to fool classifiers. The overall training process of the proposed method JUAP is shown in Algorithm 1.

4 Experiments

4.1 Implementation Details

Datasets. In our experiment, three representative image classification datasets (i.e., ImageNet [8], Chest X-Ray dataset [16], and Intel Image Classification dataset[1]) are used to validate the effectiveness of the proposed method.

Classifiers. Two representative deep neural networks are used as the classifiers, i.e., ResNet18 [12] and DenseNet121 [14]. We directly use the pre-trained models as the classifiers when constructing experiments on the ImageNet dataset. For other datasets, we fine-tune the pre-trained models as the target classifiers. The Top-1 accuracy attained on different datasets is summarised in Table 4.

Generators. We adopt two representative architectures to generate UAPs: ResNet generator [15] and U-Net generator [24].

Baselines. To better demonstrate the superiority of the proposed method, we use several representative methods as baselines for comparison: (1) UAP [21]: This is the first iterative method for generating UAPs. (2) GUAP [23]: This method is a typical generative method for creating UAPs (3) GUAP-C_t [23]: This method is used to generate UAPs for the targeted attack. (4) PGD [20]: This method is used to craft image-dependent perturbations. (5) R-JUAP: This is the proposed method using the ResNet generator. (6) U-JUAP: This is the proposed method using the U-Net generator.

Evaluation Metrics. Fooling Ratio (**FR**) calculates the ratio of examples that can successfully fool the classifier. **L1** metric assesses the discrepancy of attribution maps between benign and adversarial examples in L1 distance. Intersection-Over-Union (**IOU**) measures the similarity of attribution maps by calculating the area of intersection over the area of union between two images.

[1] https://www.kaggle.com/datasets/puneet6060/intel-image-classification.

Table 1. Results of fooling ratio.

		Datasets	ImageNet	X-Ray	Intel
Method	ResNet18	UAP	77.64	75.80	51.46
		GUAP	79.91	83.97	50.75
		R-JUAP-CAM	80.35	84.62	55.627
		R-JUAP-GradCAM	80.21	**84.94**	**51.71**
		R-JUAP-RTS	83.88	79.49	50.78
		U-JUAP-CAM	77.35	80.29	54.63
		U-JUAP-GradCAM	84.27	82.53	46.58
		U-JUAP-RTS	**85.00**	83.01	50.32
	DenseNet121	UAP	**78.37**	75.16	46.83
		GUAP	77.01	79.17	53.10
		R-JUAP-CAM	76.60	**83.81**	47.54
		R-JUAP-GradCAM	77.54	81.09	50.57
		R-JUAP-RTS	77.31	76.12	52.99
		U-JUAP-CAM	77.17	79.81	45.01
		U-JUAP-GradCAM	78.10	78.53	51.78
		U-JUAP-RTS	76.12	79.81	**54.06**

Table 2. Interpretation discrepancy between adversarial and benign attribution maps (Model: DenseNet121).

	Datasets	ImageNet		X-Ray		Intel	
	Metrics	L1	IOU	L1	IOU	L1	IOU
Method	UAP-CAM	0.23	0.52	0.28	0.45	0.25	0.51
	GUAP-CAM	0.18	0.59	0.25	0.46	0.20	0.53
	U-JUAP-CAM	0.17	0.63	0.22	0.53	0.18	0.59
	R-JUAP-CAM	**0.17**	**0.63**	**0.21**	**0.54**	**0.18**	**0.61**
	UAP-GradCAM	0.21	0.36	0.28	0.44	0.23	0.55
	GUAP-GradCAM	0.18	0.46	0.25	0.47	0.20	0.53
	U-JUAP-GradCAM	0.18	0.49	0.21	0.54	0.20	0.55
	R-JUAP-GradCAM	**0.17**	**0.51**	**0.21**	**0.54**	**0.20**	**0.57**
	UAP-RTS	0.10	0.68	0.13	0.72	0.13	0.61
	GUAP-RTS	0.14	0.60	0.14	0.71	0.20	0.54
	U-JUAP-RTS	0.08	0.72	0.08	0.81	0.12	0.64
	R-JUAP-RTS	**0.07**	**0.74**	**0.06**	**0.85**	**0.08**	**0.71**

4.2 Effectiveness of Attacking Classifiers

We first evaluate the effectiveness of JUAP for attacking classifiers. We summarise the FR for different classifiers on three benchmark datasets, and the results are shown in Table 1. We only report one result for UAP and GUAP since interpreters do not affect their FR. We use R-JUAP-CAM (or R-JUAP-GradCAM, and R-JUAP-RTS) and U-JUAP-CAM (or U-JUAP-GradCAM, and U-JUAP-RTS) to represent the JUAP generated by the ResNet generator and U-Net generator, respectively, where the interpreter is CAM (or GradCAM, and RTS).

From the results, it is observed that both R-JUAP and U-JUAP achieve a high FR across different target classifiers compared with other baselines, which demonstrates the effectiveness of JUAP for fooling classifiers. Although the optimization objective is complicated, it is still possible to find the optimal solution. R-JUAP and U-JUAP achieve a similar FR, which indicates that the proposed framework is robust to the architecture of the generator. Meanwhile, in most cases, R-JUAP and U-JUAP with different interpreters outperform the other baselines in the FR, indicating that the proposed framework successfully resolves the dilemma between attacking the classifier and its coupled interpreters.

4.3 Effectiveness of Attacking Interpreters

In this section, we evaluate the effectiveness of JUAP for deceiving interpreters. We first visualize some examples for qualitative comparison. Figure 3 shows some attribution maps of benign and adversarial images (produced by UAP, GUAP, U-JUAP, and R-JUAP) with respect to different interpreters (i.e., CAM, Grad-CAM, and RTS). We observe that attribution maps of U-JUAP and R-JUAP are similar to those of the benign images with respect to various interpreters. As for the other baselines, the differences in attribution maps are large, which makes the attack perceptible.

Next, we use L1 and IOU for quantitative comparison. As shown in Table 2 and Fig. 5, both R-JUAP and U-JUAP achieve high IOU scores with small L1 measure, indicating that the adversarial attribution maps of JUAP are perceptually indistinguishable from their benign counterparts.

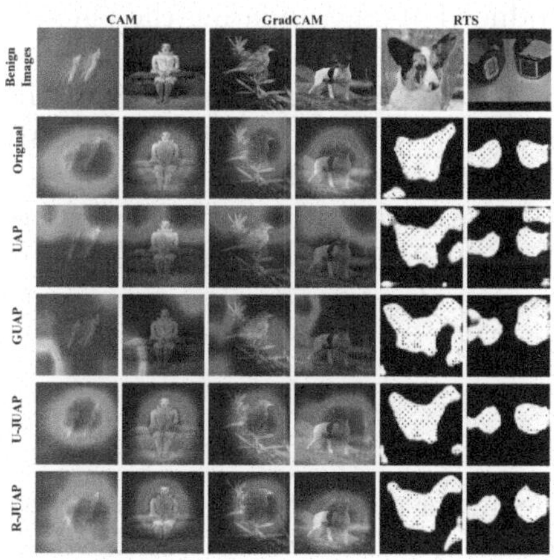

Fig. 3. Attribution maps of benign images and adversarial images with different interpreters on ResNet18.

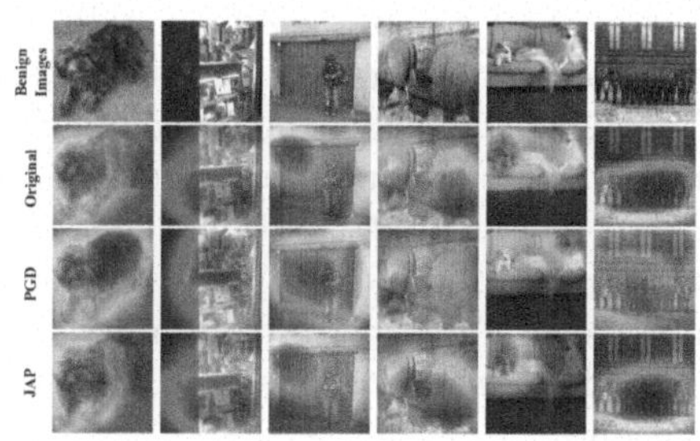

Fig. 4. Interpretation discrepancy of attribution maps between benign and adversarial examples (Model: ResNet18).

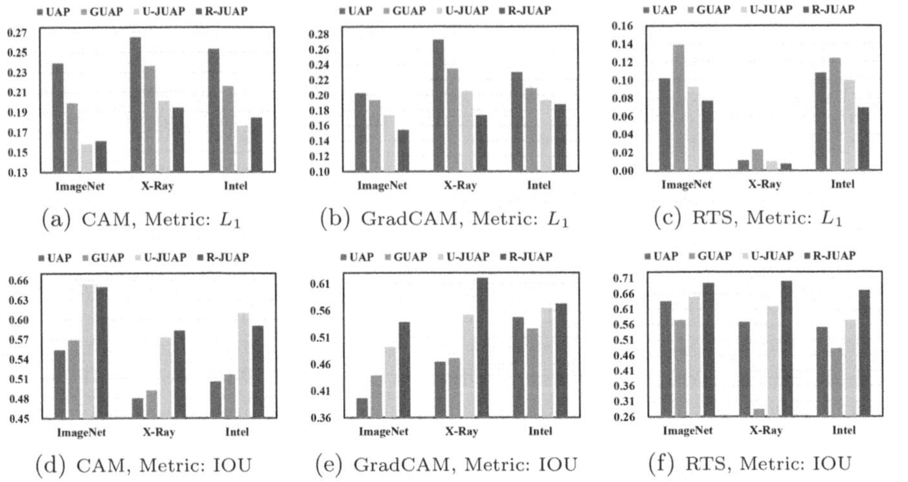

(a) CAM, Metric: L_1 (b) GradCAM, Metric: L_1 (c) RTS, Metric: L_1

(d) CAM, Metric: IOU (e) GradCAM, Metric: IOU (f) RTS, Metric: IOU

Fig. 5. Interpretation discrepancy of attribution maps between benign and adversarial examples (Model: ResNet18).

4.4 Effectiveness of Generating Image-Dependent Perturbations

Our method can be easily generalized to produce IDPs by updating the parameters of the generator for each example. To verify its performance, we use PGD [20], as the baseline for comparison, and GradCAM is exploited as the basic interpreter. We first illustrate some examples for qualitative comparison. As shown in Fig. 4, attribution maps of samples with added joint adversarial perturbations (JAP) almost remain unchanged. The quantitative results are summarized in Table 5. We can observe that JAP achieves a high FR and IOU with a small L1 measure, which further quantitatively demonstrates the above conclusion.

4.5 Model Analysis

In this section, we aim to investigate the model hyper-parameters in our proposed framework. In addition to $p = 2$ with threshold $\zeta = 2000$ in Eq. (4), here we investigate how $p = \infty$ with threshold $\zeta = 10$ affects the attacking performance. The results are summarized in Table 3. We observe that the three metrics (i.e., FR, L1 measure, and IOU score) fluctuate in a small range, which indicates that our JUAP creation is robust under different threat models.

5 Conclusion

In this work, we first find that DNN models' interpretations can be used to inspect the problematic outputs from adversarial examples caused by UAPs. Then we explore a new research problem: *whether there exist UAPs that can*

Table 3. Fooling ratio on different datasets.

Models		ResNet18			DenseNet121		
Method		FR	L1	IOU	FR	L1	IOU
L_∞-10	R-JUAP-CAM	85.32	0.12	0.64	75.50	0.13	0.61
	R-JUAP-GradCAM	78.39	0.15	0.66	78.88	0.17	0.61
	R-JUAP-RTS	80.38	**0.08**	**0.69**	76.69	**0.07**	**0.73**
	U-JUAP-CAM	81.69	0.16	0.64	78.37	0.17	0.62
	U-JUAP-GradCAM	**86.30**	0.18	0.49	**79.15**	0.18	0.47
	U-JUAP-RTS	85.44	0.09	0.64	79.06	0.09	0.68
L_2-2000	R-JUAP-CAM	80.35	0.16	0.65	76.60	0.17	0.63
	R-JUAP-GradCAM	80.21	0.15	0.54	77.54	0.17	0.51
	R-JUAP-RTS	83.88	**0.08**	**0.69**	77.31	**0.07**	**0.74**
	U-JUAP-CAM	77.35	0.15	0.65	77.17	0.17	0.63
	U-JUAP-GradCAM	84.27	0.17	0.49	**78.10**	0.18	0.49
	U-JUAP-RTS	**85.00**	0.09	0.65	76.12	0.08	0.72

Table 4. Accuracy on different datasets.

Datasets / Models	ImageNet	X-Ray	Intel
ResNet18	67.340	87.821	90.100
DenseNet121	72.100	91.506	88.604

perform a joint attack to attack DNN classifier and its interpretation simultaneously with malicious desires? We propose a novel attack framework using generators to learn UAPs to solve this problem. Our comprehensive experiments validate the effectiveness of the proposed JUAP on three real-world datasets.

Acknowledgments. The research described in this paper has been partially supported by the General Research Funds from the Hong Kong Research Grants Council (project no. PolyU 15207322, 15200023, 15206024, and 15224524), internal research funds from Hong Kong Polytechnic University (project no. P0042693, P0048625, and P0051361), and industry collaboration fund P0041282.

Table 5. Results of IDPs on ImageNet.

Target Model	Method	FR	L1	IOU
ResNet18	PGD	100.00	36.70	0.55
	JAP	100.00	**27.15**	**0.65**
DenseNet121	PGD	100.00	34.54	0.57
	JAP	100.00	**26.42**	**0.66**

References

1. Adebayo, J.: Debugging tests for model explanations. In: NIPS (2020)
2. Bastani, O.: Measuring neural net robustness with constraints. In: NIPS (2016)
3. Boopathy, A.: Proper network interpretability helps adversarial robustness in classification. In: ICLR (2020)
4. Dabkowski, P., et al.: Real time image saliency for black box classifiers. In: NIPS (2017)
5. Dai, J., Shu, L.: Fast-UAP: an algorithm for speeding up universal adversarial perturbation generation with orientation of perturbation vectors. arXiv (2019)
6. Dai, Z.: Saliency attack: Towards imperceptible black-box adversarial attack. ACM TIST (2023)
7. Das, B.C.: Security and privacy challenges of large language models: a survey. ACM Comput. Surv. (2025)
8. Deng, J.: ImageNet: a large-scale hierarchical image database. In: CVPR (2009)
9. Fan, W.: A comprehensive survey on trustworthy recommender systems. arXiv (2022)
10. Fan, W.: Adversarial attacks for black-box recommender systems via copying transferable cross-domain user profiles. TKDE (2023)
11. Fong, R.C., Vedaldi, A.: Interpretable explanations of black boxes by meaningful perturbation. In: ICCV (2017)
12. He, K.: Deep residual learning for image recognition. In: CVPR (2016)
13. Heindorf, S., Neib, D.: Assessing natural language explanations of relational graph neural networks. In: CIKM (2025)
14. Huang, G., et al.: Densely connected convolutional networks. In: CVPR (2017)
15. Johnson, J.: Perceptual losses for real-time style transfer and super-resolution. In: ECCV (2016)
16. Kermany, D.S.: Identifying medical diagnoses and treatable diseases by image-based deep learning. Cell (2018)
17. Lertvittayakumjorn, P., Toni, F.: Explanation-based human debugging of NLP models: a survey. TACL (2021)
18. Li, J.W.: Boosting adversarial transferability via relative feature importance-aware attacks. TIFS (2025)
19. Liu, H.: Trustworthy AI: a computational perspective. ACM TIST (2022)
20. Madry, A.: Towards deep learning models resistant to adversarial attacks. In: ICLR (2018)
21. Moosavi-Dezfooli, S.M., et al.: Universal adversarial perturbations. In: CVPR (2017)
22. Pan, C.: Adversarial initialization with universal adversarial perturbation: a new approach to fast adversarial training. In: AAAI (2024)
23. Poursaeed, O.: Generative adversarial perturbations. In: CVPR (2018)
24. Ronneberger, O., Fischer, P., Brox, T.: U-Net: Convolutional Networks for Biomedical Image Segmentation. In: MICCAI (2015). LNCS, vol. 9351, pp. 234–241. Springer, Cham (2015). https://doi.org/10.1007/978-3-319-24574-4_28
25. Selvaraju, R., et al.: GRAD-CAM: visual explanations from deep networks via gradient-based localization. In: ICCV (2017)
26. Simonyan, K.: Deep inside convolutional networks: visualising image classification models and saliency maps. arXiv (2013)
27. Smilkov, D., et al.: SmoothGrad: removing noise by adding noise. arXiv (2017)

28. Stallkamp, J.: Man vs. computer: benchmarking machine learning algorithms for traffic sign recognition. Neural Netw. (2012)
29. Wang, H.: A multi-type transferable method for missing link prediction in heterogeneous social networks. TKDE (2023)
30. Wei, W., Liu, L.: Trustworthy distributed ai systems: robustness, privacy, and governance. ACM Comput. Surv. (2024)
31. Zhao, Y.: On evaluating adversarial robustness of large vision-language models. In: NIPS (2024)
32. Zhou, B.: Learning deep features for discriminative localization. In: CVPR (2016)

Transferring Physical Priors into Remote Sensing Segmentation via Large Language Models

Yuxi Lu, Kunqi Li, Zhidong Li, Xiaohan Su, Biao Wu, Chenya Huang, and Bin Liang(✉)

University of Technology Sydney, Ultimo, NSW, Australia
{Yuxi.Lu,Kunqi.Li,Xiaohan.Su,Biao.Wu-2,Chenya.Huang}@student.uts.edu.au,
{Zhidong.Li,Bin.Liang}@uts.edu.au

Abstract. Semantic segmentation of remote sensing imagery is fundamental to Earth observation. Achieving accurate results requires integrating not only optical images but also physical variables such as the Digital Elevation Model (DEM), Synthetic Aperture Radar (SAR) and Normalized Difference Vegetation Index (NDVI). Recent foundation models (FMs) leverage pre-training to exploit these variables but still depend on spatially aligned data and costly retraining when involving new sensors. To overcome these limitations, we introduce a novel paradigm for integrating domain-specific physical priors into segmentation models. We first construct a Physical-Centric Knowledge Graph (PCKG) by prompting large language models to extract physical priors from 1,763 vocabularies, and use it to build a heterogeneous, spatial-aligned dataset, Phy-Sky-SA. Building on this foundation, we develop PriorSeg, a physics-aware residual refinement model trained with a joint visual-physical strategy that incorporates a novel physics-consistency loss. Experiments on heterogeneous settings demonstrate that PriorSeg improves segmentation accuracy and physical plausibility without retraining the FMs. Ablation studies verify the effectiveness of the Phy-Sky-SA dataset, the PCKG, and the physics-consistency loss.

Keywords: Large language models · Remote sensing segmentation · Physical priors

1 Introduction

Semantic segmentation in remote sensing assigns semantic labels to each pixel in satellite or aerial imagery, forming a core task in Earth observation [23]. It underpins essential applications such as land cover mapping, urban planning, and environmental monitoring [12,20].

Recent advances in deep learning have driven a shift from low-level texture recognition to high-level semantic understanding, with Foundation Models (FMs) emerging as a representative paradigm. Built upon self-supervised learning, they learn generalized visual representations from large-scale remote sensing

R. C.-W. Wong et al. (Eds.): PAKDD 2026, LNAI 16617, pp. 586–597, 2027.
https://doi.org/10.1007/978-981-92-1926-1_47

data and exhibit strong generalization in downstream tasks such as segmentation [7].

In practice, however, ground objects possess not only visual and textual attributes but also measurable physical variables that are observable by sensors, such as terrain elevation, surface reflectance, and radar backscattering. As illustrated in Fig. 1, these physical variables carry essential structural and material properties that complement visual cues and enhance semantic discrimination-particularly in visually ambiguous scenarios. For example, metal roofs and concrete buildings exhibit distinct Synthetic Aperture Radar (SAR) backscatter [16], flooded [9,10] and normal water bodies differ in Digital Elevation Model (DEM) heights [5], and healthy vegetation shows higher Normalized Difference Vegetation Index (NDVI) values than barren or built-up areas [6].

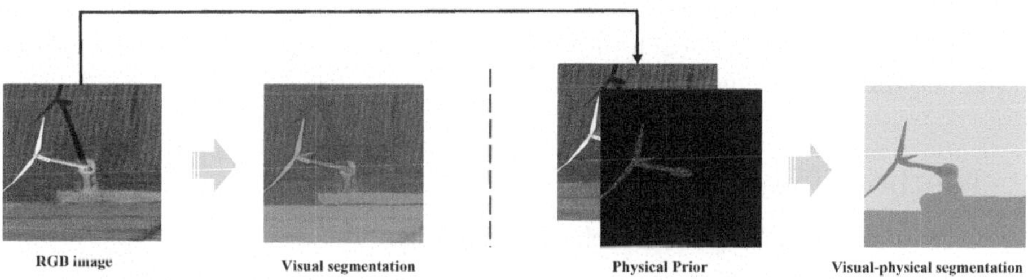

Fig. 1. Visual and visual-physical segmentation: adding the physical prior (simulated SAR) preserves the true object while preventing the shadow from being segmented.

Existing remote sensing FMs (e.g., SkySense [4], RemoteCLIP [14]) integrate spatially aligned physical variables or textual descriptions during pre-training to achieve heterogeneous data alignment via contrastive learning. Despite their strong performance, two major challenges remain: (1) they rely on large, manually aligned datasets, and (2) when involving new sensors or domains, they often require full retraining or architectural modification, limiting scalability and flexibility. This raises a key question: *Can physical priors be efficiently injected into existing FMs without manual spatial alignment or expensive retraining?*

To this end, we propose a novel paradigm for transferring physical priors into segmentation models via large language models (LLMs). We employ LLMs to extract physically plausible numerical ranges from 1,763 vocabularies for each semantic category-covering NDVI, DEM, and SAR-and organize them into a structured **Physical-Centric Knowledge Graph (PCKG)**. Based on it, we synthesize the heterogeneous dataset **Phy-Sky-SA**, whose simulated physical variables follow category-level constraints, enabling physically grounded training without manually aligned datasets.

Building on these physical priors, we introduce **PriorSeg**, a lightweight residual refinement model that learns visual-physical mappings. It attaches to any frozen foundation model and enhances segmentation consistency through structured physical reasoning. At inference, PriorSeg supports two modes: visual-only, producing physically coherent results from learned correlations; and visual-physical, leveraging available variables and the PCKG for further refinement and interpretability. Our contributions are summarized as follows:

- A novel LLM-based Physical Prior Transfer paradigm was proposed. We transfer physical priors into segmentation models via large language models, which extract domain-specific numerical ranges from 1,763 vocabularies. Based on these extracted priors, we construct the *PCKG* and *Phy-Sky-SA* dataset, enabling subsequent physically grounded training.
- We design a lightweight model named PriorSeg. It attaches to frozen foundation models and refines their predictions using visual-physical consistency, without retraining the backbone model. It supports both visual-only and visual-physical inference through integrating physical constraints.
- Across five datasets and multiple backbones, PriorSeg improves mIoU by 1.14%–6.7%. Ablation studies show that Phy-Sky-SA, the PCKG, and the physics-consistency loss each provide complementary gains, together explaining the full improvement.

2 Methodology

2.1 Transferring Physical Priors via LLMs

To incorporate physical priors into segmentation without requiring direct access to manually aligned heterogeneous data, we propose a novel method that leverages LLMs to extract physical priors and inject them into the training process. Our approach comprises two stages: (1) constructing a structured PCKG, as illustrated in Fig. 2, and (2) synthesizing a heterogeneous dataset, Phy-Sky-SA, guided by the PCKG, as shown in Fig. 3.

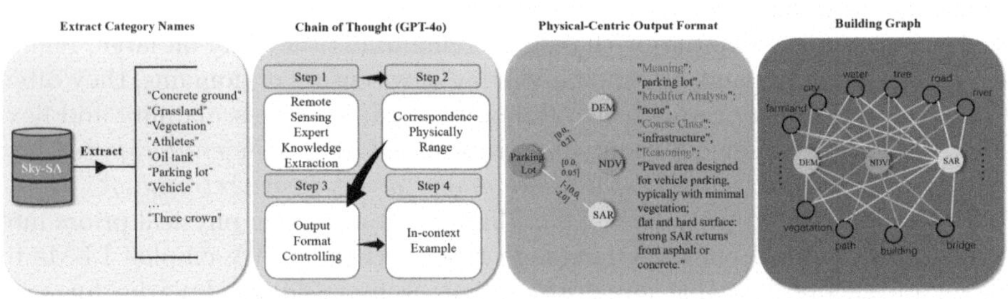

Fig. 2. Schematic of PCKG construction with GPT-4o. Category labels are prompted to the LLM, which returns NDVI, DEM, and SAR intervals $[a, b]$ plus a brief reasoning trace. The results are stored as JSON records and aggregated into a lightweight Physics-Centric Knowledge Graph that later guides synthetic-modal generation and loss design.

As shown in Fig. 2, we begin by constructing the PCKG using LLMs. The model is prompted with domain-specific instructions and prior knowledge about three widely used physical variables in remote sensing: DEM [5], NDVI [6], and SAR [16]. These variables are chosen for their broad availability, high discriminative power across land cover types, and general applicability across most semantic categories in remote sensing.

We use the large-scale segmentation dataset *Sky-SA* [24], which contains 33,776 satellite images and 183,000 mask-text pairs across 1,763 categories, as the textual foundation for category vocabularies. Using its category vocabularies, we design structured prompts that enable LLMs to extract physically plausible value ranges for each semantic class. Given a category vocabulary (e.g., "bare soil" or "urban park"), the model is asked to:

- Parse the semantic structure of the category phrase (e.g., target object and its modifiers),
- Map the phrase to a coarse physical class (e.g., vegetation, road, water),
- Infer plausible numerical intervals for NDVI, DEM, and SAR values,
- Justify each inference through step-by-step natural language reasoning.

Each entry in the PCKG is stored as a structured JSON object with the following fields: "Category", "Meaning", "Modifier Analysis", "Coarse Class", "NDVI Range", "DEM Range", "SAR Range", "Reasoning". The value ranges are defined as closed intervals with two decimal points of precision. Collectively, these entries form a lightweight knowledge base incorporating physical priors for model training and inference.

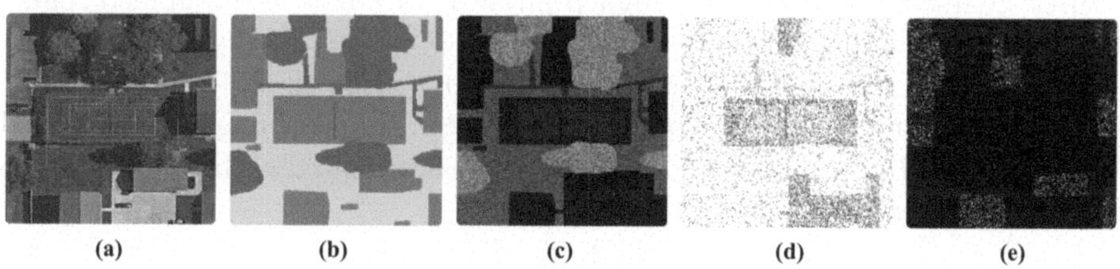

Fig. 3. Example sample from the Phy-Sky-SA dataset. From left to right: Image, GT, and the three simulated physical variables-NDVI(S), DEM(S), and SAR(S)-generated according to the PCKG, where the "(S)" denotes simulated values.

Having established the PCKG, we integrate it with the Sky-SA dataset to synthesize Phy-Sky-SA, as shown in Fig. 3. Although Sky-SA offers rich category diversity, it lacks physical annotations such as DEM, NDVI, and SAR. To address this gap, we generate simulated physical variable maps for each RGB image, guided by the category-specific ranges defined in the PCKG. This process ensures that the synthesized physical maps are pixel-aligned with the original imagery.

The use of LLM-guided prior extraction offers several advantages. It eliminates dependence on manually aligned physical measurements, enables generalization to unseen categories through semantic reasoning. The resulting Phy-Sky-SA dataset then supports training of our lightweight physics-aware refine model PriorSeg.

2.2 PriorSeg Overview

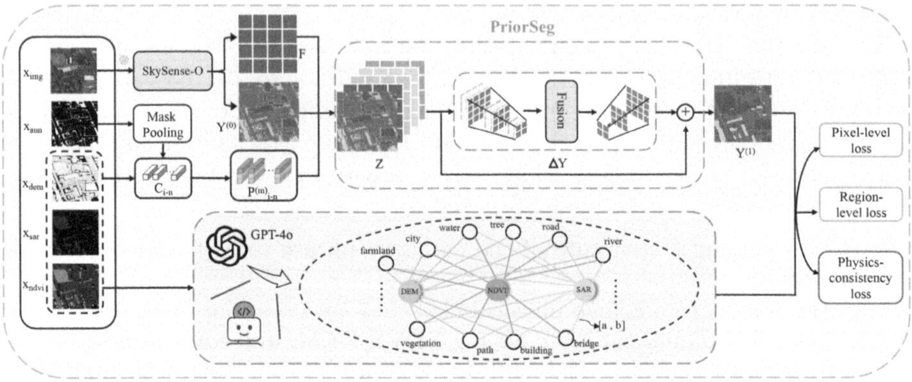

Fig. 4. Overview of the PriorSeg training framework. A frozen backbone extracts visual features and an initial mask, which are fused with optional physical variables. A residual head refines the segmentation, and three losses jointly enforce visual quality and physical consistency.

PriorSeg is a physics-aware residual refinement model that integrates visual features, coarse predictions, and aligned physical variables into a unified refinement pipeline (Fig. 4). A frozen SkySense-O backbone first produces a visual feature map F and an initial coarse mask $Y^{(0)}_{\text{pred}} \in [0,1]$ from the RGB image. Here, the subscript "pred" indicates predicted soft segmentation maps. The aligned physical rasters $P^{(m)}$ (NDVI, DEM, SAR) are concatenated with F and $Y^{(0)}_{\text{pred}}$ to form the joint tensor

$$Z = \left[F,\ Y^{(0)}_{\text{pred}},\ P^{(m)}\right],$$

which encodes visual, predictive, and physical cues.

A fusion module processes Z, and a residual head predicts a correction ΔY, yielding the refined mask

$$Y^{(1)}_{\text{pred}} = Y^{(0)}_{\text{pred}} + \Delta Y.$$

Residual prediction focuses the network on correcting the errors in $Y^{(0)}_{\text{pred}}$ instead of relearning the mask from scratch, leading to faster convergence, improved stability, and a lightweight refinement module that is easily compatible with different frozen backbones.

During training, PriorSeg is supervised by three complementary losses- pixel-level segmentation, region-level compactness, and physics-consistency- computed for each class c using the Physical-Centric Knowledge Graph (PCKG), where $[a, b]$ denotes the admissible physical interval for each class. When physical variables are unavailable, their channels are zero-padded, enabling PriorSeg to operate seamlessly in both visual-only and visual-physical modes using identical model weights.

2.3 Visual-Physical Joint Training

Training minimises a joint objective on $Y_{\text{pred}}^{(1)}$ alone: a visual layer (cross-entropy, Dice, region compactness) learns discriminative features, while a physical- consistency layer uses a hinge loss to align each region's mean physical value with its PCKG-defined interval, embedding physical priors into the network.

Pixel-Level Loss. Cross-entropy (CE) supplies dense gradients, while the Dice coefficient rewards spatial overlap and mitigates class imbalance.

$$L_{\text{seg}} = \text{CE}\big(Y_{\text{pred}}^{(1)}, Y_{\text{gt}}\big) + \alpha\,\text{Dice}\big(Y_{\text{pred}}^{(1)}, Y_{\text{gt}}\big), \tag{1}$$

where Y_{gt} is the ground-truth segmentation and α controls the trade-off between the cross-entropy and Dice terms.

Region-Level Loss. Let $\hat{Y} = \arg\max Y_{\text{pred}}^{(1)}$ and $\mathcal{R}_c = \{(x, y) \mid \hat{Y}(x, y) = c\}$, where $\mathcal{R}_c$ denotes the set of pixels predicted as class c. Define the mean visual feature $\mu_c = |\mathcal{R}_c|^{-1} \sum_{i \in \mathcal{R}_c} F_i$.

$$L_{\text{region}} = \sum_{c=1}^{C} \frac{1}{|\mathcal{R}_c|} \sum_{i \in \mathcal{R}_c} \|F_i - \mu_c\|_2^2, \tag{2}$$

This loss collapses intra-class variance, suppressing speckle noise and stabilising subsequent physics statistics.

Physics-Consistency Loss. For each variables m, the PCKG provides an admissible interval $[v_{\min}^{(m,c)}, v_{\max}^{(m,c)}]$, where c indexes the semantic classes and C is the total number of classes. Denote the mean physical value in region $\mathcal{R}_c$ by $\bar{v}_c^{(m)} = |\mathcal{R}_c|^{-1} \sum_{i \in \mathcal{R}_c} v_i^{(m)}$.

$$L_{\text{phys}}^{(m)} = \sum_{c=1}^{C} \Big[\big|\bar{v}_c^{(m)} - v_{\max}^{(m,c)}\big|_+^2 + \big|v_{\min}^{(m,c)} - \bar{v}_c^{(m)}\big|_+^2 \Big], \tag{3}$$

where $|x|_+ = \max(0, x)$. Averaging over variables yields $L_{\text{phys}} = \frac{1}{m} \sum_m L_{\text{phys}}^{(m)}$. The hinge acts only when $\bar{v}_c^{(m)}$ departs the legal range, gently steering predictions toward physical plausibility.

Total Loss. The overall objective for visualphysical joint training of PRIORSEG is

$$L_{\text{total}} = L_{\text{seg}} + \lambda_1 L_{\text{region}} + \lambda_2 L_{\text{phys}}, \tag{4}$$

with $\lambda_1 = 0.05$ and $\lambda_2 = 0.40$ tuned on the validation set.

By jointly observing Z during training, PriorSeg internalises the implicit mapping between visual features and physical rules.

2.4 Inference

PriorSeg operates in two modes, both starting from the *frozen* SkySense-O prediction $Y_{\text{pred}}^{(0)}$ and feature map F.

Visual-Only Mode. When no physical raster is available, the physics branch of PriorSeg is gated off. The refiner observes $(F, Y_{\text{pred}}^{(0)})$ and predicts a residual ΔY, yielding $Y_{\text{pred}}^{(1)} = Y_{\text{pred}}^{(0)} + \Delta Y$. The final label is $\hat{Y}_i = \arg\max_c Y_{\text{pred}}^{(1)}(i, c)$. Even without external measurements, PriorSeg relies on its learned visual-physics memory to correct visually ambiguous regions and produce physically plausible masks.

Visual-Physical Mode. If a subset $\mathcal{M}_{\text{avail}} \subseteq \{\text{NDVI}, \text{DEM}, \text{SAR}\}$ is provided, the corresponding variables $P^{(m)}$ are supplied to the physics branch. For each pixel i, class c, and variables m, let $d_i^{(m,c)}$ denote the distance between $v_i^{(m)}$ and its PCKG interval. With cap τ and tolerance σ,

$$s_i^{(m,c)} = \exp\Big[-\min\big(d_i^{(m,c)}, \tau\big)^2/\sigma^2\Big], \tag{5}$$

The attenuation over available variables is $S_i^{(c)} = \prod_{m\in\mathcal{M}_{\text{avail}}} s_i^{(m,c)}$. The refiner first produces ΔY as in the visual-only path; its output logits are then reweighted,

$$\tilde{p}_i^{(c)} = \frac{\big(Y_{\text{pred}}^{(1)}(i,c)\big)\, S_i^{(c)}}{\sum_j \big(Y_{\text{pred}}^{(1)}(i,j)\big)\, S_i^{(j)}}, \qquad \hat{Y}_i = \arg\max_c \tilde{p}_i^{(c)}. \tag{6}$$

The Gaussian factor $S_i^{(m,c)}$ down-weights classes whose measurements violate PCKG constraints, while τ prevents rare outliers from dominating. If $\mathcal{M}_{\text{avail}} = \varnothing$, then $S_i^{(c)} \equiv 1$ and the procedure degrades gracefully to visual-only mode.

With real physical variables, PriorSeg yields higher accuracy and stricter physical consistency; the *reasoning* field in the PCKG provides explicit interpretability for the applied corrections.

3 Experiments

To demonstrate that PriorSeg effectively improves the semantic segmentation accuracy of foundation models, we perform evaluations across five datasets covering diverse scenes and variables combinations, paired with different six backbone models. We observe consistent improvements of approximately 1.14% to 6.7% mIoU.

3.1 Implementation Details

We train PriorSeg model using two A100 (80 GB) GPUs. While several advanced LLMs-such as *ChatGPT* [8], *Gemini* [3], *LLaMA* [15], and *DeepSeek* [1]-offer impressive multi-modal and reasoning capabilities, we adopt *GPT-4o* for its superior performance in grounded reasoning and ease of API-based integration. Training utilizes Sky-SA (SkySense-O), a large-scale remote sensing dataset extended with additional physical variables data using a PCKG generated by GPT-4o.

Table 1. Performance comparison of six backbone models with and without the proposed PriorSeg refinement module. Results are reported as mIoU(%) on four datasets: RGB-only of OEM, iSAID, LoveDA, and RGB-Physics WHU-OPT-SAR, SEN12MS.

Model	Publication	RGB- Only OEM	RGB- Only iSAID	RGB- Only LoveDA	RGB- Phy WHU-OPT-SAR	RGB- Phy SEN12MS
SegGPT	ICCV 2023	25.19	29.17	31.40	23.42	21.84
SegGPT+PriorSeg		**27.33(+2.14)**	**32.18(+3.01)**	**33.55(+2.15)**	**29.33(+5.91)**	**27.56(+5.72)**
DINOv	CVPR 2023	23.05	25.35	25.17	22.74	20.09
DINOv+PriorSeg		**24.32(+1.27)**	**27.39(+2.04)**	**27.95(+2.78)**	**28.67(+5.93)**	**25.44(+5.35)**
SAN	CVPR 2023	24.87	11.77	27.83	25.97	21.33
SAN+PriorSeg		**27.22(+2.35)**	**15.24(+3.47)**	**30.51(+2.68)**	**32.71(+6.74)**	**26.76(+5.43)**
CAT-SEG	CVPR 2024	30.26	20.58	37.15	35.22	32.17
CAT-SEG+PriorSeg		**32.38(+2.12)**	**23.55(+2.97)**	**39.04(+1.89)**	**39.47(+4.25)**	**37.16(+4.99)**
SegEarth-OV	Arxiv 2024	40.30	21.70	36.90	31.61	30.21
SegEarth-OV+PriorSeg		**41.98(+1.68)**	**22.85(+1.15)**	**38.37(+1.47)**	**35.74(+4.13)**	**34.69(+4.48)**
SkySense-O	CVPR 2025	40.83	43.92	38.30	39.83	39.71
SkySense-O+PriorSeg		**41.97(+1.14)**	**45.23(+1.31)**	**39.72(+1.42)**	**42.98(+3.15)**	**43.10(+3.39)**

3.2 Zero-Shot Refinement Evaluation

We evaluate PriorSeg in two settings. In the *visual-only* mode, the model is tested on three external RGB benchmarks-iSAID [19], OEM [21], and LoveDA [17]-without any fine-tuning or exposure to their labels. Even without physical variables, PriorSeg consistently improves mIoU across all backbones (Table 1), indicating that its visualphysics memory generalizes from vision alone. In the *visual-physical* mode, PriorSeg is evaluated on WHU-OPT-SAR and SEN12MS, which provide real NDVI and SAR. Without retraining, it achieves the largest gains as physical variables activate PCKG-guided reasoning. As shown in Fig. 5, representative examples visually confirm these refinements.

3.3 Evaluation with Different Backbones

Because PriorSeg operates purely on the feature map and first-pass mask of a frozen backbone model, it can attach to arbitrary architectures. We test six backbones-SegGPT [18], DINOv [11], SAN [22], CAT-Seg [2], SegEarth-OV [13], and the original SkySense-O [24]. When a backbone's output visual feature shape differs from that of SkySense-O, a lightweight 1×1 adapter is inserted to match the expected tensor size; only the refiner (and, if present, the adapter) is trained. Across the four external datasets PriorSeg delivers consistent mIoU gains on every backbone (Table 1), confirming that the proposed refiner generalises well beyond its source model. The residual refiner is conservative with

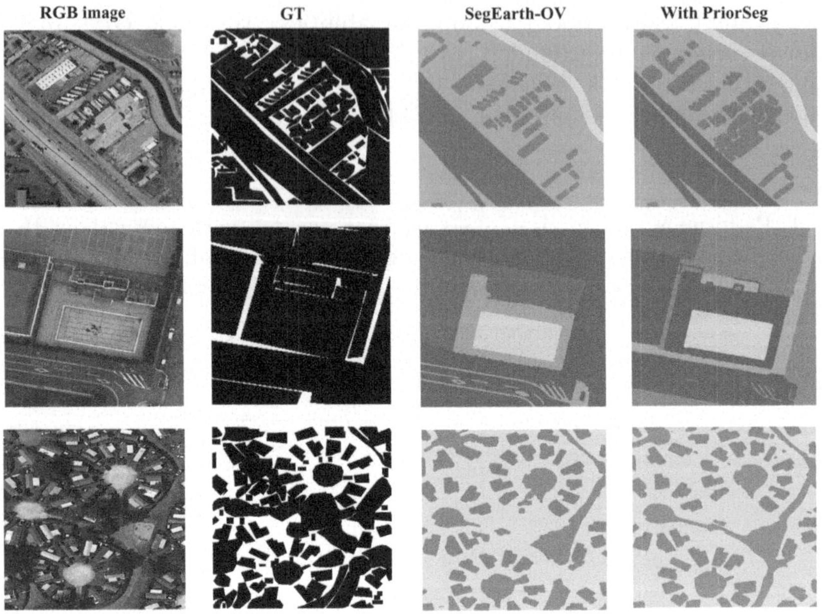

Fig. 5. Three representative visualization examples on SegEarth-OV backbone, comparing GT, SegEarth-OV predictions, and our PriorSeg-enhanced results.

respect to already correct regions. When applied to a strong baseline such as SkySense-O, which has been extensively trained on the Sky-SA dataset, PriorSeg performs only subtle adjustments on pixels whose physical readings violate the PCKG intervals or whose confidence is low. As a result, the observed gains are concentrated in areas exhibiting pronounced physical discrepancies, and the overall improvement remains moderate.

3.4 Reliability Analysis

To assess the reliability of simulated physical variables, we replicate the Phy-Sky-SA synthesis procedure on the WHU dataset, generating SAR, DEM, and NDVI variables from ground truth labels and PCKG intervals. The NDVI is computed as (NIR − Red)/(NIR + Red), while DEM data are sourced from manually preprocessed SRTM (30 m resolution) tiles covering Hubei Province (30–33°N, 108–117°E).

Figure 6 shows strong distributional overlap across NDVI, DEM, and SAR. NDVI matches most closely, DEM shows moderate variation, and SAR displays a wider natural spread. Median alignment and compact ranges confirm that PCKG-guided synthesis produces realistic physical characteristics suitable for downstream applications.

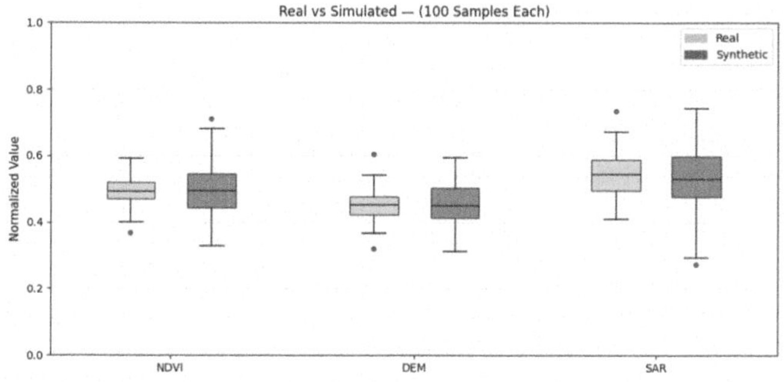

Fig. 6. Comparison between real and simulated physical variables on the WHU-OPT-SAR dataset.

Table 2. The ablation results of the SAN model on the WHU-OPT-SAR dataset, evaluating Phy-Sky-SA, PCKG, and $\mathcal{L}_{\text{phys}}$.

+Phy-Sky-SA	+PCKG	+$\mathcal{L}_{\text{phys}}$	mIoU (%)
			25.97
✓			27.69(**+1.72**)
✓	✓		29.93(**+2.24**)
✓	✓	✓	32.71(**+2.78**)

3.5 Ablation Study

Table 2 evaluates the contributions of Phy-Sky-SA, PCKG, and physics-consistency loss. Training on Phy-Sky-SA yields a 1.72% gain. Introducing the PCKG adds 2.24% by injecting pixel-wise physical logic. Adding the physics-consistency loss provides another 2.78%, penalizing visually ambiguous yet physically implausible predictions. Together, these components enable PriorSeg to leverage joint visualphysical information and deliver coherent refinement results.

4 Conclusion

We introduced a paradigm for transferring physical priors into remote sensing segmentation without requiring manually aligned datasets or retraining foundation models. Using large language models, we constructed the PCKG and the Phy-Sky-SA dataset with physically constrained NDVI, DEM, and SAR variables. Built on these priors, PriorSeg serves as a lightweight refinement module that enforces visual-physical consistency for frozen backbones. Experiments show improved segmentation accuracy and physical plausibility, and future work will incorporate more types of physical variables.

References

1. Bi, X., et al.: DeepSeek LLM: scaling open-source language models with longtermism (2024). https://doi.org/10.48550/ARXIV.2401.02954
2. Cho, S., Shin, H., Hong, S., Arnab, A., Seo, P.H., Kim, S.: CAT-Seg: cost aggregation for open-vocabulary semantic segmentation. In: Proceedings of the IEEE/CVF Conference on Computer Vision and Pattern Recognition, pp. 4113–4123 (2024)
3. Comanici, G., et al.: Gemini 2.5: pushing the frontier with advanced reasoning, multimodality, long context, and next generation agentic capabilities (2025). https://doi.org/10.48550/ARXIV.2507.06261
4. Guo, X., et al.: SkySense: a multi-modal remote sensing foundation model towards universal interpretation for earth observation imagery (2023). https://doi.org/10.48550/ARXIV.2312.10115
5. Guth, P.L., et al.: Digital elevation models: terminology and definitions. Remote Sens. **13**(18), 3581 (2021). https://doi.org/10.3390/rs13183581
6. Huang, S., Tang, L., Hupy, J.P., Wang, Y., Shao, G.: A commentary review on the use of normalized difference vegetation index (NDVI) in the era of popular remote sensing. J. For. Res. **32**(1), 1–6 (2021). https://doi.org/10.1007/s11676-020-01155-1
7. Huang, Z., et al.: A survey on remote sensing foundation models: from vision to multimodality. arXiv preprint arXiv:2503.22081 (2025)
8. Hurst, A., et al.: GPT-4o System Card (2024). https://doi.org/10.48550/ARXIV.2410.21276
9. Jia, W., Liang, B., Lu, Y., Khan, M.A., Zheng, L.: A comprehensive survey on deep learning solutions for 3D flood mapping. In: Pacific-Asia Conference on Knowledge Discovery and Data Mining, pp. 21–38. Springer (2025)
10. Jia, W., Liang, B., Lu, Y., Wilaiwongsakul, A., Khan, M.A., Zheng, L.: HOTA: hierarchical overlap-tiling aggregation for large-area 3D flood mapping. In: Asian Conference on Pattern Recognition, pp. 188–202. Springer (2025)
11. Li, F., et al.: Visual in-context prompting. In: Proceedings of the IEEE/CVF Conference on Computer Vision and Pattern Recognition, pp. 12861–12871 (2024)
12. Li, J., Huang, X., Gong, J.: Deep neural network for remote-sensing image interpretation: status and perspectives. Natl. Sci. Rev. **6**(6), 1082–1086 (2019). https://doi.org/10.1093/nsr/nwz058
13. Li, K., et al.: SegEarth-OV: towards training-free open-vocabulary segmentation for remote sensing images. In: Proceedings of the Computer Vision and Pattern Recognition Conference, pp. 10545–10556 (2025)
14. Liu, F., et al.: RemoteCLIP: a vision language foundation model for remote sensing. IEEE Trans. Geosci. Remote Sens. **62**, 1–16 (2024). https://doi.org/10.1109/TGRS.2024.3390838
15. Touvron, H., et al.: LLaMA: open and efficient foundation language models (2023). https://doi.org/10.48550/ARXIV.2302.13971
16. Tsokas, A., Rysz, M., Pardalos, P.M., Dipple, K.: SAR data applications in earth observation: an overview. Expert Syst. Appl. **205**, 117342 (2022). https://doi.org/10.1016/j.eswa.2022.117342
17. Wang, J., Zheng, Z., Ma, A., Lu, X., Zhong, Y.: LoveDa: a remote sensing land-cover dataset for domain adaptive semantic segmentation (2021). arXiv preprint arXiv:2110.08733
18. Wang, X., Zhang, X., Cao, Y., Wang, W., Shen, C., Huang, T.: SegGPT: segmenting everything in context. arXiv e-prints, arXiv–2304 (2023)

19. Waqas Zamir, S., et al.: iSAID: a large-scale dataset for instance segmentation in aerial images. In: Proceedings of the IEEE/CVF Conference on Computer Vision and Pattern Recognition Workshops, pp. 28–37 (2019)
20. Wilaiwongsakul, A., Liang, B., Jia, W., Zheng, B., Chen, F.: BARE: boundary-aware with resolution enhancement for tree crown delineation. In: Australasian Conference on Data Science and Machine Learning, pp. 302–315. Springer (2025)
21. Wu, C.H.: OEM product design in a price competition with remanufactured product. Omega **41**(2), 287–298 (2013)
22. Xu, M., Zhang, Z., Wei, F., Hu, H., Bai, X.: Side adapter network for open-vocabulary semantic segmentation. In: Proceedings of the IEEE/CVF Conference on Computer Vision and Pattern Recognition (CVPR), pp. 2945–2954 (2023)
23. Yuan, X., Shi, J., Gu, L.: A review of deep learning methods for semantic segmentation of remote sensing imagery. Expert Syst. Appl. **169**, 114417 (2021). https://doi.org/10.1016/j.eswa.2020.114417
24. Zhu, Q., et al.: SkySense-O: towards open-world remote sensing interpretation with vision-centric visual-language modeling. In: Proceedings of the Computer Vision and Pattern Recognition Conference (2025)

C^3: Capturing Consensus with Contrastive Learning in Group Recommendation

Soyoung Kim[1], Dongjun Lee[2], and Jaekwang Kim[3(✉)]

[1] Department of Applied Artificial Intelligence/Convergence Program for Social Innovation, Sungkyunkwan University, Seoul, South Korea
syfg6716@g.skku.edu

[2] Department of Electrical and Computer Engineering, Sungkyunkwan University, Suwon, South Korea
akm5825@g.skku.edu

[3] Department of Immersive Media Engineering/Convergence Program for Social Innovation, Sungkyunkwan University, Seoul, South Korea
linux@skku.edu

Abstract. Group recommendation aims to recommend tailored items to groups of users, where the key challenge is modeling a consensus that reflects member preferences. Although several existing deep learning models have achieved performance improvements, they still fail to capture consensus in various aspects: (1) Capturing consensus in small-group ($2 \sim 5$ members) recommendation systems, which align more closely with real-world scenarios, remains a significant challenge; (2) Most existing models significantly enhance the overall group performance but struggle with balancing individual and group performance. To address these issues, we propose **C**apturing **C**onsensus with **C**ontrastive Learning in Group Recommendation (C^3), which focuses on exploring the consensus behind group decision-making. A Transformer encoder is used to learn both group and user representations, and contrastive learning mitigates overfitting for users with many interactions, yielding more robust group representations. Experiments on four public datasets demonstrate that C^3 significantly outperforms state-of-the-art baselines in both user and group recommendation tasks.

Keywords: Group Recommendation · Transformer Encoder · Contrastive Learning

1 Introduction

Group activities, such as traveling with friends or dining with family, are essential in human social life, and these activities are planned through online platforms, such as Mafengwo[1] and Meetup[2].

[1] https://www.mafengwo.cn.

[2] https://www.meetup.com.

R. C.-W. Wong et al. (Eds.): PAKDD 2026, LNAI 16617, pp. 598–610, 2027.
https://doi.org/10.1007/978-981-92-1926-1_48

Traditional recommendation systems primarily focus on recommending items relevant to individual users. However, such systems are less effective in group recommendation scenarios, where group members have diverse preferences and varied interactions with items. Group recommendation involves challenges such as capturing the noise arising from varying user preferences and interactions [20]. Prior work has primarily focused on aggregating member preferences to infer group preference [1,4–7]. Early approaches use simple rules such as average [4], least misery [1], or maximum satisfaction [3]. These heuristic-based methods cannot adapt to the dynamic and diverse opinions of group members [16]. With the advancement of deep learning, attention-based models have been introduced. For example, AGREE [5] utilizes attention mechanisms to dynamically adjust the influence of group members. However, assigning higher weights to users with frequent interactions lead to overfitting, especially in small-group, where recommendations become overly focus on highly interactive individuals. Recently, hypergraph neural network-based (HGNN-based) methods, which allow a single node to connect to multiple edges, have been applied to group recommendation systems. This approach is particularly suitable for scenarios involving groups composed of multiple users and has demonstrated significant performance improvements in this domain [7,16].

Despite these advancements, challenges remain. **(1) The challenge of capturing small-group (i.e., between 2 and 5 members) consensus.** Consensus reflects a group's final agreement, integrating the diverse preferences of its members and guiding decision making [16]. In this study, we regard a model as effectively capturing consensus if the group representation for the target item remains stable even when some users are randomly masked. As illustrated in Fig. 1, consider a small group that has rated visited places. Because most members frequently travel to destinations in Asia, the group's consensus preference for an overseas trip should naturally lean toward Asia. However, attention-based methods may overfit to a highly interactive member and skew recommendations toward Europe. Recent HGNN-based models have been extensively studied to capture group consensus [16,17]. ConsRec [16] was designed to comprehensively capture group consensus by using hypergraph convolutional operations, which enable the generation of rich member representations. However, most HGNN-based models exhibit performance degradation on datasets with high interaction but small-group [7,16]. This is because they fail to provide diverse recommendations that reflect the preferences of all group members.

(2) Contrastive learning without leveraging the group's original preference representation. Group-item interactions are often sparse, posing substantial challenges in effectively learning group preferences. To address this, contrastive learning has been adopted in group recommendation for data sparsity problem [20]. For instance, CubeRec [7] utilizes hypercube modeling integrated with contrastive self-supervision to address data sparsity issues. The Transformer encoder-based model GBERT [19] employs contrastive learning by generating fake groups to compare with real groups. However, the effectiveness of contrastive learning relies on high-quality data augmentation and the accurate generation of

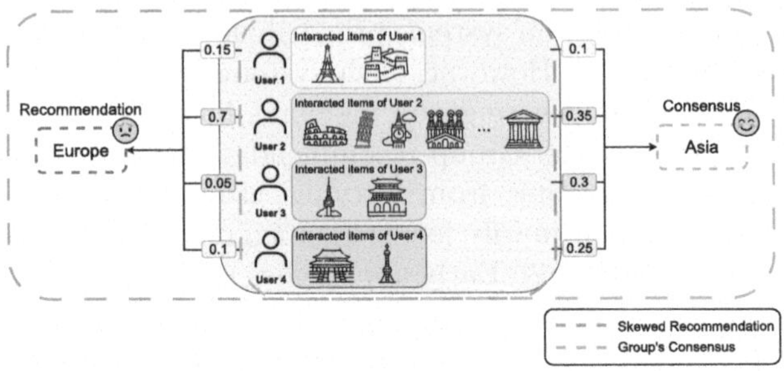

Fig. 1. Comparison of group recommendation scenarios a red-dotted example where one dominant user shifts the choice to Europe, and a blue-dotted example where full preference aggregation yields an Asia-leaning consensus. (Color figure online)

contrasting representations, making it challenging to generalize these methods to diverse group recommendation scenarios [20]. Furthermore, these methods fail to effectively utilize the representation of the original group, which can result in overfitting to the remaining users when the group size temporarily changes.

(3) Difficulty of generalization. Most group recommendation systems focus on improving group performance, even if it involves reducing recommendation performance for individual users [17]. Since group recommendation aggregates the preferences of individual users, an effective group recommendation system must not only perform well for groups but also offer accurate recommendations for individual users. It can be argued that such a model is effective and demonstrates generalization ability.

To address these challenges, we present **C**apturing **C**onsensus with **C**ontrastive Learning in Group Recommendation, namely C^3. C^3 employs a Transformer encoder to model both useritem and groupitem interactions, enabling a generalized recommendation system that mitigates performance degradation in user tasks. In particular, we design a recommendation loss with three components: positive, negative, and margin, as well as a contrastive loss based on an augmentation strategy. Positive loss emphasizes items interacted with by a user or group, with logarithmic scaling to regulate its magnitude. Negative loss suppresses predictions for non-interacted items via exponential scaling, while margin loss explicitly widens the positivenegative gap to enforce stronger separation. We also promote group consensus by creating two augmented views of each group through random user masking. In each batch, the two corrupted views form a positive pair against all others, pulling positives together and pushing negatives apart. This stabilizes group representations under member dropouts, prevents overfitting to highly active users, and better captures whole-group preferences.

2 Method

2.1 Task Definition

Let $\mathcal{U}$, $\mathcal{I}$, and $\mathcal{G}$ denote the user, item, and group sets: $\mathcal{U} = \{u_1, u_2, \ldots, u_M\}$, $\mathcal{I} = \{i_1, i_2, \ldots, i_N\}$, and $\mathcal{G} = \{g_1, g_2, \ldots, g_K\}$, where M, N, and K are their sizes. We consider two interaction types: useritem and groupitem. For group g_k, its interacted items are $\mathcal{Y}_k = \{i_1, i_2, \ldots, i|\mathcal{Y}_k|\}$ with $i_n \in \mathcal{I}$. Given a target group g_t, we predict a ranked list of items the group is likely to prefer [16].

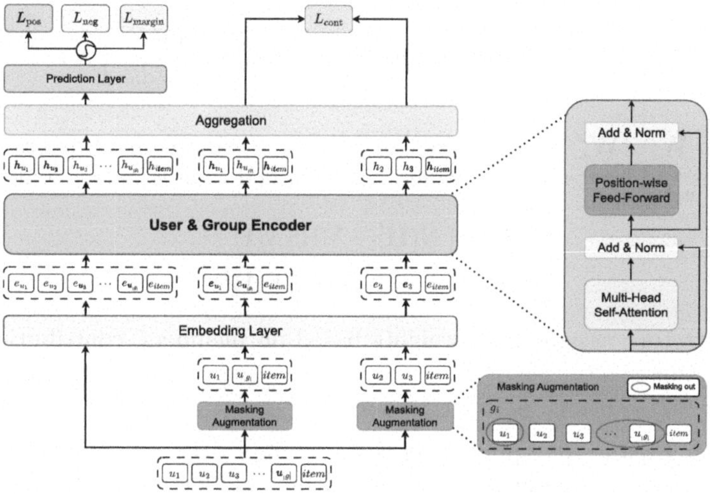

Fig. 2. Overview of our proposed C^3, consisting of the transformer encoder, margin loss, and contrastive loss.

2.2 C^3 Framework

Embedding Layer. We embed each user and item into d-dimensional vectors using $\mathbf{E}_u \in \mathbb{R}^{M \times d}$ and $\mathbf{E}_i \in \mathbb{R}^{N \times d}$. For a group $g = \{u_1^g, u_2^g, \ldots, u_{|g|}^g\}$, each member u_m^g is mapped to $\mathbf{e}_m^g$ via $\mathbf{E}_u \cdot u_m^g$, and each item to $\mathbf{e}_{\text{item}}$. The input to C^3 is the concatenation of user and item embeddings, formulated as:

$$\mathbf{H}_{g,i}^0 = \text{Concat}(\{\mathbf{e}_{u_j^g}\}_{j=1}^{|g|}, e_{\text{item}}), \tag{1}$$

where $\mathbf{H}_g^0$ represents the initial hidden state. In the case of user recommendation, where $|g| = 1$, the group consists of a single user.

User and Group Encoder. The encoder in Fig. 2 is built from stacked Transformer encoder layers [8]. Each layer contains two submodules: a multi-head self-attention (MHSA) block and a position-wise feed-forward (FF) network. MHSA uses self-attention to capture dependencies among tokens in a sequence, and its effectiveness has been widely validated in prior work. In our model, MHSA is used to model interactions between group members and candidate item, enabling the encoder to learn representations that reflect group preference dynamics:

$$\begin{aligned} \mathrm{MHSA}(\mathbf{H}^l) &= \mathrm{Concat}(\mathrm{head}_1, \ldots, \mathrm{head}_h)\mathbf{W}^O, \\ \text{where, } \mathrm{head}_i &= \mathrm{Attention}(\mathbf{H}^l\mathbf{W}_i^Q, \mathbf{H}^l\mathbf{W}_i^K, \mathbf{H}^l\mathbf{W}_i^V), \\ \mathrm{Attention}(\mathbf{Q}, \mathbf{K}, \mathbf{V}) &= \mathrm{softmax}\left(\frac{\mathbf{Q}\mathbf{K}^\top}{\sqrt{d_k}}\right)\mathbf{V}, \end{aligned} \tag{2}$$

Here, $\mathbf{W}_i^Q$, $\mathbf{W}_i^K$, $\mathbf{W}_i^V \in \mathbb{R}^{d \times \frac{d}{h}}$, $\mathbf{W}^O \in \mathbb{R}^{d \times d}$ are trainable parameters. Residual connections and layer normalization [2] are applied as in standard Transformers.

$$\begin{aligned} \tilde{\mathbf{H}}^l &= \mathrm{LN}(\mathbf{H}^l + \mathrm{MHSA}(\mathbf{H}^l)), \\ \mathbf{H}^{l+1} &= \mathrm{LN}(\tilde{\mathbf{H}}^l + \mathrm{FF}(\tilde{\mathbf{H}}^l)), \end{aligned} \tag{3}$$

This architecture assigns high weights based on members' contribution to the final prediction.

Prediction Layer. The prediction layer estimates the probability that a user or group will prefer an item. The encoder outputs hidden vectors for the members and the item, which are merged into a single representation via mean pooling:

$$\mathbf{h}_{g,i} = \frac{1}{|g| + 1}\left(\sum_{j=1}^{|g|} \mathbf{h}_{u_j} + \mathbf{h}_{item}\right), \tag{4}$$

where $\mathbf{h}_{g,i}$ denotes the aggregated group representation. We then apply a linear layer followed by a sigmoid to obtain the interaction score:

$$s_{g,i} = \sigma(\mathbf{W}\mathbf{h}_{g,i} + \mathbf{b}) \tag{5}$$

2.3 Optimization for Recommendation Task

We treat items interacted with by a user or group as positive, and all others as negative. For training, we use a recommendation loss composed of positive, negative, and margin terms, defined as follows. The positive loss encourages high probability for positive items:

$$\mathcal{L}_{\mathrm{pos}} = \frac{1}{|\mathcal{P}|} \sum_{g \in \mathcal{G}, i \in \mathcal{P}} - \log(s_{g,i} + \epsilon), \tag{6}$$

where $\mathcal{P}$ is the set of positive items, and ϵ is a negligible constant for numerical stability. Logarithmic scaling is applied to this loss function to ensure that lower scores assigned to positive items result in higher penalties. Negative loss penalizes predictions for negative items, thus ensuring that negative items receive lower probability in the predictions.

$$\mathcal{L}_{\text{neg}} = \frac{1}{|\mathcal{N}|} \sum_{g \in \mathcal{G}, j \in \mathcal{N}} \left[\exp(s_{g,j}) - 1\right], \tag{7}$$

$\mathcal{N}$ is the set of negative samples. Additionally, margin loss enforces a difference between the predictions of positive and negative samples, ensuring that positive items rank higher than negative items in the predictions:

$$\mathcal{L}_{\text{margin}} = \frac{1}{|\mathcal{P}|} \sum_{g \in \mathcal{G}, p \in \mathcal{P}} \frac{1}{|\mathcal{N}|} \sum_{n \in \mathcal{N}} \max\left(0, \delta - (s_{g,p} - s_{g,n})\right), \tag{8}$$

δ is the margin hyperparameter. Unlike Bayesian Personalized Ranking (BPR) [14], which only adjusts pairwise item ordering, proposed losses adjust predicted probabilities to clearly distinguish positive from negative items, thereby reflecting absolute scores. Moreover, the margin term encourages the model to maintain a relative gap between positive and negative probabilities. Finally, the total loss is computed as follows:

$$\mathcal{L}_{\text{main}} = \alpha\left(\mathcal{L}_{\text{pos}} + \mathcal{L}_{\text{neg}}\right) + (1-\alpha)\mathcal{L}_{\text{margin}} \tag{9}$$

where α is a hyperparameter that mediates the balance between two losses.

2.4 Contrastive Learning

Augmentation. A group consists of multiple users whose preferences are aggregated with a encoder. However, since self-attention favors users with stronger interactions, the model may overweight highly active members and produce biased recommendations. To address this, we design a masking augmentation that preserves members' preferences and produces robust representations even with missing users. In training, we randomly mask users and generate two independent augmented views per group. The two views from the same original group constitute a positive pair, while views from different groups are treated as negatives. This augmentation is formulated as:

$$g' = g \setminus \mathcal{M}, \quad \mathcal{M} \subseteq g, \quad |\mathcal{M}| = \lfloor r \cdot |g| \rfloor \tag{10}$$

g' represents the augmented group. $\mathcal{M}$ denotes the selected subset of g for masking, and r indicates the masking ratio. To distinguish between augmented samples, for the i-th group g_i, the corresponding augmented samples are denoted as g'_{2j} and g'_{2j+1}. In this module, we randomly select a subset of $\mathcal{M}$ for masking. This randomness prevents the learned representations from overfitting to specific users and helps avoid trivial collapse in contrastive learning. Additionally, we introduce a threshold hyperparameter to regulate the augmentation. Augmentation is applied only to groups above a size threshold to avoid excessive distortion in very small groups.

Self-supervised Learning Signal. As discussed in the previous section, augmented samples pass through all layers to obtain the hidden representations $\mathbf{h}_{g'_{2j}}$ and $\mathbf{h}_{g'_{2j+1}}$. Then, we compute the contrastive loss using the InfoNCE [13]:

$$\mathcal{L}_{\textbf{Cont}}(g'_{2j}, g'_{2j+1}) = -\log\frac{\exp(\text{sim}(\mathbf{h}_{g'_{2j}}, \mathbf{h}_{g'_{2j+1}})/\tau)}{\sum_{k=1}^{2B} \mathbb{1}_{[j\neq k]}\exp(\text{sim}(\mathbf{h}_{g'_{2j}}, \mathbf{h}_{g'_{k}})/\tau)} \tag{11}$$

Table 1. The statistics of the datasets.

Dataset	#Users	#Items	#Groups	#U-I interactions	#G-I interactions	Avg. group size
Mafengwo	5,275	1,513	995	39,761	3,595	7.19
CAMRa2011	602	7,710	290	116,344	145,068	2.08
MovieLens	943	1,682	5,000	99,057	88,705	4.27
MafengwoS	11,027	1,236	1,215	8,237	2,468	12.34

where B is the batch size and τ is the temperature. This loss pulls positive pairs together and pushes negatives apart within each mini-batch, enabling the encoder to learn similar representations for augmented groups with removed users and thus maintain stable group representations even when highly engaged members are masked. Group-preferred items should reflect the consensus of all members. Therefore, even if excluding some users changes the top-ranked item as group composition varies, the model should still assign high scores to previously preferred items. This loss is incorporated into main loss with a scaling factor β:

$$\mathcal{L} = \mathcal{L}_{\text{main}} + \beta \cdot \mathcal{L}_{\text{cont}} \tag{12}$$

3 Experiments

3.1 Experimental Setup

Datasets. Mafengwo is a tourism platform where users record visited locations and form travel groups. CAMRa2011 [5] includes household movie ratings, containing group preferences. MovieLens, designed in previous group recommendation research [20], is constructed by randomly selecting users as members of a group. MafengwoS [16] is a reconstructed Mafengwo dataset that includes semantic details such as item names. Table 1 summarizes the dataset statistics.

Evaluation Metrics. Following prior settings [5,6], We evaluate the top-K recommendation performance using hit ratio at K (HR@K) and normalized discounted cumulative gain at K (NDCG@K) [10]. We reports results for HR@1/5/10 and NDCG@5/10. Best performance is in bold and second-best is underlined (Table 2).

Baselines. We evaluate our model[3] against state-of-the-art baselines:

Classical Neural Network-Based Model: (1) **NCF** [9] treats each group as a single virtual user for making predictions.

Attention-Based Models: (1) **AGREE** [5] employs an attention mechanism to dynamically aggregate user preferences within a group. (2) **GroupIM** [15] aggregates user preferences via attention mechanism and applies self-supervised learning to address data sparsity.

Graph Neural Network (GNN)-Based Models: (1) **S^2-HHGR** [18] employs hierarchical hypergraph to capture interactions within and across groups. (2) **CubeRec** [7] uses hypercubes to adaptively aggregate group members' interests through geometric expressiveness. (3) **ConsRec** [16] captures group consensus by jointly modeling member, item, and group perspectives. (4) **AlignGroup** [17] captures group consensus via hypergraph and leverages self-supervised learning to reduce the gap between group consensus and individual preferences. DHMAE [20] is excluded due to an issue that produced incorrect predictions[4].

Table 2. Performance comparison over all baselines on group recommendation task.

Datasets	Metrics	NCF	AGREE	GroupIM	S^2-HHGR	CubeRec	ConsRec	AlignGroup	C^3	Improv.
Mafengwo	HR@1	0.3242	0.4563	0.3387	0.6809	0.6312	0.6231	0.6744	**0.8613**	27.71%
	HR@5	0.4291	0.7045	0.6412	0.7568	0.8533	0.8824	**0.9548**	0.8864	–
	HR@10	0.6181	0.7769	0.7367	0.7779	0.9025	0.9056	**0.9628**	0.9115	–
	NDCG@5	0.3405	0.5892	0.4986	0.7322	0.7572	0.7697	0.8343	**0.8711**	4.41%
	NDCG@10	0.4020	0.6126	0.5295	0.7391	0.7734	0.7794	0.8369	**0.8796**	5.10%
CAMRa2011	HR@1	0.1957	0.3097	0.2083	0.1600	0.2110	0.1966	0.8048	**0.9255**	15.00%
	HR@5	0.5803	0.5910	0.6152	0.6131	0.6435	0.6366	0.8062	**0.9262**	14.88%
	HR@10	0.7693	0.7807	0.7993	0.8152	0.8262	0.8145	0.8324	**0.9269**	11.35%
	NDCG@5	0.3896	0.4016	0.4164	0.3882	0.4334	0.4218	0.8055	**0.9258**	14.93%
	NDCG@10	0.4448	0.4530	0.4763	0.4547	0.4932	0.4793	0.8135	**0.9260**	13.83%
MovieLens	HR@1	0.2230	0.4349	0.1512	0.0280	0.3220	0.4546	0.7624	**0.9258**	21.43%
	HR@5	0.3991	0.7816	0.6177	0.2151	0.7282	0.7615	0.8268	**0.9266**	12.07%
	HR@10	0.5886	0.8871	0.8232	0.3622	0.8615	0.8531	0.8914	**0.9318**	4.53%
	NDCG@5	0.3899	0.6176	0.3869	0.1203	0.5378	0.6213	0.7941	**0.9261**	16.62%
	NDCG@10	0.4561	0.6519	0.4545	0.1675	0.5812	0.6512	0.8148	**0.9278**	13.87%
MafengwoS	HR@1	0.0366	0.1581	0.2526	0.0516	0.4089	0.3436	0.3471	**0.4227**	3.37%
	HR@5	0.0728	0.4485	0.5464	0.1787	0.6289	0.6443	0.6392	**0.7354**	14.14%
	HR@10	0.1965	0.5997	0.6632	0.2698	0.6993	0.7106	0.7680	**0.8076**	5.16%
	NDCG@5	0.0978	0.3062	0.4038	0.1169	0.5052	0.5051	0.5012	**0.5771**	14.23%
	NDCG@10	0.1064	0.3555	0.4422	0.1464	0.5482	0.5362	0.5436	**0.6012**	9.67%

[3] The code is available on https://github.com/soso-young/C3.
[4] https://github.com/ICharlotteI/DHMAE/issues/3.

Table 3. Performance comparison of all methods on the user recommendation task.

Datasets	Metrics	NCF	AGREE	GroupIM	S^2-HHGR	CubeRec	ConsRec	AlignGroup	C^3	Improv.
Mafengwo	HR@1	0.2386	0.2816	0.2406	0.2497	0.0393	0.6009	0.6693	**0.9282**	38.68%
	HR@5	0.6363	0.6790	0.6237	0.6761	0.1887	0.7720	0.8033	**0.9373**	16.68%
	HR@10	0.7417	0.7834	0.7674	0.7976	0.3478	0.8381	0.8541	**0.9521**	11.47%
	NDCG@5	0.5432	0.4951	0.4447	0.4781	0.1121	0.6877	0.7377	**0.9321**	26.35%
	NDCG@10	0.5733	0.5293	0.4911	0.5176	0.1636	0.7095	0.7541	**0.9368**	24.23%
CAMRa2011	HR@1	0.3285	0.3568	0.2113	0.1741	0.1641	0.2199	0.8209	**0.9485**	15.54%
	HR@5	0.6119	0.6243	0.6229	0.6375	0.6276	0.6774	0.8239	**0.9485**	15.12%
	HR@10	0.7894	0.7967	0.7993	0.8239	0.8215	0.8515	0.8348	**0.9502**	11.59%
	NDCG@5	0.4018	0.4217	0.4234	0.4105	0.4054	0.4531	0.8222	**0.9485**	15.36%
	NDCG@10	0.4535	0.4827	0.4810	0.4718	0.4686	0.5100	0.8256	**0.9490**	14.95%
MovieLens	HR@1	0.0258	0.0817	0.0477	0.0668	0.0371	0.1644	0.4677	**0.6723**	43.75%
	HR@5	0.1278	0.3128	0.2238	0.3044	0.1474	0.3139	0.4783	**0.6734**	40.79%
	HR@10	0.2869	0.4836	0.3701	0.4899	0.2566	0.4846	0.5281	**0.6851**	29.73%
	NDCG@5	0.0775	0.1955	0.1329	0.1825	0.0918	0.2354	0.4722	**0.6729**	42.50%
	NDCG@10	0.1926	0.2507	0.1793	0.2425	0.1269	0.2902	0.4878	**0.6766**	38.70%
MafengwoS	HR@1	0.0046	0.1225	0.1004	0.0783	0.0735	0.1434	0.0741	**0.2915**	103.28%
	HR@5	0.0929	0.3554	0.3220	0.2903	0.2127	0.3811	0.2784	**0.3967**	4.09%
	HR@10	0.1565	0.5137	0.4851	0.4361	0.3345	0.5054	0.4265	**0.5538**	7.81%
	NDCG@5	0.0688	0.2419	0.2124	0.1843	0.1430	0.2645	0.1766	**0.3398**	28.47%
	NDCG@10	0.0894	0.2926	0.2649	0.2318	0.1826	0.3043	0.2242	**0.3904**	28.29%

Table 4. Ablation study on the contribution of our framework's loss functions.

Task	Dataset	Metrics	w/o. Margin	w/o. Cont	C^3
Group	**CAMRa2011**	HR@10	0.8903	0.9110	**0.9269**
		NDCG@10	0.8846	0.9082	**0.9260**
	MovieLens	HR@10	0.9022	0.9163	**0.9318**
		NDCG@10	0.8804	0.9055	**0.9278**
User	**CAMRa2011**	HR@10	0.9173	0.9286	**0.9502**
		NDCG@10	0.9188	0.9249	**0.9490**
	MovieLens	HR@10	0.6066	0.6617	**0.6851**
		NDCG@10	0.5873	0.6546	**0.6766**

Implementation Details. We optimize our method with Adam [11]. The embedding dimension sets to 32, and the model uses 3 layers with a 0.2 dropout rate. We set $\tau = 1.0$, margin $\delta = 1$, and $\alpha = 0.5$. The threshold is tuned from $\{3, 5, 7, 9\}$, the mask ratio from $\{0.2, 0.4, 0.6, 0.8\}$, and β from $\{0.025, 0.05, 0.075, 0.1\}$. We adopt baseline hyperparameters from the original papers.

3.2 Overall Performance Comparison

Group recommendation task. C^3 achieves significant improvements in group recommendation performance, particularly in @1 and the NDCG metrics. Furthermore, the improvements are particularly evident on small-group datasets such as CAMRa2011 and MovieLens. Our approach learns through masking group members to capture the diverse preferences of all users within the group. It indicates that learning the preferences of all users more uniformly, rather than relying on specific individual, is crucial to precisely modeling group representation. In contrast, GNN-based models exhibit a significant decline in performance across nearly all metrics on small-group datasets. This suggests that GNN are well-suited for group scenarios; however, their performance degrades when groups are small, as the reduced nodeedge connectivity limits their effectiveness.

User Recommendation Task. In the user recommendation task,(illustrated in Table 3), C^3 demonstrates outstanding performance across all metrics and datasets. The Transformer architecture is key to this result. Unlike a Transformer model [19] designed to take only user embeddings as input, our model takes both user and item inputs. This design enables the model, when learning user representations, to capture a user's individual preferences and that user's preferences within the group, allowing the two tasks to complement each other. It is noted that robust user representations improve group modeling and recommendation performance for both users and groups. Thus, C^3 can be considered a generalized group recommendation system (Table 4).

3.3 Ablation Study

Without Margin Loss (w/o. Margin). Margin loss showed the largest improvement, with 5.38% in group and 15.21% in user, respectively. Since margin loss focuses on maximizing the interval between positive and negative items, it directly impacts the ranking list. Specifically, it showed significant improvements in user recommendation.

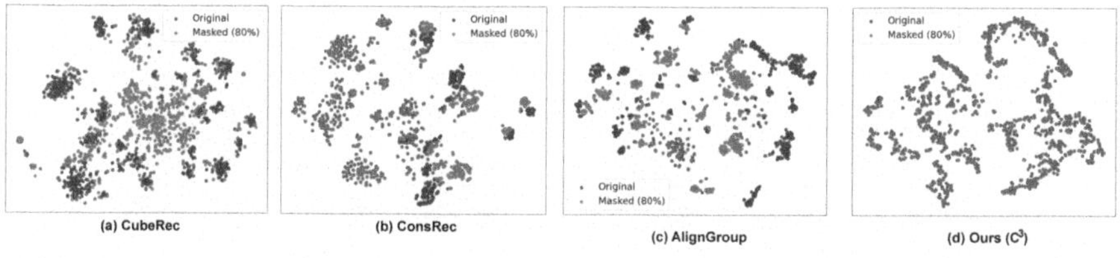

Fig. 3. Visualization of the original representations (blue dots) and masked representations (red dots), where 80% of random users in a group are removed on Mafengwo. (Color figure online)

Without Contrastive Loss (w/o. Cont). Our contrastive loss improves performance by 2.46% for groups and 3.54% for users. Although designed to capture diverse group preferences, its gain in user recommendation likely stems from the Transformer. The Transformer inherently assigns attention to interactive members through relationship among user(s) and item, while contrastive loss encourages learning on less interactive members, leading to enhanced user representation. Overall, these losses strengthen the efficiency of C^3.

3.4 Capturing a Consensus

This evaluation demonstrates the extent to which the model preserves the robustness of the group representation, which represents the aggregated preferences of group members for the target item. To illustrate this, we visualize group embeddings using t-SNE [12] comparing original groups with versions where 80% of users are removed. We experiment with models designed to capture group consensus (ConsRec [16] and AlignGroup [17]) and a self-supervised learning-based model (CubeRec [7]). As shown in Fig. 3, ConsRec and AlignGroup show minimal drift under user removal, while CubeRec preserves some structure but with noticeable changes. In contrast, C^3 produces representations nearly identical to the originals, demonstrating that it reflects consensus in recommendations.

3.5 Effect of Different Group Sizes

In group recommendation, different group sizes affect performance, so robustness across sizes is essential [7]. We compare C^3 with four baselines on the Mafengwo, categorizing group sizes following the CubeRec [7] definition of small groups (i.e., 2∼5 members). As shown in Fig. 4, the baselines perform worst on small groups and improve with larger sizes, while C^3 achieves the best performance on small groups and also improves for groups with 10 or more members, demonstrating robustness. A decline for 6∼9 members groups likely stems from their small proportion in the dataset, where even minor errors cause noticeable drops.

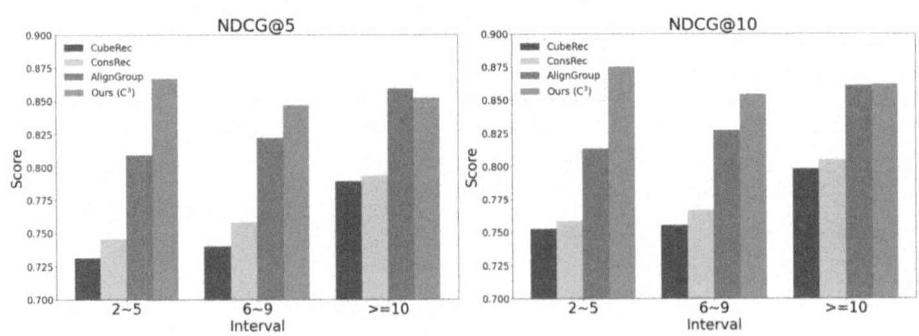

Fig. 4. NDCG@K comparison across group sizes on the Mafengwo dataset.

4 Conclusion

In this paper, we introduce C^3, a group recommendation method that captures group consensus using a Transformer encoder. Our method not only enhances group recommendation performance but also improves user recommendation performance, contributing to a more generalized group recommendation system. Additionally, we design a recommendation loss and a contrastive loss to keep group representations robust, preventing the model from focusing too much on highly interactive members and helping it better reflect diverse preferences. Extensive experiments on four public datasets demonstrate the effectiveness of C^3.

Acknowledgments. This research was supported by the Basic Science Research Program of the National Research Foundation (NRF) funded by the Korean government (MSIT) (No. IITP-2026-RS-2024-00346737); and by three additional grants from the Institute for Information & Communications Technology Planning & Evaluation (IITP) funded by the Ministry of Science and ICT (MSIT), Korea, through the Global Scholars Invitation Program (No. IITP-2026-RS-2024-00459638), the Graduate School of Metaverse Convergence at Sungkyun-kwan University (No. IITP-2026-RS-2023-00254129), and the ICT Challenge and Advanced Network of HRD (ICAN) support program (No. IITP-2026-RS-2023-00259497).

Disclosure of Interests. The authors have no competing interests to declare that are relevant to the content of this article.

References

1. Amer-Yahia, S., Roy, S.B., Chawlat, A., Das, G., Yu, C.: Group recommendation: semantics and efficiency. Proc. VLDB Endowment **2**(1), 754–765 (2009)
2. Ba, J.L.: Layer normalization. arXiv preprint arXiv:1607.06450 (2016)
3. Baltrunas, L., Makcinskas, T., Ricci, F.: Group recommendations with rank aggregation and collaborative filtering. In: Proceedings of the fourth ACM Conference on Recommender Systems, pp. 119–126 (2010)
4. Boratto, L., Carta, S.: State-of-the-art in group recommendation and new approaches for automatic identification of groups. In: Information Retrieval and Mining in Distributed Environments, pp. 1–20. Springer (2011)
5. Cao, D., He, X., Miao, L., An, Y., Yang, C., Hong, R.: Attentive group recommendation. In: The 41st International ACM SIGIR Conference on Research & Development in Information Retrieval, pp. 645–654 (2018)
6. Cao, D., He, X., Miao, L., Xiao, G., Chen, H., Xu, J.: Social-enhanced attentive group recommendation. IEEE Trans. Knowl. Data Eng. **33**(3), 1195–1209 (2019)
7. Chen, T., Yin, H., Long, J., Nguyen, Q.V.H., Wang, Y., Wang, M.: Thinking inside the box: learning hypercube representations for group recommendation. In: Proceedings of the 45th International ACM SIGIR Conference on Research and Development in Information Retrieval, pp. 1664–1673 (2022)
8. Devlin, J.: Bert: Pre-training of deep bidirectional transformers for language understanding. arXiv preprint arXiv:1810.04805 (2018)

9. He, X., Liao, L., Zhang, H., Nie, L., Hu, X., Chua, T.S.: Neural collaborative filtering. In: Proceedings of the 26th International Conference on World Wide Web, pp. 173–182 (2017)
10. Järvelin, K., Kekäläinen, J.: Cumulated gain-based evaluation of ir techniques. ACM Trans. Inf. Syst. (TOIS) **20**(4), 422–446 (2002)
11. Kingma, D.P.: Adam: a method for stochastic optimization. arXiv preprint arXiv:1412.6980 (2014)
12. Van der Maaten, L., Hinton, G.: Visualizing data using t-sne. Journal of machine learning research **9**(11) (2008)
13. Oord, A.V.D., Li, Y., Vinyals, O.: Representation learning with contrastive predictive coding. arXiv preprint arXiv:1807.03748 (2018)
14. Rendle, S., Freudenthaler, C., Gantner, Z., Schmidt-Thieme, L.: Bpr: Bayesian personalized ranking from implicit feedback. arXiv preprint arXiv:1205.2618 (2012)
15. Sankar, A., Wu, Y., Wu, Y., Zhang, W., Yang, H., Sundaram, H.: Groupim: a mutual information maximization framework for neural group recommendation. In: Proceedings of the 43rd International ACM SIGIR Conference on Research and Development in Information Retrieval, pp. 1279–1288 (2020)
16. Wu, X., et al.: Consrec: learning consensus behind interactions for group recommendation. In: Proceedings of the ACM Web Conference 2023, pp. 240–250 (2023)
17. Xu, J., Chen, Z., Li, J., Yang, S., Wang, H., Ngai, E.C.: Aligngroup: learning and aligning group consensus with member preferences for group recommendation. In: Proceedings of the 33rd ACM International Conference on Information and Knowledge Management, pp. 2682–2691 (2024)
18. Zhang, J., Gao, M., Yu, J., Guo, L., Li, J., Yin, H.: Double-scale self-supervised hypergraph learning for group recommendation. In: Proceedings of the 30th ACM International Conference on Information & Knowledge Management, pp. 2557–2567 (2021)
19. Zhang, S., Zheng, N., Wang, D.: Gbert: pre-training user representations for ephemeral group recommendation. In: Proceedings of the 31st ACM International Conference on Information & Knowledge Management, pp. 2631–2639 (2022)
20. Zhao, Y., Zhang, H., Bai, Q., Nie, C., Yuan, X.: Dhmae: a disentangled hypergraph masked autoencoder for group recommendation. In: Proceedings of the 47th International ACM SIGIR Conference on Research and Development in Information Retrieval, pp. 914–923 (2024)

Learn to Shade: Deep Assumption-Free Modeling for First-Price Auctions

Abhishek Mungoli(✉), Raja Subramaniam, Vishwath Parthasarathy, Jayanta Pal, and Narayan Bhamidipati

InMobi, Bengaluru, India
{abhishek.mungoli,raja.subramaniam,vishwath.parthasarathy,jayanta.pal, narayan.bhamidipati}@inmobi.com

Abstract. Bid shading is essential for real-time bidding systems operating in first-price auctions, where bidders must strategically reduce bids below their true valuation to avoid overpaying for impressions they could win more cheaply. Unlike second-price auctions-where truthful bidding is optimal-the shift of major exchanges to first-price auctions has made shading a critical capability for modern demand-side platforms (DSPs), especially performance DSPs operating with tight margins. Prior work typically estimates win-rate distributions and applies Surplus Max to select the bid that maximizes expected surplus, but most existing approaches impose strong parametric assumptions or rely on heuristics, limiting robustness in heterogeneous and volatile auction environments. We introduce a fully assumption-free deep learning framework for win-rate modeling that achieves state-of-the-art performance. To our knowledge, this is the first method to treat win-rate estimation as a time-series prediction task. Our architecture combines LSTM-based temporal modeling with feedforward contextual encoders in a hybrid ensemble and uses 20 quantile-regression heads to construct a calibrated empirical CDF without post-processing. Deployed at billion-scale in InMobi's DSP production system, the model yields a 10% lift in win rate, a 4.5% improvement in surplus, and consistent cost-efficiency gains, including reductions of 3.2%, 4.2%, and 3.1% in eCPM, eCPC, and eCPI, respectively.

1 Introduction

Real-time bidding (RTB) [15] enables automated, millisecond-latency auctions for digital impressions, forming a core component of modern programmatic advertising. Demand-Side Platforms (DSPs) bid on behalf of advertisers, Supply-Side Platforms (SSPs) manage publisher inventory, and ad exchanges facilitate bidding across millions of requests per second. User, device, publisher, and contextual signals flow through the pipeline to inform automated bidding decisions [20,21].

Until 2019–2020, second-price auctions dominated RTB. With major platforms-most notably Google Authorized Buyers [8]-shifting to first-price auctions, bidding strategy changed fundamentally. In second-price auctions, bidding

R. C.-W. Wong et al. (Eds.): PAKDD 2026, LNAI 16617, pp. 611–623, 2027.
https://doi.org/10.1007/978-981-92-1926-1_49

truthfully is optimal; in first-price auctions, bidders must "shade" bids to avoid paying their full valuation. Auction theory shows such bid shading is essential [9,26]. In practice, shading is intertwined with pacing, budget constraints, and performance optimization [1,17].

Two broad families of shading strategies exist:

- **Direct shading**: predicting a shading ratio or multiplicative discount applied to the valuation.
- **Two-step bidding (TSB)**: estimating the win-rate distribution, then applying surplus maximization to obtain an optimal bid.

Direct methods are simple but often unstable. TSB methods decouple win modeling from bid optimization but rely heavily on the quality of the estimated win-rate curve. Predicting clearing prices directly is difficult due to volatility and heterogeneity across publishers, formats, and markets. Win-rate estimation, by contrast, is smoother and more stable, making it a better input for surplus computation.

However, most existing win-rate models assume a parametric form (e.g., log-normal [2], Gaussian [18], Gamma [25]) or rely on heuristic binning approaches [23]. These assumptions often fail to capture the diverse distributions observed across billions of auctions.

Contributions. We introduce **DEEP-MHQR**, the first win-rate modeling approach that:

- treats win-rate estimation as a *time-series forecasting* task,
- uses a hybrid ensemble of LSTM (recurring patterns) and feedforward networks (sparse or irregular auctions),
- applies 20 quantile-regression heads to directly approximate the entire CDF,
- requires no distributional assumptions or post-processing.

We further derive a closed-form bid optimizer over piecewise-linear CDF segments, enabling efficient surplus maximization even under non-unimodal surplus curves. Our model is deployed in a production DSP and delivers significant cost and performance gains. The paper is organized as follows: Sect. 2 reviews prior work; Sect. 3 details the modeling and optimization framework; Sect. 4 presents offline and online results; Sect. 5 outlines future extensions; and Sect. 6 concludes.

2 Related Work

Bid shading approaches can be broadly grouped into (i) *direct* methods, which predict a shading ratio [6], and (ii) *two-step bidding (TSB)* methods [12,24]. Direct approaches (e.g., [6]) optimize a penalty-weighted loss to learn the optimal bid ratio, but they do not explicitly model win probabilities. TSB methods first estimate the bid-dependent win-rate distribution and then perform surplus maximization, providing a clearer treatment of risk-reward trade-offs.

Pan et al. [12] proposed a censored logistic regression model using $\log(b)$ as a monotonic feature, which is suitable for limited feedback but suboptimal for modern non-censored settings. Zhou et al. [24] addressed this by fitting parametric distributions-Log-Normal [2], Gaussian [18], Gamma [25]-and using their CDFs as win-rate curves. However, real auction landscapes deviate from these assumed forms [23], limiting robustness.

Non-parametric alternatives avoid predefined distributional assumptions. ADM [11] predicts bucketed price distributions using a Neighborhood Likelihood Loss to unify censored and observed outcomes. DLF [13] models temporal auction patterns using RNNs, while Link Structures [19] exploit relational dependencies across auctions. These methods flexibly capture empirical distributions but rely on bucketization or structural heuristics.

In contrast, we use multi-head quantile regression to directly estimate $\Pr(b > \hat{b} \mid x)$ in a fully non-censored setting. Quantile predictions form a smooth empirical CDF without assuming specific parametric families or predefined buckets. Here, b is the submitted bid, $\hat{b}$ the clearing price, x contextual auction features, and p the corresponding win probability. Our hybrid LSTM-feedforward ensemble with enforced quantile monotonicity yields calibrated, assumption-free win-rate curves well suited for surplus-maximizing bid selection.

For more complex settings, Gong et al. [7] proposed a three-tower model jointly predicting CTR, win-rate, and shading ratio, primarily for multi-slot display environments [3,5,7,10].

Another important axis of distinction is *parametric* vs. *non-parametric*. Many TSB variants-e.g., Pan, Zhou, and Gong-are parametric [7,12,24], while MEOW [23] is non-parametric, optimizing surplus within impression bins. However, binning may miss fine-grained auction variations unless heavily customized.

Finally, most existing techniques are *offline* approaches [7,12,23,24]. Liu et al. [16] proposed the first adaptive, active-learning-based shading framework [4,14,22], exploring uncertain bids under budget constraints.

Our work complements these efforts by providing an assumption-free, calibrated, time-series-aware win-rate estimator that integrates seamlessly into surplus-maximizing bidding.

3 Modeling and Optimization Framework

This section presents our unified framework for estimating clearing-price distributions and selecting surplus-maximizing bids in first-price auctions. We describe the hybrid architecture, multi-head quantile regression, empirical CDF construction, and our closed-form bid optimizer. The goal is to learn the conditional win-rate curve $\hat{F}(b \mid x)$ without assuming any parametric form (Table 1).

Table 1. Notation for auction modeling and bid optimization.

Symbol	Description
V	True value of the ad opportunity (e.g., CTR, CVR, pacing signal)
b	Submitted bid
$\hat{b}$	Clearing price (minimum winning bid)
$S(b; V, \hat{b})$	Surplus $(V - b)\mathbf{1}(b > \hat{b})$
s	Expected surplus $\mathbb{E}_{\hat{b}}[S(b; V, \hat{b})]$
b^*	Surplus-maximizing bid
x	Contextual auction features
$q_p(x)$	Predicted bid achieving win probability p
$\hat{F}(b \mid x)$	Empirical CDF formed by quantiles
M_{LSTM}	LSTM expert (temporal patterns)
M_{FF}	Feedforward expert (contextual features)
M_{ens}	Mixture-of-experts ensemble gate
Q_{reg}	Multi-head quantile regressors (20 heads)
θ	Model parameters

3.1 Notation

3.2 Modeling Approach

We estimate the conditional win-rate $\Pr(b > \hat{b} \mid x)$ through a hybrid ensemble of LSTM and feedforward networks. Each expert outputs 20 quantile bids, which are merged via a learned gating mechanism to produce a smooth empirical CDF $\hat{F}(b \mid x)$.

Model Architecture. LSTM Expert (M_{LSTM}). Designed for recurring auctions with strong temporal structure. A single 25-unit LSTM encodes lagged clearing prices, followed by shared layers and 20 quantile heads. An L_2 penalty of 0.01 controls overfitting.

Feedforward Expert (M_{FF}). Used for sparse or irregular auctions. A 3-layer ReLU MLP (64→128→64) with BatchNorm and dropout (0.2–0.3) processes contextual features. Categorical embeddings use $\min(50, \lfloor n/2 \rfloor)$ dimensions. Outputs 20 quantiles.

Ensemble Gate (M_{ens}). A lightweight 16-unit ReLU → 2-way softmax gate produces mixture weights

$$q_p(x) = \alpha_{\mathrm{LSTM}} q_p^{\mathrm{LSTM}}(x) + \alpha_{\mathrm{FF}}\, q_p^{\mathrm{FF}}(x).$$

Monotonicity Layer. A projection layer enforces $q_1 \leq \cdots \leq q_{20}$ to eliminate quantile crossing (Fig. 1).

Training Objective. Each Quantile Head Minimizes the Standard Pinball Loss:

$$L_p = \sum_i \max\Big[p(\hat{b}_i - q_p(x_i)),\ (1-p)(q_p(x_i) - \hat{b}_i)\Big],$$

and the joint objective is $L_{\text{total}} = \sum_{p \in P} L_p$. Multi-head training enforces calibration across the full win-rate curve.

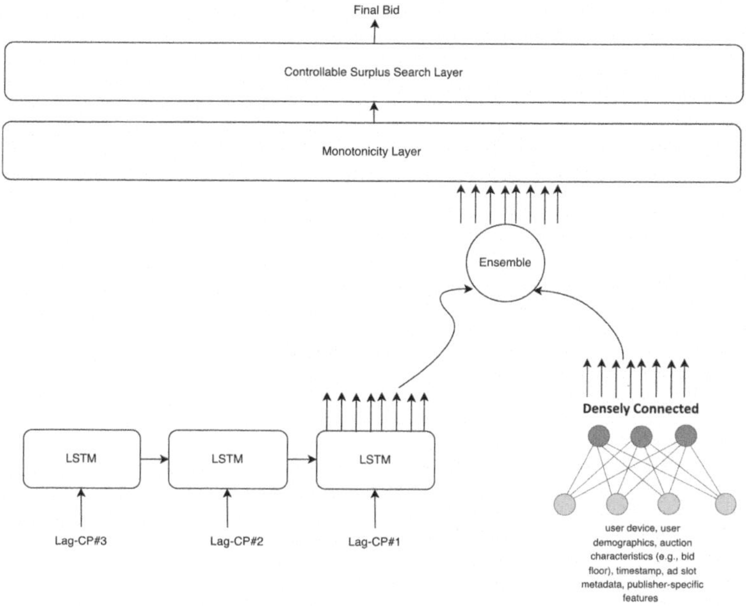

Fig. 1. Hybrid LSTM-feedforward architecture with multi-head quantiles and learned gating.

Generalizability to Censored Settings. Although trained mainly on non-censored auctions, the model generalizes naturally to censored or partially observed cases. When clearing-price history is missing (e.g., missing clearing prices when the DSP loses or when the exchange does not return them), the LSTM expert receives zero or sparse lags and is down-weighted by the ensemble gate, shifting reliance to the feedforward expert, which exploits contextual signals (bid floors, publisher/placement patterns, device features, temporal encodings). If surrogate temporal traces from related exchanges or similar publisher–user cohorts are available, they can be supplied as substitute lags to preserve temporal structure. Thus, without changing the loss or adding censor-specific mechanisms, the mixture-of-experts architecture provides a smooth fallback path that maintains robustness under both censored and non-censored conditions.

3.3 Surplus Maximization

Given the empirical CDF, expected surplus is:

$$\mathbb{E}_{\hat{b}|x}[S(b; V, \hat{b})] = (V - b)\, \hat{F}(b \mid x). \tag{1}$$

We select the optimal bid:

$$b^* = \arg \max_{b \in (0,V)} (V - b)\, \hat{F}(b \mid x).$$

3.4 Non-unimodality of Surplus

Contrary to prior assumptions of unimodality (which permit golden-section search), empirical surplus curves can be multi-modal. Table 2 and Fig. 2 illustrate a case with two distinct optima.

Table 2. Example surplus values for different bids.

b	Win Prob.	Surplus
1	0.10	1.90
9	0.45	4.95
10	0.51	**5.10**
14	0.85	**5.10**
18	0.96	1.92

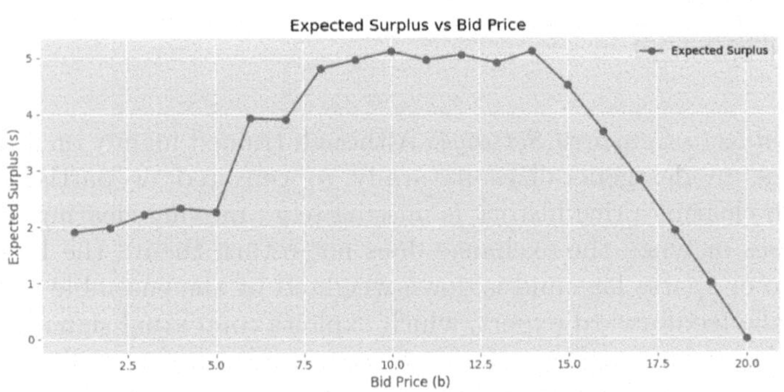

Fig. 2. Example surplus curve for $V = 20$ showing multiple local maxima.

3.5 Closed-Form Optimization Across Quantile Segments

Between consecutive quantiles (q_{p_1}, q_{p_2}), we assume the win-rate varies linearly with the bid, yielding a piecewise-linear approximation of $\hat{F}(b \mid x)$. Thus,

$$w(b) = ab + c, \qquad a = \frac{p_2 - p_1}{q_{p_2} - q_{p_1}}, \qquad c = p_1 - a q_{p_1}.$$

Surplus within the segment is:

$$s(b) = (V - b)(ab + c),$$

a quadratic with closed-form maximizer:

$$b^* = \frac{V}{2} + \frac{q_{p_1}}{2} - \frac{p_1}{2a}.$$

We evaluate this critical point and both segment endpoints for all 19 intervals and take the global maximum. This guarantees correctness even under multi-modal surplus landscapes.

Computational Complexity. Inference requires $\mathcal{O}(A + PB)$ time, where A is feature computation and B the per-head forward cost. The interval search is $\mathcal{O}(P)$, making the overall process linear in the number of quantile heads. This makes the number of output heads P the dominant factor in runtime cost (Fig. 3).

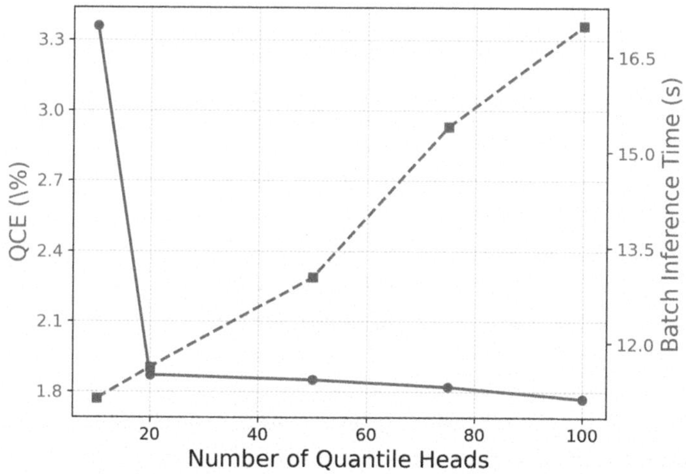

Fig. 3. Quantile Calibration Error (left) and latency (right) vs. number of quantile heads P.

Experiments with $P \in \{10, 20, 50, 75, 100\}$ show diminishing calibration improvements beyond $P = 20$ while latency increases sharply. We therefore deploy with $P = 20$.

3.6 Component vs. Ensemble Performance

Table 3. Component vs. Ensemble Performance (MAE for Q50).

Condition	LSTM	Dense NN	Ensemble	%Cases
Overall	0.560	0.620	**0.530**	100%
0 lags CP available	3.230	2.860	**2.830**	3.1%
1 lag CP available	1.460	1.810	**1.450**	4.1%
2 lags CP available	1.180	1.380	**1.160**	6.2%
3 lags CP available	0.359	0.420	**0.358**	86.5%

In cases where clearing-price lags are sufficiently available, the LSTM expert leverages temporal patterns to outperform the Dense NN component. Conversely, when clearing-price history is sparse (e.g., 0 lags), the Dense NN outperforms the LSTM by relying more heavily on contextual features such as bid floors, publisher dynamics, and device signals. The ensemble consistently outperforms both individual experts by combining the strengths of each, demonstrating the model's robustness in censored or partially observed settings (Tables 3 and 4).

3.7 Performance vs Dataset Size

Table 4. Model Performance Across Dataset Sizes.

Data Points	MAE(Q50)	QCE(%)
100K	0.656	2.92
1M	0.642	2.11
10M	0.640	1.90
20M	0.637	1.75
25M	**0.63621**	**1.72**
50M+	**0.63620**	**1.72**

Performance plateaus beyond $\approx$ 25M samples, validating our use of a 7-day rolling window ($\approx$ 25M impressions) for daily retraining. Dataset construction details appear in Sect. 4.2.

4 Experiments

4.1 Evaluation Objectives

We evaluate the proposed assumption-free multi-head quantile model through both offline simulations and online traffic experiments along three dimensions:

1. **Calibration and robustness of win-rate predictions:** We compare against standard parametric distributions (truncated normal, log-normal, exponential, gamma) [2,18,25] and non-parametric baselines such as MEOW [23]. Evaluation is performed on a strictly time-held-out validation set, measuring how well predicted quantile bids achieve their target win probabilities on unseen auctions.
2. **Economic efficiency in budget-constrained offline simulations:** We measure key economic signals-including *premium paid* (overpayment above clearing price) and *surplus savings* (difference between valuation and paid price)-under identical budget constraints that terminate bidding when spend limits are reached. This setup mirrors real DSP behavior and ensures fair comparison across bidding strategies.
3. **Impact on downstream business metrics in online A/B tests:** We measure eCPM, eCPC, and eCPI, standard KPIs for performance-driven advertising, to assess real-world efficiency relative to the production baseline.

Together, these axes evaluate statistical calibration, economic efficiency, and real-world business impact.

4.2 Dataset Creation

We construct the training and evaluation corpus from large-scale bid-request logs collected over 10 consecutive days (7 for training, 3 for validation). Each record corresponds to a first-price auction and contains the contextual features and the observed clearing price.

- **Winning auctions:** The exchange returns the second-highest competing bid.
- **Losing auctions:** The highest bid that won the auction is returned, representing the minimum winning threshold.

The dataset spans multiple pricing types (CPM, CPC, CPI), geographic regions, devices, OS types, and ad formats (banner, video, native).

Each auction record includes structured features:

- **User features:** device, OS, demographic segments, and interest categories.
- **Auction features:** publisher and placement IDs, bid floor, slot metadata, time-of-day and day-of-week encodings.
- **Publisher dynamics:** rolling-window fill-rate, historical eCPM, and recent DSP win rate.
- **Temporal features:** lagged clearing prices and bid floors over multiple time windows.

A strictly chronological split ensures evaluation only on unseen, forward-in-time data, mitigating temporal leakage and reflecting realistic RTB market variation.

4.3 Evaluation Metrics

We use both calibration-oriented ML metrics and business KPIs. Table 5 summarizes key metrics:

Table 5. Evaluation metrics for calibration and bidding performance.

Metric	Description
QCE	Quantile calibration error: deviation between observed win rate and target quantile.
Win Rate	Proportion of auctions won.
Surplus (%)	$(V - b)/V$ for winning bids.
Premium (%)	$(b - \hat{b})/b$ for winning bids.
ECPI/ECPC/ECPM	Standard performance KPIs: spend per install/click/impressions.
Budget Duration	Time to exhaust allocated budget.

4.4 Experiment Variants

We benchmark the following win-rate modeling approaches:

- **Parametric fits** [2,18,25]: TN, LN, EXP, and GAMMA.
- **MEOW_TWEAKED PROD**: the current production non-parametric baseline [23].
- **DEEP-MHQR**: our hybrid (LSTM + dense) ensemble with multi-head quantile regression.

All variants are integrated into the same Surplus Max bidding pipeline.

4.5 Offline Results

Offline evaluation uses a time-split test set and fixed advertiser-campaign budgets. For each variant, bids are generated via Surplus Max using the predicted win-rate curve.

Table 6. Offline simulation results across calibration and economic metrics.

Variant	QCE	Win (%)	Premium (%)	Surplus (%)	Budget Hrs
TN	10.53	16.1	21.1	42.1	12.1
LN	4.65	18.9	18.1	45.3	14.2
EXP	12.04	14.2	24.1	40.1	9.6
GAMMA	8.00	17.6	19.2	43.4	13.8
MEOW_TWEAKED PROD	3.74	19.2	18.7	45.8	14.5
DEEP-MHQR	**1.72**	**21.1**	**17.3**	**47.1**	**15.1**

Results are summarized in Table 6:

Our method achieves the lowest QCE (1.72%), highest surplus (47.1%), best win rate (21.1%), and lowest premium (17.3%), while also extending budget duration-indicating strong pacing efficiency.

Figure 4 visualizes the QCE across all variants, highlighting the calibration superiority of the proposed DEEP-MHQR model.

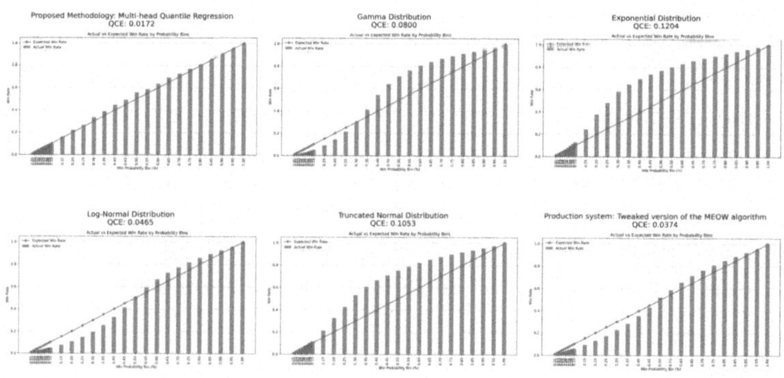

Fig. 4. Quantile Calibration Error (QCE) across all evaluated variants. Lower is better.

4.6 Online Results

We further performed randomized A/B testing on live traffic using equal budget splits across matching advertiser-campaign pairs. Each model predicted a win-rate curve, and Surplus Max produced the final bid.

Table 7 shows performance relative to the production baseline:

DEEP-MHQR delivers consistent lifts across all KPIs: +9.8% win rate, +4.5% surplus, and meaningful reductions in eCPM (–3.2%), eCPC (–4.2%), and eCPI (–3.1%), confirming substantial real-world value.

Table 7. Online A/B performance (percentage change relative to production baseline).

Variant	WinRate	Spend	Surplus	eCPM	eCPC	eCPI
TN	–4.5	–1.2	–6.1	+2.3	+3.4	+1.6
LN	+1.2	–0.2	–.2	+0.5	+1.2	+2.3
EXP	–8.2	+0.5	–10.5	+5.6	+7.3	+4.8
GAMMA	–1.5	–0.7	–6.9	+4.3	+4.9	+3.5
DEEP-MHQR	**+9.8**	**+0.2**	**+4.5**	**–3.2**	**–4.2**	**–3.1**

4.7 Online Inference

The model is fully deployed and scaled in InMobi's distributed real-time serving environment. Requests are batched over 3 ms windows ($\approx$ 100 requests per batch) and served via the Triton Inference Server. End-to-end latency is 11 ms (P95) and 13 ms (P99). Multiple serving nodes (16 CPU cores, 128 GB RAM each) collectively sustain approximately 30M QPS in production.

5 Future Directions

We highlight two immediate extensions. First, we plan to evaluate model behavior across finer-grained data slices (e.g., user cohorts, exchanges, ad formats, app categories) to identify segments with residual error and inform targeted feature or architecture refinements. Second, we aim to develop a context-adaptive surplus objective: the win-cost trade-off may vary with campaign goals, budget pressure, and market conditions, and incorporating real-time feedback could enable dynamic adjustment of the surplus-maximization strategy.

6 Conclusion

We introduced **DEEP-MHQR**, an assumption-free hybrid deep learning framework for win-rate modeling in first-price auctions. By combining LSTM-based temporal signals, feedforward contextual encoders, and multi-head quantile regression, the model produces calibrated win-rate curves that directly support surplus-maximizing bidding. Extensive offline evaluation and online A/B testing demonstrate consistent gains over parametric and production-grade baselines, including higher win rates, lower premiums, and improved surplus under real-world budget constraints.

References

1. Cai, H., et al.: Real-time bidding by reinforcement learning. In: WSDM (2017)
2. Cui, Y., Zhang, R., Li, W., Mao, J.: Bid landscape forecasting in online ad exchange marketplace. In: KDD (2011)

3. Sarma, D., Gujar, A., Narahari, S., Y.: Multi-armed bandit mechanisms for multi-slot sponsored search auctions (2010)
4. Dasarathy, G., Nowak, R., Zhu, X.: S2: An efficient graph-based active learning algorithm, p. COLT. (2015)
5. Deng, X., Sun, Y., Yin, M., Zhou, Y.: Mechanism design for multi-slot ads auction in sponsored search markets. In: FAW (2010)
6. Gligorijevic, D., et al.: Bid shading in the brave new world of first-price auctions. In: CIKM (2020)
7. Gong, Z., et al.: Mebs: multi-task end-to-end bid shading for multi-slot display advertising. In: CIKM (2023)
8. Google authorized buyers: real-time bidding protocol updates - march **13**, 2019 (2019)
9. Hortaçsu, A., Kastl, J., Zhang, A.: Bid shading and bidder surplus in the us treasury auction system. Am. Econ. Rev. (2018)
10. Hosanagar, K., Abhishek, V.: Optimal bidding in multi-item multi-slot sponsored search auctions. Oper. Res. (2013)
11. Li, X., Zhang, M.M., Wang, Z., Tong, Y.: Arbitrary distribution modeling with censorship in rtb. In: KDD (2022)
12. Pan, S., Kitts, B., Zhou, T., He, H., Shetty, B., Flores, A., Gligorijevic, D., Pan, J., Mao, T., Gultekin, S., Zhang, J.: Bid shading by win-rate estimation and surplus maximization (2020)
13. Ren, K., Qin, J., Zheng, L., Yang, Z., Zhang, W., Yu, Y.: Deep landscape forecasting for real-time bidding. In: KDD (2019)
14. Settles, B.: Active Learning Literature Survey. University of Wisconsin (2010)
15. Wang, J., Zhang, W., Yuan, S.: Display advertising with real-time bidding and behavioural targeting. CoRR (2016)
16. Wang, Z., Zheng, Z., Kang, Y., Huang, J.: Cost-effective active learning for bid exploration in online advertising. In: WSDM (2024)
17. Wu, D., et al.: Budget constrained bidding by model-free rl in display advertising. In: CIKM (2018)
18. Wu, W., Yeh, M.Y., Chen, M.S.: Predicting winning price in real time bidding with censored data. In: KDD (2015)
19. Wu, W., Yeh, M.Y., Chen, M.S.: Deep censored learning of the winning price in rtb. In: KDD (2018)
20. Yuan, S., Wang, J., Zhao, X.: Real-time bidding for online advertising: measurement and analysis. In: ADKDD (2013)
21. Yuan, Y., Li, J., Qin, R.: A survey on real time bidding advertising. In: SOLA (2014)
22. Zhang, J., Katz-Samuels, J., Nowak, R.: Galaxy: Graph-based active learning at the extreme (2022)
23. Zhang, W., et al.: Meow: a space-efficient nonparametric bid shading algorithm. In: KDD (2021)
24. Zhou, T., et al.: An efficient deep distribution network for bid shading in first-price auctions. In: KDD (2021)
25. Zhu, W.Y., Shih, W.Y., Lee, Y.H., Peng, W.C., Huang, J.L.: A gamma-based regression for winning price estimation in rtb advertising. IEEE Big Data (2017)
26. Zulehner, C.: Bidding behavior in sequential cattle auctions. Int. J. Ind. Organ. (2009)

Correction to: Data Science: Foundations and Applications

Raymond Chi-Wing Wong, Hanghang Tong, Hua Lu, James Kwok, Flora Salim, Yuanfeng Song, and Man Lung Yiu

Correction to:
R. C.-W. Wong et al. (Eds.): ***Data Science: Foundations and Applications*****, LNAI 16617, https://doi.org/10.1007/978-981-92-1926-1**

The book was published with an incorrect volume number, which has been corrected to 16617.

The updated version of this book can be found at https://doi.org/10.1007/978-981-92-1926-1

R. C.-W. Wong et al. (Eds.): PAKDD 2026, LNAI 16617, p. C1, 2027.
https://doi.org/10.1007/978-981-92-1926-1_50

Author Index

R. C.-W. Wong et al. (Eds.): PAKDD 2026, LNAI 16617, pp. 625–627, 2027.
https://doi.org/10.1007/978-981-92-1926-1

The manufacturer's authorised representative in the EU is Springer Nature Customer Service Centre GmbH, Europaplatz 3, 69115 Heidelberg, Germany. If you have any concerns regarding our products, please contact ProductSafety@springernature.com

Printed and bound by CPI Group (UK) Ltd, Croydon, CR0 4YY
21/09/2026
02219987-0013